CIVIL WAR COLLECTOR'S ENCYCLOPEDIA

Volumes I & II

Complete & Unabridged in
This Double Volume

by Francis A. Lord

BLUE & GREY PRESS

CIVIL WAR COLLECTOR'S ENCYCLOPEDIA
Volumes I and II

This edition published in 1995 by
BLUE & GREY PRESS
by permission and in conjunction with
Morningside House, Inc., under an agreement between
Morningside House and Francis A. Lord, copyright holder.

Blue & Grey Press
A division of Book Sales, Inc.
114 Northfield Avenue
Edison, New Jersey 08837

ISBN 0-7858-0467-6

Library of Congress Catalog Card Number: 63-14636

MANUFACTURED IN THE UNITED STATES OF AMERICA

VOLUME I

To

My wife, MARJORIE T. LORD

and

My mentor, COLONEL W. S. NYE,

whose patience and encouragement
have contributed so much, and
whose suggestions have
added so materially!

FOREWORD

IN the preparation of this encyclopedia the author has used extensively the literature on specialized subjects pertinent to this study as well as the manuals and books of instruction published just before and throughout the war. Obviously this written material is of value only if supplemented by actual specimens now included in museums and private collections. Of invaluable assistance have been the many consultations and discussions with collectors and experts in many specialized fields.

This encyclopedia has been prepared for experts and novices alike. Collectors and students of the Civil War period have long been aware of the great variety of artifacts produced for military or naval use by both sides in the war. An effort has been made to include every item that would be of interest to the individual collector. There are some exceptions: Although a number of quite rare articles are described, others have been omitted because data on them is lacking or their very rarity makes it unlikely that they will be available to any but a few collectors. Owing to the limitations of space and the impracticability of giving definitive coverage in any publication except a full book, currency, stamps, and pictorial mailing covers are not included. For example, any work that describes only a few stamps would be worthless. It must be all or none. Fortunately these specialties are covered in complete works on those subjects. Similarly bulky items such as railroad rolling stock, large cannon, boats, camp and barrack equipment, and many types of vehicles have been omitted except that in some instances they are referred to briefly as background information and to make certain lists complete. An example of this is pontoon bridging equipment.

It must be emphasized that while the list of various articles is as complete as possible, there is no definitive treatment of each. Unnecessary repetition would result if the author had attempted to duplicate such thorough studies as Peterson on American swords or Fuller on the rifled musket. However, an up-to-date bibliography of such individual studies has been compiled for those who wish to read at greater length on their particular interests. Where good studies of certain items are already in existence I have merely outlined such items in compact form, with brief descriptions, because their complete exclusion from this book would detract from its encyclopedic character and intent.

The encyclopedia includes both military and also those non-military items which were used by fighting men of both sides at the front. In this respect, especially, this work is unique, since up to now there has not appeared any ready reference work which includes such nonregulation items.

Both Federal and Confederate basic types of equipment and weapons are included. It is impossible to describe every variation. However, to assist in identifying questionable items, separate lists of U.S. and C.S. makers have been appended at the back of the book.

The bewildering variety of weapons and equipment used in the war staggers even those who have studied the war intensively for years. One of the reasons for the great variety was the need to get something—anything— in the hands of the men as quickly as possible. In the equipping of a volunteer regiment for active service, neither the state nor national authorities appeared to take the leading part. First came the family friends with several scores of "absolutely indispensable" articles, such as thimbles, scissors, papers of pins, needle books with all sizes of needles, several spools of thread, big balls of yarn for darning—some went so far as to put in a bundle of patches, buttons, bandages, these were a few of the motherly, wifely, or sisterly tokens tucked away in the soldier's knapsack. Then outside friends brought their offerings, among them cases of medicine for self-doctoring; tourniquets for the stoppage of blood flow; havelocks, handerchiefs, etc. Masculine admirers who had a sanguinary idea of soldiering—for others—contributed their addition to the outfit in the shape of enormous pocket knives containing a complete kit of tools; dirks; revolvers with bullet moulds and powder flasks. A knife-fork-spoon contrivance was a trophy for the more favored ones. Yet this was only a beginning. While in camp in the state, soldiers' money was obtained easily and expended lavishly. Innumerable, useless knick-knacks, were laid in store. One of the favorite articles was the steel-plated vest, a garment into which a pair of heavy iron breastplates were to be slipped when going into action, at other times to be carried in the knapsack.

Camps were constantly thronged by visitors and friends bringing all manner of gifts, useful and useless—all varieties of pastry and delicacies, towels and soap, blankets and hammocks, handkerchiefs and needle books, tobacco, pipes, and pills. A Connecticut officer was even given a gallon jug of molasses. Portable writing desks, water filters, Bowie knives, and a score of other contrivances had been invented, declared to be absolutely indispensable to health and comfort, and were provided in great numbers. Volunteers were urged to carry a rubber blanket, extra shirts, an extra pair of shoes and socks, and a variety of cooking utensils. These, with paper and envelopes, pocket-album, and a Testament, made, with musket and equipments, a load from 120 to 150 pounds. Most recruits undertook to carry this burden. The veteran, content with blanket, canteen, haversack, tin cup, and jackknife, smiled at the pack under which he perspired in his early days of soldiering. He laughed in later years at the advice of "an old soldier" who told the volunteer: "Let your beard grow. March always in cotton stockings, but have a pair of woollen ones to put on when you stop. Wash your whole body every day." How easy to do this on a march in Virginia or Georgia! And how invigorating in open air after creeping out of a "dog-tent" on a December morning in Falmouth! One veteran urged the soldiers to avoid "oily meat and strong coffee!"

In 1861, many soldiers were presented with a copy of the *Soldier's Pocket Health Companion,* a book which listed 25 different items every soldier should have. Among these were the following:

6 linen pocket handkerchiefs
2-6 yards of white flannel
1 yard linen
1 pair slippers
1 small box lard
1 small bottle peppermint
1 paper cayenne pepper

This helpful book pointed out that every soldier should provide himself with all 25 items and "store them away in one corner of his knapsack—they will occupy but little room."!

Certainly one of the most commonly observed phenomena of 1861-1865 was the disparity in equipment, not only between Union and Confederate forces, but also between individual units of the better-equipped Union forces. For example, the historian of the 4th Iowa Cavalry wrote:

"The armament of the regiment was very poor. A few men had Colt's navy revolvers. The clumsy (infantry) rifles were still in the hands of those men who had not the hardihood or ingenuity to 'lose' them. Some had revolvers of the Starr and other bad kinds, many had the single-barrelled holster-pistols, with ramrods, of the pattern in use in the Mexican War, while all had the awkwardly long and very heavy dragoon sabre, as old as the century. Every man saw and, what was much worse, *felt* the inefficiency of the arms."

Inefficient as many Civil War arms were—especially some imported weapons—it must be emphasized that they were made to kill with, and still are dangerous and should be handled like modern arms—carefully! For purposes of safety as well as for preventing breakage, do not "snap" the hammer just to hear it click. It is also extremely important to realize that any explosive projectile or device, regardless of age, and if still loaded, should not be tampered with or exposed to intense heat. An ordnance expert should unload or deactivate such projectiles.

Where the term "tin" is used, it is in the generic sense. Actually, "tin" in the Civil War was usually thin iron covered with a tinning process. For example, in the *History of the 13th New Hampshire Infantry* (p. 530) we read: "Half a canteen unsoldered by heat, and held in a split stick, makes an excellent little frying-pan; the *tin* soon burns off, leaving only the *thin iron.*"

Troops on the "Blackberry Raid," July 13, 1863, near Yorktown, Virginia, hid their knapsacks in the woods, but took another route on their return from the raid, and as a result, the knapsacks "and their varied contents snugly tucked under boards, brush and hedges, await the effect of time, or the future collector of useless relics!"

Although space limitations have prevented the inclusion of all types and variants of the articles described herein, I do not doubt that many of these, of which we are currently unaware, will be discovered. One of the purposes of this book is to flush them out of hiding.

Rockville, Maryland
July 1, 1963

—Francis A. Lord

ABOUT THE AUTHOR

Dr. Francis A. Lord was born December 8, 1911, in Los Angeles, California of New England parents. His grandfather and two great grandfathers fought in the Federal Army during the Civil War.

The author is the third generation of his name to enlist in the army at the age of 18 years, from the state of New Hampshire. Lord left high school to enlist as a private in the 5th U. S. Infantry the day after his 18th birthday. His grandfather enlisted at 18 to serve in the Civil War and an uncle enlisted at 18 to serve in the Spanish-American War.

Graduated from the University of Massachusetts in 1936 the author received his M.A. from Michigan State University in 1938 and his Ph.D. from the University of Michigan in 1948. With a major in American History, Dr. Lord taught at Lawrence Institute of Technology from 1940 through 1946 except for intervening Army service, and at Mississippi College from 1948 through 1951. Since that time he has been a research analyst with the United States Government.

His military career includes service with the 5th U. S. Infantry and 3rd U. S. Cavalry before World War II and 4½ years as an intelligence officer in World War II. Much of his war service was spent as an interrogator of German prisoners of war. For his services with O.S.S. he was awarded the Commendation Medal for duty in the European Theater of Operations 1944-1945.

Dr. Lord has written extensively on the Civil War. His definitive study of the Federal fighting man *They Fought For The Union* was published in 1960. In addition to numerous articles for periodicals he writes a regular column on arms and equipment for *Civil War Times Illustrated,* and is in constant demand as a lecturer on the Civil War period.

The author is a fellow of the Society of Military Collectors and Historians, a member of the American Historical Association, the Advisory Council, U. S. Civil War Centennial Commission, and the Cosmos Club of Washington, D. C. He is married, has three children, and resides at Bethesda, Md.

ACKNOWLEDGMENTS

Every effort has been made to consult museums and collections, as well as individuals to insure as complete an encyclopedia as possible. In his research the author has been accorded very substantial cooperation from collectors who have permitted their items to be photographed. In each case credit is given. Where no mention is made of repository or collection, the item of equipment depicted is from the author's collection.

The author gratefully expresses his sincere appreciation to the following individuals whose assistance has contributed very substantially to this book:

Colonel W. S. Nye, who edited the entire manuscript. Not only is Bill Nye a valued friend but his keen sense of literary style coupled with his extensive military knowledge and experience as a professional soldier have made this (and many other) books possible. Such unselfish help can only be adequately appreciated by those who have worked with him.

I am greatly indebted for the extensive assistance and invaluable advice rendered by Norm Flayderman, whose collection is very probably the best in the country. Photographs of items from Norm's collection are found throughout this book; his expert knowledge is equally omnipresent. Sincere thanks also to Ray Riling for permission to reproduce illustrations from his beautiful and valuable book, *Uniforms and Dress of the Army and Navy of the Confederate States of America* (Phila., 1960).

Much information on medical items was furnished by an esteemed friend, Dr. John L. Margreiter of St. Louis, Missouri. John is one of many combat veterans who have studied the Civil War as a hobby.

Among the unsung heroes (in this case, heroines) whose sensible advice and cheerful cooperative spirit are too often taken for granted are three staff members of the National Archives in Washington, D. C. The author welcomes this opportunity to thank Miss Josephine Cobb, Miss Sara Jackson, and Mrs. Eddie Stokes. The assistance of Frederick P. Todd and Gerald C. Stowe, of the West Point Museum is deeply appreciated.

The following collectors have been especially generous in permitting the use of items to be photographed for use in this book:

William A. Albaugh, III, Falls Church, Virginia
Mrs. Prentiss Bassett, Cambridge, New York
Craig Caba, Harrisburg, Pennsylvania
George G. Christman, Spring Lake, Michigan
Richard N. Ferris, Boonville, New York
Sydney C. Kerksis, Pensacola, Florida
Stephen M. Millett, Columbus, Ohio
William A. Miner, Dansville, New York
Bernard Mitchell, Falls Church, Virginia
Harold Peterson, Arlington, Virginia
William Prinz, Wheaton, Maryland
Ray Riling, Philadelphia, Pennsylvania
James A. Shutt, Columbus, Ohio

Two collectors have aided substantially with excellent drawings of items of equipment. These men—Robert L. Miller, Arlington, Virginia, and Mike McAfee, Athens, Ohio, were always ready to make drawings for this book at times when photographs were difficult or impossible to obtain.

Dr. Louis Walton Sipley, Director of the American Museum of Photography in Philadelphia, Pennsylvania, aided me greatly in preparation of the section on "Pictures."

Greatly appreciated also, has been the expert assistance on military buttons from Alphaeus H. Albert of Hightstown, New Jersey, to whom credit is extended for the material on buttons in the Appendix.

The author is especially indebted to Herschel C. Logan of Salina, Kansas, for his fine drawings of small arms ammunition. The enthusiasm and knowledge of Mr. Logan are exceptional; he is the unusual combination of artist and scholar.

My hearty thanks go to my wife, who typed the manuscript, and to Mr. R. Grey Smith, Fairfax, Virginia, who photographed some items in my collection for use in this book.

In the corrections and changes which appear in this second printing, the author has been assisted by many people, both in this Country and abroad. He is especially indebted to the following for specific additions and corrections:

Mrs. M. Bearss, Vicksburg, Mississippi
Michael Brewer, Wood-Ridge, N. J.
Bernard T. Doane, Chevy Chase, Md.
Arnold C. Franks, Jr., Everett, Washington
Al Gross, Cleveland, Ohio
L. James Halberstadt, Williamsburg, Mass.
Fritz Haselberger, Hackettstown, N. J.
A. L. Honeycutt, Jr., Fort Fisher, N. C.
Sidney C. Kerksis, Pensacola, Fla.
H. Michael Madaus, Milwaukee, Wisc.
Lt. Col. John H. Magruder, Marine Corps Museum, Quantico, Va.
Ken Mattern, Havertown, Pa.
Carol Ruckdeschel, Atlanta, Ga.
Tom Staats, Milwaukee, Wisc.
Bruce Stevens, Berwyn, Ill.

F.A.L.

TOPIC ARRANGEMENT

This book is designed in the form of a modified encyclopedia, in which the major topics are in alphabetic order. Grouped under these principal headings are, in most cases, one or more subtopics which, though in alphabetic order within that major grouping, are not in alphabetic order insofar as the entire book is concerned. The reason for this is to show what articles pertain to each major heading. For example, the major topic ACCOUTERMENTS includes such subtopics as CARTRIDGE BOX, BELT, SCABBARD, etc. However, to further assist the reader in quickly finding a particular item in the text, an abbreviated index is furnished at the end of the book, in which all items are in alphabetic order, with a certain amount of cross indexing where items might be known under more than one name.

In the text, major items or topics are titled with large capital letters, viz: ACCOUTERMENTS; subtopics or included items within such major headings are titled in italic capitals, small capitals, or capitals and lower case, italics, depending on the number of breakdowns required; viz: *ACCOUTERMENTS, INFANTRY,* BAYONET SCABBARD, *Emerson Bayonet Scabbard* (page 1).

Material is cross-referenced for quick location of major individual topics. To locate a maker or contractor's name, look under the item in the text proper and also under the lists of patentees, contractors, and dealers which appear at the end of the book.

Civil War Collectors Encyclopedia

Additions And Corrections

to

Volume One

Since publication of the first edition of *Collectors Encyclopedia,* the following additions and corrections have been submitted by the readers. The author is sincerely appreciative of these contributions.

Major H. C. Cooper, Dahlgren, Virginia.
Subject: Button Makers (P. 339)
Federal Eagle button with shield "A". Marked:
Wm. H. Smith & Co.
New York
Federal Eagle button with shield "R". Marked:
Schuyler H & Co.
New York
New York State button marked:
Steele & Johnson
Federal Eagle button with shield "F". Marked:
Horstmann, New York

Roy Hill, Savannah, Georgia.
Subject: Intrenching bayonet (P. 144)
Acquired in North Carolina an intrenching bayonet with an overall length of 10 1/2 inches which may well have been made for a .54 caliber rifle. "The bayonet is very crudely made . . ."

Ronald B. Johnson, Racine, Wisconsin.
Subject: Carbine sling snap-hook (P. 338)
Has a carbine sling snap-hook marked on the roller frame:
T. J. Shepard Chicopee, Mass.

Henry B. Pennell, Santa Barbara, California.
Subject: Incorrect caption (P. 308)
This caption should read: Federal Cavalry Sergeant Major.

Tom Staats, Milwaukee, Wisconsin.
Subject: Cap box. (P. 337)
Has a cap box marked:
J. Davy Co.

Bruce Stevens, Berwyn, Illinois.
Subject: Revolver holster (P. 123)
Has a holster similar to the one to the extreme left of the picture. Marked:
W. Kinsey & Co.
Newark, N.J.

ACCOUTERMENTS. This term includes items of equipment, other than weapons and clothing, carried by the soldier, sailor, or Marine. (In the Civil War the common spelling was "accoutrements.") Generally the term applied to the articles carried on or by the belt, and included the belt, cartridge box, cap box, and bayonet scabbard. Accouterments differed for the three combat branches of the Army—infantry, cavalry, and artillery. Details are given under appropriate headings. The canteen, haversack, and knapsack were usually excluded from the term "accouterments." For component items see: Belt, Cartridge-Box; Belt, Waist; Belt, Sword, Shoulder; Box,

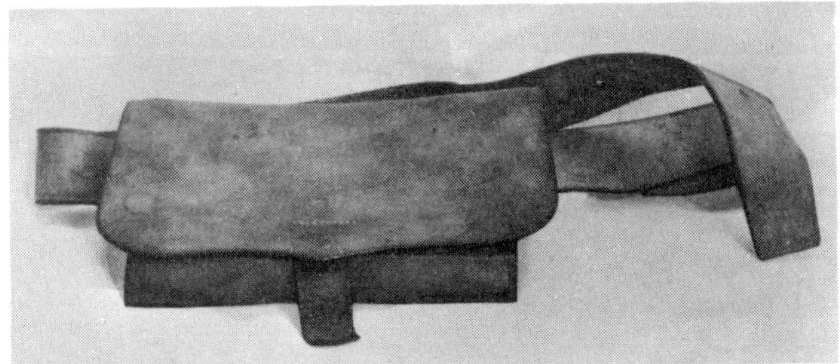

Artillery belt and fuze pouch.

Cap; Box, Cartridge; Scabbard, Bayonet; Sling, Cartridge-Box; and Sling, Gun.

ACCOUTERMENTS, ARTILLERY. (See also ARTILLERY). For items common to all arms, see *ACCOUTERMENTS, INFANTRY.* Artillery accouterments were much more varied than in either the infantry or cavalry since artillerymen had to carry special items for servicing their cannon. Most artillerymen wore a leather waist belt on which were carried a short sword or artillery saber, pistol and holster, cap box, and a fuze pouch. An artilleryman also carried a pendulum hausse and wore a gunner's haversack over his shoulder.

ACCOUTERMENTS, CAVALRY. Cavalry accouterments consisted of two belts and the articles (excluding weapons) attached to them. To the waist belt (saber belt) was attached a cartridge box for carbine ammunition, a pistol box for revolver ammunition, and a cap box; also the saber in its scabbard and the revolver in its holster. To the carbine sling (or belt) was attached, by a swivel, the carbine.

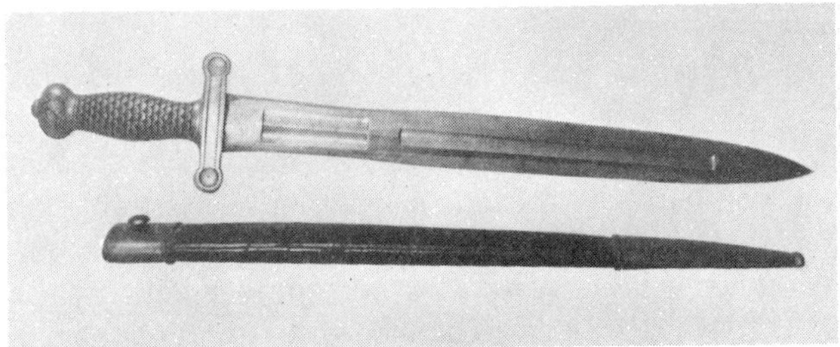

Artillery short sword.

Artillery gunner's haversack.

CARTRIDGE BOX. Some cavalry used the *Blakeslee Cartridge Box* (Patent No. 45,469), patented December 20, 1864, by Erastus Blakeslee, Plymouth, Conn. This box contained one or more removable tubes filled with fixed ammunition, by which a magazine arm like Spencer's could be replenished or the cartridges could be gotten out singly. A side pouch was attached for other ammunition.

MANN'S ACCOUTERMENTS. These were designed to replace the earlier cavalry accouterments, but only came into limited use late in the war. This new equipment combined the cartridge box, pistol box, and cap box in one unit, and enabled the trooper to carry

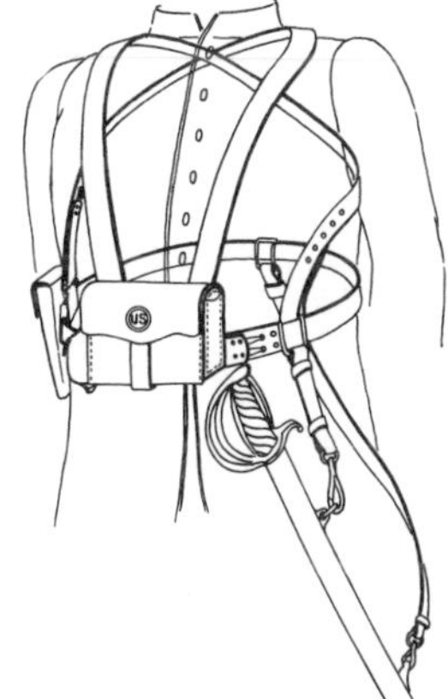

Mann's accouterments. (National Archives)

more than double the amount of ammunition held by the old boxes. It transferred, by two broad belts, the weight from the man's waist to his shoulders. Unfortunately this improved type of equipment was never generally adopted; therefore many cavalrymen, using the old equipment, suffered rupture, hemorrhoids, weak back, and diarrhea from the weight of the ammunition and heavy arms attached to the waist.

Confederate belt and buckle. Imported through the blockade. (Drawing by Mike McAfee)

ACCOUTERMENTS, CONFEDERATE. Since the Confederacy was short of leather it was necessary to import leather equipments and also to find substitute material. One of the substitutes was prepared cotton cloth, stitched together in three or four thicknessess. Instead of brass, lead and wood were used. (See Confederate Makers)

Belts. Two types of Confederate belts are illustrated, one of them being imported from England.

Cap Box. Confederate cap boxes are very rare, especially those marked CS, like that shown in the accompanying photograph. Made similar to the U.S. cap box, it shows high-quality craftsmanship, may possibly have been manufactured in England but more likely was made in the South. Has an impressed CS in an oval cartouche. Cap boxes of this type are susceptible of being forged, but such fakes are easily distinguishable. Note the squarish appearance of the flap on the authentic one illustrated. Almost identical to the US type, but has a different design bearing the CS.

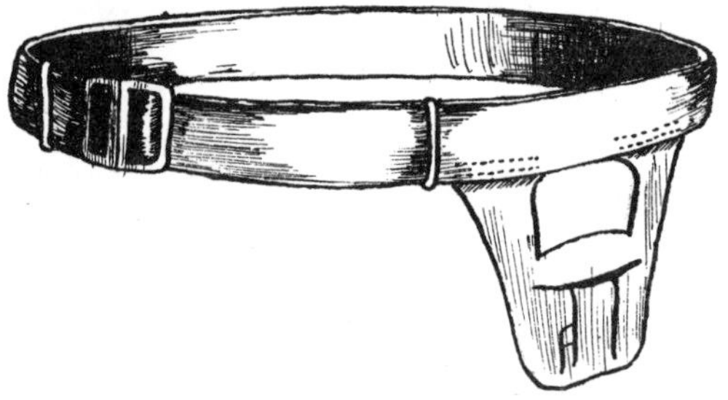

Confederate artillery belt. (Drawing by Mike McAfee)

Confederate cap box or pouch, made similar to U.S. Shows high quality craftsmanship, may possibly have been manufactured in England but more likely in the South. Impressed design "CS" in oval cartouche.

Cartridge Box. Many cartridge boxes used by Confederates were imported from England as part of the equipments used with Enfield muskets and rifles. Shown here is such a box. There is also illustrated an original Confederate-manufactured pouch for infantry, with the original cross shoulder strap. It has generally the same proportions as the U.S. issue but the leather is of different quality and it is extremely rough on the inside. The outside is smooth black leather with the original impressed oval design CS. The letters themselves are impressed in the leather as differentiated from the U.S. model, in which the U.S. seems to stand out slightly. This Confederate box also has a lead fastening button. The original wide-stitched, black waterproofed-linen cross shoulder-strap is still affixed. It shows a spot where once there was a circular plate, now missing.

Confederate cap pouch with different impressed design but also bears "CS" lettering. Almost identical to U.S. type. (Norm Flayderman)

ACCOUTERMENTS, INFANTRY. Consisted of a cartridge-box belt, to which were attached the following; cartridge-box sling, cartridge box, cap box, bayonet scabbard, and canteen (not an accouterment). Sergeants and musicians wore a waist belt. Noncommissioned officers wore a sword shoulder belt.

Bayonet Scabbard. There were two infantry bayonet scabbards:

Above are five of a series of photos made for the Quartermaster, U.S. Army to illustrate clothing and equipment of the Civil War and postwar period. Upper left, artillery private with infantry equipment; upper right, Ordnance sergeant with miscellaneous arms and equipment; lower left, infantry corporal with infantry equipment; center, cavalry accouterments, Spencer carbine, and sling; lower right, artillery short sword worn by artillery sergeant. (Smithsonian Institution)

Enfield cartridge box, dated 1861.

Rare Confederate cartridge box, for infantry. (Norm Flayderman)

Emerson Bayonet Scabbard (Patent No. 36,209). Patented August 19, 1862 by J. E. Emerson, Trenton, N. J. "As a new article of manufacture (Emerson patented) an angular bayonet scabbard, constructed of steel."

Gaylord Bayonet Scabbard (Patent No. 28,269). Patented May, 1860 by Emerson Gaylord, Chicopee, Mass.

Cap Box. Four types of containers or holders for percussion caps were in use by the infantry:

Harvey Cap Box (Patent No. 43,497). Patented July 12, 1864 by Thomas Harvey, Baltimore, Md. This cap box involved the use of an annular cap holder freely movable within a circular or cylindrical case, with teeth on its interior surface, thus permitting the caps to come in succession opposite the ejection opening in the case.

Lamb Cap Box (Patent No. 40,487). Patented November 3, 1863 by Thomas Lamb, Hamilton, Mich. A "cap holder," consisting of two notched revolving plates joined at their centers, with the portions of plate between the notches being flexible and forming studs on which the caps were placed.

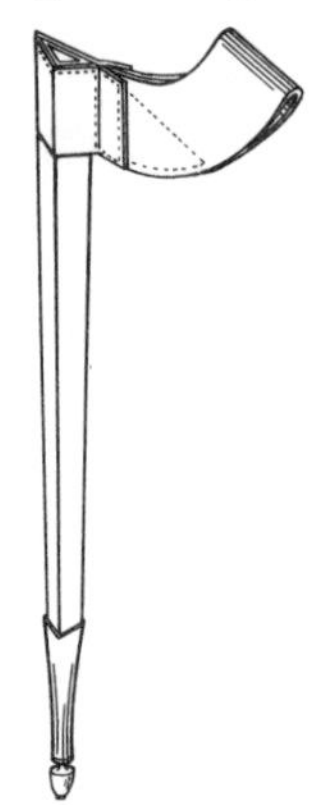

Gaylord bayonet scabbard. (National Archives)

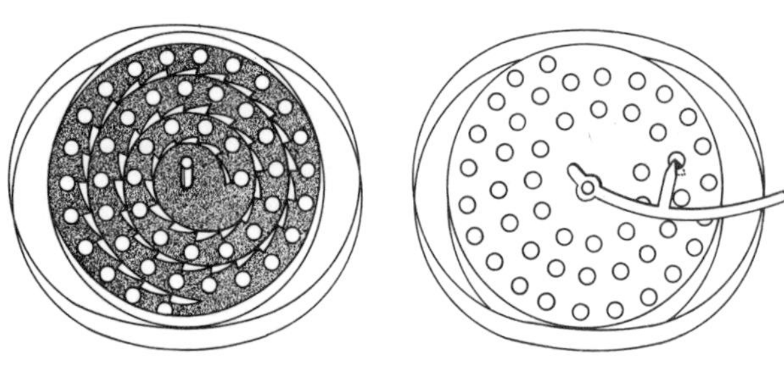

Warren's cap box.

Pickett Percussion Cap Holder (Patent No. 47[illegible]). Patented April 4, 1865 by Rufus S. Pickett, New Haven, Conn. The caps were arranged in a row around the interior of an oblong box upon an endless belt extended between a small pulley and a ratchet wheel. The ratchet wheel was revolved by means of a thumb dog passing through the back of the box, so as to drive forward one cap at every movement of the dog.

Warren Cap Box (Patent No. 41,655). Patented February 16, 1864 by J. T. Warren, Stafford, N. Y. This invention involved a spirally revolving disc within a case operated by a small lever, which by a ratchet movement brought the percussion caps in succession

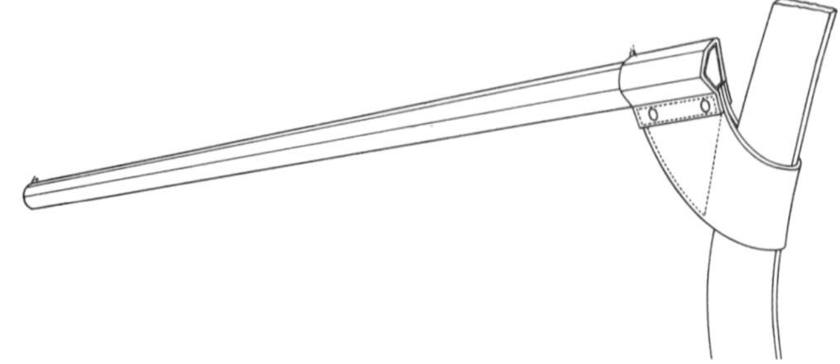

Emerson bayonet scabbard. (National Archives)

Bennett's cartridge box. (National Archives)

opposite an opening where, by means of a spring, a cap was thrown out into a cup-shaped mouth so as to enable it to be readily seized by the hand of the soldier.

Cartridge Box. Eleven different types of patented cartridge boxes were in use by the infantry, as follows:

Bennett Cartridge Box (Patent No. 37,485). Patented January 27, 1863 by Augustus A. Bennett, Cincinnati, Ohio. The cover opened automatically through the use of one or more springs "suitably located."

Bush Cartridge Box (Patent No. 37,216). Patented December 23, 1862 by Francis Bush, Boston, Mass. A metallic box containing the cartridges was placed in

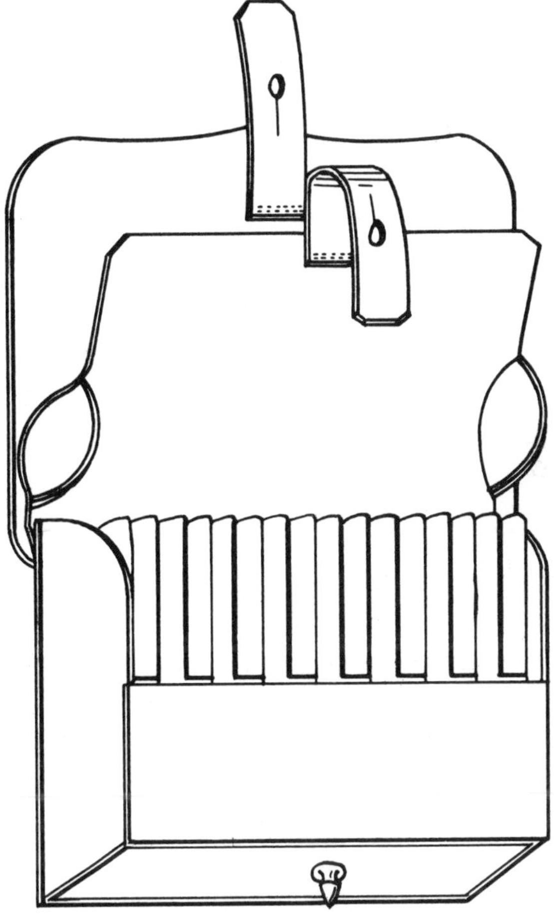
Smith cartridge box. (National Archives)

the cartridge box. The box was open at the top only, thus providing the box with one or more sliding boxes resting on the bottom of the main box.

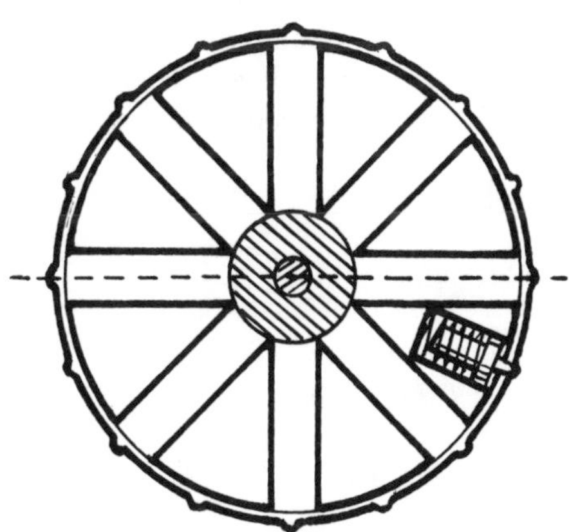
Domis' cartridge box. (National Archives)

Domis Cartridge Box (Patent No. 34,820). Patented April 1, 1862 by Adam Domis, New York, N. Y. This cartridge box had a cylindrical revolving case provided with a series of chambers to receive cartridges, and equipped with a spring strap enabling the soldier to stop the revolving case at the desired interval.

Hirschbuhl Cartridge Box. (Patent No. 34,423). Patented February 18, 1862 by J. J. Hirschbuhl, Louisville, Ky. Compartments were arranged within an outer case for carrying the different articles of ammunition, including a compartment for a powder flask. Separate boxes were attached to one side by hinges, opening outwards to hold bullets, percussion caps, and balls.

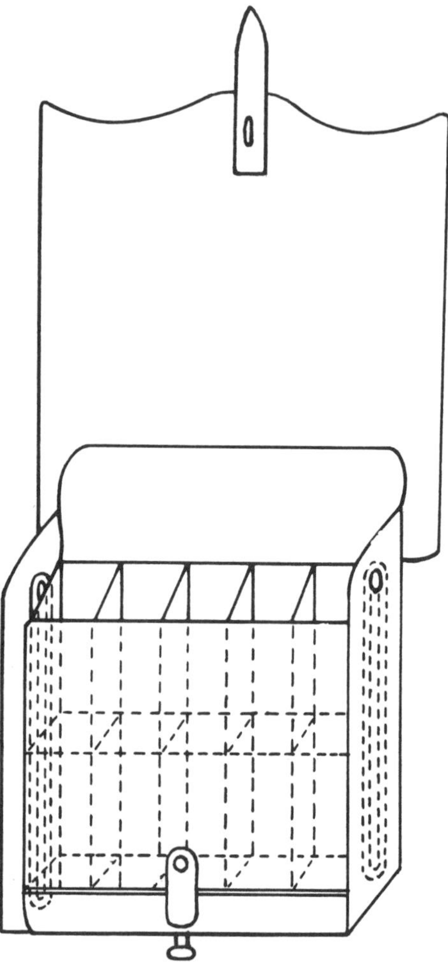

Warren's cartridge box. (National Archives)

Nonregulation or Militia Cartridge Boxes (see Militia Equipments).

Pease Cartridge Box (Patent No. 50,730). Patented October 31, 1865 by John Pease, Boston, Mass. In this invention, the cartridge box was provided with a compartment at the bottom, opening at the sides and covered by protecting flaps for the purpose of conveniently holding bullet patches, swabs, or cloths, oil bottle, etc.; and also with a cap pouch in front.

Smith Cartridge Box (Patent No. 31,680). Patented March 12, 1861 by J. S. Smith, Brooklyn, N. Y. The case of the cartridge box was constructed in a series of

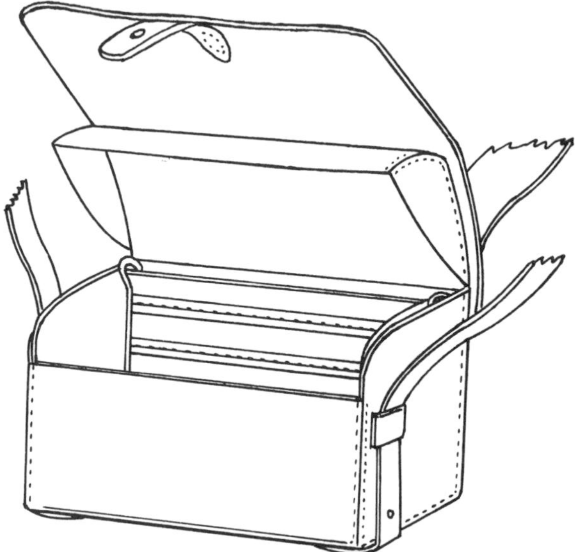

Weston's cartridge box. (National Archives)

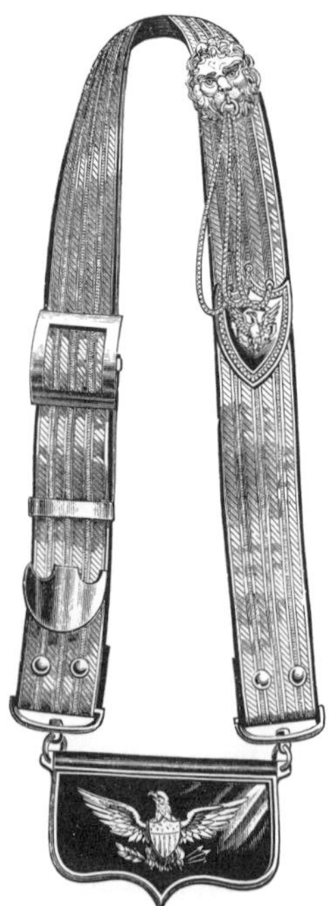

Militia equipments—officer's belt and cartridge box. (Norm Flayderman)

Militia equipments—belt, box, scabbard. (Norm Flayderman)

two vertical tubes of sufficient height to receive two cartridges, one on top of the other.

Warren Cartridge Box (Patent No. 43,373). Patented June 28, 1864 by J. T. Warren, Stafford, N. Y. The inner tin cartridge box had two compartments, one above the other, each being subdivided. When the upper part was emptied, the case could be rotated or turned upside down by means of two pivots on the

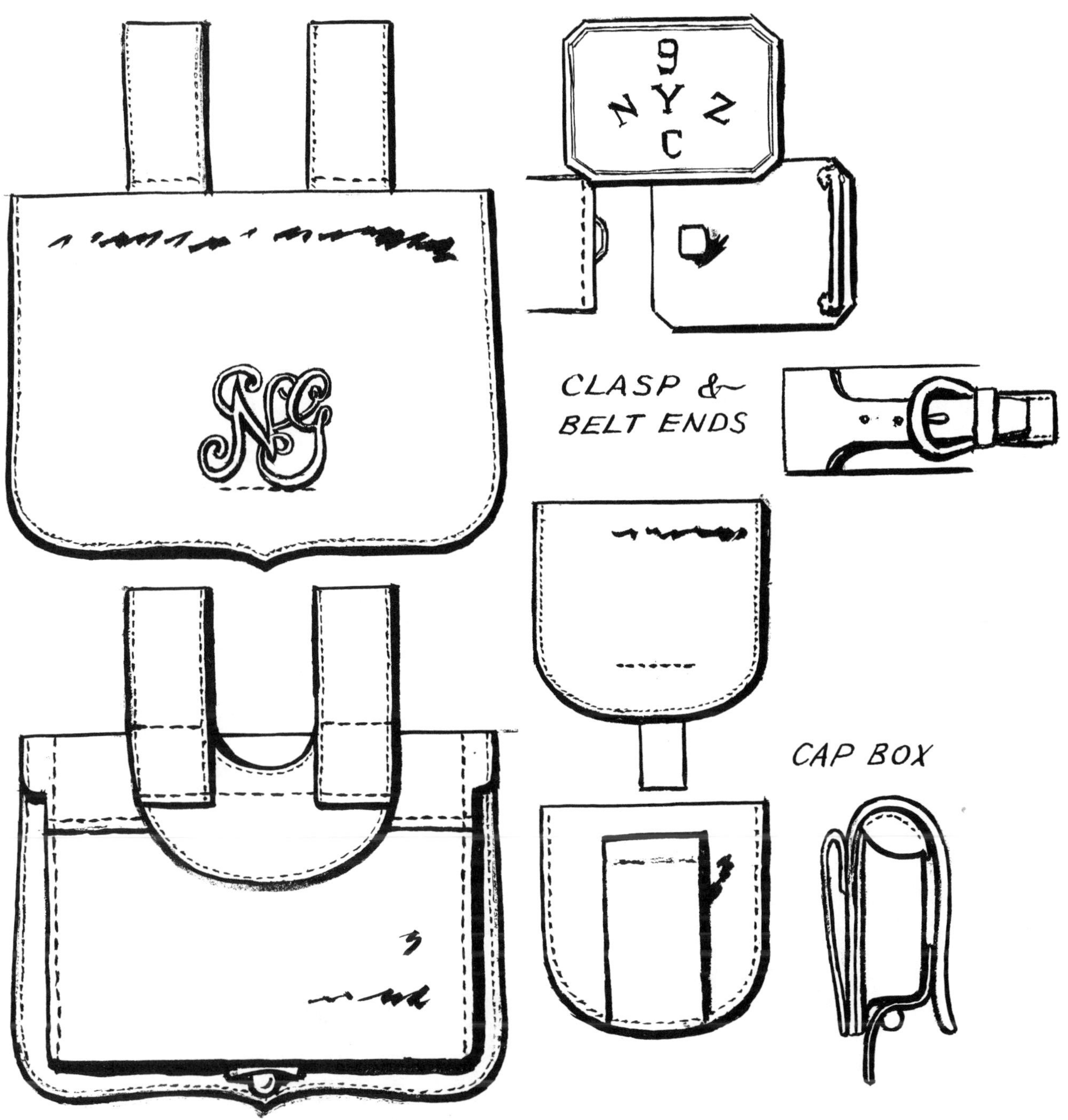

CARTRIDGE BOX - SINGLE TIN-TOP IN 4 SECTIONS

Equipments of Hawkins' Zouaves, worn by Sergeant Samuel L. Malcolm, Co. C, 9th N.Y. Inf. Author's collection. (Drawings by Robert L. Miller)

leather box and two slots by the tin case, without detaching it from the leather box.

Warren and Chesebrough Cartridge Box (Patent No 44,999). Patented November 8, 1864 by J. T. Warren, Stafford, N.Y., and R. A. Chesebrough, New York, N.Y. A circular revolving box with a suitable circular case similar to those commonly employed for holding percussion caps, and provided with chambers for holding both cartridges and caps.

Weston Cartridge Box (Patent No. 43,539). Patented July 12, 1864 by Horace S. Weston, Akron, Ohio. This invention involved the arranging of a horizontal series of sharp blades at the back of the cartridge box. These blades actuated by a spring block, cut the paper ends of the cartridge rows.

White Cartridge Box (Patent No. 46,411). Patented February 14, 1865 by Martin V. B. White, Troy, N.Y. This cartridge box was narrow, elongated, and curved, adapted to the side of the soldier. The box was provided with an apron at its bottom, upon which the cartridges were placed standing in one or more rows. By means of a coiled spring the cartridges were constantly pulled forward, so as to always present one at the front opening of the box.

Wilson Cartridge Box. (Patent No. 26,402). Patented December 6, 1859 by John W. Wilson, Washington, D.C. Had a cartridge-box fastening composed of a hinged lever and spring. The spring served to hold the lever open or closed.

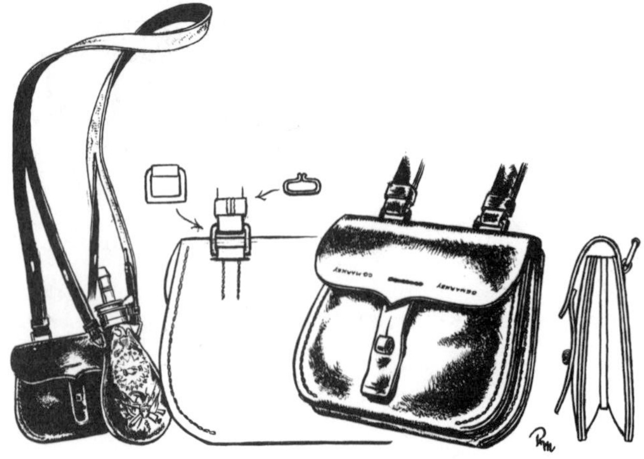

Rifleman's pouch and flask. (Robert L. Miller)

Mann's Accouterments (Patent No. 40,849). Patented December 8, 1863, by W. D. Mann, Detroit, Michigan, this improvement was made by slinging the accouterments so that the cartridge box was worn in front, thus acting as a counterbalance to the other accouterments.

Militia Equipments. Various state militia units had their own accouterments, usually nonregulation, and designed for dress affairs such as ceremonies and official social occasions.

Ninth New York Infantry (Hawkins' Zouaves) Equipments. Those shown in the drawing were used by Sergeant Samuel L. Malcolm, Company C, 9th New York Infantry. He enlisted May 4, 1861, and fought at Big Bethel, Roanoke Island, and Antietam. His uniform is shown in the section on uniforms and clothing.

Rifleman's Flask and Pouch. The *U.S. Ordnance Regulations* for 1834 provided for copper powder flasks and pouches for riflemen. Although these accouterments became obsolete in 1857 it is probable that some were used in the early part of the war. These accouterments were last mentioned in the 1850 *Ordnance Manual* but omitted in the 1861 edition.

Rifleman's Waist Belt for Sword Bayonet. The illustration shows the waist belt for riflemen armed either with the 1841 Mississippi Rifle or the Model 1855

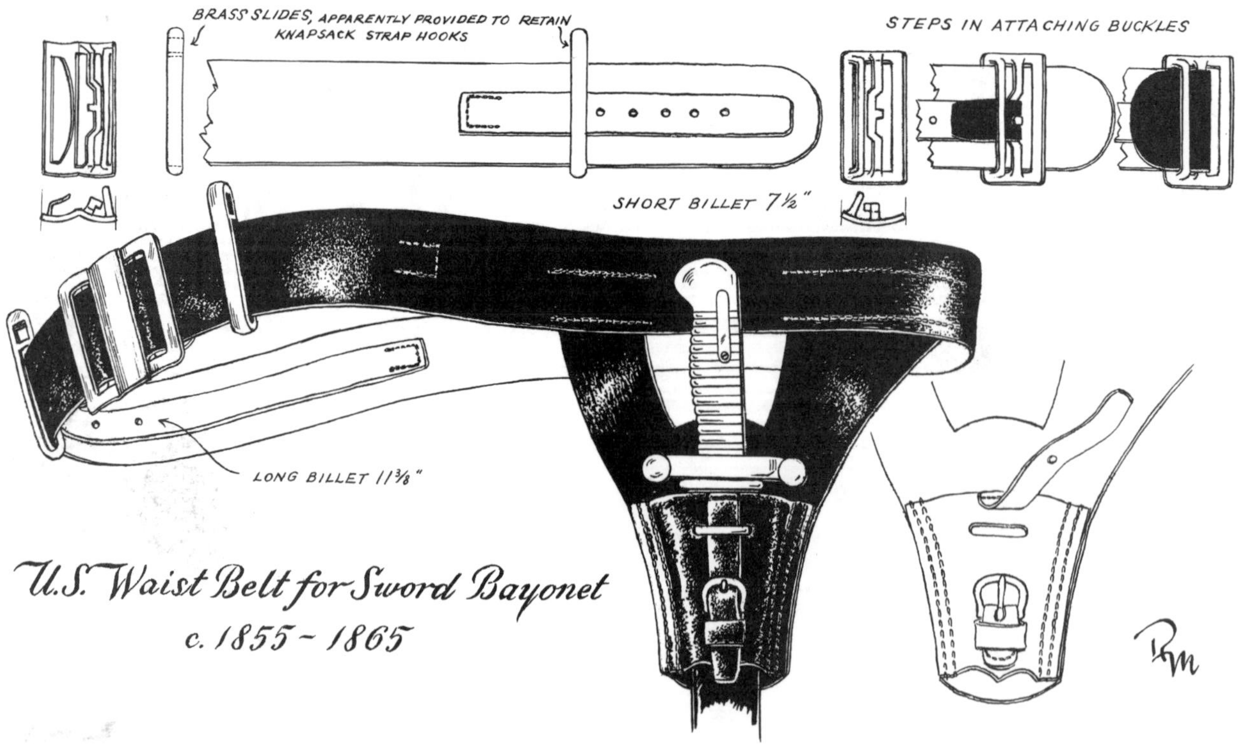

Rifleman's waist belt. (Robert L. Miller)

Manufacture of ammunition. Filling cartridges at the arsenal at Watertown, Mass. (Harpers)

Manufacture of artillery ammunition. (Harpers)

Naval accouterments. Note the pistols, cutlasses, and cartridge boxes. Note also the Marine's accouterments. (National Archives)

Rifle. It has been definitely established that some of these belts were used in the field during the war, since the buckles have been found on Civil War battlefields.

ACCOUTERMENTS, U.S. MARINE CORPS. The following descriptions of Marine Corps accouterments are extracted from U.S.M.C. Regulations.

Belt. All enlisted men shall wear white waist belts of the French pattern, with the French clasp and knapsack sliding slings; the cartridge box to be attached to the belt by a frog, also sliding on the belt: Non-commissioned Officers wearing swords, as also Musicians, will wear their swords in a sliding frog.

Drum sling. White webbing, provided with a brass drum-stick carriage.

Knapsack. Of cow-skin (black), and to be made and slung, according to pattern in the Quartermaster's Department, Headquarters.

Haversack. Of same material, size, and form, as those issued to the United States Army.

Canteen. Same as used in United States Army.

Musket sling. The Musket Slings to be of black leather; muskets will not be put into the hands of troops without the slings.

The Knapsack, Haversack, Canteens, and Musket Slings will be served out on charge, and receipted for by an officer, as are arms and other equipments. Knapsacks, haversacks, and canteens will be kept in the store-room on shipboard, and put in the hands of the troops when occasion requires.

ACCOUTERMENTS, U.S. NAVY. Naval accouterments varied depending on the service required of their wearers. In the Civil War, sailors were employed in amphibious or landing operations, where they fought as infantry (as at Fort Fisher), and at other times as gun crews on men of war. Boarding axes, cutlasses, and pikes were issued to such forces as well as to crews of vessels who might be used in boarding operations. (See *Boarding Axe and Holder, Swords and Sabers,* and *Boarding Pike.*)

Belt. Made of buff leather, 47 inches long, 2 inches wide, with a japanned black metal buckle.

Cap Box. Identical with the infantry cap box except that the letters USN are stamped on the flap.

Cartridge box, Navy (Musket). Black bridle leather, similar in size and shape to the U.S. Infantry cartridge box, but equipped with a single wide carrying loop and stamped USN on the flap.

Cartridge Box (Revolver). Similar to the Navy cartridge box except smaller (5½ inches long and 4 inches high), and furnished with a tin liner for revolver ammunition. Has a pouch for caps sewn on the box under the flap, marked "Navy Yard, Phila. 1863."

Fuze Box. Black leather, 4½ inches wide, 3½ inches tall, and 2 inches deep. Contains a tin box with hinged cover. Marked on flap "Navy Yard, Phila. 1862."

Four-wheel ambulance. Zouaves drilling in removing the wounded. Note officer apparently reaching for the wine bottle in the ambulance (see Bottle, Liquor). (Library of Congress)

AIGUILLETTE (cord and tassel). An ornamental tagged cord worn on the uniform. In the Federal service a red aiguillette was worn as part of the dress uniform of light artillerymen. (See Uniforms and Clothing—Light Artillery uniform).

AMBROTYPE (See Pictures).

AMBULANCE. The standard Army ambulance was a stout spring wagon having a leather-covered stuffed seat running the length of the vehicle on each side. Hinged to the inner sides of these seats was a third upholstered seat which could be let down so that three patients could lie down lengthwise of the vehicle. In

Aiguillette. (Norm Flayderman)

Navy gun crew. Note the "powder monkey" with right hand ready to remove top of pass box. (National Archives)

Navy accouterments. Left to right: cap box, fuze box, pistol cartridge box, musket cartridge box.

the rear of each ambulance was a water keg, and in front, under the driver's seat, was a supply of beef stock and medicines. On each outer side of the ambulance was hung a canvas-covered litter or stretcher. The whole vehicle was covered with white canvas supported on bows.

Two years before the war a War Department board had tested, in New Mexico, two-wheeled and four-wheeled ambulances. Both were favorably reported on, but the two-wheeled vehicle was considered the best for badly wounded men. During the war, however, the four-wheeled ambulance was found to be the best for field service. The two-wheelers were mainly used for transportation of senior officers for pleasure in garrison or in the field when they were incapacitated for horseback riding. Especially in Washington could one see ranking officers riding about in these "official" cabs. Medical wagons were also used in the field. The allotment of ambulances, as prescribed by General Meade for the Army of the Potomac in the fall of 1863, was three per regiment of infantry, two per cavalry regiment, and one per artillery battery.

McKEAN AMBULANCE (Patent No. 44,643). Patented October 11, 1861 by Edwin R. McKean, Washington, D.C. McKean's patent description emphasized the arrangement of fans to be actuated by the motion of the carriage; also, certain conveniences such as a water supply for the patients; ventilation; and stretchers to run on rollers so the patients could be raised and moved into the vehicle with ease and comfort.

AMMUNITION, ARTILLERY. See PROJECTILES.

AMMUNITION BOX. Made of white pine boards, dovetailed and nailed together, and finished with wooden handles nailed to the ends of the box. The lid was fastened with six 1.75-inch screws. These ammunition boxes were painted different colors to indicate the kind of cartridges they contained. Each box was marked on each end with the number and kind of cartridges, and on the inside of the cover with the place and date of manufacture.

Cartridges were packed in the ammunition boxes, 1,000 per box. Five tiers of bundles of cartridges were laid flat in a single row along each side of the box, the rest were placed on edge, the caps alternately up and down. Blank cartridges were packed 2,000 to a box.

MUSKET, RIFLE, AND CARBINE AMMUNITION BOX. The ammunition box shown here has the following dimensions: length 14¼ inches, width 10 inches, depth (with cover) 7 inches. Marked: "1,000 Ball Cartridges Sharps Carbine Cal. .52 1864."

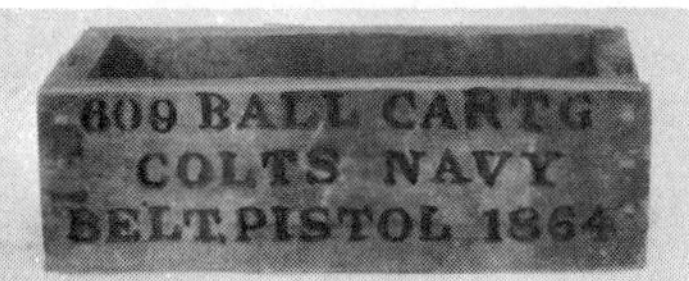

Ammunition box. Held 600 rounds of Colt pistol ammunition.

PISTOL AMMUNITION Box. Dimensions: length 13¼ inches, width 5⅝ inches, depth (without cover) 4⅛ inches; marked: "600 Ball Cartg. Colts Navy Belt Pistol 1864" on one side. On the reverse side of the box is the marking: "Watervliet Arsenal."

Ammunition boxes. Sergeant Thomas Lawrence, Co. F, 22nd N.Y. Infantry (left), and an assistant, preparing to issue ammunition for the regiment's caliber .577 Enfields. (National Archives)

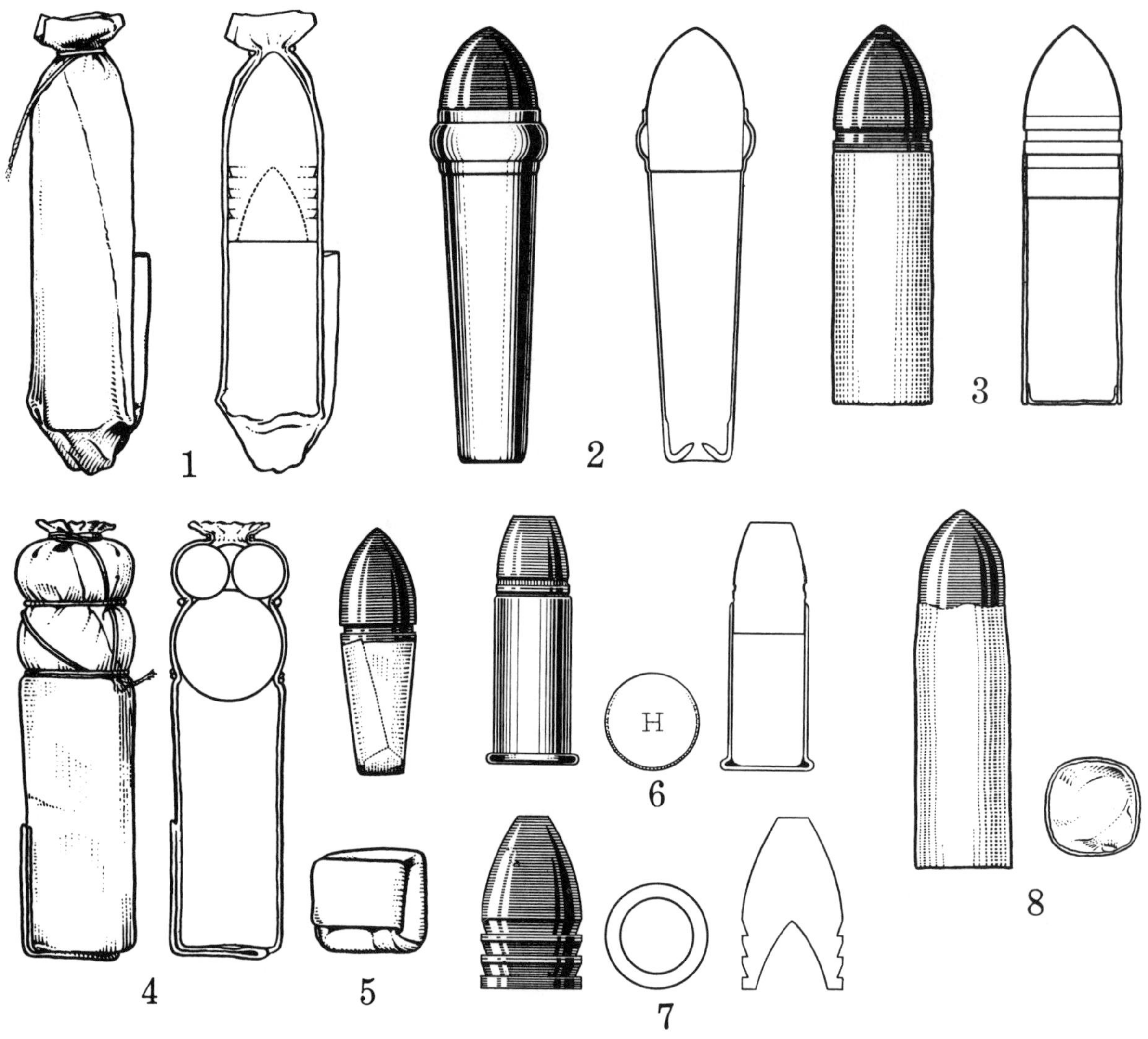

Small arms ammunition. (Herschel C. Logan)

1. Caliber .58 paper cartridge
2. Caliber .54 Burnside brass case
3. Caliber .52 Sharps linen case
4. Caliber .69 buck and ball paper cartridge
5. Caliber .44 Colt revolver paper cartridge
6. Caliber .44 Henry flat ball with copper case
7. Caliber .58 Minié ball
8. Caliber .54 Starr linen cartridge

AMMUNITION, SMALL ARMS. The large number of calibers used during the war greatly intensified the problem of supply. An ordnance expert said: "Our muskets and carbines range in caliber from .40 to .61. Twenty different calibers of ammunition, from .44 to .69 were furnished the Burnside expedition; and, lest one transport carrying all of one caliber should be lost, each vessel had to be supplied with an assorted cargo made of certain proportions of the whole. In 1861, when every tyro knew that a breech-loader was best—in fact nobody but an idiot or an officer of our Ordnance Department would ever decide otherwise—the Chief of Ordnance had stated that 'a Harper's Ferry smooth bore muzzle-loading gun, with buck and ball, was the best arm that could be placed in the hands of a soldier,' and asserted he would have no such gun as a breech-loader in service because 'it would require a mule to carry the ammunition for each soldier—it would be shot away so fast!' "

BUCK AND BALL. The caliber .69 muskets used a round ball, or a round ball with three buckshot called "buck and ball." This was effective only up to 200 yards and as soon as the smoothbores could be rifled the Minié bullet was used instead. However, buck and ball cartridge boxes have been found at Spotsylvania, showing that they were used as late as 1864.

EXPENDITURES. Troops advancing to meet the enemy were issued 20 extra rounds of ammunition per man, carried in the pockets. But if there were a few severe marches before battle, these last 20 rounds were often thrown away particularly by new men, to lessen the load they already were carrying. This statement is supported by many reports of major engagements during which regiments and even brigades were withdrawn because of an early expenditure of their ammunition.

At Murfreesboro it was estimated that it took 27 cannon shots or 145 bullets to hit one Confederate, whereas at Gainesville, Va., in August 1862, an average of 100 bullets were required to hit each Confederate.

Capt. Samuel Fiske, of the 14th Connecticut of Hancock's II Corps noted the contrast between Federal and Confederate troops in use of ammunition. Fiske, later killed at The Battle of the Wilderness, commented that the Federals "have been taught to load and fire as rapidly as possible, three or four times a minute; they go into the business with all fury, every man vying with his neighbor as to the number of cartridges he can ram into his piece, and spit out of it. The smoke arises in a minute or two, so you can see nothing where to aim. By and by the guns get heated, and won't go off, and the cartridges begin to give out. Meanwhile, the rebels, lying quietly a hundred or two yards in front, crouching on the ground or behind trees, answer our fire very leisurely, as they get a chance for a good aim (about one shot to our three hundred), hitting about as many as we do, and waiting for the mild tornado of ammunition to pass over their heads; and when our burst of fighting is pretty much over, they have only commenced. If I had charge of a regiment or brigade, I'd put every man in the guard-house who could be proved to have fired more than twenty rounds in any one battle. I wouldn't let them carry more than their cartridge-box full (forty rounds)."

MINIÉ BALL. The Minié bullet was the contribution of Captain Claude Etienne Minié of the French Army, who in 1848 perfected a bullet which revolutionized warfare. The U.S. Army adopted the principle in 1855. The bullet was the usual elongated shape but was hollowed at the base for about one-third of its length. When the gun was fired, the gasses forced the lead into the riflings of the barrel. This bullet was more effective than the old caliber .69 ammunition because instead of the soldier having to insert the powder and ball separately into the barrel, the Minié bullet and powder were encased together in a paper cover which was inserted into the barrel at one count. The Minié bullet, used extensively in the caliber .58 rifle muskets, had great smashing power. For example, at Cold Harbor, the First Sergeant of Company A, 2d New Hampshire Infantry was wounded in the right arm by a Minié bullet which shattered the bone into 23 pieces.

SPECIAL TYPES OF BULLETS

Explosive Bullets. The employment of explosive bullets in warfare was widely discussed from an ethical point of view, particularly after the Civil War. Both Union and Confederate soldiers claimed the other used explosive bullets in battle on various occasions. The Medical Department, U.S. Army listed 130 cases of wounds attributed to explosive bullets. The records of the Ordnance Office, U.S. Army, show that 33,350 "explosive bullets" or "musket shells" were issued to the troops in 1863. Over 10,000 rounds were abandoned on the field for want of transportation. It is probable that they fell into the hands of the Confederates, accounting in a measure for the 130 wounded referred to above. No doubt wounds were erroneously attributed to explosive bullets, since under certain conditions the conventional bullet was capable of inflicting extensive bone and tissue damage, owing to its tumbling in the air and also compressing the body fluids with a disruptive effect.

No doubt some Federal troops did use explosive bullets. In June, 1863, they were issued to the 2d New Hampshire Infantry. The regimental history notes that on June 8 "Forty rounds of cartridges per man were distributed this morning. The balls were called musket shells—an explosive bullet—and woe to the Johnny that stops one!"

The regiment marched on to Gettysburg where it soon came under artillery fire. Many men were hit and several cartridge boxes were exploded. A shell struck and burst on the box of a corporal of Company C. The cartridges were driven into his body and exploded, and for 30 seconds the "musket shells" were exploding in his quivering form. Death was mercifully quick. The next moment a fragment of shell exploded the cartridge box of a sergeant. He instantly tore off the box hanging by his side, thus escaping with only a severe wound.

The 2d New Hampshire had its first experience with explosive bullets at Glendale on the Peninsula, when

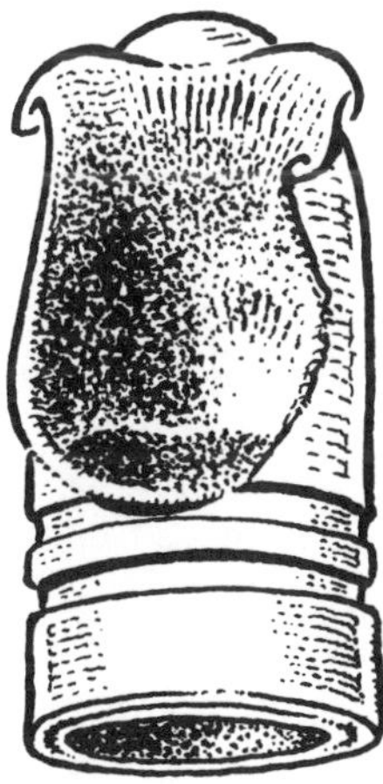

Explosive bullet from Seven Days' Battle before Richmond 1862. (Herschel C. Logan)

their opponents used them. The regiment was in line of battle about dusk when enemy pickets began firing at the men. "For a time the men were a good bit puzzled to account for sharp reports which were heard in every direction—to the rear, overhead—everywhere. In connection with the deepening gloom, the manifestation was decidedly uncanny. The mystery was solved, however, when a bullet, cutting across the breast of Captain Sayles, suddenly exploded, inflicting a painful lacerated wound."

Explosive bullet. Cross section. (Herschel C. Logan)

The Gardiner explosive bullet was a cylindro-conoidal projectile of lead, made in two sizes: the larger, of caliber .58, weighing 451 grains; the smaller, of caliber .54, weighing 363 grains. Within the interior was placed an accurately fitting acorn-shaped chamber filled with fulminate, communicating with a 1¼ sec. time fuze, which was exposed to the charge at the rear of the missile. The fuze was ignited by the discharge of the piece. The bursting charge was sufficient to rend the bullet and transform it into a jagged dangerous missile. If the bullet penetrated the body before exploding, its effects were still more destructive.

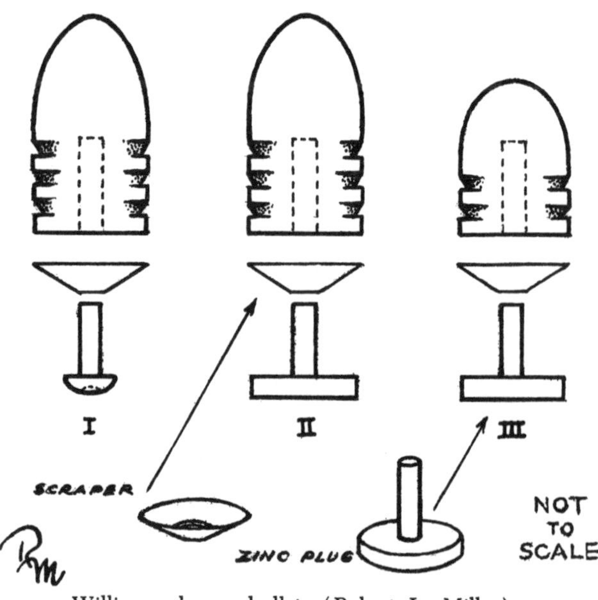

Williams cleaner bullet. (Robert L. Miller)

Shaler Bullet (Reuben Shaler's Patent, August 12, 1862). This unique 3-piece bullet was issued in 1863 on an experimental basis. There were 6 variants of the Shaler bullet. To date five types have been found, of which the one shown here is the scarcest. The well-known expert, Herschel C. Logan, in a letter to the author, said: "The Shaler bullet was to serve as sort of a 'buck and ball' idea . . . that is, it was hoped that the three pieces would separate and fly off towards the target . . . but with a more pronounced velocity. In actual practice it didn't work too well and so not too many of them were made . . . hence the top rarity today."

Williams Bullet (Patent No. 37,145). This bullet was patented December 9, 1862 by Elijah D. Williams of Philadelphia, Pennsylvania. Called the "Williams elongated bullet," it consisted of the combination expand-bullet of a headed pin and a concave expanding disc, the disc having its concave side against the base of the bullet and the pin entering the cavity thereof, and operating to produce the flattening of the disc by which it was caused to expand against the walls of and enter the rifling of the gun.

TABULATION OF TYPES

Muzzle-loading weapons

Type	*Caliber*
Round ball	.69
Buck and ball	.69
Buckshot	.69
Blank	.69
Hall carbine	.64
Pistol	.54
Conical ball	.69
Minié ball	.58
Williams' Patent	.574
Shaler Patent	.574
Confederate	.577
Enfield	.577
Gardiner's "Explosive"	.54 .58

Revolvers

Type	*Caliber and Model*
Adams	.36
Allen and Wheelock	.44 Army
	.36 Navy
Beal	.44 Army
	.36 Navy
Colt	.44 Army
	.36 Navy
Joslyn	.44

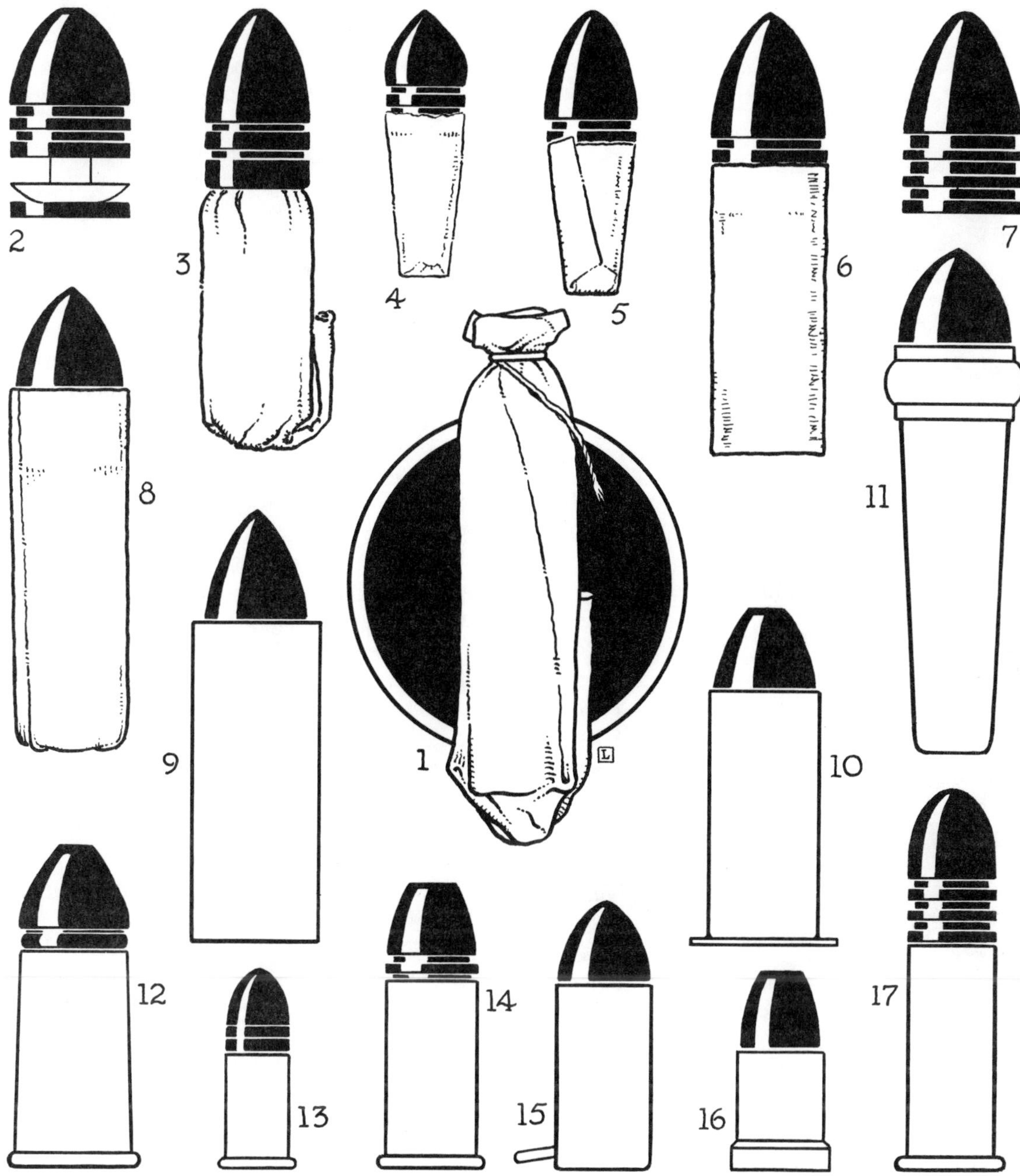

Principal types of small arms ammunition. (Herschel C. Logan)

1. The paper encased .58 caliber Minié ball was the most widely used of all Civil War small arms ammunition.
2. Williams bore-cleaning bullet. One or more was put in every package of .58 caliber ammunition.
3. Confederate .577 caliber with the paper cylinder containing powder inserted in the base of the bullet, rather than around.
4. .36 Colt combustible envelope cartridge for the Colt navy revolver.
5. .44 Combustible envelope cartridge. Used in the .44 caliber revolvers.
6. Most noted of the combustible cartridges was the .52 caliber linen-cased Sharps. Over sixteen million of the cartridges were purchased during the war.
7. Best known bullet of the war was the .58 caliber Minié ball.
8. Brass and paper cased .50 caliber Gallager used in the carbine by that name.
9. .50 caliber rubber-cased Smith. A tiny hole in the base permitted the flash from a percussion cap to ignite the powder charge.
10. The Maynard .50 caliber cartridge had a brass case with a large head, in which was a tiny hole for detonating the powder charge.
11. Most unusual in shape, the .54 caliber Burnside cartridge looked more like a small ice cream cone than a cartridge. It also was separately primed, that is, fired, by a percussion cap.
12. Another widely used cartridge, the No. 56/52 Spencer. The Spencer rifle was one of the first repeating arms to use a self-priming, rimfire cartridge.
13. Though not a martial arm, many of the Smith & Wesson No. 2 army revolvers were carried by men and officers alike. It used this early .32 caliber rimfire cartridge.
14. The Henry rifle, forerunner of the Winchester repeating rifle, used this .44 Henry cartridge. Rimfire with copper case.
15. The imported French Lefaucheux revolvers used this pin-fire cartridge of 12mm caliber.
16. Another foreign revolver imported for use in the war was the French Perrin. Though resembling a rimfire it had an inside primer and was center-fire. Caliber was 12mm.
17. The Remington .46 caliber rimfire cartridge used in the Remington carbine.

Revolvers

Type	*Caliber and Model*
LeFaucheux	12-mm
Perrin	12-mm
Pettingill	{.44 Army .36 Navy}
Prescott	.38 Navy
Rafael	12-mm
Remington	{.44 Army .36 Navy}
Rogers & Spencer	.44
Savage	.36 Navy
Smith & Wesson	.32
Starr	{.44 Army .36 Navy}
Whitney	.36 Navy

Rifles and Carbines

Type	*Caliber*	*Material*
Ball	.50	Copper
Ballard	.46, .54, .56	Copper
Burnside	.54	Brass
Colt	.44, .56	Paper
Cosmopolitan	.52	Linen
Gallagher	.54	Paper
Gibbs	.54	{Paper Linen}
Greene	.54	Paper
Hall (rifle)	.52	Paper
Hall–North	.52	Paper
Henry	.44, .46	Copper
Jenks	.52, .54	Linen
Joslyn	.56	Copper
Lindner	.58	Paper
Maynard	.50	Brass
Merrill	.54	Paper
Palmer	.52	Copper
Remington	.46	Copper
Schroeder	.53	Paper
Sharps	.52	{Paper Linen}
Sharps and Hankins	.52	Copper
Smith	.50	{Paper Rubber}
Spencer	.52, .56	Copper
Starr	.54	Copper
Warner	.50	Copper
Wesson	.44	Copper

ANVIL. Both the Army and the Navy used anvils of the type illustrated. Army units carried in the field both anvils and portable forges, but most of the horseshoeing was done by blacksmiths enlisted as farriers. The anvil shown here is 14 inches long (at top), 6¼ inches high, and weighs 33 pounds. The Navy used anvils for repair work aboard ships. One specimen examined is stamped with an eagle and anchor; it is 19 inches long, 9 inches high, and weighs 95 pounds.

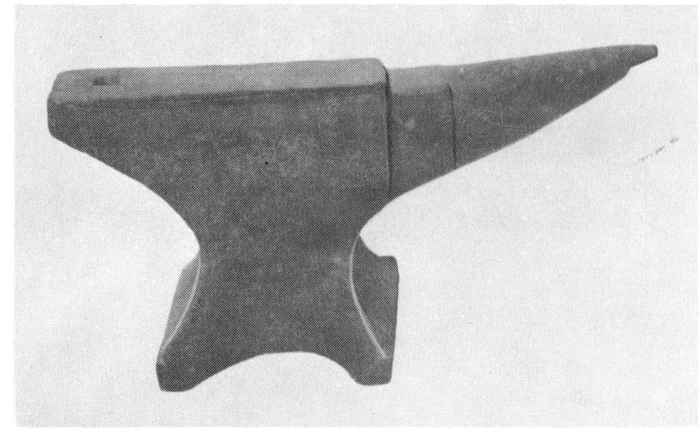

U. S. Army anvil.

APPENDAGES. According to Scott's *Military Dictionary,* the appendages for the Model 1855 Rifle Musket consisted of: Wiper, ball-screw, screw driver, spring vice, tompion, spare cone, tumbler, and wire punch. These appendages were also used for the later model rifle muskets, including the 1861, 1863, and 1864 models. According to Scott, "each soldier should have a screw-driver and a wiper, and each squad of ten a wire and a tumbler punch, and a spring vise." It was forbidden to use other tools in taking arms apart or assembling them. *The Army and Navy Journal* for February 27, 1864, described a gun cleaner, the invention of P. F. Carr, Company "B," 14th Indiana Volunteers. The cleaner consisted of a cylindrical plunger, encased in India rubber, or other soft elastic material, coated with emery. The cleaner was fitted with a screw and nut, by which it could be expanded

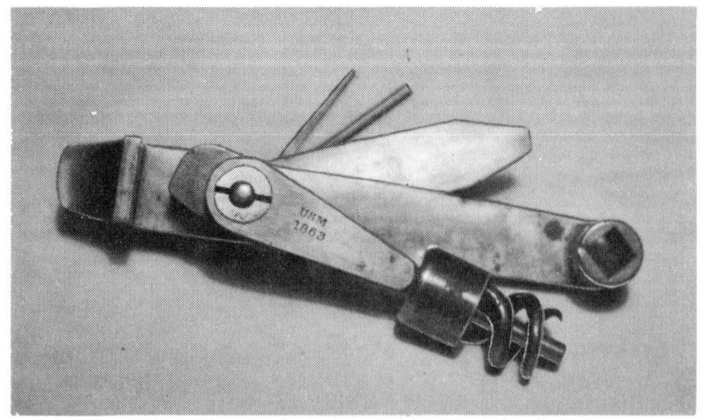

Rare model appendage. Marked "USM-1863," meaning U.S. Model 1863. All parts, marked "USM." Overall length 4 inches. Only two removable pieces are the worm and the ball remover. These are affixed to the end of the ramrod on the gun itself. It has the following tools (contained on the piece itself): Nipple wrench; screwdriver; pick; tumbler punch; large punch, which may be used also as mainspring vise. (Norm Flayderman)

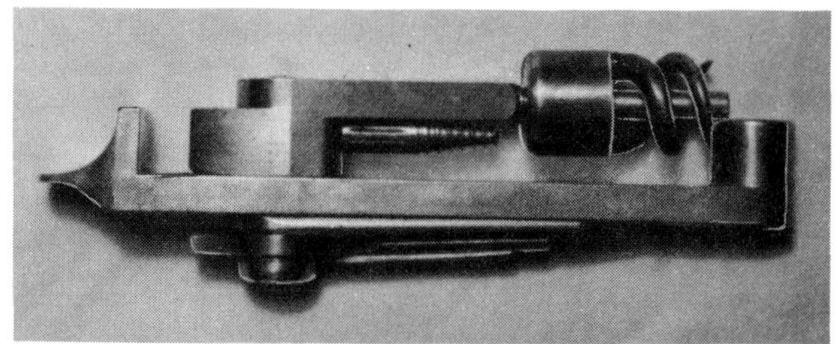

Experimental all-purpose appendage made at Springfield Arsenal for the caliber .58 rifle musket. (Norm Flayderman)

circumferentially to make it fit as tightly as desired in the base of the musket, and was equipped with a screwed socket, by which it is screwed to the ramrod when the gun is being cleaned.

In the illustration is an experimental all-purpose appendage tool made at Springfield Arsenal for the caliber .58 rifle musket. This is the only one of its type that has come to the attention of the author.

Ball Screw (Patent No. 46,220). Patented February 7, 1865 by Arthur de Witzleben, of Washington, D.C. This is a bullet extractor, having two spring jaws with auger-like points. The patentee claimed originality in forming on the inside of these points a projecting edge or screw-like thread. This device more effectively prevented the bullet from slipping from the grasp of the spring jaws.

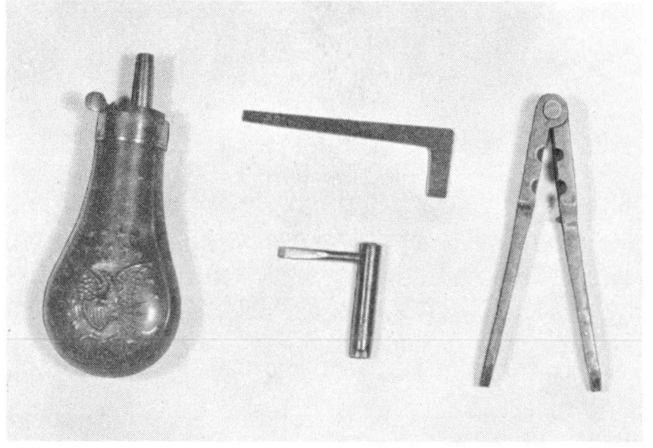

Appendages and accessories. Left, pistol flask; center, top, screwdriver; center, bottom, combination screwdriver and nipple wrench; right, bullet mold.

Carbine Appendage. An all-steel appendage consisting of a screwdriver, bullet mold, and a rear sight screwdriver. Total length, 8¼ inches. Marked 36 on top. There were other types, including one for the Burnside carbine.

Cone Picker. A small pointed wire was issued to the infantry soldier for the purpose of cleaning the cone vent of his musket. (see Accouterments)

Tompion. This is a device for plugging the muzzle of a gun that is not in use.

ARMOR, BODY. Steel breastplates worn by soldiers as protection against small arms fire. Sold by sutlers and commercial firms. Also called "Iron Vests."

ARMS CHEST (Rifle musket). Made of well-seasoned white pine boards 1 inch thick. Inner dimensions: 59.25 inches, width 16 inches; depth 13.25 inches. Capacity: 20 rifle muskets. The Model 1855 rifle was packed in a chest the same as for the rifle muskets but with the following dimensions: Length 50.2 inches; width 17.5 inches; depth 13.5 inches.

Weight of Boxes of Arms and Appendages, Packed

20 muskets	Model 1855		286 lbs.
20 muskets	Model 1855	for sea voyage	301 lbs.
20 muskets	Model 1842		285 lbs.
20 muskets	Model 1842	for sea voyage	300 lbs.
20 rifles	Model 1855		321 lbs.

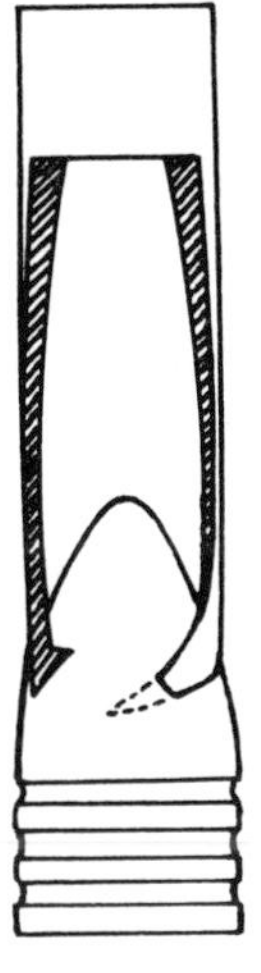

Witzleben's bullet extractor, patent February 7, 1865. (National Archives)

ARTILLERY. Artillery used by land forces during the Civil War may be classified according to its tactical employment as field, garrison, and siege artillery. The most popular fieldpiece was the Napoleon, model 1857, 12-pounder gun-howitzer, which could be fired from 2 to 4 times a minute. Although the Napoleon, a smooth-bore cannon, was very effective at short range, the rifled cannon, because of greater range and accuracy, were especially effective against such large

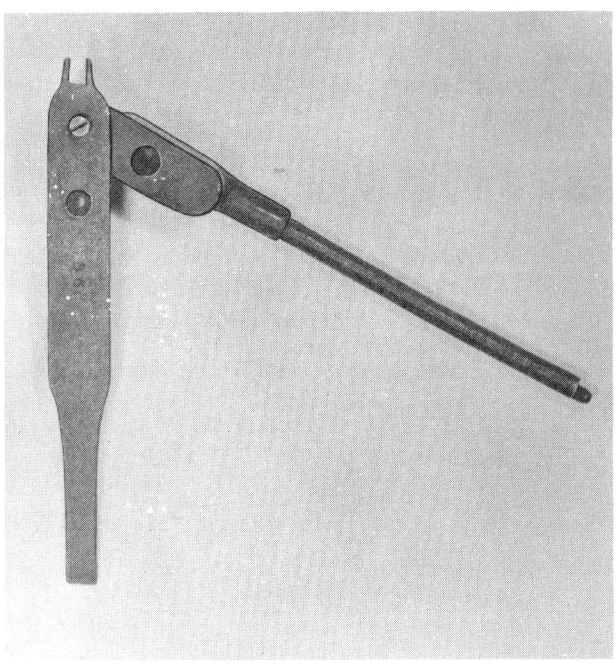

Carbine appendage.

masonry fortifications as Pulaski and Sumter. The most popular rifled cannon were the Parrott and Rodman.

Some breech-loaders were used, most of them imported from England. Among these were the famous Whitworth, as well as the Blakeley and Armstrong.

Field artillery ranged from 6-pounders to 32-pounders in smoothbores and from 2.56 inch Wiard (a 6-pounder) to the 3-inch types.

Siege and garrison artillery ranged from 4.2 inch to 10-inch pieces, while seacoast artillery ranged from 5-inch (the 80-pounder Whitworth rifle) to the 15-inch Columbiad. The largest of the seacoast cannon had a 20-inch bore. However, this monster cannon saw little if any actual service and the largest cannon actually used were probably the 15-inch Columbiad, and such pieces as the 300-pounder Parrott and the 13-inch mortar. Maximum ranges of Civil War siege cannon were: the 80-pounder Whitworth rifle, 7,700 yards; the 10-inch mortar, 4,200 yards; and the 13-inch mortar, 4,300 yards.

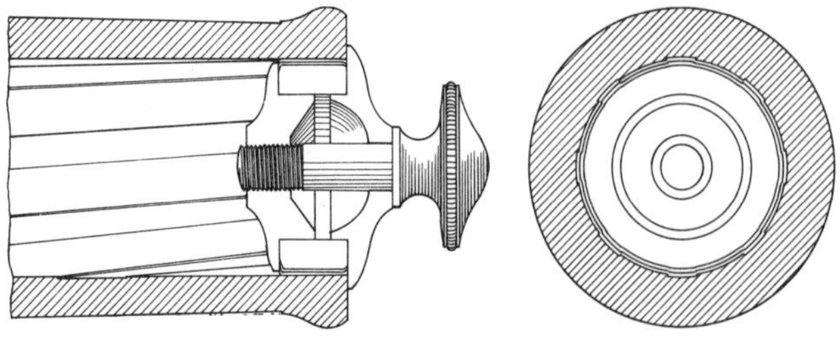

Wilmott tompion (Patent No. 40,720). Patented November 24, 1863 by George R. Wilmott, Meriden, Connecticut. It consisted of two disks, in one of which the thread of the bolt caught, and against the other of which the bolt impinged. Between the disks was a rubber ring covered with a soft fabric which pressed against the inside of the bore of the gun by the action of the screw drawing the threads together. Many other types were used during the war.

Traditionalism in the Army Ordnance Department, and lack of cooperation between the Army and Navy, delayed progress in the design and development of modern artillery materiel during the Civil War. The best evidence of this is that the United States Army continued to employ and manufacture muzzle-loading cannon despite the fact that breech-loaders had been invented and were being built in Europe. A discussion of this is contained in a report of a Joint Congressional Committee on Ordnance in February, 1869:

"The difficulty [in conducting experiments in the Ordnance Department] appears to have been two-fold; first, the ordnance officers, knowing their positions secure to them for life, have not felt the incentive to exertion and improvement which stimulates men not in government employ, and they have become attached to routine and to the traditions of their corps, jealous of innovation and new ideas, and slow to adopt improvements. An illustration of this is found in the fact that the late war was fought with muzzle-loading guns, (with the exception of carbines for cavalry), although a variety of excellent breech-loaders were urged upon the attention of the government constantly, and the honor was reserved for Prussia, with a weapon inferior to many American inventions, to demonstrate the immeasurable superiority of breech-loading guns. In the second place, these officers, educated to a specialty and proud of their positions, come to look upon themselves as possessing all the knowledge extant upon the subject of ordnance, and regard citizen inventors and mechanics who offer improvements in .arms as ignorant and designing persons, and pretentious innovators, who have no claim to consideration. Instead of encouraging the inventive talent of the country, these officers seem to have constantly discouraged it, and many complaints of improper and oppressive treatment have been laid before the committee . . . Another difficulty that has retarded progress in the science of ordnance has been the fact that prominent officers have been inventors of arms, and have possessed sufficient influence to secure the adoption and retention in service of their inventions frequently without due regard to the question of real merit, and to the prejudice of other and better devices brought forward by citizens, or developed in other countries. A further difficulty, calling for a remedy, lies in the want of cooperation between the war and navy ordnance bureaus. Great diversity exists in the practice of the two branches of the service respecting the arms adopted, and the manner of proving, mounting and using the same. The

Heavy artillery in Fort Totten, one of the defenses of Washington, D.C. These were 32-pdr. columbiads. (Library of Congress)

Another battery at Fort Totten, showing the crude methods of laying the guns for direction and range. (elevation). (Library of Congress)

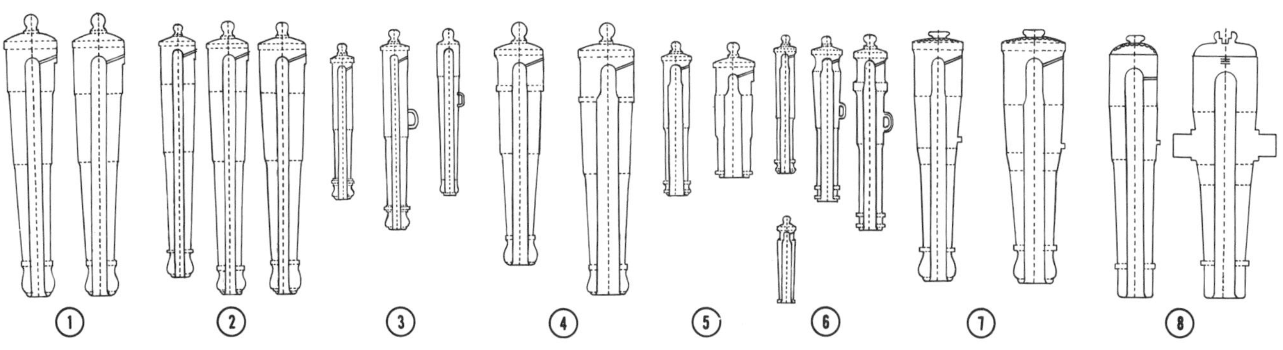

Guns and howitzers.

1. Seacoast guns, 32 and 42-pdrs.
2. Siege and garrison guns, 12, 18, and 24-pdrs.
3. Field guns, 6 and 12-pdrs.
4. Seacoast howitzers, 8 and 10-inch
5. Siege and garrison howitzers, 24-pdr.
6. Field howitzers, 12, 24, and 32-pdrs.
7. Columbiads, 8 and 10-inch
8. New Columbiads, 8 and 10-inch.

Guns and mortars.

1. 3-inch field gun, rifled
2. Siege howitzer
3. 4.5-inch siege gun, rifled
4. 8-inch siege mortar
5. 10-inch siege mortar
6. Coehorn mortar
7. 10-inch seacoast mortar
8. 13-inch seacoast mortar

calibers, models, chambers and ammunition of the navy guns are entirely unlike those in use in the army. For example, the navy 12-pounder boat howitzer has a caliber of 3.4 inches, while the army 12-pounder guns are of calibers 3.0, 3.2, 3.67, and 3.8 inches. The chamber of the navy gun is of parabolic form, while the army gun either has a cycloidal chamber or none at all. The models of the two guns are entirely different, so that neither could be used on the carriage of the other; the army guns being furnished with trunnions, and the navy gun having, in some cases, the loop and loop-bolt of the old carronade. The system of sighting is also different. A gunner in one arm of the service, without special instruction, could not use a gun belonging to the other; one being graduated to seconds of time of the flight of the shot, and the other to degrees of elevation. The navy has 8, 9, 11, and 13-inch smooth bores, while the army guns are of the calibers of 6, 8, 10 and 12-inches. In the guns of the two branches of the service there is no uniformity, in either rifle or smooth-bore in the 20 calibers adopted below the caliber of the 32-pounders. It is impossible to use navy ammunition in an army gun or army ammunition in a navy gun. Cooperation between the army and navy while in active service is thus greatly restricted, and in some cases has been entirely prevented. Offensive operations on the part of a joint expedition of the two might be brought to an end by the want of projectiles for the land forces, while the ships of the navy possessed a surplus of the very articles required, which could not be used for the land forces."

AMMUNITION, ARTILLERY

FUZES. A fuze was a device for detonating a shell or case shot. Fuzes were classified as *Time, Concussion, and Percussion.* The time fuze was composed of a case of paper, wood, or metal, enclosing a burning composition. It was cut or bored to a length proportional to the intended range of the shell, so that it would detonate the bursting charge just as the shell struck the ground or, if desired, in the air above the target.

In 1860 the United States used three kinds of time fuzes—the mortar fuze, the Bormann and the seacoast fuze. Other types early in the war were the Bickford and the Gomez Patent Electric Safety Fuze.

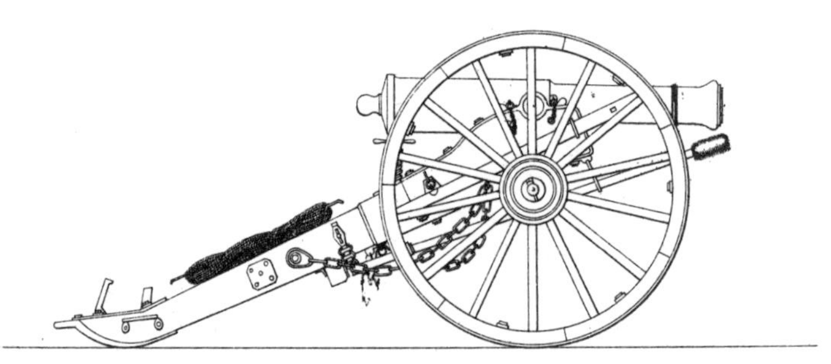

Field carriage.

CANISTER, CASE SHOT, SOLID SHOT, AND SHELLS. See PROJECTILES.

CANNON TYPES, ARMY. In addition to their classification by tactical employment, cannon used by the Army may be classified by the type of bore, by the method of loading, and by the type of trajectory:

CLASSIFIED BY BORE.

Smoothbores. Like other nations the United States possessed many smoothbore cannon before the war. This pre-war smoothbore was gradually superseded by the new pattern 12-pounder, or "Napoleon" as it was familiarly called. This was a gun-howitzer of about 1,200 pounds weight, with a diameter of 4.62 inches, made of gun metal, and whose projectiles—all spherical—were solid shot, case-shot, shell and canister. For service, its ammunition was all "fixed"; that is, the powder charge was attached to the projectile. The fuzes for its hollow projectiles were all "time" fuzes of the peculiar pattern known as the "Bormann." The charge of powder for these guns was 2½ pounds. The gun was mounted generally on the old pattern 24-pounder howitzer carriage, with a slight alteration in the elevating screw bed. For all distances up to 1,500 yards this gun was extremely effective; and with case-shot at 800 yards or canister at 200 yards it was considered to be irresistible.

Rifled Cannon. The first appearance of rifled cannon in any quantity in the U. S. was near the outbreak of hostilities when the Federal artillery was equipped with 300 wrought-iron 3-inch guns. This "12-pounder," which fired a 10-pound projectile, gave excellent results. The cannon which proved most effective in siege work was the invention of Robert P. Parrott. His cast-iron guns can be seen today in the battlefield parks. Parrotts were made in 10-, 20-, 30-, 60-, 100-, 200-, and 300-pounder calibers, one foundry making 1,700 of them during the war.

In 1860 about half of the pre-war smoothbores were scheduled to be converted to rifled pieces. The early U.S. rifles had a muzzle velocity about the same as the smoothbore, but whereas the round shot of the smoothbore lost speed so rapidly that at 2,000 yards its striking velocity was only about 1/3 of the muzzle velocity, the more streamlined rifle projectile lost speed much more slowly. The rifle had to be served more carefully than the smoothbore. Rifling grooves were cleaned with a moist sponge, and sometimes oiled with another sponge. Lead-coated projectiles like the James, which tended to foul the grooves of the piece, made it necessary to scrape the rifle grooves after every half dozen shots, although guns using brass-banded projectiles did not require the extra operation. With all muzzle-loading rifles, the projectile had to be pushed close home to the powder charge; otherwise the blast would not fully expand its rotating band, the projectile would not take the grooves, and would "tumble" after leaving the gun, with an utter loss of range and accuracy.

Types of heavy artillery. A Confederate battery at Vicksburg. (Kean Archives)

A Federal 3-inch rifled gun, showing the accessories. Bearded officer is Capt. John C. Tidball, 2d U.S. Artillery. (Library of Congress)

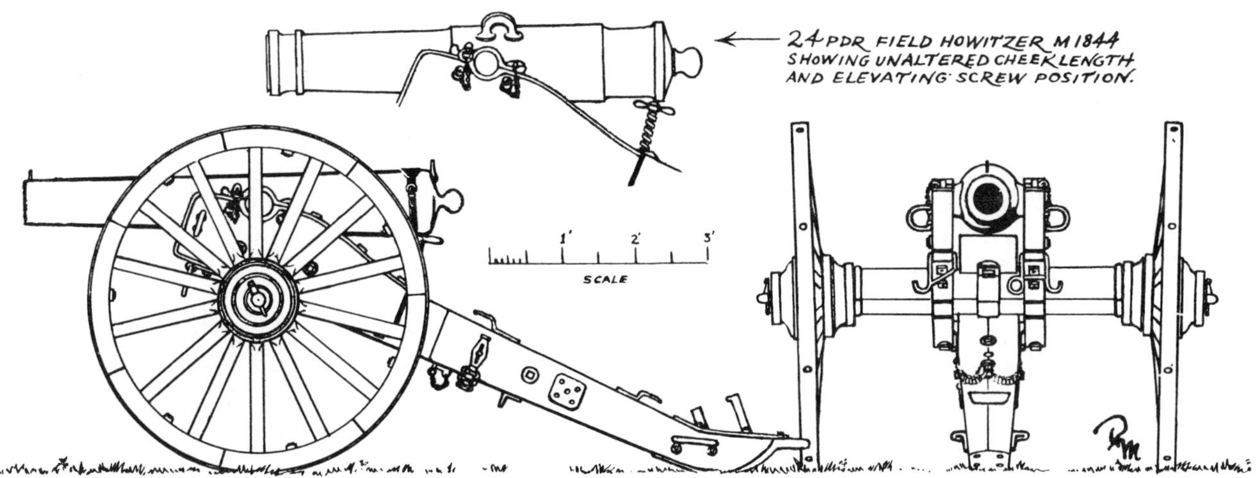

Standard field piece, the Napoleon. (Robert L. Miller)

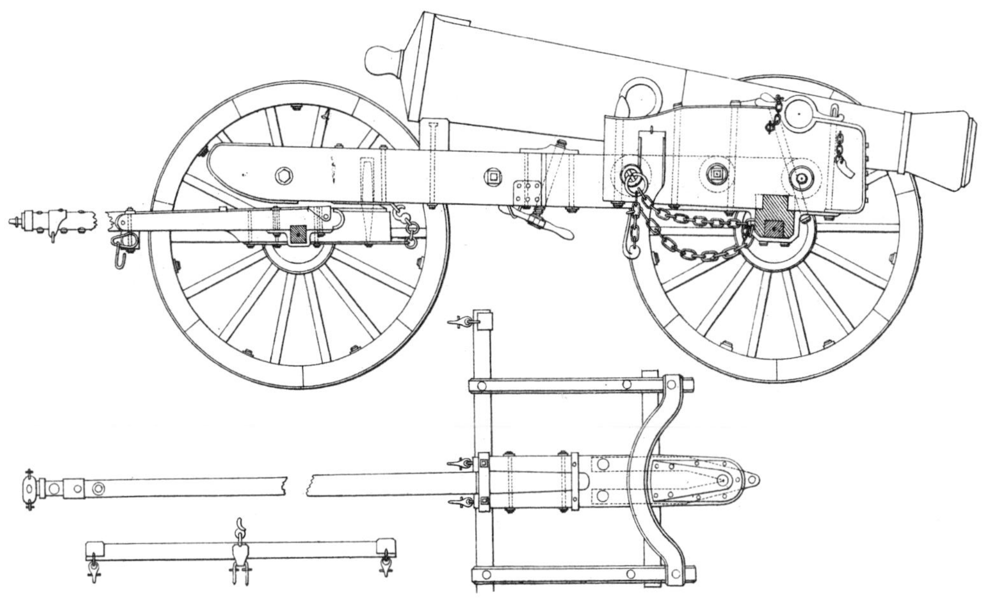

Siege carriage.

Guns and howitzers took their denominations from the weight of their solid shot in round numbers, including the 42-pounder; larger pieces, rifle guns, and mortars took their denominations from the diameter of the bore.

In siege operations the rifles showed the way to a new era. The first really effective use of rifles was in siege operations at Fort Pulaski in 1862. Using 10 rifles and 26 smoothbores, General Gillmore breached the 7½-foot-thick brick walls in little more than 24 hours. Yet his batteries were a mile away from the target! The next year, 1863, Gillmore used 100-, 200-, and 300-pounder Parrott rifles against Fort Sumter. The range and accuracy of these rifles startled the military world. A 30-pounder (4.2 inch) Parrott had an amazing carry of 8,453 yards with 80-pound hollow shot.

The rifled field guns most generally used in the U. S. service were the Parrott 10-pounder (2.9-inch caliber) and the regulation wrought-iron 3-inch gun. The range of rifled field guns at 12-13 degrees (the maximum elevation which their carriages permitted) was from 3,000 to 3,500 yards, or about 1.75 to 2 miles. With higher elevations, readily achieved by methods known to the artillerists, ranges of 4,000, 5,000, or even 6,000 yards (more than 3¼ miles) could be obtained.

A 3-inch rifle was also made by John Griffen in Pennsylvania. The unusual feature of this artillery piece of the 1850's was the making of a gun out of wrought iron and being bored afterwards. The Griffen gun was appreciably lighter than the contemporary bronze 6-pounder and withstood very severe tests. During the Civil War the Federal Government bought some 1,400 which were made by the Phoenix Iron Company. A Griffen gun is reported to have fired the opening artillery shot at Gettysburg.

One of the most important fieldpieces of the war was the 3-inch steel or wrought-iron gun, which was made in large quantities. Many fired the Hotchkiss and Schenkl projectiles (see PROJECTILES).

Parrott's 20, and 30-pounders (3.64-inch and 4.2-inch bore) were considered to be among the best of the heavier rifled pieces. But large rifles had grave defects, the most serious of which was the unequal and uncertain life of the piece. Some of the most valuable batteries on Morris Island (1863) were disabled by the bursting of the barrels at a very early stage in the operations. In January 1865 the bursting of six 100-pounder Parrotts on the vessels of the Wilmington fleet caused the U. S. Naval Ordnance Department to suspend further orders for this type of cannon until a board should discover the cause of the bursting of these guns. At Charleston harbor Gillmore had six 200-pounder and seventeen 100-pounder Parrotts explode during the siege.

Parrott, however, pointed out that his smaller guns, 30-pounder and smaller, had been found to be perfectly satisfactory.

Several of the larger rifled cannon became widely known for their unusual size, employment, and from their nicknames. Among these were the "Swamp

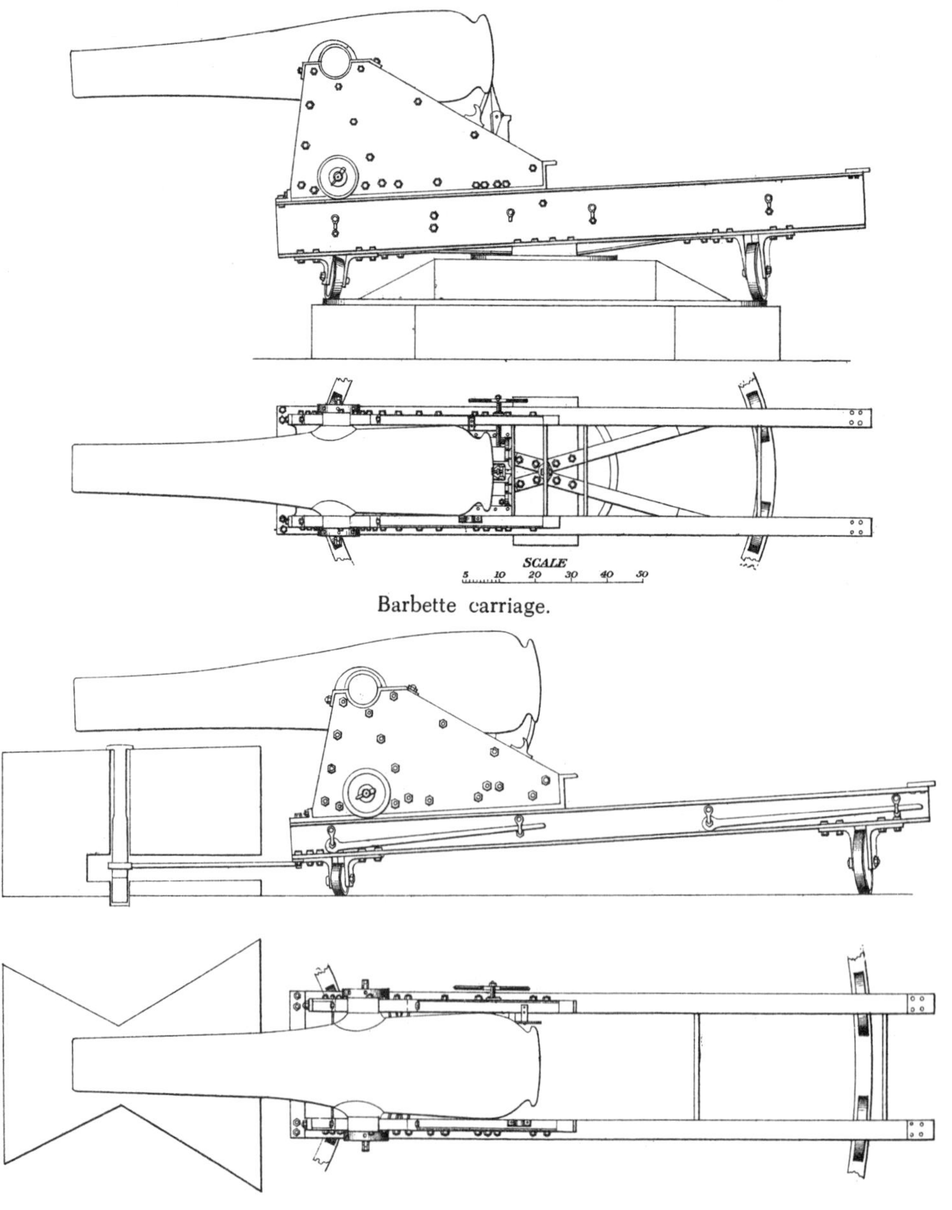

Barbette carriage.

Casemate carriage.

Whistling Dick. (Library of Congress)

Angel" and "Whistling Dick." The former was an 8-inch 200-pounder Parrott rifle located on Morris Island at the mouth of Charleston harbor. The city itself, 7,900 yards from the weapon, was the target. At 1:30 on the morning of August 22, 1863, the first shell, with percussion fuze, was fired from the "Swamp Angel." The noise made by bells and whistles in the middle of the night told the Federal soldiers that the shell had fallen in the city. Sixteen shells were fired that early morning hour. Twelve of the shells fired were of R. P. Parrott's own construction at the West Point foundry, and filled with a fluid composition, and the other four shells were filled with "Short's Solidified Greek Fire." (See GREEK FIRE)

From 1 p.m. August 21, 1863, when initial preparations were made for emplacing the gun, two Confederate 10-inch Columbiads and two 10-inch seacoast mortars were trying to prevent the manning of the gun, and, after it had commenced firing, to silence it. But they did little damage to the battery and none to the men. The mortar shells, with long-time fuzes, did not explode until they had buried themselves in the mud; and the shells from the Columbiads, which burst in front of the parapet, did no damage.

The "Swamp Angel" was purchased after the war and sent to Trenton, N.J. to be melted, but having been identified, was set up on a granite monument in that city on the corner of Perry and Clinton streets.

"Whistling Dick," a rifled Confederate 18-pounder, was made at Tredegar Works and used in the defense of Vicksburg. Originally a smoothbore but later rifled, its projectiles gave off a peculiar whistling sound in their flight. Another well-known Vicksburg cannon was a 7.44-in. Blakely rifle known as the "Widow Blakely."

CLASSIFIED BY METHOD OF LOADING. Most of the cannon used during the Civil War were *muzzle-loaders,* mainly because the Chief of Ordnance, General Ripley, was not interested in *breech-loaders.* A few types of the latter were offered for trial, one of which was a breech-loading iron field piece, about 4½ feet long, with a 2-inch bore. Five ounces of powder were sufficient to send the gun's 4-pound projectile about 2½ miles. This model of breech-loading cannon was very rapid in operation, and could be fired 100 times in 6 minutes without over-heating.

Whitworth of Manchester, England, constructed several rifled breech-loading cannon of various calibers. His 3-pounder gun, 208 pounds in weight, with a caliber of 1.5 inches, a charge of 8 oz. of powder, and an elevation of 35 degrees, projected its projectile to a distance of more than 5½ miles, and this with remarkable accuracy. Whitworth applied the same principles to his cannon which had been so successful in his small arms—using a very long projectile, 3½ diameters in length, so that the air resistance would be as low as possible. To overcome the tendency of so long a projectile to turn over in its flight, a rapid rotation to the projectile's flight was insured by the hexagonal bore.

The sunken British blockade runner *Modern Greece* recently (1962) yielded several cases of 12-pounder Whitworth bolts. This vessel went down off Fort Fisher June 27, 1862.

Some breech loaders are difficult to identify today. For example on March 1, 1862, the 7th Illinois Cavalry captured three guns from Jeff Thompson near Sikestown, Missouri. These guns had 1¼-inch bore and were breech loaders.

The Federals manufactured a 300-pound breech-loading cannon of 1½-inch bore on the B. F. Joslyn principle. In April 1861 two of these guns were assigned to Ellsworth's Zouaves, hence the name *Ellsworth Guns*. Fremont received 20 of the guns in 1862 and such Confederate leaders as Morgan also used them after they had been captured in battle.

CLASSIFIED BY TYPE OF TRAJECTORY. Cannon may be designated as guns, howitzers, or mortars, depending on whether their trajectories (path of the projectile through the air) are relative flat, medium, or high-angle. The flat-trajectory weapons (guns) usually have higher muzzle velocities than the other two types.

Guns. The gun secured its high velocity by means of heavy propelling charges, from ¼ to ½ the weight of the projectile, and by longer tubes, which gave the expanding gases of the propellant a longer time in which to act on the projectile. Usually the gun was of smaller caliber than a howitzer or mortar that fired the same weight of projectile, but because of its length and the thickness of the breech, necessary to withstand the force of the propelling charge, it usually was heavier. Guns were always designated by the weight of the solid projectiles they fired, there being seven types:

Field guns: 6 and 12 pounders. The 6-pounders were used chiefly by horse artillery, which served with cavalry and thus had to secure maximum mobility. The 12-pounder was the standard for light artillery supporting the infantry.

Siege and garrison guns: 12-, 18-, and 24-pounders.

Seacoast guns: 32- and 42-pounders, used mainly in defense of harbors, against naval attack.

Howitzers. Except for mountain and field howitzers, this weapon usually was of larger caliber than the gun, but lobbed its projectiles higher in the air, and had a shorter range. They were effective against personnel behind shelter, as a hill, which the flat-trajectory weapon could not reach. Classified according to the caliber in inches or the weight of the projectile, howitzers were of four categories:

Whitworth gun. (National Archives)

The British-made Whitworth cannon, sold to the Confederacy. One of the few successful breechloading cannon used during the Civil War. (Harpers)

The Blakely 3.5-inch steel rifled field gun, also made in England and bought by the Confederacy. (West Point Museum collections)

Federal railway mortar. (National Archives)

Mountain: 12-pounders
Field: 12-, 24-, and 32-pounders
Siege and garrison: 8-inch and 24-pounders
Seacoast: 8- and 10-inch

Columbiads. A special type of howitzer, the Columbiad was of larger caliber than the ordinary cannon, and was used for throwing solid shot, shells, spherical case, and canister. Calibers were the 8-inch, 10-inch, and 15-inch. All were of cast-iron except the fieldpieces, which were of bronze.

Mortars. The mortar was a short-tube weapon of large caliber, used for crushing fortifications or setting fire to them. It was the weight of the projectile rather than its velocity that produced the effect. There were seven types, as follows:

Heavy, seacoast, 10- and 13-inch
Light, siege and garrison, 8- and 10-inch
Stone, 16-inch
Coehorn, 5.82-inch (24-pounder)
Eprouvette, 5.65 inch (24-pounder)

Mortar projectiles were formidable; the 13-inch mortar fired a 200-pound shell. During the siege of Petersburg, the Federals used "The Dictator," which had special wrought-iron beds with a pair of rollers. In spite of their high trajectory, mortars could range well over a mile.

The Federals also used a small (24-pounder) antipersonnel mortar called the Coehorn. Named for the Hollander, Baron Menno van Coehorn (1641-1704), the developer of a small portable mortar, this mortar was an important weapon in the Mexican war, but was not used in the Civil War to any extent until the spring of 1864. The Chief of Artillery of the Army of the Potomac, Brig. Gen. Henry J. Hunt, took 8 Coehorn mortars with the army in the operations against Richmond, and they saw extensive use in the Petersburg area. By the first of April, 1865, the Army of the Potomac had about 40 Coehorns.

Cannon Types, Navy. As with the Army during the war, the U.S. Navy also used many types and calibers of cannon. The main types and calibers are listed here. The Confederacy used much the same types of weapons with the addition of such pieces as the Brooke rifle, especially the 4.2 inch, 7-inch, and 8-inch models. Ranges of most of the Civil War naval cannon varied from 1,000 to 4,000 yards.

Main Types of Naval Cannon (Shell)

Caliber in inches	*Weight of projectile in pounds*
Guns	
8-inch	51.5
9-inch	72.5
10-inch	103.0
11-inch	136.0
15-inch	350.0
Guns (shot) and Howitzers	
4.62 (12-pounder)	10
5.82 (24-pounder)	20
6.4 (32-pounder)	26 shell 32 shot
Guns (rifled)	
3.40 (12-pounder)	12
3.67 (20-pounder Parrott)	19
4.00 (20-pounder Dahlgren)	20
4.20 (30-pounder)	29
5.30 (60-pounder)	50
6.40 (100-pounder)	100
8.00 (150-pounder)	155
Mortars	
13.0-inch	200

CANNON MANUFACTURE. At the start of the war all artillery pieces were made at privately-owned foundries and afterwards inspected and proved by Ordnance Department officers detailed for the purpose. The foundries making cannon in 1860 were:

West Point Foundry (near Cold Spring, N. Y.)
Fort Pitt Foundry (near Pittsburgh, Pa.)
Tredegar Foundry (near Richmond, Va.)
Algers Foundry (near Boston, Mass.)
Ames Foundry (near Chicopee, Mass.)

All cannon were required to be weighed and to be marked as follows: The number of the gun, and the initials of the inspector's name, on the face of the muzzle; the numbers in a separate series for each kind and caliber at each foundry; the initial letters of the name of the founder and of the foundry, on the end of the right trunnion; the year of fabrication on the end

Federal railway gun. (National Archives)

of the left trunnion; the foundry number on the end of the right rimbase, above the trunnion; the weight of the piece in pounds on the base of the breech; the letters U. S. on the upper surface of the piece, near the end of the reinforce.

FIELD ARTILLERY EQUIPMENT. Field artillery equipment includes the devices for laying and firing the piece, for loading, cleaning, and repairing the weapons, and miscellaneous tools and articles used in the battery.

Ammunition Chest. This chest, for the 6-pounder gun, consisted of eight partitions of poplar wood, four in each half, perpendicular to the sides of the chest. A tray, for holding implements, rested on the partitions in the left half of the chest.

Ammunition carried in each chest

Kind	*No.*	*Weight*
Shot, fixed	25	190
Spherical case, fixed	20	140
Canisters, fixed	5	42
Spare cartridges 1¼ lb.	2	2.6
Friction primers	75	.97
Slow-match-yard	2	.38
Portfires	2	.57
Total no. of rounds	50	
		376.52

Weights and dimensions varied with other types of guns.

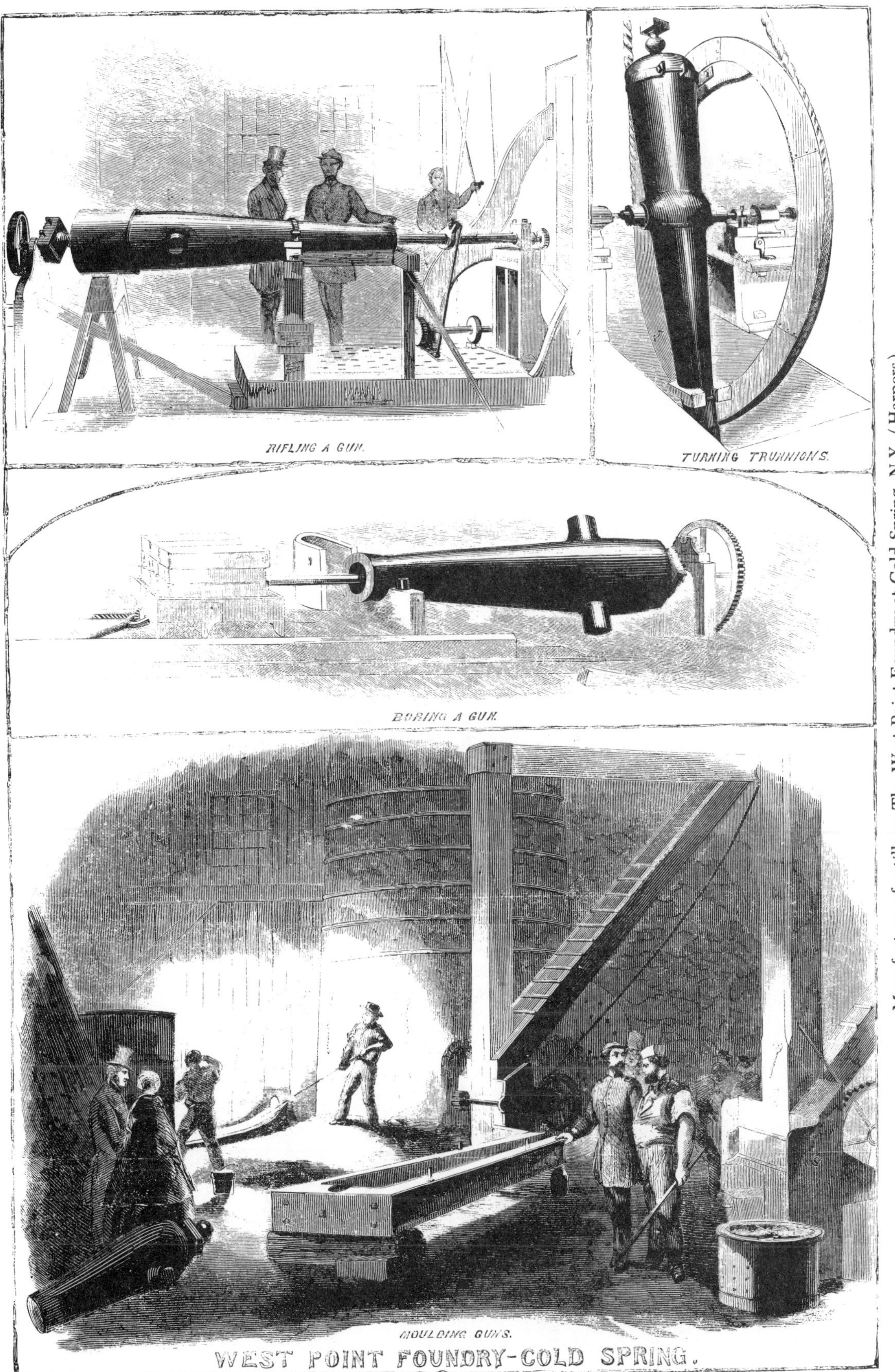

Manufacture of artillery. The West Point Foundry at Cold Spring, N.Y. (Harpers)

The finished product of the Cold Spring armory—a 10-pdr. Parrott. (Library of Congress)

Equipment for Carriages

Caisson Accessories and Tools:

Item	*No.*	*Weight, lbs.*
Felling axe	1	6.0
Pickaxe	1	6.5
Shovel, long handle	1	4.75
Spare handspike	1	7.25
Spare pole	1	25.30
Spare wheel	1	180.00
Tar bucket	1	7.00
Tarpaulin, large	1	37.75
Tow hooks	2	1.20
Watering bucket, leather	2	16.00
Gun or Howitzer Accessories and Tools:		
Fuze cutter	1	
Gunner's gimlet	1	.20
Gunner's haversack	2	3.72
Gunner's pincers	1	.85
Handspike	2	14.50
Hausse	1	.65
Lanyard for friction primer	1	.08
Priming wire	1	.08
Prolonge	1	12.5
Sponge and rammer	2	
Sponge bucket	1	10.00
Sponge cover	2	.24
Tar bucket	1	7.00
Tarpaulin, large	1	37.75
Thumb stalls	2	.01
Tow hooks	1	.60
Tube pouch	2	1.80
Vent cover	1	.20
Vent pouch	1	.08
Water bucket, leather	2	16.00
Worm and staff	½	3.6

Horse Equipments, Artillery. See also HORSE EQUIPMENTS. A complete set of artillery harness consisted of headgear, saddles, and valise. Draft harness differed according to use, whether for the wheel or lead horses. One whip was allowed for each driver, and one leg guard for each driver of wheel horses.

Artillery saddles were equipped with brass stirrups as contrasted with iron or leather hooded stirrups for cavalry and mounted officers of the other services. The valise-saddle was similar to the driver's saddle except for minor variations in dimensions and the addition of two valise straps.

The valise was of thick bridle leather, cylindrical in shape, 18 inches long, with a flat bottom, and had round leather handles at both ends.

For draft horses the collars were of two sizes, 17 inches and 20 inches. Hames were of iron, painted black, while the traces consisted of a leather trace with a chain and toggle attached to each end. Breeching was of thick harness leather. A pole pad was placed on the end of the pole to prevent the swing horses from being injured by the pole. The whip, of rawhide, was about 30 inches long. Leg guards and nose bags were also issued to artillery units. Mountain artillery had a specially-designed packsaddle for carrying the tube, carriage, and ammunition chests. The harness complete consisted of the headgear, packsaddle, which was the same for packing the gun carriage or chests, the crupper, breeching, breaststrap, lashing girth, and rope.

McMurray and Topham Saddle Valise (Patent No. 47,028) patented March 28, 1865 by Robert McMurray and James T. Topham, Washington, D. C. This consisted of a cylindrical valise to fit close behind the saddle, made without any seams exposed to rain, and riveted together so as to dispense with stitching.

Wilkinson Artillery Valise (Patent No. 47,829) patented May 23, 1865, by Warren H. Wilkinson, Springfield, Massachusetts. This consisted of a valise made with a hollow to fit to and upon the top surface of the saddle of the horse. The valise had side fastenings and bottom straps.

Implements, Fire Control (Aiming Devices). These devices were used to lay the piece for direction and range.

Breech Sight. This consisted of an upright piece of sheet brass supported on a foot piece, the lower side of which was curved to fit on the base ring of the gun on which the sight was used.

Cannon Sight, Patent No. 46329. Patented February 14, 1865 by James Brady, Philadelphia, Pa. This was a pendulum sight having two graduated standard bars and one sliding extension bar between the standards, it being fixed in one and sliding on the other end, and made adjustable, resembling the letter T supported at its extremities.

Chock. A small wedge, with a handle in the side, used for chocking the wheels of permanently fixed carriages, when the piece had been laid for direction.

Gunner's Calipers. Made of sheet-brass, with steel points. The graduations showed diameters of the bores of guns and the calibers of projectiles. See also Implements for Loading Shells.

Gunner's level. An instrument for determining the highest points of the base ring and muzzle, preparatory to the use of the breech sight and tangent scale. It consisted of an upright of sheet brass, supported on two feet, the line joining the bottom points being perpendicular to the direction of a sliding pointer, which moved up and down in sockets on the upright.

Gunner's Perpendicular. Made of sheet brass, the

Cannon at Hilton Head, S.C. (Western Reserve Historical Society)

lower part of which was cut in the form of a crescent, the points being of steel. A small spirit level was fastened to one side of the plate, parallel to the line joining the points of the crescent, and a slide was fastened to the same side of the plate, perpendicular to the axis of the level. The instrument was useful in marking the points of sight on siege guns and mortars when the platform was not level.

Handspike. Used for giving the horizontal direction to the piece. That for the field pieces, called a *trail handspike,* was round, and conical shaped at the large end, to fit into the pointing rings. Other types were the *roller handspike* and the *truck handspike.* The *maneuvering handspike* was longer than the trial handspike and was designed for service with siege and garrison carriages. It differed somewhat in shape from the trail handspike, being octagonal in the middle, and, for mechanical maneuvers, the large end was made square, and, at the end, tapered off on one side so as to allow its entrance under a weight in getting a purchase. For these heavy siege and garrison artillery pieces, the handspike was shod with iron. All handspikes were made of well-seasoned hickory or tough oak.

The *trail handspike* for field carriages was 53 inches long; the *maneuvering handspike* for garrison and seacoast carriages was 66 inches long; for siege and other heavy work it was 84 inches long of 12 pounds weight. The *shod handspike* was especially useful in servicing mortars, and casemate and barbette carriages; the *truck handspike* was for casemate carriages (wrought iron); the *roller handspike* was for casemate carriages. The trail handspike was made of iron, 1-inch round, the point being conical. Total length, 34 inches.

Pendulum-Hausse. Since the tangent scale and breech sight gave the proper elevation to the piece only when the gun's trunnions were horizontal, the pendulum-hause was used as a corrective for a faulty position of the trunnions. In this way, the necessity for a gunner's level or new sighting points was obviated.

The pendulum-hausse consisted of an upright piece of sheet brass, like the breech sight, and had a movable slider and scale, similarly arranged. At the lower end was a bulb, filled with lead. The scale passed through a slit in a piece of steel and was connected with it by a brass screw, which served as a point on which the scale vibrated laterally; the slit was long enough to allow the scale to assume a vertical position, in any ordinary cases of unevenness of the ground on which the gun carriage might be situated.

Quadrant, of wood or metal, was used for mortars or long artillery pieces, for which the ordinary breech sight and tangent scale were not sufficiently developed. The quadrant consisted of a quarter of a circle fixed to a long arm. The edge of the circle was divided into degrees, and the inclination of the arm to the horizon was determined by a plummet which was fastened at the center of the curve.

Quoin. A large wedge, used in place of an elevating screw, under the chase of mortars and the breech of short howitzers, to keep them in the proper position when elevating. It had a handle in the large end, by which it was moved.

Tangent scale. This was made of sheet brass with a flange along the lower edge, which was cut to fit the base ring of the piece. The upper edge was cut in steps, each *rise* representing the tangent of ¼ degree to a radius equal to the distance between the highest points of the breech and muzzle, measured parallel to the axis. In the middle of each step a notch was placed to assist in sighting. When the piece was sighted by these different notches, the axis was at an elevation indicated by the degrees and minutes under the notches. The tangent scale had fallen into disuse and was, to a large extent, replaced by the pendulum-hausse or breech sight, being preferred as more convenient in form.

IMPLEMENTS FOR LOADING SHELLS. Shells were not issued nor transported loaded, but were loaded and fuzed at the battery position.

Gunner's Calipers. Made of sheet brass with steel points. The two branches were connected by a brass pivot, fastened on the upper side by a washer and screw. The scale in inches and divisions on the edge was used for measuring lengths of fuzes. Calipers were also used to measure the diameter of shot and the caliber of guns.

Funnel. This item, made of sheet copper, was used

Confederate field artillery materiel. Guns, caissons, limbers captured at Richmond in 1865. Note battery wagon in foreground. (U.S. Army Photograph)

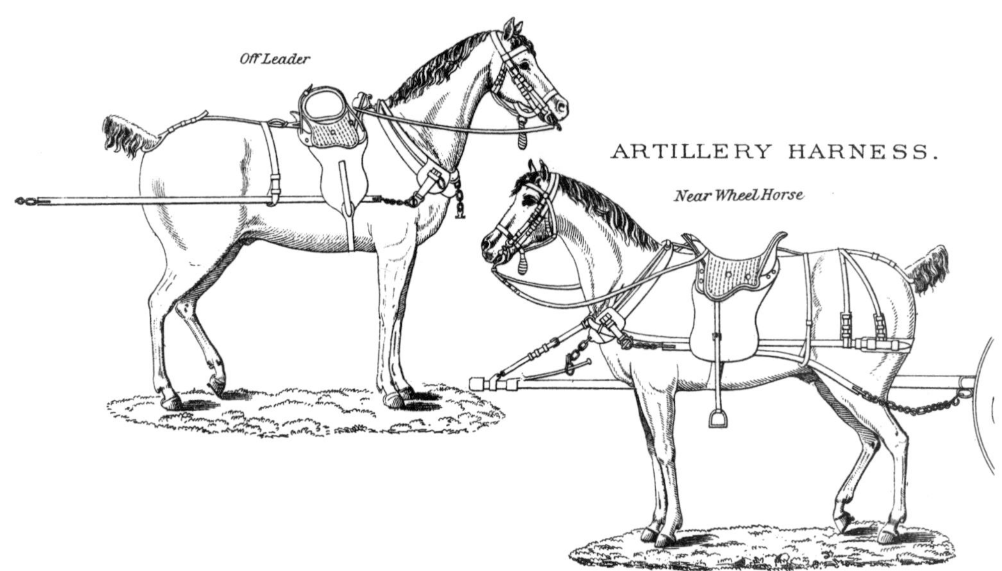

Field artillery harness and saddle.

for pouring the charges from the powder measure into the shell. It was of an ordinary funnel shape, the upper edge being turned over and outwards to stiffen it.

Fuze Auger. After fuzes were set in position it sometimes became necessary to reduce the length of the composition column; for this the fuze auger was employed. It consisted of a steel bit fastened in a wooden handle, at the lower end of which was a brass socket, with a bar, under which the graduated limb of the slider moved. The bit fit into the slider and, by means of a steel thumbscrew, was fastened to it for any required position. The position of the slider, which determined the depth to which the auger bored, was regulated by a scale attached to it by a screw.

Fuze Extractor. Was used for extracting wooden fuzes from the fuze hole when they had been too firmly driven to be withdrawn in any other way. It consisted of an inner screw and stem of steel, riveted to an iron handle, and was contained in a hollow steel screw, which worked up and down by means of an iron nut with two handles. To extract a fuze the bottom of the frame was placed on the shell over the fuze head, and the inner screw screwed into the fuze by means of the upper handle. The handles of the nut were then turned, which raised the hollow screw and with it the inner screw and the fuze.

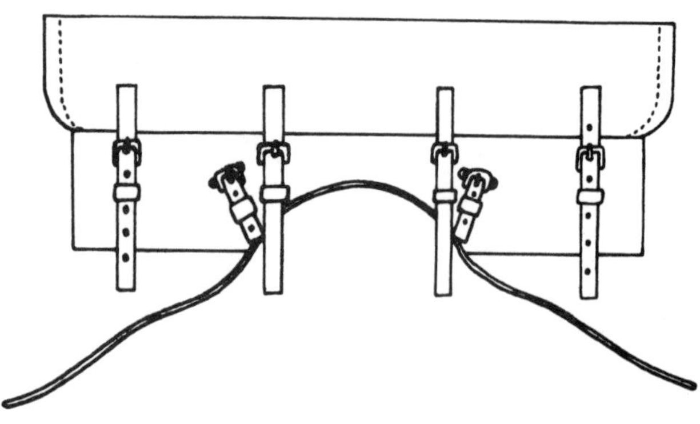

Wilkinson's artillery valise. (U.S. Patent Office)

Fuze Mallet. Used for setting the fuze home. It was cylindrical in shape, with a hand on one end, and was turned out of one piece of dogwood, oak, or other hard wood.

Fuze Saw. This saw was issued for cutting wooden fuze to the proper length. It was a common 10-inch tenon saw.

Fuze-setter. Used for setting wooden fuzes in the fuze hole. It was made of brass; the bottom was countersunk and cup-shaped to prevent it from slipping off the head of the fuze.

Portfire Cutter. A device for cutting portfires to place in the shells or for other purposes. It was simply a strong pair of steel scissors, with an indentation 1 inch wide and .4 inches deep in one of the blades to hold the portfire.

Powder Measure. Used for measuring, not only the charges for shells, but also those for the pieces themselves. For the latter, when extreme accuracy was required, it was necessary to weigh the charges. Powder measures were made of sheet copper and were cylindrical in shape. The bottom was made with a flange, turned downwards, and was soldered to the sides.

Shell Plug-Screw. This implement was used for extracting the corks or wooden plugs with which fuze holes were stopped. It was made of iron, and consisted of a ring 2 inches in diameter to which was fastened a strong screw.

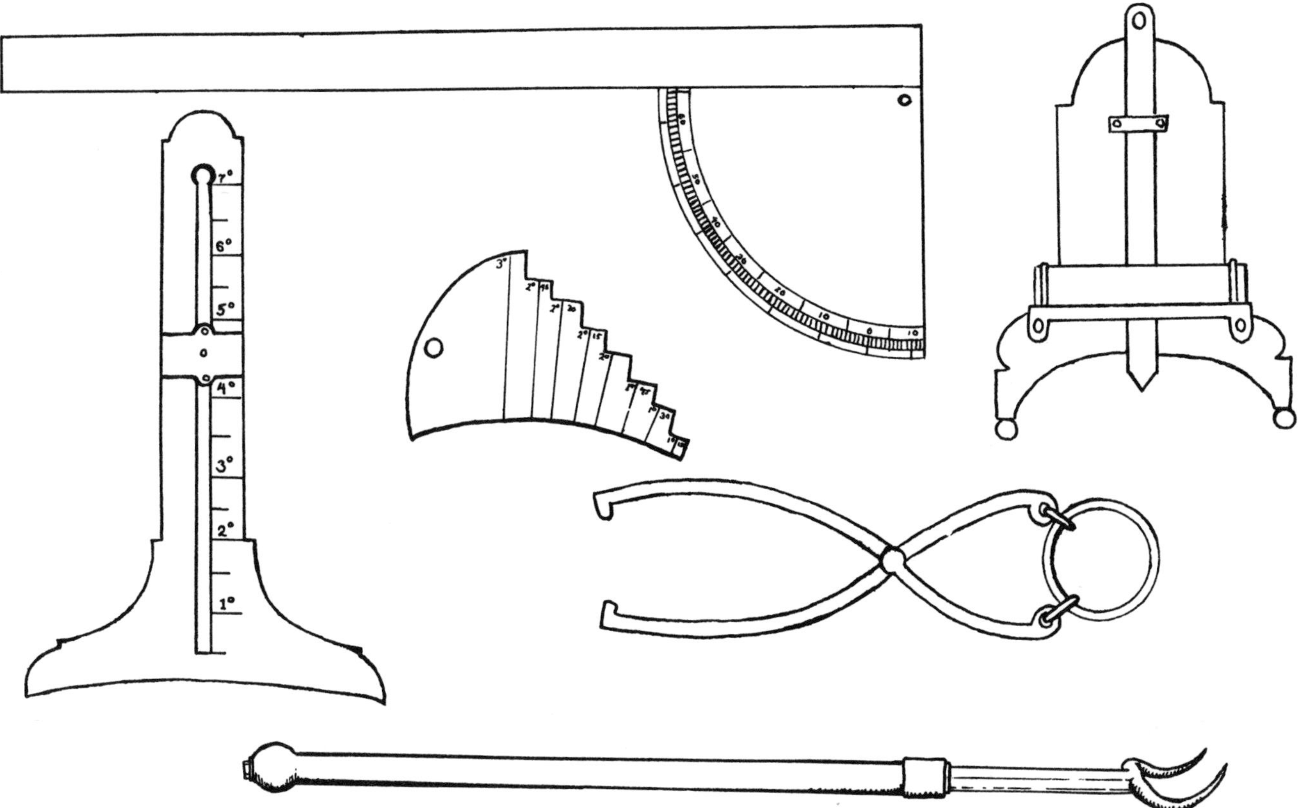

Artillery implements: top, left to right, breechsight, tangent scale, gunner's quadrant, gunner's level. Below: loading tongs. Botton: fork for hot shot. (Drawings by Mike McAfee)

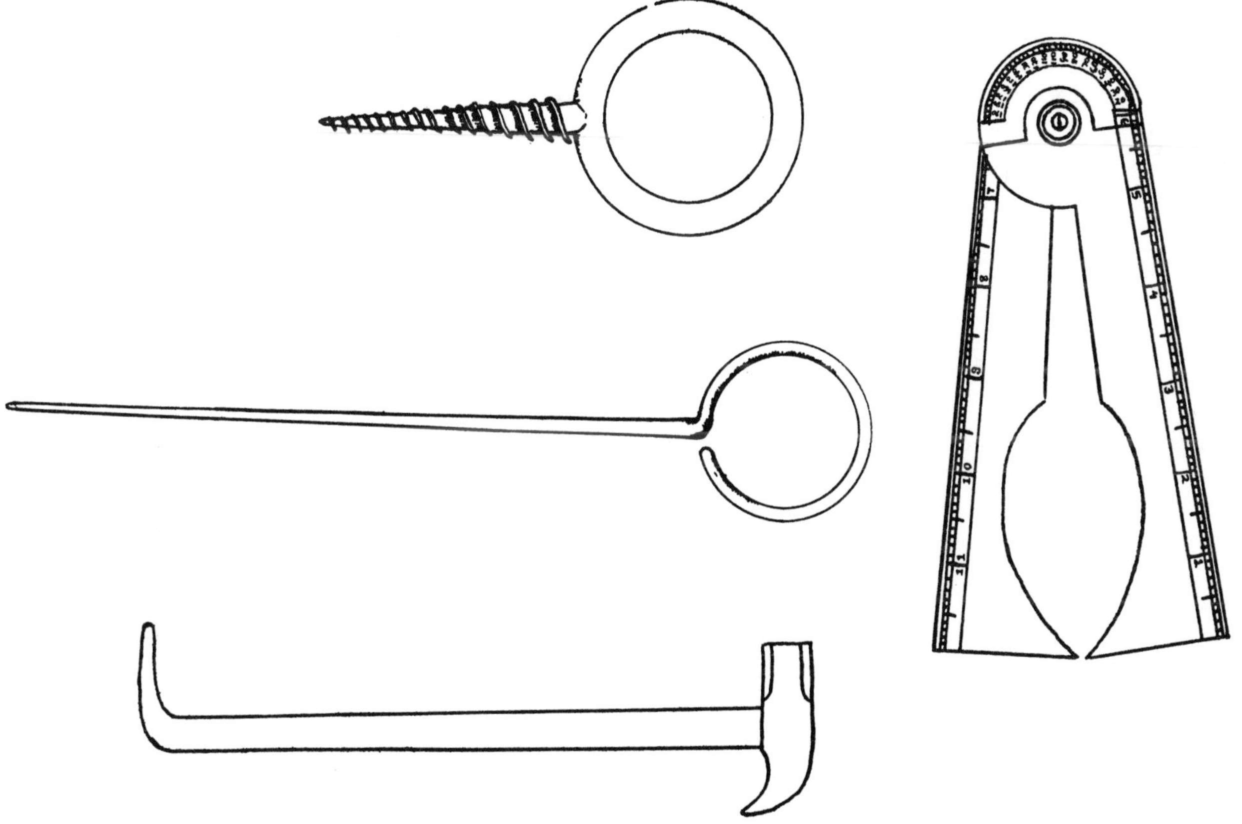

Artillery implements: left, top to bottom, shell plug, screw priming-wire, tow-hook. Right, gunner's calipers. (Mike McAfee)

IMPLEMENTS FOR LOADING THE PIECE

Budge Barrel. A strong oak barrel, bound with copper hoops. To protect the cartridges placed in it and also to permit easy access to the cartridges, it had a cover made of bag leather, the lower edge of which was fastened under the top hoop by copper nails, and the rivets which held the hoop. The mouth was drawn together by a double cord passing through holes in the leather near the upper edge. The budge barrel

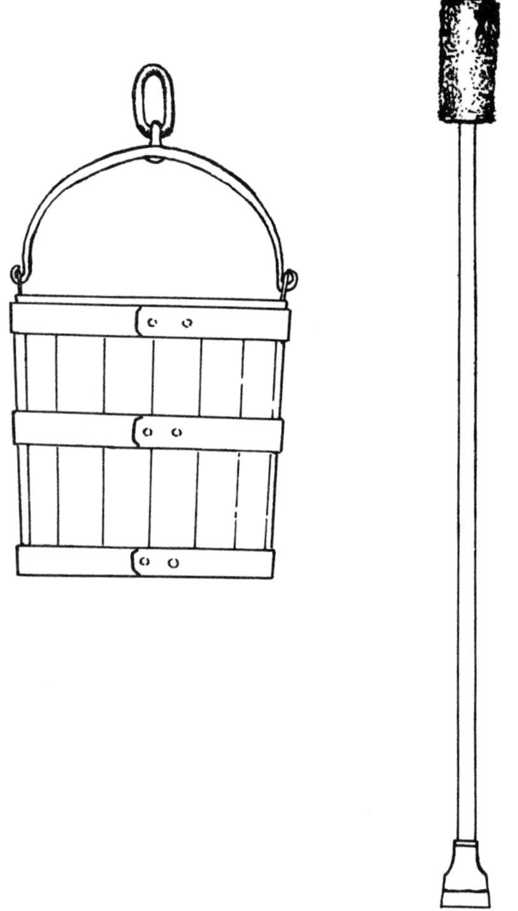

Artillery implements: left, water bucket; right, sponge staff. (Mike McAfee)

was used to carry cartridges from the magazine to the batteries for the purpose of distributing them to the pieces, by means of the haversacks or pass-boxes.

Common Ladle. To unload projectiles from cannon when firing of the cannon was not desired, a common ladle was used. It consisted of a ladle-head, made of the same kind of wood and in the same way as a rammer-head, and the ladle proper, which was of sheet brass, fastened to the head with copper nails. Ladle-staves were made like those for rammers and sponges and were fastened to the heads in the same way, with wooden pins.

Dredging Box. To render the fuzes of mortar shell more certain of taking fire, meal powder was sprinkled

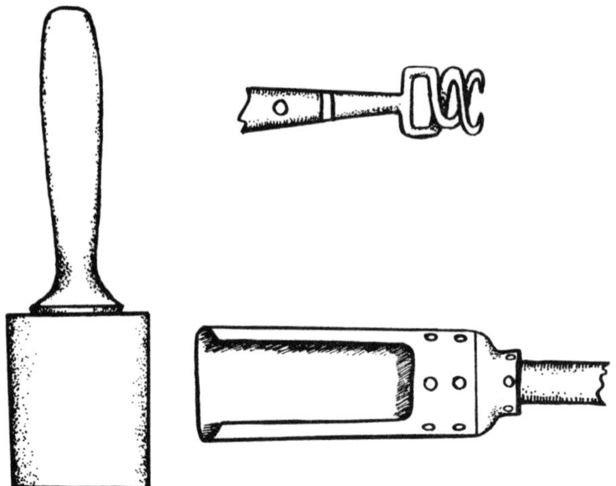

Artillery implements: left, fuze-mallet; right top, worm; right bottom, ladle. (Mike McAfee)

over them, after the shell had been placed in the mortar, from a dredging box. It was made of sheet copper. The top fitted over the box and was pierced with holes for the escape of the powder.

Haversack. A device to prevent accidents while the cartridges were being carried to the guns. For this purpose haversacks were used with field pieces and mortars, and sometimes with larger guns. The gunner's haversack was made of russet bag leather, the front and back being connected by gussets which formed the ends and bottoms and allowed the bag to be folded flat. The flap was of the same piece as the back, folds down, and was fastened to the front by a buckle and strap. A billet and a bucklestrap, sewed to the back of the bag, formed the shoulder-belt.

Hot-shot Fork. A hot shot projectile required special implements for getting it from the furnace, carrying it to the pieces, or placing it in the muzzle. The fork was made of iron, sometimes fastened to a wooden handle and was used to take the shot out of the furnace. It had two prongs which curved inward and upward so as to retain the shot between them when once in position.

Ladle. For carrying the shot to the artillery piece there were two kinds of ladles. The first consisted of a ring and stem of iron, fastened to a wooden handle two feet long. The inner top edge of the ring was grooved out to receive the shot. The other ladle, for carrying the largest shot, consisted of a similar ring, to which stems were fixed for connecting one single and one double handle, so that two men could be used to carry the shot, the double handle preventing the ladle from turning over.

Loading Tongs. For inserting the propelling charge and shell in such pieces as the 8-inch siege howitzer. Formed of two arms so hinged together that the bent ends of the short arms would enter the ears of the

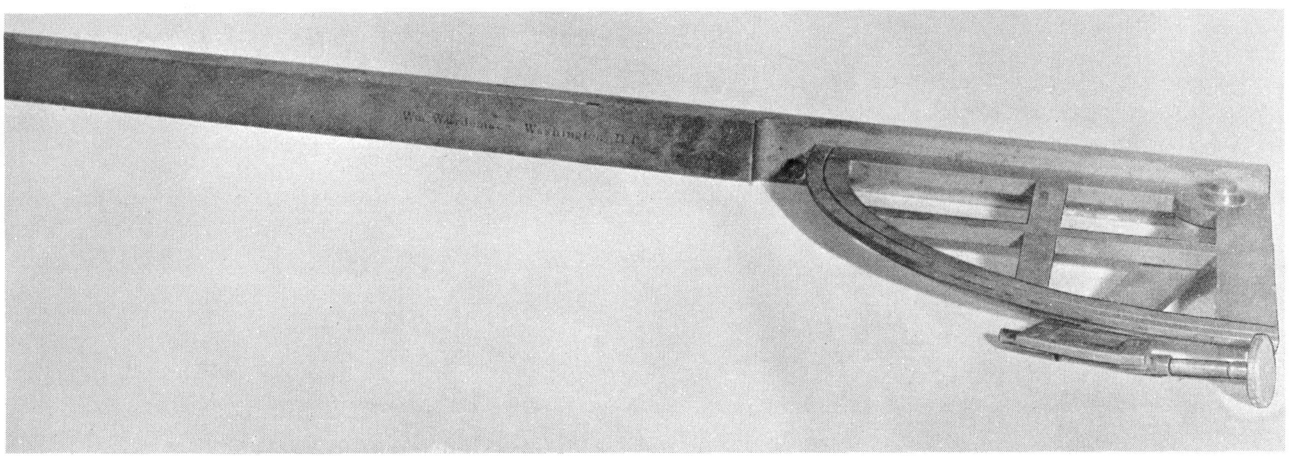

Gunner's brass quadrant, marked "Wm. Wuerdemann, Washington, D.C." Length 29½ inches.

shell, and the grooved and widened ends of the long ones would clasp between them the cartridge.

Pass Box. Used to carry the cartridges to guns in garrison or sieges. It was made of white pine, the sides and ends dove-tailed together, and the bottom let in between the sides, and nailed to them and the ends. The top was fastened on with two butt hinges, and kept closed by a strong hook and staple. A wooden handle was fastened with screws diagonally on one end, and was used to carry the box.

Rammer. The rammer head was cylindrical in shape, made of beech, elm, or other hard wood, and had the corners at the large end slightly rounded. It was bored to receive the tenon of the staff, to which it was fastened with a wooden pin; and around the neck was placed a copper band.

Scraper. This implement was used to scrape the residue of powder from the bore of mortars and howitzers and remove it from the piece. It consisted of a handle of iron, having a scraper at one end, and a spoon for collecting dirt at the other, both being made of steel.

Shell Hooks. Used for mortar and other heavy shells which were difficult to handle. Shell hooks consisted of two bent iron arms connected by a pivot, one end of each was bent inwards to enter the ear of the shell, while the other ends were joined to a handspike ring by two small rings. A handspike was run through the large ring, and the lower ends of the arms adjusted to the ears of the shell, these ends approached each other, taking hold of the shell as soon as the handspike was raised.

Sponge. Made of woolen yarn,woven into a warp of hemp or flax-thread. This made a tissue about half an inch thick, sewed up in the form of a bag, which fitted the sponge head, to which it was fastened with copper nails driven into the inner end of the head, near the staff. A strip of leather was put under the head of the nails to prevent them from tearing out. For the Coehorn mortar the sponge was attached to a short staff, no rammer or sponge-heads being used. For the Columbiads, separate woolen sponges were provided for wiping the chamber and the bore. Stiff hair brushes were also occasionally used with these pieces in order to clean them more easily and thoroughly.

Sponge-covers. To protect and preserve the sponges. They were made of strong linen or canvas and painted. The diameter of the bag was equal to that of the bore of the gun, and the length was sufficient to allow the mouth to be drawn together, around the staff, by means of a cord inserted in the hem. A loop of canvas sewed to the bottom served as a handle by which to pull the cover off. Covers were marked with the caliber of the piece to which they belonged.

Sponge-head. This was cylindrical, the corners at both ends being slightly rounded, and was bored out to receive the tenon of the staff to which it was fastened with two wooden pins. It was made of poplar, elm, or similar wood.

Tongs. To pick up any shot which might fall upon the ground, iron tongs were used. They consisted of two arms joined by a pivot, each arm at its lower end being fastened to a semicircular piece which clasped firmly under the shot when the handles were closed.

Worm. This was made of iron, twisted as shown in the illustration, with a socket to receive the staff to which it was fastened with an iron rivet. There were two main sizes—one for siege and garrison guns, the other for field artillery. Worms were used for withdrawing cartridges, rags, and debris from artillery pieces.

IMPLEMENTS FOR PRIMING AND FIRING

Friction Primer. This was the device most generally used in the Federal service for firing artillery pieces. This primer consisted of a short tube of metal inserted

Artillery implements: top, gunner's pincers; bottom left, tar bucket; bottom right, sponge bucket. (Mike McAfee)

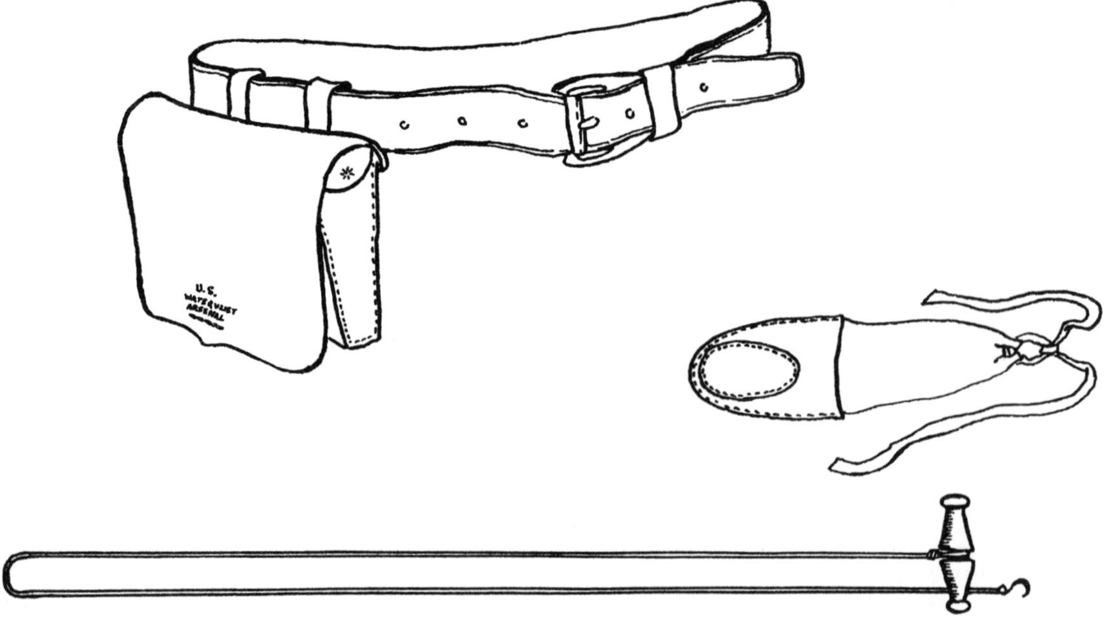

Artillery implements: top, tube-pouch; center, thumb-stall; bottom, lanyard. (Mike McAfee)

into a hole near the top of a longer tube, and soldered in that position. The short tube was lined with a composition made by mixing together one part of "chlorate of potassa and two parts of sulphurate of antimony," moistened with gum water. A serrated wire passed through the short tube and a hole opposite to it in the side of the long tube. The long tube was filled with musket powder, its upper end being covered with shellac-varnish blackened with lamp black, and its lower end closed with shoemaker's wax and dipped into varnish.

A great advantage of the friction tube was that it gave the enemy at night no clue to the position of the piece, as did the lighted port-fire or slow-match.

The friction primer for cannon was a small brass tube filled with gunpowder, which was ignited by drawing a rough wire briskly through friction composition, contained in a smaller tube inserted into the first near the top and soldered at right angles to it. A lanyard, with a hook attached, was used to ignite the primer. Friction primers were put up in bundles of 10 each, wrapped in waterproof paper; 10 bundles were packed in a tin box; 100 tin boxes were packed in a box made of 1-inch white pine boards, dovetailed.

Gunner's Gimlet. Of the same shape and size as the priming wire except that at the point a small screw was formed. It was used for boring out plugs which may have been inserted in the vent or the stems of priming tubes which may have become wedged in there.

Gunner's pincers. If the obstruction in the vent projected beyond the surface of the gun, or had a head, it could be withdrawn with the gunner's pincers, which were made of iron with steel jaws. One end of the arms had a clasp for drawing nails.

Lanyard and Hook. The almost universal method of firing cannon was by means of friction tubes, the only implement required being a lanyard, or cord of suitable length fixed at one end to a wooden handle on which it was wound when not in use, and having at the other end a small hook which entered the eye of the friction tube. When quick-match was used for priming, it was usually ignited by using a piece of lighted slow-match held in a linstock, which was a short staff of oak or ash with a pointed ferrule to stick in the ground, and near the head a hole through which passed the end of the slow-match. The lanyard was used to pull the primer only and not with slow- or quick-match. The lanyard was a piece of strong line,

Pass boxes: left, Navy; right, Army.

Navy pass box. Marked "Patern Navy Yard, Boston 1864 IX inch."

about .2 inches thick, 12 feet long. To one end of the lanyard was attached a small iron hook, with an eye for the line, and attached to the other end was a wooden toggle, .75 inches in diameter and 4 inches long.

Priming Tube. A small pipe, with a cup at one end, and filled with a composition for firing the cannon.

Priming Wire. Used for pricking the cartridge before priming when the quill or metal tubes were used. It was made of wire, slightly less in diameter than the vent, sloping to a point at one end, and at the other bent into a circle, which served as a handle as well as preventing it from slipping through the loop on the tube pouch where it was carried when not in use.

Quick-match. Made of cotton yarn such as was used in candle wicks. One yard of quick-match burned in the open air in 13 seconds. A quick-match inclosed in tubes burned more rapidly than in the open air, and more so in proportion as the tubes were progressively smaller in size.

Slow-match. Made of hemp, flax, or cotton rope, with three strands slightly twisted. Cotton rope well twisted formed a good match without any preparation, and burned 4½ inches an hour.

Thumb stall. Made of buckskin, with the pad stuffed with hair, and a string at the end also of buckskin, to tie around the wrist. The thumb stall was used to stop securely the vent while the piece was being loaded.

Tube Pouch. Used to hold friction tubes, lanyard, and thumb stall, and to carry the priming wire and gunner's gimlet. The sides and ends were made of russet sole leather. It had two covers, the inner one having end pieces sewed to it which shut over the ends of the pouch. The outer one or "flap" was of the same piece as the back, and was fastened down by a strap to a brass button riveted to the bottom of the pouch. It was provided with a waist-belt, which passed through two loops sewed to the back of the pouch. Two small loops sewed to the inside of the flap served for carrying the priming wire and the gimlet.

Vent Cover. Made of black bridle leather and used to strap over and protect the vent of a piece. A pin of copper or brass, fastened by two rivets, entered the vent to prevent the cover from slipping. It was fastened to the piece by a buckle and strap, the latter passing around the breech, with the length depending on the size of the gun.

Vent Punch. When obstructions could not be removed by the gunner's gimlet, the vent punch was used, especially if an iron plug had been inserted. The vent punch was a short wire, cut off square at one end and with the other brazed into an iron head. The head had a hole through which a nail or piece of wire could be inserted, to aid in withdrawing the punch from the vent.

MISCELLANEOUS EQUIPMENT FOR FIELD ARTILLERY BATTERIES

Drag Rope. A 4-inch hemp rope, with a thimble worked into each end, one of the thimbles carrying a hook. Six handles, made of oak or ash, were put in between the strands of the rope, and lashed with marline. It was used to aid in extricating carriages from different positions, by the men, for dragging pieces, and similar functions. The drag rope was 28 feet long.

Men's Harness. Made of 4-inch hemp rope, with two thimbles and a hook like the drag rope. Six loops, made of bag leather, were attached to the rope in pairs, by means of knots worked in the rope, or by leather collars sewed to it with strong twine. As implied by its name, it was used for harnessing the men to the pieces, under circumstances when horses could not be used; as, for example, in dragging the guns up very steep ascents. The men's harness was 18 feet long.

Parbuckle. A 4-inch rope, 12 feet long, with a hook at one end and a loop at the other. To parbuckle a gun meant to roll it in either direction from the spot on which it rested. However, if the ground was horizontal, handspikes only were necessary to move the gun.

Prolonge. Made of 3½ inch hemp rope. A toggle was

fastened to one end by three rings and a "thimble," which was worked into the rope; another "thimble" held a hook at the other end of the rope; the splice at each end was served with marline. The prolonge was used with field pieces to attach the gun to the limber when firing during a retreat, or advancing, instead of limbering up; for the same purpose in crossing ditches; for coupling a piece to a limber, for righting carriages when upset, and for other purposes. The prolonge was 26 feet 7 inches long, and was carried wound around the prolonge hooks on the trail of the piece.

Sponge Bucket. Made of sheet iron. The top and bottom were turned over the sides and fastened with rivets. Sometimes the bottom was fastened to the sides by a double fold and stiffened with a hoop shrunk on above the seam. It had a "float" made of wood and which served as a cover to the bucket. The handle of the float was attached by two rivets and was connected with the handle of the bucket by two rings and a chain. A toggle was fastened to the top of the handle by two links and a swivel and was used to attach the bucket to the eye of the axle strap on the gun carriage. This bucket held water in which the sponge was dipped when washing out the cannon.

Tar Bucket. Made of sheet iron in the same manner as the sponge bucket. The cover was kept shut by means of a stud riveted into the top of the bucket. It was provided with a hook and chains and was used for carrying tar along with the guns, for use on marches during hot weather. Tar was mixed with the axle grease to prevent the grease from melting.

Tow Hook. Made of round iron, with a hook at one end, and a small hammer welded to the other. It was used for unpacking the ammunition chests of field carriages. The hammer was used for making any repairs on the strapped shot and shell and fixed ammunition, as found necessary in the field.

Water Bucket. Before 1860 this was usually of wood but during the war was made of leather, the seams sewed and riveted together, and the whole painted. This was a much lighter and more durable utensil than the old wooden water buckets, although the wooden water buckets were still used for garrison service.

FIELD ARTILLERY MATERIEL. In its broadest sense, *materiel* encompasses all types of military equipment, as differentiated from *personnel.* But the artilleryman usually thinks of materiel as including only his cannon and wheeled vehicles. The wheeled materiel includes the gun carriages, each with its caisson, and each gun and caisson having a limber. There were six different carriages in the field artillery, each having the same sized wheels and the same kind of limber. Thus the limbers and wheels were interchangeable within these types. The 6-pounder gun and the 12-pounder howitzer used the same carriage; the 24-pounder carriage was once used also by the 9-pounder gun; and the carriage for the 12-pounder gun and the 32-pounder howitzer were the same. Each battery also had a battery wagon, in which certain tools and equipment were carried, and a traveling forge.

CAISSON. An ammunition cart for mobile artillery. When coupled to its limber the caisson became a four-wheeled vehicle. The number of rounds of ammunition carried by each caisson and its limber was as follows:

Type of Cannon	*No. of Rounds*
6-pounder gun	150
12-pounder gun	96
12-pounder howitzer	117
24-pounder howitzer	69
32-pounder howitzer	45

The number of caissons with field batteries were: with a battery of 12-pounders, 8 caissons for guns and 4 for howitzers; and with a battery of 6-pounders, 4 for guns, and 2 for howitzers.

LIMBER. The limber is often confused with the caisson but actually was a two-wheeled vehicle similar in general appearance but instead of carrying projectiles the "chest" contained tools and items necessary for firing the cannon. When the battery was actually firing, the limber was about 10 yards behind the cannon. The gun limber was the fore part of a mobile gun carriage to which horses were attached. The same limber was used for all field carriages.

AXES AND HATCHETS (ARMY).

The axes and hatchets which have survived the century since the War, and the surprisingly large number which have been found on battlefields and camp sites demonstrate two facts about them. First of all, they were very plentiful as one would expect in view of the woody terrain in which the armies operated. Secondly, the Civil War types of axes and hatchets were very similar to those in use today. Axes were issued to pioneer troops and units assigned to "slashing" forests in areas around fortifications. Moreover, many soldiers bought camp hatchets for their own use in the field. An axe head in the author's collection is 9¾ inches from blade to hammer surface, with the extreme blade length of 9¼ inches. It is marked: "D. Simmons, Cohoes, N.Y. Cast Steel Warranted."

AXES

AXE, CAMP. An axe head found on the battlefield of Champions Hill, Mississippi is typical of the army

Pioneer soldier, equipped with axe. Photograph taken about 1862. (Smithsonian Institution)

axe used extensively in all theaters. Length of head, 8 inches; width of blade, 4½ inches.

AXE, PIONEERS. No markings. Total length, 36 inches; width of blade from cutting edge to hammer surface, 10 inches.

AXE, SPLITTING. Wooden handle, painted black. Total length, 28 inches; length of axe head from blade to hammer surface, 8 inches; width of blade, 2¾ inches.

AXE HOLDER. Most axes were issued without holders. However, the author has one made of russet leather. It is 10 inches long, 6 inches wide, and is equipped with straps. This axe holder is marked: "Axe Sling. January 1863."

HATCHET, ARMY. Two types of hatchet heads have been recovered from campsites and battlefields in recent years. These show clearly that there has been practically no change in design and size of hatchets in the past 100 years. A fairly rare type was found on the battlefield of Spotsylvania. Part of the original handle is still present. Length of head from blade to hammer, 6 inches. More common is a second type, known as "camp hatchet," which varied slightly in size although the shape was the same. A specimen in the author's collection, 4¾ inches long, was found at Spotsylvania, while another one, from The Wilderness, is slightly narrower.

BACTERIOLOGICAL WARFARE. When Lieutenant Charles W. Randall, 17th Vermont Infantry, had his health permanently impaired by smallpox, it was believed that he caught the disease from infected clothing. This clothing, consisting of undergarments, had been purchased at a store in Washington which afterward came under suspicion as a place of consignment for the "infection scheme suggested by Dr. Blackburn of Kentucky." The lieutenant died shortly after the war. (See "The Youngest Officer in the War," in *Stories of Our Soldiers,* p. 229. Boston Journal Newspaper Company, Boston, 1893.) It has not been possible to verify the allegation. Pollution of wells by throwing dead animals in them was not infrequent.

BADGES, CORPS. Corps badges were worn by Federal troops in the various theaters of war. To increase esprit de corps and for a ready recognition of corps and divisions in the various armies, a system of badges for the various corps was adopted. The idea first originated with General Philip Kearny,

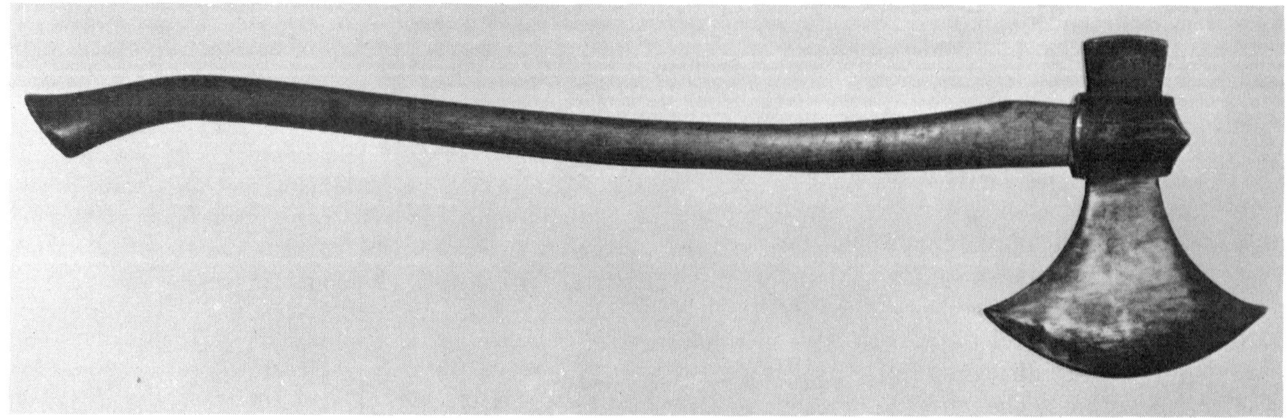

Pioneer's axe.

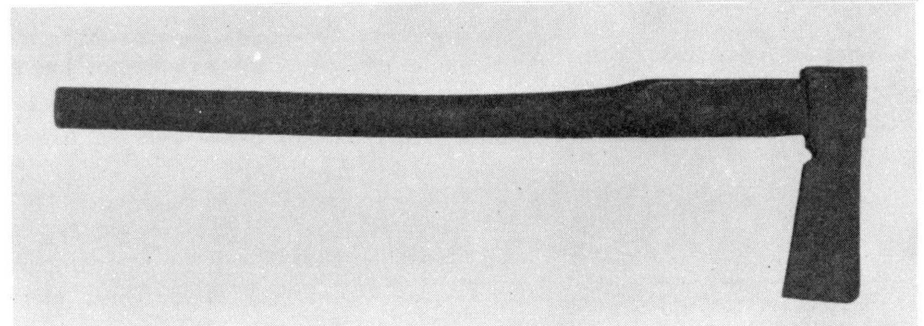

Splitting axe.

who had the soldiers of his division wear a red patch to distinguish them from other troops. The idea of corps badges to be worn throughout the Army of the Potomac was suggested to Hooker by his Chief of Staff, General Daniel Butterfield, who devised the badges in detail. Butterfield's biographer has told us how the different badges came to be selected. The design for the First Army Corps was a disc, "the first thing thought of." A patch or lozenge was reserved for the Third Army Corps, as Kearny's division was in that corps. For the Second Army Corps the trefoil was chosen, as a sort of shamrock, there being many troops of Irish origin in that corps. The order for the first corps badges (Army of the Potomac, March 21, 1863) was prompted by the need of ready recognition of corps and divisions to prevent injustice by reports of straggling and misconduct through mistakes as to their organization. The Chief Quartermaster was directed to furnish without delay the badges to officers and men.

The idea of corps badges was taken to the Western armies by the transfer of the Eleventh and Twelfth Army Corps from the Army of the Potomac to Tennessee in 1863. When these corps arrived at Chattanooga they were wearing their corps badges. Rivalry between them and the Western corps was strong and the contrast in neatness of dress between the two sections was marked. One of the Easterners asked an Irishman of the Western troops what his corps badge was. The Westerner slapped his cartridge box and replied: "This is my corps badge." As a result of this incident, his unit, the Fifteenth Army Corps, adopted the cartridge box with the words "Forty Rounds" as their corps badge. Only two (Thirteenth and Twenty-first) of the 25 corps failed to adopt badges in the Federal Army.

The badges were cloth and were worn either on the cap or left side of the hat. There appears to have been no continuous government issue of these badges; the men bought them from sutlers or made them from the lining cloth of their overcoats. In some armies at least, badges were furnished by division headquarters. The original badges for the Army of the Potomac were ordered on March 24, 1863 by number for color and style of pattern to be made in Philadelphia. Moreover, dies for cutting badges were issued the various corps of the Army of the Potomac, while the Department of West Virginia also requested punches for field use in cutting its corps badges. The corps emblems were used everywhere—being painted on ambulances, wagons, and other materiel, as well as being worn by the men. Most of the metal corps badges were sold by sutlers. In addition to brass and tin, silver badges, engraved with the soldier's name, company, and regiment were popular. These fancy badges were widely advertised in *Harper's Weekly*, *Leslie's*, and *The Army and Navy Journal*. One soldier considered his corps badges as possessing the power to protect him from all Reb missiles. But, whether cloth, tin, brass, or silver, corps badges actually worn during the war are very scarce today and most collectors consider themselves fortunate if they have any at all. The Confederacy did not have corps badges.

BAG, CARPET. Most carpet bags were made for civilian use but some were made primarily for sale to soldiers. Two carpet bags in my possession are equipped with locks which are identical with many dug up on various battlefields in Virginia. Apparently some soldiers brought carpet bags to camp with them on enlisting or returning from furlough. The two carpet bags in the author's collection, differing in size and color, are as follows: The larger is 15½ by 15½ inches. The smaller is 13½ by 12 inches. Both are of very brilliant multi-colored carpet material and equipped with the locks mentioned above.

BAG, POWDER (Cartridge-Bags). According to Gibbon: "The cartridge-bag should be made of wildbore, merino, or bombazette, which should be composed entirely of wool, free from any mixture of thread or cotton, which would be apt to retain fire in the piece. The texture and sewing should be close enough to prevent the powder sifting through. Untwilled stuff is to be preferred. Flannel may be used when the other materials cannot be obtained."

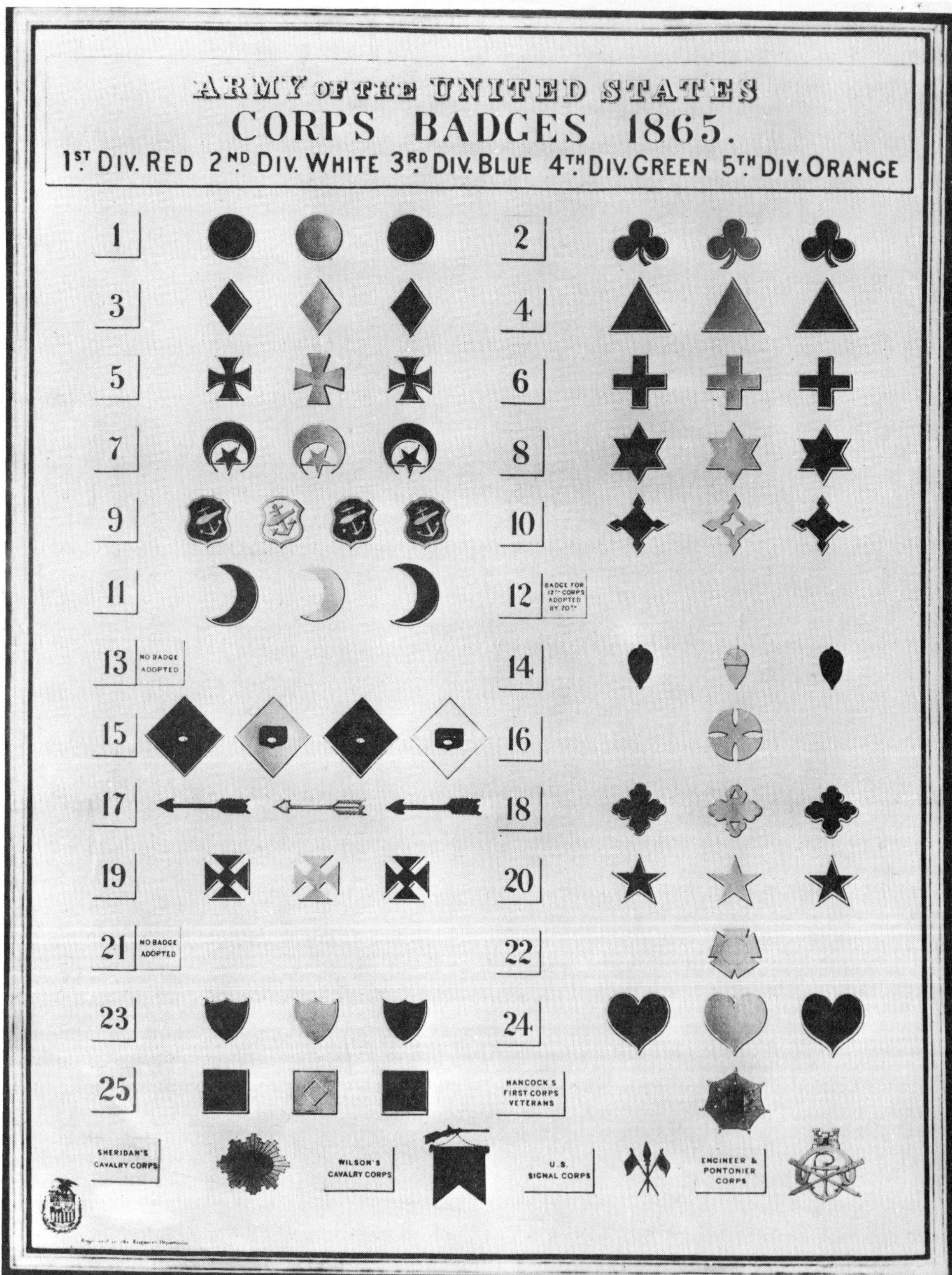

Corps badges of the Federal Army. (National Archives)

Bags to be used with fixed ammunition were not stitched all the way to the top. They were tested for size by being filled and then passed through the shot-gauge of their caliber. Because of the wide range of calibers used in the war there is likewise a wide range in size of powder bags. Many colors were used including a tartan supposedly imported from England for Confederate use.

BAKE OVEN, FIELD. Various types and sizes of field bake ovens were used by regiments when they first went in the field. Most if not all were of private manufacture and differed widely from state to state. Bake ovens soon disappeared from the "impedimenta" of units in the field, and after 1862 were used mainly by troops at draft rendezvous and similar rear echelon units. The author has a field stove found at Antietam after the battle. Stoves and ovens that are known definitely to have seen service in the war are excessively rare.

BAKE OVEN, MOBILE. Early in the war there was an attempt to supply the troops with soft bread while they were engaged in active campaigning. As a result, several hundred huge bakeovens on wheels were issued to troops in the field. These mobile ovens, together with mules, drivers, and trained bakers, were assigned one such unit per regiment. "At first the boys thought they were a great thing, and they were—for the contractor who furnished them." The ovens functioned fairly well but the quality of bread produced went from bad to worse. Sometimes the unwieldy ovens would stick in the mud and not reach camp until midnight; "or the baker would so far forget his duty to his suffering country as to get drunk, and then there would be no bread, good or

Carpet bag. Used by a Maine soldier during the war.

Federal balloon *Intrepid* being inflated during the Battle of Fair Oaks. (National Archives)

bad." Hardtack was much more portable and dependable. One by one the ponderous oven vehicles got out of repair, or were overturned and wrecked, or were abandoned as a useless incumbrance. By the fall of 1862 they had practically disappeared.

BALL AND CHAIN. While the ball and chain was used for both Army and Navy prisoners, the very weight of the apparatus itself restricted its use to the more permanent prisons and places of confinement in the rear areas. Moreover, the ball and chain was used only in the more desperate cases or on prisoners under confinement for very serious offenses. Prisoners confined for lesser offenses were generally not shackled in any way but were confined in buildings or tents under armed guard. The only specimen available for study is a ball and chain weighing 33 pounds. The chain is 53 inches long. No markings.

BALLOONS. In order to identify clearly the Federal balloons, some were marked with red, white, and blue bunting. The *Constitution* was decorated with a large portrait of George Washington; the *Union* had a gigantic spread-eagle and the Stars and Stripes; while the *Intrepid* bore its name conspicuously on its side.

By January 1862, Lowe had 7 balloons in operation, and on the Peninsula his balloon corps used mobile field generators. McClellan permitted the addition of a telegraphic train to the Balloon Corps. By means of this telegraph, Lowe participated in the first use of artillery fire direction with aerial observation in American history. The Balloon Corps was disbanded just before Gettysburg.

Ball and chain and hand and leg irons.

BALL SCREW. See APPENDAGES.

BAR-SHOT. See CHAIN-SHOT and PROJECTILES.

BASEBALL. See RECREATIONAL EQUIPMENT.

BASIN. Some officers and a few enlisted men used basins during their early months of service, but

Army basin.

such luxuries soon disappeared at the front. The basin shown here is of tin, 10¼ inches in diameter, and 2½ inches deep.

BATON. See MUSICAL INSTRUMENTS.

BATTERY WAGON. See TELEGRAPH EQUIPMENT. Compact portable electric batteries and telegraph sets were occasionally transported in ambulances, called "Battery Wagons" constructed for the purpose. However, more often the telegraph station was set up under tent flies in close proximity to the commanding general's headquarters.

BAYONETS. Most muskets and rifles were equipped with either a socket or saber bayonet, depending on the model and make. All U.S. regulation muskets and rifles except the Model 1841 rifle, 1855 rifle, and Remington 1863 rifle used the socket bayonet. The Plymouth rifle used either a saber bayonet or the famous Dahlgren knife bayonet. The non-regulation Merrill and Sharps rifles were also equipped with saber bayonets. Most troops disliked the saber bayonet because it was too unwieldy; as a result, saber bayonets saw comparatively limited use. It is interesting to note that a correspondent of the *Army and Navy Journal* recommended the adoption of a knife bayonet with a blade 10 or 12 inches long, since a weapon of that size could be used either as a bayonet or a knife.

The angular or socket bayonet was a "savage looking thing" with three fluted sides and a needle-sharp point. Most recruits had an abiding faith in the efficacy of the bayonet, having read harrowing descriptions of the devastation wrought by the bayonet in charges on the enemy. There is no doubt that some bayonet wounds were given and received on both sides during the war. But the number of men who received bayonet wounds was very small. There

Battery wagon used by Signal Corps in the field. Petersburg, 1864. (National Archives)

were many surgeons of extensive combat experience in dressing stations and field hospitals who never dressed a bayonet wound.

None can deny the psychological effect of a bayonet charge, but usually one side or the other broke before the men closed in enough to use the bayonet effectively. However, some units with ambitious officers spent a great deal of time and perspiration in learning the bayonet drill. "This drill was a Frenchy affair—with its *parry, prime, 'se-conde,' tierce, high quarte, lunge, blow with the butt*—all of which kept the men jumping around like so many animated frogs . . .

the models of U.S. regulation bayonets. The most common saber bayonet was the one designed for the Fayetteville rifle, but it, like most Confederate bayonets, is unmarked. Probably the most common Confederate triangular bayonet was made at the Richmond Armory. These bayonets have slim blades. Only the tips are steel—the rest of the bayonet is made of iron. Some bayonet scabbards were locally made, but the Confederacy also imported large numbers as part of the equipment used with such weapons as the Enfield. Shown here are two types of Enfield bayonets with their scabbards.

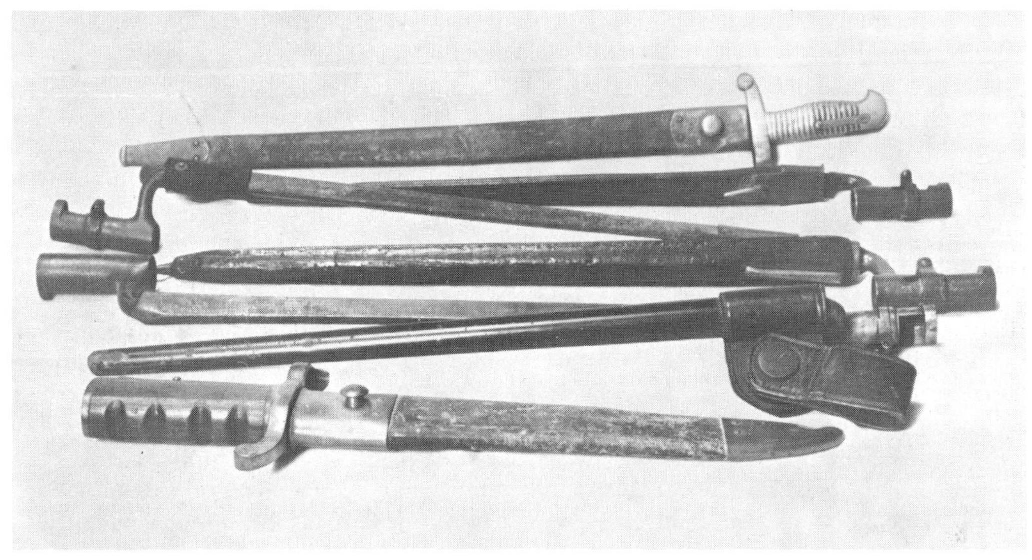

Types of Civil War bayonets.

Perhaps they fight on these scientific principles in France, but in our war nobody ever heard any of these commands given in battle. An officer who attempted to put the drill into actual practice would have been sent to the rear and clothed in a strait jacket."

One of the most universal uses of the bayonet was for pounding the kernels of coffee in a tin cup. Another very common use of the bayonet was as a candlestick. The bayonet also was employed to dig up vegetables or as a tent pin.

Bayonet Attachment (Patent No. 45,901) Patented January 10, 1865 by Hiram Berdan of New York, N.Y. The shank of the bayonet was shorter than usual, and the holding stud, or end of the barrel, was so located as to bring the blade directly over the ramrod, which was pushed up under the blade or shank, and thus the locking clasp or ring was better secured.

Bayonet Scabbard. See ACCOUTERMENTS.

Bayonet Trowel. See INTRENCHING TOOLS.

Confederate Bayonets. The Confederates copied

Dahlgren Bayonet. The Navy was the first to adopt a knife bayonet in the United States. Credit for this innovation belongs to Admiral John A. Dahlgren who in 1856 pointed out the need for a bowie knife type of bayonet for hand-to-hand fighting, and a heavy tool for cutting away damaged naval tackle. Dahlgren devised a heavy bayonet which was officially adopted and was used with the so-called Plymouth rifle, another weapon manufactured according to Dahlgren's specifications. These new bowie bayonets were made under contract by the Ames Manufacturing Company at Chicopee Falls, Massachusetts, and were unique in the history of American naval weapons.

Sawtooth Bayonet. Although no weapon of this type was issued extensively, if at all, by either Federal or Confederate ordnance departments, such bayonets had been in use in some European armies since 1809, and perhaps a few were imported for the Civil War. On October 29, 1864, a captain of the Maryland Artillery proposed the adoption of a saw-tooth bayonet.

He believed that combining the saw and bayonet in a single weapon would be useful to engineer and pontonnier units. The sawtooth bayonet, as patented in 1864, was called a "fascine-knife." The blade was so shaped that it was broader at the point than at the hilt, and therefore could be used with greater force as a hatchet. The back had teeth filed into it so it could be used as a saw. This bayonet was attached to the rifle, as any saber bayonet, and was therefore no hindrance to firing, while the point was sharp enough to serve very well for a thrust.

long as the rest of us, carrying all our gear, they wouldn't try 'to preachify ter the soljers.'"

Testaments were given to soldiers by both Northern and Southern tract societies, religious organizations, and relatives or friends. Due to the substantial number of soldiers of foreign extraction, especially in the Federal armies, New Testaments and other religious texts were published in German, French, and other foreign languages, as well as English.

Testaments and religious literature, especially tracts, were scattered among the soldiers by the thousands,

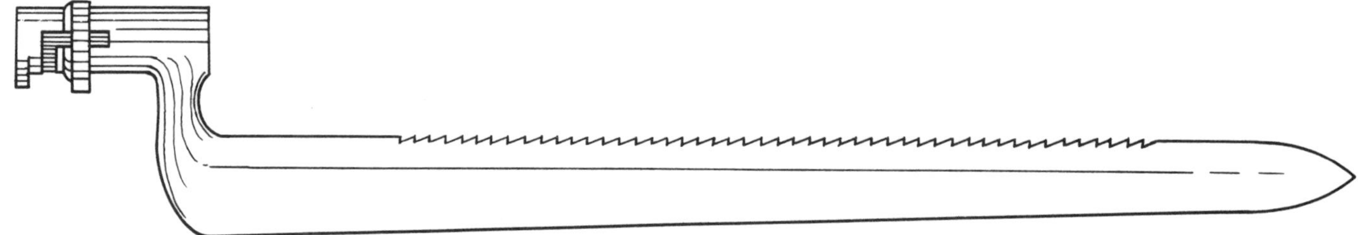

Alexander's saw bayonet, patent Nov. 15, 1864. (National Archives)

and probably were helpful in improving the morals of many men. But there were many cases similar to the Massachusetts soldier who complained that when his regiment arrived in New York, en route to the seat of war, the men were presented with "a plate of thin soup and a Testament." Such incidents were illustrative of mistaken philanthropy that was expended upon the Army by well-intentioned individuals. Many religious zealots often labored under the delusion that the armed services were composed of bad men altogether. Testaments were generally appreciated and very often carried throughout the war, but tracts were so written as to defeat their own purpose and were usually thrown away, often without being read at all.

SAWTOOTH BAYONET (Patent No. 45,009). This bayonet was patented November 15, 1864 by F. W. Alexander of Baltimore, Maryland. It was a flat or saber bayonet, provided with sawteeth on one edge so that it could be used as a knife or saw.

SLIDING BAYONET (Patent No. 35,760). Patented July 1, 1862 by James Jenkinson of Brooklyn, New York. Jenkinson's bayonet was "so constructed and applied as to admit of its being readily advanced in the act of lowering the piece to *charge bayonet* and readily retracted in the act of restoring the piece to a vertical position." The bayonet was held in its advanced position by means of a spring catch.

BELT. See ACCOUTERMENTS.

BELT PLATE. See BUCKLES.

BIBLE AND TESTAMENT. The Federal Government gave free transportation to Christian Commission delegates who carried their Bibles, Testaments, tracts, and books to troops in the battle areas. One delegate in a few months distributed 106 hymn books, 379 soldier's books of various kinds, 94 copies of parts of the Scriptures, 1,773 religious papers, and 3,652 pages of tracts. During 1864 alone the Commission distributed 569,794 Bibles and Testaments, 4,815,923 hymns and psalm books, and 13,681,342 pages of tracts.

When preparing for a long march, the soldiers often tried to give away their Bibles. They often gave them to the chaplains, who also picked Bibles and Testaments up from the ground where the soldiers had dropped them. When it came to choosing between blisters and Bibles, it did not take long to reach a conclusion. When reproved by their chaplains the men would respond: "If chaplains had to march as

BLACKING. Most commanders required their men to keep their boots and shoes well blackened, but did not provide blacking. Usually a box of blacking was given to soldiers before they started for the front and, after arrival, they purchased blacking from sutlers. The shoe brush was separate and difficult to pack, while often the box of blacking was carried in the pocket.

Leather equipment, both accouterments and footwear, was kept in good appearance by the blacking which men bought out of their own pockets. The only example of Civil War surviving blacking known to the author is the corroded remains of a box from the Wilderness battlefield. The tin can is 2¾ inches in diameter and about ⅝ inch in depth. The can still has the blacking in it. William G. Gavin found a can of blacking approximately twice the size of the one described above.

BLANKETS. Blankets were "all alike and there was

no choice," either for individuals or branch of service. Many soldiers considered them much the same as the horse blankets used back home on the farm. They were made of coarse material and had a large U.S. in the middle. Blankets were usually woolen, gray in color, and the U.S., in black, was 4 inches long. The regulation army blanket was 7 feet long, 5½ feet wide, and weighed 5 pounds. Confederate blankets were much less uniform in color and size; often Confederate soldiers used pieces of carpet as blankets, and often had nothing at all.

Most Federal soldiers were provided with both a woolen and a rubber blanket. When they retired after tattoo roll call, they did not strip to the skin, but usually took off coat and boots and perhaps the vest. Some, however, stripped to their flannels, and donning a smoking cap, would turn in. There were a few in every regiment who never took off anything, day or night, unless compelled to do so. It was common for soldiers to make an undersheet of the rubber blanket, the lining side up.

Blankets were normally issued to the men before leaving their home state. But in August, 1862 the sudden call for volunteers and militia had exhausted the market supply of blankets fit for military purposes. Therefore, the U.S. War Department, by General Order No. 121, advised all citizens who might volunteer or be drafted to take blankets with them to their rendezvous camp in their home state. These blankets were to be of "good, stout, wool."

Blanket Sling (Patent No. 35,002). Patented April 15, 1862, by Joseph Short of Salem, Massachusetts. This sling for carrying blanket or overcoat consisted of an arrangement of straps by which an overcoat or blanket, when rolled up compactly, could be carried just above the small of the back in a comfortable fashion.

BLOUSE. See UNIFORMS AND CLOTHING.

BOARDING AXE. Tables of allowances of Ordnance Equipments and Stores, U.S. Navy, 1864, provided for battle axes (i.e. boarding axes or hatchets) as follows:

Ship of the Line	170
Frigate	92
Sloop of War	20-60
Brig	10
Screw Steamer	10-110
Side-wheel Steamer	10-60

The number of battle axes furnished a vessel was determined by its complement of seamen.

The specimen illustrated here is marked "U.S. Navy. J.M. VICAR CAST STEEL."

Dimensions: Length, 16¼ inches, width of blade to hammer head 6¾ inches. Wooden handle. Two nail-pulling slots in blade.

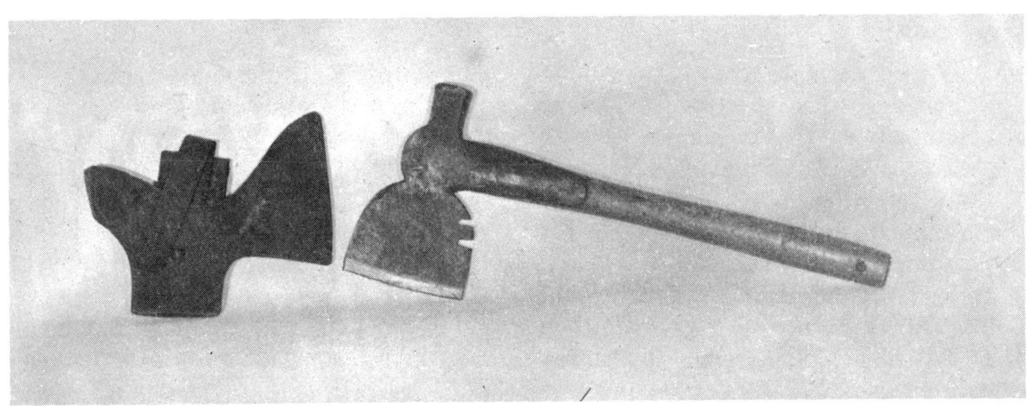

Boarding axe and holder.

A smaller boarding axe (handle is broken off) is only 6½ inches wide from edge of blade to tip of hammer. Marked: "No. 2 D. SIMMONS & CO. COHOES, N.Y. Warranted Cast Steel."

Probably there also were French boarding axes imported for use in the war since several specimens have been found in accumulations of Civil War surplus. These are usually marked with an anchor.

Boarding Axe Holder. Made of black bridle leather, 7¾ inches long, with loop for attaching to the belt. Marked "U.S.N. Boston."

BOARDING PIKE. In addition to small arms, cutlasses, and boarding axes, Civil War fighting ships also carried boarding pikes. Those in the author's collection are generally similar in shape and design but differ somewhat in dimensions of the metal tip. The length of the pike is 8 feet but the metal tips are 7, 9, and 12 inches. Side-straps for holding the metal tip in the pole vary from 6 inches to 24 inches. An original specimen, unchanged in any respect from the war period, has a staff painted white with a red tip.

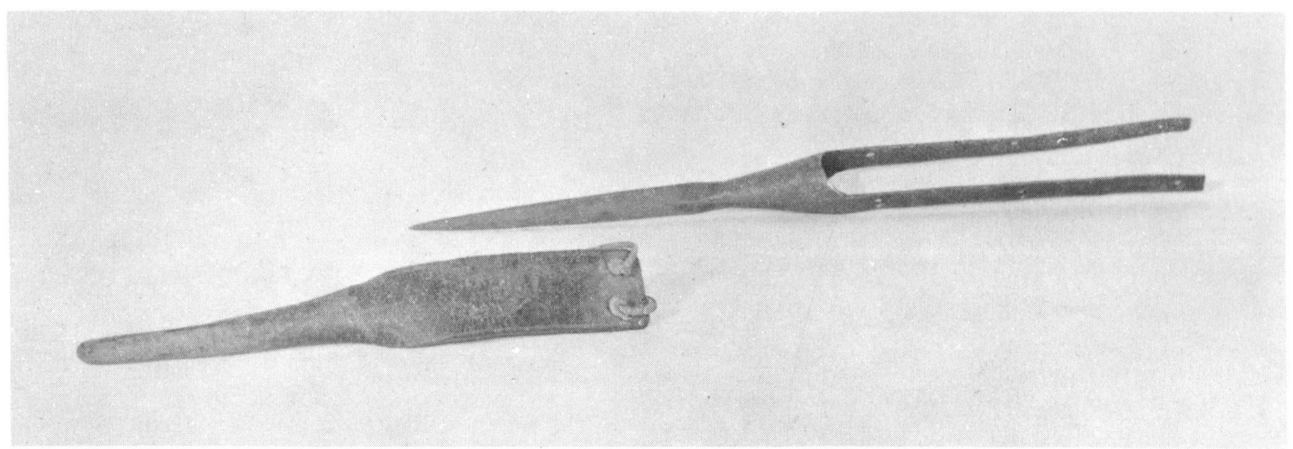

Boarding pike and holder.

No markings have been found on any specimens examined.

According to *Ordnance Instructions* U.S. Navy, "one-fourth of the number of men composing a gun's crew (rejecting fractions and the Powderman or Boy), and all the men of the Master's division on the spar-deck, except those designated as Boarders and those at the wheel and conn are to be Pikemen." One boarding pike for each gun on covered decks was always "to be kept triced up conveniently near it" to be used by the Powderman or any other person left at the gun to guard the port. Pikemen were to be covered by the Marines with their bayonets fixed.

In case of an attack by enemy boarders, "the Pikemen should arrange themselves in rear of those armed with swords (cutlasses), and in situations which will allow them to rest the points of their pikes on the hammocks or rail, and cover that part of the ship and the parts where the assault is expected. The Marines, with their muskets loaded and bayonets fixed, may be formed behind the Pikemen."

BOARDING PIKE SHEATH. Made of black bridle leather 10¾ inches long, and equipped with strong cord for tying around the pike staff. Marked: "Navy Yard, N.Y. 1864."

BODY ARMOR. Although the Government never issued armor of any sort, sutlers and private dealers sold iron vests to many recruits. These vests were so heavy that they were soon thrown away and in the few cases where they were worn in battle they failed to live up to expectations. One such breastplate (probably discarded by a Confederate soldier) was worn by a Federal soldier until he was severely wounded. He then gave it to a comrade who was killed by a minie ball which struck the breastplate near its lower border and passed through it carrying pieces of the plate into the abdomen. A typical advertisement for one of these soldiers' bulletproof vests stressed that it had been "repeatedly and thoroughly tested with pistol bullets at 10 paces, rifle bullets at 40 rods, by many army officers and was approved and worn by them." Simple and light, it was "guaranteed" to save thousands.

BOMB-SHELL. See also PROJECTILES. The shell thrown by a mortar was called a "bomb-shell"; and the shelters made for magazines, etc. should be "bomb-proof."

BOOKS. See RECREATIONAL EQUIPMENT.

BOOTEES. See UNIFORMS AND CLOTHING.

BOOTJACK. A device used to hold the boot while the foot is being drawn out of it. Advertisements for bootjacks appeared in journals of the war era and there are homemade specimens in collections today.

BOOTS. See UNIFORMS AND CLOTHING.

BOTTLE, LIQUOR. Although beer was popular among the troops, the most common intoxicant was definitely whiskey. An officer writing in the *Army and Navy Journal* for February 11, 1865, pointed out that "a very large proportion of the whiskey furnished by the Commissariat is used by the officers (who) can almost invariably get as much as they want, though enlisted men cannot. Indeed, I have known the supply of whiskey to be abundant when the public animals were starving for forage and the troops were on half rations. The Navy does without whiskey. Why cannot the Army?"

Although called the "whiskey ration," whiskey was only supplied by the Government to enlisted men on rare occasions and then usually by orders of the Medical Department. Whiskey was usually issued only after a strenuous march, heavy fighting, or in cold rainy or snowy weather. Captain N. D. Preston, 10th New York Cavalry, stated that his brigade commander ordered a light issue of whiskey for the troops—"the first and only regular issue of whiskey I ever made or know of being made to an enlisted man." But most observers

Body armor. (Norm Flayderman)

have recorded much more frequent and liberal supplying of whiskey. Certainly the large number of bottles still being found in old campsites would indicate that a relatively substantial quantity of whiskey was consumed by soldiers during the war. These bottles were of all conceivable shapes and sizes. Beer was also popular with the men. Frequently officers carried whiskey flasks with them in the field.

A sample specimen of a liquor bottle is made of dark, almost black glass, and is 9½ inches tall and 2½ inches in diameter. All bottles in this photograph except the beer bottle were found at headquarters of 3rd Cavalry Division, Army of the Potomac, in Virginia. None of these bottles is marked. Also shown is a large wicker-covered wine bottle of pale colored glass, 15¼ inches tall, 6 inches in diameter. It is equipped with a wooden base to insure its remaining upright. Also a smaller wicker-covered wine bottle, also of pale colored glass 10 inches tall and 4 inches in diameter. The beer bottle illustrated is made of medium-brown colored heavy glass, 11½ inches tall and 3 inches in diameter. Marked on bottom of bottle: "C. MILW."

BOWIE KNIFE. See KNIFE.

BOX, DITTY. Made of sandalwood with a hinged gutta-percha cover, embossed with stars, flags, can-

Liquor and beer bottles. Left to right: wine bottle, beer bottle, large and small wicker-covered wine bottles.

non, anchor, etc. Dimensions: 3¼ inches tall, 4¾ inches wide, and 4¾ inches deep. This box is identical with another box except for the embossing on the cover, whose motif is agriculture, i.e. plow, sheaf of wheat, corn tassels, etc. However both boxes were used in the war. On the inside of the cover of the second box is pasted the original label as follows: "From Moses Ulman and Sons. The Old Reliable one price, Clothiers and Merchant Tailors, OPP. the Court House, Williamsport, Pa." These boxes were originally collar boxes but were used to carry small items in during the early months of soldiering.

BRASSES. A term used by troops when referring to their brass ornaments on uniforms and equipment. Specifically, this meant waist belt plate, cartridge box belt plate, cartridge box plate, shoulder belt plate ("eagle"), headgear letters and numbers, buttons, and shoulder scales.

BREECH SIGHT. See ARTILLERY.

BRICOLE. See also ARTILLERY. Men's harness for dragging guns. Length 18 feet. Was used for harnessing men to guns when horses could not be used.

BRIDLE. See HORSE EQUIPMENTS.

BRIDOON. See HORSE EQUIPMENTS.

BRUSH, HORSE. See HORSE EQUIPMENTS.

BUCKLES. See also ACCOUTERMENTS and UNIFORMS AND CLOTHING. The waist belt was fastened by a belt plate, usually oval in shape and with the letters U.S. or C.S. in block letters in the center of the buckle. Some regiments, both Federal and Reb, wore their State letters, e.g. N.C., S.C.,

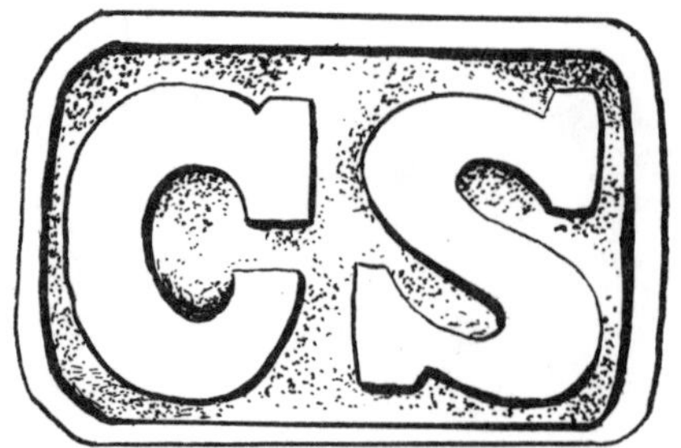

Some Confederate buckles. (Mike McAfee)

Federal officer's buckles. Center buckle, the most common of the three types shown here, was 2 inches wide. (Norm Flayderman)

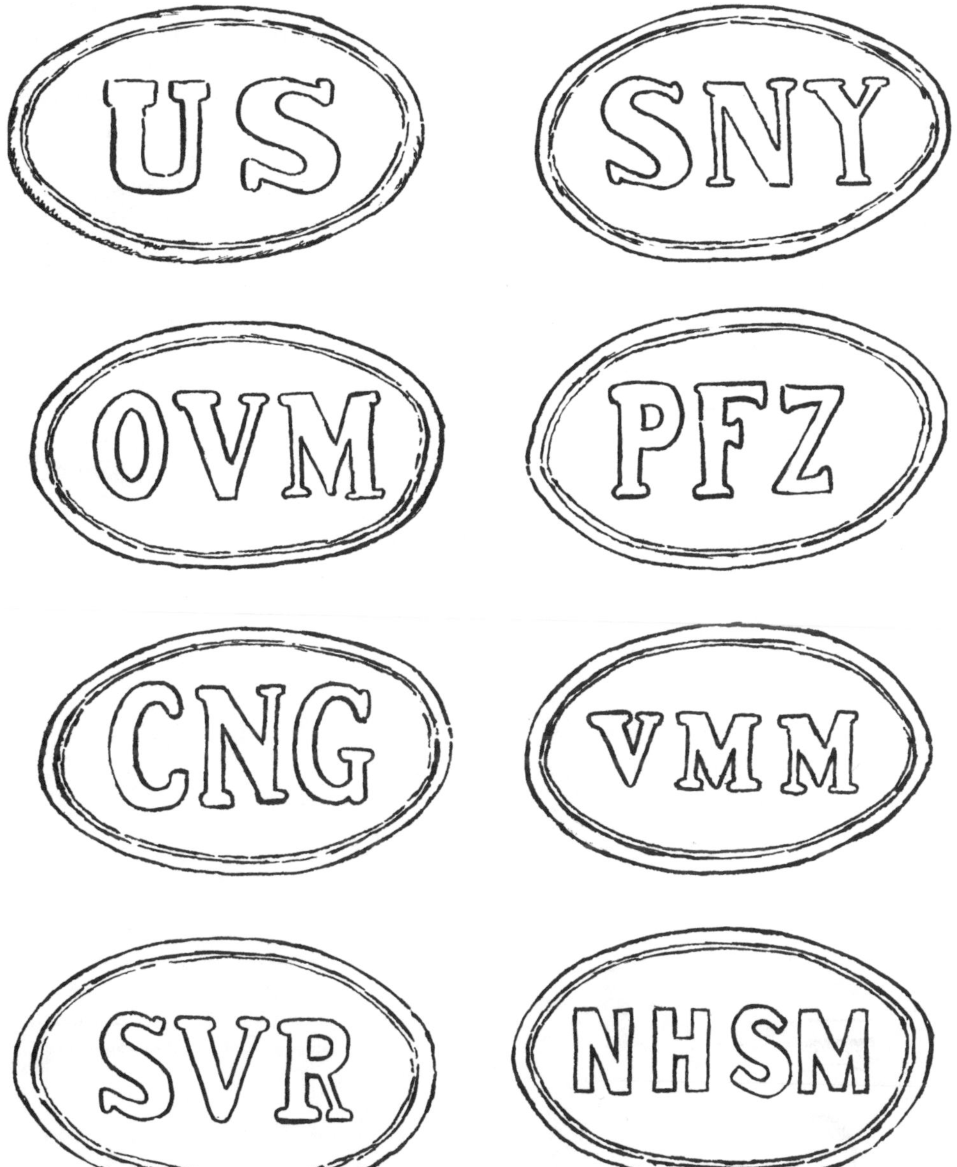

Some Federal buckles: Left row: top to bottom: U.S., OVM (Ohio Volunteer Militia); CNG (Connecticut National Guard); SVR (not identified; possibly worn by a member of Sons of Veterans Reserve). Right row: top to bottom: SNY (State of New York); PFZ (Philadelphia Fire Zouaves); VMM (Volunteer Militia of Maine); NHSM (New Hampshire State Militia). (Drawings by Mike McAfee)

S.N.Y. (New York), O.V.M. (Ohio Volunteer Militia). When the 10th Maine Infantry left for the front, October 6, 1861, it wore accouterments which had V.M.M. (Volunteer Maine Militia) instead of U.S. as belt buckles and cartridge box plates. It is in this field of belt buckles and box plates that much of the unethical misrepresentation as to genuineness of relics is being carried on. Collectors should be very cautious about the "unquestioned authenticity" of such items and should check with recognized specialists before spending the inflated prices asked. NCO's and musicians in the Federal service wore buckles of similar shape and motif to those of commissioned officers. In the Confederate service the variety of such rectangular buckles with State seals or letters is extensive. No specimen of U.S. Marine Corps buckles are available but officers buckles apparently were similar to Army officers' buckles.

BUDGE BARREL. See ARTILLERY.

BUGLE. See MUSICAL INSTRUMENTS.

BULLET MOLD. Individual bullet molds for the several calibers of small arms were in fairly extensive use, especially the molds for revolvers. These molds were often included as part of the cased set of revolvers, along with the other appendages. Some "gang molds" were used, although most small ammunition as used by both sides was made in government arsenals and issued to troops in ammunition boxes—all ready for use. The specimen shown was patented May 20, 1862 by C. B. Tatham of Brooklyn, N.Y. A machine for casting minie balls, it was contrived to "insure the centrality of the hole in the base of the ball, and . . . a sound casting."

BUTTONS, ARMY, U.S.

Enlisted Men. Buttons for enlisted men were yellow, and of the same pattern as for artillery officers except that the letter in the shield was omitted.

According to some expert collectors, the regulation buttons, made of hard rubber and marked with Goodyear's pattern of 1851, were used by Berdan's sharpshooters. The rubber buttons did not glisten in the sun as did the regulation uniform buttons of the line units. Therefore, these unusual rubber buttons were ideally suited for use on the sharpshooters' uniforms, and were probably so used.

It should also be pointed out that many regiments, especially in the early months of the war, wore buttons with their state seals on them. Many of these buttons have been recovered from battlefields and campsites. For identification of such buttons see INSIGNIA.

Medical Cadets. Same as for officers of the General Staff.

Musicians. The evidence available indicates that

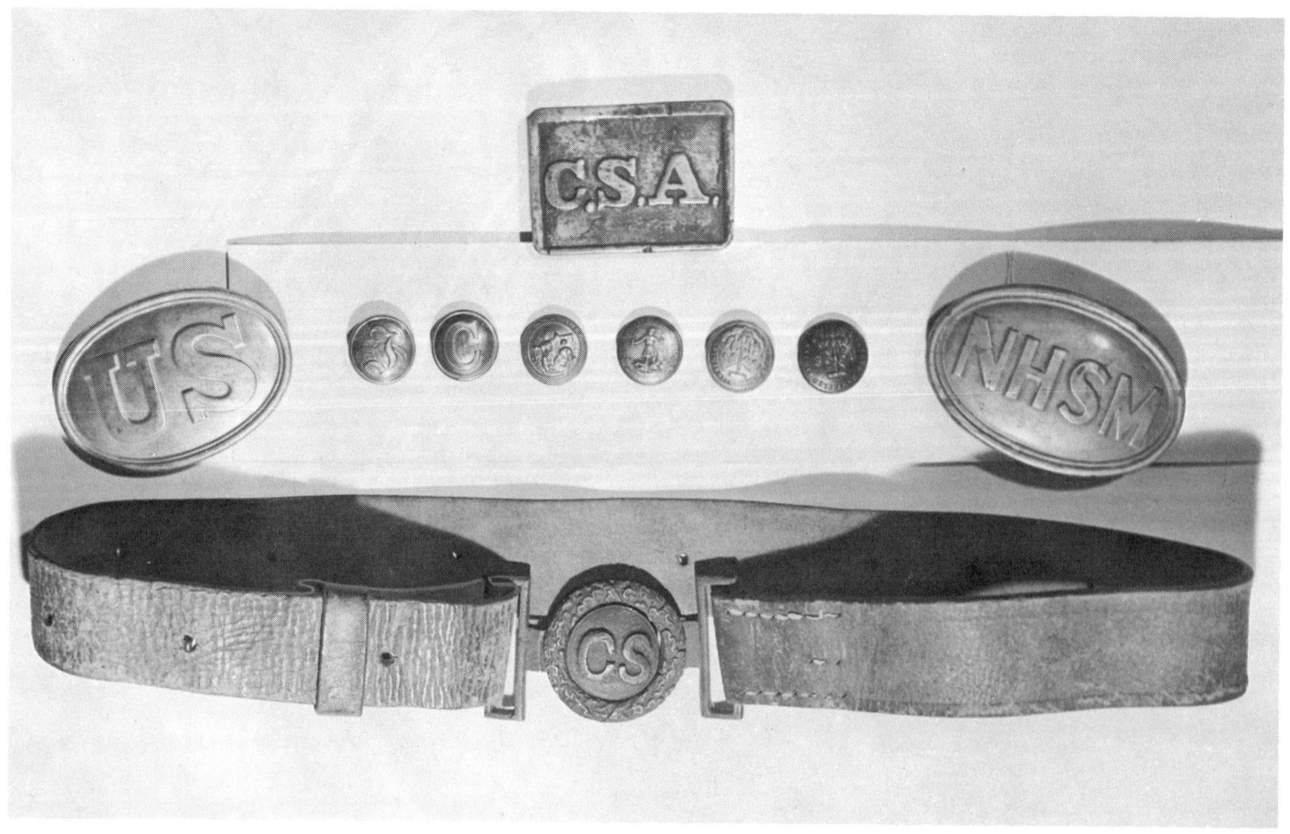

Buckles and buttons from the Norm Flayderman collection.

Buckle of the 114th Pa. Infantry of Collis' Zouaves (Zouaves d'Afrique). (Robert L. Miller)

the three-string lyre insignia was used on musicians' buttons in the Civil War. Such a button was found on a battlefield near Fredericksburg, Va. The records of the button manufacturers, Scovill Manufacturing Company, show that they were making this type of button as early as 1860. The four-string lyre, however, is postwar.

OFFICERS.

Aides-de-Camp. Were authorized to wear the button of the General Staff or of their regiment or branch of service, at their option.

Combat Arms—Artillery, Cavalry, Infantry. The button was gilt, convex. The device on the shield was a spread eagle with the letter A for artillery, C for cavalry, or I for infantry. The large button was ⅞-inch in exterior diameter, the small one was ½-inch.

Corps of Engineers. Gilt, 9/10 of an inch in exterior diameter, slightly convex; a raised bright rim, 1/30 inch wide; device, an eagle holding in his beak a scroll, with the word "Essayons," a bastion with embrasures in the distance surrounded by water, with a rising sun. The figures to be of dead gold upon a bright field. Small buttons were of the same form and device, and 55/100 of an inch in exterior diameter.

Corps of Topographical Engineers. Gilt, ⅞-inch exterior diameter, convex and solid; device the shield of the United States, occupying one-half the diameter and the letters T.E. in old English characters the other half; small buttons, ½-inch in diameter, device and form the same.

U.S. Regulation buttons. Top row, left to right: Infantry, Artillery, Cavalry, Dragoons, Rifles. Bottom row, left to right: Veteran Volunteers, Engineers, Ordnance, Staff, Topographical Engineers. (Mike McAfee)

Confederate Buttons, With Backmarks listed. (Courtesy Sidney C. Kerksis)

1. General Staff. "Firmin & Sons/163 Strand London/13 Donduit St."
2. General Staff. "Extra Superb."
3. General Staff. "H T & B/Manchester."
4. General Staff. "H T & B/Manchester."
5. General Staff. No backmark, Confederate manufacture.
6. General Staff. No backmark, Confederate manufacture.
7. Adjutant Generals Department. "G & Cie Paris."
8. Navy. "Courtney & Tennent/Charleston/S.C."
9. Navy. "Courtney & Tennent/Charleston/S.C."
10. Navy. "Rivet'd & Solder'd."
11. Navy, composition four-hold sew-through. "Courtney & Tennent/Charleston/S.C./Manton's Patent."
12. Navy. "E. M. Lewis & Co./Richmond Va." Confederate manufacture.
13. General Service. "Superior Quality."
14. General Service. No backmark, solid cast. Confederate manufacture.
15. Infantry. "Superior Quality."
16. Infantry. "S. Isaacs Campbell & Co/London/71 Jermyn St."
17. Infantry. "E. M. Lewis & Co/Richmond Va." Confederate manufacture.
18. Infantry. No backmark, solid case. Confederate manufacture.
19. Artillery. "H T & B/Manchester."
20. Artillery. "Halfmann & Taylor/Montgomery."
21. Artillery. "E. M. Lewis & Co/Richmond Va." Confederate manufacture.
22. Cavalry. "Superior Quality."
23. Cavalry. "S. Isaacs Campbell & Co/London/71 Jermyn St."
24. Cavalry. No backmark, Confederate manufacture.
25. Engineers. "H T & B/Manchester."
26. Engineers. "Van Wart Son & Co."
27. Engineers. "Extra Rich/Quality."
28. Riflemen. "W. Dowler/Superior Quality."
29. Riflemen. "Van Wart Son & Co."
30. Riflemen. "Halfmann & Taylor/Montgomery."

General officers and officers of the General Staff. Gilt, convex, with spread eagle and stars, and plain border; large size, ⅞ of an inch in exterior diameter; small size, ½ inch.

Ordnance Department. Gilt, convex, plain border cross cannon and bomb-shell, with a circular scroll over and across the cannon, containing the words "Ordnance Corps." Large size, ⅞ inch; small size, ½ inch.

BUTTONS, ARMY, C.S. The following is according to the C.S.A. Regulations of 1861.

ENLISTED MEN

Artillery. Yellow, convex, large raised letter *A* in the center; ¾-inch in exterior diameter.

Other Enlisted Men. Same as for Artillery, except that the number of the regiment, in large figures, will be substituted for the letter *A*.

OFFICERS

Aides-de-Camp. Allowed to wear the button of the General Staff, or of their regiments or branch of service, at their option.

Combat Arms—Artillery, Infantry, Riflemen, and Cavalry. Gilt, convex, plain, with large raised letter in the center; A for Artillery; I for Infantry; R for Rifleman; C for Cavalry; large size, ⅞-inch in exterior diameter; small size, ½-inch.

General Officers and officers of the General Staff. Bright gilt, rounded at the edge, convex, raised eagle in the center, with stars surrounding it; large size, 1 inch in exterior diameter; small size, ½-inch.

Corps of Engineers. Same as for the General Staff, except that, in place of the eagle and stars, there will be a raised E in German text.

BUTTONS, NAVY (U.S.). Gilt, convex, of 3 sizes in exterior diameter: *large* (7/8 inch); *medium* (7/10 inch); *small* (9/16 inch). Each size had the same device, that of an anchor.

BUTTONS, NAVY (C.S.—1862 Regulations). Buttons of three sizes; large, medium, and small, and all of the same device, as per pattern.

BUTTON BOARD. These useful items, made of both wood and metal, were used to protect the cloth while shining buttons on the overcoat, blouse, and dress coat. A wooden one used by Dwight Bradley, Co. B 37th Massachusetts Infantry (Ferris Collection), is 8¼ inches long, with a 5½-inch slot for the buttons.

Chest for company records. Used by Co. E, 60th Indiana Infantry.

A wooden button board in the author's collection is 10 inches long, with a 6-inch slot. Likewise, a brass button board in the author's collection is crudely stamped as follows: "Corpal C.V. LAVAN Co. C.1st BAT.ENGS." This button board, of heavy brass, is 3¾ inches long, 2¼ inches wide, and has a 2⅜ inches slot.

CAISSON. See ARTILLERY—FIELD ARTILLERY MATERIEL.

CALIFORNIA FURNACE. See STOVES.

CALTRAP (or CALTROP). See CROWS FEET.

CAMP EQUIPMENT. Under this category are in-

Officer's tent furniture. Note camp stool, table, shawl, candle, etc. (National Archives)

Camp equipment. Except in active campaigns when the armies were moving frequently, Sibley tents were used to make winter huts. Note that each tent, housing a squad, has a cook stove; evidently in this unit, messing was by tent or squad. (National Archives)

Interior of an officers' winter hut. No issue equipment is in evidence, all the furniture being homemade. (Library of Congress)

cluded much of the baggage and impedimenta which accompanied new troops to the field, as well as such bulky objects as trunks and similar items. Federal and Confederate soldiers in 1861 often took along with them large trunks, boxes, chests, and folding cots and tables for use in the field. However, when both armies stripped down for active campaigning, such non-essentials were left behind or destroyed in the interests of mobility and speed on the march. Most of these cumbersome items were either shipped home or left in storage in the last city or town in which the troops had been stationed. For example, a notice in the *Army and Navy Journal* for September 23, 1865 informed its readers that during the war an immense quantity of regimental and private property, contained in boxes, chests, trunks, valises, etc., belonging to officers and men of the military service had accumulated in the warehouses in Washington. There were boxes marked for General Sedgwick, killed in the Wilderness, General Bayard, killed at Fredericksburg, and many others. The notice stated that all items not called for after November 10, 1865 would be sold at auction to the highest bidder.

Chest for Company Records. Made of pine wood with rope handles. Dimensions: 25½ inches long, 17½ inches wide, 11¼ inches high. Painted on front of chest:

Company Books & Papers,
Co. "E" 60th Ind. Vols.

The 60th Indiana, commanded by Richard Owen, was closely associated with the New Harmony, Indiana communal experiments. Most of the regiment was captured in the fall of 1862. The men were paroled and took a very effective part in the entire Vicksburg campaign. The unit later served under Banks in the Red River campaign.

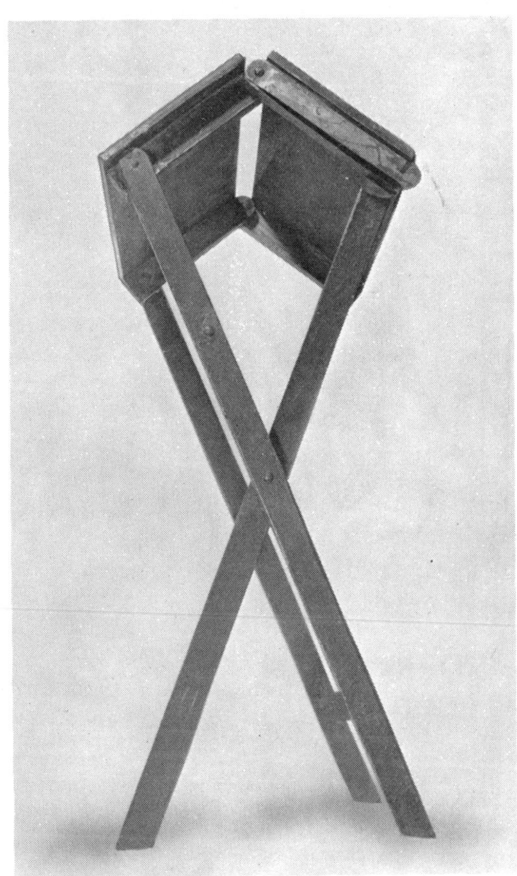

Collapsible camp table. Used by a soldier in Baker's 1st D.C. Cavalry.

Cot, Camp. Contained in a wooden trunk, metal-bound, covered with handsomely-tooled leather. Dimensions: 23 inches long, 19 inches wide, 13½ inches tall. The trunk opens up, permitting a canvas cot, 6 feet 7 inches long and 1½ feet wide, to be set up on folding wooden legs. The trunk bears the original owner's name as follows:

1st Lt. Solomon F. Linsley
15th Conn. Inf.

Stool, Camp. In the author's collection is a wooden camp stool, painted black, with a heavy carpet-

Canvas-covered trunk. Used by E. W. Barstow, 3d Mass. Heavy Artillery.

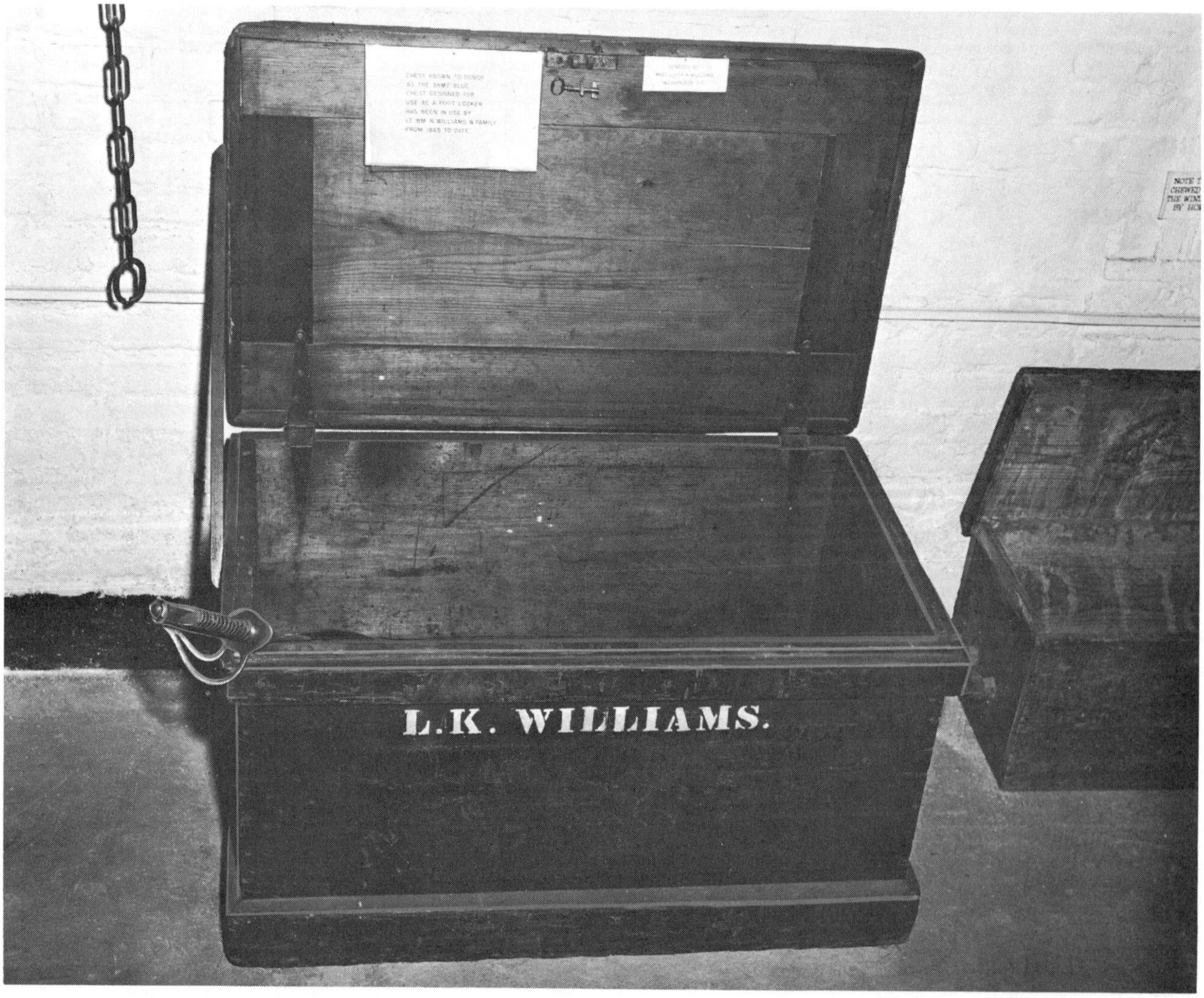

Wooden footlocker. (Photograph courtesy of Col. John W. Gorn, 3d U.S. Infantry, Fort Myer, Va.)

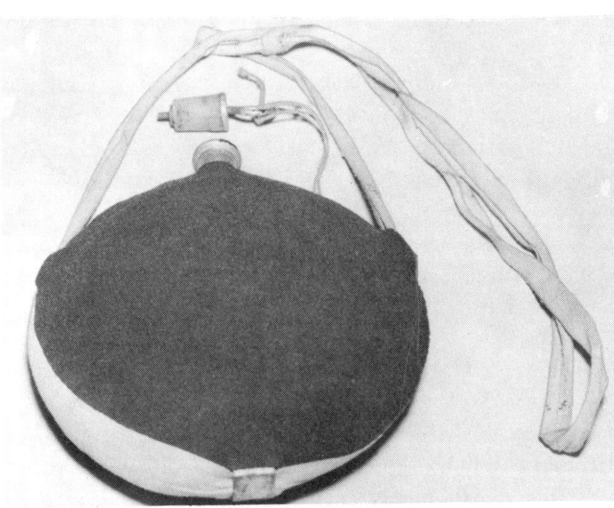

Regulation U.S. canteen. (James A. Shutt)

material seat. Folds into a compass of 23½ inches by 19 inches. When unfolded it is 30 inches high. Used by Major Charles O. Brigham, 1st Connecticut Heavy Artillery. During his regiment's shelling of enemy positions at Fredericksburg, December 13, 1862, Brigham sat on this stool while observing the battle.

TRUNK, OFFICERS. Canvas covered with leather handles. Dimensions: 30½ inches long, 17 inches wide, 17¼ inches tall at highest part of the trunk. Marked in black letters on end of trunk:

E. W. BARSTOW
5th Artillery
U. S. A.

Elijah W. Barstow was a 2d Lt. in the 5th Artillery in May 1866. He used this trunk also when he was a 1st Lt. in the 3d Massachusetts Heavy Artillery during the war. Barstow died in 1867.

FOOTLOCKER used by 1st Lt. Wm. N. Williams, 6th Indiana Infantry, Courtesy of his daughter, Miss Lucia K. Williams, Washington, D. C. whose name appears on the footlocker. As a baby Miss Williams slept in this footlocker when her father, an officer of the 3rd U. S. Infantry, was stationed in the west, fighting Indians.

CANDLE. See LIGHTING EQUIPMENT.

CANDLESTICK. See LIGHTING EQUIPMENT.

CANDLE TRIMMER. See LIGHTING EQUIPMENT.

CANISTER. See PROJECTILES.

CANNON. See ARTILLERY.

CANTEEN. The U.S. Regulation canteen, shown in the illustration, was made of tin, with an outer covering of dark blue woolen cloth stitched together around the outer radius of the canteen. It had a cork stopper with a metal cap over the top and extending ⅛ inch down the sides; also a metal ring on top with stem through the center of cork with nut and washer on bottom. Overall length of cork with metal cap, 1¼ inches; top, ¾ inch in diameter; metal ring, ⅛ inch in diameter with 1⅛ inch outside diameter. Tan cloth strap 1 inch wide passing through three metal loops, one on each side and one on bottom on outer radius of canteen. Overall size, 8 inches in diameter, 2¾ inches thick at center, tapering to ¼ inch at outer

Non-regulation canteen made of heavy leather, riveted at sides, and with a pewter top. (Norm Flayderman)

Combination canteen and mess outfit.

edges. Neck for stopper, ¾ inch high, with rolled top edge 1 inch in diameter overall.

Federal soldiers also purchased or were given non-regulation canteens, a number of which are illustrated.

CANTEENS, CONFEDERATE. Many Confederate volunteers in 1861 used clay jugs, straw or leather-covered bottles, and all sorts of home-made "water bottles." Tinsmiths made various types of canteens, varying in size and shape. However, it is obvious that many Confederate soldiers used captured Yankee canteens. The Confederate Museum at Richmond has several interesting types of Confederate canteens. One of the most unique is a brown porcelain canteen shaped like a doughnut. This canteen was carried in the Revolutionary War as well as the Civil War. The typical C.S. tin canteen was simply designed and constructed. The spout of the C.S. tin canteen was always made of tin, while Federal canteens generally had pewter spouts. Also extensively used was the wood canteen made in several places in the South during the war.

Non-regulation canteen with three compartments. (Norm Flayderman)

CAP. See UNIFORMS AND CLOTHING.

CAP BOX. See ACCOUTERMENTS.

CAP CONTAINERS. Most of these were made of tin, marked with the makers' names, and were about 2 inches in diameter. In depth they ranged from ½ inch to about 2 inches. A typical marking was:

250
Hicks
Waterproof
U. S. Musket Caps
Am. Flask & Cap Co.
Waterbury
Conn.

Percussion caps were also wrapped in cartridge papers and included in the 10-cartridge packets issued to the soldier.

CARCASS. See PROJECTILES.

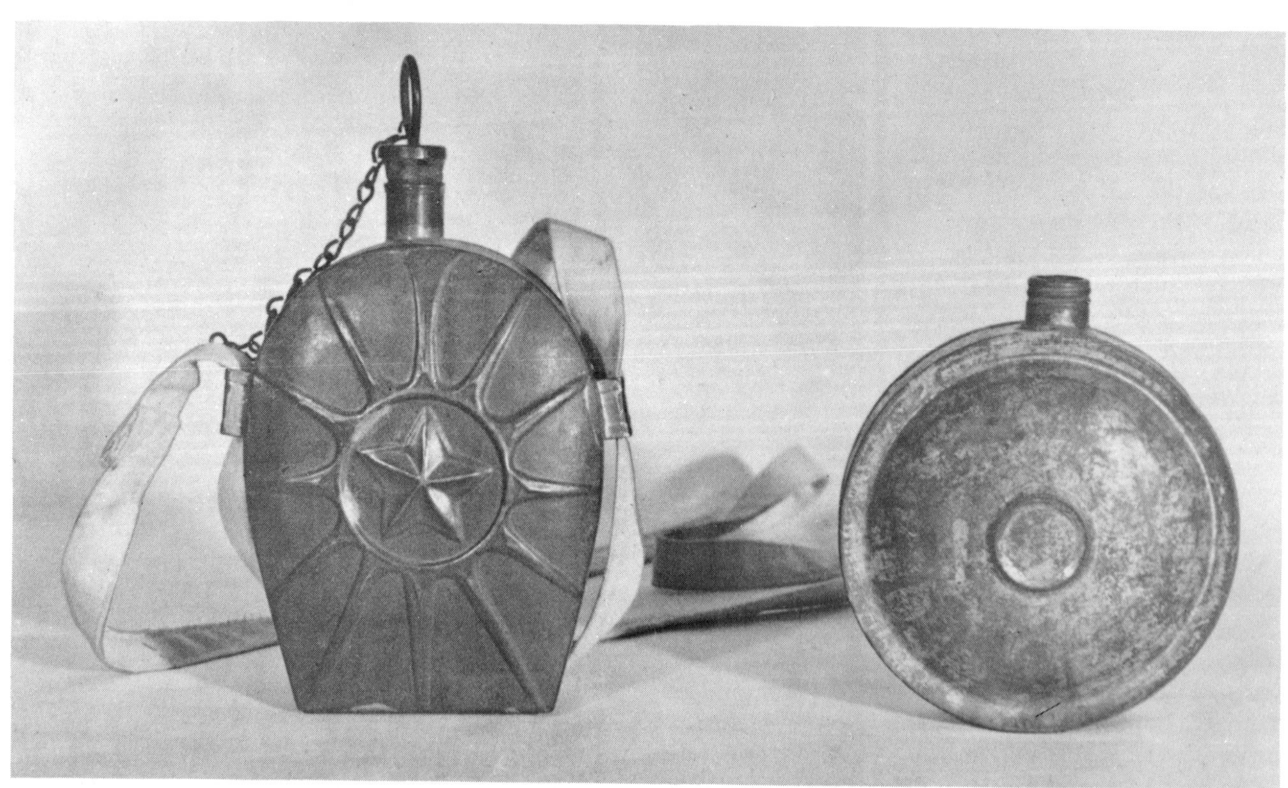

Non-regulation canteens. The round canteen on the right was carried by a soldier from Galena, Ill., named Hudson.

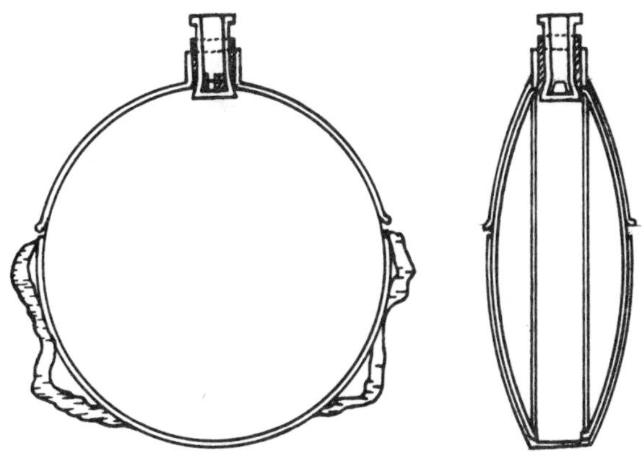

Farciot's canteen. Patented Jan. 31, 1865. (National Archives)

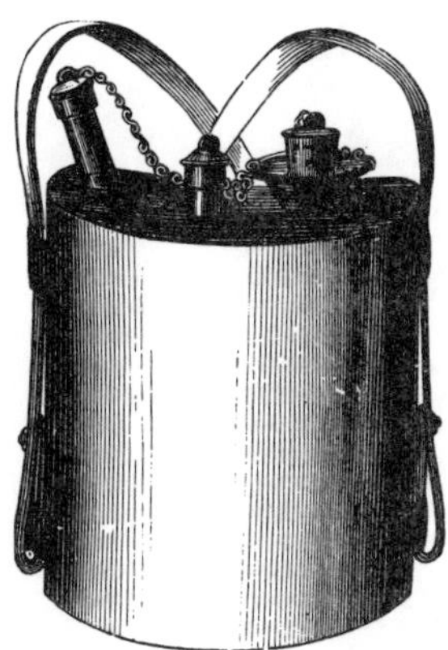

Water-filter canteen, originally cloth-covered. Norm Flayderman)

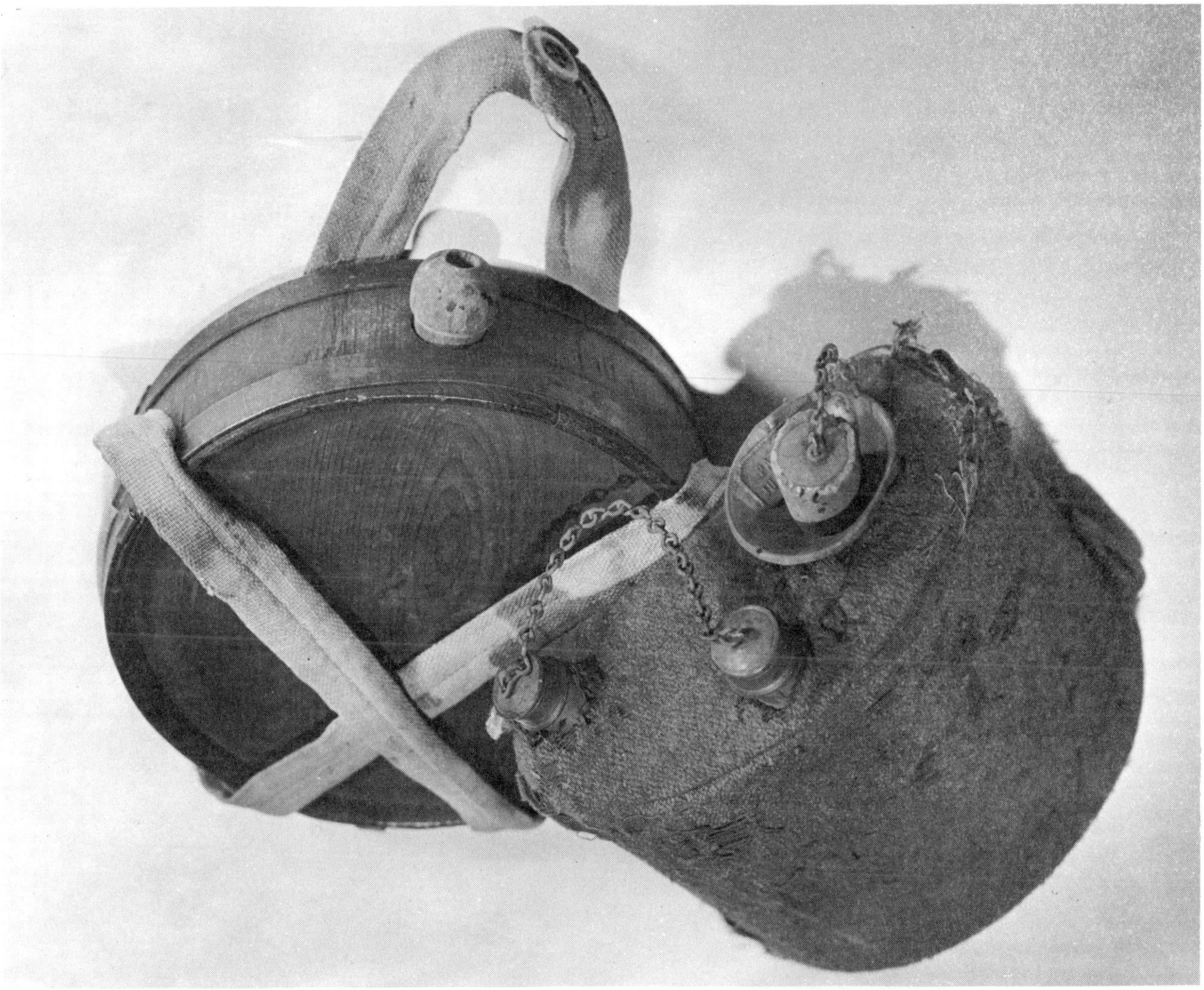

Standard-type Confederate wood canteen with original linen strap. The other is a water purifying Union issue canteen. The center container is merely a narrow cylindrical compartment containing extra filters, probably charcoal. Water is poured in the right side, filters through a section in the center and is supposedly purified when used through the left spout. Has a brass patent, label, and wool covering.

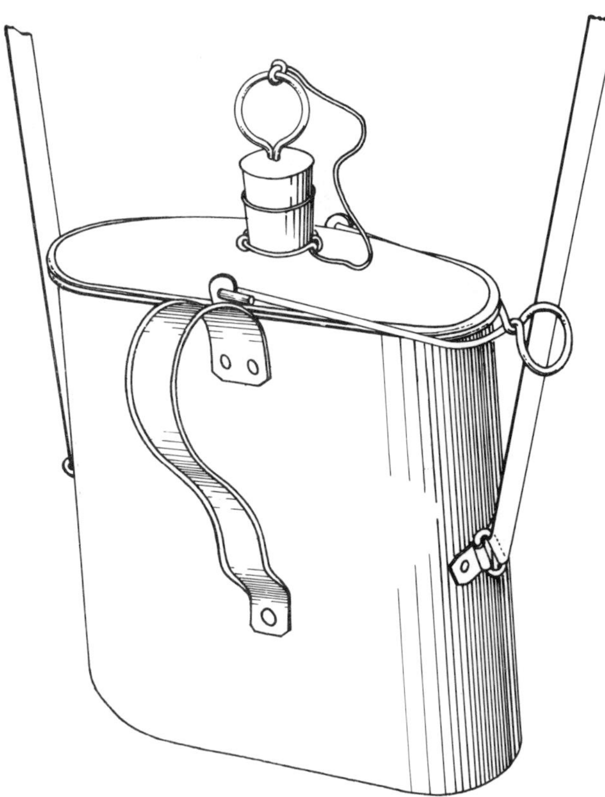

Trowbridge, U.S. Army. This "cooking canteen" served as a boiler. It consisted of a bottle inclosed in a cup. (National Archives)

Wooden canteen brought home by Lt. James Gillette, 4th Maryland Infantry (US). (Courtesy Mrs. Prentiss Bassett. Photo by Woodruff, Cambridge, N.Y.)

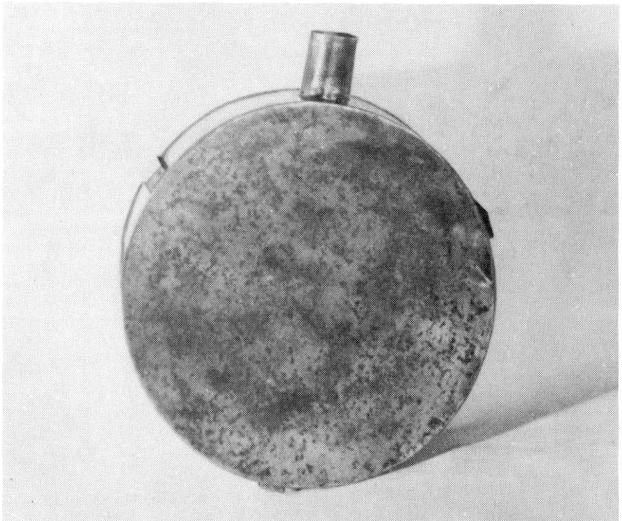

Typical Confederate tin canteen. Six inches in diameter and two inches thick, with three tin loops for the carrying strap.

CARBINE. See SHOULDER WEAPONS.

CARBINE SLING. See ACCOUTERMENTS.

CARBINE SOCKET. See HORSE EQUIPMENT.

CARDS, PLAYING. See RECREATIONAL EQUIPMENT.

CARTE DE VISITE. See PICTURES.

CARTRIDGE TEARER. (Patent No. 37,171.) Patented December 16, 1862 by Daniel Kelly of Grand Rapids, Michigan. This device consisted of a metal wing or band, fitted tightly to the band of the gun near the muzzle, and provided with two horns, between which was a tooth, made in the same piece and projecting radially from it, the horns being at such a distance apart as to receive between them the fold of the paper which closed the cartridge.

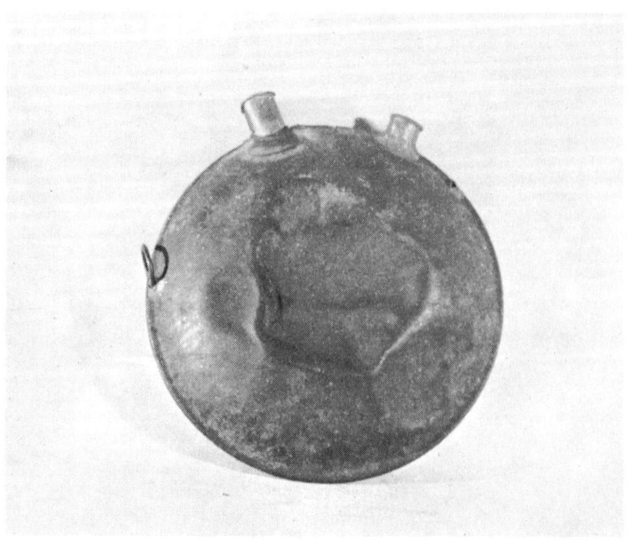

Double-spout canteen. Original cloth cover is gone. Not identified, and no markings.

Confederate cedarwood canteen carried by A. J. Bethune, Co. E, 45th Alabama Infantry, whose initials are on the side shown. Captured by W. Zimmerman, 50th Indiana Infantry, whose initials are also carved on the side.

CARVINGS. See RELICS AND SOUVENIRS.

CASKET. A sad but important part of each soldier's war experience was the burial of his comrades who were killed in battle or died of disease. Some regiments refused to permit strangers to bury their men, hoping for better treatment if their turn should come. In the majority of cases, soldiers killed in battle were buried in their blankets unless there was time to get boards and make coffins, which was seldom the case. The government sent no coffins to the front but at large assembly points and at general hospitals coffins were furnished. In the earlier part of the war, when funds were available metallic caskets were used to ship the bodies home.

CAVALRY EQUIPMENT. See HORSE EQUIPMENT.

Arms. See CARBINE; PIKES; REVOLVERS; RIFLE; SWORDS AND SABERS. Illustrative of the variety of arms issued cavalry regiment was the experience of the 4th Iowa Cavalry. Carbines were first issued to this regiment. Only 40 could be obtained and they were divided among several companies. These weapons were Hall carbines, an inferior gun of limited range, taking a paper cartridge, but, since they were breech-loaders, the men were eager to get them. But the weapons of the regiment were still very poor. A few men had Colt Navy revolvers. The clumsy Austrian infantry rifles, issued when the regiment was first outfitted, were still in the hands of men who had not had the hardihood or ingenuity to "lose" them. Some men had revolvers of the Starr and other

Cap containers. Left to right: Maynard primers, cap containers. In foreground—pistol flask carried by Sergeant Joshua Grafham, 1st D.C. Cav.

inferior types; many had the single-barrelled holster pistols, with ramrods, such as had been used in the Mexican War, while all had the awkwardly long and very heavy dragoon saber. Every man saw and, what was much worse, *felt* the inefficiency of the arms.

An Eastern regiment was in even worse shape. Men of the 10th New York Cavalry drew everything on the list of cavalry equipment just prior to the first march of the new regiment. The list included watering bridles, lariat ropes, and picket pins. Many men had extra blankets, nice large quilts presented by some fond mother or maiden aunt, sabers and belts, together with the straps that passed over the shoulder, carbines and slings, pockets full of cartridges, nose-bags and extra little bags for carrying oats, haversacks, canteens, and spurs, some of the latter being of the Mexican pattern, as large as windmills. They also carried curry-combs, brushes, ponchos, shelter tents, overcoats, frying pans, cups, and coffee pots. And when the regiment attempted to mount, "such a rattling, jungling, jerking, scrabbling, cursing was never heard before." On the march many of these overloaded recruits did not overtake their regiments until the next day.

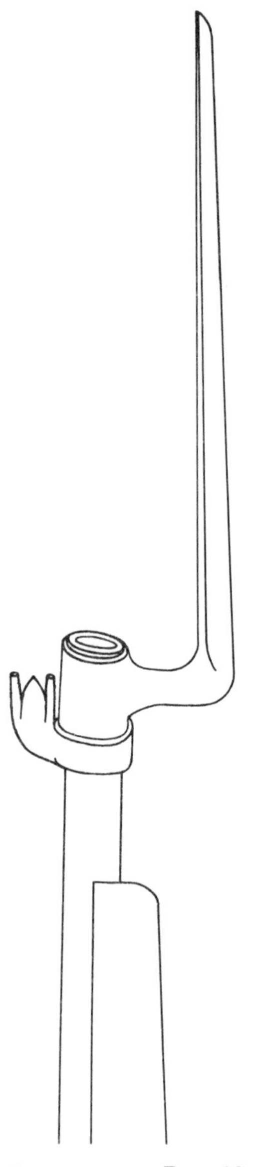

Kelly's cartridge tearer, patent Dec. 16, 1862. (National Archives)

Eventually most Federal cavalry units were reasonably well and uniformly equipped, but Confederate troopers used whatever they could get. The marked superiority of Confederate cavalry up to June 1863 was due, in part at least, to their superior mobility. Their opponents were overloaded with unnecessary equippage.

In general, Confederate cavalrymen preferred the revolver over the saber, in contrast to Federal cavalry. Moreover, many Confederate cavalrymen were armed with short Enfield rifles and musketoons, cut-down infantry muskets, sporting rifles, and shotguns.

Cavalry Horse Equipments. A complete set of horse equipments for cavalry consisted of a bridle, a watering bridle, curry comb, halter, horse brush, lariat, link, nose bag, picket pin, saddle, saddle bags, saddle blanket, surcingle, and spurs.

Bridle. Made of black leather, and consisted of a headstall, bit, and pair of reins. There were 4 varieties of bits, all alike below the mouth piece. Shown in the photograph is an all-brass horse bit for officers of staff rank. These are among the most elaborate of any in collections today. The very large lead-backed brass side rosettes have a relief eagle design. The chain is brass. The watering bridle consisted of a bit and a pair of reins.

Curry comb. Iron, japanned black. Consisted of a body of sheet iron, the top and bottom edges turned at right angles, forming two rows of teeth, three double rows of teeth riveted to the body by six rivets; crossbar, riveted to the top by two rivets; handle-shank; handle (wood) turned and painted; and a sheet-iron ferrule. Dimensions: Length 4 inches, width 4.75 inches, thickness .75 inch, length of handle 4 inches, weight .75 pound.

Halter. Consisted of two cheek-pieces, sewed, one end to two square loops, and the other to two cheek-rings, two standing loops for the toggles of the watering bridle, a crown-piece, buckle and chape, nose-band, chin strap, throat strap, hitching-strap ring, and billet.

Horse brush. Consisted of a maple body in which were inserted Russia bristles; cover, glued and fastened to the body by eight screws; and a hand strap.

Dimensions 9.25 inches long, 4 inches wide, .5 inch thick; handstrap 2 inches wide; weight .57 pound.

Lariat. Made of the best hemp rope, 1.25 inches thick. Was 30 feet long, of four strands, with an eye spliced in one end and the other end wrapped with twine. Weight 2.38 pounds.

Link. Consisted of a strap with a spring hook at one end and a buckle and billet at the other. Weight .2 pound.

of seat; No. 2, 11½ inches of seat; No. 3, 12 inches of seat.

The carbine-thimble was buckled to the D-ring on the off side of the saddle.

Saddle-Bags. The saddle bags consisted of 2 pouches and 1 seat, the ends of the seat being sewed to the pouches.

Saddle-Blanket. Was of pure wool, close woven, of stout yarn of an indigo-blue color, with an orange

Cavalry horse equipments.

Nose Bag. Consisted of a body of strong linen or cotton duck, a bottom of harness leather, and a head strap. Width of bag at top, 15 inches; height, 15 inches.

Picket-Pin. Iron, painted black. The parts were the body, neck, head, swell, point, lariat ring around the neck, 8-shaped, the larger opening for the lariat. Dimensions: Length, 14 inches, diameter at swell, 4 inches. Weight of pin, 1.25 pounds.

Saddle. All the leather was black bridle or harness leather, and the buckles were malleable iron, blued. The saddle consisted of a tree, saddle skirts, stirrups, stirrup leathers, girth, girth-strap, surcingle, and crupper. There were three sizes to the trees, varying in the length of the seat as follows: No. 1, 11 inches

border 3 inches wide, 3 inches from the edge. The letters U.S., 6 inches high, of orange color, were in the center of the blanket. Dimensions: 75 inches long, 67 inches wide. Weight 3.1875 pounds.

Spurs (Brass). Consisted of 2 spurs, 2 rowels, 2 rivets, 2 spur straps, 2 roller-buckles, 2 standing loops. Weight of pair of spurs and straps .57 pound.

CHAIN. See ENGINEER EQUIPMENT.

CHAIN SHOT. Consisted of two cannon balls connected by a chain. The motion of rotation of these projectiles in flight was expected to render them useful in cutting the masts and riggings of war vessels; but their flight was inaccurate. When the means of connecting the two cannon balls was a bar of iron instead of a chain, they were called *Bar shot.*

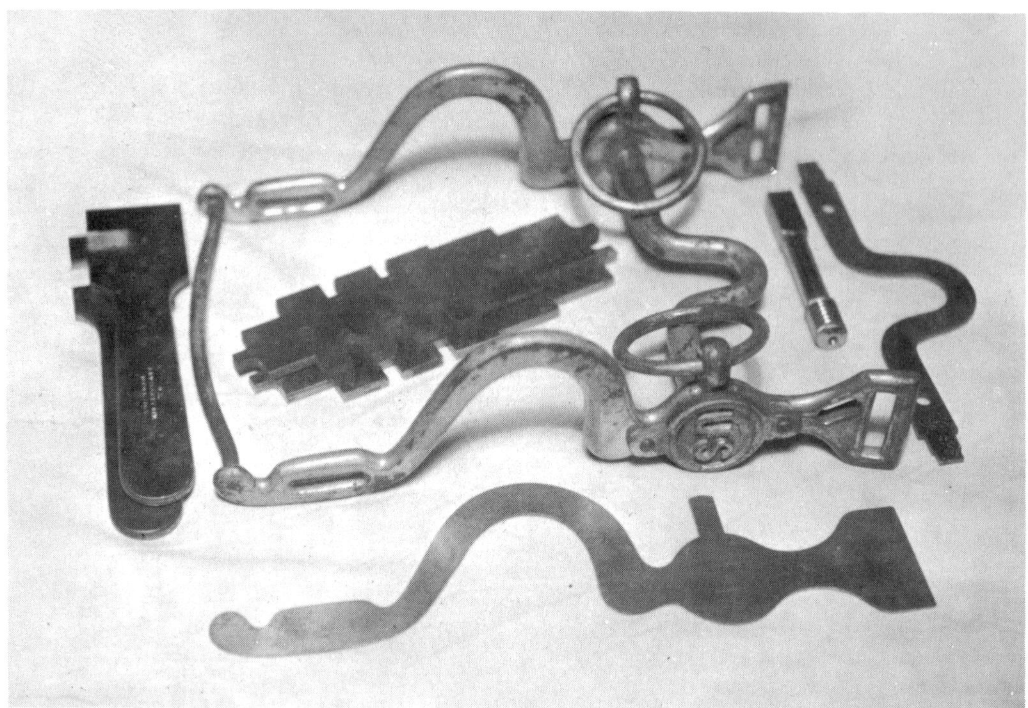

This photograph shows the standard Civil War Federal horse bit. It is marked 'U.S.." Also included in the photograph are the original arsenal inspector's gauges for this model bit. Each of the gauges bears markings "U.S. Artillery Bit M 1863." (Norm Flayderman)

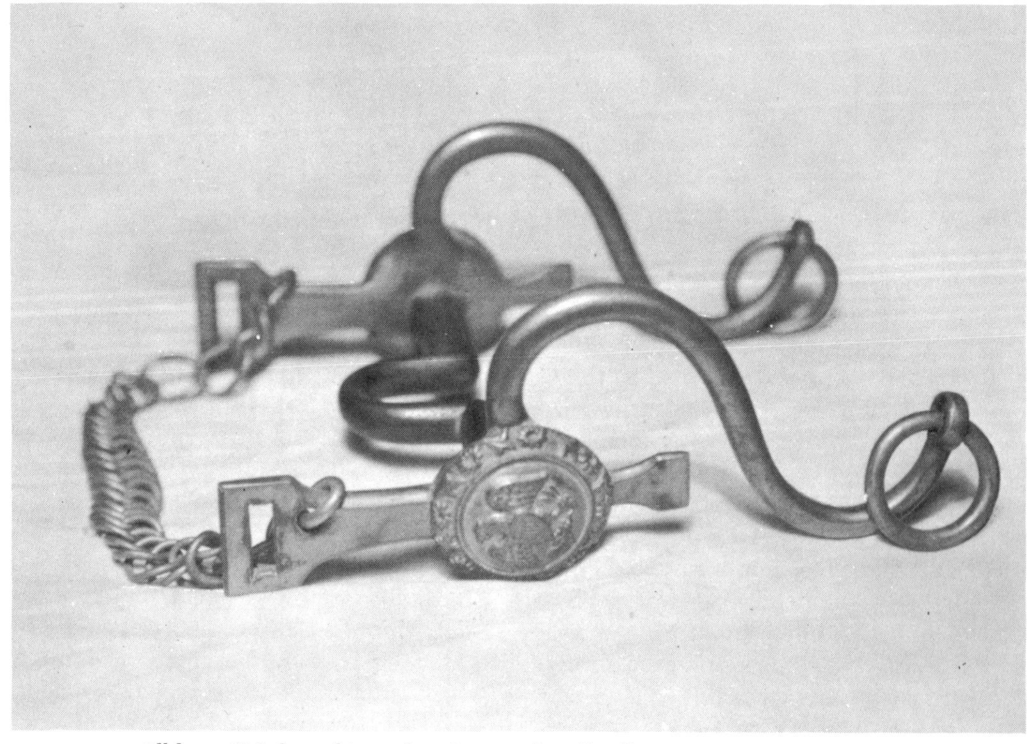

All-brass U.S. horse bit used on horses of staff officers. (Norm Flayderman)

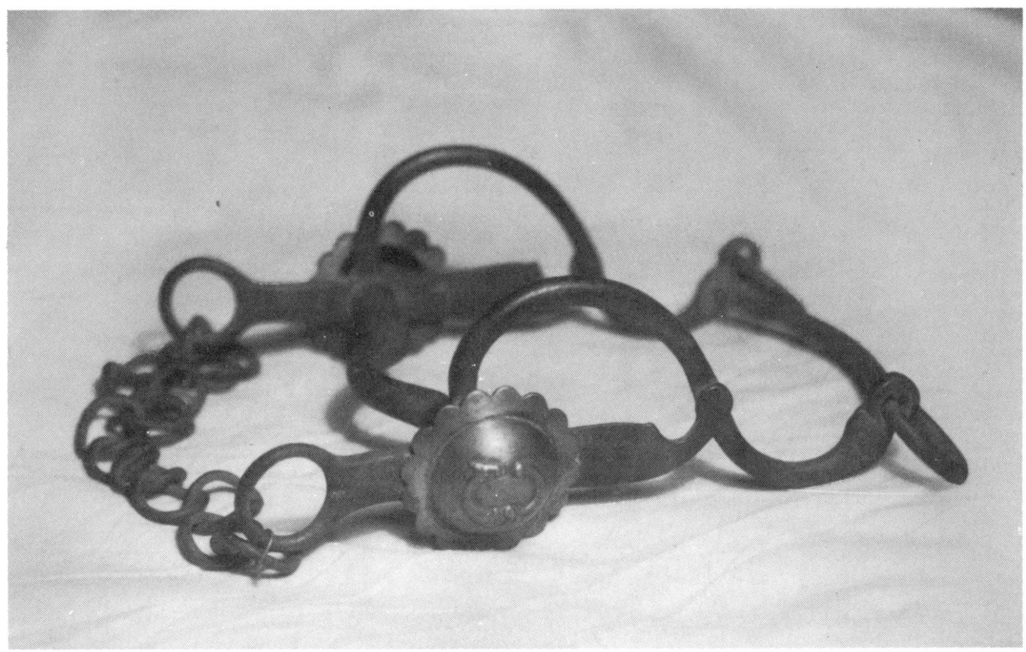

Confederate bit shown here was probably for an officer's mount. It is iron with very large brass side rosettes bearing relief letter "C." (Norm Flayderman)

CHAIR. See CAMP EQUIPMENT.

CHAPEAU DE BRAS. A dress hat, worn mainly by Naval officers, which could be folded flat and carried under the arm. A few officers of the Army, like General Winfield Scott, wore the chapeau de bras, but it was not in general use during 1861-1865.

CHECKERS. See RECREATIONAL EQUIPMENT.

CHESS. See RECREATIONAL EQUIPMENT.

CHEMICAL WARFARE. In May 1862 a New York school teacher, John W. Doughty, wrote President Lincoln proposing the use of heavy shells filled with liquid chlorine, which would expand into a choking gas many times its original volume. The inventor explained to Lincoln that since the gas was denser than air, the gas would sink irresistibly into trenches and bomb proofs. There is no evidence that Lincoln ever received this letter.

CHEVRAC. A woolen saddle blanket over buckram, and leather bound. See HORSE EQUIPMENT.

CHEVRONS, U.S.

ARMY. The rank of noncommissioned officers was indicated by chevrons above the elbows of both sleeves of the uniform coat and overcoat. They were of silk or worsted binding ½ inch wide and of the same color as the edging on the coat (see UNIFORMS); points of chevrons down.

Corporal. Two bars in worsted.

First Sergeant. Three bars and a lozenge, in worsted.

Hospital Steward. A half chevron of the following description: Of emerald green cloth, 1¾ inches wide, running obliquely downward from the outer to the inner seam of the sleeve, and at an angle of about 30 degrees with a horizontal, parallel to, and ⅛ of an inch from, both the upper and lower edge, an embroidery of yellow silk ⅛ inch wide, and in the center a cauduceus 2 inches long, embroidered also with yellow silk, the head toward the outer seam of the sleeve.

Ordnance Sergeant. Three bars and a tie, in silk.

Pioneer. Two crossed hatchets of cloth, same color and material as the edging of the collar, to be sewed on each arm above the elbow in the place indicated for a chevron (those of the corporal to be just above and resting on the chevron), the head of the hatchet upward, its edge outward, of the following dimensions, viz: Handle–4½ inches long, 1/4 to 1/3 of an inch wide. Hatchet–2 inches long, 1 inch wide at the edge.

Sergeant. Three bars, in worsted.

Sergeant Major. Three bars in an arc, in silk.

Service (length of service). To indicate service, all noncommissioned officers, musicians, and privates, who had served faithfully for the term of 5 years, would wear as a mark of distinction, upon both sleeves of the uniform coat, below the elbow, a diagonal half chevron, ½ inch wide, extending from seam to seam, the front end nearest the cuff, and ½ inch above the point of the cuff, to be of the same color as the edging on the coat. In like manner, an additional half chevron, above and parallel to the first, for every subsequent 5 years of faithful service; distance between each chevron ¼ of an inch. Service in war was to be indicated by a light or sky blue stripe on each side

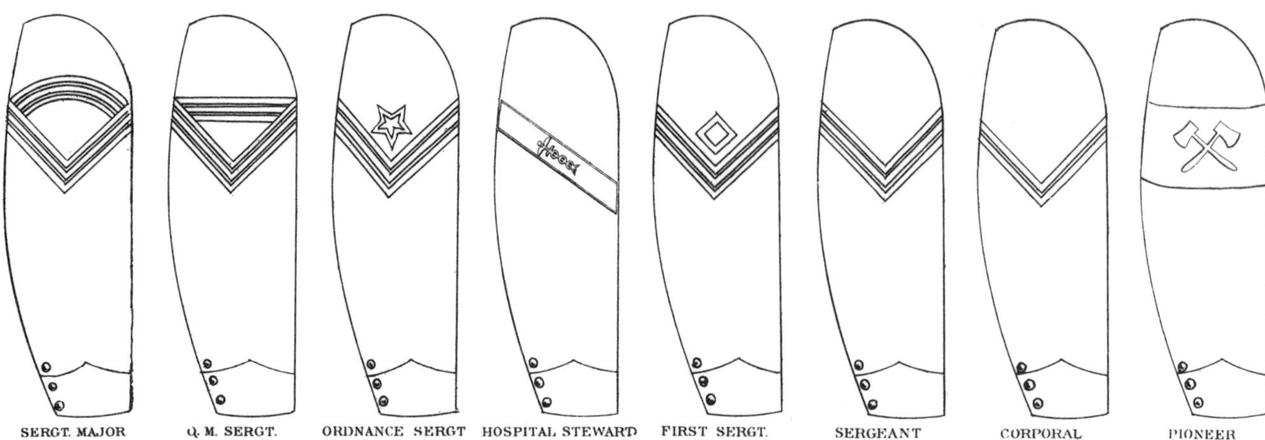

Chevrons as worn by the Federal Army. (Norm Flayderman)

of the chevron for artillery, and a red stripe for all other branches of service, the stripe to be ⅛ inch wide.

CHEVRONS, CONFEDERATE. The rank of a non-commissioned officer was shown by chevrons on both sleeves of the uniform tunic and overcoat, above the elbow; they were of silk or worsted binding ½ the edging of the tunic; the points were down.

First Sergeant. Three bars and a lozenge in worsted.

Corporal. Two bars in worsted.

Ordnance Sergeant. Three bars and a star in silk.

Quartermaster Sergeant. Three bars and a tie in silk.

Sergeant. Three bars in worsted.

Sergeant Major. Three bars and an arc in silk.

MARINE CORPS (US). Regulations provided that the chevrons would be worn on the uniform coat above the elbow, points up. The material was of yellow silk lace, ½ inch wide, and as described below.

Corporal. Same as for sergeants (see below) except that the chevrons had two bars each.

Drum-Major. Three bars and a tie, with a star in the center, on a scarlet ground.

First Sergeant. A chevron of yellow worsted lace ½ inch wide, placed above the elbow, point up, with three bars and a lozenge, edged with scarlet.

Quartermaster-Sergeant. Same as first sergeant, except that it had three bars and a tie, on scarlet ground.

Sergeant. Same as first sergeant except that the lozenge was omitted.

Sergeant-Major. Same as first sergeant except that it had three bars and an arc, on scarlet ground.

CHOCK. See ARTILLERY.

CIPHER DISC. See SIGNAL EQUIPMENT.

COAT. See UNIFORMS AND CLOTHING.

COAT OF ARMS. See INSIGNIA.

COEHORN. See CANNON.

COFFEE MILL. Some of the veteran troops had coffee mills but such items were not issued. The soldiers of 1861 were accustomed to confiscating them whenever found. But because these coffee mills were cumbersome, most soldiers pounded out their coffee by means of a regulation triangular bayonet and a tin cup. A real rarity of the war is the Sharps carbine coffee mill. This ingenious adaptation of the patch box as a coffee mill was not extensively made. Apparently the handle was easily lost; moreover, ground coffee was usually issued or the soldiers found other ways of crushing their coffee beans.

COFFEE POT. See MESS EQUIPMENT.

COLORS. See FLAGS, COLORS, GUIDONS.

COLUMBIAD. See ARTILLERY.

COMB. Combs were not issued; the men bought them. Those existing today which are known to have

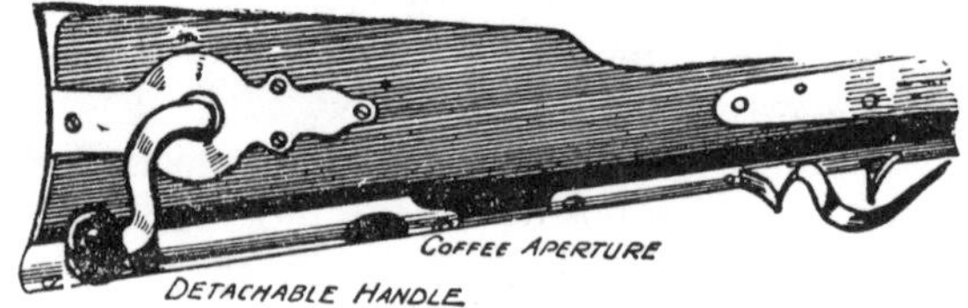

Sharps coffee mill. Francis Bannerman Sons

been used in the Civil War were small folding combs. Probably straight combs were more generally used, but the author has seen only a few, and believes that most of them were carried over into civil life after the war and were not preserved as relics.

COMMISSARY. This was the department that provided food to the troops; it was also a common synonym for whiskey.

COMMISSION. See DOCUMENTS.

COMMISSION CASE. Officers' commissions were mailed by the state authorities to recipients in the field; or sometimes the governor or his representative delivered them personally. No cases were provided; consequently if an officer wished to preserve his commission in such a container he bought one. Most such cases sold during the Civil War were of japanned tin, usually without markings. Shown here is a case that belonged to Gen. Charles Ewing. It is of japanned tin, 17 inches long, 2⅜ inches in diameter, and marked in gold letters: *Commission of Charles Ewing, Brigadier General U.S. Volunteers.*

COMPASS, PRISMATIC. See ENGINEER EQUIPMENT.

has two very small religious objects, including a crucifix 1 inch long, carried by Thomas J. Prescott, 1st New Mexico Cavalry, during the war. Many Catholics carried similar objects.

CRUTCHES. Crutches varied in size and design. Four are shown here. The longer ones are 4 feet in length while the shortest is 3 feet 8½ inches. All are crudely made of wood.

CUP. See MESS EQUIPMENT.

Commission case. Used by Brig. Gen. Charles Ewing, U.S. Vol.

COMPASS, SHIP. See NAVIGATION INSTRUMENTS.

CONE, PICK. See APPENDAGES, CONE PICKER.

CONFEDERATE PATENTS. See APPENDIX.

CORPS BADGES. See BADGES, CORPS.

COT, FOLDING. See CAMP EQUIPMENT.

CRAVAT. See UNIFORMS AND CLOTHING. Sometimes called stocks, regulation cravats were of leather for men and black cloth for officers. However photographs show that individuals wore cravats of different colors and sizes.

CROW'S FEET. Iron-pointed stars or stout nails that had sharp points uppermost when lying on the ground. They were strewn in front of enemy cavalry or on terrain which hostile cavalry might pass. A sort of Civil War static booby trap.

CRUCIFIX. Paul Nachtrab II of Colorado Springs

CURRY COMB. See HORSE EQUIPMENT.

CUTLASS. See SWORDS AND SABERS.

DAGUERREOTYPE. See PICTURES.

DAHLGREN BAYONET. See BAYONETS.

DESK, FIELD. See also CAMP EQUIPMENT.

DIARY. Many officers and soldiers of both armies kept diaries. Fortunately many of these day-to-day accounts have been preserved and afford us a much clearer and more intimate understanding of the emotions and less-heralded events of the war. Shown here is the diary of Color Sergeant Francis H. Buffum, 14th New Hampshire Infantry. Many diaries resemble this one-pocket size, bound in black leather, with the year stamped in gold on the outside flap.

DICE. See RECREATIONAL EQUIPMENT.

DIPPER. See MESS EQUIPMENT.

DIRIGIBLE. On July 5, 1864 Solomon Andrews of

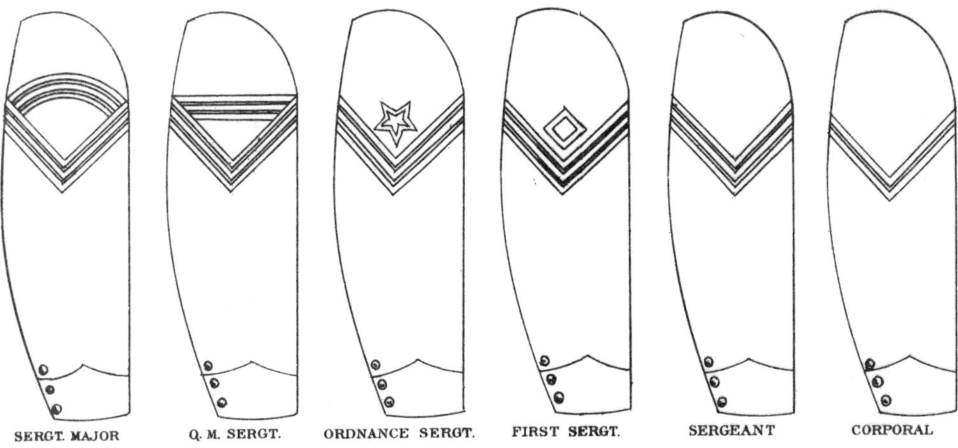

Confederate chevrons.

Perth Amboy, N. J. was granted Patent No. 43,449 for an "elliptical balloon" which could be steered in any direction.

DISCHARGE. See DOCUMENTS.

DISPATCH CASE. Although few dispatch cases were believed to have been made, they were used by all three services; one displayed at a Gettysburg museum has a carrying strap, is of black bridle leather, and is approximately the size of World War II Marine Corps dispatch cases. (See also SABRETASCHE, this being a type of dispatch case.) The author's collection contains an Army dispatch case that differs from that in the museum at Gettysburg, but was also carried during the war. It is of black bridle leather, 11 inches long, 8¼ inches wide, tapering to 7¾ inches at the bottom. The carrying strap, also of black bridle leather, is 51 inches long with a black painted buckle. The only markings are the stamped letters "J.B." which probably are the initials of an inspector.

Crucifix carried by Thomas J. Prescott, 1st N. Mex. Cavalry. This crucifix, only one inch high, was carried in a small brass container.

DIVIDERS, ENGINEER'S. See ENGINEER EQUIPMENT.

DOCUMENTS (Administrative Forms). By War Department General Order No. 13, Feb. 11, 1862, the following forms were a six-months supply for each regiment:

- 1 Guard Report Book
- 1 Consolidated Morning Report Book
- 10 Company Morning Report Books
- 100 Consolidated Morning Reports
- 2 List of Rolls, Returns, etc. to be made out by Company Commander
- 6 Field and Staff Muster Rolls
- 18 Field and Staff Muster and Pay Rolls
- 6 Muster Rolls of Hospital
- 18 Muster and Pay Rolls, Hospital
- 60 Company Muster Rolls
- 180 Company Muster and Pay Rolls
- 12 Regimental Returns
- 60 Company Monthly Returns
- 20 Returns of Men Joined Company
- 6 Quarterly Regimental Return of Deceased Soldiers
- 30 Quarterly Company Returns of Deceased Soldiers
- 2 Annual Returns of Casualties
- 40 Descriptive Lists
- 100 Non-Commissioned Officers' Warrants

The following documents are considered to be representative of the more important ones in use during the war:

- Commission
- Discharge
- Parole
- Proclamation
- Pass
- Warrant

Confederate documents, although rarer, were similar to U.S. types but generally printed on much inferior paper.

DOG TAG. See IDENTIFICATION DISCS.

DOG TENT. See TENT.

DOMINOES. See RECREATIONAL EQUIPMENT.

DRAG-ROPE. See ARTILLERY.

DRAWERS. See UNIFORMS AND CLOTHING.

DREDGING BOX. See ARTILLERY.

DRILL WEAPONS. While some unit commanders confined their training activities to loading and firing,

Crutches used by Federal soldiers.

others paid considerable attention to bayonet, saber, or cutlass drill, depending on the arm of the service. Much of the enthusiasm for bayonet drill was engendered by the Zouave emphasis on the use of the bayonet and by McClellan's report on the Crimean War, together with his resulting manual of the bayonet written some ten years before the war.

Shown here the more common drill weapons of the 1861-1865 era: drill musket, fencing rifle, fencing bayonets, and drill cutlass. Of semi-military significance are the fencing foil and mask which were sold by some private dealers to interested officers and men.

Navy dispatch case.

BAYONET, FENCING. (Patent No. 36,081). Patented August 5, 1862 by John G. Ernst of York, Pennsylvania. A "removable bayonet guard," composed of a soft elastic ball fastened to a socket of a hard material, provided with a slotted flange on the outside to receive the ends of a strap, and with ears on the inside which served to secure the ball to the socket. By means of straps this guard could be fastened on a bayonet when the soldiers used the bayonet in fencing exercises.

On Dec. 23, 1862 Ernst took out another patent, No. 37,222. This was for a bayonet scabbard and guard. Fitting closely around the neck of the bayonet and against the shoulder of the blade was an elongated link or ring, one end of which was attached to a spring secured within the scabbard. To the lower end of the scabbard was secured, by a socket, a ball of India-rubber or other elastic material, which constituted a guard for the point of the bayonet.

DRUM. See MUSICAL INSTRUMENTS.

EMBALMER. Metallic caskets, "air tight, indestructible, and free from encroachments of vermin or water" were advertised by commercial firms. Embalmers did a thriving business during the war and their ghastly advertisements met the eye of visitors in Washington and other large cities as well as at the front. At times rival embalmers would send their teams along the front handing out handbills headed, "The Honored Dead." One firm charged $50 to embalm an officer and $25 for an enlisted man. Later these prices were raised to $80 and $30 respectively. The embalmed bodies certainly looked lifelike. They were placed in long boxes, lined with zinc, on the lid of which was written the name of the deceased and the address of his parents.

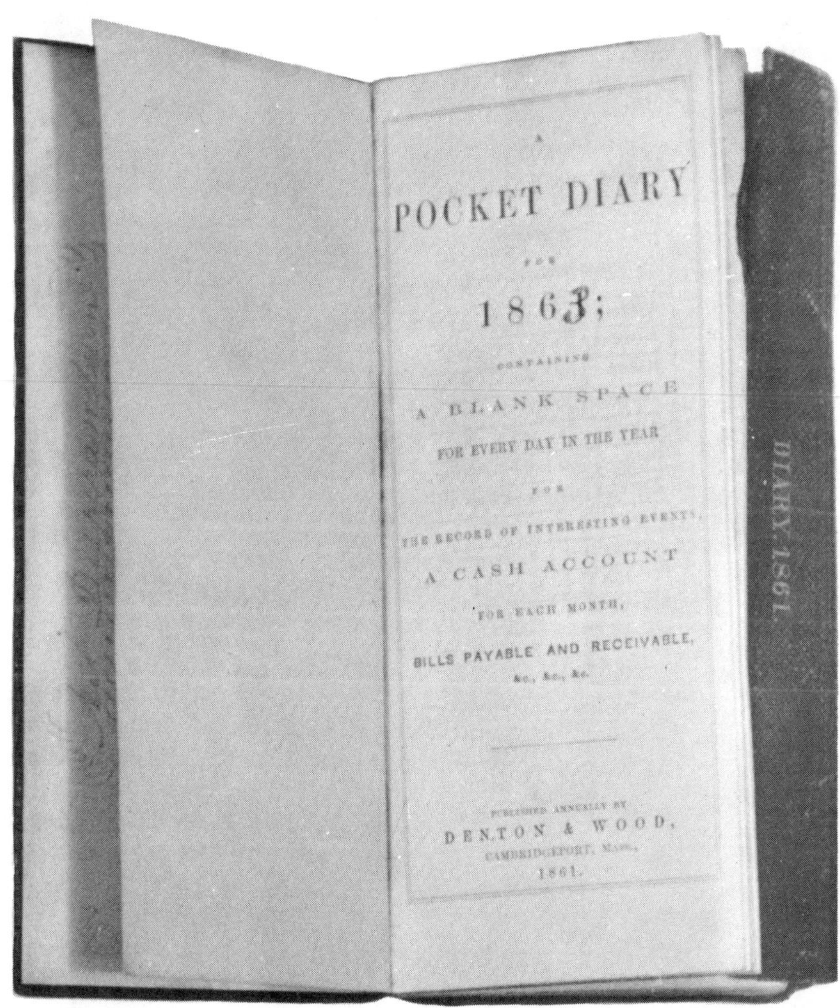

Diary carried by Color Sergeant Francis H. Buffum, 14th N.H. Infantry.

Pennsylvania, SS:

A. G. Curtin

IN THE NAME & BY THE AUTHORITY OF THE

Commonwealth of Pennsylvania

ANDREW G. CURTIN

GOVERNOR OF THE SAID COMMONWEALTH.

To all to whom these Presents shall Come, Sends Greeting:

Know Ye, That Isaiah Conley of the County of Bedford

Having been duly appointed by me, the said ANDREW G. CURTIN,

First Lieutenant of Company G of the 101st Regiment,

Infantry--Pennsylvania Volunteers,

Mustered into the service of the United States, for the defence of the General Government, I do commission him to rank as such from the Twenty first day of January Anno Domini one thousand eight hundred and sixty-three

He is therefore carefully and diligently to discharge the duty of First Lieutenant by doing and performing all manner of things thereunto belonging.

This Commission to continue in force, until the same shall be lawfully determined or annulled.

Given under my Hand and the Great Seal of the State, at Harrisburg this Fourteenth day of February in the year of our Lord one thousand eight hundred and sixty-three and of the Commonwealth the eighty-seventh.

By the Governor:

Dep. SECRETARY OF THE COMMONWEALTH.

Commission of 1st Lt. Isaiah Conley, 101st Pa. Inf.

BY HIS EXCELLENCY

WILLIAM A. BUCKINGHAM,

Governor of the State of Connecticut,

A PROCLAMATION.

Citizens of Connecticut: You are again called upon to rally to the support of our Government. In the name of our common country, I call upon you to enroll your names for the immediate formation of six or more Regiments of Infantry, to be used in suppressing the rebellion. Our troops may be held in check, and our sons die on the battle-field, but the cause of civil liberty must be advanced, the supremacy of the Government must be maintained. Prompt and decisive action will be economy in time and money. By delay, our armies, and even the nation may be imperilled. The rebellion, contending with the desperation of a wicked and hopeless cause, must be met with equal energy. Close your manufactories and work-shops,—turn aside from your farms and your business,—leave for awhile your families and your homes,—meet face to face the enemies of your liberties. Haste, and you will rescue many noble men now struggling against superior numbers, and speedily secure the blessings of peace and good government.

Given under my hand and the seal of the State, at New Haven, this, the third day
L. S. *of July, in the year of our Lord one thousand eight hundred and sixty-two.*

WILLIAM A. BUCKINGHAM.

By His Excellency's command.
J. HAMMOND TRUMBULL, *Secretary of State.*

Proclamation by the Governor of Connecticut calling for six regiments of infantry 1862.

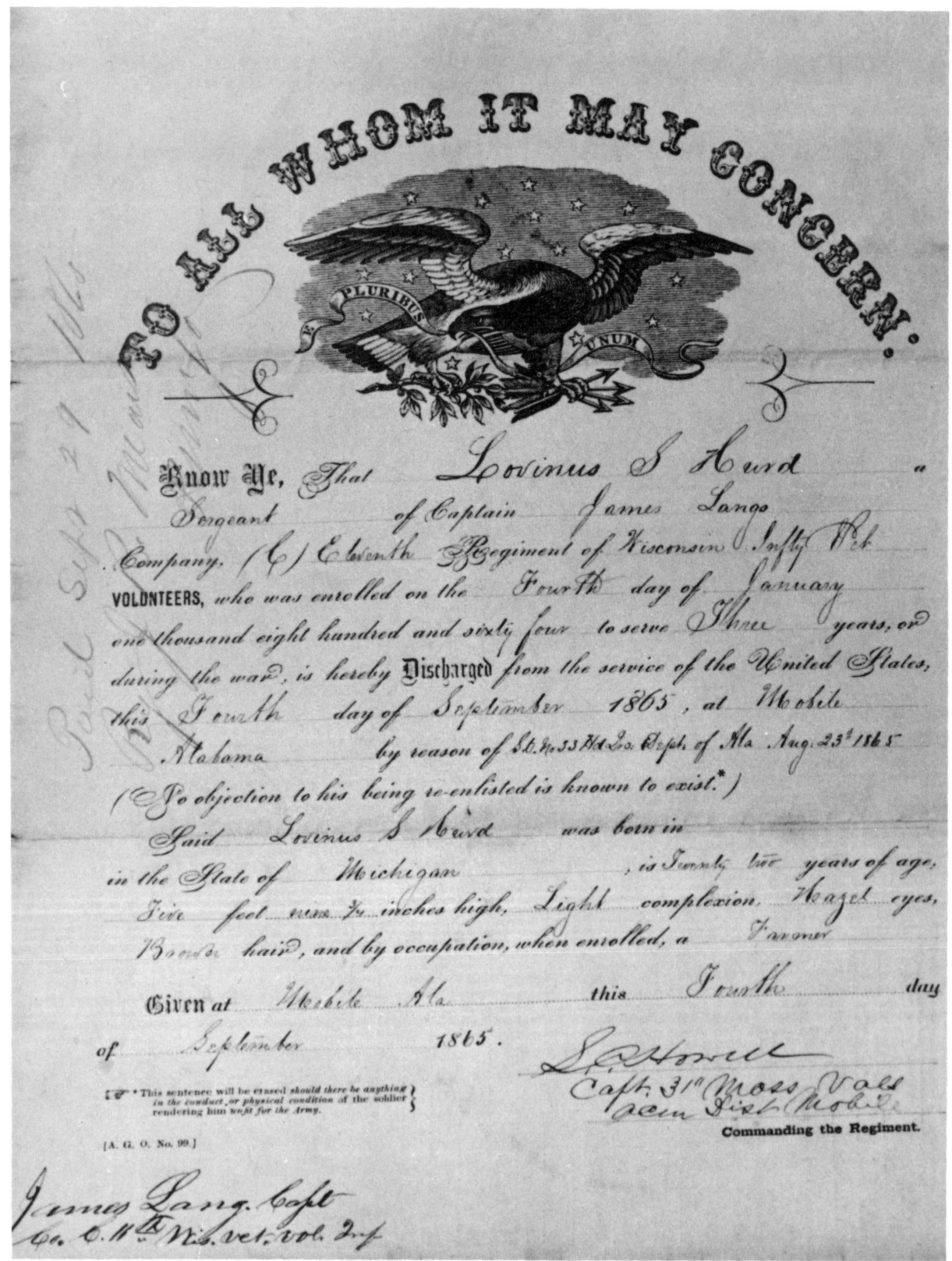

TO ALL WHOM IT MAY CONCERN.

E PLURIBUS UNUM

Know Ye, That Lovinus S Hurd a Sergeant of Captain James Lange Company, (C) Eleventh Regiment of Wisconsin Infty Vet VOLUNTEERS, who was enrolled on the Fourth day of January one thousand eight hundred and sixty four to serve Three years, or during the war, is hereby Discharged from the service of the United States, this Fourth day of September 1865, at Mobile Alabama by reason of S.O. No. 33 Hd Qrs Dept. of Ala Aug. 23d 1865

(No objection to his being re-enlisted is known to exist.*)

Said Lovinus S Hurd was born in in the State of Michigan, is Twenty two years of age, Five feet nine ½ inches high, Light complexion, Hazel eyes, Brown hair, and by occupation, when enrolled, a Farmer

Given at Mobile Ala this Fourth day of September 1865.

S. C. Howell
Capt. 31st Mass Vols
Com Dist Mobile
Commanding the Regiment.

*This sentence will be erased should there be anything in the conduct, or physical condition of the soldier rendering him unfit for the Army.

[A. G. O. No. 99.]

James Lang. Capt
Co. C. 11th Wis. vet. vol. Inf

Discharge of Lovinus S. Hurd, Co., C, 11th Wisc. Inf.

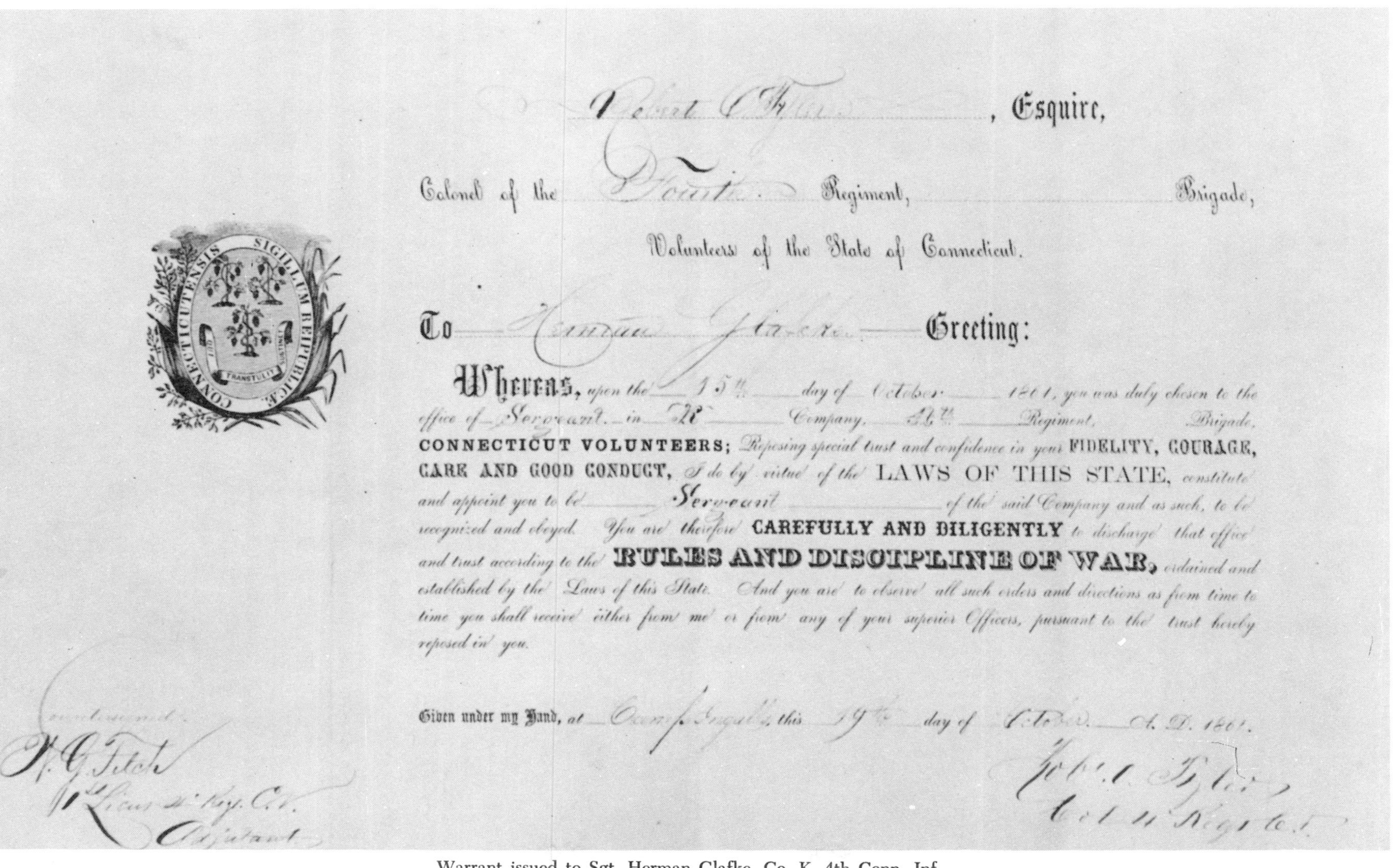

Robert C. Tyler, **Esquire,**

Colonel of the Fourth Regiment, Brigade,

Volunteers of the State of Connecticut.

To Herman Glafke **Greeting:**

Whereas, upon the 15th day of October 1861, you was duly chosen to the office of Sergeant in K Company, 4th Regiment, Brigade, **CONNECTICUT VOLUNTEERS;** Reposing special trust and confidence in your **FIDELITY, COURAGE, CARE AND GOOD CONDUCT,** I do by virtue of the LAWS OF THIS STATE, constitute and appoint you to be Sergeant of the said Company and as such, to be recognized and obeyed. You are therefore **CAREFULLY AND DILIGENTLY** to discharge that office and trust according to the **RULES AND DISCIPLINE OF WAR,** ordained and established by the Laws of this State. And you are to observe all such orders and directions as from time to time you shall receive either from me or from any of your superior Officers, pursuant to the trust hereby reposed in you.

Given under my Hand, at Camp Ingalls this 19th day of Octo. A. D. 1861.

Robt. C. Tyler
Col 4th Regt C.V.

Countersigned:
H. G. Fitch
1st Lieut 4th Reg. C.V.
Adjutant

Warrant issued to Sgt. Herman Glafke, Co. K, 4th Conn. Inf.

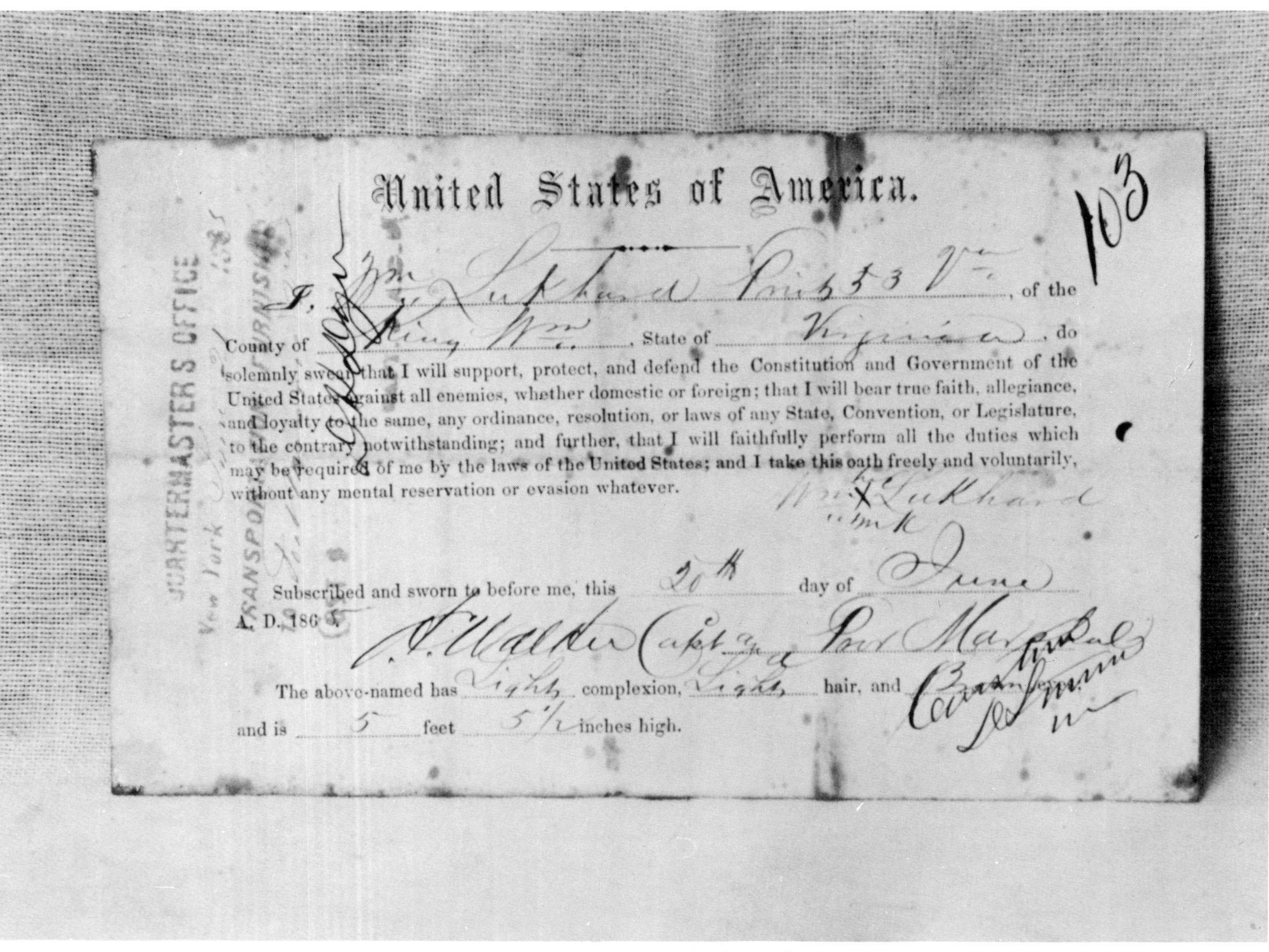

United States of America.

I, Wm Lukhard Pvt 53 Va, of the County of King Wm, State of Virginia, do solemnly swear that I will support, protect, and defend the Constitution and Government of the United States against all enemies, whether domestic or foreign; that I will bear true faith, allegiance, and loyalty to the same, any ordinance, resolution, or laws of any State, Convention, or Legislature, to the contrary notwithstanding; and further, that I will faithfully perform all the duties which may be required of me by the laws of the United States; and I take this oath freely and voluntarily, without any mental reservation or evasion whatever.

Wm X Lukhard
mk

Subscribed and sworn to before me, this 20th day of June A. D. 1865

A. Walker Capt & Pro Marshal

The above-named has Light complexion, Light hair, and [illegible] eyes; and is 5 feet 5 1/2 inches high.

QUARTERMASTER S OFFICE
New York
TRANSPORTATION FURNISHED

Oath of allegiance of soldier of 53d Va. Inf.

ENGINEER EQUIPMENT. The Corps of Engineers was charged with planning, staking out, and constructing permanent and field fortifications; construction and maintenance of various communications facilities including waterways, harbors, and roads; bridge construction and repair, including the building of temporary bridges from improvised materials and by means of pontoon trains; reconnaissance and staking out of defensive positions for the field forces; and many other construction projects necessary for the movement and supply of troops in the field. The Corps of Topographical Engineers, which until 1863 were a part of the Corps of Engineers, were responsible for the survey, drafting, and reproduction of maps. With a few exceptions, the equipment used by the engineers was similar to or identical with that used by civilian engineers of that period. The most notable exceptions were in pontoon bridge equipment and in field mapping and reproduction. Engineer troops, usually called pioneers in the Confederate Army, also accompanied the field forces to assist them in clearing fields of fire, constructing field works, repairing routes, crossing streams, and installing heavy ordnance.

BRIDGING EQUIPMENT. Engineers and pioneers were trained to use improvised materials of whatever was available in constructing bridges. Such materials included lumber, cut timber, canal boats, ferries, rafts, and the like. But they also had, in limited quantity—especially scarce in the Confederate Army—equipment called pontoon trains for throwing floating bridges quickly across streams and other bodies of water.

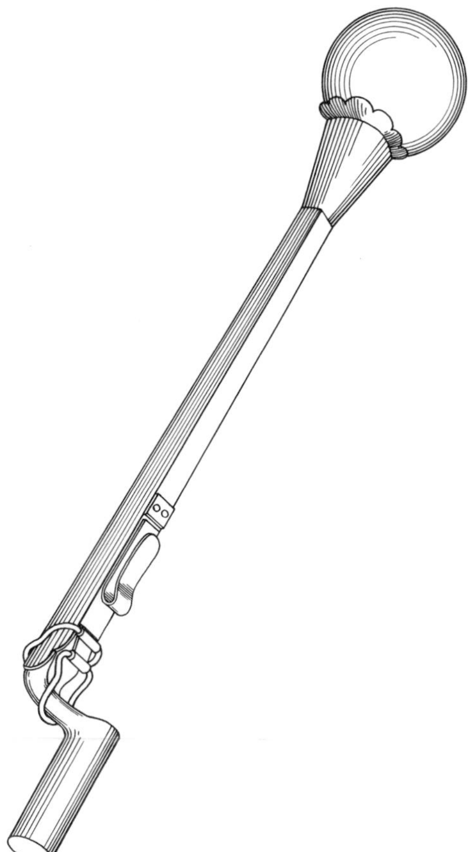

Ernst's fencing bayonet, patented Aug. 5, 1862. (National Archives)

PONTOON BRIDGES. Pontoon trains were modelled after the French wooden trains and the Russian canvas trains. The wooden pontoons were heavier and more suitable for bridges that required strength and some permanence. The small canvas pontoons were more portable, and were generally used with the field armies in most theaters of operations. The balks and chess were carried in wagons somewhat similarly to present-day pre-cut lumber for building houses. The pontoon frames were covered with canvas paulins. These canvas pontoons were less suitable in rough water such as the lower reaches of the James and Potomac Rivers. The heavy wooden pontoons were also better for constructing floating docks or approaches to wharves. Pontoons of both kinds could also be used to ferry troops across a stream or from ship to shore in river crossings or amphibious operations. Illustrated here

Completed pontoon bridge. (National Archives)

are components of the issue equipment of the U.S. Army during the Civil War.

Blanket Boats. Herman Haupt developed a very simple, practical, and useful plan for crossing streams by means of boats each constructed of a single rubber blanket. Such a boat was capable of carrying a soldier, knapsack, arms, and accouterments, with only 4 inches of displacement. The size of some of the common rubber blankets was 6 by 4.75 feet, but Haupt would have preferred that they be 7 x 5. The rubber blanket covered a frame made of round sticks, 1 inch and 1½ inch in diameter. Several of these boats lashed together and covered with poles could be used to form a raft, on which wagons could be ferried across a stream. However, for artillery, rafts of wagon bodies, or something possessing greater flotation power were employed.

Haupt also developed rafts of casks, floating arks, which could be used as floating docks, warehouses, and transports.

India-Rubber Pontoons. These were developed by George W. Cullum, Corps of Engineers, U. S. Army, and were used first in the Mexican War. These pontoons were made of double India-rubber cloth, and consisted each of three tangent cylinders, peaked at both extremities like the ends of a canoe, which were firmly united together by two strong India-rubber ligaments along their lines of contact, and widening into a connecting web towards the ends. The whole thus formed a single boat 20 feet long and 5 feet broad, of great bouyancy and stability, and because of its form and lightness it presented but trifling resistance to the water.

Each cylinder (including its peaked extremities) was 20 feet long, 20 inches in diameter, and was divided into three distinct air-tight compartments, each of which had its own inflating nozzle. The middle compartment occupied the whole width of the roadway of the bridge, but the ends of it were placed sufficiently within the ends of the chesses (or cross boards) to be secure from injury—especially from shot—except in rare cases. The end compartments were exposed, but, if pierced, could be quickly repaired by means of India-rubber patches.

Inflating bellows were used for inflation and the pontoons. Pontoons were moored by a light anchor, weighing 45 pounds. To work the position of the anchor, a buoy was fastened to the anchor by means of a buoy line. These pontoons held a weight of 7,000 pounds safely.

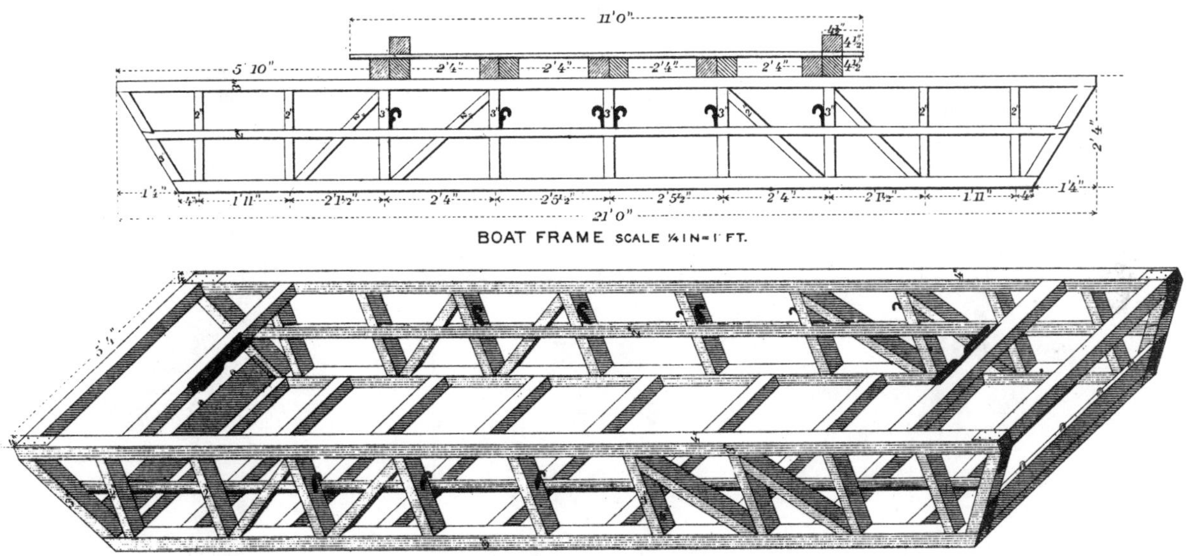

Frame for canvas pontoon.

Wooden pontoons. More commonly used than India-rubber boats were bateaux. The bateau was a flat-bottomed wooden boat, 31 feet long weighing 1,455 pounds. It was transported on specially constructed wagon frames and could be carried to the water by 16-20 men hoisting it on their shoulders.

A mooring boat was flatter than a bateau, to permit its passing under the bridge flooring, but similar in all other respects.

Railway Bridges, Floating. These were built, put together in sections along the shore, then towed into position and secured by piles or anchors. Such a bridge, constructed by Haupt, sank only 5 inches under the weight of a 25-ton locomotive.

Trestle Bridge. Bridges of this type, made of round sticks cut in the immediate area, were widely used.

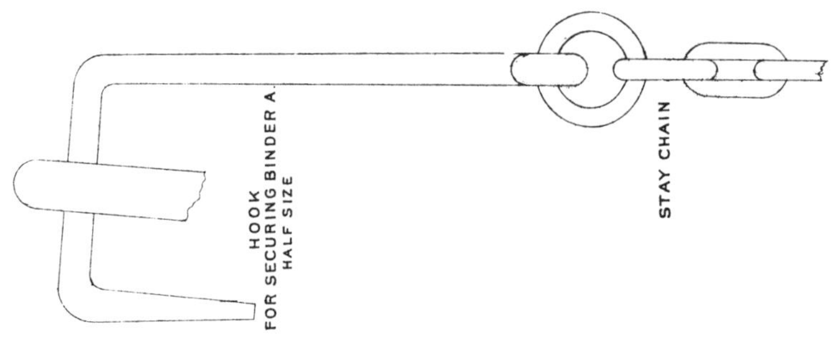

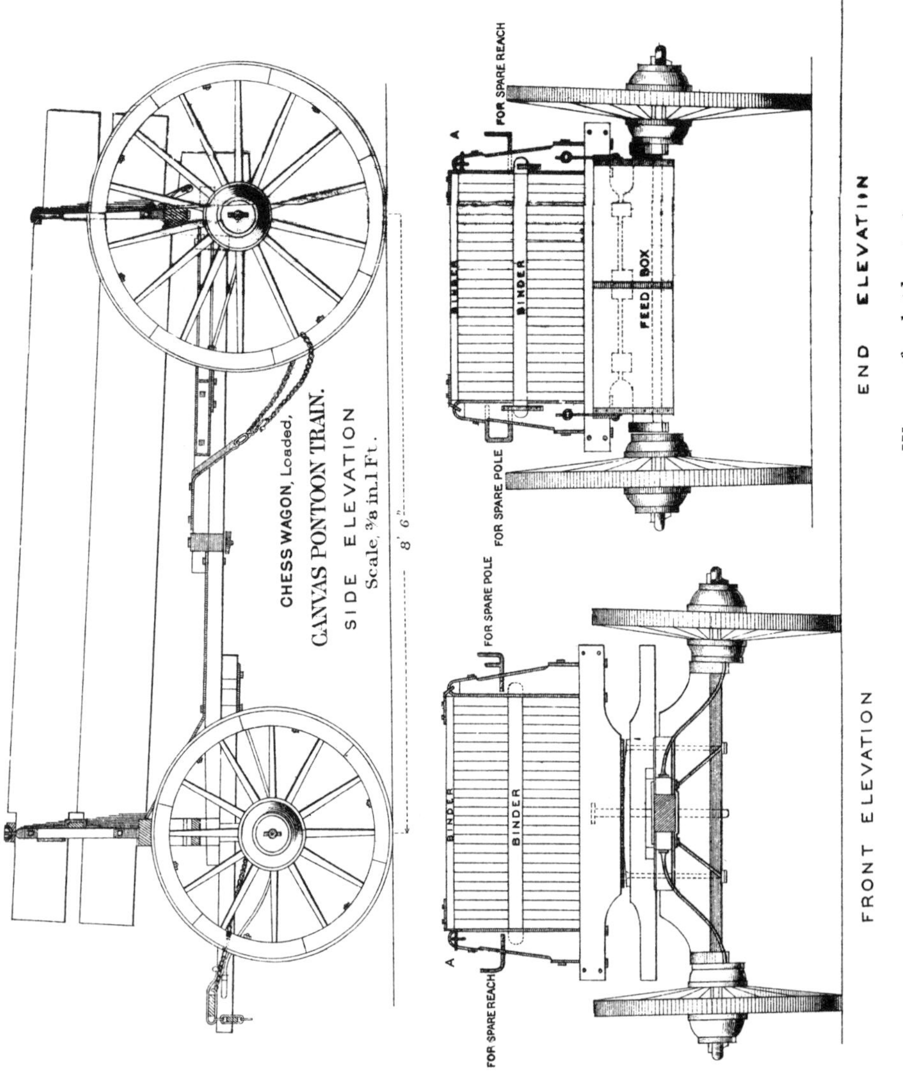

Wagons for bridge train.

This type of bridge could be constructed rapidly with no high degree of skill required by the builders. When the height was too great for single trestles, they were erected in two or more tiers.

Herman Haupt built a trestle bridge over Potomac Creek in 9 working days, using round sticks cut from the neighboring woods. His untrained crew built this bridge in 4 stories; it was 80 feet high and about 400 feet long.

Wire Suspension Bridge. Such bridges were constructed and used, especially after 1862, by the Federals. These bridges were of 200 foot span, single track, 5 feet 8-inch wide, and designed to carry a load of 30 pounds per square foot. This type of bridge using 200 foot span, was anchored by suspension cables attached to trees or solid ground 50 feet back of the suspension tower.

In addition to suspension bridges, the Federals used portable arched truss bridges for military roads.

MAPS. Until mid-1863 the production and reproduction of maps in the Federal Army was a function of the Topographical Engineers; subsequently the Corps of Topographical Engineers became a branch of the Corps of Engineers. The topographical engineers, in addition to mapping, made surveys for frontier defense and positions for fortifications and siege artillery, reconnaissance of routes through which the mobile forces had to pass, and examination of routes of communication on land and water for supplies and troop movements. They supervised the construction of military roads and bridges. In the Confederate Army the situation was generally analogous, though with the field forces some of the work done by engineers was the responsibility of pioneers units which were formed from combat troops who were given special training. The survey for and production of maps was, however, a specialty, and in some cases, notably that of Jed Hotchkiss, the work was done by civilian engineers attached to the field forces. It is not generally known that Hotchkiss was a civilian until late in the war—though he is usually referred to as "Captain," and even "Major."

In the U.S. Army the Topographic Engineers were given some assistance by the Coast Survey (now U.S. Geological Survey) under its capable superintendent, Alexander D. Bache, aided by civilian engineers.

During the last year of the war the Topographic Engineers furnished 20,938 sheets of maps to the field forces.

MAP CASES. Two samples of cases for carrying maps in the field are shown here. The shorter case, of tin, is the type which saw extensive use in the war by officers and engineer units. Length 20½ inches, diameter 2½ inches. Carried by Surgeon Eli N. Love, 5th West Virginia Cavalry.

The other case is much more elaborate. It is of wood with brass ends, 26 inches long and 2 inches in diameter. The case is equipped with a leather carrying handle and was used by a New York officer.

MAP REPRODUCTION. When armies were in the field at great distance from base of operations, it was essential that each large unit have a complete map re-

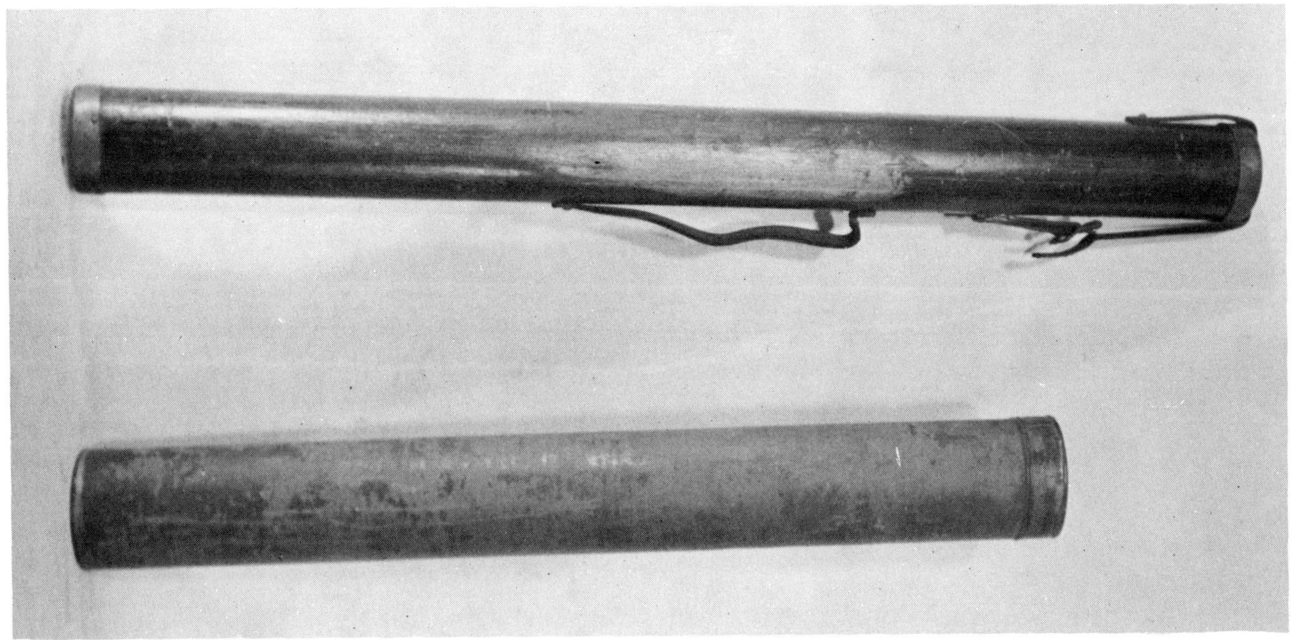

Map cases. Top, wooden case used by a New York officer. Bottom, tin case used by Surgeon Eli N. Love, 5th West Virginia Cavalry.

production establishment of its own. In the west, the office of chief topographical engineer had a printing press, two lithographic presses, and one photographic establishment with complete arrangements for map mounting and a full complement of draftsmen and assistants.

During the first year of the war, maps were reproduced by photography but unless a very fine and expensive lens was used, the various sheets were distorted at the borders, which prevented the sections from being joined accurately. Other disadvantages of the photographical maps were that they faded when exposed to sunlight and copies could not be made at night or in the rain. Much superior maps were reproduced from lithographic stones and presses which were, however, too heavy for transportation in an active campaign and were used only in the rear echelons.

The best device used was a photo-printing outfit which used a system of chemical baths. The printing was done by tracing the required map on thin paper and laying it over a sheet coated with nitrate of silver. The sun's rays passing through the tissue paper blackened the prepared paper except under the ink lines, thus making a white map on a black ground. As new information came in, the maps were altered; occasionally there would be several editions of the same map in a day. In addition to survey, data for maps were obtained by interrogation of refugees, spies, prisoners and "any and all persons familiar with the country in front of us." Copies for the cavalry were printed directly on muslin, as such maps could be washed clean whenever soiled and could not be injured by hard service. Many officers sent handkerchiefs to the topographical engineer office and had maps printed on them.

SURVEY AND DRAFTING EQUIPMENT.

CHAINS. The surveyor's chain was a measuring instrument consisting of 100 wire rods or links. Each of these links was 7.92 inches long (Gunter's chain), or 12 inches long (engineer's chain). The chain shown here is an engineer's chain used in the war and marked as follows on one handle: "Keuffel and Esser Co. New York 6411"; on the other handle "Tested KNE 100—FEET STEEL NO. 12." Both 50-foot and 100-foot chains were used, the former being more common.

COMPASSES. Compasses were comparatively rare although it is known that engineer units and some individual line officers and scouts used them. The author has a brass specimen, with a carrying ring, that is 1½ inches in diameter. This compass was actually used in the war but its only marking is "Made in France."

Box Compass. This was used extensively by the engineers during the war. It was graduated zero to 360 degrees, the numbers increasing in a clockwise direction. The north and south line was parallel to the side on which the cover was hinged.

Prismatic or Schmalcalder Compass. This compass could be held in the hand but was more accurate and convenient when mounted on a tripod or a single staff. This compass consisted of a box and a card with needle attached, and a pivot which supported both needle and card. A sight-vane had a thread to direct the line of sight and a reflector to enable observations of objects above the horizon. The card was graduated in different instruments, some from zero to 90 degrees; some from zero to 180 degrees and back to zero; and others had 4 quadrants, each from zero to 90 degrees.

Dividers. The engineer dividers shown here was

Engineer's chain made by Keuffel & Esser, New York.

found at Petersburg, Va. It is of steel, and when closed is 5¼ inches long.

Levels. Leveling instruments were of two types: The *Water-Level* consisted of a ~~cylindrical~~ brass tube, bent at its extremities so as to form two arms at right angles to its length. In these arms were set two glass vials. The tube was mounted on a tripod, and could be rotated around its vertical axis so as to make a circuit of the horizon. The *Y Spirit Level* consisted of an

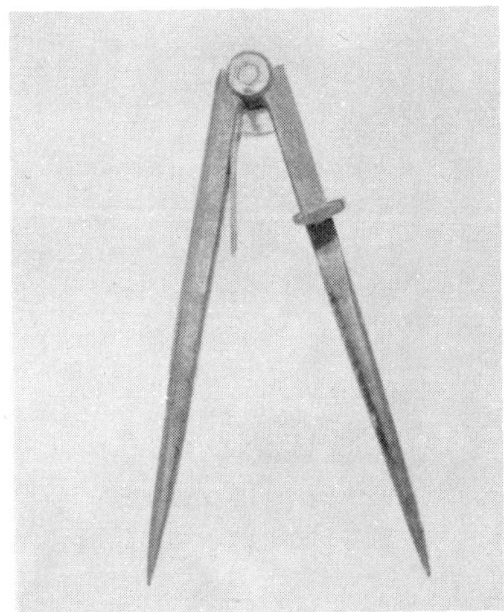

Engineer's dividers found at Petersburg.

achromatic telescope mounted in Y's, and had a reticle in the principal focus of the eye-glass. The reticle consisted of two spiders' lines, at right angles to each other, fastened at their extremities in separate slides. A spirit bubble was used in this instrument.

Other levels used during the war were Burrel's Reflecting Level, Captain Livet's Level, Mason's Level, Slope Level, and Burnier's Slope Level—all of which are described in the technical manuals of the period.

Odometer. This instrument was a small brass circular box containing a series of cogwheels, which regulated the motion of an index on a dial-plate upon its exterior, which recorded the number of revolutions of a wheel to which the box was attached by straps. The odometer measured distance; the length of the perimeter of the wheel, multiplied by the number of revolutions, gave the distance passed over.

Plane Table. This consisted of a board to hold paper, a tripod to furnish a support, and the intermediate arrangement of different constructions which were utilized to level the board. A common type during the Civil War was 16 inches square with its upper edge rabbeted to receive a boxwood frame which was placed on the board and was used to stretch and hold the drawing paper on the board. One face of the frame was graduated from zero to 360 degrees in order to measure angles. The reverse side of the frame was usually divided into equal parts, as inches and tenths. Also used with the plane table was a compass-box to serve as a check on accuracy, a brass ruler, and occasionally a sight vane or telescope to direct the line of sight.

Protractor. Used for measuring angles on the plane table or drafting board. A rectangular protractor was most commonly used, arranged with a scale. The favorite make was Abbott's, which differed from the ordinary rectanglar protractor in that it was graduated differently. Abbott's ran from zero to 180 degrees on one side, and from 180 to 360 degrees on the other side.

Ruler. Two types of rulers were used:

Parallel Ruler. Two strips of oak, painted black, each 15 inches long, and connected by two brass swivels. Length completely shut, 29⅜ inches.

Straight-Edge Ruler. For drawing straight lines.

Sextant. A surveying instrument, involving the optical principle of a ray of light reflected once by each of two plane reflectors, in a plane normal to their intersection, and was deviated from its original direction by an angular amount equal to twice the angle of the reflectors.

The pocket sextant differed in arrangement from the larger type, but was similar in principle. The index and horizon glasses were enclosed in a brass box of 2-3 inches diameter. The top of the sextant unscrewed and could be screwed on the bottom for a handle. The

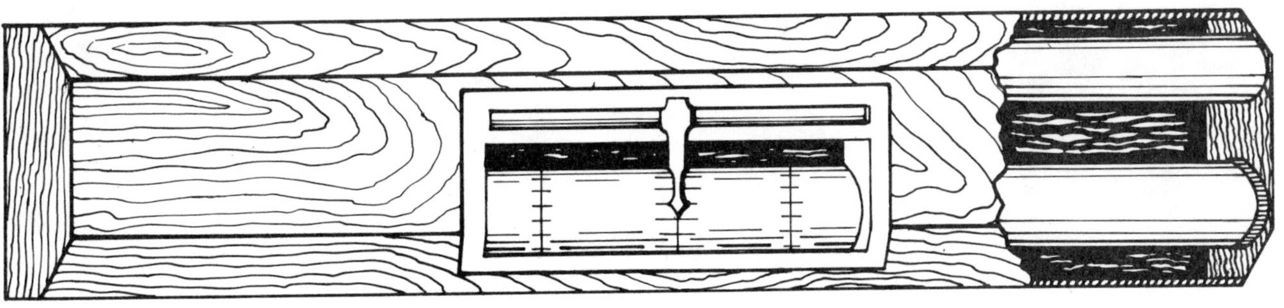

Wood's parallel ruler, patented Nov. 14, 1865. (National Archives)

Topographical engineers at their plotting table, on the Peninsula in 1862. At the left is an engineer level on a tripod. The instrument at the right, also on a tripod, is concealed by the man's hand. (National Archives)

box protected the glasses from all ordinary chances of injury or displacement.

STADIA. This consisted of a telescope with two horizontal hairs in or near the principal focus of the eyeglass. When used with a graduated stick, the distance to an object could be determined.

THEODOLITE. This was the best instrument for measuring angles and bearings in the field. When firmly mounted, on a table, stand, or tripod, and carefully adjusted, it read angles to within a few seconds, using a vernier. For ordinary rapid field survey, instruments of less precision were used, such as the sextant, compass, and plane table.

EPAULETTES, UNITED STATES UNIFORMS

ARMY. All officers having military rank were required to wear an epaulette on each shoulder. They could be dispensed with when the officer was not on duty or on such duties as drill, inspections of barracks and hospitals, on courts of inquiry and boards, inspection of articles, supervision of working parties and fatigue details, and upon the march except when there was an immediate expectation of meeting the enemy; also when the overcoat was worn.

General Officers. The epaulette was of gold, with solid crescent. The insignia of rank was worn on the strap, as shown, the stars being silver embroidered. Lieutenant generals and the Major General commanding the Army wore three stars, other major generals two, and brigadiers one.

Regimental Officers. In addition to insignia of rank, these officers wore their regimental number embroidered in gold, within a circlet of embroidered silver, upon cloth of the following colors: Artillery, scarlet; infantry, light blue; cavalry, yellow.

Staff. Staff officers wore letters or emblems denoting their branch of service, as follows: Medical Department, a laurel wreath embroidered in gold, and within the wreath in old English the letters M.S. (Medical Staff). The Pay Department emblem was the same as for the Medical Department except that the letters were P.D. The Corps of Engineers wore a turreted castle of silver. The Corps of Topographical Engineers wore a shield embroidered in gold, and below it the letters T.E. embroidered in old English. The Ordnance Department was shown by a shell and flame embroidered in silver.

MARINE CORPS

Commandant. Gold, with solid crescent; device of the Corps; a bugle of solid silver, containing the letter M within the ring of the bugle; bugle and letter same size as that worn on the undress cap. This device was placed within the crescent; on the center of the strap, a silver embroidered star one and one-eighth inches

Officer's epaulette, 3½ inches long, ½ inch diameter. (Norm Flayderman)

Insignia of branch on epaulette—Ordnance. (Norm Flayderman)

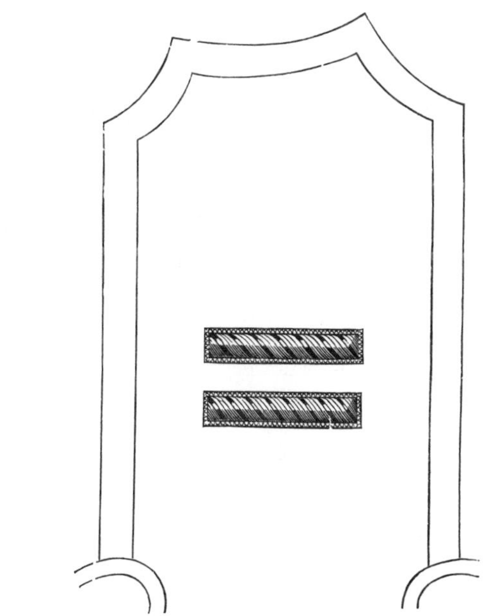

Insignia of rank on shoulder strap of epaulette—captain. (Norm Flayderman)

Navy epaulette, captain. (Norm Flayderman)

in diameter, dead and bright bullion one-half inch in diameter, and three and one-half inches long.

Colonel. Same as for the Commandant, substituting a silver embroidered spread-eagle for the star upon the strap.

and two and one-half inches long; and substituting for the star two silver embroidered bars.

First-Lieutenant. Same as for the Commandant, except that the bullion was only one-eighth of an inch in diameter, and two and one-half inches long; and substituting for the star one embroidered silver bar.

Second-Lieutenant. Same as for a First-Lieutenant, omitting the silver embroidered bar. Epaulettes were only worn in full dress.

Enlisted Men. Yellow metal crescent, and scale strap, with yellow worsted bullion; the bullion was removable in order to clean the metal.

Sergeant-Major, Quartermaster-Sergeant, Drum-Major, and Chief Musicians. Bullion three and one-half inches long and three-eighths of an inch in diameter.

Sergeants. Same as for Sergeant-Major, except the bullion was only one-quarter of an inch in diameter.

Epaulette box of a lieutenant of the 51st New York.

Lieutenant-Colonel. Same as for the Commandant, substituting for the star, a silver embroidered leaf upon the strap.

Major. Same as for the Commandant, without the star on the center of the strap.

Captain. Same as for the Commandant, except that the bullion was only one-fourth of an inch in diameter,

Corporal. Same as for Sergeant-Major, except that the bullion was only one-sixteenth of an inch in diameter.

Private. Same as for Corporals.

Navy. Epaulettes to be of gold, bullion and finish, with rank designation of silver as follows:

Captain. An eagle and anchor 2⅝ inches long, with

a silver embroidered star above, 1⅛ inches in diameter. The senior Captain in the Navy and the Commander-in-Chief of a Squadron will have on the epaulette an additional star, 1 inch in diameter—the centers of the stars to be separated 1½ inch.

Commander. Two crossed foul anchors, 2 inches long from crown to ring.

Lieutenant. One foul anchor 2 inches long.

Master. Plain epaulette as the one for a lieutenant.

Surgeon, Passed Assistant Surgeon, and Assistant Surgeon. Epaulettes with solid smooth crescents with the letters M.D. in old English characters embroidered in silver, in the middle of the frog. The senior Surgeon of the Navy and the "Surgeon of the Fleet," had a silver embroidered rosette on the epaulette above the letters. The senior and other Pursers had the same as senior and other surgeons, with the letters P.D. in old English characters, embroidered in silver in the middle of the frog.

Chief Engineer. Same as for a Master, except that the epaulette was of silver lace, with the letter "E", ¾ inch long, in old English character embroidered in gold on the frog, and the crescents were smooth and solid.

PATENTED EPAULETTE (Patent No. 23,620). Patented April 12, 1859 by James S. Smith of New York, N.Y. This early type of epaulette, which was widely used in the war, was an "improvement in epaulettes, featuring an adjuster."

EPAULETTE BOX. Dress eqaulettes came in either cardboard boxes or, more commonly, in japànned tin containers with a metal carrying handle attached to the cover of the box.

EPROUVETTE. An apparatus to test the projectile force of gunpowder. This method was adopted by establishing at the Washington Arsenal a cannon pendulum and a musket pendulum, which were used for testing samples of powder sent from powder factories. The eprouvette showed the initial velocity of a projectile fired from a cannon or musket.

EYE GLASSES. Some of the older men wore eyeglasses. Especially interesting is the fact that some sun glasses also were used. These sun glasses were similar in size and shape to the regular eyeglasses, but the glass was coated with a heavy blue material to reflect the sun. In the Gavin collection is a photograph of Capt. T. B. Griffith, Co. B, 3d Massachusetts Infantry, wearing this type of dark glasses.

EXPLOSIVE BULLETS. See AMMUNITION, SMALL ARMS.

FERROTYPE. See PICTURES.

FIFE. See MUSICAL INSTRUMENTS.

FIRE BALL. See PROJECTILES.

FLAGS; COLORS AND STANDARDS; ENSIGNS; GUIDONS. "Flag" is the general name to designate an emblem or device on light cloth to indicate nationality or some lower organizational level. The colors used in the Flag of the United States are traditionally white for purity and innocence, red for valor, and blue for vigilance, perseverance, and justice. Four different names for the United States flag are in use in the military service: flag, color, standard, and ensign. In general the term "flag" is applicable regardless of size and use, but the other three terms have special uses as follows: (1) A *color,* during the Civil War, was the national, state, or regimental flag carried by dismounted units, the President, and certain general officers; (2) a *standard* was a flag of the same type as specified in the foregoing, carried by mounted units; and (3) an *ensign* was the flag flown on ships and boats.

Ordinarily, the term flag applied only to those displayed from buildings, headquarters, and the like, and not those carried by troops.

Bunting, in the national colors, was used for decorating buildings, review stands, and the like, but was not referred to as "flags."

Flags, colors, standards, and guidons had tips or finials of every conceivable variety. Brass was the usual metal; however, the design varied from an eagle with outstretched wings to espontoons, halberts, and spheres. The spear point was probably the most common finial used during the war.

At the outbreak of war the United States flag had 33 stars. The arrangement of these stars varied greatly, including such patterns as a huge star or an anchor. The flag over Sumter in April 1861 had a star arrangement of 7 vertical lines as follows: 5-3-5-7-5-3-5. However, the most common arrangement apparently was 5 horizontal lines of stars, from top to bottom as follows: 7-7-5-7-7.

COLORS AND STANDARDS. Today colors and standards are used by troops only during ceremonies, but during the Civil War they were also carried into battle. Each regiment had a color guard composed of men of exceptionally fine physique and demonstrated courage. The guard consisted of four men, two carrying the colors and two acting as guards. There were repeated instances of mortally wounded color bearers desperately trying to hold the colors aloft and refusing to give them up except to another member of the color guard or until death relaxed their stubborn hold. The colors often served as a rallying point for the regiment.

Battle Streamers. On Washington's birthday, 1862, the U.S. War Department ordered that units would carry, attached to their colors, by means of streamers attached to the staff, the names of battles in which they were participants. The order, which contributed substantially to esprit de corps among combat units, said in part: "It is expected that troops so distinguished will regard their colors as representing the honor of their corps—to be lost only with their lives; and . . . those not yet entitled to such a distinc-

National Standard of the 2d U.S. Artillery, used in Civil War. (West Point Museum collection)

Presentation flag. (Norm Flayderman)

Regimental color, 6th U.S. Infantry. (West Point Museum collection)

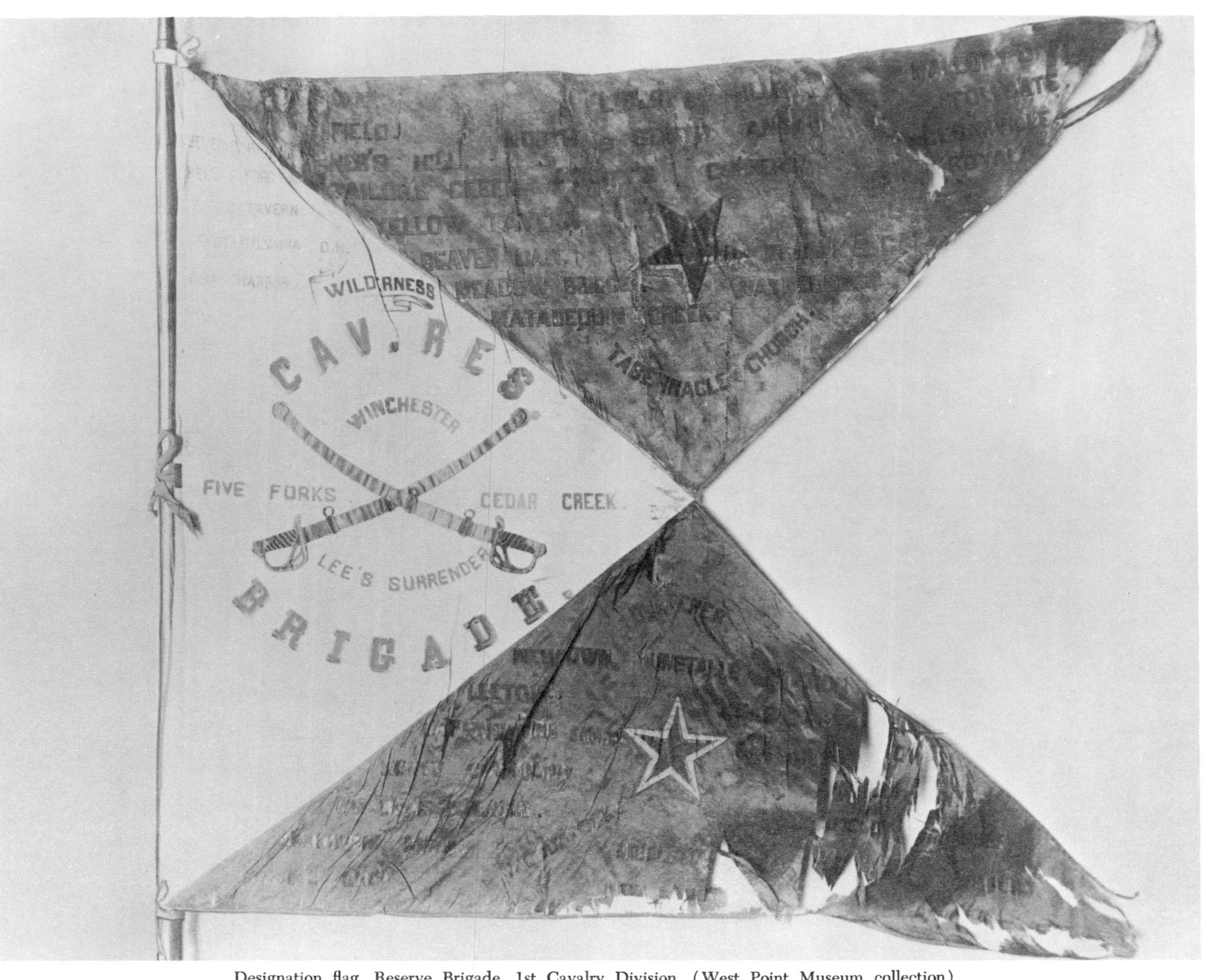

Designation flag, Reserve Brigade, 1st Cavalry Division. (West Point Museum collection)

Color of 1st Battalion, 11th Infantry. Carried in 21 battles. (West Point Museum collection)

Battle flag of Battery K, 1st U.S. Artillery. (West Point Museum collection)

Ohio flag of undetermined origin, but owned in post-war years by veterans of the 35th Ohio Infantry. (Stephen M. Millett)

tion will not rest satisfied until they have won it by their discipline and courage."

Colors, Regular Army. Each regiment of infantry had two silken colors. The National color or Stars and Stripes had the number and name of the regiment embroidered in silver on the center stripe. The regimental color was blue with the arms of the United States embroidered in silk on the center. The name of the regiment was on a scroll, underneath the eagle. Size of each color was 6 feet 6 inches fly, and 6 feet deep on the pike. The length of the pike, including spear and ferrule, was 9 feet 10 inches. The fringe was yellow while the cords and tassels were blue and white silk intermixed.

Each regiment of artillery had two silken colors. The National color was similar to the garrison flag. The number and name of the regiment was embroidered in gold on the center stripe. The Regimental color was yellow, the same dimensions as the regiment's National color, bearing in the center two crossed cannon, with the letters U.S. above, and the number of the regiment below; fringe, yellow. Each color was 6 feet 6 inches fly, and 6 feet deep on the pike. The pike, including the spear and ferrule, was 9 feet 10 inches in length. Cords and tassels were red and yellow silk intermixed.

Colors and Standards, Volunteers and Militia. State regimental colors differed from Regular Army colors in that the coat of arms of the United States on the Regular Army regimental flags was replaced by the state coat of arms. State regimental colors were generally purchased from local contractors and presented to the regiment in impressive ceremonies just before leaving the state for the seat of war. Usually some prominent local dignitary or a lady, in a flowery patriotic speech presented the colors to the regiment whose colonel received them in a speech of appreciation assuring the donors that the regiment would guard the colors with their lives. The colors were beautiful affairs and extremely expensive. For example, the state flag of the 10th Massachusetts Infantry, made by Thomas G. Savory of Boston, was trimmed with yellow silk fringe and mounted with gold cord and tassels and represented an outlay of $275.00. The accompanying Union banner was a worthy companion, of regulation size presenting in silk the red, white and blue.

Holders and Carriers. Both regimental and state colors and standards were carried in leather socket-type carriers, as illustrated.

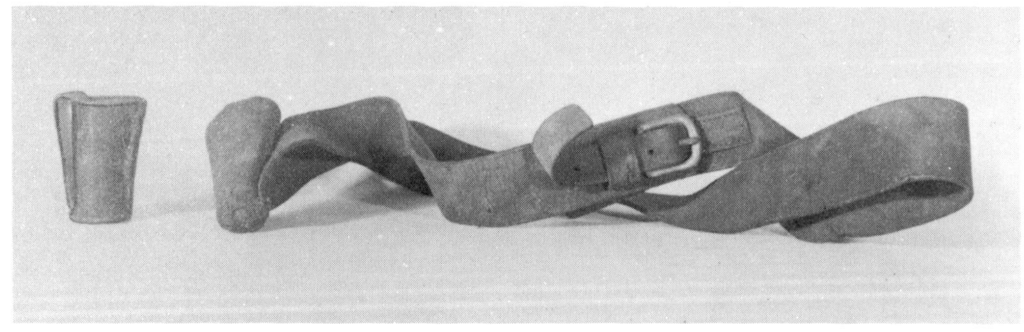

Flag holder.

Standards and Guidons of Mounted Regiments. Each regiment was provided with a silk standard, and each company with a silk guidon. The standard bore the arms of the United States, embroidered in silk, on a blue ground, with the number and name of the regiment in a scroll underneath the eagle. The flag of the standard was 2 feet 5 inches wide, and 2 feet 3 inches on the lance, and was edged with yellow silk fringe.

FLAGS

Camp Colors. Camp colors were of bunting, 18 inches square, white for infantry, and red for artillery,

Cavalry guidon. Co. E, 2d Massachusetts Cavalry. (West Point Museum collection)

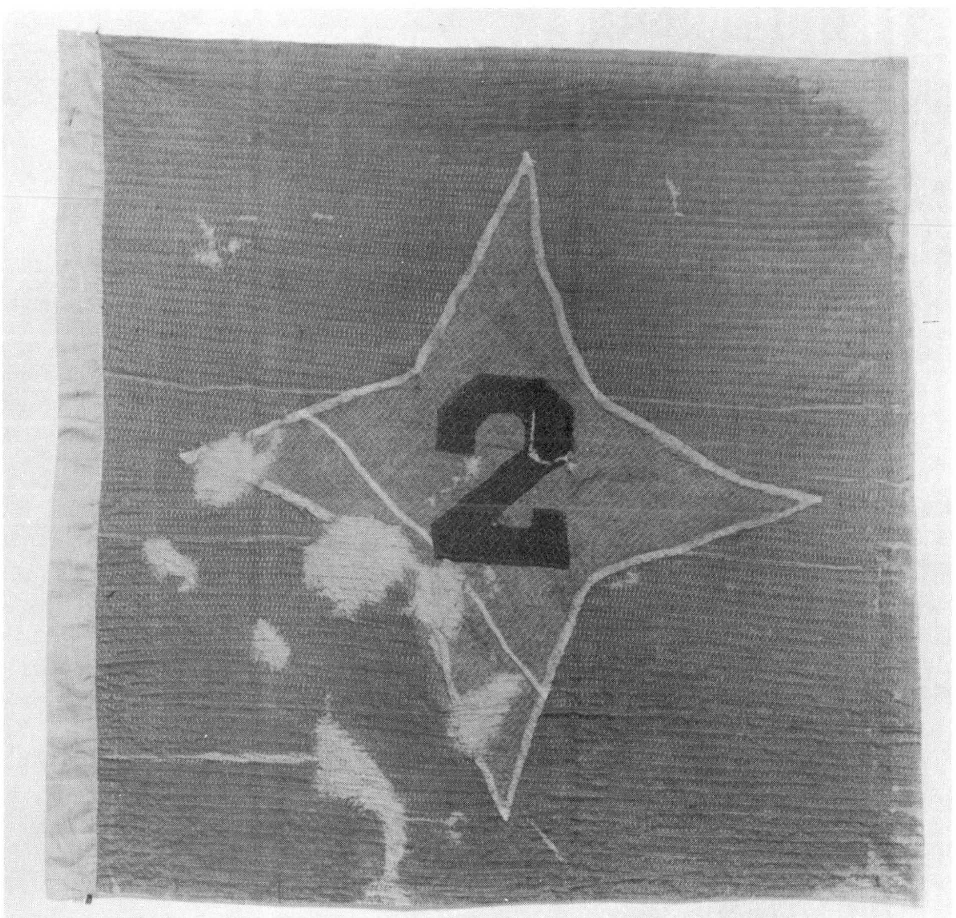

Flag of 2d Division, 19th Army Corps.

with the number of the regiment on them. The pole was 8 feet long.

Confederate Flags. The Confederacy had four flags. The first, adopted March 4, 1861, consisted of two horizontal red stripes with a white stripe in between. This flag had seven white stars in a circle on a blue field.

However, this flag was easily confused with the U.S. Stars and Stripes and after 1st Bull Run a second flag was adopted. This flag was red with a blue St. Andrew's cross containing thirteen white stars.

A National Flag was adopted May 1, 1863, to replace the Stars and Bars. This new flag was white with the battle flag in the upper right quarter.

A fourth flag, adopted March 4, 1865, by adding a broad vertical bar to the edge of the National Flag. This was done because when the old National Flag was furled, too much white showed and it somewhat resembled a flag of surrender or flag of truce.

Garrison Flag. The garrison flag was the national flag. It was made of bunting, 36 feet fly and 20 feet hoist, in 13 horizontal stripes of equal breadth, alternately red and white, beginning with the red. In the upper quarter, near the staff, was the Union, composed of a number of white stars, equal to the number of states, on a blue field, one-third the length of the flag, extending to the lower edge of the fourth red stripe from the top.

Headquarters Flag. In addition to the national and regimental flags, the military forces of the U.S. had distinctive flags for armies, corps, divisions, and brigades. For the flags of army corps, the central theme was the insignia of the corps itself. Divisions were indicated by colors as follows: First Division—red; Second Division—white; Third Division—blue; Fourth Division—green. Brigades were indicated by a numerical designation.

Confederate flags. Left, Flag of 4th Division, 19th Army Corps. Right, Flag of the Confederate States of America. This was the flag that was superseded by the more familiar "Stars and Bars."

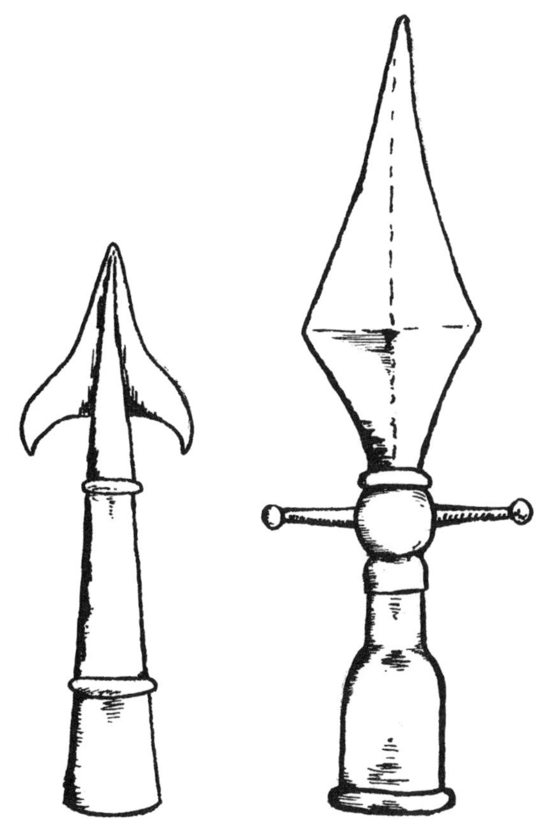

Spear-heads for battle flags. (Drawn by Mike McAffee)

Hospital Flags. Early in January 1864, the U.S. War Department established hospital and ambulance flags for the Army as follows: General Hospitals—yellow bunting 9 by 5 feet, with the letter H, 24 inches long, of green bunting, in the center; Post and Field Hospitals—yellow bunting, 6 by 4 feet, with letter 24 inches long, of green bunting, in the center; ambulances and guidons to mark the way to field hospitals—yellow bunting 28 by 14 inches, with a border, one inch deep of green.

Miscellaneous Flags. As today, there were many other flags used during the war for various purposes including presentation to local units or for display at home. There was a bewildering variety of design and size in these unofficial flags, many of which can be seen in collections and museums today. Most of the regimental colors of the war were silk and today are in very poor condition. In addition to the damage wrought by enemy shot and shell, the silk itself has deteriorated and many flags are now little more than a few brittle fragments of silk attached to the wooden staffs. According to reliable sources, nothing can be done to halt the deterioration of the flags since the material (silk) is especially susceptible to disintegration.

Navy Flags. Flags of the U.S. Navy varied according to the rank of the fleet or unit commander. The flag of a rear admiral was rectangular, plain, blue, and was to be "worn at the mizzen." If two or more rear admirals in command afloat should meet, or be in the presence of each other, the senior only was to "wear" the flag of blue; the next in seniority was to "wear" it of red; and any other officers of similar rank were to "wear" it of white. Rear admirals, and especially lesser officers, "wore broad pendants."

A divisional mark and the mark of a senior officer present were both to be triangular in shape, with a middle part of a different color from the rest, in the form of a wedge, the base occupying one-third the whole hoist or head, and the point extending to the extremity of the fly. For a First Division—blue, white, blue; for a Second Division—red, white, red; for a Third Division—white, blue, white; for a Senior Officer Present—white, red, white.

Recruiting Flags. Similar to the garrison flag except smaller—9 3/4 feet by 4 1/3 feet.

Storm Flags. Similar to the garrison flag except for size: 20 feet by 10 feet.

Guidons. In the early months of the war, some companies and batteries used guidons presented before they left their states for the front. Sometimes, these guidons were sent to troops already in the field. On June 14, 1862, Battery F, 1st Rhode Island Light Artillery was presented with two guidons, one for parade and one for drill, by friends of the battery commander.

Eagle shield from the staff of a regimental standard.

The flag of the guidon was swallow-tailed, 3 feet 5 inches from the lance to the end of the swallow-tail; 15 inches to the fork of the swallow-tail, and 2 feet 3 inches on the lance. The guidon was half red and half white, dividing at the fork, the red above. On the red, the letters U.S. were in white; and on the white, the letter of the company was in red. The lace of the standards and guidons were 9 feet long, including spear and ferrule.

FLAME THROWERS. See also GREEK FIRE. Alfred Berney, in his demonstration of incendiary shells to Lincoln and Stanton on May 9, 1863, also showed the Federal leaders a flame-thrower. Berney squirted fire from a hand pump on a woodpile. He then played a stream of fire on 300 gallons of his fluid which represented the amount thrown in a minute from the nozzle of a steam pump. The black pool blazed up and fire billowed into the twilight. No known use was made of this invention during the Civil War.

Flag tip of a Maine battleflag.

FLASK, POWDER. For rifleman's flask see ACCOUTERMENTS. Most of the ammunition used in the war was fixed ammunition, i.e. fabricated in government arsenals and issued to troops in the field all ready for use. However, especially in the early part of the war, some powder flasks were used by riflemen, and many of the pistol flasks were given or purchased by officers and men to be used with their revolvers. The photograph shows an example of the "pocket" or pistol flask as used in the war. It should be emphasized that many other types, both military and non-military, were used by individuals on an unofficial basis. In fact, reports exist which indicate that some of the less fortunate Confederate soldiers from rural areas even carried powder horns in the early months of the war.

FLASK, WHISKEY. Shown in the accompanying photograph is a flask which was actually carried during the war and was worn by its owner at the Battle of Antietam. Personal reminiscences and histories are replete with instances of individuals fortifying themselves with "a pull at their flask," whether on the march or in combat. Most of these flasks were taken to the front from home; after arrival at the seat of war officers and men drew their whiskey ration in their tin cups or canteens, or purchased bottles of whiskey from the regimental sutlers.

FOOD.

Hardtack. Officially called hard bread, this was a plain flour and water biscuit. In size this cracker was 3⅛ by 2⅞ inches and nearly half an inch thick.

Although these biscuits were issued to organizations by weight, they were dealt out to the men by number, 9 constituting a ration in some regiments and 10 in others; but there were often enough for those who wanted more, since some men, especially in camp, did not draw them. Although nutritious, hardtack was often very hard or wormy. At other times the biscuits were wet or mouldy. Hardtack was put up in wooden boxes. It was a common sight to see thousands of boxes of hardtack piled up at railroad

Pistol flask. Made in sizes 2 oz., 4 oz., (Navy), 6 oz. (Navy), 8 oz. (Navy). (Norm Flayderman)

stations, where they usually were not covered as protection from the rain or snow.

There were many ways in which hardtack could be made somewhat more palatable. Naturally, many men ate the hardtack just as it was issued. Often it was soaked in coffee—this certainly was the most common method, and often constituted the whole meal, especially in the field. However, there were many ways of preparing hardtack. Often it was crumbed in soups. Some men crumbed the hardtack in cold water and then fried the crums in the juice and fat of meat. A dish called "Skillygalee" was prepared by soaking hardtack in cold water, then frying it in pork fat, salted to taste. This was indigestible enough to satisfy the cravings of the most ambitious dyspeptic. Others toasted their hardtack and, no matter how badly it was charred, ate it eagerly as they thought that well-toasted hardtack was good for weak bowels. Condensed milk and sugar were used whenever available. Condensed milk was of two well-known brands—*Lewis* and *Borden.*

The hardtack shown here was brought home from the war by Assistant Surgeon Robert Elmer, 23rd New Jersey, Infantry.

INSTANT COFFEE. Instant coffee is not a modern-day invention but actually was introduced during the Civil War to make the Federal soldier's rations less

Whiskey flask. Carried at Antietam.

Hardtack. Brought home in 1865 by Asst. Surgeon Robert Elmer, 23rd N. Jersey Inf.

bulky. One account mentions General Grant as having tested it first. According to files in the National Archives, instant coffee was prepared in paste form and contained milk and sugar, a "convenience" unfortunately not provided by present day brands.

The soldier's rations were carried in a canvas haversack slung over the right shoulder and resting on the left hip. The Government haversack was better than those made by private firms; the regulation type had an inside lining which kept the rations from contact with the canvas, but usually these linings soon disappeared as the men cut them up for gun cleaners. Coffee and sugar rations were sometimes issued in small cotton bags and the haversack soon became quite odorous with its mixture of bacon, pork, salt junk, sugar, coffee, tea, desiccated vegetables, rice, bits of yesterday's dinner, and old scraps husbanded with miserly care against a day of want sure to come.

FOOTBALL. See RECREATIONAL EQUIPMENT.

FORK, HOT-SHOT. See ARTILLERY.

FOUGASSE. Charges of gunpowder were frequently placed at the bottom of a pit or shaft dug in the ground over which an enemy must pass to the attack. The main difficulty in using fougasses was to explode them at the instant when the enemy was passing over the pit.

Britannia liquor flask. Hogskin covered; made in sizes: 1 pint, 1¼ pint, 1½ pint. (Norm Flayderman)

FRICTION PRIMER. See ARTILLERY.

FRYING PAN. See MESS EQUIPMENT.

FUNNEL. See ARTILLERY.

FURLOUGH. See DOCUMENTS.

FUZE. See ARTILLERY.

FUZE-AUGER. See ARTILLERY.

FUZE-EXTRACTOR. See ARTILLERY.

FUZE-MALLET. See ARTILLERY.

FUZE-SAW. See ARTILLERY.

FUZE-SETTER. See ARTILLERY.

GAITERS. See UNIFORMS AND CLOTHING.

GLASSES, FIELD. See OPTICAL INSTRUMENTS.

GLOVES and GAUNTLETS. Troops in garrison were required to wear white gloves, often called "Berlin gloves" when appearing in formal dress parade at ceremonies.

Mittens and gloves worn for warmth were generally purchased by the individual soldier or knitted at home by parents or local organizations.

Part of the dress uniform of officers consisted of gauntlets, many of which were of elaborate design as shown in the accompanying photograph. Since both gloves and gauntlets had a utilitarian value after the war comparatively few specimens have survived to the present day.

U.S. Army Regulations provided that general officers and staff officers would wear buff or white gloves, while officers of artillery, infantry, cavalry, dragoons, and riflemen could wear white only. The Marine Corps regulations also called for white gloves.

GRAPE SHOT. See PROJECTILES.

GRAPPLING IRON. Consisted of from four to six branches bent and pointed, with a ring at the root. A rope being fastened through this ring, and any object at which the grappling iron was thrown, could be held fast or dragged closer.

GREEK FIRE, HOT SHOT, INCENDIARIES.

Greek Fire. In a few instances, at least, the Federals used Greek Fire as an incendiary against their adversaries. One of these occasions was during the siege of Charleston in 1863. However, its employment there led to such complaint as to its barbarity that further use of it during the war was very limited. It was on August 22, 1863, during the siege of Charleston, that the Federals' "Swamp Angel" fired 12 Parrott shells filled with a fluid composition and four other shells filled with "Short's Solidified Greek Fire." The Confederate commander in Charleston, General

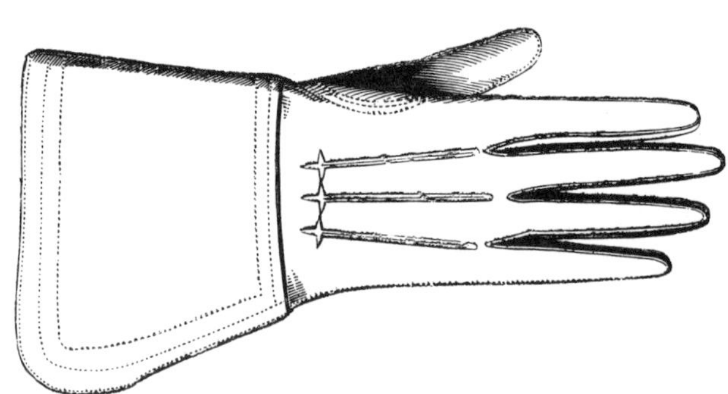

Officer's gauntlets, buff or white. (Norm Flayderman)

P. G. T. Beauregard, at once wrote the Federal commander, General Q. A. Gillmore, that his firing "a number of the most destructive missiles ever used in war into the midst of a city taken unawares and filled with sleeping women and children [would] give you a bad eminence in history." The Federal general replied, and on August 23d twenty more shells filled with Greek Fire, were fired from the gun in the marsh, i.e., the Swamp Angel. Six of these shells exploded in the gun, doubtless shortening the life of the piece to some extent. On the 36th discharge of the Swamp Angel, the breech blew out.

Apparently some of the Northern military experts

Officer's gauntlets, embroidered. (Norm Flayderman)

were skeptical about the use of Greek Fire because the semi-official military journal *United States Service Magazine* for January 1864 said in part: "The attempt of Mr. Levi Short of Philadelphia to introduce into the department of the South, an effective combustible agent, designed to be employed in the bombardment of Charleston, is one of the many recent efforts to introduce inflammables into the warfare. We are not apprised of the composition of Mr. Short's invention, but it may safely be asserted that five out of every six of the shells loaded with his preparation, either from attrition of the particles in the rotary motion of the shell, or from some other cause, burst in the gun, or just in front of it; and it is a matter of extreme doubt whether a single shell thus charged ever reached the city."

However, we do know that some regimental histories attest to the use of Greek Fire at Charleston. Several inventors attempted to sell the Federal Government their version of Greek Fire compound. On one occasion, Lincoln was an interested observer of a demonstration of Greek Fire in which two 13-inch shells charged with it were exploded. Each shell spewed fire 40-50 feet in the air and covered the ground over a 50-foot radius with a blaze lasting several minutes.

General B. F. Butler took 100 of them along with him on his expedition against New Orleans. Whether he used them is not clear from available records. The Confederates used Greek Fire in arson operations in New York City, e.g. the burning of Barnum's museum. Probably their use of it was not extensive

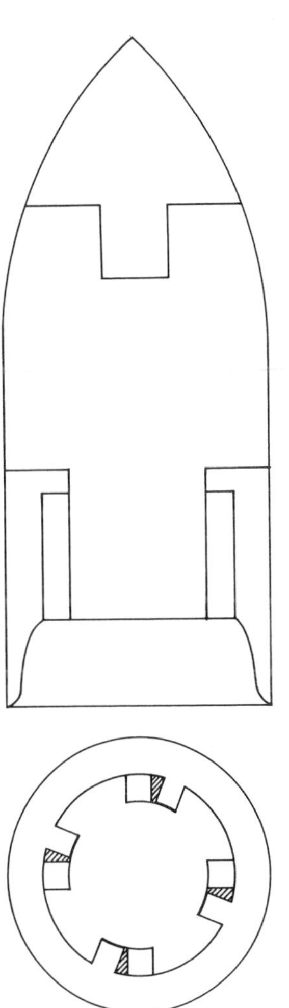

James' hot shot projectile. Patent Jan. 21, 1862. (National Archives)

since Greek Fire is primarily an offensive weapon used against such targets as towns and cities, and the Southern forces were normally defending, not attacking such targets. Greek Fire as used by the Federals at Morris Island in 1863, was furnished in tin tubes closed at one end, about 3 inches long by ¾ of an inch in diameter. These were covered with one thickness of paper similar to cartridge paper. This was folded over the ends of the tube, that part covering the open end having upon it a priming of

Hanes and Ketchum Grenades.

powder and coal tar. The directions for using were to put as many in a shell as it would hold, then fill with powder and shake it down. These tubes did not give satisfactory results. Mr. Short, the inventor, therefore visited Morris Island and changed the method of filling, first putting in considerable powder. He also covered some tubes with several thicknesses of cartridge paper and others with several layers of muslin. Greek Fire was only used at the Marsh Battery, or Swamp Angel, but the shells burst prematurely and their effectiveness was questionable. Apparently 40 to 50 tubes were enclosed in a shell which was itself enclosed in an ordinary service shell, exploding in the usual manner.

Hot Shot Shell. (Patent No. 34,207). Patented January 21, 1862 by Charles T. James of Providence, Rhode Island. The separate point of the projectile could be removed so that the body of the projectile could be heated, and the point put on while cold. This resulted in a projectile which had penetrating power combined with the capability of setting fire to enemy targets.

Incendiaries.

Incendiary Shells. An incendiary shell was invented by Alfred Berney, whose demonstration before Lincoln of his shell's effectiveness resulted in an order for 1,000 of them. Both Lincoln and Stanton watched the demonstration, May 9, 1863. As they watched, the inventor sent a woodpile flying into the air in a burst of smoke and flame and detonated two shells in the middle of the wood to suggest their effect on an enemy position.

Shell, liquid fire (Patent No. 36,934). Patented November 11, 1862 by Alfred Berney of Jersey City, New Jersey.

This projectile was formed of a hollow shell, through the center of which passed a tube which contained the bursting charge of powder. The cavity surrounding the tube was filled with a composition of benzole, crude petroleum, coal tar, turpentine, distilled petroleum, residuum, and coal oil from coal tar.

GRENADES.

Grenades, Artillery. See PROJECTILES.

Grenades, Hand. Scott's *Military Dictionary* (1864 edition) defined a hand grenade as a "small shell about 2½ inches in diameter, which, being set on fire by means of a short fuze and cast among the enemy's troops, causes great damage by its explosion." According to Scott, these grenades could be thrown 26 yards. Rampart grenades were larger and were used to roll down ramparts. However, Gibbon's *Artillerist's Manual* (1860) stated that any kind of shell, unfit for firing either from being defective in form or solidity could be used for the purpose. Six-pounder spherical case shot could be used as hand grenades.

Both North and South used hand grenades fairly extensively in siege operations. At Vicksburg the Confederates filled glass bottles with powder and balls, with fuzes in the open ends. At Port Hudson Federal soldiers improvised hand grenades from 6-pounder shells. In the defense of fortifications the smaller grenades could be thrown by hand into the head of a sap, trench, or covered way, or upon attackers or besiegers mounting a breach in the works. Larger types, made of artillery shells, could be rolled over the parapet into the defender's trench. In the assault on Port Hudson, June 14, 1863, the skirmishers, from the 8th New Hampshire and 4th Wisconsin, were deployed at intervals of two paces. They were followed by five companies from the 4th Massachusetts and 110th New York, armed with hand grenades. The order for the attack specified: "The hand grenade men carry their pieces on their backs and carry each one grenade. They will march three paces in rear of their line of skirmishers. Having thrown their grenades they will go on as skirmishers. The skirmishers will clamber upon the parapet followed by the carriers of hand grenades, which will be thrown over into the works as soon as the skirmishers are on the outer slopes of the parapets."

The results, according to the Confederates, were not too good. In some instances the Federal skirmishers succeeded in getting to the trenches and throwing their grenades over the parapets. Many grenades failed to explode or were thrown back at the assaulting units. The entire engagement lasted about four hours, with heavy losses to the attackers.

Adams Hand Grenade. (Patent No. 45,806). Patented January 10, 1865 by John S. Adams of Taunton, Mass. A friction or cannon primer was securely attached to the time fuze inserted in the grenade, a hook which was attached to a strap secured to the wrist being inserted into a loop formed on the end of the friction primer. When the grenade was thrown the hook activated the friction primer just after the grenade left the hand, and thus ignited the time fuze.

Hanes ("Excelsior") Hand Grenade (Patent No. 36,295). Patented August 26, 1862 by W. W. Hanes, Covington, Ky. This was a cast-iron sphere with an inner and an outer shell. The outer shell was 3½ inches in diameter and the inner shell 2½ inches. The inner shell contained the powder, and on its outside were screwed 14 nipples which took the regular musket percussion caps. The outside shell, which was in two sections screwed together, formed the hammer to the percussion caps on the nipples attached to the inside shell. The inside shell was separated from the outside shell by a cushion to prevent the percussion caps from coming into contact with the outside shell, until it was desired to be exploded by striking some object with sufficient force to cause the cushion to yield, causing the percussion caps to come in contact with the inside of the outside or surrounding shell. When the grenade struck an object, at least one of the 14 caps was sure to receive the impact and thus explode the shell. Since the outer shell was in two parts, these parts would break up into many destructive fragments. But this grenade was so dangerous to handle that only a very few were ever made.

Ketchum Hand Grenade. (Patent No. 33,089). Patented August 20, 1861 by William F. Ketchum of Buffalo, New York, this was the most common hand grenade of the Civil War. It was of elongated form and expanding at the center, cast with an opening at each end into one of which was fitted a tube of soft metal with a flange at the outer end and a nipple for holding a percussion cap. The charge

Hanes Excelsior Hand Grenade. (Drawn by Mike McAfee). (Courtesy of Francis Bannerman & Sons)

was then placed in the shell, and when the grenade was to be used a stick with four wings of pasteboard, to be used as a guide, like the tail on a rocket, was inserted in the end opposite the cap. In the cap tube was a plunger which exploded the percussion cap when the outer end of the tube struck a resisting object. To prevent accidental discharge, the plunger which communicated the shock to the percussion cap was not inserted until the moment before the grenade was thrown.

Ketchum one-pounder hand grenades have been found at Vicksburg, but U.S. Ordnance Memorandum No. 1 (1865) lists this grenade as being furnished in 1-, 2-, 3-, and 4-pound weights.

Naval Hand Grenades. It is known that the Navy used hand grenades because the Naval *Ordnance Instructions* for 1864 lists 3- and 5-pound hand grenades as being available for regular issue on board ship.

GUIDONS. See FLAGS, COLORS, GUIDONS.

GUIDON CARRIER. Brass, 4¾ inches long, with one end to hold a guidon staff and the other to affix, on a caliber .58 musket, by means of a locking ring, exactly like a triangular bayonet.

GUN. See ARTILLERY and CANNON.

GUN CAPPER. Patented October 29, 1861, by Edgar D. Seely of Brookline, Massachusetts, this was a metal tube in which a cap receptacle was inserted. The receptacle had one end filled with a piece through which an eyebolt passed into the end of the cap receiver. At the other end the cap receiver projected beyond the end of the case, and its sides were formed into spring nippers to retain and deliver each cap. In the end of the follower nearest the eyebolt screw was fixed a spring of rubber or elastic cord, which passed over a stop or pulley connected to the receiver near its nipper end, and from thence passed along the length of the receiver to the other end. By means of a guide the implement was used to cap the gun, the fingers being guided by touch.

These cappers were actually tried out in the field. In December, 1864 the Ordnance Department sent a supply of them to the best regiment in the XIX Army Corps for trial. The corps commander, Major General W. H. Emory, selected the 116th New York Infantry as the "best regiment." After a trial, however, the regimental commander submitted an adverse report and shortly thereafter received the following letter from General Sheridan dated February 5, 1865:

"Your report on Seely's gun cappers' for infantry, has been received at this office, and forwarded to the War Department, with the following endorsement: 'Respectfully forwarded to Brig. Gen'l A. R. Dyer, Chief of Ordnance, Washington, D. C. The regiment of Col. Love enjoys the reputation of being the best in the Nineteenth Army Corps, and the colonel states that the men do not want these gun cappers, as they consider them worthless. I forward the report of this efficient officer with no further comment than that his opinions are endorsed by me fully.' "

"P. H. Sheridan
Maj. Gen'l. Comd'g."

The Seely gun capper was of solid brass, 7¼ inches long, ¾ inch deep, and ½ inch wide. Marked as follows:

E. D. Seely
Pat'd Oct. 20, 1861
made by
S.E. and J.N. Root
Bristol, Ct.

Another gun capper, maker unknown, was recently discovered with several identical specimens but due to lack of any markings on the specimens or pertinent literature details on this type of gun capper are not available. The main part of the capper is round (diameter 2¾ inches) while there is a nozzle projection extending from the circular part of the capper. Total length 4 inches. This extremely well-made gun capper is of brass.

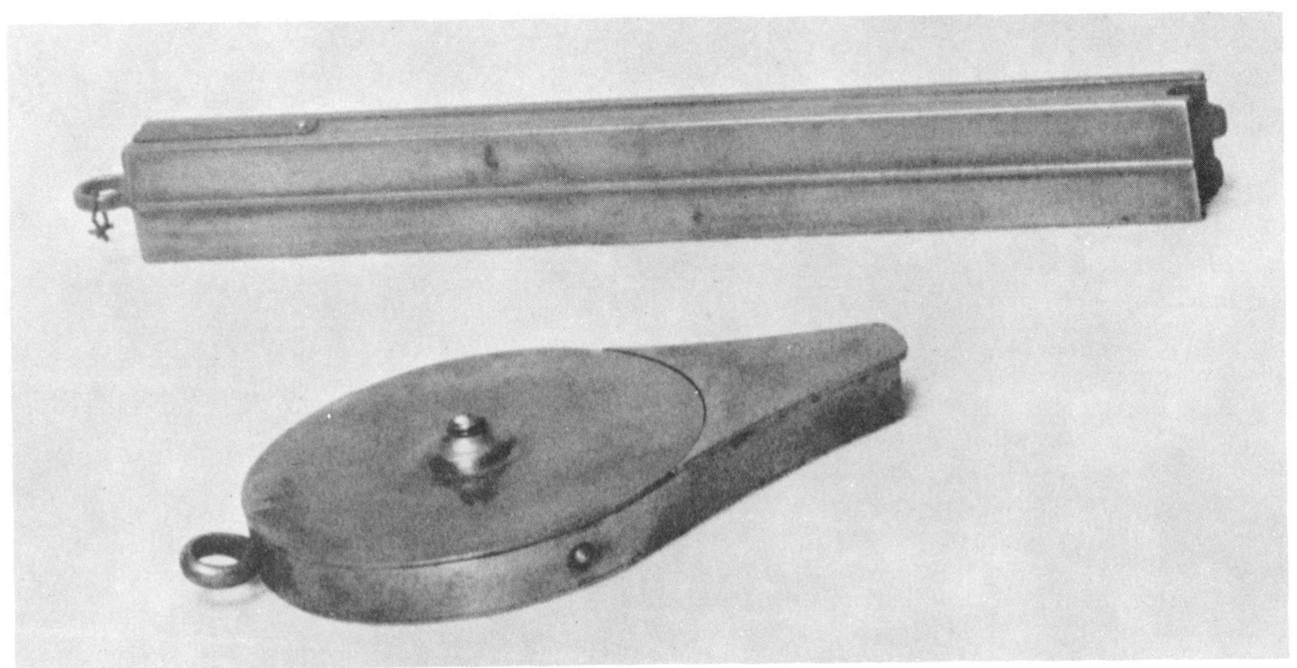

Gun cappers. Top: Seely gun capper. Bottom: Gun capper by unknown maker.

GUNNER'S CALIPERS. See ARTILLERY.

GUNNER'S GIMLET. See ARTILLERY.

GUNNER'S LEVEL. See ARTILLERY.

GUNNER'S PINCERS. See ARTILLERY.

GUN SLING. Although many photographs of Civil War soldiers show men armed with muskets not equipped with gun slings, it is known that slings were normally issued. Moreover, photographs of gun slings on muskets are common. Two main types of slings, shown here, were used extensively.

British Enfield Gun Sling. Light canvas material, 30 inches long, with 2 leather loops, and a heavy wire hook on the end. Many of this type were used by Confederate troops.

U.S. GUN SLING. Russet leather, 38½ inches long, with 2 loops and a brass hook on the end.

HAIR BRUSH. Soldiers have left numerous references to hair brushes among their lists of personal effects or purchases but the author has never seen one. No doubt they were of ordinary commercial pattern.

HALTER. See HORSE EQUIPMENT and CAVALRY EQUIPMENT.

HAND IRONS. See BALL AND CHAIN. Recalcitrant prisoners, both in the Army and Navy, were often confined in irons. Often these hand irons were used in conjunction with leg irons and sometimes with the ball and chain. Artillery soldiers, sentenced to severe punishment were tied on the spare wheel on a caisson, while infantry soldiers were bucked and gagged. The soldier undergoing such punishment was forced into a sitting position, a musket placed under his legs, and his hands placed under the musket and tied. Then a bayonet would be put across his mouth and held in position by rope tied behind his head. In some cases soldiers guilty of such violations of discipline as insolence or drunkenness were tied up by their thumbs, a severe punishment indeed.

Hand irons consisted of two steel cuffs, each locked by means of a very small key. The cuffs, joined to each other by a 3-link steel chain, could be adjusted to different wrist sizes. Total length when extended—9 inches.

HANDKERCHIEF. In the Ferris collection is a hand blocked cotton handkerchief, carried in the war by Daniel Heyden, Co. E 149th New York Infantry. The dominant color is red, with white circular designs spread throughout. The size is 25 by 22 inches.

HANDSPIKE. See ARTILLERY.

HARDTACK. See FOOD.

HAT. See UNIFORMS AND CLOTHING.

HAT BOX. While probably not in very extensive use, tin box containers for both Navy chapeau de bras and Army dress hats are known to have been used. These hat boxes are of the same type of japanned tin which is characteristic of the containers for officers' epaulettes.

HATCHET. See AXES AND HATCHETS.

HAVELOCK. One of the first "necessities" which some of the earlier troops wore to the field was the havelock. This was a "foreign contraption" invented before the war, and derived its name from the English general who distinguished himself in the war in India in 1857 where they were worn. The havelock was a simple covering of white linen for the cap, with a cape depending for the protection of the neck from the sun. The havelocks may have been very essential to the comfort of British troops in India, but, while whole regiments went to war with them in 1861, they never proved themselves, and very few survived three months of active service. Those that did survive were put to good use as patches for cleaning the bores of rifles and muskets.

The havelock fever raged mainly in the early months of the war. English journals having stated that in 1857, during the suppression of the rebellion in India, the soldiers used with advantage the havelock. The home folks went very enthusiastically into making them for the soldiers. Many soldiers were provided with as many as two, and a Connecticut company received six per man.

HAVERSACK. When in the field each soldier carried his rations in a haversack, made of canvas, cloth, leather, or similar material. The haversack was slung over the right shoulder and rested on the left hip with the tin cup usually buckled on the outside. Many officers purchased leather haversacks of elaborate design, often a shiny, patent leather item which would hold only one day's rations. These fancy affairs had a convenient pocket in which the officer might carry a flask—for medicinal purposes—while his reserve supplies were transported by wagon or upon the broad shoulders of his servant, usually a loyal and rugged "contraband."

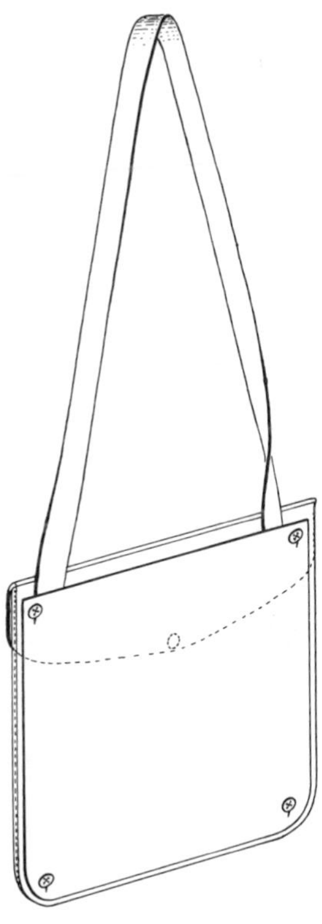

Keech's haversack. Patented Sept. 22, 1863. (National Archives)

Gun slings. Top: U.S. russet leather sling. Bottom: C. S. canvas sling.

Officer's haversack. Carried by Capt. E. H. Barstow, 3d Mass. Heavy Artillery.

The regulation haversacks were often marked with the number and name of the regiment, the company letter, and the soldier's company number. This regulation haversack was better made than those sold by private firms. The regulation type had an inside lining which kept the rations from contact with the outer haversack lining covering, but these linings soon disappeared as the men cut them up for gun cleaners. Coffee and sugar rations were sometimes carried in small individual bags inside the haversack, but the haversack itself soon became quite odorous with its mixture of stale parts of bacon and other rations.

From the haversacks now in museums and collections, and from the descriptions furnished by veterans of the war, we know that there were many types of haversacks but apparently there were two main types issued: canvas and black oilcloth. All types held about a peck although varying in size. One of the most common issue types was about 13 inches long, 12½ inches wide, and was carried by a 32-inch strap sewn on the haversack itself. This strap was about 1¾ inches wide.

In theory all haversacks were waterproof, but once they became well worn they were no better than cloth for keeping water out. A penetrating rain was sure to make a mess of the contents. Although the canvas and cloth types were issued white, a short period of active service made them black. As one soldier put it: "By the time one of these [white canvas haversacks] had been in use for a few weeks as a receptacle for chunks of fat bacon and fresh meat, damp sugar tied up in a rag—perhaps a piece of an old shirt—potatoes and other vegetables that might be picked up along the route, it took on the color of a printing office towel. It would have been alike offensive to the eyes and nose of a fastidious person."

A veteran soon became accustomed to the looks and odors of his haversack and thought nothing about using it with equanimity. At the halt he would drop by the roadside, draw his grimy and well-greased haversack around in front of him, and "from its dark and odorous recesses bring forth what tasted better to him than the daintiest morsel to the palate of an epicure." Recruits were initially distressed at the obvious lack of refined living which the haversack represented, but then, they were equally appalled at the retrogression in table manners exhibited by the veterans. A few days association with their new comrades-in-arms and with hunger soon brought them around, and they too concentrated on food, not appearances.

Occasionally a soldier would attempt to wash his haversack but due to lack of adequate laundry facilities and a stubborn amalgamation of the haversack lining with its varied contents, he soon gave up. In fact, the only superiority of the black haversack was that the effects of use were not so readily apparent to the eye; grease and dirt were there, but not so obviously. As far as the nose was concerned, there was no difference. The Government haversack outlasted a dozen of the fancy types sold by the sutlers. One of the worthwhile equipment items was the small tin box strapped to the knapsack for carrying rations. Because of their utilitarian value, comparatively few haversacks have survived. Many were used after the war by school children to carry books in and by adults for use around the farm and home.

Keech's Haversack (Patent No. 40,047). Patented September 22, 1863, by Thomas Keech of New York City, New York. This was a haversack made of duck "or other textile fabric," with a detachable sidepiece of waterproof material, to preserve the clothes from contact with the soiled side of the haversack.

HAVERSACK, CONFEDERATE. If Confederates carried haversacks at all, they carried a simple, homemade affair of canvas, leather, or cloth, in which they stored their meager allowance of corn pone or goober peas. Often enough, however, the Confederate infantry soldier carried neither knapsack nor haversack. Actually, the average Confederate soldier in 1864 and 1865 carried only one of each essential item, hat, coat, pants, etc., and his "baggage" was usually wrapped up in the inevitable blanket roll. As General Richard Ewell correctly phrased it: "The road to glory can not be followed with much baggage."

HAVERSACK, GUNNER'S. See ARTILLERY.

HEADBOARD. In April 1862, each Federal commanding general was directed to reserve plots of ground near each battlefield and to inter therein the remains of the dead. Each grave was to be marked with a headboard bearing a number corresponding with a register to be kept of the burial ground. However, many soldiers on both sides were buried where they fell, by comrades who marked their graves with boards on which were inscribed the soldier's name, regiment, and state. These boards were respected by everybody and made it easier for parents to find their sons' remains. But the wood soon rotted away and as a result very few headboards have survived.

HELICOPTER. What apparently was a steam-driven helicopter was nearly completed, with encouraging results, when construction was stopped by Benjamin F. Butler's departure from active service in the war. The author knows no further details concerning this steam driven helicopter.

HOLSTER, PISTOL. Holsters were of two general types—those worn on the belt and the double holsters worn by mounted men attached to the saddle pommel. The belt holsters varied according to the size and

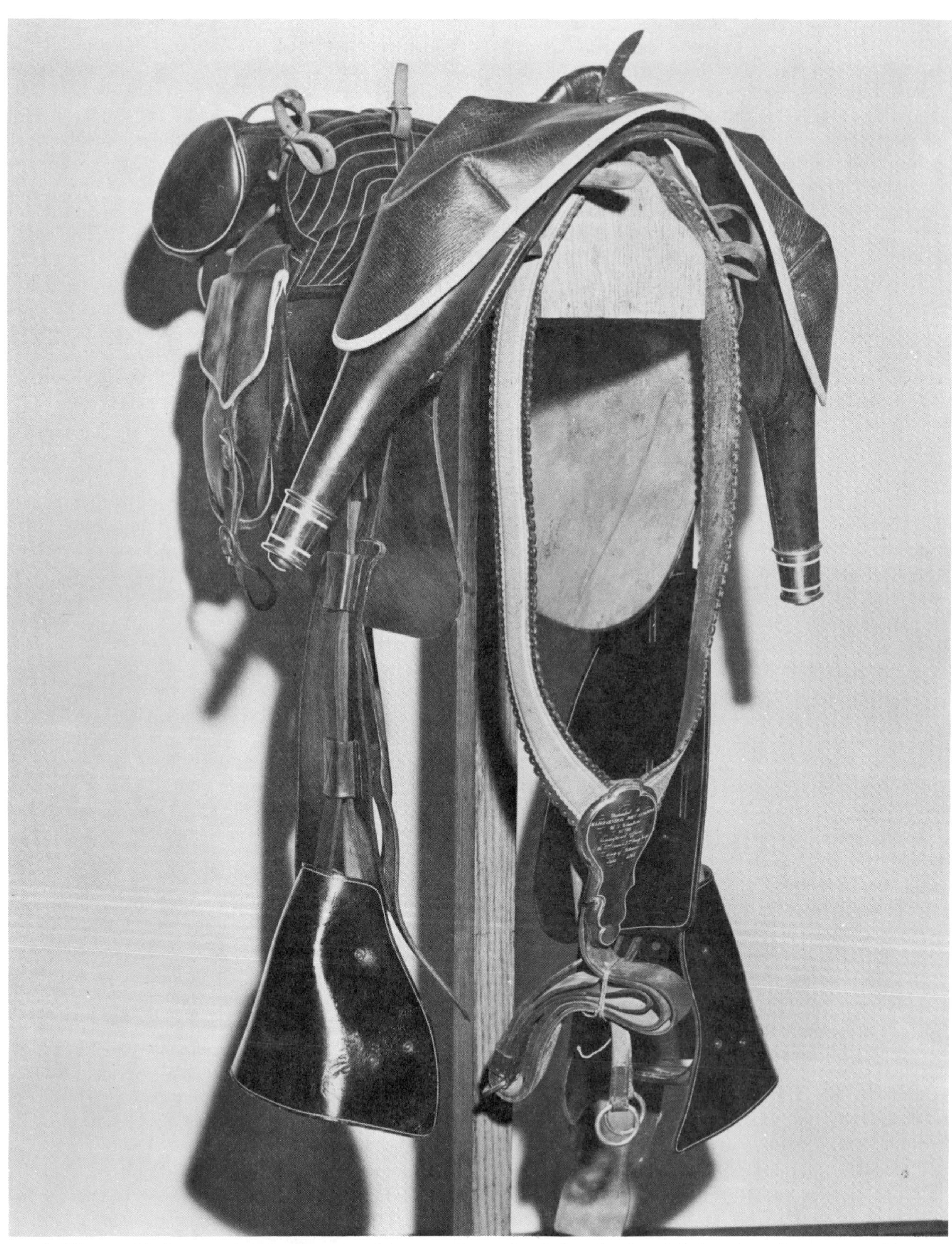

Saddle, pistol holsters, and saddle bags owned by Maj. Gen. John Sedgwick when killed at Spotsylvania Court House. (West Point Museum collection)

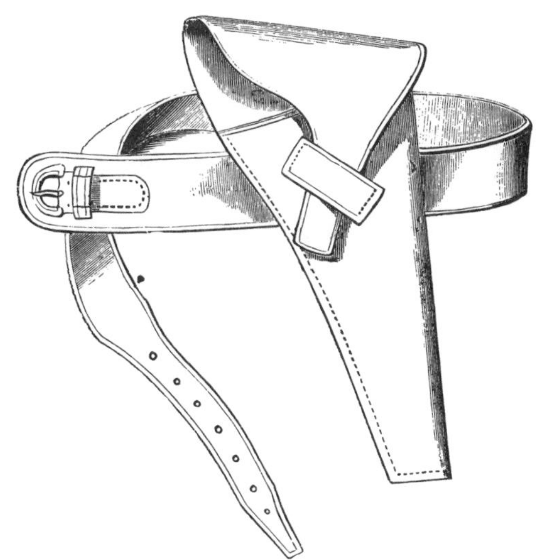

Pistol holster. (Norm Flayderman)

model of the pistol or revolver which it held.

HOLSTER, PISTOL (Patent No. 38,213). Patented April 21, 1863 by Augustus A. Bennett of Cincinnati, Ohio. This invention consisted of an automatically operated flap, which secured and covered the pistol by a spring.

HOOF CLEANER. The two-pronged hoof cleaner was used by General Turner Ashby, C.S.A. until he was killed in action at Harrisonburg, Va., June 6, 1862. It is 5½ inches long and made of steel. The other hoof cleaner also has a hammer attachment. The hook itself can be used as a rasp in shoeing horses. Length 6½ inches, neither cleaner has any markings.

HORN. See MUSICAL INSTRUMENTS.

HORSE EQUIPMENTS. See also ARTILLERY and CAVALRY EQUIPMENTS.

ARTILLERY VALISE. Made of black bridle leather 17½ inches long 7½ inches wide at the widest place, and 7¼ inches tall. A heavy leather flap 20 inches long and 12½ inches wide extends well over the front of the valise. The valise is lined with denim cloth, has leather carrying handles, and three straps on the cover for securing the valise. Each end of the valise is marked: "U.S. Watervliet Arsenal, G".

BRIDOON. The snaffle and rein of a military bridle which acts independently of the bit, at the pleasure of the rider.

JENIFER SADDLE (Patent No. 28,867). Patented June 26, 1860 by Walter H. Jenifer of Baltimore, Md. an "improved military saddle utilizing a flat English seat."

SPENCER SADDLE (Patent No. 34,320). Patented February 4, 1862, by Robert Spencer of Brooklyn, New York. This invention was designed to secure a firm seat to the rider, the front pieces being intended to prevent the rider from being thrown forward over the saddle, thus obviating the ill effects caused by the

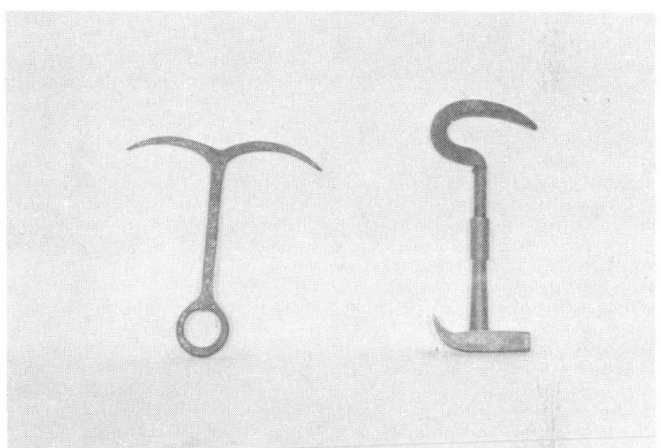

Hoof cleaners. Left: cleaner used by Gen. Turner Ashby, CSA. Right: U.S. issue hoof cleaner.

Group of revolver holsters.

ordinary pommel under similar circumstances.

SPURS. For all mounted officer spurs were of gilt or some yellow metal. For enlisted men—yellow metal. U.S. Marine Corps Regulations provided that spurs for all mounted officers would be of gilt or other yellow metal.

U.S. ARMY REGULATION HORSE FURNITURE AND EQUIPMENT. The following paragraphs are quoted from the Regulations:

General Officers and General Staff.

Housing for General Officers—to be worn over the saddle; of dark blue cloth, trimmed with two rows of gold lace, the outer row one inch and five-eighths wide, the inner row two inches and one-fourth; to be made full, so as to cover the horse's haunches and forehands, and to bear on each flank corner the following ornaments, distinctive of rank, to wit: for the *Major-General Commanding the Army*—a gold-embroidered spread eagle and three stars; for other *Major-Generals*—a gold-embroidered spread eagle and two stars; for a *Brigadier-General*—a gold-embroidered spread eagle and one star.

Saddle-cloth for General Staff Officers—dark blue cloth, of sufficient length to cover the saddle and holsters, and one foot ten inches in depth, with an edging of gold lace one inch wide.

Surcingle—blue web.

Bridle—black leather; bent branch bit, with gilt bosses; the front and roses yellow.

Collar—yellow.

Holsters—black leather, with gilt mountings.

Stirrups—gilt or yellow metal.

Officers of the Corps of Engineers and Topographical Engineers. The same as for General Staff officers. In time of actual field service, general officers and officers of the General Staff and Staff Corps are permitted to use the horse equipments provided for the mounted service.

Mounted Service. A complete set of horse equipments for mounted troops consists of 1 bridle, 1 watering bridle, 1 halter, 1 saddle, pair saddle bags, 1 saddle blanket, 1 surcingle, 1 pair spurs, 1 curry comb, 1 horse brush, 1 picket pin, and 1 lariat; 1 link and 1 nose bag when specially required.

Artillery valise marked "U.S. Watervliet Arsenal. G."

Head Gear. All leather is black bridle-leather, and the buckles are malleable iron, flat, bar buckles, blued.

Bridle. It is composed of 1 *headstall,* 1 *bit,* 1 *pair of reins.*

Headstall. 1 *crown piece,* the ends split, forming 1 *cheek strap* and 1 *throat lash billet* on one side, and on the other, 1 *cheek strap* and 1 *throat lash,* with 1 *buckle,* .625 inch, 2 *chapes* and 2 *buckles* .75 inch, sewed to the ends of cheek piece to attach the bit; 1 *brow band,* the ends doubled and sewed form 2 loops on each end through which the cheek straps and throat lash and throat lash billet pass.

Bit (shear steel, blued). 2 *branches,* S shaped, pierced at top with an *eye* for the cheek strap billet,

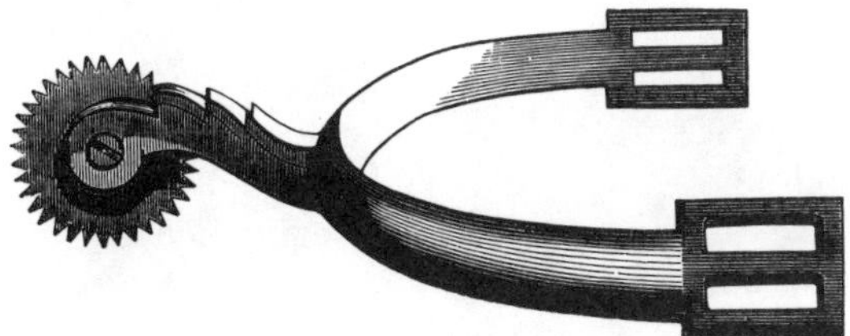

Strap Spur.

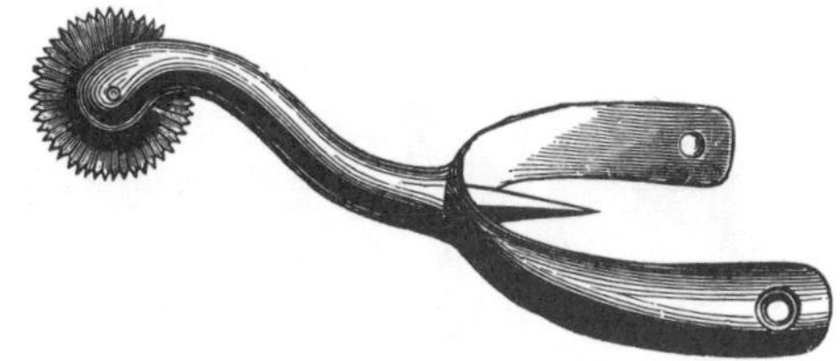

Screw-out Neck Spur.

Screw-out Neck Spur.

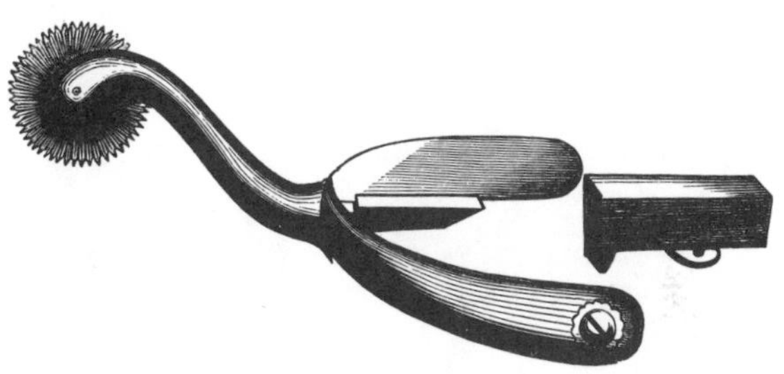

Patent Box Spur.

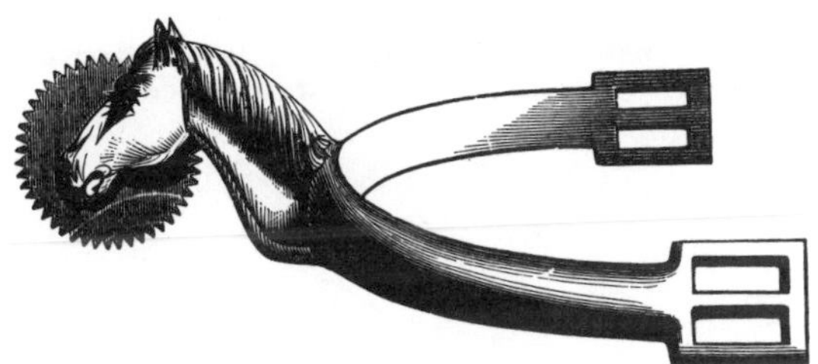

Horse-Head Strap Spur.

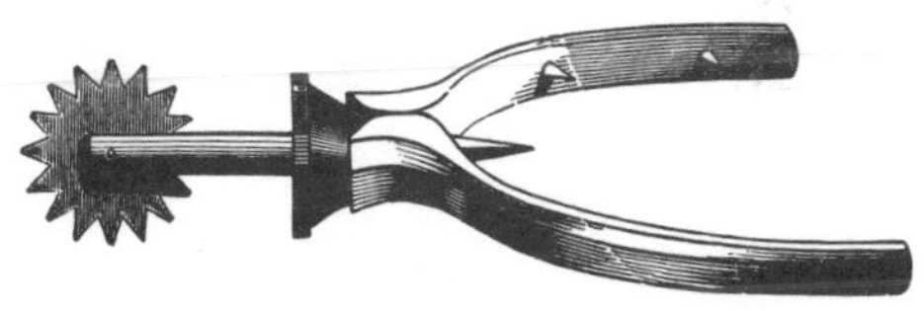

Garibaldi Steel Patent Spur.

Gilt Eagle Spur.

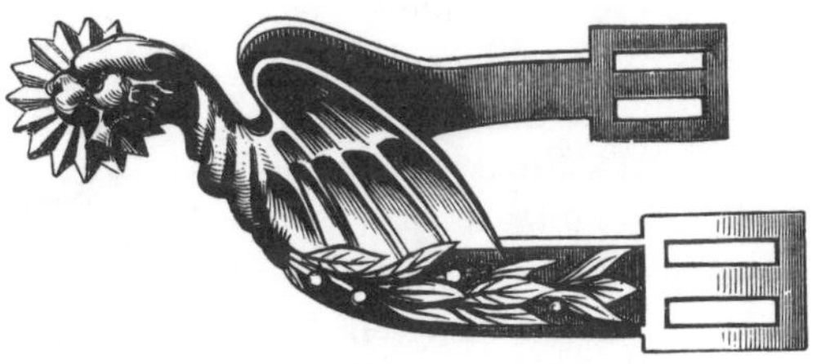

Extra Fine Dolphin Spur.

Officers' spurs. (Norm Flayderman)

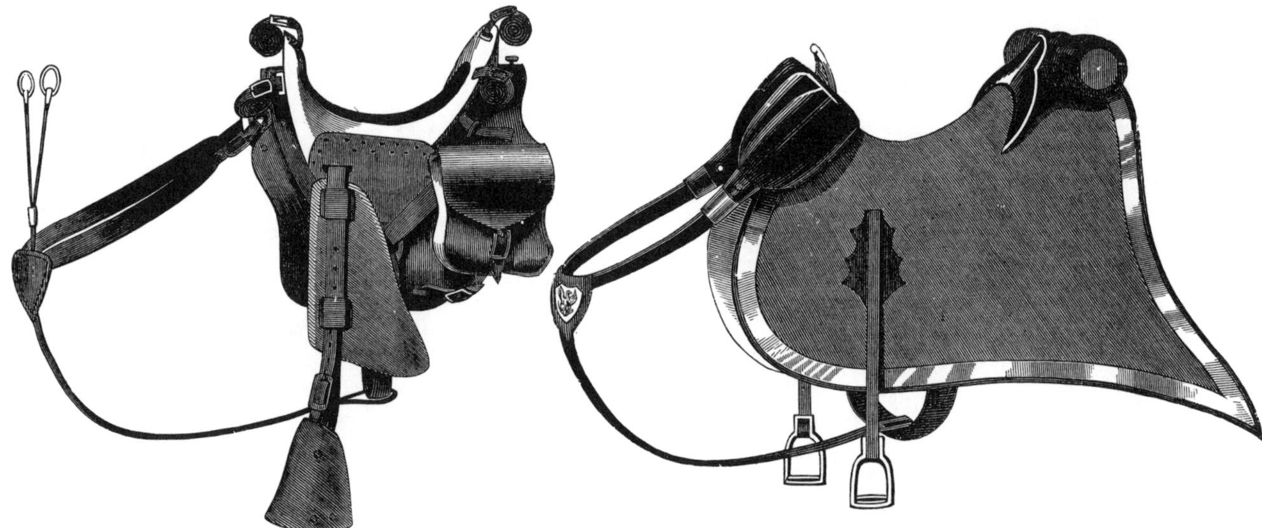

McClellan Equipments.

Saddle, Stirrups, Saddle-cloth, Holsters, Valise, and Collar, for Field and Regimental Staff Officers.

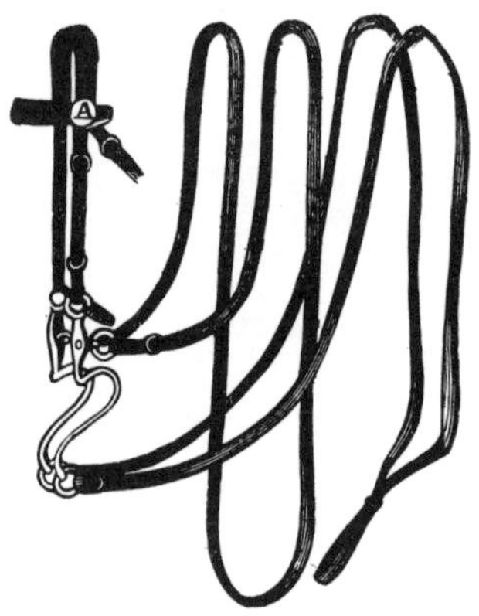

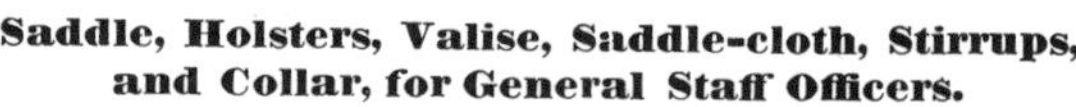

Saddle, Holsters, Valise, Saddle-cloth, Stirrups, and Collar, for General Staff Officers.

U. S. Bridle.

Bronzed U. S. Bit, with Ring.

Horse furniture. (Norm Flayderman)

and with a small hole near the eye for the curb chain, terminated at the bottom by 2 *buttons,* into which are wedded 2 *rings,* 1 inch, for the reins; 1 *mouth piece,* curved in the middle, its ends pass through the branches and are riveted to them; 1 *cross bar,* riveted to the branches near the lower ends; 2 *bosses* (cast brass), bearing the number and letter of the regiment and the letter of the company, riveted to the branches with 4 *rivets;* 1 *curb-chain hook,* steel wire, No. 10, fastened to the *near* branch; 1 *curb chain,* steel wire, No. 11, curb-chain links 0.7 inch wide, with 1 loose ring in the middle, fastened to the *off* branch by a S hook, coldshut; 1 *curb strap* (leather), fastened to the curb chain by 2 *standing loops.*

1 *curb ring* for bit No. 1 replaces the curb chain and curb strap. They are of two sizes: No. 1 has an interior diameter of 4 inches; No. 2, of 3.75 inches. The number is marked on the outside of the swell. No. 1 is the larger size.

There are four bits, differing from each other in the arch of the mouth piece, and in the distance from the mouth piece to the eye for the cheek strap. The branches are alike below the mouth piece. No. 1 is a Spanish bit, No. 2 is the next severest, and No. 4 is the mildest. Height of arch is 2½ inches in No. 1, 2 inches in No. 2, 1½ inches in No. 3, and ½ inch in No. 4. The distance between the branches is 4.5 inches in all the bits.

Reins. Two *reins* sewed together at one end, the other ends sewed to the rings of the bit.

Watering Bridle. Composed of 1 bit and 1 pair of reins.

Bit (wrought iron, blued). Two *mouth-piece sides* united in the middle by a loop hinge; their ends are pierced with 2 holes to receive 2 *rings* 1.7 inches diameter for the reins. Two *chains and toggles,* 3 links, each 1 inch × 0.55 inch, welded in the rein rings.

Halter. Consists of 2 *cheek pieces,* sewed at one end to 2 *square loops* 1.6 inches diameter, and the other to 2 *cheek rings* 1.6 inches diameter; 2 *standing loops* for the toggles of the watering bridle sewed to the cheek piece near to the square loops; 1 *crown piece* sewed to the *off* cheek ring, 1 buckle 1.12 inches, and *chape* sewed to the near cheek ring; 1 *nose band,* the ends sewed to the square loops; 1 *chin strap,* the ends sewed to the square loops and passing loose through the hitching-strap ring; 1 *throat strap,* folded on itself making two thicknesses, and forming at top a loop for the throat band to pass through, and embracing in the fold at the other end 1 *bolt* which holds 1 *hitching-strap ring;* 1 *throat band* passes loose through the loop in the throat strap, and is sewed to the cheek rings; 1 *hitching strap* 6½ feet long, 1 *buckle* 1.25 inches, and 1 *standing loop,* 1 *billet* sewed to the buckle end by the same seam which holds the buckle.

Saddle. All the *leather* is black bridle or harness leather, and the buckles are blued malleable iron. The *saddle* is composed of 1 *tree,* 2 *saddle skirts,* 2 *stirrups,* 1 *girth* and *girth strap,* 1 *surcingle,* 1 *crupper.*

Saddle Tree.

Wood (beech). One *pommel* made of 2 pieces framed together at top and glued; 1 *cantle* formed of 2 pieces like the pommel; 2 *side bars* (poplar), each made of 3 pieces glued together; they are glued to the pommel and cantle, and fastened by 2 *rivets,* 2 *burrs,* and 4 *nails,* the burrs let in on the under side; 1 *strap mortise* in the pommel, 3 *strap mortises* in the cantle.

There are three sizes of trees, varying in the length of the seat. The number is marked on the pommel ornament.

No. 1.	11 inches length of seat.	15 per cent.
No. 2.	11½ " "	50 "
No. 3.	12 " "	35 "

Iron. One *pommel arc* 0.1 inch thick, with three small holes on top, fastened to the side bars by 4 *rivets;* 1 *pommel plate* 0.1 inch thick, semicircular, fastened to the front of the pommel by 4 *rivets;* 1 *cantle arc* 0.1 inch thick, with three small holes on top, fastened to the side bars by 4 rivets; 1 *cantle plate* 0.1 inch thick, fastened to the rear of the cantle by 4 *rivets;* 2 *stirrup loops* hinged in 2 *holdfasts* which are fastened to the side bars by 6 *rivets.*

The tree is painted with one coat of white lead. It is covered with the best quality kip skin raw hide, put on wet, sewed with thongs of the same, and held in place by stitches through the wood along the junction of the pommel and cantle with the side bars. The seams are made on the edges of the side bars, where they will not chafe the horse or rider.

2 *crupper rings,* held by staples driven into the front ends of side bars; 2 *foot staples* for coat straps, fastened to the front of the pommel by 4 *brass screws,* ¾ inch; 2 *crupper rings* (japanned black), fastened by staples driven into the rear ends of side bars; 2 *foot staples,* fastened to the rear of cantle by 4 brass screws, ¾ inch; 1 *guard plate,* 1 *pommel ornament* shield-shaped (sheet brass), fastened to the pommel, each, by 3 brass screw pins; 6 *guard plates,* fastened to the cantle by 12 *screw pins;* 2 *foot staples,* fastened on the back strap by 4 *brass screws,* ¾ inch; 1 *saddle-bag stud,* fastened on the back strap to the cantle arc by 2 copper rivets.

Two Saddle Skirts (thick harness leather), fastened to the side bars by 38 brass screws, ¾ inch; 2 *stay loops* for the saddle-bag straps, sewed to the rear edge of the skirts.

Two Stirrups (hickory or oak), made of one piece bent, the ends separated by 1 *transom* and fastened by 2 *iron rivets,* each, 4 *burrs;* 2 *leather hoods,* fastened to the stirrups by 12 *copper rivets and burrs*—distance of hood from rear to stirrup, 6 inches; 2 *stirrup straps,* 2 *brass buckles,* 1.375 inches, 2 *sliding loops* pass through the stirrup loops and through a hole cut in the skirts; 2 *sweat leathers,* each has 2 *standing loops.*

Girth. Two *girth straps* pass over the pommel and cantle arcs, to which are fastened by 4 *copper rivets* and 4 *burrs;* they are fastened to the side bars by 4 *brass screws,* ¾ inch; the ends are sewed into 2 D rings, 1.85 inches; 2 *girth billets,* sewed to the straight side of the D rings; 1 *girth,* 4.5 inches, blue woolen webbing; 1 *chape,* 1 *buckle,* 2 inches, 1 *standing loop,* and 1 *safe* on the off end; and 1 *chape,* 1 *buckle,* 1.5 inches, 1 D *ring,* 1.85 inches, 1 *standing loop,* 1 *safe* on the near side; 1 *standing loop* on the middle.

Six Coat Straps, 6 *buckles,* 0.625 inch and stops. They pass through the mortises in the pommel and cantle and the foot staples.

One Carbine Socket, 1 *strap,* 1 *buckle,* 0.75 inch, sewed to the socket. The socket is buckled on the D ring on the off side of the saddle.

One Surcingle, 3.25 inches, blue woolen webbing; 1 *chape,* 1 *buckle,* 1.5 inches, 1 *standing loop* on one end, and 1 *billet* on the other; 1 *billet* lining sewed over the end of webbing to the billet; 2 *standing loops* near the buckle end.

Crupper. One *dock,* made of a single piece and stuffed with hair, the ends sewed to the body of the crupper; 1 *body,* split at one end, has sewed to it 1 *chape,* 1 *ring,* 1.25 inches, 2 *back straps*—each has one buckle, 0.75 inch, and 2 *sliding loops*—they pass through the rings of the side bars and the ring on the body of the crupper.

Saddle Bags (bag leather). They are composed of 2 *pouches* and 1 *seat;* the ends of the seat are sewed to the pouches. Each pouch has 1 *back,* sewed to the gusset and upper part of inner front with a *welt;* 1 *gusset,* sewed to the back and to 1 *outer* and 1 *inner front* with a *welt;* 1 *flap,* sewed to the top of the back and to the seat by 2 seams; 1 *flap billet,* sewed to the point of the flap; 1 *chape* and 1 *buckle,* 0.625 inch, sewed to the outer front; 1 *billet,* 1 *buckle,* 0.625 inch, sewed to the chape. The seat is sewed to the pouch by the same seams which join the flap to the back of the pouch. It has 2 *holes* for the foot staples and 1 *hole* for the saddle-bag stud; 2 *key straps,* sewed to the seat near its ends; 4 *lacing thongs* for the pouches.

Saddle Blanket. To be of pure wool, close woven, of stout yarns of an indigo-blue color, with an orange border 3 inches wide, 3 inches from the edge. The letters U.S., 6 inches high, of orange color, in the centre of the blanket. Dimensions: 75 inches long, 67 inches wide; weight, 3.1875 pounds; variation allowed

U.S. Artillery brass stirrups.

Collection of cavalry rosettes, martingale hearts, and a copper star from a militia shako.

in weight, 0.1875 pounds.

SPURS (brass). Two *spurs*, 2 *rowels*, 2 *rivets*, 2 *spur straps*, 19 inches long, 2 *roller buckles*, 0.625 inch, 2 *standing loops*.

Length of heel for No. 1, 3½ inches; for No. 2, 3¼ inches–inside measure.

Width of heel for No. 1, 3¼ inches; for No. 2, 3 inches–inside measure.

Length of shank to centre of rowel, 1 inch.

Diameter of rowel, 0.85 inch.

ONE HORSE BRUSH. One *body* (maple), Russia bristles; 1 *cover*, glued and fastened to the body by 8 brass screws; 1 *hand strap*, fair leather, fastened to the sides of the body by 6 screws; 2 *leather washers* under the heads of screws. *Dimensions:* Body, 9.25 inches long, 4 inches wide, 0.5 inch thick; cover, 0.1 inch thick; bristles project 0.9 inch; hand strap, 2 inches wide.

ONE CURRY-COMB. Iron, japanned black. The pattern of "Carpenter's, No. 333." One *body* (sheet-iron, 0.4), the top and bottom edges turned at right angles, forming two rows of teeth; 3 *double rows* of teeth, riveted to the body by *six rivets;* 1 *cross bar,* riveted across the top by 2 rivets; 1 *handle shank,* riveted to the body by 3 rivets; 1 *handle* (wood), turned and painted, passes over the shank and is held by the riveted end of the shank; 1 *ferrule,* sheet-iron. *Dimensions:* Length, 4 inches; width, 4.75 inches; thickness, 0.75 inch; length of handle, 4 inches; weight, 0.84 pound.

ONE PICKET PIN (iron, painted black). The parts are: *the body, the neck, the head, the swell, the point;* 1 *lariat ring* around the neck, 8-shaped, the larger opening for the lariat. *Dimensions:* Length, 14 inches; diameter at swell, 4 inches from point, 0.75 inch; at neck, 0.5 inch; at head, 1 inch; lariat ring, 0.2 inch wire, welded, interior diameter, 1 inch; weight of pin, 1.29 pounds.

ONE LARIAT. Best hemp 1¼-inch rope, 30 feet long, of 4 strands; an eye spliced in one end, the other end whipped with small twine; weight, 2.38 pounds.

ONE LINK. One *strap,* embracing in the fold at one end 1 *spring hook,* and at the other 1 *buckle,* 0.75 inch, and 1 *billet.*

ONE NOSE BAG. Same as for Light Artillery.

WHIP. Made of heavy braided strips of black bridle leather, about 4 feet in length, and has a carrying loop of leather on the heavy end. The whip is also equipped with a brass hook attachment for wearing on the belt when the whip is not being used. No markings.

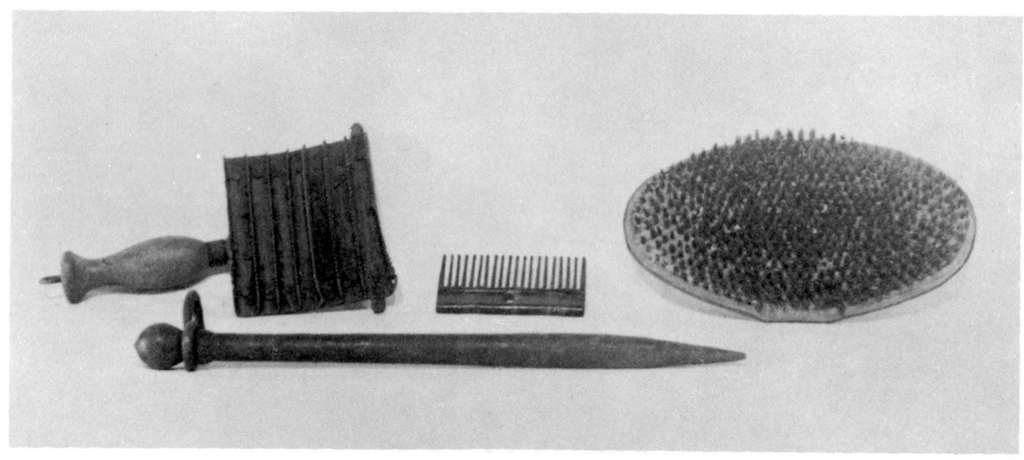

Curry comb, mane comb, brush, and picket pin.

HOSPITAL CAR. Several types of improvised cars were used but one of the best was fitted up late in 1862 by the Philadelphia Railroad Company. The internal arrangements were similar to sleeping cars except that the berths slid in and out; each of these berths with its patient could be carried like a stretcher by two men. Each hospital car had 51 of these berths, and a seat at each end for an attendant. It was provided with a stove on which soups could be cooked, a water tank and locker, and a convenient toilet.

HOT SHOT. See PROJECTILES.

HOUSEWIFE. Each soldier mended his own clothes, or did not mend them at all, just as he thought best. However, no man hired it done. Many men had their "housewife" or its equivalent. A housewife contained the necessary needles, yarn, thimble, which was furnished by some mother, sister, sweetheart or, more rarely, by a Soldier's Aid Society. Most soldiers put off mending their clothes or darning their socks until they could either draw the clothing they needed or perhaps could "find" the articles they

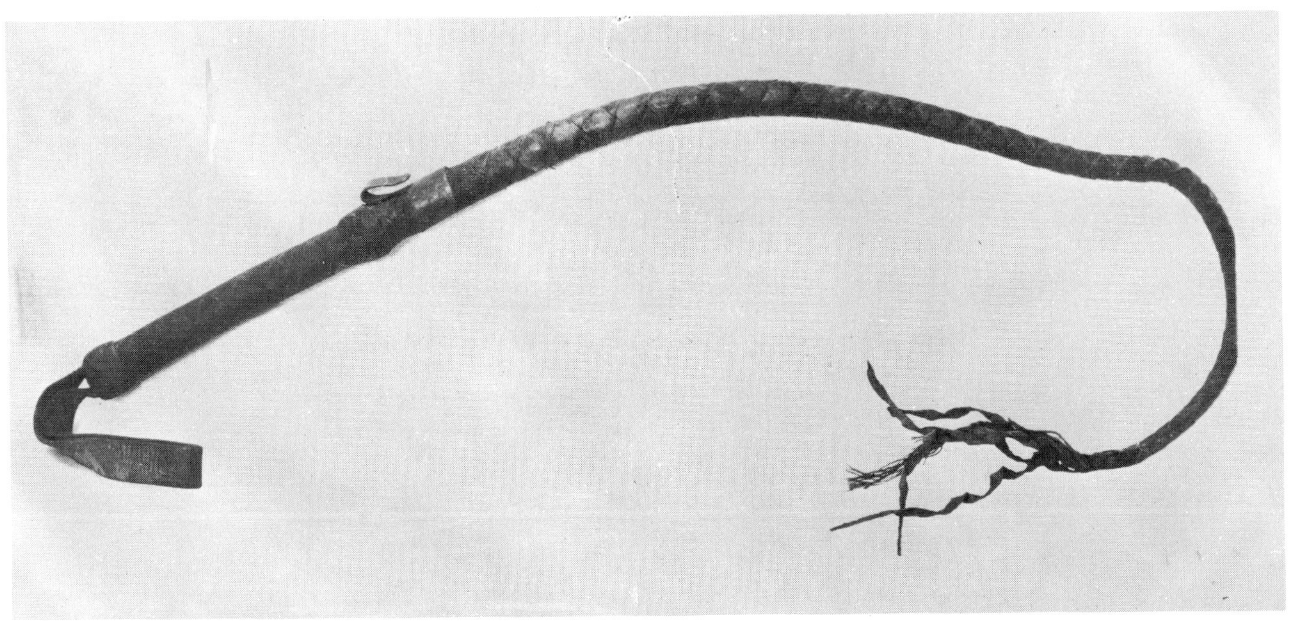

Whip.

needed which a careless soldier may have left unguarded for a few moments. The speediest method of mending a hole in the socks was that of tying a string around the hole. Then there were the men who, having arranged a checkerboard of stitches over the holes, as they had seen their mothers do, had not sufficient time or patience to fill in the squares, with the inevitable result that "both heels and toes looked through the bars only a few hours before breaking jail again."

Some men were kept furnished with homemade socks that had been knit, perhaps, by mother or grandmother. Such socks wore well. But the men did not attempt to repair the socks drawn from the Government as these socks were too often of the shoddiest material and were simply not worth repairing.

A sample housewife is of brown leather trimmed with blue cloth and tied with blue cloth tape. This housewife has inner pockets, in one of which are still remaining two army buttons and some blue thread. In another pocket is a blue pin cushion with pins stuck in it. This particular housewife is 3 by 3 inches but housewives were made in all sizes and shapes.

Of different shape is a smaller housewife, also of brown leather, with a cylindrically shaped pin cushion, and with needles stuck in a piece of white cloth sewed into the inside of the housewife. This housewife is 3½ inches long, 1¼ inches thick, and has brown laces sewed on the housewife which can be wrapped around the housewife and tied.

A square housewife 2½ by 2¾ inches, of brown leather, has the usual needles and pincushion plus a thimble which is inserted in a recess within the pincushion. A wide brown silk tab is sewed on the cover of the housewife for tying.

Also shown is a Navy sewing kit. This unusual item is a hollow wood container, designed to hold needles and thread. Due to its length—6½ inches—this kit may have been used for the large needles used in repairing sails.

HOUSINGS. The cloth covering for saddles prescribed as part of the uniform of the Army in regulations.

IDENTIFICATION DISCS. Generally speaking, soldiers in combat had no means of being identified if they were killed in combat. On several occasions men going into combat improvised means of identification which their Government failed to provide. At

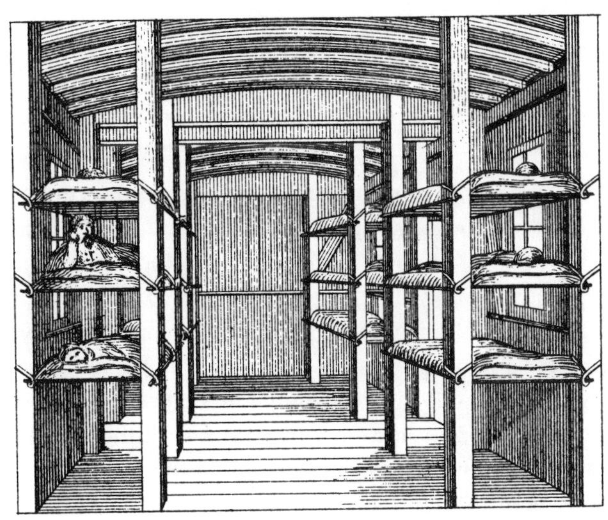

Improvised hospital car.

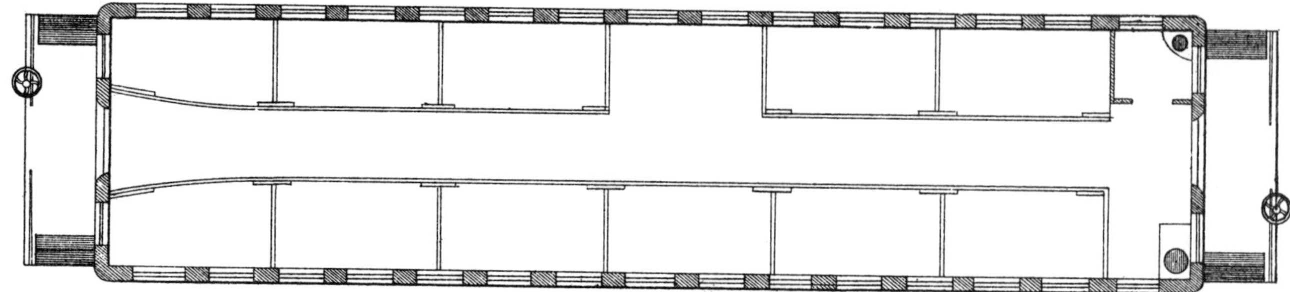

Horizontal plan of one of the hospital cars of the Army of the Cumberland.

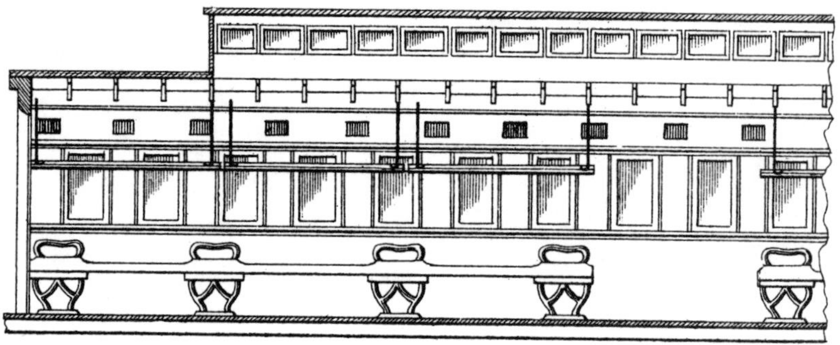

Side elevation of one of the hospital cars constructed under Dr. Cooper's supervision.

Cooper's hospital car.

Marye's Heights, Mine Run, and Cold Harbor, in preparation for what they knew was a hopeless attack, Federals cut slips of paper and pinned them to the backs of their coats, so that their dead bodies could be identified on the field. Many of these slips of paper were useful before the day was over. Thus some soldiers on their own initiative made reasonably sure of their identification in case they became casualties. Often such items of equipment as haversacks and knapsacks were stenciled with the owner's name and regiment. Occasionally a soldier would scratch his name and unit in the back of the brass U.S. buckle of his waist belt. Notebooks, diaries, and letters from home were invaluable in identifying a man killed in battle.

The more farsighted soldiers provided themselves with items sold by private concerns before leaving their home state, or purchased them from enterprising sutlers on arrival at the theater of war. These items were of two general types. The first type, the more expensive, was widely advertised in *Harper's Weekly, Leslie's* and other popular periodicals and newspapers. This type was a pin, usually of gold or silver, and quite ornate. Generally these pins were shaped to suggest branch of service and were engraved with the soldier's name and unit. Often the pin was in the shape of the army corps badge but must not be confused with the corps badges as issued by the Government for wear on hat or cap. The privately purchased badges were usually worn on the coat.

The second type of identification markers were similar to the "dog tags" of World War I and early World War II pattern, but were of brass or lead instead of aluminum. These tags had a hole for attaching by string around the neck. There were several variations of these tags. Usually they had on one side an eagle or shield and such phrases as "War for the Union," or "Liberty, Union, and Equality." The other side had the soldier's name and unit and sometimes a list of battles in which he had participated. Lettering was machine stamped. On one occasion, at least, nearly an entire regiment went into an active campaign with this type of identification disc. In July 1864, the 14th New Hampshire Infantry, passing through Charlestown, West Virginia, on its way to the Shenandoah Valley, purchased many of these brass discs from a sutler who had set up his tent by the roadside. He stamped each disc purchased with men's name, company, and regiment.

The lead discs included on one side such legends as "Gen. Geo. B. McClellan, U.S.A.," and "First in the hearts of his soldiers" or the New York State coat of arms with "Union and Constitution" and "N.Y.S. Vols." with the dates "1776" and "1861". The soldier's name and regiment were stamped on the reverse side.

Investigation into official records and museums has not disclosed any reference to an official issuance of identification media of any kind to Federal troops in the Civil War.

There were a few Confederate identification discs used. The Flayderman collection includes one which is stamped:

Lieut. J.H. Counts
Co. "G"
13th S.C. Regt.
McGowan's Brig.
Wilcox Div.
A.P. Hill's Corps
R.E. Lee's Army

INCENDIARY SHELL. See GREEK FIRE and PROJECTILES.

INFERNAL MACHINES. See MINES AND TORPEDOES.

INK. See WRITING EQUIPMENT.

INSIGNIA. See also EPAULETTES and SHOULDER STRAPS.

CONFEDERATE (INSIGNIA OF RANK). On the sleeve of the tunic, rank was distinguished by an ornament of gold braid extending around the seam of the cuff, and up the outside of the arm to the bend of the elbow. Had 1 braid for lieutenants; 2 for captains; 3 for field officers; and 4 for general officers. The braid was ⅛ inch wide.

On the front part of the collar of the tunic, the rank of officers was distinguished as follows:

General Officers. A wreath, with 3 stars enclosed, embroidered in gold. The edge of the wreath was ¾ inch from the front edge of the collar; the stars to be arranged horizontally; the center to be 1¼ inches in exterior diameter, and the others ¾ inch in diameter.

Colonel. Three stars, embroidered in gold, arranged horizontally, and dividing equally the vertical space of the collar. Each star was 1¼ inches in exterior diameter; the front star ¾ inch from the edge of the collar.

Lieutenant Colonel. Two stars of same material, size, and arrangement as for a colonel.

Major. One star of same material and size as for a colonel, placed ¾ inch from edge of collar, and dividing the vertical space.

Captain. Three horizontal bars, embroidered in gold; each ½ inch wide; the upper bar 3 inches long; the front edge of the bars inclined to correspond with the angle of the collar, ¾ inch from the edge; the line of the back edges were vertical.

First Lieutenant. Two horizontal bars of same material and size as for captains, and dividing equally the vertical space of collar.

Second Lieutenant. One horizontal bar of same

Housewives. Dimensions of housewives left to right are: 3½ inches by 1¼ inches; 2½ inches by 2¾ inches; 3 inches by 3 inches. In the foreground is a Navy sewing kit.

material and size as for the center bar of captain, and dividing equally the vertical space of collar.

FEDERAL

ARMY INSIGNIA OF RANK. See also UNIFORMS AND CLOTHING. Worn on the shoulder straps. Lieutenant generals, one silver star; major generals, two silver stars; brigadier generals, one silver star;

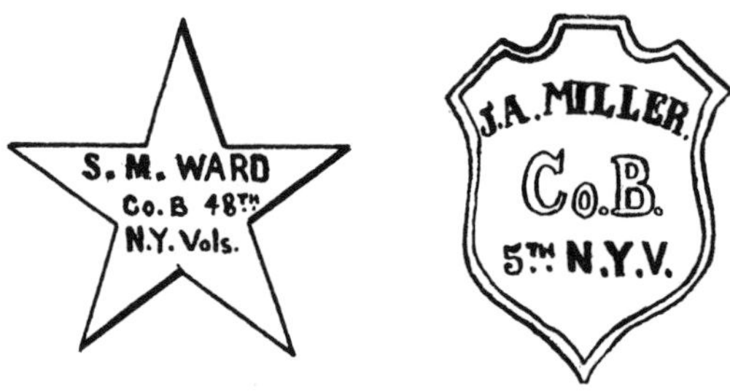

Types of identification pins sold to soldiers by commercial firms. Note the corps motif in each. (Drawn by Mike McAfee)

colonels, silver eagle; lieutenant colonel, silver maple leaf; major, gilt or gold maple leaf; captain, two silver bars; first lieutenant, one silver bar; second lieutenant, nothing on shoulder strap; brevet second lieutenant, same as second lieutenant.

ARMY INSIGNIA OF BRANCH OR SPECIAL UNIT. Branches of service were indicated by insignia on the cap or hat, trimming on the coat, and piping on the trousers. These were: Scarlet for Artillery; sky-blue for Infantry; yellow for Cavalry and Engineers. The insignia worn on the cap or hat were: crossed cannons for Artillery; a bugle for Infantry; crossed sabers for Cavalry; a turreted castle for Engineers; a shield with the letters "T.E." in old English Characters for Topographical Engineers; crossed flags for the Signal Corps; and a bursting bomb for the Ordnance Department.

Soldiers also wore their regimental number and company letter on their headgear; later in the war their corps badges (1863-1865) tended to displace all other insignia on caps or hats.

Ambulance Corps. The designating insignia for members of the Ambulance Corps in the Army of the Potomac was: Sergeants—a green band 1¼ inches wide around the cap, and inverted chevrons of the same color on each arm, above the elbow; privates, the same kind of band and a half chevron of the same material.

Berdan's Sharpshooters. At least one member of Berdan's 1st U.S. Sharpshooters wore the letters U.S.S.S. on his forage cap. But veterans scoffed at the wearer and pointed out that the letters stood for "Unfortunate Soldiers Sadly Sold." The wearer of the insignia was a boastful officer whom the men did not respect.

Coat of Arms (State). Each state had its own coat of arms, and with many, especially the Southern states, the coat of arms were very prominently displayed. This was true not only of battle flags, but also of the design on belt buckles, cartridge box plates, and especially buttons. For an aid in identifying such objects, the various state seals or coat of arms are given here. It should be emphasized that these illustrations pertain to the state coats of arms as they were officially authorized during the 1861-1865 period. Several states have made changes in their coat of arms since 1865. The accompanying illustrations should be of assistance in determining actual Civil War use or at least in indicating possible Civil War use since

Identification disks. Left to right: worn by James Nichols, Co. E, 30th New York Infantry; wooden object carried at 1st Bull Run by Leman C. Miner, Co. A, 3d Conn. Infantry. In the foreground is an unusually small "dog tag" worn by Sergeant John Wright, Co. H, 61st Ohio Infantry.

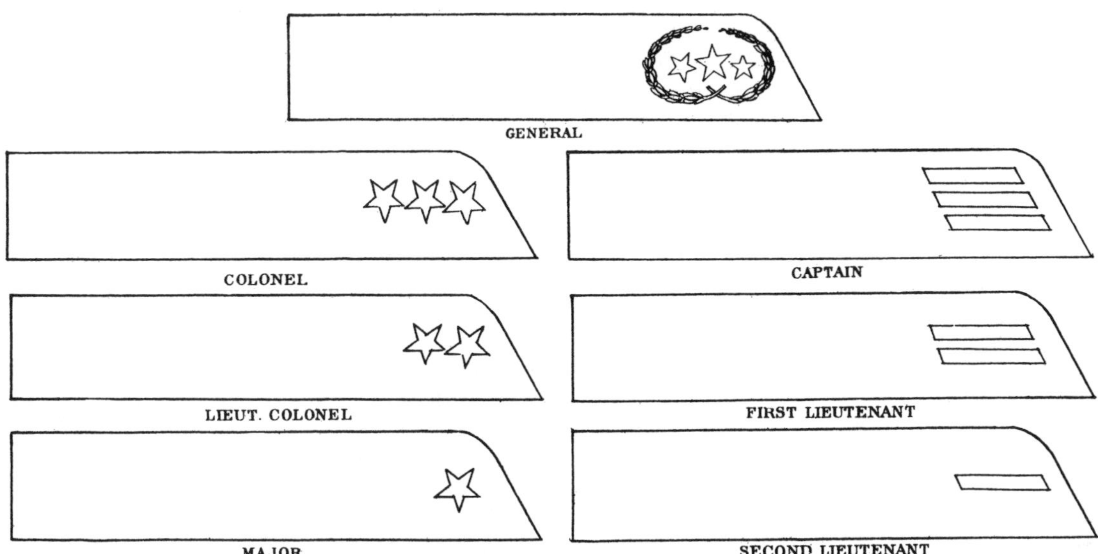

Confederate collar insignia of rank.

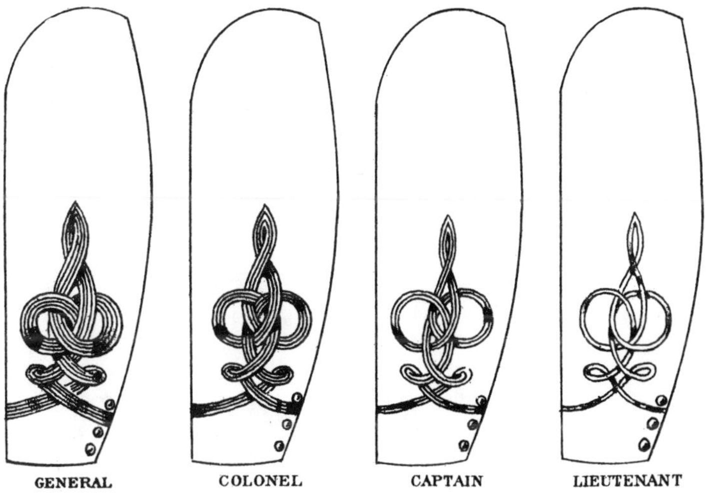

Confederate sleeve insignia of rank.

many states continued to use the same insignia after the war. Also, in the case of buttons, the name of the maker is often a good clue as to when the buttons were actually made.

In addition to Federal and state insignia of various kinds, some regiments had distinctive insignia of their own. An example was the insignia of "Corcoran's Regiment" of Irish soldiers in Meagher's Irish Brigade. This regiment, the 69th New York Infantry, lost 259 in killed alone; it lost more men in action, killed and wounded, than any other infantry regiment from the state of New York.

Coat of Arms. (U.S.). Army Regulations defined "Arms of the United States" as follows: Paleways of thirteen pieces, argent and gules; a chief, azure; the escutcheon on the breast of the American eagle displayed, proper, holding in his dexter talon an olive-branch, and in his sinister a bundle of thirteen arrows, all proper; and in his beak a scroll, inscribed with this motto: 'E. Pluribus Unum.' For the crest: over the head of the eagle, which appears above the escutcheon, a glory breaking through a cloud, propet, and surrounding thirteen stars, forming a constellation, argent, and on an azure field.

Federal insignia of rank worn on shoulder straps.

Insignia for branches of Service. Top: left to right: infantry, ordnance, engineers. Bottom: Artillery, cavalry. (Drawn by Mike McAfee)

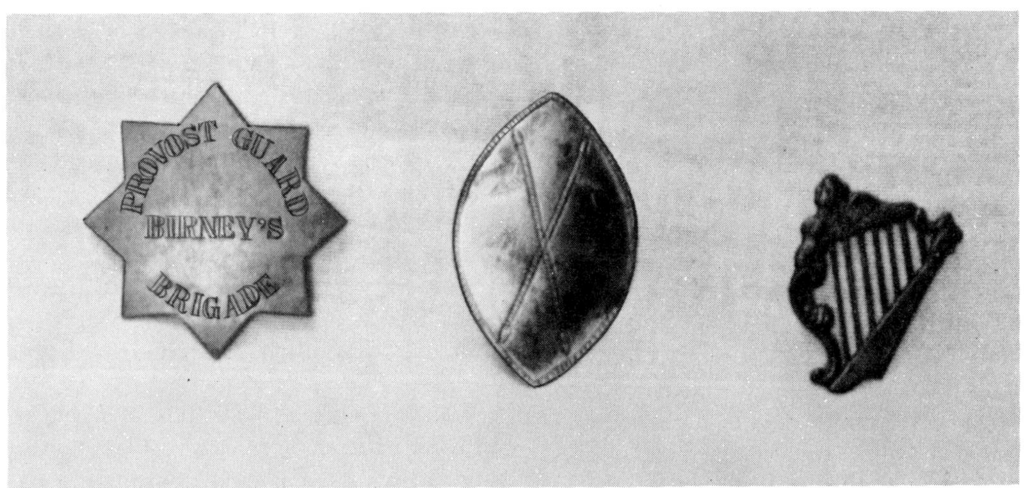

Insignia left to right: Provost Guard, Birney's Brigade; Rush's Lancers; Corcoran's Legion (Irish units).

UNITED STATES.

U.S. coat of arms. (Norm Flayderman)

Regimental colors carried the arms of the United States, and the eagle motif was very commonly used as decoration for various items of military equipment.

Military Aeronautics. Although members of the Federal Balloon Corps were rated as civilian employees, and accordingly wore civilian clothes, a few attempted to wear "B.C." (Balloon Corps) or "A.D." (Aeronautic Department), as insignia on their headgear. These insignia were not officially sanctioned and the aeronauts soon discarded them as they only provoked amusement.

Military Telegraph Service. As with the Balloon Corps, members of the U.S. Military Telegraph Corps were civilians and therefore, not authorized any distinguishing insignia. Nominally under the Quartermaster Department, the telegraphers actually comprised a separate, elite organization of highly-specialized civilians. Some of the personnel wore officers' uniforms but without any insignia of rank. In many cases this was necessitated by the ill feeling of Army personnel toward the telegraphers who were well paid and exempt from military draft. However, an exception was made by General Order No. 51, Dept. of the Cumberland, whereby telegraphers were authorized to wear a dark blue uniform with commissioned officers' cap but without any ornament. Buttons for this uniform were to be those worn by officers of the General Staff.

Musicians. Apparently the motif of a lyre in a wreath was used to a limited extent as musicians' insignia. Buttons with insignia which some well-informed collectors and students believe to have been in fairly general use by musicians during the war do exist. There is no official data available to corroborate this.

Pioneer Corps. Some regiments had a pioneer corps with a distinctive insignia. Such a regiment, the 148th Pa. Infantry, had its own pioneer corps of ten picked men, whose main qualification was to be first-class axemen. In addition to their axes they had digging tools.

Rush's Lancers. The 6th Pennsylvania Cavalry (Rush's Lancers) wore the regulation uniform, including crossed sabers; on the preceding page is shown an insignia peculiar to the 6th Pennsylvania.

Signal Corps. Officers were detailed to the Signal Corps from line units and often continued to wear the insignia of their original branch of service. However, the insignia of crossed flags, as we know it today, was the insignia of the Signal Corps during the war.

MAINE.

NEW HAMPSHIRE.

VERMONT.

MASSACHUSETTS.

RHODE ISLAND.

CONNECTICUT.

State coats of arms. (Norm Flayderman)

State coats of arms. (Norm Flayderman)

State coats of arms. (Norm Flayderman)

ARKANSAS.

TENNESSEE.

CALIFORNIA.

OREGON.

State coats of arms. (Norm Flayderman)

U.S. Military Railroads. Except for the temporary detailing of line units to railroad construction, personnel of the USMRR were civilians. Accordingly, no military insignia was authorized for them.

MARINE CORPS. (Quoted from Regulations). (Insignia of rank is same as for Army).

Hat Ornament

Company Officers.—A United States Shield within a half wreath; resting upon the centre of the shield, a bugle and the letter M; the letter to be placed within the ring of the bugle, and to just fit that ring; the letter to be of *solid white metal, fastened on to the shield;* the shield, bugle and wreath to be of *yellow metal, heavily gilt.*

Enlisted Men.—Same as for Company Officers, except that the shield, bugle, and half wreath will not be gilt, but kept bright. The letter M will be of *white metal, like that on the ornament of the officer's cap.*

Ornament

Officers.—A gold embroidered bugle, two and one-quarter inches long, and one and five-sixteenths greatest width; solid silver or plated M within the centre of the ring of the bugle, the letter to be made with an eye on the back, like a button, that it may be removed and cleaned; bugle to be embroidered on scarlet cloth, which will be trimmed off, so as to present a margin of one-eighth of an inch, following the line of the embroidery.

For Enlisted Men.—For all enlisted men, a bugle of yellow metal same size as that of the officer, the letter M in white metal; the letter to rest on a circular piece of red leather; both bugle and letter to be fastened with eyes and rings, on leather strips. The undress cap to be provided with a water-proof cover, according to pattern sent to Quartermaster's Department.

Pompon

For all Company Officers.—Of gold net, two inches in height, and one and one-half inches in diameter, to be made over a cork foundation, of elliptical form; the pompon to be fixed to a wire loop, three inches long, and, when attached to the cap, to pitch forward in a line parallel with the rear slope of the cap; between the top of the shield in the ornament and the base of the pompon, a hemisphere of yellow metal, heavily gilt.

For Enlisted Men, except the Drum-Major.—A red worsted ball, five inches in circumference; when attached to the cap, to pitch forward in a line parallel with the rear of the slope of the cap. Between the top of the shield, in the ornament, and the base of the pompon, a hemisphere of yellow metal, to be kept bright, with a red leather ground just under the knot, above the shield on the uniform cap, extending out and scolloped, or cut in points so as to give effect.

For the Drum-Major.—Same as for enlisted men, except it shall be ten inches in circumference, to be fixed on a ring, the ring on a loop.

The uniform cap ornament, and pompon, will not

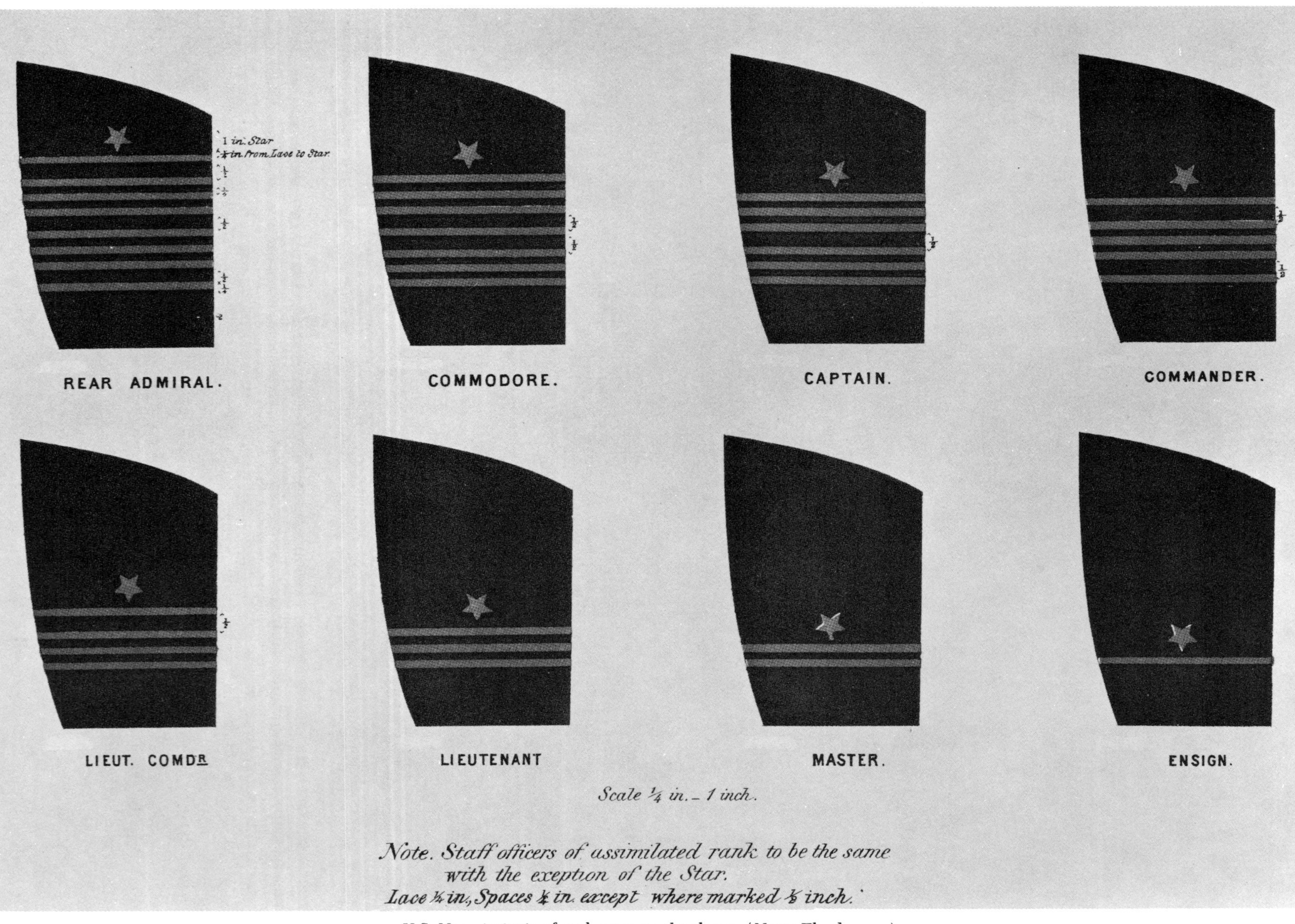

U.S. Navy insignia of rank worn on the sleeve. (Norm Flayderman)

be issued to enlisted men as part of the cap and clothing allowance, but will be served out *on charge,* to be returned at the expiration of each enlistment, and to be receipted for by an officer, as are arms and accoutrements.

Navy Cuff and Sleeve Ornaments. The lace on the cuffs and sleeves is to be navy gold lace, a quarter of an inch wide, and to be placed a quarter of an inch apart, except where a half is hereinafter designated, the first strip being below but joining the cuff seam, and the others distributed in groups upwardly.

For a Rear-Admiral, eight strips, with half an inch space between first and second, fourth and fifth, and seventh and eighth.

For a Commodore, seven strips, with half an inch space between third and fourth, fourth and fifth.

For a Captain, six strips, with half an inch space between third and fourth.

For a Commander, five strips, with half an inch space between first and second, fourth and fifth.

For a Lieutenant-Commander, four strips, with half an inch space between third and fourth.

mate, at $40 per month, the star without the lace, and in the same position as the star on the sleeves of an ensign.

The cuff and sleeve ornaments of the *staff officers* are to be the same as for the *line officers* with whom they assimilate, respectively, in rank, except the gold star, which is to be worn by *line officers* only.

No other officers are entitled to the ornaments above described.

INTRENCHING TOOLS. According to Scott's *Military Dictionary* "Pioneers [are] soldiers sometimes detailed from the different companies of a regiment and formed under a noncommissioned officer, furnished with saws, felling axes, spades, mattocks, pickaxes, and bill hooks. Their services are very important, and no regiment is well fitted for service without pioneers completely equipped."

Section 750 of the 1861 *U.S. Army Regulations* defined pioneers as working parties attached to convoys to mend roads, remove obstacles, and erect defenses. "The convoys should always be provided with spare wheels, poles, axles, etc."

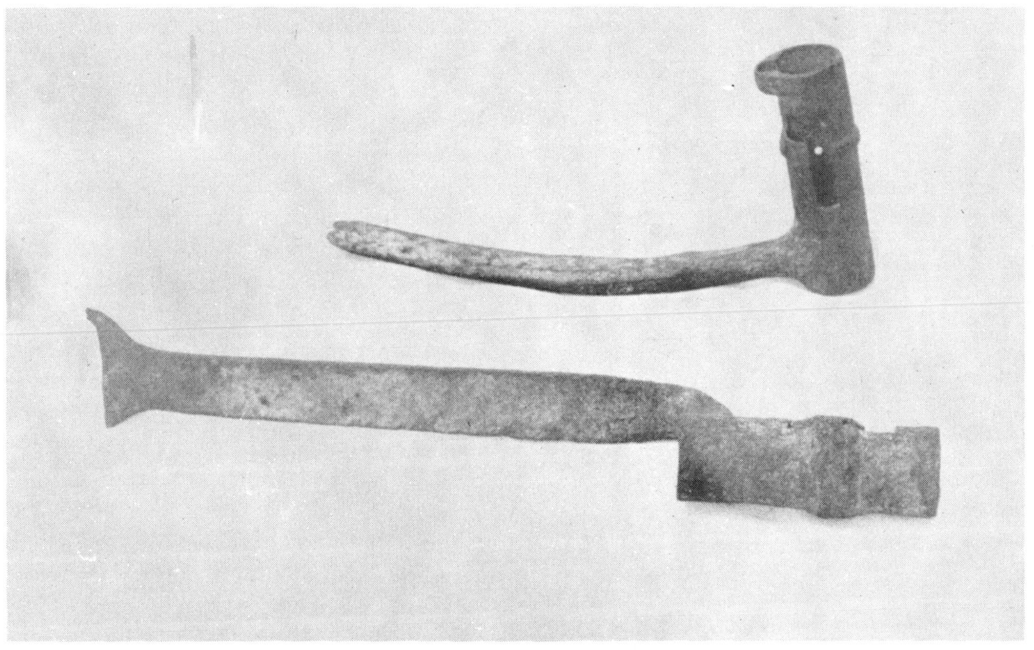

Intrenching bayonets dug up at Kernstown, Va.

For a Lieutenant, three strips; for a *Master,* two strips; and for an *Ensign,* one strip.

On the upper side of each sleeve, above the lace and midway the seams, is to be worn a star of five rays, embroidered in gold, and one inch in diameter, with one of its rays directly downwards, the point thereof being a quarter of an inch from the upper edge of the lace.

For a midshipman, boatswain, gunner, and *master's*

In addition to pioneers, line troops, often whole regiments, were detailed to work on fortifications, and in combat to prepare their own positions for defense. Such troops were issued intrenching tools of the type shown in the illustrations.

ARTILLERY SHOVEL. This was 4 feet 6¾ inches long overall, with the shovel 10 inches wide at its widest part. There was a ring attached to the handle at a point 9 inches from the end.

INTRENCHING BAYONETS. Shown here are two very unusual specimens of intrenching tools dug up on the battlefield of Kernstown. Apparently these tools were experimental types, issued to some unit of Banks' army and were left during his retreat from Jackson's forces. Both are cal. 58 musket bayonets adapted for digging purposes. The adze type of tool has a blade 6 inches long, while the remnant of spade-type tool has a blade 7 inches long. The author has never seen any other items like the two pictured here.

SHOVELS AND SPADES. A shovel shorter than the artillery shovel, and straighter, probably was in more common use. It is shorter and lighter. If carried in bulk, these shovels were much better adapted to field service. All metal parts are painted black. Width of shovel at widest point–8½ inches.

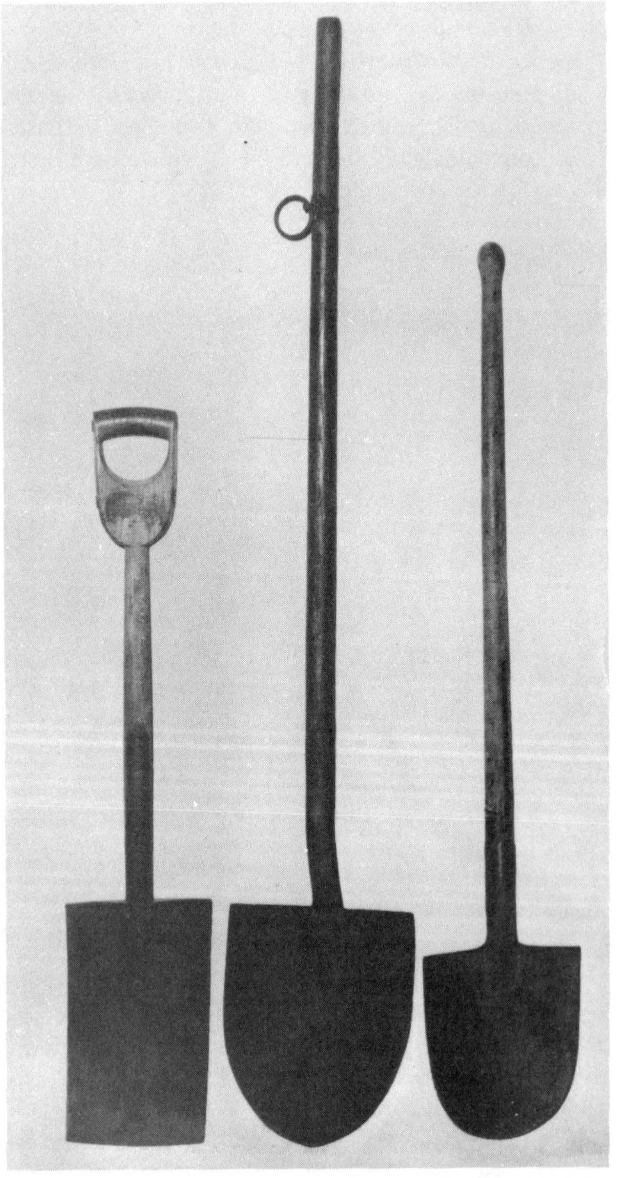

Shovels and spades. Left to right: infantry spade; artillery shovel (4 feet 6¾ inches long); common shovel (3 feet 8½ inches long).

The spade illustrated, probably designed for infantry use in trenches, is 3 feet long. The spade proper is 7 inches wide. All metal parts are painted black.

All three types have been found on battlefields, especially in the East.

KEPI. Forage Cap–See Uniforms and Clothing.

KETTLES. Mess or camp kettles were cylindrical in shape and made of heavy sheet iron. They were generally from 13 to 15 inches high, and varied in diameter from 7 to 12 inches. However, the only specimen seen by the author is 11½ inches tall with a 9-inch inside diameter. This kettle is in the Robert L. Miller collection. All camp kettles were about the same height but came in three or four sizes so that they could be conveniently "nested" for transportation. They rapidly fell victims to the exigencies of active service. These kettles were made by contract. Some became leaky from causes known only to the firm which made them. Other kettles were run over by wagons and the soldiers kicked them about the camp. During the last year of the war thousands of soldiers did not so much as see one camp kettle for months at a time. A little ingenuity and activity in foraging for adequate substitutes for the cumbersome camp or mess kettles usually sufficed. By 1864 most soldiers used their tin cups or half canteens in lieu of the regulation kettle. Also, many soldiers appropriated the pot-bellied kettles they found at most farm houses as they moved into Southern territory. In some of the more rural areas of the South these kettles are still being used.

KNAPSACK. In addition to his accouterments, haversack, and canteen, the Civil War soldier was also issued a knapsack. This was worn on the back and was made of painted canvas, often with the owner's company letter and regimental number stencilled on the back. This canvas material resembled non-porous plasters, and when the knapsacks were strapped on the soldier's back, all clothing was closely bound about his chest and shoulders–a most vicious combination for hard marching in hot weather. Many knapsacks had wooden frames; the top boards pressed directly on the shoulder blades. Rubber-covered knapsacks protected their contents from moisture but were even more uncomfortable than canvas under a hot sun. Observers commented on the baggy appearance of the knapsacks and the fact that they slipped down too far toward the small of the back. One observer observed that "the hardiest packhorses in the world would break down under the heavy, sagging, illy-adjusted loads borne by our soldiers!"

Much of the difficulty with the regulation knapsacks could have been avoided if the men had packed

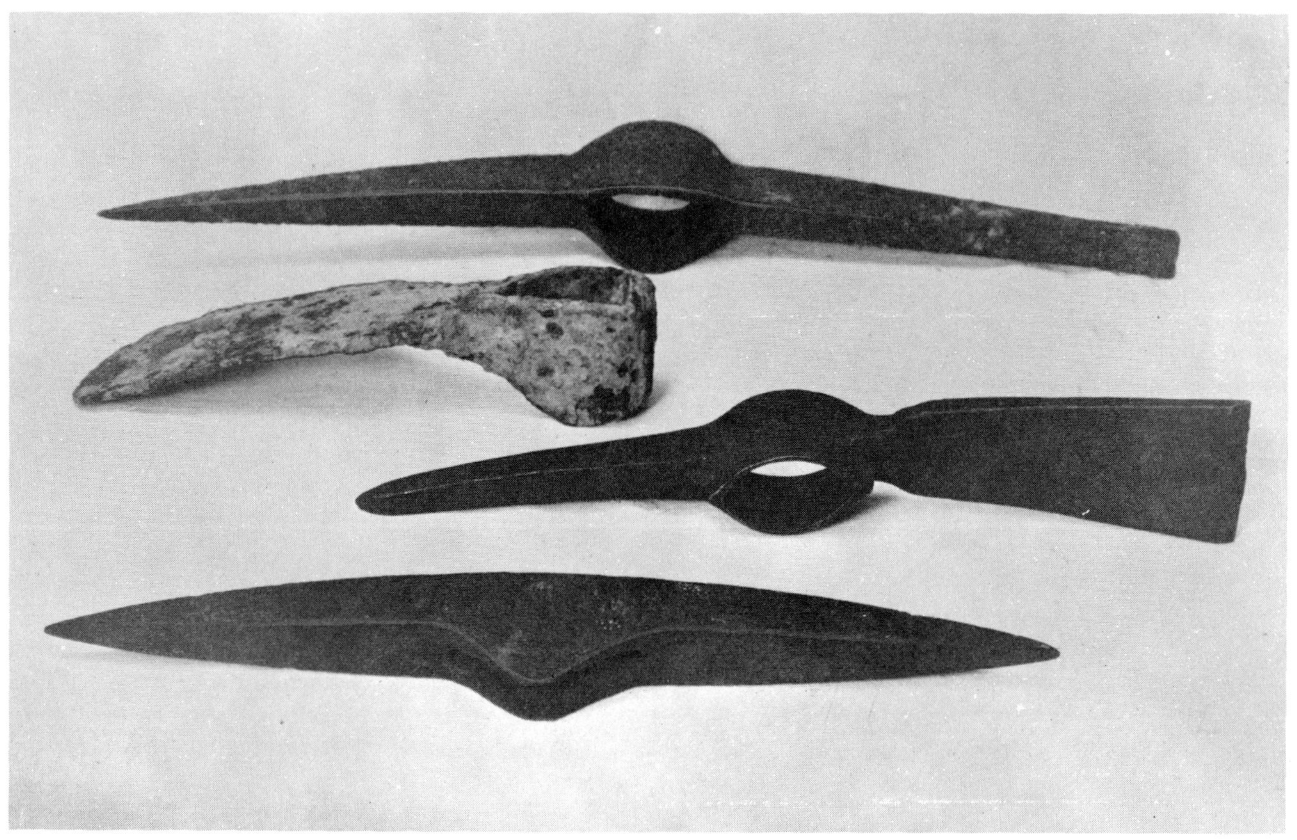

Digging tools. Top to bottom: pick from Cold Harbor, Virginia battlefield. Two feet long. Mattock from camp of the U.S. 2d Corps at Falmouth, Virginia. Length 11½ inches. Adze from Falmouth, Virginia. Length 12½ inches. Pick, painted black. Length 16 inches.

them only with those items necessary for their comfort. These would have included a double wool blanket, half a shelter tent, and a rubber blanket. Some units, like the 4th New Jersey Infantry, late in the war, turned in their knapsacks, cartridge boxes, and belts, receiving in exchange the Mann accouterment. (See ACCOUTERMENT) Colonel W. D. Mann, designer of this accouterment, resigned his commission in the 7th Michigan Cavalry and went to Washington early in 1864, where he persuaded the Ordnance Department of the worth of his improved system of cavalry and infantry accouterments. The Government soon gave large orders for their manufacture and most of the regiments which used them apparently liked them, mainly because the suspenders arrangement kept the weight of the accouterment off their loins or kidneys.

Even after many of the non-essentials had been eliminated, Federal troops still carried unduly heavy and bulky knapsacks. In the Chancellorville campaign many Federal soldiers carried both overcoat and blanket although it was intended that only one or the other should be taken. One Confederate division commander reported that "the enemy abandoned such a large number of knapsacks in retreating to his works that when this division began its homeward march in the rain it was thoroughly equipped with oil cloths and shelter tents of the best quality.

The experience gained at Chancellorsville convinced the Quartermaster General and corps commanders of the Army of the Potomac that the knapsack was an unnecessary encumbrance which should be replaced by the blanket roll. At Chancellorsville the Army of the Potomac lost about 25 percent of its knapsacks. In the V Corps it was about 30 percent; in the XI and XII Corps it was about 50 percent. Even though knapsacks were carried by some regiments in the field all through the war, they were usually stored before setting out on an active campaign and their place taken by a blanket. This blanket, with a change of underclothing in it, was rolled into a cylinder and slung across the left shoulder and crossing to the right hip, was tied together by a string.

When troops were in the field the soldier carried his own ammunition and rations. The total weight carried by each Federal soldier averaged 45 pounds, which included the knapsack, haversack, change of underclothing, overcoat or blanket, arms and accouterments, and one half a shelter tent. Eight days' short rations were carried on the person, 40 rounds of am-

Camp scene showing types of kettles in common use during the war. Notice the camp bucket, crude table, coffee pot, and cups. (Library of Congress)

munition in the cartridge box, and 20 rounds in the man's pockets. Weights of knapsacks varied greatly. A sergeant in Berdan's Sharpshooters carried a knapsack, which, fully loaded, weighed 28 pounds. Occasionally there were reports of men carrying 70 pounds in their knapsacks. But normally no such back-breaking, side-splitting weight was carried by the soldiers—unless some unfortunate was working out a sentence, walking a beat under guard thus loaded in lieu of the ball and chain, or log substitutes for thumb-tying, the stocks, and other fairly severe punishments. No shoddy knapsack would hold together with a 70-pound load in it.

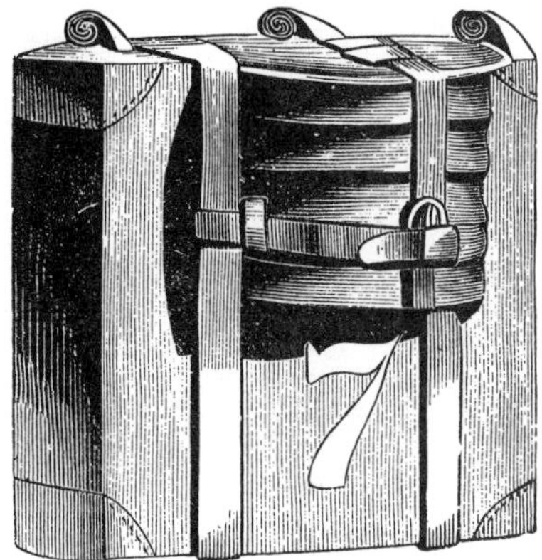

National Guard knapsack. As used by the 7th New York and other militia regiments. (Norm Flayderman)

In light marching order the knapsack, if carried at all, had little more in it or on top than a rolled blanket, sometimes extra rations, and the balance of 60 rounds of ammunition that couldn't go in a 40-round cartridge box. At other times the knapsack varied all the way from that carried by a new outfit to the smallest possible kit or supply of extras, mainly underclothing, poncho or rubber blanket, and woolen blanket. The overcoats were turned in at the beginning of a spring campaign. All told, the 10 pound musket, 40 rounds of ammunition, canteen of water, haversack packed with hardtack, coffee, sugar, and pork broiled or raw, would add up to about 40 pounds, including accouterments. The man, however, tended to leave enough in camp so that when they took the road their knapsack weighed about 15 pounds.

Berdan's sharpshooters carried a knapsack of hair-covered calfskin, with cooking kit attached. This was considered the best in use, as it was the best-looking outfit of all, very durable and complete.

The 83d Pennsylvania Infantry had a unique knapsack, which had been imported from France early in the war. There was no other regiment in the Federal service with this type knapsack, according to a statement of one of the survivors of the 83d. The knapsack was made of calfskin tanned with the hair on. Incidentally, the author's grandfather, a member of the 14th New Hampshire Infantry, saw a Confederate soldier at the Battle of Winchester (September 19, 1864) wearing a similar knapsack. Apparently the Confederates either imported the same type of knapsack or used a similar type made in the South during the war.

Shown in the drawing is one of the most common type of knapsack carried during the war.

ACCESSORIES

Knapsack Collar (Patent No. 37,146). Patented December 16, 1862 by James E. Atwood of Washington, D. C. Consisted of attaching to the upper edge of a knapsack a heavy leather collar made to fit closely around the neck, with ends extending down in front, to which straps could be attached.

Knapsack Sling (Patent No. 37,893). Patented March 17, 1863 by D. W. C. Baxter, Philadelphia, Pa. This improvement was designed to prevent pressure of the knapsack on the small of the back and the arms by supporting the knapsack by strips of wood extending from the shoulder to the hips.

Knapsack Sling (Patent No. 46,410). Patented February 14, 1865 by J. T. Warren, Stafford, N.Y. This invention consists in the construction of metallic slings, having a back strap below and yielding straps or loops above, attached to the knapsack to conform to the shape and size of the shoulders.

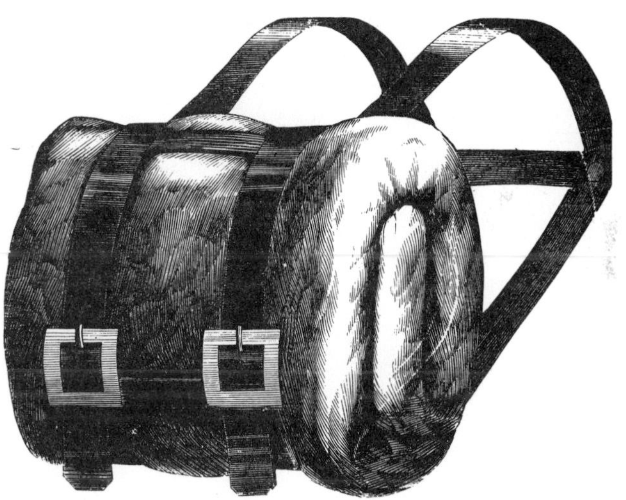

Overcoat sling made of enameled leather. (Norm Flayderman)

Coat Sling (Patent No. 37,029). Patented November 28, 1862, by D. F. Drake, Somerville, Mass. This coat sling was made with a brace strap combined with a back plate and shoulder straps, so arranged as to go across the back and below the shoulder blades and connecting upward to the shoulder straps.

Knapsack Strap Slide (Patent No. 47,958). Patented May 30, 1865 by George D. Kellogg, Troy, N.Y. This contrivance, called a "Shoulder Strap Slide," involved a slotting of each of the shoulder straps attached to the waist belt which cross on the back of the shoulders. By means of a stud, which adapts itself to the point of crossing, the knapsack adapts itself to the motion of the soldier's body as he moves.

Knapsack Supporter (Patent No. 46,886). Patented March 21, 1865, by Adam Dickey, Cincinnati, Ohio. This invention consists of a method of relieving the soldier of the backward pulling upon the shoulders caused by the knapsack.

Buchanan Knapsack (Patent No. 25,625) Patented October 4, 1859 by Robert C. Buchanan, U. S. Army. A knapsack of ordinary shape but equipped with yokes for the shoulders.

Clark Knapsack (Patent No. 37,936). Patented March 17, 1863 by Augustus N. Clark of Boston, Mass. To the lower side of the knapsack a strap was buckled, which passed up the front side and then split into two sections, passed to the upper edge, where they ran over guides, and from them over the shoulders, and across the breast.

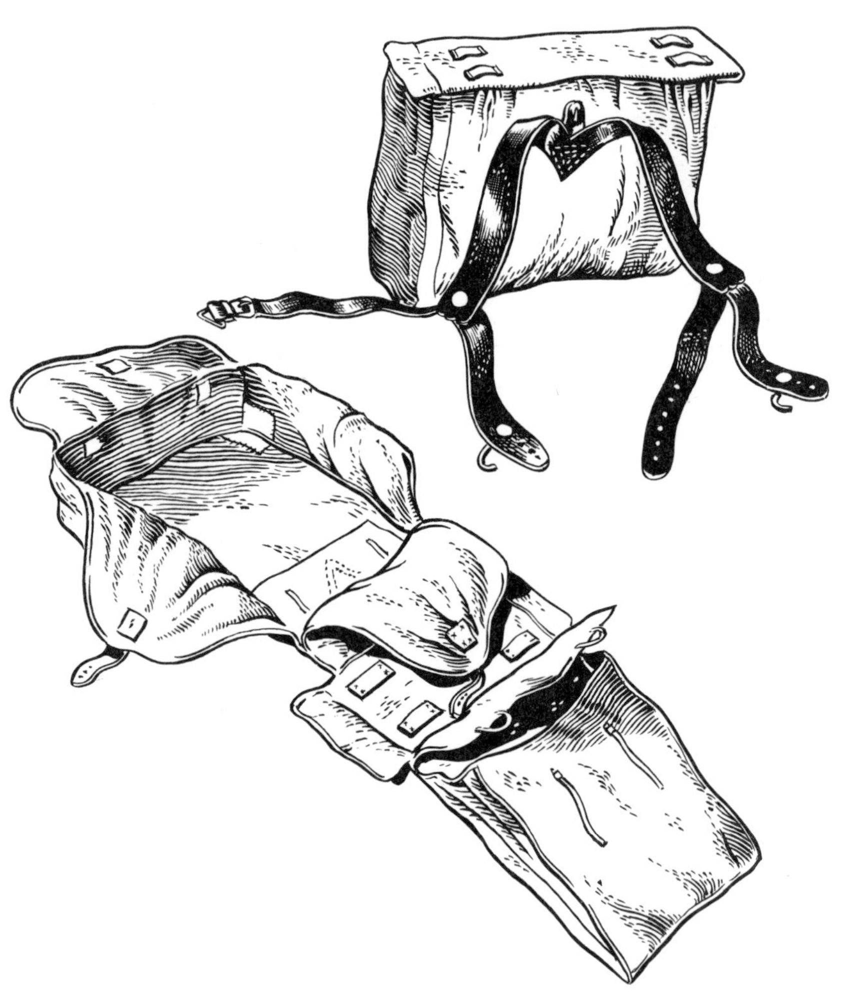

Knapsack. (James A. Shutt)

Types of Federal Knapsacks. Although the general design of knapsacks tended to be similar there is almost literally no end of variations. The more common variations are given below.

Bondy Knapsack (Patent No. 34,560). Patented March 4, 1862, by Joseph Bondy of New York, N.Y. The device was designed to be attached to knapsacks made with stretchers instead of frames, the object being to draw the knapsack close to the shoulders and in proper position on the back.

Griffiths Knapsack (Patent No. 23,979). Patented May 10, 1859 by William Griffiths of Philadelphia, Pa. Knapsack with the inner frame capable of being removed, folded into a compact form, permitting the knapsack to be rolled up into a cylinder.

Joubert Knapsack (Patent No. 39,150). Patented July 7, 1863 by Louis Joubert of Paris, France. This knapsack combined all the parts necessary to make a litter, shelter half, while keeping the size and weight of the knapsack equivalent to issue knapsacks.

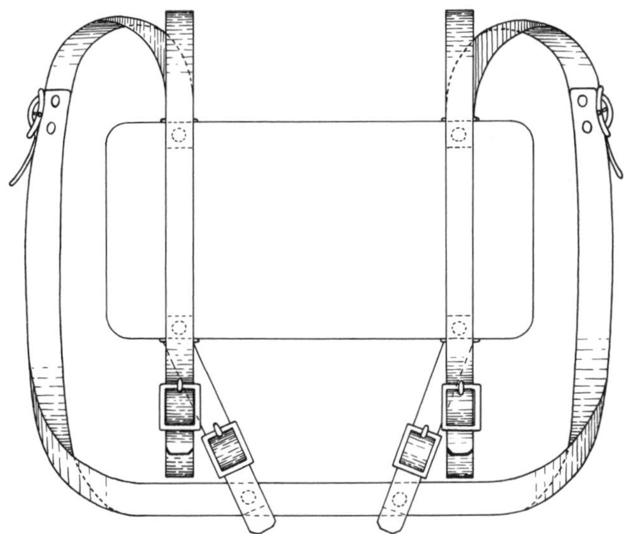

Drake's coat sling. (National Archives)

Miles Knapsack (Patent No. 34,260). Patented January 28, 1862 by Thomas Miles of Philadelphia, Pa. This device was designed to economize cost and weight, simplify the means of holding the knapsack upon the back, and dispense with all breast straps.

Rider's Tent-Knapsack. Consisted of a piece of gutta-percha 5¼ feet long, and 3¾ feet wide, with double edges on one side, and brass studs and button-holes along the edges, and straps and buckles on the fourth side. The whole outfit weighed 3 pounds. It had 2 sticks, each 3¾ feet long and 1¼ inches in diameter, and a small cord. When used as a knapsack, the clothing was packed in a cotton bag, and the gutta-percha folded around it, lapping at the ends.

When used as a shelter, the sheet, composed of 4 knapsacks, was 10½ feet long and 7⅓ feet wide and when pitched on a rope 4⅓ feet above the ground, covered a horizontal space 6½ feet wide and 7⅓ feet long, and would accommodate 5 men comfortably and could be made to shelter 7. The sheet could also be used on the ground in lieu of the rubber blanket.

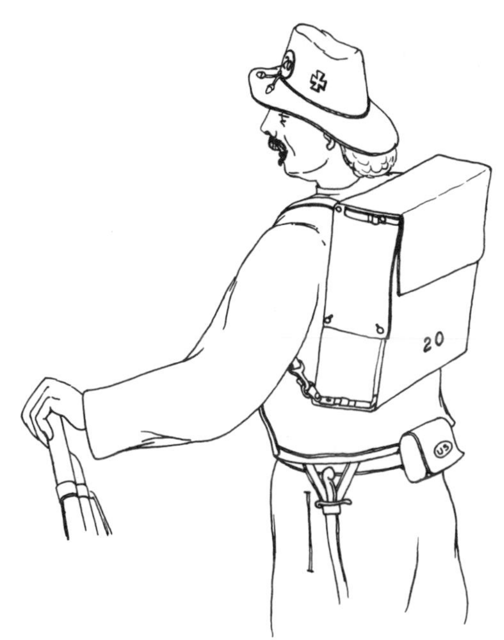

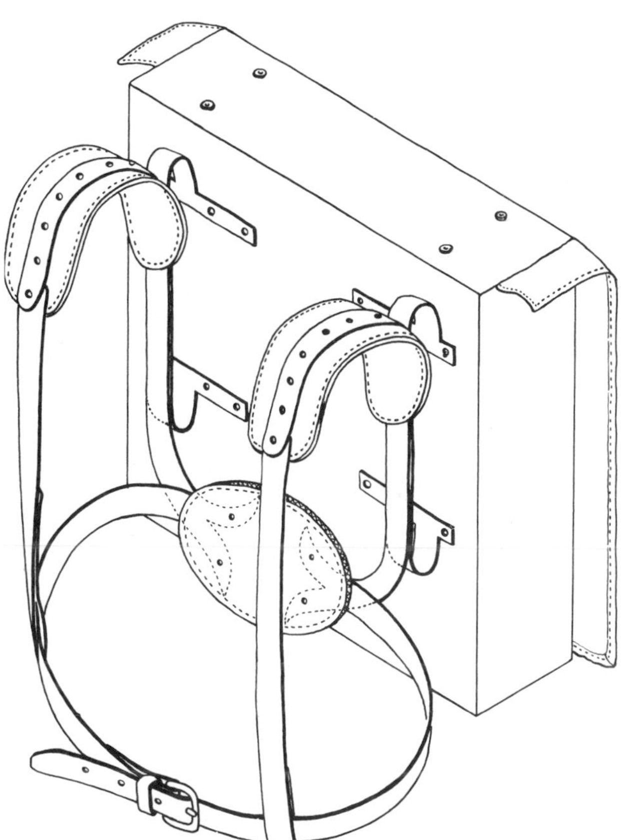

Sweeney and Hooton's knapsack. Patent Feb. 4, 1862. (National Archives)

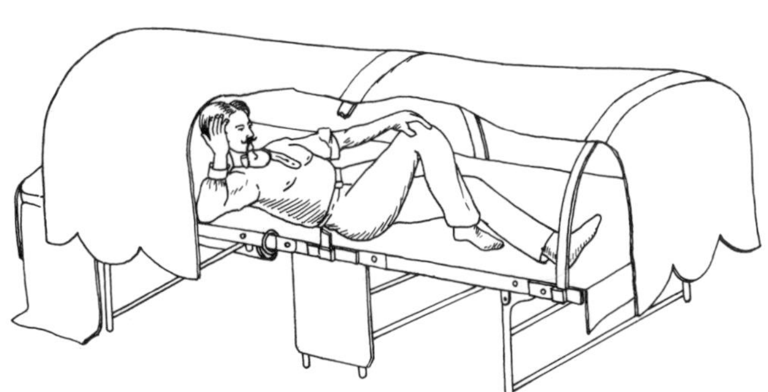

Weber's knapsack. Patent Jan. 31, 1865. (National Archives)

Rush Knapsack (Patent No. 34,778). Patented March 25, 1862 by John Rush of Philadelphia, Pa. The frame of the knapsack was made of two parts hinged together. At the thick end of one part were pivoted two arms, which, when extended, rested upon the edge of the knapsack, and served to hold the canvas for forming a bed.

Short Knapsack (Patent No. 34,272). Patented January 28, 1862 by Joseph Short of Boston, Mass. The uniqueness of this knapsack was the arrangement of the straps, permitting the top of the knapsack to fall away from contact with the shoulders and spine of the wearer, allowing ventilation of the back and shoulders.

On December 16, 1862, Short was granted Patent No. 37,203. This was an improvement of the knapsack for which a patent was granted to Short January 28, 1862. It consisted of a strap arrangement connected with a neck band or yoke and "steady pins" at the bottom of the knapsack to prevent it swaying sideways while the soldier walked rapidly or ran. In Short's patent knapsack the wooden strips were curved, thin and light, and not fastened together, but easily adjusted. Short knapsacks were supplied to some regiments.

Southward Knapsack (Patent No. 38,701). Patented May 26, 1863 by E. F. Southward of Boston, Mass. The purpose of this invention was to construct the knapsack so that, without increasing its bulk or weight, it could be adapted as a litter, bed, hammock, or shelter tent.

Sues Knapsack (Patent No. 42,805). Patented May 17, 1864 by A. William Sues of New York, N.Y. This invention involved the use of a pair of suspending straps which passed over the shoulder, in connection with shorter straps attached to the top of the knapsack, and to the ends of the knapsack for varying the position of the knapsack.

Sweeney and Hooton Knapsack (Patent No. 34,336). Patented February 4, 1862 by C. E. Sweeney and W. H. Hooton of Charlestown, Mass. This device was designed to prevent the knapsack coming in immediate contact with the back, "thus avoiding heat and consequent fatigue."

Weber, Wharton, and Snyder Knapsack (Patent No. 46,195). Patented January 31, 1865 by Jacob Weber, New York, N. Y.; Wm. Wharton, Jr., Philadelphia, Pa.; and Ira B. Snyder, New York, N.Y. This invention consists of a knapsack which was capable of being changed into a couch merely by opening it, being a light metallic frame covered with waterproof material.

Wood's Knapsack (Patent No. 42,895). Patented May 24, 1864 by Oliver Evans Woods, Philadephia, Pa. This invention consisted of the arrangement of a system of straps with rings and hooks which could be attached to the knapsack for the purpose of carrying the gun, and counterbalancing the bearings of the knapsack and gun when attached. On November 8, 1864, Woods was granted Patent No. 44,993 as follows: A frame knapsack so constructed that the leather of the knapsack proper projected beyond the frame in such a way that the frame did not come in contact with the soldier's body. Also, the haversack was suspended from the knapsack by means of hooked straps.

Sues knapsack. Patent May 17, 1864. (National Archives)

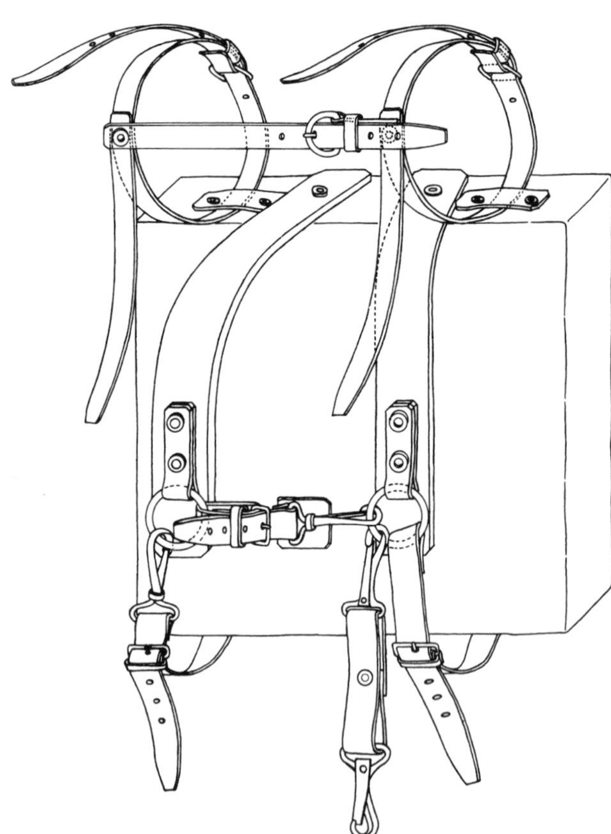

Wood's knapsack. Patent May 24, 1864. (National Archives)

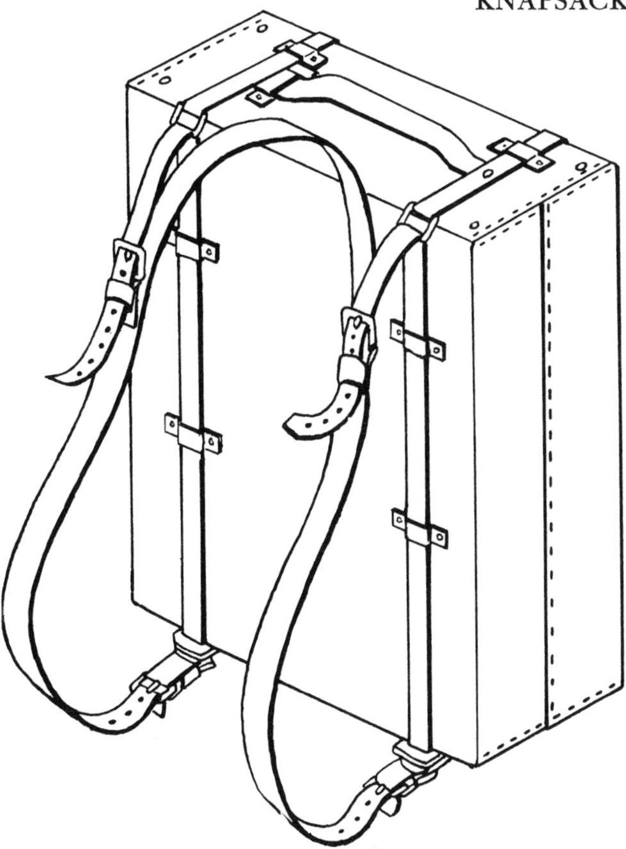
Short's improved knapsack. (National Archives)

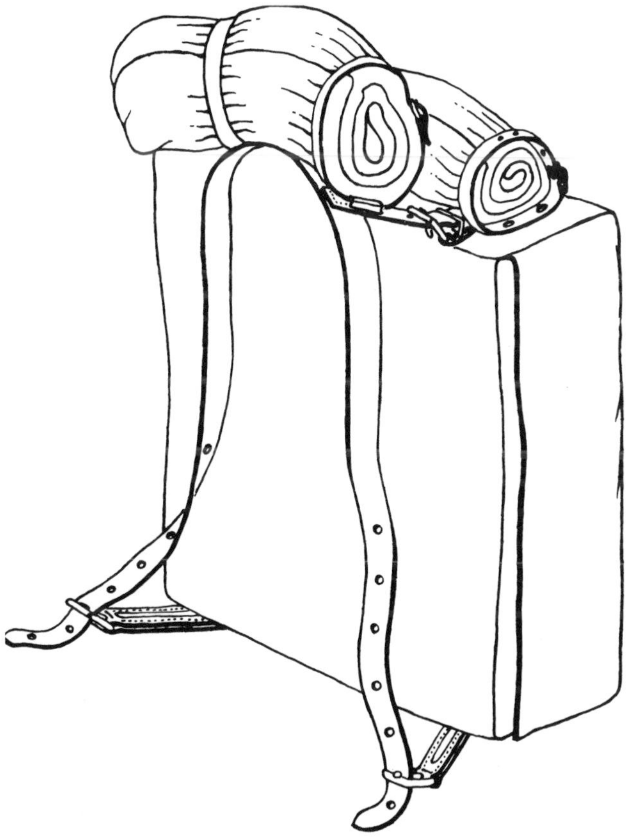
Short's knapsack. (National Archives)

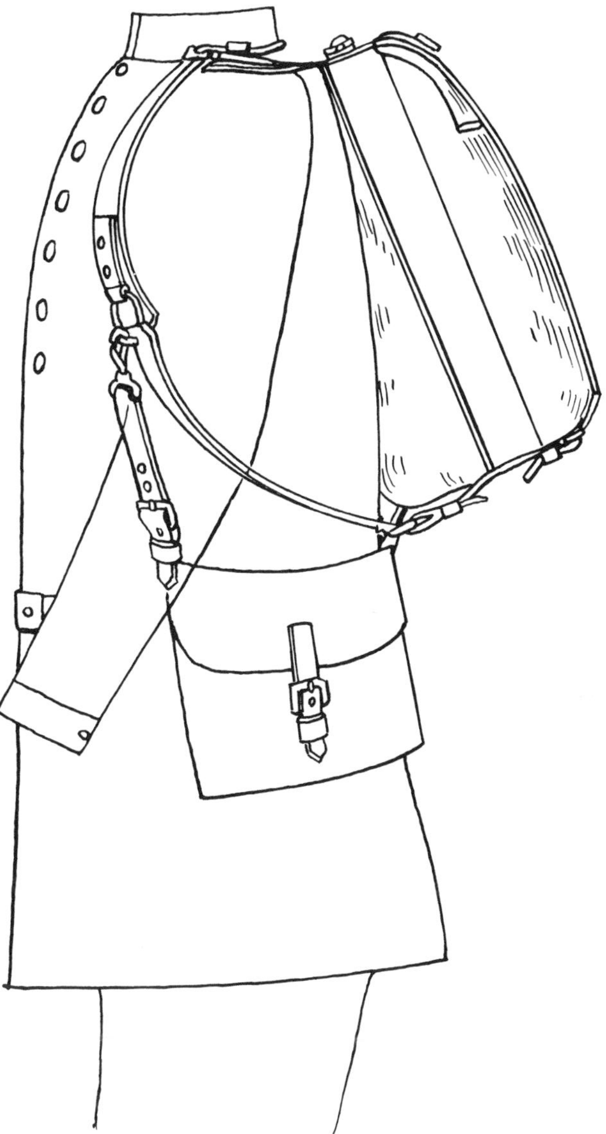
Woods' knapsack. (National Archives)

CONFEDERATE KNAPSACKS. Many Confederate soldiers used homemade cloth satchels in lieu of the military knapsack. However, Confederates used knapsacks only to a limited extent after 1862. Southern soldiers sent home their daguerreotypes and other nonessentials, and wrapped all their real necessities into a blanket, tied the ends together, covered it with a Yankee "rubber blanket" and slung it over the left shoulder, from whence it crossed over to the right hip.

KNAPSACK, HOSPITAL. See MEDICAL EQUIPMENT.

KNIVES

Bowie Knives. Early in the war many volunteers on both sides were presented with bowie knives of various patterns and lengths. They were more popular with Southern troops than with Northern, but even the

Federals used them. On one occasion the local pastor made a presentation speech in donating these bowie knives to a group of Federal volunteers. To emphasize his remarks the doctor of divinity drew one of the knives from its sheath and held it up before the "tearful and shuddering audience," exhorting the men to "Strike 'til the last armed foe expires." Although one of the volunteers made an impassioned speech in reply, and assured the donors that those blades would never be dishonored, the knives were never used "except to saw slices of bacon, chop off chickens' heads, or cut sticks to hold the coffee pots over the fire."

Shown in the illustration is a Yankee knife picked up on the battlefield of South Mountain a few days after the battle. Bone handle, leather scabbard tipped with metal. Total length in scabbard—11 inches. Length of handle—4 inches. Blade is marked with etchings and "The Land of the Free—Home of the Brave" and maker's name: "Manson, Sheffield."

The town of Ashby, Massachusetts presented every one of its residents with a bowie knife when he enlisted. Relatives and friends gave soldiers these knives on leaving for the war. But veterans recalled that the knives were soon abandoned, especially by Federal soldiers, who found that their own issue equipment was sufficient. However, Confederate soldiers were not so well armed, and, therefore, the bowie knife remained popular with them.

Northern soldiers generally carried English-made knives while Confederates relied more on homemade products. Mounted men particularly favored pocket knives with stone hooks to help care for their horses' hooves on the march; and corkscrews were always useful to a foraging soldier.

The bowie knife was standard equipment with many Confederate soldiers who termed all sheath knives "bowies" no matter their size. In official parlance, bowie knives were called "side knives." Bowie knives were made in almost limitless sizes and shapes. Some states like Georgia purchased large numbers of the knives from over a hundred different makers. These knives had 18-inch blades, weighing about 3 pounds each. Very few bowie knives were marked. (See CONFEDERATE CONTRACTORS, in Appendix)

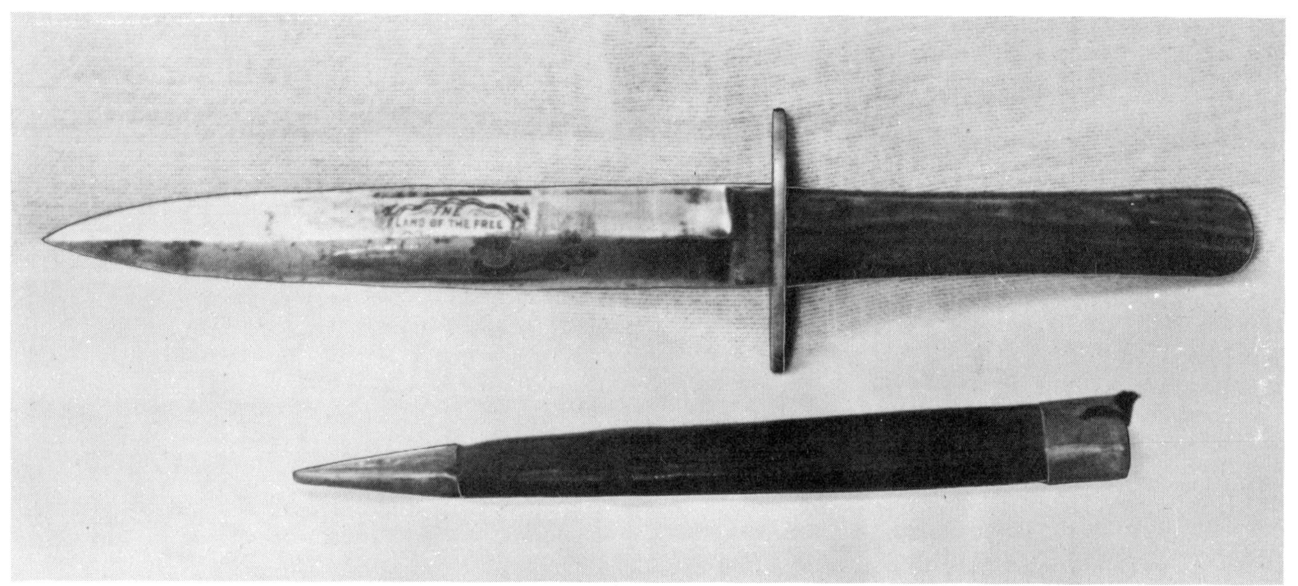

Yankee bowie knife from the Battle of South Mountain.

Mess Knives, Forks, Spoons. Since the individual states furnished their men with knives, forks and spoons made under contract, and these contracts varied widely from state to state, the net result was a wide diversity in the quality and dimensions of the items issued to the volunteers. The result is a complete lack of uniformity. Among the knives, forks, and spoons whose use in the war is completely authenticated, the following types and dimensions have appeared:

Knives. Type A—length 8¾ inches. Marked on blade "U.S.A." all metal. Type B—length 8¾ to 9½ inches. Wooden handles. No markings. Type C—length 8¾ to

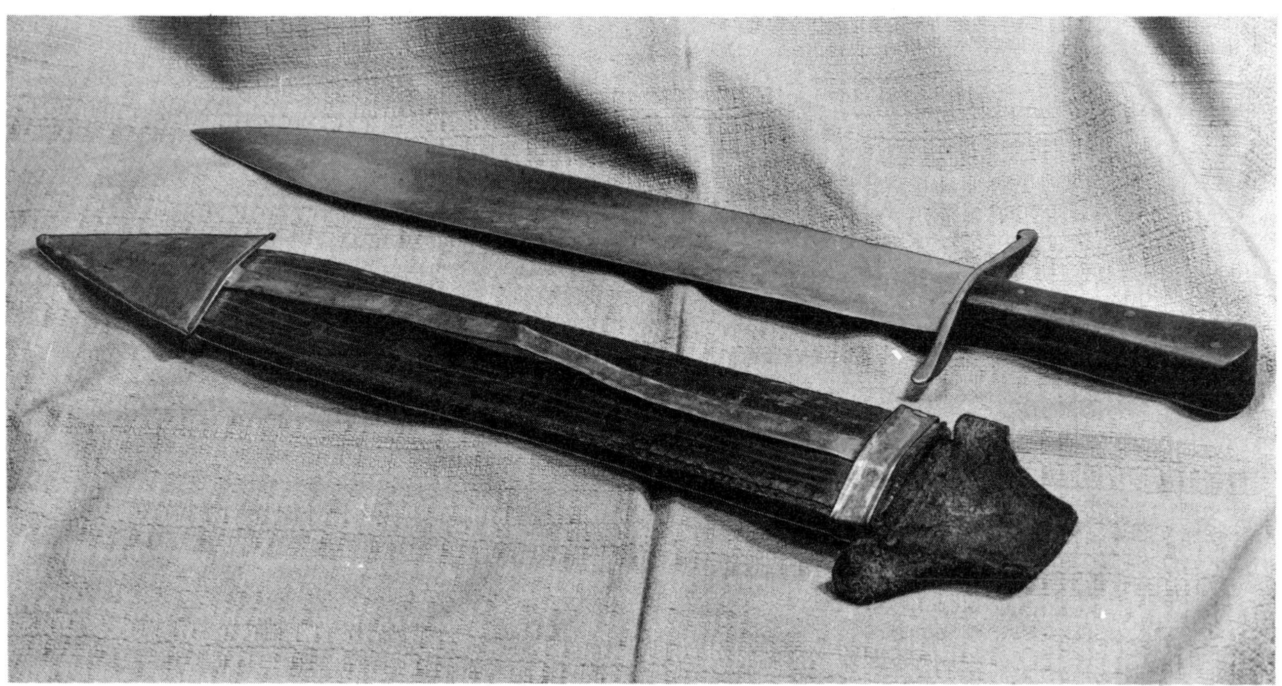

Confederate bowie knife found, bloodstained, in house in Murfreesboro after Battle of Stone's River. Presented to West Point Museum by Maj Gen. George H. Thomas. (West Point Museum collections)

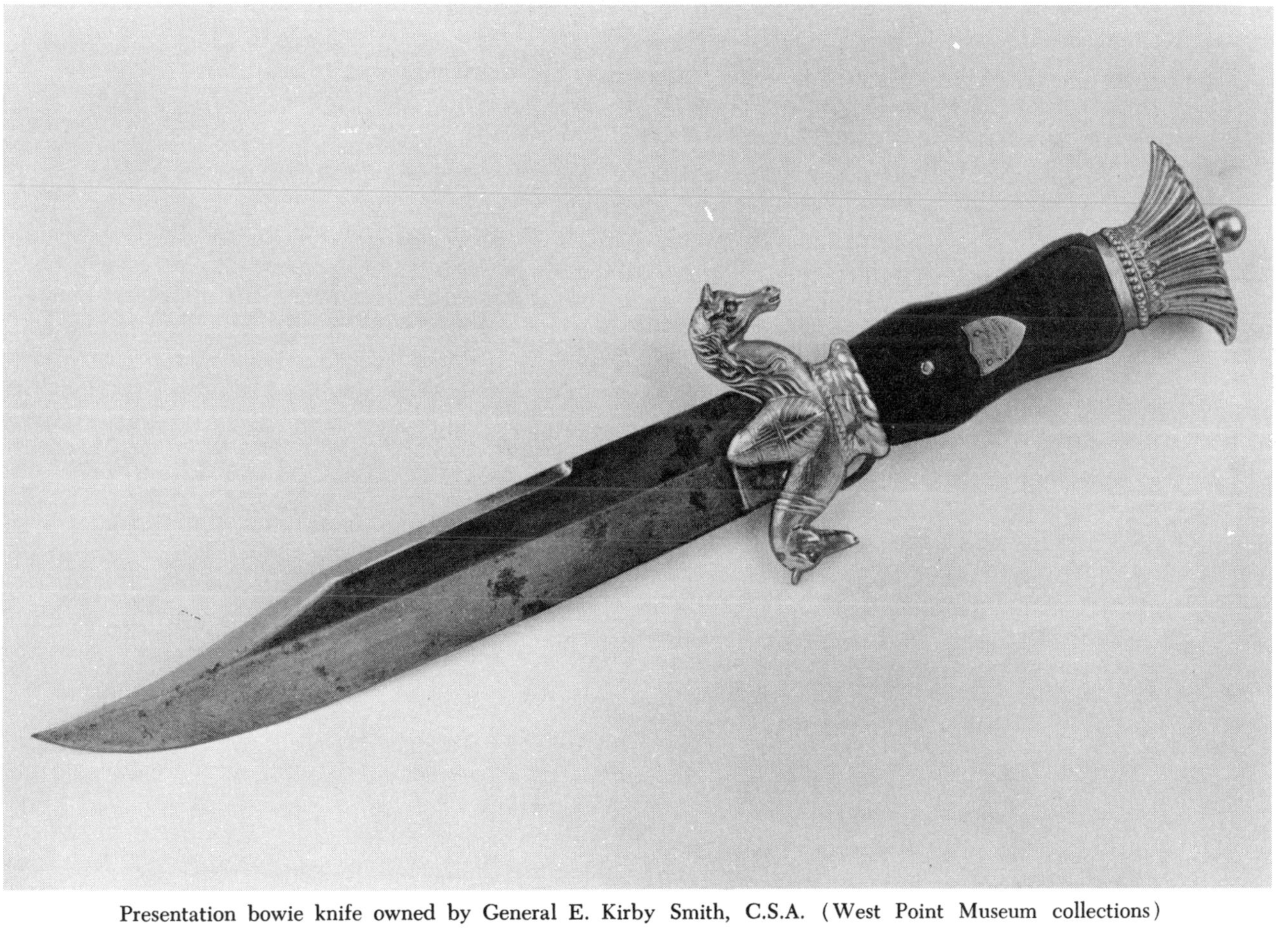

Presentation bowie knife owned by General E. Kirby Smith, C.S.A. (West Point Museum collections)

Knives, forks, and a spoon used during the war. The knife on the extreme left is a U.S. Navy knife. The spoon was used by a prisoner at Libby Prison.

9½ inches. Bone handles. No markings.

Forks. Type A—a three-tined fork, length 7⅝ inches, all metal. Type B—a three-tined fork, length 6 inches. Wooden handles, held by two rivets. This fork was used by a Michigan soldier. Type C—a four-tined fork, much wider than types A and B. No markings. Length 7½ inches. Type D—a two-tined fork, length 6⅝ to 7 inches. Wooden handles. No markings.

Spoons. A pewter spoon used at Libby Prison is only 5¾ inches long. However most of the spoons recovered from battlefields and campsites approximate 8 inches in length, are wide bowled and made of tin.

Three specimen mess knives, forks, and spoons are:

Mess Knife. A knife carried by Daniel Heyden, Co. "E", 149th New York Infantry has an overall length of 9½ inches. The wood handle is fastened to the 6-inch blade with three rivets. Blade is marked "Sanderson" and "Sheffield." (Ferris collection)

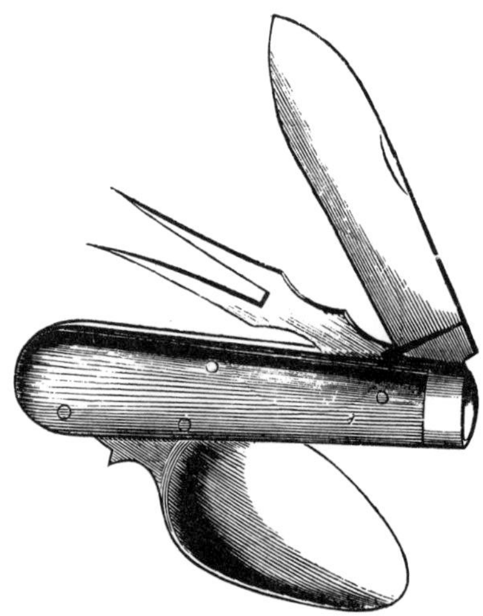

Type of knife-fork-spoon combination sold by commercial firms to Federal soldiers. (Norm Flayderman)

Fork. The Ferris collection has a 3-tine fork, 6⅝ inches long, with a wood handle carried by Daniel Heyden, Co "E", 149th New York Infantry.

Spoon. The Ferris collection has a heavy tin spoon carried by Daniel Heyden, Co. "E", 149th New York Infantry. This spoon is 8¼ inches long and 1¾ inches wide at the widest part of the bowl.

NAVY KNIVES.

Jack Knife. Most sailors carried clasp knives for cutting and splicing ropes and other odd jobs requiring a cutting blade. Whittling or carving was one of a sailor's principal amusements during long months at sea. And if a man became tangled in a running line, a good knife often meant the difference between life and death. In the Navy these clasp knives were issued to seamen during the Civil War.

Mess Knives. One specimen is silver plated, length 8⅝ inches. Floral designs on handle, and also the letters "USN" and an anchor. This knife was probably for the officers' mess.

PATENTED COMBINATIONS. Among the many devices to catch the money of the soldiers a few were really valuable. One of these was an ingenious combination of knife, fork, and spoon which when not in use, could be folded up into small compass and carried in the haversack or pocket. Many soldiers bought them despite the fact that the government supplied eating utensils. One soldier bought a knife-fork-spoon combination even though his mother had fitted him out with cutlery. This turned out to be the best of all his investments, doing him good service long after the pretty knife and fork his mother gave him had gone the way of all things in the Army.

Cables Knife-Fork-Spoon Combination (Patent No. 34,712). Patented March 18, 1862 by J. H. Cables of the American Knife Company, Plymouth Hollow, Conn. The knife and fork when joined together were held by headed pins on the inner scale of the fork handle, which fit into keyhole-shaped slots in the inner scale of the knife handle.

Hardie and Hayward Knife-Fork-Spoon Combination (Patent No. 34,098). Patented January 7, 1862 by J. W. Hardie, New York, N.Y. and A. S. Hayward, Boston, Mass. The handle of the knife, a single piece of metal, with the blade so shaped as to receive therein the fork and spoon handles was the distinguishing characteristic of this patent.

Neill Knife-Fork-Spoon Combination (Patent No. 34,069). Patented January 7, 1862 by Arthur Neill, Boston, Mass. The knife, fork, and spoon were so made that either of the first named could in conjunction with the last mentioned, form a receptacle for the knife or fork.

Thorpe Knife-Fork Combination (Patent No. 46,832). Patented March 14, 1865 by T. B. Thorpe, New York, N.Y. This is a combined pocket knife and fork, the handle being arranged in two parts, one holding the knife, the other the fork, so as to be disconnected and used separately.

Knife-Fork-Spoon Combination. Three common types are described here. The most common type always has a brass spoon and either a knife or fork as well. A few have both. Of 9 specimens of this type in the author's collection, 8 are 4½ inches long, and the other, supposedly Confederate, is 3¾ inches long. A specimen is marked "A Bland."

A second type has the knife combining with the fork-spoon unit. This is the Richards patent of July 23, 1861 and so marked.

The third type is similar to the second except that the whole unit is shorter (7½ inches as compared to 9½ inches when assembled), and the material is apparently a cheaper quality metal. This third type, moreover, has the knife, fork, and spoon as three separate pieces, rather than having the spoon and fork combined as in the second type. This third type is marked:

Group of mess gear. (Herschel C. Logan)

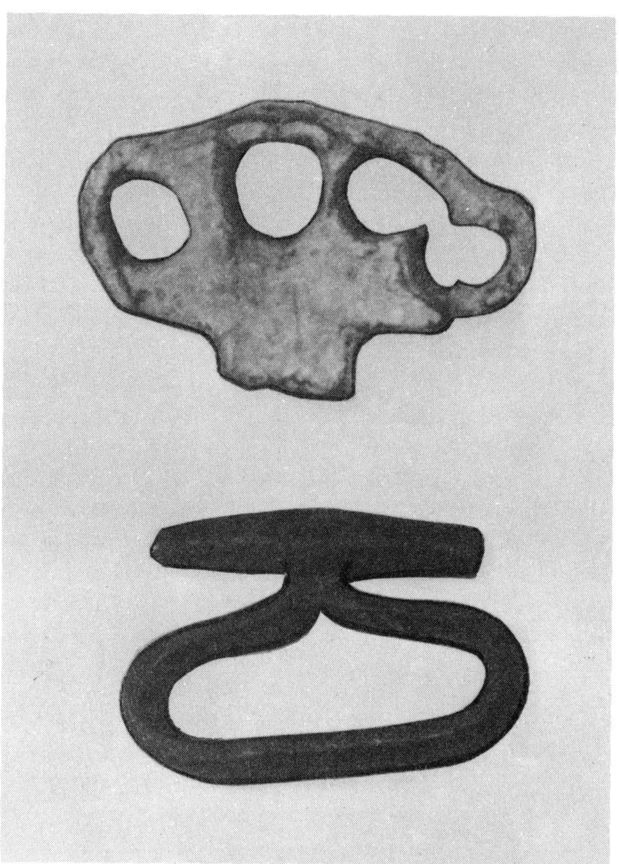

Lead and iron knuckles. At the top are lead knuckles from the battlefield of Big Black River, Mississippi. Bottom: Iron knuckles, from a Confederate soldier at Gettysburg.

"Norman Ely & Co.
Phila.
Patent Feb. 4, 186?"

KNUCKLES, lead and iron. Men occasionally took lead or iron and maybe brass, knuckles into battle with them. Shown here are two which were used in combat: lead knuckles from the battlefield of Big Black River, Mississippi, and iron knuckles, made by a blacksmith, taken off a Confederate soldier at Gettysburg.

LADLE. See ARTILLERY.

LAMP. See LIGHTING EQUIPMENT.

LANCE. Much confusion exists in the minds of the average student and even some collectors as to the use of the lance during the Civil War. Often a pike or even a guidon is mistakenly called a lance by the non-collector. However, while few lances were used, such weapons were carried by a few units.

On the Confederate side much of the reference to lances consisted of suggestions and recommendations as to the weapon's usefulness. Major General John B. Magruder and Lieutenant Colonel (later General) Richard Ewell went on record as favoring the lance as a weapon for some cavalry units. Magruder pointed out that the lance "can be made by any carpenter and ordinary blacksmith . . . and . . . [is] more efficient than the saber." As early as February 1862, the Secretary of War, Judah P. Benjamin, announced that the government would accept lancers and would provide the lance. An order for 1,000 lances was placed but the Confederate Government never implemented Benjamin's announcement so far as can be ascertained. In March 1862, Texas announced that a Colonel James P. Morgan had been commissioned to raise a regiment of lancers. Possibly this was done since lances with Confederate pennons have appeared in collections and, according to tradition, "were carried by a regiment of Texas lancers."

In Virginia a company of lancers actually existed. On January 3, 1862, Confederate artilleryman George Neese recorded in his diary that on that day "a company of our Cavalry passed us armed with lances, which consisted of a steel spear about ten inches long mounted on a wooden shaft about eight feet long."

On the Federal side, several foreign soldiers of fortune attempted to raise lancer regiments, including a Colonel Smolenska (a Pole) and Colonel Pleyel (a German). Moreover, Colonel Arthur Rankin, a Canadian, recruited eight companies for a regiment, the 1st United States Lancers. Rankin's outfit, however, and the others as well, never received lances but functioned as normal cavalry units, armed with the regulation saber, carbine, and revolver.

Nevertheless under the urging of McClellan, one regiment, the 6th Pennsylvania Cavalry, was issued lances and actually used them in combat until 1863. This regiment, known as "Rush's Lancers," were equipped with a lance about nine feet long with an eleven-inch, three-edged blade. The staff was of Norway fir, about one and one quarter inches in diameter with ferrule and counterpoise at the heel—the whole weighing four pounds, thirteen ounces. The people of Philadelphia purchased 1,000 scarlet swallow-tailed pennons for the lances. Naturally, this unique outfit attracted a great deal of attention, and was a favorite subject for both the photographer and the artist.

Although popular with spectators and officers, the men hated the clumsy weapon, in which they felt no confidence. One of Rush's lancers pointed out that while "the officers like . . . [the lance] . . . the men do not, and the officers wouldn't if they had to use them." Actually the heavily wooded terrain in which the regiment operated during much of its service was extremely unfavorable for using lances at all. The regimental historian tells us that since "our weapon . . . [was] unfitted for any service but the charge, we were held only to resist attack from the enemy." On one occasion when Rush's Lancers were attacked

View of Upper Section

View of Lower Section

Ready for use.

View of Stick Closed, forming one pair.

Brass candlesticks. (Norm Flayderman)

by a Virginia cavalry regiment, the Lancers broke in disorder, leaving many of its lances as trophies to the enemy. As a Confederate eyewitness pointed out: "Their sudden and total discomfiture furnished a striking proof of the fact that this weapon, formidable enough in the hand of one accustomed to wield it, is a downright absurdity and encumbrance to the inexperienced."

Apparently the Federals believed this also, for in 1863, the 6th Pennsylvania Cavalry turned in its lances, and fought the rest of the war with sabers and revolvers.

LANTERN. See LIGHTING EQUIPMENT.

LANYARD AND HOOK. See ARTILLERY.

LARIAT. See HORSE EQUIPMENTS.

LEGGINGS. See UNIFORMS AND CLOTHING.

LEG IRONS. See BALL AND CHAIN. Leg irons were often used with hand irons on prisoners, both military and naval, under arrest for serious infractions of regulations and military law. Although unmarked, these leg irons were apparently made by the same manufacturer as the hand irons described in this book. The steel cuffs, each locked by a small key, were joined by a 12-link chain. These leg irons could be adjusted to different ankle sizes. Total length when extended, 20¾ inches.

LIGHT BALL. (See PROJECTILES).

LIGHTING EQUIPMENT. For lighting his hut or tent the soldier was issued candles in limited quantities; at first long ones, which had to be cut for distribution, but later in the war only short candles were issued.

The Government did not issue candlesticks of any kind. However, soldiers used their bayonets; the bayonet shank was the candlestick of the rank and file who used the bayonet which, in the case of the infantry, was always available and just "filled the bill." To a limited extent potatoes were used also, but they were too valuable to come into general use. Quite often the candle was set up on a box in its own drippings.

CANDLESTICKS. Several types made by private concerns were sold by sutlers.

Alexander Candlestick (Patent No. 34,045). Patented January 7, 1862 by Charles Alexander, Washington,

U.S. tin lanterns using candles for lighting.

D. C., this invention consisted of inserting a socket in the bottom of a common drinking cup, so as to hold the candle when the cup was inverted.

Lyman Candlestick (Patent No. 41,226). Patented January 12, 1864 by Alfred E. Lyman, Williamsburg, Mass. The candleholder was for use in tents and shops. It consisted of two semi-circular parts, one of which was movable and could be adjusted at varying distances from the other by means of a set screw passing through a slot in the moveable piece. The candleholder had a bracket to serve as an extension holder.

LAMPS AND LANTERNS. When candles were not available, soldiers often improvised a "slush lamp" made by filling a sardine box with cook-house grease, and inserting a piece of rag in one corner for a wick. The "lamp" was then suspended by a piece of baling wire from the ridgepole of the hut or tent.

Various types of lanterns were used, but the most common were those using a candle and those using kerosene oil. Many of both were purchased by soldiers from non-military sources. Some were made under contract.

Lantern. Heavy tin, painted black, with an isinglass opening to show light given off by a candle. The taller lantern is 14¾ inches tall and 5 inches in diameter. The shorter lantern is 11½ inches tall and 5½ inches in diameter. It is marked "U.S." in front in white letters. Both lanterns contain their original candles.

The third lantern shown here has a carrying handle on the lantern proper. It is black painted tin, 11½ inches tall and 4½ inches in diameter.

Field Kerosene Lamp. Tin lamp with brass fittings. The base measures 4⅞ inches in diameter. Shade is missing. No markings.

Oil Lamp. Equipped with a small rope in the nozzle for a wick. Dimensions: 2½ inches tall, 1½ inches in diameter, with a 3-inch spout. Carried by a wire loop on the belt. No markings.

Oil lamp. A crudely made metal lamp from Rappahannock Station, Virginia.

LIMBER. See ARTILLERY.

LINSTOCK. See ARTILLERY.

LINK. See HORSE EQUIPMENTS.

LIQUID FIRE. See GREEK FIRE.

MACHINE CANNON AND MACHINE GUNS.

AGER COFFEE MILL. The Federals had a machine gun called the Ager or "Coffee Mill" gun, so named because it was crank-operated with a hopper feed so that it closely resembled a kitchen coffee grinder. The caliber was .58 and the gun was purposely made not to exceed a speed of 120 shots per minute, since it used only a single barrel. The heat from rapid firing was considered a serious drawback. Later the inventor added an ingenious cooling device. Maximum range was 1,000 yards. The Ager gun was a very advanced weapon for the Civil War era. But there was little military demand for a machine gun, since the Ordnance authorities condemned such weapons as requiring too much ammunition ever to be practical. However, machine guns were used in battle in a few isolated instances. Lincoln rather liked the idea of adopting the Ager gun but was not supported by his ordnance chief.

BARNES MACHINE CANNON. The U. S. Patent Office on July 8, 1856, issued to C. E. Barnes (Lowell, Massachusetts) a patent for a crank-operated machine cannon. This weapon had many original improvements, and was the forerunner of a series of crank-operated weapons. The rate of fire depended solely on the speed with which the crank was turned. Far ahead of its time, the development of this weapon would have given the United States Army a reliable machine gun at the outbreak of war in 1861. Other inventors came up with variations and improvements, including a patent in 1861 by Ezra Ripley of Troy, New York. Still another was the ingenious Williams rapid fire gun, which proved not to be practical.

Model of Williams rapid fire gun. (West Point Museum collections)

GATLING GUN. A third and very important machine gun was the famous Gatling gun, the logical outgrowth of the trends portrayed in Ager and other earlier guns. The Gatling gun is the prototype of one of the most remarkable firing mechanisms of all ordnance history and its inventor is generally credited with being the father of the machine gun. The 1862 Gatling gun was fundamentally the Ager principle, improved by the multibarrel arrangements of the

Ripley gun. As early as 1862, a model of Gatling's gun was exhibited before thousands of people in Indianapolis. Among them was Governor Morton of Indiana, who wrote to the Assistant Secretary of War telling him of the weapon's unusual performance, and suggesting that Gatling's gun be permitted officially to prove its worth. Nothing was done by the Government but Gatling continued to improve his gun, including the use of copper-cased rim-fire ammunition. The Gatling's rate of fire was 250-300 rounds per minute.

On one of his trips to Washington, Gatling met the Army Chief of Ordnance and asked that the weapon be given tests with a view of adopting it. This was not done but a few days later one of Gatling's representatives interested General B. F. Butler by means of a successful demonstration of the gun. Butler immediately purchased 12 guns, paying $12,000 for the weapons, complete with 12,000 rounds of ammunition, and personally directed their use during the siege of Petersburg. The Navy adopted the Gatling in 1862, but the Army waited until August 24, 1866.

Gatling gun. (West Point Museum)

Gatling's gun was used successfully on a small scale in the Franco-Prussian war, while the much publicized rapid-firing weapons of European origin were being proved failures in many cases. For more than 40 years thereafter, the Gatling gun was used by practically every major power and influenced world events in no small manner.

Requa Battery. The Requa Battery, built in 1861 by the Billinghurst Company, Rochester, N. Y., interested the Federal authorities. This weapon, of .58 caliber, was publicly demonstrated in front of the New York Stock Exchange in the hope of interesting investors. The gun had 25 barrels, mounted flat on a light metal platform. The sliding breech mechanism was operated by a lever, and charging was accomplished by means of cartridges held in special clips. This gun was known as the "covered bridge" gun. During the Civil War many of the important crossings over streams were in the form of a wooden bridge with roof and sides. As those covered bridges were usually long and narrow, a Requa machine gun in the hands of an alert crew could break up a quick charge by the enemy, either on horse or afoot. The 25 barrels could be adjusted to the necessary height and width of the bridges. With a crew of 3 men, the weapon could be fired at the rate of 7 volleys or 175 shots per minute. The effective range was 1,300 yards. In the field the Requa battery had its limitations. Dampness in the unprotected powder train would render it useless. It was not adaptable for offensive service, but it was effective on the defense, using restricted fields of fire. Soldiers of the 3d New Hampshire Infantry on August 25, 1863, in the firing on Fort Sumter noted that "the Requa Batteries . . . opened as if to drive the Rebels out. They fired so rapidly that their ammunition failed." According to observers these guns, served by three-man crews, would be fired seven times a minute. They were used chiefly on the flanks of the firing line and "the boys called them the 'Mosquito Batteries'."

Requa-Billinghurst machine gun. (West Point Museum collections)

MANTLET. A musket-proof shield, sometimes used for the protection of engineer troops or riflemen dur-the attack of a fortress.

Hunter Portable Shield for Rifleman (Patent No. 36,781). Patented October 28, 1862 by Thomas Hunter, New York, N. Y. This device consisted of a shot-proof shield, portable, and capable of being set up in any desirable location so as to protect one or more riflemen, and to afford a convenient rest for their rifles while taking aim. Hunter's device could be folded up for transportation and could be converted into a bedstead or table.

MANUALS

Army. Certain volumes of training literature and Army regulations were published by commercial concerns, notably D. Van Nostrand, of New York, whose advertisement in Harpers Weekly, May 4, 1861 listed the military books published and sold by this firm. Among their texts were the famous *Infantry Tactics* by Winfield Scott, 3 volumes for $2.50, and Capt. John Gibbon's *The Artillerist's Manual,* which sold for $5. Harper and Brothers, New York, published and sold an *Army Regulations.* Most Army official manuals were issued, as prescribed in General Orders No. 13, February 11, 1862, in the following quantities to each regiment, as appropriate to the arm concerned: 35 Army Regulations, 35 Tactics Manuals, 30 Manuals on Bayonet Exercise, 30 Manuals on Target Practice, and 30 Manuals on Outpost Duty. The following were also commonly used manuals:

Ordnance Manual, 1862 edition.
Army Officers' Pocket Companion (William P. Craighill)
Gilham's Manual (William Gilham)
Treatise on the Camp and March (Henry D. Grafton)
A System of Target Practice (Henry Heth)
Customs of the Service (August V. Kautz)
Advanced-Guard, Out-Post and Detachment Service of Troops (D. H. Mahan)
Manual of Bayonet Exercise (George B. McClellan)
Military Dictionary (H. L. Scott)
Field Manual of Courts-Martial (Henry Coppee)
Manual for Engineer Troops (J. C. Duane)
Treatise on Field Fortifications (D. H. Mahan)

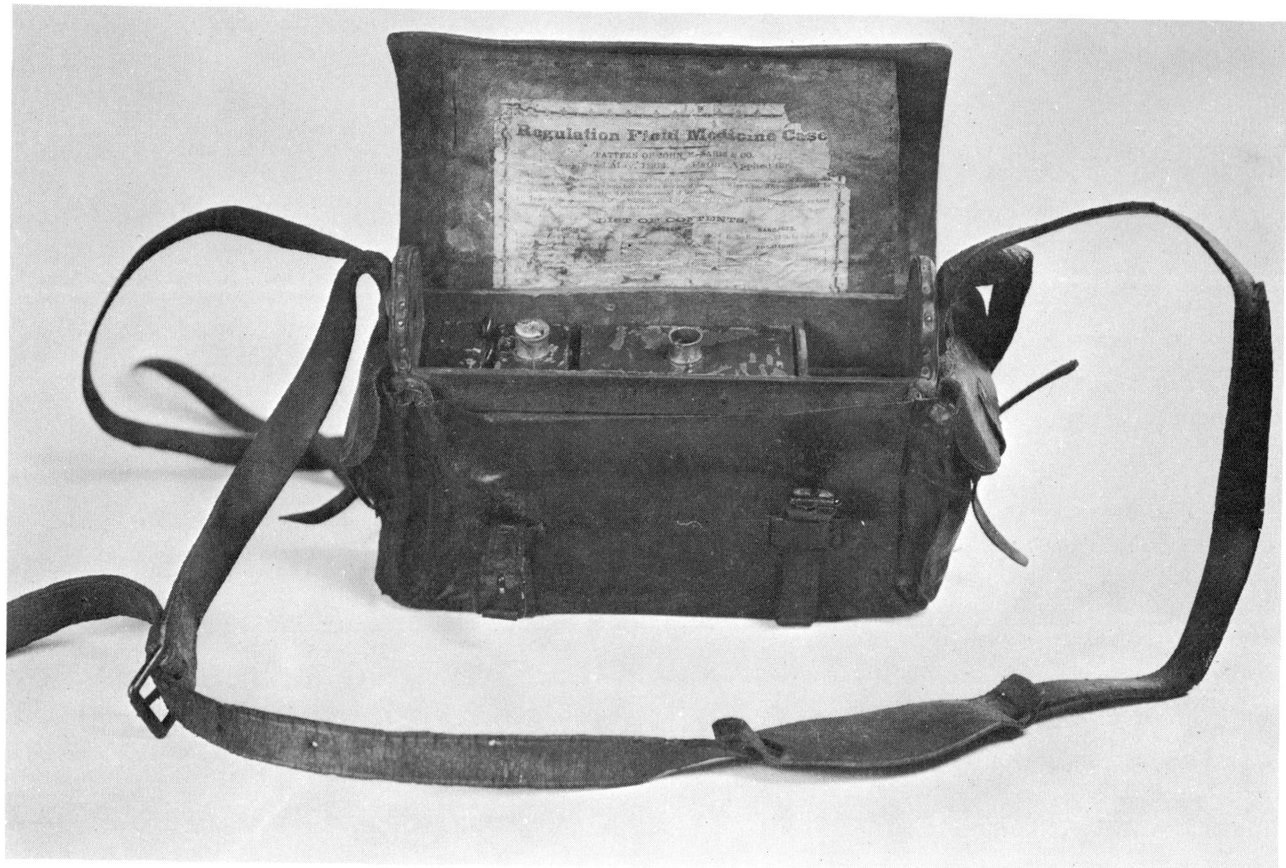

Field medical case or knapsack carried by surgeon's orderly. (Herschel C. Logan)

Camp and Outpost Duty (David Butterfield)
Infantry Tactics (Silas Casey)
Rifle and Light Infantry Tactics (W. J. Hardee)
Infantry Tactics (Winfield Scott)
Cavalry Tactics (The Poinsett or 1841 tactics)
Cavalry Tactics (Philip St. George Cooke)
Instructions for Field Artillery (Robert Anderson)
The Artillerists' Manual (John Gibbon)
Hand-Book of Artillery (Joseph Roberts)

(For a detailed list of U. S. manuals of the Civil War see Francis Lord's *They Fought for the Union.*)

CONFEDERATE. Most Confederate manuals were copies of U. S. manuals with title-pages changed.

NAVY

Seamanship (S. A. Luce)
Squadron Tactics under Steam (Foxhall A. Parker)
Manual of Naval Tactics (James H. Ward)
Gunnery Instructions (Edward Barrett)
Gunnery Catechism (J. D. Brandt)
Artillery Afloat and Ashore (William H. Parker)

MAP. See ENGINEER EQUIPMENT.

MAP CASE. See ENGINEER EQUIPMENT.

MARTINGALE. See HORSE EQUIPMENTS.

MATCHES. See also LIGHTING EQUIPMENT. A soldier of the 36th Wisconsin Infantry, quoted in the regimental history, noted that it took but five minutes for each soldier to break up a rail and get a fire started. But where 50,000 men got their fire he never could understand because "there was never a match issued by the government that I knew of." Other regiments, however, were issued matches.

Matches came in cards or singly. Some in the author's collection are of pine, 2½ inches long, with very small red tips.

MATCH BOX. Although matches were items of government issue they were issued in bulk with no means of protecting them from being ruined by the weather. Accordingly some soldiers used tin match boxes which they purchased at home or from stores near their camps. One in the author's collection is of heavy tin, oval in shape, 3¼ inches long, 2¼ inches wide. A unique match box is a small tin box in the shape of a knapsack. The box is gilt and marked on the cover: "Knapsack Matches, Licensed." On the back side is the name of the maker—the "United Machine and Supply Co. N. Y."

MATTOCK. See Intrenching Tools.

MAYNARD PRIMER. To increase the rate of fire

of percussion weapons a dentist, Doctor Maynard, had invented a primer tape some twenty years before the war. Model 1855 weapons were manufactured with the intent of using his primer. The principle was good; with each cocking of the gun a fresh primer was pushed up over the nipple of the gun in position for use. But the primers frequently failed to explode the cartridge, and percussion caps were resorted to again and used throughout the war. One of the main complaints about the Maynard primer was that dampness rendered it useless.

The container for Maynard Primers was a Japanned tin container 2¾ inches tall and 1 inch in diameter.

MEDICAL EQUIPMENT

Hospital Knapsack. In combat the regimental surgeon was accompanied by a hospital orderly who carried a limited supply of anaesthetics, styptics, stimulants, and anodynes, and material for primary dressings. This hospital knapsack was of the model of 1859. It was made of light wood, 18 inches tall, 15 inches wide, and 7½ inches deep. Later the wood knapsack was replaced by one of wickerwork, covered with canvas or enamelled cloth. Weight when filled, 18 pounds. This knapsack was in general use in the first year of the war.

"New Regulation" Hospital Knapsack. In 1862 a new type appeared with modifications of the 1859 model. The new type was 16 inches tall, 12½ inches wide, and 6 inches deep. The contents were packed in drawers, which were more accessible than in the 1859 model and less liable to become disarranged or broken. The weight when packed was nearly 20 pounds. This 1862 knapsack was too heavy and cumbersome to be carried by the surgeon himself, and when entrusted to others was apt to be lost in battle.

McEvoy Hospital Knapsack (Patent No. 34,117). Patented January 7, 1862 by John McEvoy, New York, N. Y. Made of wicker-work, with partitions and doors, covered with waterproof material. Contained medicines, lint, bandages, splints, and surgical instruments.

Field Case, Model of 1863. In the early part of 1863 Medical Inspector R. H. Coolidge, U.S.A. arranged a field case or "companion" to take the place of the knapsack. It was designed to be carried by the surgeon himself. The "companion" was a leather case, 13 inches long, 6 inches wide, and 7½ inches deep; it was supported by a strap passing over the shoulder and with a waist strap to steady it when carried.

Litters, Hand. From 1861 to 1865 the Federal Government used 52,489 hand litters of various types. The most common were: Saterlee, Halstead, Sanitary Commission, and Schell. There also proposed or used to

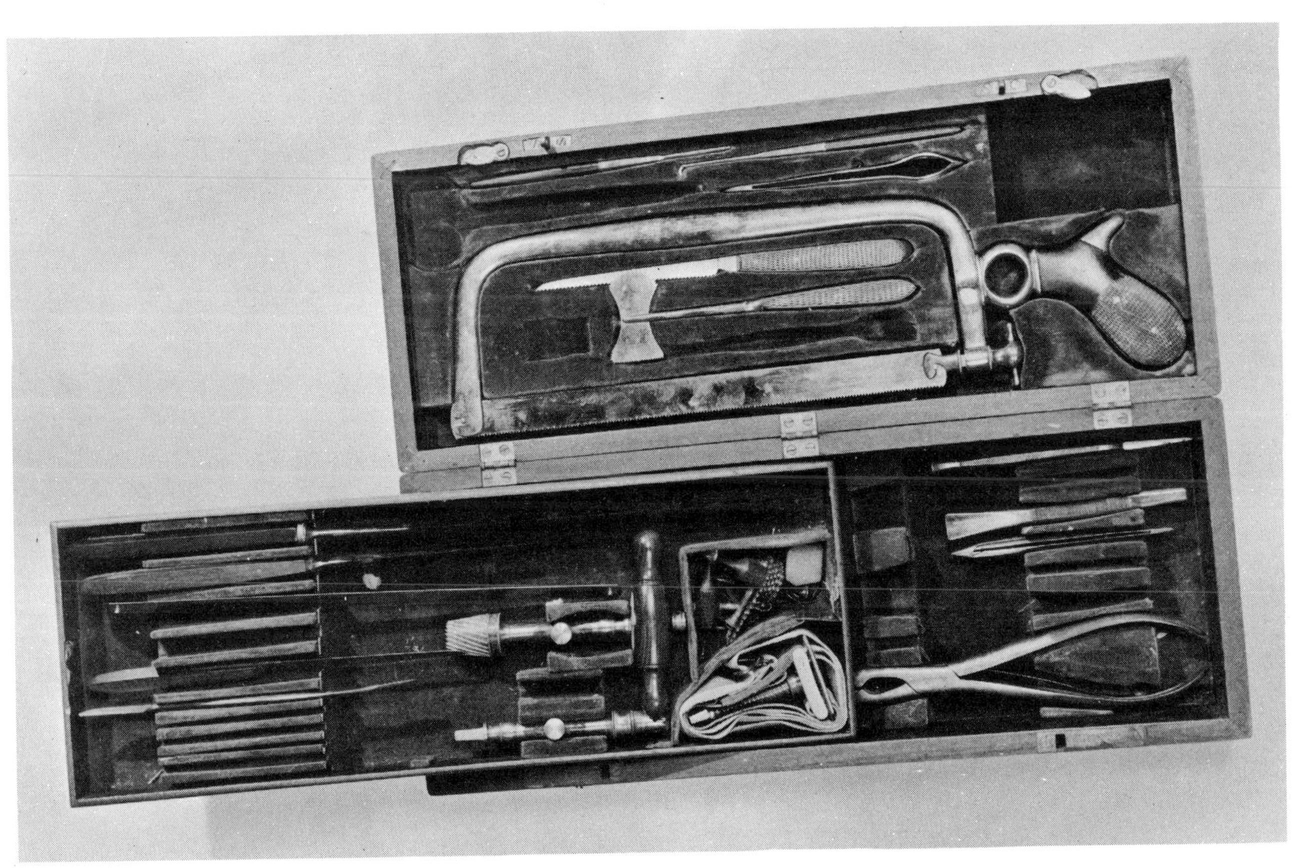

Surgeon's kit used in the Civil War. Used by Surgeon Albert L. Barnard. (Dr. John L. Margreiter, St. Louis)

Hospital steward with medicine bottles and mortar and pestle. 1862. (Smithsonian Institution)

some extent a hand-litter carriage, two-horse litter, and the cacolet. Dimensions of litters were as follows:

Type	*Dimensions*	*Weight*
Saterlee (canvas)	5 feet, 10 inches long	
	27 inches wide	24½
Halstead (canvas)	5 feet, 11 inches long	
	23½ inches wide	23¾
Confederate (duck cloth)		
Schell (canvas)	6 feet 2 inches long	

MEDICAL CANTEENS. These canteens are definitely established as having been used in the war, and the assumption is that they are medical canteens, used for carrying water to the wounded.

Large tin canteen. This was 9½ inches tall, 8½ inches in diameter, and 4¼ inches thick. Loops for large carrying strap. No markings.

Pewter canteen. A canteen 6¾ inches tall (excluding spout), 9½ inches wide, and 1⅝ inches thick. Canteen is curved to fit the body and probably originally had a cloth cover since there are no carrying loops on the canteen. Marked:

Compton & Co.
C & M
1861

Tin canteen. This was similar to the pewter canteen described above except it has two loops for a carrying strap. This unmarked canteen is 8 inches tall, 12 inches long, and 1¼ inches thick.

MEDICINES. Medicines were made by private companies and, especially late in the war, by government establishments. One of the largest of the government suppliers was the Medical Purveying Depot at Astoria, Long Island, N. Y.

MEDICINE PANNIER. The hospital medicine chest, mess chest, and bulky hospital supplies were transported in wagons of the supply train and were often inaccessible when required. As a substitute for these, the pannier was provided, containing the most necessary medicines, dressings, and appliances. These pan-

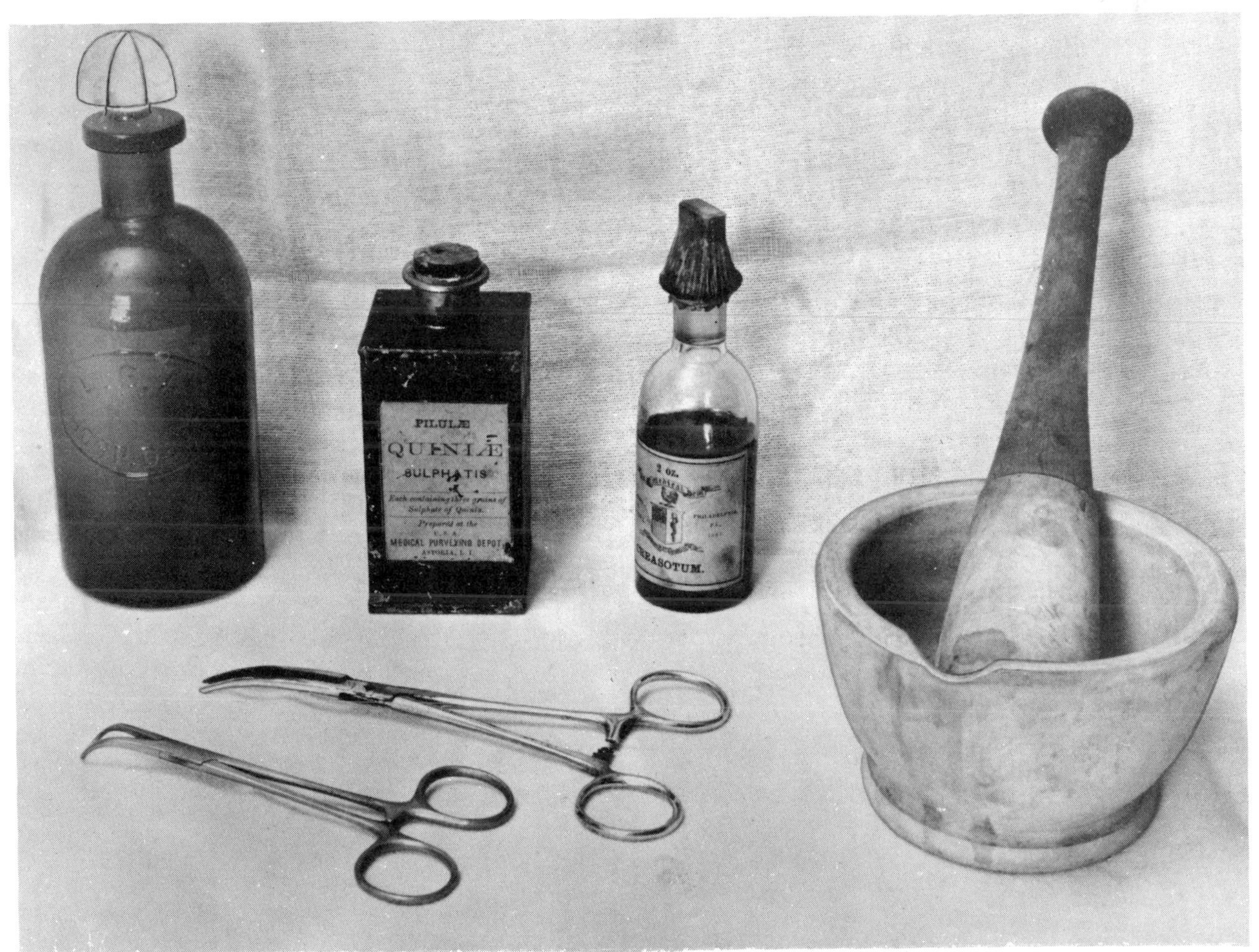

Medical supplies, Left to right: medical bottle marked "USA Hosp. Dept."; medical can marked "pilulae quiniae sulphatis"; medical bottle (with original contents) marked "Creasotum"; mortar and pestle. In the foreground are two bullet forceps.

niers were designed to be carried on the backs of pack animals, but were found to be inconveniently heavy to be carried in this manner. Accordingly, they were generally carried in one of the ambulance wagons and filled from the medicine chest as required. The wood box, bound with iron, adopted as the Army pannier was designed by Dr. Squibb of Brooklyn, N. Y. and measured 21⅛ inches long, 11⅝ inches wide, and 11⅜ inches deep. It weighed, when filled, 88 pounds. The medicines were well packed in japanned tin bottles and boxes, and room was left for an adequate supply of dressing material. The pannier had two compartments.

MEDICINE WAGON. In the early part of the war medical supplies and instruments were carried in heavy Army wagons. In March 1862, a medicine wagon was constructed by E. Hayes and Company in accordance with plans and instructions of Surgeon Jonathan Letterman, U. S. Army. In November 1862, Mr. J. Dunton designed a medicine wagon, but it was reported officially as unsatisfactory, November 3, 1862. In June 1864 the Army adopted the Autenrieth medical wagon. An improved wagon, recommended by the Medical Department and constructed at Government shops, was adopted during the last year of the war.

SURGICAL INSTRUMENTS

Pocket Case (Army). Pocket cases were of various sizes, according to the number and kind of instruments which they contained. The pocket cases were often adapted to the wishes of prominent surgeons as, for example:

Dr. Willard Parker's Pocket Case.

Dr. Wm. H. Van Buren's Pocket Case.

These small cases were 5 inches long and 2½ inches wide. They contained:

1 scalpel and sharp bistoury, spring back
1 scalpel and blunt bistoury, spring back
1 tenaculum and tenotomy knife, spring back
1 double catheter
1 pr. silver probes
1 exploring needle
1 pr. straight scissors
1 artery forceps
1 silver director with spoon
Needles, silk; and silver wire in the pocket.

Pocket Case (Navy). The surgeons of the U. S. Navy had a small case, comparable to a pocket case, containing the following instruments:

Medical canteens. Left: pewter canteen marked "Compton & Co., C & M 1861"; center: large tin canteen; right: tin medical canteen from Maine.

Mess equipment. Coffee pot used by Co. E, 53d Pa. Inf.; cup and plate used by Peter J. Keck, Co. E, 115th N.Y. Inf.; knife-fork-spoon combination from The Wilderness battlefield; camp basin.

4 scalpels
1 sharp bistoury
1 blunt-pointed bistoury
1 hernia bistoury
1 aneurism needle
1 tenaculum
1 artery forceps
1 pr. scissors
6 small needles
1 bullet forceps
1 curved trocar
1 straight trocar
1 plated syringe with fittings for hydrocele and the ear
1 hone
1 probe

General Case. This case contained a variety of instruments sufficient for any emergency in practice. A complete case included instruments for amputating, trephining, hernia, lithotomy, etc. Various general cases were in use, manufactured by instrument makers according to the plans of different surgeons. Among these were:

Dr. James R. Wood's General Operating Case.
Dr. Willard Parker Compact Case.
Field case of Dr. Frank H. Hamilton of New York.

Dr. Henry S. Hewitt, brigade surgeon, U.S. Army devised a general case which he called a "brigade," that contained, in compact and portable form, a large and useful assortment of instruments for the army surgeon.

Regimental Surgeon's Medical Outfit. The regimental surgeon in the U.S. Army was provided with a general operating case, in addition to special cases for amputation, trephining, and exsection, containing the following instruments:

1 small amputating knife
1 small catling

Coffee boiler used by Daniel Heyden, Co. E, 149th N.Y. Inf. (Richard N. Ferris)

3 bistouries
1 hernia knife
3 scalpels
1 cataract knife
1 cataract needle
1 tenaculum
1 double hook

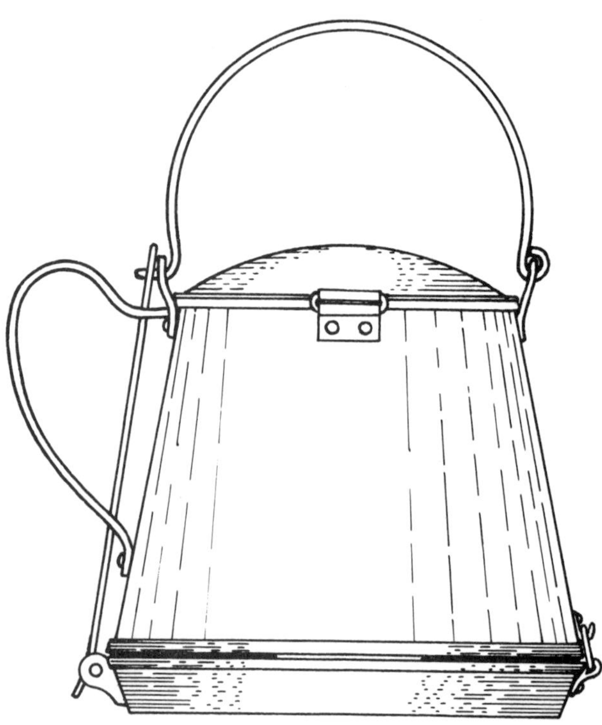

Blakeslee's mess kit. (National Archives)

6 steel bougies, silvered, double curve, Nos. 1 and 2, 3 and 4, 5 and 6, 7 and 8, 9 and 10, 11, 12
6 wax bougies Nos. 2, 4, 6, 8, 10
3 silver catheters, No. 3, 6, 9
6 gum elastic catheters, Nos. 1, 3, 5, 7, 9, 11
1 Metacarpal saw
1 trocar
1 Ball forceps
1 Gullet forceps
1 Artery forceps
1 Dressing forceps
2 Scissors, straight and curved
1 Artery Needle, with four points
12 Surgeon's Needles
1 Tourniquet
2 mahogany cases, brass-bound
1 Gutta Percha pouch

MEN'S HARNESS. See ARTILLERY.

Coffee pots.

MESS CHEST. The U. S. Army used a mess chest manufactured by T. Morris Perot and Company, 314 Vine Street, Philadelphia, Pa., whose advertisement claims that these chests were largely used by the Medical Department of the Federal Army during the war and were highly appreciated by the surgeons and other officers who used them, since these chests were the most compact available for carrying the articles necessary in a mess chest. Each chest contained the ordinary articles of a mess chest, such as camp kettles, mess pans, tea kettle, coffee and tea pot, tin cups and tumblers, frying pan, gridiron, cans for tea, coffee, sugar, and butter, plates, knives and forks, cook's knife, spoons, ladles, etc. Also included were a sheet iron stove, a tin oven, and a box lantern. The chest when opened made a good table.

MESS EQUIPMENT. A soldier's personal mess equipment consisted of his tin "dipper" or cup, tin plate, knife, fork, and spoon. However, camp mess equipment included the larger cooking utensils and other more cumbersome items which are discussed under CAMP EQUIPMENT.

In the photograph are shown a plate and cup carried by Corporal Peter Keck, Co. E 115th New York Infantry, who was wounded at Olustee, Florida, February 20, 1864.

In a regular camp, camp kettles were used, in quantity sufficient for a mess of six or eight men, but on a march and in bivouac each man was provided with a small tin cup (usually made by himself from an empty fruit can) in which he could make a quart of coffee for one or two men. This crude utensil was seen hanging to every belt or saddle on a march, and three or four times a day, if halts were made long enough, or opportunity offered, small fires were started and water set on for making coffee.

Boiler, Coffee. This item of mess equipment was ideal for the field; it was not as cumbersome as the large coffee pots but somewhat larger than the issue tin cup. Fitted with a wire carrying handle, it has a hinged cover, is 5½ inches tall and 4½ inches in diameter. Carried by Dwight Bradley, Co. "B" 37th Massachusetts Infantry (Ferris collection).

Coffee Pots

Blakeslee Coffee Pot–Frying Pan combination (Patent No. 46,210). Patented February 7, 1865 by Erastus Blakeslee, New Haven, Conn. This mess kit consisted of fastening a frying pan to the bottom of a camp coffee pot by passing the handle of the pan up through a hole made in the bottom of the coffee pot, and then securing it at the upper end for convenience of transportation.

Copper Coffee Pot. One specimen was 10¾ inches tall, diameter at bottom is 6¾ inches; diameter at top 4¼ inches. No markings. Top lid is missing. Another Copper pot had a wood carrying handle, and copper handle on rear of pot for ease in pouring. This pot is 9¾ inches tall, 9¾ inches in diameter at the bottom, and 7¼ inches at the top. Marked: "E 53." It was used by Co. E 53d Pa. Infantry at Gettysburg and elsewhere.

Cups

Baritt Cup (Patent No. 40,017). Patented September 22, 1863 by Charles L. Baritt, New York, N.Y. This invention consisted of a strainer or filterer for use inside the cup, a "new article of manufacture" according to its inventor.

Tin Cups. Several types are known:

(a) A tin cup or "dipper": Held from a pint to a quart. But this was soon replaced by a pint or quart preserve can with an improvised wire bail as a handle. This was the typical coffee-boiler of the private soldier and had the advantage of being easily replaced when lost, as canned goods were in very general use by commissioned officers and hospitals. Besides this, each man was generally supplied with a small tin cup as a drinking cup for his coffee and water.

Types of cups used in Civil War. (Robert L. Miller)

Cup used by Daniel Heyden. (Richard N. Ferris)

(b) Tin Cup: This type of cup or "dipper" was very commonly used during the war. Dimensions were 4 inches high, diameter 4¼ inches.

(c) Cup: Made of heavy tin, 2¾ inches tall and 5 inches in diameter. Carried by Daniel Heyden, Co. E 149th New York Infantry (Ferris Collection).

(d) A cup in the Shutt collection is tin, 4 inches in diameter, 4 inches high, with 3/16 inch bead rolled around top and bottom edges. The bottom is soldered on, and the handle 1⅛ inches wide tapers to ¾ inch at the bottom, rivetted to the body top where handle passes the lip of body. (Also shown are two mess plates and a knife, fork, spoon assemblage.)

Cup, Folding: Carried by Sergeant H. Dwight Grant. Co. I, 117th New York Infantry. Cup is 2⅝ inches in diameter at the widest part (the top), and consists of 4 sections which fold into each other and fit into a metal carrying can, equipped with a cover. (Ferris collection.)

Baritt Cup (Patent No. 40,017). Patented September 22, 1863 by Charles L. Baritt, New York, N.Y. This invention consisted of a strainer or filter for use inside the cup, a "new article of manufacture" according to its inventor.

Field Mess Chest, C.S. Pine chest 27¾ inches long, 13½ inches wide, and 13 inches tall. Equipped with wooden handles by which it was carried by the camp servant of Major Thomas Foster, C.S.A.

Field Mess Chest U.S. Generals often had elaborate mess outfits. In April 1864, General E. W. Hincks, U.S. Army, was using a mess chest which not only contained cooking utensils, table settings for six and camp stools, but also, when opened, formed a table with legs.

Certainly one of the most elaborate was the mess chest of Major General Benjamin F. Butler. It contained a complete set of silver plates, cups, etc. and silver cutlery from Tiffany. Dimensions 30½ inches long, 16¼ inches wide, and 18½ inches tall. The chest is wood, well-made with felt linings and iron mountings. On the lid of the chest is a brass plate with the inscription:

Benj. F. Butler
Maj. Gen'l. U.S.V.

Frying Pan. Called "creepers" by some Massachusetts troops, these were usually of thin wrought iron. They were of different sizes, and were sold by sutlers. It was a common sight on the march to see them carried aloft on a musket, to which they were tied, or tucked beneath the straps of the knapsack. But most soldiers made their own frying pans—much lighter than those sold by the sutlers. The men used their ingenuity in making these improvised frying pans. Often men by the score could be seen frying food in their tin plates. And frequently an old canteen was unsoldered, its concave sides mustered into active duty as two frying pans, each half held in the jaws of a split stick. Sometimes more enterprising men would rivet a section of barrel hoop on the canteen-half and would have a frying pan which would last for months.

A metal frying pan dug up on the battlefield of Chancellorsville is illustrated. This pan is exactly the same as others in the author's collection which were found in Virginia battlefields. Dimensions: 8¾ inches in diameter; 7½ inch handle with a hole in the end of the handle for hanging the frying pan on a nail.

Tin Plate. The Ferris collection has a heavy tin plate carried by Daniel Heyden, Co. E, 149th New York Infantry. This plate is 9 inches in diameter.

Meat Can. On November 28, 1863, the *Army and Navy Journal*, in an article on "Infantry Equipments" pointed out that "coffee and sugar rations are sometimes dealt out on the march in small cotton bags, one to each man, and are so kept clear of the meat and hardtack. Another praiseworthy device is the small

Cup, mess plates, and knife, fork, and spoon used in Civil War. (James A. Shutt)

tin box strapped to the knapsack for the same purpose."

Mess Pan. A mess pan was generally about 6 inches high and 12 inches in diameter at the top. Each mess pan held nearly 6 quarts. Mess pans were made out of tin and sheet iron. Three sizes were common. The largest was of heavy tin, painted light blue, 11½ inches in diameter, and 5¼ inches deep. The medium and smallest pans were of the same design, of light tan with metal loops for hanging up. The dimensions of the medium were: diameter—8 inches; depth—2½ inches. The smallest pan was 6½ inches in diameter and 2¼ inches deep.

Porcelain cup used by officers' mess of 5th Illinois Cavalry; folding cup used by a New York soldier.

PLATES

Farciot Canteen, Plates, Cup, and Funnel (Patent No. 46,095). Patented January 31, 1865 by Charles O. Farciot, Philadelphia, Pa. This invention consists in combining with a canteen one or two plates, leaving spaces between the canteen and plates for food, and also providing a funnel which holds the dishes in position, and is also useful for filling the canteen and as a drinking cup.

MINES AND TORPEDOES. During the Civil War these terms were practically synonymous, a torpedo being what today would be called a mine or a bomb.

LAND MINES. Booby traps and mined areas were used by the Confederates as early as their defense of Yorktown in the spring of 1862. In this defense they used booby traps which were buried in the ground or attached to objects above ground. These "torpedoes," as they were called, exploded on contact. At Yorktown, Chaplain James J. Marks of the 63d Pennsylvania Infantry saw one of these booby traps go off, thus demonstrating the "devilish ingenuity" of the constructors of these lethal instruments. A soldier of a New York regiment, while getting water at a spring, saw a pocket knife lying on the ground. Picking it up, the soldier found a cord tied to it. Without any suspicion he gave it a pull and the next instant was torn into fragments, since the cord had been fastened to the mechanism of a concealed torpedo, and the slight pull had exploded it. These torpedoes were actually shells, buried in such a way that only the capped nipple was at the surface of the ground; when stepped on they would explode. Other Federal officers and men stated they witnessed the explosion of concealed shells at Yorktown, which were shells buried in the woods, fields, and even the fortifications themselves. The shells were the ordinary 8 or 10-inch mortar or Columbiad shells, filled with powder, and buried a few inches below the surface of the ground, and so arranged with some fulminate, or with the ordinary artillery friction primer, that they exploded by being trod upon or otherwise disturbed.

General McClellan was so incensed over the use of such "infernal machines" that he had a number of Confederate prisoners go over the ground and completely remove the buried torpedoes. Of course these prisoners ran great risks, but none were injured, as they well knew where the torpedoes were hidden.

Mess pan. Dimensions, diameter, 8 inches, depth 2½ inches.

Confederate newspapers roasted McClellan, calling such handling of prisoners of war as cruel, barbarous, and completely unwarranted by the usages of war.

The originator of this use of anti-personnel mines appears to have been General G. J. Rains, C.S. Army, whose brigade was assigned rearguard duty on the march from Williamsburg toward Richmond. Hotly pressed by advancing Federals, Rains came upon a broken ammunition wagon containing some loaded shells. Four of these shells, equipped with sensitive fuze primers were planted in the Confederate rear, near some trees cut down as obstructions to the road. A body of Federal cavalry came upon these buried shells which exploded with terrific effect. As a result of this incident, Rains' immediate superior, General Longstreet, took Rains to task in an official communication, pointing out that he (Longstreet) wished this practice of "putting shells or torpedoes behind you" to cease, as he did not consider it a "proper or effective method of war." Rains was unconvinced, insisted on the legality of his actions, and continued to advocate the use of booby traps as a legitimate employment in warfare. However, the whole matter eventually got to the C.S. Secretary of War, G. W. Randolph, who sided with Longstreet. In this Federal advance on the Williamsburg road, several soldiers of the units which preceded Hooker in line of march had been blown up by what the men termed "infernal contrivances." By the time Hooker's division arrived many of the unexploded torpedoes had been located and were marked by little red flags or guarded by sentries stationed to warn off the men from the advancing units as they came up. There was but little straggling from the ranks, as safety lay in following the path where others had gone uninjured.

Apparently there was somewhat of a hiatus in the use of these contrivances until the closing months of the war. But at Fort Fisher (January 1865), the Confederates again used mine fields. They buried several large "torpedoes" in the sand over which an attacking force would have to pass. Wires had been attached to each torpedo and, in turn, connected to a "magnetic" battery inside the fort. Had not a Federal naval shell exploded and severed the connecting wire, the Federals would have lost many more men than they actually did in the assault. Whereas the mines at Yorktown had been individually located and could be detonated only by direct contact with an individual stepping on them, the minefield at Fort Fisher was connected in a detonation pattern with a master switch inside the fort.

Also in December, 1864 around the outer ditch of Fort McAllister the Confederates buried 7-inch shells just below the surface, which exploded if stepped on. Several Federals were killed or mangled by these "subterranean torpedoes." General Sherman forced a Confederate officer to make his men dig these shells up.

The Federals also used booby traps, but on a much lesser scale than their adversaries. This was natural since the South was on the defensive and therefore employed more defensive devices than the attacking Federals. Booby traps were used by Sherman's men during the Atlanta Campaign. A participant described how men of the 100th Indiana Infantry used sledge hammers, picks, etc. to wreck the rail line. They then placed in the area several shells which exploded by contact and which would prevent any enemy troops from removing the wrecked rails or other items of railroad equipment which Sherman's men had buried in the ground.

Torpedo, Coal. Under the leadership of Captain Thomas E. Courtenay of the Confederate Secret Service, there was developed a deadly device known as the "coal torpedo." This was a hollow metal casting which resembled a lump of coal and, when filled with powder, was secreted in the coal bunker of an enemy vessel. A variation of the coal torpedo used against river steamers was a piece of wood, hollowed out and filled with powder, which was put in piles of cord wood commonly used as fuel during the war. According to Courtenay his coal torpedo did much damage and demonstrated "beyond a doubt that iron-steel built steam vessels can be more easily destroyed than by cannon or conical shell." However, actual statistics on effectiveness of the coal or wood torpedo are lacking. Their use does demonstrate the ingenuity of the Confederate ordnance and secret service personnel.

Torpedo, Land. (Known also as "Sub-terra torpedo" and "Sensitive shell"). More than 60 torpedoes were planted in front of Fort Wagner, arranged with an apparatus intended to be exploded by the tread of the men forming an assaulting column.

Three types were used. The first, of which there were about 20, consisted of a loaded 24-pounder shell. In its fuze hole was firmly fixed a wooden plug with a small hole through it. Extending into the powder of the shell through this hole was a fuze enlarged at its upper end into a ball containing the explosive composition which rested on the plug. Over all, enveloping the shell, was a cylindrical box of thin tin, painted black. The bottom of this box rested on the cap. This apparatus was buried fuze hole up, the explosive composition being even with the surface of the ground. A slight pressure, as a footstep on the box, would explode the shell.

The second type consisted of 10-gallon kegs, the ends of which were extended by conical additions.

Confederate 24-pounder land torpedo. (Sydney C. Kerksis)

This peculiar shape, the same as the floating torpedoes, indicates that originally they were intended for use against Federal shipping.

The third type, of which only three were found, consisted of a large 15-inch naval shell, buried like a small shell, with a metallic explosive apparatus. (The following description and illustration are contributed by Mr. Sydney Kerksis whose research both on and off Civil War battlefields have been of inestimable value to Civil War collectors and historians.)

Recently five Confederate land torpedoes were found on a Southern battlefield. The five are all common artillery shells; they are 24- and 32-pounder spherical shells, and a 10-inch mortar shell. The

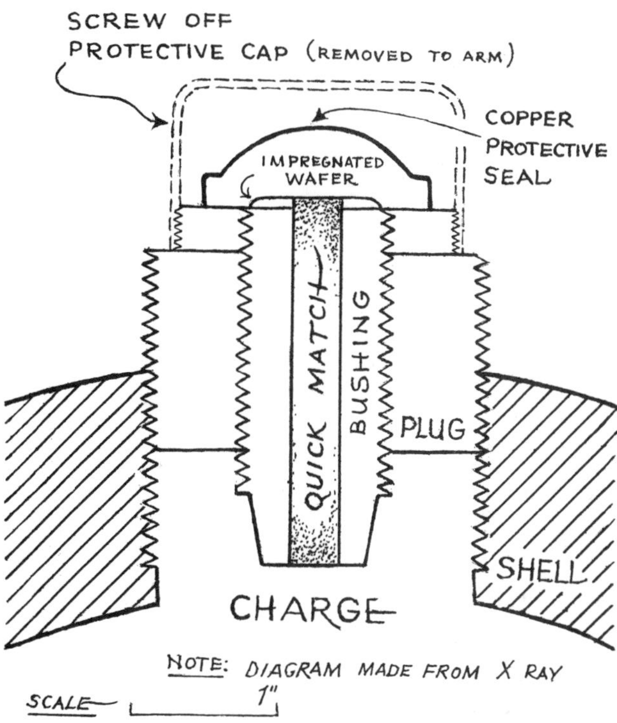

Fuze for 24-pounder torpedo. (Sydney C. Kerksis)

accompanying illustration shows one of the 24-pounders.

The fuzes, designed by Brigadier General G. J. Rains, C.S. Army, were chemical in nature and designed to be ignited by contact or pressure. The chemical composition was: Chlorate of potassium—50%; sulpheret of antimony—30%; and pulverized glass—20%. The fuze was activated by the crushing downward of the very thin metal foil protective cap by the weight of a man stepping upon it. The mechanism of the fuze device was simple—consisting of a large threaded fitting, which contained a center bushing as fitted into an altered artillery shell. All parts of the fuze and the adapter were of cupric metal, probably copper, very typical of Confederate devices of this nature.

On August 9, 1864, a time bomb placed in an ammunition ship at City Point set off an explosion which wrecked much of the surrounding wharf area, killed and wounded nearly a hundred men, and narrowly missed killing the Federal commanding general. The time bomb consisted of a clockwork type of mechanism set in a small box filled with explosives.

NAVAL TORPEDOES AND TORPEDO BOATS

TORPEDOES. As far back as the American Revolution, torpedoes were invented for use with submarines. Robert Fulton developed a system of torpedoes in the early 19th century, and the Russians used contact-exploding submarine and land mines in the Crimean

War. In the Civil War torpedoes and mines were developed even further and, in time, were recognized as of genuine military value, especially in defensive operations. Robert Fulton placed a 5-pounder gun in a water-tight box, only the muzzle, which was protected by a water-tight tompion, protruding outside. This apparatus was placed in water 3 feet down, and the gun was fired by a live coal dropped upon the cannon vent through a tin tube. The shot from the cannon travelled 40 feet and imbedded itself in the mud. In another attempt, Fulton was able to drive a shot through pine logs 11½ inches thick at a distance of 12 feet. The British in 1864 believed that these and later experiments were of great importance, "threatening a total revolution in the method of naval warfare."

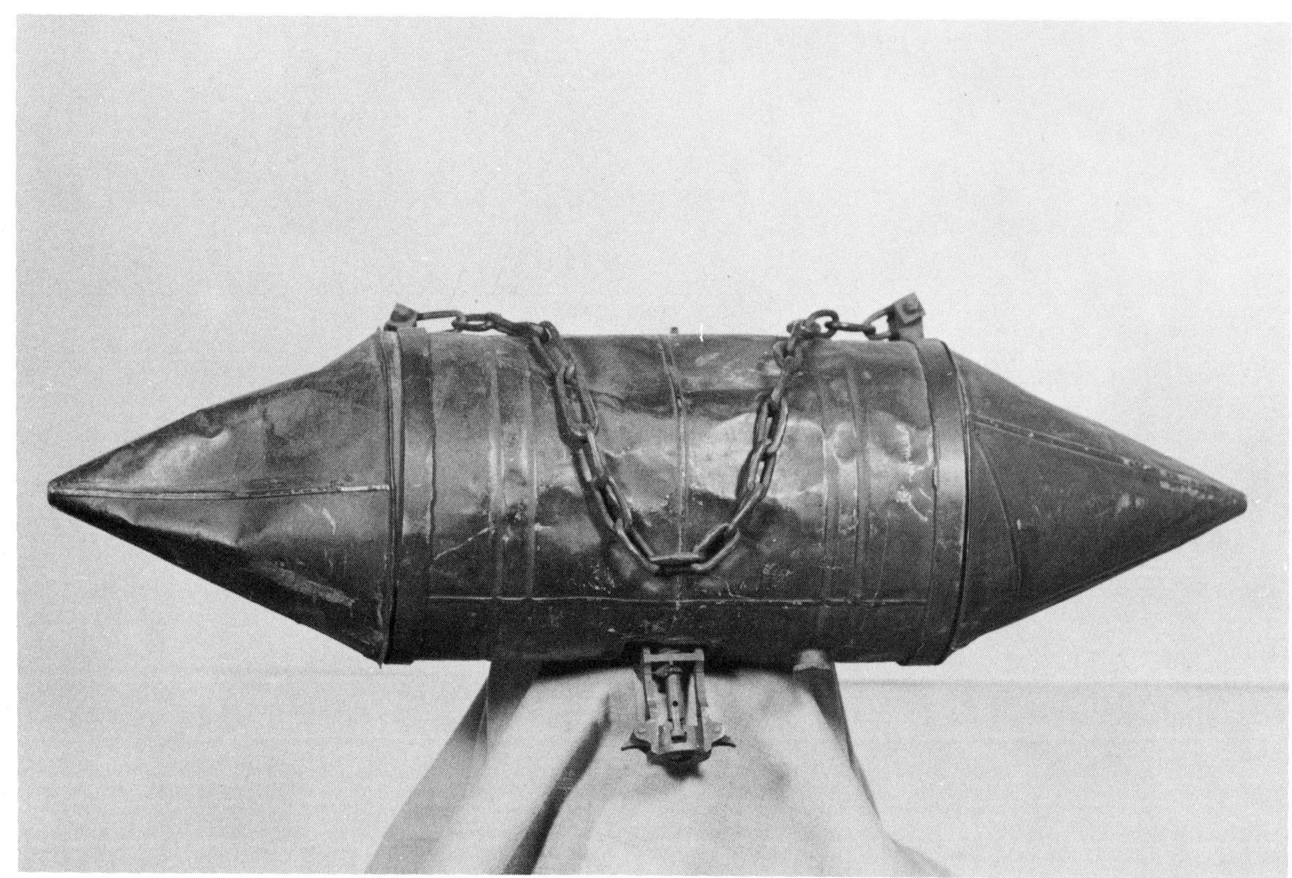

Confederate torpedo (mine). (West Point Museum collections)

The Confederacy, as the adversary which was mainly concerned with defence, established a torpedo bureau early in the war, and the Federals adopted the torpedo about the middle of 1863.

Naval torpedoes, used almost from the very beginning of the war, consisted mainly of cylinders of boiler iron filled with powder and suspended beneath floating casks or barrels. They varied from the Singer torpedo of 50-100 pounds to large iron boiler torpedoes of 2,000 pounds. The latter type was designed to be set off electrically from land. One such torpedo sank a 542-ton gunboat in the James River on May 6, 1864.

Although the Confederates definitely tended to dominate the scene so far as torpedoes were concerned the Federals had their moments as well. In October 1864, William B. Cushing, in one of the most daring attacks of Naval history, sank the powerful Confederate ironclad ram, the *Albemarle,* by means of a torpedo detonated under the hull. Cushing's launch was equipped with a 14-foot spar which was hinged to the launch's bow, and could be raised or lowered by a windlass. This spar held the torpedo, which differed from the ordinary spar torpedo as used by the Confederates. Cushing had his torpedo placed well under the hull of the *Albemarle* by lowering the spar. When in position, a line was pulled which actuated a pin and released the torpedo. The ejected torpedo then floated up, nestled against the bottom of the ship, and, when another line was pulled, the torpedo's firing mechanism was actuated, permitting a large grapeshot to fall on the cap, setting off the explosion. The *Albemarle* sank in a short time because of the gaping hole caused by Cushing's torpedo.

Confederate mine. (West Point Museum collections)

Confederate mine. (West Point Museum collections)

Projectiles and mines. (National Archives)

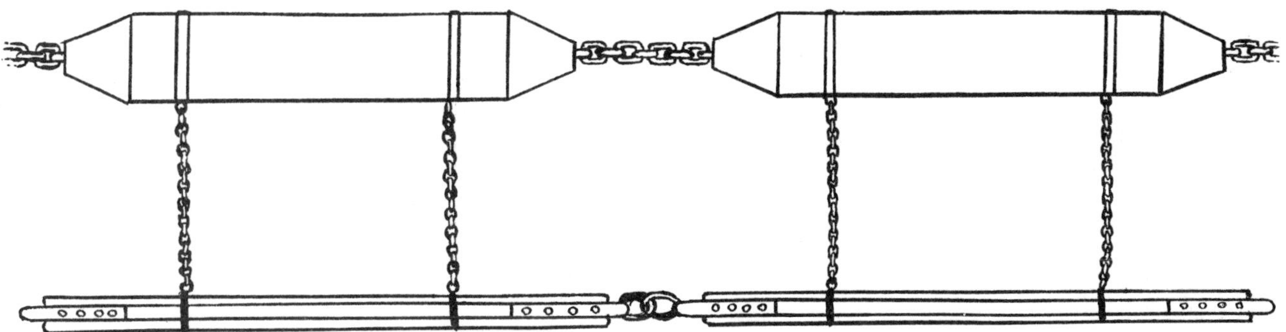

Confederate boom. (Mike McAfee)

The Federal Navy used some ironclads during the siege of Charleston. Because these ironclads were practically invulnerable to shot or shell, the Confederate leaders looked about for other means to attack them successfully. Considerable ingenuity and resourcefulness were displayed by the city's defenders in their attempts to destroy elements of the blockading squadron. Torpedoes (we call them mines today) were planted in the harbor.

Even more spectacular, however, were the attempts to sink Federal men of war by submarine attacks. It was decided to attack the Federal admiral's ship, *New Ironsides,* the "most powerful vessel in the world," in 1863. The attack was made on October 5. The next day the Federal ordnance expert Admiral Dahlgren described the attack. Much of Dahlgren's information was given by a survivor of the submarine which made the attack. The man was pulled out of the water and, although badly shaken by his experience, was still able to tell what happened. The Confederate submarine which made the attack was about 50 feet long and shaped like a cigar. It was 5-6 feet in diameter and equipped with an engine which could drive the "cigar" at a speed of 8-10 knots. At the bow was a bar ten feet long, with a torpedo at the end holding 60 pounds of powder, with four nipples to act by percussion. The submarine had a crew of four men who stood on the floor of the submarine with their heads out of the hatch, which projected part way out of the water. They left Charleston at dusk, passed the Federal blockading vessels in the dark, then turned back and attacked the *New Ironsides.*

The captain of the submarine was also picked up after the attack. Although the torpedo did some damage to the *New Ironsides,* there was insufficient power in the explosion to sink the powerful vessel. (However the next year a Confederate "submarine" did succeed in sinking the Federal vessel *Housatonic.*)

The Confederates were fairly successful with their mines. On January 15, 1865, the Federal monitor *Patapsco* was sunk by a mine in the channel off Fort Sumter. The vessel struck and exploded a large mine or group of mines about thirty feet from the bow and on the port side. The *Patapsco's* captain immediately gave the order to start the pumps, but too late. The whole forward part of the vessel was already submerged, and since there was no chance of saving his ship, the captain gave the order to man the boats. But even before this could be done, the vessel had sunk to the top of its turret. So rapidly did the *Patapsco* sink that 62 officers and men were lost. The Federal commander had known that his vessel was in dangerous waters and his ship had her "torpedo-fenders" and netting as usual around her. Moreover, three boats with drags had preceded her "searching to some depth" the water which the *Patapsco* passed

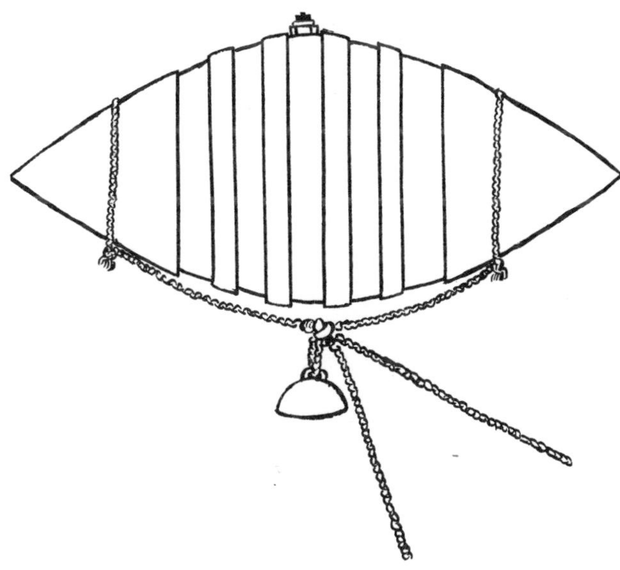

Confederate barrel mine. (Drawn by Mike McAfee)

over, while steam-tugs and several boats "were in different positions on the bow, beam and quarter."

Barrel Torpedo. This type of mine was used against shipping. In January 1865, the Confederates placed 16 barrel torpedoes between Fort Sumter and Moultrie, extending across the main ship channel. They were anchored with a single mushroom anchor to each, with sufficient length of rope to leave them 4-5 feet below the surface of the water at low tide. In addition, the Confederates employed large "boiler-iron torpedoes," and "torpedo rafts," which consisted of 4 round logs 60 feet long, with cast-iron torpedoes attached. These torpedoes held from 25-50 pounds of powder. The rafts were anchored in such a way that the torpedoes were 3 feet below the water at low tide.

Sea Mines. Captain F. D. Fee, of the Confederate Engineers, was employed in building torpedoes to be placed in Charleston harbor, because he believed their employment against the Federal naval units was the best way to combat the naval superiority possessed by the United States. The Confederates also believed that a large number of small boats suitable for torpedo service, capable of making simultaneous attacks, would be effective, especially if the element of surprise could be achieved.

Submarine Torpedo. In December 1862, Pascal Plant, who had offered the North a rocket-driven submarine the previous spring, demonstrated his rocket-driven submarine torpedo to the Secretary of the Navy. In the demonstration, two of Plant's torpedoes were fired from a scow anchored in the Potomac River. One of the torpedoes plunged into the mud and exploded; the other veered off suddenly at a 60 degree angle and sank a small schooner, the *Diana*, this being the first known instance of a self-propelled torpedo sinking a ship. A later demonstration was less spectacular but equally unsuccessful and terminated the Navy's interest in Plant's submarine torpedo.

TORPEDO BOATS.

Confederate. The Confederates used two general types, the ram and the submarine. The *David* was a type of ram. This little cigar-shaped boat was built at private expense, and was carried by rail to Charleston since she drew so much water it would have been impossible to get her over the bar, and consequently was only fit for harbor defense. The *David* was ballasted so as to float deeply in the water, and all above the water was painted the most invisible color—bluish. The torpedo was made of copper, containing about 100 pounds of rifle powder, and provided with 4 sensitive tubes of lead containing an explosive mixture. This torpedo was carried by means of a hollow iron shaft projecting about 14 feet ahead of the boat and 6-7 feet below the surface of the water. The *David* also had an armament of 4 double-barrel shotguns, 4 navy revolvers, and 4 cork life preservers.

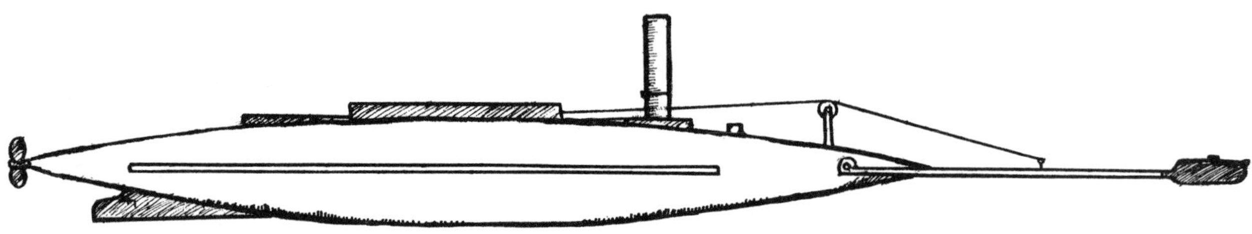

Confederate torpedo boat *David.* (Mike McAfee)

Another Confederate ram is discussed in the *Army and Navy Journal* for April 30, 1864, which in describing the Confederate attack on Plymouth, North Carolina, narrates how a Confederate ram silently ran down the river, eluded a Federal shore battery, and struck its prow into the starboard side of the Federal vessel *Southfield*, which sank in 10 minutes. The ram then proceeded to drive off the Federal gunboats and shelled the defences around Plymouth.

This ram was similar to the *Merrimac*—with a length of 150 feet, breadth of beam 40 feet, depth at hole 12 feet. Built of 16-inch timber and clad with iron plates or railroad iron, it carried 2 or 3 Whitworth 20-pounders. The vessel sat low in the water and was of slow speed, from 4 to 6 knots an hour.

The *Hunley* was a Confederate submarine built in Mobile, Ala. in 1863 and designed by Horace L. Hunley and two associates. Experimentation with this submarine took a toll of 36 lives, all volunteers. On February 17, 1864, with Lt. George E. Dixon and a crew of six, the *Hunley*, using a spear-head torpedo on the end of a spar, sank the Federal vessel *Housatonic*. The *Hunley* went down in this operation and is still resting by its victim, the *Housatonic*, in Charleston Harbor.

Federal. The *Army and Navy Journal* for September 17, 1864, describes a new torpedo boat, the invention of Chief Engineer Wood, U.S.N. The boat was a wooden vessel, 75 feet long, 20 feet beam, and with 7 feet depth of hold. It had iron plating sufficiently thick and strong to withstand shot and shell.

Sitting low in the water at all times, the vessel floated only 20 inches above the water when not in the vicinity of the enemy, and when approaching a hostile vessel only the crown of her deck was visible. The *Army and Navy Journal* gave the speed of the vessel as 12 miles per hour.

MIRROR, ARMY. Tin or pewter case—3 inches in diameter, with a small tin loop for hanging on a nail or twig in the field. It also has a tin extension to enable it to stand upright on a level surface. These mirrors are decorated with floral designs and more rarely, with patriotic symbols. Carried by Daniel Heyden, Company "E" 149th N.Y. Infantry. (Ferris collection).

MITTENS. Mittens were not an item of government issue although many soldiers bought them in stores or from sutlers. Relatives and friends at home often included hand-knit mittens in their boxes to the men at the front. Sometimes civilian patrons or officers supplied the men of a whole unit with mittens or gloves. The wealthy and patriotic General James Wadsworth donated a pair of warm woolen gloves to every man in his brigade.

MORTAR. See also CANNON and ARTILLERY. According to Scott's Military Dictionary of 1864, the following mortars were used in the U.S. service:

Type	*Weight*	*Total length in inches*
13-inch	11,500	53
10-inch (heavy)	5,775	46
10-inch (light)	1,852	28
8-inch (light)	930	22.5
Brass stone	1,500	31.55
Brass coehorn 24-pounder	164	16.32
Iron eprouvette	220	12.85

Mortars were mounted on beds. Siege mortars were placed on a platform of wood made of 6 sleepers, 18 deck planks, and 72 dowels, fastened with 12 iron eye-bolts.

MOUNTAIN ARTILLERY. The mountain howitzer weighed 220 pounds, with a whole length 37.21 inches, diameter of bore 4.62 inches. Range 500 yards at an elevation of 2 degrees 30 minutes. According to elevation the range varied from 150 to 1,000 yards. A battery of six mountain howitzers required 33 horses or mules. A mountain howitzer ammunition chest would carry about 700 musket ball cartridges for muskets, besides 8 rounds for the howitzer.

MUCKET. Nickname used by soldiers of the 83d Pennsylvania Infantry, and probably other units as well, for a small tin kettle of 3-pint capacity, used for making coffee in the field. These kettles were equipped with covers, and probably were not kettles, but large mess cups.

MUG, TABLE. See MESS EQUIPMENT.

MUSIC. See also MUSICAL INSTRUMENTS. Most regiments had particular tents or huts in which vocal or instrumental music was a feature of the evening's recreation. There was probably not a regiment that did not boast at least one violinist, one banjoist, and a bones player in its ranks—not to mention many other instruments currently popular. No matter how amateurish were the performers, they were certain to be the center of an interested audience. The usual medley of comic songs and Negro melodies comprised the greater part of the entertainment. If space permitted, a jig or clog dance was stepped out on a hardtack box or improvised platform.

Regiments had their own bands although the Federal regimental bands were mustered out in the fall of 1862, and henceforth brigade and higher units furnished the bands for Federal troops. Also, many units had fife and drum corps made up of personnel from the regiments themselves.

In the early part of the war regiments often hired civilian bands to accompany them to the front; in other units bandsmen were enlisted to serve as such. The majority of band instruments used by bands were made by private concerns. Therefore it is extremely difficult to authenticate any instrument as having been definitely used from 1861 to 1865. (See list of band-instruments dealers in Appendix.)

MUSIC, SHEET. The Civil War is characterized by a great number of patriotic and sentimental songs on both sides. A surprisingly large amount of sheet music is one of our legacies of the 1861-1865 period. In the four years of the war a few excellent songs appeared and a much larger amount of sentimental and usually dolorous songs were published. Often the music to songs of the period was published with colored covers emphasizing patriotic motifs and decorated with scenes of camp and battlefield. The list of Civil War songs is indeed a long one. Shown here is a typical example of the sheet music which was so popular with both troops at the front and their relatives and friends at home.

The example shown is typical of the sheet music produced by both sides throughout the war. Usually the song appeared in 4-6 pages with the front cover decorated in color or black and white with patriotic emblems. Size of each page, 13¼ by 10 inches. At the bottom of the cover is printed: "Entered according to Act of Congress in the year 1862; by A. C. Peters and Bro. in the Clerk's Office of the Dist. Court of the U.S. for the Southern District of Ohio." On the

The USS Resolute sweeping Confederate floating mines from the Potomac River in July 1861. (Frank Leslie's)

Patriotic sheet music, 1862.

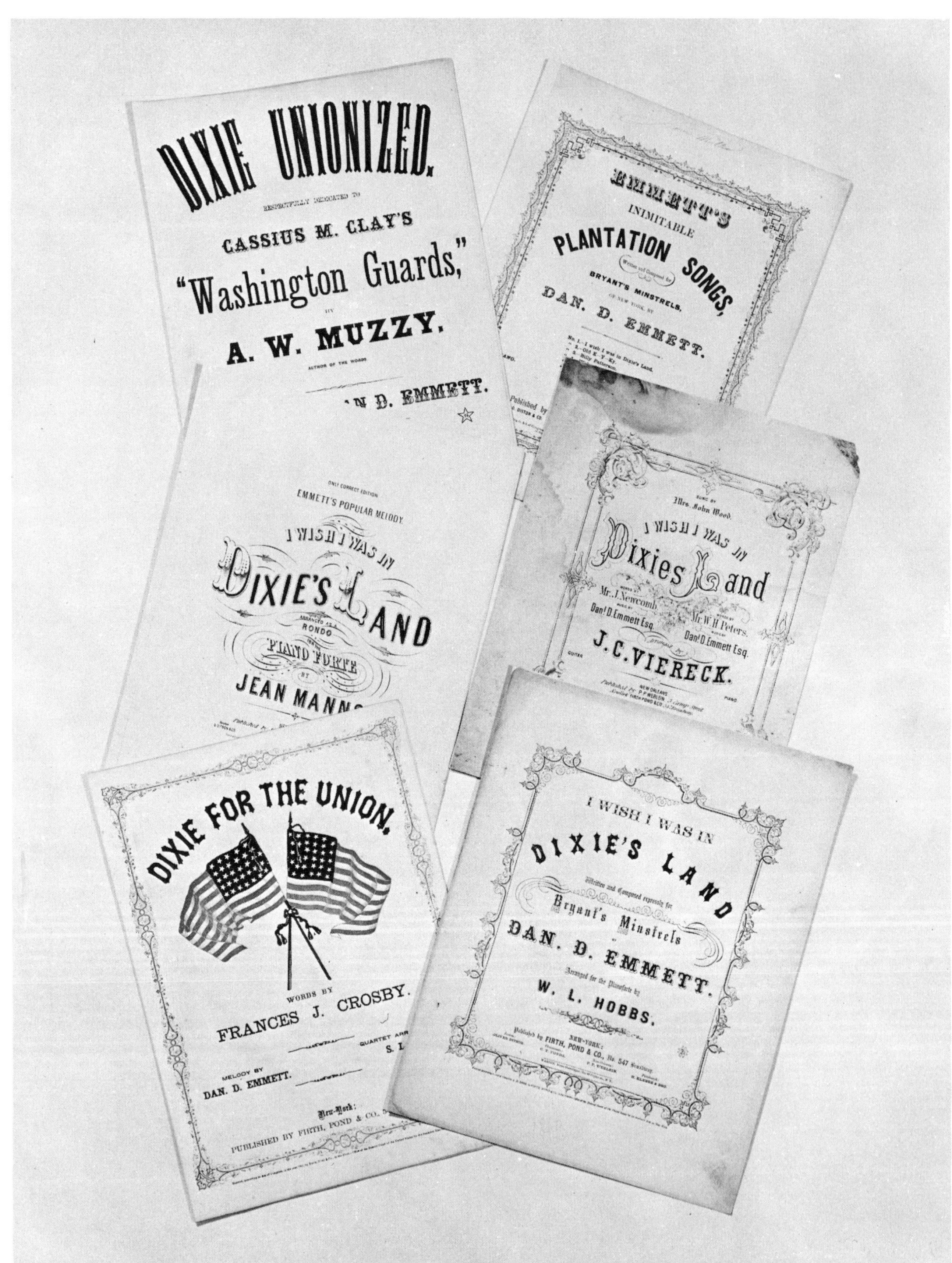

Sheet music of the Civil War period.

cover also are listed other songs published by this company at prices from 25 to 50 cents.

MUSICAL INSTRUMENTS

BATON, DRUM MAJOR'S. This beautiful baton is of rosewood and has brass tips on both ends. Running the length of the wood section is a decorative worsted cord. Total length, 46 inches. The diameter of the bulb-head of the baton is 3¾ inches. No markings, but was used by a Maine soldier in the war.

Drum major's baton. No markings. Used by a Maine soldier in the war.

BUGLE, ARTILLERY. Made by Horstmann and so marked. Made of copper with brass mouthpiece. Length, 15½ inches. Diameter of horn, 5⅝ inches.

BUGLE, CAVALRY. This short copper bugle has no markings but is decorated with the American eagle coat of arms. Total length 10¼ inches. Diameter of horn 3¾ inches. Bugles of many types were used by both sides but Federal bugles usually had a brass reinforcement band around the end out of which the sound came.

BUGLE, INFANTRY. Copper with brass trimming and mouthpiece. Length overall–18½ inches. Diameter of horn, 5½ inches. No markings.

DRUMS. By Army Regulations drums were to be decorated by the U.S. coat of arms, painted on the drum itself. However, available photographs and contemporary sketches show conclusively that many if not most, military drums were devoid of any insignia or other types of decoration. Most of the drums which were used in the war and whose authenticity is unquestioned, now possessed by collectors and museums, do not have any decoration on them, except, perhaps, tacks or nails arranged in the design of a 5-pointed star.

Some military drums carried by state units in the early months of the war were decorated with the state coat of arms, but this was exceptional.

The principal musician of Co. C 36th Wisconsin Infantry kept his drum after the war and would bring it to every reunion. As one veteran expressed it: "No doubt when we are all together in the great future reunion, he will be drumming and looking both ways (he is cross-eyed) to see if we are all present or accounted for."

DRUM-SLING. White webbing. Provided with a brass drumstick carrier, according to pattern.

FIFE. Although regimental bands generally disappeared after the fall of 1862, fife and drum corps tended to remain and be heard throughout the rest

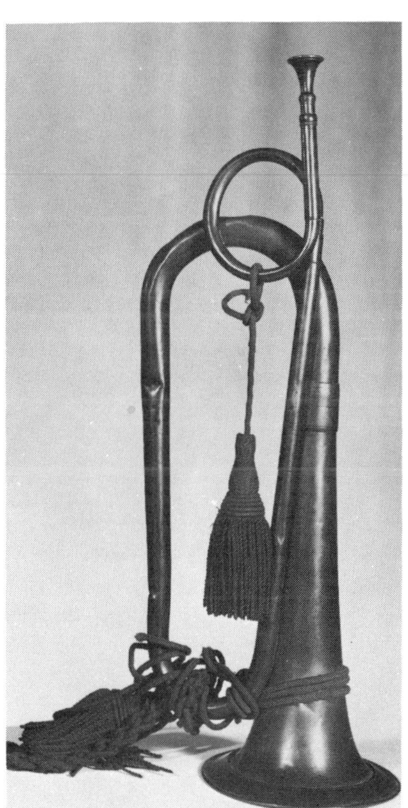

Bugle used in Custer's division to sound the last charge at Appomattox. (West Point Museum collections)

Federal fife and drum corps. (National Archives)

Musical instruments. Top to bottom: U.S. Regulation bugle (brass); drum; fife. (Norm Flayderman)

of the war. There was no finer inspiration for the men at the front than the first burst, crash, and roll of reveille, when a good fife and drum corps, with melodious shrill fifes rallied upon the color line and roused an entire regiment. The effect was intensified when, in a great army stretching out for miles, a single bugle-note gave the signal, and then, as by magic, from every direction broke out the accelerating roll of drums, the screech of fifes, and the blare of bugles.

Specimens examined ranged in length from 15¼ to 17 inches. Every fife has 6 small holes on one end and a larger hole on the other. Most fifes are rosewood, with silver tips; however, some are maple with brass tips. The author has a rosewood fife 17 inches long, silver-mounted, and marked: "Geo. Cloos, Crosby."

Horns. Of all musical instruments used in the war, horns are most difficult to identify as authentic. Drums, fifes, and bugles were used much more extensively since drum and fife corps (and the inevitable buglers!) were in service for the whole four years. Much uncertainty as to Civil War horns has also arisen because of the popularity of brass bands after 1865, when similar horns were used. Shown here are specimens of horns known to have seen service in the field 1861-1865.

Brass instruments used by Civil War bands were constructed so that the bell pointed back over the musician's shoulder. The band music was played for the benefit of the marching column which followed the band. The bands were not for the amusement of the spectators as they are today. Also, there was an absence of woodwind instruments, used to such a great extent in present-day bands.

MUSKET. See SHOULDER WEAPONS.

MUSKETOON. See SHOULDER WEAPONS.

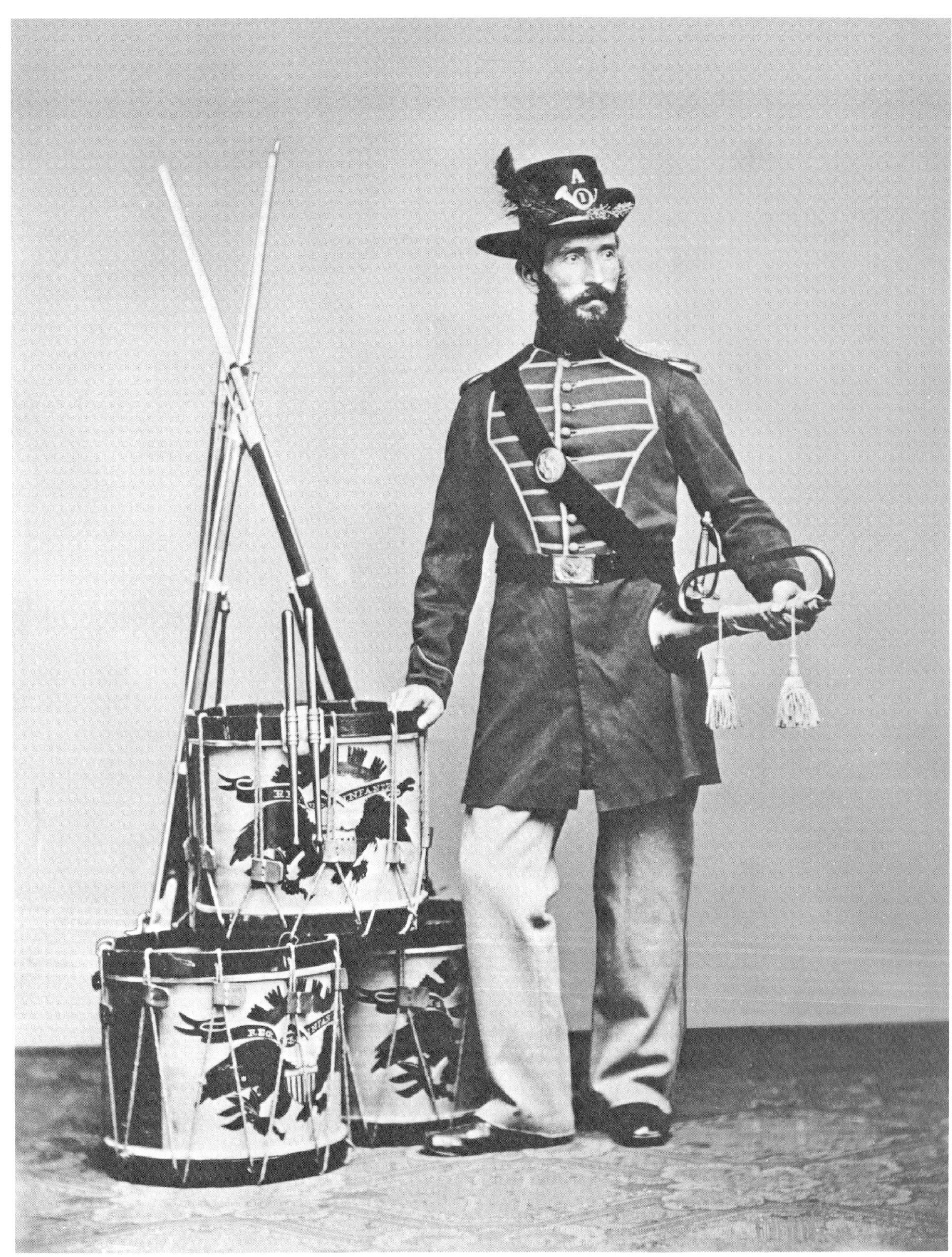

Federal infantry bugler. Note drums and drum stick holder. (Smithsonian Institution)

Federal artillery drummer. Note drum sling and drum stick holder attached to the sling. (Smithsonian Institution)

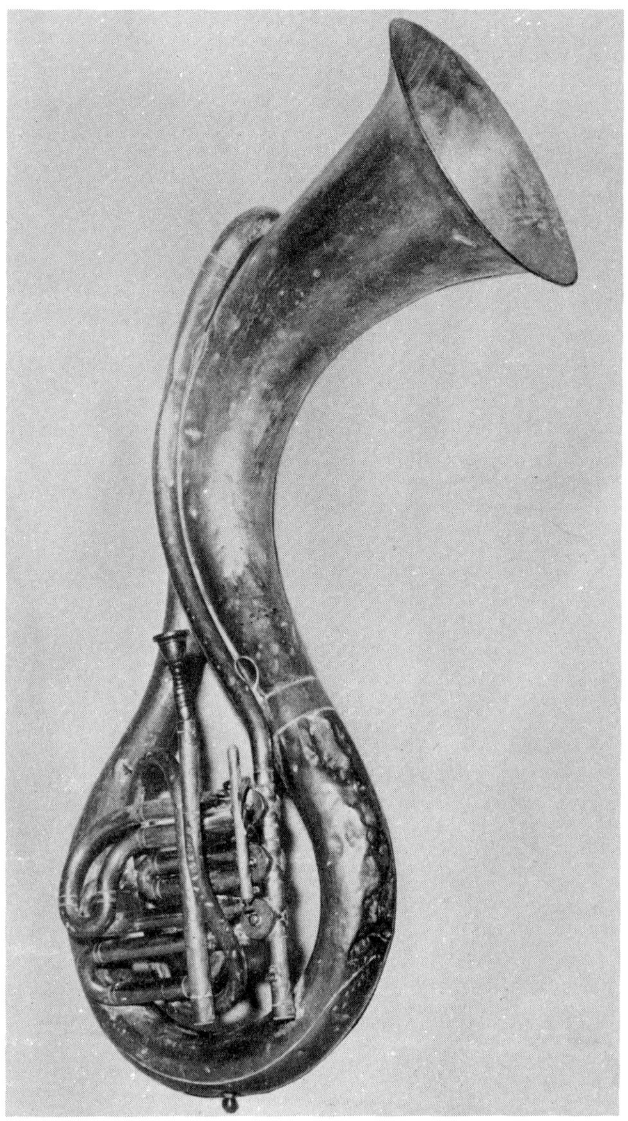

Large brass horn. Silver trimmings. 40 inches long with a 11½ inch diameter at the bell. (From Antietam battlefield)

NAIL BALL. See PROJECTILES.

NAVIGATION INSTRUMENTS. The navigation instruments used by both sides were made chiefly by private concerns, many in the North, France, and Great Britain. It is difficult to definitely establish Civil War use except by tradition. Markings on Civil War navigation instruments usually only assist in establishing maker and place of manufacture.

SEXTANT. Enclosed in a wooden case 15 by 12¾ inches. Top of case is marked "B 3." This sextant was used on the same ship as the ship's compass described below. The sextant is English made and has written instructions for its use, issued by the Admiralty March 16, 1858, and pasted on the inside of the cover.

A smaller sextant, used by the commander of a ship at Mobile Bay has the following dimensions: 11 inches wide, 9¼ inches deep, and 3¾ inches deep. The cover is not marked, nor are there any markings on the sextant itself.

SHIP'S COMPASS. Box is 8¾ inches on each side and 2¼ inches deep. The cover is marked: "BNC. E. B 90", and also has the compass directions "N" for North and "S" for South stamped in the wood.

SHIP'S FLOATING COMPASS. This compass, taken from a Confederate blockade runner, is 11¼ inches tall, 8¾ inches wide, and 7½ inches deep at the bottom. A hinged door has a glass window for reading the compass. Moreover, the compass can be read at night by a brass oil lantern which can be attached to the side of the wooden case of the compass. The floating compass is marked only with the number 1441.

NECK STOCK. See UNIFORMS AND CLOTHING.

NEGRO BROGANS. This term is frequently encountered in descriptions of Federal contracts with shoe manufacturers for Army footware. Extensive

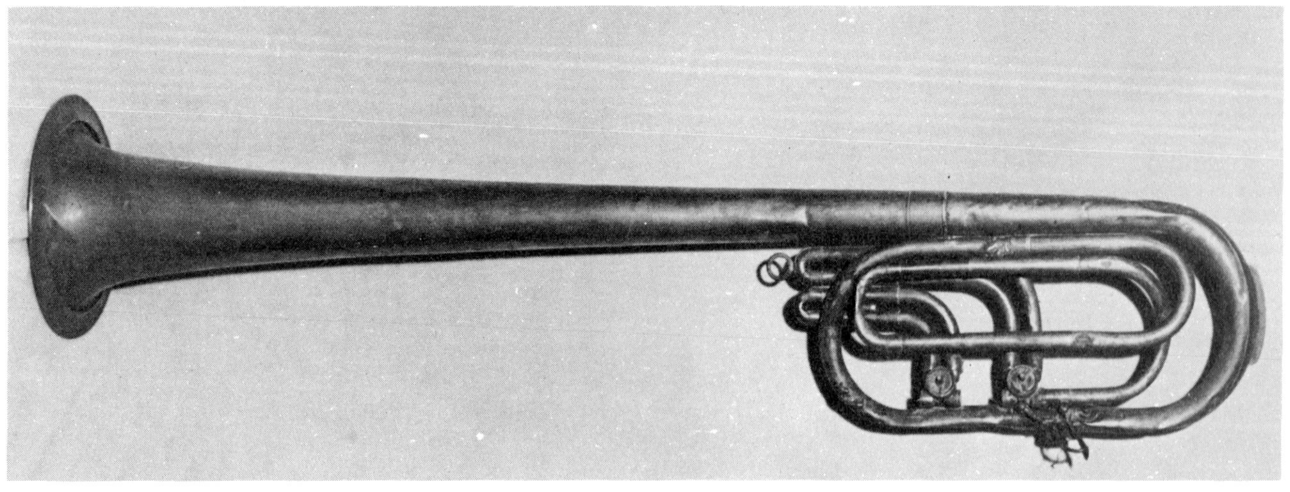

Straight brass horn, 40 inches long with a 7¾ inch diameter at the bell. All brass with steel mouthpiece. Marked on shield: "John F. Stratton, New York."

Ship's compass.

Floating compass taken off a blockade runner.

research has failed to locate any other reference to "Negro Brogans." It is possible that the term applied to the type of Army shoes which resembled the shoes worn by Negroes on the plantations.

NEWSPAPERS. See RECREATIONAL EQUIPMENT.

NEW TESTAMENT. See BIBLES AND TESTAMENTS.

NIGHT CAP. As with shawls, some of the men, usually older soldiers and officers, brought to the field their habit of wearing a night cap to bed. No specimen available.

NIPPLE PROTECTOR. To protect one of the most fragile—and essential—parts of the musket,—the nipple, a nipple protector was issued with each Enfield rifle musket or rifle. Since this was the only weapon so protected, men armed with other weapons often made their own nipple protectors. In some cases this involved making a crude nipple protector from a Minie bullet. Since lead is easily cut, this was probably the most practical solution.

NIPPLE WRENCH. See APPENDAGES.

NOSE BAG. See HORSE EQUIPMENTS.

OPTICAL INSTRUMENTS. Optical instruments included telescopes and field glasses. Many of these were made in France and Great Britain. However, unlike Civil War navigation instruments, the optical

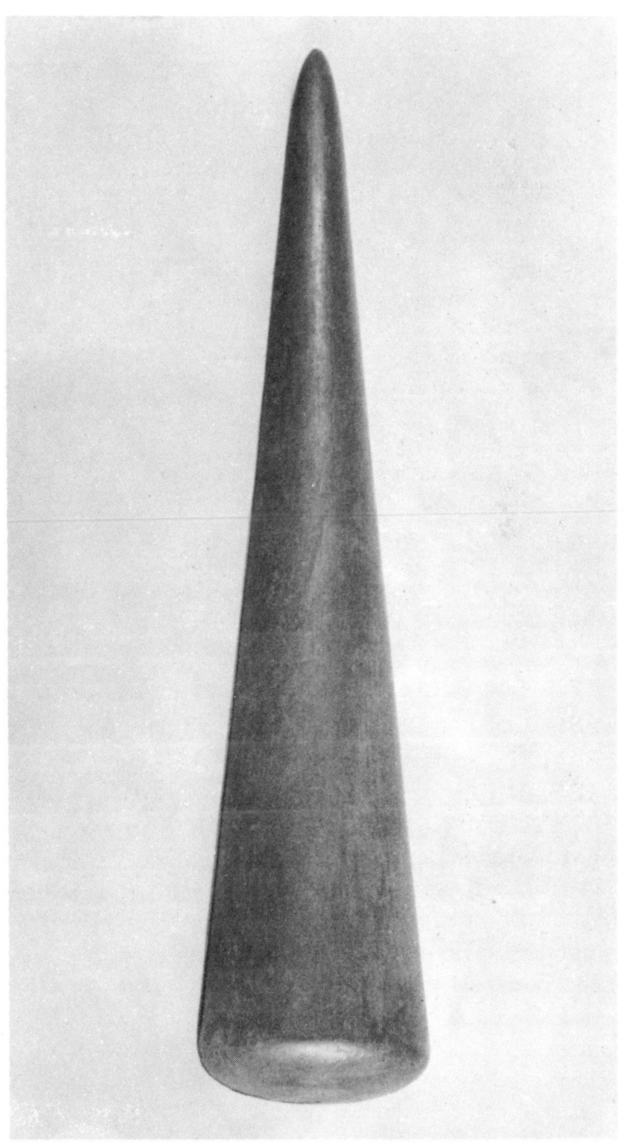

Marlinspike. Used by sailors to separate strands of rope. Made of heavy wood (probably oak or mahogany). Weight 4 pounds. Length 18 inches. Diameter at thick end, 3¾ inches.

instruments bear such markings as U.S. Army, U.S. Navy, etc.

NAVAL TELESCOPE. In metal case 17 inches long with loops for carrying straps. Telescope is brass bound; case is mahogany. Length extended, 3 feet; closed, 16½ inches. Three sections. No markings. Used by Captain Percival Eddy, U.S.N., at the Battle of Mobile Bay.

SMALL BRASS TELESCOPE. The author knows of two of these that were carried during the war. The one shown here is in 4 sections. Length extended, 6¼ inches; closed, 2¼ inches. No markings.

SMALL FIELD TELESCOPE. Leather covered with silver mountings. Length when closed, 9¾ inches; when open, 22 inches. No markings.

An Enfield rifle nipple protector with brass chain and nipple protector, made from a Minié bullet. (From Fredericksburg battlefield)

ORDNANCE TOOLS. Shown here are two original tools—a plane and clamp—used in a U.S. Ordnance plant during the war. Such items are very rare.

ORNAMENT, HAT. See INSIGNIA.

OVERCOAT. See UNIFORMS AND CLOTHING.

PAROLE. See DOCUMENTS.

PASS. See DOCUMENTS.

PASS BOX. See ARTILLERY.

PEN. See WRITING EQUIPMENT.

PENCIL. See WRITING EQUIPMENT.

PENDULUM HAUSSE. See ARTILLERY.

PERCUSSION BULLETS. See AMMUNITION, SMALL ARMS.

PERCUSSION CAP. With the exception of such rifles as the Spencer, which used a metallic cartridge, all muskets, rifle muskets, and rifles were fired with either percussion caps or the Maynard Primer. The percussion caps were carried in the cap box (or cap pouch) on the soldier's belt. Twelve percussion caps were issued per every ten cartridges. Loading was slow with these small caps, as they were easily dropped while being placed on the nipple of the gun. The percussion cap for small arms was made of copper. It was slightly conical, with a rim at the open end; it had four slits, extending about half the height of the cap. The cap was charged with fulminate of mercury, mixed with half its weight of nitre, the object of the nitre being to render the fulminate less explosive and to give body to the flame. To protect the percussion powder from moisture and also to prevent it from falling out, it was covered over, in each cap, with a drop of pure shellac varnish. Percussion caps for small arms were formed by a machine which cut a blank from a sheet of copper, and transferred it to a die in which the cap was shaped by means of a punch.

PHOTOGRAPH. See PICTURES.

PICK. See INTRENCHING TOOLS.

PICKET PIN. See HORSE EQUIPMENTS.

PICTURES. Much of the interest in the war has been due to the large number of photographs which have survived to make the contest live for later generations. Prior to the Mexican and Crimean Wars combat was shown by artists' concepts, that is, by paintings and drawings. These served only to give interested students a second hand portrayal of men and events, who were often portrayed in a completely unrealistic or exaggerated fashion. Actual photographs, by the thousands, were made from 1861 to 1865, and the war will always seem very real and close to us and future generations. While much credit belongs to Brady (1823-1896) it must not be forgotten that hundreds of photographers in villages and cities were

Field glasses. (Norm Flayderman)

available to take pictures of the country boys in their brand new "soldier suits." Some of these photographs which have survived are labelled with the subjects' names, but many are unmarked.

AMBROTYPE. Invented in 1854 by James Ambrose Cutting of Boston, and his partner, Isaac Rehn of Philadelphia. This process produced by the collodion process a photographic positive on glass which when backed up with black wax, paint, paper, or velvet gave a positive image. The picture was not marred by the double reflection, so annoying in the daguerreotype. The process spread rapidly throughout the country, it being simpler and cheaper to make than the daguerreotype. The outstanding characteristic of ambrotypes was the absence of reflection; the ambrotype when held in the hand could be moved in any direction or held at any angle and the photographic image would look the same.

Ambrotypes were made the same sizes as daguerreotypes and so were sold with the same mats, preserves, and cases. This causes much of the modern misconception concerning which is which.

CARTE DE VISITE. A form of paper portrait which was extremely popular was the card photograph or carte-de-visite. The original idea of these cards was that suggested by their name, i.e. visiting cards. The individual's photograph appeared instead of his or her printed name. The first printed reference to the production of these cards in the United States was in the list of exhibits at the 1858 Exhibition of the Franklin Institute in Philadelphia. From 1860 to 1866 the carte-de-visite fad spread like wildfire. Edward Anthony in 1861 placed on the market an album for storing and preserving these in the home.

DAGUERROTYPE. A photograph on a silver or a copper plate covered with silver. One of the first photographic processes, the daguerrotype was invented by Louis J. M. Daguerre and announced to the world in 1839. Through the 1840's and 1850's "daguerreotype saloons" were established in many urban centers in the U.S. Daguerreotypes were usually sold in attractive cases, often of gutta-purcha, and embossed with decorative designs, including military symbols such as crossed cannon and the American flag. Because of their expense, daguerreotypes were not as commonly sought after by the common soldier as either ambrotypes or tintypes. However, many soldiers did carry to the front daguerreotypes of their wives, children, or sweethearts. Such a daguerreotype is shown here. This specimen was recently dug up on the battlefield of Chancellorsville at the spot where Jackson struck the exposed flank of the hapless XI Corps. Who the woman was, no one can tell, but very probably she was the wife or girl friend of one of the Federal soldiers who became an early casualty on the fateful May 3d. Although the picture was in the ground for nearly 100 years, it is remarkably well preserved.

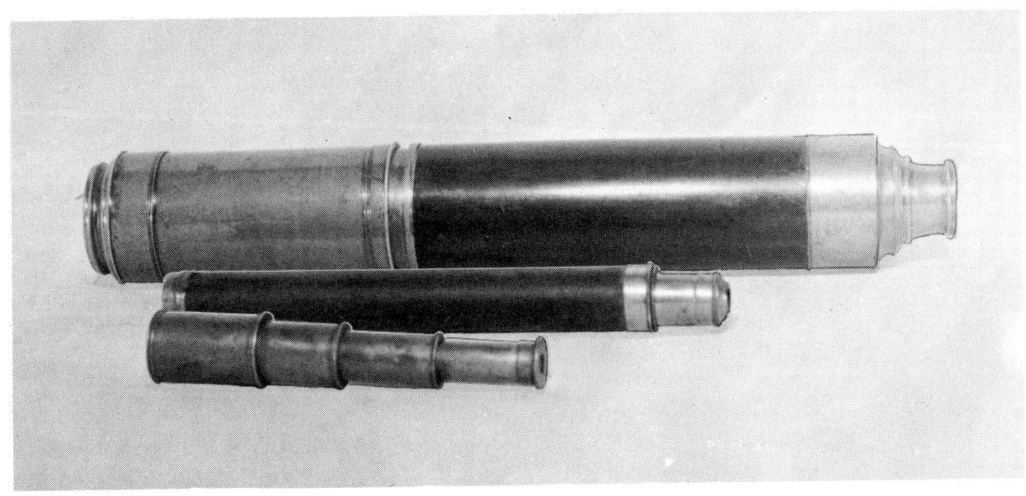

Telescopes. Top: Naval telescope used by Capt. Percival Eddy, USN.; center: small field telescope; bottom: small brass telescope.

For the collector who wishes to distinguish a daguerreotype from later forms of photographs sold in similar cases, the following test can always be made. The quickest and surest method of identifying a true daguerreotype is to hold it in one hand, move it through various angles—and, in so doing, it will be observed that sometimes the photographic image is clearly seen and in others only shiny metal is seen. This is because the mirror surface of the daguerreotype is only coated in spots, while the remainder of the surface holds the reflection characteristic of a true mirror and will reflect light from various toned surfaces in the same manner as the ordinary mirror. Dag-

U.S. Ordnance tools. Plane marked "Ord Dept."

uerreotypes were made in various sizes, the most common being the 1/6 size, the silver plate of which measured 2¾ x 3¼ inches.

Since daguerreotypes are direct pictures, the original are reversed as in the case of an individual seeing himself in a mirror.

Restoration of daguerreotypes to almost original condition is possible. However, it is a special chemical process requiring great care and there are only a few laboratories competent to do such work. In no case should a cloth, brush, or finger be brought into contact with the face of the daguerreotype if the glass has been removed. The result may be the complete destruction of the image with no chance for future restoration.

PHOTOGRAPHS. War photography existed before the Civil War, and in that war Brady was only one of numerous photographers behind the Federal lines. Alexander Gardner the Scotchman who taught Brady the wet-collodian process, Timothy H. O'Sullivan, T. C. Roche, Geo. M. Barnard, and Capt. A. T. Russell being a few of the others. Prominent Confederate photographers were George S. Cook of Charleston, S.C. and A. D. Lytle of Baton Rouge, La. It is probable that Lytle deserves credit for being the first to use photography for military purposes because he often worked behind the Federal lines and sent his negatives back to Confederate headquarters for military study.

STEREOSCOPIC VIEWS. Popular with the home folks were stereoscopic views of the war. One of the main dealers in them was the E. and H. T. Anthony and Company of 501 Broadway, New York City. In the *Army and Navy Journal* for April 15, 1865, this company advertised stereoscopic views of the war "obtained at a great expense and forming a complete Photographic History of the Great Union Contest." Some of the views mentioned were those of Bull Run, Yorktown, Hanover Junction, and Fort Morgan.

TINTYPES. The ambrotype was not two years old when a U.S. patent was issued (February 19, 1856) to Professor Hamilton L. Smith of Kenyon College (Ohio) for a process of making "photographic pictures on japanned surfaces." Among the surfaces specified was japanned iron. The tintype was also known as the melainotype and ferrotype. Eventually the latter name became most used but the popular name by which they were, and still are, called was "tintypes."

At first the tintypes were made in similar sizes and cases as the daguerreotype and ambrotype. However, the cost of producing them became so cheap that photographers went after customers who would only spend a quarter or dollar to have their pictures taken. The cases were dispensed with and the tintypes put in simple paper case. The very small pictures of this type were extremely popular. They were not much larger than a dime in size and were offered in simple paper mats.

Where a tintype (or melainotype or ferrotype) has been mounted on a case it is difficult to distinguish it from an ambrotype. A certain method is to remove it from the case. If the picture is on metal then it be-

Daguerreotype dug up at Chancellorsville. (Ray Whipp, Silver Spring, Maryland.)

longs to the tintype group; if on glass, it is an ambrotype.

While most of us have forgotten the origin of the old saying "Not on your tintype" we do know that the wide use of the term indicates the popularity of tintypes during the war. The tintype was another evidence of experimentation with various photographic processes in the years preceding the war. This variation, called a ferrotype, was a positive photograph taken on a sensitized sheet of enameled tin or iron. Although probably not as numerous as Brady's carte de visites or the daguerreotypes, the many specimens extant attest to the popularity of the tintype.

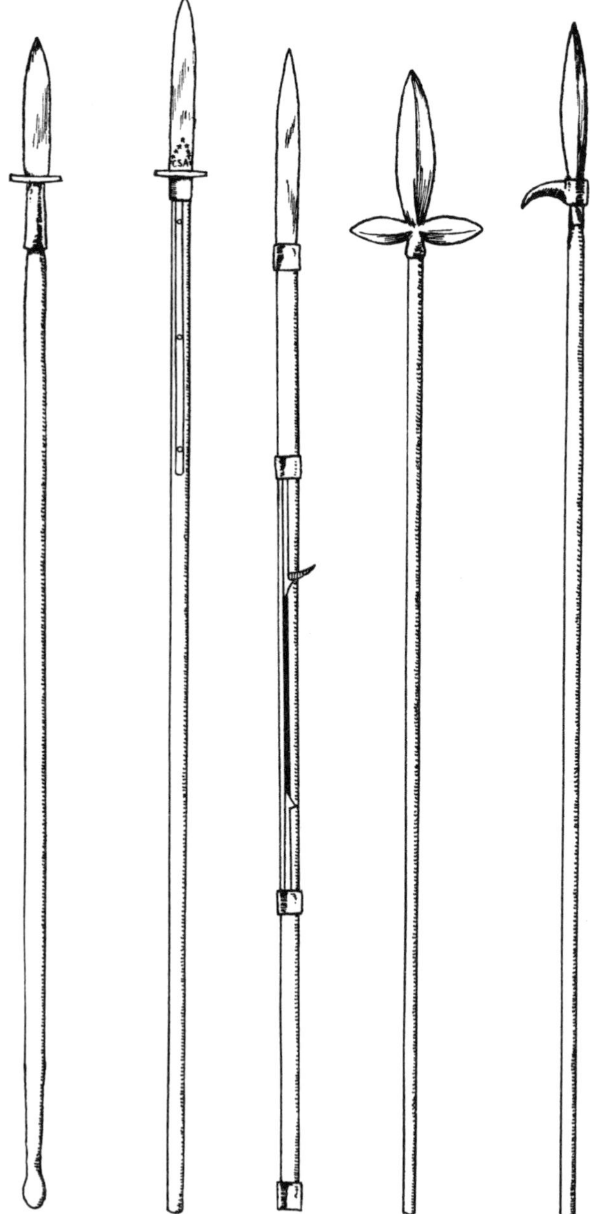

Pikes. Left to right: "John Brown Pike"; "Georgia Pike"; Georgia "bridle cutting pike." Francis Bannerman Sons. Drawn by Mike McAfee)

PIKES. Except for John Brown's weapons, pikes used during the Civil War were locally manufactured weapons for Confederate use. The first Confederate pikes were made by Ross Winans of Baltimore. So far as states were concerned, most of the pikes were turned out in Georgia, to be used against the invading forces under Sherman. One of the makers of Georgia pikes was Samuel Griswold, who turned out a clover leaf type of pike, as did H. Stevens. A Captain Franz Reuter of Louisiana invented a pike consisting of a scythe blade on a 10-foot pole; the pike had a sharp hook at the base of the blade. Alabama appropriated money for a pike with a keen two-edged steel head like a bowie knife.

A noted authority on Confederate weapons, William A. Albaugh III, points out that the average soldier in the Confederacy would have nothing to do with pikes, hence they were used mainly for drill. A few pikes were used by a Confederate artillery unit, DeGournay's Heavy Artillery, during the Seven Days' Battles around Richmond. Pikes shown in illustration: No. 1. "John Brown pike" made under contract by Charles Blair of Collinsville, Conn. and Charles Hart of Unionville, Conn.

No. 2. "Georgia Pike" decorated with "C.S.A." and 11 stars. The ash pole is 7 feet long and has a 1-foot blade, 1.75 inches wide, weight 5 lbs.

No. 3. Several variations of this model pike were made. Its main feature was a collapsible blade (varying in length from 10 to 14 inches), which could be recessed in the pole when not in use.

No. 4. Georgia "clover leaf pike." The ash pole was 6 feet long, with a 10-inch blade. Each side blade was 3.25 inches long. Weight about 4 pounds.

No. 5. Georgia "Bridle Cutting Pike," which consisted of a 7-foot ash pole with a 12.5-inch blade. The side hook was 5.5 inches long. Weight 4.5 pounds.

PIPES. See also RELICS AND SOUVENIRS.

One method of passing time in camp which was carried on very extensively was the making of pipes and rings for souvenirs of a camp or, more rarely, a battlefield. The pipes were made from the root of the mountain laurel, when available, or otherwise from some other type of wood. The pipes were often surprisingly well made, ornamented with the badges of the various corps, either in relief or inlaid.

PISTOL. See REVOLVERS.

PISTOL CARBINE. See SHOULDER WEAPONS.

PLATE, TIN. See MESS EQUIPMENT.

POMMEL BAG. See HORSE EQUIPMENTS.

POMPOM. See INSIGNIA.

PONCHO. Made of rubberized cloth or coated fabric, much the same as the knapsack and haversack.

Federal poncho, 1862. (Smithsonian Institution)

Size was 45 inches by 79 inches, with brass eyelets along the outer edges. It was slit in the center so that it could be drawn over the head; the slit was reinforced with double thickness cloth and double-stitched. Weight 3 lbs. All outer edges were hemmed, and eyelets reinforced with double thickness of cloth.

Another type of poncho was made of unbleached muslin coated with vulcanized India-rubber, 60 inches wide and 71 inches, having an opening in the center lengthwise of the poncho, through which the head passed, with a lap 3 inches wide and 16 inches long. The poncho was used in lieu of the rubber or "gum" blanket, although many men used the term "gum blanket" for poncho. Actually, the gum or rubber blanket was not a poncho and could not be worn as such.

Ponchos shielded the wearer from the rain and also were handy for wrapping around a quarter of pork or mutton smuggled into camp. About half the ponchos, after they had been in service a few months, had checker boards pencilled or painted on them and the other half had the necessary squares and figures for "Chuck-a-Luck," "Sweat," "Honest John," and other fascinating games that tended to impoverish those who were addicted to them.

PONTOON. See ENGINEER EQUIPMENT.

PORTFIRE. See ARTILLERY.

PORTFIRE CUTTER. See ARTILLERY.

POSTERS. The collection of Civil War "broadsides" and posters is a complete collecting field in itself. Shown here are two examples of posters, but the variety is almost limitless. These appeals for enlisting were posted in prominent places and were directed to local citizenry to "join up" with a specific unit being raised in their locality. Such posters were usually printed in very small numbers and used only a few weeks or months at most. As a result, Civil War posters and broadsides are rare.

POWDER CONTAINER. Although most ammunition used in the war was fixed, there was some use made of canned powder. Powder used during the war was stored in cans and barrels, both metal and wood. The illustration shows an example of each type of container.

POWDER BARREL, METAL. Tin, 11½ inches tall and 9½ inches in diameter. Painted green and red. Metal stopper for hole at top of can which is marked: "Patent July 12, 1859." On the bottom of the barrel is pasted a paper bearing the inscription: "Hazard Powder Company, Hazardville, Conn. U.S. Government Warranted proof. Cannon." This paper also has a design of crossed cannons.

POWDER BARREL, WOOD. This was 13 inches tall and 10½ inches in diameter. Wrapped top and bottom with wooden strips, 4 at each end. Top has a wooden plug which screws into the hole used for emptying powder from the barrel. Marked on top: "FFF GLAZED" and "10821 E." Marked on bottom of barrel: "Laflin and Rand Powder Co. New York."

POWDER MEASURE. See ARTILLERY.

PRIMING WIRE. See ARTILLERY.

PROJECTILES.

CONFEDERATE PROJECTILES. The Confederates used many types of rotation systems for their projectiles as well as various types of fuzes, including imported types. The Confederates also used copies or adaptations such Federal projectiles as the Hotchkiss, Schenkl, Dyer, Sawyer, etc. A typical Confederate projectile was the ratchet sabot, some of which were made by Brooke.

Armstrong. Imported from England, these were fired from a breechloading cannon. They were lead-coated, shunt types, with studs to engage the rifling.

Blakely. Imported from England, these projectiles used a lead sabot to engage the rifling. Large-caliber Blakely guns also fired projectiles made with flanges to correspond with the grooves in the bore of the cannon.

Reed. Similar to the U.S. Parrott type. The Reed projectile had an expanding ring of soft metal at the base of the projectile to give a rotation to the projectile in flight.

Whitworth. The Whitworth gun, imported from England, was a breechloader that fired a hexagonal projectile made so as to fit the interior of the bore. Both shell and solid shot were used.

FEDERAL PROJECTILES. General description of types used:

Canister Shot. Cylindrical tin cases with iron heads, of caliber suitable for different types of cannon, filled with cast-iron balls arranged in four tiers and packed in with dry sawdust. Canister was used at ranges not exceeding 400 yards, but was most destructive at from 100-200 yards.

Case Shot. Small balls enclosed in a case which, when broken by the shock of the discharge in the piece, or by a charge of powder within the case, exploding during the flight of the case, scatters the balls. The kinds of case shot used were: grapeshot, canister shot, and spherical case.

Carcass. A spherical shell with three additional holes of the same dimensions as the fuze hole, pierced at equal distances apart in the upper hemisphere of the shell, and filled with a composition which burned with intense power for 8-10 minutes. The flame issuing from the holes set fire to everything combustible within its reach. The carcass was used in bombard-

WAR MEETING!

IN

KINGSVILLE!

At TOWN HALL,

Saturday Evening, August 2d.

A. S. HALL,

Colonel of the 105 Ohio Regiment, and

L. S. SHERMAN, Esq.,

Will address the people as above stated, upon the all absorbing topic of the day, viz: the raising of additional troops to assist in using up the rebellion. Rally, men, and save the country! Our homes are in danger. We have no homes without a country.

By order of Military Committee.

Poster calling for a "War Meeting" in Ohio 1862.

ments, setting fire to shipping, etc., and was fired from cannon like a cannon shell.

Chain Shot. Two round shot held together by a chain. The motion of rotation of these projectiles in flight would have made them valuable for cutting masts and riggings of ships, if the flight of chain shot had not been so inaccurate. When the means of connecting the round shot was a bar of iron instead of a chain, the projectile was called *Bar shot.*

bottom, and put into a canvas bag and then quilted around with a strong cord.

Grenades. A grenade was a shell thrown by hand; or by large caliber mortars, and ignited as are other shells by means of a fuze. The two main types were hand grenades and rampart grenades. For hand grenades it was possible to use 6-pounder spherical case if the patent hand grenades were not available (see also GRENADES). Grenades were useful in the

Powder containers.

Fire Ball. An oval projectile formed of sacks of canvas filled with combustible composition which emitted a bright flame. It was used to light up the enemy's works, and was loaded with a shell.

Grapeshot. A stand of grapeshot consisted of 9 shot, put together by means of 2 cast-iron plates, 2 rings, and a bolt and nut.

The projectile was attached by straps of tin to a wooden sabot, to which was also attached the cartridge bag containing the charge. This was the method for making a round of fixed ammunition for the guns, the 12-pounder howitzer, and the mountain howitzer. The cartridge for the 24- and 32-pounder howitzers was not attached to the sabot, but to a cartridge block, and was separate from the projectile.

By 1863, if not earlier, the use of grapeshot in the Federal Army had been discontinued, canister being more effective and easier to fabricate. Old pattern grapeshot, often called "quilted grapeshot" probably was continued in use by the Navy throughout the war. These shot were made by placing the balls in tiers around an iron pin attached to an iron tompion at the

defense of works. Smaller grenades could be thrown by hand into trenches, covered approaches or at besiegers mounting a breach; the larger grenades could be rolled over the parapet.

Hot Shot. See also Hot-Shot Fork, under ARTILLERY. The charges for hot shot were from ¼ to 1/6 the weight of the shot. With small velocities, the shot split and splintered the wood, so as to make it favorable for burning. With great velocity, the projectile sank deep into the wood, was deprived of air by the closing of the hole, and charred instead of burning the surrounding wood. It was not efficient if penetration was deeper than 10-12 inches. Red-hot shot did not set fire to the wood until some time after penetration.

Light Ball. The same as a fire ball except it had no shell in it, and was used to light up one's own works.

Nail Ball. A round projectile with an iron pin projecting from it, to prevent its turning in the bore of the piece.

Shell. A hollow sphere of cast iron, containing powder which was ignited by means of a fuze. When fired at troops the shell was so prepared as to explode over the heads of the enemy troops, or, if the terrain was favorable for ricochets, shell was fired a little in front of hostile troop. When fired at works or buildings the shell was expected to explode after penetration.

Smoke Ball. A hollow paper sphere similar to a light ball, filled with a composition which emitted a dense, nauseous smoke. The smoke ball was used to suffocate enemy miners at work, or to conceal one's own operations. The smoke ball burned from 25-30 minutes.

Solid Shot. A solid sphere of cast iron, almost exclusively used by guns. The gun itself usually derived its denomination from the weight of the shot, as 6-pounder, 12-pounder, etc.

Spherical Case Shot. A thin shell of cast iron containing a number of musket balls and a charge of powder sufficient to burst it. A fuze was fixed to it as in an ordinary shell, by which the charge was ignited and the shell burst at any particular instant.

A spherical case shot, when loaded ready for use, had about the same specific gravity as a solid shot, and therefore, when fired with the service charge of powder, its range and velocity was about equal to that of a solid shot of the same caliber.

The spherical case mostly used for field service was the 12-pounder and contained, when loaded, 90 bullets. Its bursting charge was 1 oz. of powder and it weighed 11.75 lbs. Its rupture could be made to take place at any point in its flight and was, therefore, superior to grape or canister. Spherical case should not have been used at any distance under 500 yards; the spherical case shot from a rifled cannon was said to be effective at over 2,000 yards. Spherical case possessed all the advantages of canister shot and, additionally, could be used at ranges beyond the reach of canister.

Tier Shot. Another term for grapeshot, but a term not very extensively used during the war.

FIELD ARTILLERY PROJECTILES. Ammunition for smoothbore field artillery consisted of five basic types of projectiles. For long-range work, solid shot, explosive shell, and spherical case were used, and solid shot was employed more often than not. There was always the chance that a projectile of this type might sweep down a line of men or hit a column head on. Shell, because of its black powder bursting charge, did not shatter; sometimes there were only two fragments. The most effective long-range projectile was spherical case, if its fuze worked properly. When the small bursting charge could be exploded a few yards in front of and above the target, the individual balls would hit in a fairly dense pattern. Eventually the Napoleon became practically the only active smoothbore field piece. The ammunition for this weapon consisted of all three long range types.

For close work a tin can of iron or lead balls called canister was by far the most effective. The maximum range for canister before 1861 was theoretically about 300 yards; however, Federal canister in particular, because of its lead balls, would do damage at a greater range. Grapeshot, larger than canister, was effective at 700 yards and beyond.

For field pieces the projectile was attached to a block of wood called a *sabot.* In field guns and the 12-pounder field and mountain howitzers the projectile and cartridge were attached to the same sabot, and was then known as a round of fixed ammunition. In the 24- and 32-pounder field howitzers the projectile was separate from the charge. Instead the cartridge was attached to a block of wood called the cartridge-block, with the purpose of giving a finish to the cartridge and filling the chamber.

Sabots for shot and spherical-case for guns each had one groove for attaching the cartridge; sabots for gun canisters and for the 12-pounder howitzer shells, spherical-case, and canisters had two grooves. Sabots for the 24- and 32-pounder howitzers had no grooves, but were furnished with handles made of cord, which passed through two holes in the sabot, and fastened by knots on the inside. Projectiles for field service were fastened to the sabot by straps of sheet tin or of strong canvas, when tin or sheet iron could not be procured.

The U.S. *Ordnance Manual* 1861, lists the following projectiles for field and mountain service:

Canister: 6- and 12-pounder gun, and 12-, 24-, and 32-pounder howitzer and mountain howitzer.

Shell: 12-pounder gun–12-, 24-, 32-pounder howitzer and mountain howitzer.

Shot: 6- and 12-pounder guns.

Spherical Case Shot: 6- and 12-pounder guns, and 12-, 24-, and 32-pounder howitzer and mountain howitzer.

PROLONGE. See ARTILLERY.

PUP TENT. See TENT.

QUADRANT, GUNNER's. See ARTILLERY.

QUOIN. See ARTILLERY.

RAMMER. See ARTILLERY.

RATTLE, ALARM. The Navy used wooden rattles on board ship to call the crew to their posts at times of emergency. These rattles were either permanently fixed or were carried by hand as shown in the illustration. Some of these alarm rattles were very similar to the gas alarm rattles used in France in World War I. *Ordnance Instructions, U.S. Navy* prescribed that alarm rattles for calling boarders were to be made like those used by watchmen, of white oak or some similar wood "Rattle, 12 inches long; ratchet, 2 inches in diameter; spring, one inch in

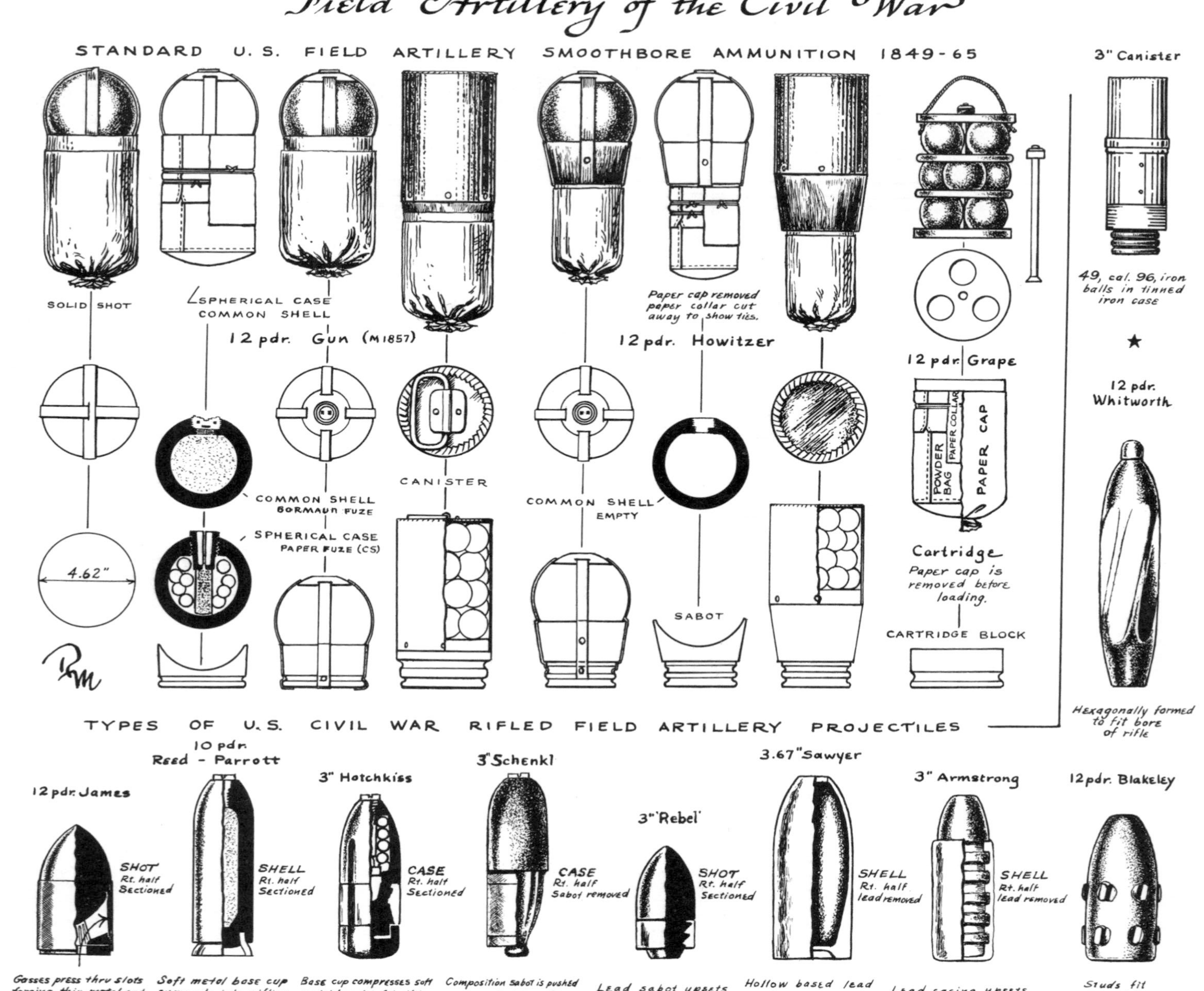

Artillery projectiles. (Robert Miller)

Recreational equipment. Confederate homemade playing cards.

Federal soldiers indulging in a wholesome, recreational outdoor sport—poker. Officers lying nearby are reading letters or the daily paper, another common recreation

width and of sufficient thickness and elasticity to produce the requisite sound. Weight enough should be given to the butt to cause it to revolve round the handle with ease. Fixed rattles of greater power will be attached to suitable places on each deck."

RECREATIONAL EQUIPMENT.

Books and Newspapers. Reading was a pastime quite generally indulged in, and there was no novel so dull, trashy, or sensational as not to find someone so bored with nothing to do that he would not wade through it. Many soldiers never read so much in their lives, nor ever read so much again, as they did in the service. Some soldiers were critical that the Christian Commission did not do more in the way of supplying good literature to the men. Had the Commission done so, maintained these men, there would have been much less gambling and sleeping away of daylight than there was.

Cards: Various games of cards were often played by soldiers of both sides. Many men played for money. Cribbage and euchre were favorite games. The evenings in camp were less occupied in games than were the off-duty hours in the daytime; partly, perhaps, because the tents or huts were rather dimly lighted, and partly because of a surfeit of such recreation in daylight. In general, the evenings were the time of sociability and reminiscence. This was the "visiting time" of soldiers both within the regiment and with the men of other regiments. The American Card Company sold the "Union Playing Cards" which consisted of the following suits: Eagles, Shields, Stars, and Flags. A colonel stood for a king, The Goddess of Liberty for a queen, and a major for a jack. According to the *Frank Leslie* advertisement "The Union Playing Cards are the first and only genuine American Cards ever produced . . . and are rapidly taking the place of cards bearing foreign emblems."

Illustrated here are examples of Union and also Federal playing cards. The Confederate playing cards have a stand-of-arms design, while the cards themselves each bears a portrait of a different Confederate general or cabinet member. The Union flag has 35 stars. Colors are red, white, and blue.

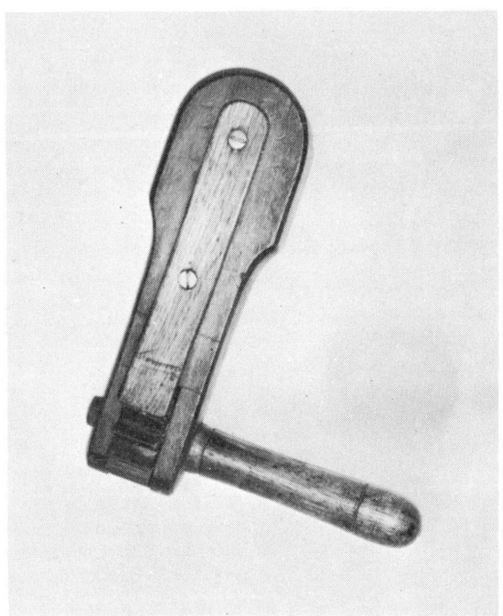

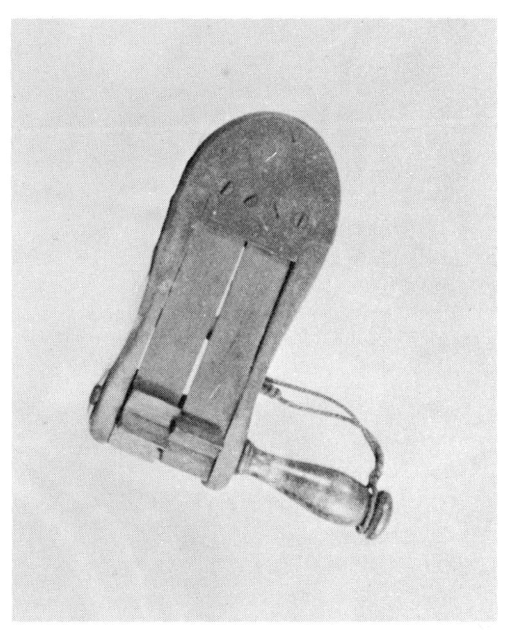

Navy alarm rattles. The rattle on the left is shown through courtesy of Herschel C. Logan.

Poker was a great favorite in some regiments. In the 150th Pennsylvania Infantry it became an "absorbing occupation, the private soldier yielding to its fascinations as readily as his superiors, and risking his scanty allowance as heedlessly as the latter their liberal stipend." At the various headquarters, army down to brigade, the game drew in staff officers who frequently lost or won, in a single night, several months' pay.

Checkers and Chess: Checkers was a popular game among both soldiers and sailors, Backgammon less so, while Chess was only rarely played. There were some soldiers and sailors who rarely joined in any game. In this class were the illiterate members of the unit or crew. Of course they did not read nor write; they rarely played cards; but were usually satisfied to lie on their blankets, talk with one another, or watch the playing.

Chuck-or-Luck: One of the most popular gambling

Card playing in the field. Two Federal sergeants playing cards, aided by a young drummer boy and the First Sergeant as kibitzers. (National Archives)

Playing cards. Top to bottom: Confederate playing cards. Left side shows backs, which is a stand of arms design. Cards themselves each bear a portrait of a different Confederate general or cabinet figure in the upper left corner denoting card value. Original and of the period. Backs in full red, white and blue colors. Two different decks Civil War playing cards. These are enclosed in boxes and boxes only are showing. (Norm Flayderman)

games which kept more men on their knees than did the chaplains. The officers had a similar game called "Sweat-Board," in which the stakes were much higher. After the men had been visited by the paymaster, they set up their Chuck-or-Luck bands. At each "bank" there would be some 10-20 men, down on their knees, laying their money on certain figures laid out on a board or, more often, a rubber blanket, while a "banker" threw the dice.

Dice: Specimens found are crude and of much smaller size than in common use today.

Dominoes: Photograph shows dominoes used during the war. They are crudely made, but the numbers found definitely indicates that dominoes was popular in the 1860's.

Games of Prisoners. In prison the men improvised games. Federal officers at Belle Isle played chess, checkers, dominoes, and cards. Chess was played on a card marked out on the floor, with chessmen made of beef bones. Checkers were played in like manner with buttons and wooden men. Games of cards were going on constantly, especially euchre, whist, and bluff. The greasy, worn cards were guarded carefully as they were invaluable to men desperately in need of recreation. Dominoes were also popular.

REVOLVERS. Just prior to the war several types of revolvers were developed and patented. Probably the best known of the types in use was the Colt revolver, which monopolized the field for some time, but others soon came into demand, such as Remington, Smith and Wesson, and Whitney. Thousands of revolvers were sold monthly, and the new recruit who did not possess a revolver either by his own purchase, or as a present from solicitous relative, admiring friends, or enthusiastic business associates, was something of a curiosity. Along with the pistol went a flask and bullet mould. It was not realized by the soldier or donors that by the time the government had provided him with the necessary arms, ammunition, and equipment, he would then be loaded with about all he could bear, without adding a personal armory and magazine. Veteran troops did not unduly burden themselves by adding revolvers to their load. The troops of 1861 and 1862 took out hundreds of revolvers only to lose them, give them away, or throw them away. Since many regiments were forbidden by their colonels to wear revolvers, a large number of revolvers were sent back to the North.

In some cases, whole companies were recipients of revolvers as gifts. Such a lucky outfit was Co. D 2d Conn. Inf., in May 1861.

Confederate Revolvers. The Southern armies used captured, Confederate-made, and imported revolvers.

Confederate-Made. Manufacturers of revolvers in the South were:

- Thomas W. Cofer, Portsmouth, Va.
- Columbus (Ga.) Firearms Manufacturing Company.
- Dance Brothers and Park, Columbia, Texas.
- Griswold and Gunnison or Griswold and Grier, Griswold, Ga.
- J. and F. Garrett and Co. Greensboro, N.C.
- J. Gerald, Alabama.
- Leech and Rigdon, Greensboro, N.C.
- Marshall, Texas.
- Richmond copy—U.S. Model 1842.
- Rigdon and Ansley, Augusta, Va.
- Schneider and Glassick, Memphis, Tenn.
- Shawk and McLanahan, St. Louis, Mo.
- Samuel Sutherland, Richmond, Va.
- Spiller and Burr, Atlanta, Ga.
- Tucker and Sherrod, Lancaster, Texas.
- Wm. Glaze and Company, Columbia, S.C.

Imports.

- Deane
- French pin fire
- Kerr
- Le Mat—made in France
- Tranter

Federal Revolvers. In the North the three most popular revolvers were the Colt army, the Colt navy, and the Remington. Their dimensions were:

Colt Army Revolver—6 shot, caliber .44; length 14 inches, weight 2.69 pounds; weight of projectile 260 grains; weight of charge 30 grams. This was the principal revolver of the war, over 100,000 being furnished to the Federal Government during the years 1861 to 1863 inclusive. Probably double that number were used before the end of the conflict.

Colt Navy Revolver—6 shot, caliber .36. Length 13 inches, weight 2.63 pounds, weight of projectile 125 grains, weight of charge 14 grains, muzzle velocity 760 feet per second.

Remington Army Revolver—6 shot, caliber .44. Length 13.75 inches, weight 2.88 pounds, weight of projectile 260 grains, weight of charge 30 grains.

Totals Procured, All Types. The Atlas to the *Official Records* shows the following revolvers in its pictures of representative weapons used by the North: Allen, Colt, Joslyn, LeFauchaux, and Remington. However, the Federal Government purchased the following revolvers during the war. (It should be emphasized, also, that many individuals and local organizations also purchased these and other types of revolvers and pistols.) This list includes only weapons bought by the U.S. Government:

Make	*Caliber*	*Number Purchased*
Adam	.44	415
Allen	.44	536
Beal	.36, .44	2,814
Colt (Army)	.44	129,730
Colt (Navy)	.36	17,010
Colt (Pocket)	.31	17,010
Joslyn	.44	1,100
Perrin	.44	2,001
Pettingill	.435	2,001
Le Faucheux (Army)	.43	12,374
Le Faucheux (Navy)	.35	12,374
Rafael	.41	978
Remington (Army)	.44	125,314
Remington (Navy)	.36	4,901
Rogers and Spencer	.44	5,000
Savage	.36	14,287
Starr	.36, .44	47,952
Whitney	.36	11,214

The Government also purchased 100 horse pistols and 100 foreign pistols.

Confederate imported revolver—Kerr 5-shot, double action, caliber .44 or .45. (West Point Museum collections)

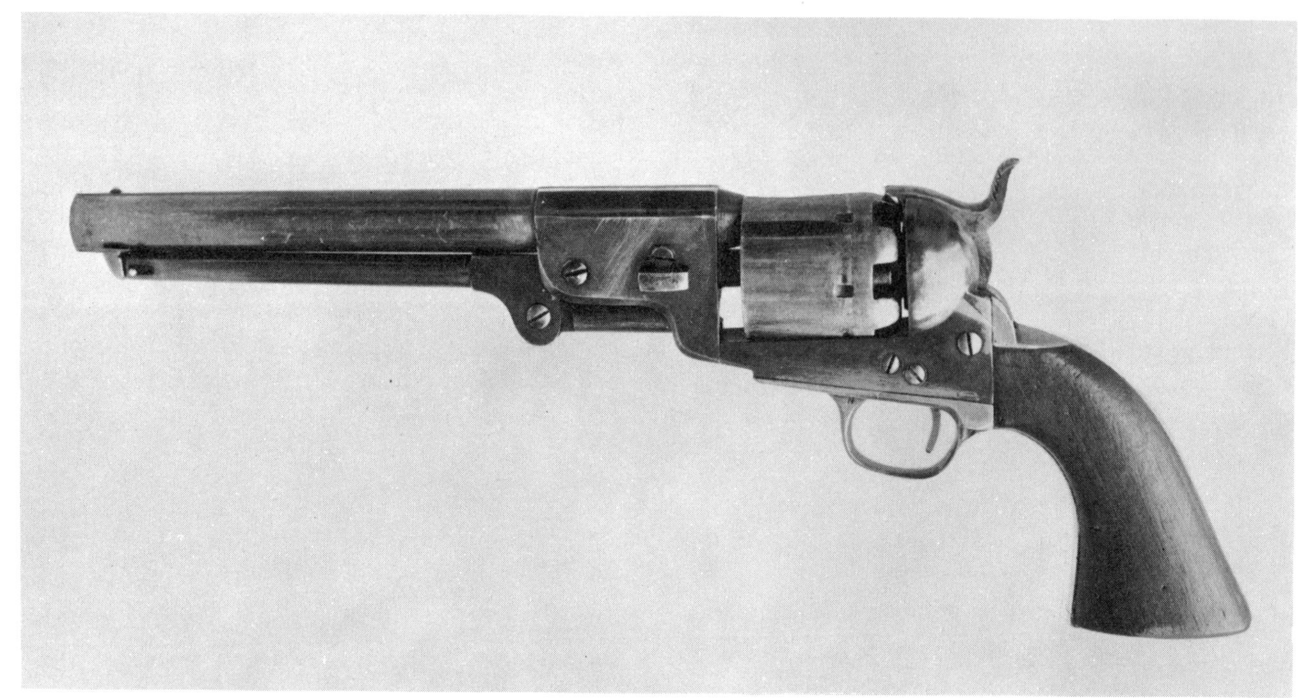

Confederate Leech and Rigdon revolver, caliber .36. (West Point Museum collections)

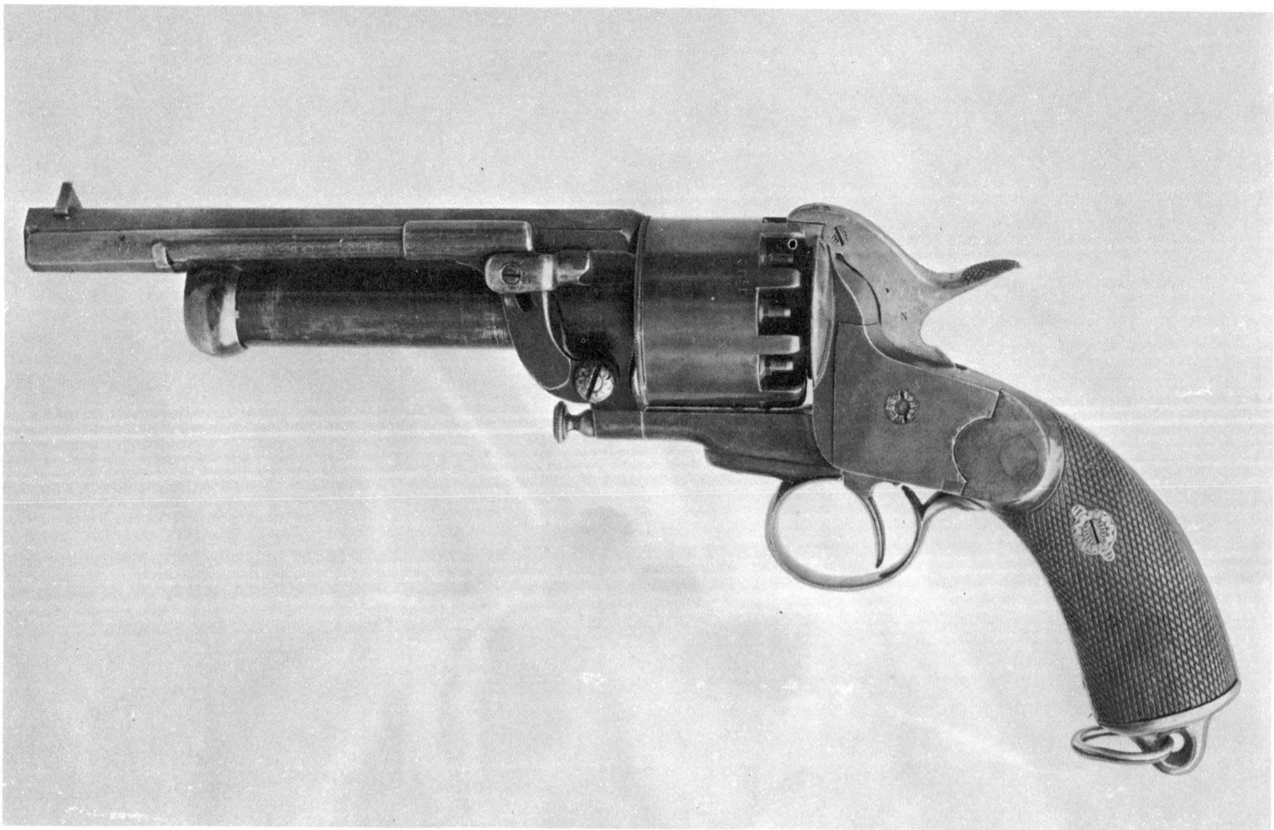

Confederate imported Le Mat revolver. (West Point Museum collections)

Confederate imported Tranter revolver. (Norm Flayderman)

Federal Adams revolver—5-shot, double action, caliber .44. (West Point Museum collections)

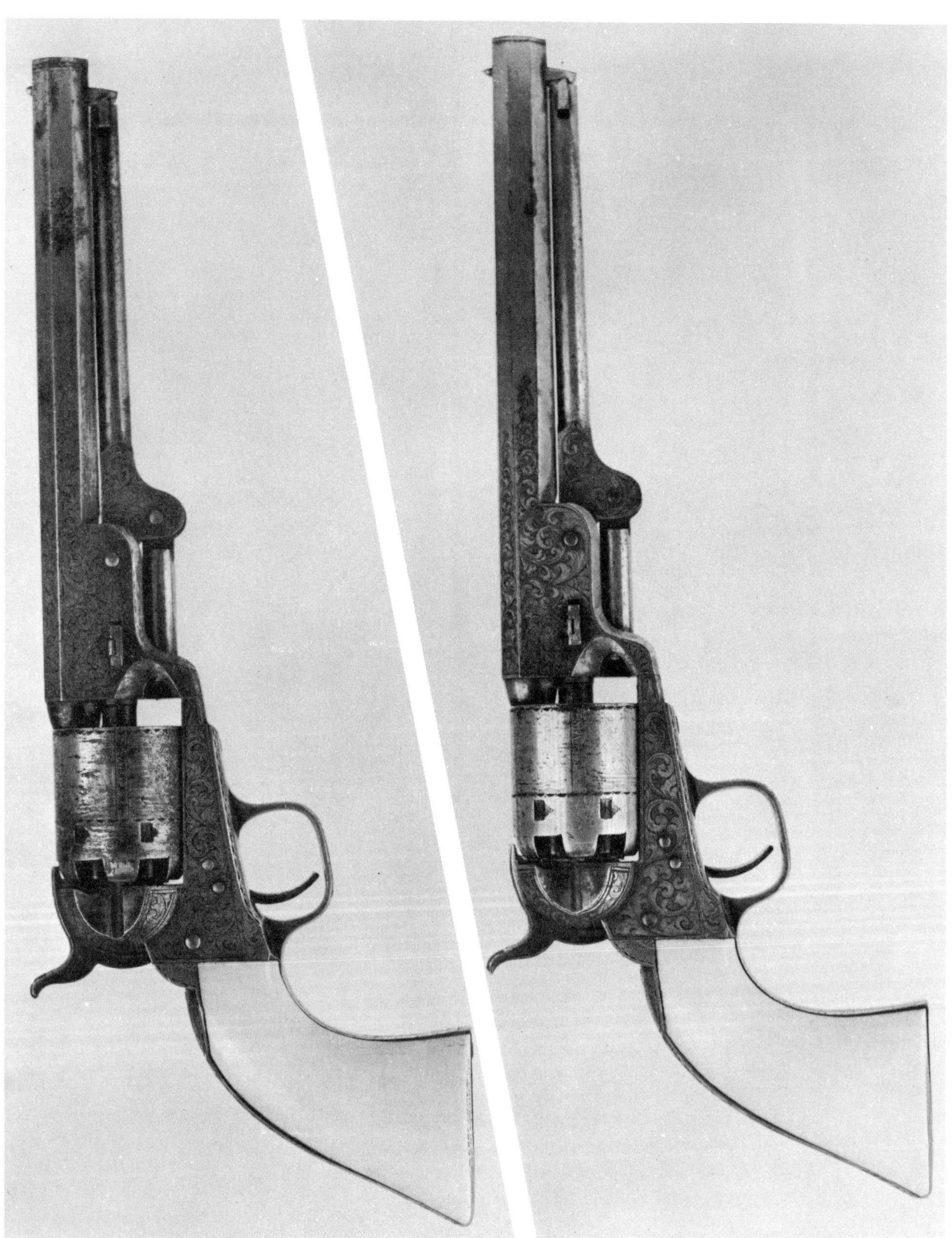

Pair of Colt's navy revolvers. (West Point Museum collections)

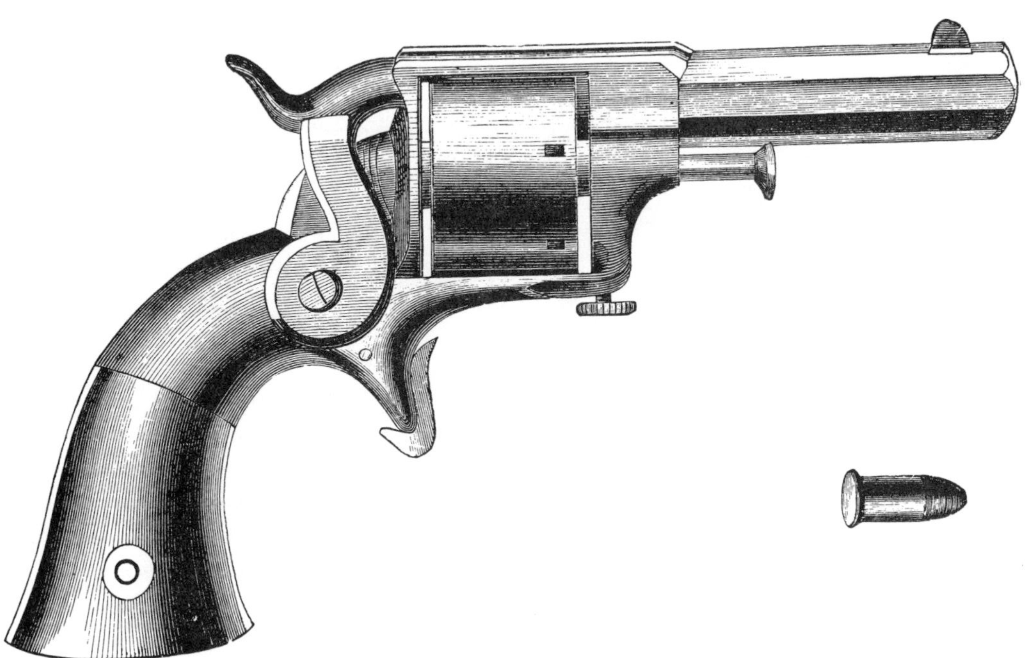

Allen revolver. (Norm Flayderman)

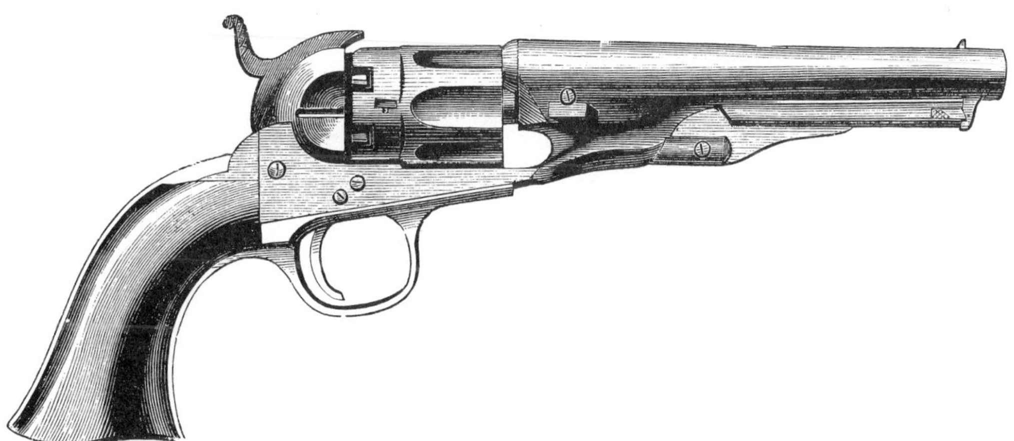

Colt's new patent revolver. (Norm Flayderman)

Colt's army revolver, 1860. (West Point Museum collections)

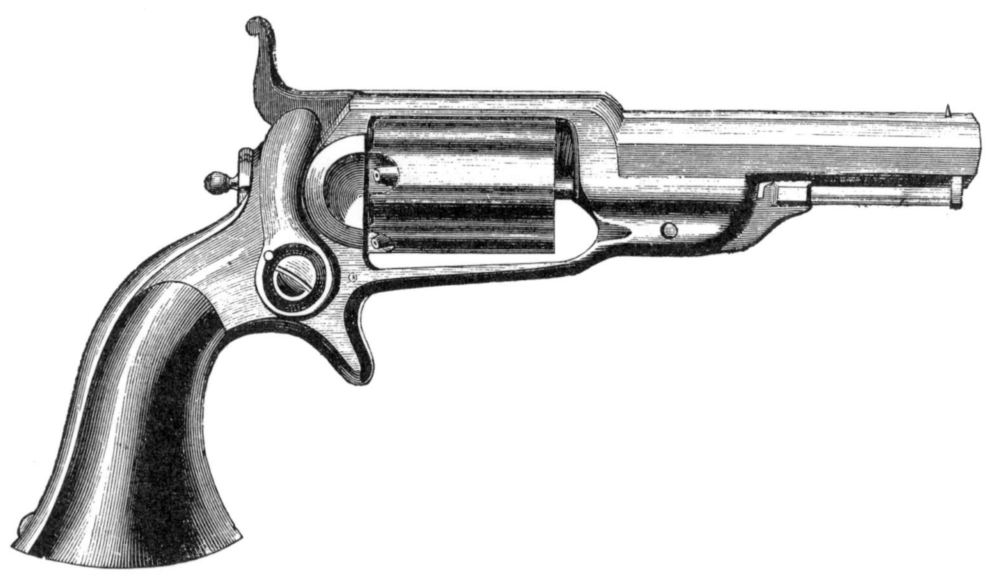

Colt's new model. (Norm Flayderman)

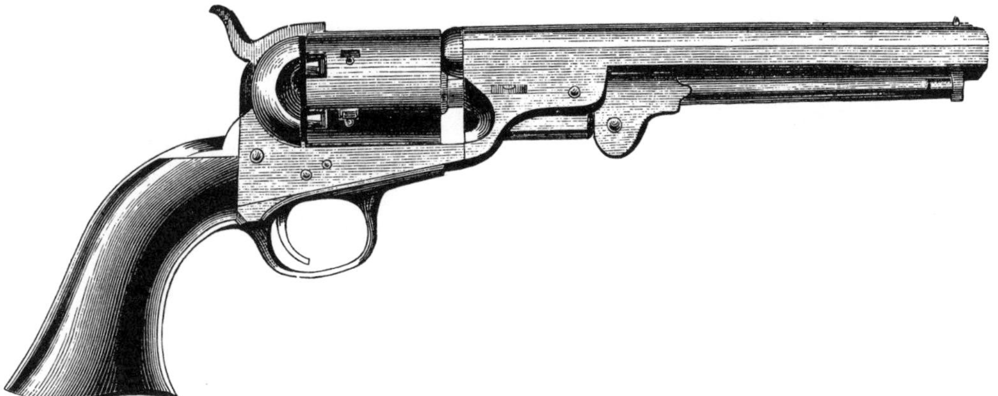

Colt's old model. (Norm Flayderman)

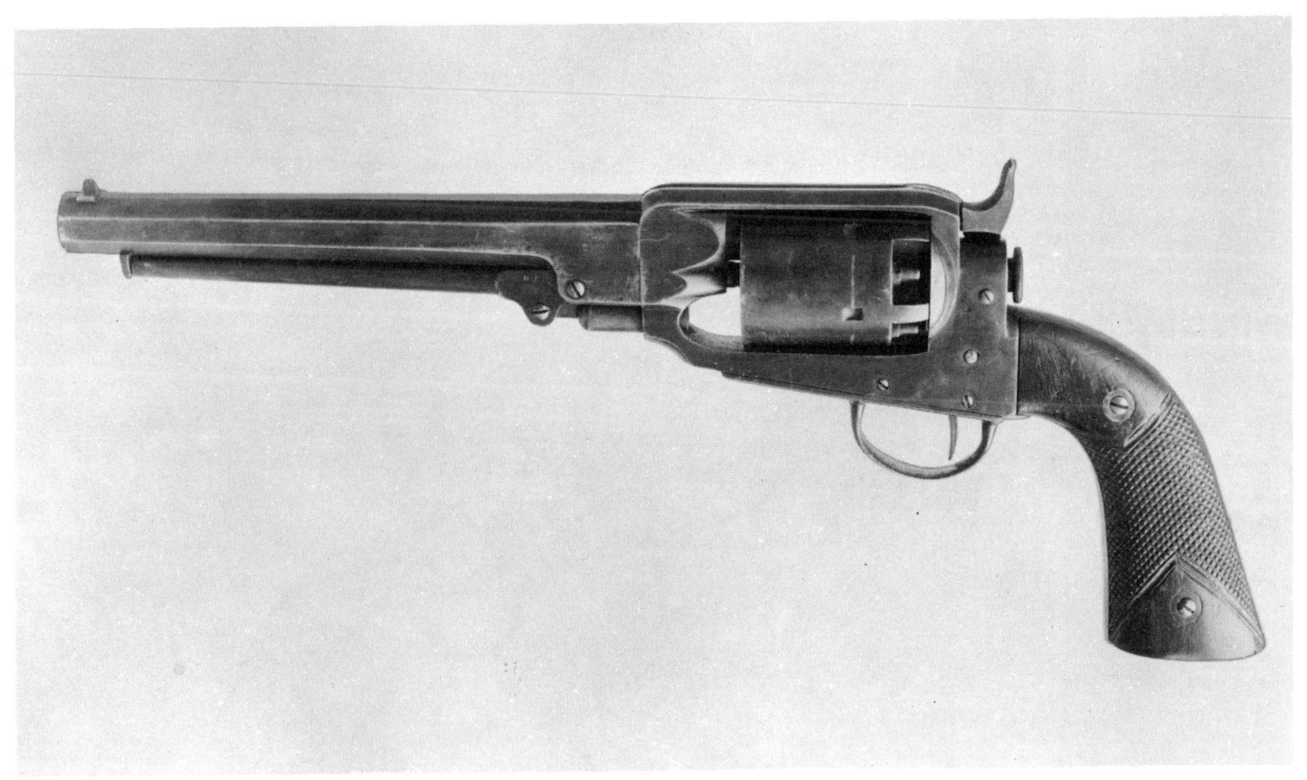

Joslyn revolver. (Norm Flayderman)

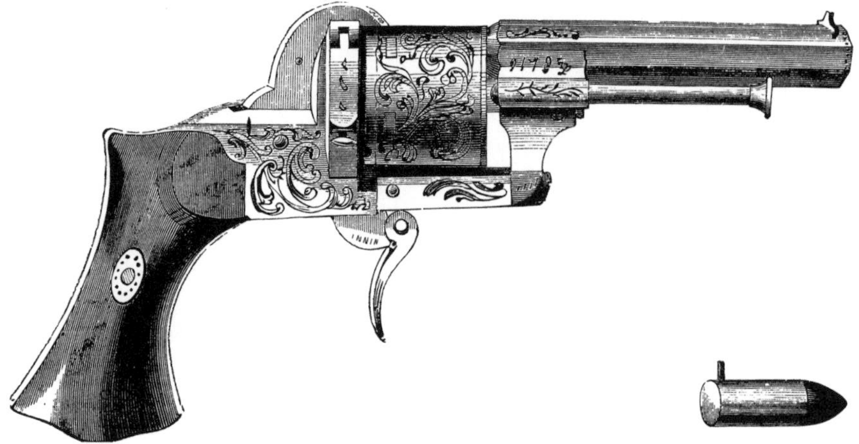

Lefaucheux revolver. (Norm Flayderman)

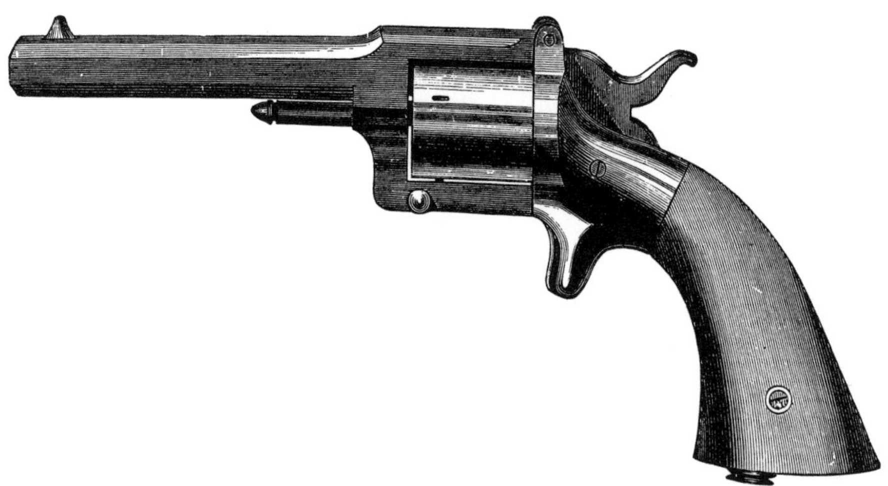

Pond's patent metal cartridge revolver. (Norm Flayderman)

Remington's navy revolver.

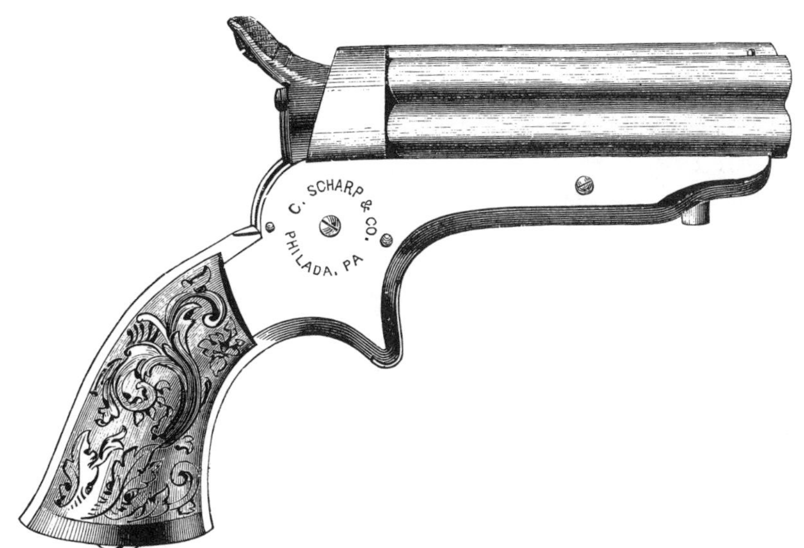

Sharps pistol. This 4-shot pocket pistol was the most popular pistol made by C. Sharps & Co. of Philadelphia. (Norm Flayderman)

Rider's revolver. (Norm Flayderman)

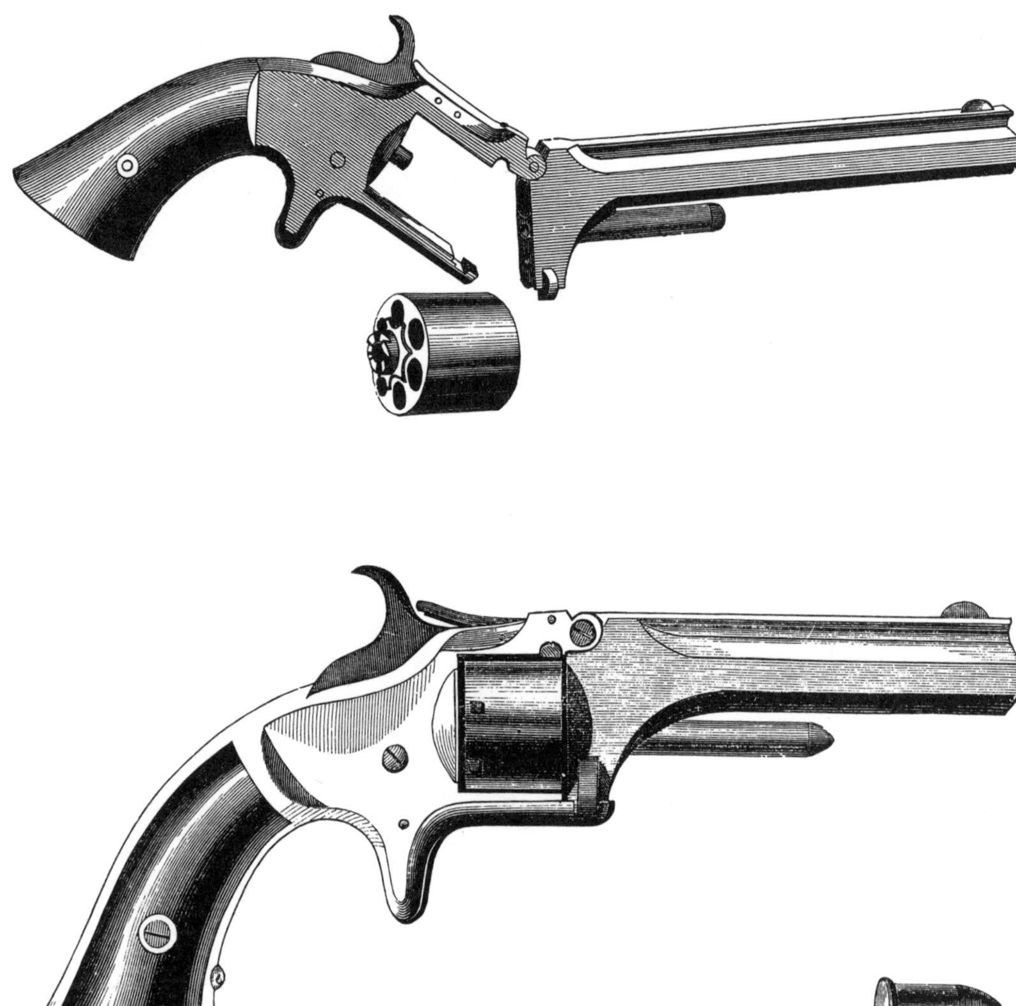

Smith and Wesson revolver. (Norm Flayderman)

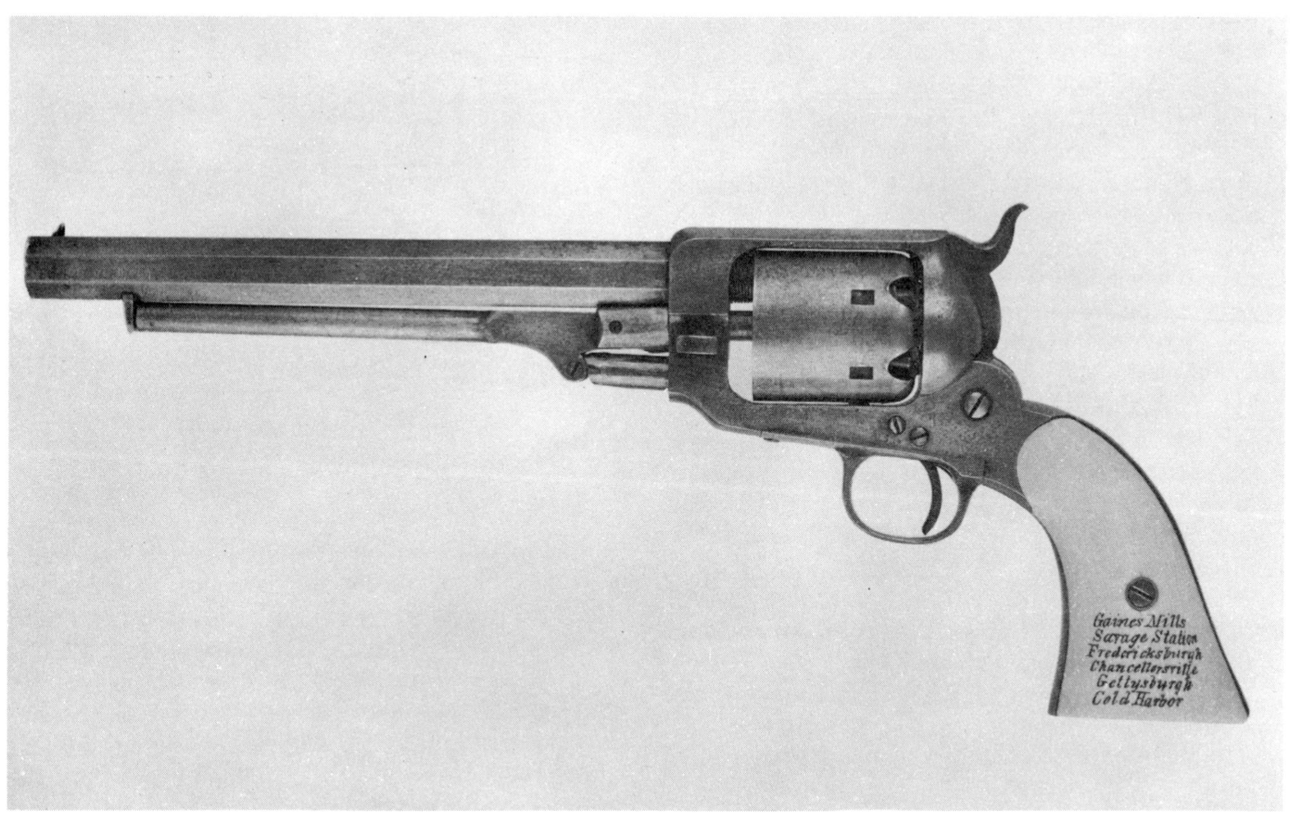

Whitney navy, 6-shot, single-action, cailber .36. The captain in the Army of the Potomac who owned this revolver was killed in action. (West Point Museum collections)

Starr revolver, caliber .44. (West Point Museum collections)

RIFLE. See SHOULDER WEAPONS.

RIFLE MUSKET. See SHOULDER WEAPONS.

RINGS. See RELICS AND SOUVENIRS.

ROCKET LAUNCHER. War rockets during the war were usually fired either from tubes or troughs mounted on portable stands, or on light carriages.

ROCKET LAUNCHER (HALE). Total length, 4 feet 10½ inches. External diameter of bore, 3 inches. Length of each bipod leg, 37 inches. The elevation sight is set off in numbers 1 to 8 with 2¼ inches between each two numbers. Total weight of launcher and legs, 30 pounds. No markings.

ROCKET, SIGNAL. See SIGNAL EQUIPMENT

ROCKETS, WAR. The standard Hale rockets were the 2¼ inch, weighing 6 pounds; and the 3¼ inch, weighing 16 pounds. The fixed shell weighed 9.2 pounds, the spherical case 11 pounds, and the canister 11.2 pounds.

Most of the rockets used in the war were Hale's, in which steadiness in flight was given by rotation of the rocket produced by three small vents placed at the base of the head of the rocket. Hale's rocket was improved during the war by placing three tangential vents in a plane passing through the center of gravity of the rocket, and at right angles to the axis. This was done by dividing the rocket case into two distinct parts by a perforated partition. The composition in the front part furnished the gas for rotation, and that in the rear the gas for propulsion.

War rockets. Top, Hale; bottom, Congreve. (Mike McAfee drawing)

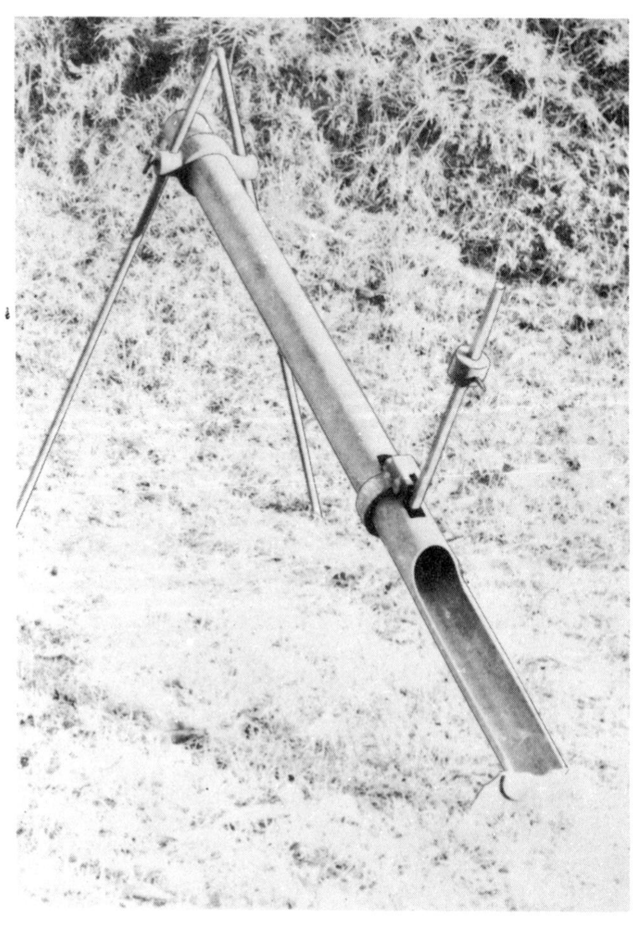

Rocket launcher.

At an angle of 4 to 5 degrees the range of these rockets was from 500 to 600 yards; and with an angle of 47 degrees the range of the smaller rocket was 1,760 yards and the larger was 2,200 yards. The Hale rocket used in the Federal service consisted of (1) a sheet iron case lined with paper and charged with rocket composition; (2) a cast iron cylindro-conoidal head, with a small cavity communicating with the bore of the rocket, and pierced with three holes, oblique to the surface, for the escape of gas; and (3) a wrought iron plug welded into the rear end of the case, and having a hole in its axis for the escape of gas.

The composition was pressed solid in the case by means of a powerful press, and the bore of the rocket was drilled and reamed out to the proper size. The sizes of rockets were indicated by the interior diameter of the cases.

Dimensions:

Whole length of rocket 16.9 inches.
Length of the finished case 14.2 inches.
Exterior diameter of case 3.25 inches.
Interior diameter of case 3.00 inches.
Weight of rocket, complete 14.00 lbs.

Hale's differed from any other rocket in having no guide stick. This was a great improvement, but the great difficulty in rocket-firing was to get them started in the right direction and keep them that way.

There were also two sizes of Congreve rockets, which were made of sheet iron, lined with paper or wood veneer. The head was of cast iron and could be either a solid shot or a fuzed shell.

Relics and captured items. Metropolitan Fair, New York, 1864. (National Archives)

Congreve's rocket, like the ordinary sky rocket of the period, had a directing stick, but instead of being tied to the outside of the case, it was inserted in a socket placed directly in rear of the case, the flame escaping through holes. This modification was introduced by Sir William Congreve, who was the first individual in modern times to make use of metal cases, although he was not the inventor of the rocket which had been known from time immemorial in China and India.

Hale's rockets saw some combat use in the war, but Hale's offer to come over from England and make rockets for the Union was refused. However, in 1861 a Major Thomas W. Lion, late of the British Army, arrived at Albany, New York, and organized a "rocket battalion" to use, in the field, a rocket of his invention. His "rocket gun" was a breechloading field piece, intended mainly for setting fire to buildings. Lion claimed his gun had a range of over three miles, but it did not perform well in tests. Accordingly the "rocket battalion" turned in their rocket guns, received conventional 6-pounder field pieces in return, and served through the war as the 24th New York Battery. Members of the unit stated that the Lion rocket was intended to be an improvement on the Congreve rocket. However, Lion's rocket had one fault which proved too great to overcome—the uncertainty of direction that the rocket would take. This meant it could come back towards the gun crew and, at best, it was impossible to tell exactly where it was going. Members of the rocket battalion regretted that the pioneer organization of this "wonderful arm of the service" never was permitted to fight with its original armament of rockets.

Confederate canteen. Battlefield pickup. (Herschel C. Logan)

ROSETTE, CAVALRY. Ornamental insignia on each side of horses' bridles, usually marked "U.S." (or "C" for Confederates), as used by mounted troops in the war. See HORSE EQUIPMENT.

RULER, PARALLEL. On November 1865, W. L. Woods of Washington, D.C. was granted a patent (No. 59,980) for a type of parallel ruler which had seen service during the war. This invention consisted of providing the rollers of an ordinary parallel ruler with scales, which, in connection with an index on the edge of an opening made in the surface of the ruler over the rollers, indicated the distance which the ruler was moved.

RELICS AND SOUVENIRS. Even during the war soldiers on both sides exchanged buttons, canteens, and other items. Many men sent captured articles home and included items of their own uniforms and equipments as souvenirs to relatives and friends. Civilians who visited the front picked up battlefield relices and sent them home. After the war a thriving business was carried on by Southern natives who picked up literally tons of buckles, bullets, projectiles, and weapons and sold them to Northern veterans who made pilgrimages to the battlefields where their units fought. To this accumulation of artifacts have recently been added large collections of metal items recovered by eager buffs using such modern contraptions as mine detectors. During the current Centennial observance many Civil War items have been rediscovered in family attics and even public museums. The traffic in Civil War relics, especially Confederate artifacts, has become so lucrative that unscrupulous dealers have duplicated rare items and foisted them on unsuspecting collectors. In many cases the replicas are so well made that an expert should be consulted before buying Civil War relics. This is especially true of Confederate buckles, buttons, and weapons.

Relics ranged from skulls to Bibles. Some soldiers of the 148th Pennsylvania Infantry, in passing over the battlefield of Second Manassas, found skulls in great numbers. "These we took up and wiggled out some teeth preferring those with gold fillings for momentoes. All the skulls we examined were remains of very young men, many having every tooth sound. In some of the skulls the third molars were still absent, showing that the soldiers were still under eighteen years of age." And after Gettysburg it was a rare occurrence to find a dead soldier who had not been robbed by the "battlefield bandit" or robber of the dead. Generally the pockets were cut open and thoroughly rifled through the incision. The battlefield robbers were well known by the large amounts of money they had, and the watches, pocketbooks, pocket knives, and other valuable trinkets they offered for sale after the battle. All regiments had them.

During truces between the lines, soldiers of both sides often swapped canteens, buttons, and even belt buckles and insignia. Some men were always looking for souvenirs, not only from the battlefield but also from occupied buildings, homes, libraries, and even state archives. During the war captured enemy weapons and equipment were displayed at the various fairs which were organized to raise money for soldiers and relief agencies. After the war there was a regular traffic in battlefield pickups, such as buckles, bullets, canteens, projectiles, bayonets, and other articles. The interest in these relics has been intensified during the present Centennial, abetted by the rich finds turned up by hundreds of relic hunters using mine detectors to find pieces heretofore hidden under the ground.

Buckles. Civil War diaries, reminiscences, and

Relic buckles. Top to bottom: Chancellorsville, Wilderness, Chancellorsville.

regimental histories contain many references to individuals who were saved from death by New Testaments, blanket rolls, or decks of cards which stopped bullets. However, here are three belt buckles, two of which show clearly that *their owners* were not so fortunate, while the fate of the third owner is not too clear. All three of these buckles were recovered from battlefields and illustrate the inviting target which brightly polished brasses presented to the enemy. Since the eagle ornament was worn over the middle of the chest and the belt buckle over the stomach, it can be easily seen that their wearers were mortally wounded or killed outright.

Bullets. One of the most common, and certainly one of the most interesting, phases of Civil War collecting is to be found in the assembling of a representative collection of Civil War small arms ammunition. For a comparatively small outlay of money, coupled with persistent search on battlefields, it is possible to put together a varied collection of bullets which will prompt further interest and research. There is literally almost no end to the types and calibers of Civil War musket, rifle, and pistol ammunition, and the surface has only been scratched. The general types, of course, have been covered in recent publications, but collectors are still coming up with specimens which baffle even the most knowledgeable experts. Today many dealers sell Minie balls, both genuine and replicas. Perhaps the most interesting relics of this type are in the West Point Museum. They have one or more specimens where two bullets met in midair and were mashed together.

Carvings. In winter quarters or in quiet sectors soldiers were making pipes and rings as mementoes of a camp or battlefield. Often mountain laurel root was used for making pipes, which also would often be decorated with a corps badge, either inlaid or in relief. The rings were made of dried horn, roof, in fact, from bone of any sort. Sometimes rings were carved from large gutta-percha buttons sent from home.

The illustration shows two carved military pipes. The longer one with relief eagle carving bears a

Carved wooden chain.

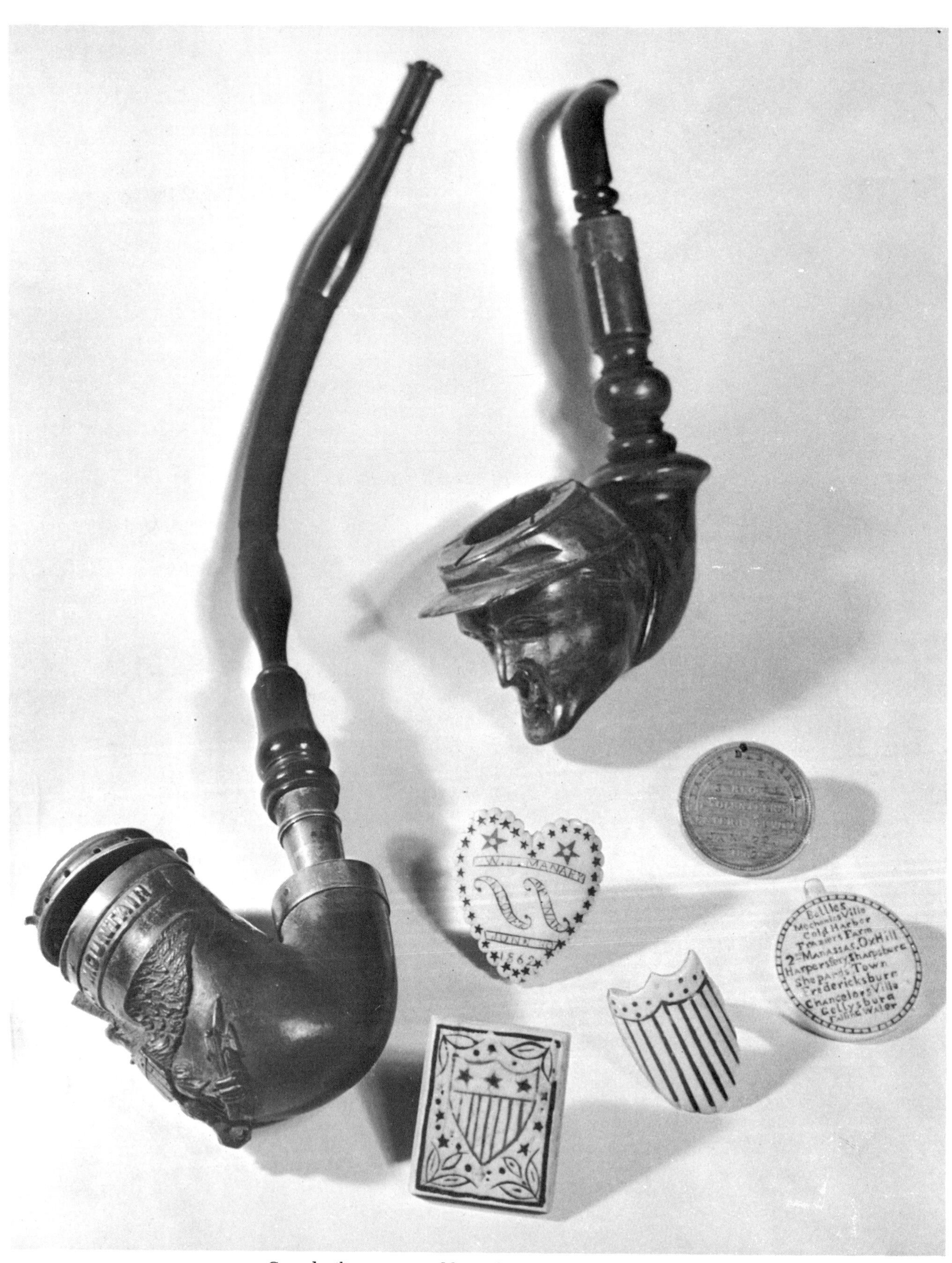

Carved military pipes and bone objects. (Norm Flayderman)

Relic muskets. An 1862 Springfield from Antietam, and (below) remnants of a Model 1861 musket from Bloody Angle at Spotsylvania.

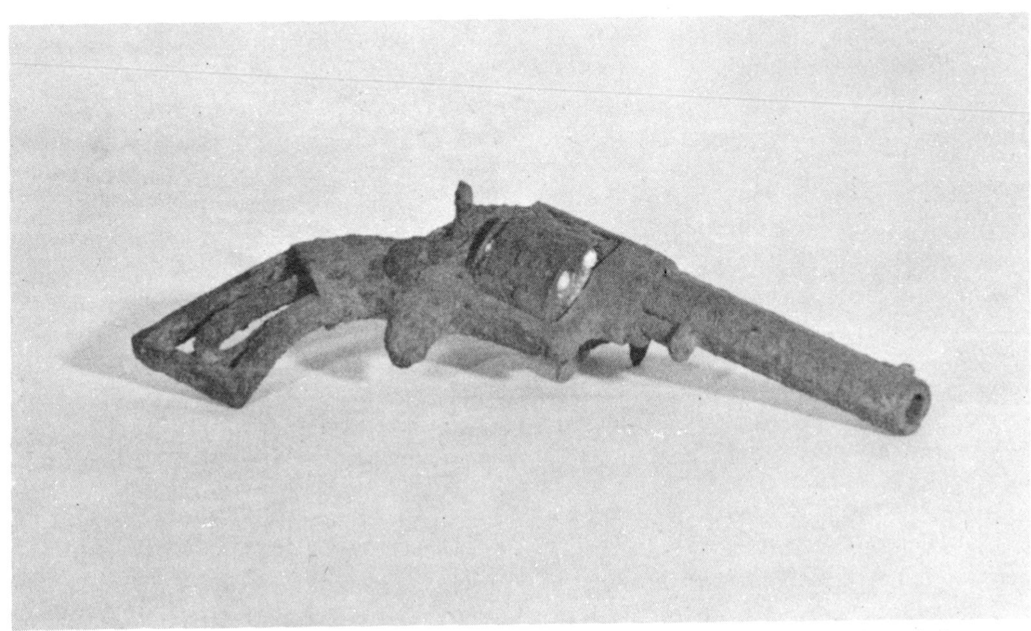

Relic revolver. Dug up at the battlefield of Balls Bluff. Note the rounds still in the cylinder.

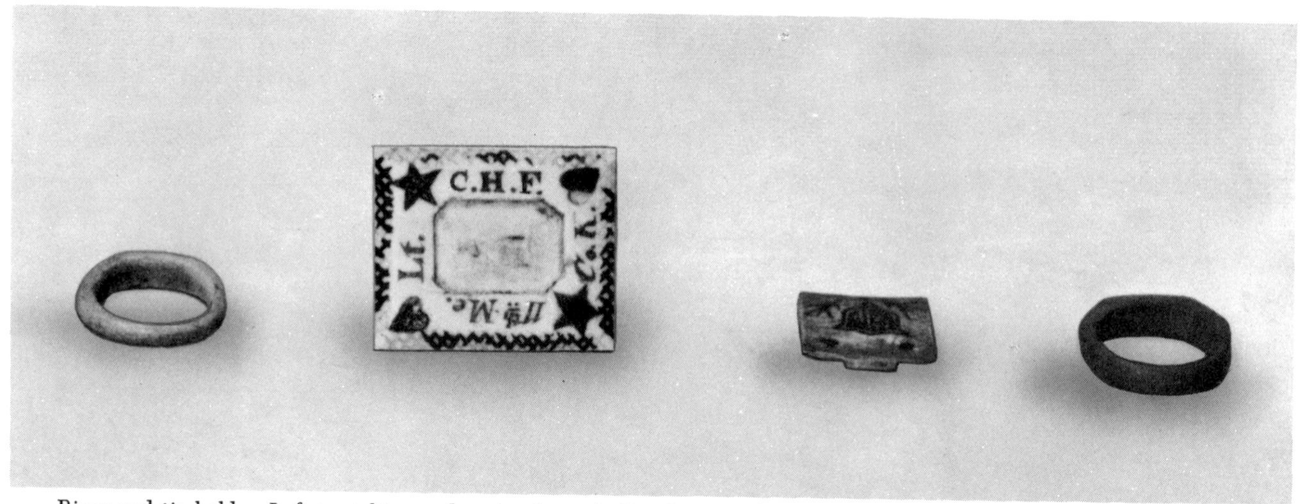

Rings and tie holder. Left to right: wooden ring from the Pemberton oak tree at Vicksburg, carved by a soldier of the 12th Michigan Infantry; bone tie holder made by a Federal prisoner at Libby prison; bone ring made by Lt. C. H. Foster, Co. K, 11th Maine Infantry; bone ring.

presentation inscription from a captain to a major on the silver cover, and also bears relief wording "Lookout Mountain." The smaller pipe is the emaciated head of a Civil War soldier with cap. It was probably carved by a prisoner of war in a prison camp, to represent the hard life there. The face is obviously gaunt and half-starved.

The three shield-shaped items are carved bone neckerchief slides as carved by prisoners of war. The very fancy one with the name "W. J. Manary, etc." actually bears the inscription "Prisoner of War" and the date June 1862. Upper right is a round brass disc, a Union identification tag. Lower right is a circular bone carved Confederate officer's identification tag. The reverse side (not shown) gives full details of his name, regiment, etc.

This wooden chain was made by a soldier while in winter camp. It is hand carved from pine wood, 12 inches long, and consists of 48 individual interlocking pieces of wood.

Muskets. Relics can logically be divided into three categories. The first includes those items which were either taken home by veterans in 1865 or were deposited in government arsenals and storehouses after the war. Items of this category are in better condition than the other two categories. The second category includes items picked up on the field shortly after the fighting ended and are in a fairly good state of preservation. The example shown here is an 1862 Springfield musket picked up on the field of Antietam shortly after the battle. The third category includes those items, chiefly metal, which have been plowed up or dug up where they have lain under the surface of the ground for the past hundred years. Illustrative of this category is the Model 1861 musket shown here which was dug up recently at the Bloody Angle at Spotsylvania. A large proportion of muskets dug up in recent years on Civil War battlefields are found to be loaded. In one case known to the author, a Virginia farmer was killed while heating one of these barrels preparatory to using it to repair an iron fence on his farm. The heating exploded the charge in the barrel and the Minié ball hit the farmer squarely in the forehead, killing him instantly.

Projectiles. Projectiles of the war are the same whether unused or found a century after the war ended. With the exception of some rust and pitting, their exterior appearance is the same as appears in photographs of projectiles taken during the war. And what is especially important to note is that internally they are the same too! The powder will still function and individuals handling Civil War projectiles (other than solid shot) must exercise a very real caution since these projectiles can and do explode. When the author's home burned in 1951 his Civil War projectiles exploded, even those which had lain in the ground for 100 years. The firemen thought another war had started. Common sense dictates that all projectiles which still contain powder should be deactivated by an ordnance expert. Especially dangerous is the attempt by amateurs to remove the metal fuze from projectiles. Let experts do this for you. Remember that although the powder may be wet, it can dry out and is then very sensitive to heat or sudden shock. The author knows of one instance where a family found two projectiles on their farm in Mississippi, used these projectiles as andirons in the fireplace of their cabin, and later returned with mixed emotions to see the entire end of the cabin blown off by the explosion of the "harmless" projectiles! Fortunately, they had left the cabin after starting a fire in the fireplace.

Rings. Rings were often carved as mementos of a camp, battlefield, or prison. Due to the long periods of monotony, especially in prison camps, the men had the time and incentive to devote a lot of time to such time-killers as carving rings or other small objects.

SABRETASCHE. From the German *Sabel,* a saber, and *Tasche,* a pocket. The sabretasche, occasionally part of the accouterments of a cavalry or staff officer, was a leather pouch, suspended at the left side from the sword belt or by a shoulder sling. It was used for carrying maps and papers.

Sabretasche. (Norm Flayderman)

SADDLE. See HORSE EQUIPMENTS.

SADDLE BAGS. See HORSE EQUIPMENTS.

SADDLE BLANKET. See HORSE EQUIPMENTS.

SAFETY GUARD FOR FIREARMS (Patent No. 46,100). Patented January 31, 1865 by H. E. Gibbon, Brooklyn, N.Y. Consisted in providing the hammer with a toothed or ratchet arc, into which a spring pawl engages, and thereby holds up the hammer from striking.

SASH. See UNIFORMS AND CLOTHING.

SCISSORS AND SHEARS. Examples in collections show practically no differences from those in use today.

SCRAPER. See ARTILLERY.

SCREW DRIVER. See APPENDAGES.

SHAVING EQUIPMENT. Nearly every unit had at least one barber in camp. Many of these had never barbered in civilian life, but took it up to earn extra cash. Many soldiers in both armies never used the razor in the service, but allowed a shrubby straggling growth of hair and beard to grow, as if to camouflage themselves from the enemy. Certainly the many photographs and daguerreotypes of the soldiers of the '60's prove that beards were the style, especially for the older men. However many more men carried their own shaving equipment and shaved themselves, frequently shedding some blood for their country in the process. But there was still a large number who, either from lack of skill in use of the razor, or from want of inclination, preferred to patronize the camp barber.

Shaving equipment.

Shaving cups.

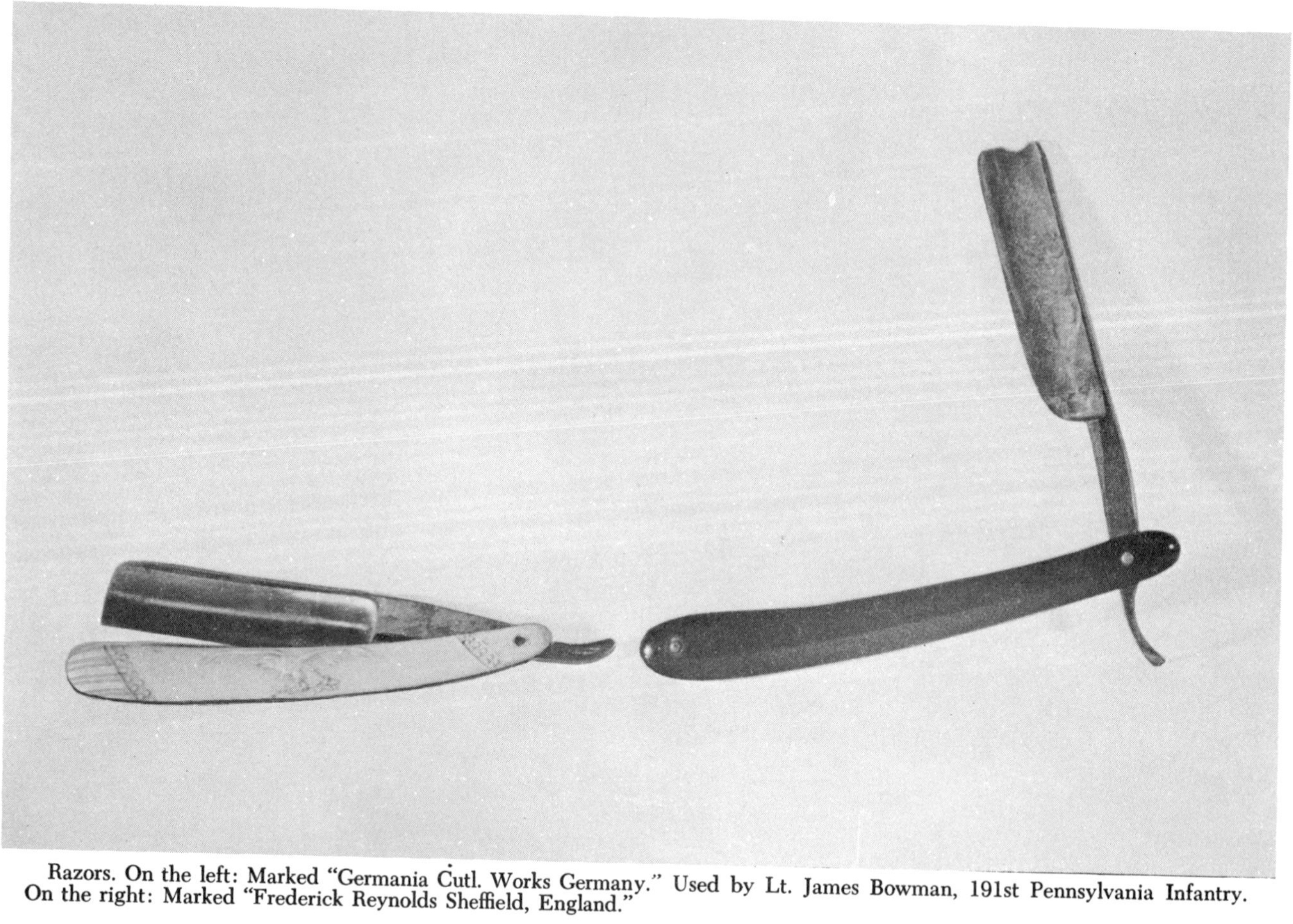

Razors. On the left: Marked "Germania Cutl. Works Germany." Used by Lt. James Bowman, 191st Pennsylvania Infantry. On the right: Marked "Frederick Reynolds Sheffield, England."

This individual plied his vocation inside a tent in cold or stormy weather, but in clement weather he was to be seen in rear of his tent. His improvised chair consisted of four stakes driven into the ground, two long ones for the back legs, and two shorter ones for the front. On these legs was placed a crude wooden platform on which his victims sat.

Shaving equipment, as carried by men in the field, consisted of a straight razor, a strap, and a round mirror. These mirrors were often decorated with eagle designs or other patriotic symbols. Some men used tin shaving mugs.

SHAVING CUP. Both these unmarked shaving cups consist of the cup proper with a slot for holding the razor strop, and a small removable cup for holding the soap and making the lather. The cup proper holds the hot (or, in the field, cold) water. The taller shaving cup is 4¼ inches tall, 3 inches in diameter, and was a type used by commissioned officers. The shorter cup, 3¾ inches tall, 3 inches in diameter, was found in Strasburg, Virginia.

SHAWL. When in winter quarters, fortunate headquarters officer personnel, and occasionally company officers as well, permitted themselves the luxury of wearing a shawl in the evening or in their tents in cold weather. Apparently few officers used shawls and even fewer of their men. However some shawls saw service. One specimen preserved today is made of light brown wool, with fringes on both ends. It looks very similar to a blanket but is made of finer material, and much larger. Dimensions: 5-1/2 feet wide by 11-1/3 feet long. Used by 1st Lt. William S. Ames, 38th U.S. Colored Troops.

SHEET, BED. One of the rarest of Civil War items, a sheet in the author's collection is stamped: "Hosp. Dept. U.S.A." The original label states that it was used in a Federal hospital in Annapolis, Maryland. The sheet is made of heavy cotton, 8¼ feet long and 5 feet wide.

SHELL. See PROJECTILES.

SHELL-HOOKS. See ARTILLERY.

SHELL PLUG-SCREW. See ARTILLERY.

SHIRT. See UNIFORMS AND CLOTHING.

SHOES. See UNIFORMS AND CLOTHING.

SHOT GAUGE. See ARTILLERY.

SHOULDER KNOTS, MARINE CORPS. See also EPAULETTES. All officers wore on each shoulder of the undress coat, and undress white linen coat, a shoulder knot, of fine gold cord three-sixteenths of an inch in diameter, the shoulder knot consisting of a twisted strap, and an end of a clover leaf shape. The clover leaf end was lined with scarlet cloth, showing through the openings; the twisted strap was also lined, only so as to show through the openings; there was no cushion under the end which rests on the shoulder and the twisted strap extending from thence up to the coat collar. The knot was fastened by a small Marine button, and tags at the collar. At the shoulder were two tags; tags to pass through the cloth of the coat and tie on the inside.

Commandant. Four cords in the twisted strap and clover leaf end, with a silver embroidered star in the center of the clover leaf.

Colonel. Same as for the commandant, substituting a silver embroidered spread eagle for the star.

Lieutenant-Colonel. Same as for the commandant, substituting a silver embroidered leaf for the star.

Major. Same as for the commandant, but without any device.

Captain. Of three cords, with two silver embroidered bars in the clover leaf ends.

First Lieutenant. Same as for captains, omitting one of the bars.

Second Lieutenant. Same as for captains, but without any device.

SHOULDER SCALES. Light-artillerymen, cavalry troops, and even some NCO's, musicians, and privates of infantry units went to the front decorated with brass scales on their shoulders, but finding an utter absence of such ornaments on the persons of soldiers who had

Shoulder scales. (Norm Flayderman)

ILLUSTRATED CATALOGUE OF MILITARY GOODS. 51

Russian, or Artillery Shoulder Knots.

No. 70.

Gold Knots, without ornaments, for Major.
do. do. Silver Emb'd Leaf, for Lt.-Col.
do. do. do. do. Eagle, for Colonel.

No. 69.

Gold Knots, Three Rows, without ornament, for 2d Lieutenant.
do. do. with One Silver Emb'd Bar, for 1st Lieutenant.
do. do. with Two do. do. Bars, for Captain.

No. 71.

Gold Knots, Fancy Cord.

Shoulder knots. (Norm Flayderman)

seen combat service, and feeling sensitive about being known as raw troops, they soon disposed of these decorations. However, such heavy artillery regiments as the 1st Maine Heavy Artillery, which joined Grant as infantry in the 1864 campaign, wore shoulder scales into action at Spotsylvania. Theoretically, shoulder scales were worn to ward off the blows of a saber aimed by cavalrymen; practically, however, it is doubtful if they ever served such a purpose. At least three types have been identified.

These scales were made of stamped brass and were attached to the coat by means of wing stud sewed to the coat on top of the shoulder next to the collar. This stud fitted through a T slot on the scale and turned 90 degrees so as to prevent the scale from falling off.

SHOULDER STRAPS.

ARMY

Major-General Commanding the Army. (Similar shoulder straps were worn by the Lieutenant General, 1864-1865.) Dark blue cloth, 1⅜ inches wide by 4 inches long; bordered with an embroidery of gold ¼ inch wide; three silver-embroidered stars of five rays, one star on the center of the strap, and one on each side equidistant between the center and the outer edge of the strap; the center star to be the largest.

All Other Major Generals. The same as for the Major General Commanding the Army, except that there were two stars instead of three; the center of each star being 1 inch from the outer edge of the gold embroidery on the ends of the strap; both stars were of the same size.

Brigadier General. The same as for a major general, except that there was one star instead of two; the center of the star being equidistant from the outer edge of the embroidery on the ends of the strap.

Colonel. The same size as for a major general, and bordered in like manner with an embroidery of gold; a silver-embroidered spread eagle on the center of the strap, 2 inches between the tips of the wings, having in the right talon an olive branch, and in the left a bundle of arrows; an escutcheon on the breast, as represented in the arms of the United States; cloth of the strap as follows: for the *General Staff and Staff Corps*—dark blue; *Artillery*—scarlet; *Infantry*—light or sky blue; *Cavalry*—yellow.

Lieutenant Colonel. The same as for a colonel, according to branch of service, omitting the eagle and substituting a silver-embroidered leaf at each end, each leaf extending ⅝ of an inch from the end border of the strap.

Major. The same as for a colonel according to branch of service, omitting the eagle, and substituting a gold-embroidered leaf at each end, each leaf extending ⅝ of an inch from the end border of the strap.

Captain. The same as for a colonel, according to branch of service, omitting the eagle and substituting at each end two gold-embroidered bars of the same width as the border, placed parallel to the ends of the strap; the distance between them and from the border equal to the width of the border.

First Lieutenant. The same as for a colonel, according to branch of service, omitting the eagle, and substituting at each end one gold-embroidered bar of the same width as the border, placed parallel to the ends of the strap, at a distance from the border equal to its width.

Second Lieutenant. The same as for a colonel, according to branch of service, omitting the eagle.

Brevet Second Lieutenant. The same as for a second lieutenant.

Medical Cadet. A strip of gold lace 3 inches long, ½ inch wide placed in the middle of a strap of green cloth 3¾ inches long by 1¼ inches wide.

The shoulder strap was worn whenever the epaulette was not.

NAVY, U.S. (Quoted from U.S. Navy Regulations). All shoulder straps, except for gunners, boatswains, carpenters, and sailmakers, are to be of navy-blue cloth, four inches and a quarter long, and one inch and a half wide, including the border, which is to be a quarter of an inch wide, and embroidered in gold.

The centre and end ornaments, or distinctions of the line and staff, and indications of rank, are to be embroidered in gold or in silver, as hereinafter designated, and are to be as follows:

Line officers. For a *Rear-Admiral*—A silver foul anchor in the centre, in a horizontal position, and a silver star of five rays at each end.

Commodore. A silver star, embroidered on a gold foul anchor, in the centre.

Captain. A silver spread eagle, resting on a silver plain anchor, in the centre.

Commander. A silver foul anchor in the centre, and a silver oak leaf at each end.

Lieutenant-Commander. A silver foul anchor in the centre, and a gold oak leaf at each end.

Lieutenant. A silver foul anchor in the centre, and two gold bars at each end.

Master. A silver foul anchor in the centre, and a gold bar at each end.

Ensign. A silver foul anchor in the centre.

Staff officers are to wear shoulder straps of the same description as prescribed for *line officers* with whom they assimilate, respectively, in rank, with the following exceptions as to centre devices.

In the *Medical Corps,* the anchor is omitted; in the *Paymaster's Corps,* an oak sprig, in silver, is substi-

Shoulder Straps for Officers—Exact Size of U. S. Regulation.

Length of Strap, 4 inches—Width, 1⅜ inches—Width of Embroidery, ¼ inch.
FOR GENERAL STAFF OFFICERS—on Dark Blue Cloth.
FOR INFANTRY, OFFICERS—on Saxony Blue Cloth.
FOR ARTILLERY OFFICERS—on Scarlet Cloth.
FOR RIFLE OFFICERS—on Green Cloth.
FOR CAVALRY OFFICERS—on Yellow Cloth.
FOR DRAGOON OFFICERS—on Orange Cloth.

No. 84. GENERAL-IN-CHIEF—3 Silver Embroidered Stars.

No. 85. MAJOR-GENERAL—2 Silver Embroidered Stars.

No. 86. BRIGADIER-GENERAL—1 Silver Embroidered Star.

No. 87. COLONEL—Silver Embroidered Eagle.

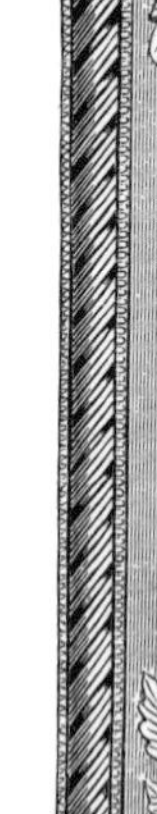

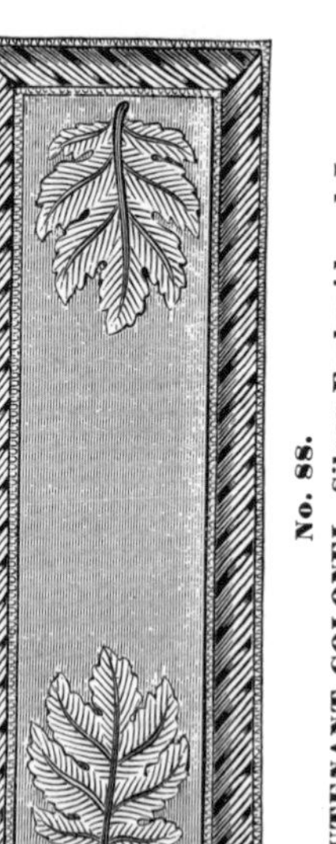

No. 88. LIEUTENANT-COLONEL—Silver Embroidered Leaves.

No. 89. MAJOR—Gold Embroidered Leaves.

U.S. Army shoulder straps. (Norm Flayderman)

Shoulder Straps for Officers—Exact Size of U. S. Regulation.

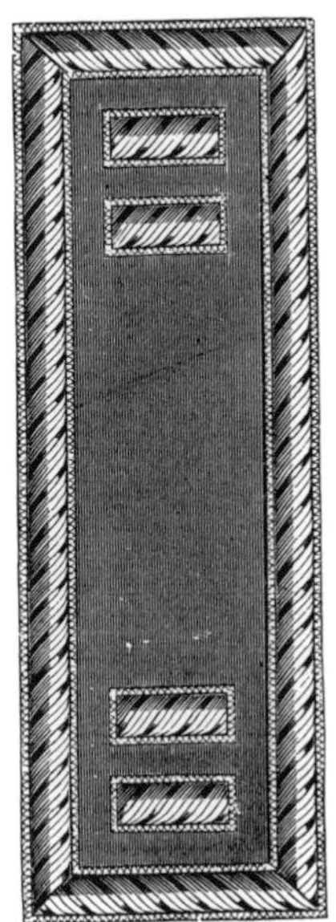

No. 90.
CAPTAIN—2 Gold Embroidered Bars at each end.

No. 91.
1st LIEUTENANT—1 Gold Emb'd Bar at each end.

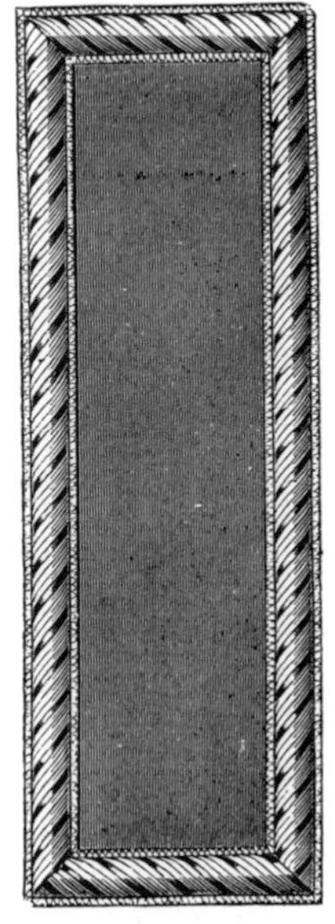

No. 92.
2d LIEUTENANT.

Shoulder Straps—Extra Rich.

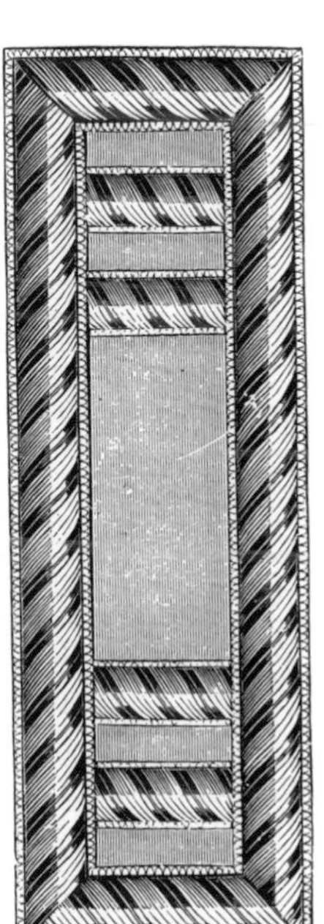

No. 93.
CAPTAIN—2 Gold Embroidered Bars at each end.
One Row Extra Rich.

No. 94.
1st LIEUTENANT—1 Gold Embroidered Bar at each end.
One Row Extra Rich.

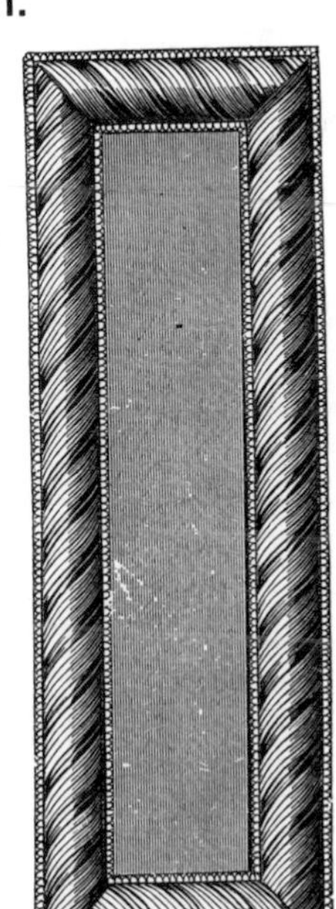

No. 95.
2d LIEUTENANT.
One Row Extra Rich.

U.S. Army shoulder straps. (Norm Flayderman)

tuted; in the *Engineer Corps*, a device of four oak leaves, in silver, in the form of a cross, is substituted; for *Professors of Mathematics*, the letter 𝔓, in silver relief, on plain gold circle, is substituted; for *Naval Constructors*, a live-oak sprig is substituted; for *Chaplains*, a silver cross is substituted; for *Secretaries*, the letter 𝔖, in silver, is substituted.

Midshipmen, Third Assistant Engineers, and *Clerks*, are not to wear straps.

Gunners, boatswains, carpenters, and *sailmakers*, are to have shoulder straps of plain gold lace, four inches long, and three-quarters of an inch wide, the *boatswain* to have the letter 𝔅, and the *carpenter* the letter ℭ, embroidered in silver, midway upon their straps.

For the exact dimensions and form of the devices, and the manner of arranging them, see plates, by which the officers will be guided.

NAVY, C.S. (From 1862 Regulations)

Flag Officer. Sky-blue cloth, edged with black, 4 inches long and 1⅜ inches wide, bordered with an embroidery of gold ¼ inch wide with 4 stars in line at equal distances, the two on the ends 6/10 an inch in diameter, and the two intermediate 6/8 inch in diameter.

Captain. Same as for a flag officer, except that there shall be 3 stars at equal distances, each 6/10 inch in diameter.

Commander. Same as for a captain, except that there shall be but 2 stars.

Lieutenant. Same as for a commander, except that there shall be but 1 star, in the center.

Master. Same as for a lieutenant, except that there shall be no star.

Passed Midshipman. A strip of gold lace 4 inches long and ½ inch wide.

Surgeon (Over 12 years standing). Same as for a master, except that they shall be of black cloth, with 2 sprigs of olive, crossed, embroidered in gold in the center.

Surgeon (Under 12 years standing). Same, except there shall be but 1 sprig of olive.

Passed Assistant Surgeon. Same as for a surgeon, except that instead of sprigs of olive, there shall be an olive leaf embroidered in gold on each end.

Assistant Surgeon. Same as for a passed assistant surgeon, without the leaves.

Paymaster (Over 12 years standing). Same as for a surgeon of over 12 years standing, except that the straps shall be of dark green cloth.

Paymaster (Under 12 years standing). Same as for a surgeon of under 12 years standing, except that the straps shall be of dark green cloth.

Assistant Paymaster. Same as for an assistant surgeon, except that the straps shall be of dark green cloth.

Chief Engineer (Over 12 years standing). Same as for a master, except that there shall be 2 sprigs of live oak embroidered in gold in the center, and the straps shall be of dark blue cloth.

Chief Engineer (Under 12 years standing). Same, except that there shall be but one sprig of live oak.

PATENTED SHOULDER STRAPS

Evans (Patent No. 37,143). Patented December 9, 1862 by George G. Evans, Philadelphia, Penn. Consisted of a border plate or frame, a detachable back plate, and other attachments, to enable the shoulder strap to be readily connected with and disconnected from the shoulder part of the coat.

Robinson Shoulder Strap (Patent No. 37,056). Patented December 2, 1862 by Gideon Robinson, New York, N.Y. This invention consisted of forming the border of the shoulder strap of wire by coiling the latter upon a mandril of half-round shape.

WEARING THE SHOULDER STRAP. The *Army and Navy Journal* for September 24, 1864, pointed out the confusion resulting from the similar insignia for major and lieutenant colonel—being "hard to distinguish at any distance, or after dark." One writer suggested: for a lieutenant colonel, a shield with crossed swords in the center; for a major, a gold shield with crossed halberts. These insignia would be in the center of the shoulder straps, not at the ends.

Miniature insignia of rank were permitted in lieu of the conspicuous shoulder straps. Captain E. A. Flint, 1st Massachusetts Cavalry (shown in the photograph on cavalry equipment) is wearing the 4-button enlisted men's blouse with miniature officer's insignia.

But the Federal Government even went further. By General Order No. 286, November 22, 1864, the War Department permitted officers in the field to dispense with shoulder straps altogether. The designation of rank, however, was to be worn. Officers also were permitted by this order to wear overcoats of the same color and shape of those of the enlisted men. No ornaments were required to be worn on the overcoats, hats, or forage caps, nor were sashes or epaulettes required to be worn in the future. The sensible order undoubtedly saved many lives.

SCHUYLER, HARTLEY & GRAHAM. NEW-YORK.

ADMIRAL.

Nº 266. 4¼ Anchor in length ⅞. Stars in diam.r ⅞. From center of Star to end of Strap ⅞. Width of Border ⅛ in.

COMMODORE.

Nº 267. 4¼ Anchor in length ⅞. Star in diam.r ⅞.

CAPTAIN.

Nº 268. 4¼

COMMANDER.

Nº 269. 4¼ Leaf in length ⅝. Stalk of leaf from end of Strap ⅜. Length of Anchor ⅞.

LIEUTENANT COMMANDER.

Nº 270. 4¼ Leaf in length ⅝. Stalk of leaf from end of Strap ⅜. Length of Anchor ⅞.

LIEUTENANT

Nº 271. 4¼ Bars 2/10ths wide, ½ in. long. " 4/10ths from end to Strap. Space between bars 1/10th. Anchor ⅞ths long.

MASTER.

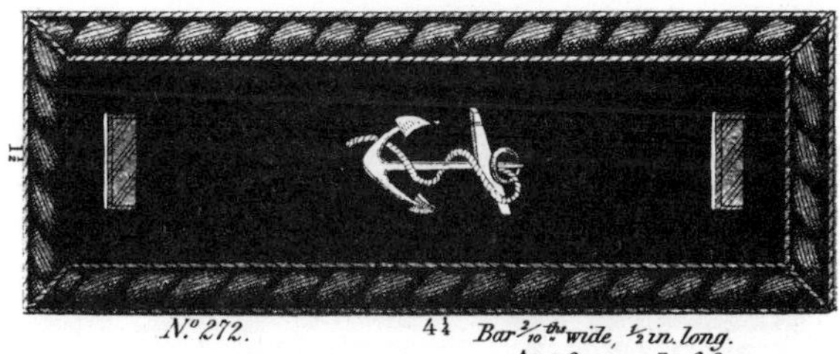

Nº 272. 4¼ Bar 2/10ths wide, ½ in. long. " 3/10 " from end of Strap. Anchor ⅞ths long.

ENSIGN.

Nº 273. 4¼ Anchor in length ⅞ths

U.S. Naval officers' shoulder straps. (Norm Flayderman)

SCHUYLER, HARTLEY & GRAHAM. NEW-YORK.

CHIEF OF BUREAU OF PROVⁿ & CLOTHING.

No. 274. 4¼ *Length of Oak Sprig $1\frac{1}{4}$ in.*
Star in diamr. $\frac{7}{8}$
Width of Border $\frac{1}{2}$.

FLEET PAYMASTERS & PAYMASTER AFTER 15 YEARS.

No. 276. *Eagle from tip to tip 2 in.*
Length of Oak Sprig $1\frac{1}{10}$th

PAYMASTERS, AFTER 1ST FIVE YEARS.

No. 278. *Length of Oak Sprig $1\frac{1}{4}$.*
End leaf in length $\frac{5}{8}$.
Stalk of leaf from end of strap $\frac{3}{8}$.

PAYMASTERS, 1ST FIVE YEARS.

No. 280. *Length of Oak Sprig $1\frac{1}{4}$.*
End leaf in length $\frac{5}{8}$.
Stalk of leaf from end of Strap $\frac{3}{8}$.

ASSISTANT PAYMASTER.

No. 282. *Length of Oak Sprig $1\frac{1}{4}$.*
Bar $\frac{2}{10}$ths wide, $\frac{1}{2}$ in. long.
" $\frac{3}{10}$ths from end of Strap.

CHIEF OF BUREAU OF CONSTRUCTION.

No. 275 *Spread of live oak leaves $1\frac{7}{10}$ths*
Star in diamr. $\frac{7}{8}$.

NAVAL CONSTRUCTORS OF MORE THAN 20 YEARS.

No. 277. *Eagle 2 in. from tip to tip.*
Length of live oak sprig $\frac{9}{10}$ths"

NAVAL CONSTRUCTORS OF MORE THAN 12 YEARS.

No. 279. *Spread of live oak leaves $1\frac{1}{10}$th*
End leaf in length $\frac{5}{8}$.
Stalk of leaf from end of Strap $\frac{3}{8}$

NAVAL CONSTRUCTORS OF LESS THAN 12 YEARS.

No. 281. *Spread of live oak leaves $1\frac{1}{10}$th*
End leaf in length $\frac{5}{8}$.
Stalk of leaf from end of Strap $\frac{3}{8}$.

ASSISTT NAVAL CONSTRUCTOR.

No. 283. *Spread of live oak leaves $1\frac{1}{10}$th.*
Bar $\frac{2}{10}$ths wide, $\frac{1}{2}$ in. long.
" $\frac{3}{10}$" from end of Strap

Naval shoulder straps. (Norm Flayderman)

SCHUYLER, HARTLEY & GRAHAM. NEW-YORK.

CHIEF OF BUREAU OF MEDICINE & SURGERY.

No. 284. 4¼ *Star in diam.r 7/8.*
Width of Border 1/4.

FLEET SURGEONS & SURGEONS AFTER 15 YEARS.

No. 285. 4¼ *Eagle 2 in. from tip to tip.*

SURGEONS AFTER 1ST FIVE YEARS.

No. 286. 4¼ *Leaf in length 5/8.*
Stalk of leaf from end of Strap 3/8.

SURGEONS 1ST FIVE YEARS.

No. 287. 4¼ *Leaf in length 5/8*
Stalk of leaf from end of Strap 3/8.

PASSED ASSIST.T SURGEONS.

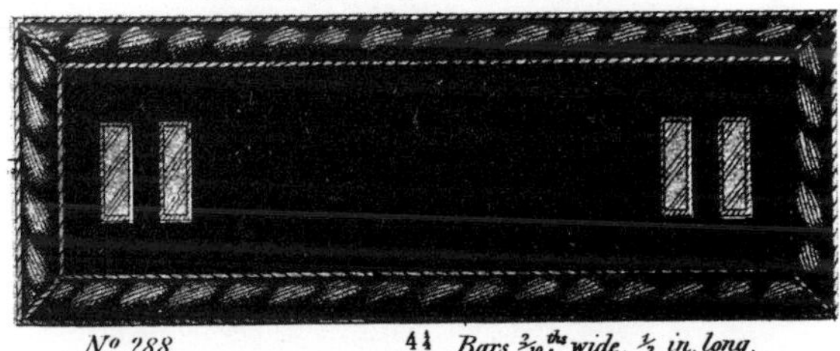

No. 288. 4¼ *Bars 2/10ths wide, 1/2 in. long.*
" 4/10ths from end of Strap.
Space between bars 1/10th

ASSISTANT SURGEONS.

No. 289. 4¼ *Bar 2/10ths wide, 1/2 in. long.*
" 4/10ths from end of Strap.

CHAPLAINS OF MORE THAN 12 YEARS.

No. 290. 4¼

CHAPLAINS OF LESS THAN 12 YEARS.

No. 291. 4¼ *Length of Cross 7/8.*
" of Leaf 5/8ths
Stalk of Leaf from end Strap 7/8.

Naval shoulder straps. (Norm Flayderman)

SCHUYLER, HARTLEY & GRAHAM. NEW-YORK.

CHIEF OF BUREAU OF STEAM ENGINEERING.

No. 292. 4¼ Center Ornament 1 in. long.
Star in diam.r 7/8 ths
Border 1/4 in.

FLEET ENGINEERS & CHIEF ENGINEERS AFTER 15 YEARS.

No. 293. Eagle 2 in. from tip to tip.
Spread of leaves 1¼ in.

CHIEF ENGINEERS AFTER 1ST FIVE YEARS.

No. 294. Leaf in length 5/8.
Stalk of leaf from end of Strap 3/8.

CHIEF ENGINEERS 1ST FIVE YEARS.

No. 295. Leaf in length 5/8.
Stalk of leaf from end of Strap 3/8.

1ST ASSIST ENGINEERS.

No. 296. Bar 3/10 ths wide, 1/8 in. long.
4/10 ths from end of Strap.

2D ASSIST ENGINEERS.

No. 297 Center Ornament 1 in. long.

PROFESSORS OF LESS THAN 12 YEARS.

No. 298 Plain center circle 5/8 ths in. diam.r
with letter in relief.
PROFESSOR OVER 12 YEARS.— same but Silver in place of Gold Emb.d Leaves.

SECRETARIES.

No. 299. Bars 2/10 ths wide, 1/2 in. long
" 4/10 " from end of Strap.
Space between bars 1/10 th

Naval shoulder straps. (Norm Flayderman)

SHOULDER WEAPONS. In this topic, "shoulder weapons" are divided into two main categories: muskets (including rifle-muskets) and rifles, and carbines.

CARBINES

CONFEDERATE

Domestic

Alexander Breech-loading Carbine
Confederate Sharps
Confederate Dropping-Breech Carbine
Confederate Rising-Breech Carbine
Fayetteville Pistol Carbine
D.C. Hodgkins and Sons, Macon, Ga.
J.P. Murray, Columbus, Ga.
Morse Breechloading Carbine
Perry
S.C. Robinson, Richmond, Va.
Tarpley

Imports

Enfield Carbine
LeMat Revolving Carbine
Terry Bolt-Action Carbine

FEDERAL. Several makers of rifles also made carbines, utilizing the same firing mechanism in both. In some cases, e.g. the Henry, the weapon appeared in only one size; while in others, such as the Sharps and Spencer, both rifle and carbine were produced.

The following carbines were illustrated in the Atlas to the *Official Records* and were very probably considered to have been the most common types in general use by the Federal forces:

Burnside
Henry
Maynard
Merrill
Remington
Sharps
Smith
Starr

Sharps Carbine. The *Army and Navy Journal* maintained that Sharp's carbines were the favorite cavalry carbine through admitting that upon this subject there is a diversity of opinion, each commander having some pet arm which he thinks superior to any other." Its characteristics were:

Breech-loading
Caliber .52
Length 37½ inches
Weight 8 lbs.
Weight of projectile 475 grains
Weight of charge 50 grams

Spencer Carbine. The *Army and Navy Journal* later maintained that within the last 18 months (written in 1865) there had been a decided improvement in carbines. It was commonly conceded that the Spencer carbine, or rifle, "is, by all odds, the best shooting weapon ever issued to mounted men." Its characteristics:

Repeater—7 shot
Caliber .52
Length 39 inches
Weight 8¼ lbs.
Weight of projectile 385 grains
Weight of charge 48 grains

Custer's and Merritt's divisions at Cedar Creek totalled 20 regiments. At least 10 were armed with the Spencer carbine:

5th, 6th, 7th Michigan Cavalry
1st New York Dragoons
2d Massachusetts Cavalry
1st Connecticut Cavalry
3d New Jersey Cavalry
5th New York Cavalry
2d Ohio Cavalry
18th Pennsylvania Cavalry

The other regiments were armed with single-shot carbines as follows:

4th, 6th, 8th, 9th, 22d New York Cavalry
1st, 2d, 5th, U.S. Regular Cavalry
3d Indiana Cavalry (companies)
1st New Hampshire Cavalry
1st Vermont Cavalry

The 9th New York Cavalry, originally supplied with Sharps carbines, were issued the Sharps and Hankins carbines, which used a metallic cartridge. The men preferred them to the Sharps. They found the Sharps and Hankins carbine "much more reliable and efficient" than either the Sharps or the Burnside. The 11th New York Cavalry (Scott's "Nine Hundred") also was armed with the Sharps and Hankins carbine.

Wesson Carbine. Single shot, caliber .44, rim-fire. Total length 39¼ inches. Weight 5 pounds 12 ounces. The carbine is marked "F.Wesson's Patent Oct. 25, 1859 & Nov. 11, 1862" and "B. Kitteredge & Co., Cincinnati, O."

As was often the case during the war, the term "rifle" was used to apply to a carbine. Hence, many references were to "Wesson Rifles," when carbines were meant. "Wesson rifles" were widely advertised in *Frank Leslie's Illustrated Newspaper*, where the manufacturer, B. Kitteredge and Company of Cincinnati, Ohio stated that: "We have furnished our Wesson's Rifles as follows:

"State of Kentucky	1,366
"State of Indiana	760
"Colonel Ripley	150
"Colonel Collins	220"

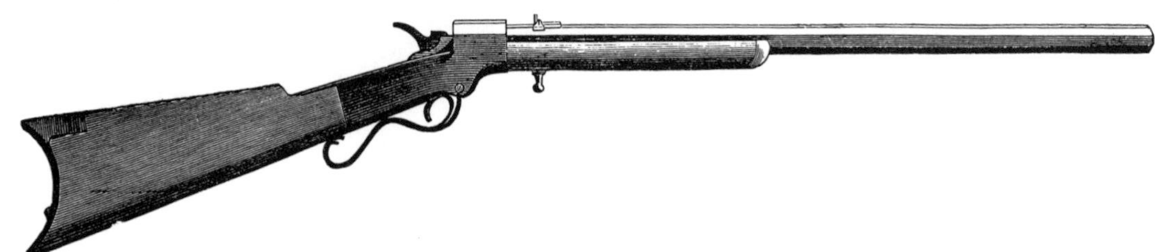

Ballard's breechloading rifle. (Norm Flayderman)

Burnside's patent breechloading carbine. (Norm Flayderman)

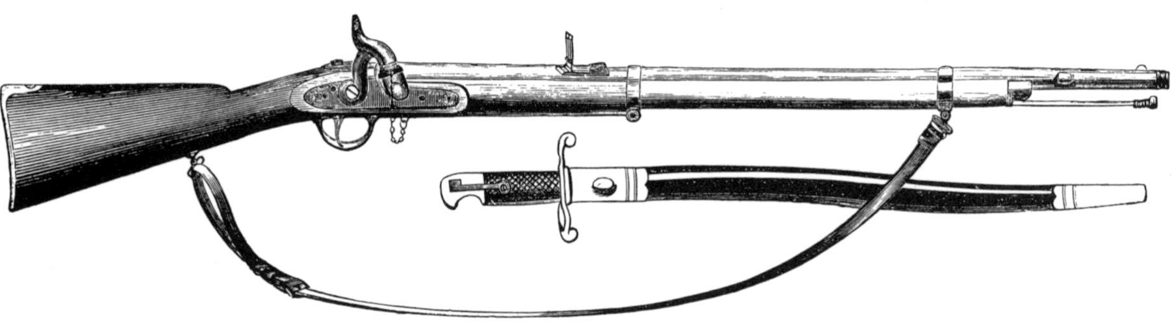

Enfield rifle. (Norm Flayderman)

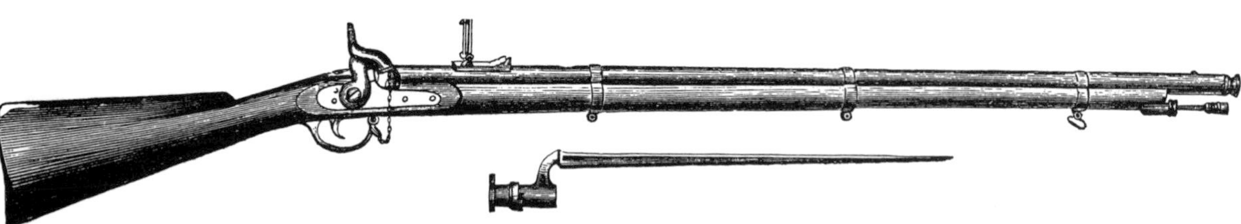

Enfield rifle. (Norm Flayderman)

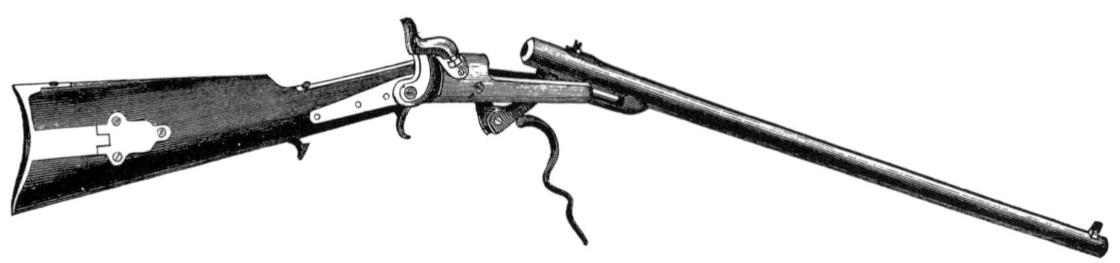

Gallagher breechloading carbine, caliber .52. (Norm Flayderman)

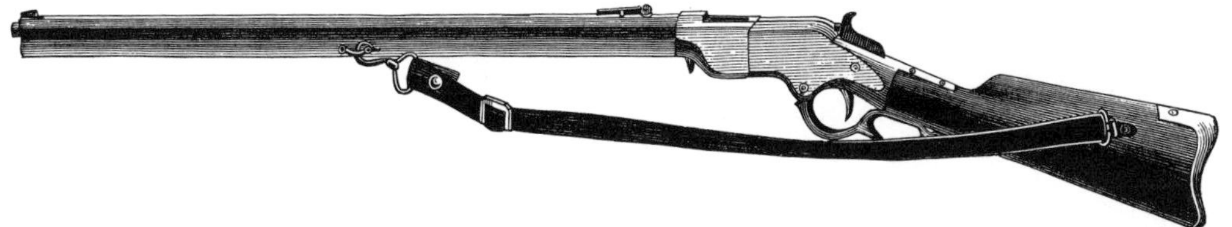

Henry rifle, caliber .44. (Norm Flayderman)

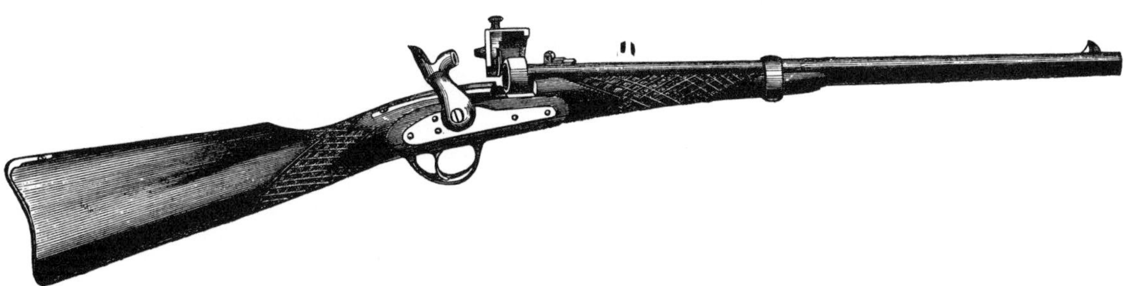

Joslyn carbine. (Norm Flayderman)

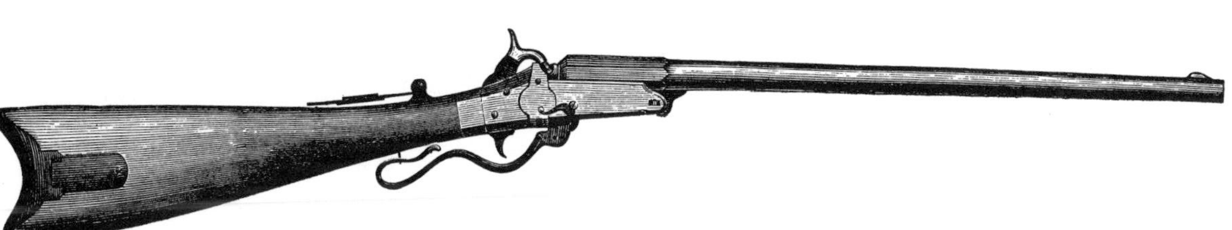

Maynard's carbine. (Norm Flayderman)

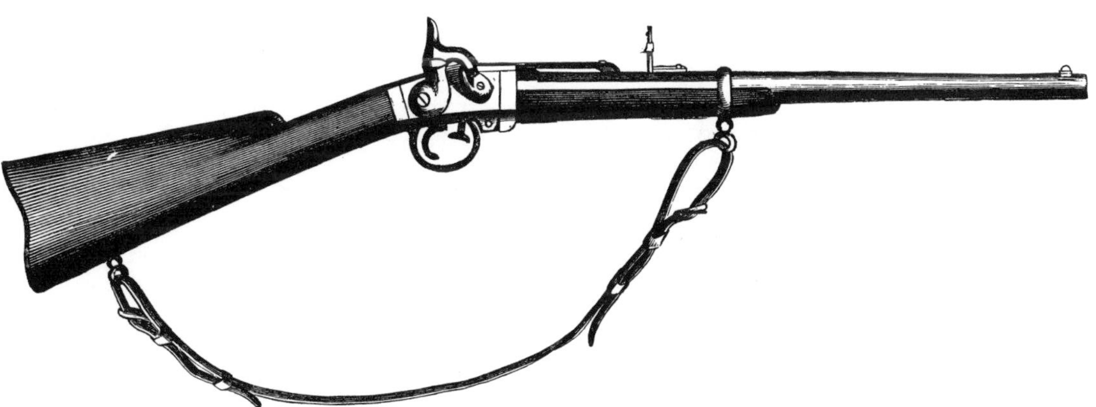

Smith's patent breechloading carbine, caliber .50. (Norm Flayderman)

Also included as recipients of Wesson rifles were companies from Kansas, Illinois, Indiana, Ohio, and Missouri. Colonel M. S. Grant of the 1st Kansas Cavalry added a testimonial about the superiority in accuracy of the Wesson rifles over the infantry standard arm.

TYPES ISSUED. The following types of carbines were issued by the U.S. Government:

Ball	Caliber .44 Caliber .50
Ballard	Caliber .44 Caliber .54
Burnside	Caliber .54
Cosmopolitan	Caliber .50
Gallagher	Caliber .51
Gibbs	Caliber .52
Hall	Caliber .64
Joslyn	Caliber .54
Lindner	Caliber .57
Maynard	Caliber .50
Merrill	Caliber .54
Palmer	Caliber .44 Caliber .50
Remington	Caliber .46
Sharps	Caliber .52
Smith	Caliber .50
Spencer	Caliber .52
Starr	Caliber .54
Warner	Caliber .50
Wesson	Caliber .44

In addition, other carbines, both foreign and American-made, saw use during the war. Among these were:

Austrian
Colt
Greene
Jenks
Lee
Merrill-Latrobe
Sharps and Hawkins
Symmes

CONFEDERATE MUSKETS, RIFLE MUSKETS, AND RIFLES

ARMORIES, C.S. The ingenuity of the South in devising new weapons and fabricating known types of muskets and rifles almost entirely "from scratch" contrasts sharply with the inexcusable conservatism of such Northern ordnance personnel as Chief of Ordnance Ripley.

Apart from captured Federal weapons, and they were many, and small numbers turned out by a large number of local gunsmiths—the following were the most significant of the many Confederate armories and makers of arms:

Cook and Brother, Athens, Ga.
Fayetteville (N.C.) Armory
Palmetto Armory, Columbia, S.C.
Richmond Armory, Richmond, Va.
Tallassee Armory, Tallassee, Ala.
Tyler, Texas Armory
Virginia Manufactory

ARMORIES, PRIVATE

Asheville, N.C.
Blunt
Davis and Bozeman, Ala.
D.C. Hodgkins and Son, Macon, Ga.
Dickson, Nelson and Co. Alabama
Ga. Armory
H.C. Lamb & Co., Jamestown, N.C.
John B. Read, Tuscaloosa, Ala.
J. P. Murray, Columbus, Ga.
McElwaine Co., Holly Springs, Mississippi
Mendenhall, Jones and Gardner, Greensboro, N.C.
Pulaski Gun Factory, Pulaski, Tenn.

IMPORTS

Austrian Rifle
British Sharpshooters Rifle
Brunswick Rifle—Model 1835
Enfield Rifled Musket—Model 1858
Enfield Short Rifle
Enfield Rifled Musketoon
Enfield Officer's Model Rifle
Kerr Rifle
Whitworth Rifle
Wilson Breech-Loading Rifle

Enfield Rifle Musket, C.S. Was quite accurate up to 1,000 yards. The North imported over 400,000, and the South found it to be one of its most effective imports as well. Generally speaking, it was the most popular of the Confederate-used long arms, and certainly one of the most popular also with Federals.

FEDERAL MUSKETS AND RIFLE MUSKETS. In 1861, according to the U.S. Ordnance Manual, the following long arms adopted for service were:

Rifle musket, model 1855
Musket, model 1842
Cadet musket, model 1858. The Cadet Musket, model 1858 was identical with the rifle musket of 1855 except the Cadet Musket was shorter.
Rifle, model 1855
Rifle, model 1842, reamed out to .58 inch
Pistol carbine, model 1855

No model had yet been adopted for a carbine for the cavalry service; several patterns were then in the hands of the troops for trial.

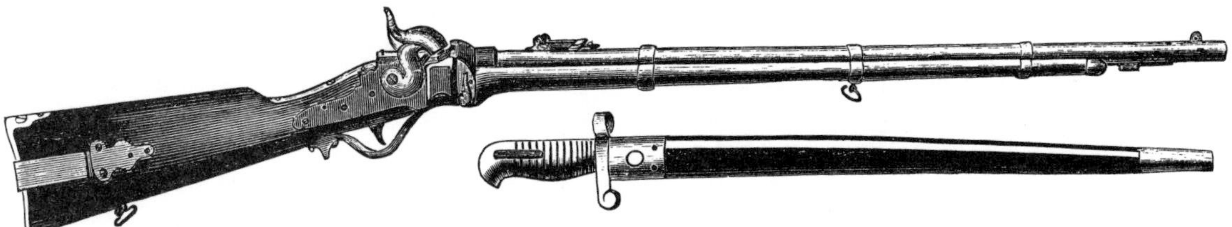

Sharps rifle. (Norm Flayderman)

Spencer's breechloading carbine. (Norm Flayderman)

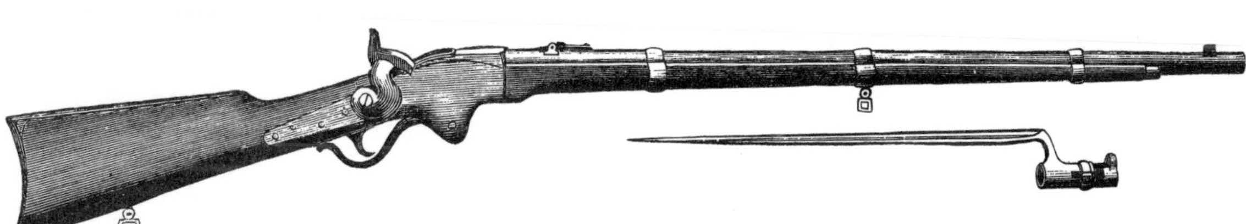

Spencer's breechloading rifle musket. (Norm Flayderman)

F. Wesson breechloading rifle. (Norm Flayderman)

A repeating pistol was issued to the cavalry and to the light artillery.

It is significant that the Atlas to the *Official Records* shows the following long arms, and it is reasonable to conclude that the rifles and muskets so depicted were among the most commonly used by the Federal forces:

Springfield
Enfield
Harpers Ferry Rifle
Austrian
Belgian
Jager (with sword bayonet)
Ballard
Spencer

In the early months of the war it was customary to issue rifles to the flanking companies of infantry regiments. The flanking companies were the leading company and rear company on the march, and the flank companies in line of battle. In the case of the 2d Connecticut Infantry the flanking companies were issued Sharps rifles while the other eight companies received Enfield muskets.

Rate of Fire. Scott's *Military Dictionary* states that "in cases of emergency, firing with two bullets might be effectively employed against masses of infantry and cavalry, if the distance does not exceed 300 yards." Muzzle-loading small arms can be discharged two or three times in a minute, and breech-loading arms about ten times.

When two oblong bullets are fired from the new rifle-musket, or altered rifle, with the ordinary service charge of 60 grains, they separate from each other and from the plane of fire about 4 feet in a distance of 200 yards.

Waste of Ammunition. By an examination of the 27,574 muskets picked up after Gettysburg, it was found that 24,000 were loaded. Of these, 12,000 contained 2 loads each, and 6,000 (over 20 percent) were charged with from 3 to 10 loads each. One musket had in it 23 loads, each charge being put down in regular order.

Shiny Muskets Aided the Enemy. A Federal soldier, writing from Petersburg the year following the end of the war, pointed out the poor judgment in Federal units of keeping their firearms brightly polished: "Many ex-Rebel officers now bear witness to the fact that the movements of our Federal forces were often made known to them by the sheen from our burnished gun-barrels." The author cited specifically Fredericksburg, where the moon was reflected on Federal gun barrels as they moved into position; at Second Bull Run where they glittered through the dust; and at Petersburg where the Confederates "were often made aware of our movements to the left by the light that played above our moving columns, when they could not see the troops at all." The author asks a question which is relevant: "What better mark could possibly be desired than blue uniforms and burnished gun-barrels? Why would it not, then, be better to have a bronzed or blued barrel . . .?" As a matter of fact, many of the imported arms, especially the Enfield, were either browned or blued, but regulation-conscious regimental commanders had them use emery cloth until the barrels were "good and shiny." And often the men did this on their own.

Because both sides needed desperately "anything that will shoot," in the early part of the war obsolete weapons were called back into service. This was true even with flintlocks, especially in some Confederate units. The regulation U.S. weapons listed in the accompanying table were used by both sides. Weights do not include bayonets unless otherwise stated.

Muskets and Rifles (U.S. Regulation). Springfield Armory was the only government armory in operation in the North after the abandonment of the armory at Harper's Ferry in April, 1861. The output of the armory at Springfield was so meager that it was necessary to arm many volunteers of 1861 and 1862 with older models of United States weapons. The best of these were the model 1855 rifle, model 1855 rifle musket, model 1841 rifle, and model 1842 musket. All of these were percussion weapons. The model 1855 arms were caliber .58; the model 1841 rifle (also known as the Mississippi Rifle, Windsor Rifle, Jager Rifle) was caliber .54; the model 1842 musket was caliber .69. Also extensively used in the early part of the war were the 1816 and 1835 models of flintlock muskets that were converted to percussion shortly before and during the war to meet the pressing need for arms. These weapons also were caliber .69.

The Model 1842 Percussion Musket, known also as the Harpers' Ferry Musket, was widely used. It was caliber .69, smoothbore musket weighing slightly over 9 pounds. This musket fired a 1-ounce spherical ball. As late as the Battle of Monocacy, July 9, 1864, the 9th New York Heavy Artillery, serving as infantry, was armed with Harper's Ferry muskets, smoothbore, using buck and ball ammunition. One member of this regiment went into the battle with one of these muskets which even lacked "a tube for the hammer to strike upon."

U.S. Rifle, Model 1841. Caliber .54. Total length 48¾ inches. Weight 9¾ pounds. The furniture of this weapon is brass, polished bright. Many of these 1841 rifles were re-rifled to correspond with the .58 caliber of the 1855 rifle musket, and were equipped with longer range sights and provided with a long saber bayonet. The Model 1841 Rifle was also called the

"Yager," (from *JAEGER*—German for huntsman); "Mississippi" (from use of the weapon by Davis' Mississippi regiment in the Mexican War); and "Windsor," from Windsor, Vermont, where some of these rifles were made under contract.

The 7th Maine Infantry was armed with "Windsor rifles, with plenty of brass trimmings to keep clean, and sabre bayonets. Very proud we were of them, and when we come to use them we found they shot pretty straight. Cumbersome as the sabre bayonets were, they were good to dig shelter with, and several times I have seen their long leveled lines carry consternation to the gray-clothed foe."

In 1855 the U.S. Government came out with a new model rifle and a rifle musket. The single shot, muzzle-loading rifle, known also as the Harper's Ferry Rifle, had the following specifications:

Caliber .58
Length 49.37 inches
Weight 9½ pounds
Muzzle velocity 910 ft. per sec.
Weight of projectile 550 grains
Weight of charge 60 grains

The Model 1855 Rifle Musket was a single-shot muzzle-loading weapon with the following characteristics:

Caliber .58
Length 56 inches
Weight 9.9 lbs.
Muzzle velocity 960 ft. per second
Weight of projectile 550 grains
Weight of charge 60 grains

U.S. Rifle-Musket, Model 1861. The Model 1861 Springfield rifle musket was the principal weapon of the Civil War. By the end of 1863, most Federal infantrymen were armed with this weapon or the Enfield. The Springfield was a percussion rifle 58½ inches long, muzzle-loading, caliber .58. The rifle barrel was 40 inches long; the pitch in the rifling was one turn in 6 feet; there were 3 grooves each 3/10 of an inch wide, .005 of an inch deep at the muzzle,

Model	*Smooth or Rifled*	*Caliber*	*Length in inches*	*Weight in Pounds*	*Bayonet*
1817 Flintlock Rifle. Some converted to percussion	R	.54	51.25	10.25	......
1819 Flintlock Rifle. Later models of rifles and carbines were percussion. "Hall's Breechloader"	R	.53	52.75	10.25	Angular
1822 Flintlock musket. Converted to percussion in 1840's and 1850's	S	.69	57.7	9.33	Angular
1841 Percussion Rifle	R	.54	48.75	9.75	Saber & Angular
1842 Percussion Musket	S	.69	57.75	9.20	Angular
1842 Cadet Musket	S	.54	55.25	8.50	Angular
1842 Musketoons					
Cavalry	S	.69	41.0	7.22	......
Artillery	S	.69	41.0	7.70 (with bayonet)	Angular
Sappers and miners	S	.69	41.0	9.35 (with bayonet)	Saber
1855 Pistol carbine	R	.58	17.75 (pistol only)	3.8 (pistol only)	
1855 Carbine	R	.54	36.75	...	......
1855 Rifle musket	R	.58	59.8	9.18	Angular
1855 Rifle	R	.58	49.3	9.93	Saber
1861 Rifle musket	R	.58	56.0	9.75 (with bayonet)	Angular
(Models 1863 and 1864 rifled muskets had same dimensions as model 1861 rifled musket).					
1861 Navy Rifle (Plymouth)	R	.69	50.0	12.0 (with bayonet)	Saber or knife bayonet
1862 "Zouave" Rifle	R	.58	49	9.37	Saber
1863 Double Rifle musket (Lindsay)	R	.58	56	9.0	Angular

U.S. flintlock musket. (Norm Flayderman)

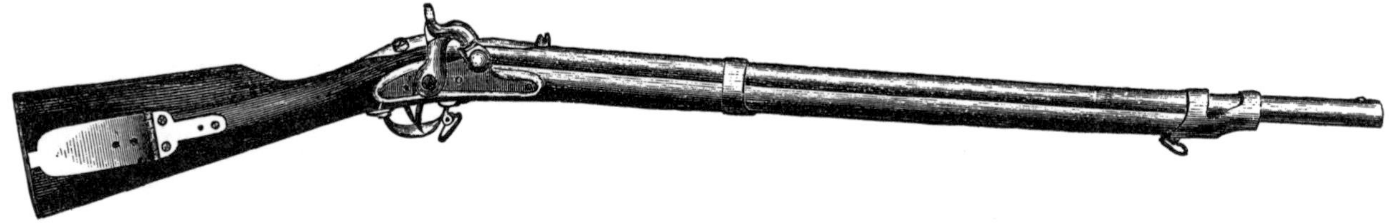

U.S. or Mississippi rifle. (Norm Flayderman)

increasing regularly in depth to .15 at the breech. This rifle, with its 18-inch socket bayonet, weighed 9.75 pounds. The ammunition used was a hollow-based cylindro-conical bullet of 500 grains; muzzle velocity was 950 foot seconds. This compares with 2,300 foot seconds for the famous 1903 Springfield which saw so much use in World War I and later, as well as the Garand rifle of World War II.

Including the bayonet and ramrod and other appendages, there were 53 pieces in the model 1861 Springfield, which in 1861 cost $14.93 to manufacture. All parts were interchangeable. In the 1863 and 1864 variations of the 1861 model slight improvements were made but the model 1861 rifle musket remained, practically unchanged, as the basic infantry weapon of the war. One of the interesting changes was the abolition of band springs in 1863 and their re-appearance in 1864. Men in the field found that the bands tended to "jump" loose without the band springs when their guns were fired.

It is interesting to note that, in addition to the American contractors, model 1861 muskets were made by Manton in England and by firms in Germany. Several of the contract arms are extremely rare today since foreign contractors made only a few muskets.

While the Civil War musket as produced at Springfield or in the many contractors' factories seems very old and quaintly ineffectual as compared with such weapons as the Garand of today, the Boys in Blue and their adversaries were quite impressed by its appearance and performance. On November 23, 1862, a corporal in the 52d Massachusetts Volunteers wrote as follows: "Our guns were issued to us the other day, beautiful pieces; of the most improved pattern—the Springfield rifled musket . . . Mine is behind me now, dark black—walnut stock, well oiled, so that the beauty of the wood is brought out, hollowed at the base, and smoothly fitted with steel, to correspond exactly to the curve of the shoulder, against which I shall have to press it many and many a time. The spring of the lock, just stiff and just limber enough; the eagle and stamp of the Government pressed into the steel [lock] plate; barrel, long and glistening—bound into its bed by gleaming rings—long and straight and so bright, that when I present arms, and bring it before my face, I can see the nose and spectacles and the heavy beard on lip and chin, which already the camp is beginning to develop. Then the bayonet, straight and tapering, dazzling under a sunray, grooved delicately—as if it were meant to illustrate problems in conic sections—smooth to the finger as a surface of glass, and coming to a point sharp as a needle."

An interesting weapon which appeared during the war but one which probably was not used was the U.S. Rifle Model 1862, Remington. This weapon incorporated the best features of the Model 1841 and Model 1855 rifles.

Even more unique was the Lindsay rifle musket. This unusual weapon was caliber .58 and similar in appearance to the Model 1863 rifled musket. The unusual feature is that the weapon functions by a single trigger which operates two centrally hung hammers. The trigger works perfectly, and irrespective of the position of the hammers, the right-hand hammer always falls first. The fire from the cone of the right hammer communicated with the forward charge of powder, the rear charge which is fired by the left hammer acting as a gas check for the forward charge.

Although 1,000 of these muskets were delivered to the War Department on August 16, 1864, the arms proved a failure. The long channel connecting the cone with the forward charge of powder became blocked with fouling, and occasionally the forward charge leaked past the bullet of the rear charge firing both simultaneously. A specimen was dug up recently at Petersburg. The weapon is marked "Lindsay Patent Oct. 9, 1860".

Even the Navy had its own specially-designed rifle although unquestionably the Navy used Army weapons as well. The Whitney Navy Rifle Model 1861-Plymouth was caliber .69 with a total length of 50 inches. It was made for Navy use and used a 22-inch saber bayonet or the famous Dahlgren knife bayonet.

Contractors for U.S. Rifled Musket Models 1861, 1863, 1864, Caliber. 58:

Contract Date	*Contractor's Name*	*Number Delivered*
Dec. 26, 1861	Sarson & Roberts	5,140
Dec. 26, 1861	A.M. Burt	11,495
Dec. 26, 1861	J.T. Hodge	10,500
Dec. 26, 1861	Eagle Manufacturing Co.	20,000
April 1, 1864	Norwich Arms Co.	10,000
October 18, 1864	Norwich Arms Co.	15,000
Dec. 24, 1861	C.B. Hoard	1,500
Dec. 1, 1863	C.B. Hoard	11,300
July 13, 1861	Alfred Jenks & Son	25,000
Oct. 7, 1861	Alfred Jenks & Son	19,000
Dec. 15, 1863	Alfred Jenks & Son	48,000
Feb. 1, 1865	Alfred Jenks & Son	6,000
January 7, 1862	James Mulholland	5,502
January 7, 1862	William Mason	30,000
July 13, 1861 Nov. 26, 1861	Providence Tool Co. Providence Tool Co.	38,000
May 1, 1864	Providence Tool Co.	32,000
July 11, 1861 Oct. 7, 1861	Lamson, Goodnow & Yale	50,000
January 7, 1862	Amoskeag Manufacturing Co.	10,001
Nov. 5, 1863	Amoskeag Manufacturing Co.	15,000
January 6, 1865	Amoskeag Manufacturing Co.	2,000
September 28, 1863	Parker, Snow & Co.	15,000
October 11, 1861 Nov. 26, 1861	C.D. Schubarth	9,500
Dec. 7, 1861	Wm. Muir & Co.	30,000
Dec. 26, 1861	J.D. Mowry	10,000
Nov. 27, 1863	J.D. Mowry	2,000
April 6, 1864	J.D. Mowry	10,000
October 17, 1863	Eli Whitney	15,001
September 9, 1862	Savage Arms Co.	13,500
Feb. 25, 1864	Savage Arms Co.	12,000
Nov. 6, 1861	W.W. Welch	16,000
January 12, 1864	W.W. Welch	1,000
Dec. 14, 1863	E. Remington & Son	40,000
June 10, 1863	Edward Robinson	12,000
Dec. 29, 1863	Edward Robinson	4,000
Feb. 23, 1864	Edward Robinson	8,000
Oct. 4, 1864	Edward Robinson	6,000
July 5, 1861	Colt's Patent Fire Arms Co.	25,000
June 5, 1863	Colt's Patent Fire Arms Co.	12,500
March 19, 1864	Colt's Patent Fire Arms Co.	37,500
	Total	643,439

Foreign Muskets and Rifles Imported by the Federal Government. To supplement domestic weapons the Government and the various States made extensive purchases of foreign weapons. Probably the most widely used of these, next to the Enfield and Austrian weapons, were the Belgian muskets. These guns were of uneven caliber and crooked barrels. The recoil was fearful and the men detested them. They soon gained the nickname of "European stove-pipes" by men who found them unreliable in battle. The English and Belgian sources were insufficient and agents purchased from the little German states all their old-fashioned arms, which those states hastened to get rid of at a price which enabled them to replace their obsolete weapons with the new breech-loading needle guns. "In short, the refuse of all Europe passed into the hands of the American volunteers." Included in this debris were thousands of Austrian and Prussian muskets. These weapons were heavy, clumsy, and slow of fire. An examination of a shipment of 3,000 Austrian guns by the Adjutant General of the Army revealed that only 500 could be used.

At least one Western regiment, perhaps more, was armed with Russian muskets, caliber .72. In fact, it appears that the Western units were discriminated against in the procuring of the better models of weapons, although McClellan wrote the Secretary of War in October 1861, that his infantry regiments were "to a considerable extent" armed with unserviceable weapons. McClellan maintained that many good arms intended for the Army of the Potomac had gone "elsewhere." The general did not specify where these weapons were sent. Apparently they did not go to the Department of the Missouri as we find General Sherman complaining of the old condemned muskets with which he was forced to arm his men. At Vicksburg the Federals captured 60,000 muskets that were so far superior to their own that their altered flintlocks and Belgian muskets were exchanged for the better weapons. Some Western troops carried antiquated weapons until after Chickamauga.

The following types of foreign weapons were issued by the Federal Government to troops. The list would be even greater if all the State, local, and dealers in military supplies were included.

Austrian	—Caliber .54
Belgian	—Caliber .69
	Caliber .71
Boker (Austrian with quadrangular bayonet)—	
	Caliber .70
Enfield	—Caliber .577
French	—Caliber .71
Jaeger	—Caliber .54
Prussian	—Caliber. .69
(rifled &	Caliber .70
smoothbore)	Caliber .71
Suhl	—Caliber .71
Tower	—Caliber .71

There were other foreign smooth-bore muskets ranging in caliber from .69 to .79.

Burnside breechloading carbine, caliber .54. (West Point Museum collections)

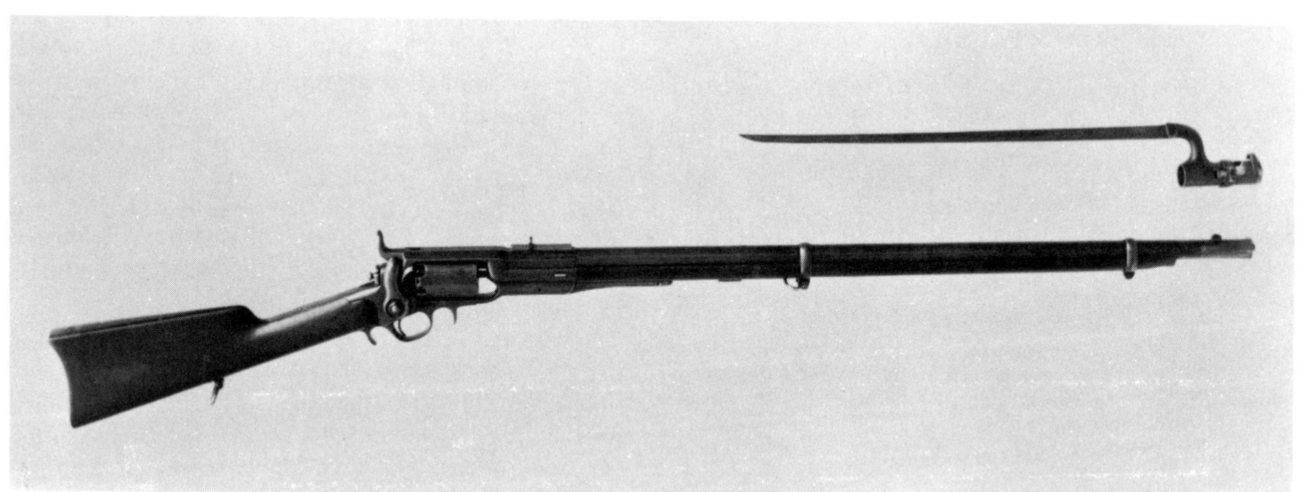

Colt 6-shot musket, caliber .44. (West Point Museum collections)

English Enfield, Model 1863, caliber .577. (West Point Museum collections)

Austrian Rifle and Muskets. These were fairly good weapons, of calibers .54 to .69. The rifles were better made and much more accurate than the muskets, which were heavy, clumsy, and slow of fire. Austrian weapons were widely used by both sides in the war.

Enfield Rifle Musket. The Enfield musket model 1853 (and the model 1858), was one of the best of the foreign arms. It was made chiefly at the government armory at Enfield, England, where shortly before the war machinery had been installed which was a direct copy of that in the United States armory at Springfield, Massachusetts. The Enfield musket was 3/1000 of an inch smaller in caliber than the Springfield (caliber .58); the difference was small enough so as not to prevent the use of caliber .577 ammunition in the Springfield rifle. The Enfield was sighted to 1,100 yards but it was believed by at least one observer that this sighting was excessive since the Enfield was not accurate beyond 700 yards.

A common mistake of many students of the period (and some collectors as well) is to assume that only the South used the Enfield. Actually, a study of the reports of State Adjutant Generals in the North shows conclusively that many Federal regiments were issued the Enfield. For example, of the 136 New York regiments receiving infantry weapons in 1861-1862, almost half (57) were issued the long Enfield musket, while another three regiments received the short Enfield rifle. As a matter of record, the U. S. Government purchased 428,000 Enfields in the early months of the war while the Confederacy received some 400,000 during 1861-1862.

The Enfield was slightly lighter than the Springfield, and, according to contemporary accounts, was "a beautiful arm and presented a natty appearance." The Enfield weighed 8 pounds, 14½ ounces; length about 54 inches; length of barrel 39 inches; diameter of bore .577; number of grooves 3; pitch of grooves 1 turn in 6 feet 6 inches; diameter of bullet .568; weight of bullet 530 grains; charge of powder about 70 grains. The Enfield when fired at 500 yards had a mean deviation of only 2¼ feet.

But some officers did not like the Enfield musket. On December 30, 1861, General William F. Smith told an investigating committee that he preferred the Springfield to the Enfield and gave his reasons. The general pointed out that the Enfield rifles which the U.S. brought in to this country were not made by the British government or for the British government. They were "exceedingly rough, and tear the men's hands to pieces when they are going through the manual." They had sharp points; the stock was rough; the workmanship would not compare with that of our own rifle, ie. the Springfield. According to General Smith the Enfield rifles were all made by hand, and if the men, in the hurry of the moment, happened to exchange bayonets, there were many rifles which could not be used with bayonets. "No bayonet, as a general thing, will go on any rifle, except the one it is intended for. But in the case of the Springfield rifles, any one bayonet will fit them all."

We must concede that the general was correct in criticizing the lack of interchangeability of parts in the Enfield arms. But other officers and men of the war have left unquestioned testimony that the Enfield was an excellent weapon, well-made and accurate. Certainly the many Enfields now reposing in museums and private collections give definite evidence of excellent workmanship. The men who used them in battle swore by them.

The London Armory Company, caliber .58 Enfield rifled musket, marked "LAC 1862," etc. was exclusively supplied under contract to the Confederacy.

Enfield Rifle (short model). This model of imported weapon was very popular with the Confederates, and to a lesser extent, with the Federal troops as well. It was designed for use by riflemen, much the same as the U.S. Model 1855 rifle was to be issued to light infantry and rifle units. Like its U.S. counterpart, it was equipped with a sword bayonet. A corporal of the 5th Rhode Island Battalion, in describing the recruiting for his unit, stated that the recruiting posters announced that his battalion was to be used exclusively for coast service and would be armed with short "English Rifles" and "French Boarding Swords." But, as it turned out, the unit was equipped with the short Enfield rifles, caliber .577, with heavy sword bayonets (the "French Boarding Swords" of the recruiting posters). Although these bayonets were imposing enough when fixed, they made the pieces top-heavy and more awkward to handle than the ordinary bayonet, not being so well balanced. After the unit had been in service some 8 months, these short Enfields were exchanged for the long Enfields, which were equipped with the common triangular bayonets.

Vincennes Rifle. This was a heavy, cumbersome, awkward musket, caliber .69, which was equipped with a large sword bayonet. According to a report submitted by the 148th Pennsylvania Infantry in November, 1862:

"The caliber of the piece may be reckoned as .69, although the bore is so irregular that, whilst in some instances, .69 caliber ammunition fits the bore tightly, in others it falls from the muzzle to the breach. In many instances in firing at a target at 250 yards the balls fall short, without even penetrating the ground. The locks are of soft iron and many of them are already unserviceable from wear. The workmanship,

Gerdom rifle. (West Point Museum collections)

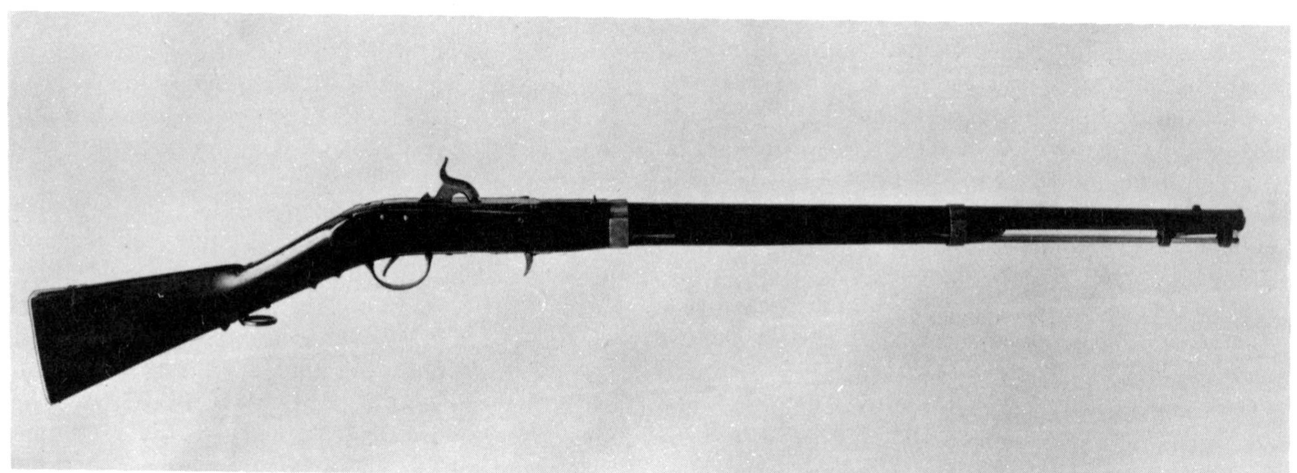

Hall carbine, breechloading, caliber .52. (West Point Museum collections)

Sharps box-lock breechloader. (West Point Museum collections)

both in the wood and iron, is extremely rough and the piece very heavy. The bayonet is a formidable sword bayonet. The rifling of the piece is very shallow and adds nothing to the accuracy or effectiveness of the weapons. Altogether, the weapon is very inefficient and unreliable."

Hall Rifle. Patented in 1811 by J. H. Hall. The first breechloader adopted by the U.S. Made in many models, caliber .53. Used to some extent in the early part of the war.

Long Arms (Breechloaders). Even as late as 1863, the Federal Army was officially using 79 different models of rifles and muskets and over 20 models of carbines. A similar situation existed among the Confederate troops.

The best single-shot breechloader was the Sharps, while the best repeaters were the Henry and Spencer. The historian of Berdan's sharpshooters says flatly that "the open-sighted Sharps rifle . . . was the best breech-loading gun (made during the war) . . . It was a perfectly safe and reliable arm, combining accuracy with rapidity, just what a skirmish line needed for effective work." However, many other reports indicate the Sharps had gas leakage at the breech.

A soldier, writing the *Army and Navy Journal* the day before Christmas, 1864, in an article on "Breech-Loading Rifles," complimented the *Journal* for favoring the issue of breechloaders. He wrote in part:

"If those in authority have any doubts as to the propriety of thus adding to our efficiency, let them come to the front armed with one Springfield musket, and oppose themselves to an equal number of Rebs, armed with repeaters or breechloaders. If they can stand that, let them go to the picket line, and while fumbling for a cap and trying to get it on the cone one of these cold days, offer themselves as a target to some fellow on the other side who has nothing to do but cock his piece and blaze away. If they don't throw down their bungling, slow-shooting gun in disgust, they may be excused for indulging in remarks not complimentary to those who compel them to the unequal contest. The objection has been urged that we fire too many shots with our present muzzle-loaders, and consequently it would be folly to add to the waste of ammunition by affording us greater ease or facility in loading. Do our good friends ever reflect that the loss of time in loading is the great *cause* of haste, and consequent inaccuracy in firing?"

Breech-loading rifles were issued by the Government to some regiments late in the war. Early in the war some states had equipped a few of their regiments with breech-loading weapons. The best of the single-shot breechloaders were the Ballard, Merrill, and Sharps rifles. All were excellent weapons and the Sharps especially was in great demand. It was used by Berdan's sharpshooters in the Army of the Potomac and was issued to the flank companies of the Connecticut regiments as well as to other state units. Three types of breech-loading repeating rifles were in use by volunteer infantry regiments 1863, 1864, and 1865. The most generally used of these was the Spencer rifle, which had excellent range and accuracy. The Spencer was a seven-shooter and because of the amount of ammunition it consumed in action, received an unfavorable report from the Chief of Ornance in 1861. This rifle, however, fully justified itself in combat. Another repeater that was very effective but was used mainly in the last year of the war was the Henry 16-shot repeater. This weapon was found most extensively in the West where the men purchased their own at the cost of about three months' pay. Another type of repeating rifle, although used in fewer numbers than either the Spencer or Henry, was the Colt revolving rifle. This weapon, like the Colt revolver, was made with either five or six chambers. The bullet was forced into seven grooves which formed a spiral and which became steadily more contracted as it approached the muzzle of the rifle. The result was a long-range rifle which was formidable in practical hands but considerable time was required in reloading. Some complaint was made that all of the chambers had a tendency to go off at once.

General Rosecrans believed in the Colt rifle, however, and in 1863, asked for 5,000 of them believing that five or six chambers were better than one. The inventor of this rifle, Samuel Colt, was commissioned colonel in May 1861, and ordered to raise a regiment to be known as the 1st Connecticut Revolving Rifles. Colt's regiment was to be armed with his revolving rifles; each man was to be over six feet tall and a good marksman. The regiment was disbanded in a few weeks over administrative questions. The cost of the Colt rifles was $45 while such foreign weapons as the Belgian, Austrian, and Prussian muskets were $6 or $10 depending on whether they were smoothbore or rifled.

Ballard Rifle, Model 1861. Single shot, caliber .56 rim-fire, 30-inch round rifled barrel. Total length 45½ inches. Patented November 5, 1861, Patent No. 33,631. These arms were also made in .45 caliber, and also calibers .46 and .54 during 1862-1863.

Colt Revolving Rifle Model 1855. The early civilian method of fastening a shoulder stock on the heavy barrel revolvers and making a serviceable repeating shoulder arm led the Colt company to apply the same idea to a full-fledged rifle. Consequently, the 1855 model revolving rifle was produced. It became the first repeating rifle adopted by the armed services of

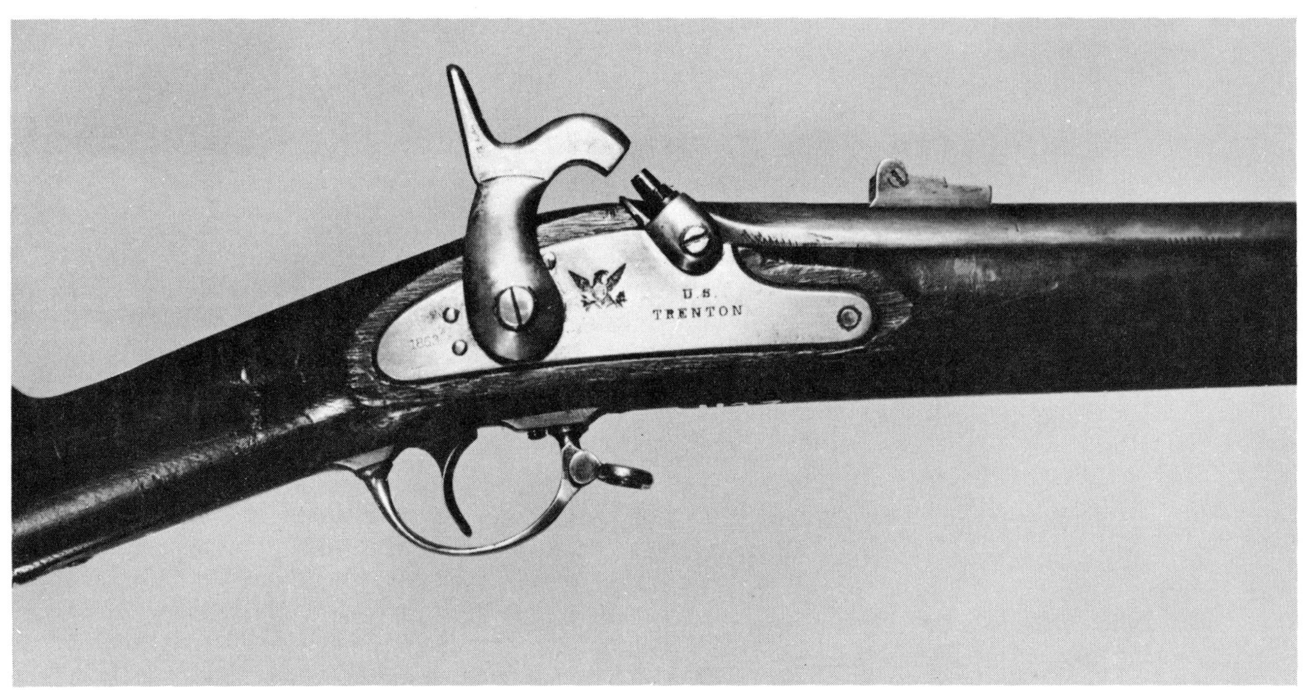

Trenton rifle, Model 1863. (West Point Museum collections)

U.S. Springfield rifle musket, Model 1855. (West Point Museum collections)

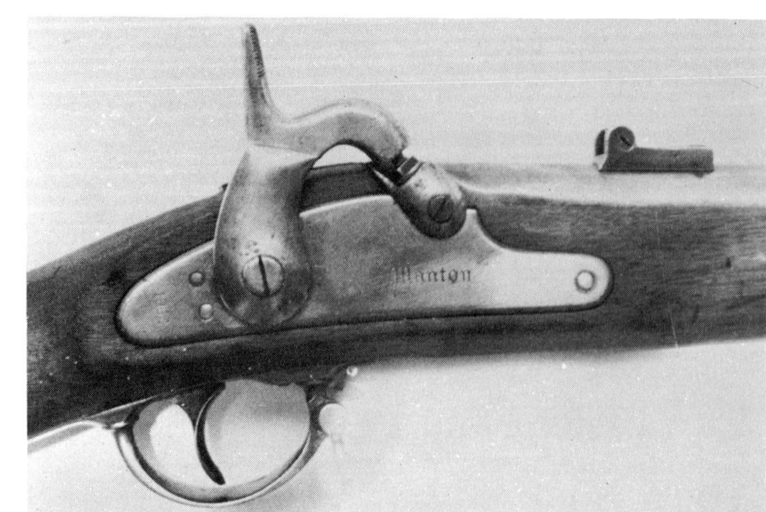

Manton contract rifle musket. (Author's collection)

the United States. This rifle was made in several barrel lengths for the Army and Navy. Although the patent for the mechanism was taken out in 1855, there was no production of the weapon until 1857 because kinks had to be removed in the locking, unlocking, and turning of the cylinder.

In 1857 the Government purchased 101 Colt revolving rifles at $50 each, and another lot of 300, and appurtenances at $42.50 each. Both rifles and carbines, some equipped with sword bayonets, were purchased in 1858, and 1859, the rifle still at $42.50. During the Civil War these arms were also purchased by the Navy at $44 and by the several states for their militia units. The type which saw most use was probably the five-shot caliber .56 military model, although many individuals, especially officers, purchased the caliber .36 sporting model.

A thousand Colt revolving rifles were issued to Colonel Hiram Berdan's First U.S. Sharpshooters shortly before the launching of McClellan's Peninsula campaign. Generally speaking, Colt's rifles were not popular with the Sharpshooters, who claimed that there was danger of all chambers exploding at once. Moreover, the chambers heated up rapidly when used continuously. On May 7, 1862, while the Berdan Sharpshooters were in front of Yorktown, they exchanged their Colt revolving rifles for Sharps rifles. Colonel Berdan, however, considered the Colt weapon to be a "very superior weapon," especially for skirmishes.

But even in the South Colt had difficulty selling his revolving rifle. As one of his agents said: "I could sell a great number if I had the proper confidence in them . . . Last trial (was) before General Gist at Union, South Carolina. Took all the evening to pick the powder and pieces of lead out of my face. No use telling a person to hold their head back, might as well tell them to hold it under their arm."

Colt's revolving rifle never became popular and after its brief use with Berdan's Sharpshooters it started to decline long before it ever enjoyed a real period of success.

Soldiers of all branches were exceedingly unhappy over the flash and the loud report so close to the face and the fearful recoil when several chambers went off at once. But, even more seriously, there was one major weakness which definitely precluded any extensive adoption of this weapon for the service. During firing the heavy rifle barrel had to be supported by hand. This had not been necessary in a revolver equipped with a shoulder stock. Sometimes loose powder from a faulty cap or gas leak would cause other chambers to be ignited. When this happened, the soldier using the piece lost his hand or the portion of his arm that happened to be in front of the exploding cylinder. One such accident in a regiment destroyed not only confidence in the weapon, but the morale of soldiers and officers alike. The total failure of the Army's official attempt to introduce a repeating shoulder weapon into the service gave the conservative element a chance to point out the inevitable disaster that always follows any such departure from what has proved successful over the years. Finally a board of officers met. After hearing all the evidence they ordered that the Colt use be discontinued and the pieces sold for whatever price could be obtained. The highest bid was 42¢ a rifle!

The U.S. Government made very few purchases of Colt revolving rifles during the war. In addition to the 1,000 purchased for Berdan's men, the records indicate only 2,725 purchased in late 1862 and early 1863. It is doubtful if any agency, Government or local, purchased Colt revolving rifles after February 1863. But dealers in the North continued to offer them for sale to individual soldiers and small units. During the war, the Colt armory furnished the Government with 386,417 revolvers but only about 7,000 revolving rifles.

According to contemporary observers it was an unusually accurate weapon, and it certainly was regrettable that the designers of the Colt rifle were not able to remove the unpleasant and dangerous characteristics of the piece. Had they done so the U.S. Government might well have had an efficient repeating weapon as standard issue for troops at the beginning of the Civil War.

Greene Rifle, Model 1857. Breech-loading, percussion, caliber .54 with oval bore. Length 52¾ inches. Weight without bayonet 10 pounds. The interesting feature of this rifle is its bolt action loading mechanism. This action was patented November 17, 1857 by Lieutenant Colonel J. Durrell Greene, U.S. Army Patent No. 18,634.

Henry Rifle, Model 1860

Repeater—12-shot
Caliber .44
Length 43½ inches
Weight 9¼ lbs.
Weight of projectile—216 grains
Weight of charge—25 grains

The Henry rifle was probably the best all-round rifle that saw service in the war and it was patented in 1860. It was the first magazine rifle which the Federal army used in any quantity at all. The Government purchased 1,731 Henry rifles and 4,610,400 cartridges from July 23, 1863 to November 7, 1865. These arms were also purchased by several states to arm militia companies. About 10,000 are believed to have been made. But most of the rifles were used because the

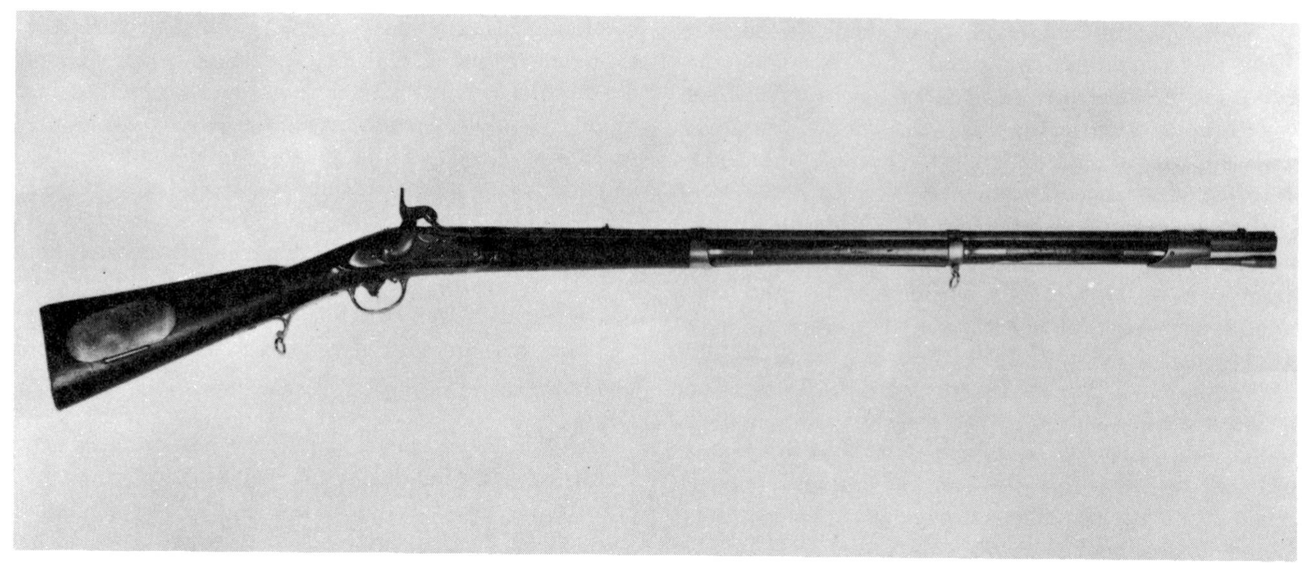

U.S. Starr muzzleloading rifle. (West Point Museum collections)

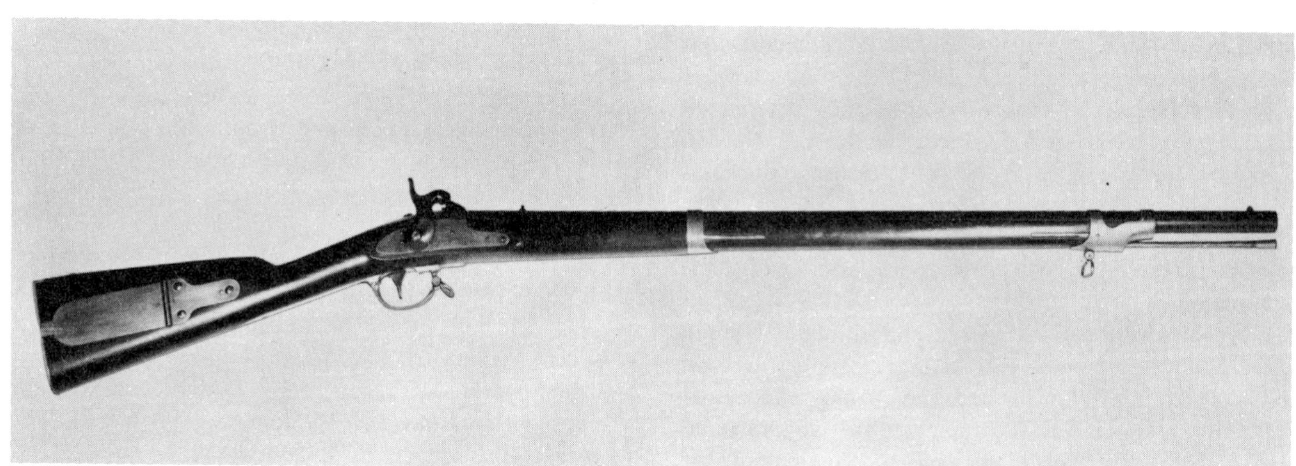

U.S. Whitney muzzleloading rifle. (West Point Museum collections)

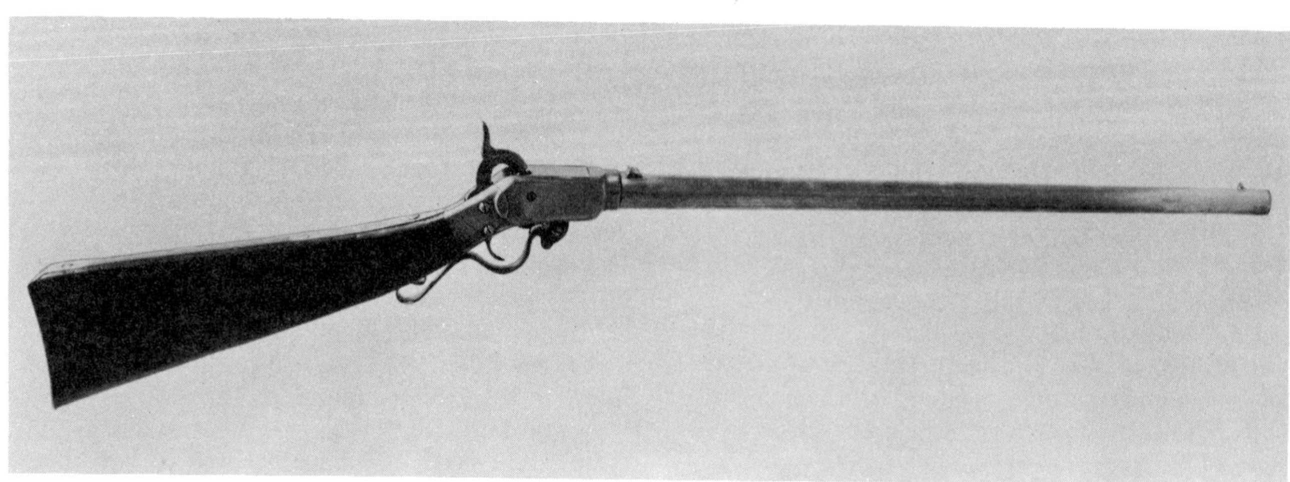

Perry's Confederate carbine. (West Point Museum collections)

men saw their superiority over the single shot muzzle-loader and bought them out of their own pockets. In fact, the Government was so determined in its refusal to accept the Henry repeating rifle that it informed the makers of the gun that their weapons would not be accepted unless the manufacturers would arm a whole regiment, and keep it supplied at the company's expense.

Members of Birge's Sharpshooters (66th Illinois Infantry) replaced their target rifles and purchased the Henry rifle at their own expense. The rifle cost the men $50 apiece. Thus, the men owned their own guns but the Government furnished the cartridges. Another Illinois regiment, the 7th Infantry, was also armed with the Henry, obtained by the men at their own expense. The regimental historian of the 7th commented that the sacrifice of the men in buying their Henrys was "worthy of loyal commendation." It was also a very wise sacrifice! The color guard of this regiment was equipped with the Henry. The 7th Illinois fought brilliantly under Sherman. Another regiment which used the Henry rifle was the 97th Indiana Infantry. When men were wounded they often sold their rifles to men from other units who were delighted to acquire such an excellent weapon. These Western regiments demonstrated the usefulness of the Henry rifle in combat but it was only late in the war that a beneficial change was made in the office of Federal Chief of Ordnance. The new man saw the value of a weapon that could be fired in a prone position and also used as a copper-cased cartridge which rainy weather didn't affect. One of the "might have beens" of the war was in the minds of Confederate generals like E. P. Alexander, who believed that had the Federal infantry been armed from the first with even the breechloaders available in 1861, the war would have been terminated within a year.

Using a caliber .44 Henry rim-fire ammunition, the Henry had a long tubular magazine under the barrel, holding 15 rim-fire cartridges loaded from the front. The piece was operated by lowering the trigger guard lever, which mechanically slid the carrier block backwards, cocked the hammer, extracted and ejected the empty shell, and on its return to closed position, pushed the next round into the chamber. In 1866, Winchester Repeating Arms Company took over the New Haven Arms Company which had produced the Henry Rifle.

Merrill Rifle, Model 1858. Breech-loading percussion, caliber .54. Total length 48½ inches, weight 9 pounds. Used a saber bayonet. The lock is marked "J.H. Merrill Balto.", "Pat. July 1858", "April 9, May 21-28-61". The top of the operating lever is marked "J.H. Merrill, Balto.", "Pat. July 1858".

Nye Improvement in Breech-Loading Firearms (Patent No. 37,356). Patented January 6, 1863 by John C. Nye, Cincinnati, Ohio. This "improvement in breech-loading firearms" was an attached stud to the rear end of the "gate," which activated the plunger, and thus broke the adhesion caused by firing.

Sharps Rifle

Breechloading
Caliber .52
Length 47 inches
Weight 8¾ lbs.
Weight of projectile—475 grains
Weight of charge—50 grains

A total of 9,141 Sharps rifles were purchased by the U.S. Government during the war. This is in contrast to the 80,000 Sharps carbines purchased by the Government during the war. Each Sharps rifle cost $36.15.

Spencer Rifle Model 1860

Repeater—7 shot
Length 47 inches
Caliber .52
Weight 10 lbs.
Weight of projectile—385 grains
Weight of charge—48 grains

Although Spencers were made in both rifle and carbine models, carbines were much more extensively produced and even some infantry regiments were issued carbines. The 7th Connecticut Infantry was issued Spencer carbines on November 19, 1863 and the infantrymen had to learn a new manual of arms. These Spencer carbines were good for 7 shots "as fast as the handle could be worked." After the men had become used to working the mechanisms of their Spencers they could get a shot every 3-4 seconds. At Olustee, Florida, February 20, 1864, although outnumbered, the regiment assisted in breaking up a massed attack; "they pumped the bullets out of these rifles with astonishing rapidity" . . . the enemy "retreated in disorder to their lines leaving their path strewn with dead and wounded."

If there was a single cartridge in the magazine the Spencer never missed fire, and an average trained marksman could fire the 7 rounds in 12 seconds. "Its range is enormous. It will throw a ball with fair accuracy 2,000 yards (over a mile) and at a distance of 150 feet will penetrate through 13 inches of timber."

Volcanic Rifle. Charles King, while serving as an aide in 1861, carried a "Volcanic Rifle." King describes this weapon as "the pigmy progenitor of the Winchester—a thing that fired a bullet the size of a marrowfat from one end, and singed off your eyebrows at the other owing to some imperfection in the gas-check, a thing he lent to everybody who wanted to try it,

Richmond Confederate musketoon. (West Point Museum collections)

Richmond Confederate muzzleloading musket, caliber .69. (West Point Museum collections)

secure in the conviction that he wouldn't want it again."

Only a few Volcanic rifles were made, because the Volcanic Repeating Arms Company became insolvent in 1857.

Sharpshooters Rifle. This rifle, as used by some members of Berdan's sharpshooters, was a target rifle, weighing from 15 to 30 pounds, and was generally shot from a rest. Many were equipped with strong telescopic sights which "were powerful magnifiers, so much so that a small object, not distinguishable to the naked eye, could be seen at a long distance." These heavy rifles, whether equipped with telescopic or globe sights, were of great value before permanent or semi-permanent fortifications, but were useless for the mobility required in skirmishing.

The sharpshooters acted as individuals—professional snipers—who, equipped with rations, water, and ammunition, sallied forth in the morning to the front line where, hidden in the foliage of trees, they looked for such vital targets as officers and artillerymen.

The following incident which occurred in November, 1863, in the area of the 10th New York Cavalry, was only typical of many. An artillery officer complained that a Confederate sharpshooter was picking off his men and horses. The sharpshooter detailed to "get" the Confederate was "a tall, stooping, ungainly-looking specimen . . . (who carried) an immense rifle (with a long telescope-sight running the entire length of the barrel) over his shoulder. He shambled along under cover of the trees until he passed just beyond the skirmish line. Stationed behind a large tree, he watched intently a tree near the bridge which crossed the little stream in our front, along which the rebel line extended. Presently he brought the immense rifle to his shoulder, the report of its discharge was blended with those of the carbines on either flank, and those who had been watching the proceedings saw a man fall from the tree . . . A few moments later the rebels fell back, and as a part of the Regiment passed the spot in pursuit, the lifeless form of the rebel sharpshooter was seen lying as he had fallen, a victim of the barbarous mode of warfare which he himself had chosen."

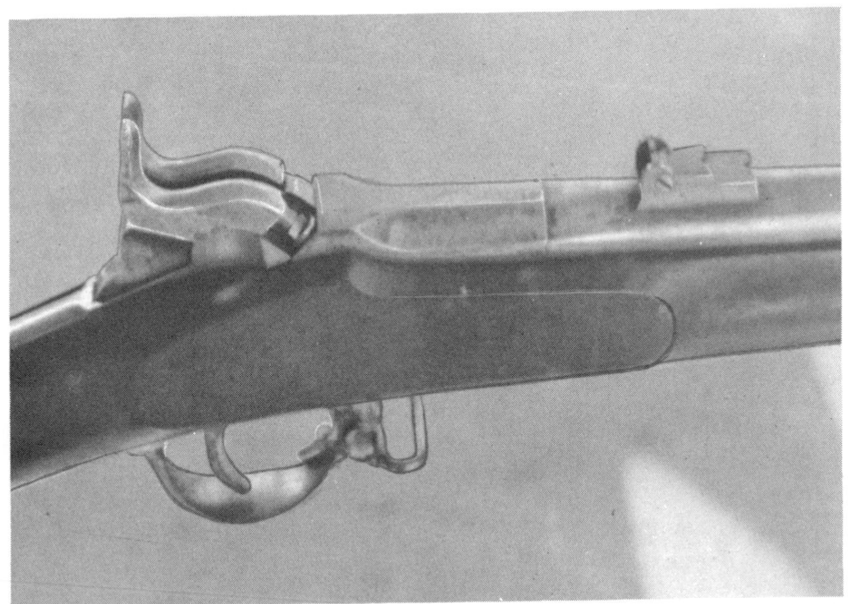

Hammer arrangement of the Lindsay rifle musket.

SHOVELS AND SPADES. See INTRENCHING TOOLS.

SIGNAL EQUIPMENT. An officer, probably General Albert Myer, writing to the *Army and Navy Journal,* October 7, 1865, in looking back on the Signal Corps operations observed: "our signals and theirs were substantially the same, and no system of visible signals has yet been invented which can not be decyphered by an expert." Most signal equipment was comparatively simple and easily carried.

APPARATUS. Every signal officer was expected to have in his possession a full set of signal apparatus ready for immediate use. A regulation set of signal equipments, when packed complete, was composed of three elements—the kit, the canteen, and the haversack.

Canteen. Made of copper, with one seam, and soldered, capable of containing one gallon of turpentine or other burning fluid.

Haversack. This contained wicking, wind-matches,

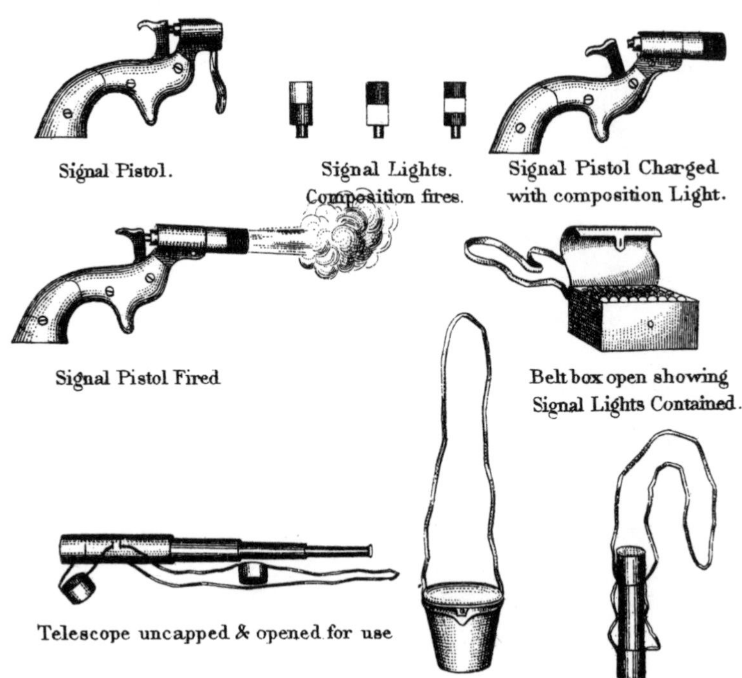

Signal apparatus.

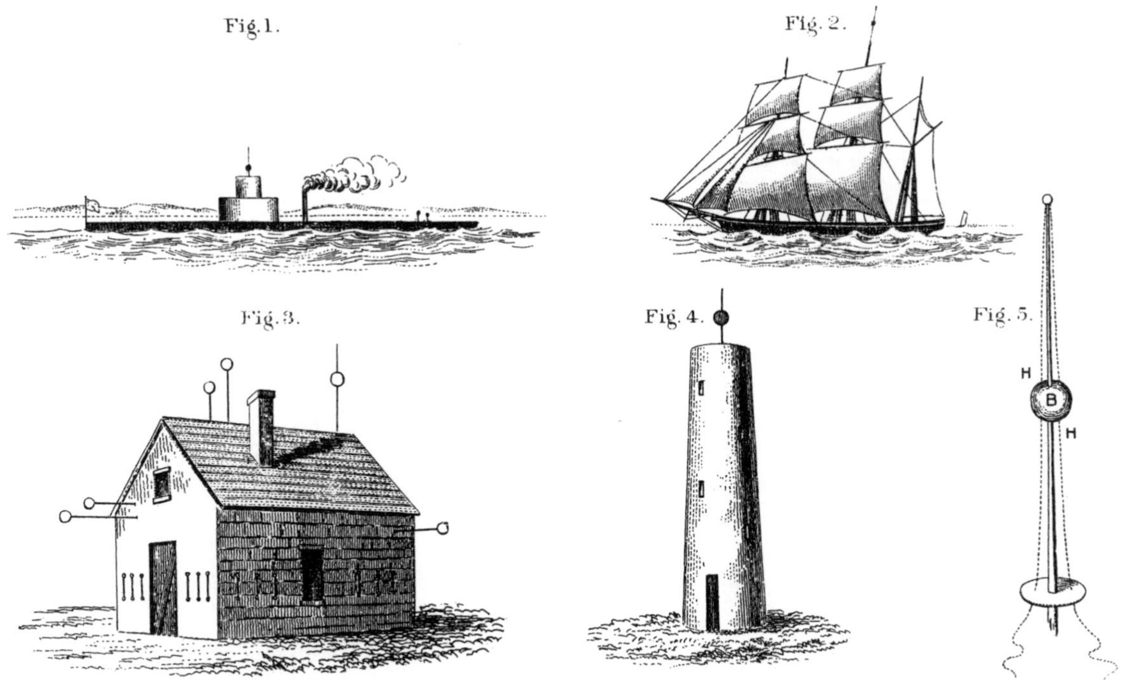

Visual signal equipment.

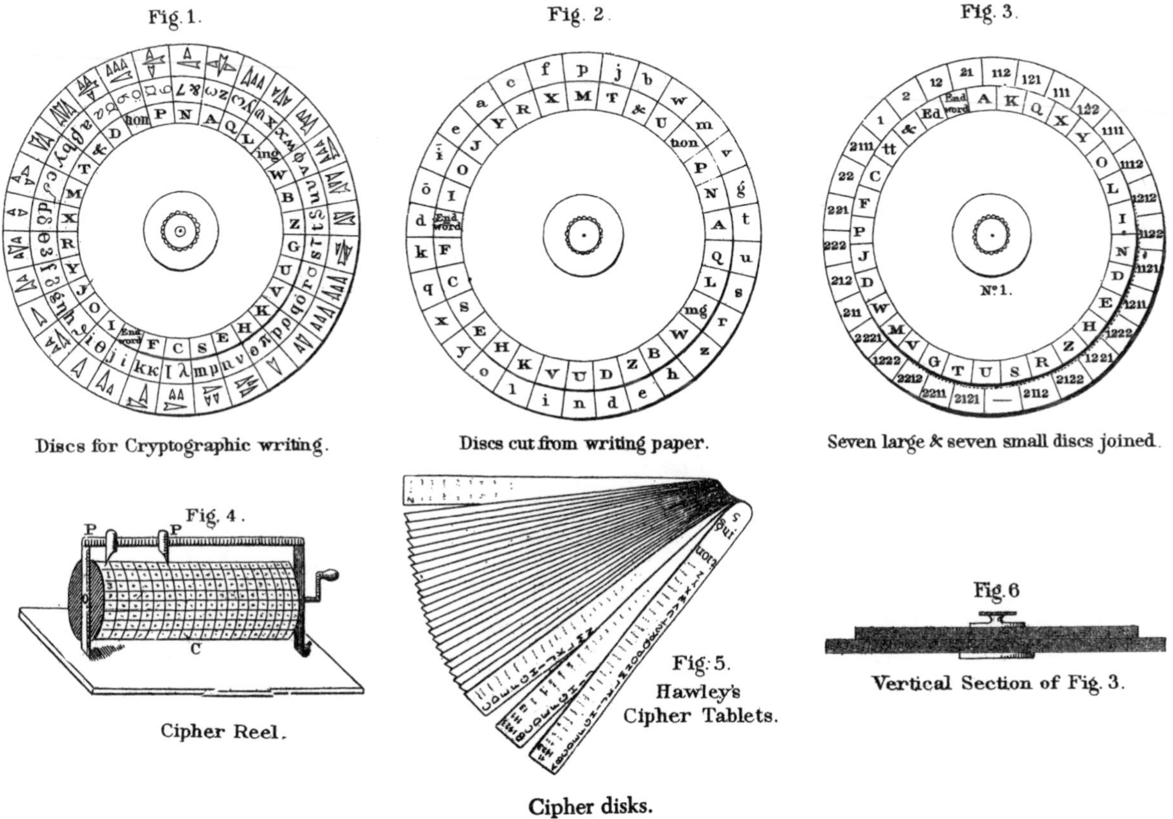

Cipher disks.

pliers, and shears for trimming the torch, a small funnel for filling the torch, two-flame-shades, and a wind-shade.

Kit. This canvas signal-case contained the signal staff, flags, torch-case, torches, and wormer. These were all compactly rolled together and bound by straps. A wormer is a screw used when the torch wick is accidentally drawn so far into the tube of the torch that it cannot be seized by pliers.

The signal staff, was of hickory, and made in 4 joints, each 4 feet long, tapering as a whole from 1¼ inches at the butt to ½ inch at the tip. The joints were ferruled at the ends with brass, and fitted to be joined together similarly to fishing rods. The third joint was guarded with brass for 6 inches at its upper end, to protect it from the flames of the torch, which was attached, when in use, to this joint. The tip or fourth joint was the one to which the flag was attached for day signals. When in use, two or more joints of the staff were fitted together.

The signal flags were made of cotton or linen. There were 7 of these as follows:

1. Six-foot white, square with a center consisting of a 2-foot red square.
2. Six-foot black, with white square in the center.
3. Four-foot white, with 16-inch red square at the center.
4. Four-foot black, with 16-inch white square at the center.
5. Four-foot red, with 16-inch white square at the center.
6. Two-foot white, with 8-inch red square at the center.
7. Two-foot red, with 8-inch white square at the center.

All of these flags were fitted with tapes for tying them to the staff. Tapes were 1 foot apart.

The kit-case, canteen, and haversack were fitted with shoulder-slings or straps for carrying. The service can was a 5-gallon strong copper can, with rolled seams hard soldered. The nozzle was fitted with a screw cap to prevent leakage.

Cipher Disk. A small disk of cardboard on which was written or printed the letters of the alphabet in irregular sequence and arranged around the circumference of the disk.

Compass. Officers of the Signal Corps were furnished with a good pocket compass, which was found to be very useful in reconnaissance and in locating signal stations, both friendly and hostile.

Field-Glass (also known as binocular-glass or marine glass). This had a low magnifying power but an extensive field of view. The field glass was used in sweeping the landscape to find the tents of the enemy, his wagons, artillery, pickets, and other objects, to be

Fig. 2.

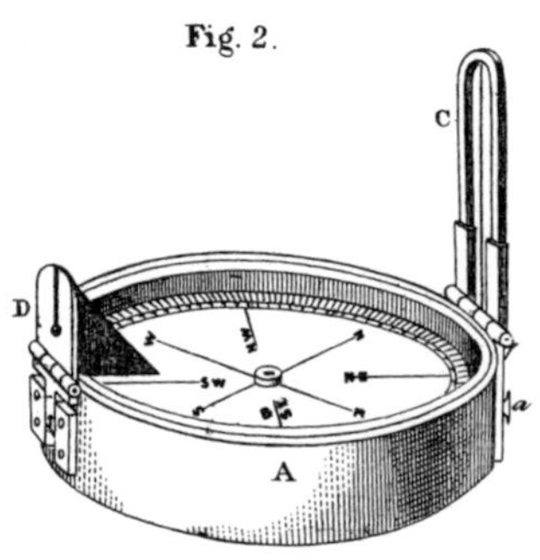

Prismatic Compass.

Fig. 3.

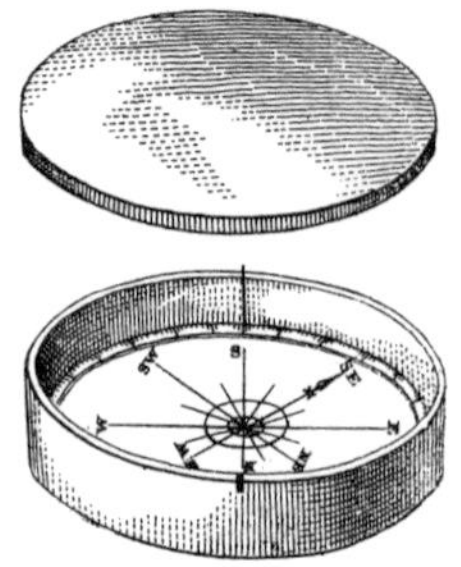

Pocket Compass.

Compass.

afterward more closely examined with the telescope. The field glass was also very useful on shipboard or in boats, where the motion interfered with the use of the telescope. It was excellent for reading signals at short ranges of 5 miles or less, although signals were frequently read at the distance of ten miles.

Flags, Signal. See *Kit*, under Apparatus.

Pistol, Signal. Army and Navy Models. Both used the percussion cap as with the revolvers but for cartridges the "Composition Fires" were used. "Composition Fires" were pyrotechnic compositions which burned with great intensity of light and color. The colors red, white, and green were found to be best suited for signalling. These signal cartridges were fired by the explosion of the percussion cap on the signal pistol. The colors of the cartridges were indicated by the colors painted on the outside of the cases or shells. The U.S. Government purchased 348 signal pistols during the war.

Signal cartridges were prepared on the principle of the Coston lights and were constructed so as to be fired by the explosion of the percussion cap on the signal pistol. The colors on the cases of signal cartridges indicated colors which would be used. Apparently, there was a series of ten different lights, but more normally in the field the main colors, as stated above, were red, white, and green. These, of course, were used in various combinations, according to a predetermined code. Generally, all message signals consisted of two lights each, as, for example:

White and Red—Enemy approaching
White and White—Enemy retreating

and so on.

Rockets, Signal. Paper or pasteboard cylinder filled with a charge, and with quick fuzes and correctly-timed fuze, were used. With these signal rockets a "quick-match" was commonly used. A yard of this quick-match burned 12 seconds. Time of ignition of the rockets could be arranged by cutting off proportional lengths of the fuze. Signal rockets attained great elevation and generally could be seen up to a horizontal range of 8 miles. However they were not very successful in wooded terrain, for the rockets rose above the trees, thus necessitating the presence of observers above the trees (in towers or on mountains). Also, occasionally when clouds hung low, rockets threw out their stars above the clouds and thus could not be seen. Signal rockets were fired from a frame or stand or occasionally against a fence or post.

Signal rockets as furnished by the U.S. Army Ordnance Department were generally made with sticks attached, or in readiness to be attached, by means of twine or wire.

Brass bound with leather covering. Loops to hold a carrying strap. Length closed, 10¼ inches; open, 31 inches. Marked in script letters: "U.S.A. Signal Telescope. JAS. W. QUEEN, Phila."

TORCH, SIGNAL. Torches could be read at night at 8 miles, rarely, at 25 miles.

Case. The torch-case was a piece of rubber cloth about 3 feet long by 2½ feet wide, fitted on one side with pouches, in which the torches were inserted.

Flying-torch. A copper cylinder, 18 inches long and 2 inches in diameter; it was closed at the lower end, with the exception of a nozzle, through which it could be filled, and which closed with a screw cap; it was open at the wick end, and on its sides, at this end were four openings, 1 inch long and ½ inch broad, which opened into the wick.

Foot-torch. A copper cylinder, 18 inches long and 2 inches in diameter, and was similar in form to the flying-torch. Each torch was equipped with a flame-

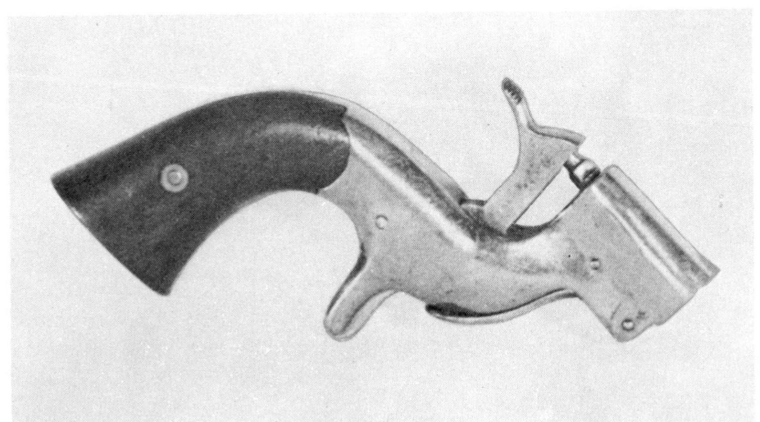

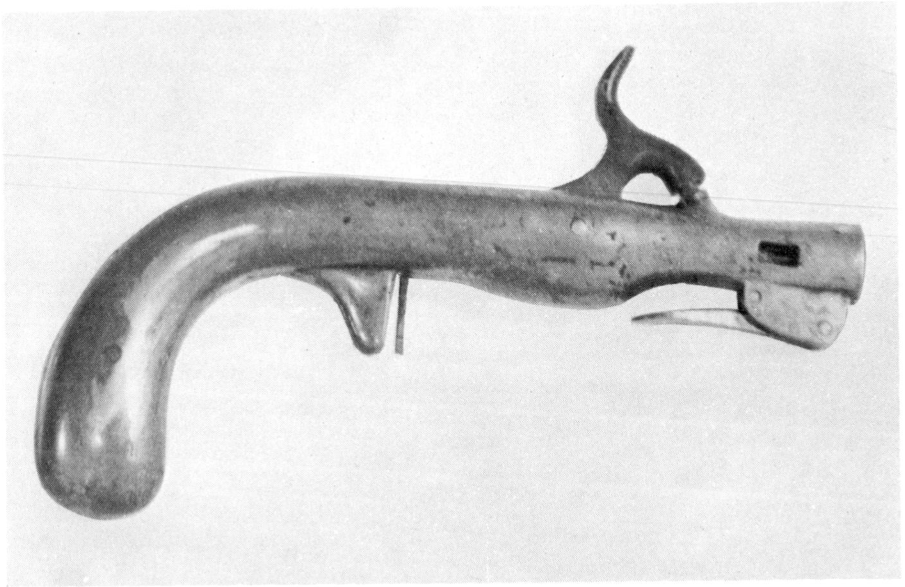

Signal pistols. Upper, Army signal pistol dated 1862. Lower, Navy signal pistol dated 1863.

TELESCOPE, SIGNAL. The Signal Corps telescope was considered to be the best in general use. This telescope was 30-power and had a focal length of 26 inches. The tube was cased in leather. The draw was of four joints, bronzed black, in order that there might be no glitter to attract the enemy. The telescope had leather caps for both ends and was carried by a strong leather strap. Specimen:

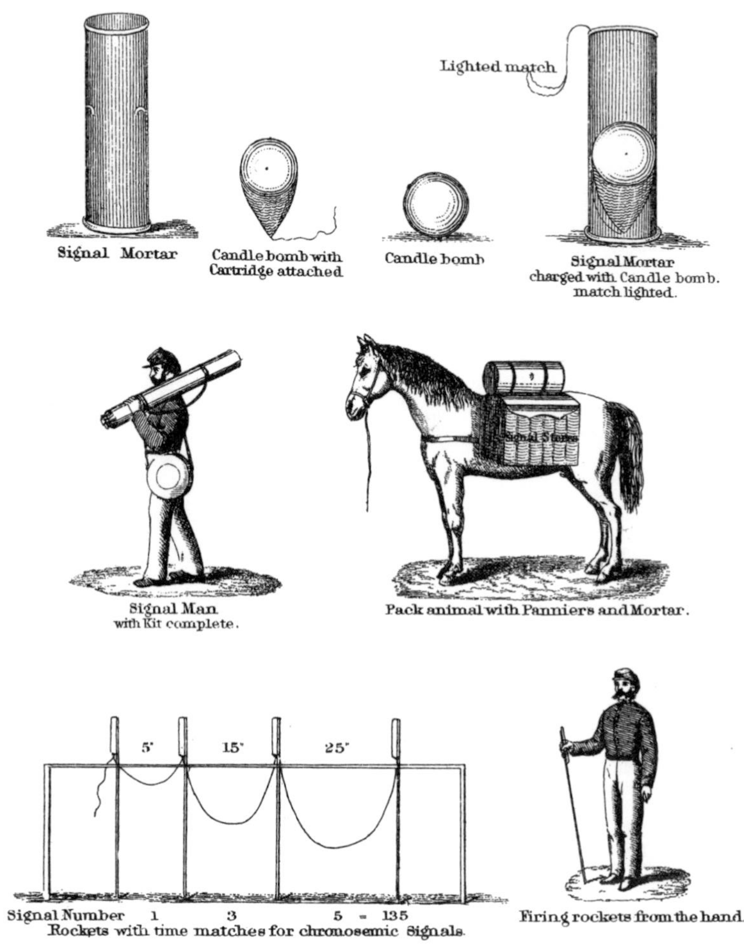

Rocket head and stick

Signal rockets.

Signal lantern.

shade and a wind-shade.

SIGNAL FLAGS. See SIGNAL EQUIPMENT.

SIGNAL PISTOL. See SIGNAL EQUIPMENT.

SIGNAL TORCH. See SIGNAL EQUIPMENT.

SMALL ARMS. A collective term for shoulder and hand weapons. This included all weapons of small caliber operated or carried by hand, for example, rifles, muskets, pistols, revolvers, and machine guns. See the appropriate headings.

SMOKE BALL. See PROJECTILES.

SOAP AND SOAP BOX. Soap, like candles, was a regular item of issue. Quality varied with makers and contractors, but for the most part, the soap was of the "rough and ready" type, similar to coarse laundry soap of today. Fancy toilet soap made a good present to soldiers and sailors, who also were given non-issue soap boxes, often fancy in design. Shown here is an example of soap box used by a soldier, and a more elaborate gutta-percha navy soap box.

SOAP BOX, ARMY. Consists of two parts of wood which screw into each other. In the top part is a mirror; in the bottom part is a pewter liner which held the soap. It is 1½ inches tall—when assembled—and 3¼ inches in diameter. The original tag carries the inscription: "Soap box that Edward T. Mapes carried all through the War of the Rebellion."

SOAP BOX, NAVY. Beautiful gutta-percha box, marked on the top with an anchor, the letters "U.S.N.," and the motto "Don't give up the ship." In addition to room for the soap there is also a mirror on the inside of the cover. Dimensions of this round box are 3 inches in diameter and 1½ inches deep.

SOCKS. See UNIFORMS AND CLOTHING.

SOLID SHOT. See PROJECTILES.

SPHERICAL CASE SHOT. See PROJECTILES.

SPONGE BUCKET. See ARTILLERY.

SPRING VISE. See APPENDAGES.

SPURS. See HORSE EQUIPMENT.

SPUR CARRIER (Patent No. 45,776). Patented January 3, 1865, by E. P. Watson, New York, N.Y. A metallic plate was provided with a projecting flange and screw holes. This plate was attached to a boot-heel so that the flange would prevent the bottoms of the trousers from getting under the boot-heel, would furnish a foot hold for drawing off the boot, and would serve as a support for spurs.

STADIA. See also ENGINEER EQUIPMENT. A stadia was a metal (brass or silver) instrument for measuring distance, given as a prize in competitive marksmanship with the rifle, musket, or carbine. A company prize was a brass stadia; a regimental prize was a silver stadia. Illustrated are: Brass Stadia. 5¼ inches long, marked "U.S. Stadia" and "Frankford Arsenal," with graduated scale on both sides. Obverse for infantry and reverse for cavalry, so marked with brass chain for carrying and original cord with lead ball (which was held between the teeth for gauging distance). The silver stadia on the right is a fancy presentation type, marked "Frankford Arsenal" and the name of the maker "George W. Simons, Philadelphia."

STENCIL. Many organizations required their members to stencil items of equipment and clothing with the owner's name. Such marking often included the company number, a fact which is disconcerting to collectors because it makes more difficult the establishing of the original owner's unit. Often, for example, an item will be stencilled with a man's name, his company, and his company number. And, in lucky cases, the company number will be omitted but the regimental number will be present.

Individual soldiers, North and South, often had their own stencils, usually of brass, with name, company, and regiment. These often served to identify the soldier if he became a casualty. Such a stencil is shown here.

Stencils were of brass with the letters cut out. These varied in size but the most common was about 3¼ by 1½. A specimen in the author's collection be-

U.S. Navy signal equipment: telescope and signal flags. (Library of Congress)

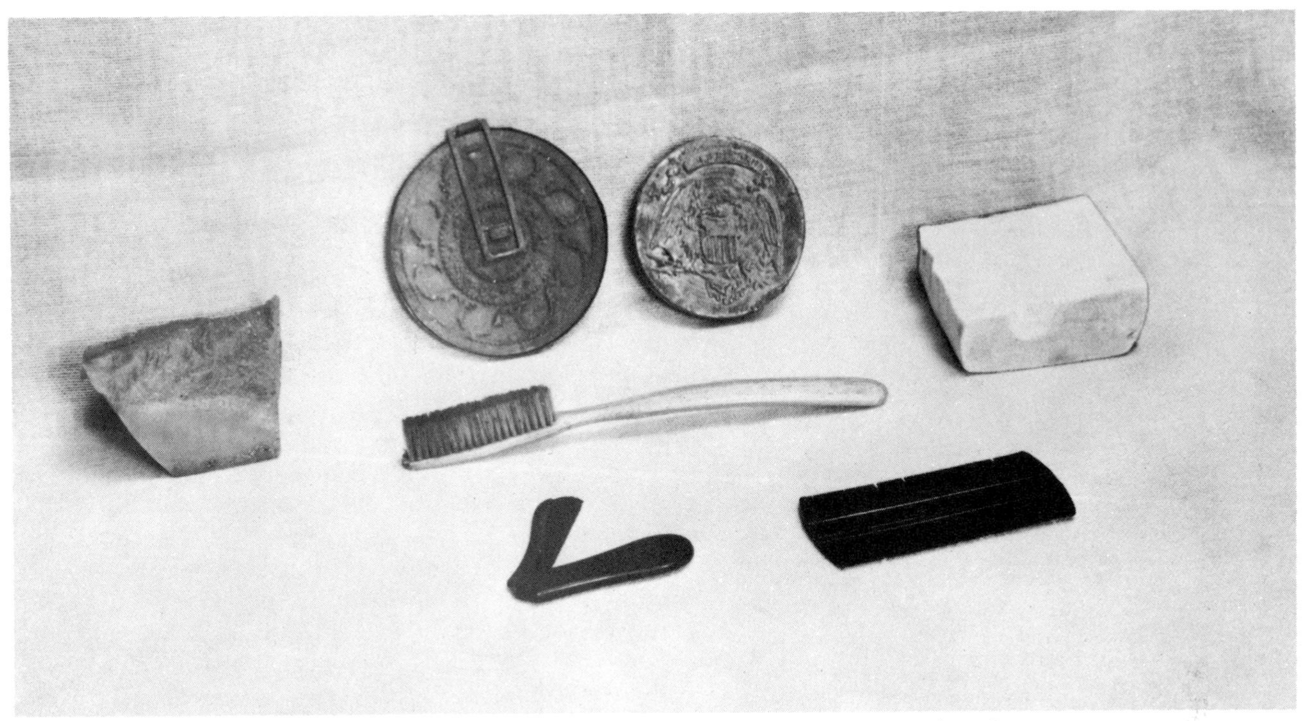

Soap actually used in the Civil War. Army mirrors, toothbrush, and combs

Soap box, Navy.

longed to E. B. KILBEY Co. K 1st Maine Heavy Artillery. An officer's stencil is 5½ by 1⅞ inches and belonged to Captain Charles H. Paull, Co. G 4th Massachusetts Volunteers.

A battlefield find is a 2 x 1⅛ brass stencil found at White Oak Swamp battlefield on the Peninsula. It belonged to H. G. MORGAN, CO. E 85th New York Infantry.

Another stencil, also of brass, in the author's collection is 3 x 1¼ inches and was the means of identifying its owner who was killed in action. The soldier was S. A. MILLER, Co. G 57th Indiana Infantry. Miller was killed at Peach Tree Creek, Georgia.

STIRRUPS. See HORSE EQUIPMENTS.

STOVE, CAMP. While the Sibley stove was the most commonly used, a wide variety existed among the different units, both North and South. The large, cumbersome types were used mainly in rear echelons or at large headquarters, but after 1862 stoves were used infrequently, and after the 1864 campaign opened they were rarely seen. In barracks and hospitals, of course, they saw extensive use throughout the war.

HOPE STOVE (Patent No. 37,399). Patented January 13, 1863, Castleton, Vermont. This stove consisted of a box top of sheet metal, provided with holes

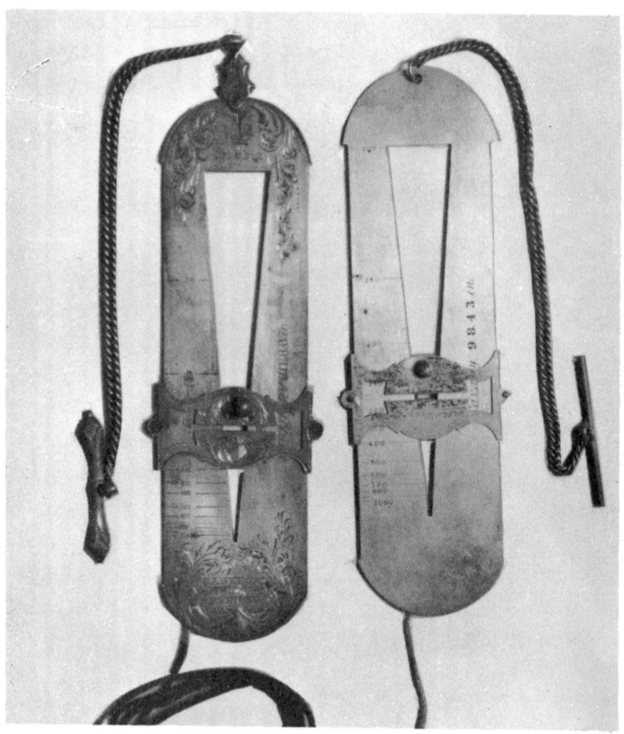

Stadia. Left: Standard issue all-brass stadia sight. 5¼ inches overall. Marked "Frankford Arsenal." Also "U.S. Stadia, etc.," graduated scale both sides. Obverse for infantry; reverse for cavalry—so marked with brass chain for carrying and original cord with lead ball (which was held between teeth) for gauging distance. Right: identical to above but the fancy solid silver fully engraved presentation type which was given as prizes. This one also marked "Frankford Arsenal" like above but also bears marks of "George W. Simons, Philadelphia," who obviously made it. (Norm Flayderman)

for the chimney and for a kettle. The stove was designed to use over a trench cut in the ground.

Sibley Stove. See also Sibley Tent under TENT. This cone-shaped stove was used in conjunction with the tent of the same name. The stove pipe was connected with the stove proper, which stood beneath the tripod supporting the tent. A chain hung from the fork of the tripod, with a hook on which a kettle could be hung. During the war the Federal Army used about 16,000 Sibley stoves. The Sibley stove was an airtight cylinder 30 inches tall, with an 18-inch base diameter, 5 sections of pipe tapering from 5 down to 4 inches, a hinge or slide door 8 inches high, 6 inches wide, and 8 inches from the bottom. This model weighed 30 pounds. There were also specifications for 25- and 18-pound models.

Smith Stove (Patent No. 37,926). Patented March 17, 1863 by Lowell H. Smith, Owensville, Ohio. This stove was made of sections which fit into each other. When the outer section was raised and supported on logs, the other sections slipped out in telescope fashion.

Soyer's New Field Stove. This stove consumed not more than 12 to 15 pounds of fuel. Thus, allowing 20 stoves to a regiment, the consumption would be 300 pounds per 1,000 men. Coal also could be used. Salt beef, pork, Irish stew, stewed beef, tea, coffee, and cocoa could be prepared in these stoves.

Williams Stove (Patent No. 34,385). Patented February 11, 1862 by J. S. Williams, Philadelphia, Penn. Consisted of outer and inner casings in two pieces hinged to each other. A detachable cover, provided with two flanges, fit over the upper edges of the outer casing.

Woodbury Stove (Patent No. 34,457). Patented February 18, 1862 by S. D. Woodbury, Lynn, Mass. This stove could be disassembled and compactly packed. It consisted of a fire chamber in two sections and had a sectioned stovepipe of tapering pieces.

Although not strictly a stove but more correctly a method of heating was the "California furnace" used by some units. Some Massachusetts troops in 1861, and probably other troops as well, heated their tents by running a string of pipe underground from a pit in the center. The fire was built in the pit. Occasionally water would drown out the fire and flood the California furnace.

STRETCHER OR HAND LITTER. See MEDICAL EQUIPMENT.

SUBMARINE. See *Torpedo Boat* in MINES AND TORPEDOES.

Stencils. Left to right: Stencil of S. A. Miller, Co. G, 57th Indiana Infantry; Captain Charles H. Paull, Co. G, 4th Mass. Infantry; E. B. Kilbey, Co. K, 1st Maine Heavy artillery.

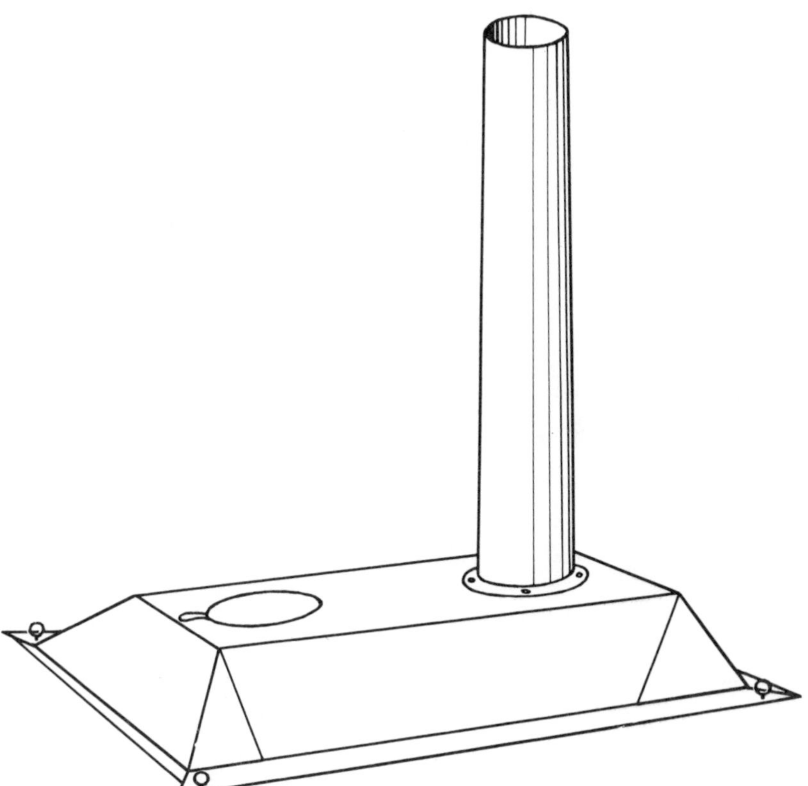

Hope's camp stove, patent Jan. 13, 1863. (National Archives)

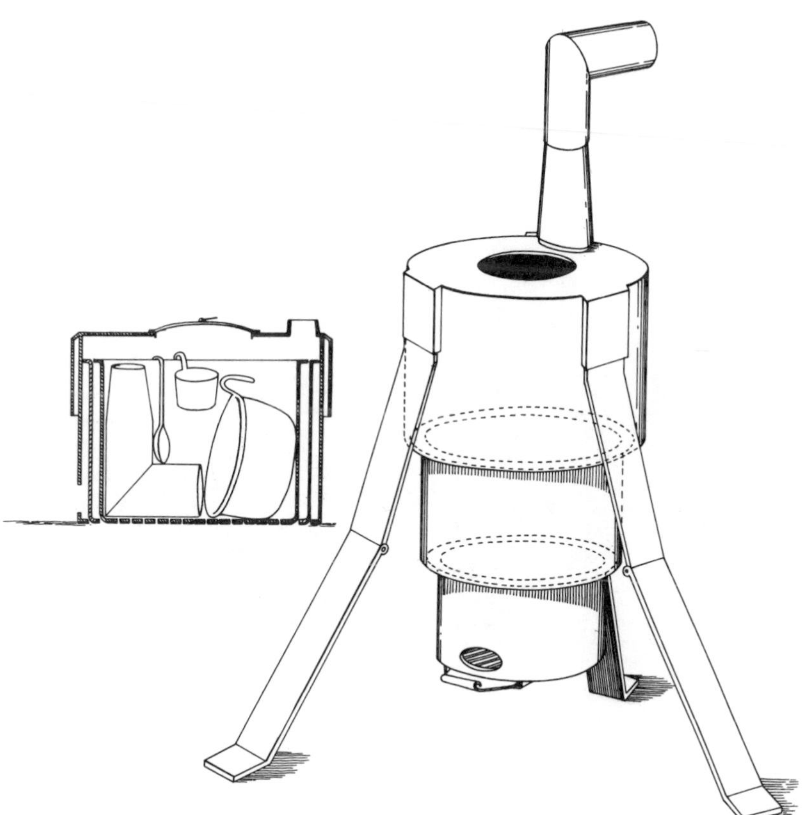

Smith's camp stove. Patent March 17, 1863. (National Archives)

Artist's conception of Confederate submarine. Drawing from *Harpers Weekly* labeled "Submarine Infernal Machine Intended to Destroy the *Minnesota.*"

The *Intelligent Whale,* Federal Navy's contribution to submarining in the late months of the Civil War. There is no record that this land-bound monster (still on exhibit at the Brooklyn Navy Yard) ever operated on land or under the water. (National Archives)

Sibley stove.

SURCINGLE. See HORSE EQUIPMENTS.

SUSPENDERS. See UNIFORMS AND CLOTHING.

SUTLER. Most regiments had sutlers at some time in their service. These sutlers used their own chits and tokens when money was not plentiful among the men. Shown here is a chit of the regimental sutler of the 11th New York Cavalry ("Scott's Nine Hundred"). J. R. Bostwick served this regiment as regimental sutler throughout the entire war. He kept a large variety of goods that soldiers required, such as gloves, blacking, polishing materials, thread, needles, pipes, tobacco, and cigars. He charged a good price for his wares, but the prices were not exorbitant, considering the risks which he took. He furnished the officers' mess for a while and had money to lend for a fair rate of interest; he trusted the men for two dollars' worth of tickets per month, to be paid on the first pay day, and would give a still longer credit if a soldier asked for it. It was the general belief that the sutler made a good deal of money out of the regiment, but he also lost considerable money in unpaid debts. Probably no one but the sutler himself knew what the actual profits were.

A chit of the sutler of the 84th Pa. Vols., Allen and Co., is also shown.

SWORD BELT.

CONFEDERATE SWORD BELT. For all officers, a waist belt, not less than 1½ inches, nor more than 2 inches wide; to be worn over the sash; the sword to be suspended from it by slings of the same material as the belt, with a hook attached to the belt upon which the sword may be hung.

General Officers. Russian leather, with 3 stripes of gold embroidery; the slings embroidered on both sides.

All Other Officers. Plain, black leather.

All Noncommissioned Officers. Plain, black leather.

CONFEDERATE SWORD BELT PLATE

All Officers and enlisted men. Gilt, rectangular; 2 inches wide, with a raised bright rim; a silver wreath of laurel encircling the "arms of the Confederate States."

Sword Knot. Of plaited leather, with tassels.

Sash. General officers: Buff silk net, with silk bullion fringe ends; sash to go twice around the waist, and to tie behind the left hip; pendant part not to extend more than 18 inches below the tie.

Officers of the General Staff and Engineers, and of the Artillery and Infantry: Red silk net.

Officers of the Cavalry: Yellow silk net.

Medical Officers: Green silk net.

All sashes to have silk bullion fringe ends; to go around the waist, and to tie as for general officers.

Sergeants: Of worsted, with worsted bullion fringe ends: red for artillery and infantry, and yellow for

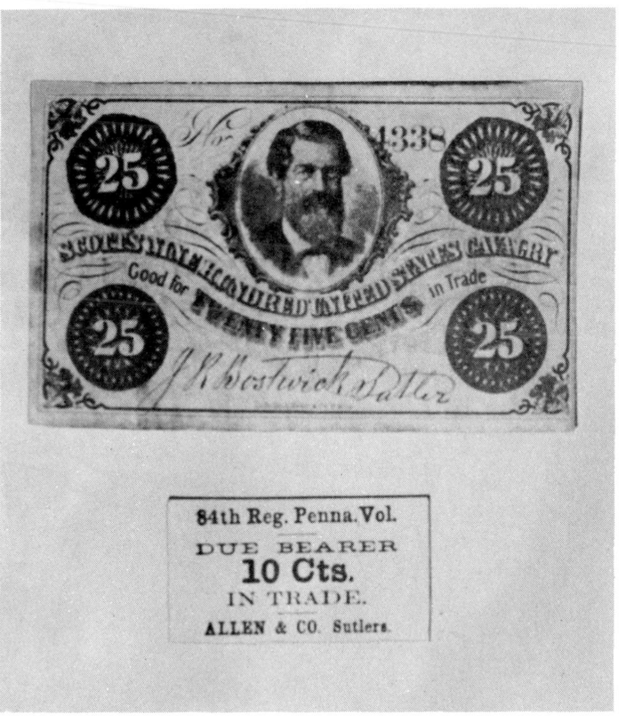

Sutler currency and "chits."

Presentation sword in sword case. Metropolitan Fair, New York 1864. (National Archives)

U.S. Navy sword belt and buckle. (Norm Flayderman)

cavalry. Sashes to go twice around the waist, and to tie as above specified.

FEDERAL SWORD BELTS (Regulations)

ARMY SWORD BELT

All Officers. A waist belt not less than one and one-half inch nor more than two inches wide; to be worn over the sash; the sword to be suspended from it by slings, of the same material as the belt, with a hook attached to the belt, upon which the sword may be hung.

General Officers. Russia leather, with three stripes of gold embroidery; the slings embroidered on both sides.

Other Officers. Black leather, plain.

Noncommissioned Officers. Black leather, plain.

MARINE CORPS.

All Officers. A waist belt of not less than one and one-half inches, nor more than two inches wide to be worn over the sash; the sword to be suspended from it by slings of the same material as the belt, with a hook attached to the belt, upon which the sword may be hung.

The Commandant. Of Russia leather, with three stripes of gold embroidery; the slings embroidered on both sides; or the same belt as to be immediately prescribed for all other officers.

All Other Officers. Of white glazed leather.

NAVY. A belt of plain black glazed leather, not less than one inch and a half nor more than two inches wide, with slings of the same not less than one-half nor more than three-quarters of an inch wide, and hook in the forward ring to suspend the sword. Belt-plate of yellow gilt in front, two inches in diameter, as per pattern. The belt to be worn over the coat.

SWORD AND SABER KNOTS

ARMY

General Officers. Gold cord with acorn.

Other Officers. Gold lace strap with gold bullion tassel.

MARINE CORPS. Gold lace strap with gold bullion tassel.

NAVY (1852 Regulation).

Captain and Commander. Blue and gold cord, 24 inches long, including the tassel; gold and blue slide; tassel of 12 gold bullions, 1¾ inches long, enclosing fine blue bullions, with basket-worked head.

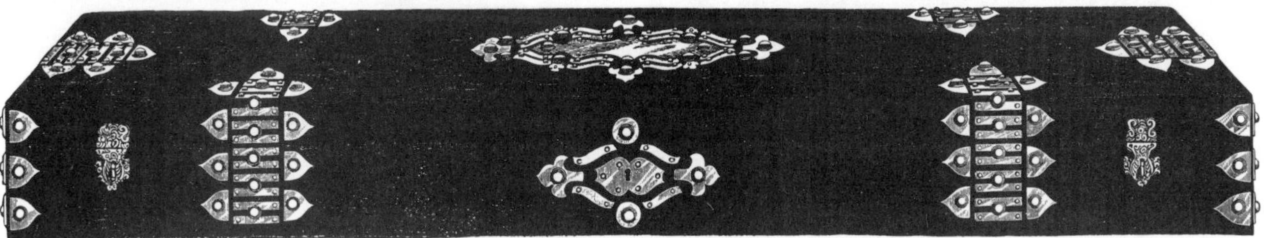

Sword case. (Norm Flayderman)

Sword Knots.

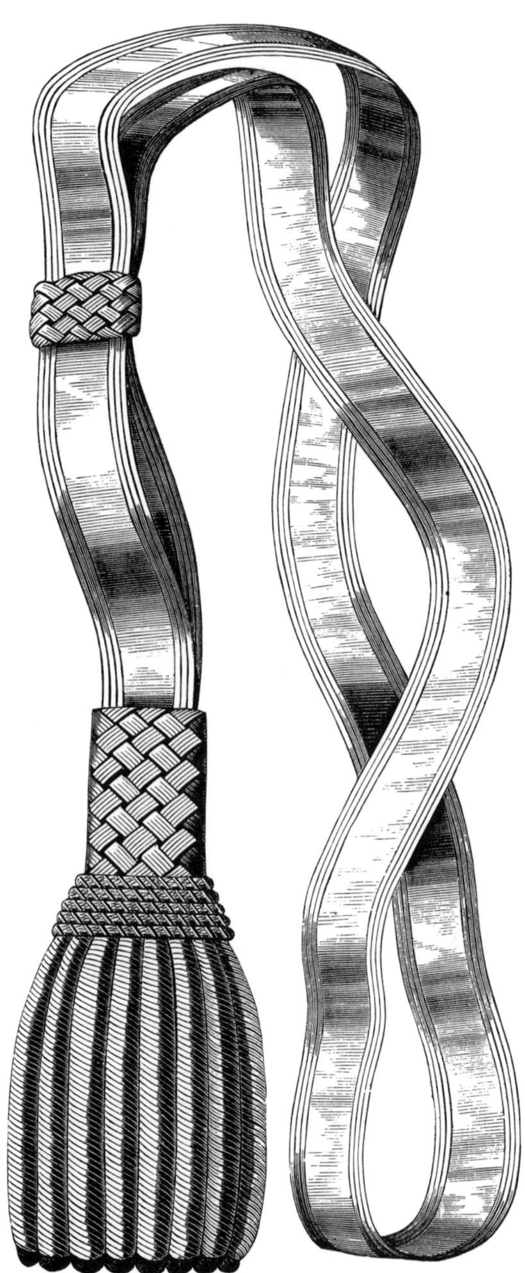

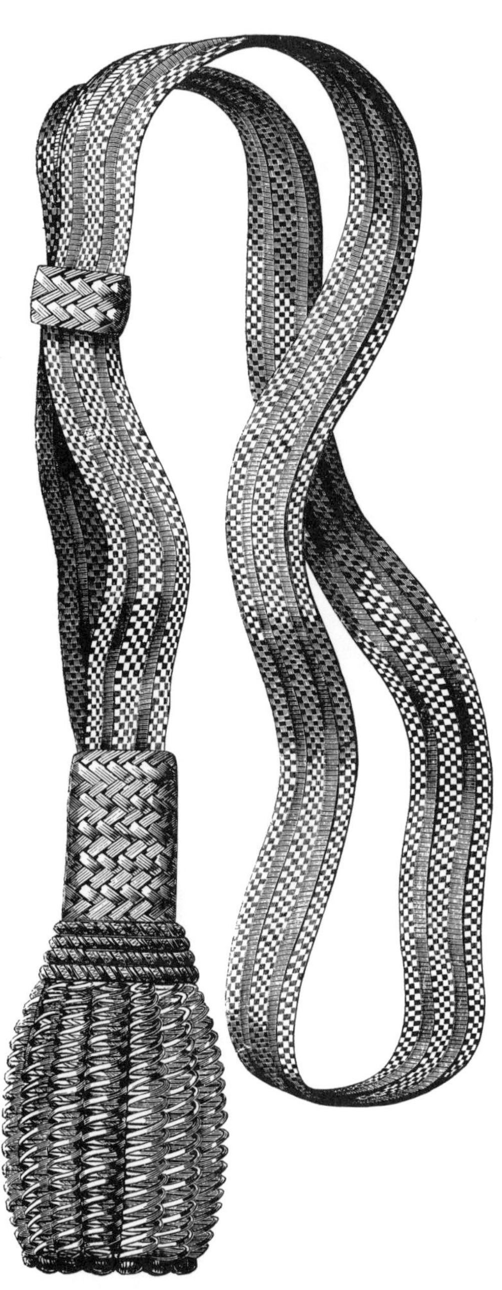

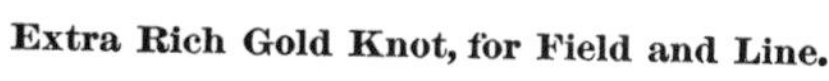

No. 38.

Extra Rich Gold Knot, for Field and Line.

No. 39.

U. S. Regulation, for Field and Line.

Sword knots. U.S. Navy. (Norm Flayderman)

Other Commissioned Officers. An epaulette of gold lace, ½ inch wide, and 18 inches long, including the tassel; gold slide; tassel of 12 gold bullions, 1¾ inches long, with basket-worked head.

SWORDS AND SABERS

CONFEDERATE SWORDS. Swords and other edged weapons were made at so many local establishments, including village blacksmiths shops, that it is absolutely impossible to list them all. Not only were all types of U.S. edged weapons copied widely by the Confederates, but there were also extensive importations from abroad. Some of the leading domestic makers:

Boyle & Gamble, Richmond
Mitchell & Tyler Co., Richmond
Kraft, Goldschmidt & Kraft, Columbia, S.C.
Leech & Rigdon Co. (Memphis Novelty Works)
L. Harman & Bro., Columbus, Ga.
W. J. McElroy, Macon, Ga.
Thomas Griswold & Co., New Orleans, La.
College Hill Arsenal, Nashville, Tenn.
Nashville Plow Works, Nashville, Tenn.
Wm. Glaze & Co., Columbia, S.C.
Dufilho, New Orleans, La.
E. J. Johnston & Co., Macon, Ga.
Louis Froelich, Kenansville, N.C.
Halfman & Taylor, Montgomery, Ala.
James Conning, Mobile, Ala.
Boyle, Gamble & Mac Fee, Richmond, Va.
Robert Mole & Co., Birmingham, England
Isaac's & Co., London
Campbell & Co., London, England

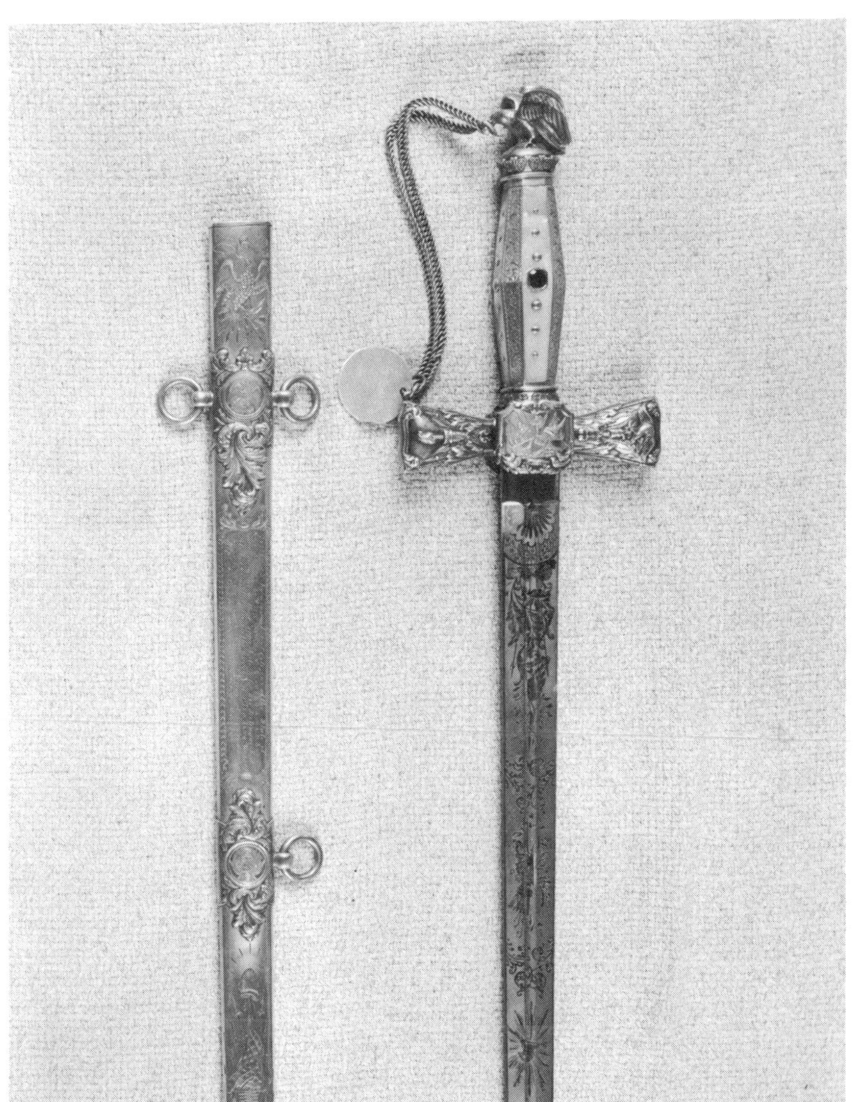

Presentation sword of Maj. Gen. Samuel G. French. (West Point Museum collections)

FEDERAL SWORDS AND SABERS. During the Civil War most swords were designed for use as well as for decoration. They designated rank, and in some instances the branch of service. Sword and sword belt were worn upon all occasions of duty without exception. When on foot, the saber was to be suspended from the hook attached to the belt. When not on military duty, officers could wear swords of honor, or the prescribed sword, with a scabbard, gilt, or of leather with gilt mountings.

ARMY SWORDS, SABERS, AND SCABBARDS.

General Officers—straight sword, gilt hilt, ilver grip, brass or steel scabbard.

Officers of the Adjutant-General's, Inspector-General's, Quartermaster's, and Subsistence Departments, Corps of Engineers, Topographical Engineers, Ordnance, the Judge-Advocate of the Army, Aides-de-Camp, Field Officers of Artillery, Infantry and Foot Riflemen, and for the Light Artillery—the sword of the pattern adopted by the War Department, April 9, 1850; or the one described in General Orders No. 21, of August 28, 1860, for officers therein designated.

Medical and Pay Departments—small sword and scabbard, according to pattern in the Surgeon-General's office.

Medical Cadets—the sword and belt and plate will be the same as for non-commissioned officers.

Officers of Cavalry—saber and scabbard now in use, according to pattern in the Ordnance Department.

Artillery, Infantry, and Foot Riflemen, except the field officers—the sword of the pattern adopted by the War Department, April 9, 1850.

The sword and sword-belt will be worn upon all occasions of duty, without exception.

When on foot, the saber will be suspended from the hook attached to the belt.

When not on military duty, officers may wear swords of honor, or the prescribed sword, with a scabbard, gilt, or of leather with gilt mountings.

According to the U.S. *Ordnance Manual* 1861, the following swords and sabers were regulation:

	Overall length in scabbard
Cavalry saber	43.25
Light cavalry saber	42.35
Light Artillery saber	38.6
Fort Artillery sword	26.0
Non-commissioned officer's sword	38.75
Musician's sword	32.75
Saber for staff and field officer	39.4
Sword for officers of the staff and staff corps	
Sword for foot officers	37.85
Saber for cavalry officers	

Commissioned officers of the Federal Army wore swords of almost limitless variety and quality. In addition to many types of militia officers' swords, the following were regulation types:

Staff and Field Officer's Sword. Adopted April 9, 1850, for all staff officers and for field officers of infantry, artillery, and riflemen. Its use was mandatory until 1860 when the frail staff and field officers' sword of that date became optional. Officers who desired a real weapon, however, continued to use it until the end of the war.

Corps of Engineers' Swords. The Engineers wore the 1850 models of foot and field officers' swords during the war. However, the Topographical Engineers wore their own model (1839 pattern) until their Corps was abolished in 1863. The sword was marked with "T.E." (Topographical Engineers) and corresponded exactly to the 1833 dragoon saber.

Medical Staff Swords. Adopted in 1840 and was worn by U.S. Army Medical Officers until 1902. There are minor variations of this sword. Early specimens had heavy blades, usually elliptical in cross section while post-Civil War specimens usually had light and frail blades diamond-shaped in cross section.

Pay Department Swords. These were similar to those carried by the Medical Department. The Pay Department sword of 1840 was exactly the same as that prescribed for the Medical Staff, except that the "M.S." (Medical Staff) was replaced by "P.D." (Pay Department).

Noncommissioned Officers' Sword. This sword, adopted by the War Department in 1840, was based principally upon a French pattern but was also reminiscent of some models used by Great Britain. It is a handsome and graceful appearing weapon, but somewhat heavy in the hilt and poorly balanced. Nevertheless, it was worn by American sergeants for over 70 years which included such great conflicts as the Mexican War, Civil War, and Spanish American War. The author saw them used as late as the 1930's by C.M.T.C. and R.O.T.C. units.

Musicians' Sword. The musicians' sword was not merely for decoration, but was issued to bandsmen who accompanied combat troops on the battlefield. There was always the possibility that bandsmen, functioning as stretcher bearers, might have to defend themselves against an enemy attack. The musicians' sword adopted by the War Department in 1840 was essentially the same as the noncommissioned officers' sword adopted at the same time. The only differences between the two were that the musician's sword did not have the double counter-guard and its blade was 4 inches shorter.

Artillery Saber. In 1840 the War Department

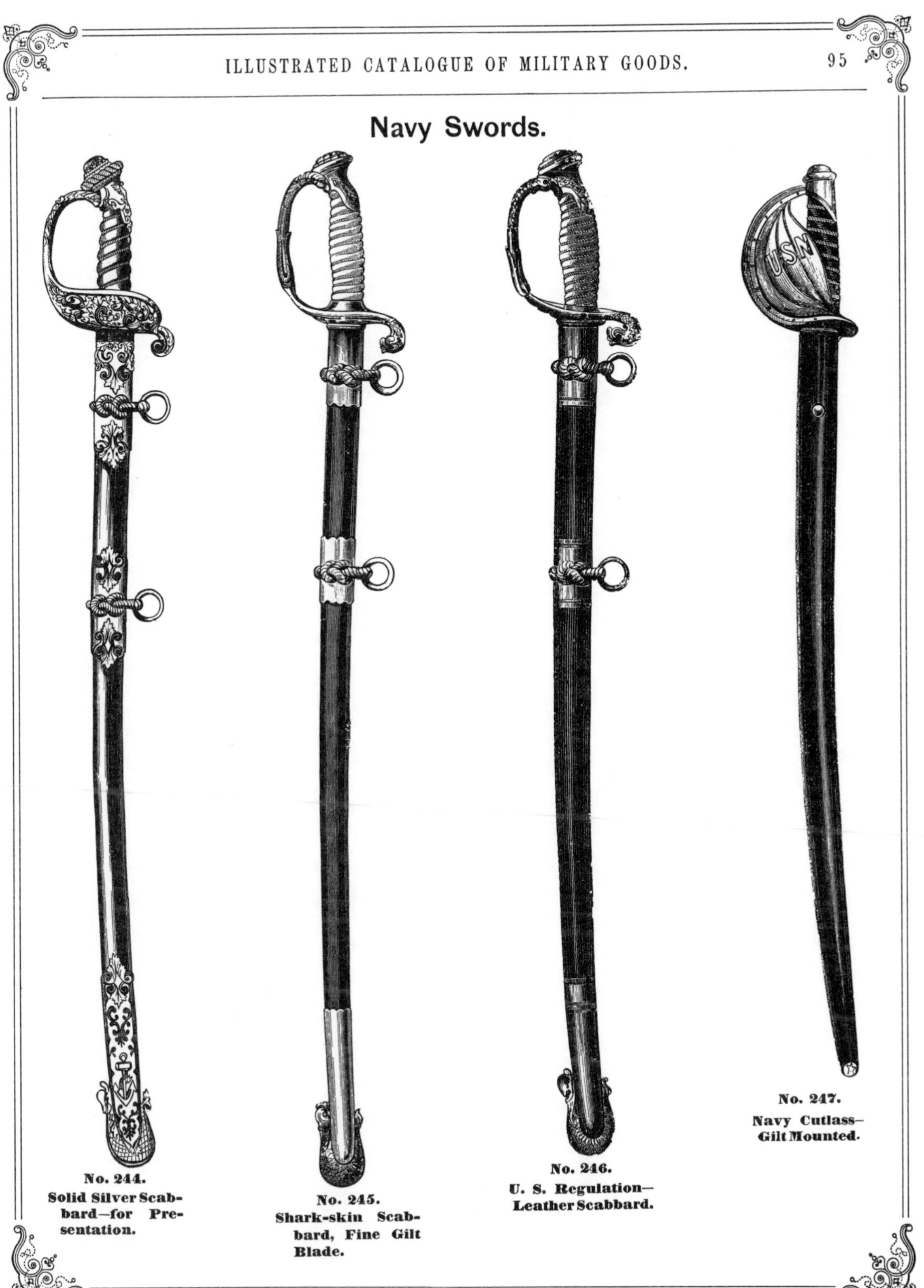

U.S. Navy swords. (Norm Flayderman)

Field telegraph station. Army of the Potomac, 1864. Note the wire reel on the wagon, used for laying wire. (National Archives)

adopted a special saber for artillerymen, based upon a French pattern, for the light artillery companies of the regular artillery regiments. A handsome and essentially serviceable weapon, it remained regulation for about half a century.

Officers' Artillery Saber. This saber was exactly like the enlisted men's weapon, but had some decoration on the hilt and blade.

Cavalry Saber. In 1840 the War Department adopted a new model saber for the Army's three dragoon regiments. This saber, closely following the French 1822 model, won the name of "Old Wristbreaker" from the men who used it. About 1860 a light saber was introduced for cavalry. This new model had a narrower blade and was much lighter than the 1840 model, many of which were also used in the war. In addition to American-made sabers, the Federal Government during 1861-1862 purchased sabers from many sources, both domestic and foreign. Most of the domestic products followed the current official models exactly.

Saber Contracts 1861

Mansfield, Lamb & Co., Smithfield, R.I.
Herman Boker & Co., New York
David J. Millard, Claysville, N.Y.
Tomes, Son & McIlvaine, New York
J. Meyer
James T. Ames, Chicopee, Mass.
T. & E. Schliefflin, Phila.
Horstmann & Brothers, Phila.
Philip S. Justice, Phila.
H. G. Leisenring, Phila
T. Kessman, New York

Marine Corps Sword. Marine Corps officers' swords are now very scarce for the Civil War period. Prior to 1859, officers of the U.S. Marine Corps wore the characteristic Marine Corps sword with the grips shaped in the Mameluke pattern. In 1859 the Marine Corps officers were ordered to abandon their distinctive swords in favor of the model 1850 foot officers' sword then worn by the infantry of the Army. The following were prescribed by regulations:

Commandant.—Either a sword of honor, presented by the General Government, or that of a State, or the sword prescribed for all other officers.

All other Officers.—The sword of the pattern adopted by the War Department, April 9th, 1850.

For Enlisted Men.—Same as U.S. Infantry.

Navy Swords. In 1852 the U.S. Navy Department adopted a sword which with only very minor variations was to be worn as long as swords continued to be a part of the uniform of the U.S. Navy. Also used in the war was a non-regulation sword of English design. The Navy regulations specified that "for all officers there shall be a cut-and-thrust blade, not less than twenty-six nor more than twenty-nine inches long; half-basket hilt; grip, white. Scabbards of black leather; mountings of yellow gilt, and all as per pattern."

Cutlass. About the beginning of the Civil War, a new model naval cutlass was adopted by the Navy Department. The traditional date of 1860 has been accepted tentatively as the year this new model appeared. The new weapon was patterned after an earlier French model and it was still found on some American naval vessels as late as 1942.

An officers' cutlass, similar to the weapon issued to seamen aboard ship, was worn by officers (perhaps by chief petty officers as well), although this weapon was not prescribed by regulations for either officers or chief petty officers.

SWORD CASE. Presentation swords were occasionally shipped to the recipient in the ornate type of sword case shown here.

TABLE, FOLDING. See CAMP EQUIPMENT.

TALMA. See UNIFORMS AND CLOTHING.

TANGENT SCALE. See ARTILLERY.

TAR BUCKET. See ARTILLERY.

TELEGRAPH EQUIPMENT. Both Confederate and Federal telegraph services became well developed during the war. It was soon apparent that the advantage which the telegraph possessed over other communication media was that it was unaffected by heavy fog or mist, and, of course, the elements of time and distance. The Federal Military Telegraph Service devised a field telegraph system consisting of reels of insulated cable strong enough to resist cannon wheels. These reels, carried on the backs of mules, played out the wire over the fields where it was raised on lances or on trees. Compact portable electric batteries were transported in Battery Wagons constructed for the purpose, but frequently set up under tent flies in close proximity to the commander's headquarters.

Both sides used code with fairly simple coding devices, a few of which have survived the war. Only a very few items actually used in the telegraph service exist today, either in museums or in private collections. Much of the materiel was used up in the expansion of telegraph services after 1865.

In the early part of the war some Federals used 40 of the "Beardslee's Patent Magneto-electric Field-telegraph machines" but by October 1863 this machine was found to be unsatisfactory for field use. Thereafter the U. S. Military Telegraph Department used the Beardslee machine very little, if at all.

TENTS. The U.S. Army traditionally used tents of different kinds in semi-permanent camps as well as in the field. The Confederates rarely used tents, except

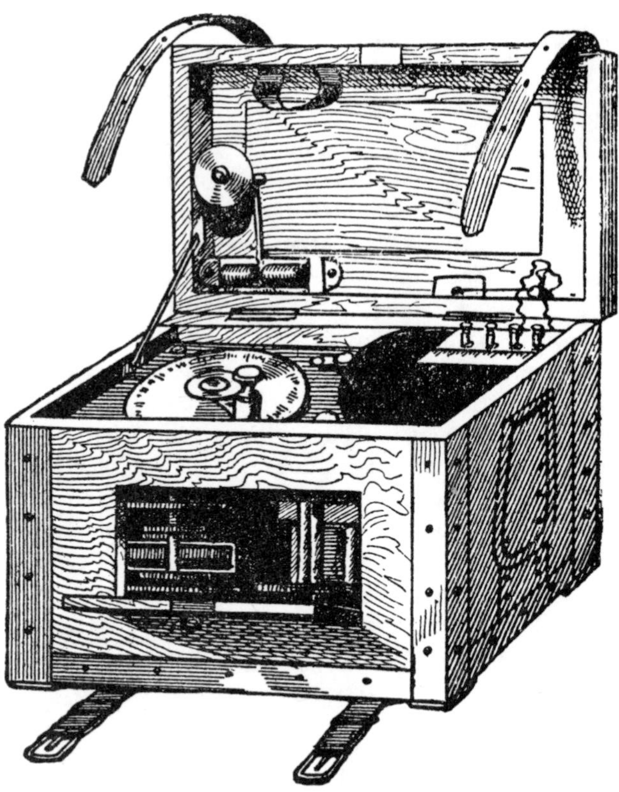

Telegraph set. Francis Bannerman Sons.

for a few senior officers; the tents they used were ordinary wall tents of the same pattern as used in the Federal Army, and often were captured equipment.

A Tents. The "A" Tent or Wedge Tent, one of the most commonly used tents, was a canvas tent stretched over a horizontal bar about 6 feet long, which was supported on two upright posts about 6 feet long each. When pitched this tent covered about 50 square feet. The name of these tents was derived from the fact that the end of one of these tents resembled the Roman letter A, and because of the resemblance to a wedge.

This type of tent usually held 4 men, but were often occupied by 5 and sometimes 6. When so occupied at night, it was necessary that all turn over at the same time, for 5 or 6 men were a tight fit in the restricted space, unless "spooned" together. These tents when stockaded were quite spacious and comfortable.

The A tents were in general use by the state and also the national government in first two years of the war, but like the Sibley, they required too much wagon transportation to take along for use in the field. Accordingly, they were turned over to camps of instruction, rendezvous depots, and to troops permanently located in or near important military centers or stations.

Brecht Tent (Patent No. 36,685). Patented October 14, 1862, by T. C. Brecht, U. S. Army, Washington, D. C. Brecht's tent was a combination tent, cloak, and bed. It consisted of a sheet of water- and air-tight fabric doubled so it could be inflated and thus form a bed or mattress. It could be used as a tent or cloak when not inflated.

Hospital or Wall Tent. This type of tent differed from others in that it had 4 upright sides or walls. To this fact it owed its name, while it got the name "hospital tent" because it frequently was used as field hospital tent. Because of the increased height, the wall tent was much more comfortable than any of the other types; the men could stand erect and move about in them with considerable freedom. Hospital or wall tents were made of different sizes. Those used in field hospitals were quite large, accommodating from 6-20 patients. Often two of these tents were joined by ripping the central seam in the two ends that came in contact. By looping back the flaps thus liberated, the tents were joined together. The new long double-tent thus had a central corridor running its entire length between a double row of cots.

The hospital tent in most general use during the war was 14 feet 6 inches by 14 feet, and 11 feet high in the center, with walls 4 feet 6 inches. They were supplemented by a fly 21 feet 6 inches by 14 feet. Each of these was designed to accommodate 8 patients comfortably. Army Regulations assigned to each regiment 3 hospital tents, 1 Sibley, and 1 "A" or Wedge Tent.

The smaller size of wall tent was in general use by

C. S. telegraph message reel. Made entirely of wood. From Virginia.

Tentage. To the left front is a shelter or "pup" tent. In rear are several small wall tents. Back of the "laundryman" are winter huts, two with improvised stick-and-mud chimneys. (National Archives)

A typical base camp, showing various types of tents—pup tents, A-tents, Sibleys, and wall tents. There are also several picket lines for animals, and parks of escort wagons. This is McClellan's base at White House, on the Pamunkey. (Library of Congress)

Hospital tent.

commissioned officers. While the Army of the Potomac was on the Peninsula, McClellan issued a General Order (August 10, 1862) prescribing wall tents for general, field, and staff officers, while each line officer was allowed a single shelter tent. Some of these wall tents were equipped with a fly.

Johns Tent-Knapsack (Patent No. 23,582). Patented April 12, 1859 by William B. Johns, U. S. Army. This was a tent-knapsack so constructed as to be entirely separated from its slings, which could be hooked together so as to permit the knapsack to function as a shelter tent or to hold the soldier's kit while on the march.

Poncho Tent. These were invented by Horace Day. His establishment at 33d and 3d Avenue, New York City, sold these tents retail for $10 each if waterproofed with rubber, and for $6.50 each if treated with enamel paint. Many believed the poncho tent preferable to the rubber blanket and warmer than the shelter tent. The poncho tent weighed 7 pounds. It consisted of 3 rubber blankets convertible into a sleeping tent capable of housing three men.

Shelter Tent. The most common of all tents, especially after the first year of the war, was the shelter tent, known also as dog tent, pup tent, or *Tente d'Abri.* A veteran believed the tent was called a dog tent because, when pitched, it would only comfortably accommodate a dog, and a small one at that. This tent was invented late in 1861 or early 1862. Most of these tents were made of cotton drilling, although

Shelter tent.

ones made of light duck and even rubber were reported. These tents were pitched by infantry as follows:

Two muskets with bayonets fixed were stuck erect into the ground the width of a half shelter apart. A guy rope which went with every half shelter was stretched between the trigger guards of the muskets, and over this as a ridge pole the tent was pitched very quickly.

Artillerymen pitched their shelter tents over a horizontal bar supported by two uprights. The framework was made from thin fence rails or saplings cut for the purpose. As with the A tents, the shelter tents were stockaded when the men went into winter quarters, if wood was not available for building huts. During the first year of the war the Federal Army used over 300,000 shelter tents. Dimensions: 5 feet 2

Sibley tent.

inches by 4 feet 8 inches (according to the 3d New Hampshire Infantry historian). Dimensions 1864—length 5 feet 6 inches; width 5 feet 5 inches. Made of cotton duck, with 9 metallic (tinned, galvanized or zinc) top buttons, and 7 metallic end buttons. There were 23 button holes on each shelter half along the upper and side edges, with 3 loops at lower corners and foot of seam, of 6-thread manila line, small, soft, and pliable. Guy lines, one with each shelter half, 6 feet 10 inches in length, of 6-thread manila line, were furnished. The above specifications from General Order No. 60, Quartermaster General's Office, 12

December 1864, gives the dimensions of the shelter half as issued in the last months of the war.

Day Shelter Tent. An excellent tent, made of gutta-percha cloth, was designed by Horace Day, which in some respects was superior to the Rider tent-knapsack, but neither of these tents saw much use by the Federal service.

SIBLEY TENT OR BELL TENT. This tent was invented by Henry H. Sibley in 1857. Sibley, a West Point graduate, accompanied Fremont on an exploration in the West, where Sibley noted the advantages of the Indian *teepee*—a wigwam made of poles covered with skins and with a fire in the center. Sibley joined the Confederate Army, rose to the rank of brigadier general, but his name is remembered chiefly because of the tent named after him. About twenty years after the war the claim was made that Sibley did not invent his tent, but this is probably not correct. Sibley patented his tent in 1858. The War Department contracted to pay him $5 royalty for every tent manufactured, but after Sibley entered the Confederate service, the U. S. Government refused to pay the royalty and also refused to hear the claim made by his family after his death.

On account of its resemblance to a huge bell the Sibley tent was sometimes called a "Bell Tent." The Sibley tent was 18 feet in diameter and 12 feet high, was supported by a single pole which rested on an iron tripod, by means of which the tent could be tightened or slackened at will. At the top of the tent was a circular opening, about a foot in diameter, which served the double purpose of ventilation and of passing a stove pipe through in cool weather. This stovepipe connected with the famous Sibley stove (described under STOVES). A small piece of canvas, called a cap, to which was attached two long guys, covered the opening at the top in stormy weather.

These tents were comfortable for 12 men, but the tents were much too cumbersome for active operations in the field. They went out of field service in 1862, and were used thereafter only in camps of instruction and similar semi-permanent assembly areas and camps in the rear areas. When stockaded these tents would accommodate 20 men.

During the war the Federal Army used 43,958 Sibley tents.

Shown in the illustration is a view of a Sibley tent and stove drawn by Herbert E. Valentine, Co. F 23rd Mass. Inf.

A twist of tobacco. This tobacco was among the effects of Captain John C. Macomber 6th Vermont Infantry, killed at The Wilderness, May 5, 1864.

TENTE d'ABRI. See TENT.

THIMBLE. Some soldiers did not take "housewives" with them but did accept thimble, needle, and thread as being sufficient for repairing their uniforms, clothing, and sewing on buttons.

Thimble. Steel, ⅝ inches tall and ¾ inches in diameter at the base tapering to ⅝ inches in diameter at the top. Was carried by Private Andrew J. Cure, Co. I, 23d New York Infantry from May 13, 1861 to his discharge on May 22, 1863.

THROGS. See UNIFORMS AND CLOTHING. A throg is a braid loop fastener for an overcoat. Same as a "frog."

THUMB-STALL. See ARTILLERY.

TIER SHOT. See PROJECTILES.

TIGE ARMS. Sometimes called "pillar breech arms," these were arms with a stem of steel screwed into the middle of the breech pin, around which a charge of powder was placed. The ball entered free and rested on the point of the pin which was tempered. A few blows with a heavy ramrod forced the ball to fill the grooves of the rifled arm. This invention was an improvement by Capt. Thouvenin on Delvignes' plan of having a chamber for the powder smaller than the bore. Capt. Minié's invention superseded the tige arms, by means of a bullet which was forced to fill the grooves by the action of the charge itself at the instant of explosion.

TINTYPE. See PICTURES.

TOBACCO. Most every soldier smoked tobacco, which was not always easy to get, especially when money was scarce or when there was no sutler. One of the most common makes of tobacco was *Kinikinic* which cost a dollar a pound.

In addition to pipe tobacco and chewing tobacco, cigars were popular. Grant was only one of many inveterate cigar smokers.

TOBACCO CAN. Tobacco was issued both in plug form and also as cut tobacco ready for smoking. The latter type was carried in any container available.

TONGS, LOADING. See ARTILLERY.

TOOTHBRUSH. Toothbrushes have changed but little from the war to the present day. Shown in the photograph is one carried in the war as well as handles of others which were excavated and whose bristles had rotted away in the ground.

TORPEDOES. See MINES AND TORPEDOES.

TOURNIQUET. There is little written information on tourniquets available to assist the collector or student. However, many specimens of Civil War tourniquets have survived.

Lambert Tourniquet (Patent No. 34,112). Patented January 7, 1862 by Thomas S. Lambert, Peekskill, New York. This tourniquet featured the combination of an elastic band with a non-elastic one, and with the pads for securing them in place and for making pressure. Wings were attached to the pads to permit collateral circulation.

Also shown here is a full package of regulation issue Civil War field tourniquets. Markings can be seen in photo. The other tourniquet is shown with the original tin container in which it was issued. Bears patent markings on metal plate on tourniquet itself "Lambert Patent–January 1862."

TOW HOOK. See ARTILLERY.

TROUSERS. See UNIFORMS AND CLOTHING.

TROWEL BAYONET. See INTRENCHING TOOLS.

TRUNK. See CAMP EQUIPMENT.

TUBE POUCH. See ARTILLERY.

TUMBLER PUNCH. See APPENDAGES.

UNIFORMS, CONFEDERATE. Confederate *Army Regulations* prescribed regulation uniforms for the various branches of service. Only a few fortunate Con-

Two types of field tourniquets including (on right) the Lambert tourniquet container. (Norm Flayderman)

federates wore uniforms of the type prescribed by Regulations in 1861 and 1862, and fewer still in the later years of the war. Many of the 1861 volunteers wore militia uniforms or a varied assortment of homespun clothing made locally. The Confederate Government was never able to furnish enough uniforms, and the problem was solved only at the state level, if it was solved even there. Many Southern volunteers were told to furnish their own uniforms. Often a local company wore uniforms made by local tailors or purchased by the company commander. Colors ranged from the gaudy outfits of the Louisiana Zouaves to the yellowish brown called "butternut." Butternut must have been very common as the color used since Federals referred to their opponents as "butternuts." The color was the result of dyeing uniforms with a solution of copperas and walnut hulls. Second in terminology to "butternuts" was the term "gray jackets" which is indicative of the extensive use of the short-waisted jacket of gray. Most Confederates wore hats although caps were prescribed by regulations. Trousers were usually gray, but shirts were all colors and all materials. Many were made by relatives and sent to the soldiers.

As with their enemies, the Confederates had little use for leather cravats and havelocks, especially after 1861. Also, the Southerners soon discovered that shoes were much better for marching than boots.

Although Confederate authorities attempted to prevent the men from wearing Federal uniforms, they only met with indifferent success. Shoes, shirts, underwear, hats, and even complete uniforms were stripped

INFANTRY. UNIFORMS OF REGULAR CONFEDERATE TROOPS. CAVALRY. ARTILLERY.

Volunteer Infantry of Virginia. 1st Regiment Maryland Line. South Carolina Light Infantry. Hampton Legion. Rockingham Battery Artillery. Gentlemen of the Road Independent Cavalry.

UNIFORMS

Louisiana Zouaves. Washington Artillery of New Orleans. Mississippi Rifles. Heavy Infantry of Georgia. Alabama Light Infantry. Marine Battery, Manassas Junction.

Iorse Cavalry. Dragoon Guards, 14th Regt., Va. Cavalry. Mounted Rifles, North Carolina. Virginia Cadets. Greyson Dare-devils. Kentucky Rifle Brigade. Tennessee Sharp-shooters.

ERATE ARMY.

Confederate staff officers.

from Federal dead or prisoners and worn by men who needed them. This was especially true of "Yankee overcoats." In some commands the men dyed their captured clothing.

Much of the Confederate problem of supplying uniforms would have been solved if each state would have looked on the problem as a national not a state problem. While Lee's men were shivering during the last winter of the war, the Governor of North Carolina refused to release 92,000 uniforms, blankets, and other necessities to the general cause. And this refusal came at a time when the North Carolina troops were all well uniformed!

Regulations for Confederate uniforms as prescribed here were promulgated in 1861 and 1862. As all collectors and students of the war know, these uniforms were not typical of the outfits worn by Johnny Reb throughout the war. Confederates wore anything they could get—homespun clothing, captured Federal items, and just clothing. But the ideal is outlined here—as it was laid down officially by the nascent Confederate War Department in those early months of the war.

The topics that follow are either extracts from Confederate Army, Marine Corps, and Army uniform regulations or are based on the regulations.

ARMY. (From C. S. Regulations, 1861)

COAT (or "Tunic"). All officers shall wear a tunic of gray cloth, known as cadet gray, the skirt to extend halfway between the hip and the knee, double breasted for all grades.

Brigadier General. Two rows of buttons on the breast, eight in each row, placed in pairs; the distance between the rows 4 inches at top and 3 inches at bottom; stand-up collar, to rise no higher than to permit the chin to turn freely over it; to hook in front at the bottom, and slope thence up and backward, at an angle of 30 degrees, on each side; cuffs 2½ inches deep on the underside, there to be buttoned with 3 small buttons, and sloped upwards to a point at a distance of 4 inches from the end of the sleeve; pockets in the

Confederate Army uniforms.

folds of the skirt, with one button at the hip and one at the end of each pocket, making four buttons on the back and skirt of the tunic, the hip buttons to range with the lowest breast buttons.

Colonel. Same as for a Brigadier General, except that there will be only 7 buttons in each row on the breast, placed at equal distances.

Lieutenant Colonel, Major, Captain, and Lieutenant. Same as for a Colonel.

Enlisted Men. The uniform coat shall be a double breasted tunic of gray cloth, known as cadet gray, with the skirt extending halfway between the hip and the knee; two rows of buttons on the breast, 7 in each row; the distance between the rows 4 inches at top and 3 inches at bottom; stand-up collar to rise no higher than to permit the chin to turn freely over it; to hook in front at the bottom, and slope thence backwards at an angle of 30 degrees on each side; cuffs 2½ inches deep at the underseam, to button with two small buttons, and to be slightly pointed on the upper part of the arm; pockets in the folds of the skirts. The collars and cuffs to be of the color prescribed for facings for the respective arms of service, and the edges of the tunic to be trimmed throughout with the same colored cloth. Narrow lining in the skirts of the tunic of gray material.

Facings. The facings for General officers, and for officers of the Adjutant General's Department, Quartermaster General's Department, Commissary General's Department, and the Engineers will be buff. The tunic for all officers to be edged throughout with the facings designated: Medical Department—black; Artillery—red; Cavalry—yellow; Infantry—light blue.

For fatigue purposes, a light gray blouse, double breasted, with two rows of small buttons, 7 in each row; small, turnover collar, may be issued to the troops.

TROUSERS. The uniform trousers for officers and enlisted men will be of cloth throughout the year; made loose, and to spread well over the foot; of light (or

Confederate Army uniforms.

sky) blue color for regimental officers and enlisted men; and of dark blue cloth for all other officers; reinforced for the Cavalry.

General Officers. 2 stripes of gold lace on the outer seam, ⅛ inch apart, and each ⅝ inches wide.

Officers of the Adjutant General's Department, the Quartermaster General's Department, the Commissary General's Department and the Corps of Engineers. 1 stripe of gold lace on the outer seam, 1¼ inches wide.

Medical Department. A black velvet stripe, 1¼ inches wide, with a gold cord on each edge of the stripe.

Regimental Officers. A strip of cloth on the outer seam, 1¼ inches wide; color according to corps; for artillery—red; cavalry—yellow; infantry—dark blue.

Non-commissioned staff of regiments and all sergeants. A stripe of cotton webbing or braid on the outer seam, 1¼ inches wide; color according to arm of service.

All other enlisted men. Plain.

Overcoats for Enlisted Men.

Mounted Men. Cadet gray cloth; stand-up collar; double breasted; cape to reach to the cuff of the coat, when the arm is extended, and to button all the way up; number of buttons—18.

Footmen. Cadet gray cloth; stand-up collar; double breasted; cape to reach to the elbows, when the arm is extended, and to button all the way up; number of buttons—18. For the present (1861), to be a talma, with sleeves, of water-proof material; black.

Headgear, Officers.

Chapeau, or cocked hat. Will be worn by General officers and officers of the General.

Staff and Corp of Engineers. Chapeau will be of the French pattern.

Forage Cap for officers. A cap similar in form to that of the French kepi.

Uniform Cap. According to pattern to be deposited in the Office of the Quartermaster General.

Confederate Army uniforms.

Pompom. For artillery–red; infantry–light blue; cavalry–yellow.

On January 24, 1862, the Confederate War Department issued an Order specifying changes in the braid of the forage cap for the Army of the Confederate States. These changes were as follows:

Forage Cap–pattern. Of the form known as the French kepi; to be made of cloth.

General Officers and Officers of the General Staff and Engineers. Dark blue band, sides, and crown.

Artillery. Dark blue band; sides and crown red.

Infantry. Dark blue band; sides and crown light blue.

Cavalry. Dark blue band; sides and crown yellow.

MARKS ON CAP TO DISTINGUISH RANK.

General Officer. 4 gold braids.

Field Officer. 3 gold braids.

Captain. 2 gold braids.

Lieutenant. 1 gold braid.

Braid to extend from the band on the front, back and both sides to the top of the cap–and the center of the crown to be embroidered with the same number of braids.

HEADGEAR, ENLISTED MEN. Cap to be of same pattern [as officers'] band of dark blue and arms of service to be distinguished by the colors of the sides and crown–artillery, red; infantry, light blue; cavalry, yellow. The number of the regiment will be worn in front, in yellow metal.

In hot weather, a white duck, or linen cover, known as a havelock, will be worn–the apron to fall behind, so as to protect the ears and neck from the rays of the sun. In winter, in bad weather, an oil skin cover will be worn, with an apron to fall over the coat collar.

CRAVAT, OR STOCK.

All Officers. Black, when a cravat is worn, the tie not to be visible at the opening of the collar.

CRAVAT, ENLISTED MEN. Black leather.

BOOTS. (C. S.)

All Officers. Ankle or Jefferson.

Confederate Navy officers. (Ray Riling)

Enlisted Men of Cavalry. Ankle and Jefferson.

All other enlisted men. Jefferson.

SPURS.

All mounted officers. Yellow metal or gilt.

ENLISTED MOUNTED MEN. Yellow metal.

GLOVES.

General officers and officers of the General Staff and Staff Corps. Buff or white.

Officers of Artillery, Infantry, Cavalry. White.

MARINE CORPS, CONFEDERATE. The C. S. Marine Corps uniform was, in general, the same as the dress uniform of the C. S. Army. It consisted of a double breasted coat of cadet gray, with high collar and a double row of brass buttons—7 on each side—and sky-blue trousers. The coat was decorated with elaborately woven epaulettes of gold braid, and the collar was marked with bars in gold braid to indicate rank. The sash was crimson. Buttons were those made in the North for the "old corps," i.e. the U. S. Marine Corps.

NAVY, CONFEDERATE. (From 1862 Regulations).

COAT.

Flag Officer. A frock coat of steel grey cloth, faced with the same and lined with black silk serge, double breasted, with 2 rows of large Navy buttons on the breast, 9 in each row, placed 4½ inches apart from eye to eye at top, and 2½ inches at bottom. Rolling collar, full skirts, commencing at the top of the hip bone and descending 4/5 thence towards the knee, with one button behind on each hip and one near the bottom of each fold. The cuffs to be 2½ inches deep, with one strip of gold lace ½ inch wide below the seam, but joining it; three strips of lace of the same width on the sleeves above the cuffs, separated by a space of ⅜ of an inch from each other, the upper one with a loop 3 inches long, and a strip of lace ½ inch wide, from the lower button to the end of the cuffs on the upper side of the opening, and four small sized navy buttons in the opening.

Captain. Same as for a flag officer, except that there shall be but three strips of lace around the sleeve and cuff, including the looped strip.

Commander. Same as for a captain, except that there shall be but two strips of lace around the sleeve and cuff, including the looped strip, and three small buttons in the opening.

Lieutenant. Same as for a commander except that the cuffs shall have but one strip of gold lace, looped, around the upper edge.

Master. Same as for a lieutenant, except that the cuffs shall have but one strip of lace ¼ inch wide, without a loop, around the upper edge.

Passed Midshipman. Same as for a master, except that the cuffs shall have, instead of lace, three medium-sized Navy buttons around the upper edge.

Midshipman. Same as for a passed midshipman, except that medium-sized buttons shall be substituted for the large buttons.

COAT (Undress or "Civil Officers").

Surgeon (over 12 years standing). Frock coat of steel gray cloth, faced with the same, double breasted, rolling collar, with two rows of large Navy buttons on the breast, 9 in each row, proportioned for body and skirts the same as for a captain, skirts lined with black silk serge, one button behind on each hip, and one near the bottom of each fold of the skirts. Cuffs the same as for a commander, except that a plain strip of lace shall be substituted for the loop.

Surgeon (less than 12 years standing). Same, except there shall be one strip of lace around the cuff and sleeve.

Passed Assistant Surgeon. Same as for a Surgeon of less than 12 years standing, except that the lace on the cuff shall be ¼ inch wide.

Assistant Surgeon. Same as for a surgeon, except that instead of lace there shall be three medium-sized buttons on the cuff.

Paymaster (over 12 years standing). Same as prescribed for a surgeon over 12 years standing.

Paymaster (under 12 years standing) Same as for a surgeon of less than 12 years.

Chief Engineer (over 12 years standing). Same as for a surgeon of more than 12 years.

First Assistant Engineer. Same as for a Chief Engineer, except that there shall be but one strip of lace on the cuff ¼ inch wide.

Second and Third Assistant Engineer. Same as for a first assistant engineer, except that instead of lace the cuffs shall have three medium-sized buttons around the upper edge.

Chaplain. Same as for a surgeon, except it shall be single breasted, with one row of 9 large Navy buttons on the breast. The cuffs plain with three small buttons in the opening.

Professor and Commodore's Secretary. Same as for a chaplain, except that there shall be but 8 buttons on the breast.

Clerk. Same as for a secretary, except there shall be but 6 buttons on the breast.

VEST FOR ALL OFFICERS. Steel grey or white, single breasted, standing collar, with 9 small buttons in front, and not to show below the coat.

TROUSERS FOR ALL OFFICERS. Steel grey cloth or white drill, made loose to spread well over the foot and to be worn over boots or shoes.

SUMMER FROCK COAT. In the summer or in tropical

climates, officers may wear frock coats and trousers of steel grey summer cloth of the style and pattern herein prescribed, with medium size navy buttons.

JACKET. May be worn as service dress by all officers when at sea, except when at general muster. To be of steel grey cloth or white drill linen with the same double breasted, rolling collar, same number of small-size buttons on breast as for undress coat, open fly sleeve with four small buttons in the opening, with shoulder straps for appropriate grades.

HEADGEAR.

Caps. Steel grey cloth, to be not less than 3½ inches, nor more than 4 inches in height, and not more than 10 nor less than 9½ inches at top, with patent leather visor, to be worn by all officers in service dress.

Flag Officer. The device shall be a foul anchor in an open wreath of live oak leaves, with 4 stars above the anchor, embroidered in gold, on the front of the cap above a band of gold lace 1¾ inches wide.

Captain. Same as for a flag officer, except that there shall be but 3 stars above the anchor, and the gold band shall be 1½ inches wide.

Commander. Same as for captain, except there shall be but 2 stars.

Lieutenant. Same as for a commander, except that there shall be but one star.

Master. Same as for a lieutenant, except that there shall be no star.

Passed Midshipman. A foul anchor without the wreath.

Surgeon (over 12 years standing). A wreath of olive leaves with 3 stars, 4/10 inch in diameter, embroidered in gold, on the front of the cap, above a band of gold lace 1¼ inches wide.

Surgeon (under 12 years standing). Same, except that there shall be 2 stars.

Passed Assistant Surgeon. Same as for a surgeon, except that there shall be but 1 star.

Assistant Surgeon. Same as for a surgeon, except that there shall be no star.

Paymaster (over 12 years standing). Same as for a surgeon of over 12 years standing.

Paymaster (Under 12 years). Same as for a surgeon of less than 12 years.

Assistant Paymaster. Same as for an assistant surgeon.

Chief Engineer (Over 12 years standing). Same as for a surgeon of over 12 years, except that the letter "E" in old English character shall be embroidered in gold below the stars.

Chief Engineer (Under 12 years). Same, except that there shall be but 2 stars.

Second and Third Assistant Engineers. Same as for a first assistant engineer, except that there shall be no stars.

STRAW HATS. In summer or in tropical climates, officers may, except at general muster, wear white straw hats. The body of the hat to be 6 inches in height, and the rim 3½ inches wide.

OVERCOATS. For all officers shall be of steel grey cloth, double breasted, rolling collar, skirts to descend 3 inches below the knee, the same number of Navy buttons, and similarly arranged as for undress coat. No buttons to be worn on the cuffs or pocket flaps. Officers entitled to shoulder straps will wear the same on their overcoats as directed for undress coats. Grey cloth cloaks may be worn in boats.

UNIFORM FOR PETTY OFFICERS AND CREW.

Boatswain's Mate, Gunner Mate, Carpenter Mate, Sailmaker Mate, Ship's Steward, Ship's Cook. Will wear embroidered in black silk on the right sleeve of their grey jackets above the elbow in front, a foul anchor on not more than 3 inches length. The same device embroidered blue to be worn on the sleeves of their white frocks in summer. All other petty officers, except officers' stewards and yeomen will wear the same device on their left sleeves.

The outside clothing for petty officers, firemen and coal-heavers, seamen, ordinary seamen, landsmen, and boys for muster, shall consist of grey cloth jackets and trousers, or grey woolen frocks with white duck cuffs and collars, black hats, black silk neckerchiefs and shoes, or boots in cold weather. In warm weather it shall consist of white frocks and trousers, black or white hats, as the commander may for the occasion direct, having proper regard for the comfort of the crew; black silk neckerchiefs and shoes. The collars and cuffs to be lined with blue cotton cloth, and stitched round with thread. Thick grey caps without visors may be worn by the crew at sea, except on holidays or at muster.

Boatswain, Gunner, Carpenter, Sailmaker. Shall be of steel grey cloth, lined with the same; rolling collar, double breasted, two rows of large navy buttons on the breast, 8 in each row; pointed pocket flaps, with three large buttons underneath each, showing one-half their diameter; 3 medium size buttons around each cuff, and 2 small ones in each opening; 1 button behind on each hip; 1 in the middle of each fold, and 1 in each fold near the bottom of the skirt. On each side of the collar to have one loop of ¾ wide gold lace, to show 1½ inch wide and 4 inches long, with a small sized navy button in the point of each loop.

UNIFORMS, UNITED STATES. The following topics concerning U.S. uniforms are either extracted from the appropriate service regulations or based thereon.

Federal officer (General Joseph Hooker) in uniform of a major general. (National Archives)

ARMY. Several states such as New York, Connecticut, and Ohio had their own uniform regulations for their troops. The buttons of these, and other states were designed to give prominence to the state coat of arms. Moreover, their belt buckles and cartridge box plates were so designed and lettered with the definite aim of emphasizing and keeping prominent the "catchy" letter and figure symbols which had made household names of some of these early militia regiments.

On the other hand, the great majority of Federal troops wore uniforms very specifically prescribed in *Army Regulations* 1861 (Sections 1442-1635), and these specifications are the main reference for this section of the *Collector's Encyclopedia.*

COAT, OFFICER. All officers shall wear a frock coat of dark blue cloth, the skirt to extend from two-thirds to three-fourths of the distance from the top of the hip to the bend of the knee; single breasted for captains and lieutenants; double-breasted for all other ranks.

Major General. Two rows of buttons on the breast, nine in each row, placed by threes; the distance between each row, 5½ inches at top, and 3½ inches at bottom; stand-up collar, to rise no higher than to permit the chin to turn freely over it, to hook in front at the bottom, and slope up and backward at a 30-degree angle on each side; cuffs 2½ inches deep to go around the sleeves parallel with the lower edge, and to button with three small buttons at the under seam; pockets in the folds of the skirts, with one button at the hip, and one at the end of each pocket, making four buttons on the back and skirt of the coat, the hip button to range with the lowest buttons on the breast; collar and cuffs to be of dark blue velvet, lining of the coat black.

Federal officers' uniforms. Left to right: infantry colonel, artillery captain, cavalry major—all in full dress.

Federal officer in field uniform.

Federal infantryman. Model is dressed as a private, Company A, 1st U.S. Infantry. (Smithsonian Institution)

Brigadier General. The same as for a major general, except that there will be only eight buttons in each row on the breast, placed in pairs.

Colonel. The same as for a major general, except that there will be only seven buttons in each row on the breast, placed at equal distances; collar and cuffs of the same color and material as the coat.

Lieutenant Colonel. The same as for a colonel.

Major. The same as for a colonel.

Captain. The same as for a colonel, except that there will be only one row of nine buttons on the breast, placed at equal distances.

First Lieutenant. The same as for a captain.

Second Lieutenant. The same as for a captain.

Brevet Second Lieutenant. The same as for a captain.

Medical Cadet. The same as for a brevet second lieutenant.

Light Artillery. A round jacket of dark blue cloth, trimmed with scarlet, with the Russian shoulder knot, the prescribed insignia of rank to be worked in silver in the center of the knot, may be worn on undress duty by officers of Light Artillery.

COAT, ENLISTED. All enlisted foot soldiers will wear a single-breasted frock coat of dark blue cloth, without plaits, with a skirt extending one-half the distance from the top of the hip to the bend of the knee; one row of nine buttons on the breast, placed at equal distances; stand-up collar to rise no higher than to permit the chin to turn freely over it, to hook in front at the bottom and then to slope up and backward at a 30-degree angle on each side; cuffs pointed according to pattern, and to button with two small buttons at the under seams; collar and cuffs edged with a cord or welt of cloth as follows to wit:

Scarlet for artillery
Sky-blue for infantry
Yellow for engineers
Crimson for ordnance and Hospital Stewards

On each shoulder a metallic scale according to pattern; narrow lining for skirt of the coat of the same color and material as the coat; pockets in the folds of the skirts with one button at each hip to range with the lowest buttons on the breast; no buttons at the ends of the pockets. All enlisted men of the cavalry and light artillery shall wear a uniform jacket of dark blue cloth, with one row of 12 small buttons on the breast placed at equal distances; stand-up collar to rise no higher than to permit the chin to turn freely over it, to hook in front at the bottom, and to slope the same as the coat collar; on the collar, on each side, two blind button holes of lace, ⅜ inch wide, one small button on the button hole, lower button hole extending back 4 inches, upper button hole 3½ inches; top button and front ends of collar bound with lace ⅜ inches wide, and a strip of the same extending down the front and around the lower edge of the jacket; the back seam laced with the same, and on the cuff a point of the same shape as that on the coat, but formed of the lace; jacket to extend to the waist, and to be lined with white flannel; two small buttons at the under seam of the cuff, as on the coat cuff; one hook and eye at the bottom of the collar; color of lace (worsted), yellow for cavalry and scarlet for light artillery.

Musicians. The same as for other enlisted men of their respective branches of service, with the addition of a facing of lace ⅜ inch wide on the front of the coat or jacket, made in the following manner; bars of ⅜ inch worsted lace placed on a line with each button 6½ inches wide at the bottom, and thence gradually expanding upward to the last button, counting from the waist up, and contracting from thence to the bottom of the collar, where it will be 6½ inches wide, with a strip of the same lace following the bars at their outer extremity—the whole presenting something of what is called the herring-bone form; the color of the lace facing to correspond with the color of the trimming of the branch of service.

Fatigue Uniform. A sack coat of dark blue flannel extending half-way down the thigh, and made loose, without sleeve or body lining, falling collar, inside pocket on the left side, 4 coat buttons down the front.

Recruit Uniform. The sack coat will be made with sleeve and body lining, the latter of flannel.

Dress Coat. The dress coat was worn by company grade officers and enlisted men and merits special discussion for that reason. Many soldiers considered the dress coat as one of their major delusions on joining the service. The dress coat was a close, tight-fitting garment, with an impressive row of brass buttons extending up to the chin, and a stiff standing collar. The sleeves were small and left little freedom of movement to the arms. The coat was worn only on formal occasions; in the early part of the war it was considered as indispensable at dress parade, inspection or review. On such occasions every button had to be buttoned and when the mercury was in the 90's the coat was a terrible sweatbox. Not a breath of air could reach the sweltering body. On the first march the dress coats disappeared rapidly. They were thrown away to lighten knapsacks and ease aching shoulders, or were traded off to the Negroes for chickens and other eatables.

The regulations specified: Single breasted frock coat of dark blue cloth, made without pleats. Skirt extended one half the distance from the top of the hip to the bend of the knee. One row of 9 buttons on the breast equally spaced. A stand up collar which rose no higher than to permit the chin to turn freely over it, hooking up in front at the bottom of the collar only, and then the collar sloping up and backward at a 30-degree angle on each side. The cuffs were pointed and buttoned with two small buttons at the under seam. Collar and cuffs were edged with cord or welt of the color of the branch of service of the wearer. On each shoulder a metallic scale was to be worn (see SCALES, SHOULDER). The lining of the coat was of the same color and material as the coat itself; pockets were in the folds of the skirt, with one button at each hip to range with the lowest button on the breast. There were no buttons at the ends of the pockets.

Sack Coat. Of dark blue flannel, extending half the distance down the thigh. Made loose with or without body or sleeve lining. Falling collar of double thickness cloth, edges turned under and stitched along outer edge. Four brass eagle buttons evenly spaced down front, no buttons on sleeve cuffs. Cuff split on rear seam for height of cuff, edges turned in and stitched along outer edge, also stitched along top of cuff on inside of sleeve to form a bead to outline top of cuff. All outside edges turned under and stitched. Sleeve seam at rear, edges turned inside and stitched on inside.

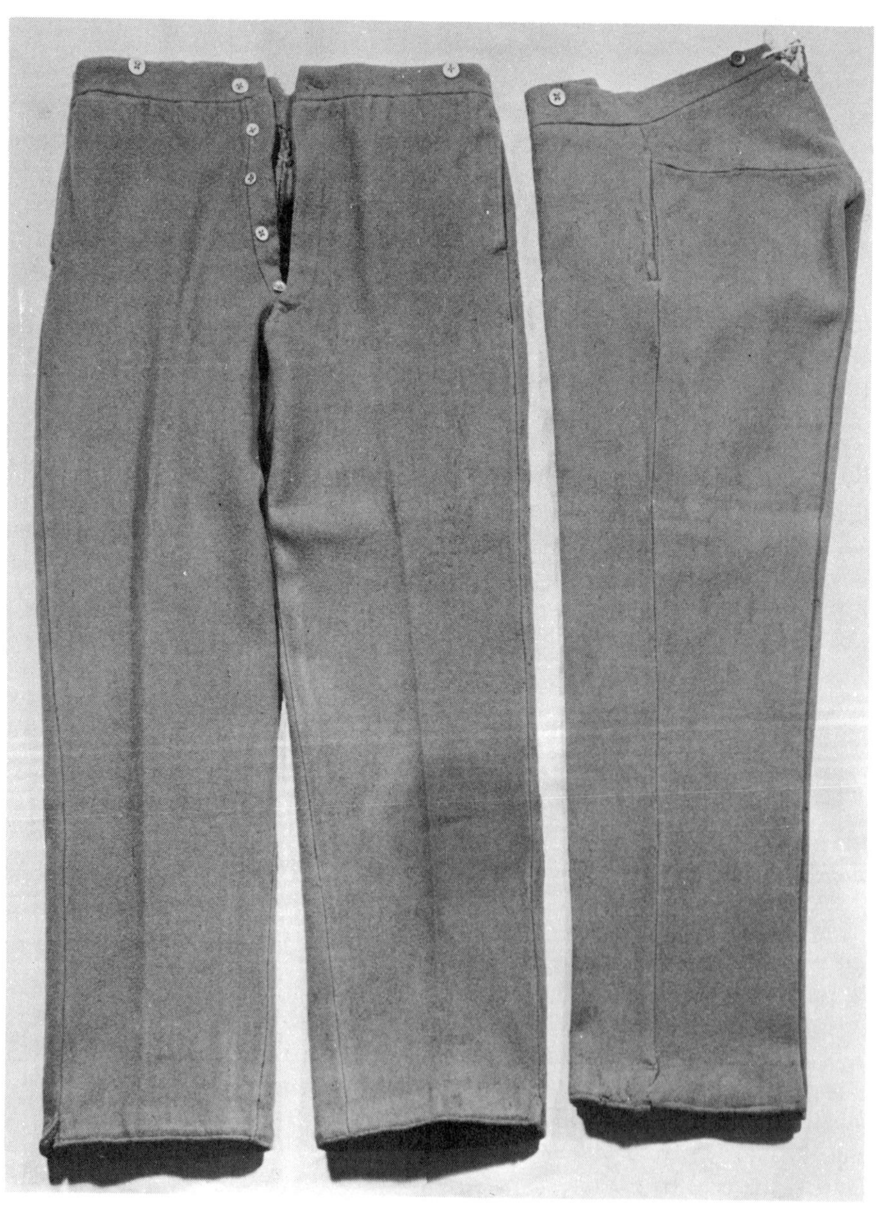

U.S. Army trousers. Sky-blue kersey. Note the absence of cuffs on bottom of trousers. Buttons for suspenders worn universally by all ranks. (James A. Shutt)

Overcoat frogs. (Norm Flayderman)

TROUSERS.

General Officers and Officers of the Ordnance Dept. Dark blue cloth, plain without stripe, welt, or cord down the outer seam.

Officers of the General Staff and Staff Corps except the Ordnance Dept. Dark blue cloth, with a gold cord ⅛ inch in diameter, along the outer seam.

Regimental Officers. Dark blue cloth, with a welt let into the outer seam, ⅛ inch in diameter, of colors corresponding to the branch of service, viz: cavalry, yellow; artillery, scarlet; infantry, sky-blue.

Medical Cadets. Same as for officers of the General Staff, except a welt of buff cloth, instead of a gold cord.

Enlisted Men Except Companies of Light Artillery. Dark blue cloth (however, General Order No. 108, Headquarters of the Army, December 16, 1861, authorized sky-blue as the color. Very few enlisted men wore dark blue trousers.) Sergeants, with a stripe 1½ inches wide; corporals, with a stripe ½ inch wide, of worsted lace, down and over the outer seam, of the color of the respective branch of service; ordnance sergeants and hospital stewards, strips of crimson lace 1½ inches wide. Privates, plain without stripe or welt. Companies of artillery, equipped as light artillery, sky-blue cloth.

All trousers to be made loose, without plaits, and to spread well over the boot; to be reinforced for all enlisted mounted men.

OVERCOAT, OFFICERS. A "cloak coat" of dark blue cloth, closing by means of four frog buttons of black silk and loops of black silk cord down the breast, and at the throat by a long loop a éschelle, without tassel or plate, on the left side, and a black silk frog button on the right; cord for the loops 15/100 inch in diameter; back, a single piece, slit up from the bottom, from 15 to 17 inches, according to the height of the wearer, and closing at will, by buttons, and button holes cut in a concealed flap; collar of the same color and material as the coat, rounded at the edges, and to stand or fall; when standing, to be about 5 inches high; sleeves loose, of a single piece, and round at the bottom, without cuff or slit; lining, woolen; around the front and lower border, the edges of pockets, the edges of sleeves, collar, and slit in the back a flat braid of black silk ½ inch wide; and around each frog button on the breast, a knot 2¼ inches in diameter of black silk cord, 7/100 inch in diameter; cape of the same color and material as the coat, removable at the pleasure of the wearer, and reaching to the cuff of the coat sleeve when the arm is extended; coat to extend down the leg from 6-8 inches below the knee, according to height. To indicate rank, there will be on both sleeves near the lower edge, a knot of flat black silk braid not exceeding ⅛ inch in width, composed as follows:

General: 5 braids, double knot
Colonel: 5 braids, single knot
Lt. Colonel: 4 braids, single knot
Major: 3 braids, single knot
Captain: 2 braids, single knot
1st Lieutenant: 1 braid, single knot

Badges Worn on Sleeve of Overcoat, to designate Rank.

No. 141.

HOSPITAL STEWARD'S Chevrons—Silk, Embroidered on Green Cloth.

No. 142.

1st LIEUTENANT — One Braid—⅛ inch Black Silk Braid.

No. 143.

CAPTAIN—Two Braids.

No. 144.

MAJOR—Three Braids.

No. 145.

LIEUTENANT-COLONEL—Four Braids.

No. 146.

COLONEL—Five Braids.

No. 147.

GENERAL—Five Braids.

Sleeve braid denoting rank as worn by the Federal Army. (Norm Flayderman)

Federal cavalry uniforms. Maj. Gen. David McM. Gregg, commanding the 2d Cavalry Division, and his staff. (Library of Congress)

Federal cavalry uniforms. Note the various types of headgear, including a straw hat, made popular by Pleasonton. Left to right, Maj. Benj. Ludlow, Col. Ulric Dahlgren, Lt. Col. Joseph Dickinson (wearing the straw hat), Count Zeppelin (German military observer), and Lt. Col. Rosencrantz. (Kean Archives)

2nd Lieutenant and Brevet Second Lieutenant: plain sleeve, without knot or ornament.

OVERCOAT, ENLISTED MEN.

Mounted Troops: sky-blue cloth; stand-and-fall collar; double-breasted; cape to reach down to the cuff of the coat when the arm is extended, and to button all the way up; buttons, yellow, the same as is used by the artillery, etc., omitting the letter in the shield.

All other Enlisted Men. Sky-blue cloth; stand-up collar; single-breasted; cape to reach down to the elbows when the arm is extended, and to button all the way up; buttons, yellow, the same as is used by the artillery, etc., omitting the letter in the shield.

Infantry Overcoat. (Based on the regulations) Sky-blue kersey, burlap lining in the coat down to the waist. Skirts of coat were left unlined. Sleeves were lined with a coarse linen or burlap. Bottom of skirt was not hemmed. A standing collar, made of two layers of cloth with burlap between, and hooking from cape to chin with three hooks and eyes. A two-piece half belt was sewn in back, and was decorated with two large buttons. The cuffs on the sleeves were each 5½ inches deep and left loose so as to turn down over the hand. The coat was single breasted with five large buttons in front and six smaller buttons on the cape. The cape was unlined, but had a ⅞-inch hem at the bottom edge. The cape was approximately 14 inches long in back. The coat itself extended to half the distance of the calves of the legs. The back was 45 inches long for the average size. Back seam was split up 12 inches from the bottom edge.

Cavalry. A gutta-percha talma, or cloak extending to the knee, with long sleeves.

Talma. A talma was a long cape or cloak worn by both men and women. The term as used in the Civil War applied to the overcoat as worn by mounted men, although apparently it was sometimes used in reference to a military cloak in general.

HATS. In general, the forage cap appears to have been more popular with Eastern troops than with Western units, where the hat was worn extensively. The "Jeff Davis" hat was heavy, hot, and uncomfortable and many soldiers "lost" them as soon as possible. However, one of the few units in the Army of the Potomac which did wear them throughout the war was the famous Iron Brigade. Its commander had the men wear their hats as a distinguishing mark of his brigade, and the enemy could recognize, always with respect, "those black-hatted fellows." The 16th New York Infantry wore straw hats on the Peninsula in June 1862, but such divergence from regulations was not long permitted, and was exceptional. The 3d New Hampshire Infantry in 1861 wore a helmet quite similar in appearance to the pith helmet worn in tropical countries today. In addition, to the U. S. regulation "chapeau de bras," which was worn only rarely, the two most commonly worn hats were the U. S. felt hat (the Hardee or Jeff Davis), and the modified version of the Hardee hat known as the "Burnside Pattern Felt Hat," which actually was a modified form of the Jeff Davis Hat. However, the Burnside hat was not worn nearly as often or by as many individuals as was the regulation Jeff Davis hat.

Hat, Officers. Of best black felt. The dimensions of medium size to be as follows: width of brim, 3¼ inches; height of crown, 6¼ inches; oval of tip, ½ inch; taper of crown, ¾ inch. The binding to be ½-inch deep of best black ribbed silk.

Hat, Enlisted Men's. Of black felt, same shape and size as for officers with double row of stitching, instead of binding, around the edge. To agree in quality with the pattern deposited in the clothing arsenal.

Hat, Medical Cadets. Will wear a forage cap according to pattern.

Hat Trimmings, General Officers. Gold cord, with acorn-shaped ends. The brim of the hat looped up on the right side, and fastened with an eagle attached to the side of the hat; three black ostrich feathers on the left side; a gold embroidered wreath in front, on black velvet ground, encircling the letters U.S. in silver, old English characters.

Officers of the Adjutant General's, Inspector-General's, Quartermaster's, Subsistence, Medical and Pay Department and the Judge Advocate, Above the Rank of Captain. The same as for general officers, except the cord, which will be of black silk and gold.

Same Departments, Below the Rank of Field Officers. The same as for field officers, except that there will be but two feathers.

Officers of the Corps of Engineers. The same as for the General Staff, except the ornament in front, which will be a gold embroidered wreath of laurel and palm, encircling a silver turreted castle on black velvet ground.

Officers of the Topographical Engineers. The same as for the General Staff, except the ornament in front which will be a gold embroidered wreath of oak leaves, encircling a gold embroidered shield, on black velvet ground.

Officers of the Ordnance Dept. The same as for the General Staff, except the ornament in front, which will be a gold embroidered shell and flame, on black velvet ground.

Officers of Cavalry. The same as for the General Staff, except the ornament in front, which will be two gold embroidered sabers, crossed, edges upward, on black velvet ground, with the number of the regiment in silver in the upper angle.

Federal infantry overcoat. (Smithsonian Institution)

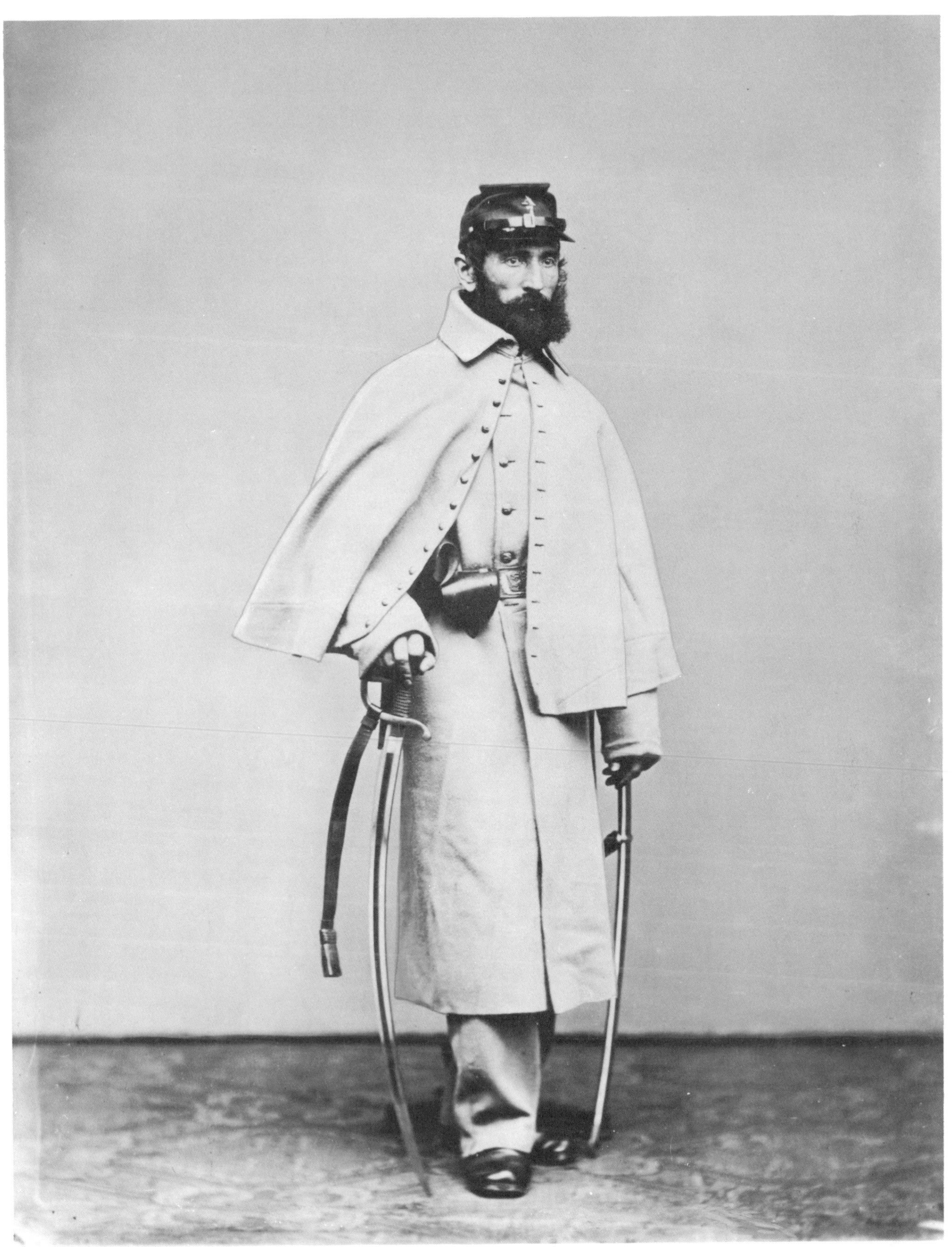

Overcoat for Federal mounted troops. (Smithsonian Institution)

48 SCHUYLER, HARTLEY & GRAHAM'S

Chapeaux, Hats, and Caps.

No. 56.

U. S. A. Regulation Chapeau.

No. 57.
U. S. Felt Hat.

No. 58.
Fatigue Cap, with Oiled Silk Cover.

No. 59.
Fatigue Cap, with Gold, or Silk Braid.

No. 60.
Burnside Pattern Felt Hat.

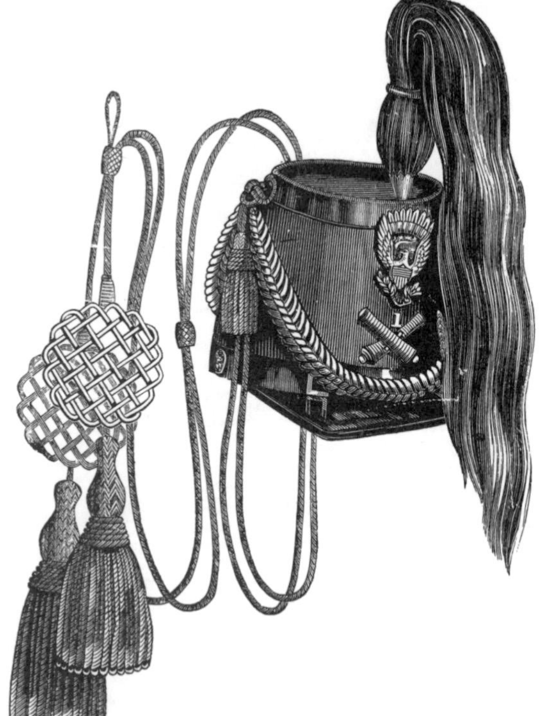

No. 60½.
Artillery Cap.

1234567890

No. 61.
Plated Metal Figures, for Officers' Caps.

ABCDE
FGHIK

No. 62.
Company Letters, Brass or Plated.
Company Figures, do. do.

Types of Federal Army headgear. (Norm Flayderman)

Officers of Artillery. The same as for the General Staff except the ornament in front which will be gold embroidered cross cannon, on black velvet ground, with the number of the regiment in silver at the intersection of the cross cannon.

Officers of Infantry. The same as for artillery, except the ornament in front, which will be a gold embroidered bugle, on black velvet ground, with the number of the regiment in silver within the bend.

Enlisted Men, except Companies of Light Artillery. The same as for officers of the respective corps, except that there will be but one feather, the cord will be of worsted, of the same color as that of the facing of the branch of service, 3/16-inch in diameter, running three times through a slide of the same material, and terminating with two tassels, not less than 2 inches long, on the side of the hat opposite the feather. The insignia of branch of service, in brass, in front of the hat, corresponding with those prescribed for officers, with the number of regiment, ⅝ inch long, in brass, and letter of company, 1 inch, in brass, arranged over insignia.

Hospital Stewards. The cord will be of buff and green mixed. The wreath in front of brass, with the letters U.S. in Roman, of white metal. Brim to be looped up to side of hat with a brass eagle, having a hook attached to the bottom to secure the brim—on the right side for mounted men and left side for foot men. The feathers to be worn on the side opposite the loop. All the trimmings of the hat are to be made so that they can be detached; but the eagle, badge of branch of service, and letter of company, are to be always worn.

Companies of Artillery, Equipped as Light Artillery. The old pattern uniform cap, with red horsehair plume, cord and tassel.

Light Artillery Uniform Hat. Lt. Philip S. Chase, Battery F, 1st Rhode Island Light Artillery, believed that it was very rare when a volunteer battery secured the full regulation light artillery uniform which included the horsehair plume, the cord over the shoulders, the rosette on the breast and tassels. Lt. Chase remarked after the war that he "never happened to see another during my term of service, and never saw ours but once after we left North Carolina."

Officers of the General Staff and Staff Corps. May wear, at their option, a light French chapeau, either stiff crown or flat, according to the pattern deposited in the Adjutant General's office. Officers below the rank of field offices to wear but two feathers.

Forage Caps. For fatigue purposes, forage caps, of pattern in Quartermaster General's Office: dark blue cloth, with a welt of the same around the crown, and yellow metal letters in front to designate companies. (Often however, enlisted men wore regimental numbers, badge of branch of service, or corps badges.) Commissioned officers could wear forage caps of the same pattern, with the distinctive ornament of the branch of service and regiment in front. (Officers also wore corps badges after their authorization in 1863.)

Some officers and many soldiers wore the forage cap copied after the French "kepi." The "McClellan cap" was a fairly faithful copy of the French kepi, but the "bummers cap" was as "shapeless as a feed bag" and not attractive at all. It had a leather visor which curled up when dry and drooped when wet. Nevertheless, this ungainly and unsightly headgear was roomy enough in the top for a wet sponge, green leaves, or a handkerchief.

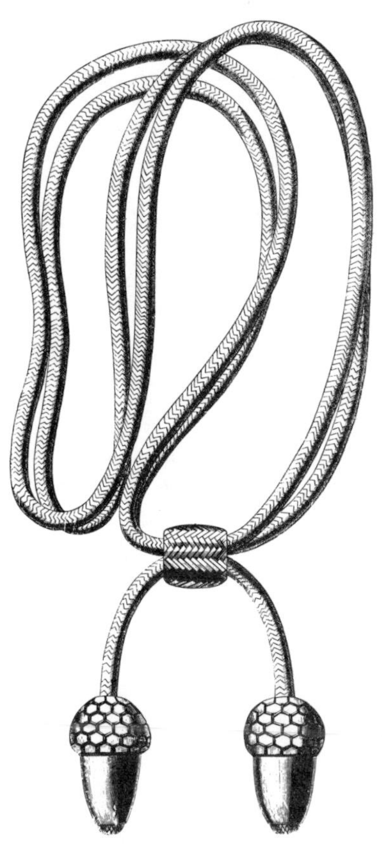

Officer's hat cord. (Norm Flayderman)

Light Artillery Shako. In the catalog of Schuyler, Hartley and Graham the ornaments on this shako differ from those shown in the photograph from the Smithsonian Institution. The latter photograph dates from early in the war, probably 1862, while the catalog was printed in 1864. This may explain the following differences: In the catalog illustration the eagle resembles the eagle on the Hardee hat and the plume holder is a plain cup. But in the Smithsonian photograph the eagle resembles those worn in the 1830's as does the plume holder. It is probable, therefore, that the early shakos, i.e. 1861-1862, were trimmed with left-over 1830 insignia, while the later shakos, i.e. 1864, used plainer and more recent insignia, such as the Hardee eagle.

CRAVAT OR STOCK

Officers. Black. When a cravat was worn, the tie was not to be visible at the opening of the collar.

Enlisted men. Black leather, according to pattern. Early in the war soldiers had to wear these leather collars to force them to hold their heads erect. These "dog collars," as the men dubbed them, were pieces of stiff upper leather, about 2 inches wide in the middle and tapering to 1 inch at the ends, which were fastened by buckles. Like the havelocks, these leather collars soon disappeared and are very rare today.

SASH

General Officers. Buff, net, with silk bullion fringe ends; sash to go twice around the waist, and to tie behind the left hip, pendant part not to extend more than 18 inches below the tie.

Officers of Adjutant-General's, Inspector-General's, Quartermaster's and Subsistence Departments, Corps of Engineers, Topographical Engineers, Ordnance, Artillery, Infantry, Cavalry, and the Judge Advocate of the Army. Crimson silk net.

Officers of the Medical Department. Medium or emerald green silk net, with silk bullion fringe ends; to go around the waist and tie as for general officers.

Sergeant Majors, Quartermaster Sergeants, Ordnance Sergeants, Hospital Stewards, First Sergeants, Principal or Chief Musicians, and Chief Buglers. Red worsted sash, with worsted bullion fringe ends; to go twice around the waist, and to tie behind the left hip, pendant part not to extend more than 18 inches below the tie.

The sash will be worn over the coat on all occasions of duty of every description, except stable and fatigue. The sash will be worn, by "Officers of the Day," across the body, scarf fashion, from the right shoulder to the left side, instead of around the waist, tying behind the left hip as prescribed.

BOOTS AND SHOES

Officers. Ankle or Jefferson.

Enlisted Men of Cavalry and Light Artillery. Ankle and Jefferson, rights and lefts, according to pattern.

Enlisted Men of Artillery, Infantry, Engineers, Ordnance. Jefferson, rights and lefts, according to pattern. While boots were generally of fine quality, their use tended to be confined to mounted personnel, including mounted officers of infantry regiments. Foot troops soon discovered that boots are not practical for long foot marches. Generally, the "bootees" or shoes issued to the troops were better than civilian boots and shoes. These bootees, also called "mudscows" and "gunboats" by the men, were low-cut, stitched, very light, and often the soles were very cheap, very broad, and the heels broad and low. Although the quality of shoes varied, the average life of a pair of contractor's shoes was from twenty to thirty days. Some paper-soled shoes were issued while others were so thin that they were only good on dry ground. The shoes worn by the Federal troops were square-toed, as were the boots worn by many officers and most mounted men.

Boots, rubber. Rubber boots were worn by some men but they were not an item of issue. Their use was limited to a comparatively small number of individuals; no specimens are available for description.

Shoes. As late as June 6, 1864, or only a month after the campaign was well under way, actual marching had worn out 50,000 pairs of shoes in the Army of the Potomac alone.

Leggings or Gaiters. Goodyear Leggings (Patent No. 34,160). Patented January 14, 1862 by Henry B. Goodyear, New Haven, Conn. As a new article of manufacture, this legging or "gaiter" was wholly or partially elastic, made of vulcanized India-rubber. Leather and canvas leggins were worn by a few units.

MISCELLANEOUS UNIFORMS

Military Store-keeper. A citizen's frock-coat of blue cloth, with buttons of the branch or service to which attached; round black hat; trousers and vest, plain, white or dark blue; cravat or stock, black.

Band Members. Bandsmen will wear the uniform of the regiment or branch of service to which they belong. The commanding officer may, at the expense of the branch of service, sanctioned by the Council of Administration, make such additions in ornaments as he may judge proper.

Signal Officer. By General Order No. 32, U.S. War Dept. June 15, 1861 the uniform and dress were to be that of a major of the General Staff.

Chaplain. By General Order No. 102, U. S. War Department, November 25, 1861, the uniform for chaplains of the Army was to be a plain, black frock coat with standing collar, and one row of 9 black buttons; plain black trousers; black felt hat, or Army forage cap, without ornament. On occasions of ceremony, a plain chapeau de bras could be worn. On August 25, 1864, the War Department (General Order No. 247) modified the uniform for Chaplains as follows: Herring bone of black braid to be around the buttons and button holes of the coat; the headgear was to be decorated with a gold embroidered wreath in front, on black velvet ground, encircling the letters U.S. in silver, old English Characters.

Federal cavalry bugler. (Smithsonian Institution)

Federal artillery sergeant. (Smithsonian Institution)

Federal light artilleryman. The shako saw very limited service, especially in the field. (Smithsonian Institution)

Invalid Corps, Officers. By War Department General Order No. 158, May 29, 1863, the following uniform was adopted for officers of the Invalid Corps: Frock Coat: of sky-blue cloth, with dark-blue velvet collar and cuffs—in all other respects, according to the present pattern for officers of infantry. Shoulder straps: According to present regulations, but worked on dark-blue velvet. Trousers: of sky-blue cloth, with double stripe of dark-blue cloth down the outer seam, each stripe ½ inch wide, with space between of ⅜ of an inch.

Enlisted Men. By War Department General Order No. 124, May 15, 1863, the following uniform was adopted for the enlisted men of the Invalid Corps: Jacket of sky-blue kersey, with dark-blue trimmings, cut like the jacket for U. S. Cavalry, to come well down on the loins and abdomen. Trousers: Present regulation, sky-blue. Forage Cap: present regulation.

Officers of Brevet Rank. General officers and colonels having the brevet rank of general officers may, on occasions of ceremony, and when not serving with troops, wear the "dress" and "undress" prescribed by existing regulations.

Officers Below the Rank of Colonel Having Brevet Rank. They will wear the epaulettes and shoulder straps distinctive of their Army rank. In all other respects, their uniform and dress will be that of their respective regiments, branch or service, and according to their commissions in the same. Officers above the rank of lieutenant colonel by ordinary commission, having brevet rank, may wear the uniform of their respective regiment or branch of service, or that of general officers, according to their brevet rank.

Officers are permitted to wear a plain dark blue body-coat, with the button designating their respective branch of service, regiment, without any other mark or ornament upon it. Such a coat, however, is not to be considered as a dress for any military purpose. In like manner, officers are permitted to wear a buff, white or blue vest, with the small buttons of their arm, service, or regiment.

Officers serving with mounted troops are allowed to wear, for stable duty, a plain dark blue cloth jacket, with 1 or 2 rows of buttons down the front, according to rank; stand-up collar, sloped in front as that of the uniform coat; shoulder straps according to rank, but no other ornament.

SPECIAL UNITS

Berdan's Sharpshooters. Uniform was of fine material and consisted of a dark green coat and cap with

Shoes or "bootees." These shoes of the "Jefferson pattern" are of heavy leather, with the rough side to the outside. No grommets in lace holes. Laces of rawhide. Squared box toe, heavy leather sole and heel. (Smithsonian Institution)

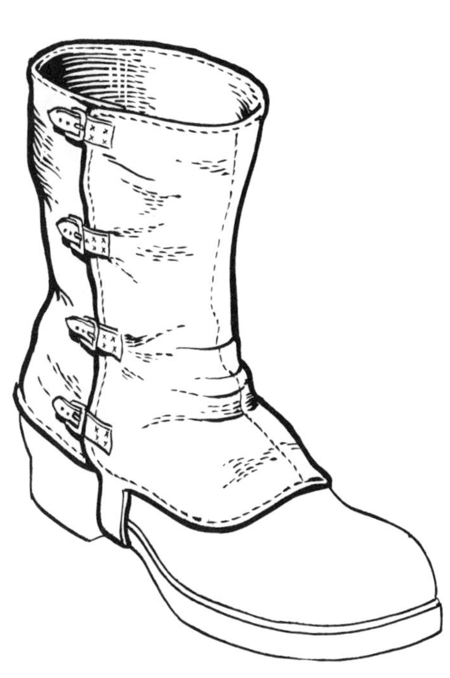

Gaiter and shirt. The gaiter is of leather and extended from top of the shoe to slightly above the calf of the leg. The shirts were usually made of flannel. (James A. Shutt)

black plume, light blue trousers (afterward exchanged for green ones), and leather leggings. Because of their unique outfit the Sharpshooters were known far and wide as the "Green Coats." Each man wore for a time, mainly while on outpost duty or in bad weather, what was called a Havelock, a gray, round hat with a wide, black visor. These were good enough around Washington far within the Federal lines, but after the men first saw combat, these hats were discarded as endangering men to fire from the rear. Also, the gray felt seamless overcoats were abandoned, although they shed the rain well, only to become stiff as a board when they finally became thoroughly wet. Apparently the Sharpshooters had distinctive buttons on their uniforms. These buttons, made of hard rubber, were decorated with the usual eagle, but due to lack of luster were much more suitable for sharpshooters than the metallic buttons worn by the line units.

Bucktails. Closely associated with the Sharpshooters were the "Bucktails" (13th Pennsylvania Reserves and the 1st Pennsylvania Rifles) who wore bucktails in their forage caps.

Garibaldi Guards (39th New York Infantry). They wore a very dark greenish-blue uniform, with a flat-brimmed round-top hat set off with cock's feathers.

Zouave Uniforms. Among the Zouave units were the "Salem Zouaves" (8th Mass. Vol. Militia); 146th New York Infantry; "Duryee's Zouaves" (5th New York Infantry); "Wilson's Zouaves" (6th New York Infantry); 4th Michigan Infantry (Canadian caps without visors and short leggings). The 44th New York Infantry "Ellsworth's Avengers") wore a modified Zouave uniform.

Most of the Zouave regiments were from Eastern states, the majority coming from the state of New York. A few Zouave regiments were raised in the Mid-West. In addition to the 4th Michigan Infantry, another early regiment was the 11th Indiana Infantry, "Wallace's Zouaves." As its colonel, the famous author-soldier, Lew Wallace, pointed out: "There was nothing of the flashy, Algerian colors in the uniform . . . no red fez . . . no red breeches, no red or yellow sash with tassels big as early cabbages. Our outfit was of the tamest gray twilled goods, not unlike home-made jeans, and a visor cap. French in pattern, its top of red cloth not larger than the palm of one's hand; a blue flannel shirt with open neck; a jacket, Greekish in form, edged with narrow binding . . . breeches baggy, but not petticoated; button gaiters connecting below the knees with the breeches, and strapped over the shoe."

Zouave officers generally wore a modified Zouave uniform. Federal Army Zouave officers wore a braided jacket of the same general color and cut as that worn by the enlisted men of their regiment. In the 165th New York Infantry the officers wore a braided jacket a cap, vest, and scarlet trousers. The jacket was adorned with gold braid and small sleeve buttons.

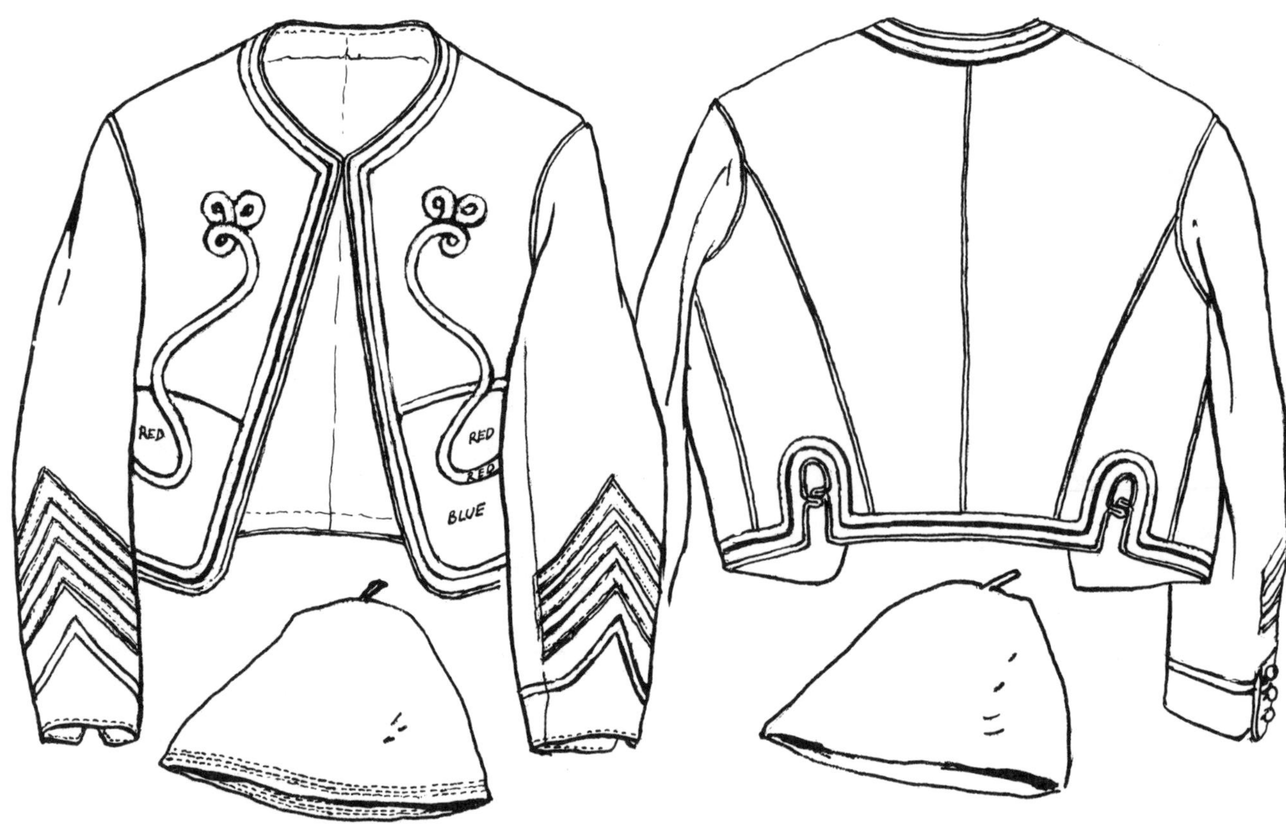

Zouave jacket and fez worn by Sergeant Samuel L. Malcolm, Co. C, 9th N.Y. Infantry (Hawkins' Zouaves). See "Accouterments" for illustration of the equipments used by Sergeant Malcolm. Author's collection. (drawn by Robert L. Miller)

83d Pennsylvania Infantry. This regiment was rewarded for its proficiency in drill by being issued by the U. S. Government, not by the State of Pennsylvania, French Zouave uniforms specially imported for this purpose. The uniform was of the Chasseur de Vincennes, consisting of a shako, "two tasteful suits," dress and fatigue, with cloak, two pairs of shoes, two pairs of white gloves, two nightcaps, and a little bag containing brushes, combs, needles, and thread.

155th Pennsylvania Infantry. This regiment was unique in that early in 1864 it was outfitted with Zouave uniform imported from France. This unusual move was done by official order of the Government as a reward for the high efficiency achieved by the regiment in drill and tactics. The exchange to the Zouave uniform from the plain blue infantry uniform was enjoyed immensely by the 155th Infantry, not only on account of their having earned the recognition, but also because of the real attractiveness of the uniform, plus greater comfort. The uniform was wide—very wide, dark blue knee-pants; with material enough in one pair to make two pairs of ordinary trousers, and shaped somewhat like the bloomer costume worn by women years ago. Next came the jacket of the same heavy dark blue material as the knee-pants, and trimmed with yellow at the collar and the wrists and down the fronts. A feature of the uniform was the red flannel sash fully 10 feet long and about 10 inches wide. The sash was trimmed with yellow, and was wound around the waist of the soldier, adding much to the comfort of the men. Footgear consisted of white canvas leggings, which came down over the shoes, and were buckled along the sides and around the ankles, reaching halfway to the knees, where the breeches were fitted into them. Lastly, the most impressive part of the uniform was the turban. It was composed of a sash of white flannel about a foot wide and ten feet long, which was nicely wound, so as to set or fit on a red fez skull cap, to which was attached a blue tassel. This turban was seldom worn except on dress parades or dress occasions; but the red fez cap with the tassel was always worn on fatigue or other duties. While this uniform had its advantages on the march and was comfortable on other occasions, at times it had drawbacks. For example, if its wearers straggled, the unusual uniform distinguished them from all other soldiers, and aided in their detection. The ever-vigilant provost guards easily knew the camp locations of the stragglers, and could identify the Zouaves by their peculiar uniform, whereas, if they had been dressed in the ordinary regulation uniform, they would have escaped arrest.

Militia uniform. A drummer boy, Gilbert J. Marbury, Co. H, 22d N.Y. Infantry standing at the trail of a Napoleon field piece. Harpers Ferry, 1862. (National Archives)

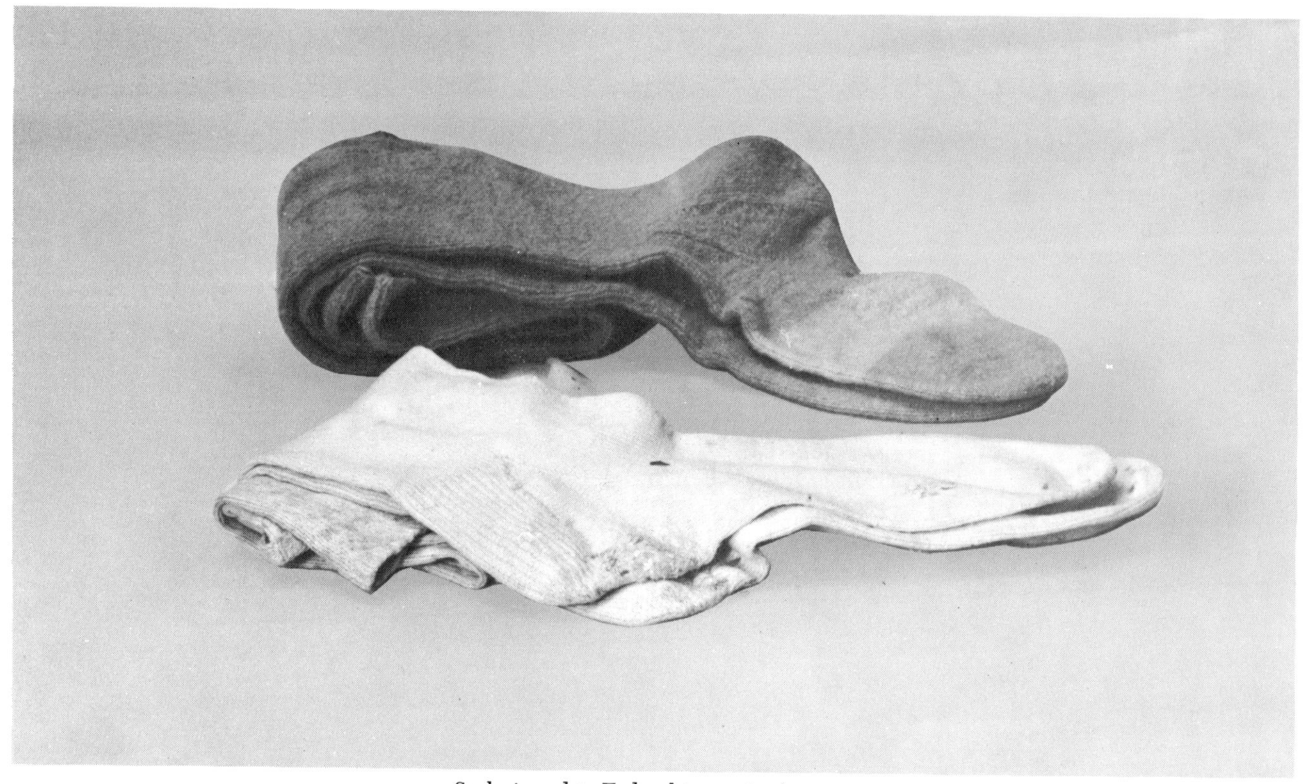

Socks issued to Federal troops in the war.

Ellsworth's "Chicago Zouaves," 1859. A bright red chasseur cap with gold braid; light blue shirt with moire antique facings; dark blue jacket with orange and red trimmings; brass bell buttons, placed as close together as possible; a red sash and loose red trousers; russet leather leggings, buttoned over the trousers, reaching from ankle halfway to the knee; and white waist belt. The jacket did not button, was cut low in the neck, without collar. Easy-fitting, high laced shoes with thick broad soles were worn, thus making up a remarkably brilliant as well as comfortable uniform.

14th Brooklyn. In 1860 the 14th New York State Militia adopted the French chasseur uniform, consisting of red pants, white leggings, blue jacket, with broad red chevrons and shoulder knots, and cap with blue band, red above the blue top. During the war the 14th New York was known as "the red-legged devils," or "Brooklyn Fourteenth."

Philadelphia Fire Zouaves (Baxter's 72d Pennsylvania Infantry, also known as the 3d California). This was another Zouave regiment which was raised in 1861. Of a total of 1,600 men, it lost 988 in killed, wounded, death by disease, and missing in action. The uniform was a modified Zouave, consisting primarily of Zouave trousers and leggings, but retaining regulation cap rather than the fez. Of especial interest to collectors is the unique cartridge box plate, in two sizes, marked with the block letters PFZ.

Birney's Zouaves (23d Pennsylvania Infantry). They wore a dark blue Zouave uniform, which wore out in six months and then the unit was issued the regulation uniform.

Hawkin's Zouaves (9th New York Infantry). This uniform was of Army blue, the trousers slightly full, plaited at the waist, with a magenta braid down the outer seam; jacket and vest with magenta trimmings, a sash of the same color of woolen material, wide enough to cover the abdomen of the wearer; white leggings, and red fez with a blue tassel. "It was totally different from the uniforms issued by the United States authorities, and no nattier one was worn by any body of troops in the service."

11th New York Fire Zouaves. The 11th New York Infantry, "Fire Zouaves," at First Bull Run wore dark-blue trousers with socks covering the trouser bottoms; red flannel shirts with the silver badge of the New York Fire Department; blue jackets, elaborately trimmed with braid; red fez caps with blue tassels; and a blue sash around the waist.

Collis' Zouaves. This Federal Zouave regiment, permitted to wear its unique uniform throughout the war, was the 114th Pennsylvania Infantry, and preserved its identity as a Zouave regiment until the close of the war. There were other Zouave regiments, but as soon as their uniforms became badly worn, these other regiments were usually required to wear the regulation uniform. The uniform of the 114th Pennsylvania was: red pants, Zouave jacket, white leggings, blue sash around the waist, and white turban. This uniform perked up the pride of the new recruits, and gave the regiment an imposing and warlike appearance. The material for these uniforms was all imported from France, and special arrangements were made to secure a sufficient supply to replenish the uniforms during the whole term of service.

Militia Uniforms. The limitations of space prevent the inclusion of practically limitless variety of militia uniforms worn by both sides in the early months of the war.

The most photographed Federal militia unit was the 7th Regiment, New York State Militia, which wore a grey uniform, the low kepi of the Civil War period, heavy knapsack with mess kit, blanket, and wide white belts with N. G. (National Guard) on belt plate and cartridge box plate. The 7th Regiment was somewhat typical of the many militia units which went into active service in 1861 in all sections of the country. Many officers got their basic training in these half social-half military outfits; the 7th alone furnished over 500 officers to the Federal Army.

Clothing, Army.

Stable Frock. As prescribed by 1861 regulations.

Canvas Overalls. For Engineer Soldiers: of white cotton; one garment to cover the whole of the body below the waist, the breast, the shoulders, and the arms; sleeves loose, to allow a free play of the arms, with narrow wristband buttoning with one button; overalls to fasten at the neck behind with two buttons, and at the waist behind with buckle and tongue.

Socks and Drawers. No information could be found to give a description of either of these items. A letter from the General Services Administration of the National Archives, dated June 18, 1957, said in part:

"An examination of the records of the Office of the Quartermaster General in the National Archives has failed to disclose any specifications for stockings prior to 1877 or specifications for underdrawers prior to 1883." The only mention of socks and drawers in the 1861 *Army Regulations* is that they should be "the same as now furnished."

Because of their utilitarian value to men after leaving the service, socks and underwear were worn out in post-1865 civilian wear and very few specimens are available for examination today. Army socks were often of shoddy material and, once worn, were not worth repairing. In appearance they were remarkably similar to the elbow of a stove-pipe; "nor did the likeness end here, for, while the stove-pipe is open at both ends, so were the socks within forty-eight hours after putting them on." The custom of rolling the trousers snugly at the ankle and hauling the gray woolen sock, legging-wise, over them became fairly universal. The socks themselves were well made, but many men preferred those knitted at home, principally, because "the Government socks . . . were evidently modelled for a race of gorillas." Long socks were best for long marching.

Underwear. Generally of good quality, and consisted of "mud-colored shirts and drawers" of flannel material. In the Ferris collection there is a pair of red flannel drawers worn during the war. They are 42 inches long, 33 inches around the waist, and can be buttoned at the ankles. On February 13, 1862, a medical doctor, C. H. Allen of Cambridgeport, Massachusetts, wrote the Quartermaster General about a new pattern "Union Drawers." He shipped a specimen to prove his contention that his "Union Drawers" could be adjusted to fit any size soldier. According to Allen's claim his drawers would allow freedom of motion in walking, running, jumping, crouching, and swimming. In unusual exposure, as at night, or in riding horseback, two pairs could be worn comfortably.

Shirt. Many Confederate shirts were homespun while Federals were issued flannel shirts, generally three a year.

MARINE CORPS UNIFORMS, U.S. (USMC Regulations)

Coat, Full Dress, Officers. All officers shall wear, in full dress, a double-breasted frock coat, of dark blue cloth, the skirt to extend three-fourths of the distance from the top of the hip to the bend of the knee.

For the Commandant. Two rows of large size Marine buttons on the breast, eight in each row, placed in pairs; the distance between each row, five and one-half inches at top, and three and one-half inches at bottom; standing collar, to rise no higher than to permit the chin to turn freely over it; to hook in front at the bottom, and slope thence up and backward, at an angle of thirty degrees on each side, making the total opening in front an angle of sixty degrees; two loops of half-inch gold lace on each side of the collar, with one small Marine button at the end of each loop; the bottom loop four and one-half inches long, the upper loop not to extend further back than the bottom loop, and the front of both loops to slope up and backward with the front of the collar, at an angle of thirty degrees; collar to be edged all around with a scarlet edging; plain round cuff, three inches deep; slash on the sleeve, six and one-half inches long, and two and one-quarter inches wide at the points, and one and nine-tenths of an inch at the narrowest part of the curve; four loops of half-inch gold lace, and four small

U.S. Marines. One of the very few known photographs of Marines during the Civil War. (Library of Congress)

Marine buttons, one in each loop, on the slash of the sleeve; the loops on the sleeve to be two inches long, and one and one-eighth of an inch wide. The slash on the sleeve to be edged with scarlet on the ends and indented edges; pockets with three-pointed side edges in the folds of the skirt; one button at the hip, one at the centre of the pocket opening, and one at the bottom, making six buttons on the back and skirt of the coat; the side edges to have one point on the centre of the edge, and to curve thence up and down to the top and bottom, corresponding with the slash on the sleeves; the side edges to be edged with scarlet on the ends and indented edges; lining of the coat, black.

For Field Officers. Same as for the Commandant, except that there shall be eight buttons in each row, placed at equal distances.

For Captains. Same as for field officers, except that there shall be but three loops of gold lace, and three small Marine buttons on the sleeve, and the slash shortened to correspond with the reduction in the number of loops.

For Lieutenants. Same as for Captains, except that there shall be but two loops and small Marine buttons on the sleeve, and the slash shortened to correspond with the reduction in the number of loops.

COAT, FULL DRESS, ENLISTED MEN'S.

For Sergeant-Major, Quartermaster-Sergeant, Drum-Major and Chief Musicians. Two rows of large size Marine buttons on the breast, seven in each row, placed at equal distances; the distance between each row, five and one-half inches at top, and three and one-half inches at bottom; standing collar, to rise no higher than to permit the chin to turn freely over it; to hook in front at the bottom, and slope thence up and backward at an angle of thirty degrees on each side, making the total opening in front an angle of sixty degrees; two loops of yellow worsted half-inch lace on each side of the collar, with one small Marine button at the end of each loop; the bottom loop four and one-half inches long; the upper loop not to extend further back than the bottom loop, and the front of both loops to slope up and backwards, with the front of the collar, at an angle of thirty degrees; collar to be edged all around with a scarlet edging, except those of the Drum-Major, Chief Musicians, and Musicians, which will be edged all around with white; plain round cuff, three inches deep; slash on the sleeve to be six inches long, and two and one-quarter inches wide at the points, and one and nine-tenths of an inch at the narrowest part of the curve; three loops of yellow worsted half-inch lace, and three small Marine buttons, one in the centre of each loop, on the slash of the sleeve; loops on the sleeve two inches long, and one inch and one-eighth wide; the slashed flap on the sleeve to be edged with scarlet on the ends and indented edges; those of the Drum-Major, Chief Musicians, and Musicians, to be edged with white; pockets with three-pointed edges in the fold of the skirt, one button at the hip, one at the centre of the pocket opening, and one at the bottom, making six buttons on the back and skirt of the coat; the pocket side edges to have one point at the centre of the edge, and to curve thence up and down to the top and bottom, corresponding with slash on the sleeve; the pocket side edges to be edged with scarlet on the ends and indented edges; those of the Drum-Major, Chief Musicians, and Musicians, to be edged with white. Lining of the coat, black. Skirts, full.

For Sergeants. Same as for Sergeant-Major, except that there shall be but two loops, and two small Marine buttons on the slash of the sleeve, and that the slash shall be shortened to correspond with the reduction of the number of loops.

For Corporals. Same as for Sergeants.

For Privates. Same as for Corporals.

The uniform of all enlisted men, except the Drum-Major, Chief Musicians, and Musicians, shall be a double-breasted frock coat, of dark indigo blue cloth, with skirt extending three fourths of the distance from the top of the hip to the bend of the knee. Skirts, full.

For Drum-Major, Chief Musicians, and Musicians. A scarlet, *cochineal* dyed, cloth, double-breasted frock coat, with skirt extending three-fourths of the distance from the top of the hip to the bend of the knee.

For Musicians. Same as for Privates, except that the coat shall be of *scarlet, cochineal* dyed, cloth, and the collar slashes on the sleeves, and the pocket side edges on the skirt, shall be edged with white, skirts, full.

TROUSERS. The uniform trousers, for both officers and enlisted men, shall, in cold weather, be of cloth, with French pockets, made loose, and to spread well over the boot, of white and light blue mixed, commonly called sky-blue mixture.

Officers *not* serving in line with troops, may wear dark blue cloth trousers, with a welt of scarlet cloth let into each outer seam.

In warm weather, the uniform trousers for both officers and enlisted men shall be of white linen. Both the cloth and linen trousers shall be cut for enlisted men as shown in plates.

The cloth for the trousers of enlisted men shall be of kersey.

Cloth trousers for Commissioned Officers shall have a welt of scarlet, three-sixteenths of an inch in diameter, let into the outer seam.

For Sergeant-Major, Quartermaster-Sergeant, Drum-Major, Chief Musicians, and Musicians, a scarlet cord, three-sixteenths of an inch in diameter, down the outer seam.

UNDRESS COAT.

Officers. For all officers, a double-breasted dark blue cloth frock coat, the skirt to extend three-fourths of the distance from the top of the hip to the bend of the knee. Skirts full.

For the Commandant. Two rows of buttons on the breast, eight in each row, placed in pairs; the distance between each row, five and one-half inches at top, and three and one-half inches at bottom; stand-up collar, to rise no higher than to permit the chin to turn freely over it; to hook at the bottom, in front, and slope thence up and backward at an angle of thirty degrees on each side, making the total opening in front an angle of sixty degrees; cuffs two and one-half inches deep, to go around the sleeve parallel with the lower edge, and to button with three small buttons at the under seam; pockets in the folds of the skirts, with one button at hip, and one at the end of each pocket, making four buttons on the back and skirt of the coat; collar and cuffs to be of dark blue velvet; lining of the coat black.

For all other Officers. Same as the Commandant, except that the buttons on the breast will be placed at equal distances; collar and cuffs of the same material and color as the coat.

For Enlisted Men. A single-breasted dark indigo blue kersey frock coat; one row of seven Marine buttons on the breast; stand-up collar (with a red welt inserted in the seam, where the collar joins the coat), to rise no higher than to permit the chin to turn freely over it, to hook in front at bottom, and slope thence up and backward at an angle of thirty degrees on each side, making the whole opening in front an angle of sixty degrees; cuffs two and one half inches deep, to go around the sleeves parallel with the lower edge, and to button with two small Marine buttons; skirt of the coat to extend from the top of the hip to the crotch of the trousers, with one button over the hip, making two buttons on the back of the coat; no pockets in the skirts; lining of the coat black. Skirts to be full. Non-commissioned Officers will wear chevrons of their grades (as prescribed in the full dress) above the elbow, points up.

FATIGUE SLACKS. All enlisted men on board of sea-going vessels will wear a flannel fatigue sack, of dark indigo blue; open half-way down the front, and buttoning with four small Marine buttons; yoke on the shoulder; the sack to extend in length half the distance from the top of the hip to the bend of the knee; small turn-down collar of the same material; sleeves like a coat sleeve, but without cuff or opening, and made larger at the wrist, to permit the free passage of the hand; seams at the side to be closed up all the way down. Non-commissioned Officers will wear the chevrons of their grade (as prescribed in the full dress) on the sleeves above the elbow, points up. No lining.

SUMMER FATIGUE COAT.

Officers. On ship board, the Summer Coat for Officers shall be of white linen, made like the blue cloth undress coat. This coat may be worn, at their pleasure, by officers visiting the shore in foreign ports, except on occasions of parade or ceremony. When this coat is worn, the shoulder knot, to be hereinafter prescribed, shall also be worn.

The fatigue sack for enlisted men shall be worn at sea in warm weather; and in the tropics, on ordinary occasions, in port also. When worn, it must be with a white shirt underneath.

CHAPEAU. The Commandant and Field Officers shall wear a chapeau (French pattern) of the following dimensions: Length from point to point, from seventeen to nineteen inches; height of front, or cock, four and three-quarter inches; back or fan, five and one-half inches; points, two and five-eighths inches wide; to be bound with black lace (silk), to show five-eighths of an inch; at each end a gold and scarlet flat tassel, of fine gold and fine scarlet silk bullion; on the front, or cock, a black uncut velvet cockade, three inches in diameter; a loop of gold, one-half inch Marine lace, with a Marine coat-button at bottom of the loop; distance between the two strips of lace forming the loop, one quarter of an inch.

PLUME.

For the Commandant. Of yellow swan feathers, bunched; length, twelve inches, drooping from a three-inch stem. Plume to be worn in a leather socket, placed inside of front or cock, four inches in advance of the gold loop.

For Field Officers. Same as for Commandant, except that it shall be of cock or vulture feathers, and that the color shall be red.

UNIFORM CAP.

Company Officers. Of fine black cloth; top, visor, and bands of fine glazed black leather; visor bound around the edges with the same; base line of cap to be *perfectly straight,* visor straight, and placed upon a continuation line; height of cap in front, from the rim under the visor, five and one-half inches; height of back six and one-half inches; difference of height between front and back, one inch; diameter of top, five and three-eighths inches; counter-sinking of top, three-eighths of an inch; width of lower black glazed leather band, one inch and one-eighth; width of upper black glazed leather band, seven-eighths of an inch; width of visor, six and three-quarter inches; depth, one inch and one-half.

Enlisted Men. Same as for Company Officers, substituting black felt for cloth. For Drum-Major, of Astracan lambskin.

FATIGUE CAP.

Officers. All officers shall wear, in undress, a dark blue cloth cap, according to pattern; black ribbed silk band one inch and five-eighths of an inch wide; three rows of black silk braid, three-sixteenths of an inch wide down each seam from the crown to the bottom; in the centre of crown a knot of the same braid, and also one row around the edge of the crown; vizor six and one-half inches wide, and one and one-half inches deep.

Enlisted Men. Same as officers, except the silk band and braid. The lining in the band and crown to be of prepared leather.

OVERCOAT.

Officers. A "cloak coat" of dark blue cloth, lined with scarlet woolen, and closing by means of our frog olive-shaped buttons, of black silk, one inch and one-eighth in length, and loops of black silk cord down the breast, and at the throat by a long loop *a echelle* without tassel or plate, on the left side, and a black silk frog button on the right; cord for the loops three-sixteenths of an inch in diameter; back a single piece, slit up from the bottom, from fifteen to seventeen inches, according to the height of the wearer, and closing at will, by buttons and button-holes in a fly-flap; collar of the same color and material as the coat, rounded at the edges, and to stand or fall; when standing, to be about five inches high; side pieces, with the pockets cut according to pattern. Sleeves loose, of a single piece, and round at the bottom without cuff or slit; the sleeves to be cut according to pattern. Around the front, the lower border, the edges of the pockets, the edges of the sleeves, collar

U.S. Navy uniform, apparently with carpenter insignia. (National Archives)

Sergeant Major Chief Musician Drum Major Musician

Full dress uniforms of Marine Corps enlisted men (1859). (Department of Defense photo. Marine Corps)

and slit in the back, a flat braid of black silk, one-half an inch wide; and around each frog button on the breast, a knot two and one-quarter inches in diameter, of black silk cord, one-sixteenth of an inch in diameter. A cape of the same color and material as the coat, removable at the pleasure of the wearer, and reaching to the edge of the coat sleeve when the arm is extended; lining of cape black; coat to extend down the leg from six to eight inches below the knee, according to height. *To indicate rank*, there will be on both sleeves, near the lower edge, a knot of flat black silk braid, one-eighth of an inch in width, and composed as follows:

For the Commandant. Of five braids, double knot.

For a Colonel. Of five braids, single knot.

For a Lieutenant-Colonel. Of four braids, single knot.

For a Major. Of three braids, single knot.

For a Captain. Of two braids, single knot.

For a First Lieutenant. Of one braid, single knot.

For a Second Lieutenant. A plain sleeve, without knot or ornament.

Enlisted Men. Of blue gray mixture, stand-up collar; single breasted, with one row of seven large Marine buttons on the breast; loose sleeves, with cuffs five inches deep; cape to be cut circularly, and to reach down in front to the upper edge of the cuff when the arm is extended, and to button all the way down in front, with five small Marine buttons. The cape to be made separate from the coat, and to be buttoned on. Non-commissioned Officers shall wear the chevrons of their grade, as prescribed for the full dress coat, on the cuffs of their overcoats.

Other Articles of Clothing.

Officers. Officers may wear a fatigue jacket of dark blue cloth, lined with scarlet, collar same as undress coat, but edged all around with one-half inch gold lace; pointed cuff, point up, six inches deep, and edged all around with half-inch gold lace, sixteen small Marine buttons in a single row in front and at the opening of the sleeve; shoulder knots will be worn with the fatigue jacket.

Enlisted Men. The flannel shirts shall be changed in color from *red* to *blue.*

The blankets to be *all wool,* and to weigh four pounds; color gray, with the letters U. S. M. in black, four inches long; blankets to be seven feet long, and five and a half feet wide; the letters U. S. M. to be placed in the centre.

Allowances of clothing for an enlistment of four years, as follows:

One uniform cap, two uniform coats, two sets of epaulette bullion, seven pairs of linen trousers, eight pairs of woolen trousers, twelve shirts, two stocks, sixteen pairs of shoes, one blanket, eight pairs of socks, eight pairs of drawers, four fatigue caps, four fatigue coats, eight blue flannel shirts, one great coat.

After a guard marches on board of a sea-going vessel, each enlisted man shall be entitled to receive the additional articles of clothing following: one great coat *(on charge, and only to be worn, under direction of Commanding Marine Officer in port, when the men are posted, or formed as a guard of honor on the quarter-deck; at all other times to be kept in the Marine Store-room; these extra coats to be worn, on post, by day only, in clear, cold weather),* and two dark blue flannel sacks.

Sash.

For the Commandant. Of buff silk net, with silk bullion fringe ends; sash to go twice around the waist, and to tie behind the left hip; pendant part not to extend more than eighteen inches below the tie.

For Field and Company Officers. Of crimson silk net to go around the waist, and tie, as for the Commandant. The Sash will be worn by "Officers of the day" across the body, scarf fashion, from the right shoulder to the left side, instead of around the waist, tying behind the left hip.

For Sergeant-Major, Quartermaster-Sergeant, Drum-Major, Chief Musicians, and First Sergeants. Of red worsted, with worsted bullion fringe ends, to go twice around the waist, and to tie behind the left hip; pendant part not to extend more than eighteen inches below the tie. The sash will be worn (over the coat) on all occasions of duty of every description, except fatigue.

Boots.

Officers. Ankle or Jefferson.

Enlisted Men. Of the pattern now furnished to the Infantry of the U. S. Army; to be made rights and lefts, and inspected before they are dressed off; the dressing to be done under the supervision of the Quartermaster's Department.

NAVY UNIFORMS, U.S. (From Regulations) The uniform of the U. S. Navy during the Civil War was that prescribed by the 1852 Uniform Regulations, its amendments, and new regulations issued in 1864. The use of sleeve lace to indicate officer rank was introduced in 1852. The trend was towards a common uniform for all officers of the Navy, line or staff, with the branch of service indicated by distinctive devices. As the Navy expanded during the war, the ranks of rear admiral, commodore, lieutenant commander, and ensign were established. These ranks were provided for as shown in the following regulations.

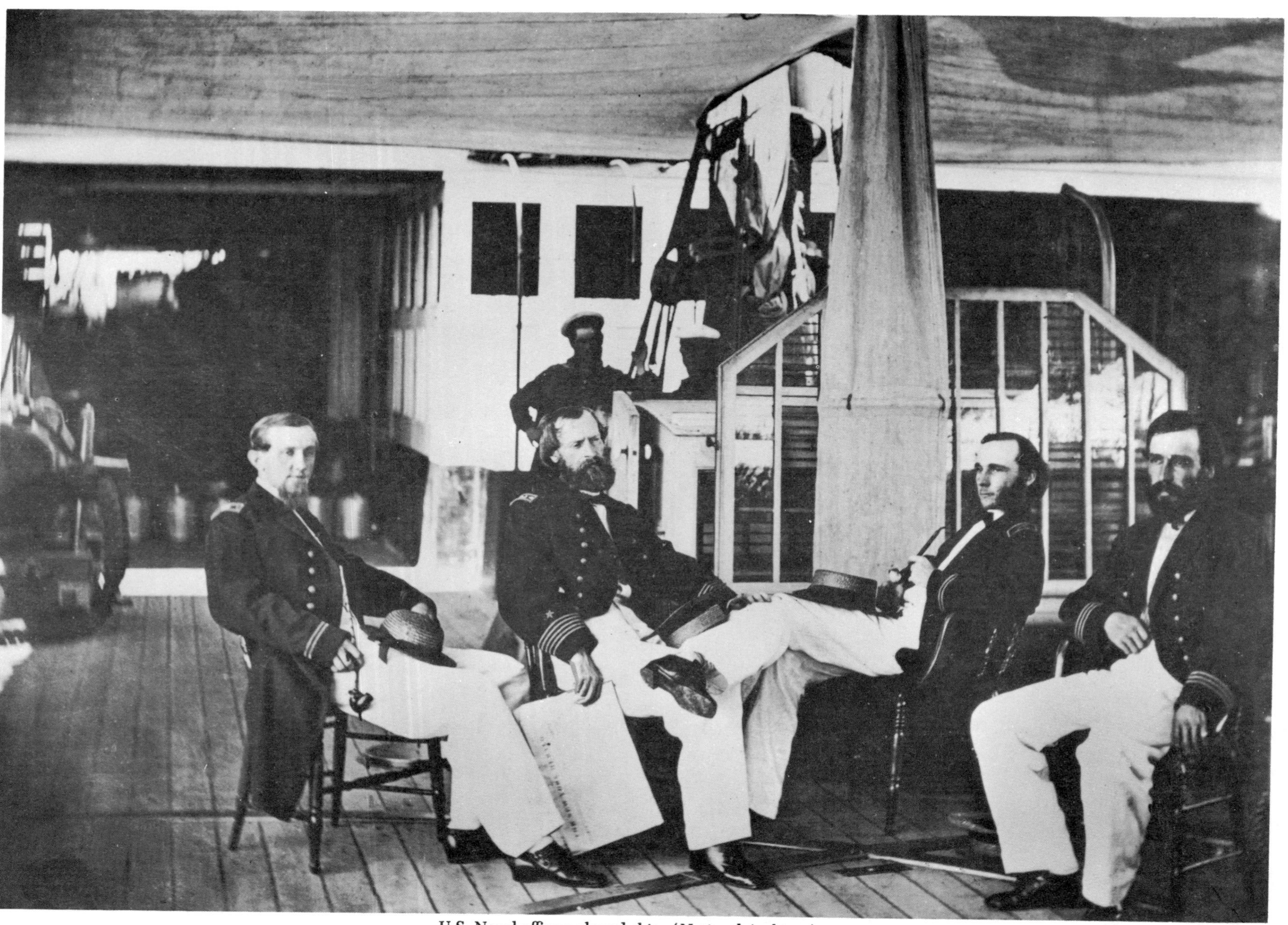

U.S. Naval officers aboard ship. (National Archives)

General Regulations

Full Dress. Frock coat, epaulettes, cocked hat, sword, and plain pantaloons; the coat to be worn fully buttoned. The epaulettes, cocked hat, and sword-knot are to be dispensed with during the war.

Undress. The same as full dress, but without cocked hat or epaulettes, and with or without sword.

Service dress. The same as undress. Swords to be worn at quarters and on leaving a navy yard or vessel on duty.

Officers are to wear their uniform, either full or undress, whenever they make official visits to the President of the United States, the Secretary of the Navy, or to foreign authorities and vessels of war; when acting as members of courts-martial, courts of inquiry, boards of examination, or of special boards, or when attending such boards as witnesses, or in any other capacity.

It is left optional with officers to wear their uniform while on duty in the Navy Department, at the Observatory, or on light-house duty ashore.

Uniform is to be worn by all officers when attached to any vessel of the navy or Coast Survey, to any navy yard or station, or to any hospital or other naval establishment, for duty, unless when absent on leave.

Officers on furlough will not wear their uniform, and officers are strictly prohibited from wearing any part of it while suspended from duty by sentence of a court-martial.

On all occasions of ceremony, abroad or in the United States, when a commanding officer may deem it necessary to order the attendance of the officers under his command, he shall be careful in such order to prescribe the particular dress to be worn.

Officers attached to vessels of the United States Navy in foreign ports will not visit the shore without being in uniform.

Officers appointed on "temporary service" are not required to supply themselves with full-dress uniforms, but are required to obtain undress uniforms and side-arms.

Officers holding executive appointments in the volunteer service of the navy are to wear the same uniform as is authorized for their respective grades in the regular service.

U.S. Naval officers' headgear. (Norm Flayderman)

Before a vessel proceeds to sea, there will be a general muster for the purpose of ascertaining whether the officers and crew are provided with the uniform prescribed by the regulations, and the commanding officer of the vessel will see that all deficiencies are supplied.

Coats

For a Rear-Admiral, Commodore, Captain, Commander, Lieutenant-Commander, Lieutenant, Master, and *Ensign,* and all *Staff Officers* of assimilated rank,

U.S. Navy uniforms. Capt. John Winslow (third from left) with officers on deck of USS *Kearsarge*. (Library of Congress)

respectively, to be as follows:

Frock coat, of navy-blue cloth, faced with the same, and lined with black silk serge; double breasted, with two rows of large navy buttons on the breast, nine in each row, placed four inches and a half apart from eye to eye at top, and two inches and a half at bottom; rolling collar; skirts to be full, commencing at the hip bone and descending four-fifths thence towards the knee, with one button behind on each hip and one near the bottom of each fold; cuffs to be closed and from two and a half to three inches deep.

For gunners, boatswains, carpenters, and *sailmakers,* the same.

For midshipmen, third assistant engineers, and *clerks,* the same, except that the buttons are to be of medium size only.

For a master's mate, receiving $40 per month, frock coat, of navy-blue cloth or flannel; rolling collar; single breasted, with nine navy buttons of medium size on the breast, one behind on each hip, one near the bottom on each fold, and none on the cuffs. They will also wear a gold star above the cuff, and the navy cap, with simply the wreath.

For masters' mates, receiving $25 per month, *yeomen, masters-at-arms, sergeants, stewards,* and *paymasters' Stewards,* blue cloth or flannel jacket, rolling collar, double breasted, with two rows of medium sized navy buttons on the breast, six in each row; and slashed sleeves, with four small sized navy buttons. They will also wear the navy cap without wreath or device.

JACKETS

Jackets may be worn as "service dress" by all officers, except at general muster, or upon special occasions of ceremony, when a different dress is prescribed by the commanding officer; to be of navy-blue cloth or navy-blue fine flannel, faced with the same, and lined with black silk serge; double or single breasted, as in the coat; rolling collar, with the same number of small sized buttons on the breast as for the coat, and with the same arrangement of lace on the cuffs, and the same shoulder straps.

In mild climates or seasons officers in "service dress" may wear the uniform made of navy-blue fine flannel. Coats to be lined with black silk serge, and furnished with navy buttons of medium size. The same may be worn on shipboard at sea, except at general muster; also on board ship in port, except at general muster, when on watch with the colors hoisted, or on occasions of ceremony, when a different dress is prescribed by the commanding officer.

DRESS FOR PETTY OFFICERS AND CREW

Boatswain's mates, gunner's mates, carpenter's mates, sailmaker's mates, and *ship's cook,* will wear, embroidered in white silk, on the right sleeve of their blue jackets, above the elbow in front, an eagle and anchor, or not more than three inches in length, with a star of one inch in diameter, one inch above. The same device, embroidered in blue, to be worn on the sleeves of their white frocks in summer.

All other petty officers, except officers' stewards, will wear the same device on their left sleeves.

The outside clothing for *petty officers, firemen,* and *coal-heavers, seamen, ordinary seamen, landsmen,* and *boys,* for muster, shall consist of blue cloth jackets and trowsers, or blue woolen frocks; black hats; black silk neckerchiefs, and shoes, or boots in cold weather. In warm weather it shall consist of white frocks and trousers; black or white hats, as the commander may for the occasion direct, having proper regard for the comfort of the crew; black silk neckerchiefs, and shoes; the collars and cuffs to be lined with blue cotton cloth, and stitched round with thread. Thick blue cloth caps, without visors, may be worn by the crew at sea, except on holidays or at muster.

It is strictly enjoined upon commandants of stations and commanding officers of the navy to see that the foregoing regulations are complied with in every respect, and to require all deviations from them to be corrected.

OVERCOATS. Shall be a caban overcoat and cape, of dark blue beaver or pilot-cloth, lined throughout with dark blue flannel; skirt to extend four inches below the knee; cape to be ten inches shorter; double breasted, with pockets in side seam, and buttons arranged as for frock coat; the cape to be made so that it can be removed at pleasure, and provided with an extra cloth collar to detach, so as to form a separate garment. On each end of the collar of the overcoat shall be the following devices: For a Rear-Admiral two silver stars; Commodore, one silver star; Captain, a silver eagle; Commander, a silver leaf; Lieutenant-Commander, a gold leaf; Lieutenant, two silver bars; Master, one silver bar; Ensign, a small gold cord on the front edge of the collar. Staff officers of corresponding assimilated rank are to wear the same designations. Stars, eagle, and bars to be parallel to the ends of the collar. The overcoats of *all other officers* than those above mentioned are to have no devices, and but seven buttons in each row.

PANTALOONS

For all officers, to be of navy-blue cloth or white drill, or for "service dress" of navy-blue fine flannel, and to be worn over the boots or shoes.

Within the tropics, white pantaloons are to be worn at all seasons, unless when otherwise authorized by the officer in command.

North of the tropics blue ones are to be worn from

the 1st of October to the 15th of May, and white ones from the 15th of May to the 1st of October; and *south* of the tropics *vice versa,* subject, however, to such exceptions as may be directed or authorized by the senior officer present in command.

VESTS

For all officers, single breasted, standing collar, with nine small navy buttons in front.

CAP AND CAP ORNAMENTS

Cap. Of dark blue cloth; top to be one-half inch greater diameter than the base; quarters one and a half inch wide between the seams; back of the band to be two inches wide between the points of the visor, with a welt half an inch from the lower edge, extending from point to point of the visor; band in front one and a half inch wide; bound, black patent leather visor, green underneath, two and a half inches wide, and rounded, as per pattern; inside of the band of heavy duck. The cap ornaments are to be worn on the band in front. During rainy weather a black cover may be worn over the cap.

Cap ornaments shall consist of a gold wreath in front, composed of oak and olive branches, three inches in width, and inclosing the following described devices:

For a Rear-Admiral. Two silver stars, each five-eighths of an inch in diameter, with their centres four-fifths of an inch apart.

For a Commodore, Captain, Commander, Lieutenant-Commander, Lieutenant, Master, and *Ensign.* A silver foul anchor, seven-eighths of an inch long, in a vertical position.

For Medical Officers. An oak leaf, in silver, nine-tenths of an inch long, in a vertical position.

For Paymasters. An oak sprig, composed of three leaves, in silver, nine-tenths of an inch in height, in a vertical position.

For Engineers. Four oak leaves, in silver, in the form of a cross, one and one-tenth of an inch horizontally, and nine-tenths of an inch vertically.

For Naval Constructors. A sprig, composed of two leaves of live-oak, in silver, in a vertical position, and with a spread of one and one-fourth of an inch.

For Chaplains. A silver cross, seven-eights of an inch in length, and one-half an inch in width, in an oblique position.

For Professors of Mathematics. The letter 𝔓, in silver, and in relief upon a plain gold circle, four-fifths of an inch in diameter,

For Secretaries. The letter 𝔖, in silver, one-half an inch in length.

For all other officers. Simply the wreath.

For more minute descriptions of the devices, and the manner of arranging them, see drawings.

STRAW HATS. In tropical climates, or during warm seasons, officers may wear white straw hats, under the same restrictions as in the case of jackets; the body of the hat to be not more than four and a half nor less than four inches in height, and the rim not more than three and a half nor less than three inches in width, with a plain band of black ribbon.

UNIFORM CIRCULAR NO. 3

Cap for Navy Officers. To be of dark-blue cloth, half an inch greater in diameter at the top than at the base; *quarters* to be one inch and a half between the seams; *outside band* to be two inches in width in the rear and one inch and a half in width in front—the points of the visor being the line of distinction, and the rear portion to have a welt half an inch from its lower edge, extending from point to point of the visor; *inside band* to be of uncolored leather, and one inch and a half wide in front and two inches wide in the rear; *linings* of the outer band to be of heavy duck, and of the cap to be of uncolored leather, which is to be sewed up with and form a part of the cap; *visor* to be of black patent leather on the upper side and bound with same, and to be green underneath; to be two inches and a half wide in front in all sizes of caps, and rounded as per pattern; the distance from point to point of the visor measuring across the cap to be the same width of the cap, and thus varying as the sizes vary; *strap* to be five eighths of an inch wide, with a gilt slide two inches from the right button, and a gilt loop the same distance from the left button; *buttons* to be placed below the welt, with their eyes passing through and secured on the inside of the cap; *cover*—during rainy weather only a black glazed silk cover may be worn over the cap, made so as to cover the visor also.

UNIFORM CIRCULAR NO. 1

Uniform of a Vice-Admiral. The Uniform of a Vice-Admiral shall be the same as that prescribed for a Rear-Admiral in the Regulation of a January 28, 1864, with the following exceptions:

Cap Ornaments. Three silver stars, instead of two, above the gold wreath—the third one equi-distant from and below the others, and partially covering a gold embroidered foul anchor, placed vertically.

Shoulder Straps. Three silver stars, instead of two—the centre one partially covering a gold foul anchor one inch in length, placed nearly horizontally, the tip of one of the rays passing through the ring of the anchor.

Sleeve Ornaments. A strip of gold lace two inches wide, with the lower edge an inch from the end of the sleeve, and two other strips of gold lace one inch wide with a space of half an inch between the wide

Naval uniforms. Gun crew on U.S. man-of-war. (National Archives)

Watch and chain. Watch of Capt. G. H. Amidon, Co. E, 4th Vermont Infantry. The chain was taken from a wounded soldier of the 93d Pa. Infantry at Gettysburg.

and narrow laces, respectively; also the gold star worn by line officers.

Overcoat Ornaments. Three silver stars on each end of the collar—two parallel with the end, the other in the rear of them—forming an equilateral triangle.

CHANGE IN SLEEVE ORNAMENTS OF REAR-ADMIRALS

The Sleeve Ornaments for a Rear-Admiral. Shall be the same as for a Vice-Admiral, except that there shall be one strip of one-inch lace, instead of two.

Sack Coats. Sack coats of Navy-blue flannel or blue cloth may be worn as "service dress" by all officers on board ship and in the United States, except at general muster or upon special occasions of ceremony, when a different dress is prescribed by the commanding officer; but never on shore, nor on board ship on duty in a foreign port. Shoulder straps and lace on the sleeves may be dispensed with on sack coats—retaining the star for line officers—in which case the designations of rank will be worn on the ends of the collar, omitting the centre ornament, except when it alone indicates rank. Sack coats shall be single-breasted, with a row of five buttons in front.

UNIFORM CIRCULAR No. 2. The regulations for the uniform of the United States Navy, approved January 28, 1864, are hereby altered and amended, so far as they relate to the uniform of Midshipmen, in the following respect, viz:

Cap Ornament. The gold wreath is abolished, and in the place thereof Midshipmen will wear a plain anchor, one inch and a quarter in length, embroidered in gold, and in a vertical position.

Jacket. To have a standing collar, one inch and a quarter high, with a plain anchor, one inch and a quarter in length, embroidered in gold, and in a horizontal position, on each end of the collar.

U. S. REVENUE CUTTER SERVICE. (From Regulations). Revenue officers are required to provide themselves with the uniforms prescribed by the Regulations, to wear them on board the vessels to which they belong, and while on duty in boarding vessels, and elsewhere.

The uniform established to distinguish the officers of the revenue cutter service is as follows:

DECK OFFICERS

Captain's Full Dress—Blue cloth frock coat, with rolling collar, double-breasted, lined with black silk, nine buttons on each lappel, two on upper part of skirt, and two on lower part of skirt; two strips of half-inch gold lace around the upper part of each cuff; two plain gold epaulettes; blue cloth Navy cap, with one band of gold lace, with ornament of Treasury shield within wreath in gold; with navy regulation sword; black silk cravat or stock; buff, blue, or white vest (according to the season), single-breasted, with nine buttons in front; blue pantaloons, with stripe of gold lace on outer seam, or white pantaloons, according to season.

Captain's Undress. Same as full dress, substituting

Infantry uniforms. These are soldiers of the 7th New York in their fancy gray uniforms much in evidence both in North and South early in the war. (National Archives)

Michigan soldiers, showing the change to a simpler garb as the war progressed. The man on the right is wearing a musician's sword, the one on the left has a bowie knife.

for the epaulettes a shoulder strap on each shoulder, of blue cloth, with raised gold edging; in the centre, two cross foul anchors; all of them to be worked in gold.

First Lieutenant's Full Dress. Same as captain, with the exception of one strip of lace on the cuff, and cap with one foul anchor, over shield, with wreath, all in gold.

Undress. The same as captain, with the same exceptions; shoulder strap to be with one foul anchor over shield, and two bars at each end; cap the same as in full dress.

Second Lieutenant. Dress and undress same as first lieutenant, omitting one bar at each end of shoulder strap.

Third Lieutenant. Dress and undress same as second lieutenant, omitting bars on shoulder straps.

ENGINEERS

Chief Engineers' Dress and Undress. Same as first lieutenant. Shoulder strap blue cloth, with raised gold edging, with gold wheel, surmounted by anchor; cap with band, with wheel surmounted by star within wreath, all in gold.

First Assistant Engineers. Same as chief engineer, substituting three buttons on cuff, in lieu of lace; shoulder strap same as chief engineer, omitting anchor; cap with gold band, with wheel inside of wreath, omitting star.

Second Assistant. Same as first assistant, omitting wheel on strap and cap.

Petty Officer's Dress. Blue cloth jacket, with nine revenue buttons on each lappel, three under each pocket flap, and three on each cuff; white or blue pantaloons (according to season).

Seaman, firemen, coal-passers, stewards, cooks, and boys, white frock, with collar and facings of blue, or blue frock (according to season); white or blue trousers; blue mustering cap or sennet hat.

VALISE, ARTILLERY. See HORSE EQUIPMENT and ARTILLERY.

VENT-COVER. See ARTILLERY.

VENT-PUNCH. See ARTILLERY.

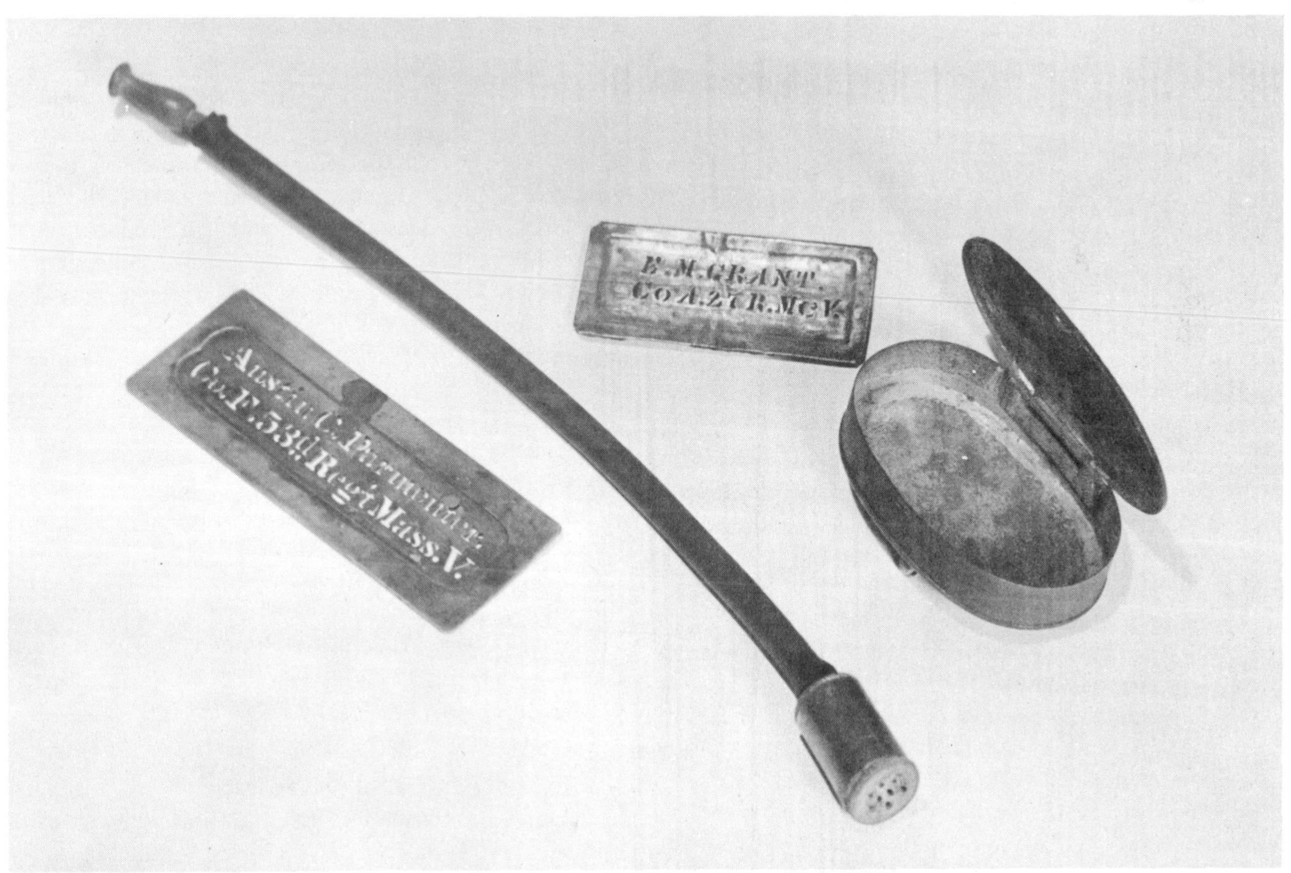

Water filter and soldiers' stencils. Depicts two small brass name stencils as used by Civil War soldiers to label their personal equipment, clothes, etc. Center one is of "E. M. Grant of 27th Maine Volunteers." One on the left to "Austin C. Parmenter of 53rd Regt., Mass. Vol." The long tube and container also shown in photo were allegedly captured from a Confederate soldier; a very old handwritten note accompanied the piece. It is a charcoal water filter. The cylindrical end with the perforated holes actually inserted in the stream, pond, etc., and water sucked through other end supposedly filtered by charcoal in center. This is the original tin container it came in. (Norm Flayderman)

VEST. See UNIFORMS AND CLOTHING.

WAGON, FIELD OFFICE. The office wagon of the XVIII Army Corps before Petersburg in 1864 had 3 panels on each side and 1 at the rear. All these panels let down to serve as desks. When they were opened, pigeon holes were disclosed, holding various papers, orders, etc. When not on the move, the wheels were removed and the desk wagon rested on wooden horses. The wagon was kept under a large tent, the rear part of which was utilized as corps headquarters.

WALLET AND MONEY BELT. Although definitely not issue items, the wallet or money belt was extensively used by soldiers during the Civil War. Apparently money belts were much less widely carried and are very rare so far as authenticated Civil War use is concerned.

WALLETS. Most wallets used were of brown leather, 4 to 4½ inches long and 2½ to 3 inches wide. Many have a wrap-around strap. In the author's collection is a wallet of finely-tooled leather 7½ inches long and 3⅝ inches wide. It belonged to Corporal H. V. Polley, 14th New Jersey Volunteers. The excellent quality of Polley's wallet is unusual. Moreover its large size rendered it cumbersome to carry in the field.

WARRANT. See DOCUMENTS.

WATCHES. During the winter of 1861-1862 the camp of the 3d New Hampshire Infantry was visited with the "watch fever," so-called, and it raged with such fury at one time that nearly every man was affected with it, and had a watch in each pocket. Many got nipped so badly by their first trade, that it also became their last one. The desire for watch trading ran so high that small groups of men could be seen hovering over dying campfires into the small hours of the morning, trading watches. The guards were finally instructed to arrest anyone who appeared like a watch fiend after taps. The fever broke after a while, as all fevers do, and soon disappeared, and with it the legion of watches, good, bad, and indifferent, that had been scattered through the regiment. Where they all came from, or where they went, no one knew.

Occasionally the men of a company would present their captain with an appropriately-engraved watch as a token of their respect and esteem. The one shown here was given to Captain G. H. Amidon, Co. E 4th Vermont Infantry. Captain Amidon was wounded at the Wilderness and at Cedar Creek. At the Wilderness his regiment lost 268 killed and wounded out of less than 500 engaged.

WATER BUCKET. See HORSE EQUIPMENTS and ARTILLERY.

WATER FILTER. The water filter had a metallic mouthpiece at one end of a guttapercha tube which was about 15 inches in length. At the other end of the tube was a suction chamber, an inch long by a half-inch in diameter with the end perforated and containing a piece of backing, functioning as a filter. Midway of the tubing was an air chamber. These filters were bought by unsuspecting soldiers early in the war, were used a few times, and then thrown away in disgust. Observers have commented on the comical sight of soldiers using their filters in muddy pools, with their eyes popping like frogs in the process. A somewhat simpler type of filter consisted of the same kind of mouthpiece, with rubber tubing attached to a small conical piece of pumice stone, through which the water was filtered. None of these filters were of any practical value and were rarely seen after the first year of the war.

Shown here is a charcoal water filter captured from a Confederate soldier. The cylindrical end with the perforated holes was inserted in the stream, pond, or puddle, and water sucked through the other end was supposedly filtered by the charcoal in the center. Photograph shows the original tin container the filter came in.

WHIP. See HORSE EQUIPMENT.

WINANS' STEAM GUN. This unique weapon was the invention of Charles S. Dickinson and was manufactured by Ross Winans, a locomotive manufacturer of Baltimore. It was claimed that this weapon could throw 200 balls a minute a distance of 2 miles; it was supposed to be bullet proof. Moreover, it was mounted on 4 wheels for mobility and supposedly could project missiles of any size from a bullet to a 100-pound cannon ball. According to the New York *Tribune*, May 4, 1861, the boiler was like that of an ordinary steam fire-engine. There was only one barrel, on a pivot, which was fed through a hopper.

The Winans' gun never was tested in battle; it was captured by the Federals May 11, 1861. The captors, members of the 6th Massachusetts Infantry, placed the gun in position to guard the viaduct over the Patuxent of the Washington branch of the B & O Railway.

WIPER. See APPENDAGES.

WORM. See ARTILLERY.

WRITING EQUIPMENT. Most men wrote letters, or had friends write for them. A few men in every unit seemed to spend all their spare time in letter writing. This was especially true in the early months of a soldier's service. Men squatted on the ground or muddy logs, about camp fires under the cold stars, whose unfathomable distances suggested to homesick warriors their far-away homes. And they

Winans Steam gun. (Harpers)

wrote home. Clumsy fingers, which had not uncorked an ink bottle since the owner's last one was shed out of the schoolhouse window years before, wrestled with exasperating pen, delusive ink, and intractable paper. Crouching in tent or stockade-bunk, in barracks, or about the crackling rail-fires, the soldiers whipped their distracted thoughts into letter composition.

At first, the soldiers used stamps on their letters, although later in the war the Government issued an order permitting soldiers to send letters without prepayment; but it was necessary to write on the outside "Soldier's Letter." A verse appeared on one of these letters ran as follows:

Soldier's letter, nary red,
Hardtack and no soft bread,
Postmaster, please put it through,
I've nary cent, but six months due.

Envelopes. There was a great variety of patriotic envelopes used in the war, and collections of these contain, in some cases, hundreds of items, all with different designs. The main motif is always patriotic, however, and the variations are endless. Many have the American eagle with a timely motto like: "The Union. It must and shall be preserved!" Others have portraits of men in the past, such as Washington, or contemporary figures like Lincoln, McClellan, Rosecrans, or Butler. The political scene was not neglected. Caricatures of Jeff Davis, Floyd, and other Confederate leaders were very common. Much rarer were envelopes with maps in bright colors. Probably the rarest of all were those envelopes made for specific units, such as the 1st Ohio Battery and the 24th Massachusetts Volunteers. Examples of these main types are shown here.

Letter writing equipment was sold in stationers at home and by sutlers at the front. The U.S. Christian Commission furnished paper and envelopes to the men free of charge. Christian Commission envelopes bear the stamp or name of the Commission and "Soldier's Letter" in one corner.

Ink. While soldiers had to buy their own ink, mainly from sutlers, ink was issued to units for official correspondence and company clerks normally used ink in filling out the forms required by regulations for each unit from company to army. Government ink was issued in glass bottles with glass stoppers.

Miscellaneous items: left to right (rear row) collapsible candlestick; inkwell; folding candlestick; pewter inkwell; collapsible candlestick. In the foreground: two lead candlesticks and a mechanical pencil. (Herschel C. Logan)

Paper and envelopes.

Paper. The stationery of the Civil War ranged from plain coarse yellow paper to excellent writing paper decorated with much the same partriotic cartoons and slogans as were the envelopes.

Pen. Most official documents and many such unofficial items as letters and diaries were written in ink. The pens used were mostly wood with steel points.

Pencil. Enough specimens are still extant for us to know that pencils have changed little in the century since the war. From the diaries and other written material dating from the war it is obvious that all soldiers who could write had pencils and used them.

Small Writing Kit (Patent No. 34,168). Patented January 14, 1862 by H. C. Small, East Limington, Maine. This invention combined a writing case and checker board in such manner that the checker board occupied but little space in the writing case. The case also had compartments for pens, ink, postage stamps, checkers in one part; envelopes, penholders, and pencil in another part.

Stamps. Before the Government permitted soldiers to send letters without charge, postage was necessary. However, due to the early disappearance of silver money in the war, postage stamps took its place as an unofficial medium of exchange. This was before paper scrip was issued by the Government as a replacement for the silver money. When soldiers left for the front they took large quantities of stamps with them, some for use on letters, but most for use as money. Many an old soldier after the war remembered his disgust on finding what a mess his stamps were in either from rain, perspiration, or compression, as he attempted, after a hot march, to get one for a letter. If he could split off one from a welded mass of perhaps a hundred or more he counted himself fortunate. Of course they could be soaked out after a while, but he would need to dry them on a hot surface later because they were so sticky.

Whittier Writing Kit (Patent No. 37,326). Patented January 6, 1863 by Horace C. Whittier, Plymouth, Mass. Consisted of a folding cylinder divided longitudinally by a joint; one-half was a box and the other half its cover. At one end of the case was an inkstand, while the rest of the case was occupied a roll, which, when extended, formed a writing tablet.

Writing Guide. This item looks like a ruler but has no graduated scale. The guide is a bit thicker than a ruler and is used as a straight-edge. Thousands of these, varying in size and type, were used during the war. All clerks, scribes, and others charged with preparing official correspondence and paperwork must have used them. In many cases where Army paperwork is displayed, note the straight lines and the fact that the lower loops of some letters have been cut off, showing that a guide was used. The guide illustrated here is especially nice; it is made of maple and beautifully painted in red and black with "Major George D. Savage–12th Regiment MHV."

Writing Kit. The Ferris Collection has a writing kit carried by Sergeant H. Dwight Grant, Co. I 117th New York Infantry. This kit is 8½ inches long, 2 inches in diameter, and rolls up into a cylinder and is tied by two strings attached to the black leather cover. Total weight–10 ounces. Marked as follows:

Patented Jan. 5, 1864
Brooks' Patent
D. B. Brooks & Brother Salem, Mass.

The Flayderman collection contains two very interesting and very scarce Civil War period collapsible/portable soldiers' writing "desks." When closed they are perfectly round-cylindrical shaped 8½" x 2" diameter. When unrolled, the wood section of the desk, which is composed of a number of fitted slats, folds out straight and a crossbar on the under side swivels open, fastens under two hooks making the desk "top" completely flat and solid. Marked on the cross piece "Patented December 24, 1861." Interesting to note that one of these is beautifully marked on the inside "B. B. Mayberry, Lowell, Mass., 15th Mass. Battery" and also "William H. Nichols, Co. E, 6th Regiment MVM." The 6th Mass. Regiment was nicknamed "The Writing Regiment" because of the unusually large amount of correspondence kept up between the boys and home.

Inkwells. Left to right: Tin inkwell from Fredericksburg; glass inkwell from Falmouth, Va.; wooden inkwell from Antietam. Silver inkwell.

Writing guide belonging to Major Savage. (Norm Flayderman)

APPENDIX

FEDERAL CONTRACTORS AND PATENTEES OF MILITARY EQUIPMENT 1861-1865

The following list, though not complete, will assist collectors by naming individuals and firms definitely identified. It is hoped that collectors and students will supply additional data for subsequent editions of this book. Some U.S. cannon and small arms have been omitted since they are covered in the discussion under the appropriate headings. Moreover, the text of this book contains the names of many individuals and firms which therefore are not included below.

ACCOUTERMENTS, KNAPSACKS, etc.

BAKER, JOHN A., 63 Walker Street, New York, N.Y. Accouterments, hatchets, kettles, mess pans.

BAKER, L. S., New York, N.Y. Cap boxes, infantry cartridge boxes.

BALDWIN, WILLIAM, 102 Broad Street, New York, N.Y. Accouterments, tents, kettles, mess pans.

BARTLETT, E., 253 Pearl Street, New York, N.Y.

BELL, J. T., New York, N.Y. Small cartridge box.

BENNETT AND VIELE, New York, N.Y.

BETTS, NICHOLS CO., 349 Broadway, New York, N.Y. Infantry equipments.

BITTER, HENRY, 19 Spruce Street, New York, N.Y. Accouterments, knapsacks.

BLACK, JOHN. Made knapsacks for New York.

BOURNE, L., JR. & CO., 2 Jacob Street, New York, N.Y.

BOYD, J. & SONS. Infantry cartridge boxes marked "Makers of Army Accoutrements, Boston."

BYRNE, GEORGE C., New York, N.Y. All types of accouterments.

CONDICT, J. E., 57 White Street, New York, N.Y. Cavalry cartridge boxes, cap boxes.

CONDICT, WOOLEY & CO., Chicago, Illinois. Horse equipments, including Grimsley-style saddle equipments; also McClellan saddles.

CONDIT, S. H. & CO., Newark, N.J.

COOPER & SON, New York, N.Y. Accouterments, kettles, mess pans, hatchets.

CORBET, H. A., St. Louis, Mo. Cap boxes.

CRANE, THEODORE T., 96 Wall Street, New York, N.Y. Knapsacks, haversacks, mess pans, kettles.

CROSSMAN, E. A. & CO., Newark, N.J. Cavalry cartridge boxes.

CROSSMAN, M. B., 258 Market Street, New York, N.Y.

CUMMINGS, J., Springfield, Mass. Cavalry cartridge boxes.

DAVY, JOSEPH. Newark, N.J. Cap boxes.

DINGEE, H. A., (Dingee of DINGEE & LORIGAN?), New York, N.Y. Cartridge boxes.

FRANKENHEIMER BROTHERS, 309 Broadway, New York, N.Y.

FRODSHAM, BRIDGE AND MORRIS LEVETT, New York, N.Y. Patent knapsack, Oct. 1, 1861.

GARRICK, THOMAS, Providence, R. I. Patent knapsack Sept. 24, 1861.

GAYLORD, E., Chicopee, Mass. Accouterments for cavalry, cap boxes.

GODWIN, JOS. H., New York, N.Y. Accouterments, tents, camp kettles, mess pans, hatchets.

GURNEE, W. S., Chicago, Ill. Accouterments and uniforms.

HAEDRICK, H. G., Philadelphia, Pa. Cap boxes.

HART, BENJ. J. AND BRO., New York, N.Y.

HARTLEY, WM. B., New York, N.Y.

HITCHCOCK, J. H., 160 Broadway, New York, N.Y.

HOOVER, CALHOUN & CO., New York, N.Y. Cavalry cartridge boxes.

HOW, JOHN, St. Louis, Mo. Horse equipments, canteens, boots, shoes, haversacks, knapsacks, uniforms.

HOWELL, T. P. AND CO. Knapsacks.

HUNT, SIMON B., New York, N.Y.

JASSATH, G., New York, N.Y.

JENNE, P. & SONS, Hartford, Conn.

JEWELL, P. & SONS, Hartford and New York, N.Y. Cartridge boxes, gun slings.

JEWETT, A. & CO. Knapsacks.

KING, D.B., Waterford, N.Y. Cartridge boxes.

KINSEY, W. & CO., Newark, N.J. Cap boxes, cavalry cartridge boxes.

KITTREDGE, B. & CO., Cincinnati, Ohio. Manufactured the metal Bennett cartridge box. Also was the manufacturer of the Wesson carbines.

LAGOWITZ, J., 19 Dey St., New York, N.Y.

LINDEN, CLARENCE, Eden Township, Illinois. Patent 36,-618, dated October 7, 1862. Patented an "air bed" which was provided with an outside cover of enameled cloth or leather. When the bed was uninflated it could be folded so as to form a knapsack and was provided with straps to be worn as such.

LONGLEY & CO., Lewiston, Maine. Cartridge and Cap boxes.

LOWDER, ROBERT, 79 Bleecker St., New York, N.Y.

LYALL, J. AND W. Knapsacks.

MANN. Cartridge boxes marked "Col. Mann's Patent. Reissued June 7th 1864 E. Gaylord, Maker, Chicopee, Mass."

McCOMB, H. S. Knapsacks and greatcoat straps.

McLAUGHLIN, J. F., Troy, N.Y.

MARKEY, C. G. Contractor for rifleman's pouch.

MERRILL, L. T., New York, N.Y. Accouterments, kettles, mess pans, hatchets.

METZGER, E., Philadelphia, Pa. Navy cap boxes, Infantry cartridge boxes.

MOONEY, JAMES E., Indianapolis, Indiana. Cartridge boxes for State of Indiana.

MORRISON, HURD & CO., 35 Chamber St., New York, N.Y.

NEECE, R., Philadelphia, Pa. Cavalry cartridge boxes.

PETERS & BENNER, Newark, N.J.

PETTY & MORRISON, 77 Chambers St., New York, N.Y. Knapsacks and straps, haversacks.

PHILLIPS, ANDREW J., 12 Cedar St., New York, N.Y.

Cartridge boxes, plates, and belts Cap boxes and cone picks.
PITTMAN, J. I., New York, N.Y. Cartridge boxes.
SCHMIDT, E. L., 211 & 213 Centre St., New York, N.Y.
SENNY, AMOS., 45 Liberty St., New York, N.Y.
SHATTUCK, W. F., Knapsacks and straps for New York.
SHEPARD, I. J. Eagle plates. Possibly an inspector.
SHORT, JOSEPH, New York, N.Y. Patent for a waterproof overcoat which can be "readily transformed into a tent, knapsack or cavalry roll." Oct. 8, 1861.
SICKLES AND CO., St. Louis, Mo. Cavalry cartridge boxes.
SIMONS, HENRY. Knapsacks.
SMITH, J. A. ADAMS, Batavia, N.Y. Accouterments, kettles, mess pans, hatchets.
SMITH, JAMES S. & CO., 15 Dutch St., New York, N.Y. Accouterments, mess pans, hatchets.
SMITH, JAMES T. & CO., 344 Broadway, New York, N.Y. Accouterments, tents, kettles, mess pans, hatchets.
SMITH, MOSES & CO., 228 W. 22nd St., New York, N.Y. Accouterments, tents, kettles, mess pans.
SMITH & GODWIN. Gun slings.
SMITH, THOMAS C., New York, N.Y. Accouterments, knapsacks, haversacks, bayonet scabbards, belts.
SPROULS, MEEKER & CO., 27 Church St., New York, N.Y. Cavalry cartridge boxes.
STERLING, STANSBURY & CO., St. Louis, Mo. Knapsacks and straps.
STERN, M., 59 Broadway, New York, N.Y.
STEVENS, F., Pearl St., New York, N.Y. Knapsacks and straps for New York.
STOKLY (?) & CO., St. Louis, Mo. Cap boxes.
STONE, ISRAEL, New York, N.Y. Knapsacks and Haversacks.
STORMS, C. S., New York, N.Y. All leather equipments.
SUTHERLAND, D. J., 120 South 17th St., Philadelphia, Pa. Accouterments, kettles, mess pans.
THAXTER, J. B. Cap box marked with this name and "HAND, ME. 1862."
TURNER & SIBLEY, Chicago, Ill. Knapsacks, haversacks, cavalry equipments.
VAN BRUNT, JAMES A., Brooklyn, N.Y. Knapsacks and haversacks.
VAN CLEVE, JOSEPH, 190 Market St., Newark, N.J. Accouterments, bayonet scabbards and frogs.
VAN RIPER, P. V. H., Paterson, N.J. Cartridge boxes.
WAGONER, F. C., 91 Liberty St., New York, N.Y. Knapsacks, haversacks.
WALEY, NATHAN, 71 Vesey St., New York, N.Y.
WATERTOWN ARSENAL. Cap boxes marked: "Watertown Arsenal" and dated 1863 and 1864.
WATKINS AND SLAUGHTER. Furnished 3000 complete sets of infantry equipment to State of Indiana.
WEATHERBY AND SON, Cincinnati, Ohio.
WIGGINS AND CO., Richmond, Indiana.
WILKESON, H. W., Springfield, Mass. Eagle plates, cavalry cartridge boxes, carbine slings.
WILKINSON, W. M. & CO., Springfield, Mass. Cavalry cartridge boxes.
WOODRUFF, BARNET & CO. (also given as WOODRUFF, BURNETT & CO.), 61 Reed St., New York, N.Y. Knapsacks.
WOODRUFF, FRENCH AND CO., 61 Reade St., New York, N.Y.
WORTHINGTON, GEO., 342 Broadway, New York, N.Y. Knapsacks.
YOUNG, S. H., Newark, N.J. Cap boxes and cartridge boxes.

AMMUNITION AND PROJECTILES

(Most artillery projectiles are discussed under PROJECTILES, ARTILLERY in the text.)

AMERICAN FLASK AND CAP CO., Waterbury, Conn. Percussion caps.
BARTHOLOW, ROBERTS. U.S. Army. Patent for improved waterproof cartridges, May 21, 1861.
BUCKEL, GEORGE AND EDWARD DORSCH. Patent for improvement in fixed cartridges, July 22, 1856.
ELEY, London.
GOLDMARK, J. "Small Ammunition manufacturer of New York." Supplied musket caps.
HICKS (see American Flask and Cap Co.).
JAMES, CHARLES T. Patent for improvement in projectiles, February 26, 1856.
JOHNSTON, ALGERNON K., Middletown, Conn. and LORENZO DOW, Topeka, Kansas. Patent for cartridges, October 1, 1861.
McMURRY, VINKLE, MEYER AND CO., St. Louis, Mo., 1861. Supplied large amounts of artillery ammunition.
MAYNARD, EDWARD. Patent for improvement in cartridges, June 17, 1856.
MONT STORM, WILLIAM, New York, N.Y. Patent for skin cartridges, October 29, 1861.
MOWREY. Foundries at St. Louis and Cincinnati. Supplied artillery projectiles.
MURRAY, STEVENSON & DAVIS, Portsmouth, Ohio. Artillery projectiles.
READ, WILLIAM & SON. Supplied cartridges and friction primers to Mass.
RIEDEL, JULIUS. Patent for improvement in cartridges, Sept. 9, 1856.
SHALER, REUBEN, Madison, Conn. Patent for cartridges, July 16, 1861.
WHITE, ROLLIN, Davenport, Iowa. Patent for cartridges, Nov. 26, 1861.

APPENDAGES AND CARTRIDGE MAKING MACHINES

ALLEN, ETHAN, Worcester, Massachusetts. Patent for making metallic cartridges, March 19, 1861.
[ANONYMOUS] Adjustable tompion marked "Patented Nov. 24, 1863."
BUTTERFIELD, JESSE S. AND SIMEON MARSHALL. Patent for improved cartridge opener, May 13, 1856.
KINSLEY, RHODOLPHUS, Springfield, Massachusetts. Patent (34,430) dated February 18, 1862. This tompion was made with the shank concave, so as to give less bearing on the inner surface of the gun. The tompion consisted of a wooden pin split in two parts for a portion of its length, and having a spring of metal or rubber inserted to force the wood against the bore of the gun.
LELONG, LOUIS AND JOHN DECAMP, Newark, N.J. Patent for gun capper, Oct. 22, 1861.
MAYNARD, EDWARD, Washington, D.C. Patent for cartridge loader April 2, 1861.
PARMENTER, FLAVEL W., Troy, N.Y. A one-time foreman of U.S. Arsenal at West Troy, N.Y. He sold a bullet-making machine to New York state.
SEELY, EDGAR D., Brookline, Massachusetts. Patent for gun capper Oct. 29, 1861.

BADGES

BALCH, C. L. AND CO., 208 Broadway, N.Y. Sold cavalry and artillery badges, as well as corps badges. Solid silver badges were $1.50; (letters in gold relief—$2.00). Solid gold badges were $5.00. For all badges, inscription of battles was 20 cents extra.
DROWNE AND MOORE, 208 Broadway, N.Y. This firm of "manufacturing jewelers" sold Army badges and "veteran pins" at $6.50 each for 18 karat gold pins, and $1.50 each for those of solid silver.
HAYWARD, B. T., 208 Broadway, New York. Solid silver badges for any corps or division in the Army, or a cavalry artillery, engineer, or pontooneer's badges with

owner's name, regiment, and company "handsomely engraved" thereon.

KEITH, R., 15 John St., New York. Corps badges and silver shields engraved with name and unit.

PHILIP, LOUIS AND CO., 609 Broadway, New York. Maker of "National Battle Pins" for the Army and Navy. These pins were of silver and in addition to a military decoration were inscribed with the soldier's company and regiment or the sailor's ship.

WARD, S. M. AND CO., 208 Broadway, New York. This firm of "manufacturing jewelers" sold "Battle Pins" with soldier or sailor's name, list of battles, and unit. Price was $1.50 for either solid silver or "fine gold plate."

BELT BUCKLES (U.S.)

BOYD AND SONS, Boston, Mass.
DINGEE, H. A., New York, N.Y.
GAYLORD, E., Chicopee, Mass.
LOWELL, W. L.
PITTMAN, J. T., New York, N.Y.
SMITH, W. H., Brooklyn, N.Y.
WILKINSON, Springfield, Mass.

BLACKING

BROWN, B. F. AND CO., Boston, Mass. "The army and navy paste blacking gives universal satisfaction. For sale throughout the Union."

BLANKETS

BEATTIE, ROBERT AND SON.
CRONIN, HUXTHAL & SEARS. Blankets—contract May 24, 1861 for New York.
CROW, McCREARY & CO., St. Louis, Mo.
DIMICK, J. W.
DUNKER, JOSEPH H. (or "DRINKER")
FIELD, BROTHER AND CO., St. Louis, Mo.
GILES, JOHN T.
HAYNES, LORD AND CO.
HIGGINS, E. S. AND CO.
HUNT, VOSE AND CO.
HUTCHINSON AND BARR.
MUIR, JAMES, ROTHSCHILD CO.
MURPHY, THOMAS.
ONTARIO WOOLEN CO.
PARKER, WILDER & CO., New York, N.Y.
PATON AND CO.
PAULE AND WALTON, St. Charles, Mo.
ROBINSON, H. & CO., Philadelphia, Pa.
STEWART, A. T. & CO.
STONE, BOWMAN & BLISS, Boston, Mass.
TURNBULL, SLADE & CO., New York, N.Y.

BOOT-JACK

WATSON, E. P., Box 773, New York, N.Y. A patent ounce spur carrier and boot-drawer.

BUTTONS, U.S.

The following is a list of the principal U.S. button manufacturers. Many buttons have the names of dealers and military outfitters but are not listed here.

DALE, T. N. & CO., New York
DRUCKER, New York
EVANS, D., Attleboro
GODDARD & BRO.
GOODYEAR (maker of rubber buttons. Also made by Novelty Rubber Co.)
HOOD, T. G., Philadelphia
HORSTMANN BROS. & CO.
MINTZER, W. G., Philadelphia
SCHUYLER, HARTLEY & GRAHAM
SCOVILL MANUFACTURING CO., Waterbury, Conn.
SIMMONS, G. W. & CO., Boston
SMITH, W. H. & CO.
STEELE & JOHNSON, Waterbury
WANAMAKER & BROWN, Philadelphia
WATERBURY BUTTON CO., 49 Chambers St., New York, N.Y., and 17 Federal Street, Boston, Mass. (also called the "Army and Navy Button Co.")

The author has also seen statements that E. A. ARMSTRONG, Detroit, Michigan, was a button dealer, perhaps a manufacturer. A musician's button found at Fredericksburg was marked "J. H. WILSON, Phil." It should be pointed out that many Civil War buttons do not have the maker's names but are merely stamped "Extra Quality" or "Superior Quality." Moreover, many buttons have no markings at all.

BUTTONS, C.S.

Some of these were dealers, not manufacturers of buttons, but these names do appear on the backs of the buttons.

BALDWIN, H. E. AND CO., New Orleans, La.
BELLENOT AND ULRICH, New Orleans, La.
CANFIELD BROTHERS AND CO., Baltimore, Md.
COURTNEY AND TENNENT, Charleston, S.C.
GMINDER, JACOB, Baltimore, Md.
HALFMANN, E., Montgomery, Ala.
HALFMANN AND TAYLOR, Montgomery, Ala.
HYDE AND GOODRICH, New Orleans, La.
KENT, PAINE AND CO., Richmond, Va.
LEWIS, E. M. AND CO., Richmond, Va.
MYERS, S. A., Richmond, Va.
MITCHELL AND TYLER, Richmond, Va.
ROUYER, C., New Orleans, La.
WENDLINGER, C., Richmond, Va.
WILDT, W., Richmond, Va.

BUTTONS, FOREIGN (USED BY C.S.A.)

BIRD, WILLIAM AND CO., London, Eng.
BUCKLEY, S. AND CO., Birmingham, Eng.
CAMPBELL, S. ISAACS AND CO., London, Eng.
CHATWIN AND SON. Birmingham, Eng.
DOWLER, WM. H., Birmingham, Eng.
FIRMIN AND SONS, London, Eng.
G & CIE (GOURDIN AND CO.), Paris, France
HAMMOND, TURNER AND BATES, Manchester, Eng.
HAMMOND, TURNER AND SONS, Birmingham, Eng.
HERBERT AND CO., London, Eng.
JENNENS AND CO., London, Eng.
SILVER, R. W. AND CO., London, Eng.
SMITH AND WRIGHT, Birmingham, Eng.
STARKEY, JOS., London, Eng.
TAIT, P., Limerick.
T. W. AND W. (TRELON, WELDON AND WEIL), Paris, France.
VAN WART SONS AND CO.
C. AND J. W. (C. AND J. WELDON), London, Eng.

CAMP EQUIPMENT

AMES, OLIVER & CO. Shovels.

ANDREWS, BENJAMIN, Philadelphia, Pa. Patent for army trunk, Nov. 5, 1861.

ASHOLD, ABEL, Garrettsville, Ohio. Patent for camp stools, Sept. 17, 1861.

ATWATER, J. H. & CO., 270-272 Pearl St., New York, N.Y. In 1861 contracted for 1500 camp kettles in nests of three—weight of 18 lbs. a nest. Also, 3000 mess pans, weight 1 lb. each.

BALL, H. W., New York, N.Y. Patent for a camp stove Nov. 5, 1861.

BELL, THOMAS M., 203 Pearl St., New York, N.Y. Camp kettles and mess pans.

CARNER, A. S., Brooklyn, N.Y. Patent for camp chest Nov. 19, 1861.

CHASE, WESLEY, Buffalo, N.Y. Patent for camp chest. Oct. 29, 1861.

CHILD, PRATT AND FOX. In 1861-1862 supplied U.S. with saddles, horse equipments, blankets, portable forges, camp kettles, mess equipment, overcoats, hatchets, knapsacks.

CONGER, WALTER M. 100,000 mess pans.

CRANE, S. G., Rochester, N.Y. Patent for camp chairs July 16, 1861.

CUSHING & MACK, Lowell, Mass. Stoves and stove pipes.

FILLEY, GILES F., St. Louis, Mo. Stoves, camp kettles, mess pans.

FILLEY, O. D., St. Louis, Mo. Tin plates and cups, camp kettles, mess pans.

HARDIE, J. W., New York, N.Y. Patent for army trunk, Nov. 5, 1861.

HARDY, PETER J., New York, N.Y. Patent for camp chair, Aug. 20, 1861.

HIGGINS, G. A., New York, N.Y. Patent for camp stove, Nov. 12, 1861.

IRWIN, C. W., St. Louis, Mo. Patent for camp chest, Dec. 17, 1861.

JEWETT, ALBERT, New York. Spades, hatchet handles, camp kettles.

JOHNSON, GEORGE W., New York. Camp kettles, mess pans.

JOHNSON, NATHANIEL, New York. Patent for camp stools, July 2, 1861.

KEMBLE, P., 29 West St., New York. Camp kettles, mess pans.

LANE, GEORGE C., Buffalo, N.Y. Patent for camp chest, Oct. 22, 1861.

LATHROP, RALPH P., Albany, N.Y. Contract with New York state for 5,000 hatchets, June 18, 1861.

MC KENZIE, DUNCAN, Brooklyn, N.Y. Patent for camp stove, Sept. 24, 1861.

MANN, HARVEY, JR., Bellefonte, Pa. Axes.

METTAM, CHARLES, New York, N.Y. Patent for camp cot, July 23, 1861.

MULLIGAN's Patent mess kettle, consisting of several parts, all fitting into one kettle. LaLANCE & GROSJEAN, 273 Pearl St., New York.

PARR, GEORGE, Buffalo, N.Y. Patent for camp chest, June 25, 1861.

PEROT, T. MORRIS & CO., 314 Vine Street, Philadelphia, Pa. Mess chest containing kettles, mess pans, tea kettle, coffee and tea pot, tin cups and tumblers, frying pan, gridiron, cans for tea, coffee, sugar, and butter, plates, knives, and works, cook's knife, spoons, ladles. Also, each chest had a large sheet-iron stove, a tin oven, and a box lantern. The chest when opened formed a table.

RYAN, JOHN B. On April 3, 1862 sent the Quartermaster General an 8-page pamphlet describing his "Army Stove" which was portable, weighed 70 lbs., and would reduce the use of cord wood since only 30 would be necessary per regiment.

SCOTT, I. & CO., 5 Cannon St., New York. Camp kettles, Mess pans.

WHITE, WILLIAM, Newark, N.J. Hatchets.

CANTEENS AND WATER FILTERS

BALDWIN AND JOHNSON, 63 Maiden Lane, New York, N.Y. Canteens, kettles, mess pans.

BARTHOLOMAE, CHARLES, New York, N.Y. Patent for a canteen, July 9, 1861.

BELL, THOMAS M., New York, N. Y. Contract of May 9, 1861 for 15,000 canteens covered with heavy cloth—strap 5½ feet long with buckle, cork attached by a nut chain.

CASE, JOHN, Philadelphia, Pa. Patent for a canteen, July 9, 1861.

COMPTON & CO. (England). Pewter Medical canteen dated 1861.

HALL, HENRY A., Boston, Mass. Patent for a portable filter with an India rubber tube, May 21, 1861.

HERBERT, SAMUEL, New York, N.Y. Patent for a canteen, Oct. 29, 1861.

JENNINGS, LEWIS, Brooklyn, N.Y. Patent for a filtering cup, Sept. 10, 1861.

MONTGOMERY, J. A., Williamsport, Pa. Patent for a canteen, Sept. 24, 1861.

MORRISON, S. G., Williamsport, Pa. Patent for a canteen, Dec. 24, 1861.

ROBBINS, GEORGE & CO., New York, N.Y. Supplied canteens, corks, and straps.

RUSSELL, STEPHEN H., Boston, Mass. Patent for a canteen filter with drinking tube, Aug. 20, 1861.

TIFFANY & CO. Supplied canteens, corks and straps.

CARBINES

Springfield musketoons, carbines and the pistol carbine—all manufactured prior to 1861—are omitted from the following list since these weapons were government made and not by contractors. Only the earliest patent date is given in the following list of carbine manufacturers.

BALL, ALBERT, Worcester, Mass. Caliber .50, patent June 23, 1863; 1,002 purchased by U.S.

BALLARD, C. H. Caliber .54; patent Nov. 5, 1861; 1,509 purchased by U.S. and many others by state militia units.

BURNSIDE, A. E., Providence, R.I. Caliber .54; patent March 25, 1856; 55,567 purchased 1861-1865.

COLT, SAMUEL, Hartford, Conn. Caliber .56; model 1855; between 5-6,000 purchased by militia 1861-1865.

GALLAGER, M. J., Savannah, Ga. Caliber .54; patent July 17, 1860; 17,728 purchased August 31, 1861—December 10, 1864.

GIBBS, L. H., New York. Caliber .54; patent Jan. 8, 1856; 1,052 purchased May 30-June 24, 1863.

GREENE, J. DURRELL. U.S. Army. Caliber .53; patent June 27, 1854; 200 purchased May 24, 1855 and others purchased from Great Britain during the Civil War.

GWYN, EDWIN AND CAMPBELL, A.C., Hamilton, Ohio. Caliber .52; patent Oct. 21, 1862; 9,342 purchased 1861-1865.

HALL, J. H., Harpers Ferry, Va. Caliber .64; model 1837; smoothbore breechloader. This basic model, with later variations, saw extensive service up through 1861.

HOWARD, CHAS. Caliber. 44; patent Oct. 28, 1862; no record of U.S. purchase.

JENKS, W. M., Chicopee Falls, Mass. Caliber .54; patent May 25, 1835; used by Navy and Cavalry units.

JOSLYN, BENJAMIN F., Worcester, Mass. Caliber .54; patent Aug. 28, 1855; 860 purchased by U.S. up to July 22, 1862, and many thousands more up through 1865.

LEE, JAMES P., Milwaukee, Wisc. Caliber .44; patent July 22, 1862; 1,000 ordered by U.S. April 18, 1965, but later cancelled.

LINDNER, EDWARD. Caliber .58; patent Mar. 29, 1859; 892 purchased.

MAYNARD, EDWARD, Washington, D.C. Caliber .50; patent May 27, 1856; 20,202 purchased 1861-1865.

MERRILL, J. H., Baltimore, Md. Caliber .54; patent July 1858; 14,695 purchased 1861-1865.

MERRILL, LATROBE AND THOMAS. Caliber .58; patent applied for Jan. 8, 1856; 170 purchased July 26, 1855.

PALMER, WM., New York. Caliber .52; patent Dec. 22, 1863; 1,001 purchased during Civil War.

PEABODY, HENRY O., Boston, Mass. Caliber .50; patent July 22, 1862; no record of purchases.

PERRY, A. D., Newark, N. J. Caliber .54; patent Jan. 16, 1855; 200 purchased April 12, 1855.

REMINGTON, Ilion, N.Y. Caliber .50 and .46; patent Dec. 23, 1863; 5,000 of cal. .46 model furnished the Govt. March 30, 1865-June 30, 1865.

SHARPS, C. Caliber .52; patent Oct. 5, 1852, 80,512 purchased 1861-65.

SHARPS AND HANKINS, Philadelphia, Pa. Caliber .52; patent July 9, 1861; used in Navy in 1866 and some issued to Cavalry regiments during Civil War.

SMITH, GILBERT, Buttermilk Falls, N.Y. Caliber .50; patent Aug. 5, 1856; 30,062 purchased 1861-1865.

SPENCER, C. M., South Manchester, Conn. Caliber .50 and .52; patent March 6, 1860; 77,181 purchased by U.S. and others by state and local organizations during Civil War.

STARR, E. T., Yonkers, N.Y. Caliber .54; patent Sept. 14, 1858; 20,601 purchased during Civil War.

SYMMES, J. C. U. S. Army. Caliber .54; patent Nov. 16, 1858; 200 purchased July 18, 1855.

TRIPLETT AND SCOTT. Caliber .50; patent Dec. 6, 1864. No record of use during Civil War.

WARNER, JAMES, Springfield, Mass. Caliber .50; patent Feb. 23, 1864; 1,501 purchased in 1864 and 2,500 purchased in 1865.

WESSON, FRANKLIN. Caliber .44; patent Nov. 11, 1862; 151 purchased by U.S. and others by state militia units during Civil War.

WILLIAMSON, DAVID, Brooklyn, N.Y. Caliber .50; patent Nov. 22, 1864; no record of purchase during the Civil War.

CARDS, PLAYING

CASWELL, H. A., 60 Nassau Street, New York, N.Y. Advertised "something new in playing cards. Love scenes. Designs from French artists." These cards could be used as ordinary playing cards but because of their elegant design "combined pleasure with amusement."

HITCHCOCK, BENJ. W. In 1862 copyrighted his "Union Cards" which were manufactured by the American Card Company, 14 Chambers St. and 165 William St., New York, N.Y.

CASKETS

FISK'S METALLIC BURIAL CASKET, W. M. RAYMOND & CO., Newtown, Long Island, N.Y.; Warerooms and office, 348 Pearl Street, New York, N.Y. The caskets were "perfectly airtight, indestructible and free from encroachments of vermin or water."

COMPASS

HUNTER, H. W., 169 William St., New York, N.Y. Maker of Hunter's Patent Army day and night pocket compass.

FIELD GLASSES AND TELESCOPES

HORN, B. H., 212 Broadway, New York. Maker of field and navy glasses, telescopes and eye glasses.

SEMMONS & CO., OPTICIANS, 669½ Broadway, New York, N.Y. Telescopes for the Army and Navy.

FLAGS, COLORS AND GUIDONS

EATON, CHARLES O. Supplied colors and guidons to Mass.

ERTLE, A. Infantry and artillery regimental colors.

EVANS AND HASSALL. Infantry and artillery camp colors.

NATIONAL FLAG DEPOT, 27 Courtlandt St., New York, N.Y.

SCHEIBLE, WILLIAM F. National and camp colors.

SEBRING, JAMES E. Recruiting, storm, garrison, hospital, ambulance flags.

SPARROW, GEORGE E. Garrison flags.

TOFT, JAMES. National colors.

GRENADES

ADAMS, JOHN S., Taunton, Mass. Patent Jan. 10, 1865.

HANES, W. W., Covington, Ky. Patent Aug. 26, 1862.

KETCHUM, WILLIAM F., Buffalo, N.Y. Patent Aug. 20, 1861.

GUNPOWDER

AMERICAN POWDER CO., South Acton, Mass.

BENNINGTON POWDER CO., Bennington, Vt.

BUCKFIELD MILLS, Paris, Maine.

CAMDEN MILLS, Camden, Maine.

DU PONT POWDER MILLS, Wilmington, Dela.

EMPIRE POWDER CO., Kingston, N.Y. and Sangerties, N.Y.

EMPIRE POWDER MILLS, Fairhaven, Vt.

FRONTIER MILLS, Xenia, Ohio.

HAZARD POWDER CO., Hazardville, Conn.

MASSACHUSETTS POWDER CO., Barre, Mass.

NEW ENGLAND COMPANY, Ware, Mass.

ORANGE POWDER CO., Newburgh, N.Y.

ORIENTAL POWDER CO., South Windham, Maine

SCHAGHTICOKE POWDER CO., Schaghticoke, N.Y.

SMITH, JOHN, Kingston, N.Y. Had a contract under date of Aug. 7, 1861.

UNION POWDER WORKS, New Durham, N.Y.

HORSE EQUIPMENTS

PALMER AND HASKELL, St. Louis (?) Mo. Supplied harness to U.S. 1861.

WATERVLIET ARSENAL. Made stirrups, artillery and cavalry equipments.

WEATHERLEY, JAMES, Cincinnati, Ohio. Supplied harness to U.S. Army 1861.

INSIGNIA

BUCKINGHAM, S. M. Brass letters and numbers, and shoulder scales.

KISSAM, D. W. Brass letters.

WILSON, Henry. Crossed sabers.

KNIFE MAKERS

AMES MANUFACTURING CO., Cabotville, Mass. and Chicopee, Mass.

BROWN AND TETLEY, Pittsburgh, Pa.

CHEVALIER, JOHN D., New York.

COLLINS AND COMPANY, Collinsville, Conn. (however, the address "Hartford" is used on Collins' products.)

CROOKS, JONATHAN.

GREAVES, W. AND SONS. Could be U.S. but address is unknown.

HASSAM, BROTHERS, Boston, Mass.

ROBY, C. AND CO. West Chelmsford and North Chelmsford, Mass.

TRYON, GEORGE W., Philadelphia, Pa.

WILLIAM ROGERS MANUFACTURING CO., Hartford, Conn.

KNIFE-FORK-SPOON COMBINATION

AMES, NATHAN, Saugus Center, Mass. Patent of Sept. 17, 1861.

RICHARDS, WM. H., Newton, Mass. Patent of July 23, 1861.

SNOW, J. P. AND CO., Hartford, Conn. and Chicago, Illinois.

WORMAN, ELY AND CO., Philadelphia, Pa. Patent of Feb. 4, 1864.

LANCE MAKERS—U.S.

BROOME, ISAAC. Contracted for 1,001 lances with the Federal Government in 1861.

MEDICAL SUPPLIES

DUNTON, J. In November 1862 designed a medical wagon which received an adverse report from a medical board on November 3, 1862.

HALSTEAD (PERHAPS MINA B.). Designed a hand litter.

HAYES, E. AND CO., Wheeling, West Virginia. In March 1862, designed a medical wagon following instructions from Surgeon Jonathan Letterman, U.S. Army.

JONES, J., New York, N.Y. In December 1862 designed a mule litter for carrying two persons in a sitting or recumbent position.

KOHLER, G. Furnished 300 mule litters to U.S. in July 1862.

LAWRENCE, BRADLEY AND PARDEE, New Haven, Conn. Patented a cacolet in 1861. Weight 131 lbs.

LUTZ AND BRIDGET. Harness-makers who, on August 20, 1861, furnished 20 sets of mule litters and cacolets to the U.S.

PEROT, T. MORRIS AND CO., 314 Vine Street, Philadelphia, Pa. Manufactured mess chests, largely used by the Medical Dept., U.S. Army, as well as medical panniers, medical knapsacks, medicine cases, and ambulances, all of which were apparently of their own pattern.

POMEROY AND CO. Designed a mule litter.

SATERLEE, R. S.. Designed a U.S. regulation hand litter.

SCHELL, HENRY S. Designed a litter in 1861. This litter could also be used as a bedstead.

SPENCER, NICHOLS AND CO. Designed an adjustable ambulance and pack saddle.

SQUIBB, E. R., M.D. In his laboratory at 149 Furman St., Brooklyn, New York, most of the medicines used by the U.S. in 1861 were made.

STEARNS. Surgeon of U.S. Army. Designed an artery clamp.

TIEMANN, GEO. & CO., 63 Chatham St., New York, N.Y. Makers of surgeons' field cases. (This is probably the the "Tiemann and Co., New York, instrument makers.")

WADE AND FORD, 85 Fulton Street, New York, N.Y. Makers of instruments and the Wood's General Operating Case.

WOODCOCK, E. P., New York, N.Y. November 1863 patented a pack-saddle for carrying litters.

MILITARY GOODS

CARRINGTON AND CO. Purchasing Agency, Army and Navy goods.

EICKE, EDWARD, 4 Courtlandt St., New York.

FOLSOM, CHARLES, 38 Maiden Lane, New York.

HORSTMANN, BROS. & CO., 5th and Cherry Sts., Philadelphia, Pa.

MILLER AND CO., 9 Maiden Lane, New York.

POLLARD, A. W. & CO., 6 Court St., Boston, Mass.

SCHUYLER, HARTLEY AND GRAHAM, 19 Maiden Lane and 22 John St., New York.

SEEBASS, BROTHERS, 17 Maiden Lane, New York.

SOMES, BROWN & CO., 2 Park Place, New York.

STADERMANN, JOHN, 292 Broadway, New York.

TIFFANY AND CO., 550-552 Broadway, New York.

TOMES, MELVAIN & CO., 6 Maiden Lane, New York.

MONEY BELT

HOWARD BELT CO., 436 Broadway, New York. The Howard Money Belt was "light, durable, elegant." It contained compartments for letters, greenbacks, and photographs. This belt, costing $2.00, "will not sweat or wet through under any circumstances."

MUSICAL INSTRUMENTS

BAKER, JOHN A., 63 Walker St., New York

BEAL, WM., Lowell, Mass. Drums.

BLUME, FRED, 208 Bowery, New York. Musical instruments and the "Excelsior Music-Book" containing patriotic songs.

BYRNE, GEORGE C., New York. Bid on contracts.

EISENBRANT, Philadelphia, Pa. Large fife has his name on it.

FIRTH, POND & CO., 547 Broadway, New York. Bid on contracts.

GETRON & ABBOTT, 149 Water St., New York. Bid on contracts.

GODWIN, JOS. H., New York.

HALL, WM. & SON, 543 Broadway, New York. Contract 1861 for drums, musical instruments, bugles, cocoa wood fifes.

HARTLEY, WM. B., New York.

HITCHCOCK, J. H., 160 Broadway, New York.

JOERDENS, J. F. M. Snare drums.

HORSTMAN BROTHERS & CO., New York and Philadelphia. Cavalry bugles.

LAFLIN, WALTER, New York. Bid on contracts.

MEIN, RICHARD. Drums.

MEACHAM & CO., Albany, N.Y. Maple wood fifes (17 inches long, brass ends).

MERRILL, L. T., New York.

PEPPER, J. W. & SON, Philadelphia, Pa. A horn bears his name.

PHILIPS, ANDREW J., 12 Cedar St., New York. Musical instruments.

ROGERS, ALEXANDER. Infantry drums.

SCHMIDT, H., 10th Near Grand., Williamsburg. Maker of military drums.

SMITH, ADAMS J.A., Batavia, N.Y.

SMITH, JAMES S. & CO., 15 Dutch St., New York.

SMITH, J. T. & CO., 344 Broadway, New York.

STRATTON, JOHN F., 105 and 107 E. 22nd St., New York. A horn bears his name. Also, cavalry bugles are found marked STRATTON & FOOTE. A military drum bearing Stratton's name is marked: "Military Band Instruments Maiden Lane, N.Y. 1860." The drum is maple with long red and black 5-point star in front.

ZOEBISHER, C. A. & SON, 163 William St., New York. Bid on contracts.

PENS

AMERICAN GOLD PEN CO., 200 Broadway, New York. Makers of gold pens.

PHOTOGRAPHS

EVANS G. G., 630 Chestnut St., Philadelphia, Pa. Specialized in "photograph card pictures and albums."

PHOTOGRAPH ALBUMS

BOWLES, SAMUEL & CO., Springfield, Mass. Sold "albums for the Army" a pocket album, holding 16 pictures, and costing 75 cents.

PIPES

POLLAK & SON, 692 Broadway, New York. Manufacturer of meerschaum pipes.

RICHARDS & CO., 97 William St., New York. Made a straight pipe similar to a large cigar holder.

PRINTING PRESS

A portable printing press was sold by J. G. COOLEY, Spruce St., New York. This press was advertised "for the Army and Navy" and was called "Cooley's Cabinet Printing Office."

RATIONS

AMERICAN DESICCATING CO., 56 South St., New York.

CHOLLET AND CO. In 1861 supplied dessicated vegetables.

NEW YORK CONDENSED MILK CO., 173 Canal St., New York. Contractor in 1861.

TILDER & CO., 98 John St., New York. Produced "Professor" Tilden's extract of coffee for soldier use.

REVOLVERS

The following list comprises the more common revolvers used by the North from 1861-1865. Both American and foreign weapons are included but very rare experimental types are omitted. Where possible, date of patent is given. In those cases where revolvers had patents renewed, only the first patent date is given. In addition, where possible, figures on Government purchases are given, but it should be pointed out that, in many cases, non-Government sales were also made, e.g. to militia units and individuals, which increased substantially the number of particular types of revolvers actually used.

There were 373,971 revolvers of nearly two dozen different makes purchased during the war. About 15,000 of these were purchased in England and Europe in 1861.

ADAMS, MASS. ARMS CO., Chicopee Falls, Mass. Patent June 3, 1856; Cal. .36 Navy Percussion Revolver, Cal. .44 Army Percussion Revolver. No record of purchases by U.S. Govt. Adams revolvers were also made in England and sold to both sides during the war.

ALLEN, ETHAN and WHEELOCK, THOMAS P., Worcester, Mass. Cal. .36 Navy Percussion Revolver, Cal. .44 Army Percussion Revolver. Patent Jan. 13, 1857. About 500 purchased by Govt. during the war for Army and and Navy.

ALSOP, C. R., Middletown, Conn. Cal. .36 Navy percussion revolver. Patent July 17, 1860. No record of purchases.

BACON MFG. CO., Norwich, Conn. Cal. .38 Navy cartridge revolver; patent Jan. 5, 1864, no record of purchases.

BEALS, FORDYCE, Ilion, N.Y. Cal. .36 Navy percussion revolver; Cal. .44 Army percussion revolver; patent Sept. 14, 1858, 12,251 purchased by Govt. during war.

BUTTERFIELD, JESSE, Philadelphia, Pa. Cal. .41 Army percussion revolver. Patent Dec. 11, 1855; no record of Govt. purchase during war.

COLT, SAMUEL, Hartford, Conn. Cal. .36 Navy percussion revolver, model 1861; 2,056 purchased by the War Dept. Feb. 17, 1862 to Jan. 20, 1863. Also used in the Federal Navy. Cal. .44 Army percussion revolver, model 1860; 107,156 furnished to the War. Dept. Jan. 4, 1861 to Nov. 10, 1863. Probably some 200,000 made during the war. Cal. .36 "Belt Model" percussion revolver model 1862. Popular with officers and men but no record of purchases available. The Colt Armory furnished the U.S. Govt. with a total of 386,417 revolvers during the war.

COOPER, JAMES M., Pittsburgh, Pa. Cal. .36 Navy percussion revolver. Patent Jan. 7, 1851, no record of purchases.

FREEMAN, AUSTIN T., Binghamton, N.Y. Cal. .44 Army percussion revolver, Patent Dec. 9, 1862. No record of purchases.

JOSYLN, B. F., Stonington, Conn. and Worcester, Mass. Cal. .44 Army percussion revolver; patent May 4, 1858; 1,100 purchased by Govt. during war.

LEAVITT, DANIEL, Hartford, Conn. Cal. .40 percussion revolver; patent April 29, 1839, no record of purchases.

LeFAUCHAUX (France and Belgium). Cal. .41 Army revolver; 12,000 purchased in 1861.

LeMAT (France and England). Cal. .44; patent 1856; used by both sides in the war.

MANHATTAN FIRE ARMS CO., Newark, N.J. Cal. .36 Navy percussion revolver; patent Dec. 27, 1859; no record of purchases.

METROPOLITAN ARMS CO., New York. Cal. .36 Navy percussion revolver; model 1859 (?). No record of purchases.

PERRIN (France). Cal. .45 Army percussion revolver; 200 purchased in 1861.

PETTINGILL, C. S., New Haven, Conn. Cal. .36 Navy percussion revolver. Cal. .44 Army percussion revolver; patent 1856. 2,001 delivered to the Govt. under contract during the war.

PLANT'S MFG. CO., New Haven, Conn. Cal. .42 Army cartridge revolver; patent July 12, 1859. No record of purchases.

POND, L. W., Worcester, Mass. Cal. .44 Army cartridge revolver; patent June 17, 1862; over 4,000 made but no record of purchases.

PRESCOTT, E. A., Worcester, Mass. Cal. .38 Navy cartridge revolver; patent Oct. 2, 1860; no record of purchase.

RAPHAEL (France). Cal. .41; 978 purchased in 1861.

REMINGTON, Ilion, N.Y. Cal. .36 Navy percussion revolver model 1861. Cal. .44 Army percussion revolver; patent Dec. 17, 1861. There were 5,000 Navy and 125,314 Army Remingtons purchased during the war.

REMINGTON-RIDER, Ilion, N.Y. Cal. .36 Navy percussion revolver, patent May 3, 1859. No record of purchases.

ROGERS AND SPENCER, Utica, N.Y. Cal. .44 Army percussion revolver; 5,000 purchased Jan. 30–Sept. 26, 1865.

SAVAGE REPEATING FIRE ARMS CO., Middletown, Conn. Cal. .36 Navy percussion revolver; patent June 17, 1856; 11,284 purchased by the Govt. during the war.

SMITH AND WESSON, Springfield, Mass. Cal. .32 Army cartridge revolver; patent April 3, 1855; 76,502 manufactured from June 1861 to 1874. No record of Govt. purchases but thousands purchased during the war by individuals who liked them.

STARR, EBEN T., New York, N.Y. Cal. .36 Navy percussion revolver, Cal. .44 Army percussion revolver; patent Jan. 15, 1856. 47,952 purchased by Govt. during war.

UNION ARMS CO., New York; Newark, N.J. Cal. .36 Navy percussion revolver. No record of purchases.

WALCH, J., New York. Cal. .36 Navy percussion revolver; patent Feb. 8, 1859; no record of purchases.

WARNER, JAMES, Springfield, Mass. Cal. .36 Navy percussion revolver. Cal. .44 Army percussion revolver; patent Jan. 7, 1851. No record of purchases.

WESSON AND LEAVITT, Chicopee Falls, Mass. Cal. .36 Navy percussion revolver. Cal. .40 Army percussion revolver; patent Nov. 26, 1850. No record of purchases.

WHITNEY, ELI, New Haven, Conn. Cal. .36 Navy percussion revolver; patent Aug. 1, 1854. 11,214 purchased by the Govt. during the war.

RIFLES AND MUSKETS

The following list excludes U.S. Government fabricated weapons, foreign arms, foreign arms made under contract e.g. Manton and German 1861 model muskets, and sharpshooters' rifles. Likewise experimental models which saw little or no actual use in the field are not included. Excellent detailed descriptions of long arms are available in published form. See bibliography for titles of such works.

AMOSKEAG MANUFACTURING CO., Manchester, N.H. Cal. .58 rifled muskets; 27,000 delivered.

BLUNT, ORISON, New York. Cal. .58 Enfield type rifled muskets. No data available on deliveries or contract.

BURT, ADDISON M., New York. Cal. .58 rifled muskets; 11,495 delivered.

COLT, SAMUEL, Hartford, Conn. Cal. .58 rifled muskets; 75,000 delivered. Cal. .44 and .56 percussion repeating rifle, model 1855; 401 delivered in 1857, and many used by militia units.

EAGLE MANUFACTURING CO., Eagleville, Mansfield, Conn. Cal. .58 rifled muskets; 5,480 delivered.

GREEN, J. DURRELL, U. S. Army. Cal. .54 breech-loading, percussion rifle, patent Nov. 17, 1857. 900 delivered.

HENRY, J. AND SON, Philadelphia, Pa. Percussion rifle (similar to U.S. model 1841 rifle). No data as to number fabricated.

HENRY, TYLER, New Haven, Conn. Cal. .44 repeating rifle; about 10,000 used by state regiments during the war.

HOARD, C. B., Watertown, N.Y. Cal. .58 rifled muskets, 12,800 delivered.

HODGE, J. T., New York. Cal. .58 rifled muskets; 10,500 delivered.

JENKS, ALFRED & SON, Philadelphia and Bridesburg, Pa. Cal. .58 rifled muskets; 98,000 delivered.

JUSTICE, P. S., Philadelphia, Pa. Cal. .69 Enfield type rifled muskets; 400 delivered in 1863.

KRIDER, J. H., Philadelphia, Pa. Cal. .58 rifle similar to U.S. model 1841 type. No data as to number fabricated.

LAMSON, GOODNOW AND YALE, Windsor, Vt. Cal. .58 rifled muskets; 50,000 delivered.

MASON, WILLIAM, Taunton, Mass. Cal. .58 rifled muskets; 30,000 delivered.

MERRILL, J. H., Baltimore, Md. Cal. .54; patent July 1858; 770 purchased between April 1862 and Nov. 1863.

MOORE, J. P., New York. Cal. .58 Enfield type rifled muskets; no data available.

MOWRY, J. D., Norwich, Conn. Cal. .58 rifled muskets; 22,000 delivered.

MUIR, WILLIAM, Windsor Locks, Conn. Cal. .58 rifled muskets; 30,000 delivered.

MULHOLLAND, JAMES, Reading, Pa. Cal. .58 rifled muskets; 5,502 delivered.

NORRIS, S. AND CLEMENT, W. T., Springfield, Mass. Cal. .58 rifled muskets; contractors to State of Mass. in 1863 for 3,000 muskets.

NORWICH ARMS CO. Cal. .58 rifled muskets; 25,000 delivered.

PARKER, SNOW AND CO., Meriden, Conn. Cal. .58 rifled muskets; 15,000 delivered.

PROVIDENCE. Cal. .58 rifled muskets, marked "Providence" exist but there is no record available to indicate the identity definitely of the contractor for this arm.

PROVIDENCE TOOL CO., Providence, R.I. Cal. .58 rifled muskets; 70,000 delivered.

REMINGTON, E., Ilion, N.Y. Cal. .58 rifled muskets; 40,000 delivered. Cal. .58 model 1862 "Zouave" rifles; 10,000 delivered.

ROBINSON, E., New York. Cal. .58 rifled muskets; 30,000 delivered.

SARSON, J. B. and ROBERTS, W. S., New York. Cal. .58 rifled muskets; 5,140 delivered.

SAVAGE, R., Middletown, Conn. Cal. .58 rifled muskets; 25,500 delivered.

SCHALK, G., Pottsville, Pa. Cal. .58 rifled muskets. Made a few arms of this type for the State of Pa. in 1861.

SCHUBARTH, CASPER D., Providence, R.I. Cal. .58 rifled musket; 9,500 delivered.

SHARPS, C., Hartford, Conn. Cal. .52 Patent Oct. 5, 1852. Breech-loading percussion rifle 9,141 purchased. Used by Berdan's Sharpshooters and some militia units.

SHARPS AND HANKINS, Philadelphia, Pa. Cal. .54 patent of 1859, no record available of number fabricated.

UNION ARMS CO., New York. Cal. .58 rifled muskets; no record of deliveries, but specimens by this contractor are in existence.

WATERS, A. H. and Co., (?) Millbury, Mass. Cal. .58 rifled muskets. It is not conclusive that the Waters Co. made the model 1861 rifled musket marked "Millbury;" no record available as to deliveries.

WELCH, W. W., Norfolk, Conn. Cal. .58 rifled muskets; 17,000 delivered.

WHITNEY, ELI, Whitneyville, Conn. Cal. .58 rifled musket; 15,001 delivered as well as some to the State of Conn. under special contract. Cal. .69 Navy Rifle, model 1861, known as the "Plymouth Rifle" no data as to deliveries.

WINDSOR LOCKS. Cal. .58 rifled muskets. No record of deliveries but specimens marked "Windsor Locks" exist today in collections.

RINGS

BEACH, E. P., 12 Maiden Lane, New York. Returning soldiers could buy this 16-carat gold ring with any of the army corps badges richly enameled in the color of each division.

HAYWARD, B. T., 208 Broadway, New York. Genuine 16-carat gold rings for every army corps.

RUBBER GOODS

BART & HICKOX, Cincinnati, Ohio. India-rubber goods.

GUTTA PERCHA CO., New York. India-rubber goods.

HAYWOOD, N. CO., Stoneham, Mass. India-rubber goods.

INDIA-RUBBER BELT CO., Park Row, New York. India-rubber goods.

PHOENIX RUBBER CO. Rubber blankets.

RUBBER CLOTHING CO., New York. Rubber blankets.

UNION RUBBER CO., New York. Rubber blankets.

SMALL ARMS (by purchase)

BOKER, HERMAN & CO. Sept. 5, 1861 contract to import over 100,000 muskets, mostly Austrian.

BOWEN, E. R., 20 Clark St., Chicago, Ill. Military goods including Henry rifles.

GREENWOOD, MILES & CO., Cincinnati, Ohio. In 1861 altered Austrian flintlock muskets for U.S.

HOWLAND & ASPINWALL. Imported arms for U.S.

JUSTICE, P. S., Philadelphia, Pa. Imported arms for U.S.

MARSTON, WILLIAM W., New York. Firearms manufacturer. Altered and rifled Hall-North carbines for U.S.

MERWIN & CO. Supplied arms to U.S.

MOOR'S J. P. SONS. Supplied arms to U.S.

SCHUYLER, HARTLEY & GRAHAM. Largest importer and dealer in arms 1861.

SIMMS AND BROTHERS. Supplied arms to U.S. 1861.

STEVENS, SIMON, New York. Altered and rifled Hall-North carbine for U.S. 1861.

TRYON, E. K. & CO., Philadelphia, Pa. Altered Austrian muskets 1861.

TYSON & CO., Philadelphia, Pa. Altered Austrian flintlock muskets, 1861.

SMOKING CASE

RIDGEWOOD MANUFACTURING CO. Made the "Ridgewood Smoking Case." This company was located at 429 Broadway, New York, and made a very attractive outfit.

SWORDS AND SABERS

AMES MANUFACTURING CO., Chicopee, Mass.

BAILEY AND CO., Philadelphia, Pa.

BALL, BLACK & CO., New York, N.Y.

BOKER, H. AND COMPANY, New York, N.Y. Name appears on cavalry sabers. In 1861 had a contract with Federal Government for cavalry sabers, light artillery sabers, officers' swords, non-coms' swords, and foot artillery swords. Bought 28,000 cavalry sabers and large number of muskets in Europe, Nov. 25, 1861.

CANFIELD AND BROTHER, Baltimore, Md.

CASTLEMAN, E., Alexandria, Va.

COLLINS AND COMPANY, Connecticut.

DISTON, HENRY AND SONS, Philadelphia, Pa.

EMERSON AND SILVER, Trenton, N.J.

EMONS AND MARSHALL, Philadelphia, Pa.

EVANS AND HASSALL, Philadelphia, Pa.

FOLSON, HENRY AND COMPANY, St. Louis, Mo.

FORST, MANN AND COMPANY. Foot artillery swords, contract, 1861.

GRUFF, J. C. AND COMPANY. Cavalry sabers, contract 1861.

HAHN, WILLIAM. Cavalry sabers.

HAMLIN, I. G., JR., Cincinnati, O.

HARTLEY, W. M. B. Cavalry sabers, contract 1861.

HEIBERGER, FRANCIS J., Washington, D.C.

HELMSFORD, W. O., Crosby, Mass.

HIRSCHBUHL, J. J., Louisville, Ky.

HORSTMANN BROTHERS & CO., Philadelphia and New York.

HUNT AND GOODWIN, Washington, D. C.

JUSTICE, PHILIP S., Philadelphia, Pa. Contracted for 5,500 cavalry sabers and 4,000 caliber .69 muskets (rifled) in Aug. 1861.

KEPMAN, T. Contracted for 1,000 sabers. Oct. 21, 1861.
LEISERING, H. G. Contracted for 20,000 cavalry sabers Sept. 19, 1861.
MAAS, C. AND SCHOVERLING. Cavalry sabers.
MANSFIELD LAMB & CO., Smithfield, R.I., contracted for 10,000 cavalry sabers Aug. 28, 1861.
MEYER, J. Contracted for 10,000 sabers Sept. 7, 1861.
MILLARD, DAVID J., Clayville, N.Y., contracted for 10,000 cavalry sabers, Dec. 13, 1861.
MINTZER, W. G., Philadelphia, Pa.
PALMER, J. C. Light artillery sabers.
PALMER AND BACHELDOR, Boston, Mass.
PROVIDENCE TOOL COMPANY, Providence, R. I.
RAPHAEL, GEORGE. Light cavalry sabers.
READ AND SON, Boston, Mass.
ROBY, C. AND CO., West Chelmsford, Mass. and North Chelmsford, Mass.
RUPRECHT, C. W. Cavalry sabers.
SACCHI, G. A. Cavalry sabers.
SAUERBIER, H., New York, N.Y., and Newark, N.J.
SCHIEFFLIN, P. AND L., New York, N.Y., Imported from Europe, by July 18, 1861, contract, 5,000 cavalry sabers, 3,000 non-coms' swords and 2,000 musicians' swords.
SCHUYLER, HARTLEY AND GRAHAM, New York, N.Y.
SHEBLE AND FISHER, Philadelphia, Pa.
SHREVE, STANWOOD, AND COMPANY, Boston, Mass.
SIMMONS, G. W. AND BROTHER, Philadelphia, Pa.
SMITH CRANE AND COMPANY. Cavalry sabers.
SYMS, W. J. AND BROTHER. Light artillery sabers.
TIFFANY AND COMPANY, New York, N.Y.
TOBEY, G. R., New York, N.Y.
TOMES, SON AND McILVAINE. Contracted for 2,000 cavalry sabers, Sept. 20, 1861.
TUSKA, P. H. Cavalry sabers and non-coms' swords. Windmuller, L., New York, N.Y.

TENTS

BETTS, E & A, Wilmington, Dela., Sibley tripods.
BOYD, THOMAS, Boston, Mass., patent for tents Aug. 27, 1861.
CHAPIN, GEORGE. Common tent poles, wall tent poles, hospital tent poles.
CLOSE, CHARLES S. Sibley tripods, poles, etc.
CURTIS, CHARLES T. Sibley tripods.
DAVIS, S. M., Lawrence, Mass., patent for tents, July 23, 1861.
DAY, HORACE. Designed a shelter tent made of gutta percha cloth.
DOLBY, L. B. M., Philadelphia, Pa., Sibley tent poles and tripods.
DOUGLASS, R. H. Tents.
ESLER & BROTHERS. Sibley tripods, tent poles.
FOX & POLHEMUS. Sibley tripods and many types of tents, mostly the "common tent."
GAYLORD, PHILIP. Common tent pins, wall tent pins, hospital tent pins.
HALL, CHARLES P. Sibley tripods.
HASKALL, ANDREW L., Boston, Mass., patent for folding tent, Sept. 24, 1861.
HEMMENWAY & BEVERIDGE. Sibley tripods. In 1861 contracted for 1,200 wedge-shaped tents. Specifications were: 7 feet long, 7 feet high, 9 feet wide; with poles, pins, slides, flys. Also contracted for 400 wall tents 9 by 9 by 9, with flys.
HITCHOCK, H. J. Tents.
JEWETT, A. & CO. Common tents (linen duck), camp kettles.
JOHNSON, WM. H. Tents.
LANDELL, JOHN H., Newark, N.J., tents and Sibley tripods.
McCOMB, HENRY S., Wilmington, Dela., Sibley tent poles and tripods.
McKEE AND ADAMS. Tents.
PALMER, L. B. & CO. Common tents.
PECK, GEORGE H., Kings Bridge, N.Y., contract May 14, 1861, for 2,000 common tents and 250 wall tents.
POOLE, J. MORTON, Wilmington, Dela., Sibley tents, poles, tripods.
PULLAN, R. B., Cumminsville, O., patent for tents, Dec. 17, 1861.
QUICK, G. C. Tents.
RANKIN, WILLIAM, New York, N.Y., patent for tents, Dec. 24, 1861.
RIDER, JOHN. Designed the "Rider's Tent-Knapsack."
SIMONS, HENRY. Sibley tripods.
TILYOU, V. Tents.
WASHBURNE & PHILBROOK, Camden, Maine. Tents.
WELLS, W. H. Tents.
WILLIAMS, E. C., Jersey City, N.J., patent for a portable tent. July 2, 1861.
WILSTACH, W. P. AND CO. Sibley poles, tripods, etc.
VANWYCK, T. J. Wall tents with flys, hospital tents with flys.

UNIFORMS AND CLOTHING

ALBRIGHT, CHARLES, Mauch Chunk, Pa., 100,000 pairs of bootees.
ARNOLD, MARTIN, AND POTTER. Bootees.
ARNOUX, ANTHONY, 531 Broadway, New York, N.Y. Overcoats, pants, jackets. Shared in contract for 15,000 Army uniforms for New York, May 27, 1861.
BALDWIN, F. B. Uniforms, overcoats.
BANISTER, J. A., Newark, N.J. Bootees.
BARNUM, CHARLES, New York, N.Y. Uniforms, overcoats.
BATCHELLER, E. & A. H. AND CO. Cavalry boots.
BAYLAN, JAMES B. Infantry trousers, blouses, cavalry jackets, artillery uniform coats.
BEINHEIMER, ADOLPH. Cavalry jackets.
BELLOWS, MARTIN, Philadelphia, Pa. 5,000 bootees.
BICTA, JOSEPH. Bootees.
BIGELOW, CHAS. D., 54 Vesey St., New York, N.Y. Bootees, shirts, socks.
BLANCHARD, LEONARD, East Abington, Mass. 4,000 bootees, cavalry boots.
BROOKS, E. A., New York, N.Y. Uniforms, overcoats, bootees.
BROWNER, H. H., Syracuse, N.Y. 50,000 bootees.
BRYANT, GEO. (or Seth?), East Bridgewater, Mass. 7,000 bootees.
BURKERT AND KOEDEL, Philadelphia, Pa. 10,000 bootees.
BUTTON, WORTHINGTON B. Infantry trousers; cavalry trousers, overcoats, jackets; artillery uniform coats; Invalid Corps jackets.
CAHILL, S., New York, N.Y. 1,000 bootees.
CANFIELD, M. B. & SON, Orange, N.J. Bootees.
CHILD, PRATT AND FOX, St. Louis, Mo. Cavalry boots, many items of Army supplies.
CHURCHILL, L. AND H., Rochester, N.Y. 5,000 bootees.
CLAFIN, WILLIAM. Cavalry boots.
CLARK, AMOS. Greatcoats, cavalry jackets.
CLARK, EZRA, JR., New York, N.Y. 5,000 bootees.
CLOUD, STEPHEN, JR., Pa. 1,000 bootees.
COBB, HENRY, Boston, Mass. 12,000 cavalry boots.
COLBURN, C. AND CO., Boston, Mass. Cavalry boots, bootees.
COMSTOCK, J. S. & CO., St. Louis, Mo. Boots, shoes.
COOK, BENJ. F. Negro brogans.
CORN, SAM'L, 59 Broadway, New York, N.Y. Army clothing.
COTRALL, J. G. & SON, Albany, N.Y. Uniforms and caps.
COUGHLAN, LANGLEY, BOICE & CO., 34 Courtland, New York, N. Y. Army clothing.
CUMMING, ALEXANDER, New York, N.Y. 75,000 bootees.
DEERING, WILLIAM. Cavalry trousers, canton flannel drawers.

DEVELIN, HUDSON & CO., New York, N.Y. Overcoats, uniforms. Made uniforms for "Mozart Regiment" (40th N.Y. Inf.).
DEXTER, J. D., New York, N.Y. Bootees.
DICKERMAN, L. & CO., Philadelphia, Pa. Bootees.
DIXON, WILLIAM T. AND BRO. Negro brogans.
DOUGLASS, M. B., Newark, N.J. Bootees.
DOWNS, H. S., Boston, Mass. Bootees, cavalry boots.
ENDERS, WILLIAM F. & CO., Boston, Mass. Uniforms.
ENOS, D. C., Philadelphia, Pa. 100,000 bootees.
EVERS, JOHN A., Philadelphia, Pa. 25,000 bootees.
FENTON, E. P. AND CO., Syracuse, N.Y. Bootees.
FOSTER, H. L. Cavalry jackets.
FOX, CHARLES, 62 Broadway, New York, N.Y. Caps.
FOX, E. W. 30,000 Army overcoats.
GARTHWAITE, J. C. Artillery and infantry uniform coats, blouses.
GEISSENDORFF, J. W. & CO., Indianapolis, Ind. Army clothing.
GILMORE, C., Raynham, Mass. Shoes for Mass.
GLASSER & BROS. Uniforms.
GODFREY, B. D., Guilford, Mass. Boots, shoes.
GOLDEN & DUNLOP, 552 Broadway, New York, N.Y. Caps.
GOLDSTEIN, B., 164 Broadway, New York, N.Y. Army clothing.
GOULD, THOMAS R., Boston, Mass. Bootees.
GRAY, W. H., Philadelphia, Pa. Patent for epaulettes, Nov. 12, 1861.
GREEN, Sharpless, Pa. Bootees.
GREEN AND BRO., St. Louis, Mo. Shoes.
HABER, ISAAC & CO. Infantry uniform coats and overcoats; artillery uniform coats; cavalry jackets and trousers.
HALL, BENEDICT & CO., New York, N.Y. Thousands of bootees, shoes.
HALL, SOUTHWICK & CO. Negro brogans.
HALLOWELL, CHARLES, Philadelphia, Pa. Bootees.
HALLOWELL, RICHARD P., Boston, Mass. Shoes, socks, underwear.
HANFORD, JOHN E., Brooklyn, N.Y. Contracted July 12, 1861 for: 40,000 sky-blue overcoats, 50,000 dark-blue infantry coats, 60,000 dark-blue pantaloons, 80,000 dark-blue sack coats, 100,000 pairs flannel drawers, 100,000 white cotton shirts.
HAZEL & CO., Philadelphia, Pa. Bootees.
HEIDELBACH, WERTHEIMER & CO. Uniforms.
HELLERMAN, WILLIAM T., Philadelphia, Pa. Bootees.
HENSELL, H. W. Sergeants' worsted sashes.
HORSTMAN BROTHERS & ALLIEN. Infantry and artillery cords and tassels.
HOW, JOHN. Uniforms, many varied items of army equipment.
HOWES, HYATT & CO., New York, N.Y. Bootees.
HUGHES, SAMUEL, Pa. Bootees.
HUNT, HOLBROOK AND BARBER, Hartford, Conn. Bootees.
HYATT, STEPHEN, New York, N.Y. Shoes.
JENKINS, LANE & SONS. Bootees.
JOHNS, WILLIAM B., Georgetown, D.C. Patent for military cloak, Oct. 22, 1861.
JONES, AARON. Stockings.
JONES, F. & N., Philadelphia, Pa. Shoes, bootees.
JONES, FREDERICK & CO., Boston, Mass. Negro brogans, bootees, cavalry boots.
JONES, WILLIAM H. Stockings.
KELLOGG, P. V. & CO., Utica, N.Y. Uniforms.
KELLOGG, PALMER P. Uniforms, overcoats.
KIMBALL, ROBINSON & CO., Boston, Mass. Cavalry boots, bootees, shoes for Co. "F" 15th Mass. Inf.
KING, D. R. & CO., Philadelphia, Pa. Bootees.
KOHNER AND BRO. Infantry overcoats.
KOLLINSKY, COLOMANNUS (et. al.) Washington, D.C. Patent for cap, Nov. 5, 1861.
LAMB, JAMES S. Uniforms.
LEE, JOSEPH. Stable frocks, canton flannel drawers, chevrons, cavalry trousers.
LEVICK, RASIN & CO., Philadelphia, Pa. Cavalry boots, bootees.
LEWIS, JOHN W., 44 Warren St., New York, N.Y. Shirts, drawers.
LIVINGSTON, BELL & CO., St. Louis, Mo. Uniforms, boots, canteens, knapsacks, Army clothing.
LONGSTREET, BRADFORD & CO. Army clothing.
LUDLOW, W. A. & J. C. Blouses.
MACK AND BROS., Cincinnati, O. Uniforms.
MANSFIELD, L. W. Knit shirts.
MARBLE, F. M., New Haven, Conn. Bootees.
MARTIN, JOHN T. Cavalry greatcoats and trousers; infantry greatcoats and trousers; artillery frock coats.
MARTIN, L. T. Infantry and cavalry trousers, blouses.
McCOMB, H. S. Bootees, leather neck stocks.
McDONALD, J. H., Albany, N.Y. Uniforms, caps.
McDOUGALL, FENTON & CO., Syracuse, N.Y. Shirts, socks.
McREA, WILLIAM H., Philadelphia, Pa. Bootees.
MEGARY, MICHAEL, Wilmington, Dela. Bootees.
MERRIAM, HENRY W. Bootees.
MERRIAM, S. S., New York, N.Y. Bootees.
METZGER, CHARLES. Cavalry hat cords and tassels.
MOORE, ROBERT, Carlisle, Pa. Bootees.
MOYER, SAMUEL D., Norristown, Pa. Bootees.
MULDOON, WILLIAM, Philadelphia, Pa. Bootees.
MUNDELL, JOHN, Philadelphia, Pa. Bootees.
MURPHY, W. J. & CO., Philadelphia, Pa. Bootees.
MURPHY & CHILDS, 50 Dey St., New York, N.Y. Caps.
MURPHY AND GRISWOLD. Forage caps, hats, trimmings.
OWENS, CHARLES H., Philadelphia, Pa. Bootees.
PARRISH, JAMES, 323 Canal St., New York, N.Y. Sold "French flannel Army shirts."
PASCAL, C. L., Philadelphia, Pa. Patent for military hat, Dec. 10, 1861.
PHILLIPS, L. J. AND I. Forage caps.
PIERCE BROS. & CO., Boston, Mass. Shirts, drawers, socks.
QUINN, HUGH. Stockings.
RANSON, W. A. & CO., New York, N.Y. Bootees.
READ, HAMILTON & CO., Newark, N. J. 10,000 bootees.
REED, NAHUM. Boots.
ROBINSON, JOHN P., Brookfield and Marlboro, Mass. and Dover, N.Y. Shoes.
ROEDEL, JACOB, Lebanon, Pa. Bootees.
ROSE, ALVIN. Flannel shirts, overcoats, canton flannel drawers.
ROSS, ALLEN, Sing Sing, N.Y. Cavalry boots, bootees.
ROTHSTEIN, H., 140 Broadway, New York, N.Y. Caps.
SAXONVILLE MILLS. Infantry overcoats.
SEAMLESS CLOTHING MANF. CO., 255 Canal St., New York, N.Y. Seamless overcoats for the Army and Navy.
SEARS, ZENAS, Boston, Mass. Bootees.
SELIGMAN, WM. AND CO., New York, N.Y. Uniforms, overcoats.
SHELDON, F. S. Uniforms.
SHELDON, J. L., Auburn, N.Y. Caps.
SHETHAR AND NICHOLS. Uniform hats.
SLADE AND COLBY. Flannel drawers.
SMITH, J. S., New York, N.Y. Patent for shoulder straps, June 18, 1861.
SMITH AND RICE. Infantry trousers.
SNYDER & CO., Philadelphia, Pa. Felt hats.
SOUTHWICK, HENRY C., Albany, N.Y. Socks.
STADLER & BROS., Cincinnati, O. Uniforms, Army clothing.
STEWART, ALEX T. Shirts, socks.
STRONG, ALEX, New York, N.Y. Bootees.
STRONG BROS. & CO., Albany, N.Y. Socks, shirts, drawers.
TALCOTT, JAMES. Stockings.
TAYLOR, JAMES, Baltimore, Md. Bootees.
TEMPLE, D. & W. Bootees.

TERHUNE, JOHN, Newark, N.J. Bootees.
TERRY, JOHN R., 397 Broadway, New York, N.Y. Caps.
TRASK, A., New York, N.Y. Bootees.
TROUNSTINE, A & J & CO. Uniforms.
TYLER, MOSES (MORRIS?), New Haven, Conn. Bootees.
VAN SICKLER & FORBY, Albany, N.Y. Uniforms, socks, shirts, drawers.
WARE, PRESTONE, Newton, Mass. Bootees.
WARE AND TAYLOR, Boston, Mass. Bootees.
WEBSTER AND CO. Bootees.
WEISS, F. W., Mount Vernon, Calif. Patent for military cloak, Dec. 10, 1861.
WHEELER, CHARLES B. Bootees.
WHIPPLE, J. F., New York, N.Y. Patent for cap, July 16, 1861.
WHITNEY, JOSEPH & CO. Negro brogans.
WHITTMORE & CO., St. Louis, Mo. Felt hats.
WICKES & STRONG. Uniforms.
WOLVERTON, G. A. & CO., Albany, N.Y. Uniforms, shoes.
WOOD, WILLARD & PRENTICE. Socks, shirts.

VAPOR BATH

TIMOLET'S SULPHUR AND MEDICATED VAPOR BATH. For the cure of rheumatism, chills, fevers, dropsy, colds, and all the diseases now prevalent among soldiers and sailors. No. 1 Carrol Place, Bleecker St., New York, N.Y.

WATCHES

AMERICAN WATCH COMPANY. To protect against imitations, the following trade marks are the only genuine ones: "American Watch Company, Waltham, Mass." "Appleton, Tracy & Co., Waltham, Mass." "P. S. Bartlett, Waltham, Mass." "Wm. Ellery, Boston, Mass."
All of these watches are made with gold or silver cases, in various sizes, and all have the name "American Watch Co." painted on the dial.
ARRANDALE & CO., 212 Broadway, New York, N.Y. Makers of "New Army Watches."
HUBBARD BROTHERS, 160 Broadway and 2 Cortlandt St., New York. Importers of "watches for the Army." These watches had an outer coating of sterling silver and an inner coating of German silver, "an imitation so faultless of solid silver as to be hardly detectable" by the most experienced judges." Cost of this watch "superbly engraved" was $35.00.
NORTON, CHARLES P. AND CO., 38 and 40 Arn Street, New York. Importers who sold an "Army watch" for $7.00; a $15.00 "European Timekeeper," an "exact imitation of a $100 gold watch used by the British army officers"; and a $30.00 "American Lever" or "Real English Duplex Stop Watch . . . for artillerists or [for] training horses."

WRITING KIT

BROOKS, D. B. & BROTHERS, Salem, Mass. Made Brooks Patent writing and toilet case for soldiers and sailors.
RITTER, A. J., Rahway, New York. Maker of a portable desk, portfolio, and checkerboard combination, containing 20 articles and weighing 12 ounces.

CONFEDERATE MAKERS, CONTRACTORS AND DEALERS

ACCOUTERMENTS AND MISCELLANEOUS MILITARY ITEMS

"A.V.C." Initials found on Alabama State buttons, buckles, and other items of equipment. A.V.C. stood for "Alabama Volunteer Corps."
AUGUSTA ARSENAL, Augusta, Ga.
BRANDS AND KORNER, Columbus, Ga. India rubber cloth, drums, fifes.
CLARK, A. W. Haversacks, cotton, 12 by 12 inches with cotton shoulder sling.
COLUMBUS ARSENAL AND ARMORY, Columbus, Ga. Infantry accouterments, and harness.
COTTRELL, S. S. AND CO., Richmond, Va. Infantry accouterments.
DARROW, J., Augusta, Ga. Artillery tube box.
GARDNER, F. J. Wooden canteens.
GARRATT AND O'HARA, Memphis, Tenn. Spurs, stirrups, belt clasps, holster trimmings, etc.
HAIMAN, L. AND BROTHER, Columbus, Ga. Belts, buckles, camp equipment, tin and sheet-iron utensils, bayonets for double-barreled rifles and shotguns, oilcloth, haversacks, cartridge boxes.
HUDSON, A. J., Charlottesville, Va. Cartridge boxes, belts, cap boxes, harness.
HUGHES, D. W., COL., Memphis, Tenn. Wooden canteens.
JEFFERIES, WILLIAM, Charlottesville, Va. Cartridge boxes, cap boxes, belts, harness.
JESSOPS WIRE FACTORY, Richmond, Va. Buckles.
KING, J. A., Mobile, Ala. Tourniquet with brass frame and screw.
MACON ARSENAL, Macon, Ga. Canteens, knapsacks, edged weapons, ammunition, cannon.
MAGEE AND GEORGE, New Orleans, La. Cartridge box.
MEISTER, J. E., Columbia, S.C. Enamelled cloth for knapsacks.
MINCHEMER, FRANCIS, Atlanta, Ga. Had a contract with Atlanta Arsenal for "C.S.A." belt plates.
MONTGOMERY ARSENAL, Montgomery, Ala. Leather goods.
SMITH AND CLEGHORN, Macon, Ga. Knapsacks, sword belts, artillery harness, saddles, leggings.
SMITH, J. W., Memphis, Tenn. Tents.
STAUNTON ORDNANCE DEPOT, Staunton, Va. Cartridge boxes and bayonet scabbards.
THOMAS, JOSEPH, Memphis, Tenn. Bullet mold.
VANLEER, SAM AND CO., Nashville, Tenn. Powder flasks and horns.
WARNER, Richmond, Va. Cartridge box.
WOOD, G. AND CO., Macon, Ga. Camp cots, camp stools, chests, and button molds.

BAYONETS

BAYSER, STEBBINS AND CO., Columbia, S.C. Had a large contract for bayonets, June 1864.
BOYLE AND GAMBLE, Richmond, Va. Bayonets, saber bayonet adapter.
BURGER AND BROTHERS, Richmond, Va.
COOK AND BROTHERS, Athens, Ga.
CONFEDERATE STATES ARMORY, Kenansville, N.C. Bayonets, lances, buttons, sabers, swords, cutlasses, infantry accouterments, knapsacks.
HILLMAN BROTHERS, Memphis, Tenn. Possibly made saber bayonets for Mississippi rifles and bayonets for double barrel shotguns.
RALEIGH BAYONET FACTORY, Raleigh, N.C.

CANNON

A. B. R. & BRO., Vicksburg, Miss. Confederate bronze howitzer.

ARCHER, DR. JUNIUS, Chesterfield County, Va. Owner of the Bellona Arsenal foundry which cast 8- and 10-inch Columbiads. Is reported to have made 12-pounder howitzers and 3-inch rifled guns.

ARK. MIL. INS. Marking on two C.S. 6-pounder brass cannon.

AUGUSTA ARSENAL, Augusta, Ga. 12-pound "Napoleons."

BARRINGER AND MORTON, Columbus, Ga. Gun carriages.

BAYLOR, JOHN R. Invented a smoothbore breech-loading cannon which was loaded with buckshot.

BRENNAN, T. N. & CO., Nashville, Tenn. 6-pounder smoothbores and 12-pounder howitzers.

BROWN'S FOUNDRY, Columbus, Ga.

CAMERON AND CO., Charleston, S.C. 12-pounders.

CARR, THOMAS, Portsmouth, Va. Cannon rifling machine.

CATO, JR., Richmond, Va. 6-pounder carriages and caissons.

CLAIBORNE MACHINE WORKS, Nashville, Tenn. 6- and 12-pounders, and siege guns up to 32-pounders.

COLUMBUS IRON WORKS, Columbus, Ga. Brass field pieces.

CONFEDERATE NAVAL WORKS, Columbus, Ga.

CUSHMAN'S FOUNDRY, Houston, Texas. Smoothbore cannon.

DEANE, F. B. JR. AND SONS, Lynchburg, Va. 12-pounder howitzers.

ELLIS AND CO., Nashville, Tenn. 6-pounder cannon.

ELLIS AND MOORE, Nashville, Tenn. Smoothbore cannon.

ETTENGER AND EDMOND, Richmond, Va. Contracted with C.S. Government to make 6-pounder carriages and caissons, and 24-pounder carriages.

FINDLAY IRON WORKS, Macon, Ga. 12-pound Napoleons.

GILLELAND, JOHN, Athens, Ga. Invented a cannon like a double-barrel shotgun which fired shot connected by a chain. But one shot went off a little ahead of the other. The cannon was a failure and only one was made.

HARRIS, R. F., Charlottesville, Va. Gun-carriages, caissons, horse shoes.

HORSMAN, A. I., New Orleans, La. 1-inch brass cannon.

HUGHES, D. W. COL., Memphis, Tenn. Invented a gun which would throw a 1.5-inch lead ball over 3 miles.

LEEDS CO., New Orleans, La. Brass breech-loader, 12-pounder Napoleons.

LIVERMORE FOUNDRY AND MACHINE CO., Memphis, Tenn.

MILLER, A. N., Savannah, Ga. Cannon, projectiles.

MULLANE, JOHN, Louisville, Ky. 6-pounder rifled cannon for cavalry. Weight 280 pounds, range 2.5-3 miles. Could be operated by 2 men.

NICHOLS, E. B., Galveston, Texas. Made cannon for the state of Texas.

NOBLE BROTHERS, Rome, Ga.

PECK, JOHN C., Atlanta, Ga. Made a rampart gun.

PHOENIX IRONWORKS, New Orleans, La. 8-inch Dahlgren navy gun.

QUINBY AND ROBINSON, Memphis, Tenn. 32-pounders.

RHAM, PHILIP, Richmond, Va. 6-pounder and 12-pounder carriages and caissons.

RICE AND WRIGHT, Florence, Ala. 24-pounder carriages, caissons, howitzers.

RICHARDS, A., Texas. 6-pounders.

SMITH, H. M., Richmond, Va. 6-pounder carriages and caissons.

STREET AND HUNGERFORD'S FOUNDRY, Memphis, Tenn. Parrott guns.

TALLBOTT AND BROTHER, Richmond, Va. 6-pounder carriages and caissons.

TAPPEY AND LUMSDEN, Petersburg, Va. In May 1861 manufactured a 5-shot revolving cannon which could be loaded "with the ease and rapidity of a Colt's revolver." Weight, about 600 lbs. Projectile, 3-inch ball, 4 lbs. in weight. The cannon was fired "with great precision" at a distance of 1200 yards.

TREDEGAR IRON WORKS, Richmond, Va. Brooke rifled cannon, a 7-inch rifle carrying a 160-pound bolt.

VAN PELT, I. AND J., Petersburg, Va. 6-pounder carriages and caissons.

WHITE, JOHN G., Macon, Ga. Gun carriages.

WOLFE, S. AND CO., New Orleans, La. 8- and 10-inch guns.

KNIVES

BAKER, JOHN, Georgia, Bowie knives.

BELL AND DAVIS, Atlanta, Ga. Bowie knife dated July 6, 1861.

BERRY, WILL, Georgia. Bowie knives.

BOYLE, GAMBLE, AND MACFEE, Richmond, Va.

BURGER AND BROTHERS, Richmond, Va.

CAMERON AND WINN, Georgia. Bowie knives.

CLARKSON AND CO., Richmond, Va.

DODGE, SIMON F., Winchester, Va. Bowie knives.

ETOWAH IRON WORKS, Etowah, Ga.

FITZPATRICK, REES, CAPT., Natchez, Miss.

FORD, J. J., Georgia.

GILLELAND, H. Made Bowie knives for Georgia.

GITTER AND MOSS, Memphis, Tenn.

GRAY, JOHN D. Bowie knives for Georgia.

HAIL, F. M., Georgia. Bowie knives.

HALL, JAMES H., Georgia. Bowie knives.

HAYNES, O. S., Georgia. Bowie knives.

HUGHES, R. J., Georgia. Bowie knives.

KNIGHT'S BLACKSMITH SHOP, Amelia, Va.

KRAFT, PETER W. Bowie knives.

LAN AND SHERMAN, Richmond, Va.

McKINSTRY, ALEXANDER. Bowie knives and Bowie-shaped pikes.

MOORE, J. W. AND L. L., Georgia. Bowie knives.

MORRISON, MURDOCH, Rockingham County, N.C. Bowie knives and pistols.

PEABODY, HIRAM, Richmond, Va.

SMITH, JOHN C., Georgia.

STATON, JOHN L., Scottsville, Va.

SUTHERLAND, Samuel, Richmond, Va.

UNION CAR WORKS, Portsmouth, Va.

UNION MANUFACTURING CO., Richmond, Va. Bowie knives and saber bayonets.

WEED, N. Made Bowie knives for Georgia.

WELCH, JAMES, Richmond, Va.

ZIMMERMAN, J. C. AND CO. Made Bowie knives for Georgia.

LANCES

READ AND DICKSON, Mississippi.

MACHINE GUN

WILLIAMS, R. S., Covington, Ky. A 1-pounder machine gun with a range of 2,000 yards. Used at Battle of Seven Pines.

MUSKETS, RIFLES AND CARBINES

BAKER, M. A., Fayetteville, N. C. Rifled muskets.

BARKER. Mississippi rifles.

BARRETT, A. R. & CO., Wytheville, Va.

BILHARTZ, HALL AND CO., Danville, Va. Carbines.

BILLUPS AND HASSELL, Pentitude, Texas. Mississippi rifles.

CHAPMAN, C. Model 1841 rifles.

CLARK AND LAMBE, Deep River, N.C. Sharpshooters' rifles.

GEORGIA ARMORY, Milledgeville, Ga.

GILLAM (or GILLIAM) AND MILLER. Mississippi rifles.

GRAY, JOHN D., Graysville, and Columbus, Ga. Mississippi rifles, Enfield rifles, carbines; also Bowie knives, pikes, sabers, wood canteens, buckets, pole slides and buttons for tents.

GREENWOOD AND GRAY, Columbus, Ga. Rifles, carbines and sabers.

HODGKINS, D. C. AND SON, Macon, Georgia. Carbines, surgical instruments, cotton goods.

HODGKINS, WALTER, Macon, Ga. Sharpshooters' rifles.
KEEN, WALKER AND CO., Danville, Va. Made carbines believed to have been the N. T. Read patent.
KREUTNER, C., Montgomery, Ala. Mississippi rifles.
LAMB AND BROTHER, Jamestown, N.C. Made 1841 model rifles.
MENDENHALL, JONES AND GARDNER, Jamestown, N.C. Mississippi rifles.
MISSISSIPPI STATE ARMORY. Carbines, chiefly Maynard type.
MORSE, GEORGE W. Breech-loading carbine.
MORSE, THOMAS. Sharpshooters' rifles.
MURRAY, JOHN P., Columbus, Ga. Mississippi rifles, musketoons, sharpshooters' rifles, model 1855 carbines.
MUSCOGEE IRON WORKS, Columbus, Ga. Small arms, saddles.
PAERSCH, ADALBERT, New Orleans, La. Invented a breech-loading musket, range 1,200 yards.
PULASKI GUN FACTORY, Pulaski, Tenn. Mississippi rifles.
ROBINSON, S. C. ARMS MANUFACTORY, Richmond, Va. Sharps model carbines.
SOUTHWESTERN FOUNDRY, Wytheville, Va. Rifles.
STATE MILITARY WORKS, Greenville, S.C. Morse carbines, muskets, and ammunition.
STURDIVANT, LEWIS G., Talladega, Ala. Rifles.
SUMNER ARMORY, Gallatin, Tenn.
SUTER, C. AND COMPANY, Selma, Ala. Rifles.
TALLASSEE ARMORY, Tallassee, Ala. Muskets and carbines.
TANNER, N. B., Bastrop, Texas. Smoothbore muskets; only one known.
TARPLEY, GARRETT AND CO., Greensboro, N.C. Tarpley carbines.
TILTON, GA. .58 caliber rifle.
TODD, GEORGE, Montgomery, Ala. Mississippi rifles.
TYLER ORDNANCE WORKS, Tyler, Texas. Rifles, canteens, ammunition, accouterments.
WALLIS AND RICE, Talladega, Ala. Mississippi rifles.
WHITESCARVER, CAMPBELL AND CO., Rusk, Texas. Mississippi rifles.
WINTER IRON WORKS, Montgomery, Ala. Mississippi rifles (See George Todd).

PIKES

ALFRED, B. B. Made pikes for Georgia.
BAKER, JOHN, Georgia. Bowie knives and pikes for Georgia.
BERRY, WILL, Georgia.
CLEVELAND, Marion, Georgia.
DORSETT, J. R., Georgia.
DUNLAP, T., Georgia.
ELDER, WILLIAM H. AND D. H. WINN, Georgia.
ESPER, JOHN, Atlanta, Ga.
EVE, J. C., Georgia.
FORD AND DUMAS, Georgia.
GRAVES, REV., Georgia. Methodist preacher who invented a pike in which an 18-inch blade was sheathed. When a spring was touched, this blade shot out sufficiently to "impale an enemy."
GRIER AND MASTERSON, Georgia.
HATCH, NASON (Georgia?).
HIGGINS, J. M. Made pikes for Georgia.
HODGSON, E. R. AND BROTHER, Georgia.
HURT, JAMES, Georgia.
HYER, F. F., Georgia.
KENT, ALFRED. Made pikes for Georgia.
LOWRY AND WILDER, Georgia.
MARSHALL, RICE AND CO., Georgia.
MARTIN, J. J. Made pikes for Georgia.
MASSEY, O. W., Georgia.
MATTHEWS, M. E., Georgia.
NISBET, T. C., Georgia.
RAINEY, W. L., Georgia.
REID, HUMPHREY, Georgia.
SCHLEY, W., Georgia.
STEVENS, H., Georgia.
TURNER AND WEBB, Georgia.
WATKINS, W. N., Georgia.
WEED, N., Georgia. Pikes and Bowie knives.
WHITE, J. G., Georgia.
WILLIAMS, E. P., Georgia.
WINANS' WORKS, Baltimore, Md.
WINN, D. H., Georgia.
WOODRUFF, D. B., Georgia.
WYMAN, G. N. AND COMPANY, Augusta, Georgia.

PORTABLE BREASTWORKS

HARTMAN, H. T., Rockbridge County, Va. Invented a portable breastworks August 21, 1861.

PROJECTILES AND AMMUNITION

ATLANTA MACHINE WORKS, Atlanta, Ga. Atlantic and North Carolina Railroad Co. was awarded a contract in February 1861 to produce "shell and shot" and to convert flintlock muskets at their shop in Newbern, N. C.
AUGUSTA ARSENAL, Augusta, Ga.
AYRES AND LITTLEPAGE, Richmond, Va. Bullet-rolling machine.
BAKER AND CO., Richmond, Va.
BOWEN AND CO., Pendleton, S.C. Powder.
CAMERON AND COMPANY, Charleston, S.C. Percussion caps.
CHURCHILL, C. B. AND CO., Natchez, Miss.
CLAIBORNE MACHINE WORKS, Nashville, Tenn. Shot and shell.
COLUMBUS IRON WORKS, Columbus, Ga.
DEANE, F. B., JR. AND SONS, Lynchburg, Va.
FISHER, W. B. AND C., Lynchburg, Va. Percussion caps.
FOSTER, CONSTANTINE, Burnet, Texas. Powder.
GWIN AND ELLSBERRY, Alabama. Supplied powder to Ala.
LITTLE ROCK ARSENAL, Little Rock, Ark. Small arms ammunition.
MAGEE, DAVID, Fredericksburg, Texas. Percussion caps made from leather and paper.
NEW ORLEANS ARSENAL, New Orleans, La. Ammunition.
NORTH CAROLINA POWDER MANUFACTURING CO., Charlotte, N.C. Capacity of 1,000 pounds per day.
OSTENDORFF AND CO., Walhalla, S.C. Powder.
PALMETTO ARMORY, Columbia, S.C. Artillery and small arms ammunition.
RALEIGH (N.C.) PERCUSSION CAP FACTORY. As early as May 1861, Professor Emmons and Charles Kuester were producing percussion caps at this establishment.
ROWAN (may be ROWIN AND MARCHBANKS), Waxahachie, Texas. Powder.
SAN ANTONIO MILLS, San Antonio, Texas. Powder.
SCHOFIELD BROTHERS, Macon, Ga. Cannon balls.
SYCAMORE POWDER MILLS, Nashville, Tenn. Percussion caps, powder.
WINSHIP AND BROTHER, Atlanta, Ga. Shot and shell.
WINTFIELD, THOMAS S., Charlotte, N.C. Explosives.
YALE, C. D., Va. Powder.

REVOLVERS

COLUMBUS FIREARMS MANUFACTURING CO., Columbus, Ga. Navy revolvers.
GARRETT, J. F. AND CO., Greensboro, N.C.
GRISWOLD AND GUNNISON, Griswoldville, Ga. "Brass-framed Colts."
HAIMAN L. AND BROTHER, Columbus, Ga.
HENLEY, W. H. Made Colt dragoon revolvers for the C.S.
LEECH AND RIGDON, Memphis, Tenn., and Columbus, Miss. Revolvers, swords, spurs and other military equipment.
MACON ARMORY, Macon, Ga. Spiller and Burr revolvers.
ROGERS, E. H., Augusta, Ga.

SCHNEIDER AND GLASSICK, Memphis, Tenn.
SHEETS, M., Shepherdstown, Va. Cal. 31 brass-framed revolvers.
SPILLER AND BURR, Richmond, Va. and Atlanta, Ga.
TUCKER, SHERRARD AND CO., Lancaster, Texas. Dragoon size imitation Colt revolvers.

SWORD MAKERS AND DEALERS

ALLEN AND DIAL, Columbia, S.C.
BASSONET, L., Mobile, Ala.
BOYLE, GAMBLE AND McFEE, Richmond, Va.
BURGER AND BROTHERS, Richmond, Va.
CHEEVE, S. C., location unknown.
CHRISTOPHER, C. J., Atlanta, Ga.
CHURCHILL, C. B. AND CO., Natchez, Miss.
COLUMBIA ARMORY, Columbia, S.C.
CONFEDERATE STATES ARMORY, Kenansville, N.C.
CONNING, JAMES, Mobile, Ala.
COOK AND BROTHER, Athens, Ga.
COURTNEY AND TENNANT, Charleston, S.C.
CRUSH AND WADE, Christiansburg, Va. (sabers).
DEWITT, A. H., Columbus, Ga. (sabers, swords, belts).
DICKSON, NELSON AND CO., Dickson, Ala. and Ga.
DODGE, SIMON F., Winchester, Va. Bowie knives.
DRISCOLL, T. D., Howardsville, Va.
DULFINO CO., New Orleans.
FREEMAN, B. P., Macon, Ga.
FROELICH, LOUIS, Wilmington, N.C.
GEORGIA ARMORY, Milledgeville, Ga.
GREEN (COLONEL OR GENERAL), Ga. Contracted with Atlanta Arsenal to make sabers. These sabers were of poor quality.
GREENWOOD AND GRAY, Columbus, Ga.
GRISWOLD, THOMAS AND CO., New Orleans.
HAIMAN, L. AND BROTHER, Columbus, Ga. (swords and sabers).
HALFMANN AND TAYLOR, Montgomery, Ala.
HALL, C., Norfolk, Va.
HAYDEN AND WHILDEN, Charleston, S.C.
HEYER, FREDERICK, Richmond, Va. Confederate naval cutlasses.
HYDE AND GOODRICH, New Orleans, La.
JOHNSTON, E. J. AND CO., Macon, Ga. Swords and cutlasses.
KEAN'S SWORD SHOP, Columbus, Ga.
KRAFT, PETER, W., Columbia, S.C.
LEECH, THOMAS S. (Memphis Novelty Works), Memphis, Tenn., Columbus, Miss., Greensboro, Ga.
MACON ARMORY, Macon, Ga.
MARSHALL, H. AND CO., Atlanta, Ga.
McELROY, W. J. AND CO., Macon, Ga. Swords, cutlasses, Bowie knives, sword belts, spurs, tin canteens, bayonets, pikes.
McKENNIE AND CO., Charlottesville, Va. (swords).
MEMPHIS NOVELTY WORKS, Memphis, Tenn. Swords, spurs, accouterments.
MITCHELL AND TYLER, Richmond, Va.
NASHVILLE PLOW WORKS, Nashville, Tenn. Made swords with "C.S.A." on the guard.
RICHMOND, C. AND CO., Memphis, Tenn.
ROWLAND. Short artillery sword.
SHARP AND HAMILTON, Nashville, Tenn. Sabers.
TREDEGAR IRON WORKS, Richmond, Va.
WALLIS, DANIEL, Talladega, Ala.
WILSON, J. C., Houston, Texas.

UNIFORMS AND CLOTHING

BAILEY, THOMAS R. AND SON, Charlottesville, Va. Shoes.
BELLENOT AND ULRICH, New Orleans, La. Louisiana state buttons.
BELLENOT, C., New Orleans, La. Louisiana State buttons.
BENTS, J. A. AND S., Baltimore, Md. Buttons.
BIRD, WM. AND CO., London, England. Buttons.
BOUIS, S. AND CO., Richmond, Va. Belt buckles.
BUCKEYE LAND FACTORY, Charlottesville, Va. Cloth for uniforms.
BUCKLEY, S. AND CO., Birmingham, England. Buttons.
CADMAN (?), Columbus, Ga. Buttons.
CANFIELD AND BROTHERS, Baltimore, Md. Maryland buttons.
CRENSHAW MILLS, Richmond, Va. Woolen uniform cloth.
DOWLER, W., Birmingham, England. Buttons.
EAGLE MANUFACTURING CO., Columbus, Ga. Cloth for uniforms, also tent cloth and India rubber cloth.
GIBBES, JAMES G., Columbia, S.C. Uniforms, hats, boots, shoes.
GODCHAUX, LEON, New Orleans, La. Louisiana State buttons.
HOPPE, F. A. AND T., Charlottesville, Va. Shoes and boots.
HOWIE, J. M., Charlotte, N.C. Buckles.
JAMESTOWN WOOLEN MILL, Old Jamestown, N.C. Cloth for uniforms.
LAVASSEUR, H., New Orleans, La. Buttons.
LEECH, JOHN AND CO., Madison County, Va. Boots and shoes.
LEWIS, E. M. AND CO., Richmond, Va. Buttons.
LOYD, W. S., Columbus, Ga. Military caps.
MICON, B. H., Tallassee, Ala. Uniform cloth.
MUNDS AND HENNING, Columbia, S.C. Shoes.
MYERS, S. A., Richmond, Va. Made Va. and N.C. buttons.
REMSEN, C. P., Columbia, S.C. Military hats.
ROTHCHILD, S., Columbus, Ga. Uniforms.
ROWYER AND LAVASSEUR, New Orleans. Buttons.
RUSH, S., Forestville, Va. Hats.
SAPPINGTON AND CO., Columbus, Ga. Shoes.
STRADTMAN, FREDERICK WM., Cahaba, Ala. Shoes.
TERRY AND JUDEN CO., New Orleans. Louisiana state buttons.
THORN, SAUL D., Columbus, Ga. Buttons and caps.
WENDLINGER, C., Richmond, Va. Virginia buttons (possibly post-Civil War).
WILT AND KLINE, Columbia, S.C. Buttons.

CONFEDERATE PATENTS, 1861-1865

One of the real finds resulting from research for this book was a complete run of the Reports of the Confederate Commissioner of Patents 1861 through 1864. It is believed that these reports have been used in only cursory fashion, if at all, by previous researchers. Great credit is due Miss Josephine Cobb and Mrs. Sara Jackson for directing attention to these Patent Reports. The following list includes all patents relevant to this study which are listed in the Confederate Commissioner's annual reports. No report for 1865 could be found and the patents themselves were not to be found in the National Archives. They probably were destroyed with other Confederate records at the end of the war. The various patents are here listed in the order in which they appeared in the original reports.

The different categories of patents are here given as they appeared in the original Reports of the Commissioner, Rufus S. Rhodes.

Year	*Category*	*Patent No.*	*Patentee*	*Date*
1861	*Mathematical instruments*			
	Machine for measuring distance	36	Alfred G. Hearn, Arkadelphia, Ark.	Sept. 10
1863	Instrument for measuring distance	162	John J. Daly, New Orleans, La.	Apr. 18
1864	Instrument for calculating distances	240	J. D. Gressit, Urbana, Va.	Apr. 15
	Leather			
1861	Stirrups	2	Charles E. Brown, Staunton, Va.	Aug. 11
1862	Wooden soled shoes	130	E. S. Collins, Aspinwall, Va.	Dec. 30
	Wooden bottom shoes	68	G. M. Rhodes and A. Bingham, Talladega, Ala.	Feb. 1
1863	Wooden soled shoes	171	Sylvester L. Burford, Lynchburg, Va.	May 21
	Wooden soled shoes	167	Robert Creugbaur, Austin, Texas	May 1
	Wooden soled shoes	195	Robert Creugbaur, Austin, Texas	Aug. 23
	Half wooden soled shoes	196	Robert Creugbaur, Austin, Texas	Aug. 28
	Spur	206	E. S. Alexander, Moorfield, Va.	Oct. 10
1864	Wooden shoe sole	264	A. F. Purejoy, Forrestville, N. C.	Nov. 22
	Household Furniture			
1861	Camp bedstead	30	Arthur E. Hall, South Quay, Va.	Oct. 7
	Camp cot	39	Henry C. Goodrich, Augusta, Ga.	Oct. 30
	Camp chest and bed combined	38	R. C. Howe, Richmond, Va.	Oct. 29
	Camp chest and bed combined	41	Wm. W. Rickenbaker, Beaufort, S. C.	Nov. 7
1862	Tent	99	S. A. LeToudal, Mobile, Ala.	July 22
	Camp cot	60	Jacob B. and W. L. Platt, Augusta, Ga.	Jan. 7
	Knapsack and tent combined	101	James E. Watson, Petersburg, Va.	July 29
1864	Combined bend and tent	246	A. D. McCoy, Livingston, Ala.	Jan. 31
	Wearing apparel			
1861	Military Cap	56	Henry Domler, Wilmington, N. C.	Dec. 14
	Lumber			
1863	Button machine	172	Alfred L. Bowen, Winchester, Va.	May 25
	Fine Arts			
1864	Photographic process for duplicating maps	227	R. S. Sanxay and A. Gomert, Richmond, Va.	Feb. 5
	Navigation and Maritime Implements			
1862	Ship of war	100	John M. Brooke, Richmond, Va.	July 29
	Reversible hook	107	John M. Brooke, Richmond, Va.	Sept. 26
	Vessel of war	98	John Cawdon, New Orleans, La.	July 22
	Submarine battery	61	J. Nichols and J. Bennett, assigners to F. Smith, Memphis, Tenn.	Jan. 8
	Submarine battery	114	James C. Patton, Petersburg, Va.	Oct. 14
	Machine for operating submarine batteries	127	J. G. Wire, New Orleans, La.	Dec. 8
	Portable flat boat	90	E. B. Stephens, assignor to J. A. VanLew, Charleston, S. C.	May 10
1863	Spar torpedo	168	F. D. Lee, Charleston, S. C.	May 4
	Submarine apparatus	211	C. Williams, St. Louis, Mo.	Oct. 28
1864	Seagoing vessel	241	F. G. Smith, Columbia, Tenn.	Apr. 18
	Submarine boat	258	C. Williams, St. Louis, Mo.	Oct. 6
	Submarine boat	261	C. Williams, St. Louis, Mo.	Oct. 25
	Firearms and Implements of war			
1861	Bullet mould	34	Joseph Thomas, Batesville, Ark.	Oct. 15
	Cannon	29	James Lynch, Petersburg, Va.	Oct. 4
	Manufacture of cannon	19	James H. Carkut (or Harkut), Natchez, Miss.	Sept. 3
	Breech-loading cannon	35	Daniel Oswalt, Cubahatchie, Ala.	Oct. 15
	Cartridges	12	Frederick J. Gardner, Newbern, N. C.	Aug. 17
	Paper cartridges	26	John R. Spillman, Warrenton, Va.	Oct. 1

Year	Category	Patent No.	Patentee	Date
1861	Device for making cartridges	27	John R. Spillman, Warrenton, Va.	Oct. 2
	Cartridge box	40	John P. Gorman, Charlestown, Va.	Oct. 2
	Breech-loading firearm	24	E. T. Ligon, Demopolis, Ala.	Sept. 27
	Percussion fuzes	23	E. D. Gotthiel and R. Mott, New Orleans, La.	Sept. 19
	Breech-loading automatic gun	8	Phidello Hall, Springfield, Texas	Aug. 10
	Breech-loading gun	21	James P. Rankin, Marion, N. C.	Sept. 14
	Breech-loading gun	1	James H. VanHouten, Savannah, Ga.	Aug. 1
	Breech-loading gun	54	John M. White, Citruille, Ala.	Dec. 7
	Lance or pike attaching to gun	11	Armand Preot, Grand Hill, Va.	Aug. 15
	Revolving pistol	9	Thomas W. Cofer, Portsmouth, Va.	Aug. 12
	Sword bayonet	18	E. Boyle, T. Gamble, E. Macfce, Richmond, Va.	Sept. 2
	Sabre lance	5	R. W. Habersham, Beaufort, S. C.	Aug. 6
1862	Percussion fuze	70	R. Archer, Richmond, Va.	Jan. 7
	Breech-loading cannon	125	M. Bridges, Memphis, Tenn.	Nov. 20
	Breech-loading firearms	111	A. J. M. T. O. Clanton, Panola, Miss.	Oct. 3
	Breech-loading firearms	91	J. W. Howlett, Greensboro, N. C.	May 10
	Projectile	106	Lucien Hopson, Lampassas, Texas	Sept. 25
	Breech-loading gun	58	Carl Laquequist, Macon, Ga.	Jan. 21
	Bullet machine	79	C. V. Littlepage, Austin, Texas	Mar. 11
	Instrument for levelling cannon	109	J. A. LeToudal, Mobile, Ala.	Sept. 29
	Mode of manufacturing scabbards	88	Augustus McBurthe, Richmond, Va.	Apr. 14
	Fuze	92	C. A. McEvoy, Richmond, Va.	May 1
	Fuze	93	C. A. McEvoy, Richmond, Va.	Apr. 23
	Fuze	123	C. A. McEvoy, Richmond, Va.	Nov. 15
	Army canteen	129	Nathaniel Nuckolls, Russel County, Ala.	Dec. 11
	Instrument for sighting cannon	84	J. C. Owing, J. H. C. Taylor, Chas. E. Stuart, Alexandria, Va.	Mar. 21
	Bullet machine	112	Wm. Spillman, Prattsville, Ala.	Oct. 3
	Firearms	96	G. J. Peterson, Marion, N. C.	May 31
	Projectile	113	Wm. S. Winfield, Springfield, Tenn.	Oct. 11
	Breech-loading cannon	121	D. R. Williams, Richmond, Va.	Nov. 5
	Machinery for traversing guns	132	Jos. A. Yates, Charleston, S. C.	Dec. 30
1863	Breech-loading firearm	163	C. W. Alexander, Moorfield, Va.	April 18
	Projectile	143	R. H. Barrett, Murfreesboro, N. C.	Jan. 26
	Projectile	160	Thomas H. Bacon, Hannibal, Mo.	April 15
	Projectile	133	Alonzo C. Chinn, Mobile, Ala.	Jan. 3
	Projectile	191	H. Conner, Mobile, Ala.	Aug. 22
	Projectile	185	Philip E. Love, Augusta, Ga.	July 22
	Fuze	174	Wm. LeRoy Browne, Ivy Depot, Va.	May 25
	Fuze	176	Isidor P. Girardy, Augusta, Ga.	June 5
	Fuze	135	C. A. McElvay, Richmond, Va.	Jan. 7
	Fuze, gauge, and cutter	182	Albert Bloomer, Richmond, Va.	July 15
	Torpedo	187	A. Barbarin, New Orleans, La.	Aug. 5
	Torpedo	197	Robert Cresezbaur, Austin, Texas	Aug. 31
	Torpedo	198	Z. McDaniel, Glasgow, Ky.	Sept. 8
	Torpedo	202	Z. McDaniel, Glasgow, Ky.	Sept. 21
	Torpedo	200	E. C. Singer, Port Lavaca, Texas	Sept. 15
	Explosive apparatus	181	Benj. M. Cook, Kinston, N. C.	July 10
	Breech-loading cannon	192	H. Conner, Mobile, Ala.	Aug. 22
	Revolving firearms	178	Asa George, Charlotte, N. C.	June 10
	Breech plug	149	D. W. Hughes, Don Juan, Ariz. Terr.	Feb. 18
	Revolving firearms	151	A. Legden, Atlanta, Ga.	Mar. 10
	Breech-loading firearms	199	Thomas Morse, Richmond, Va.	Sept. 10
	Breech-loading firearms	154	N. T. Reed, Danville, Va.	March 20
	Breech-loading firearms	148	J. H. Tarpley, Greensboro, N. C.	Feb. 14
	Cap filling machine	209	W. H. Smith, Richmond, Va.	Oct. 24
	Bullet machine	194	R. J. White and Geo. H. Lenher, Richmond, Va.	Aug. 25
	Machine for casting friction tubes	203	B. H. Washington, Hannibal, Mo.	Sept. 24
	Bullet swaging machine	212	B. H. Washington, Hannibal, Mo.	Oct. 29
	Machine for cutting and serrating friction wires	213	B. H. Washington, Hannibal, Mo.	Oct. 31
	Machine for finishing cannon	214	B. H. Washington, Hannibal, Mo.	Nov. 5
	Machine for casing cannon	218	B. H. Washington, Hannibal, Mo.	Nov. 23
	Machine for filling cartridges	161	Ellison Yerbey, Richmond, Va.	April 15
1864	Torpedo	245	A. Barbarin, New Orleans, La.	May 20
	Torpedo	257	Richard M. Harvey, New Orleans, La.	Oct. 5
	Torpedo	236	J. C. Patton and E. Cuthbert, Petersburg, Va.	Mar. 30
	Torpedo	260	J. C. Patton, Petersburg, Va.	Oct. 26
	Torpedo	255	C. Williams, St. Louis, Mo.	Sept. 6
	Torpedo	256	C. Williams, St. Louis, Mo.	Sept. 7

Year	*Category*	*Patent No.*	*Patentee*	*Date*
1864	Projectile	253	James D. Layton, Memphis, Tenn.	Aug. 25
	Projectile	226	John Scott, Ocala, Fla.	Jan. 27
	Projectile	262	D. M. Somers and H. Dabney, Lynchburg, Va.	Dec. 17
	Projectile	233	R. H. S. Thompson, New Orleans, La.	Sept. 6
	Clock torpedo	248	Wm. Moon, Richmond, Va.	July 11
	Breech-loading cannon	232	George W. Powell, Clay hill, Ala.	Feb. 29
	Gun powder steaming barrels	259	George W. Rains, Augusta, Ga.	Oct. 25
	Instrument for fixing sights to cannon	231	C. E. Stuart, Owings, Taylor, Richmond, Va.	Feb. 26
	Percussion cap rammer	266	W. N. Smith, Richmond, Va.	Jan. 6

BIBLIOGRAPHY

Newspapers and Periodicals

Frank Leslie's Illustrated Weekly, 1861-1865.
Harper's Weekly, 1861-1865.
The U. S. Army and Navy Journal and Gazette of the Regular and Volunteer Forces, 1863-1866.

Congressional Documents

Senate Ex. Document No. 16, 45th Congress, 3d Session.
Senate Report No. 183, "Sale of Arms," 42d Congress, 2d Session.
House Report No. 2, "Government Contracts," 37th Congress, 2d Session.
House Ex. Document No. 67, "Purchase of Arms," 37th Congress, 2d Session.
Rep. Com. No. 266, 40th Congress, 3d Session.
Misc. Document No. 191, 42nd Congress, 2d Session.

Official Publications—State

General Regulations for the Military Forces of N. Y., 1863. Albany, N. Y., 1863.

Official Publications—U. S. Government

War Department
General Orders, Adjutant General's Dept., 1861-1865.
Revised Regulations for the Army of the United States 1861. Philadelphia, 1862.
Ordnance Manual, 1862, Third Edition. Philadelphia, 1862.
Instructions for Making Quarterly Returns of Ordnance and Ordnance Stores. Washington, 1865.
Instruction for Field Artillery. Philadelphia, 1863.
Instruction for Heavy Artillery. Washington, 1863.
The Medical and Surgical History of the War of the Rebellion, 6 vols. Washington, 1870-1883.
Pamphlet No. 5, U. S. Medical Dept. Exhibit at International Exhibition, 1876, Philadelphia. Philadelphia, 1876.
Official Records of the Union and Confederate Armies, 128 vols. and Atlas. Washington, 1880-1901.

Navy Department

Regulations for the Government of the United States Navy. Washington, 1865.
Allowances Established for Vessels of the United States Navy, 1864. Washington 1865.
Ordnance Instructions for the United States Navy, 3d Ed., 1863. Washington, 1864.
Official Records of the Union and Confederate Navies in The War of the Rebellion, 28 vols. Washington, 1894-1927.

Books and Manuals

Abbott, Henry L., *Siege Artillery in the Campaigns against Richmond.* New York, 1867.
Albaugh, Wm. A., III, *Confederate Edged Weapons.* New York, 1961.
Albaugh, Wm. A., III and Simmons, Edward N., *Confederate Arms.* Harrisburg, Pa., 1957.
Barnes, J. S., *Submarine Warfare.* New York, 1869.
Benton, J. G., *Ordnance and Gunnery.* N. Y., 1861.
Billings, John D., *Hardtack and Coffee.* Boston, 1889.
Boatner, Mark M., *The Civil War Dictionary.* New York, 1959.
Brown, J. Willard, *The Signal Corps, U. S. A. in the War of the Rebellion.* Boston, 1896.
Bruce, Robert V., *Lincoln and the Tools of War.* Indianapolis, 1956.
Buckeridge, J. O., *Lincoln's Choice.* Harrisburg, 1956.
Casey, Silas, *Infantry Tactics*, 3 vols. Philadelphia, 1862.
Catalog-Bull Run Trader 1960-1961. Falls Church, Va., 1961.
Catalog, Francis Bannerman Sons. New York, New York, 1955.
Catalog, Schuyler, Hartley and Graham. New York, 1864.
Catalog, Starr Arms Company. New York, 1864.
Cheney, Newel, *History of the Ninth Regiment, New York Volunteer Cavalry.* Poland Center, N. Y., 1900.
Chinn, George M., *The Machine Gun*, Vol. 1. Washington, 1951.
Cooke, Philip St. George, *Cavalry Tactics.* New York, 1862.
Dahlgren, M. V., *Memoir of John A. Dahlgren.* Boston, 1882.
Duane, J. C., *Manual for Engineer Troops*, 3d Ed. New York, 1864.
Edwards, William B., *Civil War Guns*, Harrisburg, Pa., 1962.
Eldredge, D., *The Third New Hampshire.* Boston, 1893.
Fuller, Claud, *The Rifled Musket.* Harrisburg, Pa., 1958.
Fuller, Claud, *The Whitney Firearms.* Huntington, W. Va., 1946.
Fuller, Claud, and Steuart, Richard D., *Firearms of the Confederacy.* Huntington, W. Va., 1944.
Gibbon, John, *The Artillerist's Manual.* New York, 1860.
Gillmore, Q. A., *Engineer and Artillery Operations Against the Defences of Charleston Harbor in 1863.* New York, 1865. Supplementary Report to the foregoing. New York, 1868.
Gluckman, Arcadi, *United States Martial Pistols and Revolvers.* Buffalo, N. Y., 1944.
———, *United States Muskets, Rifles and Carbines.* Buffalo, N. Y., 1948.
Gluckman, Arcadi, and Satterlee, L. D., *American Gun Makers.* Harrisburg, Pa., 1953.
Gould, John M., *History of the First Tenth-Twenty-Ninth Maine Regiment.* Portland, 1871.
Graham, Mathew J., *The Ninth Regiment New York Volunteers (Hawkins' Zouaves).* New York, 1900.
Hamilton, Frank H., *A Treatise on Military Surgery and Hygiene.* New York, 1865.
Hanson, Charles E., Jr., *The Plains Rifle.* Harrisburg, 1960.
Hardee, W. J., *Rifle and Light Infantry Tactics*, 2 vols. Philadelphia, 1855.
Haupt, Herman, *Military Bridges.* New York, 1864.
Haydon, F. Stansbury, *Aeronautics in the Union and Confederate Armies*, Vol. 1. Baltimore, 1941.
Hicks, James E., *Notes on United States Ordnance*, Vol. 1. N. Y., 1940.
———, *Nathan Starr, Arms Maker.* Mt. Vernon, N. Y., 1940.
Hill, J. A., *The Story of One Regiment* (11th Maine Infantry). N. Y., 1896.
Hinman, Wilbur F., *Corporal Si Klegg and His Pard.* Cleveland, 1887.
Hyde, Thomas W., *Following the Greek Cross or, Memories of the Sixth Army Corps.* Boston, 1895.
Ingraham, Charles A., *Elmer E. Ellsworth and the Zouaves of '61.* Chicago, 1925.
Johnson, David F., *Uniform Buttons-American Armed Forces 1784-1948*, 2 vols. Watkins Glen, N. Y., 1948.
Johnson, John, *The Defense of Charleston Harbor, 1863-1865.* Charleston, S. C., 1890.
Kauffman, Henry J., *The Pennsylvania Kentucky Rifle.* Harrisburg, Pa., 1960.

King, Charles, *An Initial Experience*. Philadelphia, 1895.
Logan, Herschel C., *Cartridges*. Harrisburg, Pa., 1959.
McClellan, George B., *Regulations for the Field Service of Cavalry in Time of War*. Philadelphia, 1862.
McClellan, George B., *Manual of Bayonet Exercise*. Philadelphia, 1852.
Miller, Francis Trevelyan, *Photographic History of the Civil War*, 10 vols. New York, 1912.
Mitchell, James L., *Colt*. Harrisburg, Pa., 1959.
Myer, Albert J., *A. Manual of Signals*. New York, 1868.
Palmer, Abraham J., *The History of the Forty-Eighth Regiment, New York State Volunteers*. Brooklyn, N. Y., 1885.
Peterson, Harold, *The American Sword 1775-1945*. New Hope, Pa., 1954.
———, *American Knives*. New York, 1958.
Plum, William R., *The Military Telegraph during the Civil War in the United States*, 2 vols. Chicago, 1882.
Porter, Horace, *Campaigning with Grant*. N. Y., 1897.
Riling, Ray, *The Powder Flask Book*. New Hope, Pa., 1953.
Roberts, Joseph, *Handbook of Artillery*, 5th Ed. N. Y., 1863.
Scott, H. L., *Military Dictionary*, N. Y., 1864.
Scott, Winfield, *Infantry Tactics*, 3 vols. N. Y., 1840.
Simpson, Edward, *A Treatise on Ordnance and Naval Gunnery*, 2d Ed. N. Y., 1862.
Sipley, Louis Walton, *Collector's Guide to American Photography*. Philadelphia, 1957.
Smith, Stephen, *Hand-Book of Surgical Operations*. N. Y., 1862.
Smith, Winston O., *The Sharps Rifle*. N. Y., 1943.
Stevens, C. A., *Berdan's United States Sharpshooters in the Army of the Potomac*. St. Paul, Minn., 1892.
Wilcox, C. M., *Rifles and Rifle Practice*. N. Y., 1859.
Wiley, Bell Irvin, *The Life of Billy Yank*. Indianapolis, 1951.
———, *The Life of Johnny Reb*. Indianapolis, 1943.

CIVIL WAR COLLECTOR'S ENCYCLOPEDIA

Volume II

To

John A Marks

with whom I have spent many enjoyable hours, both in discussing "the war" and in seeking the type of objects shown in this book.

VOLUME II

Foreword

Several years after the war, a veteran listed the non-regulation items he took with him when he left Maine for the front. He could not remember everything but did recall the following: tin pail, tin pan, cup, knife, fork, spoon, woolen blanket, rubber blanket, underclothing, lanelock, portfolio, drinking tube, pencils, stencils, ink, patent pen, stationery, comb, brushed, needles and pins, a revolver with several boxes of metallic cartridges, a "murderous looking knife" (which he termed "a cross between a bush scythe and a butcher's cleaver"), money belt, and numerous patent medicines. In addition, of course, he still had his musket accounterments, etc. to carry!

The study and collecting of Civil War soldiers' "impedimenta" is a venture rich in interest and a constant source of surprise and amusement!

Acknowledgments

The author is especially indebted to Mr. William C. Davis, editor of *Civil War Times* Illustrated for permission to use my articles previously published in that magazine under the heading "Weapons and Equipment". I also want to thank Jack Magune of Worcester, Massachusetts whose cooperation and expert knowledge have aided materially in acquiring and identifying many items. Much of the photographic work has been done by Bobby Bell of Bell Studio, Lancaster, S.C. He has my sincere thanks! Also, of special value and interest are the pictures contributed by Herb Peck, Jr. of Nashville, Tennessee who has done so much in preserving the pictorial side of the war. My talented wife, Marnie, did all the photographic work on the items of the Solingen museum. She has been a constant inspiration!

Colleagues of the University of South Carolina's Institute of Archeology and Anthropology have assisted materially in several phases of the book's preparation. I would mention especially Gordon Brown for his photographs and R. Darby Erd for the eagle motif used in the brochures announcing the book's production. The Institute's Director, Dr. Robert L. Stephenson, has been most cooperative in support throughout the book's preparation, both in use of facilities and in encouragement.

I express sincere thanks to the following:

Museums

Das Heeregeschichtliche Museum - Vienna, Austria
Deutsche Klingen Museum - Solingen, Germany
H. M. Tower of London - London, England
Imperial War Museum - London, England
Smithsonian Institution - Washington, D.C.
Virginia Historical Society Collection (Battle Abbey) - Richmond, Virginia

Individuals

William A. Albaugh III, Falls Church, Va.
Ed and Margie Bearss, Arlington, Va.
Brian Bennett, Phoenix, Arizona
Ralph C. Cox, Savannah, Ga.
Tom Dickey, Atlanta, Ga.
Beverly M. DuBose, Jr., Atlanta, Ga.
Kenneth M. Eaton, Homer, N.Y.
Norm Flayderman, New Milford, Conn.
Maurice Garb, Baton Rouge, La.
Hans Gerhold, Solingen, Germany
Craddock R. Goins, Jr., Assistant Currator, Division of Military History, Smithsonian Institution
Al Gross, Cleveland, Ohio
Dr. Hanns - Ulrich Haedeke, Solingen, Germany
David C. Hannah, Rexburg, Idaho
T. Sherman Harding, Orlando, Florida
John L. Herring, Lancaster, S.C.
Gerald L. James, Keokuk, Iowa
Carol Kemph, Atlanta, Ga.
John Henry Kurtz, Los Angeles, California
Lon William Keim, M.D., Richmond, Va.
William Langlois, San Francisco, California
Herschel C. Logan, Salina, Kansas

Dr. John L. Margreiter, St. Louis, Missouri
Kendall B. Mattern, Havertown, Pa.
Clarence McGinnis, Morristown, Tenn.
Colonel Joseph B. Mitchell, Alexandria, Va.
Bill Moore, Baton Rouge, La.
James F. Moser, Jr., Orange, Va.
Harold L. Peterson, Washington, D.C.
Stanley S. Phillips, Lanham, Maryland
Robert M. Reilly, Baton Rouge, La.
Robert L. Robinson III, Savannah, Ga.
Louis G. Stockho, Vero Beach, Florida
John Walter, Brighton, Sussex, England
L. V. Warren, Memphis, Tenn.
Michael R. Woshner, Pittsburgh, Pa.

CIVIL WAR COLLECTOR'S ENCYCLOPEDIA ADDITIONS AND CORRECTIONS TO VOLUME TWO

Since publication of Volume II of *Collector's Encyclopedia,* the following additions and contributions have been submitted by the readers. The author is sincerely appreciative of these contributions.

William A. Clark; New Egypt, New Jersey. **SUBJECT:** Solingen Military Products (pp. 178-179). Kirschbaum & Bremsley used the symbol "D" as shown on page 179 (a knight's helmet) under the firm name of: C. R. KIRSCHBAUM-SOLINGEN.

Dr. E. Cantey Haile, Jr.; Columbia, South Carolina. **SUBJECT:** Bleeder (p. 9). Doctor Haile identifies this definitely to be a surgeon's "bleeder". This was a device to initiate bleeding by a spring-triggered series of small blades which penetrated the skin about ⅛ of an inch.

Richard Lucas; Rodeo, California. **SUBJECT:** Identity of Federal cavalryman on page 29. He is SUMNER A HALWAY, Co. "H", 1st Maine Cavalry. Halway (Sept. 28, 1839-Feb. 28, 1919) enlisted September 27, 1861 and was discharged for disability November 20, 1863.

Craig Margison; Riverside, California. **SUBJECT:** OLI buckle (p. 17). Cites two authorities who identify this buckle as OGLETHORPE LIGHT INFANTRY and **not** OHIO LIGHT INFANTRY.

Introduction

The purpose of this book is two-fold. First, it brings together in one volume the specialized articles which appeared in the *Civil War Times Illustrated* under the caption "Weapons and Equipment." At the request of Civil War students and collectors, and by the generous cooperation of editor William C. Davis, selected articles are now available in book form.

Secondly, the author has prepared additional articles, most of which are complete studies in themselves, while the others include supplemental material not previously covered in his basic works already published:

Civil War Collector's Encyclopedia
They Fought for the Union
Civil War Sutlers and Their Wares

It is obvious to students of the 1861-1865 period that the varied list of items used by men of both sides is almost endless, and no *complete* list and description is possible. Newly discovered items are constantly turning up. I am acutely aware of this by the hundreds of letters I receive asking me to identify unusual Civil War artifacts.

This book is the result of extensive personal research, supplemented by discussion with other Civil War collectors to insure accuracy and coverage of subject matter. It is the author's hope that this volume will assist collector and student alike and will be accorded a reception similar to that received by the first volume of *Civil War Collectors Encyclopedia.*

Unless otherwise noted, all items illustrated are from the author's collection.

A

ALARM BELL

Although the Navy issued "alarm rattles" for use on ships, the army did not provide similar devices for its land troops. But the need for some means of alerting troops to an impending attack often arose. Accordingly, both sides improvised with non-military devices of their own. In addition to sentries and outposts, some units used bells of the type shown here. The larger bell came from the camp of the 41st New York Infantry at Fredericksburg.

Description: Bronze. Height 4 inches. Diameter at bottom 4 1/4 inches; diameter at top 2 inches. The clapper is a Minie ball!

The smaller bell came from C.S. lines at Petersburg.

Description: Bronze. Height 2 3/4 inches. Diameter at bottom 3 inches; diameter at top 1 3/8 inches. The clapper is of iron.

APPENDAGES

Various types of appendages or gun tools were used by both sides. Shown here are some which were recovered by John A. Marks of Memphis, Tennessee. These came from camp sites in Tennessee and Mississippi. The tool for the caliber .56 Colt Revolving Rifle is especially rare.

ARTILLERY GUNNERS' IMPLEMENTS

Great confusion exists today among most students of the Civil War as to the terminology and use of the various implements used by gunners in firing their cannon. Accordingly, I believe a description of the implements, with a brief discussion of the use of each, will be timely and helpful. The entire question of gunner's implements is more than of academic interest, since substantial numbers of these implements have survived and are now plaguing their current owners as to what they were originally made for and how they were used.

In addition to Naval pieces, artillery of land forces during the Civil War were employed tactically as field, garrison, and siege artillery. For the purpose of describing the many gunner's implements I have divided them, according to use, into *aiming implements, loading implements*, and *firing implements.* However, it must be emphasized that some of these implements were "standard equipment" while others saw only limited use in most combat areas.

AIMING IMPLEMENTS. Certainly one of the basic implements was the *gunner's quadrant,* usually made of wood but occasionally of brass, which was used for mortars and long artillery pieces for which the ordinary breech-sight and tangent scale were not sufficiently accurate. The quadrant consisted of a quarter-circle fixed to a long arm. The edge of the circle was divided into degrees, and the inclination of the arm to the horizon was determined by a plummet which was fastened to the center of the curve.

A very much used aiming instrument was the *gunner's level,* an instrument for determining the highest points of the base-ring and muzzle, preparatory to the use of the breech-sight and tangent-scale. This level was an upright piece of sheet brass, supported on two feet, with the line joining the bottom points perpendicular to the direction of a sliding pointer, which moved up and down in sockets on the upright.

The gunner's level was an instrument for determining the highest points of the breech and muzzle of a cannon when the carriage-wheels stand on uneven ground. It is made of a brass plate, the lower edge of which is terminated by two steel points of contact. When the level is in position, the vertical slide is pressed down with the finger to mark the required point.

The *breech sight* consisted of an upright piece of sheet brass, supported on a foot piece, the lower side of which was curved to fit on the base ring of the gun on which the sight was used.

The *tangent scale* was made of sheet brass with a flange along the lower edge. The upper edge was cut in steps, with each "rise" representing the tangent of one-quarter degree to a radius equal to the distance between the highest points of the breech and muzzle, measured parallel to the axis. In the middle of each "step" a notch was placed to assist in sighting. When the cannon was sighted by these different notches, the axis was at an elevation indicated by the degrees and minutes under the notches. The tangent scale had fallen into comparative disuse by 1861 and was, to a large extent, replaced by the pendulum-hausse or breech-sight which was preferred as being more convenient in form.

The *pendulum-hausse* was used as a corrective for a faulty position of the trunnion of a cannon, thus obviating the need for a gunner's level or new sighting points. The pendulum-hausse consisted of an upright piece of sheet brass, like the breech-sight, and had a movable slider and scale. At the lower end was a bulb filled with lead. The scale passed through a slit in a piece of steel and was connected with it by a brass screw, which served as a point on which the scale vibrated laterally. The slit was long enough to allow the scale to assume a vertical position in any ordinary case of uneveness of ground on which the gun carriage might be situated.

Gunner's calipers, made of sheet brass and with steel points, had graduations showing the diameters of guns and shot.

The *gunners' perpendicular,* of sheet brass, had a

Alarm Bells

lower part cut in the form of a crescent with points of steel. A small spirit level was fastened to one side of the plate, parallel to the line joining the points of the crescent, and a slide was fastened to the same side of the plate, perpendicular to the axis of the level. This instrument was useful in marking the points of sight on siege guns and mortars, when the gun platform was not level.

A *handspike* was used for adjusting the horizontal direction of the cannon. The handspike for field pieces was termed a trail handspike and was round, with the large end conical-shaped to fit into the pointing rings on the cannon. Other types were the *roller-handspike* and the truck handspike. The *maneuvering handspike* was longer than the trail handspike and was designed for service with siege and garrison gun carriages. It differed somewhat in shape from the trail handspike, being octagonal in the middle. For moving the piece, the large end was made square and at the end tapered off to one side thus permitting its entrance under a weight in getting a purchase. For heavy siege and garrison artillery pieces the handspike was shod with iron. All handspikers were made of well-seasoned hickory or tough oak. The trail handspike for field carriages was 53 inches long; the maneuvering handspike for garrison and sea-coast carriages was 66 inches long; while the handspike for siege and other heavy cannon, was 84 inches long and weighed 12 pounds. The shod handspike was especially useful in servicing mortars, casemate and barbette carriages. The truck handspike for casemate carriages was made of wrought iron, while the *roller handspike* for casemate carriages, also of iron, was 1-inch round with a total length of 34 inches.

The *quoin*, a large wedge, was used in place of an elevating screw, under the chase of mortars and the breech of short howitzers to keep them in proper position when elevating the piece. The quoin had a handle in its large end by which it was moved. The *chock*, a smaller wedge, with a handle in the side, was used for chocking the wheels of the chassis of permanently fixed carriages, when the piece had been correctly aligned on the target.

Very little information is available on patents granted for these various aiming implements. However, a cannon sight (patent No. 46329) was granted February 14, 1865 to James Brady of Philadelphia. This cannon sight was actually a pendulum sight with two graduated standard bars and a sliding extension bar between the standards. The sliding bar was fixed in one of the standard bars while sliding on the other, was adjustable, and resembled the letter T supported at its extremities.

Pointing stakes or *wires* were used for staking out the line of direction for mortar firing. Often wooden stakes were used; a long stake for placing in the exterior slope; a short stake for the interior crest; and a medium-size stake for the rear of the mortar's platform. The *wires* were 20 inches long, and were round in shape with a 0.2 inch diameter.

LOADING IMPLEMENTS. The loading and firing of a cannon in Civil War times was rather complicated and several implements were involved in the process. The rate of fire for muzzle-loading field pieces was 2-3 rounds a minute. Naturally the rate of fire was directly proportional to the proficiency of the gun crew. In the Army of the Potomac, for instance, the gun crews were very well trained and their efficiency more than once spelled the difference between victory and defeat when that ill-fated army confronted the magnificent infantry of "Bobby" Lee.

Loading implements for Civil War cannon included the following basic items: *Rammer:* The rammer head was cylindrical in shape, of beech, elm or some other hard wood, and had the corners at the large end slightly rounded. The rammer-head was bored so as to receive the tenon of the staff, to which it was fastened by means of a wooden pin. Around the neck was placed a copper

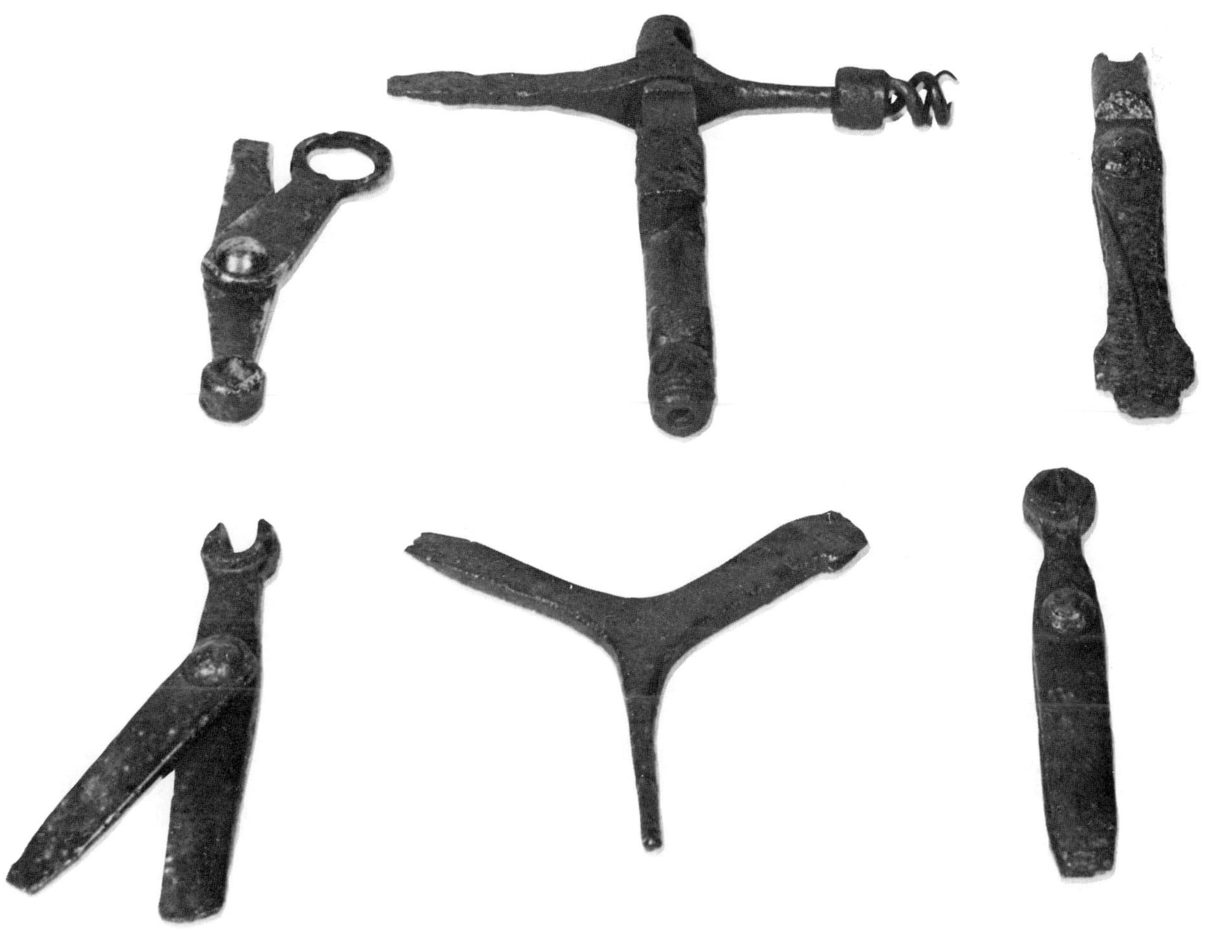

John A. Marks

Appendages
Left to Right:
Top Row: Gallager Carbine, Cal. .577 Enfield Rifle, Cal. .56 Colt Revolving Rifle
Bottom Row: Cal. .58 Springfield, Prussian Musket (?), Cal. .58 Springfield

band for strength. The sponge-head was made of poplar, elm or a similar wood. The sponge itself was a woolen yarn, woven into a warp of hemp or flax-thread, making a tissue about 1/2 inch thick, which was sewed up in the form of a bag. This bag fitted the sponge-head, to which it was fastened with copper nails driven into the inner end of the head near the staff, with a strip of leather being put under the heads of the nails to prevent them from tearing out. For the Coehorn Mortar the sponge was attached to a short staff, and no rammer or sponge-head was used. For the Columbiad, a separate woolen sponge was provided for wiping the chamber and the bore. Stiff hair brushes were also occasionally used with these pieces in order to clean them more easily and thoroughly.

Sponge covers to protect and preserve the sponges were made of strong linen or canvas. The diameter of the bag was equal to that of the bore of the gun, and the length sufficient to allow the mouth to be drawn together around the staff by means of a cord inserted in the hem. A loop of canvas sewed to the bottom served as a handle by which to pull off the cover. Covers were marked with the caliber of the piece to which they belonged.

It should be pointed out that the "rammer" was also frequently called a "sponge-staff."

The *ladle* was a copper scoop attached to the end of a staff for the purpose of withdrawing the projectile of a loaded piece. Ladles were only used for siege and seacoast cannon, as field and mountain cannon could be unloaded by raising the trail of the carriage, which permitted the projectile to slip out by its own weight.

The *worm* was a type of double corkscrew attached to a staff, and was used in field and siege cannon to withdraw a cartridge.

FIRING IMPLEMENTS. Although "fixed ammunition" was used in the Civil War, shells had to be loaded and fuses prepared. The following shell-loading, priming, and firing implements were used by artillerists as described in manuals of the period.

Various implements were used to ignite the projectiles. These were the following: *Fuse* was the means used to ignite the bursting charge of shells. Fuses were classified as *time, concussion,* and *percussion.* A fuse consisted of a highly inflammable composition enclosed in a wood, paper, or metal case.

The *gunner's haversack* was made of leather, and suspended to the side of a cannonier by a shoulderstrap. It was used to carry cartridges from the ammunition-chest to the piece.

The *pass-box* was a wooden box closed with a lid, and carried by a handle attached to one end. It took the place of the haversack in siege and sea-coast service, when the cartridge was large. (After 1861 most pass-boxes were made of leather).

The tube-pouch was a small leather pouch attached to the person of a cannonier by a waist-belt. It contained the friction-tube, layard, priming-wire, thumbstall, etc.

The *budge-barrel* was an oak barrel covered with copper hoops. To the top was attached a leather cover which was gathered with a string, after the manner of the mouth of a bag. It was employed to carry cartridges from the magazine to the battery, in siege and sea-coast services.

The priming-wire was used to prick a hole in a cartridge for the passage of the flame from the vent. It was a piece of wire, pointed at one end, and the other was formed into a ring which served as a handle.

The *thumbstall* was a buckskin cushion, attached to the finger to close the vent in sponging.

The *fuse-setter* was a brass drift for driving a wooden fuse into a shell.

The *fuse-mallet* was made of hard wood, and was used in connection with the setter.

The *fuse-saw* was a 10 inch tenon saw for cutting wooden fuses to a proper length.

The *fuse-gimlet* was a common gimlet, which could be employed in place of the saw to open a communication with the fuse composition.

The *fuse-auger* was an instrument for regulating the time of burning of a fuse.

The *fuse-rasp* was a coarse file employed in fitting a fuse-plug to a shell.

The *fuse-plug* reamer was used to enlarge the cavity of a fuse-plug, after it had been driven into a projectile, to enable it to receive a paper fuse.

The *shell-plug* screw was a wood screw with a handle; it was used to extract a plug from a fuse hole.

The *fuse-extractor* was worked by a screw, and was a more powerful instrument than the preceding; it was used for extracting wooden fuses from loaded shells.

The scraper was a slender piece of iron with a spoon at one end, and a scraper at the other, for clearing the chamber of a mortar.

The *funnel* was made of copper, and was used in pouring the bursting-charge into a shell.

The *powder-measures* were made of copper, of cylindrical form, and of various sizes, for the purpose of determining the charges of shells and cannon, by measurement.

The *lanyard* was a cord, one end of which has a small iron hook, and the other a wooden handle. It was used to explode the friction-tube with which cannon, for the land service was fired.

The gunner's pincers, gimlet, and vent-punch were instruments carried in the tube-pouch for cleaning ordinary obstructions from the vent.

The *shell-hook* was an instrument constructed to fasten upon the ears of a shell, for the purpose of lifting it to the muzzle of the piece.

AUTOMATIC PENCIL

Johann L. Faber of Bavaria, the "Father" of the lead pencil patented August 13, 1861, an automatic pencil. The principle of his pencil (patent no. 33,034), is a hole bored in a handle having a combination split tube and threaded collar (collett). The lead is held in place by the split sleeve and threaded collar much like drafting

"AUTOMATIC" LEAD PENCIL

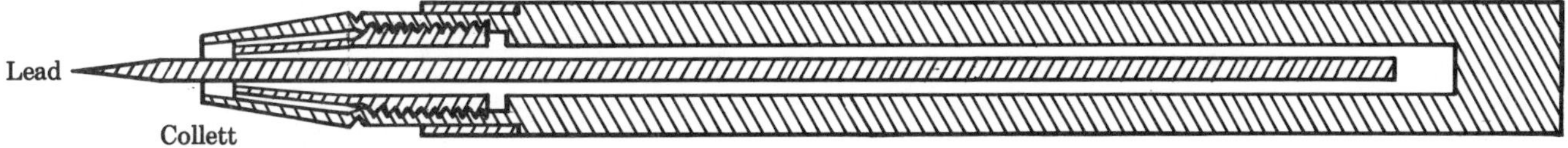

Automatic Pencil

pencils are today. A drive and holding mechanism for the lead was later added.

BALLOONS

FEDERAL BALLOONS. Military aeronauts of the Federal balloon corps enjoyed a quasi-military status which did not endear them to their military superiors. But their performance in combat was pioneer in nature and might well have been very substantial. These aeronauts were all rated as civilian employees and had no command functions of a military nature. Their families received no pensions and the aeronauts themselves were probably liable to summary execution as spies in the event of capture. They wore ordinary civilian clothes that were suitable for field service. A few attempted to wear "B.C." (Balloon Corps) or "A.D." (Aeronautic Department) as insignia on their headgear but these insignia were not official. The aeronauts soon discarded them as they only provoked amusement.

In the decade of the fifties ballooning had become widely known in the United States. Aeronauts gave exhibition flights and made ascensions at numerous county fairs and urban gatherings throughout the country, and constant publicity in the press soon popularized their work far and wide. Several of this ballooning fraternity who offered their services to the government during the war served on various fronts, both East and West. The sight of the huge gas bags with their baskets rising slowly above the ground, often subject to the enemy fire, soon became commonplace to Federal ground forces in many areas. Count Ferdinand Von Zeppelin of the Prussian Army who visited America to study the Federal employment of balloons was one of the most interested observers.

Although there were several military aeronauts in the Federal service, the chief of them all was T.S.C. Lowe who missed participation in the first battle at Bull Run because he was unable to procure men, transportation, and means for inflation of his balloon. Shortly afterwards, another aeronaut ascended 3,000 feet from the deck of a tugboat in Hampton Roads and observed the enemy beyond Newport News. Most of the balloons operated in the East, where at first they were assigned to the Corps of Topographical Engineers, and thus came under the control of the Chief Topographical Engineer of McClellan's staff. In the long inaction of the Army of the Potomac around Washington from July 1861 to March 1862, the balloon corps under Lowe operated two balloons, making ascensions above the lines to observe the enemy camps where often the observer could estimate almost down to a platoon the size of the Confederate forces by the camp fires. Often these ascensions were rendered doubly perilous because "some stupid sentinel, ignorant whether the aerial voyager was friend or enemy, would be sure to fire at the indiscreet individual who thus hovered over their heads." Such incidents convinced the aeronauts of the advisability of clearly identifying their aircraft. Accordingly, some balloons or baskets were marked with red, white, and blue bunting; the "Constitution" was decorated with a large portrait of George Washington; the "Union" had a gigantic spread eagle and the Stars and Stripes; while the "Intrepid" bore its name conspicuously on its side. By January 1862, Lowe had seven balloons in operation. On the Peninsula the balloon corps under Lowe used mobile field generators that functioned efficiently most of the time, but during the Battle of Fair Oaks it was necessary to transfer gas from one balloon to another to save time.

By means of the telegraph, Lowe participated in the first artillery fire direction with aerial observation in American history. However, the potentialities of the corps were never realized. The Chief Engineer of the Army of the Potomac disliked Lowe's freedom and found much to criticize in the civilian's conduct of purchasing supplies. There appears to be no question of Lowe's honesty, but at times the pressure of time forced him to make purchases of ballooning supplies without going through official channels. During the movement north to intercept Lee's invasion of Pennsylvania, General Hooker ordered the Signal Corps to take over the Balloon Corps and its administration but Colonel Myer protested that he had neither the men nor the appropriations with which to operate the additional branch of the service. Thereupon the balloon train was ordered back to Washington and disbanded. It is interesting to conjecture what might have happened at Gettysburg and later if the Balloon Corps had been permitted to operate throughout the remainder of the war. At least one Confederate General (E. P. Alexander) never could understand why the North abandoned balloons in 1863. "Even if the observers never saw anything, they would have been worth all they cost for the annoyance and delays they caused us in trying to keep our movements out of sight."

CONFEDERATE BALLOONS. The first mention of Confederate balloon activities seems to have been made in connection with aerial operations at Falls Church, Virginia, in June 1861. Although a Confederate signal balloon had been reported visible beyond Chain Bridge in the direction of Leesburg Pike as early as the night of July 14th, the apparatus observed on this occasion might well have been some form of pyrotechnics mistaken for a balloon, and could hardly be classified as real aeronautic activity. But during the period June 23-24, 1861, several Federal newspaper correspondents reported that the Confederates had an observation balloon up in the direction of Fairfax.

Although the Boston *Journal* declared that the supposed Confederate balloon was actually a Federal craft, the Providence *Daily Post* asserted that it was quite probable that the Confederates were using a balloon at this time, "since several aeronauts had offered their services to the Southern Government as early as May, at a considerable time previous to the offers made to the Federal Government by Professor Lowe and others." However, the Richmond papers were entirely silent on the subject of a balloon in Confederate service, but did give considerable attention to the activities of Lowe. The Richmond *Examiner* also published a notice on the potential value of balloons to both armies, stating that "the experiments already made with them in the United States in the present war, justify the belief that they will be found eminently useful." (June 26, 1861). Whether or not the Confederates actually had a balloon in operation at this time cannot be definitely determined. It can be established that some months later they did, but the exact beginning of their aeronautic operations is uncertain. On August 22, 1861, General Johnston wrote to Beauregard that "it seems to me that the balloon may be useful . . . Let us send for it; we can surely use it advantageously." From this, we can assume that the balloon referred to was one already in service elsewhere.

General Longstreet tells us that early in 1862, the Confederates gathered silk dresses and made a balloon—"a great patchwork ship of many varied hues which was ready for use in the Seven Days' campaign." But the only gas available was in Richmond, and it was the custom to inflate the balloon there, tie it securely to an engine, and run it down the York River Railroad to the desired point for ascension. But according to Longstreet "one day it was on a steamer down on the James River, when the tide went out and left the vessel and balloon high and dry on a bar. The enemy gathered it in, and with it the last silk dress in the Confederacy." This capture was "the meanest trick of the war and one that I have never yet forgiven." added "Old Pete."

Although corraborative evidence is lacking, a lieutenant of Berdan's sharpshooters reported that on April 26, 1862, his detail "fired into a rebel balloon made of an 'A' tent, and brought it down." This is claimed to have taken place during the siege of Yorktown.

BAYONETS

Most muskets and rifles were equipped with either a socket or saber bayonet, depending on the model and make. All U.S. regulation muskets and rifles except the Model 1841 rifle, 1855 rifle, and Remington 1862 rifle used the socket bayonet. The Plymouth rifle used either a saber bayonet or the famous Dahlgren knife bayonet. The nonregulation Merrill and Sharps rifles were also equipped with saber bayonets. Most troops disliked the saber bayonet because it was too unwieldy; as a result, saber bayonets saw comparatively limited use. It is interesting to note that a correspondent of the *Army and Navy Journal* recommended the adoption of a knife bayonet with a blade 10 to 12 inches long, since a weapon of that size could be used either as a bayonet or a knife.

The angular or socket bayonet was a "savage looking

thing" with three fluted sides and a needle-sharp point. Most recruits had an abiding faith in the efficacy of the bayonet, having read harrowing descriptions of the devastation wrought by the bayonet in charges on the enemy. There is no doubt that some bayonet wounds were given and received on both sides during the war. But very few men received bayonet wounds; many surgeons of extensive combat experience in dressing stations and field hospitals never dressed a bayonet wound.

As a matter of record, Federal authorities state that 246,712 actual cases of wounds were treated and of these only some 400 were men wounded by the bayonet, or less than one-sixth of 1 per cent of the total. A large proportion of the cases involving bayonet wounds had their origin in private quarrels, or were inflicted by sentinels.

None can deny the morale force of a bayonet charge, but usually one side or the other broke before the men closed in enough to use the bayonet effectively. However, some units with ambitious officers spent a great deal of time and perspiration in learning the bayonet drill. "This drill was a Frenchy affair—with its 'parry,' 'prime,' 'seconde,' 'tierce,' 'high quarte,' 'lunge'—all of which kept the men jumping around like so many animated frogs . . . Perhaps they fight on these scientific principles in France, but in 'our war' nobody ever heard any of these commands given in battle. An officer who attempted to put the drill into actual practice would have been sent to the rear and clothed in a strait-jacket."

One of the most universal uses of the bayonet was for pounding coffee beans in a tin cup. Another very common use of the bayonet was as a candlestick. The bayonet also functioned to dig up vegetables or as a tent pin in an emergency.

The Navy was the first to adopt a knife bayonet in the United States. Credit for this innovation belongs to Adm. John A. Dahlgren who in 1856 pointed out the need for a bowie knife type of bayonet for hand-to-hand fighting, and a heavy tool for cutting away damaged naval tackle. Dahlgren devised a heavy bayonet which was officially adopted and was used with the so-called Plymouth rifle, another weapon manufactured according to Dahlgren's specifications. These new bowie bayonets were made under contract by the Ames Manufacturing Company at Chicopee Falls, Mass., and were unique in the history of American Naval Small Arms.

A sliding bayonet (Patent No. 35,760) was patented July 1, 1862, by James Jenkinson of Brooklyn, New York. This "sliding bayonet" was a forerunner (as was the Hall rifle rod bayonet) of the famous rod bayonet of the 1880's and later. Jenkinson's bayonet was "so constructed and applied as to admit of its being easily advanced in the act of lowering, the piece to 'charge bayonet' and easily retracted in the act of restoring the piece to a vertical position." The bayonet was held in its advanced position by means of a spring catch.

Although no sawtooth bayonet was issued extensively, if at all, by either Federal or Confederate ordnance departments, such bayonets had been in use in some European armies since 1809, and perhaps a few were imported for the Civil War. On October 29, 1864, a captain of the Maryland Artillery proposed the adoption of a sawtooth bayonet. He believed that combining the saw and bayonet in a single weapon would be useful

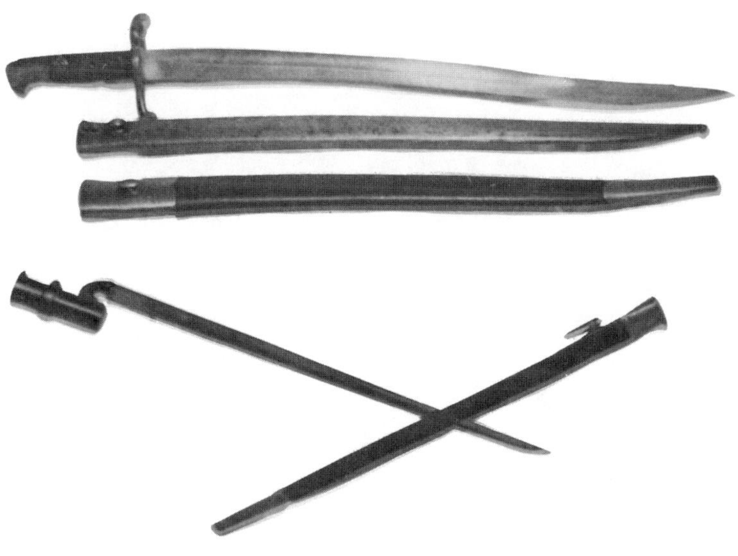

Enfield Bayonets

to engineer and pontoon bridge units. The sawtooth bayonet, as patented in 1864, was called a "fascine-knife." The blade was so shaped that it was broader at the point than at the hilt, and therefore could be used with greater force as a hatchet. The back had teeth filed into it so it could be used as a saw. This bayonet was attached to the rifle as any saber bayonet, and was therefore no hindrance to firing, while the point was sharp enough to serve very well for a thrust. This bayonet (Patent No. 45,009) was patented November 15, 1864, by F. W. Alexander of Baltimore.

The Confederates copied the models of U.S. regulation bayonets. The most common saber bayonet was the one designed for the Fayetteville rifle, but it, like most Confederate bayonets, was unmarked. Probably the most common Confederate triangular bayonet was made at the Richmond Armory. These bayonets have slim blades. Only the tips are steel—the rest of the bayonet is made of iron.

Some bayonets were locally made, but the Confederacy also imported large numbers as part of the equipment used with such weapons as the Enfield.

Shown here is the Enfield saber bayonet (top of picture) and its two types of scabbards. The 24-inch saber bayonet was used on the short Enfield musket. The metal scabbard was used mostly by artillery and naval units, at least in the British service, while the leather scabbard was used by NCO's, artillery units, and rifle regiments. Apparently such selective use of either the short musket or its bayonet scabbards was not very closely adhered to by Civil War troops. All 3-band Enfield muskets used the regular bayonet shown here, with a 17-inch blade and leather scabbard. This musket was used in great numbers by both sides during the war.

BIBLE

Shown here is a leather cover pocket *Bible*, 4 1/4 by 2 3/4 inches in size. Inside the front cover is stencilled:

Lieut. A. W. Clough
Co. H. 13th Me. Regt.

Inside the rear cover is a photograph of Clough's wife. Also shown is a photograph of Lieutenant Clough himself. The *Bible*, printed in Portland, Maine, in 1843, shows much use.

BLEEDER

Shown here is an unidentified brass object thought to be a bleeder. It was found in a Federal camp site beyond the siege lines at Savannah, Georgia. Note the eagle

Bleeder (?). Probably from a Federal Surgeon's Kit

stamped on top. Contributed by Tom Dickey of Atlanta, Georgia.

BODY ARMOR

Although the Federal Government never issued armor of any sort, sutlers and private dealers sold iron vests to many recruits during the Civil War. One dealer sold over 200 of these "iron-clad life preservers" in a single day to members of the 15th Connecticut Infantry.

"The track of the command from Washington to Arlington Heights was marked by these abandoned armor plates, the largest quantity being hurled from Long Bridge into the Potomac when the regiment was about to step on 'sacred soil,' as an offering to the gods." Another regiment, perhaps less religiously motivated than the Connecticut unit, threw their armor into the gutter in front of the White House; still another regiment waited until they got to their camping area where they either threw the breastplates away or used them for frying pans with cleft sticks for handles.

These vests were so heavy that they were soon thrown away and in the few cases where they were tried in battle they failed to live up to expectations. One such breastplate (probably discarded by a Confederate soldier) was worn by a Federal soldier until he was severely wounded. He then gave it to a comrade who was killed by a Minie ball which struck the breastplate near its lower border and passed through it carrying pieces of the plate into the abdomen.

A typical advertisement for one of these soldiers' bulletproof vests stressed that it had been "repeatedly and thoroughly tested with pistol bullets at 10 paces, rifle bullets at 40 rods, by many army officers and approved and worn by them." Simple and light, it was guaranteed to save thousands.

The Breastplates worn by Federal soldiers were of two principal types. The most popular type, the "Soldier's Bullet Proof Vest," was manufactured by G. and D. Cook and Co. of New Haven, Connecticut. It consisted of a regular black military vest, containing pockets into

Body Armor

which were inserted two thin pieces of spring steel, one on either side of the chest. When the vest was buttoned, the plates overlapped in the center. The standard infantry vest weighed 3 1/2 pounds, while a slightly heavier model for cavalry and artillery weighed 6 pounds. The second most popular type of breastplate was made by still another New Haven firm, the Atwater Armor Company. It was a far more complicated product than the Soldiers' Bullet Proof Vest and cost about twice as much. The main body of the armor consisted of four large plates held together by a keyhole and rivet system. To the button of the cuirass formed by these plates were attached hinged tasses of two leaves each. Some lives were saved by these armored vests but they passed out of use after 1862 due mainly to their bulk and weight, and the ridicule to which the wearers were subjected. There were several standing jokes about the "man in the iron stove" which never seemed to grow stale.

The equipment of an infantry soldier was burdensome without the addition of a 3 1/2 pound "bullet proof vest."

BOOBY TRAPS

Although the use of booby traps and the mining of defense areas are generally acceptable today, such practices were frowned upon by many responsible Civil War commanders. The Federals used booby traps but not to the extent their opponents did. This was natural since the Confederates were mainly on the defensive and therefore employed more defensive devices than did the attacking Federals. However, during the Atlanta campaign, Federal troops, in destroying rail lines, occasionally filled deep rail cuts with brush and tree tips, and then placed shells in these cuts to explode if the enemy attempted to clean out the cuts and get the tracks in shape again.

Booby traps and mined areas were used by the Confederates as early as their defense of Yorktown in the spring of 1862. In this defense they used booby traps which were buried in the ground or attached to objects above ground. These "torpedoes," as they were called, exploded on contact. At Yorktown, Chaplain James J. Marks of the 63rd Pennsylvania Infantry saw one of these booby traps go off, thus demonstrating the "devilish ingenuity" of the constructors of these lethal instruments. A soldier of a New York regiment, while getting water at a spring, saw a pocket knife lying on the ground. Picking it up, the soldier found a cord tied to it. Without any suspicion he gave it a pull and the next instant was torn into fragments. The cord had been fastened to the mechanism of a concealed torpedo, and the slight pull had exploded it.

Most "torpedoes" were actually shells, buried in such a way that only the capped nipple was at the surface of the ground; when stepped on they would explode. Other Federal officers and men stated they witnessed the explosion of concealed shells or torpedoes at Yorktown. These shells were buried in the woods, fields, and even the fortifications themselves. The shells were the ordinary 8- or 10-inch mortar or Columbiad shells, filled with powder, and buried a few inches below the surface of the ground, and so arranged with some fulminate, or with the ordinary artillery friction primer, that they exploded by being trod upon or otherwise disturbed.

General McClellan was so incensed over the use of such "infernal machines" that he had a number of Confederate prisoners go over the ground and completely remove the buried torpedoes. Of course these prisoners ran great risks, but none were injured, as they well knew where the torpedoes were hidden. Confederate newspapers roasted McClellan, calling such handling of prisoners of war cruel, barbarous, and completely unwarranted by the usages of war. But a Federal writer pointed out that those who castigated McClellan for misusing prisoners this way "had not a word to say against the savage barbarity of those who planted these deadly engines in the pathway of the army."

One of the originators of this so-called "barbarity" appears to have been Gen. G. J. Rains, C. S. Army, whose brigade was assigned rearguard duty on the march from Williamsburg toward Richmond. Hotly pressed by advancing Federals, Rains came upon a broken ammunition wagon containing some loaded shells. Four of these shells, equipped with sensitive fuse primers, were planted in the Confederate rear, near some trees cut down as obstructions to the road. A body of Federal cavalry came upon these buried shells which exploded with "terrific effect." As a result of this incident, Rains' immediate superior, General Longstreet, took him to task in an official communication, pointing out that he (Longstreet) wished this practice of "putting shells or torpedoes behind you" to cease, as he did not consider it a "proper or effective method of war." Rains was unconvinced, insisted on the legality of his actions, and continued to advocate the use of booby traps as a legitimate employment in warfare.

The whole matter eventually got to the C. S. Secretary of War, G. W. Randolph, who sided with Longstreet.

In this Federal advance on the Williamsburg Road, several soldiers of the units which preceded Hooker in line of march had been blown up by what the men termed "infernal contrivances." By the time Hooker's division arrived many of the unexploded torpedoes had been located and were marked by little red flags or guarded by sentries stationed to warn off the men from the advancing units as they came up. There was but little straggling from the ranks, as safety lay in following the path where others had gone uninjured.

Apparently there was somewhat of a hiatus in the use of these "infernal contrivances" until the closing months of the war. But at Fort Fisher (January, 1865), the Confederates used mine fields again. They buried several large "torpedoes" in the sand over which an attacking force would have to pass. Wires had been attached to each "torpedo" and, in turn, connected to a magnetic battery inside the fort. Had not a Federal naval shell exploded and severed the connecting wire, the Federals would have lost many more men than they actually did in the assault. Whereas the torpedoes at Yorktown were individually located and could be detonated only by direct contact with an individual stepping on them, the mine field at Fort Fisher was connected in a detonation pattern with a master switch inside the fort.

BOOT OR SHOE CLEATS

All specimens shown are metal. They were shaped to conform to the heel of the boot or shoe to which they were nailed. All have holes showing where the nails were driven.

BOTTLES

Illustrations are of bottles recovered from Civil War camp sites by Mrs. J. W. Kemph of Atlanta, Georgia.

A great variety of bottles have been found in Civil War camp sites especially in the regimental dumping areas. While some of these bottles were for use by hospitals most were containers of the popular intoxicating beverages of the period. The sale of liquor by merchants and regimental sutlers was a thriving one throughout the war. At the headquarters of such generals as Hooker and Jube Early there was ample evidence of liberal indulgence in all kinds of intoxicating liquors. Nor were the enlisted men far behind. Everything from imported champagne to locally brewed malt liquor was consumed, with whiskey probably the most popular of all.

In addition to medicine and liquor bottles, camp sites have yielded various types of patent medicine, ink and mucilage bottles to delight the bottle collector.

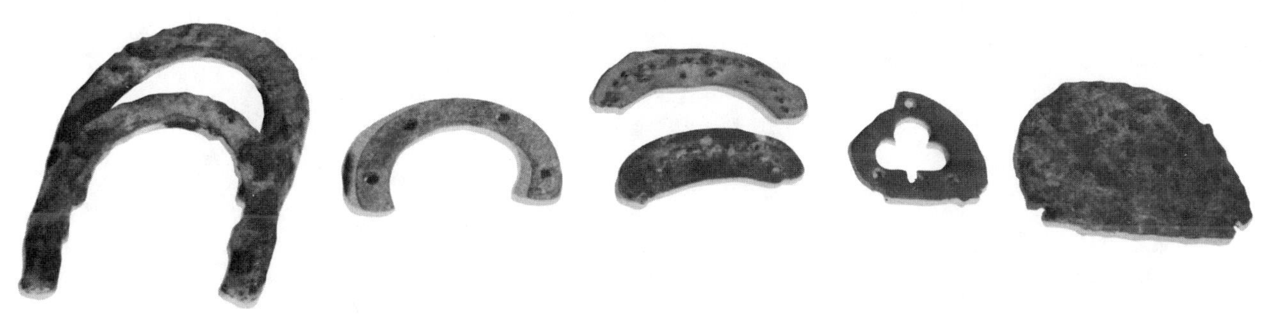

Left to right:
Two Iron Cleats. 2 3/4 inches long, 2 1/2 inches wide. From U.S. camp at Falmouth, Virginia.
Brass Cleat. 1 1/2 inches long, 2 1/8 inches wide. From C.S. camp at Orange Court House, Virginia.
Two Brass Heel Plates. From C.S. camp at Orange Court House, Virginia.
Brass Heel Cleat. 1 5/8 inches long, 1 1/2 inches wide, with 2nd Army Corps motif. From U.S. Cavalry camp at Lagrange, Tennessee.
Iron Heel Cleat. Made of thin iron. From C.S. Camp (Jeb Stuart's position) at Fredericksburg, Virginia.

J. W. Kemph Collection

Excavated Bottles

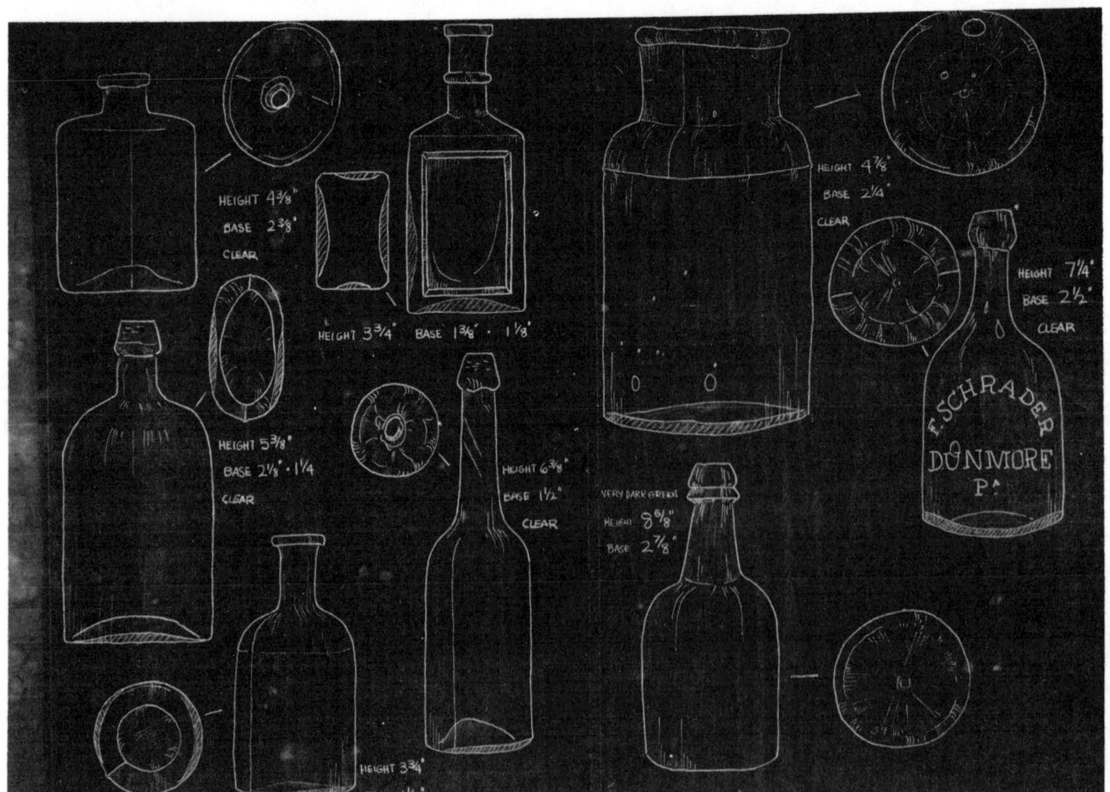

J. W. Kemph Collection

Excavated Bottles

Excavated Bottles

J. W. Kemph Collection

Civil War Bottles

J. W. Kemph Collection

Civil War Bottles

C.S. Bowie Knife

BOWIE KNIFE

The subject of bowie knives has been covered in the first volume of the *Encyclopedia.* However, the author recently acquired the Confederate specimen shown here and considers it of sufficient interest to be included in this volume. The knife is equipped with a black leather scabbard, crudely stitched, with two carrying loops. Overall length of the knife is 19 inches, with a 14 inch blade. The blade is unmarked. The wooden handle is marked as follows: On one side is—NEWBERN MARCH 14th '62—on the other—YANKEE SLAYER (!) It is interesting to note that when the 118th New York Infantry arrived in New York City on their way to the front, they were approached by hucksters "selling cast-iron knives of vicious size, inscribed *Death to Rebels* and a variety of sanguinary epithets."

BREATH FRESHENER FOR TOBACCO USERS

Breath Freshener for Tobacco Users

Breath fresheners were used by some individuals who either wanted to hide the fact they used "the weed" or to prepare for a romantic evening! Shown here is a container found in a Federal camp near Fredericksburg, Virginia. This can is of thin brass, 1 1/2 inches in diameter, and 1/4 inch thick. The cover is stamped with the head of England's Prince Albert and the words:

H. R. H. Prince Albert
Prepared By
Thomas Jackson
Cachou Aromatise

On the bottom of the can are the words:

Prince Albert's
Cachous
Th. Jackson
Inventor
and
Original
Proprietor

BRIDLE ROSETTE

Bridle rosette of Mexican design found in an 1861 Confederate camp at Lagrange, Tennessee. The material is pewter covered by silver plating. Dimensions: Diameter 2 3/4 inches; thickness 1/8 inch, but increasing to 3/8 inch at center of rose.

BUCKLES

Federal and Confederate buckles, both national and state, have been fairly extensively covered in Volume one of this *Encyclopedia* and other works. However, new specimens are being found, especially by Civil War "buffs." Shown here are examples of rare buckles used by special units in the war. Doubtless other types will be found in the future.

Bridle Rosette

L. V. Warren Collection

Cartridge Box Plates
Top: Ohio National Guard
Bottom: 114 Pennsylvania Volunteer Infantry. (Zouaves d' Afrique)

Rare Officers Buckles
Left to right:
Top Row: Penn. Vol. Militia, Fire Zouaves, Chaplain (?)
Bottom Row: Philadelphia Brigade, Philadelphia Fire Zouaves, Non-Regulation (Wilderness Battlefield)

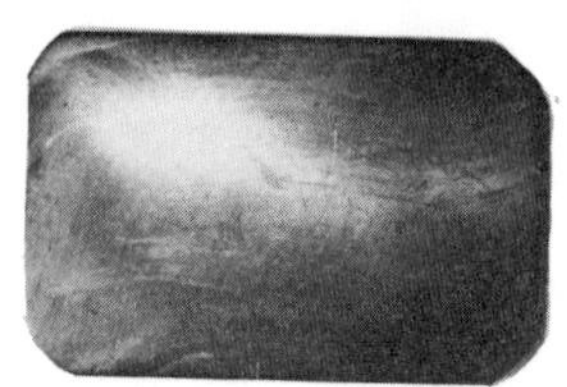

Militia Buckles. The one in upper right hand corner was worn by a member of the 9th New York Zouaves.

Top Buckle (Ohio Light Infantry?) found in section of U.S. Trenches, Savannah, Ga. Bottom Buckle is Confederate from Savannah, Ga. Both found by Robert L. Robinson III of Savannah, Georgia.

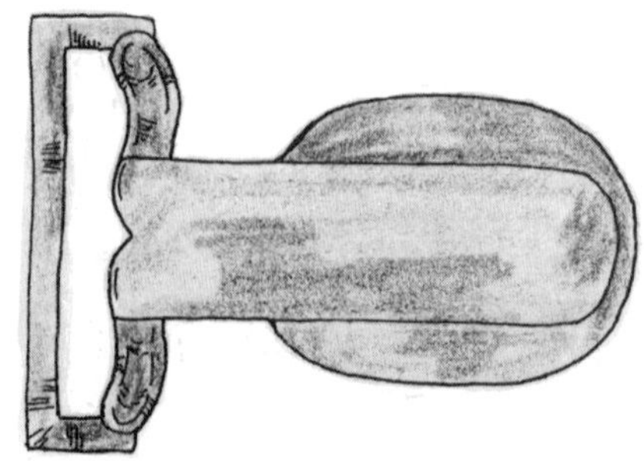

Buckle of Richardson Light Guard—an unidentified unit. Found at Hilton Head by Mrs. Carol Kemph of Atlanta, Ga.

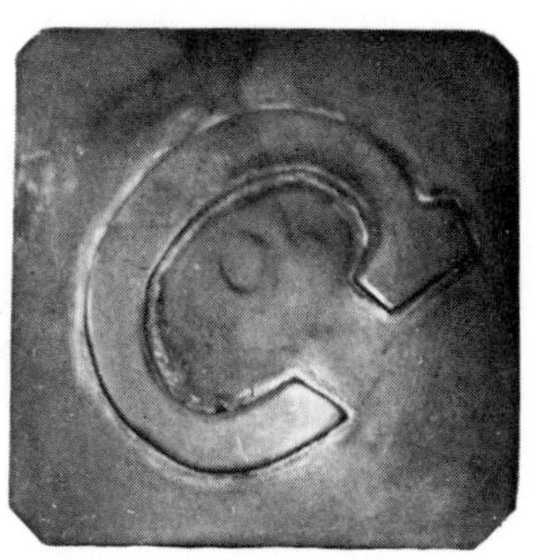

Militia Crossbelt Buckles

Belt Buckle worn by an enlisted man of the Philadelphia Fire Zouaves.

BULLET MOLD

Small arms ammunition was produced in arsenals and issued in bulk to units in the field. For example, Colt pistol ammunition was issued in wooden boxes of 600 rounds each. Musket ammunition came in 1,000 rounds per box. Only occasionally did an individual go to war with a cased revolver, including a powder flask and a bullet mold. Sharpshooters armed with sniper's rifles or hunting rifles usually brought their own bullet molds for their special caliber weapons. However, a bullet mold such as the one shown here, is especially rare. It is for the caliber .58 minie ball! Very probably it was C. S. used, since the Federals were more amply supplied with manufactured ammunition in the field.

Description: Steel. Overall length 5 5/8 inches. Caliber .58 (rifled musket).

BUTTON BOARD

It was a war of colorful uniforms and bright buttons. Soldiers spent many hours keeping these buttons shiny. Therefore, the button board was useful to protect the cloth while shining the numerous buttons on blouse,

Cal. .58 Bullet Mold

jacket, dress coat, and overcoat. These button boards were of metal or wood. A wooden one used by Dwight Bradley, Co. B 37th Massachusetts Infantry (Ferris Colbetion) is 8 1/4 inches long, with a 5 1/2 inch slot. Shown here is another wooden one-10 inches long, 1 5/8 inches wide, with a 6-inch slot. Also shown is a heavy brass button board, 3 3/4 inches long, 2 1/4 inches wide, with a 2 3/8 inch slot. It is marked:

CORPAL C. V. LAVAN
Co. C 1st BAT. ENGS.

BUTTONS

Many collectors of Civil War artifacts, as well as button collectors in general, are fascinated by the wide diversity existing among the types of uniform buttons of the 1861-1865 period. Collecting buttons is especially appealing to many individuals because buttons are often found on battlefields and also are comparatively inexpensive. Moreover, in these days of restricted space at home (as well as the singular lack of enthusiasm, by long-harassed wives, for larger relics), button collections can be exhibited without crowding the family into the woodshed.

Buttons were highly regarded as souvenirs by the Boys in Blue and their gray-clad opponents. When the opposing pickets met during a truce, an exchange of uniform buttons was not uncommon. Even before the troops left their home states, admirers, both male and female, asked and often received coat buttons from their departing heroes. Men of the 118th New York Infantry gave away so many buttons to well-wishers in Saratoga, New York, that some coats were nearly buttonless when the regiment finally entrained for Washington. One officer tells us that a demure little maiden excitedly rushed up to him saying: "Lieutenant, I'm a Philadelphia girl and if you will give me a button from your coat, I'll give you an honest patriotic kiss."

The buttons on the uniforms of the 7th Connecticut Infantry were gilt, with the state seal. These were in great demand as souvenirs. Many a young man's button reposed through the war in a velvet-lined box in his sweetheart's boudoir. Two girls, whose bold looks and actions lacked charm, accosted a man on camp guard in the 7th Connecticut: "Soldier, give us a button!"

"Really, ladies," said he, "I'll give you the rest of the uniform with pleasure, but I want to keep the buttons; they are the only ornamental part of the whole outfit."

Quite a different situation existed for Confederates at the end of the war. Many were wearing Yankee buttons, pewter buttons, and even buttons made from acorns. Often those Confederates who were still wearing uniforms having official C.S. buttons were forced to remove them if they still wished to wear the uniform until they could get civilian clothes again. We know that this was the case in certain occupied areas of the South. During the Federal occupation of Savannah, Georgia, in July 1865 a number of Confederate officers came in and surrendered. They were paroled and allowed to wear their uniforms—most of them had no other clothes—but every military insignia had to be removed. The brass buttons in particular were all cut from their coats. Some of the men wrathfully demurred, but their Federal captors were inexorable. At one time a captain of the 14th New Hampshire Infantry had a dozen of these surrendered Confederates before him, and when he started to dispossess them of the buttons with C.S.A. on them, they refused to allow it. When told that it was a matter of minus buttons or minus freedom, they agreed to cut them off. They went off wearing buttonless coats.

Occasionally, prominent Federal generals would donate buttons from their uniform coats to be sold at "soldiers' fairs" where money was raised to aid soldiers' families or for use by such philanthropic agencies as the U.S. Sanitary Commission. The author has a button from McClellan's coat and two buttons from Burnside's coat which were probably donated in this way. The Burnside buttons were made into earrings by the original purchaser.

Federal enlisted men wore either the regulation button with the eagle but no letter on the shield, or their state button. In the early months of the war many regiments wore buttons with their state seals. This was especially true of men from New York, Ohio, Massachusetts, Vermont, and Connecticut. However, most of the early volunteers wore their state buttons in 1861. By early 1863 the practice had largely disappeared. State buttons of Federal regiments have been found on battlefields up through 1864 and probably were worn up to the very end.

Regulation Federal buttons are described in the first volume of the *Encyclopedia.* In addition, some experts believe that regulation buttons made of hard rubber, and marked with Goodyear's 1851 pattern, were used by Berdan's sharpshooters. These rubber buttons do not glisten in the sun as do the brass buttons, and were better suited for the sharpshooters' uniforms. A musician's button with the three-string lyre insignia has been found on the Fredericksburg battlefield.

In contrast with their Federal counterparts, Confederate enlisted men in the combat arms (cavalry, infantry, and artillery) did wear the letter of their branch of service.

Buttons for the naval personnel of both sides came in three sizes: large, medium, and small. For the U.S. Navy the sizes were 7/8 inch in exterior diameter, 7/10 inch, and 9/16 inch. Both C.S. and U.S. naval buttons had an anchor as a device, while the Confederates also

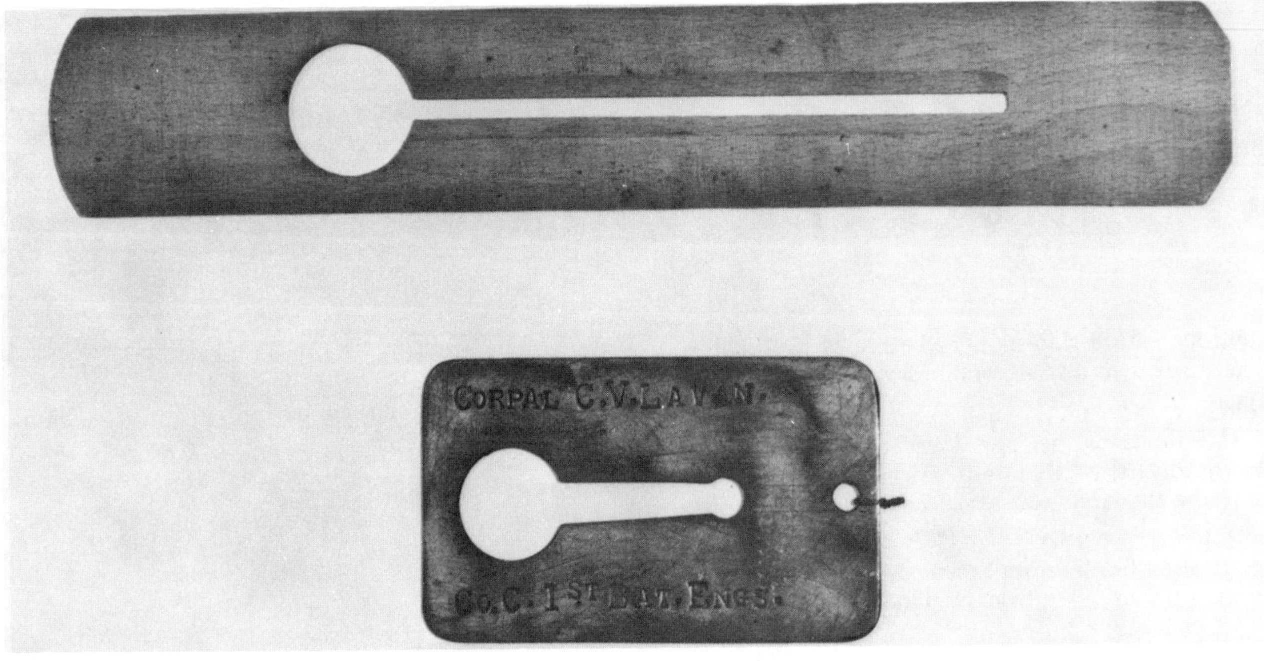

Button Boards

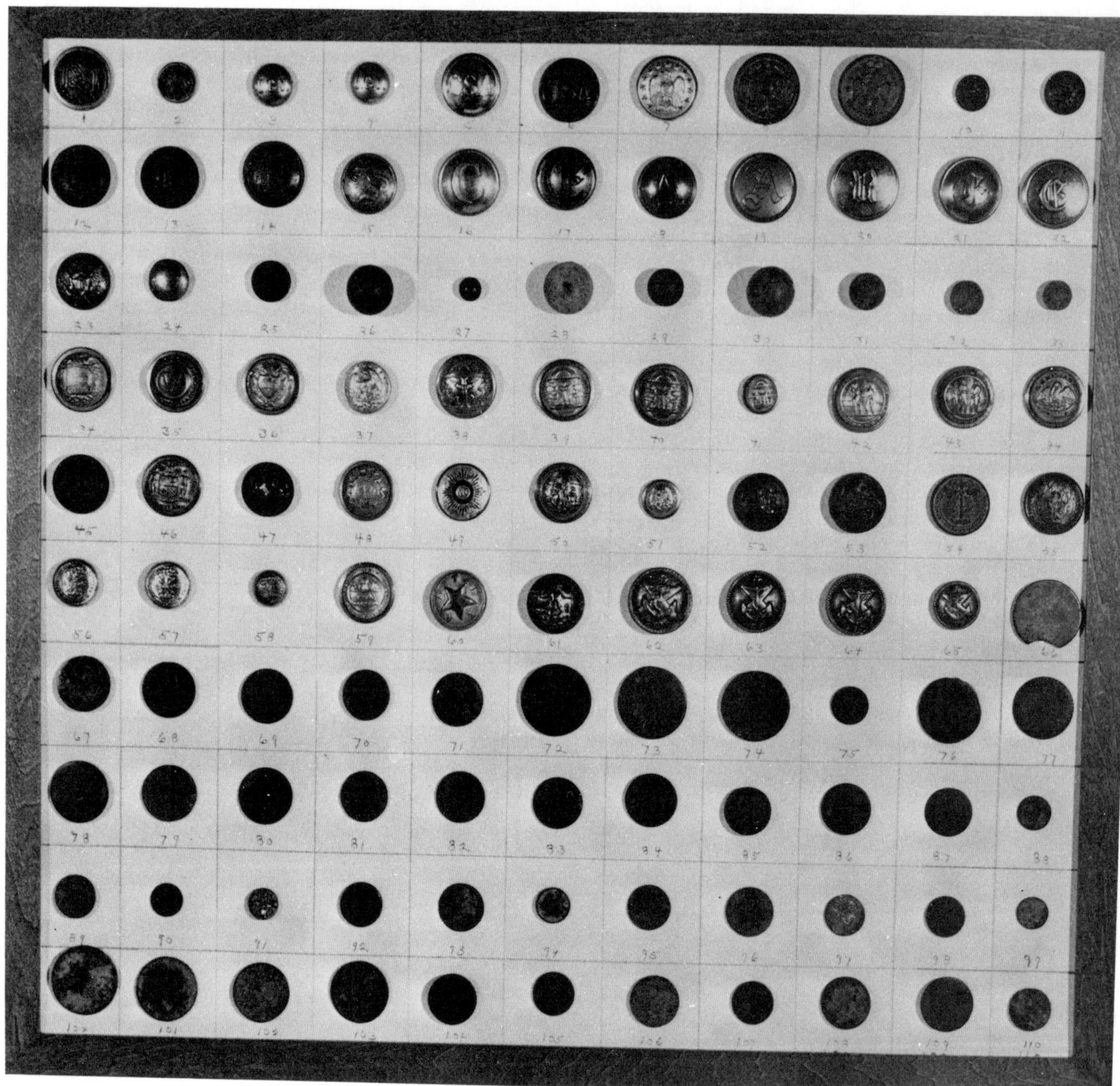
Confederate Buttons

had buttons with a ship motif. Marines of both sides also had their own distinctive buttons.

BUTTONS [*C.S.*]. Although buttons are covered in the first volume of the *Encyclopedia* this illustration shows the diversity of buttons worn by the Confederates. Note the large number of non-military buttons actually worn by C.S. military personnel.

1- 4 United Confederate Veterans
5- 6 CSA - imported from England
7 General Staff
8 General Staff - Worn by a South Carolinian
9 General Staff
10 General Staff. Battle of Port Gibson, Mississippi
11 Captured Federal button worn by a South cavalryman.
12 Infantry. Battle of Monocacy
13 Infantry. Battle of Seven Pines.
14 Infantry. Battle of Orange Court House, Va. (made of Pewter)
15 Infantry
16- 17 Cavalry
18- 19 Artillery
20 Rifleman
21- 22 Engineers

23 North Carolina. "Goldsboro Rifles" (Co. "G" 9th N.C. Inf. of Cooke's Brigade).
24 Battle of Seven Pines
25 Battle of Fredericksburg
26- 27 From C.S. trenches, Savannah, Georgia 1864
28 Jubal Early's camp of Fredericksburg, Dec. 13, 1862
29 West Point sleeve button, Battle of Blackburn's Ford, July 18, 1861
30- 33 C.S. camp at Fredericksburg. Dec. 13, 1862
34 Alabama
35 Montgomery Light Guard
36 Arkansas
37 Florida
38 Georgia. Found in a battle with five other Georgia buttons—Fredericksburg, Virginia
39- 41 Georgia
42- 43 Kentucky
44 Louisiana
45 Louisiana. C.S. made. Battle of Orange Court House, Va.
46 Maryland
47 Mississippi. Battle of Orange Court House.
48 Missouri
49 North Carolina
50 "Goldsboro Rifles" (Co. "G" 9th N.C. Infantry)
51 North Carolina
52 North Carolina. Battle of Monocacy
53 North Carolina. Battle of the Wilderness
54 South Carolina. Battle of the Wilderness
55- 58 South Carolina
59 Tennessee

Calendar

60 Texas. Worn by Charles C. Bell (later lived in Boonville, Missouri)
61 Virginia. Battle of Monocacy
62- 65 C.S. Navy. Shipped from England through the blockade
66- 71 Siege of Port Hudson
72- 73 Virginia
74- 75 C.S. camp at Dumfries, Virginia
76 C.S. from Battle of Antietam
77- 78 Virginia
79 C.S. Barracks site at Fort Fisher, NC
80 From Causten Bluff, Savannah, Georgia
81 Battle of Fort Fisher
82 Barksdale's camp site. (Mississippi Brigade). Battle of Fredericksburg
83 Battle of Mechanicsville, Va.
84 C.S. barracks site. Battle of Fort Fisher
85 Battle of Snyder's Bluff, Mississippi, Dec. 27-29, 1862
86- 88 Virginia
89- 90 Battle of Rose DHU, Georgia (near Savannah)
91 Gold tinted button from Battle of Fort Fisher
92 Camp of 6th N.C. Infantry, Dumfries, Virginia
93-110 C.S. camps in Virginia

C

CALENDAR

In the field the combat troops often lost all track of time and the day of the week. Generally speaking, the only calendars available were those in the pocket diaries carried by a proportionately small number of officers and men. These diaries, usually bound in thin black leather, were very susceptible to rainy weather. Accordingly, an enterprising individual came out with a metal (brass) permanent calendar for sale to the soldiers. Sales must have been limited since the one shown here is the only specimen known to the author. It was picked up on the battlefield of Spotsylvania.

Description: Thin brass disc 1 3/4 inches in diameter, with seven rectangular slots and a rotating inner disc. One side of the outer disc has the months while the other side has four concentric circles with numbers from 0 to 100. By rotating the inner disc it is possible to show the correct date of any month in a century. This calendar is marked:

Calendar

One Side: *COPYRIGHT SECURED ACC'D TO LAW*
Other Side: *TIPPING'S M CALENDAR*

CAMP FURNITURE

Although camp furniture has been extensively covered in the first volume of the *Encyclopedia*, recent acquisitions to the author's collection will be of interest. Shown here is the field chest of Major General Benjamin F. Butler. Known as "silver spoons" Butler it is interesting to note that this chest is equipped with silver mess gear made by Tiffany of New York. The brass plate on the chest cover is inscribed: B. F. BUTLER MAJ GEN U.S. VOLS

The camp cot used by Lieutenant Linsley is contained in a wooden trunk covered with handsomely-tooled leather. Dimensions: 23 inches long, 19 inches wide, 13 1/2 inches deep. The trunk opens up, permitting a canvas cot, 6 feet 7 inches long, to be set up on folding wooden legs.

Benjamin F. Butler's Field Chest

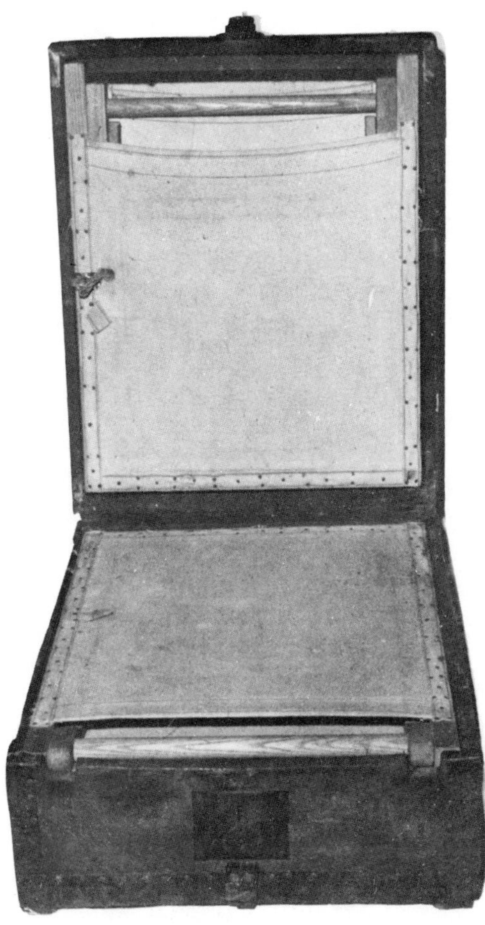

Camp Cot used by 1st Lieutenant Solomon F. Linsley, 15th Connecticut Infantry.

CAMP STOVE

Stoves of all sizes and varieties were used in Federal and Confederate camps. The illustration here is from a Civil War Advertisement of Kingsland's "army stove", sold to the troops. This stove was chosen by the U.S. Surgeon General as the best "yet devised" and as the one which should be used in all military hospitals.

CANNON

At the outbreak of war in 1861 cannon for the U.S. Army were made at the following private foundries:

Cold Springs Foundry (across the Hudson from West Point, N.Y.)
Fort Pitt Foundry (near Pittsburgh, Pa.)
Tredegar Foundry (Richmond, Va.)
Algers Foundry (near Boston, Mass.)
Ames Foundry (near Chicopee, Mass.)

All cannon were required to be inspected by a detailed Ordnance officer, then weighed, and marked as follows: The number of the gun and the initials of the inspector's name on the face of the muzzle, the numbers to be in a separate series for each type and caliber at each foundry; the initial letters of the name of the founder and of the foundry on the end of the right trunnion; the year of fabrication on the end of the left trunnion; the foundry number on the end of the right rembase, above the trunnion; the weight of the piece in pounds on the base of the breech; the letters "U.S." on the upper surface of the piece, near the end of the reinforce.

The United States had begun intensive experimentation with rifled cannon in the late 1850's and had produced a few rifled pieces by the time of the firing on Fort Sumter. In early 1861 the Federal artillery was equipped with some 300 wrought iron 3-inch guns. These guns, the famous 12-pounders, firing a 10-pound projectile, were made by wrapping sheets of boiler iron around a mandrel. The cylinder thus formed was heated and passed through rolls for welding, then cooled, bored, turned, and rifled.

However, like other major powers, the United States had large stocks of smoothbore cannon on hand in 1861. The U.S. Ordnance Board believed that conversion of these smoothbores to rifled cannon simply involved cutting grooves in the bore. In 1860 half of the pieces for the service had been scheduled for this type of conversion. A number of the old smoothbores were rebored to fire rifle projectiles of the various types which came into being prior to the adoption of a copper rotating band. Under the famous James patent, the weight of metal thrown by a cannon was virtually doubled; converted 24-, 32-, and 42-pounders were able to fire elongated shot classed respectively as 48-, 64-, and 84-pound projectiles.

At the same time that the Ordnance Board recommended conversion of smoothbores to rifles, it also urged that all large caliber iron guns be manufactured by the method developed by Captain Thomas J. Rodman, U.S. Army. This process involved casting the gun around a water-cooled core. The inner walls of the gun were thereby solidified first, being compressed by the contraction of the outer metal as it cooled down more slowly, and accordingly had much greater strength to resist explosion of the charge. The Rodman smoothbore, founded in 8-, 10-, 15-, and 20-inch calibers, was the best cast iron cannon of its day. The 20-inch Rodman, made in 1864, fired a 1,080-pound shot!

Manufacturers and designers of cannon were confronted with two basic problems: to construct a gun which would stand the heaviest charge; and to reduce the strain on the gun without reducing the velocity produced by the charge. Solid wrought iron forgings did not possess entirely the desired degrees of elasticity and hardness. Furthermore, their chief defect was lack of uniformity of the metal in casting, due to the crude process puddling, and to the numerous but indispensable welds. Low cast steel, in addition to being elastic,

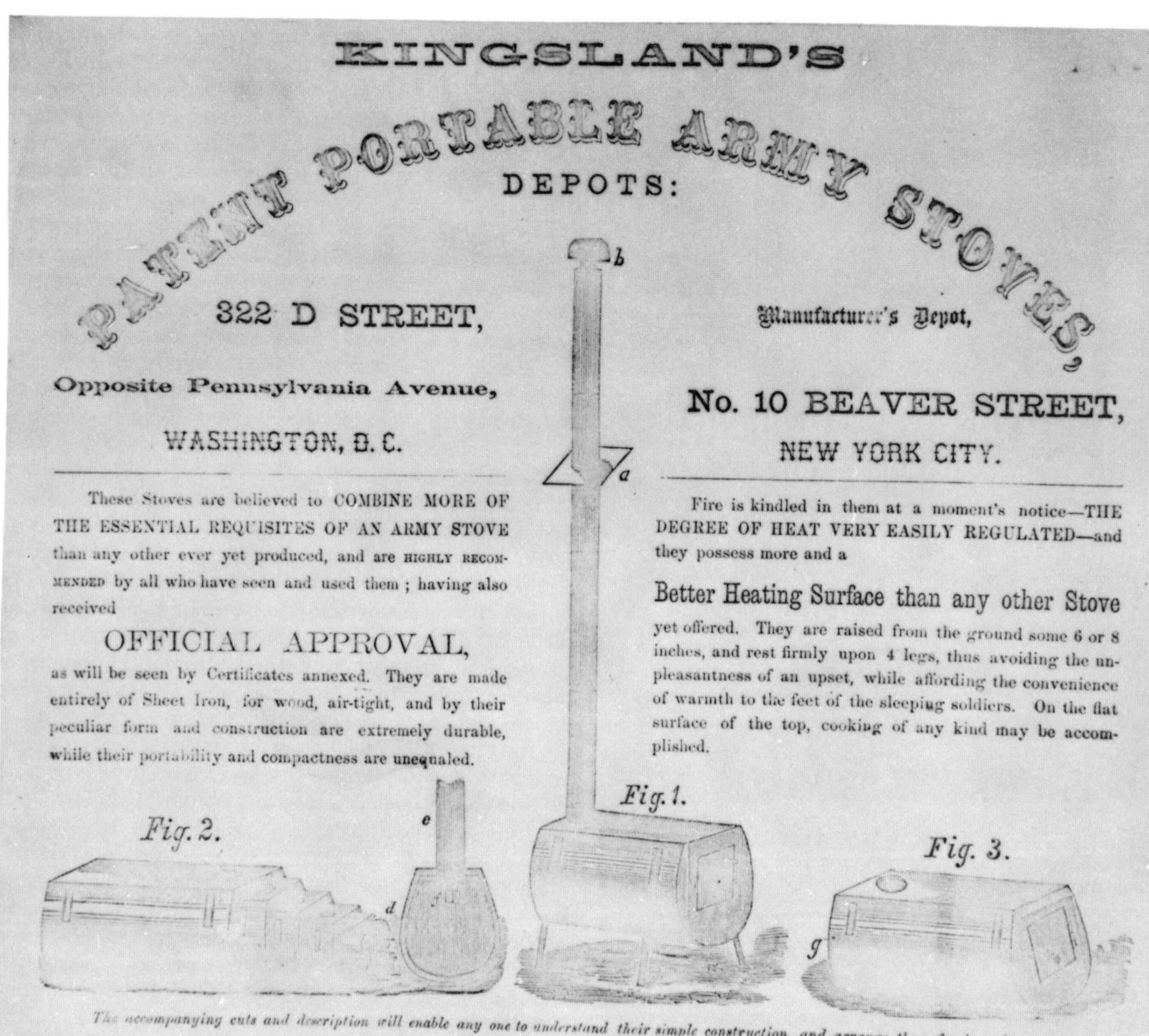

KINGSLAND'S

PATENT PORTABLE ARMY STOVES,

DEPOTS:

322 D STREET,

Opposite Pennsylvania Avenue,

WASHINGTON, D. C.

Manufacturer's Depot,

No. 10 BEAVER STREET,

NEW YORK CITY.

These Stoves are believed to COMBINE MORE OF THE ESSENTIAL REQUISITES OF AN ARMY STOVE than any other ever yet produced, and are HIGHLY RECOMMENDED by all who have seen and used them ; having also received

OFFICIAL APPROVAL,

as will be seen by Certificates annexed. They are made entirely of Sheet Iron, for wood, air-tight, and by their peculiar form and construction are extremely durable, while their portability and compactness are unequaled.

Fire is kindled in them at a moment's notice—THE DEGREE OF HEAT VERY EASILY REGULATED—and they possess more and a

Better Heating Surface than any other Stove

yet offered. They are raised from the ground some 6 or 8 inches, and rest firmly upon 4 legs, thus avoiding the unpleasantness of an upset, while affording the convenience of warmth to the feet of the sleeping soldiers. On the flat surface of the top, cooking of any kind may be accomplished.

Fig. 2. *Fig. 1.* *Fig. 3.*

b a e d g

The accompanying cuts and description will enable any one to understand their simple construction, and arrange them for immediate use.

Fig. 1 represents the stove standing complete ; *a* the tent plate, *b* the hood ; *c* the door of the stove. 4 lengths or about 7 feet of pipe accompany each stove, and the tent plate in the cut is placed about where the pipe would reach the top of tent.

Fig. 2 represents a nest of 4 of these stoves, with pipe and all the appurtenances contained in the smallest of the nest ; *d* is the end-piece of the stove removed ; *e* the shortest length of pipe, and *f* the manner in which it is secured to the stove.

Fig. 3 represents a nest of 4, closed up, ready for boxing ; *g* represents the nail-holes by which the end-pieces of the stoves are securely held in place, in addition to the iron attached on short length of pipe, marked *f*, as shown in Fig. No. 2.

A box 24x12 inches square contains one nest complete of 4, occupying 2 cubic feet, and weighing but 70 pounds to the nest.

The stoves can be made to any size and nested on the same principle—and can be made capable of heating the largest rooms.

No. 1, the largest size of the nest, 24 inches long by 12 in diameter, will cost $20.00 per nest, boxed complete.

Kingsland's Army Stove

CERTIFICATES.

SURGEON GENERAL'S OFFICE,
Washington City, D. C., Dec. 2d, 1862.

After a careful examination of Mr. Richard Kingsland's Heating and Ventilating apparatus for tents and shed hospitals, I am clearly of the opinion that it is far preferable, both in the sense of efficiency and economy, to any yet devised, and I should be glad to have it introduced into all Hospitals where they could be applied.

Signed, WILLIAM H. HAMMOND, Surgeon General U. S. A.

MEDICAL DIRECTOR'S OFFICE,
Washington City, D. C., Nov. 26th, 1862.

I have examined Kingsland's Patent Portable Army Hospital Heater and Ventilator, and recommend the apparatus as a compact, cheap, and portable method of heating and ventilating Hospital Tents.

Signed, R. O. ABBOTT, Surgeon U. S. A., Assistant Medical Director Army of the Potomac.

UNITED STATES GENERAL HOSPITAL, ARMORY SQUARE,
Washington, D. C., Nov. 21, 1862.

RICHARDS KINGSLAND,

Sir: I have the honor to inform you, in regard to your inquiries relative to the value of "Kingsland's Army Portable Stove," (patent,) as a means of heating tents in the field, and especially hospital tents, that I have put up twenty of the Stoves and thoroughly tested them, and do not hesitate to assure you that this is the most complete, compact, and desirable heating apparatus I have ever used or examined for heating tents.

Your Hospital Stoves, with ventilation, should be introduced into every Regimental Hospital in the field, and I shall at once present the matter in an official communication to the Medical Director, urging their introduction for three reasons especially, viz.:

1. Their compactness and portability.
2. Their cheapness.
3. The ease with which the heat can be regulated, and the perfect and scientific manner of ventilation it secures.

I have been connected with the Medical Department of the Army since June 1, 1861, and been on field duty constantly for 13 months, and, from necessity and a desire to make comfortable the sick soldiers in my care, have carefully studied and experimented with several of the most feasible plans of heating hospital and other tents, and do not hesitate to say that your Stoves meet every indication required to place field tents in a condition for occupation for Hospital purposes during cold weather for the winter season, and at a much less expense than the ordinary heating apparatus provided for that purpose, and the economy in fuel.

Very respectfully, your ob't servant,

Signed, D. W. BLISS, Surgeon U. S. V., in charge.

CARVER U. S. GENERAL HOSPITAL, Nov. 2 1862.

I have examined Mr. Kingsland's Patent Army Hospital Heater with great interest, and have no hesitation in expressing my opinion, that the principle of extending a drum through the length of a tent or barrack ward is an economical and effective one, preserving an equable temperature in the ward and making the smoke subserve the heating process, by passing it through the drum instead of directly through the side of the building into the open air.

I think that the principle could be advantageously applied to all Hospital tents used as long wards, and that the slight additional expense would be more than compensated by the economy in fuel.

Signed, O. A. JUDSON, Surgeon U. S. V., in charge.

UNITED STATES GENERAL HOSPITAL FINLEY.
Washington, D. C., Oct. 30th, 1862.

RICHARDS KINGSLAND, Esq.,

Sir: I am most happy to add my testimony to the value of the Army Stove and Hospital Heater and Ventilator, patented by you. The Stove, from its compactness, simplicity and low cost, fulfills all the indications of a model heating arrangement for the field, while the Hospital Heater secures ample heating power, with the fullest facilities for ventilation. Experience in the use has confirmed my first impressions of their utility, and I have no hesitation in commending them to Surgeons in the field, or in charge of hospitals, as meeting all the requirements for Army use.

Very respectfully, your obd't servant,

Signed, B. B. BREED, Surgeon U. S. A.

CAMP BARRY,
Washington, D. C., Nov. 6, 1862.

I take pleasure in expressing my admiration of Kingsland's Patent Army Ventilating Stove, having carefully examined the said Stoves as they are now arranged in the Hospital tents at Armory Square. The perfect ventilation which is secured by their

Testimonials to Kingsland's Army Stove

Camp Stove (Assembled)

Courtesy of T. Sherman Harding Orlando, Florida

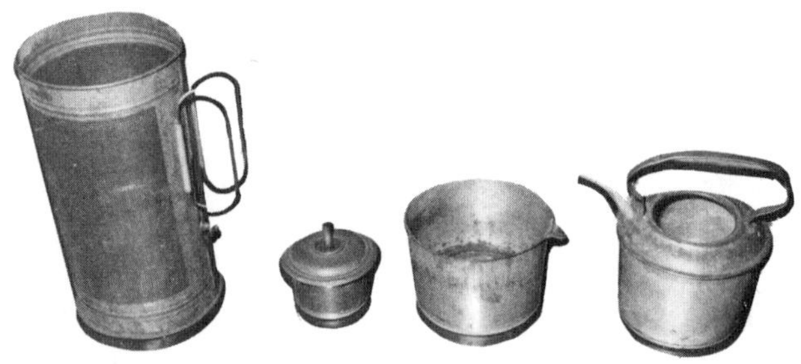

Portable Camp Alcohol Stove

hard, tenacious, and uniform, had the great advantage of being produced in large masses without flaw or weld. By the end of 1862, Krupp of Prussia was casting ingots of over 20 tons' weight and had forged cast steel cannon of 9-inch bore. Krupp was introducing the Bessemer process for producing ingots of any size at about the same cost as for wrought iron.

Cannon manufacturers found that the explosion of the powder was so instantaneous that the exterior parts of the metal did not have time to react before the inner parts were strained beyond their strength. In order to bring all parts of a great mass of metal into simultaneous tension, Blakely, and some other cannon makers, hooped an inner tube with rings having a successively higher initial tension. This resulted in all parts of the gun being strained simultaneously when it was fired. The Parrot and Whitworth cannon were constructed on this principle.

However, Wiard of New York believed that the longitudinal expansion of the inner stratum of the gun was the principal source of strain. A gun made of annular tubes solved this problem; for, if the inner tube were excessively heated, it could elongate and slip a little within those tubes surrounding it without disturbing them.

Various models of cannon were made by different processes. The Armstrong gun, used by the Confederates, was fabricated as follows: A long bar of iron, three by four inches in section, was wound into a close coil about two feet long and of the required diameter—say 18 inches. This was set on end at a welding heat under a steam hammer and "upset" into a tube which was then recessed in a lathe on the ends so as to fit into other tubes. Two tubes set end-to-end were heated to welding, squeezed together by a heavy screw passing through them, and then hammered lightly on the outside without a mandrel. (In forging, the "mandrel" was a rod used to preserve the interior form, but here refers to the spindle upon which the cannon tube was placed in shaping it in the lathe.) Other short tubes were similarly added. Five tubes of different lengths and diameters were turned and bored and shrunk over one another, without successively increasing tension, to form a gun. The breech end of the second tube from the bore was forged solid so that its grain would run parallel with the bore. A gun of this caliber cost $4,000. It was a 110-pounder rifle, 99 1/2 inches long, 7 inches bore diameter, and 27 inches maximum diameter. The gun weighed 4.33 tons.

Naturally, processes varied greatly in casting cannon. For example, the rifled guns made by Horatio Ames were constructed of wrought iron on the build-up principle. The wrought iron was in the form of rings, made by bending a bar around a mandrel and welding the ends. After turning them in a lathe, two or more of these rings were fitted one within another to form a disk. These disks were welded in succession to a concave breech piece. Some of these guns showed remarkable endurance. They were weakest against longitudinal strains.

CANTEENS

One of the basic items of equipment issued to each soldier was the canteen. This was a simple article, made of tin and covered with cloth, shaped like a flattened sphere, and had a cloth carrying strap by which it was suspended over one shoulder and rested outside the haversack against the left hip. It held about three pints.

The canteen had manifold uses, chief of which was to carry water, although it was found equally adapted to carrying other liquids. The forager also found it handy for milk, cider, molasses. In rare instances it was also used for beverages of a more vigorous character, for now and then a man found his way into the Army who was not a member in good standing of a temperance society.

A peculiarity of the canteen was that its usefulness did not end when it was no longer fit to serve in its legitimate sphere. The necessities and deprivations of active campaigning developed among the veterans a wonderful fertility of resource. Under such circumstances men become intensely practical. The condemned canteen was thrown into the fire, where the heat soon melted the

Canteen carried by Color Sergeant F. H. Buffum, 14th New Hampshire Infantry

solder by which the halves were joined. Occasionally a less patient soldier used gunpowder to blow his canteen in two. Now he had two tin basins eight or 10 inches across and in the center about two inches deep. One of these he carried in his haversack. It was not often that the latter was so full of provisions that there was not plenty of room for the basin. Its weight was nothing, and he found it useful in ways not contemplated by its designer.

The Government forgot to supply the soldiers with washbasins; hence the half canteen was a good substitute. After the soldier had finished his ablutions he would rinse the basin with water. Or, if he was too hungry for such niceties, it was a matter of small moment; he split the end of a stick for a handle, and he had a frying pan—a prime article. Tons and tons of pork were fried in the half canteen, not to mention chickens and vegetables acquired in foraging. If the soldier drew his coffee raw, the half canteen was an excellent roaster. Now and then it came in handy for cooking "flapjacks," when he chanced to get hold of something of which to make them. In the fall, when the corn in the fields was ripening, the soldier would take his half canteen, stab it outward full of bayonet holes, whereupon the convex surface made an excellent grater. Ripe hard corn was thus grated into meal, used in mush and "indescribable cakes."

For months at a time, a half canteen, and an old fruit can in which to boil coffee, comprised the soldier's entire culinary kit. The nice coffee pot and frying pan that he had long since succumbed to the vicissitudes of life in the field.

Sometimes the veteran used the half canteen for digging what we call today "fox holes." When there was no time to send to the rear for "intrenching tools," e.g. picks and shovels, the soldier loosened the ground with his bayonet and then scooped out a rifle pit with his half canteen.

The Confederate soldier carried either a tin canteen, much thicker and of different dimensions than the Federal canteen—or a cedar wood canteen. The author has one of these wooden canteens marked "A.J.B. 45 Ala Inf" and "W. Zimmerman, Co. H 50 Ind Volunteers." "A.J.B." were the initials of the original owner, A.J. Bethune, who was captured at Ackworth, Georgia, June 11, 1864, and imprisoned at Camp Morton, Indiana, where Zimmerman's regiment was on guard. The use by the Confederates of wooden canteens illustrates their industrial inferiority to the North, they being short of metal. As one would expect, Johnnie Reb did not spurn a Yankee canteen when he found one.

CARVINGS

To escape the boredom of camp life officers and men alike whiled away many hours in carving objects from bone, wood, and even lead. While the 149th New York Infantry was at Brooks Station, Virginia in 1863, the men became very proficient in making pipes, rings, and small ornaments from the roots of the laurel tree. They also carved objects from bone and inlaid them with colored sealing wax. Many friends at home treasured these souvenirs sent them from the regiment. Federal prisoners at Camp Ford, Tyler, Texas made excellent chess pieces and checkers which found a ready sale among both prisoners and guards. Confederate prisoners at Point Lookout, Maryland made souvenirs for their Federal guards. Among these items was a steam engine and train of cars made by a young Alabamian. Material used was only such as could be found in the prison itself. Tin, nails, wire and wood were the only materials used, yet a perfect locomotive was constructed. When fired up, the locomotive would actually draw the miniature train of cars around the circular track, made specially for this train. So unique and perfect was this train that a Federal officer purchased it, and sent it home to his children, paying the soldier well for it. Shown here are carved items listed according to material used.

CAVALRY ACCOUTERMENTS

Federal cavalrymen carried much unnecessary equipment until the early part of 1863 when Hooker, realizing the potential of these fast-moving troops, reorganized and refitted the mounted arm of the Army of the Potomac. In 1861-1862 each trooper carried three days' subsistence for himself and his mount, 40 rounds of carbine and 20 rounds of pistol ammunition, a haver-

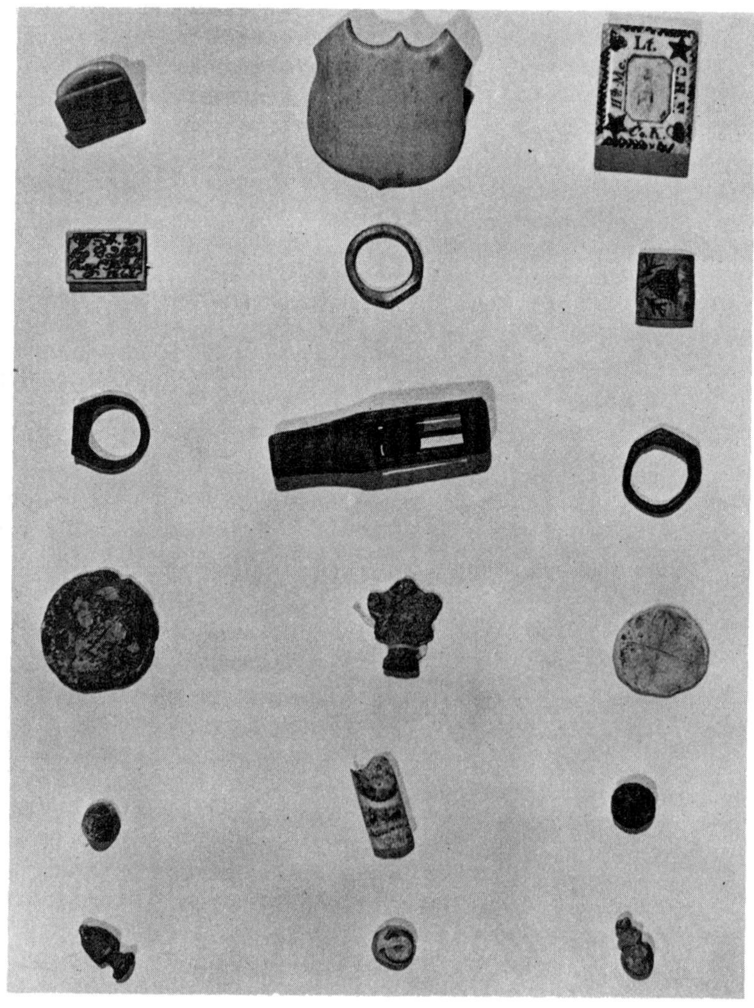

Civil War Carvings
Bone
Row 1: Soldier's carving from beef bone, 23rd Army Corps emblem, Made by Lt. C. H. Foster, 11th Maine Inf.
Row 2: Made by William Failor Co. G, 202nd Penn. Inf., Made in Libby Prison, Made in Libby Prison
Wood
Row 3: Made in Libby Prison, Bottle stopper made from a single piece of wood. Made by Cpl. Henry Brubaken, Made from Pemberton's oak. Vicksburg during the war by C.A. Perkins 12th Michigan Cav.
Lead (Games)
Row 4: C.S. poker chip, Long Bridge, Va., Chess Piece Federal camp Fredericksburg, Federal poker chip, Lagrange, Tenn.
Lead (Fishing)
Row 5: Sinker Fredericksburg 1862, Sinker Port Hudson 1863, Sinker Savannah, Ga. 1864
Lead (Military Use)
Row 6: C.S. cartridge box finial Fredericksburg, Nipple Protector Fredericksburg, C.S. cartridge box finial Wilderness

sack, canteen, tin cup, coffee pot, shelter tent, lariat, picket pin, extra horseshoes and nails, curry comb, brush, gun tools, and cleaning materials. Saddle bags and pommel bags were attached to the saddle. The load on the horse, exclusive of the rider, was about 110 pounds, and with trooper—equipped as he was with carbine, saber, and pistol—the animal had to carry at least 270 pounds. No wonder Jeb Stuart, Morgan, and Forrest rode circles around the Yankee cavalry in the early years of the war.

The uniform of the cavalryman was similar to that of the artillery except that the distinguishing color was yellow, and he wore crossed sabers on his cap or hat. The trooper's trousers were reinforced and he wore boots and spurs. Around his waist was a belt carrying a cartridge box, a cap box, saber, and revolver; and across his shoulder was a wide black leather sling to which was attached the carbine.

In the early days of the war carbines were rare, and McClellan organized the 6th Pennsylvania Cavalry as lancers owing to lack of arms. But the lance was not popular with the men of the regiment. Single-shot carbines were issued at first, but in the latter part of the war many were replaced by repeating carbines. The most commonly used single-shot carbines were the Smith, Merrill, Burnside, Sharps, and Ballard. The repeating carbines were the Colt revolving carbine, the Henry, and the Spencer. Michigan cavalry regiments were considered to be among the best in the service, and in recognition of that fact they were among the very first to receive the Spencer carbine. In addition to his carbine, the Federal soldier was commonly issued a revolver, usually either a Colt or Remington.

He used the famous McClellan saddle, which was light and comfortable and did not hurt the withers of the horse. There is dispute as to where McClellan got his inspiration for the design of this saddle; some claim that it was merely a modification of the Mexican or Texas saddle, while a member of the Army board which adopted the saddle for the United States service shortly after the war maintained that McClellan copied it from the Cossack saddle he had seen in the Crimean War. Many officers used flat saddles of the French or English type with iron stirrups. Others had the regulation McClellan saddle. Both officers and men used a curb bridle.

Much of the equipment used by Federal cavalrymen was cumbersome and useless. In time of war, except on the western plains, there was no need of lariat rope or picket pins. Generally trees were everywhere. Even watering bridles were unnecessary. The heavy leather skirts of the saddle, intended to keep the coat from getting soiled, were found superfluous. Towards the end of the war the men frequently used the saddle tree without leather skirts (they were easily unscrewed from the tree) and in order to make the saddle fit the horse better, the men would put their own blankets under the saddle, over the horse blanket, and thus prevent a saddle gall or sore, and at the same time carry their own blankets more comfortably. The heavy hooded stirrups were unsightly and unnecessary, and quickly got out of shape when wet and muddy. The wooden stirrup, without the leather, was better. Many of the bits were too severe.

Of the soldier's equipment, the rattling scabbard, with iron rings, made a ceaseless noise. Had the saber slings been fastened directly to the scabbard, the jingling would have been avoided; and on occasions, absence of this noise would have kept scouts from being detected by the enemy. The men finally learned to fasten the saber and scabbard firmly to the near side of the saddle, nearly parallel to the horse's body, and when mounted throw the left leg over it. It was then ready to be drawn when the man was mounted, yet was not in the way of the dismounted trooper, who had quite enough to do to take care of himself and his carbine in the thicket into which he so frequently had to march when skirmishing. When a man was on foot, a saber was seldom of any use, actually being in the way.

Herb Peck, Jr.

Federal Cavalry Accounterments (Soldier Unidentified)

The sabers were the model 1860 light cavalry saber, made by Ames and other contractors. In some regiments an English saber became popular. Some officers liked the long straight weapon of the French *Cent-gardes.*

By 1864, however, there was no splendor in the clothing and equipment of Federal cavalrymen and their mounts. There was something solid about the appearance of a veteran regiment of cavalry which commanded respect. When Sheridan's sunburned and weather-beaten troopers paraded in Washington in May 1865, their appearance aroused great enthusiasm.

Until 1863 Confederate cavalrymen were poorly armed and indifferently equipped. In 1861 they lacked Colt and Remington revolvers, Chicopee sabers, and good carbines. But by 1863 all men except officers carried carbines. Some of these weapons were copies of the Sharps carbine, made in Richmond, while many used the English Enfield carbine. Others used a cutdown Springfield musket or even carried infantry weapons. Confederate weapons were varied and often crude.

Confederate cavalrymen were armed with sabers of all types, usually of English make, sometimes of Austrian manufacture, and occasionally made locally. By 1863 they usually had Colt's revolvers, which they handled very skillfully, and sometimes they had C.S. imitations of Colts or such English revolvers as the Adams or Kerr. Many troopers preferred the Colt over

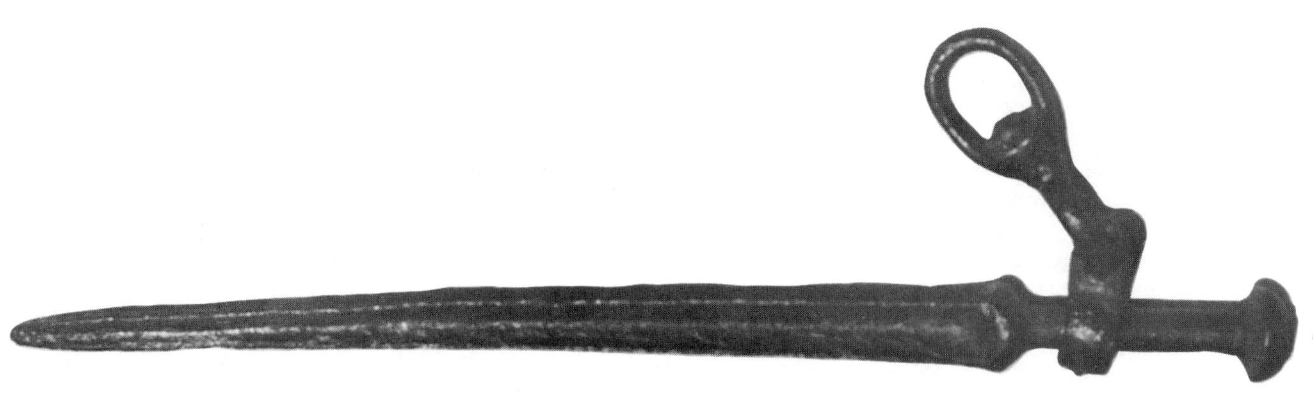
John A. Marks

Picket Pin from Hopefield, Arkansas (wrought iron, 14 1/2 inches long).

all other makes, foreign or local. Their ammunition was frequently English although the C.S. Ordnance Department was far from inactive. Often a Confederate cavalry regiment had two sharphooter companies, while the remaining companies were armed with sabers and revolvers.

At the Battle of Brandy Station in June, 1863, every Confederate cavalryman was armed with at least one, sometimes more, army or navy revolvers, and sabers. Many of the homemade saddles had been replaced by captured McClellans. After Chancellorsville, Confederate cavalry generally had a complete outfit of saddle, bridle, blankets, and weapons—all imported or locally produced, or, more generally, taken from the enemy. However, the Confederate trooper in the Western theater of war was never well equipped, possibly because his adversary in that theater likewise was the last to receive good equipment. Apparently there was a direct relationship between the Federal supply services and their ultimate recipients (the Confederate forces) in both theaters of war!

In the West, Morgan's troopers, mostly young men, were scantily equipped. In addition to their rations they carried their own ammunition, extra horseshoes (generally two), 12 nails, a blanket and "oil cloth" or overcoat. Each trooper had two Colt revolvers, a few had sabers, but most men carried double-barreled shotguns, long Enfields, Belgian, or Austrian muskets.

Generally the Confederate cavalry troopers preferred revolvers to sabers. While this undoubtedly provided greater mobility and certainly less noise, it also could result disastrously. In the 1864 Shenandoah Valley campaign General Early complained that his cavalry was armed entirely with rifles and had no sabers. The consequence was that his cavalrymen could not fight mounted and were unsuccessful in open country against large bodies of Federal cavalry. And in the West, General Joe Wheeler believed that at least one regiment of each brigade should be armed with revolvers and sabers, otherwise his force was virtually nothing but mounted infantry. Wheeler urged the adoption of the revolver and saber and a light carbine instead of such complete dependence on the rifle. He regretted that the saber had been so much overlooked; its morale effect was great. In hand-to-hand combat the necessity of the saber was "most apparent." Forrest's cavalry generally carried sabers but did not use them very often.

In the East, Mosby and his men were generally armed with the revolver; in fact, most men had two, and also carried extra cylinders to slip loaded into their revolvers when they had fired all of their original loads. Often these revolvers turned the tide of battle. At Ashby's Gap, February 19, 1865, Custer's men, armed with carbines, were at a great disadvantage in a hand-to-hand fight with Mosby's partisans. The Federals had no weapons but their carbines and these were extremely difficult to load and were actually almost useless in the

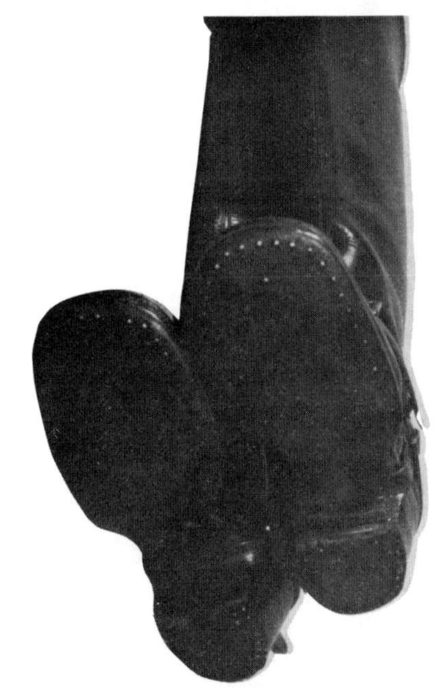

William Langlois

Cavalry Boots (C.S.)

close-in fighting. Mosby's men had very few sabers but, being well supplied with revolvers, rode up to the Federal troopers and shot them down without much resistance, since the Federals were nearly helpless once they had fired their single-shot carbines.

The Confederates learned that the saber was good for shock action except when the terrain was unfavorable, such as in wooded country. Under such conditions the revolver was substituted for the saber. However, a commander had to think and act quickly. To secure decisive results he had to make a rapid decision and take the initiative at once. A timid leader usually would fail where a bold one would succeed. In many cases, bold Confederate leaders, by means of a sudden attack, were successful and their losses were small.

Confederate cavalrymen found out that in the melee the carbine was useless against the revolver. The saber was essentially a weapon for the mounted charge, but once the action had broken down into individual combats, the revolver was vastly superior to the saber. In a man-to-man encounter, the revolver won almost every time. A good pistol shot would kill or wound his adversary before the latter could get close enough to use his saber.

CAVALRY BOOTS (C.S.)

Dark brown leather, size 7 1/2. These boots are 21 inches high in front and 17 inches high in back. Worn by Captain George A. Baxter, Co. K, 6th Virginia Cavalry. Enlisted May 21, 1861 and killed in action at Front Royal, Virginia, June 30, 1862, while leading his company in a charge. From the collection of William Langlois.

CAVALRY BUGLE (U.S.)

Brass cavalry bugle, 16 1/2 inches long. Width at bell—5 inches. Inscription on silver plate:

M. B. Strickler
Chf. Bugler
8th Reg. Penn. Cav.

Michael B. Strickler served with the 8th Pennsylvania Cavalry from October 3, 1861 to January 19, 1863. The bugle was carried in the Peninsular Campaign 1862, Antietam, Aldie, Ashby's Gap, Fredericksburg, etc. Strickler later served as a lieutenant in another regiment. From the collection of William Langlois.

William Langlois

William Langlois

Cavalry Boots (C.S.). These are other views of Capt. Baxter's Boots. Note the initials ANV—(Army of Northern Virginia)

William Langlois

Cavalry Bugle (U.S.)

CHAPLAINS BUTTON

This button was recovered from a trench in Savannah, Georgia. It is of hard rubber and therefore is probably Federal since hard rubber buttons were used by United States troops to a limited extent. This button is 3/4 inch in diameter. No maker's markings. Non-regulation since General Order No. 102, U.S. War Department, November 25, 1861, prescribed merely that Army Chaplains wear "black buttons." No Insignia of any kind, including the cross, was authorized. The author also has a fancy brass button-definitely non-military-known to have been worn by a Federal chaplain.

CHEVRONS

Noncommissioned officers' rank was shown by chevrons worn on both sleeves. Material of these chevrons was usually worsted but silk and even leather was used in contrast with United States Army chevrons today.

Description: Heavy blue worsted. The chevrons for the infantry corporal are 6 1/4 inches for each side of the chevron with a distance of 9 1/2 inches between the innertips of the chevron. The chevrons for the infantry orderly sergeant (first sergeant) are 5 3/4 inches for each side of the chevron with a distance of 8 1/4 inches between the inner tips of the chevron.

CIGAR CUTTER

Shaped like scissors with adjusting cutter. Cutter blade is held by two screws. One side marked:

WALCOTT BROTHERS, MAN'FAC

Robert L. Robinson III

Chaplain's Button

The other side is marked:

WALCOTT'S PATENT, JULY 27, 1852

Used to cut off tip of the cigar when one wishes to lay the cigar aside for a while.

Federal Army Chevrons

CLEANING ROD

Cleaning the musket was a necessary requirement of the soldier both in camp and in the field. Normally, the musket's ramrod was used for this purpose. Shown here, however, is a cleaning rod, probably issued in limited number to noncoms or artificers.

Description: Wood, probably birch. Overall length 39 3/4 inches, with a round knob at the end for holding the rod. Diameter of the knob 1 3/4 inches.

CLOTHING AND TENT ALLOTMENT AT THE FRONT (U.S.)

Although always better supplied than their adversaries, the Federals gradually learned to reduce the soldiers' packs before commencing active operations. The 10th Army Corps order shown here was issued just prior to the beginning of Grant's 1864 campaign. Written in the field, this order measures 12 1/4 by 7 5/8 inches, is a copy of the official order, and was used by the 11th Maine Infantry.

COEHORN MORTAR

One of the little-known weapons used in the Civil War was the Coehorn mortar, so named from the Dutch military engineer, Baron Van Coehorn (1641-1704), who invented it. Basically, a "Coehorn" is a small mortar, generally of 4 3/5 inches caliber. This mortar was easily manned and adjusted and used very little powder. In past wars they proved very useful in siege

Cigar Cutter

Cleaning Rod

operations, especially when grouped in large numbers. Apparently, these mortars were first used by Baron Coehorn in 1673 against the French. Some 20 were used by Oglethorpe in bombarding St. Augustine in 1740. This small portable mortar was an important weapon in the Mexican War, but was not used in the Civil War to any extent until the Spring of 1864.

The Coehorn, as used from 1861-1865, was a very small bronze mortar, designed to throw a 24-pounder shell to targets no greater than 1200 yards distant. Its weight was 164 pounds, its maximum charge was 1/2 pound of powder, and it was mounted on a wooden block, equipped with handles, so that two men could carry it easily from one part of the lines to another. Coehorns, like the light mortars of today, were employed against enemy personnel and guns which were sheltered from the fire of field pieces by the sloping terrain. They were especially effective in harrassing fire against enemy personnel. The Coehorns were so valuable to Grant that they were retained even when he sent several batteries of conventional artillery back to Washington because they impeded his war of movement in such difficult terrain as the Wilderness in Virginia.

Coehorns were fired at an angle of 45 degrees. The range depended on the powder charge. Ranges varied from 25 yards (1/2 ounce powder charge) to 1200 yards (8 ounce powder charge). The projectile weighed only 17 pounds! Experience showed that when metal friction primers were used, fragments of these primers were blown out of the touch-hole, often injuring the gun crew.

Dimensions of the 24-pounder Coehorn mortar used by the Federals were:

Bore	- 5.82 inches
Length of tube	- 16.32 inches
Weight of tube	- 164 pounds

It fired a 17 pound projectile with a .5 pound charge. This projectile carried some 1200 yards when the piece was set at 45 degrees.

It fell to the 15th New York Heavy Artillery to be one of the few units which manned Coehorn mortars in the Federal Army. This excellent German regiment was organized in New York City in the Fall of 1861. The regiment performed garrison duty in the defences of Washington until March 1864, when it joined the Army of the Potomac at the front, where it was assigned to the 5th Corps, to which it was attached throughout the remainder of the war. During its service it lost by death 8 officers and 148 enlisted men, killed and mortally wounded; 5 officers and 225 men by disease and other causes, including 63 men who died while prisoners in the hands of the enemy.

In March 1864, the regiment was assigned to the artillery arm of the Army of the Potomac under the direct command of that army's chief of artillery, Brigadier General Henry J. Hunt. At this time the 15th New York was commanded by Colonel Louis Schirmer and was equipped with the following artillery pieces: 26 Napoleans; 18 three-inch pieces; 12 ten-pounder Parrotts; 6 twenty-pounder Parrotts; and 8 twenty-four-pounder Coehorn mortars. Each of the Coehorn mortars was allocated 100 rounds of ammunition.

The regiment, after leaving Brandy Station, Virginia on May 3, 1864, crossed the Rapidan by Ely's Ford in the afternoon of the 4th, forming with the 6th New York Heavy Artillery, one brigade, commanded by Colonel J. H. Kitching. This brigade was ordered to protect the Reserve Artillery of the Army of the Potomac. On its departure from Brandy Station, the regiment consisted of 49 officers, 1,525 men present for duty (12 officers, 484 men being absent), making an aggregate of 2,070, certainly one of the largest regiments that ever took the field during the Civil War. On the 5th of May the regiment marched through Chancellorsville toward the Wilderness, and in the evening received orders to prepare to be employed as infantry in the Battle of the Wilderness, which had commenced that day. On the 6th, about 2 A.M., the 15th New York marched forward, but before a line of battle could be completed, which was difficult because of the thick undergrowth, the Confederates launched an attack on the right of the regiment, and then followed it up by attacking the center and left. Although the men of the 15th had to deploy under heavy fire, they repulsed the first attack and even pursued the retiring enemy some 200 yards. However, the Confederates moved up reinforcements and the 15th fell back in good order to the protection of heavy

Head Quarters 10th Army Corps.
Gloucester Point Va. April 20 1864

General Orders }
No. 7. }

The Clothing of each enlisted man of of this command will be immediately reduced to the following articles viz.

1 Blouse. 1 Good pair of Pants. 2 pairs of Drawers. 2 Shirts. 3 pairs of Stockings. 2 pairs of Shoes. 1 Over coat. 1 Wool Blanket. 1 Rubber Blanket.

All Clothing in excess of this allowance will be packed without delay in Company Boxes, carefully marked and turned over to the Brig. Q. M. for transportation to Norfolk Va. where it will be stored.

As fast as shelter Tents are issued the the Tents now in use by the Company officers and enlisted men will be packed marked and sent to Norfolk Va. for Storage. Co. Officers will be provided with Shelter Tents or the Officers of one Company may use the Fly of one Wall Tent instead.

By order of Brig. Gen. A. H. Terry
(sgd) A. Terry.
A. A. G.

Official
(sgd) Fred T. Mason.
Lt & A. A. A. G.
Official. T. S. Peck.
Lt. & A. A. A. Genl

I certify that the above is a true copy.
L. Lawrence
Capt. [illegible]

Clothing Allotment for the March

woods. After being relieved by elements of the 5th Corps, the 15th New York built a second line of breastworks. In the course of the fighting the regiment sustained 44 casualties.

During the fighting in the early stages of the 1864 campaign, the regimental commander complained that the regiment was not armed according to the duties it had to perform, carrying old Model 1841 rifles equipped with sword bayonets. The 15th had never received sufficient drilling as infantry, "this having been considered but a secondary part of its duty during its stay in fortifications around Washington."

About 3 P.M. on May 7th, the regiment started toward Spotsylvania Court House, and arrived about 7 A.M. on May 9. Here the Second Battalion, commanded by Major Julius Dieckmann, was detached from the regiment. This Battalion, consisting of Companies E, F, G. H. was assigned as follows: Company E to take charge of a 24-pounder Coehorn mortar battery; while Companies F, G, H were assigned to guard the reserve ammunition train of the Army of the Potomac. Also, Company B was detailed as provost guard at Brandy Station. The remaining seven companies of the regiment served throughout the war as infantry.

On June 25 these detached companies rejoined the regiment and on the 28th the regiment became part of the Federal Forces investing Petersburg. During the siege and thereafter, the 15th New York served as a unit with the Army of the Potomac. By the first of April, 1865, this army had about 40 Coehorns.

Other units which have been identified as having manned Coehorn mortars were Company K, 4th New York Heavy Artillery (attached to 18th Corps); Company C, 4th New York Heavy Artillery (attached to 5th Corps); Companies D and G, 1st Connecticut Heavy Artillery (attached to 18th Corps). These units were part of Colonel Henry L. Abbot's siege train which served with the Army of the Potomac. The siege train left Washington in the Spring of 1864, taking with it 20 Coehorn mortars and 200 rounds of ammunition per mortar. These Coehorns saw extensive action on the Petersburg front during the famous mine explosion. Their mission was to keep down the fire of the Confederates on the flanks of the Federal attacking column and to keep back Confederate reinforcements. The Federal mortars were successful in performing these missions. During the action, the Coehorns fired a total of 1037 rounds!

There can be no doubt of the value of the Coehorn mortars to the artillery arm of Grant's army. In his report of the artillery operations during May, 1864, General Hunt singled out the Coehorns for special mention. He reported that during the period May 8 - 16, these mortars were put into action wherever circumstances permitted their employment, and always with "good results."

Confederate attempts to use Coehorns were not especially successful. On August 20, 1864, they planted some Coehorn mortars within good range of the Dutch Gap Canal and kept up an intermittent fire on the Gap, but did very little damage. They lacked the Federal skill in use of Coehorns. Not one in a hundred of their shots landed on target, where Federals would have achieved a ratio of at least one in five.

When Coehorns were not available, the Federals substituted crudely-made, but effective, mortars for them. According to the chief engineer of the Federal 17th Corps at Vicksburg, it was difficult for sharpshooters to reach the Confederates by direct firing, and the artillerymen found it impossible to gauge their shells so as to have them explode immediately behind the Confederate parapets. Accordingly, the Federals constructed what they termed "Coehorn Mortars" out of gum-tree logs. These novel artillery pieces, when accurately charged with just enough powder to lift 6 or 12-pound shells over the parapets and drop them down directly behind, proved to be extremely effective.

The Confederate artillerist, General E. P. Alexander, reports that Confederates at the siege of Knoxville in 1863, rigged mortars to drop shells behind the Federal parapets and to search out areas sheltered from direct fire. These mortars were equipped with skids inclined at a 45 degree angle, one end of each skid resting on the ground, and the other on a horizontal pole supported about 6 feet from the ground by forked posts. The axle of the gun was run up on these skids, raising the wheels in the air on each side of the skids, and leaving the trail on the ground between them, until the piece had an elevation of about 60 degrees. This arrangement worked fairly well, both in Tennessee and Virginia.

The best defence against the Coehorn was the "bombproof." This shelter was used extensively around Petersburg and the Richmond defences. A bomb-proof was made of logs heavily banked with dirt, and provided with a door on the side away from the enemy. The roof was especially vulnerable to the fire of Coehorn mortars and accordingly was constructed of the heaviest logs available, covered with several feet of dirt. The interior of a bomb-proof varied in size according to the number of men whom it had to accommodate in an emergency. Some bomb-proofs were built above ground; some were holes in the ground. But, no matter how constructed, all were damp and uncomfortable, even when fireplaces were built for use in cold weather. Bomb-proofs were occupied only during periods of hostile mortar and artillery attack.

Proportionately, Coehorns and other mortars were used less than the conventional artillery pieces. The mortars were especially useful in siege operations and saw extensive use in 1864, particularly around Petersburg.

COLT REVOLVING RIFLE

The early civilian method of fastening shoulder stocks

Herb Peck, Jr.

Unidentified Federal Cavalryman armed with a Colt Revolving Carbine

on heavy barrel revolvers and making a serviceable repeating shoulder arm led the Colt Company to apply the same idea to a full fledged rifle. Consequently, the 1855 model revolving rifle was produced. It became the first repeating rifle adopted by the armed services of the United States. This rifle was made in several barrel lengths for the Army and Navy. Although the patent for the mechanism was taken out in 1855, there was no production of the weapon until 1857 because kinks had to be removed in the locking, unlocking, and turning of the cylinder.

In 1857, the Government purchased 101 Colt revolving rifles at $50 each, and another lot of 300, and appurtenances at $42.50. During the Civil War these arms were also purchased by the Navy at $44 and by the several states for their militia units. The type which saw most use was probably the five-shot caliber 1856 military model, although many individuals, especially officers, purchased the caliber .36 sporting model.

A thousand Colt revolving rifles were issued to Col. Hiram Berdan's First U.S. Sharpshooters shortly before the launching of McClellan's Peninsula campaign. Generally speaking, Colt's rifles were not popular with the sharpshooters who complained that there was danger of all chambers exploding at once. Moreover, the chambers heated up rapidly when used continuously. On May 7, 1862, while the Berdan Sharpshooters were in front of Yorktown, they exchanged their Colt revolving rifles for Sharps rifles. Colonel Berdan however, considered the Colt weapon to be a "very superior weapon," especially for skirmishers.

Gen. William S. Rosecrans, too, believed in the Colt rifle. Believing that five or six chambers were better than one, he asked for 5,000 of them in 1863.

But even in the South, Colt had difficulty selling his revolving rifle. As one of his agents said: "I could sell a great number if I had the proper confidence in them . . . Last trial (was) before General Gist at Union, South Carolina. Took all the evening to pick the powder and pieces of lead out of my face. No use telling a person to hold their head back, might as well tell them to hold it under their airm."

Colt's revolving rifle never became popular and after its brief use with Berdan's Sharpshooters it started to decline without having ever enjoyed a real period of success.

Soldiers of all branches were exceedingly unhappy over the flash and loud report so close to the face and the fearful recoil when several chambers went off at once. But, more seriously yet, there was one major weakness which definitely precluded any extensive adoption of this weapon for the service. During firing, the heavy rifle barrel had to be supported by hand. This had not been necessary in a revolver equipped with a shoulder stock. Sometimes loose powder from a faulty cap or gas leak would cause other chambers to be ignited. When this happened, the soldier using the piece lost his hand or the portion of his arm that happened to be in front of the exploding cylinder. One such accident in a regiment destroyed not only confidence in the weapon, but the morale of soldiers and officers alike. The total failure of the army's official attempt to introduce a repeating shoulder weapon into the service gave the conservative element a chance to point out the inevitable disaster that always follows any such departure from what has proved successful over the years. Finally a board of officers met. After hearing all the evidence, they ordered that the Colt use be discontinued and the pieces sold for whatever price could be obtained. The highest bid was 42 cents a rifle!

The U.S. Government made very few purchases of Colt revolving rifles during the War. In addition to the 1,000 purchased for Berdan's men, the records show 2,725 purchased in late 1862 and early 1863. It is doubtful if any agency, Federal or local, purchased Colt revolving rifles after February, 1863. But dealers in the North continued to offer them for sale to individual soldiers and small units. Samuel Colt was commissioned Colonel in May 1861 and ordered to raise a regiment to be known as the First Connecticut Revolving Rifles. Colt's regiment was to be armed with his revolving rifles, each man was to be over 6 feet tall and a good marksman. The regiment was disbanded in a few weeks over administrative questions.

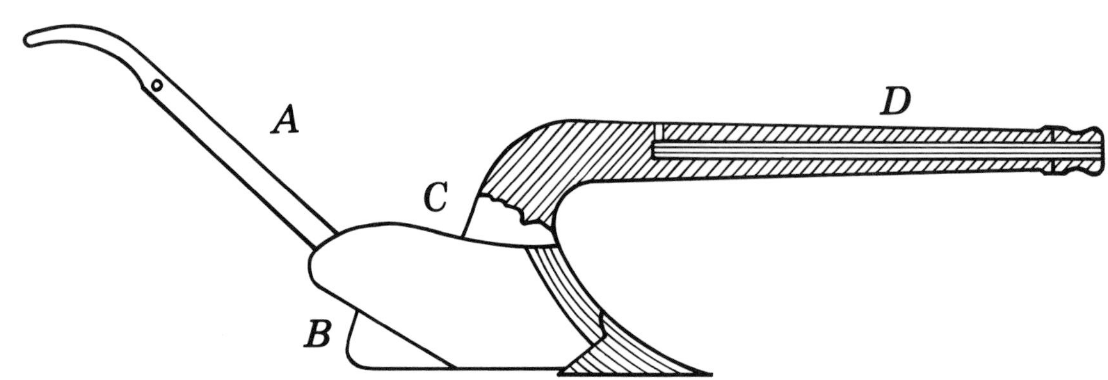

Combined Cannon and Plow

Colt's revolving rifle, like his revolver, was made with either five or six chambers. The bullet was forced into seven grooves which formed a spiral and which became steadily more contracted as it approached the muzzle of the rifle. The result was a long range rifle which was formidable in the hands of trained personnel, but considerable time was required in reloading. According to contemporary observers it was an unusually accurate weapon. It certainly was regrettable that the designers of the Colt rifle were not able to remove the unpleasant and dangerous characteristics of the piece. Had they done so, the U.S. Government might well have had an efficient repeating weapon as standard issue for troops at the beginning of the Civil War.

COMBINED CANNON AND PLOW

On June 17, 1862, C.M. French and W.H. Francher of Waterloo, New York were issued a patent (No. 35600) for a combined cannon and plow. These two men owned adjoining farms and felt the need for defense against a hostile attack while plowing their fields. They came up with the idea of a plow cast in iron, forming the barrel of a cannon in the beam of the plow. This cannon could be charged with grape or canister as with any other cannon.

A full scale model was built but several problems developed, including excess weight and coupling the muzzle of the cannon to the horse and harness. Also, the breech was too weak to take a canister charge and it split during test firing, forming a plow with two beams!

COMMISSION FOR OFFICERS

Individuals received commissions as officers either from the Government or their State. However, Army Regulations provided that officers serving *by commission* from any State took rank next *after* officers of the like grade *by commission* from the Government. The President or Secretary of War, signed commissions for officers appointed by the Government while State officers' commissions were signed by the Governor. In the early part of the war even Department commanders issued commissions!

WAR DEPARTMENT. Size 10 x 7 3/4 inches. Notice of appointment by the President of of EMORY UPTON as Second Lieutenant in the 4th U.S. Artillery. Dated May 11, 1861, and signed by Secretary of War Simon Cameron. Emory Upton, after a brilliant war service, achieved fame with the publishing of his *Military Policy of the United States.*

MILITARY DEPARTMENT. Size 9 5/8 x 7 1/2 inches. Commission as Surgeon to I. R. Duncan, 9th Kentucky Volunteers. Dated October 5, 1861. Signed by the Commanding General of the Department of the Cumberland, Robert Anderson. Anderson was the officer (as a major) in command of Fort Sumter in April 1861.

STATE. Size 14 1/4 x 12 1/4 inches. Commission as First Lieutenant to *William Warner*, 33rd Wisconsin Infantry. Dated September 12, 1862. Signed by the Governor of Wisconsin, Edward Salomon. The red seal of the State of Wisconsin is affixed to the commission.

CORPS BADGES

Federal field armies were composed of corps commanded by major generals. At full strength a corps numbered 25,000 men, but corps in the Army of the Potomac in 1863 numbered, on the average, only 16,000 men, while some were much smaller. In the Army of the Potomac each corps headquarters was designated by a headquarters flag.

In the West, there was no corps organization until October, 1862. At that time General Rosecrans established a different system of corps flags, but provisions regarding flags to designate corps headquarters were not generally adopted.

Eventually corps badges were worn proudly by troops in all theaters of war. To increase esprit and for a ready recognition of corps and divisions in the several armies, a system of badges for the various corps was

WAR DEPARTMENT,

Washington, May 11th, 1861.

Sir:

You are hereby informed that the President of the United States has appointed you Second Lieutenant in the Fourth Regiment of Artillery

in the service of the United States, to rank as such from the Sixth day of May, one thousand eight hundred and sixty one Should the Senate, at their next session, advise and consent thereto, you will be commissioned accordingly.

Immediately on receipt hereof, please to communicate to this Department, through the Adjutant General's Office, your acceptance or non-acceptance of said appointment; and, with your letter of acceptance, return to the Adjutant General of the Army the OATH herewith enclosed, properly filled up, SUBSCRIBED and ATTESTED, reporting at the same time your AGE, RESIDENCE when appointed, and the STATE in which you were BORN.

~~Should you accept, you will at once report, by letter, for orders, to~~

Simon Cameron

Secretary of War.

2d Lieutenant Emory Upton,
4th Artillery
Washington,
D.C.

Second Lieutenant's Commission for Emory Upton

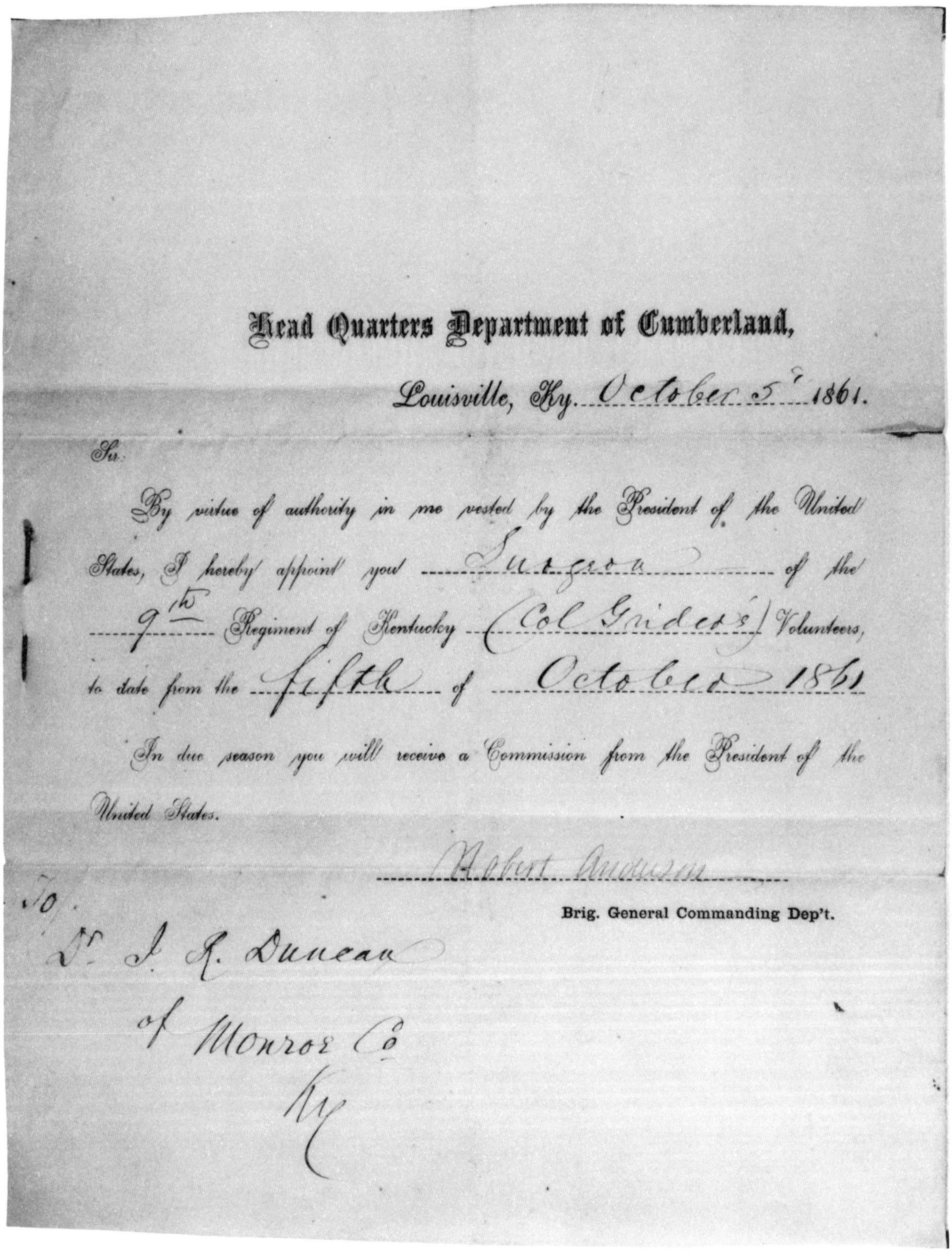

Head Quarters Department of Cumberland,

Louisville, Ky. October 5th 1861.

Sir.

By virtue of authority in me vested by the President of the United States, I hereby appoint you Surgeon of the 9th Regiment of Kentucky (Col Grider's) Volunteers, to date from the fifth of October 1861

In due season you will receive a Commission from the President of the United States.

Robert Anderson

Brig. General Commanding Dep't.

To

Dr. I. R. Duncan

of Monroe Co

Ky

Surgeon's Commission for I. R. Duncan

STATE OF WISCONSIN.

EDWARD SALOMON, GOVERNOR.

To all to whom these Presents shall Come, Greeting:

Know Ye, That reposing special trust and confidence in the Patriotism, Fidelity and Good Conduct of William Warner Wis. I have appointed and constituted, and by these Presents do appoint and constitute him First Lieutenant and Adjutant of the Thirty Third Regiment Wisconsin Volunteers with rank from September 13th 1862. And I do Hereby Authorize and empower him to execute and fulfil the duties of that office according to law; and he is required to observe and follow such orders and directions as he shall from time to time receive from the Commander-in-Chief, or any other his Superior Officer, according to the Rules and Discipline of War, and in accordance with the Constitution and Laws of this State.

In Testimony Whereof, I have hereunto subscribed my name, and caused the Great Seal of the State of Wisconsin to be affixed.

Done at Madison, this Twenty[illegible] day of September in the year of our Lord One Thousand Eight Hundred and Sixty-two.

By the Governor, Edward Salomon.

James T. Lewis
Secretary of State.

Aug. Gaylord
Adjutant General.

First Lieutenant's Commission for William Warner

adopted. The idea originated with General Philip Kearny, who had the soldiers of his division wear a red patch to distinguish them from other troops. The idea of corps badges to be worn throughout the Army of the Potomac later was suggested to Hooker by his chief of staff, General Daniel Butterfield, who devised the badges in detail.

Butterfield's biographer tells how the different badges came to be selected: "The design for the I Army Corps was a disc, the first thing thought of." A patch or lozenge was reserved for the III Army Corps, as Kearny's division was in that corps. For the II Army Corps the trefoil was chosen, as a sort of shamrock, there being many troops of Irish origin in that corps.

The order for the first corps badges (Army of the Potomac, March 21, 1863) was prompted by the need of ready recognition of corps and divisions to prevent injustice by reports of straggling and misconduct through mistakes as to identification of their organizations.

The idea of corps badges was taken to the Western armies by the transfer of the XI and XII Army Corps from the Army of the Potomac to Tennessee in 1863. When these corps arrived at Chattanooga they were wearing their corps badges. Rivalry between them and the Western corps was strong and the contrast in neatness of dress between the two sections was marked. One of the Easterners asked an Irishman of the Western troops what his corps badge was. The Westerner slapped his cartridge box and replied: "This is my corps badge." As a result of this incident, his unit, the XV Army Corps, adopted the cartridge box with the words "Forty Rounds" as their corps badge. Only two (XIII and XXI) of the 25 corps failed to adopt badges in the Federal Army.

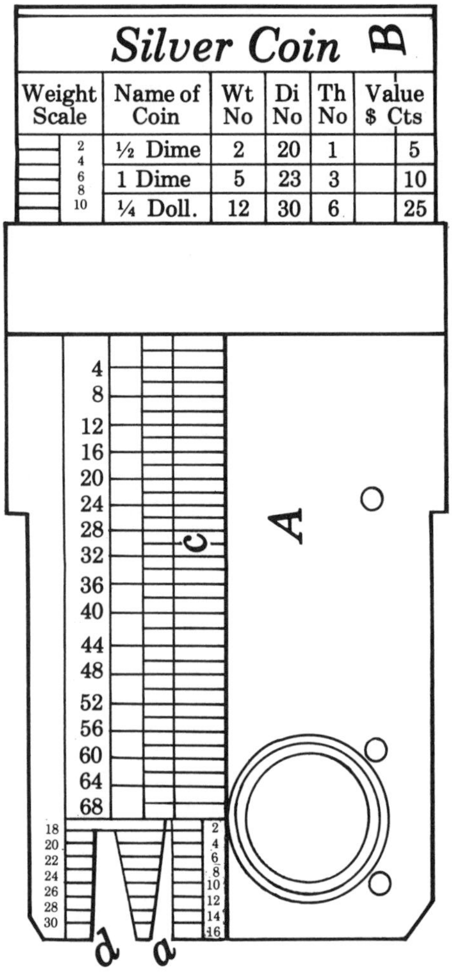

Silver Coin B					
Weight Scale	Name of Coin	Wt No	Di No	Th No	Value $ Cts
2 4	½ Dime	2	20	1	5
6 8	1 Dime	5	23	3	10
10	¼ Doll.	12	30	6	25

Al Gross

Counterfeit Coin Detector

The badges, of cloth or metal, were worn either on the cap or left side of the hat. Although the Chief Quartermaster had been directed to supply corps badges to all individuals assigned to corps, there appears to have been no regular government issue of these badges. The men bought them from sutlers or made them from the lining of their overcoats. Corps emblems were soon used everywhere—being painted on ambulances, wagons, and other material, as well as being worn by the men. Most of the metal corps badges were sold by sutlers. In addition to brass and tin, silver badges, engraved with the soldier's name, company, and regiment were popular. These fancy badges were widely advertised in *Harper's Weekly*, *Leslie's*, and *The Army and Navy Journal*. One soldier thought his corps badge had the power to protect him from all enemy missiles. That man, a private in the 14th New Hampshire Infantry of the XIX army Corps, ironically enough was killed in his regiment's first battle.

A rather unusual use of the corps emblem was that made by men of the V Army Corps, who delighted in showing the enemy that their corps had destroyed part of the Weldon Railroad. In August, 1864, these soldiers heated railroad rails, then twisted one rail over another, thus forming a Maltese cross, their corps badge. However, men of the II Corps, also active in this rail destruction, could hardly do this as the rails could not be twisted into the shape of the trefoil.

In the last two years of the war Federal corps badges were well known to friend and foe alike. When Confederate prisoners were brought into the lines of the 2nd Division of the II Corps at Bristoe Station, and saw the white trefoil of their captors, they recognized their old antagonists of Gettysburg and exclaimed: "Those damned white clubs again!"

Sometimes corps badges were a disadvantage, especially to wounded men who, in some cases, were treated only at their own corps hospitals. This happened to a I Army Corps soldier who sought treatment at an XI Corps field hospital at Gettysburg. The soldier's corps badge identified him but the surgeon finally relented and gave him too-long delayed medical assistance.

A suggestion for a distinguishing badge for Regular officers was never acted upon due to the termination of the war. However, the corps badges for Volunteers, whether the emblems were of cloth, tin, brass, or silver, were extensively worn during the war. These badges are very scarce today and most collectors consider themselves fortunate if they have even one.

COUNTERFEIT COIN DIRECTOR

Useful to paymasters and sutlers alike! Patented July 8, 1862, by W. Painter. This device consists of one or more suspended or tilted spouts inserted into a counter top or table over a drawer. Each coin must pass through the detector and is weighed and gauged. Thus a spurious coin can not pass and is detected.

CURRY COMBS AND HORSE BRUSH

Due to the large number of horses used in all theaters of operations, these essential items are frequently found, especially in camp sites. The currycombs were of steel with 8 rows of "teeth", and generally 4 3/4 by 4 inches in size. The currycomb on the left was picked up at Fredericksburg. A thin brass shield in the center of the back is marked with the American eagle and the words:

Mary...Als
Patent
New York

the handle was rusted off completely.

The center curry comb has an iron handle (the wood has rotted off) and was found in the U.S. Cavalry camp at Falmouth, Virginia.

The curry comb on the right is 5 inches long, 4 1/8 inches wide, and has a 4-inch wooden handle. This curry comb which was used with horse brush shown in the illustration is marked:

Patented
January 22, 1861

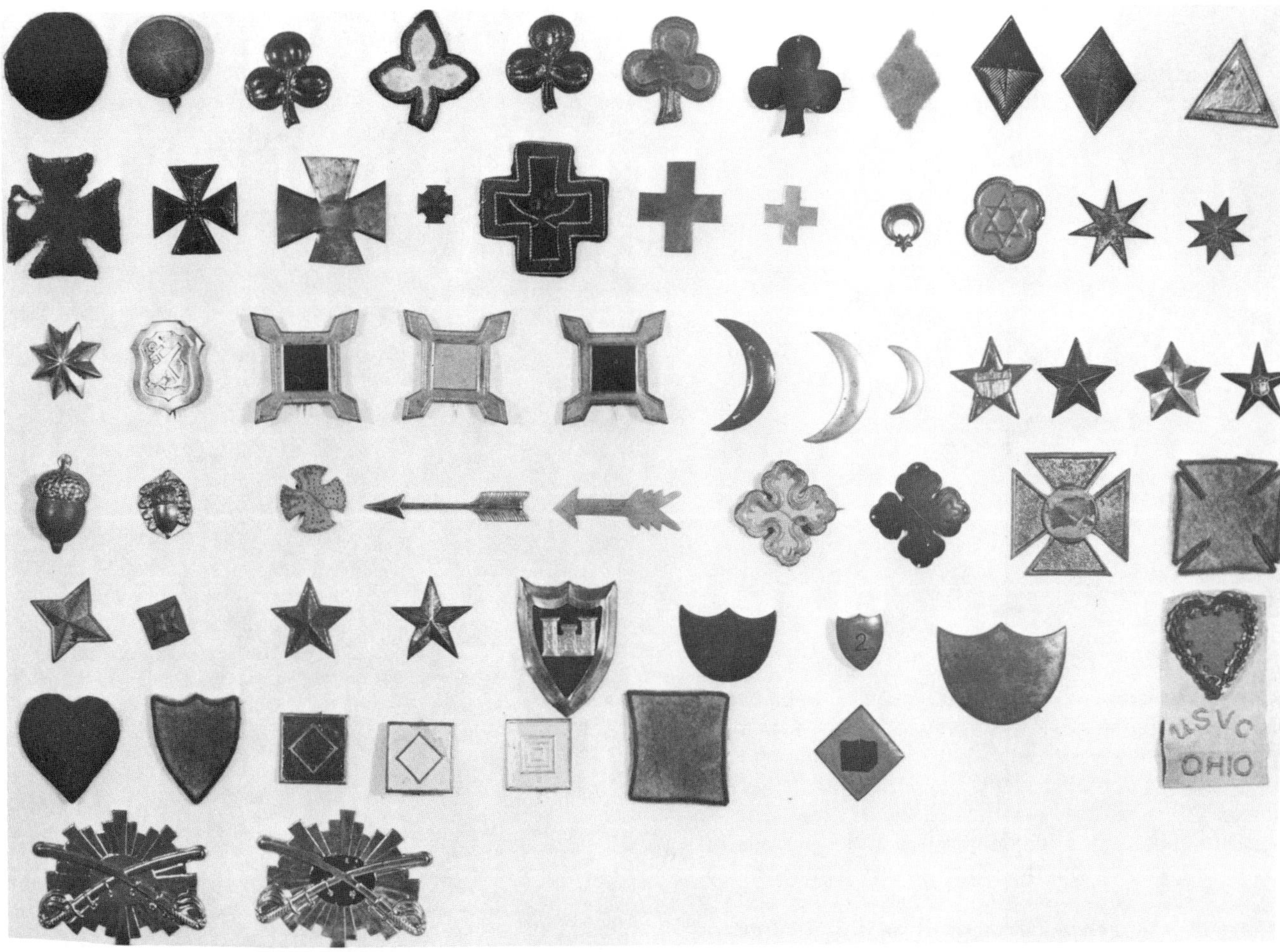

Federal Army Corps Badges

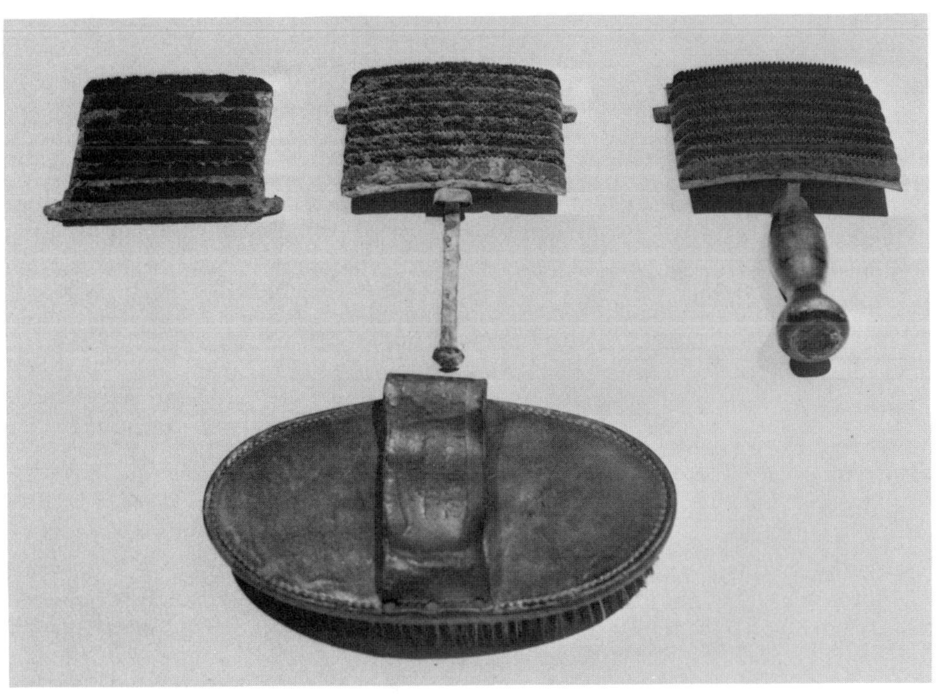

Horse Cleaning Equipment

H. M. Ruggly
Maker

The horse brush is oval in shape, 9 inches long and 4 3/4 wide in the middle. It is marked:

----Rounds
Stable Supplies
Providence, R.I.

DENTAL EQUIPMENT

A soldier needing dental service usually went to his regimental surgeon, or, less frequently, to a civilian dentist. Teeth were extracted with or without chloroform. At times dental students visited the army camps in order to practice on the teeth of the troops. Normally, these dental students were given permission to enter the camps by the camp or unit commander. Very little data is available on the practice of military dentistry during the war. There were no dental surgeons as such assigned to military units. Shown here is a civilian dentist of the Civil War era with his traveling "tooth removal kit."

Herb Peck, Jr.

Dentist of the Civil War Era

DIGGING IMPLEMENT (C.S.)

The Civil War eventually evolved into a war of intrenchments and digging trenches became a "way of life" for soldiers of both sides. The variety and number of tools used in the digging operations is almost staggering. Relic hunters are still digging up shovels, picks, mattocks and other essential digging tools. Shown here is a unique digging implement recovered from a Confederate trench at Orange Court House, Virginia. This iron implement is 12 inches long, with a 8 1/4 inch covered blade. Widest width-2 inches. The 3 3/4 inch extension to the blade obviously fitted into a wooden handle.

DITTY BOX

The ditty box and ditty bag both had the same purpose—i.e. to hold small items such as thread, needles, tobacco, etc. While the term was in more current use in the navy, many soldiers in the early months of the war did take ditty boxes with them. These boxes survived the rigors of active campaigning only briefly! Various materials were used in making these boxes.

WOOD. Size 4 3/4 x 4 1/2 inches. Gutta percha top showing crossed cannon, flags, cannon balls.

LEATHER. Size 6 1/2 x 3 1/2 inches. Has the stamped seal of the State of Massachusetts.

TIN. Size 6 3/4 x 3 1/4 inches. Japanned tin. Marked Wn. H. Horstman Company Philadelphia.

TIN. Size 5 3/4 x 3 3/4 inches. Painted green with letters A.B.M. carried in the war by a New Hampshire soldier.

C.S. Digging Instrument

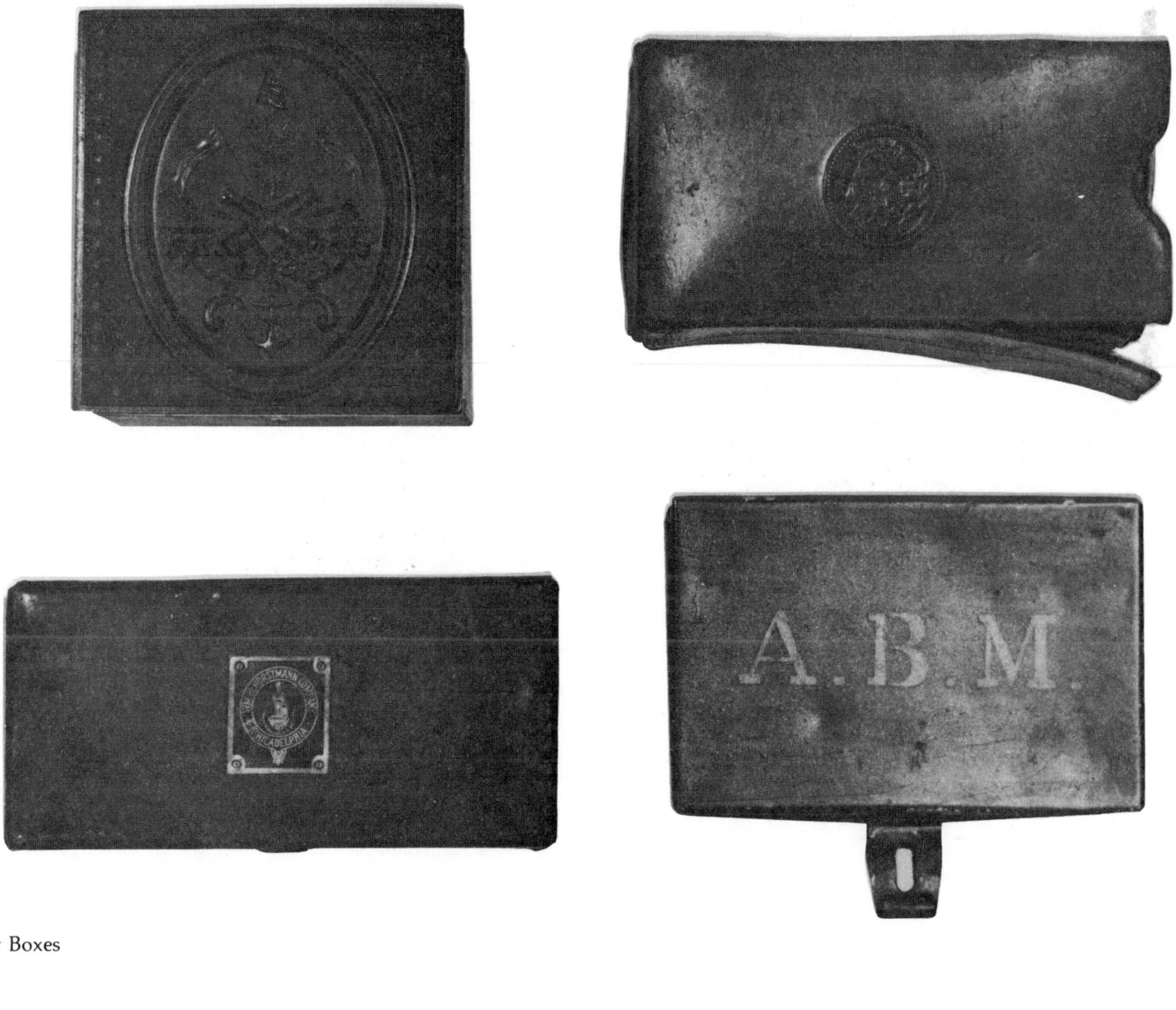

Ditty Boxes

ENFIELD MUSKET

The Enfield rifle, model 1853, was one of the best of the foreign arms. It was made originally at the government armory at Enfield, England, where shortly before the war machinery had been installed which was a direct copy of that in the United States armory at Springfield, Massachusetts. The Enfield rifle was a hundredth of an inch smaller in caliber than the Springfield (caliber .58); the difference was small enough so as not to prevent the use of caliber .577 ammunition in the Springfield rifle. The Enfield was sighted to 1,100 yards but it was believed by at least one observer that this sighting was excessive since the Enfield was not accurate beyond 700 yards.

A common mistake of many students of the period (and some collectors as well!) is to assume that only the South used the Enfield. Actually, a study of the reports of State Adjutant Generals in the North shows conclusively that many Federal regiments were issued the Enfield. For example, of the 136 New York regiments receiving infantry weapons in 1861-1862, almost half (57) were issued the long Enfield musket, while an additional three regiments received the short Enfield rifle. As a matter of record, the U.S. Government purchased 428,000 Enfields in the early months of the war while the Confederacy received some 400,000 during 1861-1862.

In contrast to the Model 1861 Springfield, which was supposed to be kept gleaming like silver, Enfield muskets were often blued or browned. The Enfield was slightly lighter in weight than the Springfield, and, according to contemporary accounts, was "a beautiful arm, and presented a natty appearance." The Enfield weighed eight pounds, 14 1/2 ounces; length about 54 inches; length of barrel 39 inches; diameter of bore .577; number of grooves, three; diameter of bullet .568; weight of bullet 530 grains; charge of powder about 70 grains. The Enfield when fired at 500 yards had a mean deviation of only 2 1/4 feet.

But some officers did not like the Enfield rifle. On Dec. 30, 1861, General William F. Smith told an investigating committee that he preferred the Springfield to the Enfield and gave his reasons. The General pointed out that the Enfield rifles which the U.S. brought into this country were not made by the British government or for the British government. They were "exceedingly rough, and tear the men's hands to pieces when they are going through the manual." They had sharp points; the stock was rough; the workmanship would not compare with that of our own rifle, i.e. the Springfield." According to General Smith the Enfield rifles were all made by hand, and if the men, in the hurry of the moment, happened to exchange bayonets, there were many rifles which could not be used with bayonets. "No bayonet, as a general thing, will go on any rifle, except the one it is intended for. But in the case of the Springfield rifles, any one bayonet will fit them all."

We must concede that the general was correct in cirticizing the lack of interchangeability of parts in the Enfields arms. But other officers and men of the war have left unquestioned testimony that the Enfield was an excellent weapon, well-made and accurate. Certainly the many Enfields now reposing in museums and private collections give definite evidence of excellent workmanship. The men who used them in battle swore by them.

ENGINEER EQUIPMENT

Since both Federal and Confederate engineers were trained at West Point, or at least, used manuals written by graduates of that institution, the methods and equipment used by both sides were essentially the same.

The Corps of Engineers was charged with planning, staking out and constructing permanent and field fortifications; construction and maintenance of various communications facilities including waterways, harbors and roads; bridge construction and repair, including the building of temporary bridges from improvised materials and by means of pontoon trains; reconnaissance and staking out of defensive positions for the field forces;

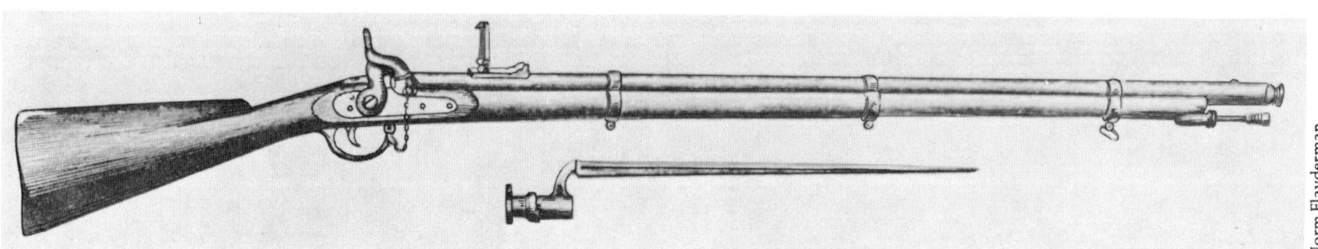

Norm Flayderman

Enfield Musket and Bayonet

Military Compasses

and many other construction projects necessary for the movement and supply of troops in the field. The Corps of Topographical Engineers of the Federal Army, which until 1863 were a part of the Corps of Engineers, were responsible for the survey, drafting, and reproduction of maps. With a few exceptions, the equipment used by the engineers was similar to or identical with that used by civilian engineers of that period. The most notable exceptions were in pontoon bridge equipment and in field mapping and reproduction. Engineer troops, usually called Pioneers in the Confederate Army, also accompanied the field forces to assist them in clearing fields of fire, constructing field works, repairing routes, crossing streams and installing heavy ordnance.

Specially trained personnel, organized as topographic engineers, made surveys for frontier defense, positions for fortifications and siege artillery, reconnaissances of routes through which the mobile forces had to pass, examination of routes of communication on land and water for supplies and troop movements. They supervised the construction of military roads and permanent bridges. They were charged with the field work, drafting, and reproduction of maps though some of this work near the coastal areas was also conducted by the U.S. Coast Survey.

The following terms and descriptions have been culled from manuals of the war period and should be of assistance in following contemporary accounts of siege and engineering operations.

The senior military engineers in both armies were mostly graduates of West Point and used the manuals published by the War Department. Officers who were nongraduates of the Military Academy were, for the most part, practising civil engineers before they entered

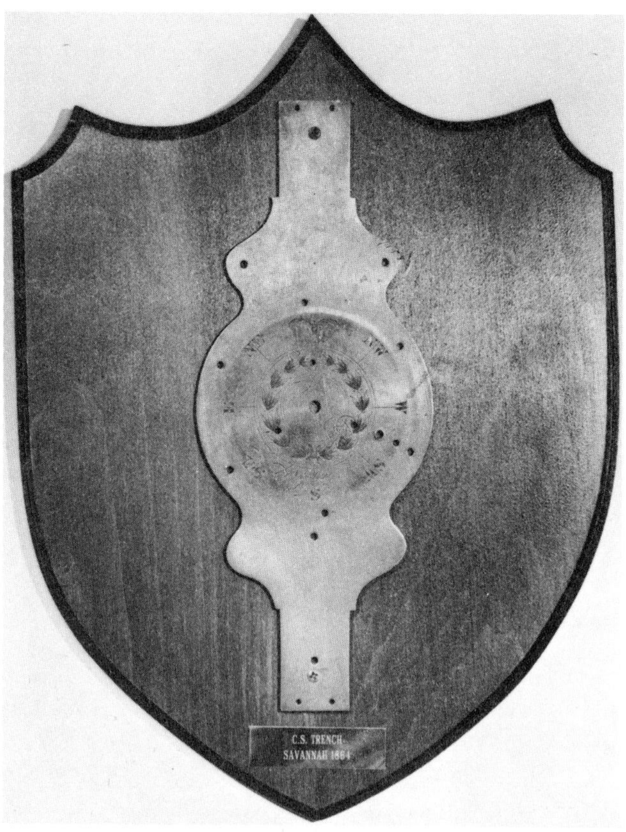

Surveying Instrument Remnant (Mounted on a Wooden Plaque). C.S. Trench, Savannah, Georgia

the armies, and generally "spoke the same language" and used the same tools as were employed in civil life—with the exception of bridging equipment.

For road building and repair, construction of field fortifications, and for mining and sapping, the common digging tools were the shovel, spade, axe, and pickax, and these differed little if any from those in use today. There were no power tools except sawmills, and these were occasionally commandeered or brought in by engineers to saw up lumber for bridge building or other purposes. There is little doubt that horsedrawn scoops and scrapers were used, especially for road building, but we have seen no pictures proving this—perhaps these devices were not regarded as noteworthy. In spite of the lack of earthmoving machinery, some very notable canals and other works were dug, largely by gangs of Negroes.

Military surveying was in no wise different from that employed in civil engineering; it was for the same purposes, and used the same instruments. For map making, the engineer ran a traverse with a transit, theodolite, or a plane table and alidade. If only rough work was possible or would suffice, the topographical engineer might measure his angles or bearings with a compass, and his distances by pacing. For example, a hasty terrain sketch might be made from the back of a horse, in which the bearings would be made with a pocket compass strapped to the operator's wrist, and the distance calculated from the time taken by his horse to walk or trot from one point to the next—he probably had made a pace scale after moving his horse several times over a measured distance. A road sketch made by such crude methods was useful where no other maps existed, and this evidently was the method employed by Jed Hotchkiss in making some of his beautifully executed but distressingly inaccurate maps. From these rough methods the engineer might progress to a much more precise system of measurements, to include even the determination of geodetic points by astronomical observations. Some of this work was done by the Coast Survey (now the Coast and Geodetic Survey) and provided a triangulation system on which accurate maps were based. To measure distances the engineers used graduated tapes and chains—either of 100 ft. or 50-ft. lengths, or used a stadia rod. Space does not permit a detailed explanation of such terms nor of the instruments employed, but specimen instruments in collections show that they were reasonably accurate, though inferior to those in use today.

The following is a list of common engineering devices used in surveying:

MILITARY SURVEYING INSTRUMENTS

Straight-edge ruler for drawing right lines.

Right-angled triangle for use with the ruler.

A pair of *dividers,* and a *protractor* were used with the *ruler* and *triangle* in the field.

A piece of tracing paper or muslin, stretched over a map, permitted the lines to be seen through it and they could be traced by a pen. *Theodolite,* the best instrument for measuring angles, could be firmly mounted, adjusted, and give angles to within a few seconds. Ordinarily, however, instruments of less precision were used in the field, including the *sextant, plane table,* and *Schmalcalder* or *prismatic compass.*

PRISMATIC or SCHMALCALDER COMPASS could be held in the hand, but was more convenient and accurate when mounted on a tripod or a single staff. This compass consisted of a box and a card with needle attached, and a pivot which supported both needle and card. A sightvane had a thread to direct the line of sight and a reflector to enable observations of objects above the horizon. The card was graduated in different instruments, some from zero to 90 degrees; some from zero to 180 degrees and back to zero; and others had 4 quadrants, each from zero to 90 degrees.

VERNIER was an auxiliary graduation which made possible the estimate of fractional portions of the smallest divisions and applied equally to linear and angular measurements.

SEXTANT was a surveying instrument, involving the optical principle of a ray of light reflected once by each of two plane reflectors, in a plane normal to their intersection, and was deviated from its original direction by an angular amount equal to twice the angle of the reflector.

pocket sextant differed in arrangement from the larger type, but was similar in principle. The index and horizon glasses were enclosed in a brass box of 2-3 inches diameter. The top of the sextant unscrewed and could be screwed on the bottom for a handle. The box protected the glasses from all ordinary chances of injury or displacement.

PLANE TABLE consisted of a board to hold paper, a tripod to furnish a support, and the intermediate arrangement of different constructions which were utilized to level the board. A common type during the Civil War was 16 inches square with its upper edge rabbeted to receive a boxwood frame which was placed on the board and was used to stretch and hold the drawing paper on the board. One face of the frame was graduated from zero to 360 degrees in order to measure angles. The reverse side of the frame was usually divided into equal parts, as inches and tenths. Also used with the plane table was a compass-box to serve as a check on accuracy, a brass ruler, and occassionally a sight vane or telescope to direct the line of sight.

CHAIN was of various lengths and was used for measurement of distances. It is known that a 100-foot chain was used during the war by military engineers, but for purposes of topography, 50-foot chains were found to be as useful as any.

ODOMETER consisted of a small brass circular box, containing a series of cogwheels, which regulated the motion of an index on a dial-plate upon its exterior, which recorded the number of revolutions of a wheel to which the box was attached by straps. The odometer measured distance; the length of the perimeter of the wheel, multiplied by the number of revolutions, gave the distance passed over.

STADIA consisted of a telescope with two horizontal hairs in or near the principal focus of the eye-glass. When used with a graduated stick, the distance to an object could be determined.

LEVELING INSTRUMENTS were of two types: Water-Level: a cylindrical brass tube, bent at its length. In these arms were set two glass vials. The tube was mounted on a tripod, and could be rotated around its vertical axis so as to make a circuit of the horizon.

Y-spirit-level consisted of an acheromatic telescope mounted in y's, and had a reticle in the principle focus of the eye-glass. The reticle consisted of two spiders' lines, at right angles to each other, fastened at their extremities in separate slides. A spirit bubble was used in this instrument.

Other levels used during the war were BUREL'S REFLECTING LEVEL, CAPTAIN LIBET'S LEVEL, MASON'S LEVEL, SLOPE-LEVEL and BURNIER'S SLOPE-LEVEL—all of which were described in manuals of the period.

COMPASS. The "box compass", extensively used by engineers in the war was graduated zero to 360 degrees, the numbers increasing in a clockwise direction. The north and south line was parallel to the side on which the cover was hinged.

PROTRACTOR. A rectangular protractor was most commonly used, arranged with a scale. The favorite make was Abbott's, which differed from the ordinary rectangular protractor in that it was graduated differently. Abbott's ran from zero to 180 degrees on one side, and from 180 to 360 degrees on the other side.

Illustrated (P. 47) are two compasses which saw military use during the war. Both were made in France and so marked. The compass on the left has a diameter of 1 1/2 inches and is 3/8 inch thick. The compass on the right has a diameter of 2 inches and is 1/2 inch thick. Both compasses are made of heavy brass. The remnant of the surveying instrument is of heavy brass, 12 1/2 inches long and 4 7/8 inches wide at the center.

It is marked: New York
Warranted

From a C.S. trench at Savannah, Georgia.

EXPLOSIVE BULLETS

The subject of the employment of explosive bullets in warfare was extensively discussed from an ethical point of view, particularly after the Civil War. Both Union and Confederate soldiers claimed the other used explosive bullets in battle on various occasions.

The Medical Department, U.S. Army listed 130 cases of wounds attributed to "explosive bullets." Records of the Ordnance Office, U.S. Army show that 33,350 Gardner's "explosive bullets" or "musket shells" were issued to the troops in the early part of the war. Over 10,000 of these were abandoned on the field for want of transportation. It is probable that these fell into the hands of the Confederates, accounting in a measure for the 130 wounded alluded to above. However, many reports of wounds attributed to explosive bullets were rendered in which it is doubtful if the bullet was actually an explosive bullet at all. Under certain conditions the conventional bullet was capable of great mutilation and of inflicting extensive bone or tissue damage.

There can be no doubt that some Federal troops used explosive bullets. In June, 1863, the 2nd New Hampshire Infantry were issued them. The regimental history notes on June 8th the following:

"Forty rounds of cartridges per man were issued this morning. The balls are called musket shells—an explosive bullet—and woe to the Johnny that stops one!"

The 2nd marched on to Gettysburg where it soon came under artillery fire. Many men were hit and several cartridge boxes were exploded. A shell struck and burst on the box of a corporal of Company "C". The cartridges were driven into his body and exploded, and for nearly half a minute the "musket shells" issued the preceding month were exploding in his quivering form. Death was mercifully quick. The next moment a fragment of shell exploded the cartridge box of a sergeant. The rapidity with which he tore off the box hanging by his side was astonishing. The sergeant escaped with a severe wound.

The 2nd New Hampshire had its first experience with explosive bullets at Glendale on the Peninsula when their opponents used them. The regiment was in line of battle about dusk when enemy pickets began firing at the men. "For a time the men were a good bit puzzled to account for the sharp reports which were heard in every direction—to the rear, overhead, everywhere. In connection with the deepening gloom, the manifestation was decidedly uncanny. The mystery was solved, however, when a bullet, cutting across the breast of Captain Sayles, suddenly exploded, inflicting a powerful lacerated wound."

The Gardner (or Gardiner) explosive bullet was a cylindroconoidal projectile of lead, made in two sizes: the larger of caliber .58, weighing 451 grains; the smaller of caliber .54, weighing 363 grains. Within the interior was placed an accurately fitting acorn-shaped chamber filled with fulminate, and communicating with a 1 1/4-second time fuze, which was exposed to the charge at the rear of the missile. The fuze was ignited by discharge of the piece. The bursting charge was sufficient to rend the bullet and transform it into a jagged dangerous missile. If it penetrated the body before exploding, its effects were still more destructive.

EXPRESS COMPANIES

Civilian shipping companies were very important in supplementing official shipments between the home front and the troops in the field. These shipments were by rail, ship and wagon. Outstanding among these shipping companies was the ubiquitous Adams Express Company and its competitors Harnden's Express and American Express Company. Shown here are specimens of vouchers for each of the three companies.

ADAMS EXPRESS COMPANY. Size 9 3/8 x 6 inches. One box sent from Philadelphia to Norfolk, Virginia, December 17, 1864.

AMERICAN EXPRESS COMPANY. Size 8 3/8 x 4 5/8 inches. One box sent from Louisville, Kentucky to Yonkers, New York, March 24, 1862.

HARNDEN'S EXPRESS. Size 8 3/4 x 5 3/4 inches. One box sent from New York on September 10, 1862 to Joseph T. Commoss, Co. A 57th New York Infantry at Tennallytown, Maryland.

EYEGLASSES

If one can judge from the thousands of Civil War Photographs available, only a few men wore eyeglasses. Or if they did, they were careful to remove their glasses before being photographed. Also, many of the soldiers were young enough to have no need of eyeglasses during the period of their enlistment. Of course some individuals wore glasses, especially those in more advanced years. Moreover, sunglasses were worn as shown in the illustration. Left to right.

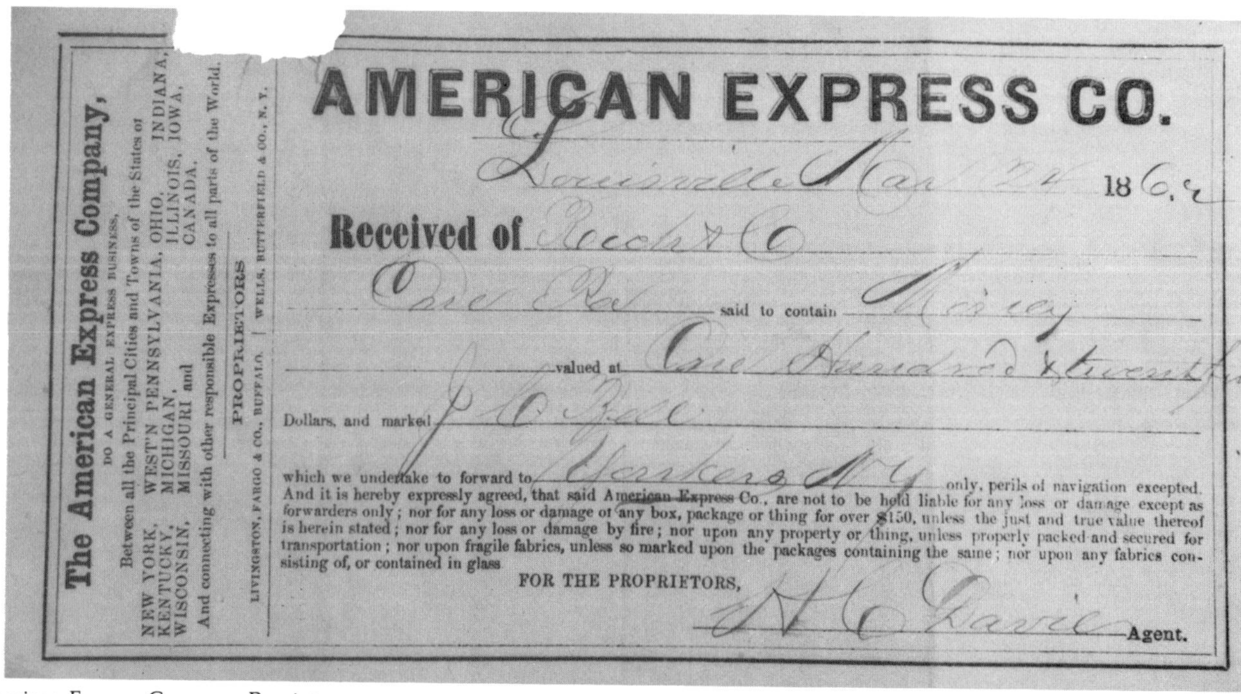

The American Express Company,
DO A GENERAL EXPRESS BUSINESS,
Between all the Principal Cities and Towns of the States of
NEW YORK, WEST'N PENNSYLVANIA, OHIO, INDIANA,
KENTUCKY, MICHIGAN, ILLINOIS, IOWA,
WISCONSIN, MISSOURI and CANADA.
And connecting with other responsible Expresses to all parts of the World.
PROPRIETORS
LIVINGSTON, FARGO & CO., BUFFALO. | WELLS, BUTTERFIELD & CO., N. Y.

AMERICAN EXPRESS CO.

18

Received of

said to contain

valued at

Dollars, and marked

which we undertake to forward to ... only, perils of navigation excepted. And it is hereby expressly agreed, that said American Express Co., are not to be held liable for any loss or damage except as forwarders only; nor for any loss or damage of any box, package or thing for over $150, unless the just and true value thereof is herein stated; nor for any loss or damage by fire; nor upon any property or thing, unless properly packed and secured for transportation; nor upon fragile fabrics, unless so marked upon the packages containing the same; nor upon any fabrics consisting of, or contained in glass

FOR THE PROPRIETORS,

Agent.

American Express Company Receipt

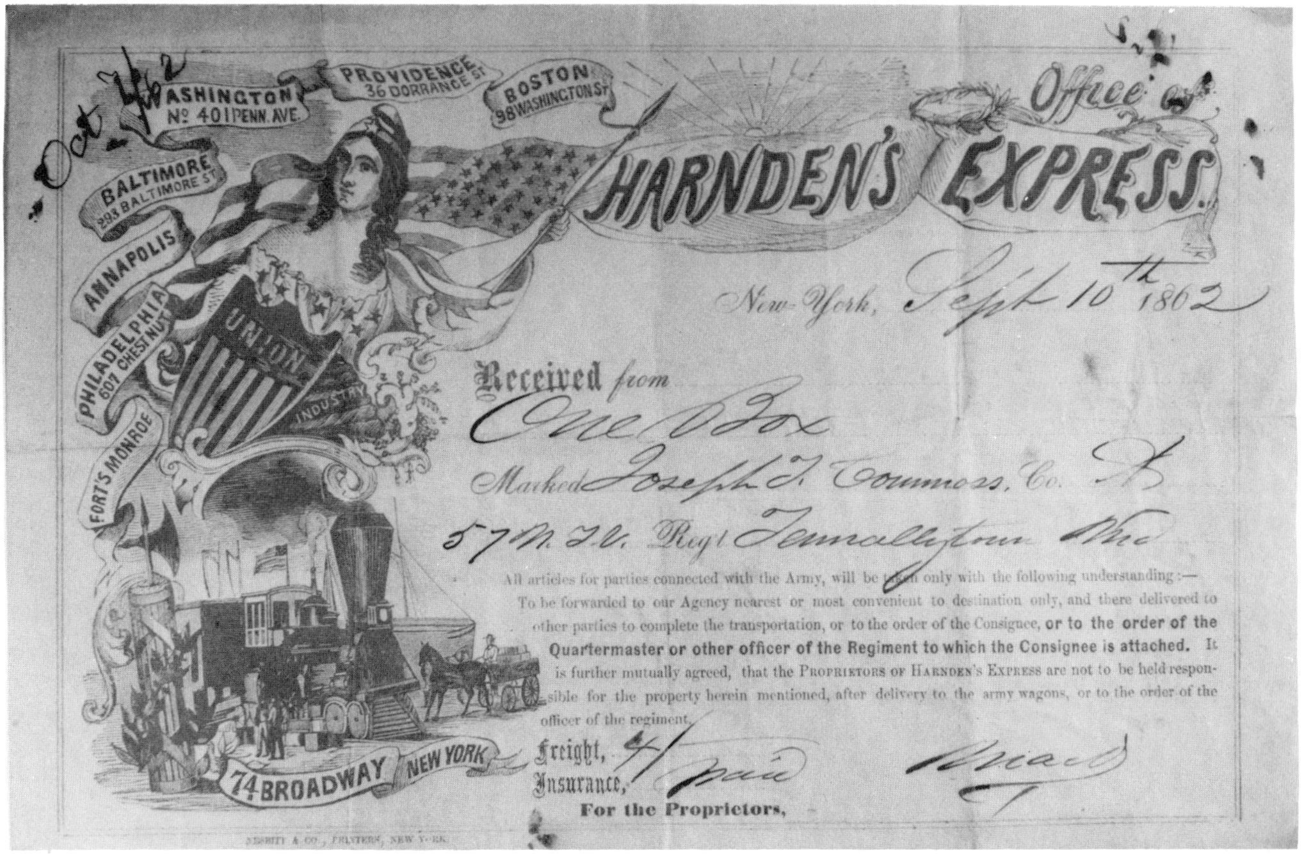

Office of
HARNDEN'S EXPRESS.

WASHINGTON No 401 PENN. AVE. · PROVIDENCE 36 DORRANCE ST. · BOSTON 98 WASHINGTON ST. · BALTIMORE 293 BALTIMORE ST. · ANNAPOLIS · PHILADELPHIA 607 CHESNUT · FORT'S MONROE · 74 BROADWAY NEW YORK

UNION · INDUSTRY

New-York, Sept 10th 1862

Received from One Box

Marked Joseph T. Commoss, Co. B

57th N.Y.V. Regt

All articles for parties connected with the Army, will be taken only with the following understanding:—
To be forwarded to our Agency nearest or most convenient to destination only, and there delivered to other parties to complete the transportation, or to the order of the Consignee, **or to the order of the Quartermaster or other officer of the Regiment to which the Consignee is attached.** It is further mutually agreed, that the PROPRIETORS OF HARNDEN'S EXPRESS are not to be held responsible for the property herein mentioned, after delivery to the army wagons, or to the order of the officer of the regiment.

Freight, 4/ paid
Insurance,
For the Proprietors,

Harnden Express Company Receipt

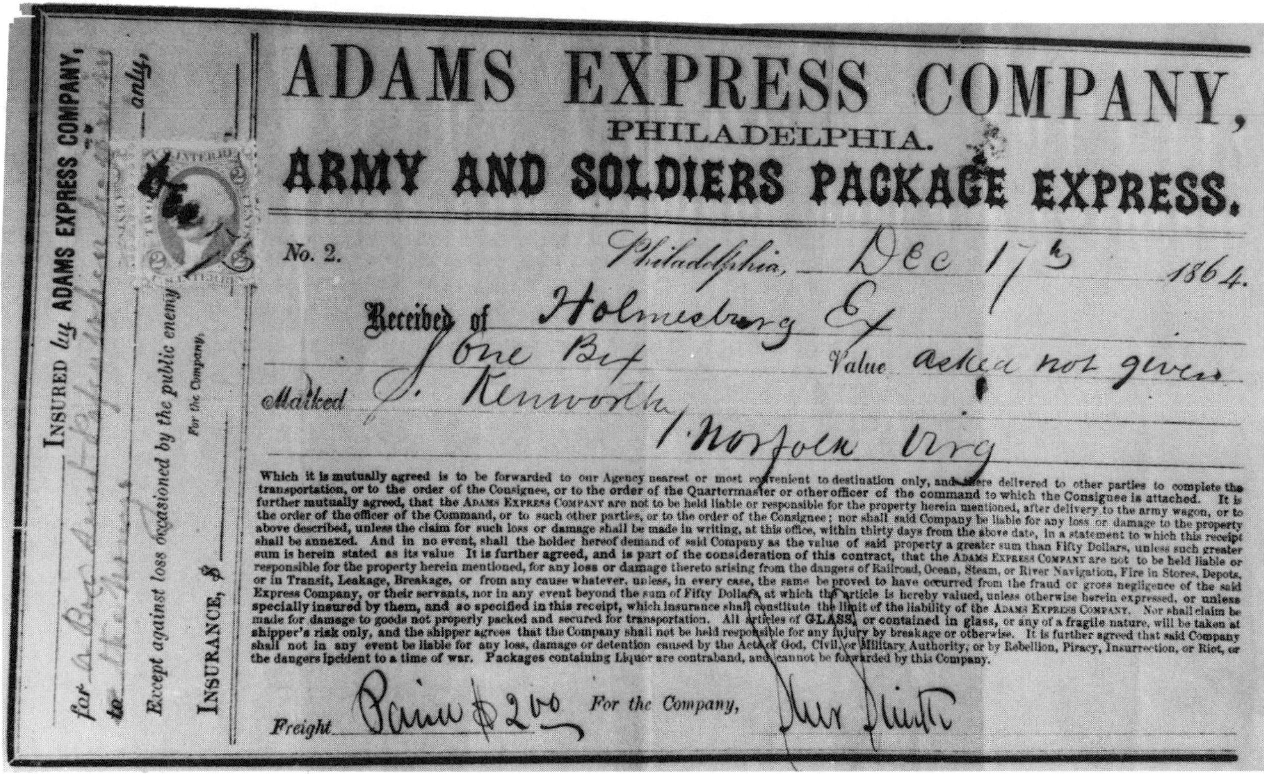

ADAMS EXPRESS COMPANY,
PHILADELPHIA.
ARMY AND SOLDIERS PACKAGE EXPRESS.

No. 2. Philadelphia, Dec 17th 1864.

Received of Holmesburg Ex

One Box Value asked not given

Marked J. Kenworth

Norfolk Virg

Which it is mutually agreed is to be forwarded to our Agency nearest or most convenient to destination only, and there delivered to other parties to complete the transportation, or to the order of the Consignee, or to the order of the Quartermaster or other officer of the command to which the Consignee is attached. It is further mutually agreed, that the ADAMS EXPRESS COMPANY are not to be held liable or responsible for the property herein mentioned, after delivery to the army wagon, or to the order of the officer of the Command, or to such other parties, or to the order of the Consignee; nor shall said Company be liable for any loss or damage to the property above described, unless the claim for such loss or damage shall be made in writing, at this office, within thirty days from the above date, in a statement to which this receipt shall be annexed. And in no event, shall the holder hereof demand of said Company as the value of said property a greater sum than Fifty Dollars, unless such greater sum is herein stated as its value. It is further agreed, and is part of the consideration of this contract, that the ADAMS EXPRESS COMPANY are not to be held liable or responsible for the property herein mentioned, for any loss or damage thereto arising from the dangers of Railroad, Ocean, Steam, or River Navigation, Fire in Stores, Depots, or in Transit, Leakage, Breakage, or from any cause whatever, unless, in every case, the same be proved to have occurred from the fraud or gross negligence of the said Express Company, or their servants, nor in any event beyond the sum of Fifty Dollars, at which the article is hereby valued, unless otherwise herein expressed, or unless specially insured by them, and so specified in this receipt, which insurance shall constitute the limit of the liability of the ADAMS EXPRESS COMPANY. Nor shall claim be made for damage to goods not properly packed and secured for transportation. All articles of GLASS, or contained in glass, or any of a fragile nature, will be taken at shipper's risk only, and the shipper agrees that the Company shall not be held responsible for any injury by breakage or otherwise. It is further agreed that said Company shall not in any event be liable for any loss, damage or detention caused by the Acts of God, Civil, or Military Authority, or by Rebellion, Piracy, Insurrection, or Riot, or the dangers incident to a time of war. Packages containing Liquor are contraband, and cannot be forwarded by this Company.

Freight Paid $2.00 *For the Company,*

INSURED by ADAMS EXPRESS COMPANY, for a Box to ___ only,
Except against loss occasioned by the public enemy.
For the Company,
INSURANCE, $

Adams Express Company Receipt

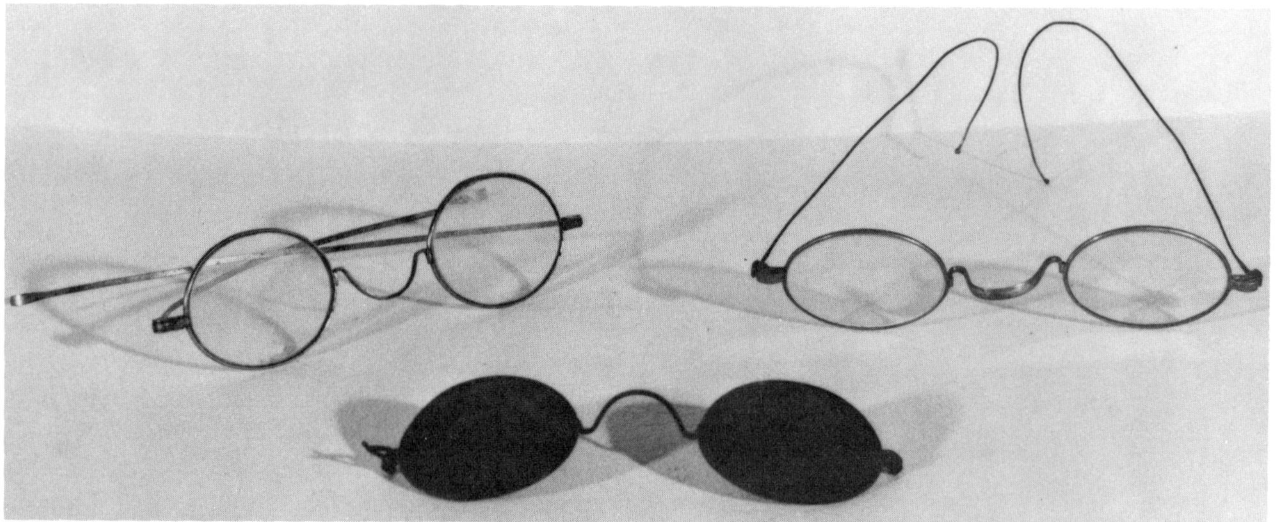

Eyeglasses

FARRIER'S TOOLS

Both armies used horses extensively throughout the war. In addition to cavalry and artillery units, field grade officers from commanding generals to infantry majors were also mounted. Thousands of draft horses and mules were necessary for the wagon trains. Accordingly, it was essential to have blacksmiths in sufficient numbers to keep these horses and mules clipped and well shod. The blacksmiths in military service were known as "Farriers". Shown here are some of the essential tools used by these farriers.

FARRIER'S TONGS. Used to clip off the ends of nails driven in to hold the shoe on the hoof. Length 12 1/4 inches. Heavy steel. From U.S. cavalry camp at Falmouth, Virginia.

HAIR CLIPPER. Works and looks exactly like a modern grass clipper. Length 12 inches. From U.S. Cavalry camp at Falmouth, Virginia.

FARRIER'S KNIFE. Used to pare hoof to fit the shoe when horse is being shod. The hook is used to remove stones, etc. which have become caught in the hoof. Ivory handle. Length 3 5/8 inches. Picked up at Gettysburg by Wagoner Thomas A. Davis, Co. F, 20th Maine Infantry.

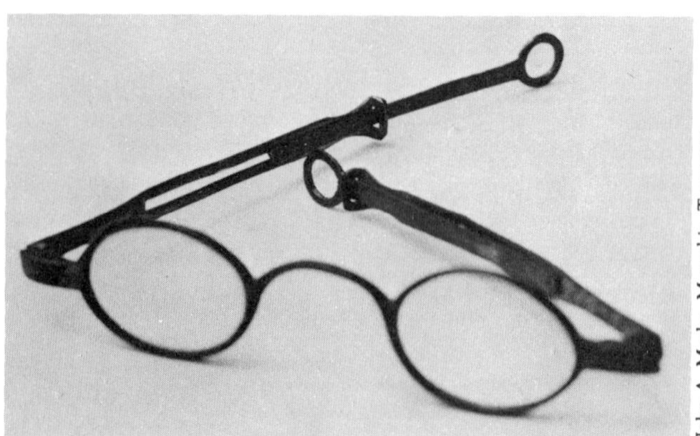

John A. Marks Memphis, Tennessee

Eyeglasses with Adjustable Bows, La Grange, Tennessee

SHOE FOR DRAFT HORSE. 6 1/2 inches long and 5 1/2 inches wide at the widest part. From a U.S. cavalry camp near Memphis, Tennessee.

SHOE FOR RIDING HORSE. Is lighter and smaller than the shoe for the draft horse. 5 1/2 inches long and 5 inches wide at the widest part. From the same cavalry camp as the shoe described above.

FIELD GLASSES

These captured field glasses were used by Preston Gochnauer, 17th Virginia Infantry. The inside of the leather cover has the following inscription in ink:

PRESTON GOCHNAUER, C.S.A.

The glasses are 6 1/2 inches long when closed. They are marked:

BARDOU & SON
PARIS

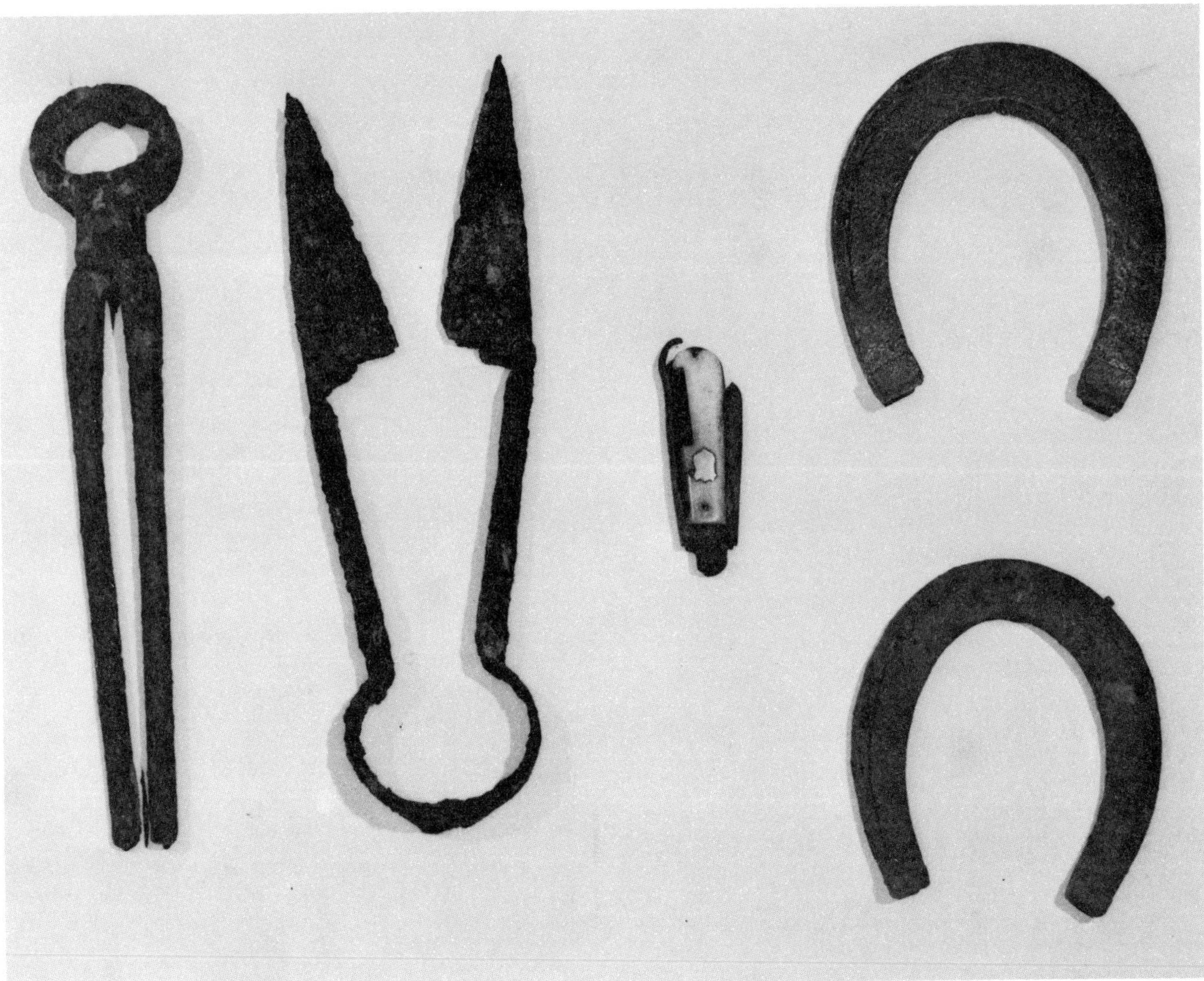

Farrier's Tools

and also

U.S. ARMY
SIGNAL GLASS
FRANCE

The black leather case has a carrying strap 60" long.

A similar field glass in the author's collection, but without any markings, has the following inscription in ink on the corner of the carrying case:

> Gen Terry used this glass in his reconnaissance of Fort Fisher.
>
> Capt. G.F. Towle
> 4th New Hampshire
> Jan. 14, 1865

FLAG HOLDERS

Every regiment had two color bearers and a few individual companies had guidon bearers. In some camps, especially in the larger and permanent camps, large garrison and headquarters flags were flown. Shown here are examples of the holders for each type.

FLAG OR COLOR CARRIER. Heavy leather carrying strap 1 3/4 inches wide and 52 inches long, with a 3-inch brass buckle for strap adjustment. The flag holder itself is of heavy brass, 3 1/2 inches tall.

GUIDON CARRIER. Thin brass, 4 3/4 inches tall. Made to fit on a caliber .58 musket barrel with locking ring as on a regular bayonet.

FLAG STAFF HOLDER. Found in an artillery position at Harper's Ferry. It is assumed that this is a flag staff holder, but no substantiation is available.

DESCRIPTION. Heavy brass, with 4 large holes at bottom and 4 smaller holes at top. Height—7 inches. Diameter of base—3 1/2 inches. Diameter of top—1 3/4 inches.

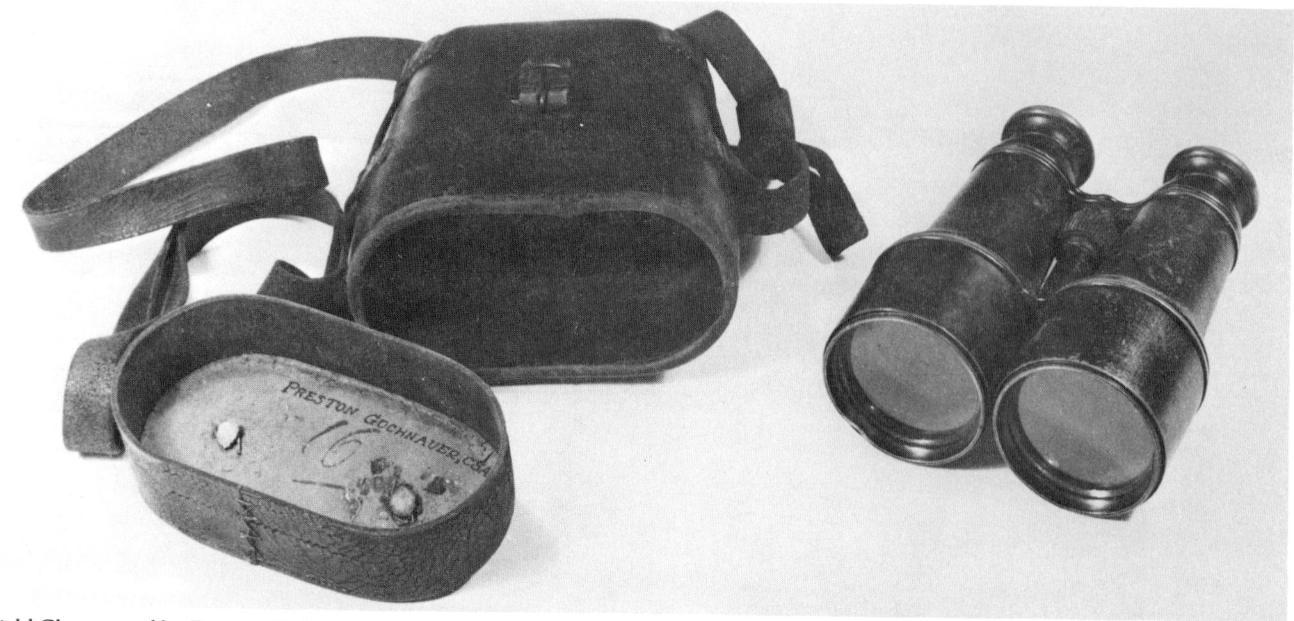

Field Glasses used by Preston Gochnauer, C.S.A.

FOOD AND FOOD CONTAINERS

Since the advent of the industrial revolution warfare has become increasingly complex. Certainly one of the baffling "variables" has been that of logistical support—including, of course, the problem of feeding hundreds of thousands of men in hostile territory. Therefore, we can subscribe to Napoleon's dictum that "an army marches on its stomach" and this dictum certainly applied to the contending armies of the Civil War.

There is surprisingly little specific information on food in Civil War literature. The best original sources are diaries and journals, and, to a very limited extent, regimental histories. Also an analysis of bones, cans, and bottles recovered from camp sites sheds additional light on types of food consumed by the troops.

Supply and transportation of rations was an extremely important aspect of the ever-present logistical problem for movement of troops. The observant French visitor to McClellan's army in 1862, the Count of Paris, was surprised at the amount of food consumed by the American soldier. The Count estimated that 2,000 wagons, drawn by 12,000 animals were strictly necessary to supply food to an army of 100,000 men and 16,000 horses at only two days' march from its base of operations.

The supplying of food to the Federal Army was the responsibility of the bureau headed by the Commissary General of Subsistence, who, in April 1861, was Colonel George Gibson. Gibson died September 29, 1861; he was succeeded by Colonel Joseph P. Taylor who died June 29, 1864; Taylor was succeeded by Brigadier General Amos B. Eaton who served to the end

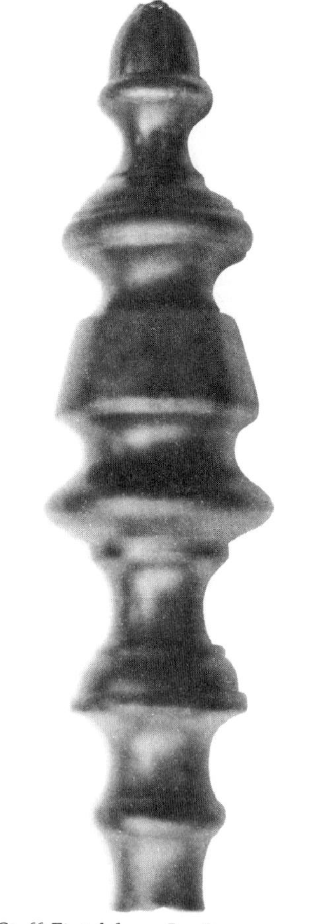
John A. Marks Memphis, Tennessee

Flag Staff Finial from La Grange, Tennessee (Cast Brass, 4 1/2 inches long)

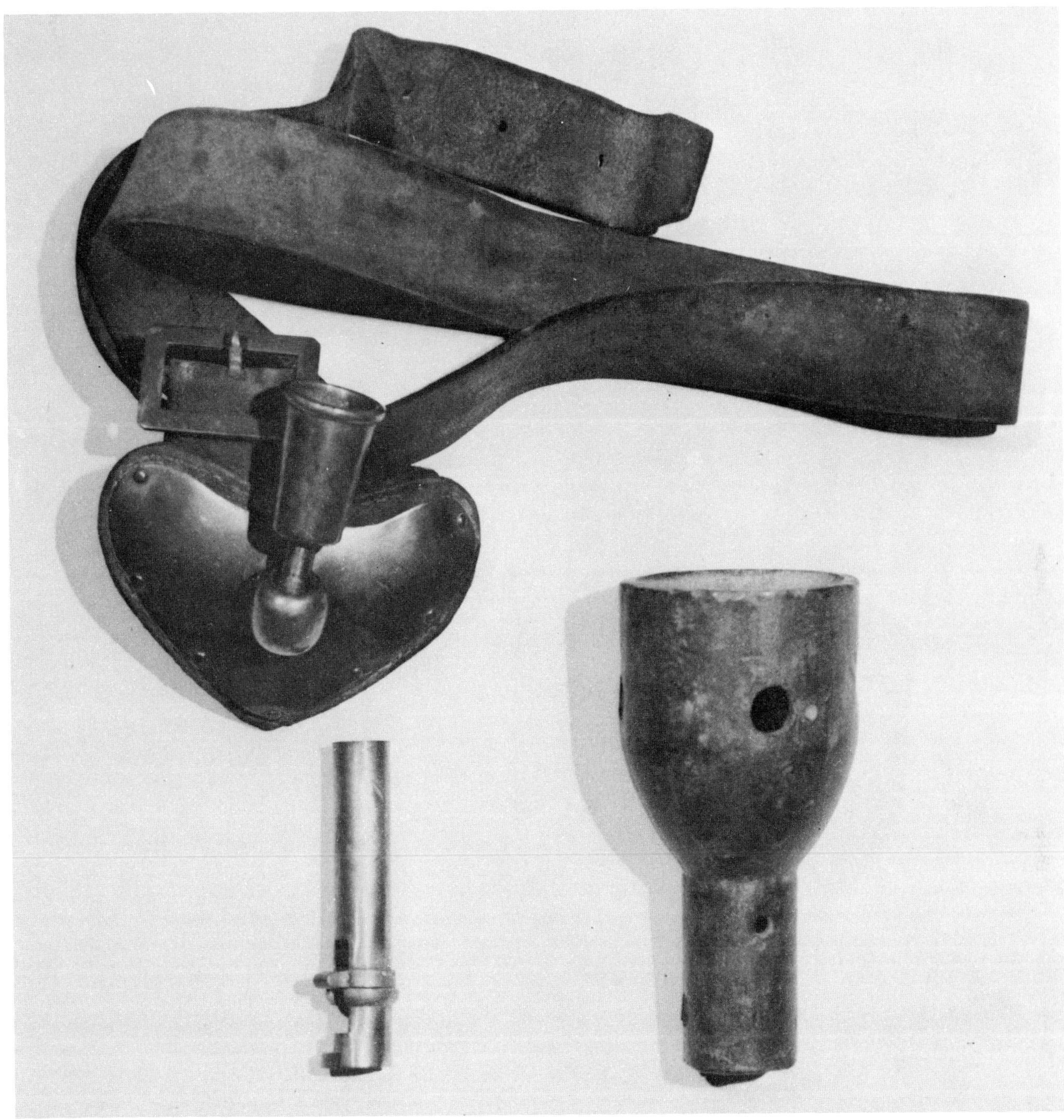

Flag Holders

of the war. (One wonders if Gibson and Taylor died from eating some of their own rations!) Eventually there were 29 officers in the Subsistence Department, aided by a commissary officer sergeant in each regiment.

Despite its small staff the Commissary Department spent $369,000,000 during the war and advertised for food in such major cities as New York, Boston, Philadelphia, St. Louis, and San Francisco.

Despite all efforts of the Subsistence Department, however, troops did not automatically receive sufficient daily rations. For example, men of the 11th Indiana Infantry during the Shenandoah Valley campaign in 1864 were "living on green bark, green apples and fresh beef without salt." In this case the lack of regular rations was due to the fact that the army had gotten far ahead of its wagons which carried the rations. During this

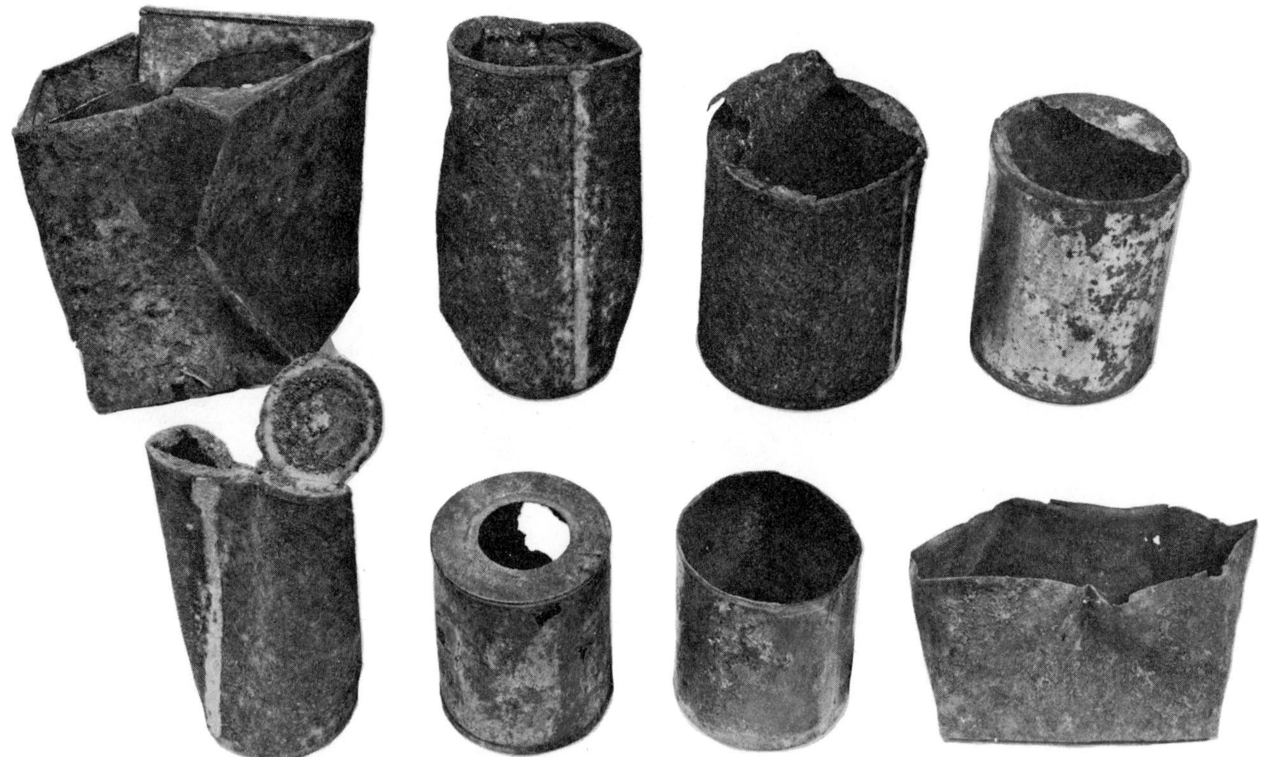

Tin Cans
Left to right:
Top Row: Tea Can Dimensions: Rectangular, 6 1/8" tall, r 1/2" on each side. From La Grange, Tennessee.

Round Can, 7" tall and 3" in diameter. Original contents—unknown. From La Grange, Tennessee.

Fruit Can, 4 7/8" tall and 4" in diameter. From La Grange, Tennessee.

Fruit Can, 4 3/4" tall and 3 1/2" in diameter. La Grange, Tennessee, (U.S. Camp).

Left to right:
Bottom Row: Can whose contents are unknown. Dimensions: 5 1/4" tall and 2 1/2" in diameter. La Grange, Tennessee.

Milk can from Brook's Station, Virginia. Dimensions: 3 1/2" tall and 3" in diameter. Originally had a removable circular top; this is missing.

Tin Can from Brook's Station, Virginia. Original contents unknown. Dimensions: 3 3/8" tall and 3" in diameter.

Heavy Tin, rectangular in shape. Dimensions: 4 3/4" long, 2 1/4" wide, and 3 1/4" tall. Original contents unknown. From camp of the 59th New York Infantry at Falmouth, Virginia.

campaign some regiments like the 12th Connecticut Infantry "were at the point of starvation."

Officers were not necessarily well fed either. During the Penninsular Campaign, General Hiram G. Berry wrote his wife [May 17, 1862]:

> I have to eat as follows: For breakfast, coffee (sometimes with, sometimes without sugar), hardbread and salt beef, occasionally a piece of tough fresh beef. I have not seen a potato or any other vegetable for many weeks, or a chicken or hen. Beef, pork and hardbread is our fare when we can get it, which is not always.

Commissioned officers did not draw rations but had a cash allowance according to rank. Like their men, they often lived on only salt pork, hardtack, and coffee. The results of such a diet as this could be seen during the war among a staggeringly large number of men. Charles Francis Adams of the 1st Massachusetts Cavalry, years after the war, wrote: "I went to the Headquarters a perfectly well man . . . but during the summer of 1864 I began slowly to break down. I now know well enough what the trouble was. I was poisoned by incessant feeding on hardtack and meat freshly killed and fried in pork-fat, and the inordinate drinking of black coffee—quarts of it, each day. We all did so; we and the medical men evincing an equal lack of either knowledge of or

Two sizes of Sardine Cans are illustrated here:
Left to right:
Can found in camp of the 59th New York Infantry (Gibbon's Division, 2nd Corps) at Falmouth, Virginia. Dimensions: 4 3/4" by 3 3/4" and 1 6/16" deep.
Can found in U.S. Camp, Atlanta, Georgia. Dimensions: 4 1/8" by 3" and 1 1/8" deep. Marked: . . . SARD . . .
. . . KNEAU

regard for the most elementary rules of hygiene . . . Even with the most iron of constitutions, it was only a question of time . . . by May, 1865, I was a mere physical wreck . . . The fact was my intestines were actually corroded with concentrated nourishment."

Even soldiers stationed in large cities often lacked good rations. When the 14th New Hampshire Infantry was garrisoning Washington in 1863, the food was so poor that men lacked the strength to do duty. The pork and bread were of poor quality nor were fresh beef or the coffee of good quality. In general, the quality of rations was not too good. For example, there was usually a sufficiency of stale beef or "salt house" as it was called, but the quality was lacking.

By Army regulations two types of rations were to be issued the troops. These were called the "Camp Ration" and the "Marching Ration". The "Camp Ration" consisted of:

22 ounces of break or flour or
1 pound of hard bread (hardtack)
Fresh beef
Beans and rice (or hominy)
1 pound of potatoes (at least 3 times a week)

A ration of tea could be substituted for a ration of coffee upon proper requisition. In hospitals fresh or preserved fruits, milk, butter and eggs were issued when possible.

The "Marching Ration" consisted of:

1 pound of hard bread (hardtack)
3/4 pound of salt pork or
1 1/4 pounds of fresh meat
Sugar, coffee, and salt

A complete list of rations was as follows:

Salt Pork
Fresh Beef
Salt Beef
Ham or Bacon (Rarely issued)
Hard Bread (Hardtack)
Soft Bread
Potatoes
Onions (only occasionally)
Flour
Beans
Salt

Split Peas
Dried Apples
Dried Peaches
Desiccated Vegetables
Coffee
Sugar
Molasses
Vinegar
Candles
Soap
Pepper

RATION CHART. Linen-backed chart showing the quantity in bulk of regular issue rations, 1 to 100,000. Size of chart 22 7/8 by 16 1/8. Marked in ink on back of the chart:

MAJOR BLAKE
PRIVATE

Food Containers
Left to right:
Tow Row: Pickle jar. Clear glass, 7 1/2" tall, 2" in diameter at the top and tapering out to 2 1/2" at the bottom. From U.S. camp at Hilton Head, South Carolina.

Same as above but only 5" tall, 1 3/4" in diameter at the top and 2" at the bottom. From Hilton Head, South Carolina.

Pickle jar from a U.S. Camp in Virginia. Light green glass. Approximately 8" tall (top is broken), square shaped, 2 3/4" on the square.

Similar to No. 3 but only about 7 1/4" tall and 2 1/4" on the square. From Hilton Head, South Carolina.

Cathedral bottle for pepper sauce. Green in color. Six-sided bottle about 6 3/4" tall. From Hilton Head, South Carolina.

Bottom Row: U.S. Navy mustard jar. Octagonal in shape, 5 3/8" tall and 1 5/8" wide at the bottom. Marked:
U.S. NAVY (On one side)
MUSTARD (On opposite side)

Mustard jar, 5" tall, 2 1/8" in diameter at each end, and wide in the middle. Marked:
MOUTARDE DIAPHANE
LOUIT FRERES & CO.

Sauce bottle, 9" tall and 2 1/2" in diameter. From a U.S. camp site in Virginia. Marked:
LONDON CLUB SAUCE
PARKER BROS.

U.S. Navy pepper jar. Exactly like No. 6 except marked:
U.S. NAVY (On one side)
PEPPER (On opposite side)

Evidently Major Blake was a commissary officer charged with issuing rations to large units, e.g. army or corps.

The following specific information has been ascertained on food items definitely identified with Civil War usage.

COFFEE. Instant coffee was introduced during the Civil War. Reportedly, it was first tried by General Grant. Instant coffee was prepared in paste form and contained milk and sugar. The purpose, of course, was to make the soldiers rations less bulky. In a petition of some fifty regiments to be allowed to use this extract of coffee with sugar and milk combined in lieu of the normal coffee and sugar ration, it was emphasized that the latter ration for 100,000 men for 20 days weighed a total of 250 tons. But if the instant coffee extract (which included sugar and milk) would be a 50% reduction in weight—"an important item on a march or advance, reducing the number of wagons . . . [by one] half".

Regular coffee was a standard item of issue in the Federal ration. A unique method of getting coffee to troops in the field is described as follows:

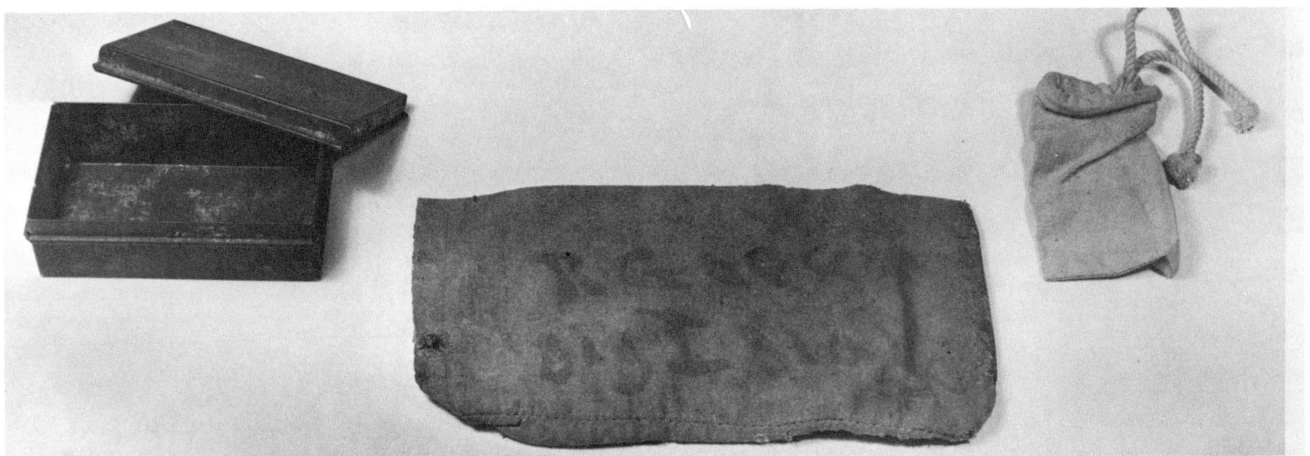

Miscellaneous Food Containers
Left to right:
Coffee Bag: Made of brown canvas, 12" long and 6" wide. Perhaps used as a ration bag. From the 1862 Peninsular campaign. Marked:
R. GOSS
BIG ISLAND

Lard Can: Made of heavy tin, 5 3/4' long, 2 15/16" inside, and 1 13/16" deep. *Probably* used for lard; was found with Civil War kitchen supplies.

Condiment Bag: Made of canvas with a heavy cord draw-string. The bag is 5 3/4" tall and 3" wide.

COFFEE WAGON. The Coffee Wagon was invented, built, and presented to the Commission, by Mr. Jacob Dunton, of Philadelphia. The following description of the wagon and its use is by Rev. C. H. Richards, one of the Delegates who rendered timely service in the Ninth and Eighteenth Corps, July 30, 1864—the day of the mine explosion and bloody repulse before Petersburg:—

"I must refer particularly to one prominent feature of their work for weary, wounded bodies on this day, which, for its novelty and usefulness, deserves especial mention. Some of the newspapers have mentioned a new Cooking Wagon, presented by the inventor to the Christian Commission, which is thoroughly *sui generis.* It is constructed somewhat like a battery caisson, so that the parts can be unlimbered and separated from each other. The 'limber' or forward part, bears a large chest which is divided into compartments to contain coffee, tea, sugar, and cornstarch, with a place, also, for two gridirons and an axe. From the rear portion rise three tall smoke-pipes above three large boilers, under which there is a place for the fire, and under the fire a box for the fuel. Each boiler will hold fourteen gallons, and it is estimated that in each one, on the march, ten gallons of tea, or coffee, or chocolate, could be made in twenty minutes, thus giving ninety gallons of nourishing drink every hour! It is truly a most ingenious and beneficient invention.

"There was a call for coffee. A party of Delegates at once volunteered to respond to the call. The fires were lighted, the water boiled, the coffee made, and soon the vehicle, drawn by two powerful horses, and attended by half a score of willing laborers, was on its way from division to division. Up the hospital avenue it rumbled and rolled, past the long rows of white tents, stopping at this cluster or that, giving to all from its generous supply. You should have seen the wondering look of the men as it passed by. They rolled themselves over to get a glimpse of it. They stretched their necks for a sight of it. The wounded heads forgot to ache, and the wounded limbs almost forgot to cry for nursing in that moment of eager curiosity. Was it a new sort of ambulance? It didn't look like one. What did those three black pipes mean, and those three glowing fires? Is it a steam fire engine, and are they going to give us a shower bath? But the savory odor that saluted their nostrils, and the delicious beverage the engine poured into their little cups, soon put the matter beyond all doubt. They soon found that there was no necromancy about it, for it had a substantial blessing for each one of them, and they gave it their blessing in return. One by one, such as were able, crowded about it with curious faces, and the wagon, as it stood steaming and glowing in the midst, was the theme of many affectionate comments. 'I say, Bill, ain't that a bully machine?' 'Yes, sir, it is the greatest institution I ever saw.' 'That's what you might call the Christian Light Artillery,' says a third. 'Good deal pleasanter ammunition in it than the Rebs sent us this morning.' 'Well, doctor,' said a Delegate to a surgeon, 'what do you think of this?' 'I thank the Lord for it. That's all I can say,' was his reply. And so, on a sudden, the new invention was crowned with the praises and benedictions of the admiring crowd. It was a

Liquor and Pop Bottles
Left to right:
Top Row: Champagne bottle. Medium green in color, 12 1/4" tall and 3 1/2" in diameter. From Fredericksburg, Virginia.

Light green wine bottle, 12 1/2" tall and 2 1/2" in diameter. From Port Hudson, Louisiana.

Amber wine bottle, 11" tall and 2 3/4" in diameter. Found in Confederate camp at Centreville, Virginia. Marked:

PATENT

Dark amber wine bottle, 9 1/2" tall and 2 1/2" in diameter. From Headquarters, 3rd Cavalry Division, Army of the Potomac.

Dark amber wine bottle, 9 1/4" tall and 2 1/2" in diameter. From Confederate prison, Johnson's Island, Ohio.

Dark amber bottle, probably for port wine. About 9" tall (top is broken), and 3 3/4" in diameter. From U.S. Camp at Hilton Head, Soutl Carolina. Marked:

CLARKE & WHITE
C
NEW YORK

Left to Right:
Middle Row: Brown and white glazed stoneware beer bottle, 8 1/4" tall and 3" in diameter. From Port Hudson, Louisiana.

Brown and white glazed stoneware beer bottle, 7 3/4" tall and 2 7/8" in diameter. From U.S. lines at Savannah, Georgia.

Dark amber beer bottle, 7 5/8" tall and 3" in diameter. From Charleston, South Carolina. Marked:

JOHANN HOFF

Greenish-blue "pop" bottle, 7 1/2" tall and 2 5/8" in diameter. Marked:

J. H. KUMP
MEMPHIS, TENN.

Bottom Row: Green bottle with rounded bottom, 9 1/8" long. From Confederate camp at Centreville, Virginia. Marked:

HENKE & MAACK

Table showing the quantity in bulk of any number of rations from 1 to 100,000.

Number of Rations.	Pork.			Beef.		Flour.			Beans.			Rice.		Coffee.		Sugar.		Whisky.			Vinegar.			Candles.		Soap.		Salt.			Number of Rations.
	Barrels.	Pounds.	Ounces.	Pounds.	Ounces.	Barrels.	Pounds.	Ounces.	Bushels.	Quarts.	Gills.	Pounds.	Ounces.	Pounds.	Ounces.	Pounds.	Ounces.	Gallons.	Quarts.	Gills.	Gallons.	Quarts.	Gills.	Pounds.	Ounces.	Pounds.	Ounces.	Bushels.	Quarts.	Gills.	
1	-	-	12	1	4	-	1	2	-	-	.64	-	1.6	-	.96	-	1.92	-	-	1	-	-	.32	-	.24	-	.64	-	-	.16	1
2	-	1	8	2	8	-	2	4	-	-	1.28	-	3.2	-	1.92	-	3.84	-	-	2	-	-	.64	-	.48	-	1.28	-	-	.32	2
3	-	2	4	3	12	-	3	6	-	-	1.92	-	4.8	-	2.88	-	5.76	-	-	3	-	-	.96	-	.72	-	1.92	-	-	.48	3
4	-	3	-	5	-	-	4	8	-	-	2.56	-	6.4	-	3.84	-	7.68	-	-	4	-	-	1.28	-	.96	-	2.56	-	-	.64	4
5	-	3	12	6	4	-	5	10	-	-	3.20	-	8.0	-	4.80	-	9.60	-	-	5	-	-	1.60	-	1.20	-	3.20	-	-	.80	5
6	-	4	8	7	8	-	6	12	-	-	3.84	-	9.6	-	5.76	-	11.52	-	-	6	-	-	1.92	-	1.44	-	3.84	-	-	.96	6
7	-	5	4	8	12	-	7	14	-	-	4.48	-	11.2	-	6.72	-	13.44	-	-	7	-	-	2.24	-	1.68	-	4.48	-	-	1.12	7
8	-	6	-	10	-	-	9	-	-	-	5.12	-	12.8	-	7.68	-	15.36	-	1	-	-	-	2.56	-	1.92	-	5.12	-	-	1.28	8
9	-	6	12	11	4	-	10	2	-	-	5.76	-	14.4	-	8.64	1	1.28	-	1	1	-	-	2.88	-	2.16	-	5.76	-	-	1.44	9
10	-	7	8	12	8	-	11	4	-	-	6.40	1	-	-	9.60	1	3.20	-	1	2	-	-	3.20	-	2.40	-	6.40	-	-	1.60	10
11	-	8	4	13	12	-	12	6	-	-	7.04	1	1.6	-	10.56	1	5.12	-	1	3	-	-	3.52	-	2.64	-	7.04	-	-	1.76	11
12	-	9	-	15	-	-	13	8	-	-	7.68	1	3.2	-	11.52	1	7.04	-	1	4	-	-	3.84	-	2.88	-	7.68	-	-	1.92	12
13	-	9	12	16	4	-	14	10	-	1	.32	1	4.8	-	12.48	1	8.96	-	1	5	-	-	4.16	-	3.12	-	8.32	-	-	2.08	13
14	-	10	8	17	8	-	15	12	-	1	.96	1	6.4	-	13.44	1	10.88	-	1	6	-	-	4.48	-	3.36	-	8.96	-	-	2.24	14
15	-	11	4	18	12	-	16	14	-	1	1.60	1	8.0	-	14.40	1	12.80	-	1	7	-	-	4.80	-	3.60	-	9.60	-	-	2.40	15
16	-	12	-	20	-	-	18	-	-	1	2.24	1	9.6	-	15.36	1	14.72	-	2	-	-	-	5.12	-	3.84	-	10.24	-	-	2.56	16
17	-	12	12	21	4	-	19	2	-	1	2.88	1	11.2	1	.32	2	.64	-	2	1	-	-	5.44	-	4.08	-	10.88	-	-	2.72	17
18	-	13	8	22	8	-	20	4	-	1	3.52	1	12.8	1	1.28	2	2.56	-	2	2	-	-	5.76	-	4.32	-	11.52	-	-	2.88	18
19	-	14	4	23	12	-	21	6	-	1	4.16	1	14.4	1	2.24	2	4.48	-	2	3	-	-	6.08	-	4.56	-	12.16	-	-	3.04	19
20	-	15	-	25	-	-	22	8	-	1	4.80	2	-	1	3.20	2	6.40	-	2	4	-	-	6.40	-	4.80	-	12.80	-	-	3.20	20
21	-	15	12	26	4	-	23	10	-	1	5.44	2	1.6	1	4.16	2	8.32	-	2	5	-	-	6.72	-	5.04	-	13.44	-	-	3.36	21
22	-	16	8	27	8	-	24	12	-	1	6.08	2	3.2	1	5.12	2	10.24	-	2	6	-	-	7.04	-	5.28	-	14.08	-	-	3.52	22
23	-	17	4	28	12	-	25	14	-	1	6.72	2	4.8	1	6.08	2	12.16	-	2	7	-	-	7.36	-	5.52	-	14.72	-	-	3.68	23
24	-	18	-	30	-	-	27	-	-	1	7.36	2	6.4	1	7.04	2	14.08	-	3	-	-	-	7.68	-	5.76	-	15.36	-	-	3.84	24
25	-	18	12	31	4	-	28	2	-	2	-	2	8.0	1	8.00	3	-	-	3	1	-	1	-	-	6.00	1	-	-	-	4.00	25
26	-	19	8	32	8	-	29	4	-	2	.64	2	9.6	1	8.96	3	1.92	-	3	2	-	1	.32	-	6.24	1	.64	-	-	4.16	26
27	-	20	4	33	12	-	30	6	-	2	1.28	2	11.2	1	9.92	3	3.84	-	3	3	-	1	.64	-	6.48	1	1.28	-	-	4.32	27
28	-	21	-	35	-	-	31	8	-	2	1.92	2	12.8	1	10.88	3	5.76	-	3	4	-	1	.96	-	6.72	1	1.92	-	-	4.48	28
29	-	21	12	36	4	-	32	10	-	2	2.56	2	14.4	1	11.84	3	7.68	-	3	5	-	1	1.28	-	6.96	1	2.56	-	-	4.64	29
30	-	22	8	37	8	-	33	12	-	2	3.20	3	-	1	12.80	3	9.60	-	3	6	-	1	1.60	-	7.20	1	3.20	-	-	4.80	30
31	-	23	4	38	12	-	34	14	-	2	3.84	3	1.6	1	13.76	3	11.52	-	3	7	-	1	1.92	-	7.44	1	3.84	-	-	4.96	31
32	-	24	-	40	-	-	36	-	-	2	4.48	3	3.2	1	14.72	3	13.44	1	-	-	-	1	2.24	-	7.68	1	4.48	-	-	5.12	32
33	-	24	12	41	4	-	37	2	-	2	5.12	3	4.8	1	15.68	3	15.36	1	-	1	-	1	2.56	-	7.92	1	5.12	-	-	5.28	33
34	-	25	8	42	8	-	38	4	-	2	5.76	3	6.4	2	.64	4	1.28	1	-	2	-	1	2.88	-	8.16	1	5.76	-	-	5.44	34
35	-	26	4	43	12	-	39	6	-	2	6.40	3	8.0	2	1.60	4	3.20	1	-	3	-	1	3.20	-	8.40	1	6.40	-	-	5.60	35
36	-	27	-	45	-	-	40	8	-	2	7.04	3	9.6	2	1.56	4	5.12	1	-	4	-	1	3.52	-	8.64	1	7.04	-	-	5.76	36
37	-	27	12	46	4	-	41	10	-	2	7.68	3	11.2	2	3.52	4	7.04	1	-	5	-	1	3.84	-	8.88	1	7.68	-	-	5.92	37
38	-	28	8	47	8	-	42	12	-	3	.32	3	12.8	2	4.48	4	8.96	1	-	6	-	1	4.16	-	9.12	1	8.32	-	-	6.08	38
39	-	29	4	48	12	-	43	14	-	3	.96	3	14.4	2	5.44	4	10.88	1	-	7	-	1	4.48	-	9.36	1	8.96	-	-	6.24	39
40	-	30	-	50	-	-	45	-	-	3	1.60	4	-	2	6.40	4	12.80	1	1	-	-	1	4.80	-	9.60	1	9.60	-	-	6.40	40
41	-	30	12	51	4	-	46	2	-	3	2.24	4	1.6	2	7.36	4	14.72	1	1	1	-	1	5.12	-	9.84	1	10.24	-	-	6.56	41
42	-	31	8	52	8	-	47	4	-	3	2.88	4	3.2	2	8.32	5	.64	1	1	2	-	1	5.44	-	10.08	1	10.88	-	-	6.72	42
43	-	32	4	53	12	-	48	6	-	3	3.52	4	4.8	2	9.28	5	2.56	1	1	3	-	1	5.76	-	10.32	1	11.52	-	-	6.88	43
44	-	33	-	55	-	-	49	8	-	3	4.16	4	6.4	2	10.24	5	4.48	1	1	4	-	1	6.08	-	10.56	1	12.16	-	-	7.04	44
45	-	33	12	56	4	-	50	10	-	3	4.80	4	8.0	2	11.20	5	6.40	1	1	5	-	1	6.40	-	10.80	1	12.80	-	-	7.20	45
46	-	34	8	57	8	-	51	12	-	3	5.44	4	9.6	2	12.16	5	8.32	1	1	6	-	1	6.72	-	11.04	1	13.44	-	-	7.36	46
47	-	35	4	58	12	-	52	14	-	3	6.08	4	11.2	2	13.12	5	10.24	1	1	7	-	1	7.04	-	11.28	1	14.08	-	-	7.52	47
48	-	36	-	60	-	-	54	-	-	3	6.72	4	12.8	2	14.08	5	12.16	1	2	-	-	1	7.36	-	11.52	1	14.72	-	-	7.68	48
49	-	36	12	61	4	-	55	2	-	3	7.36	4	14.4	2	15.04	5	14.08	1	2	1	-	1	7.68	-	11.76	1	15.36	-	-	7.84	49
50	-	37	8	62	8	-	56	4	-	4	-	5	-	3	-	6	-	1	2	2	-	2	-	-	12.00	2	-	-	1	-	50
51	-	38	4	63	12	-	57	6	-	4	.64	5	1.6	3	.96	6	1.92	1	2	3	-	2	.32	-	12.24	2	.64	-	1	.16	51
52	-	39	-	65	-	-	58	8	-	4	1.28	5	3.2	3	1.92	6	3.84	1	2	4	-	2	.64	-	12.48	2	1.28	-	1	.32	52
53	-	39	12	66	4	-	59	10	-	4	1.92	5	4.8	3	2.88	6	5.76	1	2	5	-	2	.96	-	12.72	2	1.92	-	1	.48	53
54	-	40	8	67	8	-	60	12	-	4	2.56	5	6.4	3	3.84	6	7.68	1	2	6	-	2	1.28	-	12.96	2	2.56	-	1	.64	54
55	-	41	4	68	12	-	61	14	-	4	3.20	5	8.0	3	4.80	6	9.60	1	2	7	-	2	1.60	-	13.20	2	3.20	-	1	.80	55
56	-	42	-	70	-	-	63	-	-	4	3.84	5	9.6	3	5.76	6	11.52	1	3	-	-	2	1.92	-	13.44	2	3.84	-	1	.96	56
57	-	42	12	71	4	-	64	2	-	4	4.48	5	11.2	3	6.72	6	13.44	1	3	1	-	2	2.24	-	13.68	2	4.48	-	1	1.12	57
58	-	43	8	72	8	-	65	4	-	4	5.12	5	12.8	3	7.68	6	15.36	1	3	2	-	2	2.56	-	13.92	2	5.12	-	1	1.28	58
59	-	44	4	73	12	-	66	6	-	4	5.76	5	14.4	3	8.64	7	1.28	1	3	3	-	2	2.88	-	14.16	2	5.76	-	1	1.44	59
60	-	45	-	75	-	-	67	8	-	4	6.40	6	-	3	9.60	7	3.20	1	3	4	-	2	3.20	-	14.40	2	6.40	-	1	1.60	60
61	-	45	12	76	4	-	68	10	-	4	7.04	6	1.6	3	10.56	7	5.12	1	3	5	-	2	3.52	-	14.64	2	7.04	-	1	1.76	61
62	-	46	8	77	8	-	69	12	-	4	7.68	6	3.2	3	11.52	7	7.04	1	3	6	-	2	3.84	-	14.88	2	7.68	-	1	1.92	62
63	-	47	4	78	12	-	70	14	-	5	.32	6	4.8	3	12.48	7	8.96	1	3	7	-	2	4.16	-	15.12	2	8.32	-	1	2.08	63
64	-	48	-	80	-	-	72	-	-	5	.96	6	6.4	3	13.44	7	10.88	2	-	-	-	2	4.48	-	15.36	2	8.96	-	1	2.24	64
65	-	48	12	81	4	-	73	2	-	5	1.60	6	8.0	3	14.40	7	12.80	2	-	1	-	2	4.80	-	15.60	2	9.60	-	1	2.40	65
66	-	49	8	82	8	-	74	4	-	5	2.24	6	9.6	3	15.36	7	14.72	2	-	2	-	2	5.12	-	15.84	2	10.24	-	1	2.56	66
67	-	50	4	83	12	-	75	6	-	5	2.88	6	11.2	4	.32	8	.64	2	-	3	-	2	5.44	1	.08	2	10.88	-	1	2.72	67
68	-	51	-	85	-	-	76	8	-	5	3.52	6	12.8	4	1.28	8	2.56	2	-	4	-	2	5.76	1	.32	2	11.52	-	1	2.88	68
69	-	51	12	86	4	-	77	10	-	5	4.16	6	14.4	4	2.24	8	4.48	2	-	5	-	2	6.08	1	.56	2	12.16	-	1	3.04	69
70	-	52	8	87	8	-	78	12	-	5	4.80	7	-	4	3.20	8	6.40	2	-	6	-	2	6.40	1	.80	2	12.80	-	1	3.20	70
71	-	53	4	88	12	-	79	14	-	5	5.44	7	1.6	4	4.16	8	8.32	2	-	7	-	2	6.72	1	1.04	2	13.44	-	1	3.36	71
72	-	54	-	90	-	-	81	-	-	5	6.08	7	3.2	4	5.12	8	10.24	2	1	-	-	2	7.04	1	1.28	2	14.08	-	1	3.52	72
73	-	54	12	91	4	-	82	2	-	5	6.72	7	4.8	4	6.08	8	12.16	2	1	1	-	2	7.36	1	1.52	2	14.72	-	1	3.68	73
74	-	55	8	92	8	-	83	4	-	5	7.36	7	6.4	4	7.04	8	14.08	2	1	2	-	2	7.68	1	1.76	2	15.36	-	1	3.84	74
75	-	56	4	93	12	-	84	6	-	6	-	7	8.0	4	8.00	9	-	2	1	3	-	3	-	1	2.00	3	-	-	1	4.00	75
76	-	57	-	95	-	-	85	8	-	6	.64	7	9.6	4	8.96	9	1.92	2	1	4	-	3	.32	1	2.24	3	.64	-	1	4.16	76
77	-	57	12	96	4	-	86	10	-	6	1.28	7	11.2	4	9.92	9	3.84	2	1	5	-	3	.64	1	2.48	3	1.28	-	1	4.32	77
78	-	58	8	97	8	-	87	12	-	6	1.92	7	12.8	4	10.88	9	5.76	2	1	6	-	3	.96	1	2.72	3	1.92	-	1	4.48	78
79	-	59	4	98	12	-	88	14	-	6	2.56	7	14.4	4	11.84	9	7.68	2	1	7	-	3	1.28	1	2.96	3	2.56	-	1	4.64	79
80	-	60	-	100	-	-	90	-	-	6	3.20	8	-	4	12.80	9	9.60	2	2	-	-	3	1.60	1	3.20	3	3.20	-	1	4.80	80
81	-	60	12	101	4	-	91	2	-	6	3.84	8	1.6	4	13.76	9	11.52	2	2	1	-	3	1.92	1	3.44	3	3.84	-	1	4.96	81
82	-	61	8	102	8	-	92	4	-	6	4.48	8	3.2	4	14.72	9	13.44	2	2	2	-	3	2.24	1	3.68	3	4.48	-	1	5.12	82
83	-	62	4	103	12	-	93	6	-	6	5.12	8	4.8	4	15.68	9	15.36	2	2	3	-	3	2.56	1	3.92	3	5.12	-	1	5.28	83
84	-	63	-	105	-	-	94	8	-	6	5.76	8	6.4	5	.64	10	1.28	2	2	4	-	3	2.88	1	4.16	3	5.76	-	1	5.44	84
85	-	63	12	106	4	-	95	10	-	6	6.40	8	8.0	5	1.60	10	3.20	2	2	5	-	3	3.20	1	4.40	3	6.40	-	1	5.60	85
86	-	64	8	107	8	-	96	12	-	6	7.04	8	9.6	5	2.56	10	5.12	2	2	6	-	3	3.52	1	4.64	3	7.04	-	1	5.76	86
87	-	65	4	108	12	-	97	14	-	6	7.68	8	11.2	5	3.52	10	7.04	2	2	7	-	3	3.84	1	4.88	3	7.68	-	1	5.92	87
88	-	66	-	110	-	-	99	-	-	7	.32	8	12.8	5	4.48	10	8.96	2	3	-	-	3	4.16	1	5.12	3	8.32	-	1	6.08	88
89	-	66	12	111	4	-	100	2	-	7	.96	8	14.4	5	5.44	10	10.88	2	3	1	-	3	4.48	1	5.36	3	8.96	-	1	6.24	89
90	-	67	8	112	8	-	101	4	-	7	1.60	9	-	5	6.40	10	12.80	2	3	2	-	3	4.80	1	5.60	3	9.60	-	1	6.40	90
91	-	68	4	113	12	-	102	6	-	7	2.24	9	1.6	5	7.38	10	14.72	2	3	3	-	3	5.12	1	5.84	3	10.24	-	1	6.56	91
92	-	69	-	115	-	-	103	8	-	7	2.88	9	3.2	5	8.32	11	.64	2	3	4	-	3	5.44	1	6.08	3	10.88	-	1	6.72	92
93	-	69	12	116	4	-	104	10	-	7	3.52	9	4.8	5	9.28	11	2.56	2	3	5	-	3	5.76	1	6.32	3	11.52	-	1	6.88	93
94	-	70	8	117	8	-	105	12	-	7	4.16	9	6.4	5	10.24	11	4.48	2	3	6	-	3	6.08	1	6.56	3	12.16	-	1	7.04	94
95	-	71	4	118	12	-	106	14	-	7	4.80	9	8.0	5	11.20	11	6.40	2	3	7	-	3	6.40	1	6.80	3	12.80	-	1	7.20	95
96	-	72	-	120	-	-	108	-	-	7	5.44	9	9.6	5	12.16	11	8.32	3	-	-	-	3	6.72	1	7.04	3	13.44	-	1	7.36	96
97	-	72	12	121	4	-	109	2	-	7	6.08	9	11.2	5	13.12	11	10.24	3	-	1	-	3	7.04	1	7.28	3	14.08	-	1	7.52	97
98	-	73	8	122	8	-	110	4	-	7	6.72	9	12.8	5	14.08	11	12.16	3	-	2	-	3	7.36	1	7.52	3	14.72	-	1	7.68	98
99	-	74	4	123	12	-	111	6	-	7	7.36	9	14.4	5	15.04	11	14.08	3	-	3	-	3	7.68	1	7.76	3	15.36	-	1	7.84	99
100	-	75	-	125	-	-	112	8	-	8	-	10	-	6	-	12	-	3	-	4	1	-	-	1	8.00	4	-	-	2	-	100
200	-	150	-	250	-	1	20	-	-	16	-	20	-	12	-	24	-	6	1	-	2	-	-	3	-	8	-	-	4	-	200
300	1	25	-	375	-	1	141	8	-	24	-	30	-	18	-	36	-	9	1	4	3	-	-	4	8.00	12	-	-	6	-	300
400	1	100	-	500	-	2	58	-	1	-	-	40	-	24	-	48	-	12	2	-	4	-	-	6	-	16	-	-	8	-	400
500	1	175	-	625	-	2	170	8	1	8	-	50	-	30	-	60	-	15	2	4	5	-	-	7	8.00	20	-	-	10	-	500
600	2	50	-	750	-	3	87	-	1	16	-	60	-	36	-	72	-	18	3	-	6	-	-	9	-	24	-	-	12	-	600
700	2	125	-	875	-	4	3	8	1	24	-	70	-	42	-	84	-	21	3	4	7	-	-	10	8.00	28	-	-	14	-	700
800	3	-	-	1,000	-	4	116	-	2	-	-	80	-	48	-	96	-	25	-	-	8	-	-	12	-	32	-	-	16	-	800
900	3	75	-	1,125	-	5	32	8	2	8	-	90	-	54	-	108	-	28	-	4	9	-	-	13	8.00	36	-	-	18	-	900
1,000	3	150	-	1,250	-	5	145	-	2	16	-	100	-	60	-	120	-	31	1	-	10	-	-	15	-	40	-	-	20	-	1,000
1,100	4	25	-	1,375	-	6	61	8	2	24	-	110	-	66	-	132	-	34	1	4	11	-	-	16	8.00	44	-	-	22	-	1,100
1,200	4	100	-	1,500	-	6	174	-	3	-	-	120	-	72	-	144	-	37	2	-	12	-	-	18	-	48	-	-	24	-	1,200
1,300	4	175	-	1,625	-	7	90	8	3	8	-	130	-	78	-	156	-	40	2	4	13	-	-	19	8.00	52	-	-	26	-	1,300
1,400	5	50	-	1,750	-	8	7	-	3	16	-	140	-	84	-	168	-	43	3	-	14	-	-	21	-	56	-	-	28	-	1,400
1,500	5	125	-	1,875	-	8	119	8	3	24	-	150	-	90	-	180	-	46	3	4	15	-	-	22	8.00	60	-	-	30	-	1,500
1,600	6	-	-	2,000	-	9	36	-	4	-	-	160	-	96	-	192	-	50	-	-	16	-	-	24	-	64	-	1	-	-	1,600
1,700	6	75	-	2,125	-	9	148	8	4	8	-	170	-	102	-	204	-	53	-	4	17	-	-	25	8.00	68	-	1	2	-	1,700
1,800	6	150	-	2,250	-	10	65	-	4	16	-	180	-	108	-	216	-	56	1	-	18	-	-	27	-	72	-	1	4	-	1,800
1,900	7	25	-	2,375	-	10	177	8	4	24	-	190	-	114	-	228	-	59	1	4	19	-	-	28	8.00	76	-	1	6	-	1,900
2,000	7	100	-	2,500	-	11	94	-	5	-	-	200	-	120	-	240	-	62	2	-	20	-	-	30	-	80	-	1	8	-	2,000
3,000	11	50	-	3,750	-	17	43	-	7	16	-	300	-	180	-	360	-	93	3	-	30	-	-	45	-	120	-	1	28	-	3,000
4,000	15	-	-	5,000	-	22	188	-	10	-	-	400	-	240	-	480	-	125	-	-	40	-	-	60	-	160	-	2	16	-	4,000
5,000	18	150	-	6,250	-	28	137	-	12	16	-	500	-	300	-	600	-	156	1	-	50	-	-	75	-	200	-	3	4	-	5,000
6,000	22	100	-	7,500	-	34	86	-	15	-	-	600	-	360	-	720	-	187	2	-	60	-	-	90	-	240	-	3	24	-	6,000
7,000	26	50	-	8,750	-	40	35	-	17	16	-	700	-	420	-	840	-	218	3	-	70	-	-	105	-	280	-	4	12	-	7,000
8,000	30	-	-	10,000	-	45	180	-	20	-	-	800	-	480	-	960	-	250	-	-	80	-	-	120	-	320	-	5	-	-	8,000
9,000	33	150	-	11,250	-	51	129	-	22	16	-	900	-	540	-	1,080	-	281	1	-	90	-	-	135	-	360	-	5	20	-	9,000
10,000	37	100	-	12,500	-	57	78	-	25	-	-	1,000	-	600	-	1,200	-	312	2	-	100	-	-	150	-	400	-	6	8	-	10,000
11,000	41	50	-	13,750	-	63	27	-	27	16	-	1,100	-	660	-	1,320	-	343	3	-	110	-	-	165	-	440	-	6	28	-	11,000
12,000	45	-	-	15,000	-	68	172	-	30	-	-	1,200	-	720	-	1,440	-	375	-	-	120	-	-	180	-	480	-	7	16	-	12,000
13,000	48	150	-	16,250	-	74	121	-	32	16	-	1,300	-	780	-	1,560	-	406	1	-	130	-	-	195	-	520	-	8	4	-	13,000
14,000	52	100	-	17,500	-	80	70	-	35	-	-	1,400	-	840	-	1,680	-	437	2	-	140	-	-	210	-	560	-	8	24	-	14,000
15,000	56	50	-	18,750	-	86	19	-	37	16	-	1,500	-	900	-	1,800	-	468	3	-	150	-	-	225	-	600	-	9	12	-	15,000
16,000	60	-	-	20,000	-	91	164	-	40	-	-	1,600	-	960	-	1,920	-	500	-	-	160	-	-	240	-	640	-	10	-	-	16,000
17,000	63	150	-	21,250	-	97	113	-	42	16	-	1,700	-	1,020	-	2,040	-	531	1	-	170	-	-	255	-	680	-	10	20	-	17,000
18,000	67	100	-	22,500	-	103	62	-	45	-	-	1,800	-	1,080	-	2,160	-	562	2	-	180	-	-	270	-	720	-	11	8	-	18,000
19,000	71	50	-	23,750	-	109	11	-	47	16	-	1,900	-	1,140	-	2,280	-	593	3	-	190	-	-	285	-	760	-	11	28	-	19,000
20,000	75	-	-	25,000	-	114	156	-	50	-	-	2,000	-	1,200	-	2,400	-	625	-	-	200	-	-	300	-	800	-	12	16	-	20,000
30,000	112	100	-	37,500	-	172	38	-	75	-	-	3,000	-	1,800	-	3,600	-	937	2	-	300	-	-	450	-	1,200	-	18	24	-	30,000
40,000	150	-	-	50,000	-	229	116	-	100	-	-	4,000	-	2,400	-	4,800	-	1,250	-	-	400	-	-	600	-	1,600	-	25	-	-	40,000
50,000	187	100	-	62,500	-	286	194	-	125	-	-	5,000	-	3,000	-	6,000	-	1,562	2	-	500	-	-	750	-	2,000	-	31	8	-	50,000
60,000	225	-	-	75,000	-	344	76	-	150	-	-	6,000	-	3,600	-	7,200	-	1,875	-	-	600	-	-	900	-	2,400	-	37	16	-	60,000
70,000	262	100	-	87,500	-	401	154	-	175	-	-	7,000	-	4,200	-	8,400	-	2,187	2	-	700	-	-	1,050	-	2,800	-	43	24	-	70,000
80,000	300	-	-	100,000	-	459	36	-	200	-	-	8,000	-	4,800	-	9,600	-	2,500	-	-	800	-	-	1,200	-	3,200	-	50	-	-	80,000
90,000	337	100	-	112,500	-	516	114	-	225	-	-	9,000	-	5,400	-	10,800	-	2,812	2	-	900	-	-	1,350	-	3,600	-	56	8	-	90,000
100,000	375	-	-	125,000	-	573	192	-	250	-	-	10,000	-	6,000	-	12,000	-	3,125	-	-	1,000	-	-	1,500	-	4,000	-	62	16	-	100,000
Number of Rations.	Barrels.	Pounds.	Ounces.	Pounds.	Ounces.	Barrels.	Pounds.	Ounces.	Bushels.	Quarts.	Gills.	Pounds.	Ounces.	Pounds.	Ounces.	Pounds.	Ounces.	Gallons.	Quarts.	Gills.	Gallons.	Quarts.	Gills.	Pounds.	Ounces.	Pounds.	Ounces.	Bushels.	Quarts.	Gills.	Number of Rations.
	Pork.			Beef.		Flour.			Beans.			Rice.		Coffee.		Sugar.		Whisky.			Vinegar.			Candles.		Soap.		Salt.			

NOTE.—1,000 *complete rations*, including *pork and hard bread* (pilot), occupy the bulk of 16.265 *barrels* when the ration of bread is 12 *ounces*, and 19.282 *barrels* when the ration of bread is 16 *ounces*; and 1,000 *rations*, including *pork and flour*, occupy the bulk of 11.830 *barrels*. Antiscorbutics, as potatoes, onions, beets, pickled onions, krout, molasses, &c., when required, are regulated by special instructions.

Ration Chart

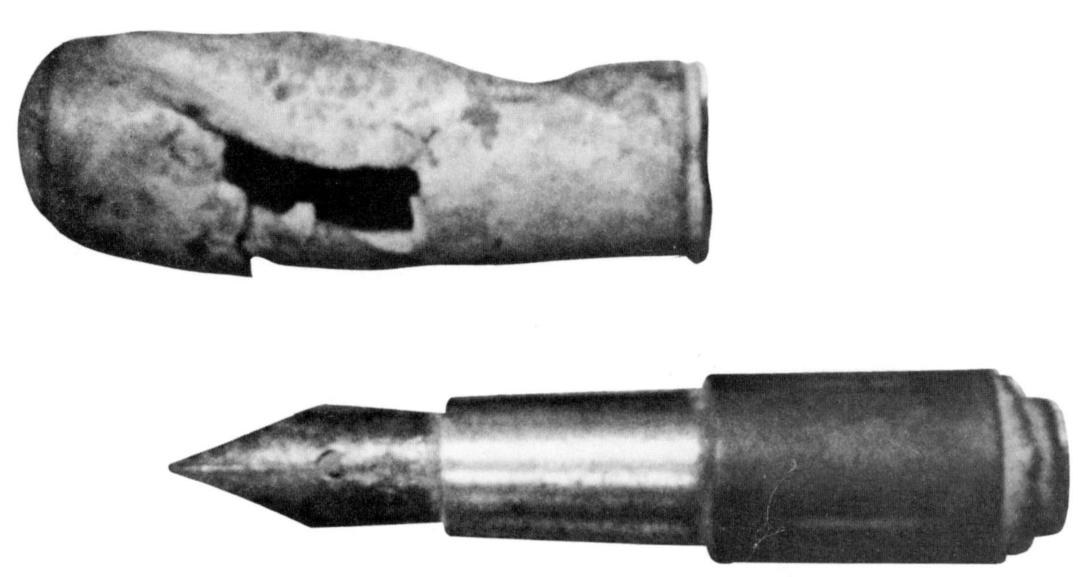

Fountain Pen. Shown here is a fountain pen dug up near Arcadia, Missouri. It was found about four inches below the ground along with several Minie balls in the camp site of the 33rd Illinois Infantry by Doctor John L. Margreiter of St. Louis, Missouri. The regiment was in this camp site until November, 1861. *Description:* Brass and an undetermined alloy, with a bladder and hard rubber cylinder. The brass cover (top of picture) is 3/8 inch thick and 1 1/2 inches long. The pen point is 1/16 inch long and marked:

EAGLE
SNAP
SHOT

marked feature in the work of the day, and must be set down as one of the 'peculiar institutions' of the Commission."

TEA. On the *Cairo* which sank in 1862, there was found the remnants of a square tin can with some tea still in the can.

HARDTACK. Officially called "hard bread" was a plain flour and water biscuit 3 1/8 by 2 7/8 inches in size and nearly half an inch thick. They were issued 9 or 10 per man from the wooden boxes which came to be such a familiar sight in camp, alongside rail lines, and on the march.

Hardtack was nutritious but often was very hard, wormy, or mouldy.

Many men soaked their hardtack in coffee or broke them up and put them in soup or stew. Others toasted their hardtack or fried it in pork fat. This latter concoction was salted to taste and was known as "Skilly Galee".

Hardtack was often months old before it was issued to the troops. The popular name for hardtack was "worm castles"! John D. Billings of the 10th Massachusetts Battery called hardtack "petrified bread honeycombed with bugs and maggots"! Mr. A. L. Tafel, noted Civil War collector, has an original piece of Civil War hardtack. It is 3 1/2 inches square and is marked:

U.S.
MARVIN'S HARDTACK

A label on this piece of hardtack says:

Army Hard-tack brot back from War July 1865 by David Williams of Co. C, 94th N.Y. Inf.

Another piece of Civil War hardtack is marked:

HOLMES & COUTTS
ARMY BREAD
NEW YORK

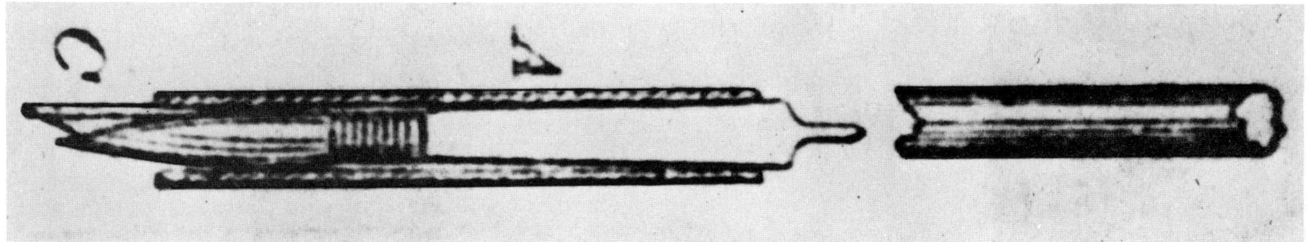
Mathers' Pen

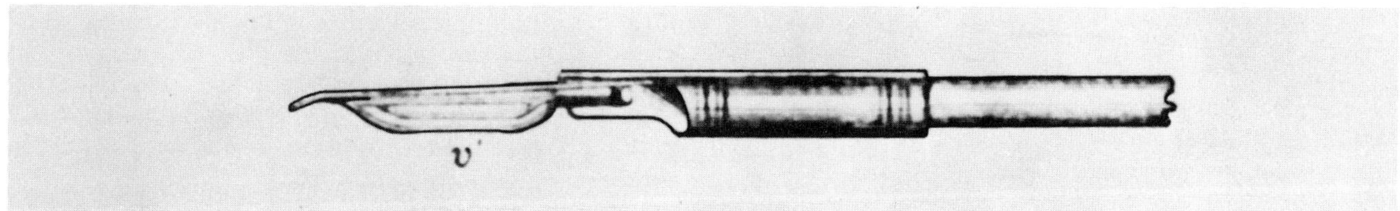
Woolley's Pen

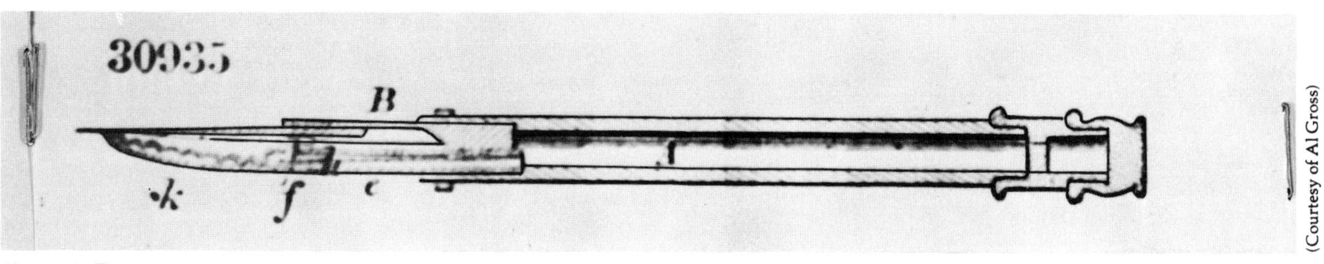

Skinner's Pen

(Courtesy of Al Gross)

Civil War Fountain Pens

FRESH BEEF. Cattle appropriated from farms along the route of march was a common source. But often the troops were in wooded areas on generally poor agricultural country and beef had to be found elsewhere. Generally beef cattle were driven along on the march and slaughtered as needed. Fresh beef was generally obtained by contract.

BEANS. Very popular with the New England regiments. However, often a unit had to set out on a march with the beans only half cooked—and the result were severe stomach aches for the men. It should be remembered that New Englanders often had beans for breakfast as well as for the other meals.

DESICCATED VEGETABLES. In June 1864, the *camp ration* was somewhat reduced but desiccated potatoes and desiccated vegetables were permitted to be substituted in the ration for beans, peas, rice or hominy. These desiccated vegetables came in sheets like pressed hops and were used as an antiscorbutic. Many men did not like them and soon the term "desecrated vegetables" was added to an ever-growing soldier vocabulary. In one regiment (the 13th New Hampshire Infantry) the desiccated vegetables issued in 1863 were "dirty, sandy, mouldy and utterly uneatable". The men paved the company streets with them.

A desiccated vegetable as issued was square, an inch thick, and apparently contained potatoes, carrots, turnips, onions, cabbage, and red peppers. These ingredients had been scalded and then pressed and dried. The idea of these was good; in fact, the ingredients were good as well. But no one could cook these with the limited cooking facilities in the field. The trouble seemed to be that each vegetable had lost its individual flavor in the cooking and vegetables were all "blended together in a nondescript sort of dish that isn't good a bit."

Apparently opinions differed on desiccated vegetables. Some regiments did like them. Normally, each man received a small piece about one ounce in weight and 2-3 inches square. These pieces looked like slabs of cheese.

WHISKEY. Although beer and wine were sold by sutlers, the only government liquor issued was whiskey.

This was done by the Commissary Department, and as a result the name "Commissary" became a soldier's term for whiskey. Whiskey was stored in large quantities at depots. Early in the war the quality was good, but later on "it was new and firey, rough and nasty to take . . . Some men let this rough whiskey simmer over a fire while others set it afire and let it burn awhile, thus getting rid of the worst part of the whiskey."

While regiments from such temperance-minded states like Maine did not get whiskey in their rations, other regiments did avail themselves of the whiskey ration. For example, in 1861, the 16th New York Infantry was allowed 1/2 gill of whiskey per man each day (a gill equals 1/4 of a pint).

WINE. All types of wine were imported in very substantial amounts as evidenced by the large numbers of bottles found at camp sites. The Navy, too, had its wine. When the *Cairo* was raised, a typical wine bottle was recovered. It is green glass, with foil on the neck.

SODA POP. The *Cairo* also had pop bottles on board. These are blue green, 7 3/4 inches tall, and marked:

J. H. KUMP
MEMPHIS

FRESH CORN. A basic item of rations for soldiers of both armies was fresh corn picked in the fields. Some soldiers brought graters from home to use this fresh corn, while other soldiers purchased graters in shops or from sutlers. When these graters were lost, the men converted canteen-halves or sardine cans into graters by punching holes in them with a nail. The fresh ears of corn were grated on the original or improvised graters by rubbing the corn off the ears until there was enough for a stew or a good old New England "hasty pudding".

However, the eating of raw corn and green applies inevitably led to chronic diarrhea, and a substantial number of soldiers—young and old—were discharged for disability for sickness arising from these causes. Many soldiers who served out their enlistments were plagued with "stomach complaints" for many years after 1865. The North Carolina soldier who "wished his bowels were in order" was only one of thousands. About 250,000 men in the Federal Army died of disease or sickness during the war. Of this number about one-fourth died of diarrhea or some other form of bowel complaint.

CARRYING OF RATIONS. Soldiers' rations were carried in a haversack slung over the right shoulder and resting on the left hip. The regulation haversack had an inside cloth lining to keep the rations from contact with the canvas outer lining, but the men soon cut up the inner lining for gun cleaners. Coffee and sugar rations were sometimes issued in small cotton bags or—more rarely—a tin ration container.

According to the November 28, 1863 issue of the *Army and Navy Journal*, coffee and sugar rations were issued in these small cotton bags to the men only on the march. Each man got one bag. The purpose of the bag was to keep the coffee and sugar separate from the meat and hardtack issue. In this article there is also reference to a small tin box strapped to the knapsack which also served to keep coffee and sugar separate from the other items issued as rations.

FOOD PREPARATION. Most men had no idea how to cook their rations and their superior officers were of little help. Non-official publications like the *Soldiers' Health Companion* advised the men to avoid strong coffee (as if that was possible!), and listed recipes for 37 soldier's dishes including lemonade and macaroni pudding!Where the men were to get the ingredients for these dishes was not mentioned.

In barracks or permanent camps food was prepared by the company cooks. On the march and at the front, men either did their own cooking, or combined in small groups to cook their rations. Some individuals and each group generally had a coffee pot, frying pan, and kettle to cook the rations.

Rations were issued uncooked and were cooked either by individuals and groups as described above or by company cooks. The company cook generally knew less about cooking than any man in the company. "Not being able to learn to drill, and too dirty to appear on inspection, he is sent to the cook house to get him out of the ranks. We were not sorry when the cook house was abolished." Such was the opinion of a soldier of the 19th Massachusetts Infantry.

Food in the hospitals was generally quite good. Most of the large general hospitals were located in large cities, near railroad depots, and the supply of food was never the problem it was in the field. A good example of food in a Federal hospital is given us by a Confederate staff officer (G. Moxley Sorrel) during a truce after the Battle of Fredericksburg.

> Here in this great kitchen were huge swinging vessels of odorous real coffee; immense chunks of fat, fresh beef of all parts of the animal; great slabs of dessicated [desiccated] vegetables, which, when thrown with knuckes of meat and good flesh into the boiling cauldron, puffed out, swelling each vegetable into something like freshness, and then with free dashes of salt and pepper, behold, a soup of strength and tastiness . . .

NAVY RATION. By Public Law No. 81, "An act to establish and regulate the Navy Ration", approved August 29, 1842, the Navy ration consisted of the following daily allowance of food for each person:

One pound of salted pork with half a pint of peas or beans; or one pound of salted beef, with half a pound of flour, and a quarter of a pound of raisins, dried apples, or other dried fruit; or one pound of salt beef, with half a pound of rice, two ounces of butter, and two ounces of cheese, together with fourteen ounces of biscuit and one quarter of an ounce of tea; and a weekly allowance of half a pound of pickles or cranberries, half a pint of molasses, and half a pint of vinegar. Fresh meat could be substituted for salt beef or pork and vegetables or sauerkraut for the other articles usually issued with the salted meats. It was permitted to substitute one pound of soft bread, or one pound of flour, or half a pound of rice for fourteen ounces of biscuit; half a pint of wine for a gill of spirits; half a pound of rice for a pint of beans or peas; half a pint of beans or peas for half a pound of rice.

No commissioned officer or midshipman, or any person under 21 years of age was permitted to draw the spirit part of the daily ration, but would be paid the value of the same in money.

The Federal Navy authorities early in the war realized that the ration described above would be insufficient for navy personnel employed for long periods of time on blockade duty. Accordingly, steps were taken to insure a regular delivery of fresh provisions to ships on blockade duty off the coast.

NON-GOVERNMENT ISSUE OF FOOD. The meagre quantity and, too often, poor quality of their rations caused soldiers and sailors to augment their food supply from other sources. Boxes of delicacies were sent by relatives and friends back home. Boxes of food were usually shoe boxes containing not only food but also other items specifically requested by the men. The food usually consisted of cakes, pies, canned jellies, turkeys, pickles, onions, chocolate, butter, sugar, sauces, pepper, and condensed milk. But in the same boxes were shipped such items as hatchets, nails, stockings, mittens, shirts, towels, sewing supplies, and shoe blacking! None of these items were furnished by the Government. Due to long delays in rail shipments, the food items quite often arrived spoiled and uneatable.

Civilian agencies like the United States Sanitary Commission sent large quantities of onions and canned fruits to the field forces in 1864 to overcome the deficiency of antiscorbutic items of the army and navy rations. Large Government bakeries were established near permanent camps, and in 1864-1865 the Federal Army was using mobile bake-ovens on wheels. As mentioned elsewhere in this book a mobile "coffee wagon" was also operating with the army in late 1864.

SUTLERS. Probably the largest (and certainly the most omnipresent) of all food suppliers were the sutlers. As described elsewhere there were literally hundreds of sutlers serving in all theaters of war, both on land and on water. These sutlers were permitted to sell fruits, dairy products, canned meats, oysters, pickles, condiments, and fish. At City Point and Bermuda Hundred in the fall of 1864, a war correspondent marveled at the ample supply of fruit, vegetables, fresh fish, figs, jellies, and wines on sale by enterprising entrepreneurs.

Due to infrequent issue of rations (which were often poor in quantity and quality) the men were forced to buy food from the sutlers. These grasping individuals sold such items as lard-filled pies, vicious patent medicines, and raw whiskey. The men grumbled constantly at the sutlers' exorbitant prices but nevertheless bought their molasses cookies (10 for 25 cents); butter and cheese (60-85 cents a pound, and a very *small* "pound" at that!). Condensed milk was 50 cents per pound can. In December, 1864, prices at City Point, Virginia were:

Can of fruit	$1.00-$1.25
Sweet potatoes	15 cents per lb.
Butter	85 cents per lb.
Cheese	60 cents per lb.
Onions	15 cents per lb.

Sutler prices in the West were about the same.

Much of the information on sutler items has come from cans and bottles recovered from camp sites or sunken ships of the Civil War era. Cans found on the *Cairo* were all sealed with a black sealing compound. This ship also had bottles of Worcestershire sauce. The bottle, cloudy green in color had distinct mold marks and is marked: WORCESTER SHIRE SAUCE around the shoulder of the bottle, LEA & PERRINS up one side of the bottle, and the letters B C A C D on the bottom. Pepper Sauce, in dark green champagne bottles, have been recovered from the *Cairo*; one can still smell the pepper! Several U.S. Navy condiment bottles have been recovered from the *Cairo*, including even a mustard paddle of round, hard wood some 5 inches long and 1/4 inch in diameter. This paddle fitted into the cork of the bottle much like the shoe blacking "dauber" of today. Tomato catsup was sold in bottles during the war. Pickled beef was sold in wooden kegs and oysters were put out in tin cans. These cans closely resembled the cans for peaches of the period and were hand-soldered.

A sutler sold the men of the 5th New Hampshire Infantry preserved pigeons which were canned. However, when the men opened the cans they found that the contents had spoiled and could not be eaten.

Condensed milk was of two well-known brands—Lewis and Borden. One gets the definite impression that the contents of the Borden can consisted of a powdered or dry substance rather than the thick liquid "condensed" or "evaporated" milk we use today.

However, sardines certainly were among the leading favorites of all foods purchased from sutlers. A rough indication of the popularity of sardines can be assumed from the fact that about 50% of all cans recovered from camp sites in the Author's collection are sardine cans. Sardine cans dated 1860 have been recovered from the

Cairo. The paper label had faded so much as to be illegible. Apparently most sardines were imported from France. They were comparatively expensive since contemporary accounts mention sardine cans usually being found around brigade (or higher) headquarters.

FOOD CONTAINERS: TIN CANS. Of 60 specimens examined, all but 2 were round. These cans were found on camp sites and battlefields in Virginia and Tennessee. A few were found at Hilton Head, South Carolina. At least 16 different sizes were found in these 60 cans with the majority 4 5/8 inches tall and 3 5/8 inches in diameter or 3 1/4 inches tall and 3 inches in diameter. However, sizes ranged from 7 inches tall and 3 inches in diameter to 1 1/2 inches tall and 2 1/2 inches in diameter. Illustrated here are a few examples of the 60 specimens examined.

CAN COVERS. A total of 57 tin can covers have been examined. These were found on camp sites and battlefields, both East and West. Four basic sizes have been noted:

Diameters of 4 1/4, 3 3/4, 3 1/2, and 3 inches. Some of these covers were made so as to come off easily, while others had to be pried off by force. A few had an easily—removed center part. However, most cans examined by this author had been crudely opened by a bayonet, knife, or hatchet.

SARDINE CANS. A total of 44 sardine cans from various battlefields and camp sites were examined. Six Confederate states are represented—Virginia, Tennessee, Georgia, Louisiana, Mississippi, and South Carolina. Of these 44 cans, 34 have the following dimensions:

Length - 4 1/4 inches
Width - 3 inches
Depth - 1 1/8 inches

The other 10 have the following dimensions:

Length - 4 1/2 inches
Width - 4 inches
Depth - 1 3/8 inches

Very few are marked; apparently the cans originally had paper labels which have completely deteriorated after a century in the ground. However, three *metal* labels have survived.

1. CAMUS SARDINES
   PARIS
   (From Hilton Head, South Carolina)
2. SARDINES A LA HUILE
   BELLE ILE
   (From Aquia Creek, Virginia)
3. DUBOIS ALLAIN
   SARDINES A L'HUILE
   PORT LOUIS PRES L'ORIENT
   (From Port Hudson, Louisiana and Aquia Creek, Virginia)

FOUNTAIN PENS

Shown (p. 63) are three patented fountain pens.

PATENT NO. 30828. Patented December 4, 1860, by Ebenezer Mathers of Fairmount, Virginia. The principle is the use of hair pencil brush or other arrangements of hair in contact with a metallic writing pen for the purpose of securing a continuous flow of ink to the pen while writing.

PATENT NO. 30851. Patented December 4, 1860, by G. W. Woolley of Philadelphia. The principle is the use of an ink-holding and controlling reservoir (V) for writing pens applied and constructed underneath the pen tip.

PATENT NO. 30935. Issued to Smith A. Skinner of West Berkshire, Vermont. A valve (f) separate from the agitator (h) with the spring pen carrier (B) is actuated under pressure to allow ink from storage (A) to flow to tip of pen and corrugated reservoir.

FRYING PANS AND GRATERS

Men purchased prying pans or made them out of canteens which had been split in half. Some soldiers took graters with them when they left home, while others made them by punching holes in their old canteens. With these improvised graters the men ground corn to a fineness in which it could be made into fried cakes. The iron frying pan shown here is 8 1/2 inches in diameter with an 11-inch handle. It was recovered off the blockade runner *Modern Greece.* A more common size of frying pan—identical in shape—has a diameter of 10 inches and has been found in several camp sites. Shown also are two relics of Fredericksburg, both made from canteens. The one on the right has a handle made by rivetting a barrel hoop section on a canteen, thus fashioning a crude frying pan. The other is a grater made by attaching a wooden handle to a canteen half.

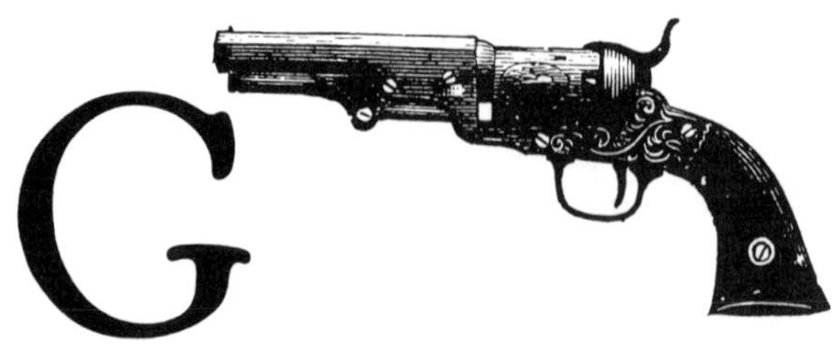

GAMES

Shown here are items used in some of the most popular games played by soldiers and sailors. Much information on these games is available in *The American Hoyle* by "Trumps", a book published in New York in 1864. The games described have not changed much since the war (1861-1865), but some terms have

Frying Pans and Grater

Robert M. Reilly

Fuse and Bullet Display. (All the bullets represent different types and calibers. They, like fuses, intrigue collectors!)

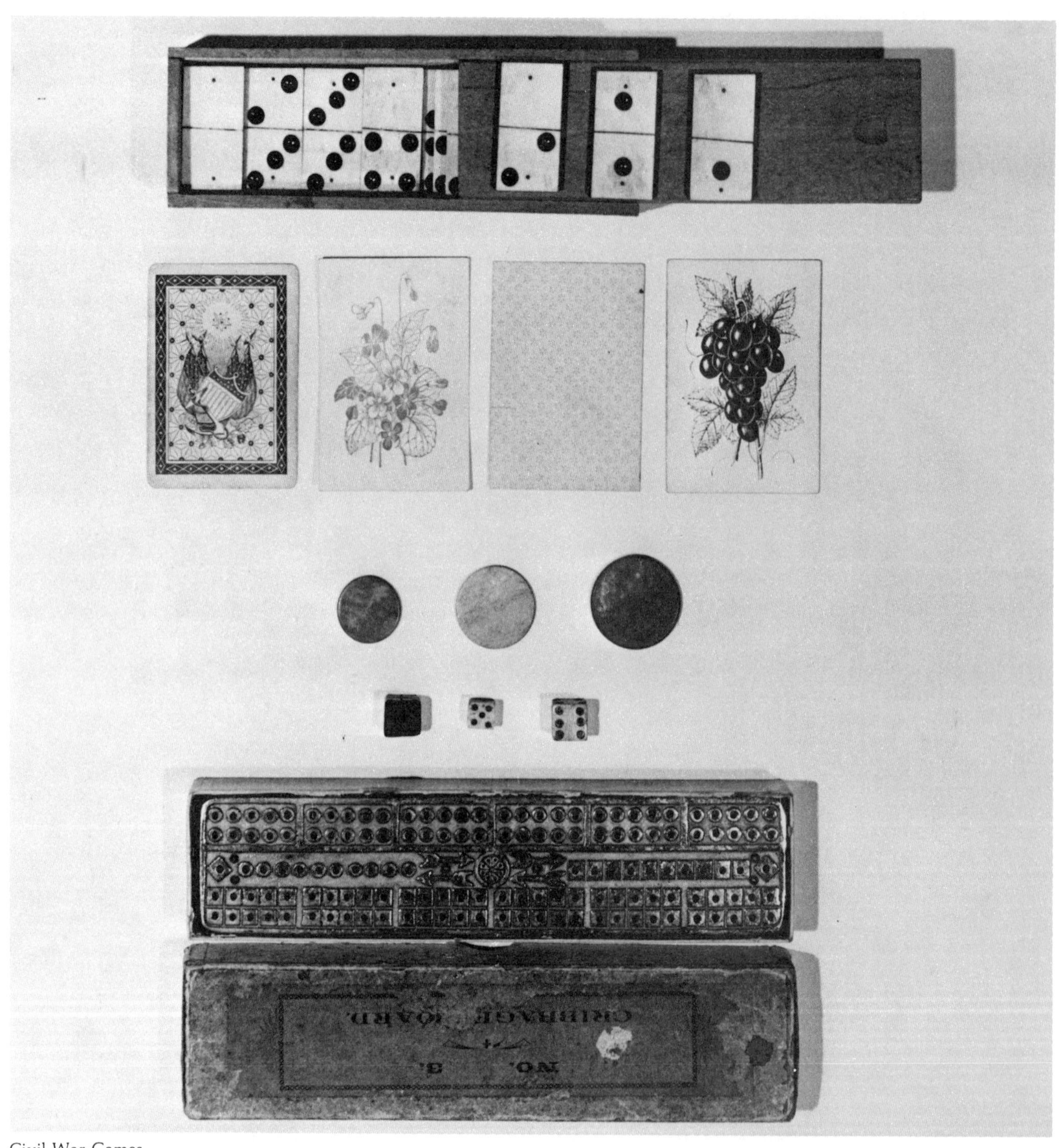

Civil War Games

changed. For example, the game of "checkers", was called "draughts", and poker was known as "poker" or "bluff". And, of course, "whist" has evolved into "bridge".

DRAUGHTS [CHECKER] BOARD. Made of cardboard, 15 x 15 1/2 inches when open. Marked:

D. S. Brown & Co.
Manufacturers of
Fine Toilet Soaps & Perfumes

Equipped with black and white wooden pieces—1 inch in diameter and marked on one side with the American eagle and on the other with:

D. S. Brown & Co.
Fine Soaps
New York

This company was active in New York during the war years.

Back of Checkerboard

Civil War Checkers

Civil War Dice and Poker Chips

Confederate Chess Set

Ken Mattern

Dice and Marbles from the grave of a Confederate Soldier, Vicksburg.

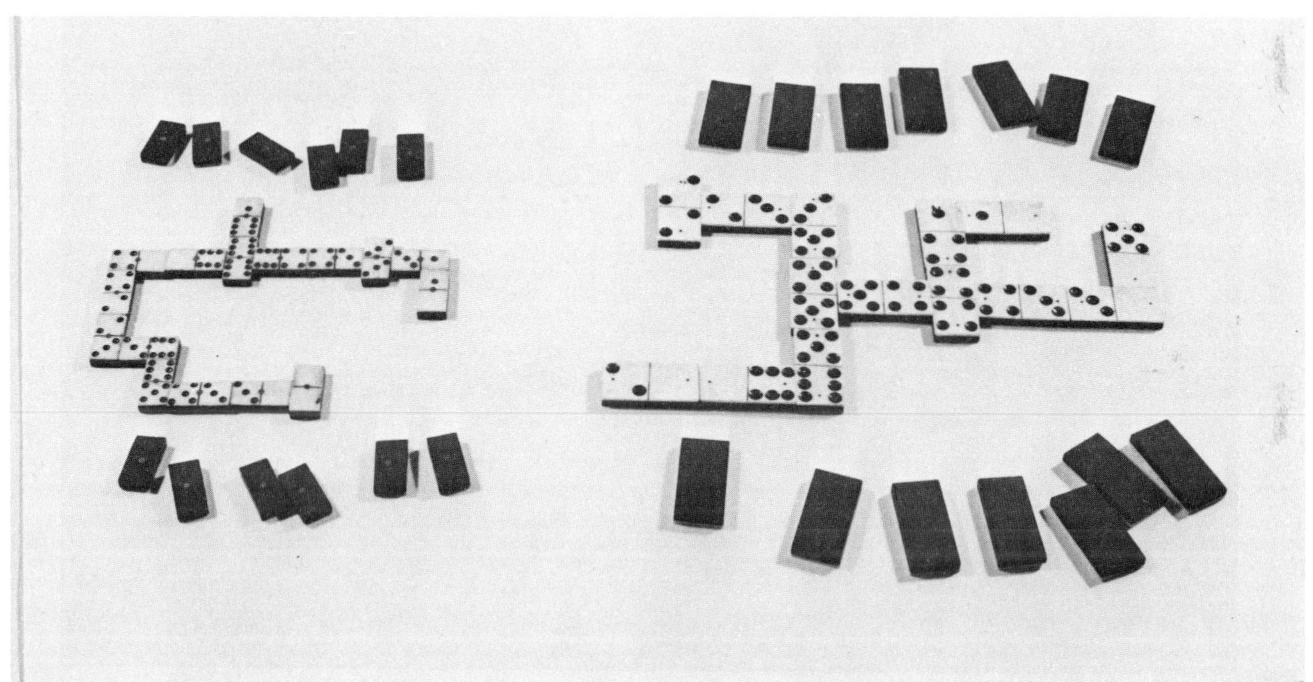

Two sets of ivory dominoes. The smaller dominoes (on the left) are 1 1/4 x 5/8 inches; the larger are 2 x 1 inches and came in a wooden box with sliding top.

CRIBBAGE BOARD. Metal top with wooden box, size 9 1/2 x 2 inches. Equipped with a cardboard box marked:

No. 3
Cribbage Board

DOMINO SET. Ivory pieces with ebony backs, carried in a wooden box with sliding cover. Size of box 7 1/2 x 2 3/8 inches. Size of each piece 2 x 1 inches.

DICE. Left to right: Ebony dice—type unknown, with lines cut on each side. 1/2 inch square. Found on battlefield of Cedar Creek, Va. Small dice—probably ivory, 5/16 inch square. Found in a fort of the "Defences of Washington".
Ivory piece 1/2 inch square found in C.S. camp, New Orleans.

POKER CHIPS. In addition to thin lead poker chips

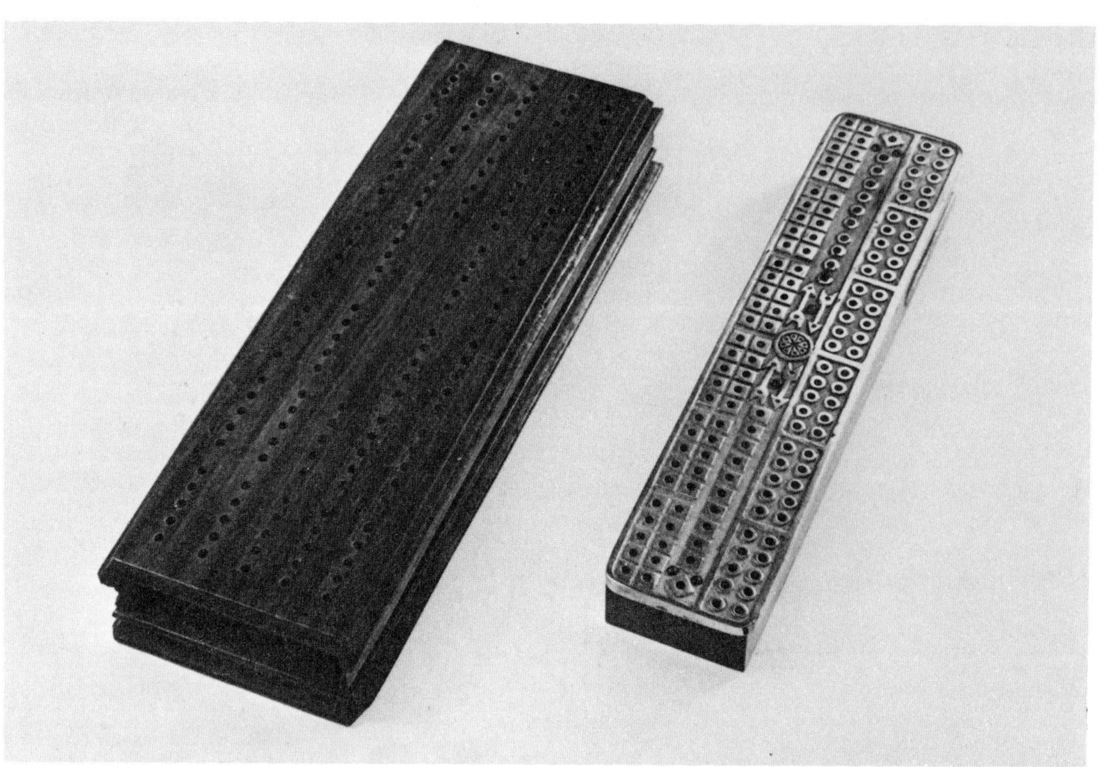

Two cribbage boards. The one on the left is of walnut and is 11 x 4 inches, while the metal one is 9 1/2x 2 1/8 inches and is marked:
No. 3 Cribbage Board

Very crude checker board. Pine wood. Probably made from a hardtack box in the field. Size is 21 x 14 3/4 inches. Marked on back:
Corp. C. Mann
Co. E 23rd Me Inf.

made by flattening bullets, the soldiers used poker chips of a material resembling plastic—possibly celluloid. Three common diameters are shown: 1, 1 1/4, 1 3/8 inches.

PLAYING CARDS: The normal size was 3 5/8 by 2 1/2 inches. Left to right:

U.S. card made by the "American Card Company".
English playing card—used by the C. S.
Card used at Libby Prison.
C. S. playing card.

CHESS SET [*C.S.*] This chess set was picked up inside the salient at Spotsylvania, May 2, 1864, by Charles Corslett of the Federal Army. The wooden chess pieces are of the following sizes: 2 7/8, 2, 1 3/4, 1 1/2, and 1 1/8 inches.

MARBLES. These dice and marbles, along with some Confederate buttons were found in a Confederate grave in Vicksburg. The dice and marbles were in the soldier's pocket.

Clay marbles have been found in Sherman's campsite (13th Corps area) in the Vicksburg area. Also five marbles were found in a Confederate campsite near Brandon, Mississippi.

[See author's article on Civil War Games in the *Sandlapper* Magazine for January-February 1975, published in Columbia, S.C.]

GARDNER POCKET KNIFE (No Picture)

On July 5, 1864, George H. Gardner of Philadelphia patented a unique pocket knife for soldiers in the field. The patent number is 43398. Gardner had served in a Pennsylvania regiment and realized the need for a combination pocket knife and musket tool. Accordingly, he designed a knife consisting of a cast handle with a spring-retained blade. A slot in the handle forms a nipple wrench while an additional blade forms a screw driver.

GREEK FIRE

"Greek Fire" refers to inflammable and destructive compositions, and was used in warfare during the Middle Ages. Probably the most notable example of its use was at the siege of Constantinople. However, as early as 429 B.C. (siege of Plataea) the Spartans used pitch and sulphur as an incendiary. Five years later (siege of Delium) a container holding pitch, sulphur, and burning charcoal was placed against the walls and fanned into flame by the use of bellows, the blast from which was conveyed through a hollow tree-trunk. A revival of the idea, using modern chemistry, was seen in the flame throwers of World War I and World War II.

In a few instances, at least, the Federals used Greek Fire as an incendiary against their adversaries. One of these occasions was during the siege of Charleston in 1863. However, its employment there led to such complaint as to its barbarity that further use of it during the war was very limited.

It was on Aug. 22, 1863, during the siege of Charleston, that the Federal's "Swamp Angel" fired 12 Parrott shells "filled with a fluid composition" and four other shells filled with "Short's Solidfied Greek Fire." The Confederate commander in Charleston, Gen. P. G. T. Beauregard, at once wrote the Federal commander, Gen. Q. A. Gillmore, that his firing "a number of the most destructive missiles ever used in war into the midst of a city taken unaware and filled with sleeping women and children (would) give you a bad eminence in history."

On August 23rd, 20 more shells, filled with Greek Fire, were fired from the gun in the marsh, i.e., the "Swamp Angel." Six of these shells exploded in the gun, doubtless shortening the life of the piece. On the 36th discharge of the "Swamp Angel," the breech blew out.

Apparently some of the Northern military experts were skeptical about the use of "Greek Fire" because the semi-official military journal *United States Service Magazine* for January, 1864 said in part:

"The attempt of Mr. Levi Short of Philadelphia to introduce into the department of the South, an effective combustible agent, designed to be employed in the bombardment of Charleston, is one of the many recent efforts to introduce inflammables into the warfare. We are not apprised of the composition of Mr. Short's invention, but it may safely be asserted that five out of every six of the shells loaded with his preparation, either from attrition of the particles in the rotary motion of the shell, or from some other cause, burst in the gun, or just in front of it; and it is a matter of extreme doubt whether a single shell thus charged ever reached the city."

However, we do know that some regimental histories attest to the use of Greek Fire at Charleston. Several inventors attempted to sell the Federal Government their version of Greek Fire compound. On one occasion, Lincoln was an interested observer of a demonstration of Greek Fire in which two 13-inch shells, charged with Greek Fire, were exploded. Each shell spewed fire 40-50 feet in the air and covered the ground over a 50-foot radius with a blaze lasting several minutes. But the

Cardboard Checkerboard made by Hill and Reed. Outside is stamped "The Defenders of the Union." Each white square has a photograph of a prominent General or official, e.g. Lincoln, Pope, Fremont, etc. Size is 15 x 15 inches.

Inlaid Wood Checker Board 16 1/4 x 16 1/4 inches square. Woods used are pine and walnut. On back of the board is the soldier who used it: J. D. Foster, Co. C 30 Massachusetts Infantry.

Cardboard Checker Board 15 1/2 x 15 1/2 inches square. Inside is marked:

D. S. Brown & Co.

Manufacturers of Fine Soaps & Perfumes

The wooden checkers are one inch in diameter with an American eagle on one side and:

D. S. Brown & Co. Fine Soaps New York

on the other.

Backgammon Game (See photograph of chess side of this set). Also found in this chess-backgammon set was the dice thrower shown here and the two small dice. Each dice is only 1/4 inch square.

Federal Chief of Ordnance (Ripley) refused to approve an order for 2,000 of the shells, of the type used in this demonstration. Nevertheless, Gen. B. F. Butler did take 100 of them along with him on his expedition against New Orleans. Whether he used them or not is not clear from available records. Nor has it been possible to determine the extent (if any) of the use of Greek Fire by the Confederates. Probably their use of it was not extensive.

GUN TOOL

The extremely rare gun tool for the Colt revolving rifle. Used by Iowa troops of Grierson's command at Lagrange, Tennessee. Total length is 4 1/8 inches; width at widest part is 3/4 inch.

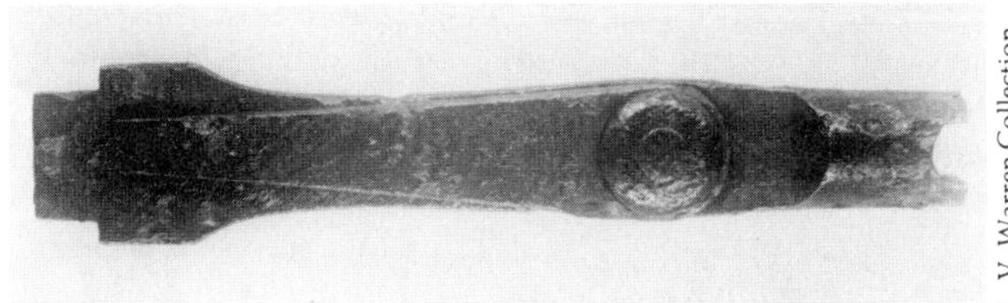

L. V. Warren Collection

Gun Tool

Collection of Norm Flayderman

Top: Confederate playing cards showing back design and nine of spades with picture of Jefferson Davis. *Bottom:* Two different decks of Civil War playing cards. These are enclosed in boxes and the boxes only are shown here.

HAND GRENADES

The most common hand grenade used during the Civil War was Ketchum's, patent of Aug. 20, 1861. It is listed in *Ordnance Memorandum* No. 1, 1865, as being of four different weights: 1, 2, 3 and 5-pounds. Also listed were 6 and 12-pound hand grenades. However, 4-pound Ketchum grenades were also produced.

The Ketchum grenade was of elongated form which expanded at the center, and was cast with an opening at each end. In one of these ends there was fitted a tube of soft metal with a flange at the outer end and a nipple for holding a percussion cap. The charge was placed in the shell, and when the grenade was to be thrown, a stick with four wings of pasteboard to be used as a guide in flight, was inserted in the other end. In the cap tube there was a plunger which exploded the percussion cap when the outer end of the tube struck a resisting object.

To prevent accidental discharge, the plunger which communicated the shock to the percussion cap was not inserted until the moment before the grenade was thrown.

Ketchum grenades have been found at Vicksburg and Port Hudson, and perhaps elsewhere. The Navy used 3- and 5-pound Ketchum grenades as regular issue on board ship, while the Army used 1-, 2-, 3-, 4-, and 5-pound Ketchum grenades.

The inventor of this grenade, William F. Ketchum of Buffalo, New York patented his invention on August 20, 1861. According to the patent description (No. 33089) the grenade was unique in the combination of the tubing and concealed cap therein, with the adjustable plunger and adjustable winged guide. Probably the monopoly of use by the Ketchum grenade was the extreme danger involved in using other competing types, such as the Hanes. It is probable that the pasteboard guide for the Ketchum grenade did not materially aid the heavy body of the grenade in flight. One wonders if perhaps the troops did not frequently throw the grenades without bothering to insert the pasteboard guide in the grenades at all! Thus far, research has not given me the answer one way or another. We do know that frequently both Federals and Confederates rolled or tossed activated artillery projectiles in lieu of grenades at their adversary. However, Ketchum hand grenades were regular ordnance issue in both the Federal Army and Navy.

In his *Military Dictionary* (1864) Scott says that a hand grenade 2 1/2 inches in diameter could be thrown about 26 yards. Ketchum's hand grenade was a small oblong percussion shell which communicated the shock to the percussion cap which was not inserted in its place until the moment before the grenade was thrown.

Another type of hand grenade was completely different. This type, known as the "Excelsior", was patented by W. W. Hanes, August 26, 1862. It was a cast-iron sphere with an inner and outer shell. The inner shell was 2 1/2 inches in diameter and contained the powder. On the outside of this inner shell were screwed 14 nipples which took the regular musket percussion caps. The outer shell was in two halves, in which was inserted the inner shell, the two halves screwing together. Before firing, percussion caps were placed on the nipples; when the grenade struck an object, at least one of the 14 percussion caps was sure to receive the impact and thus explode the shell. Since the outer shell was in two parts, these parts would break up into many destructive fragments. This projectile was so dangerous to handle that only a few were made.

HAVERSACK

When in the field each soldier carried his rations in a haversack made out of canvas, cloth, leather, or similar material. The haversack was slung over the right shoulder and rested on the left hip, with the tin cup usually buckled on the outside. Many officers purchased leather haversacks of elaborate design, often a shiny, patent leather container that would hold only one day's rations. These fancy affairs had a convenient pocket in which the officer might carry a flask—for medicinal purposes—while his reserve supplies were transported by wagon or upon the broad shoulders of his servant, usually a loyal and rugged "contraband."

The regulation (issue) haversacks were often marked with the number and name of the regiment, the company letter, and the soldier's company number. This regulation haversack was better made than those sold by private firms. It had an inside lining which kept the rations from contact with the outer haversack lining covering; but these linings soon disappeared as the men cut them up for use as gun cleaners. Coffee and sugar were sometimes carried in small individual bags inside the haversack, but the haversack itself soon became quite odorous with its mixing of stale parts of bacon and other rations.

From haversacks now in museums and collections, and from the descriptions furnished by veterans of the war, we know that there are many types of haversacks but apparently there were two main types issued: canvas and black oilcloth. All types held about a peck although varying in size. One of the most common issue types was about 13 inches long, 12 1/2 inches wide, and was carried by a 32-inch strap sewn on the haversack itself. This strap was about 1 3/4 inches wide.

In theory all haversacks were waterproof, but once they became well worn they were no better than cloth for keeping water out. A penetrating rain was sure to make a mess of the contents. Although the canvas and cloth types were issued white, a short period of active service made them nearly black. As one soldier put it: "By the time one of these (white canvas haversacks) had been in use for a few weeks as a receptacle for chunks of fat bacon and fresh meat, damp sugar tied up in a rag—perhaps a piece of an old shirt—potatoes and other vegetables that might be picked up along the route, it took on the color of a printing office towel. It would have been alike offensive to the eyes and nose of a fastidious person."

A veteran soon became accustomed to the appearance and fragrance of his haversack and used it with equanimity. At the halt he would drop by the roadside, draw his grimy and well-greased haversack around in front of him, and "from its dark and odorous receses bring forth what tasted better to him than the daintiest morsel to the palate of an epicure." Recruits were initially distressed at the obvious lack of refined living which the haversack represented, but then, they were equally appalled at the retrogression in table manners exhibited by the veterans. A few days' association with their new comrades-in-arms and with hunger soon brought them around, and they too concentrated on food, not the niceties.

Occasionally a soldier would attempt to wash his haversack, but failed for lack of laundry facilities.

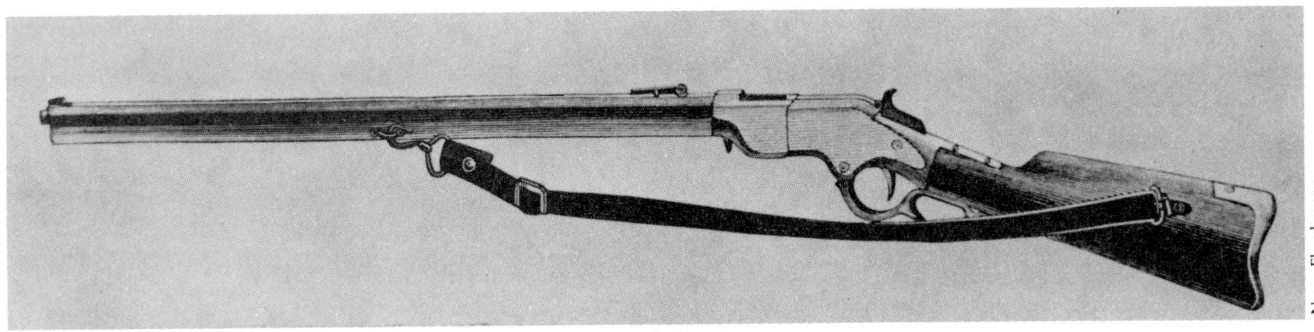
Norm Flayderman

Henry Rifle

HENRY RIFLE

One of the enigmas of the War has always been the question as to the refusal of the Federal Government to use a breech-loading rifle in large quantities. The question is both sensible and fair. Several efficient breech-loaders had been patented before April, 1861, and it is not mere hindsight to insist that they should have been officially adopted and used. It is true that some breech-loading carbines (Burnside, Smith, Gallagher and others) were used. But the best breech-loading rifles, such as the Sharps and Spencer were only used in limited numbers and the Henry, almost not at all.

The Henry deserves a second glance. It was probably the best all-around rifle that saw service in the War. Patented in 1860, it was a fine magazine rifle which the Federal army did not use in any quantity at all. The Federal Government purchased 1,731 Henry rifles and 4,610,400 cartridges from July 23, 1863 to November 7, 1865. These arms were also purchased by several states to arm militia companies. About 10,000 are believed to have been made. But most of the rifles were used because the men saw their superiority over the single shot muzzle-loader and bought them out of their own pocket. In fact, the Government was so determined in its refusal to accept the Henry repeating rifle that it informed the makers of the gun that their weapons would not be accepted unless the manufacturers would arm a whole regiment, and keep it supplied at the company's expense.

Members of Birge's Sharpshooters (66th Illinois Infantry) replaced their "target rifles" and purchased the Henry rifle at their own expense. The rifle cost the men $50.00 apiece. Thus, the men owned their own guns but the Government furnished the cartridges. Another Illinois regiment, the 7th Infantry, was also armed with the Henry, obtained by the men at their own expense. The regimental historian of the 7th commented that the sacrifice of the men in buying their Henrys was "worthy of loyal commendation." It was also a very wise sacrifice! The color guard of this regiment was equipped with the Henry. The 7th Illinois fought brilliantly under Sherman. Another regiment which used the Henry Rifle was the 97th Indiana Infantry. When men were wounded they often sold their rifles to men from other units who were delighted to acquire such an excellent weapon. These Western regiments demonstrated the usefulness of the Henry rifle in combat but it was only late in the war that a beneficial change was made in the office of Federal Chief of Ordnance.

The new man saw the value of a weapon that could be fired in a prone position and also used a copper-cased cartridge which rainy weather didn't affect. One of the "might have beens" of the war was in the minds of Confederate generals like E. P. Alexander, who believed that had the Federal infantry been armed from the first with even the breech-loaders available in 1861, the war would have been terminated within a year.

Using a caliber .44 Henry rim-fire ammunition, the Henry had a long tubular magazine under the barrel, holding 12 rim-fire cartridges loaded from the front. The piece was operated by lowering the trigger guard lever, which mechanically slid the carrier block backwards, cocked the hammer, extracted and ejected the empty shell, and on its return to closed position, pushed the next round into the chamber. Total length was 43.5 inches, and the weight was 9.25 pounds.

In 1866, Winchester Repeating Arms Company took over the New Haven Arms Company which had produced the Henry Rifle.

HORSE EQUIPMENTS

This subject has been covered in the first volume of the *Encyclopedia.* However, due to the discovery of metallic portions of the equipments in attics and on battlefields and camp sites, some typical examples are illustrated here.

MARTINGALE INSIGNIA. The martingale was used to a limited extent but was eventually discarded as non-essential. It consisted of a forked strap which passed through the noseband to the girth between the horse's forelegs. Shown here are three. The ones with the original leather portion were used by Colonel John McConnell of the 5th Illinois Cavalry. The brass portion of the martingale is 2 3/4 inches at its widest part.

In the second illustration, the three martingales are as follows:

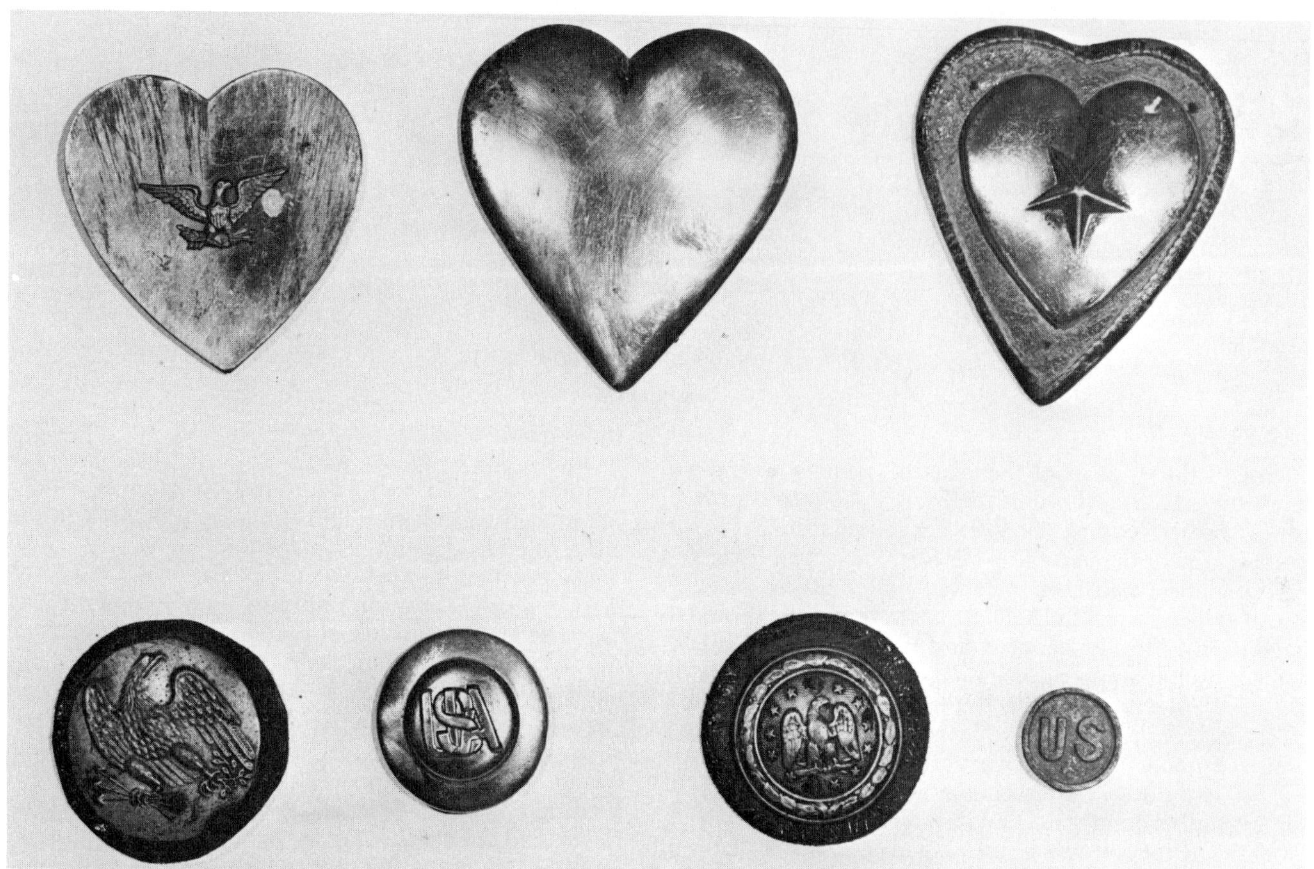

Martingales and Bridle Rosettes

The insignia with the Colonel's "eagle" is 3 1/8 inches at its widest part; the plain insignia is 3 5/8 inches at its widest part; while the insignia with the star is 2 1/2 inches at its widest part (brass portion only). The plain martingale (in the center) was the most common in use during the war.

BRIDLE ROSETTES. The two rosettes with the eagle motif are 2 3/8 and 1 3/4 inches in diameter respectively. These two were used by the same officer (Colonel John McConnell) mentioned above. The enlisted man's bridle rosette with the intertwined U.S.A. is 2 inches in diameter.

Shown also is a bridle bit rosette, 1 1/8 inches in diameter with U.S. in bold letters.

HOSPITAL TRAINS

For a considerable period of the Civil War the railway transportation of sick and wounded of the Federal as well as of the Confederate armies was carried on in the ordinary passenger and luggage cars. This transportation was generally described as having involved much severe suffering due to absence of necessary equipment and the motion of the cars. However, Dr. Letterman, Medical Director of the Army of the Potomac, mentions the moving of more than 9,000 sick and wounded in railway cars with great comfort in June 1863. This was accomplished by moving all bed patients in the beds they occupied in the hospitals and placing these beds on hay in the railway cars, and later removing these same beds carefully from the trains and placing them on transports going up the Potomac to Washington. Medical officers and supplies accompanied every train, and when required, went on the transports for the last leg of the journey. "Many of those most severely wounded, cases in which the femur was extensively fractured, assured Dr. Letterman they had not suffered . . . .up to the time of their being placed on the transports." The removal of this convoy of sick and wounded, numbering 9,025 men, began on the morning of June 12th, and before 6 p.m. on June 14th, all had left Aquia for Washington.

Towards the end of 1863, the Federal Government adopted a system of specially fitted transport cars for the lines of railway running in the directions on which the armies were operating. These railway ambulance cars were only contrived for the reception of bed patients. The external frame and general arrangement of the car itself remained unchanged from its former use as a passenger car. However, the interior of

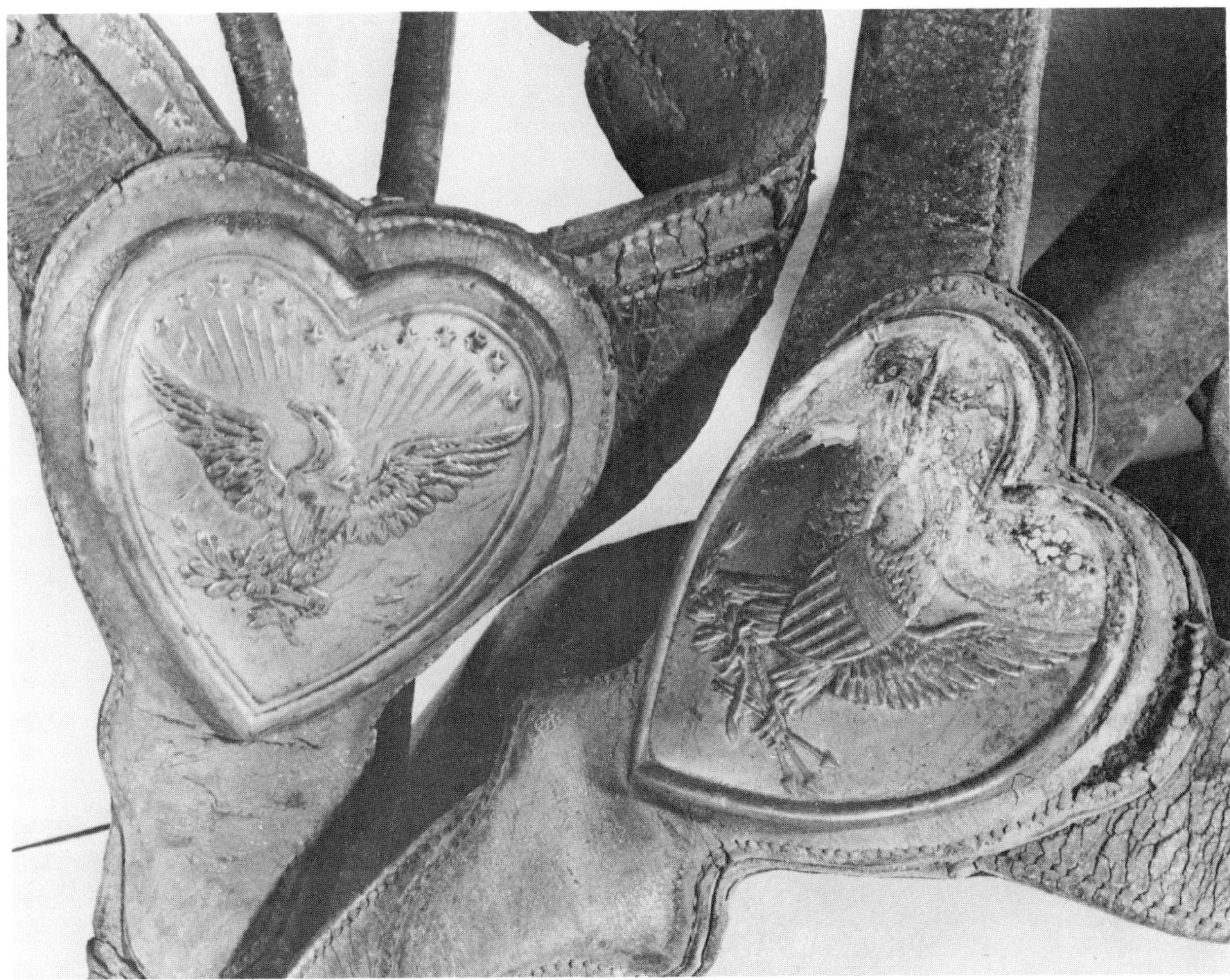

Martingales used by Colonel John McConnell

the car was altered completely. The passenger car had a door at each end and a central passage down the whole length of the car. In converting the passenger car for hospital use, the seats were removed, and standing frames erected so that stretchers could be secured to them for recumbent sick or wounded soldiers. These frames were placed at such intervals that the space between them corresponded in length to the length of the ordinary field stretcher. Each frame had strong projecting pegs, on which were placed massive circular bands of vulcanized india rubber. These india rubber bands, when suspended, held the ends of the stretcher poles.

The cars were well lighted by windows in the sides and doors of the vehicles, as well as by panes of glass along a portion of the roof which was elevated, like a skylight, above the general level. The entire interior could be quickly ventilated by opening the windows and doors, while the admission of rain was prevented by projecting eaves. Each car was furnished with a stove, so arranged that the car could be both heated and ventilated in case of severe weather preventing the windows from being opened. Good ventilation was essential since each car accommodated 32 wounded patients.

When a train of "ambulance cars" as they were called was travelling along a rail line, its nature was plainly indicated by a hospital flag near the engine, and also by the words "Hospital Train" in large letters on the car next to the engine tender.

A hospital train carried with it nearly all the equipment and medical supplies necessary for the sick and wounded as would be found in a base hospital in the rear areas. In one car was a specially arranged stove for heating water, and suited for such cooking purposes as preparation of tea and soup. A certain number of hospital attendants, as well as surgeons, accompanied the trains, and even means were supplied for verbal communication between the surgeons and attendants by speaking tubes attached along the cars. Those hospital cars furnished by the U.S. Sanitary Commission were grooved to run upon railways of different guages, so as to avoid needless transfer of patients.

Civil War Horse Bits and Spur

The method of transporting sick and wounded by rail seems to have functioned well and met with approval of everyone concerned with it. The comfort and safety which characterized the care of sick and wounded in hospital cars contrasted very sharply with the suffering experienced by patients travelling in the ordinary passenger cars. European observers soon reported favorably on the American system of hospital cars and a similar system was authorized for use in Prussia during the campaign of 1866.

HYPODERMIC INJECTOR

Found in Grierson's camp at Lagrange, Tennessee. Made of pewter, this injector is 2 1/2 inches long. The cotton pad is still intact after a century in the ground! Diameter of this injector is 9/16 of an inch.

Hypodermic Injector

IDENTIFICATION DISCS

American soldiers have used "dog tags" only since World War I. In the Civil War, troops went into combat

Attention, Soldiers!

In solid 18 k. gold, $2 50.

Every soldier should have a BADGE WITH HIS NAME MARKED DISTINCTLY upon it. The Subscribers will forward to any soldier in the Army a solid Silver Badge, with his Name, Company, and Regiment engraved upon it, on receipt of One Dollar. The above cut represents size and style of Badge furnished. It can be fastened to any garment. Adress

DROWNE & MOORE,
Manufacturing Jewelers, 208 Broadway, New York.

Cavalry and Artillery Pins in Fine Silver, with Name. Samples sent to Soldiers on receipt of $1 25; also Army Corps Badges for $1 00. Liberal discount made to agents.
E. N. FOOTE & CO.,
Manufacturers of Jewelry, 208 Broadway, New York.

Cavalry and Artillery.

Solid Silver, $1 25. Solid Silver, $1 25.

Solid 18 k. Gold, $5 00. Solid 18 k. Gold, $5 00.

Sent by mail on receipt of Price. Also all kinds Corps, Co., and Division Pins, engraved to order, by the single one, 100, or 1000, and sent to any part of the country. Terms cash in advance. Send for a circular. Address
DROWNE & MOORE,
Manufacturing Jewelers, 208 Broadway, New York.

SOLDIERS' COMPANY PINS
And Corps Badges.

Constantly on hand and Engraved to Order, and sent free on receipt of Price.

Every Co. From A. to M., solid Silver.......... $1 00
Solid Silver Letters in Gold Relief............ 1 50
Solid 18 k. Gold............................ 3 50
Solid Silver Corps Badges (plain).............. 1 00
" " " " (enameled).......... 1 50
" Gold " " " 5 00

Cavalry Badges

Terms Cash in advance. Send for a Catalogue. Address C. L. BALCH & CO., 208 Broadway, New York.

50,000 Agents Wanted.

One Agent wanted in every Regiment, Hospital, and on board every Naval Vessel. For $1, will send you as sample, with a Circular giving full instructions to Agents, either a Fine Gold Pen and Pencil, or a beautiful New Style Vest Chain, or Chatelaine Chain and Pin, or Guard Chain, or an Engraved Spring Locket, or a Seal Stone, California Diamond, or Chased Ring, or a fine Gold California Diamond Pin, or a New Style Set of Jewelry, or a solid Silver Shield, or either Army Corps Pin, with your Name, Co., and Reg., handsomely engraved upon it, or a Kearney Cross in Gold Plate; and, for 50 cents, I will send a beautiful Union League Pin, in fine Gold Plate.
B. T. HAYWARD, Manufacturing Jeweler,
Box 4876. 208 Broadway, N. Y.

Soldiers'
COMPANY PINS.

Constantly on hand and Engraved to order, and sent free on receipt of Price.

Solid Silver, $1. Solid Silver, $1.

Solid 18 k. Gold, $3 50 each.

Solid Silver, with Letters in GOLD relief, $1 50.

The above are fac-simile cuts, handsomely engraved with name and regiment—with the letter representing the Co. in BOLD RELIEF.

Corps Badges

Sent free by Mail or Express on receipt of Price.

Badges for the 1st, 2d, 3d, 5th, 6th, 11th, and 12th Army Corps.

1st Division Enameled Red, 2d Division White, 3d Division Blue.

Prices of Corps Badges.

1st Division, either Corps, Sterling Silver, enameled Red, $1 50
1st " " 16 karat Gold " 4 00
2d " " Sterling Silver " 1 00
2d " " 16 karat Gold " 4 00
3d " " Sterling Silver, enameled blue 1 50
3d " " 16 karat Gold " 4 00

Terms Cash in advance.
Send for a Catalogue.
Address J. G. PACKARD & CO.,
208 Broadway, New York.

Advertisements from Harper's Weekly. *Courtesy James Gregg, Jr.*

Identification Discs

with no assurance that, in case of death, their bodies could be identified or their ultimate fate made known to "next of kin." In the Federal Army alone there were 184,791 men captured or missing in the war. Among the missing were thousands who were buried and still remain on the records as "unknown." These men, usually strangers to the burial details, were those "who never came back." Many men who died under the surgeon's knife at field hospitals in rear areas, were only "bodies" to hospital attendants. The graves of thousands more who died in Confederate prisons are marked by one word, "unknown." When one examines regimental histories or reports of state adjutant generals, he is struck by the frequency of such entries as "never heard from" or "missing at the battle of . . ."

Much of the heartache caused by the uncertainty of a son's fate would have been spared the mother if the Government had issued some means of identification to the soldiers. On several occasions, men going into combat improvised means of identification which their Government failed to provide. At Cold Harbor, in preparation for what was obviously going to be a desperate assault, men were observed calmly writing their names and home addresses on slips of paper and pinning them on the backs of their coats, so that their dead bodies could be identified on the field. History records that many of these slips of paper were useful before the day was over.

However, some soldiers on their own initiative made reasonably sure of their identification in case they became casualities. Often such items of equipment as haversacks and knapsacks were stenciled with the owner's name and regiment. Occasionally a soldier would scratch his name and unit in the back of the brass U.S. Buckle of his waist belt. Notebooks, diaries, and letters from home were invaluable in identifying a man killed in battle.

The more farsighted (or pessimistic!) soldiers provided themselves with items sold by private concerns before leaving their home States or purchased them from enterprising sutlers on arrival at the theater of war. These items were of two general types. The first type was the more expensive and was widely advertised in *Harper's Weekly, Leslie's,* and other popular periodicals. This type was a pin, usually of gold or silver, and quite ornate. Generally these pins were shaped to suggest a branch of service and were engraved with the soldier's name and unit. Often the pin was in the shape of the army corps badge but must not be confused with the Corps badges as issued by the Government for wear on hat or cap. The privately purchased badges were usually worn on the coat.

The second type of identification markers were similar to the "dog tags" of World War I and early World War II pattern, but were of brass or lead instead of aluminum. These tags had a hole for attaching a string to be worn around the neck. There were several variations of these tags. Usually they had on one side an eagle or shield and such phrases as "War for the Union," or "Liberty, Union, and Equality." The other side had the soldier's name and unit and sometimes a list of battles in which he had participated. Lettering was machine stamped. On one occasion, at least, nearly an entire regiment went into an active campaign with this type of identification disc. In July, 1864, the 14th New Hampshire Infantry, passing through Charlestown, West Virginia on its way to the Shenandoah Valley, purchased many of these brass discs from a sutler who had set up his tent by the roadside. He stamped each disc purchased with name, company, and regiment.

The lead discs included on one side such legends as "Gen. Geo. G. McClellan, U.S.A.," and "First in the hearts of his soldiers," or the New York State coat of arms with "Union and Constitution," and "N.Y.S. Vols." with the dates "1776" and "1861." The soldier's name and regiment were stamped on the reverse side.

All the badges and discs mentioned here, and other types as well, were used by Federal soldiers during the war, but there was no official issuance of identification media of any kind to Federal troops in the Civil War.

Herb Peck, Jr.

Infantry Accouterments of an Unidentified Federal Soldier

INFANTRY ACCOUTERMENTS

Today the term "accouterments" refers to the equipment of a soldier with the exception of his weapons and clothing. In the Civil War the term "accoutrements" (as they spelled it then), or "equipments" usually applied only to the items worn on the belt. In the case of the infantry soldier this included the waist belt, cartridge box, cap box, and bayonet scabbard. The cartridge box was always included even though it usually was not worn on the belt but was carried by means of a wide strap resting on the left shoulder and passing diagonally over the body with the cartridge box proper resting on the right hip or slightly to the rear of the right hip. The black leather cartridge box held forty rounds of ammunition. Attached to the cross belt holding the cartridge box and almost directly over the heart was a brass eagle or state ornament that was decorative but, due to its polished surface, very noticeable. Soldiers found it "puzzling to explain the necessity of the breastplate, except it be to furnish a conspicuous target for the enemy." It certainly did that; the author has one with a bullet hole almost dead center in it—taken from the battlefield of Chancellorsville. The cartridge box was decorated with a brass oval shield stamped with the letters "U.S.", "C.S." or letters and insignia designating the state, e.g. Pennsylvania, Virginia, etc., but cartridge boxes made later in the war often do not have this brass plate; they merely have the letters "U.S." or "C.S." stamped into the leather. Apparently the Ordnance Departments learned their lesson in this regard! The interior of the cartridge box was divided into tin compartments which made it difficult for recruits to get out the cartridges in the excitement of combat. Veterans often carried the cartridges in their pockets, and in permanent or semipermanent positions, stacked them up in front of them on the parapet for quick use. Incidentally, the tin containers or "liners" are among the most frequently found relics by the mine detector enthusiasts today, who comb the battlefields.

In 1861 and 1862, soldiers, especially the Federals, were frequently ordered to carry 60, 80, or even 100 rounds of ammunition into combat with them. Since the cartridge boxes only held 40 rounds, it was necessary to carry the extra cartridges in the pockets where they were easily blown up by loose matches, or in the haversacks where the paper cartridges would break open, allowing the powder to mix with the coffee or sugar. As the volunteers became veterans and learned to shoot more carefully, they began to husband their ammunition and the overloading of men with surplus ammunition became a less common practice.

Some regiments in the field, and even in garrison, dispensed with the cross belt and wore the cartridge box on the waist belt. But a full box of ammunition produced an undue weight on the loins. Some commanders forbade, under penalty of a fine, the wearing of the cartridge box on the waist belt.

The waist belt was of black leather fastened by an oval belt plate similar in appearance to the plate on the cartridge box. The regulation belt plate for enlisted men was of brass, oval in shape, with "U.S." or "C.S. in large black letters in the middle. Some of the regiments, especially Confederate, wore their state letters, as for example, "N.C.,", "S.C."; "S.N.Y." :(New York), "OVM" (Ohio Volunteer Militia), and "VMM" (Volunteer Maine Militia). It is in this field of belt buckles and cartridge box plates that much of the unethical and dishonest misrepresentation as to genuineness of relics is being carried on. Every collector should be very cautious about the "unquestioned authenticity" of such items and should check carefully with recognized specialists before spending the inflated prices asked.

Non-commissioned officers wore a belt similar to commissioned officers. This belt had a rectangular belt plate with such designs as a large American eagle with floral designs or the state coat of arms in such regiments as Louisiana units. Carried on the waist belt of enlisted men were the cap box and bayonet scabbard. The cap box, containing percussion caps, was of black leather and was worn between the belt plate and the right hip.

The bayonet scabbard, usually of black leather, but occasionally of steel was suspended from the waist belt on the left side of the body. There were two main types: those for the triangular bayonets and those for the saber bayonets.

Regulations forbade the cutting of any of the belts without the captain's permission. In the early part of the war, those men in the Federal Army who cut their waist belts to get a better fit were often charged with new ones; and if a man wore his cartridge box on his waist belt (instead of using the cross belt) he was fined as much as one-fifth a month's pay. Later on many veterans wore their cartridge boxes this way. As the 150th Pennsylvania Infantry marched towards Chancellorsville a few of its members were caught in the act of removing the metallic eagle from the cross belts "but a threat of punishment put a stop to this unwarranted scheme."

Confederate soldiers and Federal troops from the west were constantly amazed at the "spit and polish" required of men in the better disciplined Army of the Potomac. In the 19th Massachusetts Infantry "dress coats with brass shoulder scales and leather neckstocks were issued, and when not drilling or on guard duty, the men spent their spare moments in cleaning "the brasses." As one of the regiment correctly put it: "If any men ever earned thirteen dollars a month, we did." It is not surprising that men who were forced to wear brightly polished items into battle finally rebelled against such stupid requirements. One of the regiments which suffered heavy losses in Burnside's blood-bath at Fredericksburg was the 13th New Hampshire. The month after the battle (January 1863) a serious disturbance, amounting almost to mutiny, arose in the regiment over wearing brasses, "a miserable, old-fashioned piece of regular army foolishness." The 13th solved the problem by burying "the entire mess of stuff" in one deep hole at midnight. As the men put it: "We came down here to put down the rebellion, not to garnish ourselves with old brass, and poor at that, and spend hour after hour in polishing it."

Of course, this was the crux of the whole problem. Discipline was essential to both armies, and one way of instilling a sense of discipline in the green troops, whether from the lumber communities of Maine or from the bayou country of Louisiana, was to insist on the minutiae of dress and equipment. But much equipment was unnecessary and, furthermore, rigid insistence on a parade-ground appearance, had no place in such terrain as the Chickahominy swamps and the men knew it. The Confederates were much more practical and realistic in this respect. They had a keener appreciation of the value of mingling with the terrain or even camouflage. But both sides kept their muskets and bayonets brightly polished with a resultant disclosure of troop positions right up to Appomattox! And this, in spite of the fact that such weapons as the British Enfield was issued either blued or browned. And, all too often, the men at once began to remove this finish and soon their muskets were "bright and shiny" all ready for an alert enemy sniper!

Since the Confederacy was short of leather it was necessary to import leather equipments and also to find substitutes. One of these substitutes was the use of prepared cotton cloth, stitched together in three or four thicknesses. Instead of brass, lead and even wood fasteners were used. Many of the cartridge boxes used by Confederates were imported from England as part of the equipments used with Enfield muskets. Confederate-made cartridge boxes and cap boxes, especially those marked "C.S." are very rare. Most Confederate equipments were militia items, imported equipments, and captured materiel—sometimes with "C.S." buckles and cartridge box plates replacing the "U.S." on the original equipments. Probably more frequently, however, was the use of Federal equipments and accouterments with no attempt to change anything. Federal-made items were generally well made and there was no time to be fussy.

Throughout the war new types of equipments and adaptations of existing items were constantly being made. Common sense asserted itself. For example, in May 1862, veteran troops on the Peninsula soon wearied of their heavy knapsacks, extra blankets, and useless knickknacks. The inventive genius of some soldier produced what was termed the "horse collar". An army blanket was spread on the ground and a few essential articles of clothing selected from the discarded knapsack and spread thereon; then the blanket and its contents were carefully and tightly rolled on, the ends brought together and firmly tied. This circular roll was put on over the head and rested on one shoulder and against the opposite side under the arm; in this manner it was easily and lightly carried. When tired of carrying it on one shoulder it would be shifted over to the other. At a halt for a few minutes it was used as a cushion to sit on. It was found to be, on fatiguing marches, a great relief from the much despised knapsack with its cutting straps and awkward, heavy back burden. Ever after, thousands of the Army of the Potomac carried their luggage of personal effects in no other way; so that the "horse collar" was a success from the start. When once settled in winter quarters new knapsacks were easily drawn from the quartermaster. In this way, commanders who adhered rigidly to regulations could have their men "correctly" equipped in winter quarters.

Other Federal units, like the 4th New Jersey Infantry, late in the war turned in their knapsacks, cartridge boxes and belts, and received in exchange the Colonel Mann accouterments. The designer of these accouterments, Colonel William D. Mann, resigned his commission in the 7th Michigan Cavalry and went to Washington early in 1864 where he persuaded the Ordnance Department of the worth of his improved system of cavalry and infantry accouterments. The Government soon gave large orders for their manufacture and most of the regiments which used them apparently liked them, mainly because the suspenders arrangement kept the weight of the accouterments off their loins or kidneys.

Surprisingly little is known of Marine Corps accouterments except in a general way. The few photographs extant which depict Marines wearing their equipments indicate that those equipments are generally similar to Army items. By Marine Corps regulations "all enlisted men . . . wore white waist belts of the French pattern with the French clasp and knapsack sliding slings; the cartridge box . . . was attached to the belt by a leather loop . . . to slide by it along the belt, the bayonet scabbard was attached to the belt by a frog also sliding on the belt . . ." These equipments appear to have been somewhat similar in general appearance to those worn by the Army during the late 1840's and during the 1850's. As with Army units, Marine NCOs and musicians wore swords. Marine Corps knapsacks were of black cow-skin, but their haversacks were of the same material, size and form, as those issued to the United States Army. Marines also used Army canteens.

INFERNAL MACHINE (C.S.)

The activities of"enemy sabotage agents" in the last two World Wars have received so much publicity that few of us realize that similar exploits were performed by a Confederae agent and companion late in the war. The Federal Army nearly lost its commanding general through the audacity of this unsung hero of the South.

On August 9, 1864, about noon, the strategic Federal supply base at City Point, Virginia, was shattered by a deafening roar. Shot and shell were hurled high in the air, almost killing General Grant and wounding one of his staff. A barge loaded with ordnance stores had blown up, killing and wounding some 200 employees and soldiers, knocking down over 600 feet of warehouses, and tearing up 180 feet of wharf. Seventy men were killed and 130 wounded by this explosion. How did it happen?

In the first place, this "accident" was not entirely unexpected. At the very moment it occured, General Sharpe, the official "spy catcher" for the Army of the Potomac, had been telling Grant and his staff that there were Confederate spies in the vital supply depot at City Point and that he had a plan for detecting and catching them. But General Sharpe was a bit too late. The explosion took place while he was outlining his plan to prevent it.

No one could figure out the cause of the disaster. Accordingly, General Grant appointed a member of his staff (General Horace Porter) as president of a board of officers to an investigation which led nowhere. Most of the witnesses present attributed the "accident" to careless handling of the ammunition by the laborers who were unloading it, although some apparently suspected that it was the work of enemy agents.

It was not until seven years after the war was over that the final truth came out. In 1872, a Virginian called on General Porter to complain that the commissioner of patents was not treating him fairly with respect to some patents. To impress General Porter, the Virginian emphasized his skill as an inventor and explained that he had devised an "infernal machine" during the war which had been very successful. This "infernal machine" had consisted of a small box filled with explosives, with a clock-work attachment which would be so set as to trigger an explosion at any given time. The Virginian explained that he and a companion, both dressed as laborers, had passed the Federal lines, and succeeded in reaching City Point, knowing this to be the base of supplies for the Federal Army operating against Richmond. By mingling with the laborers who were unloading the ammuntion, this Virginian and his companion got on board the boat, placed their "infernal machine" among the ammunition, and set the clockwork so that the explosion would occur in half an hour. This enabled them to get to a sufficient distance from the place so as not to be suspected. As a result of this occurrence, members of Grant's staff, set up an informal headquarters guard to protect their chief in the future from similar attempts at assassination.

So far as we know, there was no similar sabotage attempt made again during the war, although Grant was one of the men whom Booth picked out for assassination in April 1865.

INSIGNIA

No phase of Civil War collecting is more confusing and difficult than identification of insignia. A volume could be written on this subject alone. Regiments, and even companies, had their own distinguishing insignia; states had their coats-of-arms; militia regiments by the hundreds, on both sides of the conflict, added to the chaotic list. Here we can describe only some of the basic insignia as well as little-known badges of several of the arms and services. Lack of space prevents even mentioning the specific insignia of separate companies, battalions, and regiments.

Additionally, many militia regiments were mustered into active service for only short periods, such as thirty or ninety days. Often these units wore their traditional insignia. Some eventually adopted the regulation Army insignia but, after leaving the Federal service and reverting to the inactive status, resumed the use of their old state, local militia, or homeguard insignia. Some of these units, though small, had a long and honorable history. An example is the Philadelphia City Troop, whose lineage was from the Revolution. This was really a home-guard unit, normally responsible only to the Mayor of Philadelphia, but was mustered into the service for a few weeks in June 1863 because of the emergency caused by Lee's invasion of the state.

Specific identification of some of these units as pertaining to the Civil War is hampered because the same units continued to wear their old insignia until the Spanish-American War and even later. Even the expert can not always state definitely whether certain insignia were used before, during, or after the Civil War.

Ever since men formed groups to fight each other, they have thought it necessary to wear certain signs or insignia. These marks or emblems generally show the rank, type of service (such as branch), and special abilities of the wearer. Originally only simple designs were used, but since the 18th century they have become increasingly complex. In the past two centuries many different devices have been used, including epaulets, vari-colored cords, and cockades, buttons, badges, chevrons, stripes, and "shoulder patches."

In the Revolutionary War, generals wore ribbons across their chests. Field officers (majors, lieutenant colonels, and colonels) wore pink or red hat cockades, while company-grade officers wore yellow or green.

The term "insignia" is of Roman origin, and has come into general use only recently. Neither Scott's *Military Dictinary* of the 1860's nor Wilhelm's *Military Dictionary* of the 1880's includes it. As used today, this word *insignia* is applied to all ornaments or devices that indicate branch of service, rank, and specific military organization; e.g. divisional insignia. The more accurate use, however, is to designate the arm or branch of service, as infantry, cavalry, artillery, engineers, and so on. In this discussion the term will be used to include cap, hat, or sleeve insignia, which were worn to designate arm or branch or the service. Designations of rank (shoulder straps and chevrons), corps badges, buttons, and belt buckles will be excluded.

The insignia of the arms and services of the United States Army have followed a consistent line of develop-

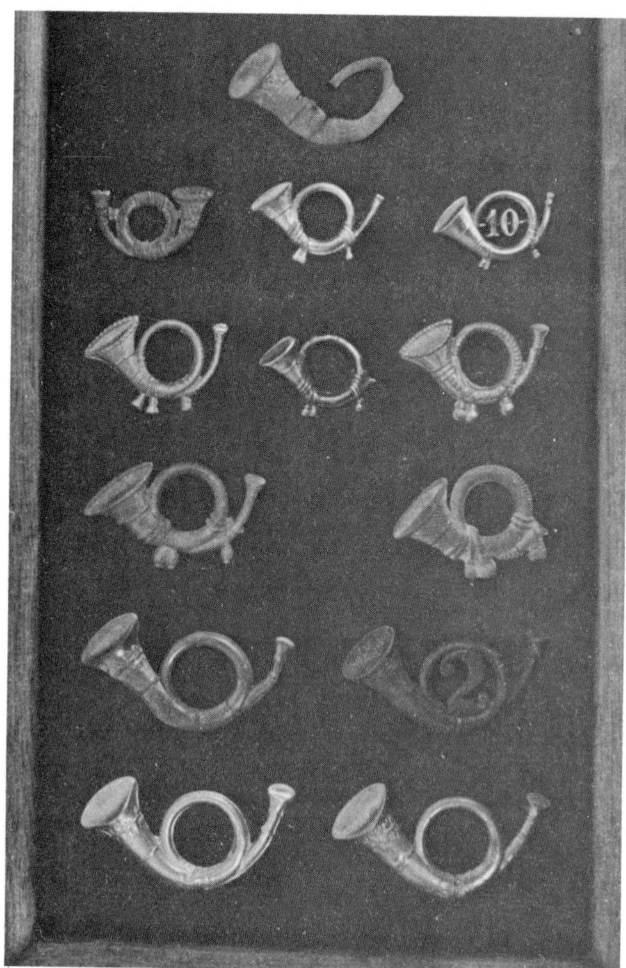

Infantry (U.S.)

Artillery (U.S.)

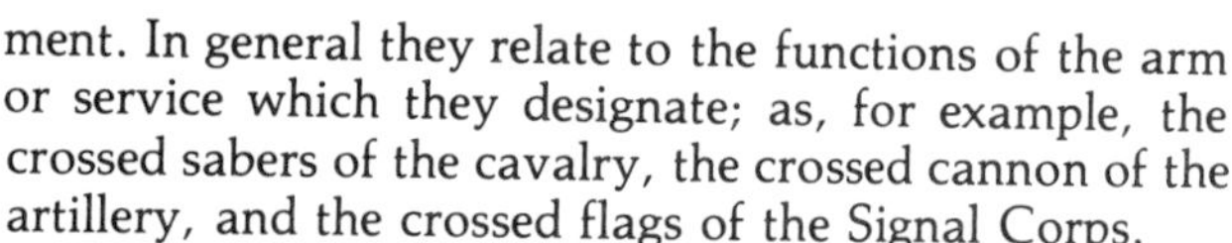
ment. In general they relate to the functions of the arm or service which they designate; as, for example, the crossed sabers of the cavalry, the crossed cannon of the artillery, and the crossed flags of the Signal Corps.

Except for many militia units with their myriad insignia, the oldest insigne was the bursting bomb of the Ordnance Department, adopted in 1832. Other insignia worn during the Civil War include the crossed cannon for artillery (1836), turreted castle for engineers (1840), crossed sabers for cavalry (1851), and the looped horn with three cords and tassels (not crossed rifles) for infantry. In 1850 the Mounted Riflemen were authorized a trumpet as insigne, but very few of these were worn during the Civil War. No Regular Army Mounted Riflemen served as such during the war, but there were a few Volunteer units of this kind, as, for example, Wilder's brigade. A few members of the 1st and 2nd U.S. Sharpshooters did wear U.S.S.S. on their caps, but this practice soon ceased. This was also true for dragoon units. Apparently the "D" on buttons was the only distinctive indicator of dragoons whether Regular or Volunteer.

Chaplains in the Federal Army wore an embroidered wreath with the U.S. in Old English letters. The Latin cross worn by Christian chaplains was not adopted until the Spanish-American War, and distinctive insignia for Jewish chaplains was not adopted until 1918. Despite persistent errors of movie studio "experts," who have their Civil War soldiers wearing crossed rifles, these insignia were not adopted for the infantry until 1875.

Many officers wore no distinctive insignia of arm or branch. Among these were all general officers, on whose hats appeared a gold-embroidered wreath on black velvet, encircling the letters "U.S." Occasionally the U.S. was replaced by the number of stars that showed the officer's rank. Officers of the Adjutant General's, Quartermaster's, Subsistence, Medical, and Pay Departments also wore the gold-embroidered wreath of oak leaves encircling a gold-embroidered shield on a black velvet background. The Topographical Engineers lost their separate identity in 1863 when they were merged with the Engineers.

The U.S.'s for officers' insignia were in Old English letters. Hospital stewards were authorized to wear a

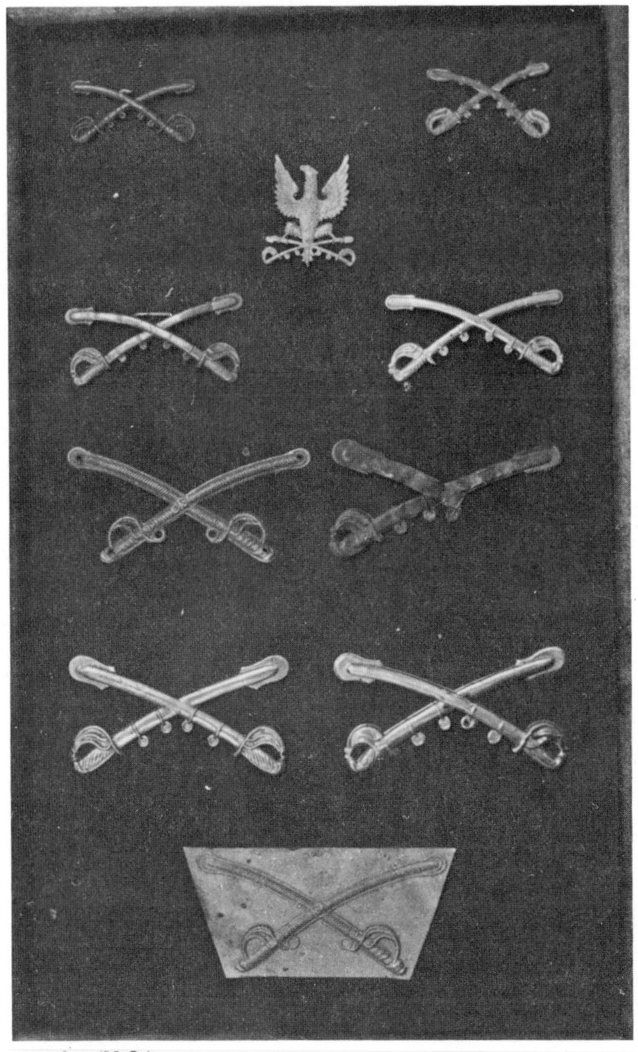

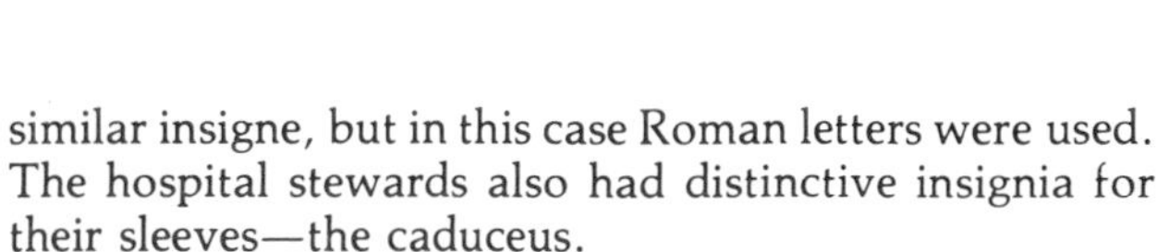

Cavalry (U.S.)

Engineers, Musicians, Pioneers, Signal, Ordnance, Lancers, Riflemen, Medical (U.S.)

similar insigne, but in this case Roman letters were used. The hospital stewards also had distinctive insignia for their sleeves—the caduceus.

Enlisted men wore either their corps badges or insignia of arm of service on their hats and caps. These were of brass, with the regimental number, 5/8-inch long, in brass and the company letter, 1-inch, in brass, arranged over the insignia of arm or service.

Branches of service were also indicated by the color of epaulets, the trimming on the coat, and the piping along the outer seam of the trousers. The basic colors were sky blue for infantry, scarlet for artillery, and yellow for cavalry.

Several other insignia received at least semi-official approval, and were extensively worn. Among these were the coats-of-arms of the individual states. Other insignia of this category, not specifically authorized by Army Regulations, but which came into fairly general use during the war, were:

Musicians: Apparently a three-stringed lyre in a wreath—used to a limited extent. Buttons with this motif have been found at Fredericksburg.

Pioneer Corps: A few regiments wore the insignia of crossed axes. In the early days of the war some regiments formed their own pioneer corps, a group of experienced woodsmen who cut slashings, built huts, and made themselves generally useful. An example was the 148th Pennsylvania Infantry.

Rush's Lancers: This unique outfit (6th Pennsylvania Cavalry) used the crossed lances as insignia. Such emblems are extremely rare.

Equally rare are the insignia of the provost guard of Birney's brigade. The Irish harp, of probable Civil War vintage supposedly was worn by Corcoran's Legion. Specimens of this badge exist in both brass and silver.

Even members of the Federal Balloon Corps wore a distinctive insignia, but not for long. A few of the aeronauts wore "B.C." (Balloon Corps) or "A.D."

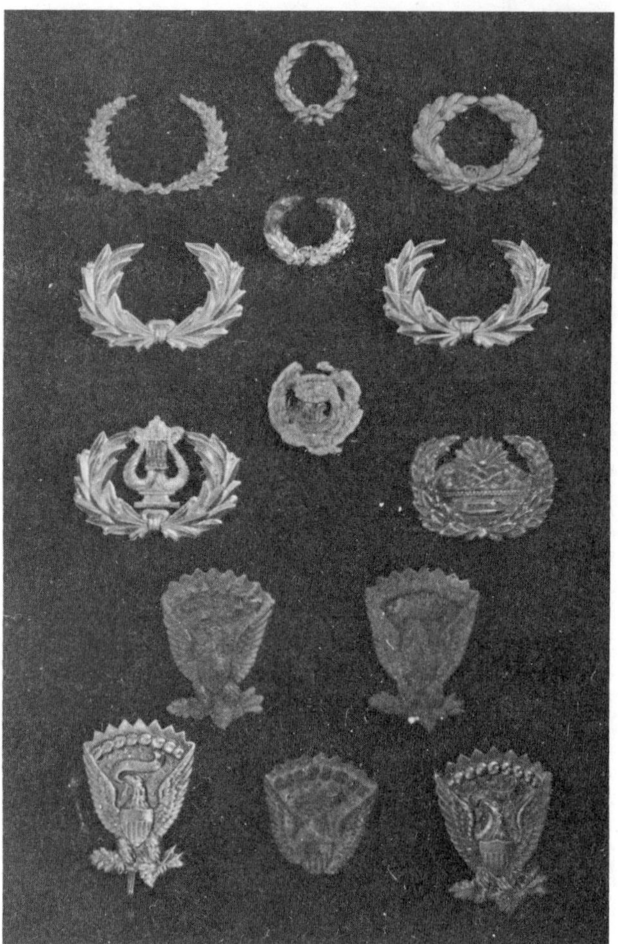

Headgear Insignia (Metal)

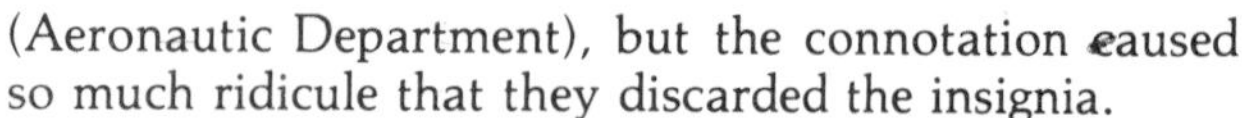

(Aeronautic Department), but the connotation caused so much ridicule that they discarded the insignia.

Sometimes the absence of insignia was significant in itself. For example, in the Department of the Cumberland, telegraph operators were authorized to wear the uniform of officers of the general staff, including staff officers' buttons and officers' caps "but without any distinctive mark or ornament."

INTRENCHING TOOLS

Yankees and Rebs, like G.I.'s of later wars disliked manual labor and especially digging intrenchments. Both sides, however, learned the necessity of "digging in." Sherman tells us in his *Memoirs* that one of Professor Mahan's maxims was that the spade is as useful in war as the musket. Sherman agreed completely, but to the spade he added the axe as being equally important.

In the early months of the war there was so much sentiment against digging intrenchments that General Lee was sneered at in the Richmond press for compelling his men to dig defensive positions. At the same time General Grant failed to provide his army with adequate protection at Shiloh, because, as he explained it, he regarded the campaign as an offensive one and had no idea that the enemy would attack.

However, eventually the men learned that their lives depended on their speed in getting up as much protection as possible. By 1864, Sherman's army in the West had completely adopted the principle of "digging in" immediately after the halt. Each man was his own engineer. After the officers had selected the general defensive line, each regiment and company fortified its own ground. A hasty barricade was constructed in case the enemy attacked at once; the front rank took all the muskets and protected the rear rank which hastened off at a double quick to collect rails, logs, rocks, in fact anything that would stop a bullet. In five minutes the men, especially if they were veteran troops, could prepare for an assault, and although outnumbered, could repulse such assault with but slight loss.

In the East, however, even as late as Cold Harbor, in June 1864, Federal skirmishers and pickets, preceding the massed formations opposing the Confederates,

Miscellaneous Insignia (U.S.)

made small rifle pits because of lack of time to dig regular intrenchments. These men should have occupied their position several hours earlier and intrenched then. Now, with only a few hundred yards separating these advanced elements from a watchful enemy, the Federals used their "tin dippers" (cups) and bayonets to dig what today we would call fox holes. One of the men was astonished "to see how much earth can be thrown up in this way in an hour." To increase protection of the men, especially from enemy snipers, "the bodies of rebel dead lying about and the bodies of some Union men also, are piled up for a barricade, but separately, also a few logs, and sand thrown upon the whole—anything to keep the rebel bullets back. A rebel shell burying and bursting in one of these horrid heaps makes a scene better imagined than described; the barricade is speedily re-arranged, however."

In occupying a position where they expected to remain for some time, whole regiments were put to work digging entrenchments usually under the direction of engineer officers of the Regular Army. The men would stack their guns within easy reach where they were ready for instant use. The implements used for digging intrenchments were shovels and picks—and sometimes axes for cutting trees to be used as "head logs."

Entrenchments before Petersburg were extremely extensive, where there were four principle Federal lines of defenses; first, the front rifle-trenches which were manned by regiments on a rotation system; second, a line of trenches about 1/4 of a mile to the rear of the first; third, a line of trenches about one mile from the front; and the fourth line about one and one-half miles from the front. All these lines are connected with approach trenches and together formed a complicated system of earth-works, trenches, rifle-pits and bomb-proofs.

Although the tools used by the Boys in Blue and Gray are not as fascinating as the weapons used, the tools *were* important and should be considered in any analysis of the equipment in use from 1861 to 1865. Regiments early in the war had selected men detailed as "pioneers," good woodsmen who preceded their units, removing such obstructions as felled trees and log barricades. Accompanying the regiment in wagons were the "intrenching tools" so often referred to in reports

Miscellaneous Cloth Insignia (U.S.)

and regimental histories. These tools consisted of shovels and picks. Some soldiers carried camp hatchets which they usually purchased from their sutlers. All these tools, shovels, picks, axes, and hatchets were very similar to the ones we use today.

However, there is evidence that intrenching tools for the individual soldier were made and used, but probably only to a limited extent. In the author's collection are two different types of digging tools, both designed to be attached to the musket. These rare specimens were dug up on the battlefield of Kernstown, Virginia. A caliber .58 trowel bayonet, long believed to have been used during the War, is now identified as having been patented about three years after Appomattox.

One aspect of the emphasis on digging intrenchments—an aspect frequently forgotten—is that many volunteer regiments were discriminated against in the construction of fortified positions. Regiments found themselves, immediately after entering the service, spending days and even weeks in constructing large entrenched camps. This was especially true of Federal regiments around Washington, St. Louis, Louisville, and Paducah. These regiments should have spent this time in drilling and target practice, but, often because of the very fact they were under good discipline, they performed a disproportionate amount of the tedious manual labor "on the fortifications." Other regiments escaped entirely, sometimes because their officers refused to enforce the long work hours and heavy labor details.

INTRENCHING BAYONET. Despite the many innovations appearing during the Civil War, there were

Kenneth M. Eaton

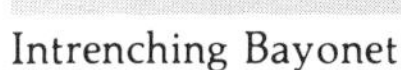

Intrenching Bayonet

some inexplicable lapses in providing essential equipment. Among these must be listed the failure to provide a light, portable intrenching tool for the foot soldier. Regimental histories, personal memoirs, journals, and diaries are replete with soldiers' complaints of the lack of tools to dig with. The lack of intrenching tools is especially surprising in a war which saw improvised earth works, fox holes, and trenches come into their own. Occasionally shovels and mattocks were available in insufficient numbers, but much more generally the soldiers had to dig with their knives, bayonets, tin plates, and even fingers.

As the war progressed entrenchments were used extensively by both sides. Soldiers learned the wisdom of "digging in" whenever time permitted. At the outbreak of the war, both sides were adverse to entrenchments, believing that manual labor detracted from the dignity of a soldier. They believed the war should be settled by a "fair, stand-up fight in the open." But by 1864 Federal and Confederate infantrymen dug themselves as much shelter as they could with the little they had to dig with. Apparently at least one inventor had developed an intrenching tool which would have been extremely useful if the Federal (or Confederate?) government had adopted it.

All we know of this intrenching tool is that it was produced (probably on a trial basis) in very small numbers. Extensive research in U.S. Patent office records of the war period had disclosed nothing on the intrenching bayonet. Nor has any reference to it been found in any contemporary work written during the war.

So far as I know, up until recently I had the only Civil War intrenching bayonets of the type shown here in the illustration. My two specimens came from the battlefield of Kernstown, Virginia several years ago. Apparently these intrenching bayonets, experimental types, were issued to some unit of Banks' army and were discarded during his retreat from Jackson's forces. Both specimens fit the caliber .58 rifle musket. One of these bayonets is an adze type of tool, with the digging portion 6 inches long, while the other bayonet has a spade-type tool 7 inches long on the digging portion.

For a long time I thought I had the only specimens of these intrenching bayonets. But recently two other Civil War collectors have sent me photographs of specimens they own. The one shown here was furnished by Kenneth M. Eaton of Homer, New York, through whose kindness it is reproduced. Another helpful collector, James F. Moser, Jr. of Orange, Virginia, has an intrenching bayonet from the Manassas-Sperryville area. He also has a cal. .58 intrenching bayonet of a sickle shape from the same area.

We are sincerely appreciative of the courteous interest of both these collectors. Some collectors have hazarded the guess that these intrenching bayonets were made by Southern farmers after the war from the regular cal. 58 bayonet. Personally I do not believe this assumption is correct. My specimens very definitely were never altered from *anything;* they were made as intrenching bayonets. This can be seen on a close examination. Maybe some written material will appear in the future telling us more about the inventor and the number produced. But *very* probably only a few were ever made and were issued on a trial basis only.

JEWELRY

Various types of jewelry were worn by officers and men of both sides throughout the war. Included in jewelry were such items as rings, watches, and lockets. Many of these items were taken home by the veterans

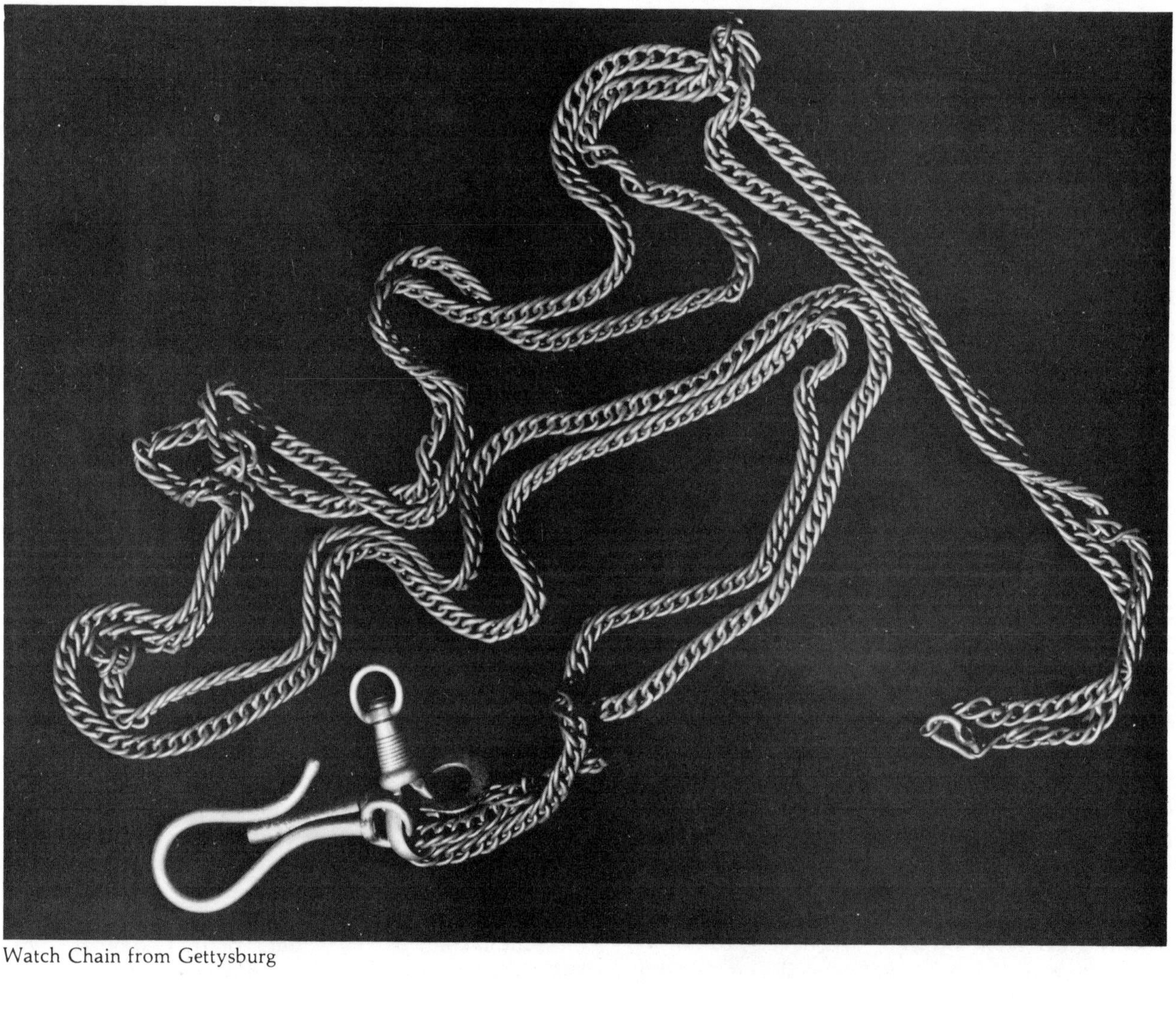

Watch Chain from Gettysburg

Civil War Jewelry

Captain G. H. Amidon's Watch (Back view)

Watch Carried by Captain G. H. Amidon 4th Vermont Infantry

but most of the items can no longer be identified as to their war association or have been lost altogether. In addition, prisoners of war often were "relieved" of their jewelry—especially watches and rings—by their captors. And, of course, items of jewelry were lost in camp, on the march, and on the battlefield.

Shown here are the following items of jewelry carried in the war.

WATCH CHAIN. Taken from a wounded comrade at Gettysburg, by Lieutenant Solomon Yeakel, 93rd Pennsylvania Infantry.

WATCH. Silver hunting case watch made by E. Howard & Son, Boston, Massachusetts. Inside the back cover is inscribed as follows:

Presented to Capt. G. H.
Amidon by Co. E
4th Regt. Vt. Vols.

In the group picture, reading left to right—top row:

Captain Amidon's watch.

Gold locket: 1 5/8 inches in diameter. Inside is an original photograph of a New Hampshire soldier.

Gold wedding ring found on the Wilderness battlefield.

Gold watch fob ornament, also found on the Wilderness battlefield.

Bottom row:

Lock of hair (originally carried in a locket). The hair belonged to "Maytie", and was carried all through the war by Corporal Davis Lippincott, Co. F, 7th Iowa Cavalry. Lippincott was 23 years of age at enlistment and "Maytie" was probably his wife or one of his children.

Back of a silver watch inscribed:

Presented to Wm. H.
Godion by the Harness
Makers under his
charge at the
Washington Arsenal
January 19th, 1865.

Gold ring with a secret hollow portion in which brief written messages were carried during the war. From South Carolina.

Silver locket with glass on both sides. From the Monocacy battlefield.

Camp Kettle used by 1st Texas Infantry

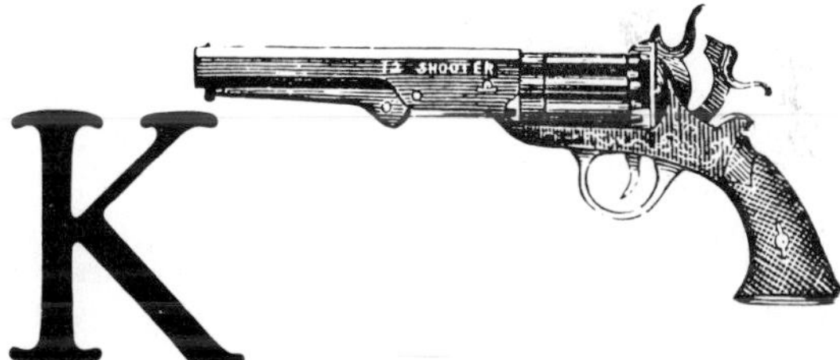

K

KETTLE (C.S.)

The types of kettles—military and civilian—used during the war are endless. Some types were discussed in the *Encyclopedia's* first volume. The one shown here is especially interesting since it has been identified as to original regimental ownership. This iron kettle weighs 10 pounds, is 9 1/4 inches wide at the middle; its top diameter is 8 1/4 inches, and it is 5 1/2 inches deep. Found on the camp site of the 1st Texas Infantry at Freestone Point, Virginia, where the regiment was encamped in September, 1861.

KNAPSACK

In addition to his accouterments, haversack, and canteen, the Civil War soldier was also issued a knapsack. This was worn on the back and was made of painted canvas, often with the owner's company letter and regimental number stencilled on the back. This canvas material resembled nonporous plasters, and when the knapsack was strapped on the soldier's back, all clothing was closely bound about his chest and shoulders—a most vicious combination for hard marching in hot weather. Many knapsacks had wooden frames, the top boards of which pressed directly on the wearer's shoulder blades. Rubber-covered knapsacks protected their contents from moisture but were even more uncomfortable than canvas under a hot sun. Observers commented on the baggy appearance of the knapsacks and the fact that they slipped down too far toward the small of the back. One observer observed that "the hardiest packhorses in the world would break down under the heavy, sagging, illy-adjusted loads borne by our soldiers!"

Much of the difficulty with the regulation knapsacks could have been avoided if the men had packed them only with essential items. These included a double wool blanket, half a shelter tent, and a rubber blanket. Some units, like the 4th New Jersey Infantry, late in the war turned in their knapsacks, cartridge boxes, and belts, receiving in exchange the Mann Accouterments. Colonel Mann, designer of this accouterment, resigned his commission in the 7th Michigan Cavalry and went to Washington early in 1864, where he persuaded the Ordnance Department of the worth of his improved system of cavalry and infantry accouterment. The Government soon gave large orders for their manufacture and most of the regiments which used them apparently liked them, mainly because the suspenders arrangement kept the weight of the accouterment off their loins or kidneys.

Even after many of the nonessentials had been eliminated, the soldiers—especially Federal troops—still carried unduly heavy and bulky knapsacks. In the Chancellorsville campaign it was intended that only one or the other should be taken. One Confederate division commander reported that "the enemy abandoned such a large number of knapsacks in retreating to his works that when this division began its homeward march in the rain it was thoroughly equipped with oil cloths and shelter tents of the best quality."

The experience gained at Chancellorsville convinced the Quartermaster General and corps commanders of the Army of the Potomac that the knapsack was an unnecessary encumbrance which should be replaced by the blanket roll. At Chancellorsville, the Army of the Potomac lost about 25 per cent of its knapsacks. In the 5th Corps it was about 30 per cent; in the 11th and 12th Corps it was about 50 per cent. Even though knapsacks were carried by some regiments in the field all through the war, they were usually stored before setting out on an active campaign and their place taken by a blanket. This blanket, with a change of underclothing in it, was rolled into a cylinder and slung across the left shoulder, and, crossing to the right hip, was tied together by a string.

When troops were in the field, the soldier carried his own ammunition and rations. The total weight carried by each Federal soldier was 45 pounds—Jackson's "foot cavalry" traveled lighter! Included in the 45 pounds were the knapsack, haversack, subsistence, and change of underclothing; overcoat or blanket, arms and accouterments, and one half a shelter tent. Eight days' short rations were carried on the person, 40 rounds of ammunition in the cartridge box, and 20 rounds in the man's pockets.

LANCE

Much confusion exists in the minds of the average student and even some collectors as to the use of the lance during the Civil War. Often a pike or even a guidon is mistakenly called a lance by the non-collector. However, while the number of lances used from 1861 to 1865 was extremely small, such weapons were used by a few units on both sides.

On the Confederate side, much of the reference to lances was in the order of suggestions and recommendations as to the weapon's usefulness. Maj. Gen. John B. Magruder and Lt. Col. (later General) Richard Ewell went on record as favoring the lance as a weapon for some cavalry units. Magruder pointed out that the lance "can be made by any carpenter and ordinary blacksmith. . .and. . .(is) more efficient than the saber." As early as February 1862, the Secretary of War, Judah P. Benjamin, announced that the government would accept lancers and would provide the lance. An order for 1,000 lances was placed but the Confederate Government never implemented Benjamin's announcement so far as can be ascertained. In March, 1862, the State of Texas announced that a Colonel James P. Morgan had been commissioned to raise a regiment of lancers. This very possibly was done since lances with Confederate pennons have appeared in collections and, according to tradition, "were carried by a regiment of Texas lancers."

In Virginia a company of lancers actually existed. On Jan. 3, 1862, Confederate artilleryman George Neese recorded in his diary that on that day "a company of our Cavalry passed us armed with lances, which consisted of a steel spear about ten inches long mounted on a wooden shaft about eight feet long."

On the Federal side, several foreign "soldiers of fortune" attempted to raise lancer regiments, including a "Colonel" Smolenska (a Pole) and "Colonel" Pleyel (a German). Moreover, Colonel Arthur Rankin, a Canadian, recruited eight companies for a regiment, the First United States Lancers, but Rankin's outfit, and the others as well, never received lances but functioned as "normal" cavalry units, armed with the regulation weapons.

However, under the urging of McClellan, one regiment, the 6th Pennsylvania Cavalry, was issued lances and actually used them in combat until 1863. This regiment, known as Rush's Lancers was equipped with a lance about nine feet long with an 11-inch, three-edged blade. The staff was of Norway fir, about one and one quarter inches in diameter with ferrule and counterpoise at the heel—the whole weighing four pounds, 13 ounces. The people of Philadelphia purchased 1,000 scarlet swallow-tailed pennons for the lances.

Although popular with spectators and officers, the men hated the clumsy weapon in which they felt no confidence. One of Rush's lancers pointed out that while "the officers like . . . (the lance) . . . the men do not, and the officers wouldn't if they had to use them." Actually the heavily wooden terrain in which the regiment operated during much of its service was extremely unfavorable for using lances at all. The regimental historian tells us that since "our weapon . . . (was) unfitted for any service but the charge, we were held only to resist attack from the enemy."

On one occasion when Rush's lancers were attacked by a Virginia cavalry regiment, the lancers broke in disorder, leaving many of its lances as trophies to the enemy. As a Confederate eyewitness well pointed out: "Their sudden and total discomfiture furnished a striking proof of the fact that this weapon, formidable enough in the hand of one accustomed to wield it, is a downright absurdity and encumbrance to the inexperienced."

Apparently the Federals believed in this also, for in 1863, the 6th Pennsylvania Cavalry turned in its lances, and fought the rest of the war with sabers and revolvers.

Civil War Hospital Lamps

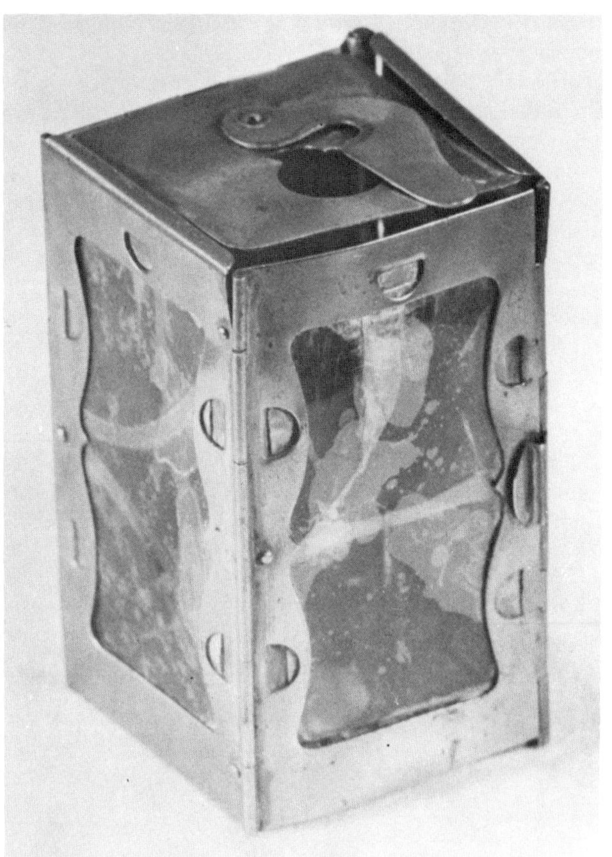
Louis G. Stockho Collection

Civil War Folding Lantern

LIGHTING EQUIPMENT

The main item used for lighting was the candle. These were issued to Federal troops, but many Southern units were unable to get them. Southern troops from the Carolinas did receive German-made candles which had been run in by blockade runners.

Men in the field used all types of candle holders and lamps—usually made of tin. Some of the varied types of lighting equipment are shown in these illustrations.

THE LINDSAY RIFLE-MUSKET

One of the most unusual weapons to appear during the Civil War was the Lindsay two-shot muzzle loading rifle musket. This innocent looking weapon had the interesting feature of firing two charges, loaded one on top of the other, from its single barrel. The inventor was John P. Lindsay, an employee of the Springfield Armory. The inventor believed that the bullet of the rear charge would act as a base and a gas check for the front charge. This principle was not new, but the ingenious lock mechanism, developed by Lindsay, involved two side-by-side centrally hung hammers, operated by a single trigger. The trigger worked perfectly, whether either hammer was cocked or both were at cock at once; in the latter case the right hammer always fell first. The fire from the cone hit by the right hammer ran along a canal to the forward charge of powder. The first from the left cone communicated directly with the charge at the rear. The rifle was patented October 9, 1860, under U.S. Patent 30,332. Its length was 56 inches, caliber .58, and had the same boring and grooving as the regular Springfield barrels of the time. In short, the Lindsay rifle was very similar in general appearance to the regulation Springfield musket, 1863 model, except, of course, for the two hammers and the absence of a lock plate.

Tradition has it that Lindsay's brother, a soldier, was killed by Indians. In the engagement the Indians employed their customary tactics of drawing the fire of the troops and then charged in overwhelming numbers before the soldiers had time to reload their single-shot weapons.

The entire company was massacred. The Lindsay two-shooter , with the appearance of a single-shooter was intended to offer the sort of surprise which would discourage repetition of such tactics.

For a long time this arm was considered an experimental product of Springfield Armory but it has now been definitely established as a contract arm. On December 17, 1863, Lindsay was granted a contract for one thousand of his muskets by the United States Government. The muskets were completed and ready for final inspection on August 12, 1864. Four days later the thousand Lindsay muskets were delivered to the War Department at the price of $25.00 each.

In addition to the "experimental trials" earlier discussed by authors in all references to the Lindsay, I discovered that the Lindsay was actually used in combat during the war. In the history of the "Corn Exchange Regiment" (118th Pennsylvania Volunteers) the author described the participation of the 16th Michigan Infantry at the Battle of Preble's Farm, September 30, 1864. According to this author, shortly before the battle "a gun of strange construction had been issued to a portion of the 16th Michigan to be tested in the first engagement. The piece had two triggers. Each trigger exploded a separate cartridge; the one farthest from the breech first, the other afterwards. At least that is what it was intended to do. As a fact, the explosion of the first cartridge always ignited the second and sometimes exploded the barrel. Such was the result of the test at Preble's Farm, and the men of the 16th Michigan who had been so unfortunate as to be allotted the new guns were seen moving along the dead and wounded replacing . . . their Lindsays with a weapon they knew all about."

So far as can be ascertained, the 16th Michigan was the only unit to use the Lindsay in actual combat. The war was nearly over when Lindsay's first contract of 1,000 guns was delivered. Even if the gun had been highly successful, it is very doubtful that the U.S. Government would have ordered any more to be made.

Oil Lamp used in a Federal Hospital

Civil War Candlesticks, Candle, and Candle Trimmer

John A. Marks Memphis, Tennessee

Iron Candle Holder from La Grange, Tennessee. (Overall length 4 inches)

The Government in 1864 and 1865 was much more interested in breechloading metallic cartridge weapons which were making all muzzleloaders obsolete.

Description

U.S. Double Rifle-Musket, Model 1863

Caliber .58, rifled with three broad lands and grooves.

Length overall 56 inches

Black walnut, oil-finished stock is 53 inches long. The 41 1/8 inch barrel is finished bright, and has an iron blade front sight atop the bayonet stud, 1 3/16 inches from the muzzle. The two-leaf rear sight is blued, and is graduated to 500 yards.

Markings

Top of the breech is marked:

LINDSAY/PATENT'D. Oct. 9, 1860 in two lines.

The socket bayonet is identical to that furnished with the regulation Model 1863 rifle-musket; it is 20 15/16 inches long, with an 18 inch blade stamped "U.S." and a 3 inch socket with clamping band.

PRINCIPLE OF OPERATION. Lindsay's patent was based on an ingenious design for the trigger assembly and the superposed charge which permitted the soldier to load two rounds into the barrel, one atop the other, and fire one at a time. Accordingly, the rear charge served as a gas check for the foremost charge.

The two hammers mounted side-by-side, each engaged its own cone. A single trigger operated both. Mechanically, this gun functioned perfectly. The pull of the trigger caused the right hammer to drop on its cone, sending a flame through a channel to the forward load. On the second pull of the trigger the left hammer dropped, sending a flame directly into the rear charge.

However, Lindsay's gun gave trouble when the channel leading to the forward load became badly fouled by repeated firing. After several rounds had been fired it was almost impossible for the flame to reach the powder, and accordingly neither charge could be ignited because the rearmost charge was still obstructed by the unfired forward charge.

One criticism was of the ever-present danger of the barrel exploding if both charges went off at the same time. However, in 1964 an owner of a Lindsay rifle-musket fired his gun 10 times, using the left hammer only. Both charges went off at once but without any damage to gun or shooter. However, the recoil was heavy!

Lindsay Rifle

LIQUOR FLASKS

Since publication of the first volume of the Collector's Encyclopedia, several different types of Civil War flasks have come to light. A few of these are illustrated here.

PRESENTATION FLASKS. Shown here are two liquor flasks, typical of the kind of personalized gifts given men leaving for the war. These flasks are of fine

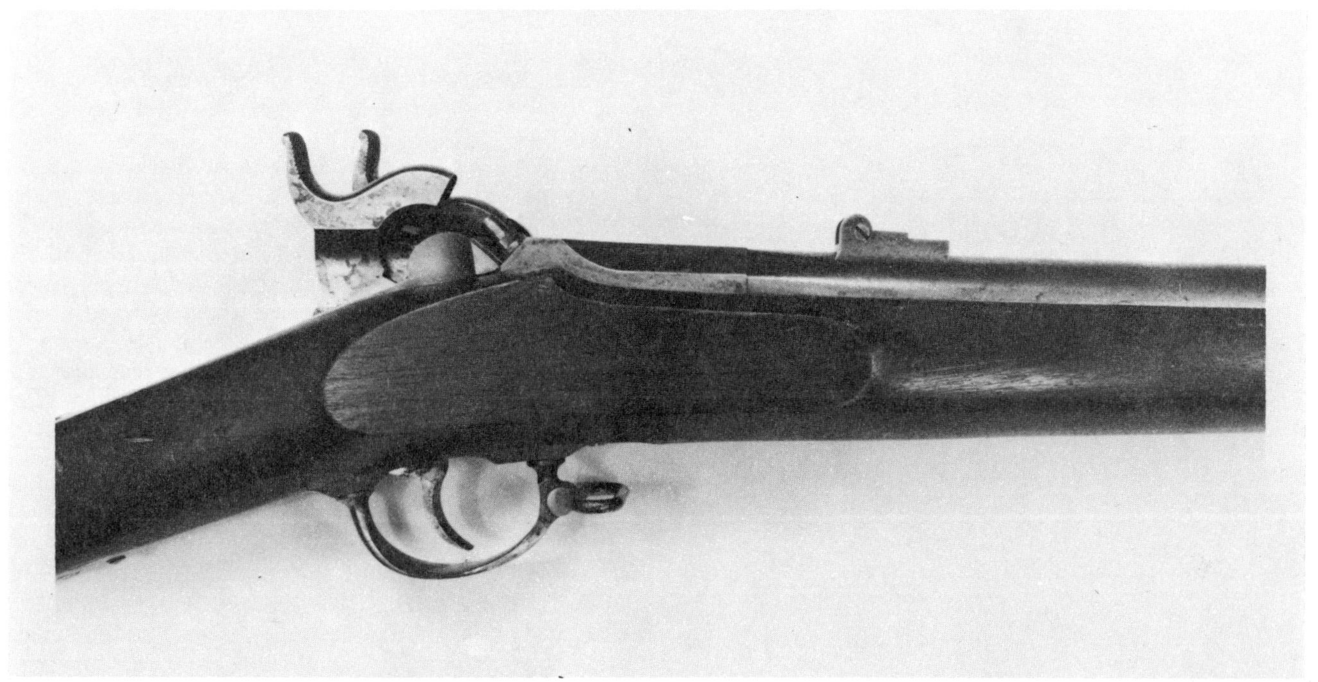

Lindsay Rifle Musket (Showing the Hammer Mechanism)

quality and undoubtedly saw use. In fact, the one used by Colonel Davis was used too much on one occasion: the good Colonel became inebriated while field officer of the day and the author's grandfather—a raw 18-year old recruit nearby shot him when he refused to halt at the picket line!

The taller flask is 6 1/2 inches tall and 3 1/4 inches wide. The top is leather carved, pewter top, and silver cup on the bottom marked: E.M. DICKINSON SHEFFIELD

The cup is engraved:

Col. P.S. Davis
39
Ms. INF
Aug. 1862

P. Stearns Davis was born in 1818. Appointed Colonel of the 39th Massachussetts Infantry. Killed at Petersburg July 11, 1864. He was a 32nd degree Mason.

The shorter flask is 5 1/2 inches tall and 2 3/4 inches wide. The top is leather carved, pewter top, with an unmarked silver cup on the bottom. There are no maker's marks on this flask.

The cup is engraved:

Maj. Josiah Hall

1st Vermont Cav.

Hall entered the service as Captain of Co. "F" 1st Vermont Cavalry, November 1, 1861. Wounded and taken prisoner at Brandy Station, paroled August 3, 1864, promoted major October 17, 1864, and Colonel May 31, 1865. Mustered out June 21, 1865.

LOCK

Although many locks of varied descriptions have been recovered from Civil War battlefields and campsites, the type shown here is the most commonly found. Of the fourteen of these in the Author's Collection, seven are from the Wilderness, three from Fredericksburg, two from Port Hudson, and one each from Chancellorsville and Chantilly. Apparently this type of lock was used mainly by Eastern units. For a long time collectors were not sure of the original use of these locks. Shown here are four different items—all definitely used in the War, and all equipped with this lock. The lock itself is of thin brass, 1 1/2 inches in diameter, and equipped with a brass key 3/4 inches long. This particular lock came from Chancellorsville. Shown here are items equipped with exactly this type of lock.

CARPET BAG. Made of multi-colored heavy material and lined with blue cotton material. It is 14 x 12 1/2 inches in size.

PORTABLE FILE FOLDER. Made of brown leather, 9 1/2 inches long, 5 inches tall, and 1 3/4 inches deep. It is divided into compartments, lettered "January AB, February CD, March EF," etc. with "Sundries" at the

Liquor Flasks
Left to right:
Top Row: Leather—Covered, pewter top used as a cup, 6 1/4 inches tall. Marked:
C. G. Bevete

Wicker—covered, pewter top, 6 1/2 inches tall. Marked:
Lt. E. P. Loring
Co. B 13 Maine Inf.

Glass, with pewter top and drinking cup fitting over the bottom of the flask. 6 inches tall. No markings.

Left to right:
Bottom Row: All pewter, rectangular in shape, 6 1/8 inches tall. Marked:
G. D. Earll
Watertown, N.Y.

Glass bottle, stamped WARRANTED FLASK, 6 1/4 inches tall. Found at Fort Ward, Defences of Washington.

Pewter, 5 inches tall. Marked:
James Dixon & Sons

Personalized Liquor Flasks

end. This folder came from Richmond, Virginia, and contained Confederate documents.

TOILET KIT. Made of black leather, 7 1/2 inches tall, 5 1/2 inches wide, and 3 1/2 inches deep. Contains soap, hair brushes, mirror, boot hooks, etc. Was carried by a Maine soldier in the War.

WRITING KIT. Made of black cardboard, 9 3/4 x 7 inches in size. Contains a penmanship manual, envelopes, etc. Carried in the War by Charles R. Cox, Co. "F" 1st. Maryland Infantry (U.S.), 2nd. Brigade, 2nd. Division, 5th. Army Corps.

MACHINE GUNS

The U.S. Patent Office on July 8, 1856, issued to C.E. Barnes (Lowell, Massachusetts) a patent for a crank-operated machine cannon. This weapon had many original improvements, and was the forerunner of a series of crank-operated weapons. The rate of fire depended solely on the speed with which the crank could be turned. This weapon was far ahead of its time. Its development would have given the United States Army a reliable machine gun at the outbreak of war in 1861. Other inventors came up with variations and improvements, including a patent in 1861 by Ezra Ripley of Troy, New York.

Federal military authorities showed an interest in a caliber .58 machine gun capable of volley fire. This weapon, the Requa battery, was built late in 1861 by the Billinghurst Company of Rochester, New York. The weapon was publicly demonstrated in front of the Stock Exchange building in New York City in the hope of interesting private investors. The gun had 25 barrels, mounted flat on a light metal platform. A sliding breech mechanism was operated by a lever; charging was accomplished by means of cartridges held in special clips. This gun was known as the "covered bridge" gun. During the Civil War many of the important crossings over streams were in the form of a wooden bridge with roof and sides. As these covered bridges were usually long and narrow, one of the Requa machine guns in the hands of an alert crew could break up a quick charge by the enemy, either on horse or foot. The 25 barrels could be adjusted to the necessary height and width of the bridge. With a crew of three men, the weapon could be fired at the rate of seven volleys of 175 shots per minute. The effective range was 1,300 yards. In the field the Requa battery had its limitations. Dampness in the unprotected powder train would render it useless. It was not adaptable for offensive service, but it was very effective in defense of restricted fields of fire.

Another machine gun used by the Federal forces was the Ager or "Coffee Mill" gun, so named because it was crank-operated with a hopper feed so that it closely resembled the kitchen coffee grinder of the period. The caliber was .58. The gun was purposely made not to exceed a speed of 120 shots per minute, since it used only a single barrel. The heat from rapid firing was considered a serious drawback. Later the inventor added an ingenious cooling device. Maximum range was 1,000 yards. The Ager gun was a very advanced weapon for the Civil War era. But there was little military demand for a machine gun; the authorities condemned such weapons as requiring too much ammunition ever to be practical. However, machine guns were used in battle in a few isolated instances. Lincoln rather liked the idea of adopting the Ager gun but was not supported by his ordnance chief.

A third and very important machine gun was the famous Gatling gun, the logical outgrowth of the trends portrayed in Ager and other earlier guns. The Gatling gun is the prototype of one of the most remarkable firing mechanisms of all ordnance history. Its inventor, Dr. Richard Gatling, is generally credited with being the father of the machine gun. The 1862 Gatling gun embodied fundamentally the Ager principle, improved by the multi-barrel arrangements of the Ripley gun. As early as 1862, a model of Dr. Gatling's gun was exhibited before thousands of people in Indianapolis. Among them was Governor Oliver P. Morton of Indiana, who wrote to the Assistant Secretary of War, telling him of the weapon's unusual performance and suggesting that Gatling's gun be permitted officially to prove its worth. Nothing was done by the government but Gatling continued to improve his gun, including the use of copper-cased rim-fire ammunition.

On one of his trips to Washington, Gatling met the Army chief of Ordnance and asked that the weapon be given tests with a view to adopting it. But the chief of ordnance refused point blank to take the gun under consideration. A few days later one of Gatling's representatives interested Gen. B.F. Butler by means of a successful demonstration of the gun. Butler used two in the Petersburg area and eight on gunboats. Winfield S. Hancock took 12 for his corps. The Navy adopted the Gatling in 1862, but the army waited until August 24, 1866. However, by then the war was over.

Gatling's gun was used successfully on a small scale in the Franco-Prussian War, while the much publicized rapid-firing weapons of European origin were being proved failures in many cases. For more than 40 years thereafter, the Gatling gun was used by practically

Lock and its Uses

every major power and influenced world events in no small manner.

THE BILLINGHURST AND REQUA "RIFLE BATTERY." On the day before the bloodiest single-day battle of the war, Antietam, September 17, 1862, William Billinghurst and J. Requa of Rochester, New York, patented their "rifle battery" or machine gun. Patent Number 36,448 was described technically as an "improvement in platoon battery." Actually it was the answer to a search by Federal military authorities for a caliber .58 machine gun capable of "volley fire." The new weapon, known as the "Requa battery," was produced late in 1861 by the Billinghurst Company of Rochester, New York. In the Civil War, a "rifle battery" usually consisted of a row of rifle barrels fixed side by side and fired in volleys.

This machine gun was crude but did have some interesting features. Charging the gun was done by means of cartridges held in special clips. These cartridges were of light steel with a base in which there was an opening in the center for ignition. They were spaced in the 25-round clip so as to mate with the open rear end of the barrels. After the breech was locked, each cartridge came opposite a channel filled with priming powder. All 25 barrels were fired simultaneously by a single nipple and percussion cap, which ignited the powder train, passing the rear hole of each cartridge. A single hammer, manually cocked and released by a lanyard, served as the firing mechanism. The Requa did not use paper cartridges inserted in the steel cases, but rather it used loose powder loaded by hand into the cylinders.

In the field the Requa battery was especially effective in defense of restricted fields of fire.

The gun saw considerable use during the siege operations against Fort Sumter and Morris Island in 1863. In fact, up to August 23rd the Requa guns "constituted the only artillery in advance of the second parallel." On several occasions the Requas were used with good effect against enemy sharpshooters and working parties. They were used chiefly at the flanks of lines of the works and were called the "Mosquito Batteries" by the line soldiers. Often infantry regiments, like the 3rd New Hampshire Volunteers, detailed about 20 men for duty with these "death producers."

On July 20, 1863 the three emplacements for Federal soldiers besieging Fort Sumter were finally finished and occupied, one, on the extreme left of the whole line, firing so as to flank the parallel and defend the entire

Mail Bag

obstacle, and two, on the right, placed between the parallel and obstacle for economy of space, and so arranged as to enfilade the beach and fire on the defenses in general. These advanced pieces were protected from hostile fire from the parallel by a traverse in their rear. The Requa guns were in embrasure, protected by a splinter-proof parapet of timber and sandbags. The fire of these guns enfiladed the beach perfectly. As additional protection, a lookout of sandbags was constructed on top of a large magazine, and a splinter-proof latrine was also provided.

Major T.B. Brooks, Assistant Engineer, Department of the South, who was stationed on Morris Island during the siege, considered the Requa machine gun to be the equivalent of a 6-pounder field gun whenever grape and canister were called for due to the exigencies of the tactical situation. Major Brooks also included spherical shot, along with grape and canister, in the categories of items which were surpassed by the Requa which, he claimed from personal observation, "possessed greater precision and much less liability to fail in producing desireable results."

In his report on the performance of Requa guns at the siege of Sumter, the Major gave additional details on the novel gun's performance. The weight of each gun, complete, was 1,382 lbs. The gun did not foul. At a 9 degree elevation the gun was effective for 1,200 yards, at which range, the barrels being separate, the bullets fanned out into an excellent cone of fire. The most effective range was about 1,300 yards, although the gun's backers claimed that it was effective up to 2,000 yards. During the siege, a total of 19 positions were constructed for the "Requa rifle batteries." These positions were built successively as the approaches advanced, and all positions were occupied by the Requa guns for longer or shorter periods of time. The platforms for the guns were of boards, 8 feet square, and well nailed to five sills, also of wood. These platforms were moved forward with the pieces. The Requa guns were the only "artillery pieces" of any kind in advance of the second parallel up to the 23rd of August, on which day 3 Coehorn mortars were moved up into the fourth parallel.

Often the Requa guns were used against concentrations of enemy personnel, and apparently with good effect. On August 25th, with 3 infantrymen per gun, the Requa batteries participated with "good effect" in a "brisk skirmish." Although the Requa gun was not really tested in defensive operations, Major Brooks believed it to be adapted to defense of earthworks, particularly in flat terrain, "where the horizontal line of dispersion (of the Requa) is more effective than the cone of dispersion of the howitzer." Major Brooks pointed out that the angle of dispersion could be varied with the Requa, but not with the howitzer. These properties, together with its short recoil, its light weight, and the fact it was a breech-loader, made it ideal for boat service, as well as siege operations.

Five of these guns were used at Morris Island during the siege. They were very effective and each took the place of 25 infantrymen. Moreover, because of the method of loading, the gun crew did not have to expose themselves, in marked contrast to the infantrymen of the line units. The Requa gun was an effective weapon, it performed well, did not foul, and should have been used extensively on the various fronts as the War progressed. However, the adamant refusal of the Federal Chief of Ordnance to be interested in new ideas doomed the Requa, along with other new weapons, to oblivion. And yet, those in the field who saw the gun in action, were emphatic in praise of its capabilities.

MAIL BAG

Delivery of mail to ships at sea, especially those on blockade duty, was slow and uncertain. The U.S.S. *Monongahela* saw extensive action during the war. It was a "steam sloop of war" and was actively engaged in the decisive battle of Mobile Bay.

DESCRIPTION: White canvas 11 inches tall and 12 1/2 inches wide, with a carrying strap 1 1/4 inches wide. The bag is marked:

USS
Monongahela

Mail
Bag

MANUALS

Federal military manuals have been extensively discussed in the author's *They Fought for the Union.* Other authors have devoted their attention to the Confederate manuals. Naturally, this material will not be duplicated here. But the manuals carried in active campaigning by a regimental commander (Colonel J.B. McCown, 63rd Illinois Infantry) are of interest. These are: *Revised Regulations for the Army of the United States* (1861); Hardee's *Tactics* (1861)—complete in one volume; Casey's *Tactics*—three volumes—(1862; Outpost and Patrol Duty (1863); and a damaged copy of *Instructions for Mustering Officers* (1863). These manuals were found in the Colonel's field desk along with files of orders and reports which he took with him on Sherman's March to the Sea.

MAPS

Civil War maps were prepared by both commercial and governmental agencies. Topographical engineers of both sides prepared maps; in fact, one of the finest cartographers of the war was Major Jedidiah Hotchkiss, topographic engineer with the Army of Northern Virginia. Federal maps were prepared by the Corps of Topographical Engineers (until 1863), the Corps of Engineers, and the U.S. Coast Survey. Shown here is a military map of NE Virginia, prepared in 1865 by the U.S. Engineers and marked with their emblem. This map is 25 x 17 3/4 inches in size and is linen-backed. It originally was folded and carried in an officer's map case.

At the outbreak of the Civil War there were few maps available to Federal commanders of the areas in which they would conduct active military operations. Most of the maps available were out-of-date, sketchy, and highly inaccurate. The basic responsibility for provision of maps to the armies was the corps of Topographical Engineers, which by act of Congress August 3, 1861, consisted of 42 officers. By the same act, the Corps of Engineers was authorized a complement of 49 officers and 600 enlisted men. These two branches of the military service performed much the same tasks, including reconnaissance, and construction of offensive and defensive positions for the army.

However, most military maps were prepared by the topographical engineers. The Corps of Topographical Engineers was absorbed by the Corps of Engineers, March 31, 1863, and became the topographical branch of that Corps. The topographical branch continued to be charged with primary responsibility for furnishing maps to the army. That it carried out this responsibility is attested to by the fact that in the last year of the war alone, the branch furnished 20,938 maps to the armies in the field.

Despite this good record, the military engineers were

Manuals

forced to get substantial assistance from the United States Coast Survey under Alexander D. Bache, aided by civilian map experts.

Confederates as well as Federals suffered from the lack of maps in the early months of the war. Naturally, the Confederates were better off than their adversaries, since the Confederates were fighting on their own terrain. Nevertheless, Lee and Jackson often were in the dark due to lack of good maps, even in Virginia. Moreover, for subordinate unit commanders, it is obvious that men from Louisiana did not know Virginia better than their counterparts from Michigan. Maps often showed roads and rivers with similar line tracings, often drawn rough approximation within the general area of their actual location.

Since most of the available maps were not sufficiently detailed or accurate, the topographical engineers made new maps by data gleaned day by day from prisoners, deserters, refugees, and local citizens. Much essential detail was obtained by personal reconnaissance, often under enemy fire. The result of these efforts was the eventual supply of maps to higher unit commanders, i.e. from army down to brigade. Regimental commanders generally had to depend on personal terrain reconnaissance themselves or on civilian maps they purchased. For example, a map of Georgia, prepared in 1859 by James R. Butt, "surveyor general," in the author's possession, was used throughout Sherman's 1864 campaign by Colonel J. B. McCown, 63rd Illinois Infantry. This map shows country lines well but lacks the detail essential for small troop movements.

When good military maps were not available, commanders often did not know how to find their way by other means. As late as Chancellorsville, Captain E.R. Monfort, Co. "F" 75th Ohio Infantry witnessed the inability of the commander of the First Division, 11th Army Corps to understand the need for terrain data. This commander was not even aware of the existence of the roads or the general topography of his area of operations. When asked by one of his ablest regimental commanders, "Do you know where you are?" he answered: "No, I don't know!" The regimental commander then went to an old resident of the area and from him got information enough to make a rough diagram and brought it to his undistrubed general. But the general still failed to appreciate the significance of the numerous roads available as necessary for the rapid movement of his command.

After First Bull Run, the Federal high command paid special attention to providing accurate maps to its commanders in the field. Due to the proximity to Washington, eastern armies initially were better served in this respect than were their western counterparts. Much of this was due to McClellan's emphasis on engineering and his support of topographical engineers under his command. In addition to the assigned

Manuals carried by Colonel J. B. McCown 63rd Illinois Infantry

engineer personnel, there were available in the volunteer regiments capable draftsmen for map-making duty. For example, one of the largest and best topographical maps which was made during the war was made by ten men of Battery "G" 2nd Pennsylvania Heavy Artillery in late 1862. These men worked under the direction of Robert Hodascowich, a graduate of the Military School of St. Petersburg, Russia. The map made quite an impression on the topographical engineers in Washington, because it was not only complete but it was also the largest known to have been made up to that time.

The provision of maps to the Eastern armies remained a constant need, especially as the troops moved into new areas. As late as the Spring of 1864, it was obvious that accurate maps of the country between the Rapidan and Richmond would have to be made for Grant's campaign. Existing maps were valueless. Accordingly, the Corps of Engineers had to start from scratch. Every road in the area of campaigning had to be surveyed and mapped. This was done and the maps were prepared and reproduced in the field and distributed as rapidly as possible. As new and more correct map data came in, the maps were revised and these revised versions issued. In this way, several editions of maps were prepared and issued, comprising surveys of an area of 730 sqauare miles. These maps were constantly being updated and corrected by instruments carried by the supply train and by comparison with maps captured from the Confederates.

At the start of Grant's 1864 campaign his army had been issued 1200 maps prepared by the Corps of Engineers. Before the siege of Petersburg had ended some 1600 more maps had been issued as a result of new surveys.

The Western armies were too far removed from Washington to be able to count on assistance from Federal Headquarters, and it was essential that each large unit have a complete map establishment of its own. Outstanding in the West was the topographical engineer staff of the Army of the Cumberland. This staff was organized under Captain N. Michler, United States Engineers, and later achieved a high state of efficiency under Colonel W. E. Merrill. An acting engineer officer

U.S. Military Map of NE Virginia 1865

was assigned to each brigade, with instructions to survey the lines of marches traversed, the lines of works erected by the brigade, its position on the battlefield, as well as corresponding works and positions of enemy troops. The data thus obtained by the brigade engineers were then sent on up to the division engineers, for preparation and consolidation before being forwarded to Corps engineer and on to the chief engineer of the Army of the Cumberland.

At many of the miliary posts in the rear areas, acting engineer officers surveyed and mapped the adjacent country.

While commanding the Army of the Cumberland, Major General Rosecrans insisted on high-level performance by his topographical engineers. In General Order No. 124 (May 31, 1863) he ordered all branches of the service to assist the topographical engineers in every way possible. In this order, the General laid down specific mapping scales as follows:

For an area of 2 miles square of less—6 inches to the mile.

For an area of over 2 and less than 4 miles—4 inches to the mile.

For an area of over 4 and less than 8 miles—2 inches to the mile.

For an area of over 8 miles square—1 inch to the mile.

The magnetic meridian and scale had to be shown on all maps.

Not only were good maps essential for military use, these maps were needed in large numbers in widely-separated areas. There were several methods employed during the war to reproduce maps. In 1861-1862, maps for field use were reproduced by photography, but maps made by this process were not satisfactory. Unless a very fine and expensive lens was used they were inaccurate at the borders; sections of a large map would not join properly; they faded when exposed to sunlight; nor could a sufficient number be made even on the best days. Because of these defects, photography gradually was replaced by lithography. However, lithographic stones and presses were too heavy to be transported in the field over prolonged periods of time. Accordingly, the lithographic process was used at large depots behind the lines. However, in a permanent rear establishment the lithographic process was of great value.

For example, the map used in Sherman's Atlanta campaign was made by this process. The map of northern Georgia, on which the Atlanta Campaign was based, was made by first enlarging the best printed map available, to the scale of one inch to the mile. With this map as a basis new information was added by extensive questionings of spies, refugees, prisoners, peddlers, and local inhabitants. After all available data had been added, the map was cut into sixteen sections and divided among the draftsmen, who worked around the clock to trace all the sections on thin paper in autographic ink. As soon as four adjacent sections were completed they were transferred to one large stone, and 200 copies were printed. When all the map had been lithographed, the map-mounters completed the work. Before the commanding generals left Chattanooga, each had received a bound copy of the map; before the enemy was encountered every brigade, division, and corps commander in Sherman's three armies had a copy. Copies for the cavalry were printed directly on muslin. Such maps could be washed clean whenever soiled, and were not injured by hard service. Individual officers often sent handkerchiefs to the engineers' office and had maps printed directly on them. Because of these maps, early provided and carefully detailed, W.E. Merrill, chief Engineer, Army of the Cumberland, believed that the army which Sherman led to Atlanta was the best supplied with maps of any that fought in the Civil War.

For use in the field, a facsimile photo-printing device was invented by Captain W.C. Margedant, 9th Ohio Volunteer Infantry. Margedant's device consisted of a light box containing several india-rubber baths, fitted into one another, and supply of the necessary chemicals. Printing was done by tracing the required map on thin paper and laying it over a sheet coated with nitrate of silver. The sun's rays passing through the tissue paper blackened the prepared paper except under the ink lines, thus making a white map on a black background. In this way, copies from the drawing-paper map could be made as often as new information came in; occasionally there would be several editions of the one map on a single day. However, the process was expensive; accordingly, the number of maps printed by this process was limited, and were issued only to the chief commanders.

Apparently, various other methods of reproducing maps were attempted during the war. On March 31, 1863,John Underwood of London, England was granted a United States patent for his "improved process of copying writings, maps, etc." (He had an earlier English patent on this process, dated April 20, 1857.)

According to the patent description (U.S. Patent No. 38,086), the map to be copied was printed with a prepared ink, and being brought into contact with prepared paper under pressure, the chemical properties of the ink and paper were such that a chemical reaction took place, and the characters on the paper were copied. The paper could be written upon with a solution of an extract of logwood, and the copying paper treated with a solution of a neutral chromate of potash. It is not known whether this process of map copying was utilized by either side during the War, but such could have been the case, since the process was patented only half way through the war.

It is interesting to note that on February 5, 1864, a Richmond, Virginia firm (R.S. Sanxay and Adolph

Gomert) were granted Patent No. 227 by the Confederate States for a "photographic process for duplicating maps." Adolph Gomert was a photographer in the 5th Louisiana Regiment. In January 1863, he was released from the Army in order to work with the R.S. Sanxay of Richmond in making copies of maps and documents for the Engineer Department of the Army. The Army furnished the men with two horses and a wagon. The men received a monthly wage from the Army and also a monthly payment for the use of their new process of copying documents by photography, patented in 1864. In addition to copying maps and documents and making occasional photographs, these men also made engraved copies of appointments and commissions for the Headquarters Staff.

MARINE CORPS HAT EMBLEM (U.S.)

Information on Marine Corps insignia is derived from the *Regulations for the Uniform and Dress of the Marine Corps of the United States* (1859). Shown here is the hat plate. On this plate was superimposed the well-known bugle (the current army designation for infantry) with an "M" to indicate Marines. The bugle and "M" are missing from the plate shown here.

Marine Corps Hat Emblem (U.S.)

MARINE CORPS SHARPSHOOTERS INSIGNIA (U.S.)

Extremely rare insignia worn by Marines stationed on shipboard as sharpshooters in the masts. Patch area: 4 inches long and 1 7/8 inches wide; actual insignia is 2 3/4 inches long and 3/4 inch wide. Colors: gold musket on a crimson background. Worn on the left shoulder above the chevron. From the collection of William Langlois.

MASCOTS AND PETS

The most famous mascot was "Old Abe," the eagle of the 8th Wisconsin Infantry. Another Wisconsin regiment (12th Infantry) had a young bear, while many regiments like the 35th Ohio Infantry, had dogs as regimental mascots. Although regiments had kittens and even goats as mascots, probably the most unique

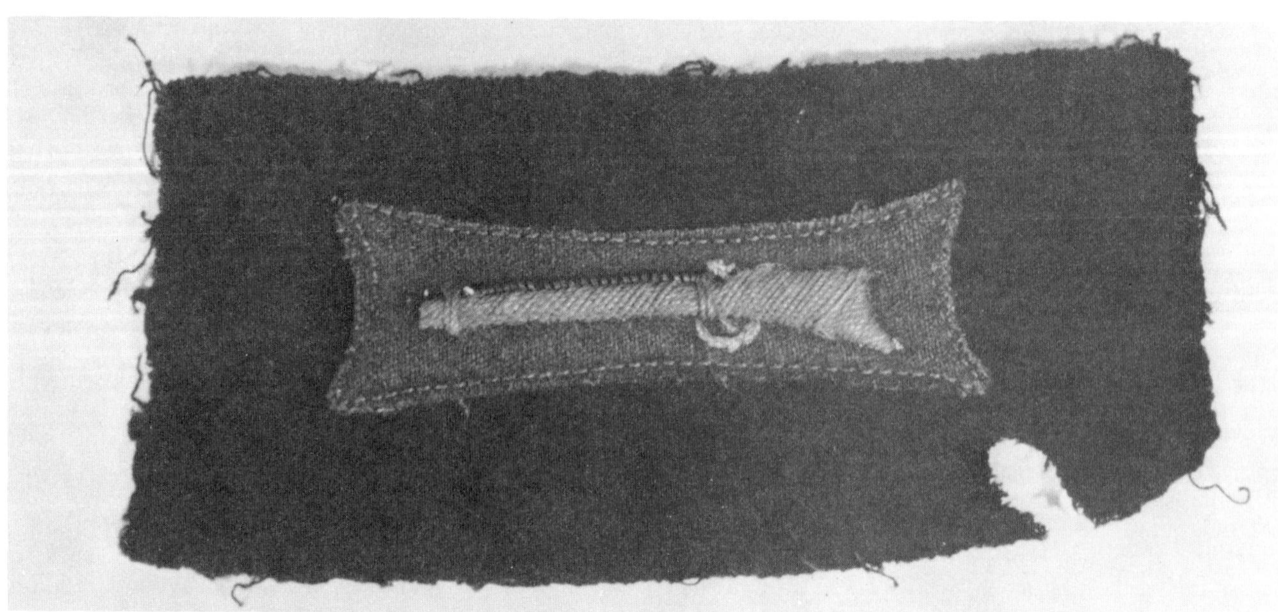

William Langlois

Marine Corps Sharpshooters Insignia (U.S.)

Library of Congress

A Mascot in Camp

was a trained pig in the 9th Connecticut Infantry. This pig, known as "Jeff Davis," was taught to stand on his hind legs, hold a pipe, etc. He put on a good show during an inspection by the commanding general who was much amused at his antics.

But most regiments like the 34th Massachusetts Infantry, had "an army" of dogs. Some howled at every bugle call; some fell in line regularly for rations; while others loitered on the outskirts of camp making a stealthy approach to the cook-house when no one was observing.

Battery "A," Chicago Light Artillery, had a "Battery dog," "Tony" by name who was wounded at Fort Donelson and Shiloh. Tony never got separated from the Battery and never got into another unit by mistake. A beautiful Newfoundland dog was found lying dead at the Antietam beside the body of W.J. Pollock, Co. "H" 20th New York Infantry. This dog had escaped death at South Mountain where he had been completely indifferent to the zip of enemy bullets around him.

The 48th New York Infantry acquired two pups as mascots. One was soon sold because he drank a can of condensed milk each meal. The other was shot dead at Cold Harbor while barking up a tree at a Confederate sharpshooter.

In the 5th Connecticut Infantry, a black and tan terrier, weighing about 15 pounds, had a peculiar respect for the commanding officer of whatever detachment or expedition he was upon. If the whole company was out, the dog kept close to the captain. If only a platoon, he kept with the sergeant. On dress parades, which he always attended, he left the company and went to the rear of the colonel and watched the parade with real dignity.

Although all soldiers looked alike, he could tell a Co. "F" man (his company) as far as he could see him from any other soldier without mistake, and he never followed others.

In battle he became highly excited and faced the enemy several feet ahead of the company line. The striking of a shell into the ground near him would make him almost wild. This dog survived the war.

MASONIC EMBLEM

Officers and men organized Masonic lodges. The community of interest between members of these lodges was remarkable. This common bond often overrode the animosities of battle. Frequently, Confederate prisoners sat in lodges with their Federal captors. Not infrequently wounded Masons gave the Masonic sign of distress and were assisted by Masons from the ranks of their enemy. Masons of both armies wore their Masonic wings and pins during their service. Shown here is a Masonic emblem large enough to be easily seen from quite a distance.

DESCRIPTION

Bright tin, 2 1/2 inches tall and 2 1/8 inches wide.

A STOLEN MASONIC EMBLEM

The lodge of Masons in which George Washington was "initiated, passed and raised," Fredericksburg, Virginia, No. 4, was pillaged in 1862, by Federal troops. The lodge safe was blown open and the records, regalia, jewels, etc., carried off. Among the articles taken, was an old jewel of solid silver in the form of a "level," highly prized by the Lodge for its antiquity. The relic was discovered some twenty years after the war in the safe of Integrity Lodge, N. 158, A.F. & A.M. of Philadelphia. It had been placed in this safe by a former member of Integrity Lodge No. 158 who had recovered it from the soldier who originally pilfered it in Fredericksburg. A note tacked to the jewel required its delivery to the Fredericksburg Lodge "when the state of Virginia should cease to be in open rebellion against the authority of the Government of the United States." The jewel was returned to the Fredericksburg Lodge.

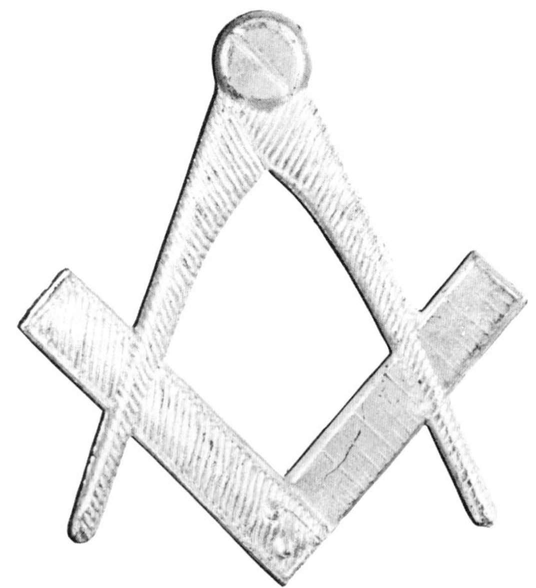

Civil War Masonic Emblem

MATCHES AND MATCH CONTAINERS

Soldiers built campfires, cooked their rations, and smoked cigars or pipes. Vast quantities of wooden matches were used up in these essential processes. Naturally, only a comparatively few of the wooden matches have survived the decades since the war. Illustrated here are some of the original matches and the containers used to keep them dry. All have a scratching surface on the bottom.

Matches Wood (pine), 2 1/2 inches long. Made from a piece of pine cut half way down for easy separation of individual matches.

Match Containers (left to right), Tin container, 2 3/4 inches long, 1 1/2 inches wide, and 3/4 inch deep. Carried by G.D. Smith, of Wayne, Maine.

Tin Container, 2 1/2 inches tall, 1 inch wide, 3/8 inch deep. Decorated with a spread eagle.

Iron Container, 2 1/4 inches long, 3/4 inch wide, and 3/8 inch deep.

Hard rubber container, 2 3/4 inches tall, 1 inch wide, and 1/2 inch deep. Marked: N.R. Co.

MESS EQUIPMENT

The bewildering variety of mess equipment of the Civil War era continues to be both a joy and a constant frustration! There just is no end to the types and variants of items now being dug up in camp and battle sites, and attics continue to yield further specimens to confound the collector. In the preparation of my *Civil War Collector's Encyclopedia* (1963) I included major types of mess items but space limitations precluded a definitive treatment. Even today a truly exhaustive treatment is not possible. However recent discoveries of other types and variants justify a new and more extended treatment.

Mess equipment divides itself naturally into two basic categories—the individual and the organizational. "Organizational equipment" was to be found in such rear installations as training and "rendezvous" camps and base hospitals. Similar equipment, especially early in the war, was also used in the field at unit headquarters from the army down to the company.

"Individual equipment" comprised those items carried by the soldier on his person. The customary mess equipment for each soldier included a tin plate, cup, and knife, fork, and spoon. If the soldier lost his cutlery he often obtained a knife—fork—spoon combination, either from home or from a sutler. It is obvious that these combinations were quite popular as evidenced by the number being found in camp sites and on battlefield. Also, the men often purchased frying pans or made them from canteens which they split in half. Some soldiers carried graters or improvised them by punching holes in canteens. These graters were used to grind corn which, in turn, were made into "Johnny cake" or pancakes.

Matches and Match Containers

Collapsible Drinking Cups
Left to right:
A 3-section cup, 2 1/2 inches in diameter at the top and 2 3/8 inches at the base. Height when fully open—3 1/8 inches. Case is of japanned tin. No markings. Carried by: Captain Luther Lawrence Co. "H" 11th Maine Infantry. Captain Lawrence died of wounds in 1864.

A 4-section cup, 2 inches in diameter at the top and 1 1/4 inches at the bottom with a base 2 1/4 inches in diameter. Height when fully open 2 1/8 inches. No markings except an American shield on the cover with 10 stars. (Mr. Gerald L. James of Chatsworth, California also has one of these in his collection and kindly shared information on this cup).

Confederate cup carried by a soldier from Charleston, South Carolina. Leather case. This 6-section cup is 2 3/8 inches in diameter at the top and 1 3/4 inches at the base. Height when fully open—2 3/4 inches. No markings.

COFFEE GRINDERS. "Hardtack and Coffee" is a term which has almost become synonymous with the Civil War ration. Naturally, coffee was of great importance and, accordingly, so are coffee grinders. Although not issued, these coffee grinders were used fairly extensively in the early part of the war. However, they were too bulky for the individual soldier to carry. Shown here are two coffee grinders. The larger is of cast iron, 4 3/4 inches wide with the box 4 3/4 inches tall. The metal base at the top is 6 inches square. No markings.

Also shown are remains of three coffee grinders used in the field. The top is from the 9th Corps area at Falmouth, Virginia. The middle piece is also from Falmouth, Virginia.

Coffee Mills

Condiment Containers

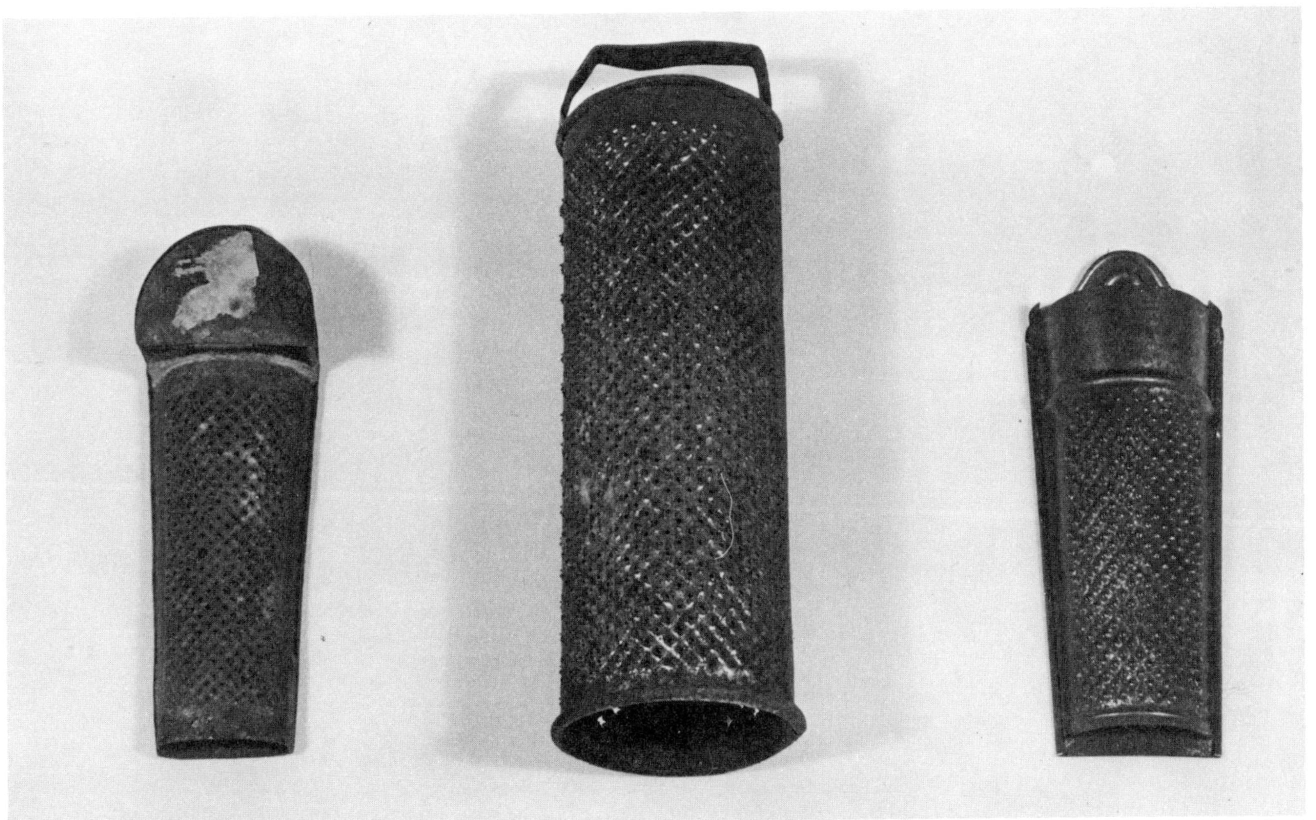

Graters
Left to right:
Grater 5 inches long, 1 3/8 inches wide at bottom and 1 3/4 inches wide at top. There is a hinged cover at the top.

A round grater, 6 1/8 inches long, 2 1/8 inches in diameter. From St. Louis, Missouri.

Grater 4 3/4 inches long, 1 5/8 inches wide at the bottom and 2 inches wide at the top. Made of Japanned tin, this grater also came from St. Louis, Missouri.

The piece on the right is from a Civil War camp at La Grange, Tennessee.

COLLAPSIBLE DRINKING CUPS. Three different types are shown here. All are nickle-plated brass.

CONDIMENT CONTAINERS. On the left a japanned tin salt shaker, 3 inches in diameter and 3 3/4 inches tall. The top has 31 perforations. No markings. On the right a heavy glass salt or pepper shaker with a pewter top with 14 perforations. No markings. This shaker is square—1 5/8 inches on a side and is 4 1/2 inches tall.

C.S. GRIDLE. This gridle was recovered in a Confederate camp at Yorktown, Virginia. The gridle is of cast iron, has three legs, and is only 3 3/4 inches tall. The 14-inch plate is completely surrounded by a 7/8 inch flange.

GRATER. Men of both armies depended largely on fresh corn picked in the fields while "living off the country." Therefore, graters were in demand for making corn meal out of the ears stripped from corn fields. Old canteens were split and the halves were punched with holes—thus improvising a crude but effective grater. Sometimes sardine tins were used for the same purpose—all that was needed was a nail and hammer!

However, graters were a common household item of the 1860's and many soldiers brought their own graters to the field. Shown here are three of the most common types. All are made of tin.

KNIFE—FORK—SPOON COMBINATIONS. One of the civilian items in use during the War which offers an almost endless variety of different types is the knife-fork-spoon combination. Shown here are ten variations. Numbers 1 and 2 are the "common" variety; of 22 specimens in the author's collection, 13 are of this type.

MESS CHEST [*C.S.*]. Made of pine, 27 3/4 inches long, 13 1/2 inches wide, and 13 inches tall. Wooden handles. Used in Virginia by Major Thomas Foster, C.S.A.

MESS PAILS. Shown here are two pails used during the war. One is made of light tin, 4 1/2 inches tall and 5 7/8 inches in diameter. The other is of heavy tin, 4 3/8

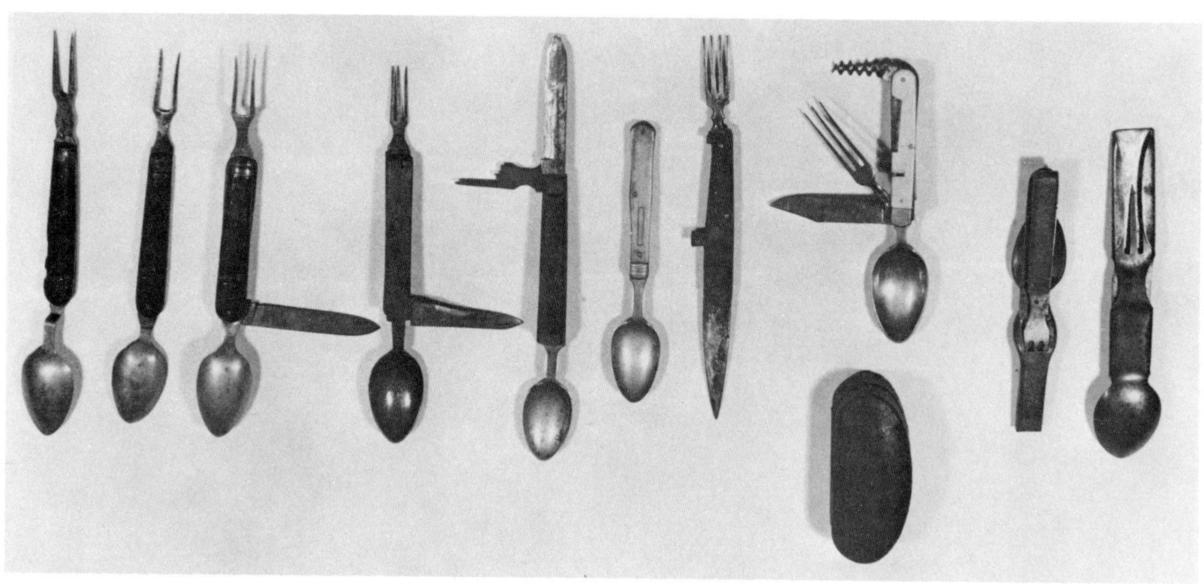

Knife-Fork-Spoon Combinations
Top to bottom:
Fork-spoon combination, a 2-tined fork. Dimensions: 4 1/2 inches closed. 11 1/4 inches open.

Fork-spoon combination. Picked up on the Wilderness battlefield. Marked:

V.A.W. Co. H 9 N.Y. Reg. 1864
2-tine fork
Dimensions: 4 1/2 inches closed. 10 1/2 inches open.

A crudely-made bone handle knife with a 3-tine fork. The 3 1/8 inch knife blade is marked: BLAND Dimensions: Closed—4 3/4 inches and open—10 1/4 inches. Used by Thomas B. Wellman in Libby Prison.

A 2-tined fork with a 3 3/4 inch knife blade marked:

KNIFE CO.
NAUGATUCK

The fork is marked:

ARMY KNIFE
UNION

Dimensions: Closed—4 3/4 inches and open—10 3/4 inches.

Another bone handle knife—fork combination. The 3-tine fork has had two tines broken off. The 3 5/8 inch knife blade is marked: . . . Sheffield. Dimensions: Closed—4 1/2 inches and open—11 3/4 inches.

An ivory handle folding spoon carried by John G. Macomber, 6th Vermont Infantry who was killed at the Wilderness, May 5, 1864. The silver spoon has proof marks. Dimensions: Closed—4 1/8 inches and open—7 1/2 inches.

A 4-tine fork item. Dimensions: Closed—4 1/2 inches and open—10 1/2 inches.

Another ivory handle combination in a velvet-lined case. This one has a 3-tine fork, a corkscrew, a spoon, and a 3 1/4 inch knife blade marked: L & G which stands for Lamson and Goodnow. Dimensions: Closed 4-inches and open 9-inches.

A knife-fork-spoon combination marked:

WORKMAN ELY & CO.
PHILA
PATENT FEB. 4, 1862

Overall length—7 1/2 inches.

Another type— Marked:

. . .RICHARDS
PATENT JULY 23, 1862

Overall length—9 1/4 inches.

C.S. Mess Chest. Used by Major Thomas Foster, C.S.A.

Mess Pails

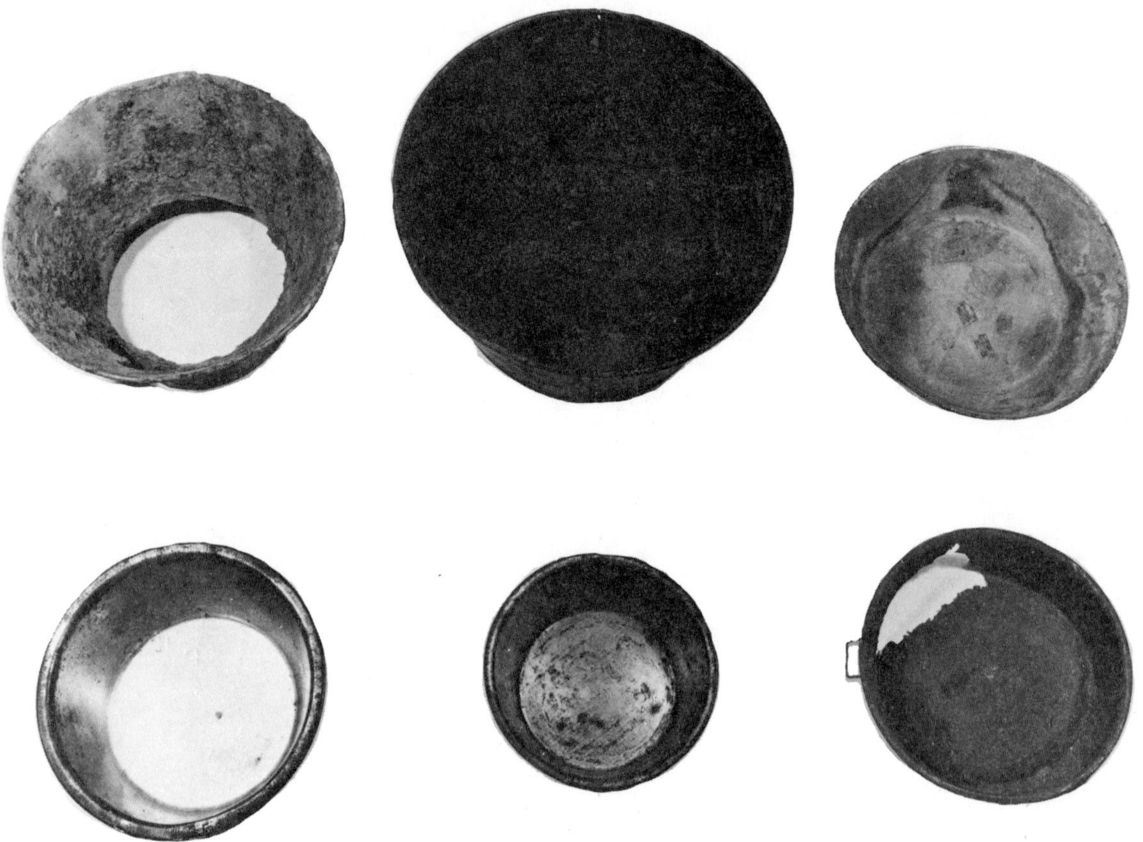

Mess Pans

Left to right:
Top Row:
Light tin, unpainted. Dimensions: 9 3/4 inches in diameter at the top and 6 inches at the bottom. Depth—4 1/2 inches. Markings: None. From camp of the 1st Texas Infantry, C.S.A. on the Potomac River, 1861.

Heavy tin, painted blue. Dimensions: 11 1/2 inches in diameter at the top and 8 inches at the bottom. Depth—5 1/4 inches. Markings: None.

Navy—Medium weight tin, unpainted. Dimensions: 8 5/8 inches in diameter at the top and 5 7/8 inches in diameter at the bottom. Depth 1 7/8 inches. Markings: None.

Left to right:
Bottom Row:
Medium weight tin, unpainted. Dimensions: 8 inches in diameter at the top and 5 3/8 inches at the bottom. Depth 2 1/2 inches. Has a metal loop for hanging up.

Medium weight tin, unpainted. Dimensions: 6 1/2 inches in diameter at the top and 4 1/2 inches at the bottom. Depth 2 1/8 inches. Markings: None.

Medium weight tin, unpainted. Dimensions: 7 3/4 inches in diameter at the top and 6 1/4 inches at the bottom. Depth 1 3/4 inches. Metal loop for hanging. Markings: None. From U.S. camp at Falmouth, Virginia.

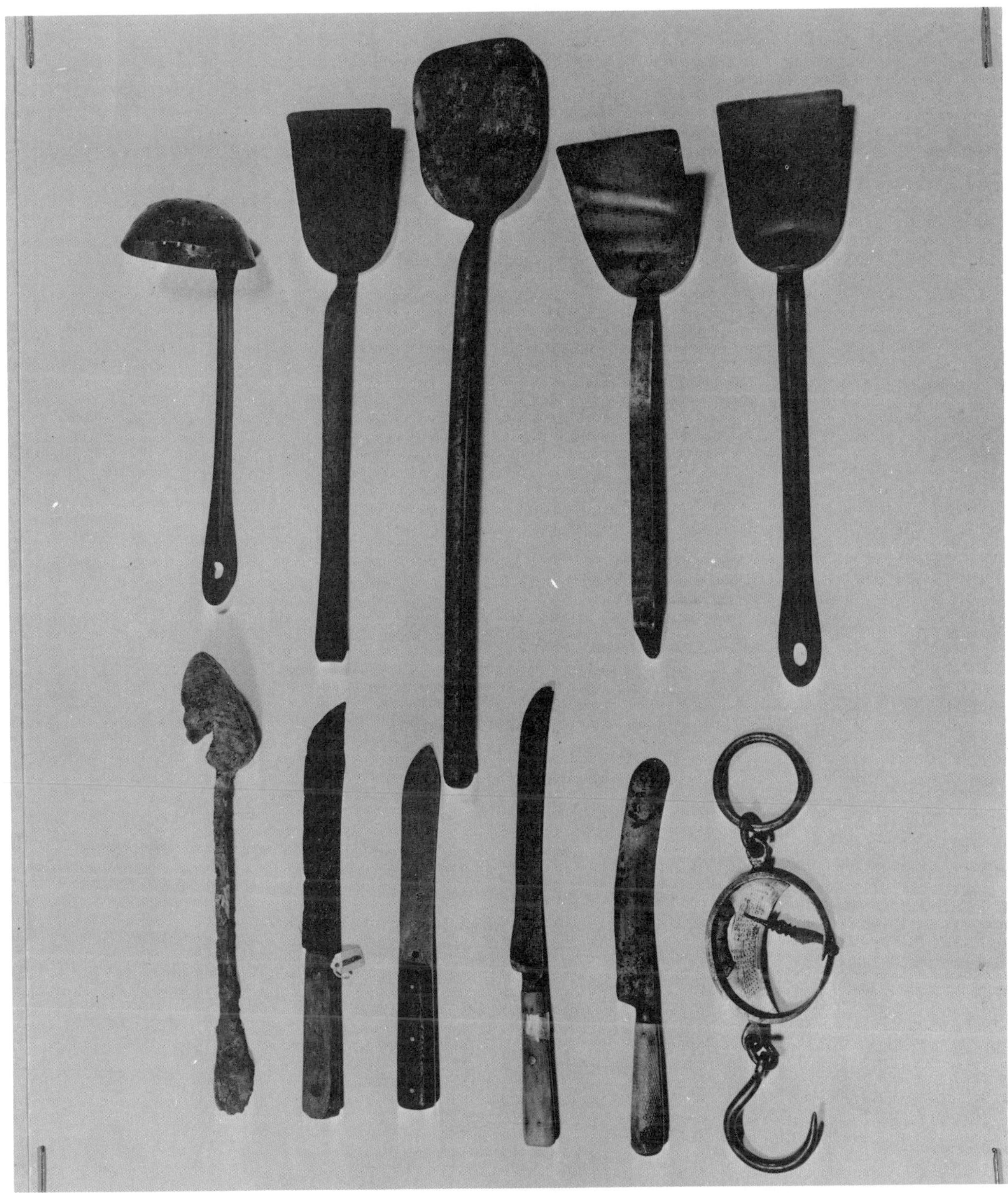

Miscellaneous Kitchenware
Left to right:
Top Row:
Tin skimmer, 11 1/4 inches long, (handle—9 3/4 inches), with a 4 3/4 inch diameter skimmer section. No markings.

Spatula, 15 1/4 inches long. Marked: 11 SEP CO.
[SEP = SEPARATE]

Spatula, 20 inches long, no markings.

Spatula, 14 inches long, no markings.

Spatula, 15 inches long, marked: 16 3

(All spatulas shown are made of iron)

Left to right:
Bottom Row:
Iron spoon, 13 3/4 inches long, from camp of the 1st Texas Infantry, C.S.A. on the Potomac River, 1861.

Kitchen knife, 10 inches long with a 6 1/8 inch blade, marked:

HANOVER CUTLERY
CO.

Wooden handle.

Kitchen knife, 11 3/4 inches long with a 7 1/8 inch blade. Picked up on the Bull Run battlefield. Wooden handle.

Kitchen knife, 12 3/8 inches long with an 8 inch blade marked:

W. & S. BUTCHER
BEST CAST STEEL

The bone handle is marked: H.J.D. Co. C 3-
From the battlefield of Kernstown, Virginia.

Kitchen knife, 10 5/8 inches long with a 6 1/2 inch blade marked: W. Dunn
Bone handle.

Metal scales, 11 3/4 inches long (at rest) marked: C. Kurtz
The scales are marked off in 20's beginning with 20 and ending with 400.

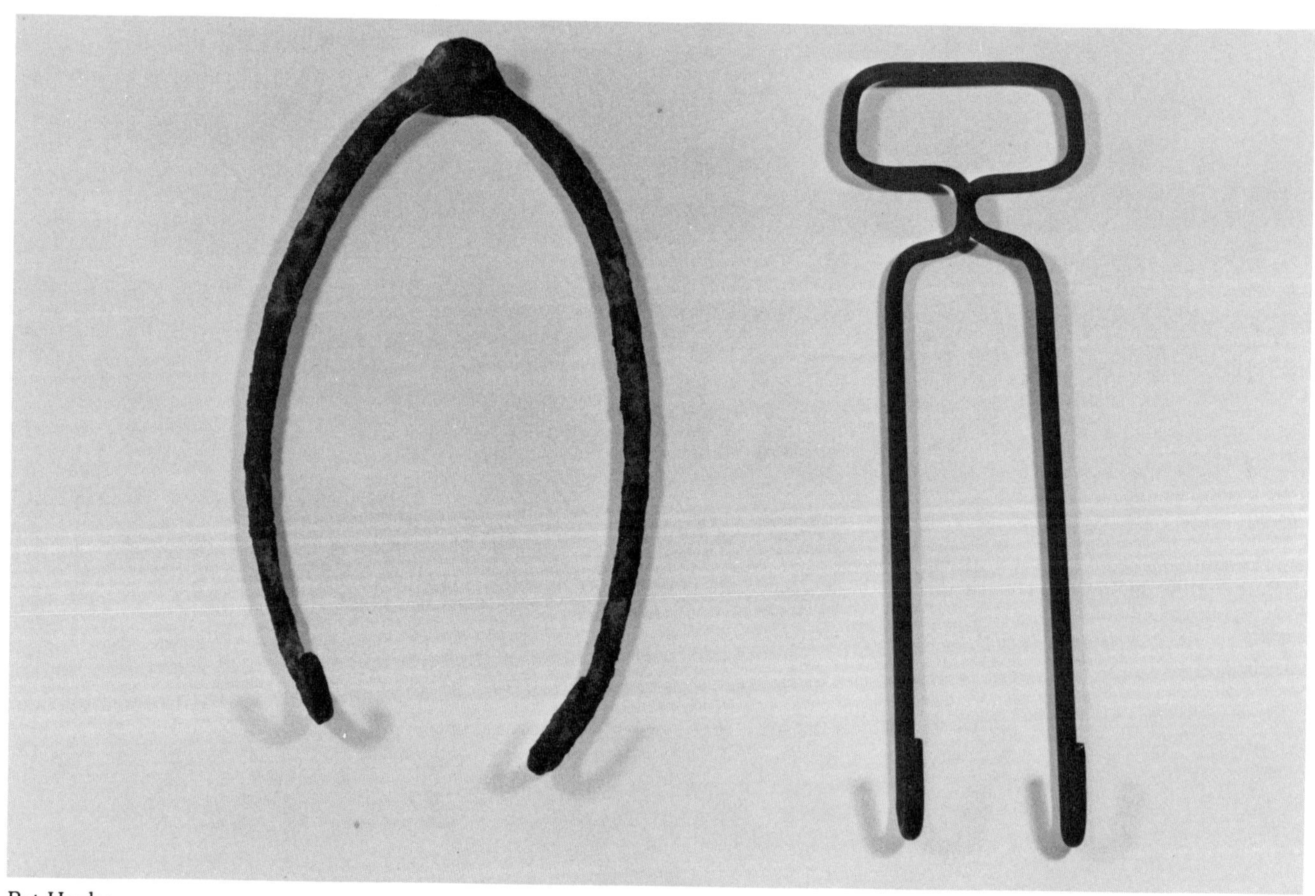

Pot Hooks
Left: Each arm of this pot hook is 13 3/4 inches long and has a hook on the end to hold a pot or kettle. From Falmouth, Virginia.
Right: Iron pot hook. Overall length—14 3/4 inches. Each hook arm is 10 1/2 inches long.

Scoops and Dippers
Left to right:
Light tin dipper, 8 inches in diameter at the top and 5 1/2 inches at the bottom. Depth—3 3/4 inches. The handle is 8 1/2 inches long. No markings.

Medium—weight tin dipper, 4 1/2 inches in diameter and 3 3/8 inches deep. The handle is 4 inches long. No markings.

Heavy tin scoop with overall length of 15 1/2 inches and width of 7 1/2 inches. Markings: 5.

C.S. Gridle

Stoves or Coffee Heaters
Both are candle-heated. Left—Author's Collection: Right—Colonel R.B. Harding's Collection.

Strainer

Individual Oil Stoves

Southern Silver Cup

inches tall and 4 3/4 inches in diameter.

MESS PANS. Although mess pans have been mentioned briefly in previous publications by the author, additional research has uncovered several new types. Accordingly, we are showing here some important variations as follows:

SOUTHERN SILVER CUP. A fine silver cup, decorated with floral designs, 3 1/4 inches tall, diameter at base 2 1/2 inches and at the top 2 3/4 inches.

Is engraved as follows:

"Taken from the
Mayor's House
Petersburg (Fredericksburg) Va.
Dec. 13, 1862
by
A.W. Gross

This cup was probably used by Gross during the war and then taken home as a souvenir of the Fredericksburg campaign.

INDIVIDUAL "STOVES" OR COFFEE HEATERS. As contrasted with the stoves used at large camp and base installations, we show here the small "stoves" or coffee heaters used to a limited extent during the war. Stove, heated by candle, made of japanned tin, 6 3/4 inches tall, 4 1/4 inches in diameter, with a removable cup 2 1/2 inches tall. No markings. The other is 9 1/4 inches tall and 5 1/4 inches in diameter. Also this still has the original cover and is *copper* with an interior tin lining. Both cups have handles similar to those on drinking cups of the period.

Shown here are two oil stoves, each carried in a tin container which is used as a holder for the coffee to be heated and as a drinking cup. The larger container is 5 inches in diameter and 2 1/2 inches high. The cover is missing. The smaller heater is 4 inches in diameter and 1 1/2 inches high.

STRAINER. Made of unpainted light-weight tin. It is unmarked with a diameter of 12 3/8 inches at the top and 10 inches at the bottom. Depth 2 1/2 inches.

Group of 4th Michigan Infantry. Note the coffee pot, tin cup, and typical 3-tine fork.

The 3rd New Hampshire Infantry at Hilton Head, S.C. 1861. Note the mess table and sundry mess gear.

The 3rd New Hampshire Infantry in camp at Hilton Head, S.C., 1861. Note the coffee mill and mess pan.

MILITARY PASSES

To supplement the military security inherent in the system of paroles and countersigns, military units often restricted the movements within their lines by means of passes. These passes were issued to specific military personnel and civilians and very often were restricted to specific roads and river crossings. Four types of passes are shown here. Note that only one required the recipient's signature! Such laxity in security is only matched by the pass for a "party of four gentlemen!" The "four gentlemen" could have been any four male adults in the Washington area.

HEADQUARTERS, FORT CORCORAN, VIRGINIA. Size 7 1/2 x 5 1/4 inches. Issued April 18, 1862, to *M. C. Corbet and wife* for passage "through to their house inside the Picket Line."

HEADQUARTERS, MILITARY DEPARTMENT OF WASHINGTON. Size 8 x 6 inches. Issued June 7, 1861, to a "Party of four gentlemen" over the Long Bridge and within the lines.

HEADQUARTERS, CITY GUARD. Size 7 1/4 x 6 inches. Issued December 20, 1861, by the Provost Marshal's office, Washington, D.C. to "*Eli Whitney* and five persons" to pass over any bridge or ferry to Virginia. Signed by Eli Whitney.

HEADQUARTERS, 104TH NEW YORK INFANTRY. Size 8 x 5 inches. Camp King near Catlett's Station, Virginia. Issued June 16, 1862, to Capt. Henry A. Wyley, 104th New York Infantry for visiting Washington, D.C. "on private business of an important nature." The pass was good for only 48 hours.

MINT DROPS CONTAINER

Made of thin brass, 1 1/4 inches in diameter and 3/8 inches deep. The top of the container is decorated with a woman's head, stars and the date 1851. The bottom of the container is decorated with an American eagle and the words:

"United States Mint Drops
Twenty."

Carried by a drummer boy of the 4th New Hampshire Infantry.

To all whom it may concern:

Head Quarters City Guard,
Provost Marshal's Office,

No 280

WASHINGTON, Dec Twentieth, 1861.

Know ye, *That the bearers,* Eli Whitney and five Persons, *have permission to pass over any bridge or ferry to Virginia, and within the lines, and back, for the purpose of* visiting friends *being subject to the inspection of guards or patrols.*

This Pass will expire Dec Twenty fifth

By command of A. PORTER, *Brig. Gen. U. S. A., Provost Marshal.*

Pass Mr Whitney and five others.

C. S. Mehaffey
Aide-de-Camp.

In availing myself of the benefits of the above pass, I do solemnly affirm that I am a true and loyal citizen of the United States; and that I will not give aid, comfort, or information to the enemies of the United States Government in any manner whatsoever.

Eli Whitney

[This Pass to be taken up at its expiration.]

A Pass that Expired Christmas Day

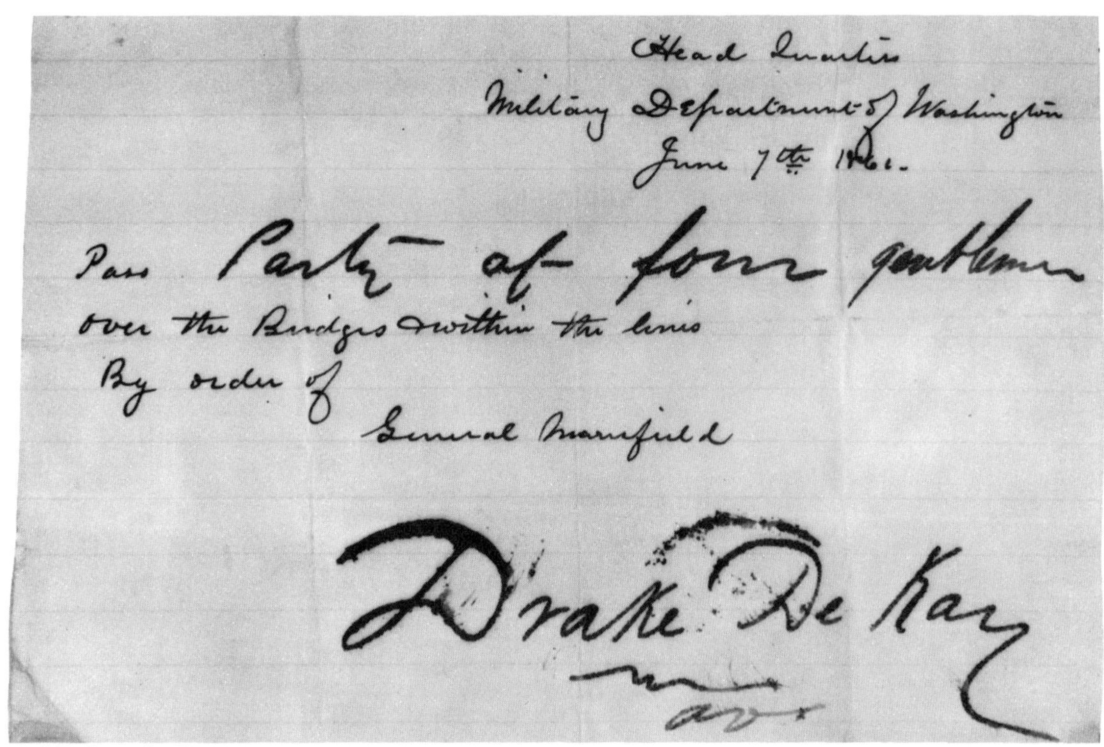

Head Quarters
Military Department of Washington
June 7th 1861.

Pass Party of four gentlemen
over the Bridges within the lines
By order of
General Mansfield

Drake De Kay
A.D.C.

A Pass Issued Early in the War

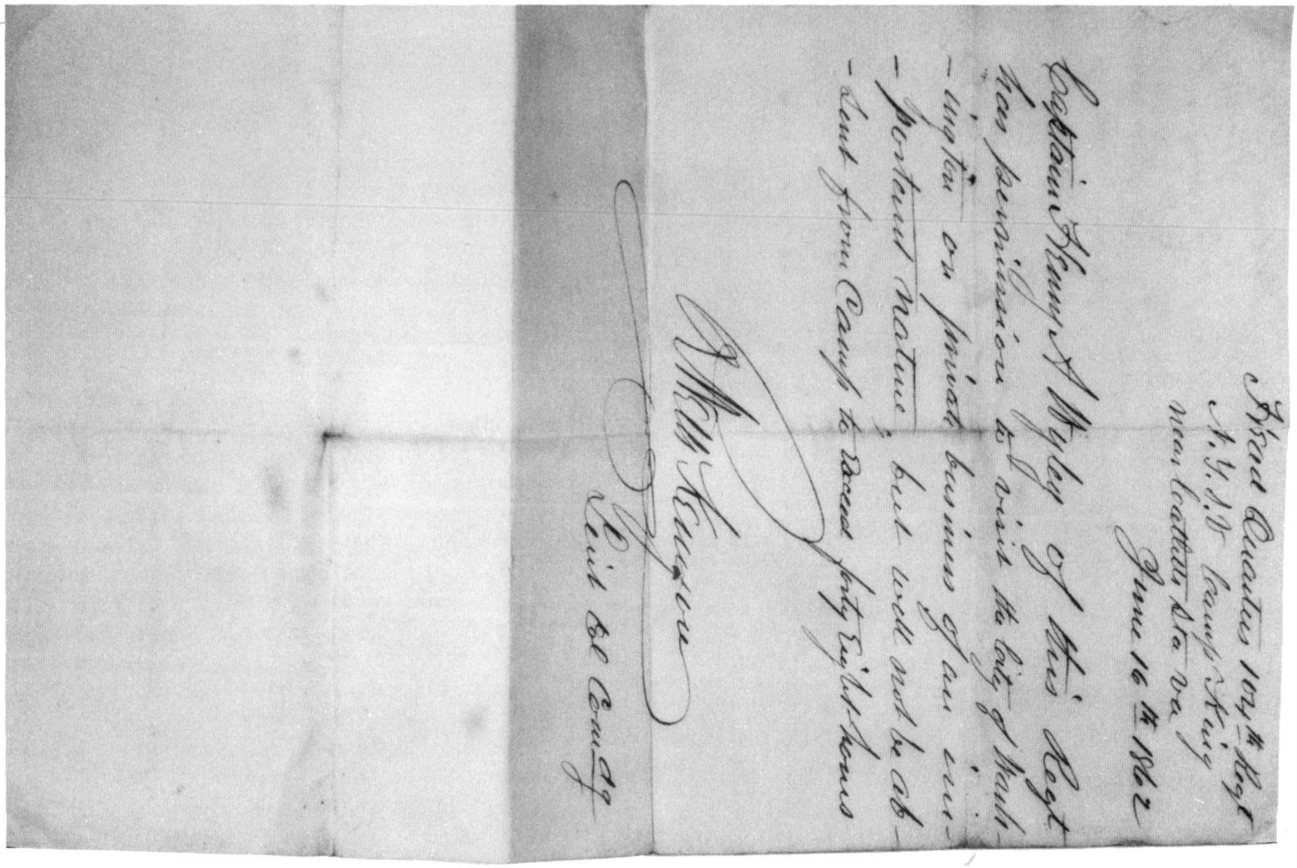

Head Quarters 104th Regt
N.Y.S.V. Camp King
near Cattletts Sta Va
June 16th 1862

Captain Henry A. Wyley of this Regt
has permission to visit the City of Washington on private business of an important nature but will not be absent from Camp to exceed forty Eight hours

Lieut Col Comdg

An Officer's Pass

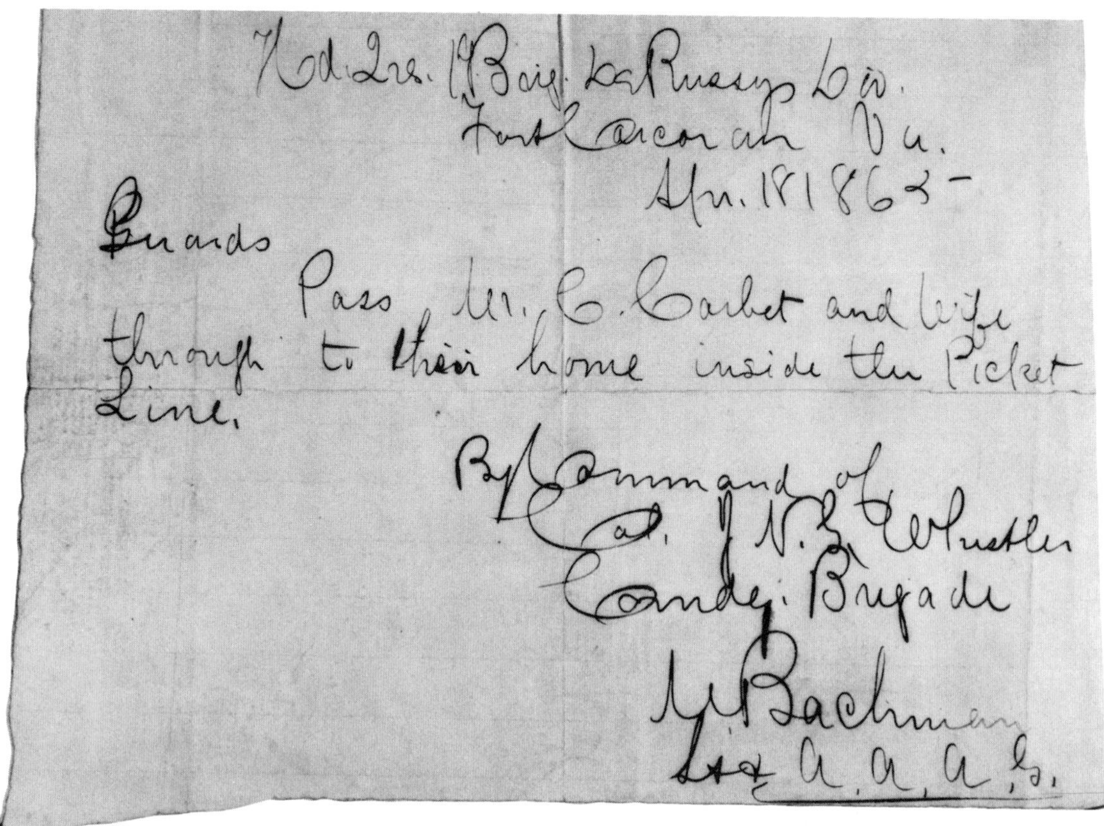

Hd. Qrs. 1st Brig. De Russy's Div.
Fort Corcoran Va.
Apr. 18 1863 –

Guards
Pass Mr. C. Corbet and Wife
through to their home inside the Picket
Line.

By Command of
Col. J. N. G. Whistler
Comdg. Brigade
M. Bachman
Lt. A. A. A. G.

Military Pass to Civilians

Mint Drops Container

THE MISSISSIPPI RIFLE

One of the most attractive and interesting of all Civil War long arms is the weapon known under many titles but most commonly as the "Mississippi Rifle." This weapon, one of the most important in United States military history, was the first regulation rifle with a percussion lock. In its day it was very generally regarded as the most accurate weapon of its type in the world. In addition to its reputation with the military it was often chosen by duellists (who had a very real interest in its accuracy)! Big game hunters swore by it.

Even before the Civil War, such regular units as the 4th U.S. Infantry used this rifle with good effect in their Indian campaigns. The regular army enlisted man believed he could hit an Indian nearly every time at ranges up to 1,000 yards with this rifle. While such shooting was probably extremely rare, the regulars were well aware of the superiority of their "Yaeger" as they termed them, to the converted flintlock muskets, especially the convered 1822 model.

The Mississippi Rifle was officially known as the U.S. Rifle Model 1841, but titles varied with localities and with troops using the weapon. The Regular Army used

Herb Peck, Jr.

Unidentified Confederate Soldier with Mississippi Rifle

such terms as Yaeger, Yager, Jaeger, Yeger, etc. depending on how close they could come to spelling the word Jaeger—the German word for rifleman. New Englanders often called the weapon the "Windsor Rifle" since large numbers were made under contract in Windsor, Vermont. Some reports and individuals referred to this weapon as the "Harper's Ferry Rifle" since the first short rifles were made at Harper's Ferry. But this was confusing because the Model 1855 short rifle was made at Harper's Ferry and the two weapon types tended to become confused in ordnance officer reports. Some called the weapon the "Whitney Rifle" because Whitney turned out this model under contract. This too was confusing because there had been Whitney contract long arms for almost a half century.

Eventually, most soldiers and observers came to use the term "Mississippi Rifle" which resulted from the issue to Jefferson Davis' First Mississippi Regiment of these rifles in 1847. Davis' rifle (made by Whitney) won such acclaim during the Mexican War that the title "Mississippi Rifle" has stuck ever since the return of that famous unit from Mexico.

During the 1850's and throughout the Civil War, the Mississippi Rifle continued to be popular with both Federals and Confederates. For example, the Mississippi Rifle, known in New England as the "Windsor Rifle" was issued to eager Federal volunteers in the early months of the war.

In August 1861, the 7th Maine Infantry was issued "Windsor Rifles," and the men received their new weapons with mixed emotions. The guns had plenty of brass trimmings to keep clean, and sabre bayonets, but their beautiful appearance made the Maine boys very proud of them. Moreover, in battle the men found that they shot "pretty straight." Cumbersome as the saber bayonets were they proved to be excellent to dig shelters with; several times in the 1862 battles on the Peninsula the long leveled line of these saber bayonets "carried consternation to the gray-clothed foe."

There is ample photographic evidence to show that the Confederates liked this arm. For example, a well-known photograph of the "Clinch Rifles" taken May 10, 1861, shows its men with this weapon. The Clinch Rifles became Company "A" of the 6th Georgia Infantry and saw action throughout the war.

One of the early Southern weapons of this type was the "Palmetto Rifle" which was very similar to the 1841 model, with a 33-inch barrel, caliber .54, and similar brass furniture. In 1852 this arm was being made at Palmetto Armory in Columbia, South Carolina by William Glaze and Company. A surprisingly large proportion of Confederate gun makers made at least a few Mississippi Rifles. Of a total of 39 identified Confederate makers of long arms, at least 14 definitely manufactured this arm. The number is probably higher since often we only know that these makers made "sharpshooters' rifles," or simply "rifles."

Throughout the war, Federals were able to bear testimony to the accuracy of this arm. At Fort Donelson, February 1862, a Confederate sharpshooter known as "Old Red Shirt," who was a remarkably excellent shot, did considerable execution among the skirmishers of the 50th Illinois Infantry. The Confederate finally was killed by a concentrated fire of his opponents and the Illinois boys moved up and got his gun. They stated that it had "shot with terrific force and made a peculiar sound." One of old Red Shirt's victims had been a Federal sergeant who staggered back to the rear with "a great hole under his left cheek bone." Old Red Shirt had used a Mississippi Rifle and was only bested by several of Birge's sharpshooters who were armed with snipers' rifles, equipped with telescopic sights.

Although sharpshooters on both sides continued to like the Mississippi Rifle, infantrymen did not like the heavy saber bayonet and preferred the triangular bayonets of the regulation 1861 rifle-musket. There is no question however, that the Mississippi Rifle saw use throughout the war, as they have been found on battle-

Missouri (C.S.) Flag

fields from 1861 through 1865.

The Mississippi Rifle, known officially as U.S. Model 1841, marked the end of the flintlock in U.S. service. After 1842, flintlocks were altered to percussion weapons, and, as every collector knows, were used in great quantities during the early years of the war. The new 1841 rifle, by using a reduced powder charge, cut down the "kick" of the larger bore muskets (the Mississippi Rifle was initially made in .54 caliber as compared to .69 caliber for the flintlock muskets.)

The barrel of the Mississippi Rifle had three grooves, one twist in six feet, decreasing from breech to muzzle. At 1,000 yards the angle of elevation was 4 degrees from 30 minutes (4 degrees 30′) as compared with 4 degrees 50′ for the altered 1822 and 1841 muskets. Initial velocity of the Mississippi Rifle was 914 feet per second. The Mississippi Rifle used the cylindro-conical ball, with three grooves around the cylinder. Weight of the ball was 500 grains. Sights were of two basic types. Some were the two-leaf type while others were the long-range type, with adjusting screw.

The walnut stock contrasted beautifully with a large patch box 7 5/8 inches long by 1 11/16 inches wide. Made by the U.S. Government at Harpers Ferry (25,296 from 1846 and 1855) and at Springfield Armory (3,200 made in 1849). This rifle was also made by contractors: Robbins & Lawrence, Windsor, Vt.; Tryon, Philadelphia, Pa.; and E. Whitney, New Haven, Conn. Confederate contractors also produced copies or modifications of this arm.

Originally this rifle had no bayonet. But in 1855 Secretary of War Jefferson Davis approved the recommendation of an ordnance board that all rifles and muskets be caliber .58. Accordingly, many 1841 rifles were re-rifled, equipped with long-range rear sights, and equipped with saber bayonets. These bayonets, with a blade 22 1/2 inches long, vary slightly in shape. But collectors have always been especially interested in the three methods used for attaching the bayonet to the rifle. The first utilized a stud on the barrel, accomplished by shortening the stock and modifying the upper band. A second method involved using a locking bar and swivel ring on the bayonet itself—the Snell bayonet—which fitted in a notch on the barrel. A third method involved the use of a split ring on the bayonet which was locked on the barrel by a tightening screw. Lastly, after 1859, the rifles were equipped with the usual socket type, triangular bayonet, the muzzle end of the barrels of some of the rifles were ground down to use the triangular bayonet.

Accouterments for the Mississippi rifle have also been of interest to collectors. The more common type used was the rifleman's belt. (Also used, but to a lesser extent, is the set of accouterments shown on page 244 of the first volume of *Collector's Encyclopedia*). These were used by Corporal Harvey H. Giles, Co. "E" 4th Maine Infantry at First Bull Run.

This weapon has to be seen to be appreciated; it is a beauty. Total length is 4 feet 1/2 inch; barrel length is 33 inches. The gun weighs 9.75 lbs. and originally was not equipped with a bayonet. The charge consisted of a half ounce round bullet and 75 grains of powder. A patch was used. The Mississippi Rifle was originally caliber .54 but in the 1850's was re-bored to .58, and used the conical, hollow base Minie ball. During and after the Civil War some Mississippi Rifles were altered to breech loaders of the Lindner, Merrill, and other systems.

Contractors for the Mississippi Rifle contributed many of the specimens to be seen in collections today. Eli Whitney contracted for 17,600 between 1842 and 1855; Tryon of Philadelphia for 5,000 in 1848; Robbins and Lawrence (predecessors or Robbins and Lawrence) had contracted for 10,000 in 1845 to be delivered over a five-year period. Probably the most prolific contractor of all was Eliphalet Remington of Ilion, N.Y. and Herkimer, N.Y., who early became involved in making the Mississippi Rifle under contract, and probably turned out some 17,500 Mississippi Rifles.

The Mississippi Rifle was being produced in the early months of the war as attested to by contracts issued in 1861-1862 for some 12,500 saber bayonets for this rifle. Many of the bayonets for the Mississippi Rifle bear no markings. Moreover, they vary considerably in appearance. All in all, the Mississippi Rifle and its varied types of bayonets, remains as one of the more interesting weapons of the war.

MISSOURI (C.S.) FLAG

This 12 Star flag, 23 1/2 inches long and 21 1/2 inches wide, is of hand sewn silk. It is cavalry size. Missouri was admitted to the Confederacy in late 1861 but was never considered to be a true member of the Confederacy because of Federal occupation of the state. Note similarity to the United States flag. Federal flags never carried less than 13 stars. This flag saw actual service and very probably drew fire from other Confederate units whose troops were too "busy" to count the number of stars. From the collection of William Langlois.

NAVAL RATING BADGES

Distinguishing sleeve insignia, known as "sleeve ornaments" were worn by Federal enlisted personnel of the Navy. Shown here are examples of these insignia. They are of thin cotton or linen and range in size from 4 x 4 inches to 3 x 3 inches.

NECKWARE

Officers wore a black cravat or tie while Federal enlisted men wore a black leather collar, but only for a short time. They soon threw these "dog collars" away! A few military personnel wore a neckerchief. Naval enlisted personnel wore black silk neckerchiefs.

ODD-BALL INVENTIONS

Among the multiplicity of inventions offered the governments of the opposing forces in the Civil War were many of very questionable value. Perhaps some of these inventions *did* have promise but ordnance officers were often too conservative to appreciate their possible usefulness. For example, several models of breech-loading cannon were offered for trial to the

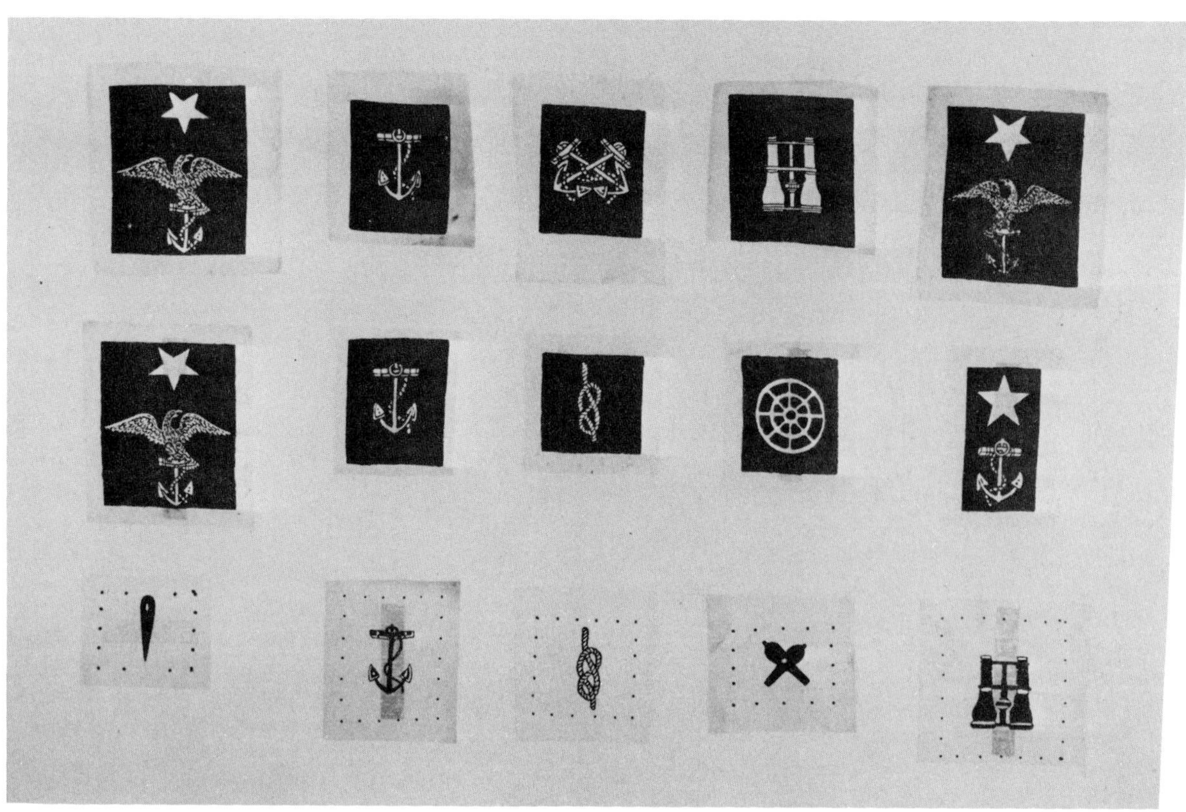

Federal Naval Rating Badges
Row 1:
Petty Officer, Coxwain to Commander of vessel and boatswain mate, Coxwain to Commander-in-chief and Captain of forecastle, Signal Quarter Master and Quarter Master, Petty Officer
Row 2:
Petty Officer, Coxwain, Captain of top, ?, Master at Arms
Row 3:
Sailmaker Mate, Coxwain, Captain of top, Gunner Mate, Signal Quarter Master

Federal Government but Ripley, Chief of Ordnance, evidenced little interest. One of these weapons, a breech-loading field piece, only 4 1/2 feet long with a 2-inch bore could send its 4-pound ball about 2 1/2 miles. This particular gun was phenomenally rapid in operation; in tests it fired a hundred rounds in six minutes and did not overheat. On the other hand, a crank, writing to the Governor of Michigan in April, 1861, urged the adoption of his weapon which operated on scientific and mechanical principles and would deliver balls on an exact range at exact intervals of 1 foot or any other spacing desired. This machine gun, according to its inventor, was more efficient than 120 men with any other small arms.

Occasionally weapons were adopted for field trial. As discussed on p. 98 the Lindsay rifled musket was issued to men of the 16th Michigan Infantry. The Lindsay had two triggers, each of which exploded a separate cartridge, the one farther from the breech first, the other afterwards. The theory was sound enough but in practice the men discovered that the explosion of the first cartridge always ignited the second. Exploded barrels could occur and, at Preble's Farm in September 1864, the men of the 16th Michigan threw away their Lindsays and picked up Springfield muzzle-loaders from the dead and wounded.

Another type of invention which was considered to be very lethal early in the war was bar or chain shot. This contraption (which incidentally had been discovered many years before the war) consisted of two balls connected by a bar of iron or chain and intended to be fired by two cannon simultaneously. The shot was supposed to take a rotary motion when fired and supposedly would have great effect against masts and rigging of vessels or against massed troops. However, in a masterpiece of understatement, Gibbon tells us that they were "very inaccurate" in their fire. Actually, it was soon learned that a simultaneous discharge of two cannon was almost impossible to achieve; and when the two cannon did not go off together, there was grave danger to the gun crews by the bar or chain shot whipping around and injuring or killing men near the guns.

An amusing device which appeared in the *Scientific*

Civil War Neckware
The Confederate officer is Captain John Murphy (unit unidentified), wearing a black tie. (Courtesy Herb Peck, Jr.)
Leather collar. Two inches wide in the middle and tapering to 1 inch width at each end.
The unidentified Confederate enlisted man is wearing a hat cord as a tie. (Courtesy Brian R. Bennett).

American as early as November 9, 1861, and later also in 1863, was for "water walkers." To overcome the logistical problems inherent in laying pontoon bridges, inventors came up with small, watertight canoes for each foot of a soldier crossing a river. The soldier was also equipped with a paddle for balance and propulsion.

Certainly one of the most prevalent fads in the early months of the War was body armor—used by soldiers in both armies. However, on the few occasions when these "iron vests" were actually tested in combat, their wearers were fortunate indeed if they survived. Nevertheless, as late as July 1864, a Wisconsin inventor was offering Lincoln a coat of mail or "Panzerhemd."

On February 14, 1865, Seth Kinman of Humboldt, California, patented an "arm supporter" for riflemen. This arm supporter was strapped around the body and could be adjusted to various sizes of men. A vertical piece was rigidly attached to the soldier's waist belt, while another piece supported the elbow, permitting free movement of the soldier while firing.

Among the Federal inventions was a metal shield for riflemen, hand-barrow type, portable breast works, and similar devices. Iron shields were suggested for troops in line of battle as well as horse-drawn iron field casemates which could be assembled in five seconds, as well as other forerunners of the tank of 1917 and 1939.

Armored locomotives, some very practical, were offered—some were actually used in the field. A unique weapon was "Winans' Steam Gun," the invention of Charles Dickinson and manufactured by Ross Winans, a Baltimore locomotive manufacturer. It was claimed that this weapon could throw 200 balls a minute for a distance of two miles. The gun was supposed to be bullet proof. It was mounted on 4 wheels for mobility and could allegedly project missiles of any size from a bullet to a 100-pound cannon ball. According to the New York *Tribune* of May 4, 1861, the boiler was similar to that of an ordinary steam fire engine. There was only one barrel, with the ammunition being fed through a hopper. The Winans' gun never was tested in battle; it was captured by the Federals May 11, 1861. The captors, members of the 6th Massachusetts Infantry, placed the naval weapon in position to guard the viaduct over the Patuxent of the Washington branch of the Baltimore and Ohio Railway.

Perhaps the whackiest invention of all was a combined plow and gun, patented June 17, 1862. Details on this odd-ball were very kindly furnished by Mr. R.V. Earle, Jr., of Indianapolis, Indiana. The inventors of this unique weapon were C.M. French and W.H.Fancher of Waterloo, New York. Their invention (patent No. 35,600) consisted of forming the beam of a plough of iron of cylindrical shape, having a bore and provided with a vent at its rear end, so that it could be used as a cannon when so desired. The object of their invention was to produce a plow equal, if not superior in point of strength and lightness to the ordinary plow, and, at the same time, to combine in its construction the elements of light ordnance, so that when the occasion should arise, the contraption could do valuable service "in the capacity of both implements." And, as Mr. Earle very sagely points out—this was better than the reverse of "beating swords into plowshares." [*See Combined Cannon and Plow*].

PAROLE AND COUNTERSIGN

In the field units put out guards to protect against surprise attack and to restrict defensive positions and camps from unauthorized entry or exit. By Army regulations a parole and countersign were issued daily from the principal headquarters of the command. The parole was given to the commissioned officers of guards; the countersign was given to the sentinels and non-commissioned officers of guards. The parole was usually in the name of a general, the countersign that of a battle. Customarily the parole and countersign were written on a small piece of paper and folded in the shape of a small triangle. The specimen shown here is a piece of white paper 5 x 4 inches and folded into a triangle with a 4-inch base and 2 1/2 inches on each side. It is dated December 1, 1862 from "Hq. U.S. Forces," Bowling Green, Kentucky. Parole is "Mitchell" and Countersign is "Huntersville." Issued by order of Brig. Gen. Granger, Commanding Post and signed by his adjutant.

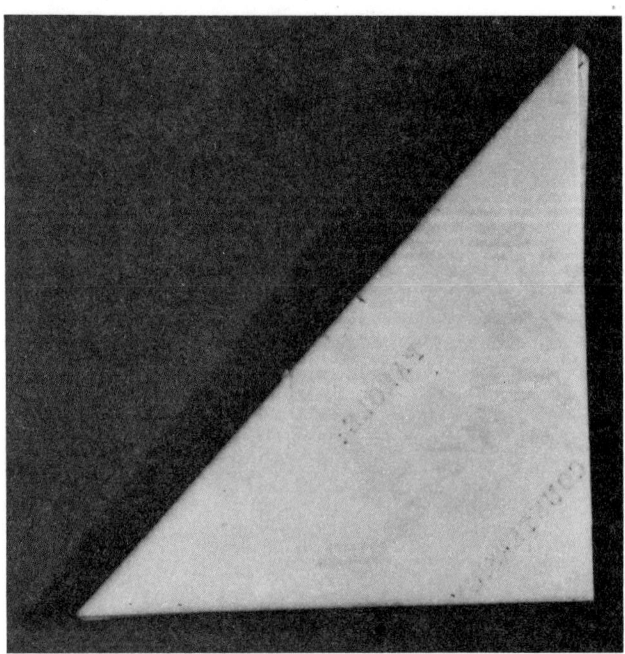

Parole and Countersign

PATRIOTIC PINS

Shown here are two rare patriotic pins recovered from a Federal camp site in Tennessee. These pins were the type presented to volunteers in the early part of the war and should not be confused with corps badges or insignia. Both are of thin brass. The round pin is 1 3/16 inches in diameter and is decorated with stars, a shield and the words:

CONSTITUTION AND UNION

The other pin is 1 inch high with an eagle and the word:

UNION

Both pins were found by John A. Marks of Memphis, Tennessee.

Patriotic Pins

John A. Marks

PICTURES

Much of the interest in the war has been due to the large number of photographs which have survived to make the contest "live" for later generations. Prior to 1861 wars were depicted only by "artists conceptions," that is, by paintings and drawings. These served only to give interested students a "second hand" portrayal of men and events, who were often depicted in a completely unrealistic or exaggerated fahion. Actual photographs, by the thousands, were taken from 1861 to 1865 and the war will always seem very real and close to us and future generations. While much credit belongs to Brady (1823-1896) it must not be forgotten that literally hundreds of photographers in village and city were available to take pictures of the country boys in their brand new "soldier suits." Some of these photographs which have survived are labeled with the subjects' names, but many are unmarked.

The main types of Civil War pictures were: daguerreotype, ambrotype, tintype, and the photograph.

DAGUERREOTYPE. A photograph on a silver or a copper plate covered with silver. One of the first photographic processes, the daguerreotype was invented by Louis J.M. Daguerre and announced to the world in 1839. Through the 1840s and 1850s "Daguerreotype saloons" were established in many urban centers in the U.S. Daguerreotypes were usually sold in attractive cases, often of gutta-percha, and embossed with decorative designs, including military symbols such as crossed cannon and the American flag. Because of their expense, daguerreotypes were not as commonly sought after by the common soldier as either ambrotypes or tintypes. However, many soldiers did carry daguerreotypes of their wives, children, or sweethearts to the front.

A daguerreotype of a young woman was dug up in quite good condition at Chancellorsville about 100 years after the battle there. At Warrenton Junction, Virginia, during the winter of 1864-1865, a daguerreotype studio carried on a brisk business. The soldiers pronounced the word "dogertype"!

For the collector who wishes to distinguish a daguerreotype from later forms of photographs sold in similar cases, the following test can always be made. The quickest and surest method of identifying a true daguerreotype is to hold it in one hand, move it through various angles—and, in so doing, it will be observed that sometimes the photographic image is clearly seen and in others only shiny metal is seen. This is so because the mirror surface of the daguerreotype is only coated in spots, while the remainder of the surface holds the reflection characteristic of a true mirror and will reflect light from various toned surfaces in the same manner as the ordinary mirror. Daguerreotypes were made in various sizes, the most common size being the 1/6 size, the silver plate of which measured 2 3/4 x 3 1/4 inches.

Since daguerreotypes are direct pictures the originals are reversed as in the case of an individual seeing himself in a mirror.

Restoration of daguerreotypes to a most original condition is possible. However, it is a special chemical process requiring great care and there are only a few laboratories competent to do such work. In no case should a cloth, brush, or finger be brought into contact with the face of the daguerreotype if the glass has been removed. The result may be the complete destruction of the image with no chance for restoration.

AMBROTYPE. The decline of the daguerreotype began in 1854 following the development of the ambrotype by Cutting of Boston and his partner, Issac Rehn of Philadelphia. This process produced a photographic negative on glass which when backed up with black wax,paint, paper or velvet gave a positive image. The picture was not marred by the double reflection, so annoying in the daguerreotype. The process spread rapidly throughout the country, it being simpler and cheaper to make than the daguerreotype. The outstanding characteristic of ambrotypes was the absence of reflection; the ambrotype when held in the hand could be moved in any direction or held at any angle and the photographic image would look the same.

Ambrotypes were made the same sizes as daguerreotypes and so were sold with the same mats, preservers and cases. This causes much of the modern misconception concerning which is which.

TINTYPES. The ambrotype was not two years old when a U.S. patent was issued (February 19, 1856) to Professor Hamilton L. Smith of Kenyon College (Ohio) for a process of making "photographic pictures on japanned surfaces." Among the surfaces specified was japanned iron. The tintype was also known as the melainotype and ferrotype. Eventually the latter name became most used but the popular name by which they were, and still are, called was "tintypes".

At first the tintypes were made in similar sizes and cases as the daguerreotype and ambrotype. However, the cost of producing them became so cheap that photographers went after customers who would only spend a quarter or dollar to have their pictures taken. The cases were dispensed with and the "tintypes" put in simple paper case. The very small pictures of this type were extremely popular. They were not much larger than a dime in size and were offered in simple paper mats.

Where a tintype (or melainotype or ferrotype) has been mounted in a case it is difficult to distinguish it from an ambrotype. A sure method is to remove it from the case. If the picture is on metal then it belongs to the tintype group, if on glass, it is an ambrotype.

While most of us have forgotten the origin of the old saying "not on your tintype" we do know that the wide use of the term indicates the popularity of tintypes during the war. The tintype was another evidence of

Types of Mid-19th Century Pictures

Upper left: daguerreotype, 3 1/4 by 4 1/4 inches. Mexican War soldier (image reversed) armed with a Kentucky rifle.

Upper right: Ambrotype, 3 1/4 by 4 1/4 inches. Federal infantry privates. One with a Springfield musket, the other with an Enfield musket! (image reversed)

Lower left: Tintype, 3 1/4 by 4 1/6 inches. Union corporal with a Mississippi Rifle. Member of the 6th Wisconsin Infantry of the "Iron Brigade". (image reversed)

Lower right: Cabinet photo, 4 by 6 inches (from glass negative) Paper mounted in cardboard mount. Indian holding a Winchester 1866 model rifle.

Herb Peck, Jr. and Some of His Pictures

experimentation with various photographic processes in the years preceding the war. This variation was a positive photgraph taken on a sensitized sheet of enameled tin or iron. Although probably not as numerous as Brady's "carte de visites" or the daguerreotypes, the many specimens extant attest to the popularity of the tintype.

CARTE DE VISITE: A form of paper portrait which was extremely popular was the card photograph of carte-de-visite. The original idea of these cards was that suggested by their name, i.e., visiting cards. The individual's photograph appeared instead of his or her printed name. The first printed reference to the production of these cards in the United States was in the list of exhibits at the 1858 Exhibition of the Franklin Institute in Philadelphia. From 1860 to 1866 the carte-de-visite fad spread like wildfire. Edward Anthony in 1861 placed on the market an album for storing and preserving these in the home.

PHOTOGRAPHS. War photography existed before the Civil War and in this war, Brady was only one of numerous photographers behind the Federal lines. Alex Gardner, the Scotchman who taught Brady the wet-collodian process, T.H. O'Sullivan, T.C. Roche, George M. Barnard and Captain A.T. Russell being a few. Prominent Confederate photographers were

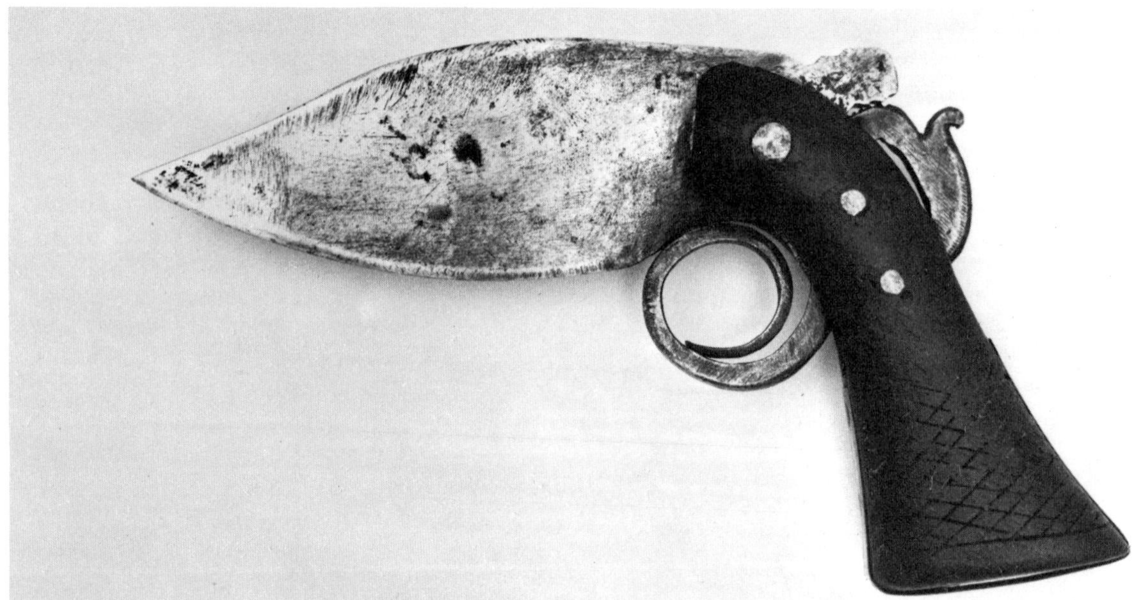

Pistol Knife (Closed)

Pistol Knife (Open)

George S. Cook of Charleston, South Carolina and A.D. Lytle of Baton Rouge. It is probable that Lytle deserves credit for being the first to use photography for military purposes because he often worked behind the Federal lines and sent his photographs back to Confederate headquarters for military study.

STEREOSCOPIC VIEWS. Popular with the home folks were stereoscopic views of the war. One of the main dealers in them was the E. and H.T. Anthony and Company of 501 Broadway, New York City. In the *Army and Navy Journal* for April 15, 1865, this company advertised stereoscopic views of the war "obtained at a great expense and forming a complete Photographic History of the Great Union Contest." Some of the views mentioned were those of Bull Run, Yorktown, Hanover Junction, and Fort Morgan.

Through the courtesy of Herb Peck, Jr. of Nashville, Tennessee, there is shown here an example of each of the four main types of pictures: daguerreotype, ambrotype, tintype, and cabinet photographs.

PISTOL KNIFE

This unusual weapon is probably C.S. made. Its entire length open is 8 1/4 inches—when closed it is 7 inches. Length of blade, 4 inches; width of blade at widest part, 1 5/8 inches. The blade is steel, the backstrap is brass, and the grips are walnut. There are no markings. Nothing is known of the past history of this weapon.

POCKET KNIVES

If one can judge from the number of specimens found in camp sites and on battlefields, just about every Yankee and Johnny Reb carried a jackknife! Shown here are ten knives used during the war.

POCKET TELESCOPE

Commanders, staff officers and engineer officers generally carried field glasses or telescopes. But some individuals purchased pocket telescopes for their own use. Such a telescope is pictured here. The black cardboard case is 3 5/8 inches long. The unmarked brass telescope is in three sections with an overall length of 6 3/4 inches.

POST-WAR SURPLUS

One of the baffling mysteries for Civil War collectors is what happened to the thousands of surplus weapons in Government arsenals after 1865. This is especially true of certain contract muskets which are known to have been made in large numbers but which are almost nonexistent in the United States today.

A partial answer is to be found in the policy of commercial dealers after the war who sold thousands upon thousands of obsolete weapons around the world. Apparently Latin American countries were among the leading customers, but underdeveloped countries all over the world purchased Civil War weapons from the United States after 1865.

ARMS ON HAND AT END OF CIVIL WAR. At the end of the war in 1865, the Federal Government found itself in possession of a large amount of muskets and other military stores, not damaged and unserviceable, but obsolete in the sense that other and improved arms were more desirable. Therefore, Congress in 1868 passed an act which permitted the Secretary of War to sell the obsolete weapons. However, no evidence disclosed that inspection or survey of weapons and ordnance stores was made. Accordingly, the breech-loaders were often sold along with muzzle-loaders.

The total number of serviceable and unserviceable arms on hand at U.S. arsenals on June 30, 1865, was 2,649,439. By June 30, 1871, this number had been reduced to 1,161,410, even though the Government had produced several thousand of the breech-loading models of rifles during the period 1865-1871.

Some weapons were retained by Federal veterans on muster-out at the end of the war. The following weapons were retained by Federal soldiers and taken home by them at muster out in 1865:

Muskets		**Revolvers**	20,046
Springfield	96,238	**Sabers**	13,645
Enfield	19,882	**NCO Swords**	974
All Others	557		
	116,677		

Rifles		**Carbines**	
Spencer	2,844	Spencer	8,289
	808	Sharps	2,549
Sharps	3,454	Burnside	392
Colt	305	Maynard	871
All Others	629	All Others	1,380
	8,040		13,481

In addition to U.S. weapons on hand in the hands of troops or in arsenals at the end of the war, there were a great many arms lying all over the country. These were "rebel arms" which had not been turned in to the U.S. Ordnance Department. The Federals had taken the "whole number of arms" after the report had been made that there were 1,300,000 on hand. Most of the untallied weapons were Enfields.

On September 21, 1866, the Ordnance Department reported to Secretary of War Stanton on ordnance stores captured from Confederate arsenals in the recent war.

In every case the captured property was placed in arsenals and depots, but due to the way in which the weapons were turned in, it was absolutely impossible to tell which were weapons turned in by Federal troops

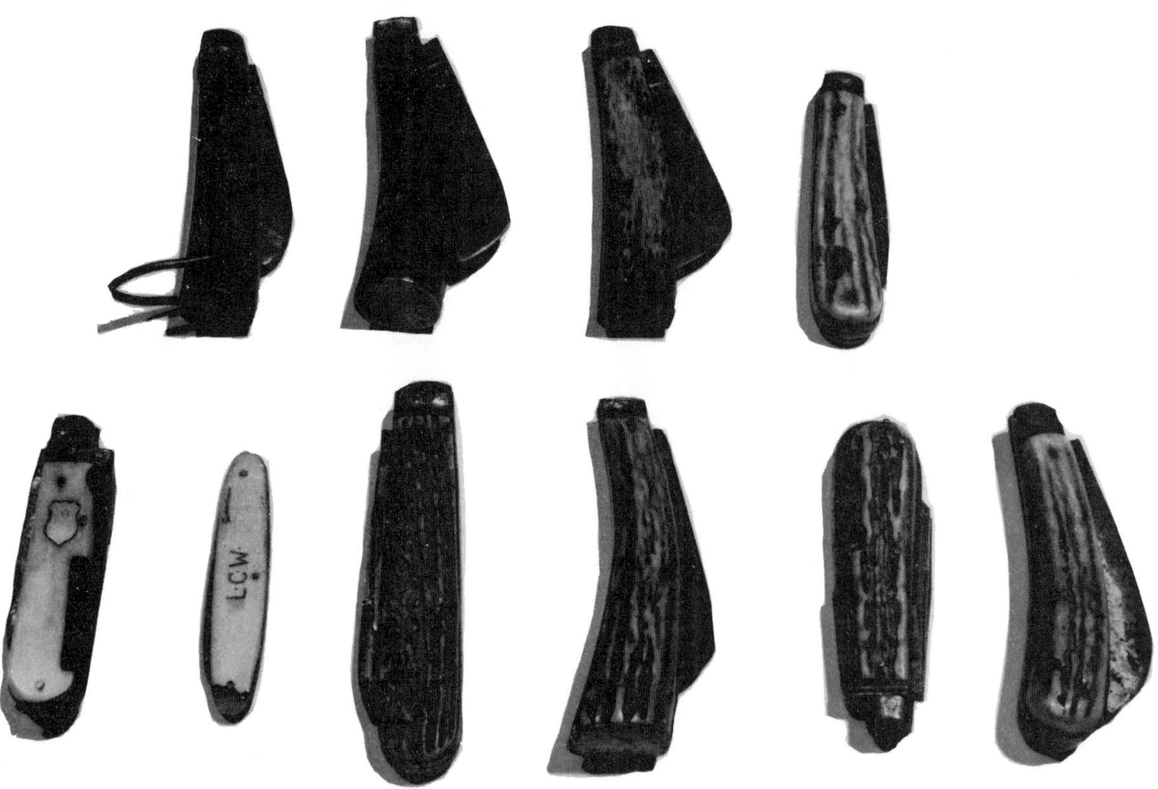

Pocket Knives
Left to right:
Top Row:
Sailor's wooden handled knife with metal loop for lanyard. 4 1/2 inches long, Marked:
Schrade Cut. Co.
Walden, New York

Sailor's wooden handled knife. From Portsmouth, N.H. 4 3/4 inches long. Marked:
Stonington Cutlery Co.

Sailor's bone handled knife used during the war by Surgeon Enoch Pearse. 4 inches long.

Jackknife. Bone-handled, 3 7/8 inches long. Marked:
George Wostenholm
Sheffield

Left to right:
Bottom Row:
Cavalryman's bone-handled knife. Also has the cleaning hook. Length 4 inches. Marked:
George Wostenholm
Sheffield

Penknife. Ivory-handled 3 1/4 inches long. Initials L.C.W. carved in handle.

Jackknife. Bone-handled, 4 3/4 inches long. Marked:
George Wostenholm
Sheffield

Sailor's bone-handled knife 4 1/2 inches long. Marked:
C11
197

Cavalryman's bone-handled knife. Has a hook for cleaning the horses' hooves.

Length 3 3/4 inches. Carried by a soldier of the 1st Maine Cavalry.

Sailor's bone-handled knife 4 1/4 inches long. Marked:
Humphrey - Radiant
Sheffield, England

The accompanying illustration shows the type of knife sold to soldiers by mail order or sutlers.

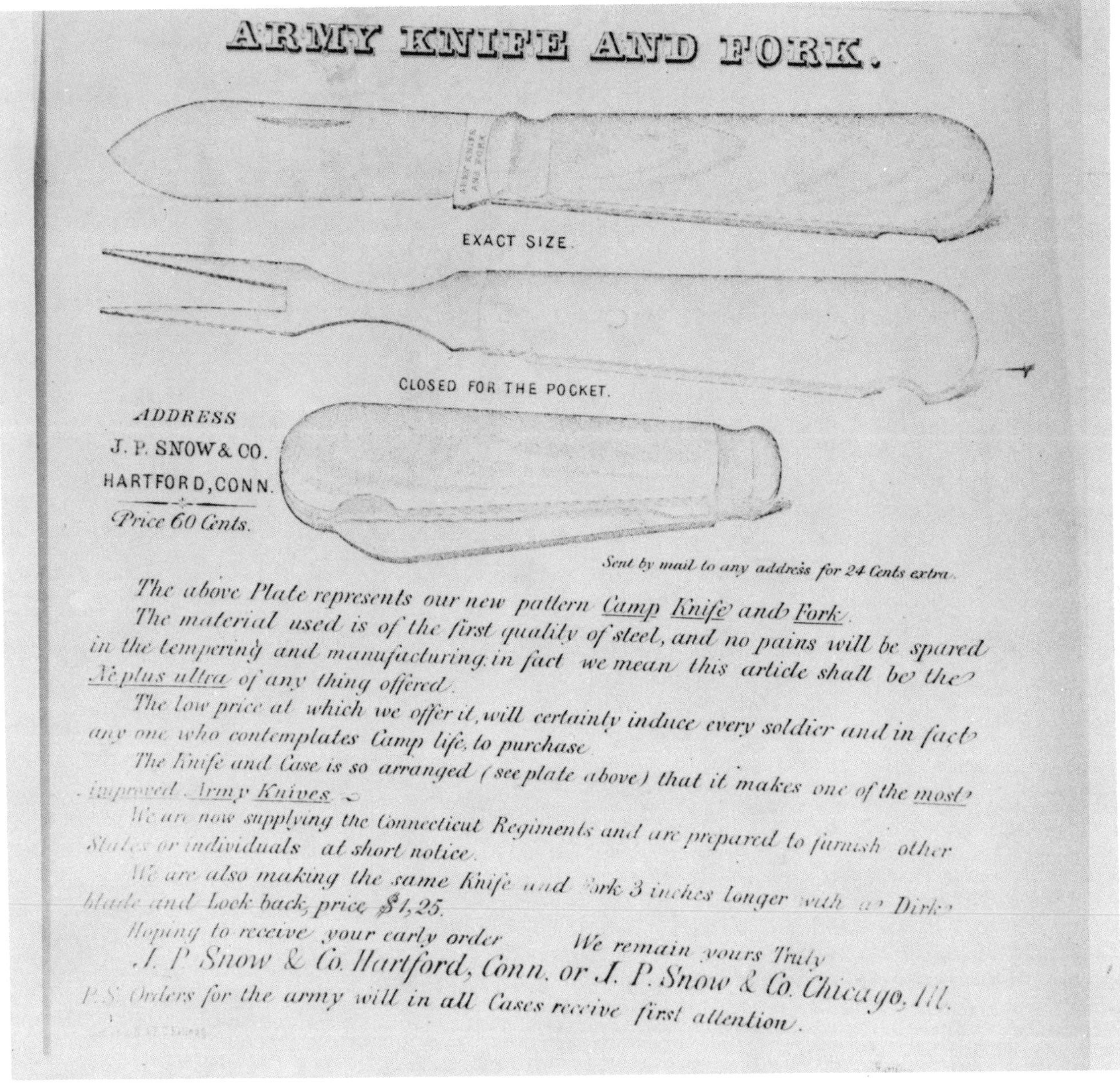

J.P. Snow's Army Knife

and which were captured arms. The amount realized from the sale of ordnance stores during the fiscal year 1865-1866, including all captured ordnance material, was $986,492.26.

The Ordnance Bureau reported that of March 1, 1872, there had been issued to the militia since January 1, 1865, the following:

Springfield muzzle-loaders, cal. 58	36,221
Smith carbines	1,000
Spencer carbines	1,719
Henry rifles	15
Revolving pistols	149
Spencer rifles	30

It is also known that about 100,000 muskets were burned in the fire which occurred at Washington arsenal in 1866.

SALE OF ARMS TO UNDERDEVELOPED COUNTRIES

In September, 1866, orders were given to send 150,000 arms from Southern arsenals to New York for storage. The purpose of this was to dispose of these weapons "with the least possible delay." On March 25, 1867, the officer in charge of the New York storage depot reported that he had 325,000 arms for sale. To sell these weapons, it had been necessary to abide by the law of 1825 which required previous inspection and

Pocket Telescope

condemnation at time of sale. Accordingly, Congress on July 20, 1868, by joint resolution, empowered the Secretary of War to dispense with said inspection and condemnation and to proceed with sales.

Before long, the United States was selling substantial numbers of weapons to France in her 1870-1871 war with Germany. The Government also sold 339,000 arms in 1869-1870 to Turkey, as well as small numbers of weapons to Liberia, Denmark and miscellaneous ordnance stores to Norway and Sweden.

At least two sales were made to Turkey—in 1869 and in 1870. The Turks probably paid $5.00 each for the ones they bought. The Turks had their own ordnance officers on hand when sales were made and invariably picked out the best muskets offered. On one occasion they rejected 42,000 muskets as not being up to their standards. The Turks were reported by a number of the committee (Logan) to have purchased 100,000 Springfields from the Prussian government for a dollar apiece.

Emerging countries during the 1870's were eager to get obsolete weapons. Japan was modeling her military forces on the French army and her military academy on West Point. Japanese infantry were being armed with the Snyder and Enfield rifles. At the armory at Yedo, muzzle-loaders were being converted to breech-loaders on the Albani pattern.

China was armed with the entire gamut of weapons from matchlocks and bows and arrows to Russian muzzle-loaders, Remington breech-loaders, and Spencers. In Tientsin the Chinese had a factory producing Remingtons, while in Canton both Remingtons and Spencers were produced.

Persia bought Colt, Smith and Wesson, Remington, and also purchased Gatting guns whenever possible.

It is extremely difficult at this late date to determine exactly how many countries were involved in these sales of arms. It is known that purchases amounting to over half a million dollars were sent directly to English firms. These firms, in turn, sold the arms to France at a profit. Involved in these sales were Enfields (which had originally come from England!) and a large stock of Spencer rifles and Spencer carbines. A major firm involved in these sales was the Valentine and Billing firm of London who agreed to sell France 70,000 Enfield muskets and bayonets at 43 francs each and 1,000 Enfield carbines with saber bayonets at 40 francs each.

The Remington Arms Company bought weapons from the U.S. Government and then sold these weapons to France, Denmark, Cuba, Spain, Sweden, the Papal Government and probably Holland and Egypt.

The evidence is also conclusive that weapons were sent to the Greeks and to the belligerents in the Chinese-Japanese War, and most Latin American countries.

A "large number of goods" went to Russia, including ammunition in the 1870's.

Major S.V. Benet, U.S. Ordnance Department, testifying March 11, 1872, admitted that the European armies were all armed with breech-loading rifles and the best they had came from the United States. He also conceded that these breech-loading weapons should not have been sold, but the United States could probably make better ones than those which had been sold.

SALE OF ARMS TO INDIANS. Certainly many of the Civil War muskets, carbines, and hand guns were sold to the Indians. For example, Sheridan tells us in his *Personal Memoirs* (Volume 2, p. 289) that Brigadier General Alfred Sully, an officer of long experience in Indian matters, commanding the District of the Arkansas in 1868, advised his agent to issue arms and ammunition to troublesome Indian warriors. Sheridan called this act of Sully a "fatal mistake" because, even while the delivery of the weapons was in progress, the Indians began raids of murder and destruction.

Ordnance Department reports of the 1870's indicate that approximately half of the weapons carried by Indians in battle were muzzle-loaders; the other half were mainly carbines, many of which were likewise "veterans of the Civil War." (See *Report* of Chief of Ordance 1879 and *Ordnance Notes,* October 1, 1879).

Indians used substantial numbers of muzzle-loading weapons in warfare. They also used bows and arrows as well as breech-loading weapons. Especially popular were such Civil War carbines as the Spencer, and Sharps.

Reports on the numbers of Civil War weapons in the hands of Indians vary greatly from tribe to tribe. However there can be no question but that the Indians, especially in the late 1860's were very glad to get the obsolete muzzle-loaders and percussion revolvers. Probably, the Indian acquisition of arms during the 1870's was mainly breech-loaders but also they bought muzzle-loaders from white traders. These traders operated under the "control" of Indian agents.

TERMS OF SALE. Arms were sold under an act of 1868 in two ways—by getting sealed proposals for the goods or by auction. The greater portion of the arms were sold by auction. An example of the sealed proposals method occurred in July 1869. The sale of 300,000 Springfields was announced to prominent dealers. Usually the sales were announced thirty days in advance and were given wide publicity in the papers.

An example of the sealed proposal method was a notice to several arms dealers that their bids would be accepted October 13, 1870, on the following:

200,000 Springfield muskets, new, cal. 58

110,000 Springfield muskets, serviceable, cal. 58 (with 150 rounds of ammunition for each gun)

40,000 Enfield muskets, new

40,000 Enfield muskets, repaired

30,000 Enfield muskets, unserviceable

As a result of this offer, the following awards were made:

AUSTIN BALDWIN & CO. 40,000 new Springfield muskets, cal. 58 at $12.30 each

110,000 cleaned and repaired Springfield muskets, cal. 58 at $9.30 each

25,000,000 cartridges, cal. .577 at $16.30 per thousand

HERMAN BOKER & CO. 50,000 new Springfield muskets, cal. 58 at $12.10 each

SCHUYLER, HARTLEY & GRAHAM. 100,000 new Springfield muskets, cal. 58 at $12.05 each

A.B. STEINBERGER. 6,300 cleaned and repaired Enfields at $5.30 each

GENERAL W.B. FRANKLIN. 30,000-40,000 new Enfields at $7.75 each

Four days later (October 17, 1870), the Ordnance office of the U.S. War Department announced it would accept sealed proposals for the following:

2,500 breech-loading muskets, cal. 58

1,000 Ball carbines cal. 50

2,500 Gallagher carbines, adapted for Spencer ammunition

4,000 Maynard carbines with 500 rounds of ammunition per gun

1,000 Palmer carbines, cal. 44 with ammunition

2,500 Warner carbines with ammunition

2,700 Joslyn carbines cal. 52 with ammunition

40,000 sets carbines accouterments

70,000 sets infantry accouterments

20,000 Starr revolvers, cal. 44, with ammunition

5,000 Rogers and Spencer revolvers, cal. 44 with ammunition

10,000 Remington army revolvers, cal. 44 with ammunition

35,000 pistol holsters

40,000 cavalry sabers

1,000 Spencer rifles

20,000 sets horse equipment

Also included were 50 batteries of field artillery, complete, with ammunition.

As early as 1869, the War Department offered for sale:

40,000 Enfield muskets, cal. 577 new

3,000 U.S. flint-lock muskets, cal. 69, serviceable

5,000 Remington carbines, cal. 44, new

15,000 Starr army revolvers, cal. 44, new

5,000 cavalry sabers, foreign, serviceable

5,000 cavalry sabers, foreign, unserviceable
Plus large amounts of powder.

The same year, the War Department offered for sale:
200,000 Springfield muskets, cal. 58
5,000 Spencer carbines, old model, cal. 52
10,000 Spencer carbine accouterments

The U. S. War Department released only limited information on weapon sales after the war. Reports of the Chief of Ordnance from 1865 to 1869 make no mention of these sales. However, in the Secretary of War report for 1870, the Chief of Ordnance reported that the War Department had been selling arms and other military items which were obsolete or unfit for issue to troops. By October 1870, more than 1,340,000 stands of small-arms had been sold since 1865; 350,000 had been sold in October alone—all at "good prices". The Chief of Ordnance reported at that time (October 1870), that if the demand for weapons continued at the current rate, the War Department would be able in a short time to dispose of the greater part of its surplus stores. "It is very desirable that this should be done, as the stores are unsuited to our wants, and the expense of keeping and preserving them is very great." The sales from July 1 to October 25, 1870, netted about $5,600,000. A year later this figure had been increased to about $10,000,000—all as a result of sales of small-arms and other ordnance stores. This accelerated sale of military supplies was due to the great demand in Europe, especially France. The proceeds of the sales, except a small sum retained to meet current expenses in preparing other stores for sale, were passed from War Department control into the Treasury. The cost of operating auctions of ordnance stores from June 30, 1870 to October 24, 1871, was $239,030. This cost also included preparation of the ordnance stores for sale and transporting them to place of sale.

An interesting example of what happened to many types of Civil War weapons can be seen in the following

SALES BY ORDNANCE DEPARTMENT, U.S. ARMY
of Cannon, Small Arms, and Ammunition - 1865-1870, inclusive

YEAR	CANNON	CARBINES	MUSKETS & RIFLES	PISTOLS	SABERS & SWORDS	ARTILLERY PROJECTILES	ROUNDS OF SMALL-ARMS AMMUNITION
1865	478	345	89,742	27	1,473	43,864	470,000
1866	433	2,089	211,243	2,523	5,940	179,188	4,210,740
1867	28	8,535	121,423	1,470	13,169	5,618	3,086,073
1868	436	12,250	96,630	1,714	6,561	7,323	5,613,749
1869	721	4,099	83,145	464	343	85,415	4,381,421
1870	549	57,568	432,476	30,472	817	20,611	58,772,821
Totals 1865-70 inclus.	2,645	84,886	1,034,659	36,670	28,303	342,019	76,534,804

Government sale of small arms which took place at Leavenworth Arsenal, Kansas, November 25, 1867. Although numbers were not given, the following types were offered for sale:

United States rifles, model 1840
United States rifle—muskets
United States smooth—bore muskets
Enfield rifle-muskets
Belgian rifle-muskets
Enfield rifles
Sappers' rifles
Austrian rifle-muskets
Austrian rifles
Prussian rifle-muskets
Colt revolving rifles
Burnside carbines
Cosmopolitan carbines
Gallagher carbines
Green carbines
Hall carbines
Joslyn carbines
Maynard carbines
Merrill carbines
Smith carbines
Starr carbines
Wesson carbines
Adams pistols
Le Faucheux pistols
Savage pistols
Starr pistols
Whitney pistols

Also sold were such items as sabers, saddles, cartridge boxes, bayonet scabbards, bayonets, harness, and artillery forges.

The most desirable muskets sold were cleaned and repaired Springfields, caliber .58; new Enfields; and every available Colt, Lawson, and Amoskeag make musket. These last-named contract muskets were the special model 1861 rifle musket.

While prices varied considerably, new Enfields cost $7.75 each, and new Springfields cost $12.05 each in several transactions. However Remington paid only $5.00 each for Springfields in September 1870. Gun collectors will wince to know that seven "old unseviceable" Colt dragoon pistols were also sold at $5.00 each!

An outstanding "disposer" of Civil War weapons for decades was the world-famous firm of Francis Bannerman Sons in New York. How many eager youngsters began their military collections by a purchase—at a modest price—of some item "from Bannerman"!This firm opened in 1865, and soon built up an incredible stock by attending auction sales, where large quantities of military goods were offered for sale by the U.S. Government. In those early decades after the Civil War it was customary with purchasing firms to buy old swords and muskets for the value *in old metal.* Old muskets would net about 7 pounds of metal. This breaking up of large numbers of old guns certainly accounts for the present scarcity of some of the early types of military weapons. This destructive practice not only prevailed in the United States but also in Europe.

Unfortunately, the U.S. Government used this method in disposing of many weapons captured from the Confederates. For example, on one occasion Bannerman made the highest bid at a Government sale on a lot of 11,000 muskets, "veterans of many wars," part of the lot surrendered at the end of the war and classified as "Rebel." The U.S. Ordnance officer refused to accept the Bannerman bid, alleging that Bannerman would repair the guns and put them in serviceable order, thus entering into competition with the obsolete guns which the Government was holding for sale. Apparently, some of those muskets dated back to the War of 1812 and even to the Revolution. It is not necessary to point out to gun collectors what value those 11,000 muskets would have today!

SALE OF ARMS DURING THE FRANCO-PRUSSIAN WAR. Early in December 1871 Carl Schurz and Charles Sumner of the U.S. Senate received information that during the Franco-Prussian war just ended "great quantities" of arms had been sold to France under circumstances that suggested corruption in the War Department and flagrant disregard of the responsibilities of a neutral. Schurz soon determined that the State Department was not involved and further, that the German government would not take advantage of any revelations to call the United States to account. Having thus provided against any possibility of foreign complications, the attack was opened.

Sumner offered a resolution proposing an inquiry and investigation concerning the sale of arms to France. Debates in Congress soon followed. A committee of investigation was appointed by the Senate but the Grant administration majority saw to it that neither Sumner nor Schurz was a member. The latter was permitted, however, to question witnesses.

The select committee was elected by the Senate and consisted of Hamlin, Carpenter, Sawyer, Ames, Harlan, Logan, and Stevenson. Hannibal Hamlin was elected by the committee as its chairman.

In May, 1872, a report was made acquitting the officials of all wrong-doing in connection with the sale of arms. Schurz, while admitting that the testimony fell short of establishing guilt by legal evidence, felt that this failure was due to the hostile attitude of the committee toward the accusers, and believed all his life that the War Department had acted recklessly and illegally.

The report of the Committee is contained in a 857-page volume entitled *Sale of Arms by Ordnance Department* (Senate Report No. 183, 42nd Congress, 2nd Session). A careful examination of the testimony is contained in this report.

The number of serviceable arms in U.S. arsenals

at the commencement of the Franco-Prussian War (June 30, 1870) was 1,151,088 including:

Spencer, Sharps, and other breech-loading rifles	5,156
Spencer, Sharps, and other breech-loading carbines	133,596
Springfield muzzle-loading muskets, caliber .58	699,134
Enfield and other muskets	193,536
Colt, Remington, and other revolvers	69,462

On April 16, 1872, the number of serviceable arms on hand at the arsenals was 682,869.

In other words, almost half a million weapons were disposed of in approximately two years. During this period the Government's arsenals were decreased by 302,063 caliber .58 Springfield muskets and by 111,256 Enfield muskets.

Prices on these weapons in July 1870 were:

Cleaned and repaired Springfields $5.00 each (price raised to $9.30 in October 1870)

Cleaned and repaired Enfields $4.00 each (Price raised to $5.30 later)

New Springfields cost from $12.05 to $12.30 in October 1870.

The leading dealer with France with E. Remington and Sons. In fact Samuel Remington, armed with letters from Gambetta and Jules Le Cesne, president of the French armament commission, served as a purchaser for the French during the war. Also, a Colonel Squire was an active purchasing agent for the French. It was reported that a ring had been formed in the United states for selling arms to the French; that the consul and his commissioner (Chauviteaux) had been members of that ring; and that outside parties, some of them American officials, had been part of it, and they had cooperated together.

Marcellus Hartley of the firm Schuyler, Hartley, and Graham sold as many as 300,000 stand of arms to foreign countries during the period 1865-1870, i.e. from Appomattox to just before the Franco-Prussian War. He also estimated he sold another 50,000 in the first year after the end of the Franco-Prussian War.

At the end of the Franco-Prussian War the rumor was going the rounds that parties in the Ordnance Bureau of the War Department had been in collusion with other parties who had made substantial profits from arms sales to the French.

Many Americans were also concerned about possible violations of neutrality by these arms sales to France. However, the German Government, knowing that "irregularities" did exist, determined to lodge no official complaint with the United States Government.

Germany also was offered weapons—a large number. But the Germans did not want them; they said they could get them cheaper by picking them up on the banks of the Loire!

The French "Second Army of the Loire" (a levee-en-masse army), during the latter phases of the Franco-Prussian War used the following:

Remingtons (including Spanish and Egyptian)
Sniders
Enfields
Sharps
Springfields
Spencers (both rifle and carbine)

The report of the general commanding the artillery brigade of this army does not specify whether the "Springfields" were muzzle or breech loaders.

However, it is known that the Breton Garde Mobiles of this army used Springfield muzzle-loading muskets in the last phases of the war—specifically at Le Mans in January 1871. It is very probable that other levee-en-masse units were similarly armed in the latter phases of the war.

POWDER BOAT

One of the few remaining entry ports still open for blackade runners in late 1864 was Wilmington, North Carolina. This "bone in the Federals' throat" was guarded by Fort Fisher. The Federal high command decided to capture this bastion by combined army-navy operations in December 1864. The method for effecting this was one suggested by Major General Benjamin F. Butler, a man with an unusual flair for novel improvisations.

Initially it was proposed to explode a floating mine containing two or three hundred tons of gunpowder. But ordnance and engineer experts rejected such a plan as unfeasible since, they contended most of the force of the mine's explosion would be vertical and not horizontal—and therefore would have little effect on the Fort.

Butler had another scheme which the experts, including Fox, Assistant Secretary of the Navy, approved. This scheme involved the use of a floating mine of great size—a powder boat. Butler got his idea from reading of the devastation wrought in England a few months earlier. On that occasion, some 150,000 pounds of gunpowder on two barges accidentally exploded with fearful effect. The noise was heard over 90 miles away, and people over 25 miles away thought it was an earthquake. The significant result—for Butler—was that the embankment was blown away for the space of 100 yards. Buildings, covering acres, were blown down and became heaps of brick, dirt and timber. The loss of these buildings and other property was about five million dollars.

On November 23, 1864, at a meeting of naval and army experts, it was decided to try Butler's plan. The effort was to be made by exploding a mass of 300 tons of gunpowder in a ship as near the Fort as it would be possible for the ship to get. Note—this would be four times the amount of powder involved in the English disaster. A formidable naval armada and veteran combat regiments were also to be used for landing and capturing the fort before the enemy could recover from the shock of explosion.

The "powder ship" selected was the *Louisiana*, an iron propeller of 295 tons, 150 feet long, 22 foot beam, and with a 8—8 1/2 foot draught when fully loaded. The masts were removed, and she was disguised as a blockade runner, having two raking smoke-stacks, one of which was real, the other a dummy. To insure having the powder as near the surface as possible, a special light deck was constructed. On this was placed a row of barrels of powder, standing on end, the upper open. The remainder of the powder was in canvas bags, holding about 60 pounds each. The whole weight of the powder was 215 tons (430,000 pounds) instead of the 300 tons originally agreed on. Three different devices were employed to ignite the fuses; a clock mechanism, candles, and slow-match. The "Gomez" fuse was used, a thin tape-like strip with an estimated burning time of a mile in four seconds.

On December 23, 1864, the *Louisiana*, under Commander A.C. Rhind, U.S. Navy, moved out and anchored within 300 yards of the northeastern salient of Fort Fisher. At 2 a.m. in the morning of December 24th the powder was exploded but with no appreciable effect on the fort. The crew, after preparing the fuses and setting fire to pine wood on the ship, had escaped by a swift boat prior to the explosion.

Reasons for the failure of Butler's "scheme" vary with the service and with the politics of the analyst. In a technical sense, we must note that the crew left the ship one hour and fifty-two minutes before the explosion took place. The whole cargo of 215 tons of gunpowder did not explode at once. Rather, there was a series of successive discharges, and a large proportion of the powder was blown away without actually igniting.

Moreover, apparently the fire set by the crew actually ignited the powder and not the complicated clock mechanism and fuse combination. The officer in charge of exploding the powder boat stated later that the explosion took place 22 minutes after the time had expired for the clock to set it off.

The fiasco also resulted in considerable anti-Butler talk on the part of both politicians and some Navy officials. While no one would presume to include B.F. Butler as the beau ideal of a combat officer, he did show imagination and willingness to try new "devices" in warfare. While the powder boat scheme was his, the Navy approved of the idea, furnished the vessel, and had control of the venture from beginning to end. In 1892 Commander James Parker, U.S. Navy told a Loyal Legion audience: "We all believed in it (the powder boat) from the admiral down, but when it proved so laughable a failure, we, of the Navy, laid its paternity upon General Butler."

PRITCHETT BULLET MOLD

Brass bullet mold for Enfield bullet, caliber .577 with Pritchett cavity. Heavy brass, 7 1/4 inches long, with no markings. Found in a Tennessee camp site by John A. Marks of Memphis, Tennessee.

PROVOST GUARDS INSIGNIA

Shown here are two rare badges worn by Federal provost guard personnel in 1862.

Description: Both badges are of brass, 2 3/4 inches tall and 2 3/4 inches wide. The Birney badge has the legend in front:

Provost Guard
Birney's
Brigade

Pritchett Bullet Mold

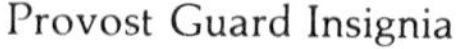

Provost Guard Insignia

The reverse side is blank. The Provost Marshal badge has the legend in front:

Provost Marshal
U.S. Army

with 89 in the center. On the reverse side is the date 1862.

The Birney badge was worn by some member of Birney's brigade which consisted of the 38th New York, 40th New York, 3rd Maine and 4th Maine regiments of volunteer infantry. General David Bell Birney (1825-1864) commanded this brigade during much of 1862. This brigade served in the 3rd Army Corps of the Army of the Potomac. Evidently, General Birney was a strong advocate of providing visible identification of units under his command. In addition to the provost guard badge depicted here, General Birney, on September 4, 1862, while in command of Kearny's old division, issued a general order requiring each officer to wear a piece of scarlet cloth on his cap. This was to support Kearny's earlier order for men of his unit to wear a round piece of scarlet cloth for purposes of identifying men of his command. Moreover, after the Battle of Chancellorsville, Birney authorized a hundred bronze medals, patterned somewhat on the Kearny medal, to be awarded as a sort of legion of honor, to such non-commissioned officers and privates of his division as especially distinguished themselves in that engagement.

An extensive search in published sources has revealed nothing on the authorization for the provost guard badges. Even the contemporary sources which have been examined show that the terms "provost guard" and "provost marshal" were used loosely and often interchangeably. Military police duty in the Federal Army was performed by the Provost Marshal General's Department from March 1863 to the end of the war. Prior to March 1863, such duty was performed by army provost marshals and their guards consisting of line units detailed for the purpose.

On February 21, 1862, Brigadier General Andrew Porter was announced as Provost Marshal of the Army of the Potomac. Under his command, "provost marshals" were appointed for each division. They were charged with suppressing marauding, including drunkenness and gambling, preserving order, apprehending deserters, issuing passes and handling complaints of citizens against the occupation troops of the Federal Army. In June, 1862, it was even ordered that provost guards would prohibit fast riding or driving of public horses and mules, except in case of necessity!

Although provost marshals were appointed in 1862 to "grand divisions", army corps, divisions, brigades and even "detachments", the badges shown here are the only ones which the writer has ever seen. Nor has he seen any illustration or description of any other badge worn by "provost guard" or "Provost marshal" personnel.

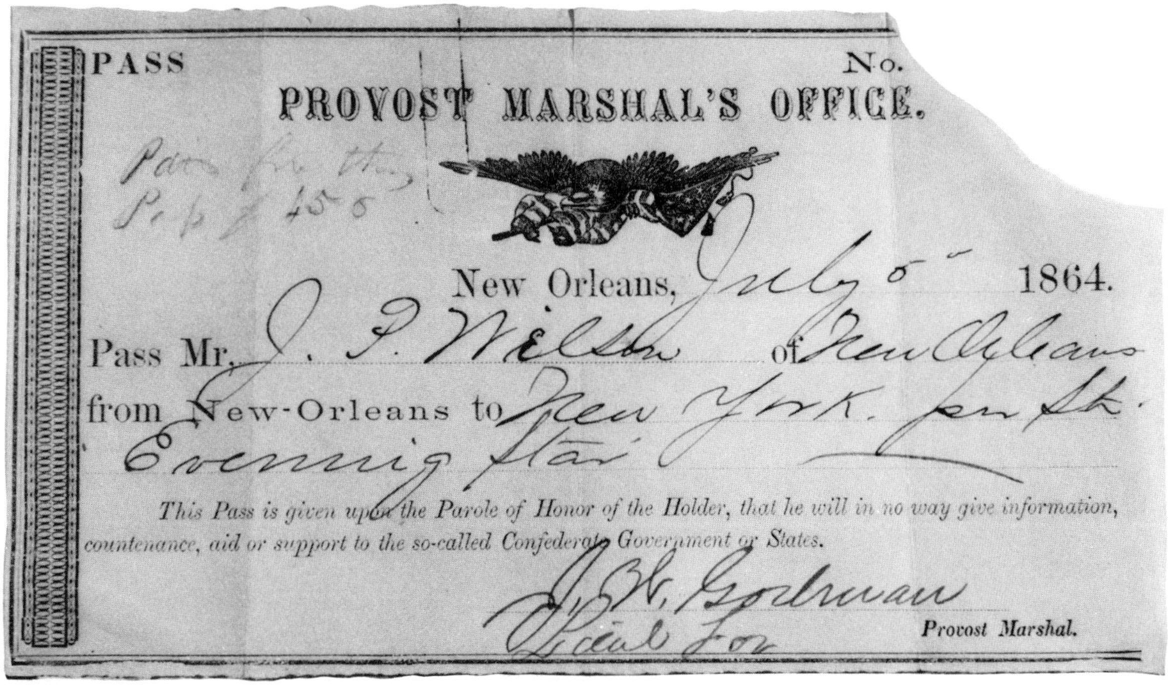

PASS No.

PROVOST MARSHAL'S OFFICE.

New Orleans, July 5th 1864.

Pass Mr. J. P. Wilson of New Orleans

from New-Orleans to New York. per Str. Evening Star

This Pass is given upon the Parole of Honor of the Holder, that he will in no way give information, countenance, aid or support to the so-called Confederate Government or States.

Provost Marshal.

Steamship Pass

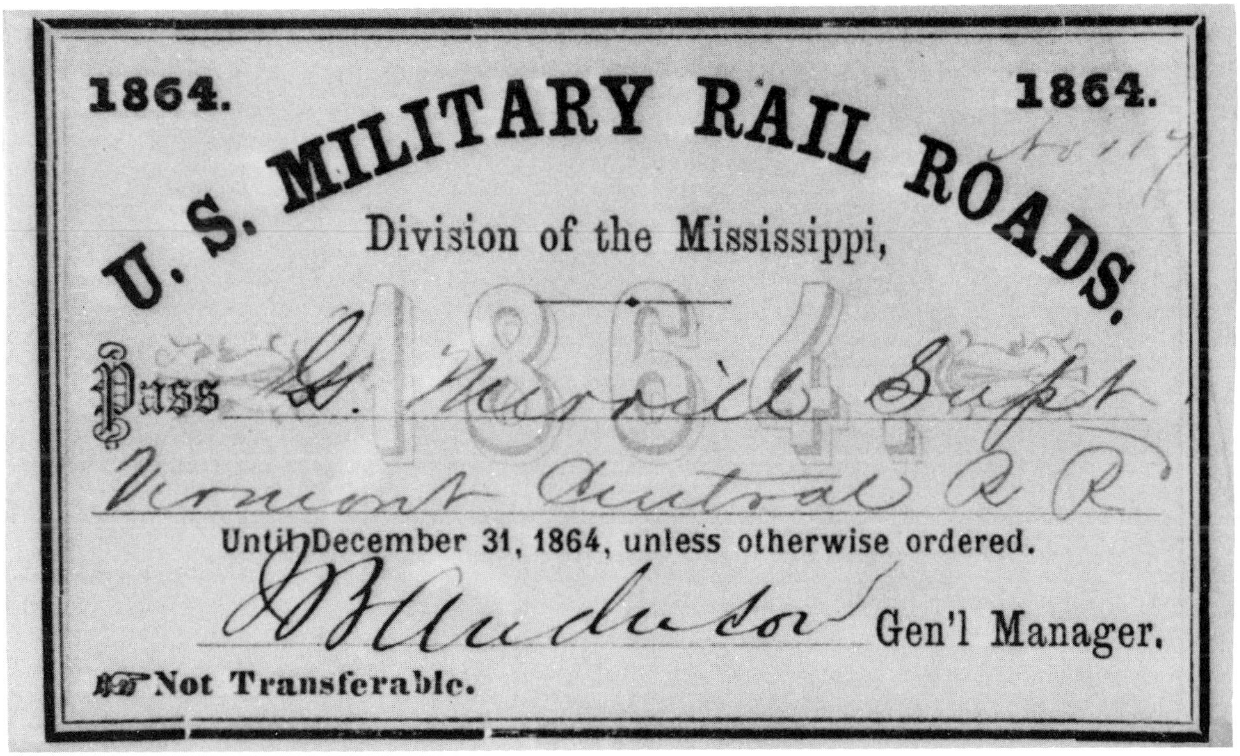

1864. **1864.**

U. S. MILITARY RAIL ROADS.

Division of the Mississippi,

Pass G. Merrill Supt Vermont Central R R

Until December 31, 1864, unless otherwise ordered.

Gen'l Manager.

Not Transferable.

U.S. Military Railroads Pass

NOT TRANSFERABLE.

UNITED STATES ARMY TRANSPORTATION.

Baltimore and Ohio Railroad Company,

Jan 24th 1865

(369) Conductor, Baltimore and Ohio Railroad, will pass Three hundred & Sixty Nine Men & 13 Horses Reg't from Benwood to Washington City on account of Government service. I have Certificate of Transportation.

John Cronin

Kelly, Hedian & Piet, print. AGENT.

U.S. Army Transportation Certificate

Issued by the Richmond & Danville R. R. Co. on the Requisition

SOLDIER'S TICKET.

No. ______	FROM
.... *Seats*	TO

Of the Quartermaster's Department of the Confederate States.

Confederate Soldier's Ticket

MEDICAL PURVEYOR'S OFFICE.

Columbia, S. C., ...186

....

Will furnish Transportation to bearer

One seat to ....and return.

Also, for..................sacks of Barks, etc.,..................lbs.

from ....to.........

....

Surg. & Med. Purveyor.

Confederate Medical Pass

RAILROAD AND STEAMSHIP PASSES

The early stages of moving to the front was usually by rail or troop ship. This was equally true for units or individuals, and also applied to movements from the front back to hospitals or home. In addition to its own rail and ship facilities the Government also contracted with rail and ship companies for the movement of men and war supplies. Illustrated here are two Confederate and three Federal transportation passes.

CONFEDERATE MEDICAL PASS. Size 4 5/8 x 3 1/2 inches. Issued at Columbia, South Carolina by the Medical Purveyor's Office.

CONFEDERATE SOLDIER'S TICKET. Size 3 1/2 x 2 inches. Issued by the C.S. Quartermaster Department as one soldier's fare on the Richmond and Danville Railroad.

U.S. ARMY TRANSPORTATION. Size 5 1/2 x 2 5/8 inches. Issued by the Baltimore and Ohio Railroad, January 24, 1865, for shipment of 369 men and 13 horses.

U.S. MILITARY RAILROADS. Size 3 1/2 x 2 1/8 inches. Issued by the U.S.M.R.R. Division of the Mississippi in 1864 to *G. Merrill,* Superintendent of the Vermont Central R.R.

STEAMSHIP PASS. Size 7 x 4 inches. Issued by the Provost Marshal's office, New Orleans, La., July 5, 1864, to *J.P. Wilson* for passage from New Orleans to New York. This passage was to be on the steamer *Evening Star.*

RELIC HUNTING

Because of the advent of many new Civil War "buffs" to the collecting fraternity, especially young people between the ages of ten and eighteen, it has been thought extremely advisable to pass on some basic cautions to the neophytes. First, and most important *never* underestimate the lethal potential of Civil War arms. It is very true that many of the muskets, especially the imported weapons, were grossly inefficient so far as accuracy and range were concerned. But it cannot be too strongly emphasized that these weapons—all of them—were made to kill with. They are still dangerous and must be handled with the same common sense care as modern arms. For purposes of

Relic Cannon Bucket from "Bloody Angle" at Spotsylvania (Height 9 1/4 inches. Diameter 8 inches)

safety—to you and your musket— do *not* snap the hammer just to hear it click. Do not allow your friends to snap the hammer, either! Not too long ago, I saw a Confederate Fayetteville musket practically ruined because an idiot just had to snap the hammer. (He broke the entire hammer assembly off). Don't permit it. It is very important to realize that any explosive projectile or device, regardless of age—if still loaded—should not be tampered with or exposed to strong heat. An Ordnance expert should be called in to unload or deactivate such projectiles.

Be very careful about restoring any Civil War weapon. The problem doesn't exist if you have an item in "mint" condition but it does occur when your item has a part or parts which are rusted or deteriorated more than the rest of the piece. Most important is the necessity of playing fair with those who inherit what we have inherited. In plain English—leave a weapon as nearly in its original condition as possible. If it was blued or browned, leave it that way. Don't "replace" rusted parts with shiny new parts from other pieces. If you do so, you are creating a composite weapon which is only illustrative of a good assembled gun which no individual ever used. Much better, I believe, is to go ahead and bring the rusted parts up to the best condition possible. But leave them on the original piece. I never have recovered from my initial shock on visiting a collector of Confederate pieces who was engaged in an indiscriminate exchanging of parts, and even substituting better parts from a box of recently purchased gun parts. Never again could he (or subsequent owners) proudly point to any one of these five pieces and say; "original—just as issued."

The most important thing that should be done with an arm is to put it in as good condition as possible without substituting parts, silverplating, or nickel plating. In fact, many collectors object to putting on a new blueing coat. Metal parts should be cleaned with steel wool or steel brush wheel, and grime and grease removed from the wood surfaces. If the wood is badly knocked about, a brilliant polish of the metal parts results in an unbalanced appearance. After all, the gun is 100 years old; it is not unreasonable to expect that it will look old! Be *very* careful not to rub down edges on the piece and not blur or obliterate any markings, including inspector's marks on the wood. If the stock of a musket has been varnished in recent years (i.e. since originally issued) remove the varnish and permit the natural wood grain to appear once more.

In restoring a weapon to the best condition possible, do not rush headlong into the job. Hasty over-cleaning, especially with abrasive wheels, can ruin your weapon literally, in a few minutes. The major problem is rust. Take the gun apart and clean each piece separately. A neutral detergent in warm water will do much to get rid of dirt. But to remove rust use either a simple abrasive as steel wool or fine emery cloth. Use wire wheels very sparingly; once a surface is scratched, much metal will have to be removed to obliterate the scratches. Many collectors use a chemical cleaner but here again, caution must be exercised. Use a mild solution and check on the metal every ten minutes to insure that the metal isn't being eaten into by the solution. Protect your eyes from any chemical solution with glasses if you wear them or, if not, weak tinted sun glasses when scrubbing a piece. Brass corrosion is easily removed by a saturated solution of vinegar and salt, and can be applied by hand. On such a soft metal as brass never use steel wool or a buffing wheel., The same is true for pewter or silver.

So far as wood is concerned, the most common threat is the powder-post beetle. This insect makes the so-called "worm holes" which are seen in the earlier Colonial and Revolutionary pieces. To end this creature's spree, use an eye dropper filled with DDT and repeat the treatment twice a day for three days. That will do the trick. Most gunstocks will be improved by treating them with linseed oil; in fact, most of them were finished originally with nothing but linseed oil.

The constant need for ethics and honesty by collectors as well as dealers must be increasingly obvious to all. We should personally set the example of 100 per cent truthfulness in describing every alteration or "improvement" we do in any item in our own collection, and should be equally insistent on the same code of ethics from others. If we do not adhere to a high standard in this regard, the authenticity of completely original and genuine items will be seriously questioned. (Some already have been). No collector worthy of the name wants a collection of mish-mash; he wants to know that every item in his collection is "right," i.e. original as when first issued to a Yank or Johnny Reb. Experience soon shows which dealers are reliable in describing their wares. They are the ones who deserve our patronage.

Hunting for battlefield relics in remote rural areas can be both rewarding and hazardous. In the early 1950's, while a college professor in Mississippi, I frequently went over the battlefields in the Vicksburg area. Much of the terrain was about as it was in 1863—primitive and very sparsely settled. Encounters with snakes, vicious hounds, and wild boars was a common experience. Usually I took a student with me. But since I did not carry a weapon for protection, I occasionally found myself in a "sticky" situation.

The first of these took place when I visited "Jefferson Davis' Island." This island, formed by the cutting through of the Mississippi River of the tract of land owned by Jefferson Davis prior to the war, was completely uninhabited except for one family. The island had become a haven for deer in hunting season, and was the romping place for wild life of all species, especially boars and cattle. A student and I landed on the island by a cub plane and at once arranged with the sole male on the island for the rental of two horses. But because of the long time taken to round up the two wild steeds, I started off alone on foot, through a maze of tangled underbrush and overgrown cotton fields. On emerging from an old foot path I was confronted by a red-nostriled bull, pawing the ground with fervor. Fortunately there was a tree close by and dropping ,my gear, I swung myself up in it exactly as the irate bull roared by under the branches. While sitting there waiting for rescue I took photographs of the irate bull but perhaps due to my precarious perch or my ravelled nerves none turned out. Eventually the student arrived with my horse and I was safe. I mounted directly from the tree not chancing another encounter with the hefty bull. It took no exception to mounted men—only those on foot.

My second experience occurred on the battlefield of Big Black River. I had ascertained the exact location of the Confederate rifle pits which were supposed to prevent a Federal crossing of the Big Black. With my terrain well in mind I sallied forth, and after driving for some time I arrived at a farm located exactly on the river where the Federal crossing was, in fact, made. Although the owner of the farm was absent, his wife gave me permission to look as much as I wanted. As an afterthought she told me to be careful not to leave gates open as the cattle were grazing in fields adjoining several fine growths of clover. This, of course, I promised to do, and jauntily went on to the field which I knew must include the major C.S. defensive positions.

My calculations were correct! I had indeed found the spot. After a few minutes digging (I had stripped my watch, keys, etc. from my wrist and pockets so as not to lose them in the diggings and had carefully laid them by a tree) I began to have extremely good results—apparently an entire regiment had left their haversacks on the one parapet on which I was working. On bending over to pick up some accouterment items I suddenly was hit with terrific force from the rear and hurled through the air until I hit the ground with substantial impact. Slightly dazed, I picked myself up and saw I was confronted by a large male goat, who, with lowered head, prepared for his next charge. I simply couldn't believe I was to be attacked for I had seen this goat innocently grazing when I first entered the field but neither of us had paid any attention to the other (so I thought).

Not yet did I sense any real danger. I attempted to "shoo" the goat away as I had always driven off cattle on the New England farm of my boyhood. The goat merely remained motionless so I bent over to continue my digging. Suddenly again, I was hit with the force of an express train but with no warning. Angry now, but not alarmed I picked myself up, seized the shovel as a baseball bat, and when the goat charged again I swung, hitting it in the face with all my strength. It was like hitting cement, but I did cut a large V-shaped flap below the eyes. The goat, thoroughly aroused now, with blood streaming from its beard, began a series of attacks which I was powerless to stop. The ground was wet from an earlier rain, I was in rubber boots and moved even slower from the battering I was absorbing. Whether by design or not, the goat gradually drove me towards the edge of a steep cliff, at the foot of which lay a scum-covered pond, alive with cottonmouth moccasin snakes.

I took cover in the scrawny trees along the top of the ridge, but the sure-footed beast relentlessly followed me. I had been hit so many times by now that I was seriously concerned about the animal knocking me into the pond.

Suddenly a brilliant idea came to my befuddled mind; if I could stand on the edge of the cliff and entice the goat to charge (not too difficult an assignment at this point) I could side-step and the animal would plunge into the pond. So I stood on the precipice side of a tree and peeked out around it and was suddenly confronted face to face with my adversary at a foot's distance. The animal now chased me down the cliff, butting me all the way. On my unceremonious arrival at the bottom of the cliff, looking around wildly for some way out of all this, I saw a large, flat-bottomed boat anchored about thirty feet off shore. The very real menace of the wild goat overcame my concern about the snakes swimming around, and I waded as fast as I could out to the boat. But, this was not my day; my boots were water-logged and I was hardly able to pick up my feet but as I tried to step into the boat it sank. I had to return to shore and climb up the cliff, stumbling slowly out of the area, with the goat hitting me at will. The goat even cleared a tall fence to keep at me.

On approaching the farm house the farmer's wife came running out with a pitchfork and attempted to hold off the goat. The enraged animal ignored her completely and charged us both repeatedly, driving itself into the tines of the pitch fork with complete indifference to pain. Eventually it attacked the owner and had to be killed.

My weary ride home was only matched by the reaction of my wife on learning of my experience. She was amused almost to the point of hysteria which bewildered me since it was not so funny to me. A local newspaper on learning of the goat attack suggested in its column that the battle be re-named "The Battle of Goat Run."Students baa-ed at me for weeks as I limped my way back to normal again. I have always shown a very real interest in the animals around a farm ever since, you can be sure.

RELIGIOUS OBJECTS

Since most soldiers on both sides came from strong religious backgrounds, they carried their Bibles, New Testaments, and religious tracts with them. Roman Catholics wore the crucifix and religious medals of their faith. Shown in the first volume of the *Encyclopedia* (page 82) is an extremely small crucifix (1 inch tall) carried through the war by Thomas Prescott, 1st New Mexico Cavalry. Recently the author acquired two variations of that crucifix as shown here. The crucifix on the left was carried by a South Carolina soldier. The containers are of brass. Also shown here are a Bible, New Testament, religious tract, and song book used during the war.

ROCKETS

ORDNANCE MEMORANDUM NO. 1 (1865) LISTS "WAR ROCKETS"

Hale's patent, consisting of 2-inch and 3-inch types. (These measurements refer to the interior diameter measurements of the case.) Scott's *Military Dictionary* defined a "war rocket" as a "projectile set in motion by a force within itself."

The Civil War rocket was composed of a strong case of paper or wrought iron, inclosing a composition of niter, charcoal, and sulpher, so proportioned as to burn slower than gunpowder. The head was either a solid shot, shell, or spherical-case shot, with the base perforated by one or more vents. The rockets used by the United States in the war were Hale's, in which steadiness in flight was given to the flight of the rocket by rotation, as in the case of the rifle bullet, around the long axis of the rocket. This rotation was produced by three small vents placed at the base of the head of the rocket.

Hale's rocket was improved during the war by placing

Religious Objects

Religious Books

three tangential vents in a plane passing through the center of gravity of the rocket, and at right angles to the axis. This was accomplished by dividing the case into two distinct parts, or rockets by a perforated partition. The compostion in the front part furnished the gas for rotation, and that in the rear the gas for propulsion. The two sizes of Hale's rockets in use were:

—2 1/4 inch (diameter of case)
—weight 6 pounds
—3 1/4 inch (diameter of case)
—weight 16 pounds.

Under an angle of from 4-5 degrees, the range of these rockets was from 500 to 600 yards; and under an angle of 77 degrees the range of the smaller rocket was 1,760 yards, and the larger was 2,200 yards.

War rockets were usually fired from tubes or troughs, mounted on portable stands or on light carriages.

Hale's rockets saw some combat use. When the war broke out, Hale's offer to come over from England and make rockets for the Union was refused; but his rockets were used.

ROYS AND LILLIENDAHL ROCKET. Despite the organization of a rocket unit and an initial enthusiasm for "war rockets" in 1861 and 1862, the North met with indifferent success with the rocket in combat. Both the Hale and Congreve rockets quickly fell into official dis-

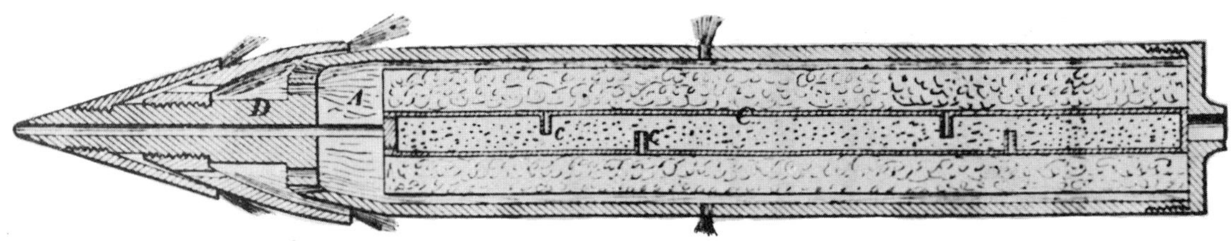

Pascal Plant Rocket

(Courtesy of Al Gross)

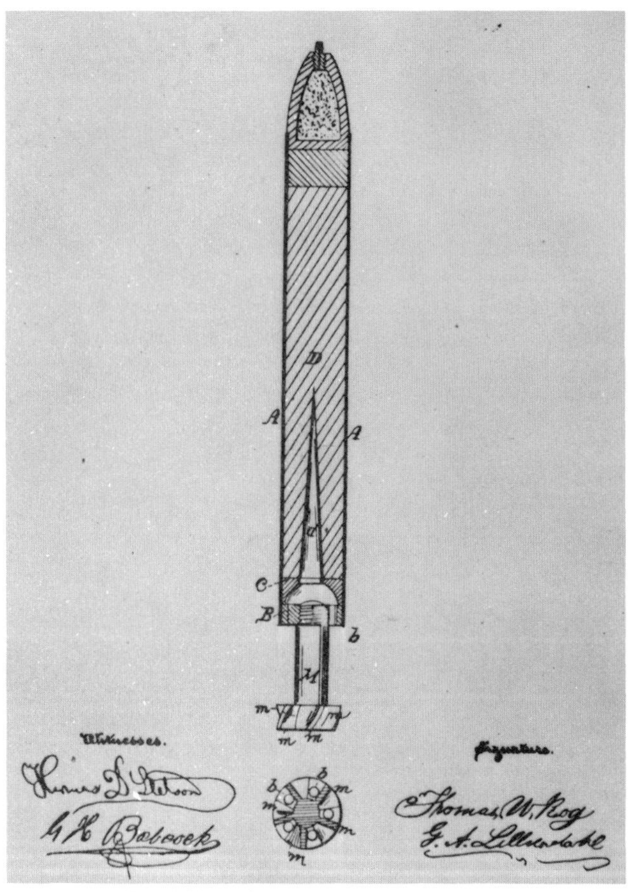

Roys and Lilliendahl Rocket

favor because they were too erratic in flight. Sometimes the rocket would double back on its course, whereupon the rocket crew quickly displayed an understandable lack of enthusiasm for their new weapon. Or, more frequently the rocket would veer off from its course and hit a target which definitely was not included in the day's firing mission.

But on July 22, 1862, two New Yorkers, Thomas W. Roys and Gustavus A. Lilliendahl, patented a rocket which successfully solved the problem of achieving controlled flight. As the inventors pointed out, ordinary rockets failed because they were constructed with gas escape vents oblique to the axis, so that the gases were projected therefrom in directions not exactly in the path of the rocket. This had been found necessary in order to give the rocket a rotary motion in flight.

In the new rocket the inventors, aware of the above problems bored holes in lines exactly parallel to the axis of the rocket, and mounted to the rear of the rocket a type of propellor. As a result the gases were emitted uniformly in the proper line to produce the maximum effect in propelling, and acted upon the propellor to produce a rotary motion to the entire projectile. Moreover, the inventors were able to achieve equal distribution of gases to the vent holes, a feature lacking in earlier rocket types.

At the forward end of the rocket was a percussion cap and a "stout" case of powder, which acted as an explosive shell on striking an object. These elements were protected from the intense heat of the burning composition by a layer of clay.

The cross section reproduced here shows A as a thin case of iron welded together, and, in turn, welded to a thick base, B, in which were bored the gas exit holes. These holes, designated by b, were of the usual size and number for rockets of the period, and were bored in lines parallel to the axis of the rocket. C was an open-topped dome to insure uniform exit of gas; D was the rocket composition, while M and m represent the propellor assembly.

The inventors claimed that their rocket performed in superior fashion to other rocket types in tests. However, the Government did not adopt it, probably because of the general distrust of rockets in general, which permeated most officialdom by mid-1862. However, according to Al Gross of Cleveland, Ohio, who kindly supplied me with a copy of the original patent, the technique disclosed is similar to today's technology in missile guidance and stabilization. The use of stabilizing devices in the exhaust stream is identical to the graphite vanes used in the Redstone Missile during several of the satellite and Mercury programs. Again, we say "There's nothing new under the sun."

FEDERAL "ROCKET BATTALION". In November, 1861, a number of New York State volunteers assembled at Fort Porter, in Buffalo. Maj. Thomas W. Lion, a former officer of the English Army, "inventor of the wonderful fire-rocket," appeared in camp and explained to the men that he wanted to form a battalion to use "his" rocket in the field. He was successful, and a rocket battalion was organized, consisting of two companies of 80 men each, under the command of Major Lion.

The battalion was armed with the Congreve rocket which, according to Major Lion, was a very effective weapon. In a speech at Albany, the major told his men that these rockets had been used with great effect in the Mexican War, "one going a mile out of its way to kill a Mexican."

As one of the soldiers sarcastically said, "I have no doubt it struck a mile from the object it was aimed at."

Claims were made that, with a little practice, a flagstaff could be hit five miles away. But the rockets were "balky," like a mule. They would go any way but the right way. The first night, after target practice with these rockets, rocket stock was low in camp.

The press made much of the "rocket gun" as being a terrifying weapon, whose principal purpose was to throw a flame of fire sufficiently large to frighten horses and thus throw the enemy's cavalry into confusion. Writers described the rocket gun as being a breech-loading fieldpiece, capable of discharging bombs, and percussion shot as well as rockets. The rockets were to be used for setting on fire buildings behind which enemy troops might be lurking. As one newspaper said, "The expansive properties of the rocket are wonderful, creating a ball of fire 15 feet in diameter, which can be thrown 5,300 yards," or over three miles.

On Jan. 24, 1862, a member of the rocket battalion, with a customary lack of security consciousness, described the rocket to his local paper as follows:

"The rockets vary from 12 to 20 inches in length and from 2 to 3 inches in diameter. The head is conical and solid iron, from 2-3 inches in length, according to the size of the rocket. The remaining portion of the rocket is a hollow iron tube, filled with a highly inflammable compound, which is ignited in the rear of the rocket by a fuze and which gives the weapon its impetus. The composition of this inflammable substance is a Government secret."

The tubes were of two types, one of drawn iron with a bore of three inches, and the other was made by combining three 4-inch rods on wires, spirally, fastened by strong bands, leaving a bore of four-to-five inches. Both types utilized a stand. Although the rockets were old and not perfectly made, the men did achieve good results with them. The wire tubes, however, proved to be the better type. Some three-inch rockets fired from the wire tubes performed magnificently. At an elevation of about 45 degrees the "fire spitter" went "direct as a bullet" for a distance of more than three miles.

Two main types of projectiles were used: solid shot; and a type of spherical case filled with musket balls and powder and exploded by a time fuze.

Organization of the rocket battalion was the same as light artillery, including gun carriages, limbers, caissons. But instead of mounting one gun on a carriage, there were four rocket tubes per carriage. Each company was to have four carriages, complete with their tubes. When drawn up in battery before an enemy infantry or cavalry regiment, each rocket was ready, spitting fire, fury, and destruction on every side, and carrying in its projectile 74 bullets, ready to burst from their shell at just the desired point, and scatter death in every direction."

The rocket guns, after a production delay of nearly four months, were turned over by the inventor and contractors to the battalion.

However, in May, 1862, a member of the battalion wrote that tests with the rockets had been unsuccessful and that the "quaint" rocket carriages had been exchanged for the substantial six-pounder carriage, and the sheet-iron tubes were exchanged for rifled cannon. These cannon were three-inch rifled pieces.

Major Lion was soon dismissed from the service for incompetence and his men eventually formed the nucleus of the 24th New York Battery. So far as most of the men were concerned, the rocket was a fizzle—yet it was an innovation and deserves more attention than it has usually received in Civil War technical literature. Apparently Major Lion had not hesitated to plead the rocket's cause before the Secretary of War and the Chief of Artillery. Much was made of the fact that the battalion was not a costly unit.

According to the men who used them, the rockets failed primarily because they were erratic as to direction. In fact, a rocket might double back on its course, and, immediately on leaving the mouth of the tube, take a counter direction and come flying into the midst of those who fired it.

According to Major Lion's statement, the rocket used by the battalion was his improvement on the Congreve rocket. But in the minds of those best acquainted with him, there were very real doubts as to whether the major knew anything at all about the science of gunnery or even about the rocket itself. Apparently the members of the battalion had high expectations and hopes in becoming "the pioneer organization of this wonderful arm of the service." Its failure certainly did not, therefore, result from lack of patriotism or interest of the members of this unique unit.

PASCAL PLANT ROCKET. This rocket, patented March 17, 1863, is remarkably similar in many respects to the 2.75 inch folding-fin aircraft rocket known as the "Mighty Mouse" developed in the early 1950's.

The 1863 rocket shown here had several unique features but the mechanics of the invention were lacking to produce an effective weapon. The rocket propellant was pressed around the center powder magazine. Discharge of the propellant gas was through openings in the conical head. Vents along the center of the rocket imparted spin to the missile.

RUBBER PRODUCTS

The process for vulcanizing rubber was patented by Charles Goodyear in 1844. Although his name appears on many items with the patent date or even as part of the maker's name, Goodyear had no part in the manufacture of these items after 1844. He held over 200 patents for applications of rubber he sold to manufacturers along with licenses to produce various rubber goods.

Waterproof boots, ponchos, coats, capes, and caps were popular in the Civil War era with civilians and soldiers alike.

The Union Medical Department made widespread use of rubber goods as shown in The Medical and Surgical History of the War of the Rebellion. These volumes list, among other things, the contents of Perot's Medicine Wagon, which include: "One self-injecting rubber syringe." Among the items listed in Autenreith's Medicine Wagon are: "Six gum-elastic catheters." A report listing certain supplies purchased during the war by the Medical Department of the Army includes: "6,486 rubber cushions with open centre, 11,724 cushions, small, for air or water, and 1144 India Rubber water beds. (These consisted of a wooden frame lined with tin, and a rubber sheet to cover it after filling with water.) Also in the medical line, the 1852 catalog of The Arnold Company of England lists India Rubber bandages, knee caps, etc.

Other rubber goods, such as whips, mail bags, life preservers, and numerous other items are known to have been used during the war. Two scarce pieces, both made of rubber over canvas, are shown. The Artillery water bucket is 10 in. diameter at the top and 9 in. high, excluding handle. It is marked 1ST BATTERY on the side and stamped on the bottom is: "Goodyear's India Rubber Glove Mfg. Co. New York." It also has the label of the dealer W.W. Wilder. The rubber blanket is 68 in. X 44 1/2 in. and is stamped "Union India Rubber Co. New York, Manufactured under Goodyear's Patent 1844. Extended 1858." It was carried by Corp. James T. Cowan, Co. E. 34th Mass. Vol. Infantry.

Courtesy of Mike Woshner

Rubber Items
Artillery Water Bucket and Rubber Blanket. Blanket has grommets around border and may have been used as a tent or shelter-half.

HARD RUBBER. The process for the manufacture of hard rubber was patented by Nelson Goodyear on May 6, 1851. Nelson died in 1852, so, like his brother Charles, he had little or no part in the actual manufacture of any items. Still, most hard rubber items of the Civil War era do contain the name "Goodyear" and patent date of 1851. Hard rubber (also called ebonite and vulcanite) grew in popularity during the 1850's and items made of the material can be found in almost every area of Civil War collecting. They have been found among soldier's personal effects as well as on battlefields and campsites.

The relatively new photography business welcomed plates made of hard rubber because of it's resistance to acids used in developing.

In the medical field, the previously mentioned Perot's Medicine Wagon contained one 8 oz. hard rubber syringe. Although there was no Dental Corps in the war, some soldiers certainly may have ended up with the hard rubber dental plates patented by Charles Goodyear, Jr. in 1855. A fine medical item, the Craig Microscope, patented in 1862, is shown with the original box. Except for the lens, mirror, and spindle shaft, it is made entirely of hard rubber. It is 5 3/4 in. high, base is 2 1/2 in. diameter and tube is 1 in. diameter. The original folder lists the price of the microscope in brass at $2.00 and in hard rubber at $2.50.

Many personal items such as pens, inkwells, combs, cups, soap boxes, and buttons were made. A few of these items are shown, along with two regulation buttons. The eagle button was used by sharpshooters as they did not glisten in the sun like the ordinary brass ones. This button was also made with the Infantry "I" in the shield. The other is a Navy overcoat button with "U S N" and anchor on front. The civilian buttons shown were popular as replacement buttons for uniforms.

Composition items, oftentimes referred to as "Gutta Percha", are similar to hard rubber and may contain hard rubber scraps, but do not enjoy it's flexibility. These items are generally rigid and break or crack easily.

The composition Confederate Navy button is the closest thing to a Confederate hard rubber item known. No other items produced by or for the Confederacy are reported.

MANUFACTURERS

RUBBER GOODS:

Congress Rubber Co—shirred goods

Roxbury India Rubber Factory—Shoes, life preservers, coats, hats

Newark India Rubber Mfg. Co.—License from Goodyear to make rubber whips.
Goodyear Metallic Rubber Shoe Co.—Rubber shoes and boots
Hartshorn and Co—Rubber shoes
The Naugatuck Co—Rubber goods
Providence Rubber Co.—Rubber goods
L. Candee and Co. New Haven, Conn.—Rubber Goods
J.R. Ford and Co, New Brunswick, N.J.—shirred goods
Boston and Lynn India Rubber Co.—Rubber cloths and blankets.

HARD RUBBER GOODS:

Meyer and Poppenhusen (1853) Hard rubber combs
Beacon Dam Co.—Hard rubber buttons, syringes and photographic supplies (1853)
New York Gutta-Percha and India Rubber Vulcanite Co. (1850's) Hard rubber items
A. G. Day Caoutchouc Co. (1850's)—Hard rubber items
Novelty Rubber Co.—Hard rubber items
India Rubber Comb Co.—Hard rubber items
Poppenhusen and Koenig (1850's) Hard rubber items

Note: shown is a hard rubber Army soap box. Dimensions: 3 1/2 inches in diameter and 1 3/8 inches high. Top shows a checkered design with a large eagle

Courtesy of Mike Woshner

Hard Rubber Items
Buttons: *Top:* Civilian buttons marked I R C Co (India Rubber Comb Co) and N R Co. (Novelty Rubber Co) and Goodyear 1851. *Bottom—Left to right:* Eagle sharpshooters button, bkmrk: N. R Co. Goodyears Pat., Navy overcoat button, bkmrk: Novelty Rubber Co. New York, Goodyear's Patent 1851, Two plain buttons worn by Chaplain Oscar Brent, 28th N.C. Inf. No bkmrk.

Personal Items
Mess Knife. Blade marked-----? CUTLERY COMPANY. Hard rubber handle marked: Goodyears Patent May 6, 1851? Niles Drinking Cup—Patented June 5th 1860; 2 1/4 in. diam. at top, 2 1/4 in. high opened. Lid keeps the cup securely closed when folded. Remains of combs found recently at Fort Mahone near Petersburg, Va. Both are marked: I R Comb Co. Goodyears Patent May 6, 1851. Mustache or Cootie Comb has initials F M carved into it. Hair comb is 3 1/2 in. long, other is 2 1/2 in.

Flasks
Left: Powder Flask believed to have been made around 1855. Marked Patented 1851-Goodyear's Brass top, iron rings. 7 1/2 in. high. Whiskey Flask with grained leather-like appearance, but all hard rubber. 5 1/4 in. high, holds 1/2 pint. Screw-on cap is marked on top: I R Comb Co. Goodyear 1851 Patented.

The Craig Microscope and original box. Disassembles into four parts for uses with direct light, larger objects, etc. Top is marked: Craig's Lens Patented Feby 18, 1862, Base is marked: GOODYEAR'S PATENT MAY 6, 1851, Spindle knob marked: N R Co. Goodyears Pat.

Salve Cans

holding a razor strop in its claws. In the eagle's beak is a banner reading *Morning Exercise.* The top of this soap box can be removed. Inside the top is a mirror. Around the inside of the top is a label reading:

Manufactured by the Novelty
Rubber Co. New Brunswick,
New Jersey under Goodyear's
Patent May 6, 1851

SALVE CANS

In addition to an astonishing variety of patent medicines, soldiers also used various lotions and salves. Illustrated here are two salve cans. The larger is of tin, 1 7/8 inches in diameter and 3/4 inch deep. The cover is decorated with military motif of a cannon, horse, soldier and the words:

Russia Salve
Redding & Co.
Boston

The smaller can is of thin brass, 3/4 inch in diameter and 3/16 inch deep. The cover is decorated with an American eagle and the words:

Preston & Merrill's Best
Lip Salve

SEWING EQUIPMENT

Sewing equipment was not supplied by the military authorities and each soldier had to provide his own. But clothing repair was a constant necessity. Soldiers bought needles and thread from commercial firms and sutlers. But most of the sewing equipment used by the soldiers came in "housewives" made by mothers and sisters at home. The "housewife" was a small cloth sewing kit, usually containing a thimble, thread, needles and extra buttons and bits of uniform cloth. In the illustration (reading left to right) are:

HOUSEWIVES. (top row-left to right) Brown leather. Contains thimble, needles, pins, pin cushion.

BROWN CLOTH. Contains thimble, pin cushion, and stencil of G. D. Smith, Wayne, Maine.

Brown leather. contains pin cushion. Carried by a New Jersey soldier.

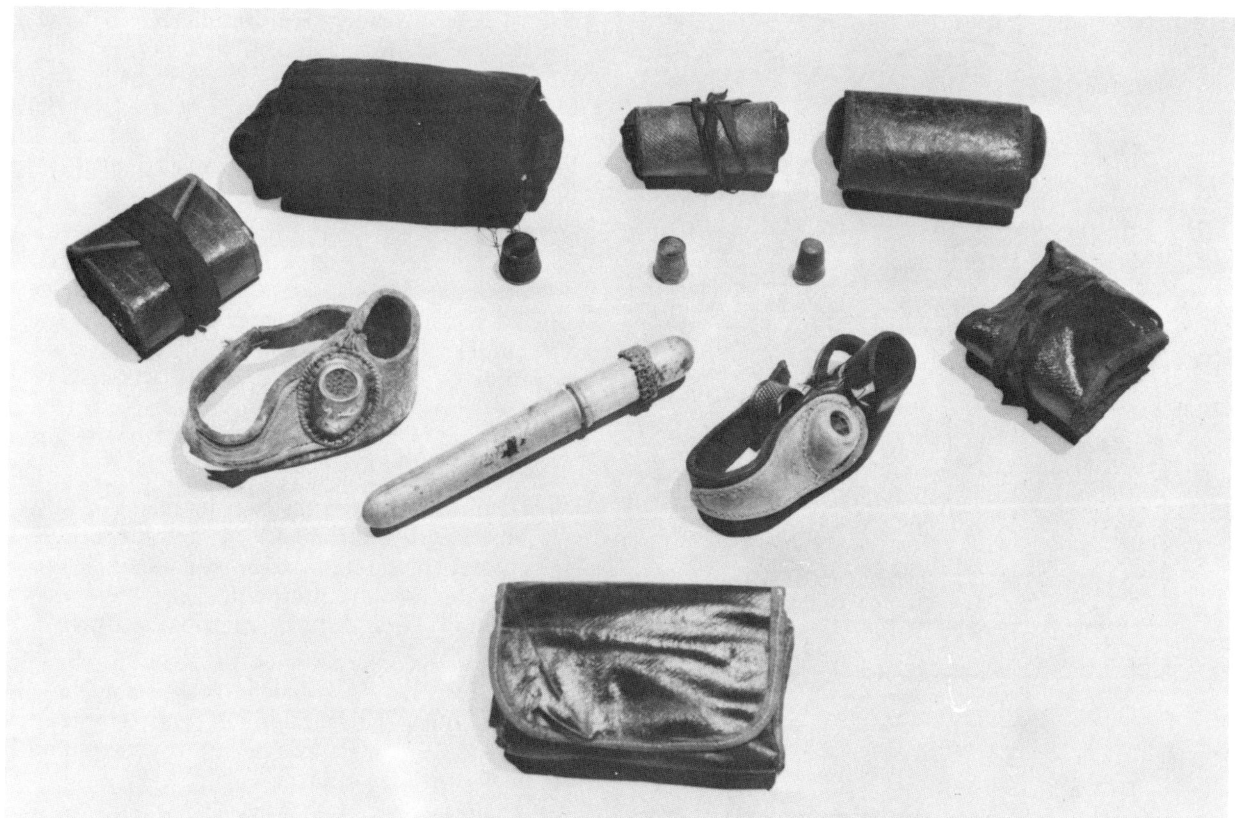

Sewing Equipment

Brown leather. Contains pin cushion and needles.
Black leather. Contains thimble, blue thread, shirt buttons.
(At bottom of illustration). Black leather. Contains thimble, needles, and pin cushion. Was carried by a New Hampshire soldier. Also shown are two Navy sewing holders and a container for the long needles used in mending sails. The three thimbles are as follows:

THIMBLES. (left to right). Carried by A. J. Cure, 23rd New York Infantry. Thimble dug up at Harper's Ferry. Thimble carried by William Read, Co. K 32nd Virginia Infantry.

HOUSEWIFE [*C.S.*]. Shown here is a Confederate housewife taken from a Confederate soldier by William G. Smith. No details are available on place of capture or units involved. The housewife is 10 3/4 inches long and 3 1/2 inches wide.

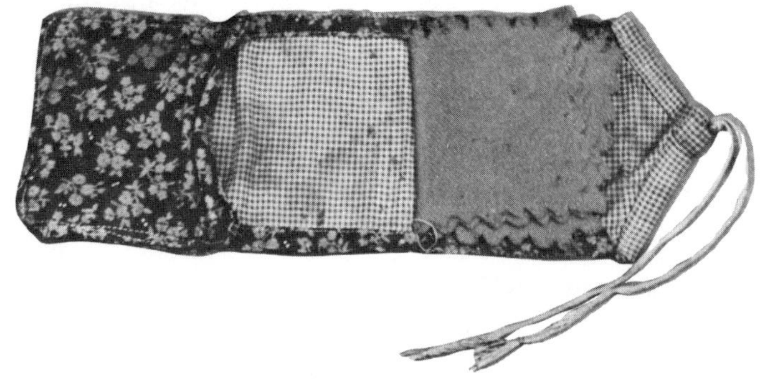

Ken Mattern

Confederate Housewife

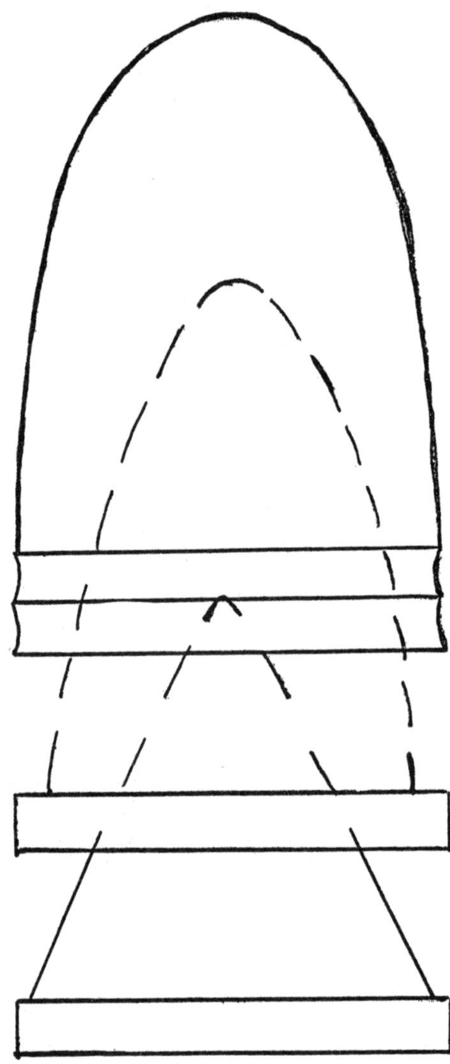

Shaler Bullet

THE SHALER BULLET

Among the many varied bullets of the Civil War, one of the most unique is the Shaler. This bullet, which separates into three parts, was caliber .58 and was issued in 1863 on an experimental basis. There were six variants of the Shaler bullet and to date five of these variants have been found. According to the well-known expert, Herschel C. Logan; "The Shaler bullet was to serve as sort of a'buck and ball' idea. . . that is, it was hoped that the three pieces would separate and fly off towards the target . . . but with a more pronounced velocity. In actual practice it didn't work too well and so not too many of them were made." There can be no question that the Shaler is one of the rare Civil War bullets.

While some authors have made passing reference to the Shaler bullet, they have discussed it in general terms only. I believe readers will be interested in the patent description of the patented *two* types of bullets. Apparently, the second was an outgrowth of the first. On July 16, 1861, only five days before First Bull Run, Reuben Shaler of Madison, Connecticut was granted Patent Number 32,844 for an "improvement in projectiles for firearms," as follows:

> In the breech of the ball or projectile is a shallow recess, into which is fitted an arched piece of metal in such a manner as to cause the pressure of the powder upon it to throw out the edges of the bullet at the breech so as to make them fit snugly against the sides of the barrel and fill the grooves, for the purpose of preventing the escape of the gas generated by the explosion.
>
> *Claim* - Providing the butt or rear end of a bullet with the flange 2, and the concave-convex spreading plate 3, so arranged as to operate in connection with each other, substantially as and for the purpose set forth.

About a year later (August 12, 1862), Reuben Shaler, backed by Ira W. Shaler (presumably a brother or some other close relative), was granted Patent Number 36,197 for "improvement in Compound Bullet for small arms" as follows:

> This projectile is composed of two or more parts, which fit the bore of the barrel, and so constructed that the forward end of each of the parts in the rear of the front one, enters a cavity in the rear of the one before it, and is formed in relation to the same in such a manner as to separate from it after leaving the barrel of the gun, and make a slight deviation in its line of flight from that of its predecessor. *Claim* - The projectile herein before described, made up of two or more parts, each of equal diameter, constructed as set forth, so as to separate from each other as stated.

This unique bullet is one of the curiosities of the Civil War. Very occasionally one of the three sections is picked up on a battlefield site. And very rarely indeed is the entire three-piece bullet found. An informal checking among Civil War collectors leads me to assume that the Shaler bullet was used mainly, if not exclusively, in the East.

SHOE BLACKING

Soldiers at home or in base camps and garrisons kept their black leather items polished. Shown here is a shoe blacking can recovered at the great base camp at Falmouth, Virginia. This camp was winter quarters for the Army of the Potomac during the 1862-1863 winter. The can is of tin, 2 11/16 inches in diameter and 1/2 inch deep.

Shoe Blacking

SHOULDER STRAPS

Federal commissioned officers wore shoulder straps to indicate rank. The various grades are discussed in the first volume of the Encyclopedia. In that volume are also shown some examples of these grades as pictured in the 1864 catalogue of Schuyler, Hartley and Graham. However, there are interesting variations in the original shoulder straps as actually worn. Accordingly, a fairly representative collection is illustrated here to show the variations.

SIGNAL EQUIPMENT

The system of signals used in both armies during the war originated with Albert J. Myer who was born in Newburg, New York. He entered the army as an assistant surgeon in 1854, and while on active duty in the west, saw the need of more rapid communications for the military service. Accordingly, he worked out a system of visual signaling which resulted in his appointment as Chief Signal Officer of the Army in 1860. Up to 1863 Myer was not only the Chief signal officer, he was the ONLY signal officer commissioned as such, while all other officers in the Federal Signal Corps were only *acting* signal officers on detached service from various line regiments. Completely on his own, Myer prepared instructional material for an organized Signal Corps which finally came into being as a recognized organization in March 1863. As early as April 1862, the Confederate Congress had passed an act to organize a signal corps. However, the C. S. organization never became an independent branch of the military service (as did its Federal counterpart), but rather was attached to the Adjutant and Inspector-General's Department. Major William Norris of General Magruder's staff was placed at the head of it.

Most signal equipment of the 1861-1865 period was simple and easily carried. Signal equipment included: *Signal Flags*, with staff 12 feet long and square flags 2 to 6 feet on each side were used. These flags, of red, white, and black, had contrasting colored squares in their centers. For example, the 6 foot white flag had a center consisting of a red 2-foot square.

For night work, torches were used. Except in fog or heavy rain these torches could be easily read at distances up to 8 miles, and often at much longer distances.

Signal Rockets were used by both sides. These rockets were fired by fuzes ignited by "quick-match." A yard of this "quick-match" similar to the "punk" we used to use to set off fire crackers, would burn twelve seconds. Signal rockets attained a substantial elevation and were generally reliable up to eight miles. But in wooded terrain these rockets, which rose above the trees, could often be seen only by observers stationed in the trees,

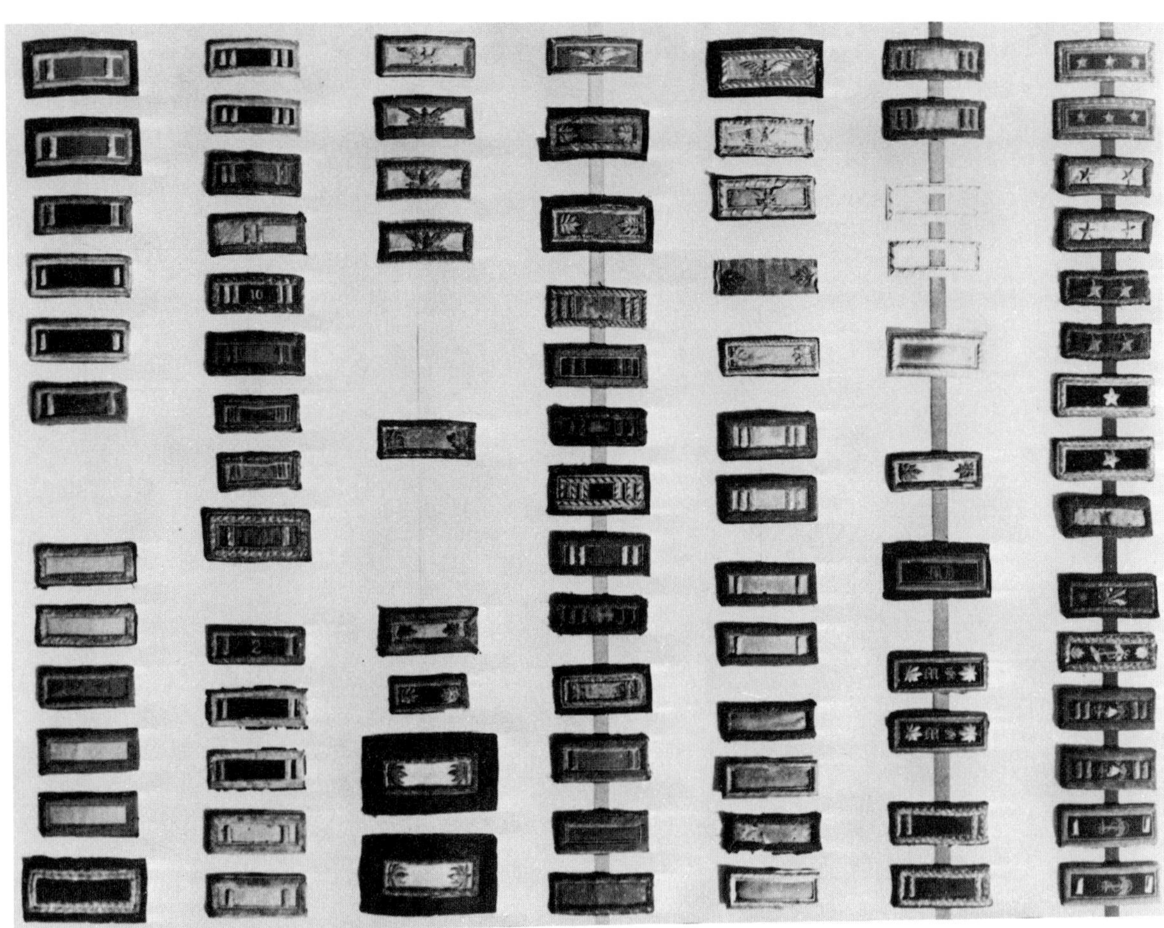

Photo by James L. Wilson, Alexandria, Va

Federal Officers Shoulder Straps
(Rows are numbered 1 to 7, reading left to right. In each row, read top to bottom)

Row 1	Infantry (Blue)
1 & 2	First Lt. Elijah Barstow Co. A, 3rd Mass. Heavy Artillery (Served as Infantry)
3	First Lt. Ohio Vols.
4,5,6	First Lt.
7 & 8	2nd Lt. Solomon Yeakel Co. K, 93rd Penn. Inf.
9	2nd Lt. from John Logan's estate
10,11,12	2nd Lt.
Row 2	Infantry (Blue)
1,2,3,4,5,6	Captain
7,8	1st Lt. John Kies Co. F, 11th Conn. Inf.
9	1st Lt. Isaiah Conley Co. G, 101st Penn. Inf.
10	1st Lt.
11, 12	1st Lt. Isaiah Conley Co. G, 101st Penn. Inf.
13, 14	1st Lt. Maine Vols.
Row 3	Infantry (Blue)
1, 2	Colonel
3, 4	Colonel Picked up at Gettysburg battlefield
5	Lt. Colonel
6, 7	Major
8, 9	Major Joseph C. Willard, Aide-de-camp
Row 4	Artillery (Red)
1	Colonel
2	Lt. Colonel
3	Major
4	Captain Elijah W. Barstow, 5th U.S. Art.
5,6,7,8,9	Captain

10, 11	First Lieutenant
12	2nd Lieutenant
13	2nd Lt. Elijah W. Barstow, Co. F, 3rd Mass. Heavy Art.
Row 5	Cavalry (Yellow)
1,2,3	Colonel
4	Lt. Colonel
5	Major
6, 7	Captain
8, 9	First Lieutenant
10,11,12,13	2nd Lieutenant
Row 6	Miscellaneous
1, 2	Capt. Samuel F. Murry, Co. F, 2nd U.S. Sharpshooters (note: these are green)
3, 4	Frames for shoulder straps
5	Blank form for shoulder strap
6	Major
7	Medical Dept.
8, 9	Major of Medical Service
10, 11	Ass't. Surgeon Robert W. Elmer 23rd New Jersey Inf.
Row 7	Miscellaneous
1, 2	Lt. Gen. Phillip Sheridan
3, 4	Maj. Gen. Phillip Sheridan
5, 6	Major General
7, 8	Brig. Gen. John M. Palmer, (Given by him to Capt. Henry Howland, Murfreesboro, Tenn., April 26, 1863).
9	Brig. Gen. Cavalry
10	Paymaster, U.S. Navy
11	Commander, U.S. Navy
12, 13	Lt., U.S. Navy
14, 15	Master, U.S. Navy

Army Signal Lantern
(Kerosene Lantern 9 inches tall. Marked: U.S. Army Signal Corps)

towers, or on mountain tops. The rockets were fired from a frame or "stand", and even from against a post or fence.

An interesting, and rare (!) item of signal equipment is the *signal pistol.* There were both Army and Navy models of this pistol, both using the percussion cap as with the revolvers, but for cartridges a "composition fire" was used. "Composition Fire" was a pyrotechnic composition which burned with great intensity of light and color. The colors red, white, and green were used. Signal cartridges were fired by the percussion cap, the colors of these cartridges were indicated by the colors painted on the outside of the cartridges themselves. The Federal Government purchased 348 signal pistols during the war; I have found no reference to their use by the Confederacy.

Each signal officer carried a regulation set of signal equipments, consisting of the kit, canteen, and haversack. The kit, or canvas signal case contained the signal staff, flags, torch case and torches. The *canteen* was made of copper, with one seam and soldered. It held one gallon of turpentine or other burning fluid. The *haversack* held wicking, wind-matches, pliers and shears for trimming the torch, a small funnel for filling the torch, two flame-shades, and a wind-shade. The kit, canteen and haversack were fitted with straps for ease in carrying.

Two types of torches were carried in these kits. The *flying-torch* was a copper cylinder, 18 inches long and 2 inches in diameter. It was closed at the lower end, with the exception of a nozzle, through which it could be filled, and which closed with a screw cap. It was open at the wick end, and on its sides. On the wick end were four openings each 1 inch long and 1/2 inch wide, which opened into the wick. The *foot-torch* was similar in dimensions and form to the *flying-torch*, but was equipped with a flame-shade and a wind-shade.

Signal officers used field glasses, usually of French manufacture, and signal telescopes. These telescopes were considered to be the best in general use. They were 30-power and had a focal length of 26 inches. The tube was cased in leather. The draw was of four joints, bronzed black, in order that there might be no glitter to attract the enemy. The telescope had leather caps for both ends and was carried by a strong leather strap. A specimen in the author's collection, used at South Mountain in 1862, is marked "U.S.A. Signal Telescope. Jas. W. Queen, Phila."

Both sides soon learned the fallacy of sending messages "in the clear," and enciphered or encoded their more important messages. Cipher discs of cardboard were used. On these discs were written or printed the letter of the alphabet in irregular sequence around the circumference of the disc. However, a Federal officer in 1865 (probably General Myer himself), in an article published in the *Army and Navy Journal*, observed that the Federal and Confederate signal systems were substantially the same, and "no system of visible signals has yet been invented which can not be decyphered by an expert."

SNIPER'S RIFLE

During the fall of 1861, Hiram Berdan was busily engaged in organizing his famous sharpshooter companies. Berdan's purpose was to bring together the best marksmen in the North and to arm them with the most reliable rifle made. With such men so armed and thoroughly equipped, it was believed that in the line of special service—which meant as snipers and skirmishers—these units would be of special usefulness in active operations. There can be no doubt that these companies, raised in the various Northern states, organized as they were in the First and Second United States Sharpshooters, killed more of the enemy than any two other Federal regiments during the war.

As soon as Berdan's proposal to form sniper companies had been accepted by the Government, printed circulars were issued by the Adjutant Generals of the individual states calling for companies of Sharpshooters and prescribing the terms on which candidates would be accepted. It was ordered that no man would be accepted who failed, at 200 yeards, to put 10 consecutive shots in a target, "with the average distance not to exceed five inches from the center of the bullseyes." Each man was allowed to use his own rifle, and, if he qualified, he could take the rifle with him to the front. For each rifle furnished and accepted, the sum of $60.00 was to be paid by the Government. However, many men did not avail themselves of the offer preferring to let the Government furnish the weapons.

Accordingly, agents of the Government made a house-to-house canvass in the districts which appeared most promising for privately owned match rifles best suited for long-range shooting. Some rifles thus obtained weighed from 15 to 30 pounds. Equipped with telescopic sights and fired from a rest, these weapons were lethal at ranges well over a mile. On one occasion a Confederate saw a Berdan sharpshooter kill a man at such a distance that the report of the rifle could not be heard. The distance was estimated at just about a mile.

One of the best of these heavy rifles was made by W. G. Langdon, a Boston watch and clock maker and expert rifleman, who in 1862 contracted to make for the Government a score of such rifles at $150.00 apiece, telescope included.

Although the heavy sniper's rifles were exceedingly cumbersome to carry on the march, they were especially valuable in siege operations where they were used against artillerymen and officers with deadly effect. The telescopic sight was "an instrument which . . . (reduced) the art of aiming to a point of mathematical certainty." Berdan's sharpshooters operated with deadly efficiency. At Chancellorsville a Confederate sharpshooter killed a colonel just in rear of the 1st New Hampshire Light Battery. Accordingly one of Berdan's sharpshooters was summoned to "fix the rebel." Members of the battery watched curiously at his manner of going to work. First he took off his cap and showed it over the earthwork. Of course, Johnnie Reb let go at it, thinking to kill the careless man under it. His bullet struck into the bank, and instantly the Federal sharpshooter ran his ramrod down the hole made by the Johnnie's ball, then lay on his back and sighted along the ramrod. He accordingly perceived from the direction that his game was in the top of a thick bushy elm tree about one hundred yards in front. It was then the work of but a few seconds to aim his long telescope rifle at that tree and "crack" she went. "Down tumbled Mr. Johnnie like a great crow out of his nest and we had no more trouble from that source."

Although some of the Berdan companies were equipped with the heavy sniper rifle, the majority used first the Colt revolving rifle, and later the Sharps breech-loading rifle. Apparently, however, snipers' rifles, equipped with telescopic sights, were used into late 1864 at least, and perhaps even later.

SOLINGEN MILITARY PRODUCTS

Civil War collectors as well as students of the 1861 - 1865 period have long been bewildered and frustrated by the almost endless variety and number of European—produced arms for *their* war. In an attempt to supplement the limited data already available in published form, I made two trips to Solingen, Germany

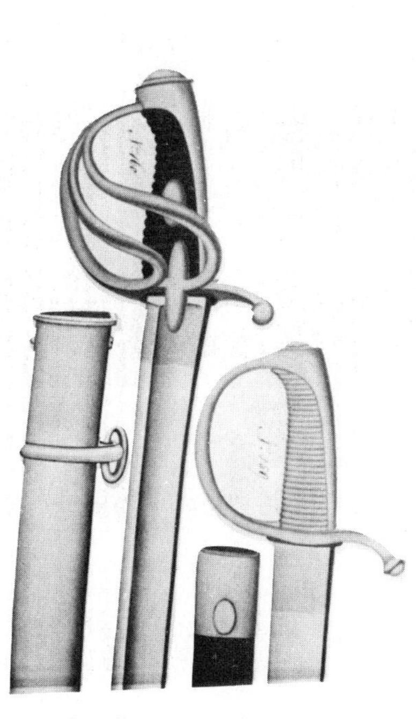

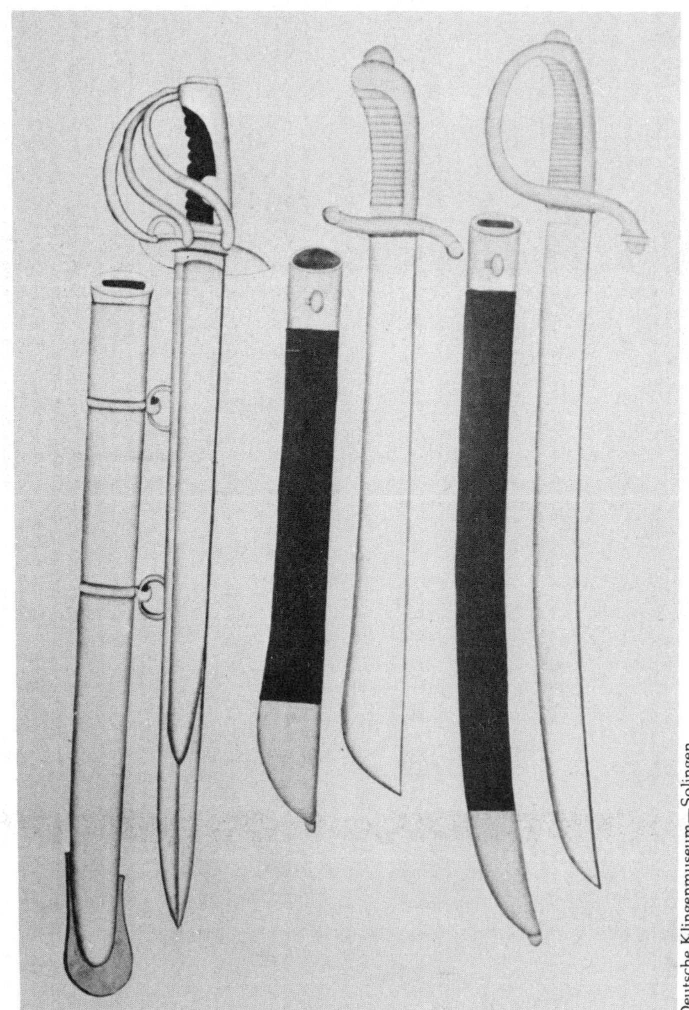

Deutsche Klingenmuseum—Solingen

Solingen Swords
Left: Wolf Fritz. *Right:* P. D. Baus

Kendall B. Mattern Collection

Non-Regulation Officer's Sword Thurmann G. F. (Solingen?)

(1968 and 1970), in order to do research in one of the most important foreign sources of military supplies for both the North and South. Because of extensive loss due to World War II and its aftermath, existing records are sparse indeed!

To supplement the information gleaned over the course of two summers in Solingen, I contacted American collectors in the States whose collections are such as to warrant the hope they could assist me in my research for this study. Although very generous in their willingness to help, their assistance was limited to a comparatively few specimens for my particular study. However, in the "acknowledgments" I am thanking each individual for the time and trouble he took to help out.

I am very especially indebted to my wife, Marjorie, who accompanied me to Solingen on both trips and who did all the photography there in preparation of this study. She photographed all the Solingen items illustrated in this study which bear the caption "Deutsche

Trademarks of Schnitzler & Kirschbaum—Solingen Maker

Deutsche Klingenmuseum—Solingen

Non-Regulation Officer's Sword P. D. Luneschloss—Solingen

Kendall B. Mattern Collection

Klingen Museum, Solingen". These photographs were made of items contained in the original archives of this museum.

Mr. John Walter of Brighton, Sussex, England was most generous with his invaluable assistance; to him, especially, I am most appreciative.

Civil War historians and collectors are well aware of the significance of Europe in furnishing both sides with military supplies from 1861-1865. A major part of the emphasis on these supplies has justly been attributed to England, France, and Austria. However, we must not neglect the extensive contribution of the firms of Solingen whose fame for quality was world famous by 1861, and who furnished both North and South with substantial quantities of their excellent products during the war.

These firms in Solingen are still carrying on their high tradition of quality products. When one mentions knives or other cutlery today, Solingen immediately comes to mind. At least 90% of the German cutlery industry is to be found in Solingen. The name of this town, stamped on millions of scissors, knives, forks and

Sword Blades of Schnitzler & Kirschbaum Solingen

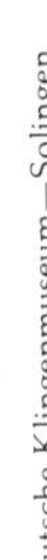

Deutsche Klingenmuseum—Solingen

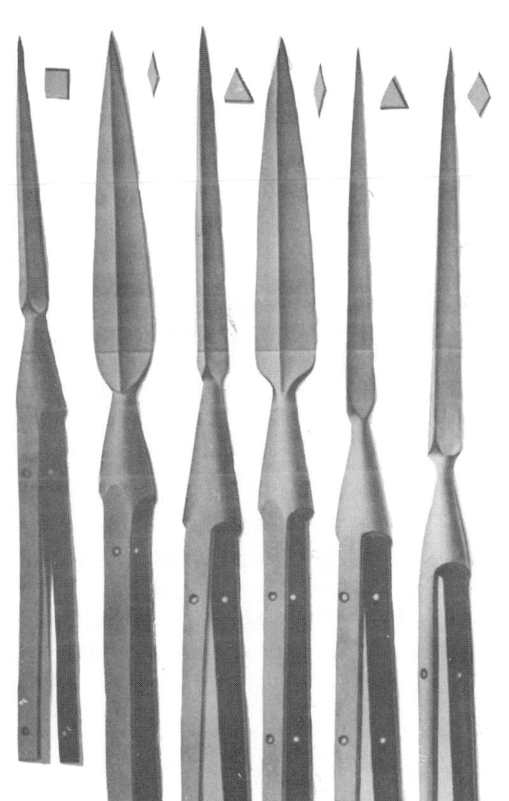

Deutsche Klingenmuseum—Solingen

Lance Heads—Wolf Fritz—Solingen

spoons, and razor blades, has become a symbol of quality throughout the world.

At least a thousand years ago, swordsmiths in the Soligen region enjoyed a well-deserved reputation. This reputation of being absolute masters of their trade has stayed with the Solingen swordsmiths right up to the present day.

Solingen is a comparatively small town, surrounded by farm areas. At the present time there are about one thousand manufacturers in the town—consisting almost entirely of small and medium-size firms. In all of Solingen there is only one firm which employs more than 1,000 people, two which employ more than 500, and about 30 which employ between 100 and 500 men. This adds up to a total of 33 large factories. The remaining 967 manufacturers employ on the average of 10 men each!

They need no smoking chimneys for their work; a network of 37 fast-running mountain streams make this an ideal location for the establishment of grinding shops.

Swordsmiths have been in Soligen for centuries. The Franks from this area early became famous for the superiority of their swords. The feature which distinguished the Frankish sword was its length and excellent balance. It was equally suitable for cutting or thrusting. These swords were made at least as early as 965 A.D.

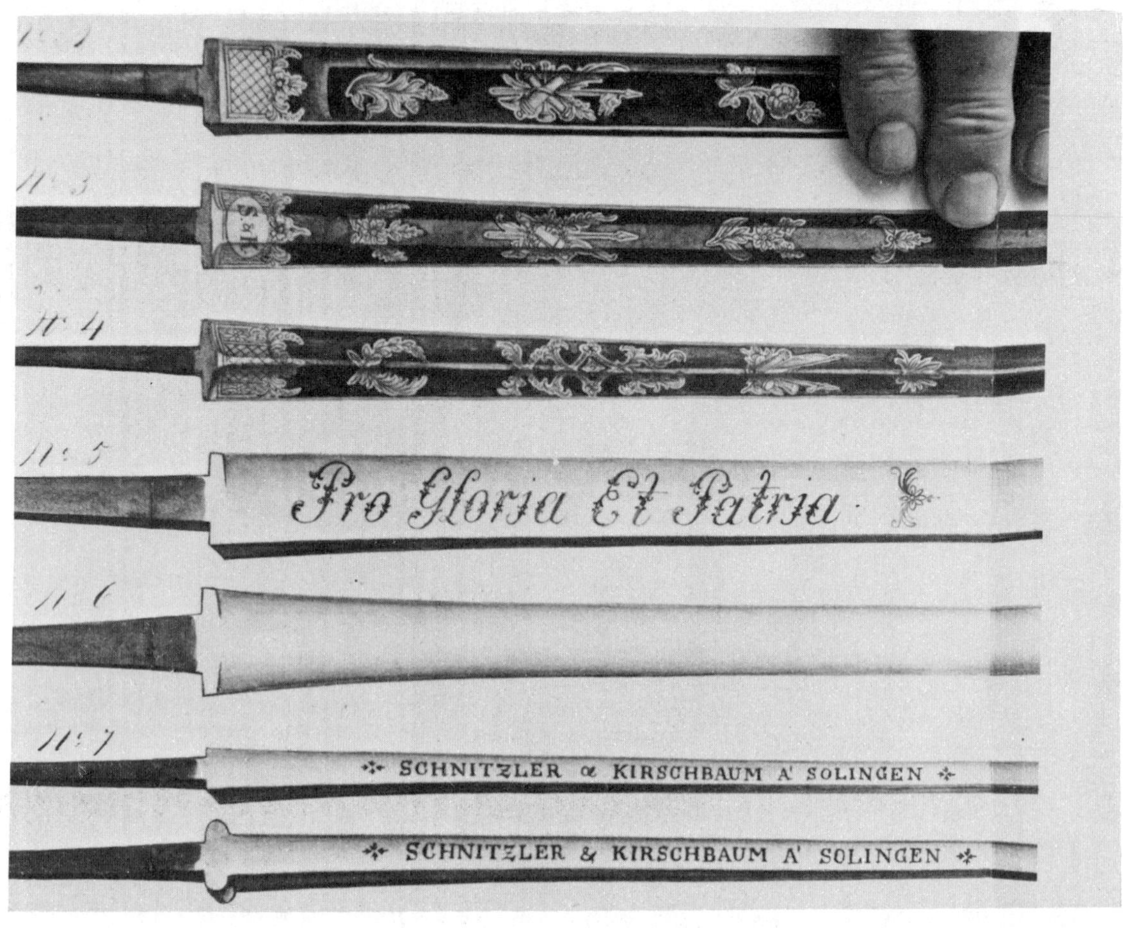

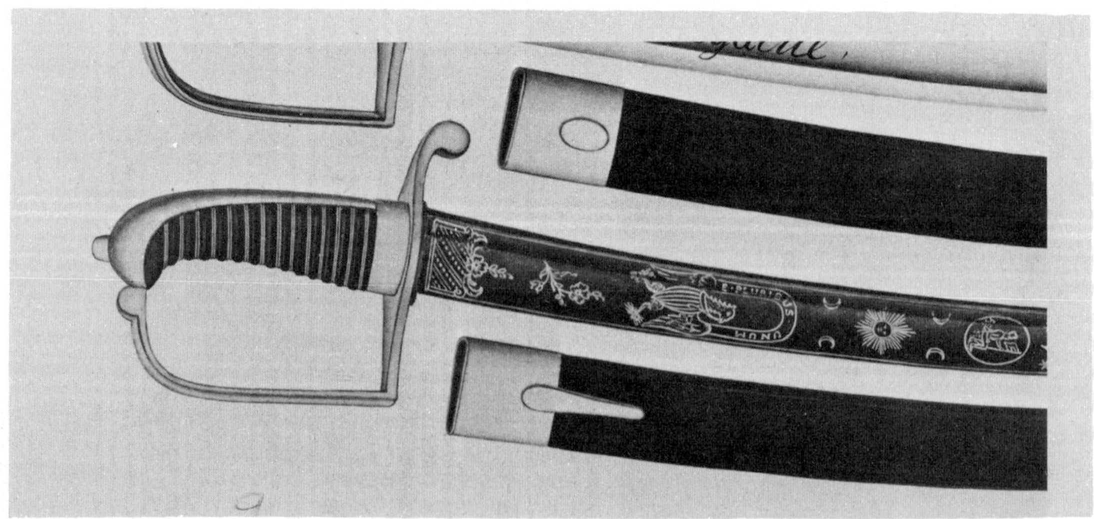

Deutsche Klingenmuseum—Solingen

Sword Blades of Schnitzler & Kirschbaum—Solingen

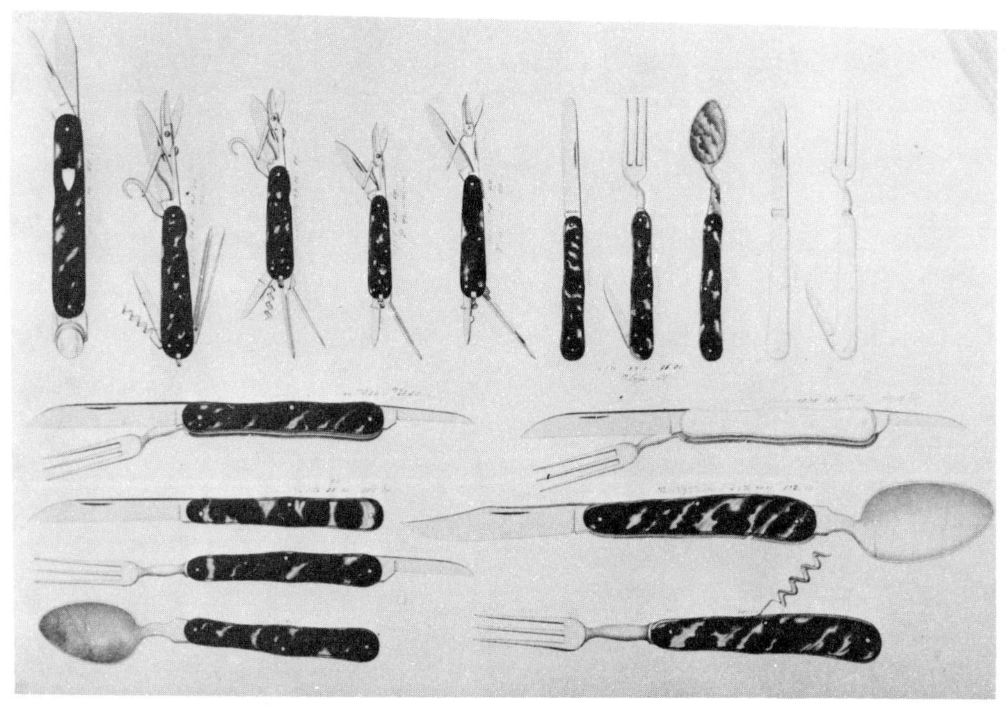

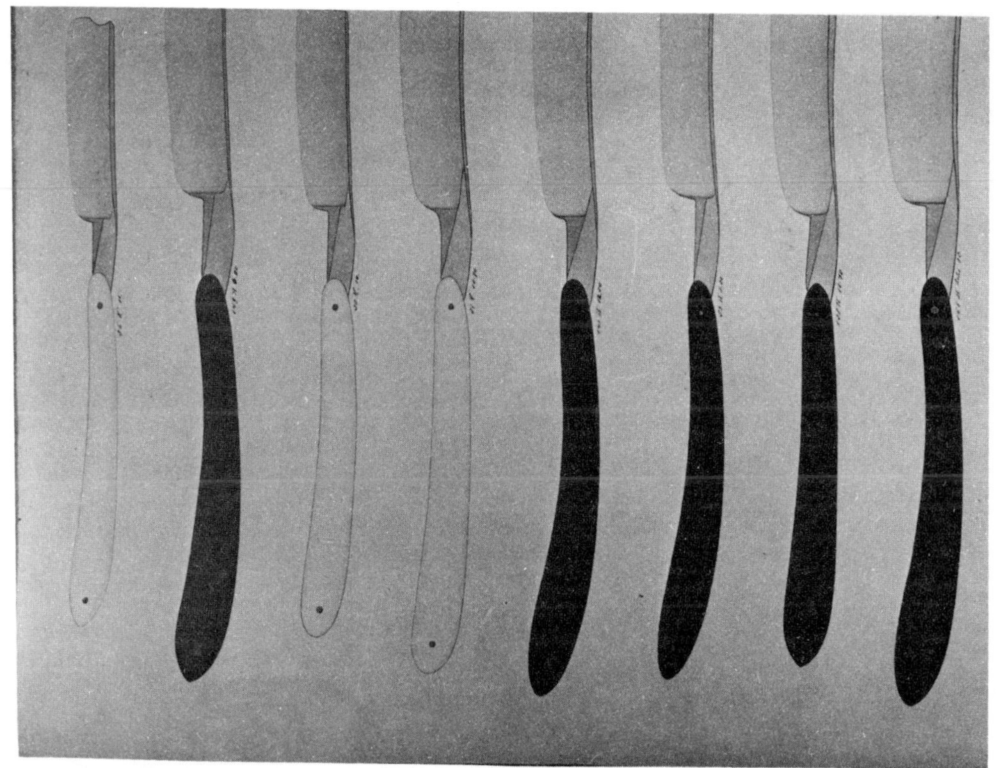

Knife-Fork-Spoon Combinations and Razors
Hermann Schulder Solingen

Deutsche Klingenmuseum—Solingen

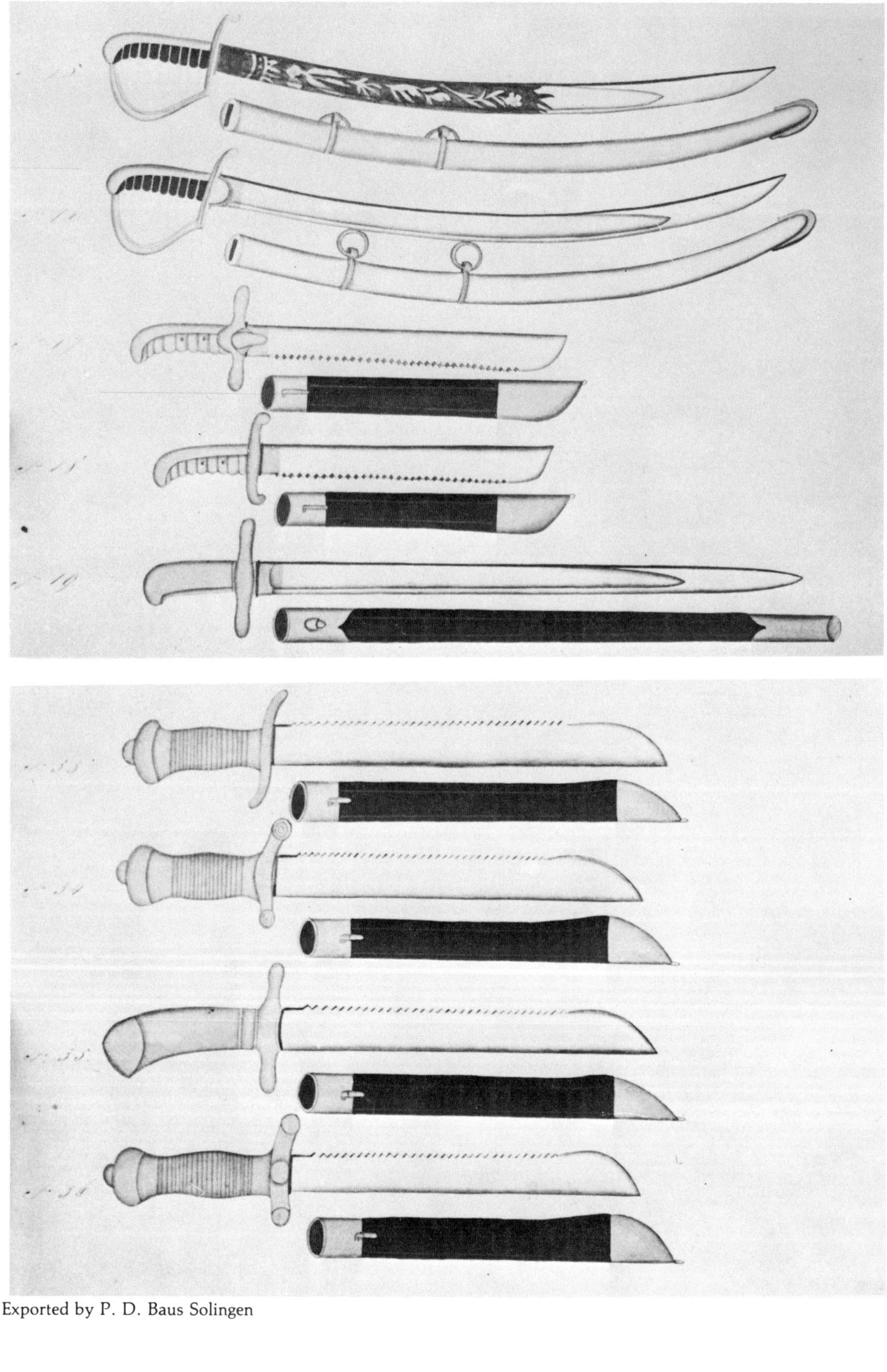

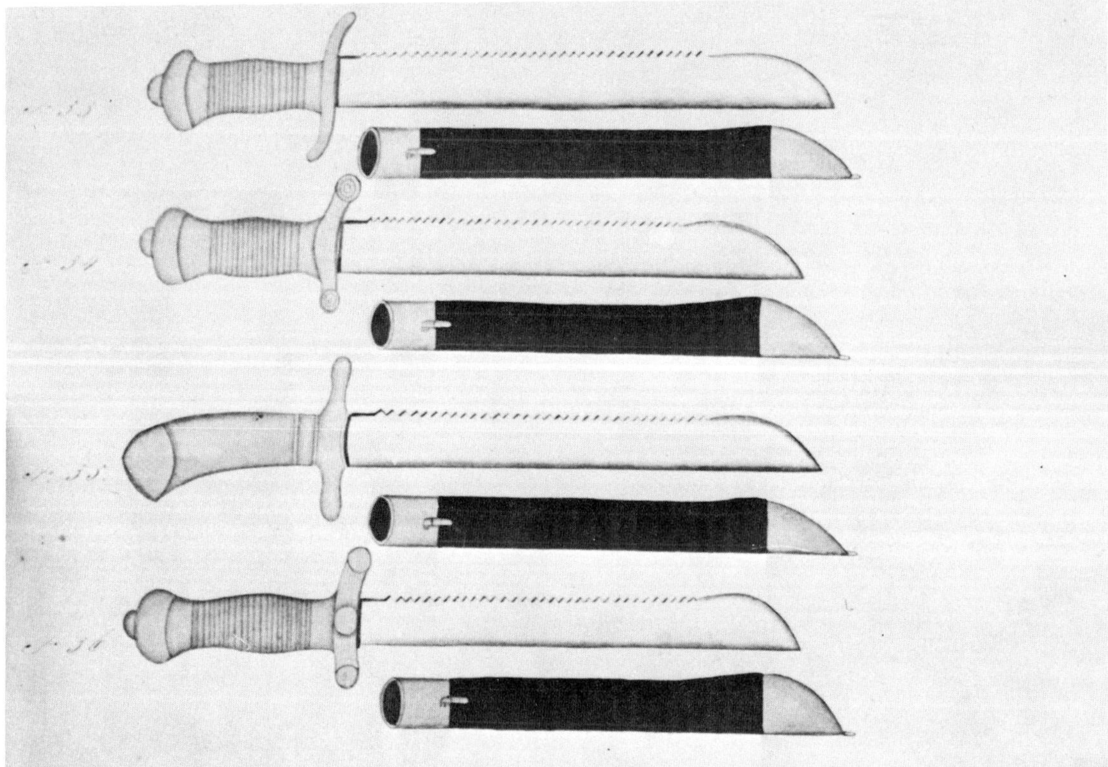

Swords Exported by P. D. Baus Solingen

Deutsche Klingenmuseum—Solingen

Letter Head of the Firm of W. Clauberg of Solingen

Deutsche Klingenmuseum—Solingen

Cavalry Officer's Saber W. Clauberg—Solingen

John L. Herring Collection

By the 13th Century the Solingen sword industry had been diversified into various crafts—swordsmiths, sword hardeners, and sword grinders. But this diversification was not sufficient to compete with the excellent English products and after the 18th Century, Solingen introduced new production methods. Since that time her reputation for quality has been second to none.

Because of the multiplicity of firms in Solingen, an established set of trade marks for the individual firms was set up and duly recorded. As early as 1684, all Solingen swordsmiths were duly entered on such a list. In time, even the name Solingen on a sword came to be practically the equivalent of a trade mark in itself.

The best source for information on makers of edged weapons imported by America during the Civil War is:

House Executive Document No. 67 (Purchase of Arms, February 12, 1861-February 1, 1862) 37th Congress, 2nd Session.

Also useful are:

Senate Committee Report No. 108, 37th Congress, 2nd Session

House Executive Document No. 99, 40th Congress, 2nd Session

Unfortunately, in none of these sources are the individual pieces described. It is known that the United States Government made foreign purchases from contractors as follows:

FIRM	DATE	ITEM
P. and L. Chiefflin	July 18, 1861	3,000 foreign non-commission officer's swords and 2,000 foreign musicians swords
Mansfield, Lamb and Company	August 28, 1861	18,000 foreign Cavalry sabers
H. Boker and Company	September 5, 1861	18,000 foreign Cavalry sabers
J. Meyer	September 7, 1861	10,000 foreign Cavalry sabers
J. T. Ames	November 1861	10,000 foreign Cavalry sabers

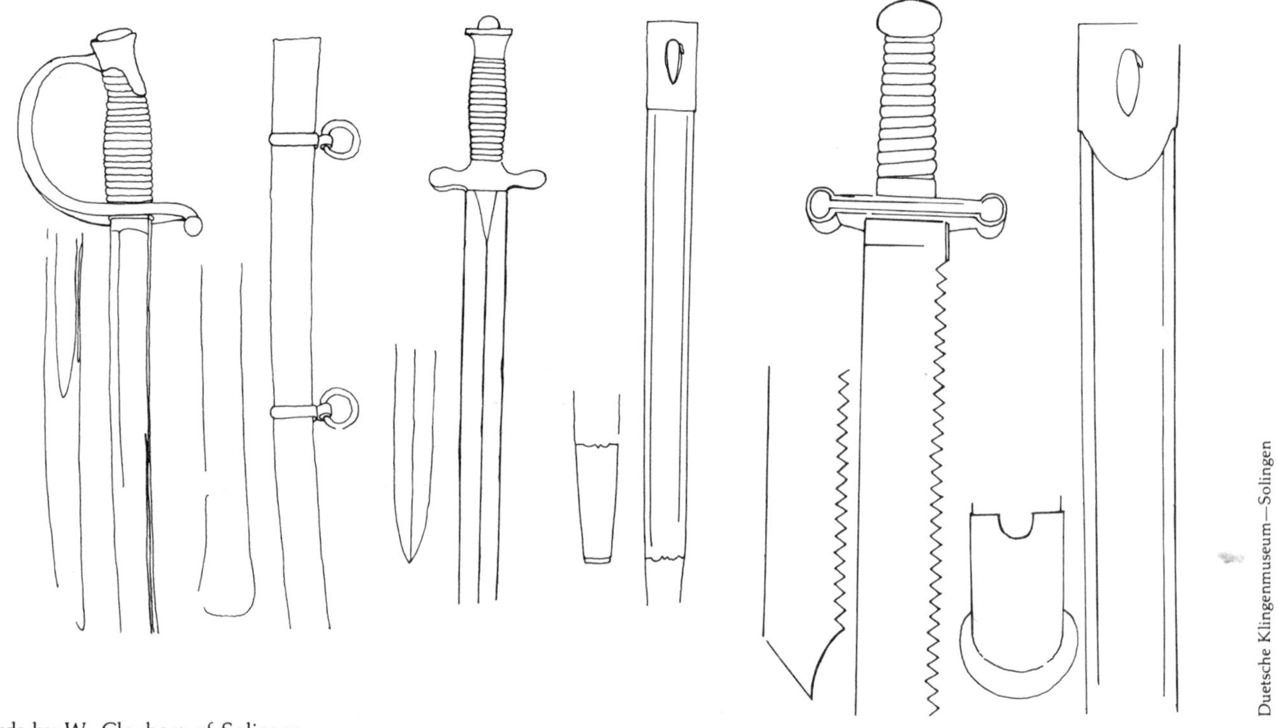
Duetsche Klingenmuseum—Solingen

Swords by W. Clauberg of Solingen
Left to right: Artillery Saber; Artillery Short Sword; Sapper's or Engineer's Short Sword.

These contracts for 1861 only. Apparently the leading importer was Hermann Boker of 50 Cliff Street in New York. He also imported from Liege, Belgium and Birmingham, England. From these and other European sources his firm imported 188,054 long arms during the Civil War.

Other important American importers were Silas Dingee (importer of Austrian weapons), and William J. Syrus and Brother. But there were many others. German exporting firms were located in Danzig, Ferlach, Herzbert, as well as several firms in Vienna, e.g. Johann and Ferdinand Fruwith, and Heiser. In Bavaria the firm of Johann Ludwig Werder was especially active as an exporter during the Civil War period. Many weapons of the Civil War are stamped with such foreign names as "Danzig," "Zella", and "Suhl". Likewise, from France came weapons stamped "St. Etienne" as well as many more from Liege, Belgium.

SOLINGEN MANUFACTURERS OF EDGED WEAPONS AND OTHER MILITARY SUPPLIES TO 1865.

P.D. Baus—Established c. 1850, sword manufacturer

J.E. Bleckmann—Founded by Johan (or Johannes) Bleckman in 1808. Not registered with the Industrie—und Handelskammer until 1931. Principally cutlery makers. Numbers of British Sabre Bayonets Pattern 1858, and Cutlass Bayonets Pattern 1860 were made—some of which probably found their way to the United States.

Trademark shown—pg. 179

(Other trademark identified as a domino—with a double one-eagle, 1808, and the legend: "Bleckmann, Bleckmann, Hammel, Er-Cu").

Wilhelm Clauberg & Co.—(1857-1970). Bayonet Manufacturers, most of their production seems to have come from the decade 1860-70 and then ceased. Trademark was a standing armoured Knight.

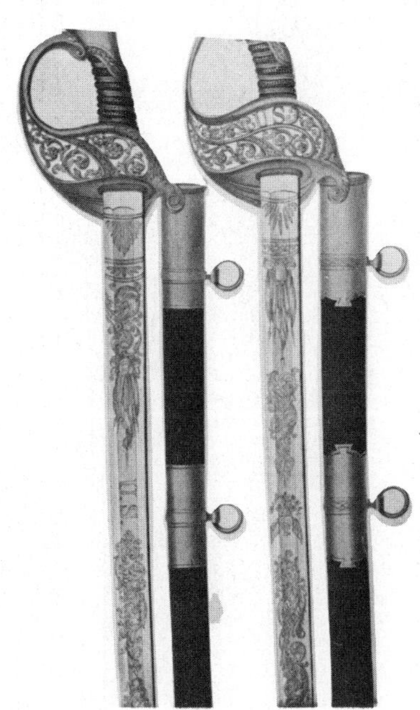
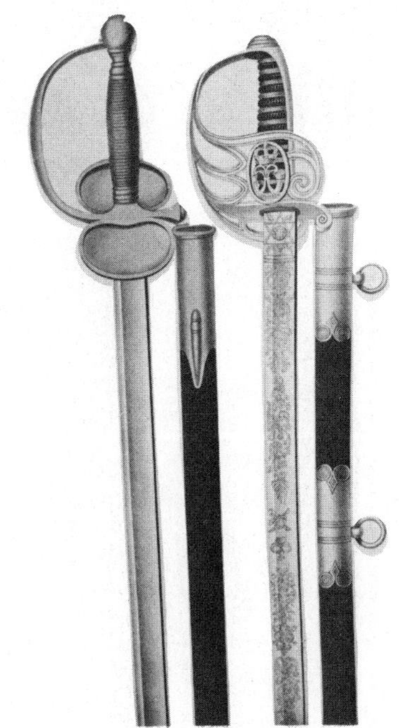
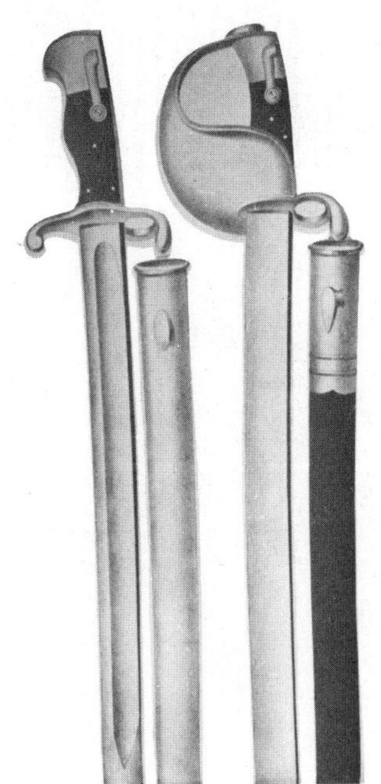
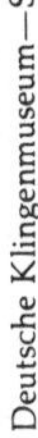

Officer's and Non-Commissioned Officer's Swords and Sword Bayonets exported by Wilhelm Hoppe of Solingen

It was one of the largest exporters of edged weapons during the 1861-1865 period. Beverly M. Dubose, Jr. of Atlanta, Georgia has two swords from this maker in his extensive collection. One of these swords is a non-regulation foot officer's sword with a very wide checkered guard containing a cast "U.S.", and the other is a two-branch guard sword. Both are marked:

W. Clauberg, Solingen—Made artillery sabers, short swords and cavalry swords. According to Harold L. Peterson, Chief Curator of the National Park Service, officers swords made by W. Clauberg and Son, were those sold through Schulyer, Hartley and Graham or Hortsmann.

Clemen and Jung—Established in 1860. A cutlery firm which made swords, daggers, as well as etched blade bayonets and swords. The earliest bayonet definitely identified (according to my information) is 1865. No trademark is recorded for this company—which used as a stamp either their name in full or the abbreviation "C & J".

Christian Cranberg—made British 1859 Cutlass Bayonets.

Wolf Fritz—Established c. 1830 (?). Made lance heads.

Gottlieb Hammesfahr & Co.—Of Solingen Foche. Founded as early as 1684, and registered on 12/11/1875. A cutlery firm, later to gain a reputation for drop-forging—they do not seem to have made any bayonets before the First World War. However, this company made knives, cutlery and scissors for export during the Civil War Period.

J.A. Henckels "Zwillingswerk" & Co.—Founded by Johann Henckels June 13, 1731. Current premises at Grunewalder Strasse 10-22 (where they have been since 1840). Registered at the Industrie—und Handelskammer zu Solingen on 5/12/1882, when the firm would permit only family members to enter their employ. Trademark was two conjoined twins ('zwillinge'). (see pg. 179)

Friedrich Abr. Herder Sohn.—The oldest of these firms, with a direct line back to 1623. Not registered with the Luhzs until 2/12/1888, premises now at Grunewalder Strasse 31. Only trademark possibly relevant to the period of the Civil War was a pair of crossed keys. (see pg. 179)

E. & F Hoerster & Co.—Founded in 1850, this seems to have been an enlargement of an earlier concern named F. Horster & Co., and the 'F Horster" stampings appear to have been used for a number of years thereafter. E & F Horster were registered with the Luhzs on 10/5/1872 as producers of "...swords, sabres, daggers, foils, etc...' Current premises at Katternberger Strasse 128 in Solingen. No trademark known; they seem always to have used the firm's full title.

F. Hoeller

S. Hoppe Sons—Swords, knives, scissors, *Trademark*—A bee hive

Wilhelm Hoppe—Made officer's and non-commis-

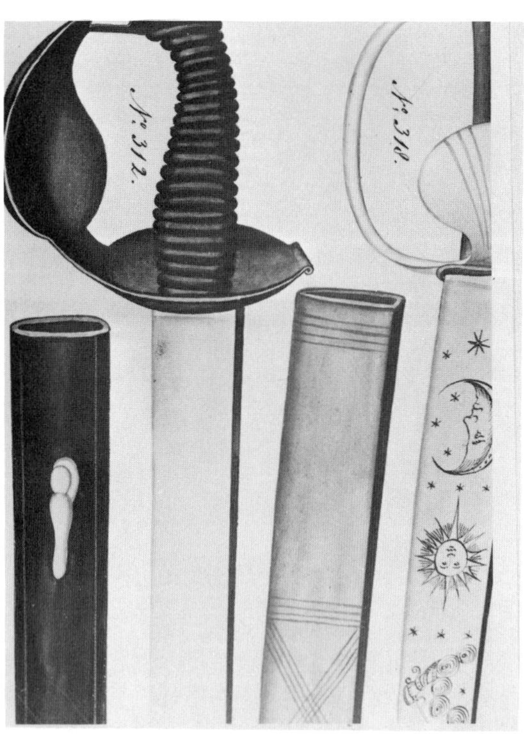

Swords of Schnitzler & Kirschmaum—Solingen

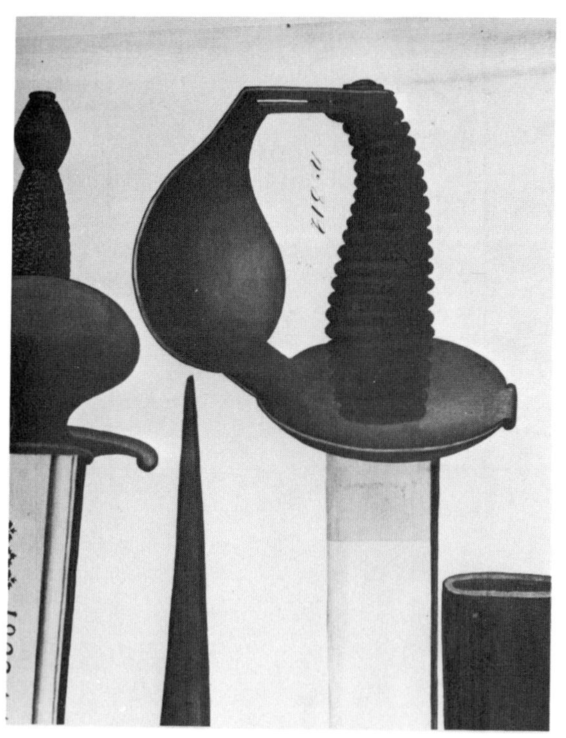
Deutsche Klingenmuseum—Solingen

sioned officer's swords as well as sword bayonets.

A. AND F Kirschbaum—Trademark—S & K

Kirschbaum & Bremshey—(predecessors of W.R. Kirschbaum & Co.) Founded in 1858 by Carol Reinhard Kirschbaum and Casper Wilhem Bremshey to produce for the British Government the Sabre Bayonet Pattern in 1858. Produced these bayonets from c. 1861-4, and then managed to get enough export orders to enable the firm to run until 1876, when Bremshey sold the machinery to Wilhelm Kirschbaum (son of Carl). The exact style of the firm's name seems a little vague, although it must be pointed out that the title W.R. Kirschbaum seems to have been used for some years prior to 1875. (see pg. 179)

Wilhelm [?] Klonne—Made British 1859 Cutlass Bayonets.

Franz Koeller & Co.—Solingen-Ohligs. Another cutlery firm, founded in 1855 and registered on 23/4/1906. Old roots in Solingen, going back to the smith Johannes Koller or Keller, Keuller (1490-1510). No trademark known in the era 1861-5.

P.D. Luneschloss & Co.—Founded 1821, ceased its production in 1945. Specialized in scissors, edged weapons and pocket knives and made bayonets for the United Kingdom, Holland, Belgium, France and the German states. (see pg. 179)

Made sword bayonets for the model 1855 Colt Revolving Rifle. Bayonets are marked with "P.D.L." in a dotted oval on one side, and "U.S." on the other.

Also made non-regulation officers' swords which were used during the Civil War. These swords are marked "P.D. Luneschloss" and "Solingen" in two lines on the blade. (Kendall B. Mattern Collection).

Friedr. Neess and Sons—Made weapons as well as iron steel products

Trademark—a skull

Schnitzler and Kirschbaum—Granted sword trademark No. 29 in 1822. Made swords, bayonets, various military supplies

Trademark—S & K

This company sent many varied types of military equipment to both North and South from 1861 to 1865. Because of the paucity of records, it is extremely difficult to list *all* types of military items which S & K produced. However, some items marked S & K which are now identified in various collections have aided materially in filling gaps on this company.

Canteens. The company made canteens marked *S & K* and *Texas.* Also located has been a Confederate Alabama tin canteen, embossed on the front with the State of Alabama and the letters *S & K* on the back. This canteen is 8 inches in diameter, 2 inches thick, and has three broad straps on the side and bottom for the carrying sling.

Belt Buckles. A brass belt buckle made by S & K has been identified. This buckle was made for the "Washington Greys" and is marked "S & K Prussia".

Sword Bayonets. The author has had an S & K sword bayonet made for the Sharps and Hankins rifle. This

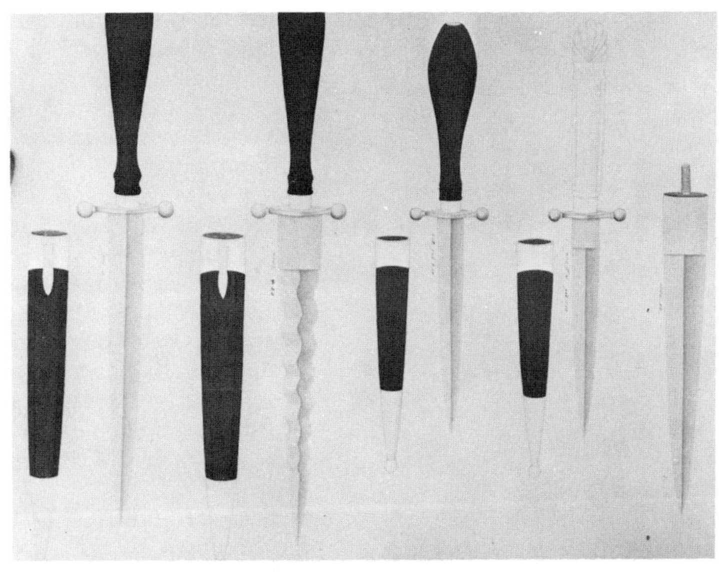

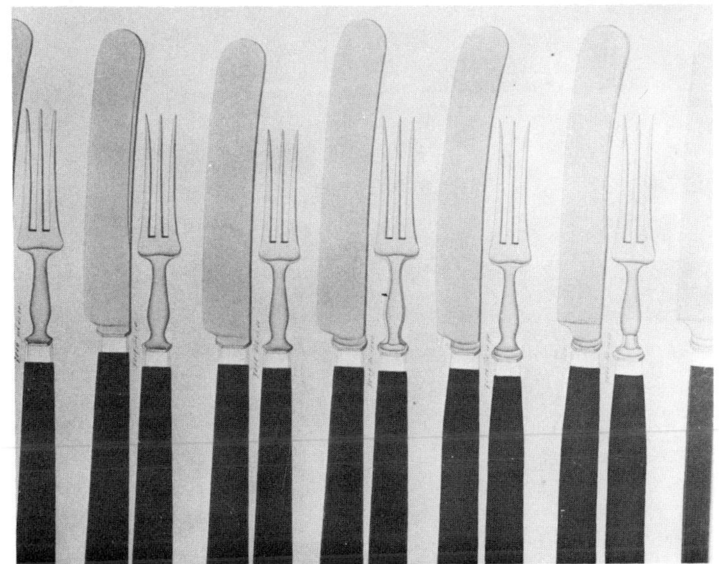

•Daggers and Cutlery Exported by Hermann Schulder 1861-1865

Trademarks of Solingen Manufacturers

A - J.E. Bleckmann
B - J.A. Henckels "Zwillingswerk" & Co.
C - Friedrich Abr. Herder Shon
D - Kirschbaum & Bremsley (predecessors of W.R. Kirschbaum & Co.)
E - P.D. Luneschdoss & Co.
F - Schitzler and Kirschbaum
G - Gebruder Weyersberg
H - Alexander Coppel & Co.

John L. Herring Collection

Model 1860 Cavalry Saber Henry Boker—Solingen

bayonet, marked S & K had a blade 24 inches long, and was probably the same as the one used with the Sharps rifle. Some of the saber bayonets for the Sharps "New Model" 1859 breech loading rifle are believed to have been manufactured by Schnitzler and Kirschbaum. These bayonets were 27 1/2 inches long, having a straight 23 inch blade.

The sword bayonet for the Colt revolving rifle and carbine was manufactured by Schnitzler and Kirschbaum. The bayonet blade was marked with an an anchor and the letters "D.C." (see pg. 179). D.C. on one side, and *S & K* on the other. Overall length of bayonet—28 3/4 inches. Length of blade 24 1/8 inches. A similar bayonet was used with the Spencer Navy rifle, model 1863. Similar also is an S & K manufactured sword bayonet for the English short sea service Enfield rifle. The Confederacy purchased these for use of their marines aboard ship.

Schnitzler and Kirschbaum made swords and bayonets for the United States Government from 1850 to 1865. It is obvious that this firm was also active in supplying individual States with military supplies during the 1861-1865 period. Among their sword contracts were contracts for model 1840 heavy cavalry sabers at the beginning of the Civil War as well as cavalry sabers with Tiffany of New York at about the same time.

As illustrated here, this company also made cutlasses, knives, and officer's swords of exceptionally fine workmanship.

Hermann Schulder. Established in 1853. Made swords, knives, razors, cutlery, daggers and knife-fork-spoon combinations.

Isaak Wester. Made cavalry sabers

Gebruder Weyersberg—The most famous of all the Solingen firms. Founded in 1787, although the family had been in the town for many years previously. Many trademarks are shown. The firm amalgamated with W.R. Kirschbaum in 1883 to form Weyersberg, Kirschbaum & Co. (see pg. 179)

SOLINGEN FIRMS POSSIBLY ENGAGED IN PRODUCTION AND SUPPLYING OF EDGED WEAPONS TO AMERICA 1861-1865

(Most of these firms specialized in iron, steel, and brass products during the period of the Civil War).

Carl Broch, Jr.

Trademark—Flying bird with legend "Premier Knife"

G. Hermann Broch

Trademark—Winged horse

Ernest Busch & Co.—Solingen. Records list their production dates, based on examined bayonets, as 1879-1922. It is possible that they were working as early as 1860 and as late as 1935. No trademark known.

Christians Brothers

Alexander Coppel & Co.—One of the more famous Solingen cutlery firms, Alexander Coppel founded the concern which bore his name in 1821. A cutlery firm, they did not turn to the volume production of edged weapons until 1872, having made scissors and pocket knives before that date. They exhibited at the Great Exhibition of 1851 (London) and were awarded the Gold Medal at the Wien Exposition of c. 1857 for their work. Later made bicycles and automobile parts until 1918. Did not resume production after 1945. (see pg. 179)

Carol Eickhorn & Co.—Despite recent reference to this company being founded in 1856, records say 1865. Hence, they are unlikely to have made any material for the Civil War.

August Evertz & Co.—Nothing known about this concern, which was working prior to 1875.

C.J. Falkenberg

Trademark—Two wine glasses and the legend "Marca Fabrica"

Robert Hartkopf

Trademark—Two winged lions

J. A. Henckels

Trademark—Two silhouetted figures between two trees

J. S. Hoelker and Company

Trademark—Tower with flag on top

W. Jung Sons—1865-1880

Jurmann, Maas and Schoverling
Kanzow and Philippi
C. G. Kratz
Trademark—anchor with "C. G. Kratz"
Hugo and Friedr. Lauterjung
Trademark—Crossed pennons and "L"
E. Luetters and Company
Trademark—Couchant lion
Mairowitz and Buscher
Trademark—A complicated design emphasizing a key, and the legend "M & B S"
Otto Mauszner
Trademark—A swan with extended wings
Eduard Muelker
Trademark—Two crossed button hooks (?)
E. & H. Neuhaus
Trademark—Coat of arms
J. A. Schmidt and Sons
Trademark—(Three are given). The main one is a three-spired church.
G. F. Thurman
A sword found on the Mine Run, Virginia battlefield is marked: "Thurman G. F." on the blade (Kendall B. Mattern Collection).
Weyersberg & Stamm.—Active 1865 to 1875. Stamping was simply "W. & St. Solingen".
Herm. Wibbeltrath
Trademark—Cross on top of a church steeple.

SOUVENIR JEWELRY

Buttons from uniforms of distinguished officers were eagerly sought after as souvenirs. Often these buttons were mounted on display cards as was done with McClellan's button shown here. Occasionally buttons were converted into articles of jewelry. Two of Burnside's buttons were made into earrings by the addition of gold clasps and worn by Mrs. Burnside. Shown here also is a ladies' hat pin made from the button from an unidentified officer's coat.

SPRINGFIELD MUSKET

Federal infantrymen were armed mainly with the Springfield Rifle Musket, model 1861, or variants of this model, i.e., the Model 1863 or 1864 rifle musket. If you have a "Civil War musket" in your collection, it very probably is a "Springfield" of this model; if not, you probably have the Enfield musket.

The Model 1861 Springfield rifle musket was the principal weapon of the Civil War. By the end of 1863, most Federal infantrymen were armed with this weapon. The Springfield was a percussion rifle 58 1/2 inches long, muzzle-loading, caliber .58. The rifle barrel was 40 inches long; the pitch in the rifling was one turn in six feet; there were three grooves each 3/10 of an inch wide, .005 of an inch deep at the muzzle, increasing regularly in depth to .15 at the breech. This rifle, with its 18-inch socket bayonet, weighed 9.75 pounds. The ammunition used was a hollow-based cylindro-conical bullet of 500 grains; muzzle velocity was 950 foot seconds. This compares with 2,300 foot seconds for the famous 1903 Springfield which saw so much use in World War I and later.

Including the bayonet, ramrod, and other appendages, there were 84 pieces in the model 1861 Springfield, which in 1861 cost $14.93 to manufacture. All parts were interchangeable. From 1861 to 1865, Springfield Armory produced 793,434 and private contractors 882,561 of these arms. In the 1863 and 1864 variations of the 1861 model slight improvements were made but the model 1861 rifle musket remained, practically unchanged, as the basic infantry weapon of the War. One of the interesting changes was the abolition of band springs in 1863 and their reappearance in 1864. Men in the field found that the bands tended to "jump" loose without the band springs when their guns were fired.

It is interesting to note that, in addition to the American contractors, model 1861 muskets were made by Manton in England and by firms in Germany.

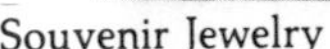
Souvenir Jewelry

Smithsonian Institution

Federal Soldier with Springfield Musket

Several of the contract arms are extremely rare today since certain contractors made only a few muskets.

While the Civil War musket as produced at Springfield or in the many contractors' factories seems very old and quaintly ineffectual as compared with such weapons as the Garand of today, the Boys in Blue and their adversaries were quite impressed by its appearance and performance. On November 23, 1862, a corporal in the 52d Massachusetts Volunteers wrote:

"Our guns were issued to us the other day, beautiful pieces; of the most improved pattern—the Springfield rifled musket . . . Mine is before me now, dark black—walnut stock, well oiled, so that the beauty of the wood is brought out, hollowed at the base, and smoothly fitted with steel, to correspond exactly to the curve of the shoulder, against which I shall have to press it many and many a time. The spring of the lock, just stiff and just limber enough; the eagle and stamp of the Government pressed into the steel (lock) plate; barrel, long and glistening— bound into its bed by gleaming rings—long and straight and so bright that when I present arms, and bring it before my face, I can see the nose and spectacles and the heavy beard on lip and chin, which already the camp is beginning to develop. Then the bayonet, straight and tapering, dazzling under a sun-ray, grooved delicately—as if it were meant to illustrate problems in conic sections—smooth to the finger as a surface of glass, and coming to a point sharp as a neddle."

The farmer boy from Iowa and the Irish immigrant from Boston were equally proud of their Model 1861 Springfields which, by regulations, were kept in excellent condition even after all other issue items had either been thrown away or had suffered from neglect. Veteran regiments were characterized by shot-rent colors and shining muskets, which were kept in excellent condition. This was also true of the equipment worn by the men. But all nonessentials had been discarded shortly after a regiment entered combat.

Although the rifle musket was the main shoulder weapon of the war, many men realized its inherent inferiority to the repeating weapons. The rifle musket could be fired two or three times a minute but breechloaders could be fired about 10 times a minute. To partially offset the slowness of fire of the muzzle-loader, two bullets were occasionally used at a time. With the ordinary service powder charge these bullets would separate about four feet from each other at a range of 200 yards.

Moreover, in the excitement of battle, many men, armed with the muzzle-loader, forgot to put a fresh percussion cap on the nipple for each firing of their weapon. An examination of the 27,574 muskets picked up after Gettysburg showed that 24,000 were still loaded. Of these, 12,000 contained two loads each and 6,000 (over 20 per cent) were charged with from three to 10 loads each. One musket had in it 23 loads, each charge being put down in regular order! In many muskets the ball had been inserted first and the powder afterwards!

Despite its beautiful appearance, the Springfield was a menace to many men because it invariably was kept brightly polished, thus destroying all attempts of its owner to conceal his position. This was not true of many Enfields and even some breechloaders which were either blued or browned. A Federal soldier after the war reported that "many ex-Rebel officers now bear witness to the fact that the movements of our Federal forces were often made known to them by the sheen from our burnished gun barrels." The soldier cited specifically Fredericksburg where the moon was reflected on Federal muskets as Burnside's men moved into position; at Second Bull Run where the muskets glittered through the dust; and at Petersburg where the Confederates "were often made aware of our movements to the left by the light that played above the moving columns, when they could not see the troops at all."

Even when blued or browned Enfield muskets were issued, regulation conscious regimental commanders had their men use emery cloth until the barrels were "good and shiny." As the soldier put it: "What better mark could possibly be desired than blue uniforms and burnished gun barrels?"

SPRINGFIELD ARMORY.

At the outbreak of the Civil War two major Federal armories (arsenals) were turning out the rifled musket. The one at Harpers Ferry was burned April 19, 1861, to prevent it from falling into Southern hands. About 15,000 muskets were destroyed along with the armory buildings. The Government therefore expanded the productive capacity of its armory at Springfield, Massachusetts, which had then an annual capacity of 25,000 muskets. This output was gradually raised to 300,000 annually by early 1865. Springfield Armory turned out 793,434 rifled muskets from January 1, 1861 to December 31, 1865. In addition, it duplicated many parts for the imported arms, especially the British Enfield and the German muskets. In his report of December 5, 1863, Secretary of War Stanton said that the excellence of arms and munitions of American manufacture supplied by the U.S. Ordnance Department was so obvious that the soldiers were no longer willing to use those of foreign manufacture.

Throughout the war, Springfield Armory hummed with increasing activity. Over 2,600 workmen were employed there at one time, working in shifts, day and night. These men were specially selected for their particular skills. The armory grounds where they worked covered an area of 72 acres surrounded by an iron fence, nine feet high. There were 15 buildings used in the manufacture of muskets and about the same number were occupied by the various armory officers and administrative personnel. However, the principal building was the arsenal—200 feet long, 70 feet wide, and three stories high—with each floor large enough to hold about 100,000 muskets.

The arsenal was used for storing muskets during the interval which elapsed from their manufacture to the time when they were shipped for storage or issue to the permanent arsenals established by the Government in various parts of the country. The storehouse, offices, and workshops were extensive buildings; the former was 800 feet long, and one of the workshops was 600 x 32 feet. The watershops, constructed of stone and brick and covering some two acres, were used forging, boring, welding, rolling, grinding, swaging, and polishing. In addition to three immense turbine waterwheels, a steam engine was installed to augment the water power.

In the manufacture of muskets, the first operation was the formation of the barrel. The barrel was run through a rolling machine, then through another set of rollers. Forty men, operating in shifts both day and night, ran the rolling mills. Each man received 4 cents for rolling a barrel. After the barrel was formed, it was bored out by machines called boring-banks; there were many of these running day and night. After the boring operation, the barrel was placed in a lathe, where the outside was turned down to proper size. A curious and interesting part of the operation of manufacturing muskets was the straightening of the barrel. Visitors were struck by the scene of hundreds of workmen standing with musket barrels held aloft in their hands, each man peering through his barrel toward one of the many windows of the building to see if it was straight.After examining the barrel, often the workman would lay it on a small anvil, give it a gentle blow with a hammer, and then check it again.

When the barrels were nearly finished, they were proved by an actual test with powder and ball. This test was carried out in a building called the "proving-house," which was very strongly built in order to contain the force of the explosions occurring when many barrels were tested simultaneously. About 1 per cent of the barrels burst during these tests. The barrels that burst were carefully examined to ascertain the causes of their defects. If it was from faulty rolling, the workman who performed the operation was charged one dollar.

There were 49 pieces used in making up a musket, all of which had to be formed and finished separately. Only two of these, the sight and cone-seat, were permanently attached to any other part, so that the musket could, at any time, be separated into 47 parts, simply by turning screws and opening springs. Most of these parts were struck in dies, and then finished by milling and filing.

Much of the manufacture was piecework, and the workmen frequently labored day and night for several consecutive days. There were instances when men worked from Monday until Thursday, day and night without any break, except an hour and a half at the morning change of shifts, one hour at noon, one at tea-time, and half an hour at midnight—four hours rest out of the twenty-four!

The numerous workmen employed were all skilled in specific jobs. Moreover, the various processes were so different that a workman employed upon one part of a musket had no knowledge of the steps by which other parts were made. Many workmen never even saw the manufacture of other parts.

The most interesting process was the fabrication of the gunstock. This was done in the old arsenal building. The wood for the stocks, black walnut, came mainly from Ohio and Canada. This was sawed into a rough semblance of a musket stock, and then passed through 17 different machines before it was completely finished and ready.

When all the various parts of the musket were finished they were assembled in a special building. Many workmen, each assigned a specific part, were kept busy assembling the muskets. Thus one man put the various parts of the lock together, then another screwed the lock into the stock. Each workman had before him on a bench the parts upon which he was working, arranged in piles, and he assembled them with "marvelous dexterity."

Springfield Armory was under the direction of a superintendent, who was charged with contracting for and purchasing all tools and materials necessary for manufacturing arms, hiring workmen, and determining their wages. He was assisted by a master armorer who managed the mechanical operations of the armory, and by a paymaster, a storekeeper, and numerous clerks.

The cost of manufacturing a musket at Springfield Armory in 1863 was $9, but the contract price paid to private companies was $20 for a weapon which was comparable to the Springfield musket in every respect.

SPUR

This spur is very probably C.S. It was found in an 1861 Confederate camp at Lagrange, Tennessee.

Width of this brass spur is 3 1/4 inches at the spot where the straps were attached. The rowel is missing but apparently was taken off as unnecessary since the rowel slot is bent to close.

STAMP AND COIN CONTAINER

Soldiers of both armies were inveterate letter writers and stamps were widely used. But stamps got wet and ruined by rain or perspiration when carried free in the pocket. This container was an answer to the problem. Because soldiers' pay was small, the loss of stamps was often a minor disaster. Accordingly, this container is a miniature safe. Money also could be kept in the container.

Description. Heavy brass, 3 1/8 inches long, 2 inches wide, and 3/4 inch deep. The hinged cover can not be opened unless all three dial settings are correct. Each dial has the numbers 1 to 12 in Roman numerals arranged clock-fashion. No one yet has been able to open this container!

STENCILS

Stencils used during the war were of two types. One type, showing an individual's name and regiment, has already been covered in the first volume of the *Encyclopedia.* Examples of this type are shown here for interest only. The second type was used in marking clothing and equipment by letter or number. Shown here are three of this type as follows:

DESCRIPTION

F. 3 1/2 x 2 1/8 inches.

3. 2 1/8 x 2 inches.

7. 2 1/8 x 2 inches. Found in the camp of the 7th Alabama Cavalry at Hall's Mill near Mobile, Alabama.

SURGEONS' KITS

Most kits used by surgeons in the War are the leather cased kits shown in the first volume of the *Encyclopedia.* Shown here are two recently acquired surgeon's kits of a fancy type. Both are mahogany cases lined in red velvet. The larger contains operating instruments made by the famous New York firm of Tiemann. This kit is 15 3/4 inches long, 5 1/4 inches wide, and 3 1/4 inches deep. The smaller kit contains such essentials as scissors and surgical thread with an inner tray holding 16 ivory-handled scalpels of varying sizes. This kit is

Courtesy of L. V. Warren
Memphis, Tennessee

Spur (C.S.)

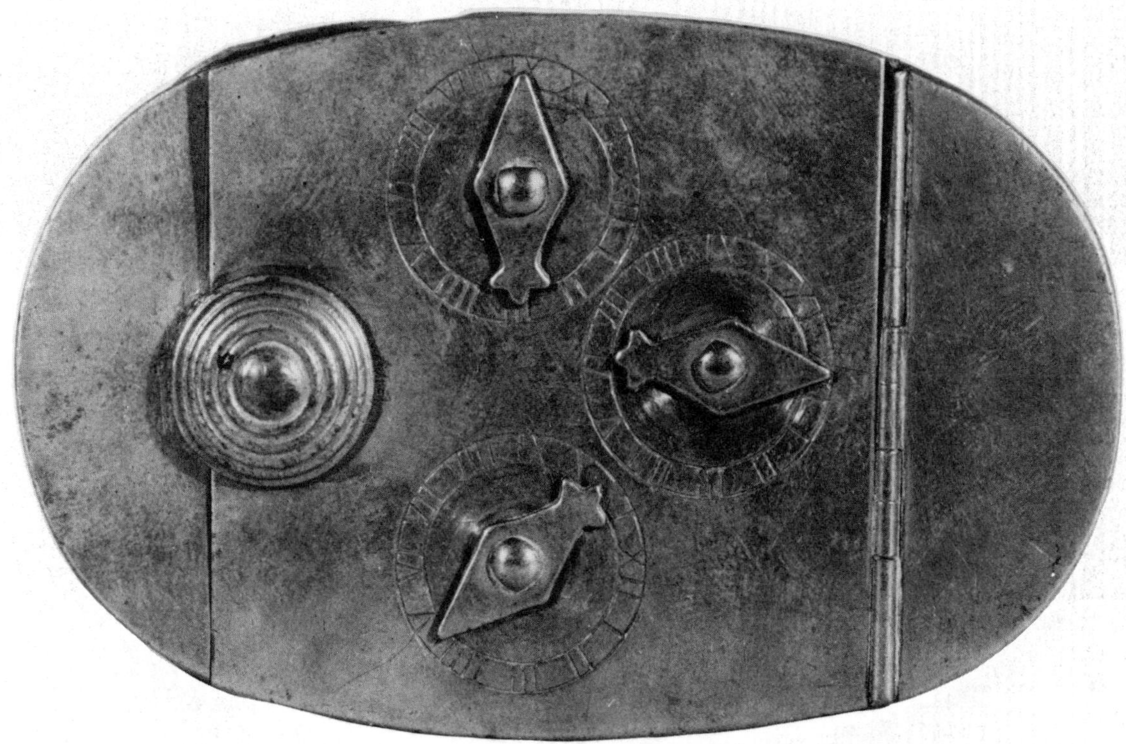

Stamp and Coin Container

Civil War Stencils

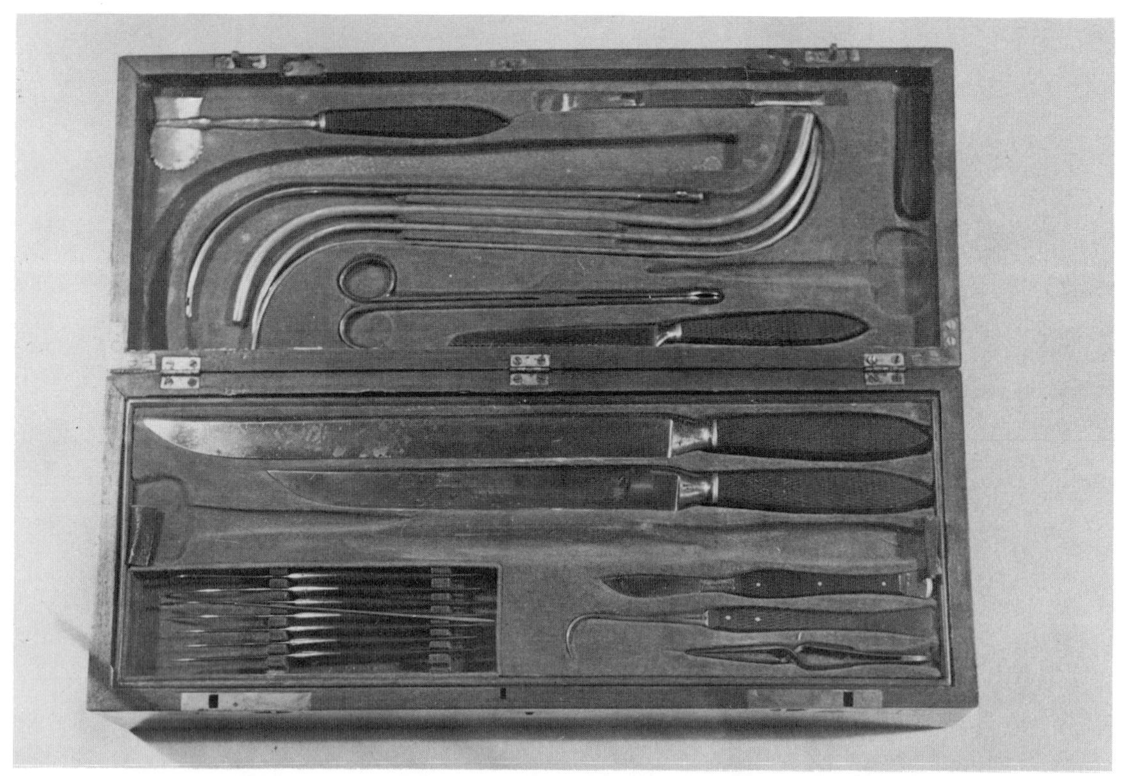

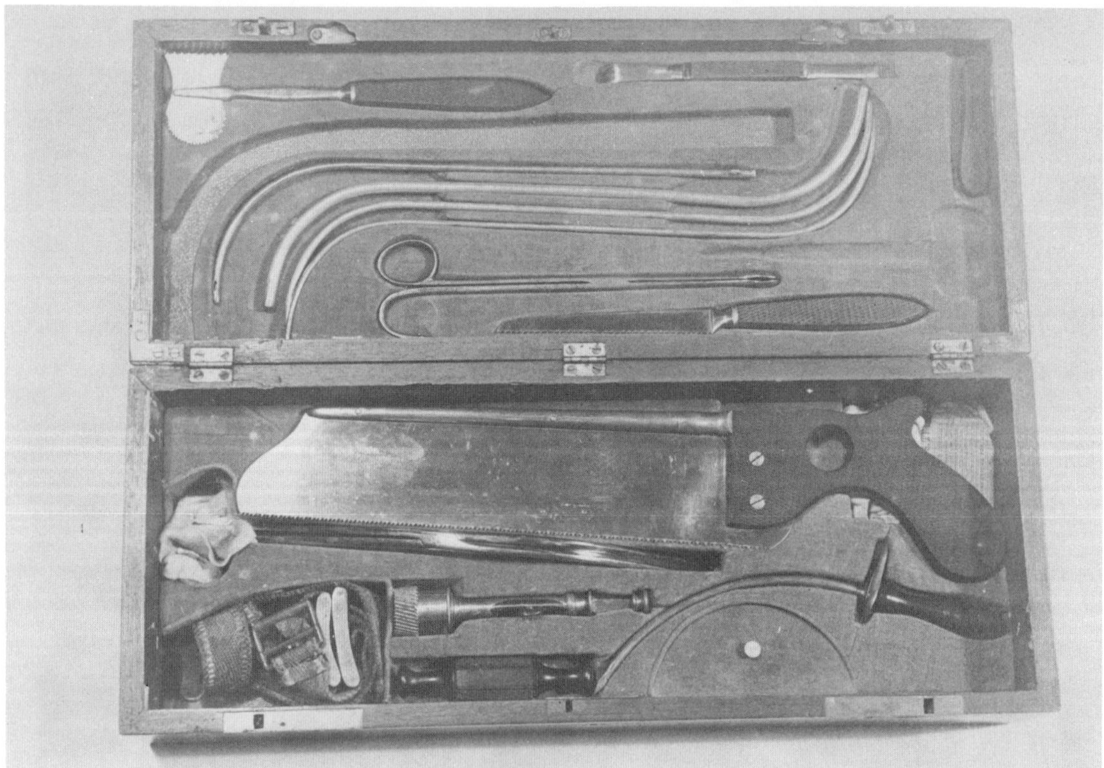

Surgeon's Kit (Open)

Surgeon's Kit (Closed) (Tiemann)

Surgeons' Kits

6 7/8 inches long, 5 3/4 inches wide, and 2 inches deep. Its instruments are marked Stod Art.

SUSPENDER BUCKLES (C.S.)

Men either wore their trousers with suspenders or without. Belts were not worn during the Civil War on trousers. Since suspenders were useful to the soldier after returning home they were soon worn out. If any survived the war they must have been very few. The author has never seen a pair of Civil War suspenders. However, buckles for suspenders did survive and are occasionally found on battlefields and in campsites. Shown here are four from three different battlefields. They vary in length from 1 1/8 to 1 1/4 inches and are about 3/4 inch wide. Reading left to right: the first two are from Longstreet's campsite at Fredericksburg, dated 1854 and 1861 respectively; the next is from a C.S. 4-gun battery position on Whitmarsh Island (near Savannah, Ga.) and dated 1858; and the last is from the position of the 16th Arkansas Infantry at Port Hudson. This buckle is marked Paris and is undated. It is possible that some of these buckles were used on the cloth belt-tab in back of the vest as they appear a bit narrow in comparison to the suspender buckles in contemporary Civil War photographs.

SWAMP ANGEL

One of the most remarkable feats of military engineering during the Civil War was the construction of a platform and firing site for the famous siege gun, the Swamp Angel, on Morris Island during the siege of Charleston in 1863. In July of that year, Maj. Gen. Quincy A. Gillmore, after an examination of the marshes on the island, was convinced that it was possible to construct an emplacement from which to fire on the city. On July 16 he directed Col. Edward W. Serrell, New York Volunteer Engineers, to select a position from which interdicting fire could be adjusted on the lower end of Charleston so that that portion of the city could be made untenable.

Colonel Serrell found that the most convenient spot was in a marsh on the left of the Federal lines, but that the ground at that position consisted of black mud, 16 to 18 feet deep, and subject to daily tidal inundation. A man walking there would sink two feet or more, but the colonel instructed a lieutenant of his regiment to survey the area and make requisition for whatever was needed for constructing a battery position and mounting the gun. The colonel believed that a cannon weighing not over 10,000 pounds could be emplaced in the selected area. However, to the lieutenant, Colonel Serrell's order seemed a tremendous joke. Accordingly, he included in his requisition a request for 1,000 men over 18 feet tall! Serrell, offended at this, haled the lieutenant before a court-martial, which found the young officer guilty of impertinence and sentenced him to be reprimanded in the presence of his men.

Nevertheless, work was begun. In the week following General Gillmore's aproval of plans for the undertaking, a road some 2 1/2 miles long was constructed to the gun site. A large detail of soldiers began to fill sand bags, while a mock battery was built some distance to the left, as a decoy to draw Confederate fire away from the Federal working parties.

At the gun site a solid foundation for the gun was made by laying down pine logs crisscross in the form of a grill or square, then driving down pilings in the center of the square. The space was filled in with planks and sandbags. Some 307 tons of timber and 812 tons of sand—a total of 13,000 filled bags— were used. By August 7, the emplacement was ready for the gun.

On August 12 the Federals carefully patrolled all the streams and inlets, using boats armed with naval howitzers, so that the soldiers could continue working. They mounted the battery. It was immediately christened the Swamp Angel by the men. The gun weighed 16,300 pounds, and fired a 175-pound projectile.

The range to the target was 8,000 yards—nearly five miles. Using an elevation of 31 degrees 30 minutes, the gun crew fired the first shell at 1:30 a.m. August 22. Firing data was calculated from the mean of several bearings taken with a pocket compass, using St. Michael's steeple as the point on which to adjust fire, since neither the city nor the steeple could be seen from the gun position. Though a very crude method of calculating data, this was probably the first instance on record in which a gun was aimed by compass at an invisible object and at such a great distance. Sixteen shells were fired during the first morning, 12 of which were filled with an incendiary material, "Short's Solid-

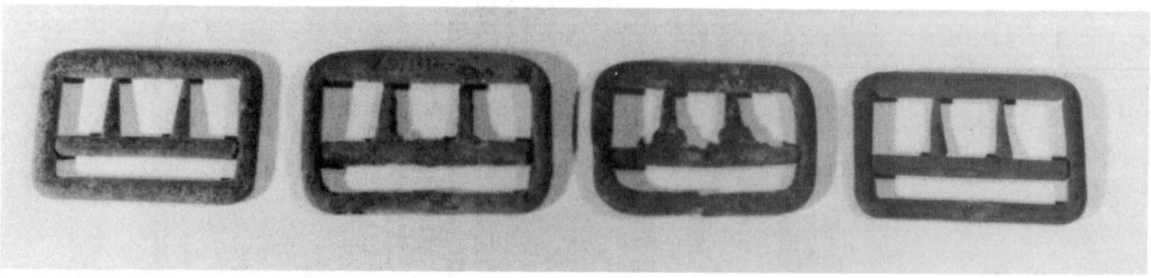

Suspender Buckles (C.S.)

ified Greek Fire." General Beauregard remonstrated bitterly against this mode of warfare, but on the following day Gillmore replied with 20 more such shells.

However, the Swamp Angel began to have its troubles. In fact, after the sixth shot the gunner reported that he could not get the priming wire down into the vent. The gun moved in its jacket, that is, in the wrought-iron band around the breech. It could still be fired, because, although the priming wire would not go down, there was still sufficient space to ignite the charge with the primer. Nevertheless the Swamp Angel was damaged beyond repair in the field, and might burst at any discharge.

The crew continued to fire but was cautioned to leave the gun's vicinity at the command "Ready" so as to be out of danger if it should burst. The number 4 man, who fired the gun, was given two lanyards tied together, that he might stand well clear, and be protected by the wall of sandbags around the gun.

At the 20th round, fired the night of the 23rd (another report says the 36th round), the gun crew commander wished to know the time of night in order to calculate the rapidity of fire. Watch in hand, he placed himself on the left side of the gun, so as to see the time by the flash of the discharge. He gave the command, "Fire." Instantly the whole battery became one sheet of flame. The Swamp Angel had burst.

The lieutenant's left ear bled from an internal injury, and his hair, eybrows, and mustache were singed. Number 4 cannoneer's hand was injured, and another member of the gun crew was severely wounded. Upon examination of the gun, it was discovered that the breech in rear of the vent had been blown loose from its jacket, and plunged through the scaffolding, on into the mud. The Swamp Angel itself had died like a soldier, face to the foe. It had pitched forward, clear out of the carriage, and rested on the ground in nearly the same posture as when ready to be fired. The projectile itself went smoothly to the city, as if nothing had happened to the gun. No wonder the Confederate batteries kept up their fire at the emplacement for two more days.

The Swamp Angel was removed later and replaced by a seacoast mortar, which was never fired.

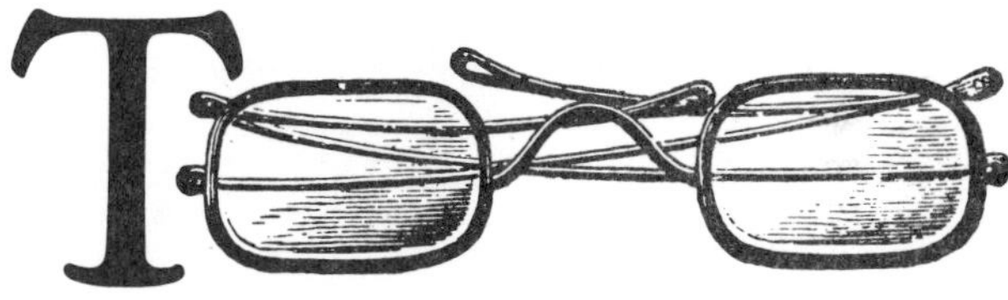

TELEGRAMS

Both civilian and military telegraph organizations functioned during the war. However, government control of the civilian telegraph companies was exercised in

WESTERN UNION TELEGRAPH COMPANY.

No. 1.] TERMS AND CONDITIONS ON WHICH MESSAGES ARE RECEIVED BY THIS COMPANY FOR TRANSMISSION.

The public are notified that, in order to guard against mistakes in the transmission of messages, every message of importance ought to be repeated, by being sent back from the station at which it is to be received, to the station from which it is orignally sent. Half the usual price for transmission will be charged for repeating the message; and while this Company will, as heretofore, use every precaution to ensure correctness, it will not be responsible for mistakes or delays in the transmission or delivery of repeated messages, beyond an amount exceeding five hundred times the amount paid for sending the message; nor will it be responsible for mistakes or delays in the transmission of unrepeated messages from whatever cause they may arise, nor for delays arising from interruptions in the working of its Telegraphs, nor for any mistake or omission of any other Company, over whose lines a message is to be sent to reach the place of destination. All messages will hereafter be received by this Company for transmission, subject to the above conditions.

A. STAGER, Gen. Sup't, Cleveland, O. I. R. ELWOOD, Sec'y, Rochester, N. Y.

To Lieut [illegible] Aug 28 186[illegible]

By Telegraph from Louisville 28 186[illegible]

Must not commence mustering until all the Companies are full return here if they will not be full in a day or two

[illegible]

Western Union Telegraph Company Telegram

The American Telegraph Company.

PRINTING AND MORSE LINES.

DIRECT TO ALL STATIONS IN THE UNITED STATES AND BRITISH PROVINCES.

OFFICES.—432 Pennsylvania Av. U. S. CAPITOL, and Willard's, The Metropolitan and National Hotels, Washington, D. C.

Terms and Conditions on which this and all Messages are received by this Company.

In order to guard against and correct as much as possible some of the errors arising from atmospheric and other causes appertaining to telegraphy, every important message should be REPEATED, by being sent back from the station at which it is to be received to the station from which it is originally sent Half the usual price will be charged for repeating the message, and while this Company in good faith will endeavor to send messages correctly and promptly, it will not be responsible for errors or delays in the transmission or delivery, nor for the non-delivery of REPEATED MESSAGES, beyond TWO HUNDRED times the sum paid for sending the message, unless a special agreement for insurance b made in writing, and the amount of risk specified on this agreement, and paid for at the time of sending the message. Nor will the Company be responsible for any error or delay in the transmission or delivery, or for the non-delivery, of ANY UNREPEATED MESSAGE, beyond the amount paid for sending the same, unless in like manner specially insured, and amount of risk stated hereon, and paid for at the time. No liability is assumed for errors in cipher or obscure messages; nor is any liability assumed by this Company for any error or neglect by any other Company over whose lines this message may be sent to reach its destination, and this Company is hereby made the agent of the sender of this message to forward it over the lines extending beyond those of this Company. No agent or employee is allowed to vary these terms, or make any other or verbal agreement, nor any promise as to the time of performance, and no one but a Superintendent is authorized to make a special agreement for insurance. These terms apply through the whole course of this message on all lines by which it may be transmitted.

CAMBRIDGE LIVINGSTON, Sec'y, **E. S. SANFORD, Pres't,**

145 BROADWAY, N. Y.

Dated Winchester Apl 20 1865.

Rec'd, Washington, Apl 20 1865, o'clock, min. M.

To Maj J. W. Nichols
Paymaster
27 Ind Ave

Please answer by telegraph the date of last payment of Sergeant John Tully Co H 2d U. S. Cavalry his time expired on the 12th inst and I cannot discharge him without date of last payment by you

James Cahill
Lieut 2d U. S. Cav.

American Telegraph Company Telegram

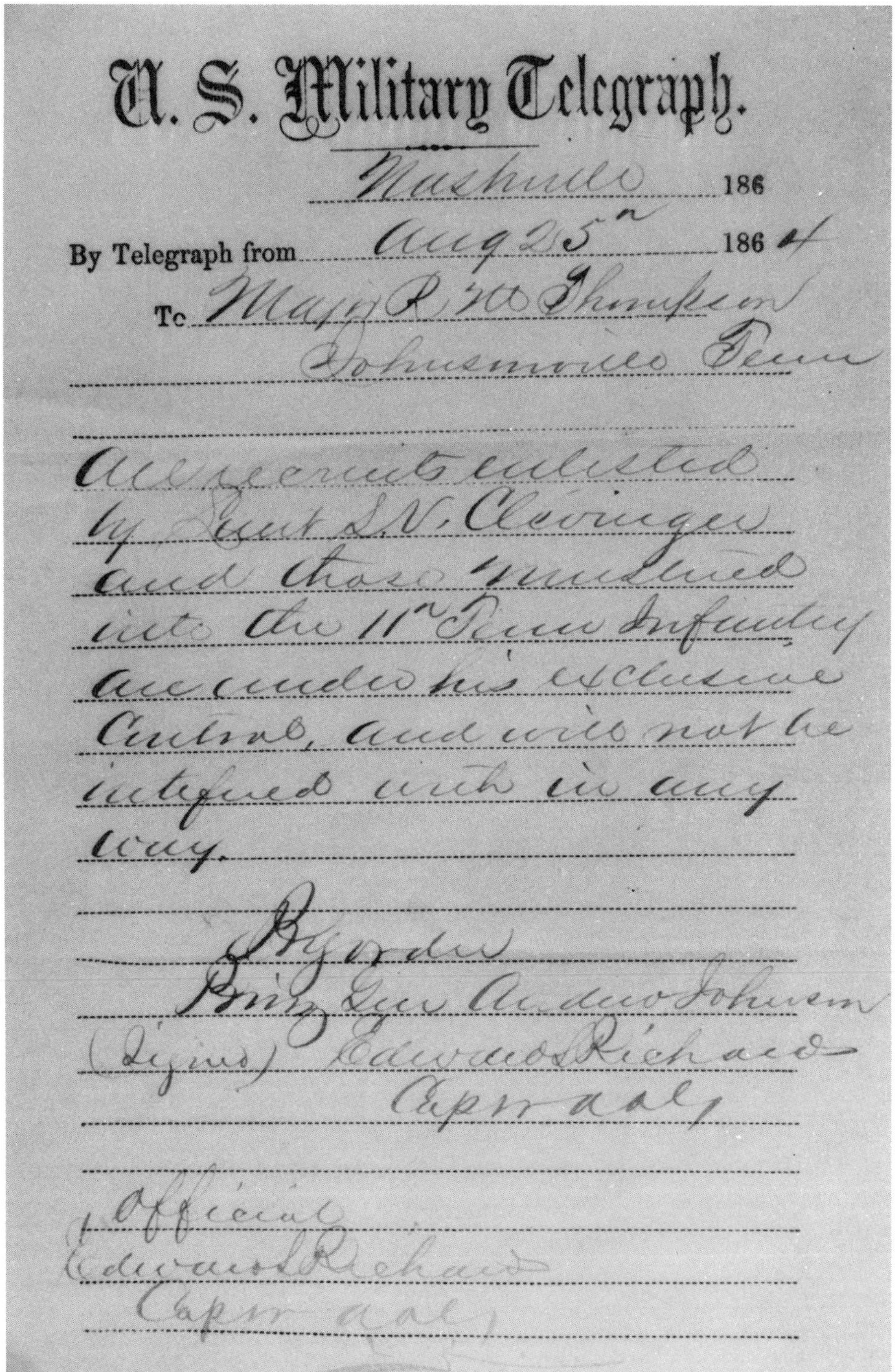

U. S. Military Telegraph.

Nashville 186

By Telegraph from Aug 25th 1864

To Maj R. W. Thompson

Johnsonville Tenn

All recruits enlisted by Lieut S. N. Clevinger and those mustered into the 11th Tenn Infantry are under his exclusive control, and will not be interfered with in any way.

By order
Brig Gen Andrew Johnson
(Signed) Edward Richards
Capt & A.D.C.

Official
Edward Richards
Capt & A.D.C.

U.S. Military Telegraph Telegram

varying degrees. In the case of the Federals, the War Department controlled the telegraph in Washington from the beginning of the war. And as early as June 1861, the field service of a military telegraph service was functioning well. Shown here are three original telegrams, two civilian and one military, but all involving military personnel.

AMERICAN TELEGRAPH COMPANY. Size 8 x 5 1/2 inches. Telegram sent from Winchester, Virginia April 20, 1865, to Washington, D.C. Sender—Lieutenant James Cahill, 2nd U.S. Cavalry. Recipient—Major J.W. Nichols.

WESTERN UNION TELEGRAPH COMPANY. Size 7 7/8 x 5 1/4 inches. Telegram sent from Louisville, Kentucky, August 28, 1862, to an unspecified destination. Sender—W. Seawall. Recipient—Lieutenant G. G. Arnett (?).

U.S. MILITARY TELEGRAPH. Size 8 1/2 x 5 1/2 inches. Telegram sent from Nashville, Tennessee, Augus 25, 1864, to Johnsonville, Tennessee. Sender—Brigadier General Andrew Johnson (later U.S. President). Recipient—Major R.M. Thompson.

C.S. TENNESSEE VOLUNTEERS BUTTON (?)

This button, with the wolf's head on it, was recently found at Bean Station, Tennessee in an area where have already appeared bullets, shells, buttons, etc. of the Civil War era. Since the material found is Confederate, it is quite possible that this unidentified button is Confederate and was worn by a Tennessee volunteer.

TENTS

Volunteer regiments of both armies were equipped with several types of tents. In the first few months of the war, most of the troops were issued the Sibley tent. This tent was a perfect cone in shape, with the apex about 12 feet above the ground. The foot of the center pole rested on an iron tripod, whose limbs straddled out like those of a "daddy longlegs." The dozen men occupying the Sibley tent slept with their feet toward the center. Despite its height, the Sibley did not permit men to stand or sit erect except at the very center. The sprawling feet of the iron tripod of the Sibley tent appeared to have been invented expressly for soldiers to stumble over at night. One soldier noted that when a burly comrade tripped over one of the legs of the tripod, his remarks were forcible but not to be repeated.

The Sibley derives its name from its inventor, Henry H. Sibley, an 1838 graduate of West Point. Sibley went with Fremont on an exploring expedition in the West and got his idea for a tent from the Indian tepee—a shelter of skins covered with long poles and with a fire in the center. During the war the Sibley tent was also called a "bell tent," due to its shape. Sibley became a brigadier general in the Confederate army but his war service was

C.S. Tennessee Volunteers Button (?)

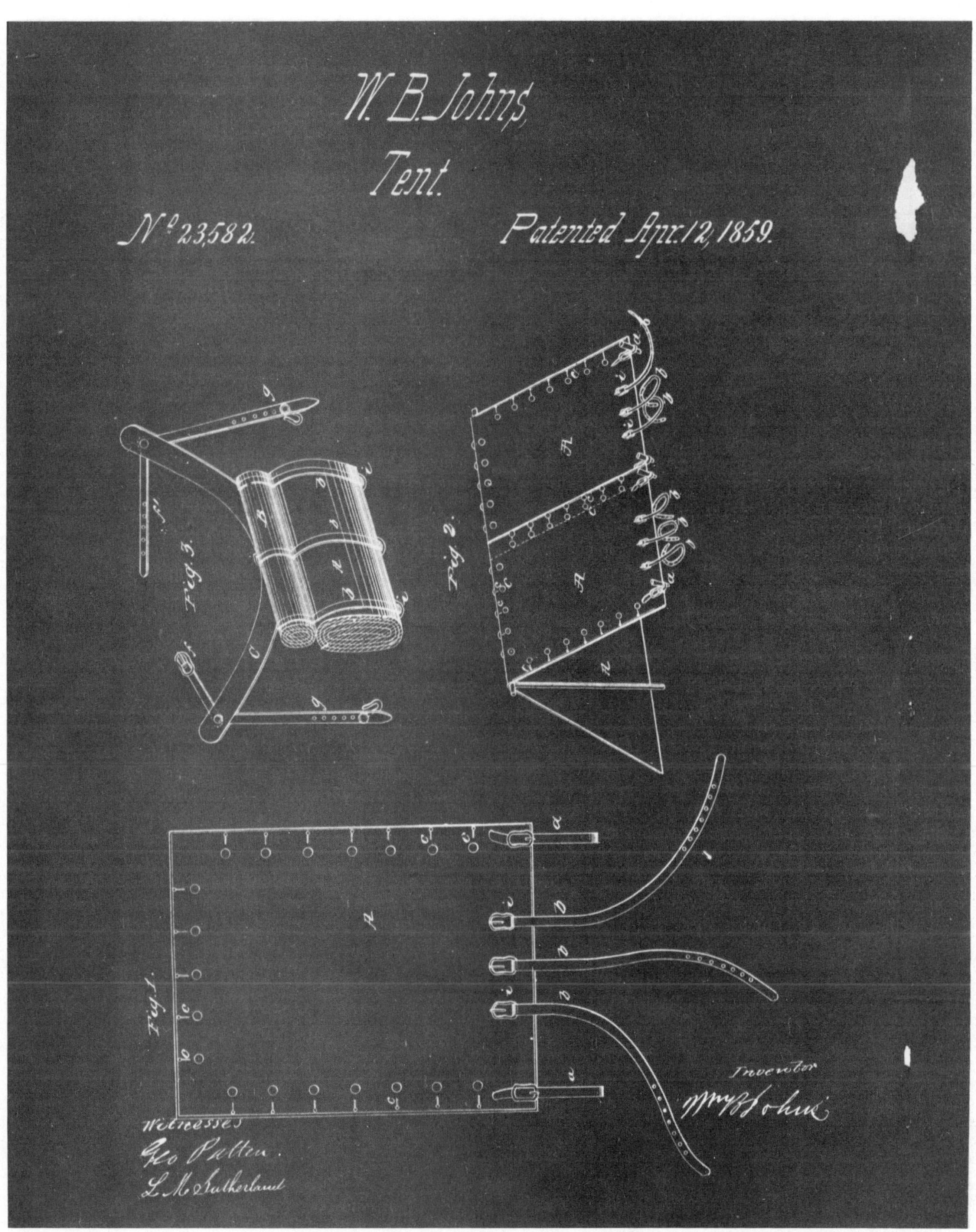

W. B. Johns Tent

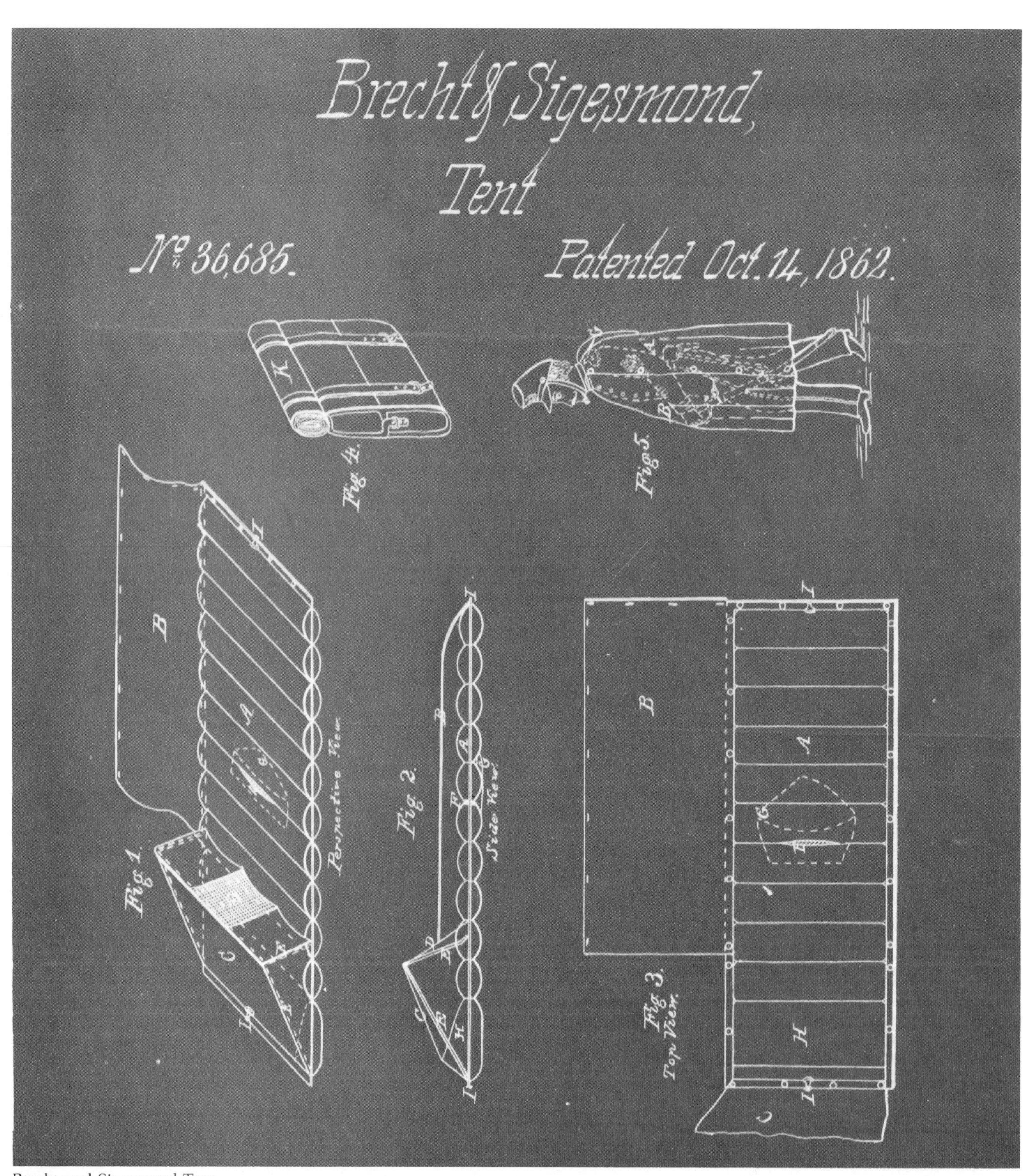

Brecht and Sigesmond Tent

not outstanding. After the war his family unsuccessfully attempted to collect money from the U.S. Government for patent infringements involved in Federal use of Sibley tents.

With the large increase of volunteer regiments sent into the field in 1862, the Sibley tents were relegated to state camps and rear echelon installations. They were too expensive and cumbersome for troops in the field. Many Sibleys with the field forces were burned because there simply were not enough wagons to transport them.

The Sibley was replaced by the "A" or "wedge" tent, a canvas structure stretched over a horizontal bar about six feet long, supported by two upright poles also about six feet high. When pitched, this tent supposedly housed four men, but often accommodated five and even six men. The "A" or "wedge" tent was used extensively throughout the war, not only by line units but also by surgeons for their patients. Often these tents were "stockaded," that is, they were placed on top of a stockade made by splitting posts in half and making an enclosure with these posts set close together. The cleft side of the posts faced inward, thus making a "clean and comely" interior.

The wall or hospital tent differed from those already described in that it had four uprights or walls, hence its name, wall tent. These tents were made in varying sizes; those used for hospital purposes housed from six to 20 patients. Often the surgeons would join two tents together, thus creating an airy hospital tent with a central corridor running the entire length between a double row of stretchers.

The most common of all tents was the shelter tent, known also as the dog tent, pup tent, or *tente d'abri.* A veteran believed the tent was called a dog tent because it could comfortably accommodate only a dog, and a small one at that. This tent appeared in the first year of the war when the Federals used over 40,000 of them. In 1864 they used about 1,500,000!

Most of the shelter tents were made of cotton drilling, although some were also made of light duck and even rubber. In size some shelter halves were 5 feet, 2 inches long by 4 feet, 8 inches wide. Each half was provided with a single row of buttons and button holes on three sides, and a pair of holes for stake loops at each corner. These tents were pitched by infantry in the following manner: Two muskets with bayonets fixed were stuck erect into the ground half the width of a shelter apart. A short guy rope which went with every shelterhalf was stretched between the trigger guards of the muskets, and over this as a ridgepole the tent was pitched very quickly.

Artillerymen pitched their shelter tents over a horizontal bar supported by two uprights. The framework was made from thin fence rails or saplings cut for the purpose. As with the "A" tents, the shelter tents were stockaded when the men went into winter quarters, if wood was not available for building huts.

The smaller tent of the early part of the war was found to be inadequate. In 1864 the U.S. Quartermaster Department provided that the shelter tent be 5 feet 6 inches long and 5 feet 5 inches wide. The material was cotton duck, with nine metallic (tinned, galvanized, or zinc) top buttons, and seven metallic end buttons. There were 23 buttonholes on each shelter half along the upper and side edges, with three loops at the lower corners.

Some shelter tents also included a three-cornered piece of cloth to close one end of the tent.

TETHER HOOK (C.S.)

Shown here is a C.S. tether hook. The tether hook, used to tether an officer's horse, came from Orange County, Virginia. The point going into the ground is 2 1/2 inches long and the width of the loop is 1 3/4 inches.

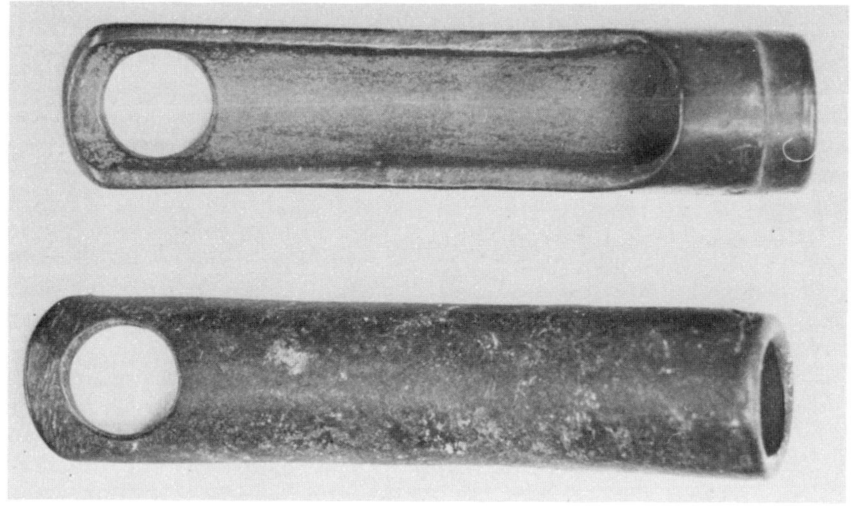

Tent Guy-Rope Holders from Hilton Head

Ken Mattern

Confederate Tether Hook

TOBACCO AND SNUFF

When we think of the tobacco of a hundred years ago, we usually think of General grant smoking cigars at Vicksburg and the Wilderness. Few people today realize that soldiers—both North and South—considered tobacco to be the most desirable item in their list of necessities.

Despite strong prejudice against the use of tobacco in many home communities, soldiers agreed with Henry T. Johns of the 49th Massachusetts Infantry that "you may preach anti-tobacco with some hope of gaining a few converts anywhere save in a wonderful solace." Tobacco went a long way toward making up the ever-present deficiency in quantity or even quality of the poor Civil War rations.

The soldiers had few means of amusement except cards and a favorite pipe tobacco. The only item the average soldier was selfish about was tobacco. Many a man would keep his tobacco hidden until he could go off in the woods where he could smoke or chew unobserved. If his comrades had known he had tobacco, his stock would have been exhausted in a few minutes.

Smoking was highly recommended by all surgeons at New Bern, North Carolina, as a preventative against "congestive chills," which caused many deaths among the troops. Tobacco was also considered beneficial in combatting other diseases in the South. The regimental surgeon of the 51st Massachusetts prescribed smoking tobacco for every man and a mixture of whiskey and quinine each morning before breakfast!

For prisoners of war tobacco was a luxury "greatly craved and almost impossible to get." If a prisoner was fortunate enough to have a plug of tobacco, he had to guard it with his life.

The arena of active operations of both armies from 1861 to 1865 was in the South and therefore in areas which included the tobacco-producing States.

The leading State in tobacco culture during the war period was Virginia. A public tobacco warehouse had been established in Richmond as early as 1730. However, up to 1861, cigars were imported mainly from Germany and Cuba. Up to 1870, cigars were handmade.

Data on ante-bellum processing of tobacco is difficult to find. Accordingly, the following excerpt from a letter of April 26, 1855, is of definite interest in this study. On that date a woman and some friends visited a tobacco "manufactory" in Richmond, and recorded her following observations:

"After quite a walk in the dust, we arrived at a large brick building. We were received by the owner of the establishment, and he explained the whole process to us. We went into a large room where there were a great many blacks at work. Saw the tobacco as it first comes to the factory—large dry leaves, that look like corn husks. It is wet in a large box, then some boys take it from there and pick out the stiff stems which grow through the middle of the leaf. They throw the good part on a table in front of this, where a man rolls a quantity together and cuts the roll in a machine, making every roll the same size. It is then passed through several pressing machines. We saw it after each pressing, and then it is packed in boxes ready for sale. The delicious thing which so many men feel they can not live without! This is only chewing tobacco. The smell was very strong, of course, and I shall now be more digusted than ever with the use of it since I have seen it mauled and rolled through so many black hands. There are 140 blacks employed here. They (each) have a certain task, a certain number of pounds a day to make for their masters. After that they work as long as they choose for themselves, and some earn a great deal in that way. One man earned enough to buy himself and his wife. They can earn more in factories than in any other way and do get money enough to enjoy themselves on Sunday!It is a pleasant kind of work, no noise of machinery like our northern factories, which is enough to deafen all the workmen. Mr. Grant asked them to sing for us and they sang several beautiful hymns. They think it is dreadful wicked to sing anything but sacred music . . . Their voices were fine, they kept good time and chorded well, though they were working all the time as fast as their hands could fly, and that was pretty fast!"

Diaries and letters of Civil War soldiers indicate that smoking and plug tobacco were used extensively by men of both sides. The smoking tobacco was purchased in paper or cloth containers or in "twist" form. Cigars were expensive and usually purchased only by officers or enlisted men who insisted on cigars regardless of the cost. Plug tobacco was a prime favorite—especially with soldiers from rural communities, while snuff seemed to have been an affectation by more opulent Northerners and in common use by many Southerners.

Northern troops usually looked to their regimental sutlers for tobacco. These sutlers were civilians who functioned as forerunners of post exchange dealers of today. Sutlers' prices for tobacco were exhorbitant and

Civil War Cigar Case

often charged as much as one dollar for a pound package of "Kinikinic" tobacco. But often soldiers would not be paid for months at a time. Also, sutlers were forbidden to accompany units during active operations at the front. As a result a war correspondent noted that men who had used tobacco every day for years had no opportunity to smoke or chew during an entire summer campaign. If any of the men had been able to find tobacco during this period, it would have cost him half a month's pay for a plug of tobacco, which the Government could issue for 25 cents. But the Government refused to handle tobacco! Accordingly, teamsters, whose trips to rear supply bases enabled them to buy tobacco, made thousands of dollars in trafficing in tobacco.

Occasionally, men received tobacco in their boxes from home. These boxes contained all kinds of "goodies", but if tobacco was included, the fortunate recipient would carefully hide his "plug" or package of tobacco, while generously sharing everything else.

Of course, the most common source of tobacco was to be found in storage in homes or warehouses in the Southern States. On the banks of the North Anna River, Virginia, Federal soldiers captured enemy soldiers in a tobacco barn; they were more thrilled with the tobacco than with their prisoners! Men of the 87th Pennsylvania Infantry, while stationed in the village of Lost River, Virginia, found in the hay of a stable some 20 boxes of chewing tobacco. These were "Lynchburg Plugs", a foot long, and highly prized. (Deeper in the hay they found two barrels of "apple jack" which soon had the men giving their officers considerable trouble before the day

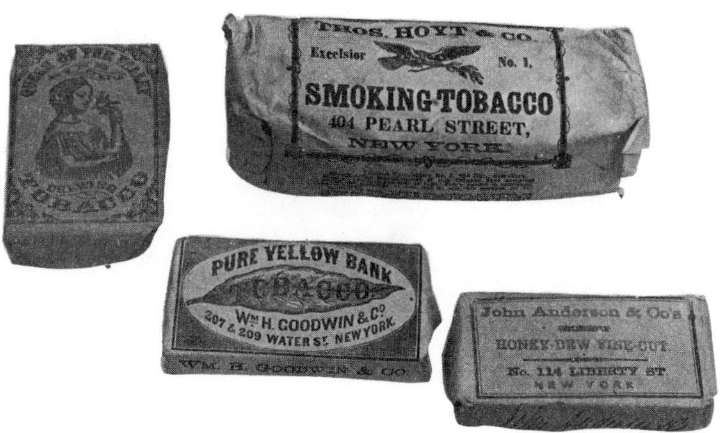

Popular Brands
Four popular brands of Civil War Tobacco

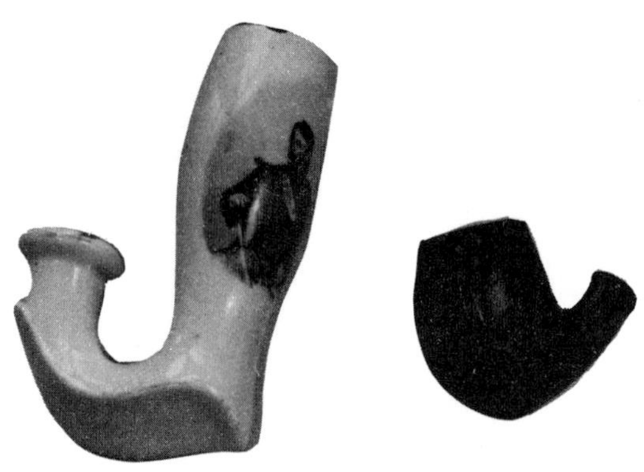

Two Pipes
The porcelain pipe on the left is reminiscent of European types, the briar pipe on the right was picked up on the Wilderness battlefield.

was over). In Suffolk, Virginia, a plantation was occupied which had in storage many hogsheads, casks, and boxes of both twist and plug tobacco.

The area around Springfield, Missouri was a very fine tobacco country. The specialty in this area was "boot-heel" tobacco made as follows: The tobacco was carefully selected, dampened, and a trace of molasses added to each leaf. A two-inch auger was then used to bore holes into hickory or walnut logs, into which a strong, loose-fitting, flat-ended plug was fitted to act as a ramrod. Then each leaf was rolled up into a wad and put into the hole; was pounded down, leaf by leaf by means of a heavy maul. After the hole was mauled nearly full a new plug was driven in to hold the tobacco down, and it stayed there all winter until needed for use. It was chopped out with an ax as needed. When taken out it could be broken up into discs, hence its name of "boot-heel". The men liked "boot-heel" very much. Chewing tobacco seemed to be a necessity with those who lived on coarse food in this region. This was especially true for those who lived on pork. As one soldier put it: Tobacco "was apparently a germicide favorable to man".

One of the curious incidents connected with the siege of Chattanooga was the complete disappearance of an immense stack of tobacco, which was stored in warehouses along the river. It is said that certain Northern men who happened to be dwelling within the limits of the Confederacy, confident of its sudden downfall, had disposed of their possessions for Confederate money, and investing the proceeds in "Long Jack" and had shipped it to Chattanooga as the point most liable to early capture by the Union forces, hoping thereby to make the exchange from Confederate currency into "greenbacks"—quickly and profitably.

There were said to be some hundreds of thousands of pounds, packed in little bales. As soon as Federals occupied the city, the owners applied for protection for their property, but the Federal commander "forgot" to put guards on the property, and it was seized by the soldiers. Years after the war, the owners sought to recover from the Federal Government pay for the tobacco with unknown results.

Obviously, the Southern soldiers had more tobacco than their enemies from Northern States. This advantage was counterbalanced by the fact that Federal soldiers had coffee and sugar—items often non-existent in Southern camps. Accordingly, soldiers of both armies very frequently used periods of truce and picket duty to do some trading. During the winter of 1862-1863, Federal and Confederate pickets carried on ex-

Snuff Box and Tobacco Can
The sterling silver snuff box was carried by Captain T. B. Crowley, 10th New Hampshire Infantry. The Tobacco can was the property of a North Carolinian.

Types of Civil War Pipes
Left to right:
Top Row: Briar pipe used at Newbern, North Carolina by "G. H." of the 45th Massachusetts Infantry; beautifully carved pipe marked "J.M.S." August 9, 1862 "Cedar Run"; handsome briar pipe marked "Lookout Mountain" with flag and shields.
Bottom Row: Pipe carved in shape of a Minie bullet; clay pipe carried by a Confederate soldier; clay pipe dug up at Antietam.

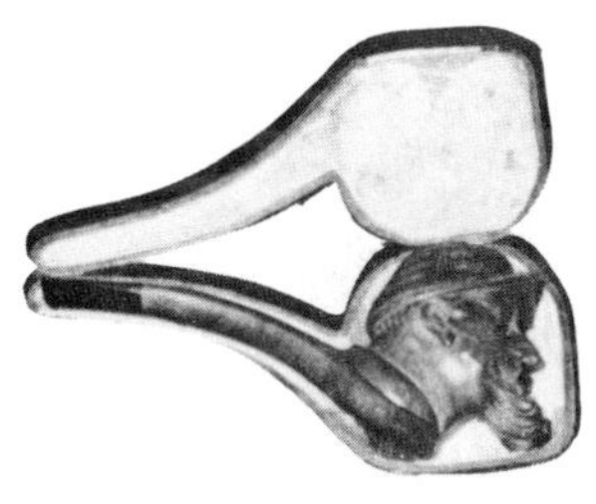

Pipe Engraved: *Capt. J.N. Jones Co. F, 6th N.H.V. 1862.*

Courtesy of T. Sherman Harding Orlando, Florida

tensive trading, despite strict orders to the contrary. Opposite the 4th New York Infantry were the 4th Georgia and 8th Alabama Regiments, who watched constantly for signals to trade from their Federal antagonists. Upon seeing the signals, the Confederates would at once prepare for business by loading themselves with cloth haversacks of tobacco, and holding them above their heads, plunge into the icy cold water, and make their way across to the Federal side of the river, sometimes passing from rock to rock, and sometimes up to their chests in water. Two generally came over at a time, and as soon as they arrived barter would commence, and in a few minutes the tobacco would be exchanged for overcoats, shoes, blankets, coffee and sugar, or any of the numerous articles plentiful with the Federals but scarce with them. Then they would at once return, both parties being satisfied with their bargains. Tobacco, in the Federal camp, was at that time worth (sutler's price) $2.50 per pound, and they would give for an overcoat which was charged to Federals at $7.50, ten pounds of navy plug tobacco, or $25.00 in value. They informed the Federals that they could draw such portion of their pay as they wished, in tobacco at $1.00 per pound, and the articles received by them in trade were of great value on their side of the river. At other places along the river pickets of both sides kept up a regular exchange by means of small, hand-made toy boats, sometimes equipped with small sails. Confederates would load up their little boat with tobacco and push it out into the river. Federals, on the other side would pull in the boat, remove the tobacco, load up the boat with coffee and sugar, and push it off to the eager Confederates.

When tobacco was not available, soldiers smoked moss taken from the trees, white oak bark, dried tea leaves, and crushed coffee beans.

The most common accessories used during the Civil War were pipes, cigars, plug tobacco, and snuff. Pipes were of all types—from common clay pipes to expensive elaborately carved pipes, often decorated with the soldier's name and unit. Many soldiers carved pipes for themselves out of briar and other woods available in their areas. Tobacco cans were very popular, while users of snuff used snuff boxes of japanned tin or even

Cavalryman's Pipe
This unusual pipe has a silver band with the owner's name engraved: Captain J. F. Vinal, 3rd Massachusetts Cavalry.

of sterling silver. But, no matter how simple or elaborate the equipment, men of both armies considered tobacco to be an absolute necessity during the monotony of camp life or battlefield dangers of America's most tragic war.

[*See author's artile "That Wonderful Solace: Virginia Tobacco in the Civil", in* Virginia Cavalcade, *Vol. XX, No. 4. Spring 1971*].

TOILET ARTICLES

In most cases, toilet articles were not items of issue to the soldiers. Whatever the soldiers used, they usually had to buy themselves. Illustrated here are types of toilet articles used during the war.

TORPEDOES

Although land mines were first used in the Civil War (during the Peninsular Campaign by Brigadier General G. J. Rains CSA), naval mines or "torpedoes" date back to the War of 1812 and perhaps earlier. Robert Fulton developed a system of naval mines in the early part of the 19th century. But in those days of hand-to-hand naval warfare, his invention was looked upon as being little less than diabolical. However, the progress of destructive weapons during the next few decades removed this aversion. In the Civil War, naval mines were developed and utilized because of their military value, especially in defensive operations. The naval mine was actually a stationary bomb-shell, intended to explode under the bottom of an enemy's ship. The mine was first used by the Russians during the Crimean War in 1854. It was found during the extensive use of naval mines in the Civil War that the damage effected by a mine exploding beneath a ship was very great; and although the failures were frequent, due to the explosion occurring at the wrong moment, the danger from the mines was always considerable. Moreover, the threat of their presence in the water often had an adverse psychological effect on the sailors, who naturally feared navigating in waters where destruction lurked at unknown points concealed from view. Probably the most famous instance of the need to overcome this natural fear was Farragut's injunction to "Damn the torpedoes. Full speed ahead!"

There were several types of naval mines in the war, but in general they could be divided into two classes—floating mines and those which were dependent on an electric current supplied from the shore. The second type was the safer for friendly ships, but was rather uncertain in action and could be used only at a moderate distance from the shore. The first type was more certain to explode, since it needed only contact with a ship to set it off, but obviously it could sink friendly ships as readily as enemy craft.

The Confederacy, as the adversary which was mainly concerned with harbor defense, established a "torpedo bureau" early in the war but the Federals, too, began to utilize naval mines about the middle of 1863. The Confederates, meanwhile, had been using mines almost from the outbreak of hostilities. These mines consisted mainly of cylinders of boiler iron filled with powder and suspended beneath floating casks or barrels. Mines varied from the "Singer torpedo" of 50-100 pounds to large iron boiler torpedoes of 2,000 pounds. The latter type was designed to be set off electrically from land. One such torpedo sank a 542-ton gunboat in the James River on May 6, 1864.

The Federals concentrated much of their attention on the "spar torpedo," like the one used by Cushing when he sank the powerful Confederate ironclad ram *Albemarle* in October 1864. Cushing's launch was equipped with a 14-foot spar which was hinged to the launch's bow and could be raised or lowered by a windlass. This spar held the torpedo which, during the action, was placed well under the hull of the *Albemarle.* Once in position, a line was pulled which actuated a pin and released the torpedo. The ejected torpedo then floated up, nestled against the bottom of the ship, and when another line was pulled, the torpedo's firing mechanism was actuated. The *Albemarle* sank in a short time because of the gaping hole made by Cushing's torpedo.

The Confederates were surprisingly successful with their mines. On January 15, 1865, the Federal monitor *Patapsco* was sunk by a mine in the channel off Fort Sumter. The vessel struck and exploded a large mine or group of mines. When his ship was hit, the Federal captain immediately gave the order to start the pumps, but even so it was too late. The whole forward part of the vessel was already submerged, and since there was no chance to save his ship, the captain gave the order to man the boats. Before even this could be done, the vessel had sunk to the top of its turret. In fact so rapidly did the *Patapsco* sink that 62 officers and men were lost.

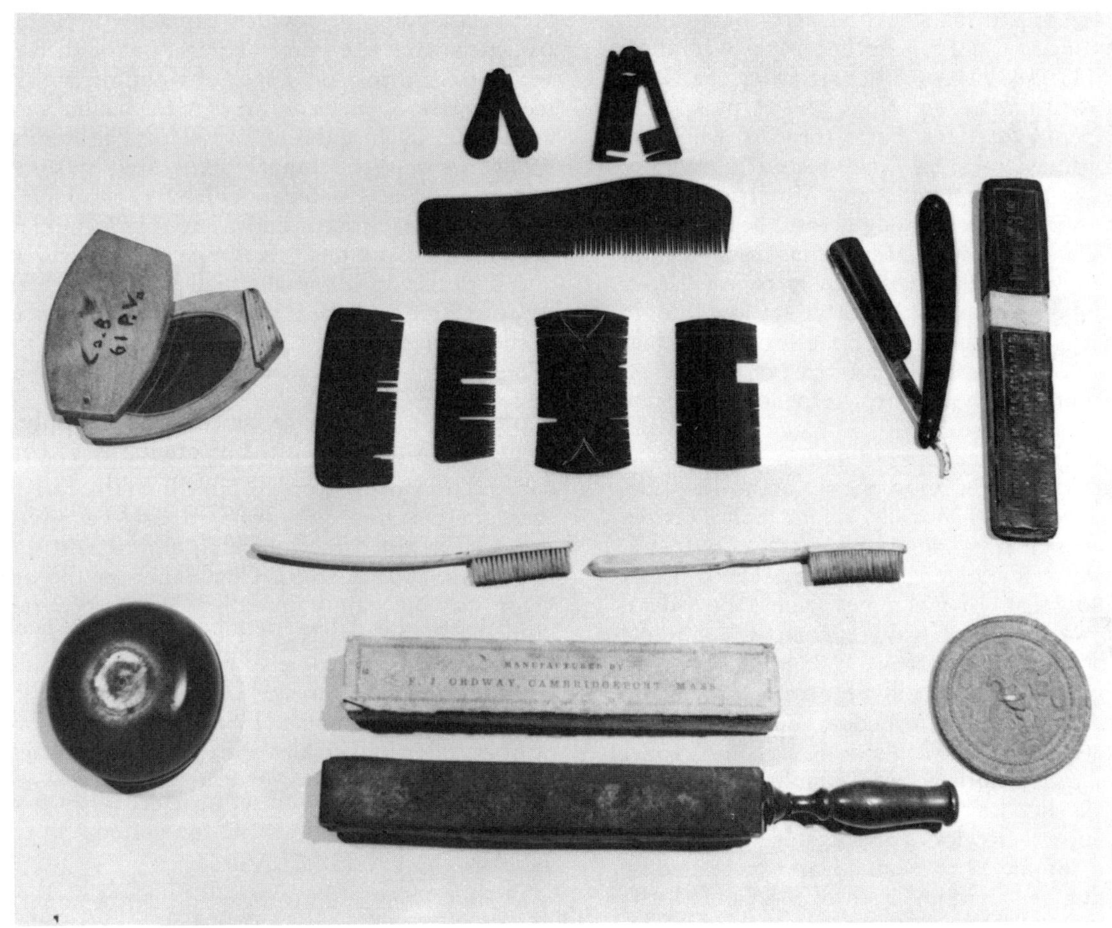

Toilet Articles

Razor
Black handle with blade decorated with American eagle and the motto "E Pluribus Unum". The black cardboard case is marked:

Frederick Reynolds
Gell Street
Sheffield, England
Price $3.00

Razor Strop
Cardboard box is marked:
The American Convex Hone and Razor Strop Combined. Manufactured for the U.S. Navy and Army.
F. J. Ordway, Cambridgeport, Mass. Used by Capt. Joseph A. Perry, Co. F. 17th Maine Infantry.

Soap Box
(Lower left corner). Made of hard wood. Small mirror inside. Carried through the war by Edward J. Mapes. Box is 3 1/4 inches in diameter.

Mirrors
(Lower right corner). Metal mirror (pewter), 3 1/8 inches in diameter. Cover has the American eagle motif. Wooden-cased mirror, 4 1/2 inches long. Marked: Co. B 61 P.V.

Toothbrushes
Both have celluloid handles and are 6 1/2 inches long. On the left—toothbrush marked: Extra Fine, Paris, France. Carried by W. L. Ames, 117th New York, Infantry. On the right—toothbrush marked: Sturtevant's Special No. 45. Carried by Surgeon Enoch Pearse, 61st Ohio Infantry.

Combs (Hard Rubber)
Navy comb, 6 7/8 inches long, marked: U.S. Navy. From the *Cairo*. (Beneath the two folding combs). Folding comb. On the left a comb 2 1/4 inches long. Carried by W. L. Ames. 117th New York Infantry. The other folding comb is 3 inches long. Straight combs. Left to right:
Marked Imperial Fine. 3 3/4 inches long.
Marked Goodyear 1851. 3 inches long.
Marked Royal Fine. 3 1/2 inches long.
Marked Goodyear Unbreakable. 3 1/4 inches long.

The Federal commander had known that his ship was in dangerous waters and his ship had her "torpedo-fenders" and netting as usual around her. Moreover, three boats with drags had preceded her searching the water through which the *Patapsco* would have to pass.

The Confederates used the "barrel torpedo" whenever possible against Federal ships. They placed 16 mines of this type between Forts Sumter and Moultrie early in 1865. These torpedoes, extending across the main ship channel, were anchored with a single mushroom anchor to each other, with sufficient length of rope to leave them four to five feet below the surface at low tide. In addition, the Confederates used boiler-iron torpedoes and "torpedo rafts." These rafts consisted of four round logs, 60 feet long, with cast iron torpedoes attached. These torpedoes held from 25 to 50 pounds of powder each. The rafts were anchored in such a way that the torpedoes were three feet below the surface at low tide. Much of the credit for the excellent mine laying carried out in Charleston Harbor should be given to Captain F. D. Lee of the Confederate Engineers. He believed firmly that the employment of naval mines against the Federal naval units was the best way to combat the naval superiority of the United States.

Rewarding research can still be done on the Confederates attempt to use torpedoes on the Federal squadron stationed in the Potomac River. In October 1862 the "Torpedo Bureau" was established in Richmond with General Rains in charge, while the "Naval Submarine Battery Service" was organized under the command of Captain M. F. Maury, later succeeded by Lieutenant Hunter Davidson, both of the Confederate Navy. It is interesting to note that General Beauregard, in command at Charleston, was among the very first to appreciate the possibilities of naval mines. When, in March 1863, his attention was called by Captain F. D. Lee to the complete success of a spar torpedo that Lee had invented, orders were immediately given to use this torpedo where possible throughout the military department of South Carolina, Georgia, and Florida. Captain Lee's spar torpedo was simply a cylinder of copper or other thin metal or wood, made water-tight, filled with 50 to 100 pounds of powder, capped with highly sensitive percussion fuzes on its conical or rounded end, the whole fixed firmly on a spar of wood or iron 25 to 30 feet long, and pushed through the water below the surface up against the enemy ship. The merits of the spar torpedo were promptly recognized by some junior officers of the Confederate Navy, although several old-line naval officers had a great contempt for such "new-fangled notions." However, youth had its way, and a flotilla of 12 small boats armed with the spar torpedo were assembled to attack Federal naval units. In a short time, every Confederate iron-clad ram was equipped with a spar torpedo, fastened to the end of a 30-foot light iron spar.

With the assistance of the State of South Carolina, Captain Lee got an appropriation of $50,000 for the construction of a strongly built boat to carry a spar torpedo. This boat was armored, and being very fast, was well adapted for attacking almost with impunity the largest Federal ships. Completion of the boat was vigorously but vainly urged by General Beauregard on both the Army and Navy Departments at Richmond. Ultimately the uncompleted boat, "a useless hulk," was left on the ways. However, though it never saw action, this torpedo ram designed by Lee was the real precursor of boats later universally adopted by the navies of the world.

TRUNK OR VALISE CLASPS

Many officers and men carried their personal belongings in trunks, valises, and carpet bags. These were not items of military issue and were usually sent home or left behind when the men went into active campaigning. Shown here are the metal clasps which have been recovered from battlefields or camp sites. Left to right:

Trunk Clasp - Brass, 2 3/4 inches long, 1 inch wide. No markings. Found on the 1862 Seven Days Battle site, near the Chickahominy River.

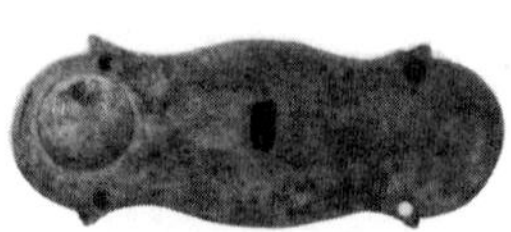

Trunk or Valise Clasps

Trunk Clasp - Brass, 2 7/8 inches long, 1 1/8 inches wide. Marked:

M. Myers & Son
Patent SGDG N. 1863
From Harrison's Landing, Virginia

Clasp - Found on writing portfolios, carpet bags, and toilet kits. Thin brass, 1 1/2 inches in diameter. No markings. Found at Port Hudson, Louisiana.

Trunk Clasp - Nickle plated. 2 1/2 by 2 1/2 inches. Marked:

Price's Patent
November 2, 1858

Found in General Hancock's bivouac at Brandy Station, Virginia. Went on a leather-covered officer's trunk. The motif is that of the Maltese Cross.

VEST

Few officers' vests survived the war. Shown here is one worn by Lieutenant A. W. Clough, Co. "H" 13th Maine Infantry. The vest is of regulation blue cloth with 4 pockets. There are 6 officers infantry buttons—each with the letter "I" in the shield. The vest can be adjusted by a narrow belt sewed on the back.

Vest

WALLETS AND COIN BAG

Four common sizes of leather wallets are shown here. The largest measures 7 1/2 by 3 3/4 inches. Inside is written in ink: Return to Capt. S. B. Sims (?). The wallet next in size measures 5 3/4 by 3 inches. Next is a heavy leather wallet 4 7/8 x 3 1/8 inches taken off the dead body of Stephen A Miller, 57th Indiana Infantry, who died of wounds received at Kenesaw Mountain. The smallest wallet shown here is 4 3/4 by 2 1/4 inches in size. It was carried by John G. Macomber, 6th Vermont Infantry, who was killed at the battle of the Wilderness, May 5, 1864. The wallet is stamped inside with:

Made by Cobb & Johnson
Lancaster, Mass.

All four wallets had wrap-around straps. The chamois money bag is 7 1/2 inches long and originally had a draw string. It has the letters LO on the bottom and was used by the Navy as a coin bag.

WHITWORTH CANNON

The Whitworth cannon is commonly thought of as a breech-loading Confederate weapon. Actually this English gun was used by the Federals as well as the Confederates.

Moreover, both breechloaders and muzzleloaders were used by the Confederates, although the Federals apparently used mainly Whitworth muzzleloaders. They did import a few Whitworth breechloaders in 1862, however. The Federals used several Whitworth 70-pounder muzzleloaders at Charleston and elsewhere; these guns had been captured from the Confederates.

Whitworth's main claim to fame has been in his excellent sniper's rifles. As with the cannon, projectile was hexagonal. Workmanship of these rifles was uniformly excellent. However, whitworth completed strongly in the Cann market as well. In May 1863, Whitworth claimed he had produced cannon in calibers from 1 1/4 to 9 inches.

But most of the interest in Joseph Whitworth today lies in his breechloading cannon, the caliber of which was 2.75 inches. The range of these guns was about five miles. Lee's army contained a battery of such guns in 1863.

The breechloading apparatus of the Whitworth consisted of a cap screwed on externally. This cap worked in a hoop which was hung by a hinge to the side of the breech. The vent was in the center of the breech assembly.

Wallets and Coin Bag

British ordnance experts believed that for practical purposes the extra range obtained by the Whitworth was of no real advantage since only slight damage could be done at an extreme range by a bolt. The British favored the Armstrong, both because of the greater caliber of the projectiles used, and because they preferred to use shells rather than solid shot.

Moreover, in spite of the apparent success of breech-loading cannon like the Whitworth, these ordnance technicians believed they were in no way superior to muzzleloaders. It was maintained that the many parts of the breech-loading cannon made it especially susceptible to damage by vibration during firing. Under no circumstances, claimed the experts, could a breech-loading cannon be as safe as a "solid" (muzzle-loading) gun. The facility of loading and rapidity of fire "amount to nothing," because the gun had to be re-laid in order to obtain accuracy of aim after every discharge. It is the laying of a gun on its target that takes time, not the loading of the piece. Moreover, said these authorities, the tendency of guns to absorb heat, developed during firing, puts a limit to extreme rapidity of fire.

Few breech-loading cannon of any type were used in the war, but one of the best was certainly the Whitworth whose pinpoint accuracy became proverbial in its day. The concept of a breech-loading cannon, as exemplified in the Whitworth, was one of many innovations introduced during the 1850's and 1860's. It was soon to be accepted as a sound, workable principle in the construction of artillery pieces.

Joseph Whitworth's inventions had brought him fame in his own country and Europe prior to the outbreak of the Civil War. He was justly recognized for his revolutionary contributions to new systems of rifling and projectiles in the field of ordnance. By 1863 Whitworth had produced steel cannon up to 5 1/2 inch (70-pounder) which had been regularly proved and adopted, and had turned out breechloading cannon up to 80-pounders. However, the 80-pounder was disabled after a short experimental test.

One of the most commonly used Whitworths was the 12-pounder muzzleloader. The average ranges of this model were as follows:

Degrees of Elevation	Range in yards
1	900
2	1,350
3	1,800
4	2,200
5	2,600
10	4,500
20	7,000
35	10,000

As early as June 1861 patriotic Northerners in Europe purchased on their own responsibility a battery of six Whitworth 12-pounder rifled cannon, with 3,000 rounds of ammunition. These cannon, complete with a machine for making 200 Whitworth projectiles per day, arrived in New York before First Bull Run.

The Confederates, too, showed a continuing interest in Whitworth cannon. On Nov. 3, 1862, the Confederate purchasing agent, James D. Bulloch, wrote from Liverpool that Whitworth was pushing hard to supersede Sir W. Armstrong from the latter's "snug berth" he had held against all competitors in England. In some of the testing experiments of Whitworth's gun, Whitworth beat out Armstrong both in range and accuracy. However, for some reason, Armstrong was favored in all these experiments. The Confederates at this time were especially interested in the Whitworth 32-pounder and the 70-pounder naval gun. Dimensions of these guns were:

32-pounder: 87 inches length of bore; 4.14 inches diameter of bore

Elevation (degrees)	Range (yards)
1	900
5	2,800
10	4,000

70-pounder: length of bore 114 inches; diameter of bore 5.5 inches

Elevation (degrees)	Range (yards)
1	1,000
5	2,900
10	5,000

Although Americans liked Whitworth's 12-pounder guns, British ordnance men paid most attention to his 120-pounder. This was a lighter gun than its major competitor (the Armstrong). Besides this advantage, Whitworth's gun was put together by hydraulic pressure as compared with the shrinkage method used by Armstrong and, generally speaking, was a much more foolproof piece. Whitworth attached great importance to annealing the steel in his cannon. After a cannon was finished in the rough, it was annealed from three to four weeks. Also, instead of shrinking on the hoops used for reinforcing the cannon tube, Whitworth tapered the inner barrel one inch in every 100 inches and forced the hoops on cold by hydrostatic pressure, with great care and accuracy. The breeches were made by solid forging. The breech-plug of the Whitworth was screwed not only into the inner tube but also into the next tube or ring.

Of the Whitworth 70-pounder muzzleloading cannon, one specimen was the subject of tests at the Washington Navy Yard by Federal ordnance experts, while several other specimens captured from the Confederates were used in the siege of Charleston and elsewhere.

The bore of Whitworth guns was usually hexagonal; the projectiles were planed by special machine-tools to fit the rifling. The twist was very sharp in order to give a sustaining rotation to the long Whitworth projectiles. One of Whitworth's important contributions was his projectile. He realized that the shape of the projectile was very important in achieving high velocity and range. By using an hexagonal projectile Whitworth increased the range. For example, with his 12-pounder,

Whitworth increased the range from the fluted cannon (2,495 yards at 7 degrees elevation) to 3,107 yards with the Whitworth 12-pounder at the same elevation. Whitworth's trajectory was flatter and its range longer. The dimensions of three basic types of Whitworth muzzleloading cannon were as follows:

Type	Bore	Length	Weight	Weight of Projectile	Length of projectile
120-pounder	7 in.	114 in.	16,000 lbs.	151 lbs.	20.5 in.
70-pounder	5.5	118 in.	8,592 lbs.	81 lbs.	19 in.
12-pounder	3 in.	104 in.	1,092 lbs.	12 lbs.	7 in.

For purposes of comparison, here is data on Whitworth's breech-loading cannon:

Bore (inches)	Powder Charge (lbs.)	Weight of Projectile	Elevation (in degrees)	Range (in yards)
3	1.75	12	2	1,250
3	1.75	12	5	2,300
3	1.75	12	10	3,780
5.2	12.00	80	5	2,600
5.2	12.00	80	7	3,490
5.2	12.00	80	10	4,400

In all cases the initial velocity was about 1,300 feet per second.

Wire Brush Cleaner

WIRE BRUSH RIFLE CLEANER

A 5-inch wire brush cleaner with threads on one end to screw on a ramrod. Quite similar to later wire brushes such as were used with the cleaning rod on the Model 1903 Springfield rifle. This specimen came from a New Jersey campsite on Falmouth Heights directly across (and north of) the Rappahannock River from Fredericksburg.

WRITING EQUIPMENT

Certainly one of the chief contributors to good morale in the Federal army was regularity in getting letters from home.

For veteran and recruit alike, the arrival of mail played a great part in soldier life—at the front or in camp. Along with the mail came packages of newspapers which were quickly distributed to the camp. In most tents the latest news brought by the leading newspapers was read in the evening and very intelligently discussed. Often, a soldier on picket duty, thinking himself unobserved, paced his beat with musket in one hand and newspaper or letter in the other.

Many regiments had newspaper men in their own ranks; often these men started a regimental newspaper on their own. Usually these papers were small affairs and ran only a few issues. One such paper, published by the 50th Illinois Infantry, was entitled *The Fiftieth,* but later was called *The Camp Prentis Register* in order to expand its range of interest and circulation. Such papers aided considerably in relieving the camps of much of the inevitable monotony incident to camp life.

In addition to newspapers, another very welcome arrival was the box of food and other desirable items from home. Usually the recipients of boxes shared their contents with less fortunate tent mates. Books, periodicals, and religious tracts were supplemented by reading matter sent by local agencies from the soldiers' home towns. So far as letter writing was concerned, many of the soldiers, North and South, indulged in extensive letter writing for the first time in their lives. Never in the Nation's history had so many letters been written as occurred during the war—a majority probably being penned by the soldiers in the field. One of the first things a soldier did after arrival in camp was to take pen or pencil and get a letter off to parents or sweetheart. Many of the older men had never learned to read or write; often letters were written for these soldiers by understanding comrades who had received instruction in the three R's. Generally, the party for whom the letter was written insisted that it be phrased "just as I would write it, you know."

Many of the requests were very amusing—both in the inimitable spelling employed and also in the substance of the letters. Usually the letters from illiterate soldiers followed a fixed sequence. First, there were the affectionate words of endearment to the wife; then words of love and warning to the children; and, lastly the writer of a letter home would get down to business. The words applicable to direct exchange of thoughts between husband and wife had already been agreed upon before the soldier ever left for the front. These words were completely comprehensible to either party, but were worse than Greek to the outsider.

Writing Equipment

On August 3, 1861, the Government passed an order which permitted all letters written by soldiers to be transmitted through the mails without prepayment of postage. However, the postage had to be paid by the recipient. Soldiers could send letters without prepayment by merely writing "Soldier's Letter" on the envelope.

A system of receipt vouchers for registered letters was established whereby the soldier could send valuable enclosures through the mail by paying a registering fee of 5 cents plus the regular postage. Trustworthy agents, often chaplains, were appointed by brigade and regimental commanders to handle these letters. For the regular mail a carpet bag was hung up in the tent of the regimental adjutant. In camp and rear areas it was often necessary to empty the bag twice a day. The 11th Massachusetts Infantry, 863 officers and men, sent an average of 4500 letters a week while in camp near Washington.

Very well organized was the postal service of the Army of the Potomac. Each regiment had a post-boy who carried the letters of his command to brigade headquarters where the mails of the different regiments were placed in one pouch and sent up to division headquarters. Cases for the letters were made of rough boards which on a march were packed away in the bottom of any army wagon.

The post-boys were usually very young enlisted men. In the 2nd Michigan Infantry one of these post "boys" turned out to be a girl who had been handling the mail for a brigade in the 9th Army Corps. She was discovered but shortly thereafter deserted.

Recently, a fountain pen of unquestioned Civil War vintage was dug up in the western area by Dr. John L. Margreiter of St. Louis. Shown here is a typical Civil War pen. Also shown is a velvet-lined case with two pens. One of the pens is of wood with a steel tip marked: Plume Lilliput, France. Blanzy Poure & Co. No. 320. The other pen is of mother-of-pearl with a gold tip. These pens were used by John G. Macomber, 6th Vermont Infantry, who was killed at the Wilderness, May 5, 1864.

PENS AND ACCESSORIES. Shown here are three pens and a pen holder—all recovered from battlefields.

Pens & Accessories
Left to right:
Light brass pen 3 inches in length—extended 5 1/4 inches in length. Chancellorsville.

Brass pen 4 1/2 inches long—extended, 5 1/4 inches. Has a brass pen point marked *California Pen*. Chancellorsville.

Brass pen holder (lid is missing). 1 1/4 inches long and 1 3/4 inches deep. One end shows a hand grasping a pen and the words: *Patented October 1856*. The other side has the number *503* and the words: *—Raynor Medalion—* Wilderness.

Silver pen, 2 7/8 inches long—when extended it is 3 1/4 inches long. Has a large brass pen point marked *Prince Albert*. Chancellorsville.

PAROLE CAMP ANNAPOLIS, M^D

Col. A. R. ROOT, Commanding

Annapolis, Md. Feb 12th 1863

Friend Vene,

It is not customary now a days for young men to let their friends and sweet hearts know who sent them their valentines but I know you will be glad to hear from me therefore I will enclose this letter in the same package with the Valentine and through the kind attention of Mr Magill I hope you will receive it by valentines day and, I shall expect an answer in two or three weeks from you stating that you received it and I am sure you will get it if the Rebs dont get it first for they are nasty boys and they fired into the

Envelope and Letter

Typical Civil War Pen

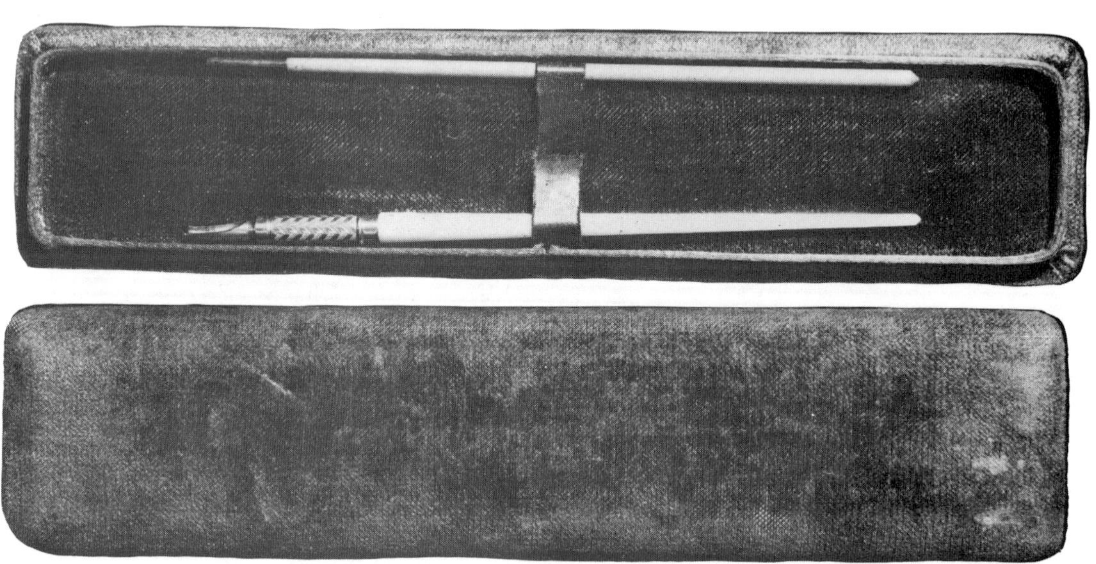

Pen Set of John G. Macomber, 6th Vermont Infantry

Bibliography

Adams, Charles Francis, *Autobiography*. Boston, 1916.

Alexander, E.P., *Military Memoirs of a Confederate*. New York, 1907.

(Anonymous), *The Twenty-Seventh Indiana . . .* N.P. 1899.

Atkins, Thomas Astley, *Yonkers in the Rebellion*. N.P. 1892.

Aubery, James M., *The Thirty-Sixth Wisconsin Volunteer Infantry*. N.P. 1900.

Brown, Alonzo L., *History of the Fourth Regiment . . . Minnesota Infantry*. St. Paul, Minn., 1892.

Brown, J. Willard, *The Signal Corps, U.S.A. in the War of the Rebellion*. Boston, 1896.

Bryant, Edwin E., *History of the Third Regiment of Wisconsin Veteran Volunteer Infantry 1861-1865*. Madison, Wisconsin, 1891.

Buel, Clarence Clough and Robert Underwood Johnson (editors), *Battles and Leaders of the Civil War*. 4 vols. New York, 1887.

Buffum, Francis H., *A Memorial of the Great Rebellion*. Boston, 1882.

Cadwell, Charles K., *The Old Sixth Regiment*. New Haven, 1875.

Cary, Eugene A., *"A Private's Recollections of Fredericksburg"* in *Personal Narratives of Events in the War of the Rebellion*. (Rhode Island) Third Series, No. 4, Providence, R.I.—1884.

Chamberlin, Thomas, *History of the 150th Pennsylvania Volunteers*. Philadelphia, 1905.

Clark, Charles M., *The History of the Thirty-Ninth Regiment Illinois Volunteer . . . Infantry*. Chicago, 1889.

Collins, Geo. C., *Memoirs of the 149th Regt. N.Y. Vol. Inft*. Syracuse, 1891.

C.S. War Department, *Regulations for the Army of the Confederate States*. Richmond, 1861.

Cunningham, John Lovell, *Three Years with the Adirondack Regiment, 118th New York Volunteers . . .* Norwood, Mass. 1920.

Duane, J.C., *Manual for Engineer Troops*. 3rd Edition. N.Y. 1864.

Eldredge, Daniel, *The Third New Hampshire . . .* Boston, 1893.

Floyd, Frederick Clark, *History of the Fortieth* [*Mozart*] *Regiment . . .* Boston, 1909.

Gates, Theodore Burr, *The Ulster Guard and the War of the Rebellion*. N.Y. 1872.

Gerrish, Theodore and John S. Hutchinson, *The Blue and the Gray*. Portland, Maine, 1883.

Gibbon, John, *The Artillerist's Manual*. N.Y. 1860.

Greene, Charles S., *Sparks from the Camp Fire*. Harrisburg, Penn. 1889.

Harper's Weekly, August 2, 1861. (article on bowie knife)

Haydon, F. Stansbury, *Aeronautics in the Union and Confederate Armies*. Vol. 1. Baltimore, 1941.

Hubert, Charles F., *History of the Fiftieth regiment Illinois volunteer infantry*. Kansas City, Mo. 1894.

Hyde, Thomas W., *Following the Greek Cross*. Boston, 1897.

Isham, Asa B., *An Historical sketch of the Seventh regiment Michigan volunteer cavalry*. N.Y. 1893.

Johns, Henry T., *Life with Forty-Ninth Massachusetts Volunteers*. Pittsfield, Mass. 1864.

Johnson, John, *The defense of Charleston Harbor . . .* Charleston, 1890.

Kimbell, Charles Bill, *History of Battery "A" First Illinois light artillery*. Chicago, 1899.

Letterman, Jonathan, *Medical Recollections of the Army of the Potomac*. N.Y. 1866.

Lincoln, William S., *Life with the Thirty-Fourth Mass. Infantry*. Worcester, Mass. 1879.

Marbaker, Thomas D., *History of the Eleventh New Jersey volunteers . . .* Trenton, 1898.

Marks, J.J., *The Peninsular Campaign in Virginia*. Philadelphia, 1864.

Marvin, Edwin E., *The Fifth regiment Connecticut volunteers*. Hartford, 1889.

Merrill, Julian Whedon, *Records of the 24th independent battery, N.Y. light artillery, U.S.V.* New York, 1870.

Murray, Thomas Hamilton, *History of the Ninth Regiment Connecticut Volunteer Infantry*. New Haven, 1903.

Nichols, James Moses, *Perry's Saints*. Boston, 1886.

Page, Charles A., *Letters of a War Correspondent*. Boston, 1899.

Pierce, C.F., *History . . . of Company C Fifty-First Massachusetts Volunteer Militia*. Worcester, 1886.

Porter, Horace, *Campaigning with Grant*. N.Y. 1897.

Prowell, George R., *History of the Eighty-Seventh Regiment Pennsylvania Volunteers*. York, Penn. 1903.

Roe, Alfred S., *The Tenth Regiment Massachusetts Volunteer Infantry*. Springfield, Mass. 1909.

Sheridan, P.H., *Personal Memoirs.* 2 vols. N.Y. 1888.

Smith, John L., *History of the Corn Exchange Regiment.* Philadelphia, 1888.

Stanyan, John M., *History of the 8th N.H. Volunteers.* Concord, N.H. 1892.

Stevens, C.A., *Berdan's United States Sharpshooters in the Army of the Potomac 1861-1865.* St. Paul, Minn. 1892.

Taylor, John C., *History of the First Connecticut Artillery.* Hartford, 1893.

Thompson, S., *Thirteenth regiment of New Hampshire volunteer infantry.* Boston, 1888.

Tilney, Robert, *My Life in the Army.* Philadelphia, 1912.

Todd, William, *The Seventy-Ninth Highlanders New York Volunteers.* Albany, N.Y. 1886.

Tourgee, Albion W., *The Story of a Thousand.* Buffalo, N.Y. 1896.

Tuson, Thomas H., *History of the First N.H. battery.* Manchester, N.H. 1878.

United States War Department, *Revised Regulations for the Army of the United States 1861.* Washington, 1861.

Ordnance Manual. Washington, 1861.

United States Navy Department, *Regulations for the Uniform of the United States Navy.* Washington, 1866.

Waitt, Ernest Linden, *History of the Nineteenth regiment Massachusetts volunteer infantry.* Salem, Mass. 1906.

Walkley, Stephen, *History of the Seventh Connecticut volunteer infantry.* Southington, Conn. 1905.

Ware, E.F., *The Lyon Campaign in Missouri.* (1st Missouri Infantry). Topeka, Kansas 1907.

Walton, Clyde C. (Editor), *The Indian War of 1864. New York, 1960.*

INDEX
TO VOLUMES I - II

A

B

C

D

E

F

G

H

I

J

K

L

M

N

O

P

Q

R

S

T

U

V

W

NOTES

NOTES

NOTES

NOTES

NOTES

NOTES

NOTES

NOTES

NOTES

Signat. I-255-261 II 165-168

NOTES